Red Hat® Enterprise Linux & Fedora™ Core 4: The Complete Reference

Richard L. Petersen

McGraw-Hill/Osborne

New York   Chicago   San Francisco
Lisbon   London   Madrid   Mexico City
Milan   New Delhi   San Juan
Seoul   Singapore   Sydney   Toronto

The McGraw·Hill Companies

McGraw-Hill/Osborne
2100 Powell Street, 10th Floor
Emeryville, California 94608
U.S.A.

To arrange bulk purchase discounts for sales promotions, premiums, or fund-raisers, please contact **McGraw-Hill**/Osborne at the above address.

Red Hat® Enterprise Linux & Fedora™ Core 4: The Complete Reference

1234567890 DOC DOC 0198765

Book p/n 0-07-226255-9 and DVD p/n 0-07-226256-7

parts of

ISBN 0-07-226154-4

Acquisitions Editor Jane Brownlow	**Proofreader** Paul Tyler
Project Editor Patty Mon	**Indexer** James Minkin
Acquisitions Coordinator Jennifer Housh	**Composition** Apollo Publishing Services
Technical Editor Ibrahim Haddad	**Series Design** Peter F. Hancik, Lyssa Wald
Copy Editor Robert Campbell	

This book was composed with Adobe® InDesign®.

To my mother,
for all her love and support
over the years

Cecelia

About the Author

Richard L. Petersen holds a M.L.I.S. in Library and Information Studies. He teaches Unix and C/C++ courses at the University of California, Berkeley

Contents at a Glance

Contents

Acknowledgments

I would like to thank all those at McGraw-Hill/Osborne who made this book a reality, particularly Jane Brownlow, acquisition editor, for her continued encouragement and analysis as well as management of such a complex project, as well as Tracy Dunkelberger, and Francis Kelly for their help on previous editions; Ibrahim Haddad, the technical editor and contributor, whose analysis and suggestions proved very insightful and helpful; Jennifer Housh, editorial assistant, who provided needed resources and helpful advice; Robert Campbell, copy editor, for an excellent job editing as well as insightful comments; and project editor Patty Mon, who incorporated the large number of features found in this book as well as coordinating the intricate task of generating the final version. Thanks also to Scott Rogers, who initiated the project.

Special thanks to Linus Torvalds, the creator of Linux, and to those who continue to develop Linux as an open, professional, and effective operating system accessible to anyone. Thanks also to the academic community whose special dedication has developed Unix as a flexible and versatile operating system. I would also like to thank professors and students at the University of California, Berkeley, for their experience and support in developing new and different ways of understanding operating system technologies.

I would also like to thank my parents, George and Cecelia, and my brothers, George, Robert, and Mark, for their support and encouragement with such a difficult project. Also Valerie and Marylou and my nieces and nephews, Aleina, Larisa, Justin, Christopher, and Dylan, for their support and deadline reminders.

Introduction

The Red Hat Fedora Core and Red Hat Enterprise Linux distributions have become major Linux distributions, bringing to the PC all the power and flexibility of a Unix workstation as well as a complete set of Internet applications and a fully functional desktop interface. This book is designed not only to be a complete reference on Linux, but also to provide clear and detailed explanations of Linux features. No prior knowledge of Unix is assumed; Linux is an operating system anyone can use.

Fedora Core and Red Hat Enterprise Linux

Red Hat has split its Linux development into two lines: Red Hat Enterprise Linux and the Fedora Project which releases Fedora Core Linux. The Red Hat Enterprise Linux product line consists of Red Hat Enterprise Linux WS (workstation), Red Hat Enterprise Linux ES (entry/mid server), and the Red Hat Enterprise Linux AS (advanced server). As a result, the enterprise family products are controlled releases from Red Hat for commercial deployments with new releases issued every two years or so. The second development line falls within the Fedora Project, an Open Source initiative supported by Red Hat. The Fedora Core releases will be issued every six months on average, incorporating the most recent development in the Linux kernel as well as supported applications. The Fedora Core release consists entirely of Open Source software. Developers from around the globe can contribute to the project by following Open Source processes, which give them freedom in promoting enhancements, new features, and new applications, while maintaining fast-paced releases in the course of rapid online development. Unlike Red Hat Enterprise Linux, the Fedora Core version of Linux is entirely free and is not a supported Red Hat product. You can download the most current version, including test betas, from **fedora.redhat.com**. The Fedora Project release replaces the original standard Red Hat Linux distribution. The Fedora Project also provides Fedora Extras, software that enhances the core collection.

The Red Hat Enterprise Linux line of products is designed for corporate, research, and business applications. These products focus on reliability, stability, and performance, in addition to supporting multiple processor architectures. They are released on a much more controlled schedule than the Fedora Project versions. What was once the low-cost consumer version of Red Hat Linux will be replaced by a scaled-down commercial Enterprise version for consumers and small business. Red Hat offers three Enterprise versions, one for the workstation and two for servers. Red Hat Enterprise Linux AS provides the highest level of support from intense mission-critical requirements for all aspect of network support, including servers, databases, and security. Red Hat Enterprise Linux ES provides a similar package, but one geared to mid-level business requirements. The Red Hat Enterprise Linux WS implements a workstation with a wide range of clients that can be used for either Red Hat Enterprise Linux ES or AS networks.

This book covers the current Fedora Core 4 release, while maintaining compatibility with Red Hat Enterprise Linux. The complete Fedora Core 4 release is provided on the DVD-ROM included with this book. This book identifies seven major Linux topics: basic setup, environments, applications, security, servers, administration, and network administration. Whereas the book details the latest administrative tools, desktops, and kernel features in the Fedora Core release, it also covers in depth the network servers, administrative tasks, and applications featured in Red Hat Enterprise Linux.

Important Developments with Fedora Core 4

With Fedora Core 4, several key changes to Linux introduced in previous releases are now incorporated as standardized and stable components of the Linux operations system. These include changes to device detection, security support, and desktop use. Some of these are listed here, with a complete listing in Chapter 1.

- There are both x86 (32-bit) and x86_64 (64-bit) versions for Fedora Core 4, as well as Apple computer versions (PPC).

- Fedora Core 4 features automatic detection and configuration of removable devices like USB printers, digital cameras, and card readers, treating CD/DVD discs as removable devices, as well as fully detecting IDE CD/DVD devices.

- GNOME now supports GUI access to all removable devices and shared directories on networked hosts, including Windows folders.

- Fedora Core 4 also provides full IPv6 network protocol support, including automatic addressing and renumbering.

- SELinux is now an integral component of Fedora Core 4, providing system-wide security. You can set different levels of control and create your own policies.

- A wide range of multimedia applications are included, such as a video player and TV viewer, along with compatible support from various multimedia applications and libraries available from **rpm.livna.org/fedora** and **freshrpms.net**, such as DVD and DivX support.

- The Red Hat Update Agent can be used to automatically update your Fedora Core 4 system and all its installed applications, from the Yum Fedora Core online repositories. You do not have to subscribe to the Red Hat Network.

- Additional popular Fedora Core compatible packages can be automatically installed from Fedora Extras. Many former Fedora Core packages, like Abiword, are now part of Fedora Extras. Use the **yum** command with the **install** option and the package name in any terminal window. An Internet connection is required. The package, along with any supporting packages, will be detected, downloaded, and installed from the Fedora Extras repository at **download.fedora.redhat.com/pub/fedora/linux/extras/4/RPMS**.

- The Xen virtualization kernel is now supported, allowing you to set up virtual machines that can run different operating systems.

- InfiniBand high-speed connections are now supported by the kernel.

- The Global File System (GFS), Red Hat's network cluster file system, is now included.

Linux Features

Of course Fedora Core 4 includes features that have become a standard part of any Linux distribution, including the desktops, Unix compatibility, network servers, and numerous software applications such as Office, multimedia, and Internet applications. GNOME and the K Desktop Environment (KDE) have become standard desktop graphical user interfaces (GUIs) for Linux, noted for their power, flexibility, and ease of use. These are complete desktop environments that are more flexible than either Windows or the Mac OS. KDE and GNOME have become the standard GUI interface for Linux systems. You can install both, run applications from one on the other, and easily switch from one to the other. Both have become integrated components of Linux, with applications and tools for every kind of task and operation. Instead of treating GNOME and KDE as separate entities, GNOME and KDE tools and applications are presented throughout the book.

Linux is also a fully functional Unix operating system. It has all the standard features of a powerful Unix system, including a complete set of Unix shells such as BASH, TCSH, and the Z shell. If you are familiar with the Unix interface, you can use any of these shells, with the same Unix commands, filters, and configuration features.

For the Internet, Linux has become a platform for very powerful network applications. With Linux, you can become a part of the Internet by creating your own Web and FTP sites. Other users can access your Linux systems, several users at the same time, using different services. You can also use very powerful GNOME, KDE, and Unix clients for mail and news. A Linux system is not limited to the Internet. You can use it on any local intranet, setting up an FTP or Web site for your network. Fedora Core 4 comes equipped with a variety of fully functional servers already installed and ready to use.

A wide array of applications operate on Fedora Core 4 and Red Hat Enterprise Linux. Numerous GNOME and KDE applications are continually released through their respective Web sites. Software released in accordance with the GNU General Public License includes professional-level applications such as programming development tools, editors and word processors, and numerous specialized applications such as those for graphics and sound. A massive amount of software is available at online Linux sites like **sourceforge.net**, where you can download Open Source applications and then easily install them onto your system.

How to Use This Book

The first two sections of the book are designed to cover tasks you will need to perform to get your system up and running. After an introduction to the working environment, including both GNOME and KDE desktops, you learn how to quickly update your system, manage users and groups, and set up your printer using the administrative tools. The software management is nearly automatic, letting you install software on your system, including applications, with just a couple of mouse clicks. Internet access can be set up for modems, DSL, wireless, and Ethernet networks with easy-to-use administrative tools that guide you every step of the way. Many people now use Linux to set up a home or local business network. The steps involved to implement a basic network can now be carried out using simple software tools. You can even install Bluetooth devices. All these topics are covered in greater detail later in the book.

Since this book is really five books in one—a user interface book, a security book, a server book, and networking book, and an administration book—how you choose to use it depends upon how you want to use your Fedora Core system. Almost all Linux operations can be carried out using either the GNOME or KDE interface. You can focus on the GNOME and KDE chapters and their corresponding tools and applications in the different chapters throughout the book. On the other hand, if you want to delve deeper into the Unix aspects of Linux, you can check out the shell chapters and the corresponding shell-based applications in other chapters. If you only want to use Linux for its Internet services, then concentrate on the Internet clients and servers. If you want to use Linux as a multiuser system servicing many users or integrate it into a local network, you can use the detailed system, file, and network administration information provided in the administration chapters. None of these tasks are in any way exclusive. If you are working in a business environment, you will probably make use of all three aspects. Single users may concentrate more on the desktops and the Internet features, whereas administrators may make more use of the security and networking features.

Section Topics

The first part of this book is designed to help you start using Fedora Core quickly. It provides an introduction to Fedora Core 4 and Red Hat Enterprise Linux along with a listing of Linux resources, including software repositories, documentation sites, newsgroups, and Linux news and development sites. The next chapter covers the streamlined installation procedure for most distributions takes about 30 minutes or less. The installation program from Red Hat provides excellent commentary, describing each step in detail. In this section you also learn the essentials of using both GNOME and KDE, along with the basic of working on the shell command line. System configuration tasks like adding printers and creating new user accounts are presented with the easiest methods, without much of the complex detail described in the administration chapters that is unnecessary for basic operations. Basic network configuration tasks are discussed such as setting up a LAN, DSL, or wireless connection to an Internet service provider (ISP). You also learn the basics of how to set up a small local network.

Part II of this book deals with environments. Here you are introduced to the different kinds of user environments available for Linux, starting with KDE and GNOME. Different features such as applets, the Panel, and configuration tools are described in detail. With either of these interfaces, you can run all your applications using icons, menus, and windows. At any time, you can open up a terminal window through which you can enter standard Linux commands on a command line. You can also choose to use just the standard Unix command line interface to run any of the standard Unix commands. Next the BASH shell and its various file, directory, and filter commands are examined.

Part III of this book discusses in detail the many office, multimedia, and Internet applications you can use on your Linux system, beginning with Office suites like OpenOffice and KOffice. The different database management systems available are also discussed, along with the Web site locations where you can download them. A variety of different text editors are also available, including several GNOME and KDE editors, as well as the Vim (enhanced Vi), gvim (graphical Vi), and GNU Emacs editors. Linux automatically installs mail, news, FTP, and Web browser applications, as well as FTP and Web servers. Both KDE and GNOME come with a full set of mail, news, and FTP clients, as well as Web browsers. There are also many independent mail clients, newsreaders, and Internet tools that you can easily install from your desktop.

Part IV demonstrates how to implement security precautions using encryption, authentication, and firewalls. Coverage of the GNU Privacy Guard (GPG) shows you how to implement public and private key-based encryption. SELinux provides comprehensive and refined control of all your network and system resources. IPsec tools let you use the IPsec protocol to encrypt and authentication network transmissions. Network security topics cover firewalls and encryption using netfilter (IPtables) to protect your system, the Secure Shell (SSH) to provide secure remote transmissions, and Kerberos to provide secure authentication.

Part V discusses Internet servers you can run on Fedora Core 4 and Red Hat Enterprise Linux, including FTP, Web, and DNS servers. Internet servers have become integrated components of most Linux systems. Both the standard vsftpd FTP server and the ProFTPD server are discussed. The Apache Web server chapter covers standard configuration directives like those for automatic indexing as well as the newer virtual host directives. Sendmail, Postfix, IMAP, and POP mail servers are covered. The INN news server, the CUPS print server, the MySQL database server, the Squid proxy server, and the ht:/Dig search server are also examined.

Part VI discusses system administration topics, including user, software, file system, system, device, and kernel administration. There are detailed descriptions of the configuration files used in administration tasks and how to make entries in them. First, basic system administration tasks are covered, such as selecting runlevels, monitoring your system, and scheduling shutdowns. Then aspects of setting up and controlling users and groups are discussed. Presentations include both the GUI tools you can use for these tasks and the underlying configurations files and commands. Software installation has been simplified with package management systems like the Red Hat Package Manager (RPM) and system-config-packages. Using, updating, and configuring the Linux kernel with its modules is covered in detail, along with procedures for installing new kernels. Different file system tasks are covered, such as mounting file systems, managing file systems with HAL and udev, and configuring RAID devices and LVM volumes. Device configuration has undergone a drastic change with the current version of Fedora Core. Devices are now automatically detected with udev and the Hardware Abstraction Layer (HAL). Fedora Core 4 has shifted to a hotplug model for managing all its devices. The udev utility will now automatically generate device interfaces, managing both fixed and removable devices using its own rules. HAL provides hotplug information about devices to applications, affording them direct access.

Part VII covers network administration, dealing with topics such as configuring remote file system access and setting up firewalls. Configuration files and features for the Domain Name System (DNS) and its BIND server are examined in detail, along with such features as virtual domains and IP aliases. IPv6 support for Internet addressing and DNS configuration is discussed in detail, showing the new IPv6 formats replacing the older IPv4 versions. You also learn how to implement your own IPv4 Dynamic Host Configuration Protocol (DHCP) server to dynamically assign hosts IP addresses, and you learn how IPv6 automatic addressing and renumbering operate. The various network file system interfaces and services such as NFS for Unix and NIS networks are presented, along with distributed network file systems like GFS. The chapter on Samba shows how to access Windows file systems and printers. Finally, an appendix covers what is available on the DVD-ROM included with this book.

Getting Started

CHAPTER

Introduction to Fedora Core and Red Hat Enterprise Linux

inux is an fast, stable, and open source operating system for PC computers and workstations that features professional-level Internet services, extensive development tools, fully functional graphical user interfaces (GUIs), and a massive number of applications ranging from office suites to multimedia applications. Linux was developed in the early 1990s by Linus Torvalds, along with other programmers around the world. As an operating system, Linux performs many of the same functions as Unix, Macintosh, Windows, and Windows NT. However, Linux is distinguished by its power and flexibility, along with being freely available. Most PC operating systems, such as Windows, began their development within the confines of small, restricted personal computers, which have only recently become more versatile machines. Such operating systems are constantly being upgraded to keep up with the ever-changing capabilities of PC hardware. Linux, on the other hand, was developed in a different context. Linux is a PC version of the Unix operating system that has been used for decades on mainframes and minicomputers and is currently the system of choice for network servers and workstations. Linux brings the speed, efficiency, scalability, and flexibility of Unix to your PC, taking advantage of all the capabilities that personal computers can now provide.

Technically, Linux consists of the operating system program, referred to as the *kernel*, which is the part originally developed by Linus Torvalds. But it has always been distributed with a massive number of software applications, ranging from network servers and security programs to office applications and development tools. Linux has evolved as part of the open source software movement, in which independent programmers joined together to provide free quality software to any user. Linux has become the premier platform for open source software, much of it developed by the Free Software Foundation's GNU project. Many of these applications are bundled as part of standard Linux distributions. Currently, thousands of open source applications are available for Linux from sites like the Open Source Development Network's (OSDN) **sourceforge.net**, the software depositories **rpmfind.net**, **rpm.livna.org**, **freshrpms.net**, KDE's **www.kde-apps.org**, and GNOME's **www.gnomefiles.org**.

Along with Linux's operating system capabilities come powerful networking features, including support for Internet, intranets, and Windows and Apple networking. As a norm, Linux distributions include fast, efficient, and stable Internet servers, such as the Web, FTP, and DNS servers, along with proxy, news, and mail servers. In other words, Linux has everything you need to set up, support, and maintain a fully functional network.

3

With both GNOME and K Desktop, Linux also provides GUI interfaces with that same level of flexibility and power. Unlike Windows and the Mac, Linux enables you to choose the interface you want and then customize it further, adding panels, applets, virtual desktops, and menus, all with full drag-and-drop capabilities and Internet-aware tools.

Linux does all this at the right price. Linux is free, including the network servers and GUI desktops. Unlike the official Unix operating system, Linux is distributed freely under a GNU General Public License as specified by the Free Software Foundation, making it available to anyone who wants to use it. GNU (the acronym stands for "GNU's Not Unix") is a project initiated and managed by the Free Software Foundation to provide free software to users, programmers, and developers. Linux is copyrighted, not public domain. However, a GNU public license has much the same effect as the software's being in the public domain. The GNU General Public License is designed to ensure Linux remains free and, at the same time, standardized. Linux is technically the operating system kernel—the core operations—and only one official Linux kernel exists. People sometimes have the mistaken impression that Linux is somehow less than a professional operating system because it is free. Linux is, in fact, a PC, workstation, and server version of Unix. Many consider it far more stable and much more powerful than Windows. This power and stability have made Linux an operating system of choice as a network server.

To appreciate Linux completely, you need to understand the special context in which the Unix operating system was developed. Unix, unlike most other operating systems, was developed in a research and academic environment. In universities, research laboratories, data centers, and enterprises, Unix is the system most often used. Its development has paralleled the entire computer and communications revolution over the past several decades. Computer professionals often developed new computer technologies on Unix, such as those developed for the Internet. Although a sophisticated system, Unix was designed from the beginning to be flexible. The Unix system itself can be easily modified to create different versions. In fact, many different vendors maintain different official versions of Unix. IBM, Sun, and Hewlett-Packard all sell and maintain their own versions of Unix. The unique demands of research programs often require that Unix be tailored to their own special needs. This inherent flexibility in the Unix design in no way detracts from its quality. In fact, this flexibility attests to the ruggedness of Unix, allowing it to adapt to practically any environment. This is the context in which Linux was developed. Linux is, in this sense, one other version of Unix—a version for the PC. The development of Linux by computer professionals working in a research-like environment reflects the way Unix versions have usually been developed. Linux is publicly licensed and free—and reflects the deep roots Unix has in academic institutions, with their sense of public service and support. Linux is a top-rate operating system accessible to everyone, free of charge.

As a way of introducing Linux, this chapter discusses Linux as an operating system, the history of Linux and Unix, the overall design of Linux, and Linux distributions. This chapter also discusses online resources for documentation, software, and newsgroups, plus Web sites with the latest news and articles on Linux. Web and FTP site listings are placed in tables for easy reference. Here you can find sites for different distributions, Linux publications, software repositories, and Linux development, as well as for office suites and commercial databases.

Red Hat Enterprise Linux and Fedora Core

Red Hat Enterprise Linux and Fedora Core are currently the most popular Linux distributions. As a company, Red Hat provides software and services to implement and support professional and commercial Linux systems. Red Hat has split its Linux development into two lines, Red Hat Enterprise Linux and the Fedora Project. Red Hat Enterprise Linux features commercial enterprise products for servers and workstations, with controlled releases issued every two years or so. The Fedora Project is an Open Source initiative whose Fedora Core release will be issued every six months on average, incorporating the most recent development in Linux operating system features as well as supported applications. Red Hat freely distributes its Fedora Core version of Linux under the GNU General Public License; the company generates income by providing professional-level support, consulting services, and training services. The Red Hat Certified Engineers (RHCE) training and certification program is designed to provided reliable and highly capable administrators and developers to maintain and customize professional-level Red Hat systems. Red Hat has forged software alliances with major companies like Oracle, IBM, Dell, and Sun.

Currently, Red Hat provides several commercial products, known as Red Hat Enterprise Linux. These include the Red Hat Enterprise Advanced Server for intensive enterprise-level tasks; Red Hat Enterprise ES, which is a version of Linux designed for small businesses and networks; and Red Hat Enterprise Workstation. Red Hat also maintains for its customers the Red Hat Network, which provides automatic updating of the operating system and software packages on your system. You can use the same Red Hat Network update tool to also automatically update Fedora Core Linux. Specialized products include the Stronghold secure Web server, versions of Linux tailored for IBM- and Itanium-based servers, and GNUPro development tools (**www.redhat.com/software/gnupro/**).

Red Hat also maintains a strong commitment to open source Linux applications. Red Hat originated the RPM package system used on several distributions, which automatically installs and removes software packages. Red Hat is also providing much of the software development for the GNOME desktop, and it is a strong supporter of KDE. GNOME and KDE are configured to appear the same, using a standardized interface called Bluecurve.

Red Hat provides an extensive set of configuration tools designed to manage tasks such as adding users, starting servers, accessing remote directories, and configuring devices such as your monitor or printer. These tools are accessible on the System Settings and Server Settings menus and windows, as well as by their names, all beginning with the term "system-config" (see Chapters 4 and 5). Of particular note is the new package management tool that lets you easily install or remove software packages, arranged in recognizable categories.

NOTE *Though Red Hat supports both the GNOME and KDE desktop interfaces, the Bluecurve interface provides the same look and feel for both desktops, integrating them into one visually similar interface, with menus, windows, and panels appearing approximately the same, though their underlying capabilities differ (see Chapters 6 and 7).*

The new release of Fedora Core and Red Hat Enterprise Linux features key updates to critical applications as well as new tools replacing former ones. Fedora Core and Red Hat Enterprise Linux include the GNOME desktop, the Apache Web server, the GNU Compiler Collection (GCC), and the GNU Java Compiler (GJC). Configuration tools, including system-config-packages for managing software and system-config-display for configuring your display hardware, have been added and others have been updated, system-config-networks, for instance, which now supports wireless networks. Fedora Core 4 and Red Hat Enterprise Linux 4 now install both the Postfix and Sendmail mail servers and let you seamlessly switch between them.

Installing Fedora Core and Red Hat Enterprise Linux has become a fairly simple process, using a graphical interface with each step displaying detailed explanations and advice. The Red Hat Enterprise Linux and Fedora Core distributions organize their installation to cater to several different uses, as a server, a workstation, and a personal desktop. The personal desktop option installs preselected software (such as office and multimedia applications) for home and personal use. It features a streamlined GNOME desktop interface. The workstation option installs desktop, office, development, and administration software. The server option installs all the standard servers, including the mail and FTP servers, along with default configurations and server administration tools. You can also elect to customize your installation, selecting your own mix of installed software.

The Fedora Core 4 distribution of Linux is available online at numerous FTP sites. The Fedora Project maintains its own FTP site at **fedora.redhat.com**, where you can download the entire current release of Fedora Core Linux, as well as updates and third-party software. Red Hat versions of Linux were designed from their inception to work on numerous hardware platforms. Currently, Red Hat Enterprise Linux supports the Sparc, Intel, and Alpha platforms. See **www.redhat.com** for more information, including extensive documentation such as Red Hat manuals, FAQs, and links to other Linux sites.

If you purchase Red Hat Enterprise Linux from Red Hat, you are entitled to online support services. Although Linux is free, Red Hat as a company specializes in support services, providing customers with its expertise in developing solutions to problems that may arise or using Linux to perform any of several possible tasks, such as e-commerce or database operations.

The Fedora Project

The Fedora Core release is maintained and developed by an Open Source project called the Fedora Project. The release consists entirely of open source software. Development is carried out using contributions from Linux developers, allowing them free rein to promote enhancements and new features. The project is designed to work much like other open source projects, with releases keeping pace with the course of rapid online development. The Fedora Core versions of Linux are entirely free. You can download the most current version, including betas, from **fedora.redhat.com**. You can update Fedora Core using the Red Hat Update Agent (RHN) to access the Fedora Core Yum repository. Updating can be supported by any one of several Fedora Core Yum repositories, which you can configure RHN to access in the **/etc/ sysconfig/ rhn/sources** configuration file. The Fedora Project release replaces the original standard Red Hat Linux version that consisted of the entry-level Red Hat release. In addition to the Fedora Core software, the Fedora Project will also provide popular compatible packages as part of the Fedora Extras and **rpm.livna.org** (see Table 1-2 later in this chapter).

Red Hat Enterprise Linux

The Red Hat Enterprise Linux line of products is designed for corporate, research, and business applications. These products focus on reliability and stability. They are released on a much more controlled schedule than the Fedora Project versions. What was once the low-cost consumer version of Red Hat Linux is replaced by a scaled-down commercial Enterprise version for consumers and small business. Red Hat offers three Enterprise versions, one for the workstation and two for servers. Red Hat Enterprise Linux AS provides the highest level of support from intense mission-critical requirements for all aspect of network support, including servers, databases, and security. Red Hat Enterprise Linux ES provides a similar package, but one geared to mid-level business requirements. The Red Hat Enterprise WS implements a workstation with a wide range of clients that can be used for either Red Hat Enterprise Linux ES or AS network.

Red Hat and Fedora Documentation

Red Hat maintains an extensive library of documentation for Red Hat Enterprise Linux as well as documentation for its older Red Hat 9 Linux. Much of the Red Hat 9 documentation is still applicable to Fedora. The documentation is freely accessible online (see Table 1-1). From the Red Hat home page, you can link to its support page, which lists the complete set of Red Hat manuals. These include the Reference Guide, the Getting Started Guide, and the Installation Guide. Tip, HOW-TO, and FAQ documents are also provided. All the Red Hat documentation is freely available under the GNU General Public License. Before installing Red Hat Enterprise Linux on your system, you may want to check the online Installation guide. This is a lengthy and detailed document that takes you through each step of the process carefully. Several dedicated Fedora Core support sites are also available to provide helpful tips and how-tos, including **fedoraforums.org**, **www.fedorafaq.org**, and **fedoranews.org**. **fedoraforums.org** is a Fedora Project–sponsored forum for end-user support. Here you can post questions and check responses for common problems. **www .fedorafaq.org** lists quick answers to some common issues like enabling MP3 support.

Fedora maintains some basic and specialized documentation, like information on understanding how udev is implemented or how SELinux is configured. For much of the documentation you will have to rely on installed documentation in **/usr/share/doc** or the man and info pages, as well as the context help button for different applications running on your desktop. Web sites for software like those for GNOME, KDE, and OpenOffice.org will provide extensive applicable documentation. On certain topics, like installation, there is no official Fedora Core documentation, though the Red Hat 9 and Enterprise installation documentation can be helpful.

Description	Reference
www.redhat.com	The Red Hat Web site
www.redhat.com/ support	The Support page for Red Hat Enterprise Linux, including links to current online documentation
fedora.redhat.com	The Fedora Project, current free open source releases
fedora.redhat.com/docs	Documentation and support tutorials for Fedora Core releases. Include FAQs for releases, specialized information like udev and SELinux.
Red Hat Reference Guide	The Red Hat Reference. **www.redhat.com/docs/manuals/linux/**
fedoraforum.org	End-user discussion support forum, endorsed by the Fedora Project. Includes FAQs and news links.
www.fedorafaq.org	Unofficial FAQ with quick help topics
fedoranews.org	Collects the latest news and developments on Fedora, as well as articles and blogs about recent changes.

TABLE 1-1   Red Hat Linux Resources

Fedora Core 4

Fedora Core 4 provides several important features. It includes the latest 2.6 kernel. Following on Fedora Core 3, there is a major change in how devices are handled by the operating system. Device interfaces are generated only for devices attached to the system, with interfaces for removable devices dynamically created as needed. For the kernel, there are both x86 (32 bit) and x86_64 (64 bit) versions, as well as Apple computer versions (PPC).

- Fedora Core 4 features automatic detection of removable devices like USB printers, digital cameras, and card readers.

- CD/DVD discs are treated as removable devices, automatically displayed and accessed when inserted.

- GNOME now supports GUI access to all removable devices and shared directories on networked hosts, including Windows folders.

- Fedora Core 4 also provides full IPv6 network protocol support, including automatic addressing and renumbering.

- SELinux is now a integral component of Fedora Core, providing system-wide security. You can set different levels of control and create your own policies.

- A wide range of multimedia applications are included, such as a video player and TV viewer, along with compatible support from various multimedia applications and libraries available from **freshrpms.net**, such as DVD and DivX support.

- With the Network Monitor, you can automatically select wireless connections.

- Information about hotplugged devices is provided to applications with the Hardware Abstraction Layer (HAL) from **freedesktop.org**. This allows applications like GNOME to easily display and manage removable devices.

- All devices are now treated logically as removable, and automatically configured by udev. Fixed devices are simply ones that cannot be removed. This feature is meant to let Linux accommodate the wide variety of devices now becoming available, such as digital cameras, USB printers, and cell phones.

- Hard disk partitions can now be implemented with the Logical Volume Manager (LVM), letting you manage your storage more easily (default for Desktop and Workstation installations). You can manage LVM volumes with system-config-lvm.

- RAID interfaces with BIOS-level drivers (fake RAID) found on most PC motherboards are now detected and supported, though you can use Linux's own software RAID to better effect.

- The Red Hat Update Agent can be used to automatically update your Fedora Core system and all its installed applications, from the Yum Fedora Core online repositories. You do not have to subscribe to the Red Hat Network.

- The office suite Office.org provides very effective office applications, featuring support for document storage standards. Evince universal document viewer displays various formats.

- CodeWeavers CrossOver Office runs Windows applications, including Office, directly in Linux windows.

- All IDE DVD/CD+-R/RW drives are now directly supported (SCSI emulation is no longer needed).

- Internet Security Protocol (IPsec) tools are now available.

- To configure the kernel, you can now use the qconf configuration tool (xconfig), which provides an effective GUI interface.

- Kernel headers, used for module source and application compilation and development, are now included with the kernel binaries and installed at **/usr/src/kernels**. The full kernel source no longer needs to be installed.

- The Fedora Core kernel source SRPM packages are now extracted to the Red Hat Build directories in **/usr/src/redhat**. The **/usr/src/linux** directory is no longer used for the kernel source. Original kernel sources in normal archives (tar) should be extracted in a user directory.

- The Xen Virtualization kernel is also provided, which allows the use of virtual machines on which you can run different operating systems adapted for use on Xen. You can also use the virtual machines to run different instances of the kernel, allowing developers and users to run and test new software without endangering the primary system.

- Fedora Core continues to refine the desktop interface, providing the latest versions of both GNOME and KDE. GNOME now uses the Clearlooks theme, based on Bluecurve.

- Updated versions of all network servers are provided, including the Apache Web server, the vsftp FTP server, the BIND DNS server, and the Samba server.

- Fedora Core has a complete range of system and network administration tools featuring easy-to-use GUI interfaces (see Chapter 4, Table 4-1).

- InfiniBand high-speed connections are now supported by the kernel. Currently used for local clusters and supercomputers, they provide transmissions at 10 gigabits per second and can go much higher.

- For software development, Fedora Core now includes the Eclipse IDE software tool.

- The Global File System (GFS) cluster file system with supporting kernel (see Chapter 40).

Fedora Core 4 Warnings

With every release certain procedures and software applications need special attention. Warnings are noted in the Release Notes located on the distribution DVD or CD-ROM, as well as on the Fedora Core Web site (**fedora.redhat.com**). With Fedora Core 4, several issues need special attention.

- Install problems may occur with LCD displays, Sony VAIO laptops, serial mice, and Ximian GNOME. Also keep in mind that the graphical install requires 128MB of memory.

- OpenSSH has a more restrictive configuration.

- The kernel source is no longer included with the distribution binaries. You have to download it separately. It no longer uses **/usr/src/linux**, but the RPM **BUILD** and **SPEC** directories in **/usr/src/redhat**. You need to specify which version of the kernel to extract (see Chapter 35).

- You can compile modules using kernel headers in the **/lib/modules/***version***/build** directory (now a link to kernel headers in the **/usr/src/kernels** directory, **source** is now a link to build).

- There is a new version of PHP with some syntax changes.

- Samba browsing of Windows shares from Gnome Nautilus file manager is prevented if your firewall is enabled and you have no Wins server set up (see Chapter 41).

- The new version of Netatalk, for accessing Macintosh systems, uses new storage methods than can result in data loss when upgrading.

- Fedora Core 4, like Fedora Core 3, now uses the X.org X Windows server instead of XFree86. Configuration and server names are different from XFree86, for instance, the **xorg.conf** configuration file and xorg server. Configuration files are still located in **/etc/X11**.

- As in recent releases, there are two Font subsystems, the older X font and the newer fontconfig. The fontconfig system supports antialiasing and will replace Xfont. The method for adding fonts is different for each system.

- Fedora Core 4 release notes now include a category for packages moved to Fedora Extras.

- The Java RPM packages from Sun have conflicts with Fedora Core 4. You should download Java packages from **jpackage.org** instead.

Operating Systems and Linux

An *operating system* is a program that manages computer hardware and software for the user. Operating systems were originally designed to perform repetitive hardware tasks, which centered around managing files, running programs, and receiving commands from the user. You interact with an operating system through a *user interface,* which allows the operating system to receive and interpret instructions sent by the user. You only need to send an instruction to the operating system to perform a task, such as reading a file or printing a document. An operating system's user interface can be as simple as entering commands on a line or as complex as selecting menus and icons on a desktop.

An operating system also manages software applications. To perform different tasks, such as editing documents or performing calculations, you need specific software applications. An *editor* is an example of a software application that enables you to edit a document, making changes and adding new text. The editor itself is a program consisting of instructions to be executed by the computer. For the program to be used, it must first be loaded into computer memory, and then its instructions are executed. The operating system controls the loading and execution of all programs, including any software applications. When you want to use an editor, simply instruct the operating system to load the editor application and execute it.

File management, program management, and user interaction are traditional features common to all operating systems. Linux, like all versions of Unix, adds two more features. Linux is a multiuser and multitasking system. As it is a *multitasking* system, you can ask the system to perform several tasks at the same time. While one task is being done, you can work on another. For example, you can edit a file while another file is being printed. You do not have to wait for the other file to finish printing before you edit. As it is a *multiuser* system, several users can log in to the system at the same time, each interacting with the system through his or her own terminal.

As a version of Unix, Linux shares that system's flexibility, a flexibility stemming from Unix's research origins. Developed by Ken Thompson at AT&T Bell Laboratories in the late 1960s and early 1970s, the Unix system incorporated many new developments in operating system design. Originally, Unix was designed as an operating system for researchers. One major goal was to create a system that could support the researchers' changing demands. To do this, Thompson had to design a system that could deal with many different kinds of tasks. Flexibility became more important than hardware efficiency. Like Unix, Linux has the advantage of being able to deal with the variety of tasks any user may face. The user is not confined to limited and rigid interactions with the operating system. Instead, the operating system is thought of as making a set of highly effective tools available to the user. This user-oriented philosophy means you can configure and program the system to meet your specific needs. With Linux, the operating system becomes an operating environment.

History of Linux and Unix

As a version of Unix, the history of Linux naturally begins with Unix. The story begins in the late 1960s, when a concerted effort to develop new operating system techniques occurred. In 1968, a consortium of researchers from General Electric, AT&T Bell Laboratories, and the Massachusetts Institute of Technology carried out a special operating system research project called MULTICS (the Multiplexed Information and Computing Service). MULTICS incorporated many new concepts in multitasking, file management, and user interaction.

Unix

In 1969, Ken Thompson, Dennis Ritchie, and the researchers at AT&T Bell Laboratories developed the Unix operating system, incorporating many of the features of the MULTICS research project. They tailored the system for the needs of a research environment, designing it to run on minicomputers. From its inception, Unix was an affordable and efficient multiuser and multitasking operating system.

The Unix system became popular at Bell Labs as more and more researchers started using the system. In 1973, Dennis Ritchie collaborated with Ken Thompson to rewrite the programming code for the Unix system in the C programming language. Unix gradually grew from one person's tailored design to a standard software product distributed by many different vendors, such as Novell and IBM. Initially, Unix was treated as a research product. The first versions of Unix were distributed free to the computer science departments of many noted universities. Throughout the 1970s, Bell Labs began issuing official versions of Unix and licensing the systems to different users. One of these users was the Computer Science department of the University of California, Berkeley. Berkeley added many new features to the system that later became standard. In 1975, Berkeley released its own version of Unix, known by its distribution arm, Berkeley Software Distribution (BSD). This BSD version of Unix became a major contender to the AT&T Bell Labs version. AT&T developed several research versions of Unix, and in 1983, it released the first commercial version, called System 3. This was later followed by System V, which became a supported commercial software product.

At the same time, the BSD version of Unix was developing through several releases. In the late 1970s, BSD Unix became the basis of a research project by the Department of

Defense's Advanced Research Projects Agency (DARPA). As a result, in 1983, Berkeley released a powerful version of Unix called BSD release 4.2. This release included sophisticated file management as well as networking features based on Internet network protocols—the same protocols now used for the Internet. BSD release 4.2 was widely distributed and adopted by many vendors, such as Sun Microsystems.

In the mid-1980s, two competing standards emerged, one based on the AT&T version of Unix and the other based on the BSD version. AT&T's Unix System Laboratories developed System V release 4. Several other companies, such as IBM and Hewlett-Packard, established the Open Software Foundation (OSF) to create their own standard version of Unix. Two commercial standard versions of Unix existed then—the OSF version and System V release 4.

Linux

Originally designed specifically for Intel-based personal computers, Linux started out as a personal project of a computer science student named Linus Torvalds at the University of Helsinki. At that time, students were making use of a program called *Minix*, which highlighted different Unix features. Minix was created by Professor Andrew Tanenbaum and widely distributed over the Internet to students around the world. Linus's intention was to create an effective PC version of Unix for Minix users. It was named Linux, and in 1991, Linus released version 0.11. Linux was widely distributed over the Internet, and in the following years, other programmers refined and added to it, incorporating most of the applications and features now found in standard Unix systems. All the major window managers have been ported to Linux. Linux has all the networking tools, such as FTP file transfer support, Web browsers, and the whole range of network services such as e-mail, the domain name service, and dynamic host configuration, along with FTP, Web, and print servers. It also has a full set of program development utilities, such as C++ compilers and debuggers. Given all its features, the Linux operating system remains small, stable, and fast. In its simplest format, Linux can run effectively on only 2MB of memory. Linux development is now supported by Open Source Labs (OSDL) at **www.osld.org**.

Although Linux has developed in the free and open environment of the Internet, it adheres to official Unix standards. Because of the proliferation of Unix versions in the previous decades, the Institute of Electrical and Electronics Engineers (IEEE) developed an independent Unix standard for the American National Standards Institute (ANSI). This new ANSI-standard Unix is called the Portable Operating System Interface for Computer Environments (POSIX). The standard defines how a Unix-like system needs to operate, specifying details such as system calls and interfaces. POSIX defines a universal standard to which all Unix versions must adhere. Most popular versions of Unix are now POSIX-compliant. Linux was developed from the beginning according to the POSIX standard. Linux also adheres to the Linux file system hierarchy standard (FHS), which specifies the location of files and directories in the Linux file structure. See **www.pathname.com/fhs** for more details.

Linux Overview

Like Unix, Linux can be generally divided into three major components: the kernel, the environment, and the file structure. The *kernel* is the core program that runs programs and manages hardware devices, such as disks and printers. The *environment* provides an interface for the user. It receives commands from the user and sends those commands to the kernel for execution. The *file structure* organizes the way files are stored on a storage device, such as a disk. Files are organized into directories. Each directory may contain any number of subdirectories, each holding files. Together, the kernel, the environment, and the file structure form the basic operating system structure. With these three, you can run programs, manage files, and interact with the system.

An environment provides an interface between the kernel and the user. It can be described as an interpreter. Such an interface interprets commands entered by the user and sends them to the kernel. Linux provides several kinds of environments: desktops, window managers, and command line shells. Each user on a Linux system has his or her own user interface. Users can tailor their environments to their own special needs, whether they be shells, window managers, or desktops. In this sense, for the user, the operating system functions more as an operating environment, which the user can control.

In Linux, files are organized into directories, much as they are in Windows. The entire Linux file system is one large interconnected set of directories, each containing files. Some directories are standard directories reserved for system use. You can create your own directories for your own files, as well as easily move files from one directory to another. You can even move entire directories, and share directories and files with other users on your system. With Linux, you can also set permissions on directories and files, allowing others to access them or restricting access to yourself alone. The directories of each user are, in fact, ultimately connected to the directories of other users. Directories are organized into a hierarchical tree structure, beginning with an initial root directory. All other directories are ultimately derived from this first root directory.

With the K Desktop Environment (KDE) and the GNU Network Object Model Environment (GNOME), Linux now has a completely integrated GUI interface. You can perform all your Linux operations entirely from either interface. KDE and GNOME are fully operational desktops supporting drag-and-drop operations, enabling you to drag icons to your desktop and to set up your own menus on an Applications panel. Both rely on an underlying X Window System, which means as long as they are both installed on your system, applications from one can run on the other desktop. The GNOME and KDE sites are particularly helpful for documentation, news, and software you can download for those desktops. Both desktops can run any X Window System program, as well as any cursor-based program such as Emacs and Vi, which were designed to work in a shell environment. At the same time, a great many applications are written just for those desktops and included with your distributions. The K Desktop has a complete set of Internet tools, along with editors and graphic, multimedia, and system applications. GNOME has slightly fewer applications, but a great many are currently in the works. Check their Web sites at **www.gnome.org** and **www.kde.org** for new applications. As new versions are released, they include new software.

Open Source Software

Linux was developed as a cooperative Open Source effort over the Internet, so no company or institution controls Linux. Software developed for Linux reflects this background. Development often takes place when Linux users decide to work on a project together. The software is posted at an Internet site, and any Linux user can then access the site and download the software. Linux software development has always operated in an Internet environment and is global in scope, enlisting programmers from around the world. The only thing you need to start a Linux-based software project is a Web site.

Most Linux software is developed as Open Source software. This means that the source code for an application is freely distributed along with the application. Programmers over the Internet can make their own contributions to a software package's development, modifying and correcting the source code. Linux is an open source operating system. Its source code is included in all its distributions and is freely available on the Internet. Many major software development efforts are also open source projects, as are the KDE and GNOME desktops along with most of their applications. The Netscape Communicator Web browser package has also become open source, with its source code freely available. The OpenOffice office suite supported by Sun is an open source project based on the StarOffice office suite (StarOffice is essentially Sun's commercial version of OpenOffice). Many of the open source applications that run on Linux have located their Web sites at SourceForge (**sourceforge.net**), which is a hosting site designed specifically to support open source projects. You can find more information about the Open Source movement at **www .opensource.org**.

Open source software is protected by public licenses. These prevent commercial companies from taking control of open source software by adding a few modifications of their own, copyrighting those changes, and selling the software as their own product. The most popular public license is the GNU General Public License provided by the Free Software Foundation. This is the license that Linux is distributed under. The GNU General Public License retains the copyright, freely licensing the software with the requirement that the software and any modifications made to it always be freely available. Other public licenses have also been created to support the demands of different kinds of open source projects. The GNU Lesser General Public License (LGPL) lets commercial applications use GNU licensed software libraries. The Qt Public License (QPL) lets open source developers use the Qt libraries essential to the KDE desktop. You can find a complete listing at **www .opensource.org**.

Linux is currently copyrighted under a GNU public license provided by the Free Software Foundation, and it is often referred to as GNU software (see **www.gnu.org**). GNU software is distributed free, provided it is freely distributed to others. GNU software has proved both reliable and effective. Many of the popular Linux utilities, such as C compilers, shells, and editors, are GNU software applications. Installed with your Linux distribution are the GNU C++ and Lisp compilers, Vi and Emacs editors, BASH and TCSH shells, as well as TeX and Ghostscript document formatters. In addition, there are many open source software projects that are licensed under the GNU General Public License (GPL). Many of these software applications are available at different Internet sites, and these are listed in Table 1-4 later in this chapter. Chapter 4 and Chapter 31 describe in detail the process of downloading software applications from Internet sites and installing them on your system.

Under the terms of the GNU General Public License, the original author retains the copyright, although anyone can modify the software and redistribute it, provided the source code is included, made public, and provided free. Also, no restriction exists on selling the software or giving it away free. One distributor could charge for the software, while another one could provide it free of charge. Major software companies are also providing Linux versions of their most popular applications. A Linux port of Sun's Java Software Development Kit (SDK) is also available through **www.blackdown.org**, though Sun now supports Linux versions directly. Oracle provides a Linux version of its Oracle database. (At present, no plans seem in the works for Microsoft applications.)

Linux Software

A great deal of Linux software is currently available from online sources. You can download applications for desktops, Internet servers, office suites, and programming packages, among others.

Software packages are distributed in compressed archives or in RPM packages. RPM packages are those archived using the Red Hat Package Manager. Compressed archives have an extension such as .tar.gz or .tar.Z, whereas RPM packages have an .rpm extension. Any RPM package that you download directly, from whatever site, can be installed easily with the click of a button using the system-config-packages tool on either the GNOME or KDE desktop. You could also download the source version and compile it directly on your system. This has become a simple process, almost as simple as installing the compiled RPM versions. Red Hat also has a large number of mirror sites from which you can download their software packages for current releases. Most Linux Internet sites that provide extensive software archives have mirror sites, such as **www.kernel.org**, that hold the new Linux kernels. If you have trouble connecting to a main FTP site, try one of its mirrors.

Fedora Core Software Repositories

For Fedora Core 4, you can update to the latest Red Hat RPM package versions of software from their Fedora Core Yum repository using the Red Hat Update Agent (see Chapter 4). For Red Hat Enterprise Linux, you can automatically download upgrades for your system using the Red Hat Network. Updates for Red Hat Enterprise Linux are handled directly by Red Hat, whereas updates for Fedora Core use Fedora Core Yum software repositories. Your Update Agent is already configured to access the standard repositories.

The Fedora Core 4 distribution provides a core selection of software ranging from office and multimedia applications to Internet servers and administration services (see Table 1-2). Many popular applications are not included, though Fedora-compliant versions are provided on associated software sites. You can obtain many popular software packages not in the core, such as BitTorrent, from the Fedora Extras repository. This is the **extra** directory located on the official Fedora Core repository and its mirrors (the **core** directory holds the Fedora Core releases). Fedora Core also provides several official repositories that are used for open source projects at **sources.redhat.com**. Due to licensing restrictions, multimedia support for popular operations like MP3, DVD, and DivX is not included with Fedora Core distributions. A Fedora Core project–associated site, **rpm.livna.org/fedora**, does provided support for these functions. Here you can download support for MP3, DVD, and DivX software. Any software you do not find here can usually be found at **freshrpms.net**, which maintains a repository for Fedora Core–compliant multimedia software. Also, again due to licensing restriction, Fedora Core does not provide support for the NTFS file system, the file system used for Windows XP, NT, and 2000 systems. There is a kernel module for Fedora Core that will give you NTFS file system access, but you need to download it separately, from **rpm .livna.org/fedora**. See Chapter 4 on how to install this support.

---

*TIP   As noted in Chapters 4 and 31, if you are downloading a large ISO image such as a DVD or CD-ROM image for Fedora Core 4, you may want to use BitTorrent. This is one of the fastest and most reliable ways to download very large files, along with **download.fedora.redhat.com**.*

Linux Software Repositories

Several centralized repositories make it easy to locate an application and find information about it. Of particular note are **sourceforge.net**, **www.gnu.org**, **rpmfind.net**, **freshrpms.net**, **www.gnomefiles.org**, and **www.kde-apps.org**. The following tables list different sites for Linux software. Repositories and archives for Linux software are listed in Table 1-3, along

URL	Internet Site
fedora.redhat.com/download	Download page for the latest Fedora Core releases
download.fedora.redhat.com/ pub/fedora/linux/core	Download site for Fedora Core releases
download.fedora.redhat.com/ pub/fedora/linux/extras	Download site for Fedora Core–compliant software not included with the official distribution
download.fedora.redhat.com/ pub/fedora/linux/core/updates	Fedora Core Yum repository for Fedora Core updates, with released and testing versions
linux.duke.edu/projects/yum	Yellowdog Updater, Modified (Yum) update tool, with listings of Yum repositories for updating Fedora Core Linux
moin.conectiva.com.br/AptRpm	APT-RPM Fedora Core repository for APT-enabled RPM packages (see Chapter 4)
rpm.livna.org/fedora	Fedora Core applications not included with the distribution due to licensing and other restrictions. Includes multimedia and NTFS support. This is an official extension of the Fedora Project.
www.freshrpms.net	Linux multimedia applications and support libraries. Specifically lists Fedora-version RPM packages.
sources.redhat.com	Open source software hosted by Red Hat
torrent.dulug.duke.edu	Fedora Core BitTorrent site for BitTorrent downloads of Fedora Core distribution ISO images

TABLE 1-2   Fedora Core and Red Hat Enterprise Linux Repositories

with several specialized sites, such as those for commercial and game software. When downloading software packages, always check to see if versions are packaged for your particular distribution. For example, **rpmfind.net**, **freshmeat.net**, and **sourceforge.net** are also good places for locating RPM packages.

Linux Office and Database Software

Many professional-level databases and office suites are now available for Linux. These include Oracle and IBM databases as well as the OpenOffice and K Office suites. Table 1-4 lists sites for office suites and databases. Many of these sites provide free personal versions of their software for Linux, and others are entirely free. You can download from them directly and install on your Linux system.

Internet Servers

One of the most important features of Linux, as of all Unix systems, is its set of Internet clients and servers. The Internet was designed and developed on Unix systems, and Internet clients and servers, such as those for FTP and the Web, were first implemented on BSD versions of Unix. DARPANET, the precursor to the Internet, was set up to link Unix systems at different universities across the nation. Linux contains a full set of Internet clients and servers, including mail, news, FTP, and Web, as well as proxy clients and servers. Sites for

URL	Internet Site
sourceforge.net	SourceForge, open source software development sites for Linux applications and software repository
www.freshrpms.net	Linux multimedia applications and support libraries
www.gnomefiles.org	GNOME applications
www.kde-apps.org	KDE software repository
freshmeat.net	New Linux software
www.linuxlinks.org	Linux links
filewatcher.com	Linux FTP site watcher
www.tldp.org/links.html	Linux links
rpmfind.net	RPM package repository
www.gnu.org	GNU archive
www.opensound.com	Open sound system drivers
www.blackdown.org	Web site for Linux Java
www.happypenguin.org	Linux Game Tome
www.linuxgames.com	Linux games

TABLE 1-3   Linux Software Archives, Repositories, and Links

Internet server software available for Linux are listed in Table 1-5. Most of these are already included on the Fedora Core 4 DVD-ROM included with this book; however, you can obtain news, documentation, and recent releases directly from the server's Web sites.

URL	Software
Database Software	
www.oracle.com	Oracle database
www.sybase.com	Sybase database
www.software.ibm.com/data/db2/linux	IBM DB2 database
www.mysql.com	MySQL database
www.ispras.ru/~kml/gss	GNU SQL database
www.postgresql.org	PostgreSQL database
www.fship.com/free.html	FlagShip (interface for xBase database files)
Office Software	
www.openoffice.org	OpenOffice
koffice.kde.org	KOffice
www.sun.com/star/staroffice	StarOffice
www.gnomefiles.org	GNOME Office and Productivity applications

TABLE 1-4   Database and Office Software

URL	Server
www.apache.org	Apache Web server
vsftpd.beasts.org	Very Secure FTP server
www.proftpd.org	ProFTPD FTP server
www.isc.org	Internet Software Consortium: BIND, INN, and DHCPD
www.sendmail.org	Sendmail mail server
www.postfix.org	Postfix mail server
www.squid.org	Squid proxy server
www.samba.org	Samba SMB (Windows network) server
www.netfilter.org	IP Tables firewall
web.mit.edu/kerberos/www	Kerberos network authentication protocol
www.openssh.com	Open Secure Shell (free version of SSH)

TABLE 1-5   Network Servers and Security

Development Resources

Linux has always provided strong support for programming languages and tools. All distributions include the GNU C and C++ compiler (gcc) with supporting tools such as make. Most distributions come with full development support for the KDE and GNOME desktops, letting you create your own GNOME and KDE applications. You can also download the Linux version of the Java Software Development Kit for creating Java programs. Perl and Tcl/Tk versions of Linux are also included with most distributions. You can download current versions from their Web sites. Table 1-6 lists different sites of interest for Linux programming.

URL	Internet Site
www.gnu.org	Linux compilers and tools (gcc)
www.tcl.tk	Tcl Developer Xchange, Tcl/Tk products
java.sun.com	Sun Java Web site
www.perl.com	Perl Web site with Perl software
developer.gnome.org	GNOME developer's Web site
developer.kde.org	Developer's library for KDE

TABLE 1-6   Linux Programming

Online Information Sources

Extensive online resources are available on almost any Linux topic. The tables in this chapter list sites where you can obtain software, display documentation, and read articles on the latest developments. Many Linux Web sites provide news, articles, and information about Linux. Several, such as **www.linuxjournal.com** and **www.linuxgazette.com**, are based on popular Linux magazines. Others, such as **www.linux.com**, **www.linuxworld .com**, and **www.linux.org**, operate as Web portals for Linux. Some specialize in particular area, such as **linuxheadquarters.com** for guides on Linux software and **www.linuxgames .com** for the latest games ported for Linux. Currently, many Linux Web sites provide news, information, and articles on Linux developments, as well as documentation, software links, and other resources. These are listed in Table 1-7.

URL	Internet Site
www.tldp.org	Web site for the Linux Documentation Project
www.lwn.net	Linux Weekly News
www.linux.com	Linux.com
www.linuxtoday.com	Linux Today
www.linuxplanet.com	Linux Planet
www.linuxfocus.org	Linux Focus
www.linuxworld.com	Linux World
www.linuxjournal.com	Linux Journal
www.linuxgazette.com	Linux Gazette
www.linuxmagazine.com	Linux Magazine
www.linux.org	Linux Online
www.li.org	Linux International Web site
www.linux.org.uk	Linux European Web site
linuxheadquarters.com	Linux guides and software
slashdot.org	Linux forum
www.opensource.org	Open source information
limestone.uoregon.edu/woven	Woven goods documentation for Linux
fedoranews.org	Latest developments for Fedora Project

TABLE 1-7   Linux Information and News Sites

Documentation

Linux documentation has also been developed over the Internet. Much of the documentation currently available for Linux can be downloaded from Internet FTP sites. A special Linux project called the Linux Documentation Project (LDP), headed by Matt Welsh, has developed a complete set of Linux manuals. The documentation is available at the LDP home site at **www.tldp.org**. Linux documents provided by the LDP are listed in Table 1-8, along with their Internet sites.

Most of the standard Linux software and documentation currently available is already included on your Fedora Core 4 DVD-ROM. HOW-TO documents are all accessible in HTML format, so you can view them easily with your Web browser. In the future, though, you may need to access Linux Internet sites directly for current information and software.

An extensive number of mirrors are maintained for the Linux Documentation Project. You can link to any of them through a variety of sources, such as the LDP home site, **www .tldp.org**, and **www.linuxjournal.org**. The documentation includes a user's guide, an introduction, and administration guides. These are available in text, PostScript, or Web page format. Table 1-8 lists these guides. You can also find briefer explanations, in what are referred to as HOW-TO documents.

Distribution Web sites, such as **www.redhat.com** and **fedora.redhat.com**, provide extensive Linux documentation and software. The **www.gnome.org** site holds documentation for the GNOME desktop, while **www.kde.org** holds documentation for the KDE desktop. The tables in this chapter list many of the available sites. You can find other sites through resource pages that hold links to other Web sites—for example, the Linux Web site on the World Wide Web at **www.tldp.org/links.html**.

Site	Web Site
www.tldp.org	LDP Web site
Guide	**Document Format**
Linux Installation and Getting Started Guide	DVI, PostScript, LaTeX, PDF, and HTML
Linux User's Guide	DVI, PostScript, HTML, LaTeX, and PDF
Linux System Administrator's Guide	PostScript, PDF, LaTeX, and HTML
Linux Network Administrator's Guide	DVI, PostScript, PDF, and HTML
Linux Programmer's Guide	DVI, PostScript, PDF, LaTeX, and HTML
The Linux Kernel	HTML, LaTeX, DVI, and PostScript
Linux Kernel Hacker's Guide	DVI, PostScript, and HTML
Linux HOWTOs	HTML, PostScript, SGML, and DVI
Linux FAQs	HTML, PostScript, and DVI
Linux Man Pages	Man page format

TABLE 1-8   Linux Documentation Project

In addition to Web sites, Linux Usenet newsgroups are also available. Through your Internet connection, you can access Linux newsgroups to read the comments of other Linux users and to post messages of your own. Several Linux newsgroups exist, each beginning with **comp.os.linux**. One of particular interest to the beginner is **comp.os.linux.help**, where you can post questions. Table 1-9 lists some of the Usenet Linux newsgroups you can check out, particularly for posting questions.

Newsgroup	Title
comp.os.linux.announce	Announcements of Linux developments
comp.os.linux.development.apps	For programmers developing Linux applications
comp.os.linux.development.system	For programmers working on the Linux operating system
comp.os.linux.hardware	Linux hardware specifications
comp.os.linux.admin	System administration questions
comp.os.linux.misc	Special questions and issues
comp.os.linux.setup	Installation problems
comp.os.linux.answers	Answers to command problems
comp.os.linux.help	Questions and answers for particular problems
comp.os.linux.networking	Linux network questions and issues
linux.dev.group	Numerous development newsgroups beginning with **linux.dev**, such as **linux.dev.admin** and **linux.dev.doc**

TABLE 1-9   Usenet Newsgroups

Installing Fedora Core 4 and Red Hat Enterprise Linux

This chapter describes the installation procedure for Fedora Core 4 Linux. The installation includes the Linux operating system, a great many Linux applications, and a complete set of network servers. Red Hat Enterprise Linux and Fedora Core use the same Anaconda installation program; it is designed to be easy to use and helpful, while at the same time efficient and brief, installing as many services and applications as possible. Detailed help panels explain each procedure, every step of the way. Certain services, such as Web server support, would ordinarily require specialized and often complex configuration operations. Red Hat Enterprise Linux and Fedora Core automatically install and provide default configurations for many of these services. A Fedora Core 4 Installation Guide is also available online.

Obtaining the CDs and DVDs

The preferred method for obtaining Fedora Core 4 is to download them from a Fedora Core mirror site. Red Hat Enterprise Linux is a commercial product whose discs Red Hat will send you. Updates can be downloaded from the Red Hat Network, now a commercial service.

A detailed description for all the Fedora download options, including all the ISO discs you will need and links to mirror sites, is available at

```
fedora.redhat.com/download
```

Check this site for the latest download procedures.
You can download directly from the Fedora download site at

```
download.fedora.redhat.com
```

The connection can be very fast with broadband DSL or cable, using an FTP client like **gFTP** (Applications | Internet menu). Web-client download with browsers like Firefox tend to be slower.

To download Fedora Core 4 for installation from a DVD/CD-ROM drive, you download the CD or DVD ISO images. These are very large files that reside in the **iso** directory on the download site and have the extension **.iso**. Once they are downloaded, you burn them to a disc using your CD or DVD writer and burner software, like **K3b** on Fedora Core (Applications | Sound & Video menu).

There are ISO images for 64-bit system support and for the standard x86 (32-bit) support. Download the appropriate one. You cannot run a 64-bit version on a x86 (32-bit) system.

You do not have to download the images to a Linux system. You can just as easily download them on a Windows system and use Windows CD/DVD burner software to make the discs.

Though you can use any FTP or Web client, such as gftp or Firefox, to download the image files, these are very large files that can take a long time to download, especially if the FTP site is very busy or if your have a slow Internet connection. The preferred alternative for such very large files is to use BitTorrent. BitTorrent is a safe distributed download operation that is ideal for large files, letting many participants download and upload the same file, building a torrent that can run very fast for all participants (three hours for a DVD binary at broadband speed). The Fedora Core 4 BitTorrent files are located at

```
torrent.linux.duke.edu
```

You will first need to install the BitTorrent client, which you can obtain from either **www .bittorrent.com** or from the Fedora Extras repository at **download.fedora.redhat.com/pub/ fedora/linux/extras**. The Fedora Extras repository splits the BitTorrent software into two packages, the bitTorrent client and its GUI interface. The most recent version will be available at the BitTorrent site, which includes all software including GUI in one distribution independent version (notice that bittorrent has two 't's and two 'r's in its spelling). See Chapter 31 for details about installing and using BitTorrent.

Installation Overview

Installing Linux involves several steps. First, you need to determine whether your computer meets the basic hardware requirements. These days, most Intel-based PC computers do. The Fedora Core 4 Installation Guide is now available at **fedora.redhat.com/docs/fedora-installguide-en/fc4/**. Check this guide before installing Fedora Core 4. It provides detailed screen examples and is geared to the x86 version (same as the DVD in this book). For Red Hat Enterprise Linux, you can use the Official Red Hat Linux x86 Installation Guide at **www.redhat.com**, on the documentation page, selecting Red Hat Enterprise Linux.

Install Sources

Red Hat supports several methods for installing Linux. You can install from a local source such as a CD-ROM or a hard disk, or from a network or Internet source. For a network or Internet source, Red Hat supports NFS, FTP, and HTTP installations. With FTP, you can install from an FTP site. With HTTP, you can install from a Web site. NFS enables you to install over a local network. For a local source, you can install from a CD-ROM or a hard disk. The DVD-ROM included with this book also operates as a boot CD-ROM. In addition, you can start the installation process by booting from your DVD-ROM, from a DOS system, or from boot disks that can then use the DVD-ROM or hard disk repository. Red Hat documentation covers each of these methods in detail. This chapter deals with the installation using the DVD-ROM provided with this book.

To select an install source, you will need to first boot the install kernel, either from a Fedora Core 4 CD or DVD disc, or from a Fedora Core CD boot image disc (you can also use VFAT USB disks and PXE servers). At the boot prompt you enter the option **linux askmethod**, as shown here:

```
boot: linux askmethod
```

Install Configurations

Fedora Core 4 currently supports three preselection install configurations: desktop, workstation, and server. They differ in the partition they will set up by default and the group of packages they will install. The desktop installs a small selection for home computer use with one GUI interface, GNOME. The workstation will add client support for servers as well as administrative tools and software development tools. The server configuration will install all the network servers, such as Web and FTP servers, as well as DHCP, Samba, and DNS servers. If you know what packages you want or if you want to install everything, you can use the custom install. This will let you choose the packages by group or individually that you want on your system, as well as let you manually configure your partitions.

- **Personal Desktop**   Home or desktop systems
- **Workstation**   Includes software development and system administration tools
- **Server**   Includes the Internet and network servers, such as the Apache Web server, FTP servers, Samba and NFS file servers, and the DNS server
- **Custom**   Select from all software packages and directly control partitioning

Install Procedures

Once the installation program begins, you simply follow the instructions, screen by screen. Most of the time, you only need to make simple selections or provide yes and no answers. The installation program progresses through several phases. First, you create Linux partitions on your hard drive, configure your network connection, and then install the software packages. After that, you can configure your X Window System for graphical user interface support. Both the X Window System and network configurations can be performed independently at a later time.

Once your system is installed, you are ready to start it and log in. Normally, you will log in using a graphical login, selecting the desktop you want and entering your username and password. Alternatively, you can log in to a simple command line interface. From the command line, you can then invoke a desktop such as GNOME or KDE that provides you with a full graphical user interface.

Installing Red Hat Enterprise Linux

Red Hat Enterprise Linux uses the same Anaconda installer that Fedora Core uses. The two installation procedures are very much the same, with few if any exceptions. Red Hat Enterprise Linux is a commercial product for which Red Hat provides direct installation support. Unlike Fedora Core, Red Hat Enterprise Linux uses a special CD boot disc of its own to start installation. You will also need the boot CD to end the install process. The install package groups may differ.

Installing Dual-Boot Systems

If you want to have another operating system on the same computer as your Linux system, you will have to configure your system to be dual-booted. The boot loader, GRUB, already supports dual-booting. Should you have both Linux and Windows systems installed on your hard disks, GRUB will let you choose to boot either the Linux system or a Windows system. Configuring dual boots can be complicated. If you want a Windows system on your computer, you should install it first if it is not already installed. Windows would overwrite the boot loader that a previous Linux system installed, cutting off access to the Linux system. Check the link for dual boots on

```
fedora.redhat.com/download
```

This references Appendix G of the Red Hat 9 manual, which is still applicable on dual boots, **www.redhat.com/docs/manuals/linux/RHL-9-Manual/install-guide/ch-x86-dualboot.html**.

Simple Graphical Direct Install with DVD/CD-ROMs

If you are installing from DVD/CD-ROMs, installation is a straightforward process. A graphical installation is very easy to use, providing full mouse support and explaining each step with detailed instructions on a help pane.

- Most systems today already meet hardware requirements and have automatic connections to the Internet (DHCP).
- They also support booting a DVD-ROM or CD-ROM disc, though this support may have to be explicitly configured in the system BIOS.
- Also, if you know how you want Linux installed on your hard disk partitions, or if you are performing a simple update that uses the same partitions, installing Fedora Core 4 is a fairly simple process. Fedora Core 4 features an automatic partitioning function that will perform the partitioning for you.
- If you choose one of the three preconfigured packaging installations, you will not even have to select packages.

For a quick installation you can simply start up the installation process, placing your DVD or CD disc in your optical drive and starting up your system. Graphical installation is a simple matter of following the instructions in each window as you progress. Many of them are self-explanatory (for LCD displays you may have to use the **nofb** option at the boot prompt).

The steps involved are as follows:

- **Media Check**   DVDs and CDs are often burned discs from downloaded ISO images. The media check can make sure your DVD/CD-ROMs are being read correctly.
- **Language Selection**   A default is chosen for you, like English, so you can usually just press Next.
- **Keyboard Configuration**   A default is chosen for you; you can usually press Next.

- **Upgrade/Install Option**   Choose whether to install or upgrade. If you already have a Fedora Core system installed, Upgrade will already be chosen.

- **Install Configurations**   Here you choose Personal, Workstation, Server, or Custom installation.

- **Disk Partitions**   For automatic partitioning you have the option of replacing any partitions already present: either all partitions or just Linux partitions (preserving any Windows partitions). You can also choose no partitions and use available free space. This is used to either preserve your old partitions or for new drives. Check the Review option to have the Disk Druid partitioning tool show your partitioning selections and let you make changes.

- **Boot Loader**   You can then configure your boot loader (GRUB). Primarily this is used to choose a different operating system such as Windows to boot by default; otherwise, you can accept the current configuration and press Next.

- **Network Configuration**   Most ISPs and routers now use DHCP, and this will be selected for you by default. Just press Next. You do have the option of entering in your own network information, including IP addresses and DNS servers.

- **Security Level**   This is the iptables firewall configuration. It will be enabled by default. Here you select the level of support you want for SELinux. Active is selected by default, but it is recommended that you change this to the Warning level until you can configure SELinux yourself. For the firewall, you can check services to allow through. Trusted interfaces allow any host connected to that interface to access all services provided by your system. They are usually used if your system operates as a server for your local network.

- **Time Zone**   Use the map to choose your time zone.

- **Root Password**   Select a password to use for the root users. This enables administrative access. Be sure to remember the password.

- **Package Installation**   For preconfigured installs, a package list will be provided. You have the option to customize it, choosing additional packages. For the Custom install, you choose the ones you want from the Package Selection screen.

- **About to Install**   At this point nothing has been done to your system. You can opt out of the installation at this point. If you click Next, then the install process will take place, making actual changes. The system will first be formatted, then packages installed, with installation progress shown, and then a post-install will perform default configurations for your packages.

- After the install, you will be asked to remove your DVD/CD-ROM and click the Exit button. This will reboot your system (do not reboot yourself).

- On reboot, you will enter a Fedora Setup Agent procedure where you will be able to set the date and time, check your sound card, and make any custom Display adjustments, even selecting a monitor or video card if they were not accurately selected. You will also be asked to create a standard user, which you can use to log in for normal use (not as root). More users can be created later.

- After Setup, your login screen will display and installation will be complete.

Hardware, Software, and Information Requirements

Before installing Linux, you must ensure that your computer meets certain minimum hardware requirements. You also need to have certain specific information ready concerning your monitor, video card, mouse, and CD-ROM drive. All the requirements are presented in detail in the following sections. Be sure to read them carefully before you begin installation. During the installation program, you need to provide responses that reflect the configuration of your computer.

Hardware Requirements

Listed here are the minimum hardware requirements for installing a standard installation of the Linux system on an Intel-based PC:

- A 32-bit or 64-bit Intel- or AMD-based personal computer. At least an Intel or compatible (AMD) Pentium-class microprocessor is required. A 400 MHz Pentium II or more is recommended for a graphical interface and 200 MHz for text. Fedora Core 4 is currently optimized for a Pentium 4.

- For 64-bit systems, be sure to use the 64-bit version of Fedora Core 4, which includes a supporting kernel.

- A CD-ROM or DVD-ROM drive (if you are using the DVD-ROM included with this book, you will need a DVD-ROM drive). Should you need to create a bootable CD-ROM, you will need a CD-RW drive.

- Normally at least 64MB RAM for text, and 192MB for a graphical interface, with 256MB recommended. For 64-bit systems, you will need 128MB for text and 256MB for graphical, with 512MB recommended. (Linux can run on as little as 12MB RAM.) At least 2.3GB free hard disk space is required for a standard installation, including applications (keep in mind that Linux can run on far less on a minimum installation, as little as 100MB and 16MB swap); 3GB to 7GB or more is recommended for a full installation (all applications). You need about 6GB to install all the software packages on most distribution CD-ROMs. The standard installation of basic software packages normally takes 3GB, plus 64MB to 512MB for swap space, depending on the amount of RAM memory you have. If you have less than 1GB of hard disk space, you can elect to perform a minimum install, installing only the Linux kernel without most of the applications. You could later install the applications you want, one at a time, using the system-config-packages tool accessible on the System Settings window.

- Hard disk requirements depend on the kind of installation you want:
  - Custom Installation (minimum): 620MB
  - Server (minimum): 1.1GB
  - Personal Desktop: 2.3GB
  - Workstation: 3.0GB
  - Custom Installation (everything): 7.5GB

- Keep in mind that the disk space requirements represent the amount of space used after installation. The install process will also require an additional amount of space for the install image (**/Fedora/base/stage2.img**) and selected RPM packages. Figure on 90MB for a minimum install and 174MB for a full installation.

Hard Drive Configuration

These days, Linux is usually run on its own hard drive, though it can also be run on a hard drive that contains a separate partition for a different operating system such as Windows.

If you want to install Linux and Windows on the same hard drive, you can use a partition management software package, such as fdisk, fips, Parted, or PartitionMagic, to set up your Windows and Linux partitions. If you have already installed Windows on your hard drive and configured it to take up the entire hard drive, you would resize its partition to free up unused space. The freed space could then be used for a Linux partition. See the Red Hat Linux x86 Installation Guide for more details.

Information Requirements

Part of adapting a powerful operating system like Linux to the PC entails making the most efficient use of the computer hardware at hand. In almost all configurations, your Linux installation process will automatically detect and configure your hardware components. Sometimes, however, particularly with older or very recent hardware, your installer may not be able to correctly identify a component. If you have such components, such as a new model monitor or video card, you should first check their manuals and take note of certain configuration settings.

You will also need to determine how you want to use hardware resources; for example, how much of your hard disk you want to devote to Linux.

CD-ROM, Hard Disk, and Mouse Information

For some older SCSI CD-ROM drives, you need the manufacturer's name and model.

Decide how much of your hard drive (in megabytes) you want to dedicate to your Linux system. If you are sharing with Windows, decide how much you want for Windows and how much for Linux.

Decide how much space you want for your swap partition. Your swap partition should be about the same size as your RAM memory, but it can work with as little as 64MB. For systems with smaller RAM configurations, the swap disk should be twice the size of the RAM. The size of the swap partition was expanded with the 2.4 kernel. Your swap partition is used by Linux as an extension of your computer's RAM.

Know what time zone you are in and to what time zone your hardware clock is set. This can be either Greenwich Mean Time (GMT), also called Universal Coordinated Time (UCT), or your local time zone.

In most cases, your mouse will be automatically detected. If you have difficulty, you may need to find the make and model of the mouse you are using. Linux supports serial, USB, PS/2, IMPS/2, and bus mice. Most mice are supported, including Microsoft, Logitech, and Mouse Systems. If you should need your mouse information, know which kind of port your mouse is using, such as PS/2, USB, or serial port. Most systems now use a USB or PS/2 port. If you use a serial port mouse, you will need to know which port it is connected to: COM1, COM2, or none.

Video and Monitor Information

Although most monitors and video cards are automatically configured during installation, you might still need to provide the manufacturer's make and model, in case the detection is wrong. Find out the manufacturer for your monitor and its model, such as Iiyama VisionMaster or Hitachi CM828. Do the same for your video card—for example, Matrox Millennium or ATI Radeon. This should be listed on the manuals or registration information provided with your computer. You can find a complete list of supported cards at **www.x11 .org**. Fedora Core now use the X11.org drivers, rather than the XFree86 ones used in previous releases.

For some of the most recent monitors and video cards, and some older, uncommon ones, you may need to provide certain hardware specifications. Having this information on hand, if possible, is advisable. At the end of the installation process, when the system enters a Setup phase after rebooting, you are presented with the opportunity to enter your own video and monitor configuration settings. You can display lists of video cards and monitors from which to choose your own. These lists are extensive. If your card or monitor is not on the list, however, you need to provide certain hardware information about them. If the configuration should fail, you can always do it later using the X Window System configuration tool, redhat-config-display. Of particular importance is the monitor information, including the vertical and horizontal refresh rates.

Network Configuration Information

If your ISP service or network uses DHCP, you will most likely not have to provide any configuration information. Most local networks, cable connections, and DSL connections now use DHCP to automatically configure hosts. Network information is provided automatically by a DHCP server. During the installation process, you will be given the option of either automatically configuring your network connection (DHCP) or entering the network information manually.

If you need to configure your network connection, you can also put configuration off until a later time and use network configuration utilities provided by your distribution to perform network configuration. All you need to do during installation is provide a hostname.

If you decide to manually configure your network connection, you will need the following information, usually obtainable from your network administrator:

- The name for your computer (this is called a hostname). Your computer will be identified by this name on the Internet. Do not use "localhost," which is reserved for special use by your system.

- The Internet Protocol (IP) address assigned to your machine. Every host on the Internet is assigned an IP address.

- Your network IP address. This address is usually similar to the IP address, but with one or more zeros at the end.

- The netmask. This is usually 255.255.255.0 for class C IP addresses. If, however, you are part of a large network, check with your network administrator.

- The broadcast address for your network, if available. Usually, your broadcast address is the same as your IP address with the number 255 used for the last number.

- The gateway IP address for your network. The gateway connects your network to a larger one like the Internet.

- The IP address of any name servers your network uses.
- The NIS domain and IP address if your network uses an NIS server.
- The Samba server if your network is connected to a Windows network.

Boot Source Options

Fedora Core 4 supports several booting options should your DVD-ROM not be bootable for some reason. Take note that floppy disk boots are no longer supported. The 2.6 kernel is too large to fit on a floppy.

- Normally you would boot from a DVD-ROM. Most systems currently support booting from a DVD-ROM drive. However, if you have an older system or DVD-ROM that will not support booting, and you can boot from a CD-ROM disc, you can create a CD-ROM boot disc, using **images/boot.iso** to burn the disc. Alternatively, you could use a USB drive or PXE network boot if these are supported for your system. Once installation begins, your DVD-ROM will be used to continue installation.

- If you are installing with CD-ROMs, most systems and CD-ROM drives are now bootable. You can use the CDs directly. If your system for some reason does not support bootable CD-ROMs, you will have to set up an alternative boot method such as a USB disk with **diskboot.img** or a PXE server.

- You can create a bootable CD-ROM disc with which to start the installation. The CD-ROM boot disc image is located in the **images** directory and is called **boot.iso**. You can also use this disc to install from alternate sources such as a hard drive or a network location such as an NFS, FTP, or Web site.

- With the **diskboot.img** file (also in the **images** directory) you can boot from small USB drives or any bootable device large enough to hold the 2.6 kernel (the size of the **diskboot.img** file, about 6MB). This is a VFAT file system. Check first if your system can boot from the USB drive.

- You can also boot from the PXE (Pre-Execution Environment) server using the **initrd.img** file in the **images/pxeboot** directory. A PXE server operates through DHCP and tftp servers off a Linux system. Check the PXE documentation file, **pxelinux.doc**, in the **/usr/share/syslinux-2.11** directory (version number may differ).

NOTE   *If you are installing from the Fedora Core 4 DVD-ROM included with this book, you will need a DVD-ROM drive on your computer to read the DVD-ROM disc. The DVD-ROM included with this book has been configured to be bootable, functioning like a boot CD-ROM. If your system supports bootable CD-ROMs, then it will boot from this DVD-ROM, letting you install your Fedora Core 4 system from the DVD-ROM directly.*

Install Methods

Fedora Core 4 supports various methods for installation. Other than the graphical install, you can user a text install or a low-resolution (lowres) graphical install, which is helpful if your graphics card was not correctly detected. If you have difficulty with detecting your hardware, you can use the noprobe option that will let you provide your own drivers, or the expert option that will let you choose all your hardware. You may also need to use **nofb** for some LCD monitors, or set **acpi=off** to disable ACPI if it stops your installation. All these options are entered at the Linux boot prompt.

- **linux text**   Use a text-based install interface employing text cursor to make selections with arrow, TAB, and ENTER keys.
- **linux lowres**   Use a low-resolution graphical interface that is video card independent.
- **linux nofb**   Disable the frame buffer (needed for some LCD monitors like Dell).
- **linux noprobe**   Do not probe hardware.
- **linux acpi=off**   Turn off ACPI, which can interfere with the install procedure.
- **linux expert**   Select all hardware.
- **linux askmethod**   Select a method of installation, as from a hard disk or a network site.
- **linux vnc**   Start a VNC install from a VNC site.
- **linux ks**=*filelocation*   Start an automated install using a kickstart configuration file.

Virtual Network Computing

A VNC (Virtual Network Computing) installation lets you boot the installation normally on the install system, and then lets the installation be managed from another Linux host, stepping through the install system's installation screen. It is a kind of remotely controlled installation, over a network connection. A VNC install requires that the host computer be running a VNC server. This is managed by the vncserver script, which can be controlled with system-config-services (System Settings | Server Settings | Services on the main menu). You can also use the **service** tool.

```
service vncserver start
```

Once vncserver is started, the host then becomes a VNC server that can access and control installations being performed on other systems. As the VNC server, the host uses the vncviewer client to interact with the installation process on the install system. The client is invoked with the **-listen** option that checks for reverse connections from a VNC server.

```
vncviewer -listen
```

The install system has to then start the installation procedure by specifying a VNC install at the boot prompt and providing the host computer IP address along with a password.

```
boot: linux vnc vncconnect=192.168.0.2 vncpassword=geo4455
```

On the install system you will have to first configure your language, keyboard, and network connection. Once you have configured the network connection for your install system, then a connection can be made to the VNC server. You can then move to the VNC host system and continue installation from there.

Automating Installation with Kickstart

Kickstart is a method for providing a predetermined installation configuration for installing Fedora Core. Instead of having a user enter responses on the install screens, the responses can be listed in a kickstart file the install process can read from. You will need to create a kickstart configuration file on a working Fedora Core system. (Kickstart configuration files have the extension .cfg.) A kickstart file is created for every Fedora Core system that holds the install responses used for that installation. It is located in the root directory at

```
/root/anaconda-ks.cfg
```

If you plan to perform the same kind of install on computers that would be configured in the same way, say on a local network with hosts that have the same hardware, you could use this kickstart file as a model for performing installations. It is a text file that you can edit, with entries for each install response, like the following for keyboard and time zone:

```
keyboard us
timezone America/LosAngeles
```

More complex responses may take options such as **network**, which uses **--device** for the device interface and **bootproto** for the boot client.

```
network --device eth0 --bootproto dhcp
```

Display configuration is more complex, specifying a video card and monitor type, which could vary. You can have the system skip this with xskip.

The first entry is the install source. This will be cdrom for a CD/DVD-ROM install. If you want to use an NFS or WEB install instead, you could place that here, specifying the server name or Web site.

You can also use the **system-config-kickstart** file to create your kickstart file. This provides a graphical interface for each install screen. To start it, enter **system-config-kickstart** in a terminal window. The help manual provides a detailed description on how to use this tool.

The name of the configuration file should be **ks.cfg**.

Once you have created your kickstart file, you can copy it to CD/DVD or to a floppy disk. You could also place the file on a local hard disk partition (such as a Windows or Linux partition), if you already have one. For a network, you could place the file on an NFS server, provided your network is running a DHCP server to enable automatic network configuration on the install computer.

When you start the installation, at the boot prompt you specify the kickstart file and its location. In the following example, the kickstart file will be located on a floppy disk as **/dev/fd0**.

```
linux ks=floppy
```

You can use **hd:***device* to specify a particular device such as a hard drive or second CD-ROM drive. For an NFS site, you would use **nfs:**.

Installing Linux

Installing Linux involves several processes, beginning with creating Linux partitions, and then loading the Linux software, configuring your X Window System interface, installing the Linux boot loader (GRUB or LILO) that will boot your system, and creating new user accounts. The installation program used on Fedora Core is a screen-based program that takes you through all these processes, step-by-step, as one continuous procedure. You can use either your mouse or the keyboard to make selections. When you finish with a screen, click the Next button at the bottom to move to the next screen. If you need to move back to the previous screen, click Back. You can also use TAB, the arrow keys, SPACEBAR, and ENTER to make selections. The installation screens will display a help panel explaining each step in detail. You have little to do other than make selections and choose options. Some screens provide a list of options from which you make a selection. In a few cases, you are asked for information you should already have if you followed the steps earlier in this chapter. Hardware components will be automatically detected and displayed as you progress. During installation, you will be able to perform administrative tasks such as configuring your network connections, creating users, and setting the time. Keep in mind that such administrative tasks can also be performed after installation. You are now ready to begin installation. The steps for each part of the procedure are delineated in the following sections. This should not take more than an hour.

The installation process will first install your Linux, including all selected packages, on your system. It will then reboot and start a Setup process to let you fine-tune certain settings, including your display settings, sound check, and time and date.

Starting the Installation Program

If your computer can boot from the DVD/CD-ROM, you can start the installation directly from the CD-ROMs or the DVD-ROM included with this book. Just place the CD-ROM in the CD-ROM drive, or the book's DVD-ROM in the DVD drive, before you start your computer. After you turn on your computer, the installation program will start up.

NOTE *To boot from a CD-ROM or DVD-ROM, you may first have to change the boot sequence setting in your computer's BIOS so that the computer will try to boot first from the CD-ROM. This requires some technical ability and knowledge of how to set your motherboard's BIOS configuration.*

The installation program will start, presenting you with an Introduction screen. After a moment, the following prompt will appear at the bottom of your screen:

```
boot:
```

Press ENTER. (If needed, you can enter boot parameters or install methods). Your system then detects your hardware, providing any configuration specifications that may be needed. For example, if you have an IDE CD-RW or DVD-RW drive, it will be configured automatically. If for some reason it cannot do so, your system will ask you to select your CD-ROM from a list. If you still have difficulty, you may have to specify the CD-ROM at the boot prompt.

```
Boot: linux hdx=cdrom
```

Replace the *x* with one of the following letters, depending on the interface the unit is connected to, and whether it is configured as master or a slave: a (first IDE controller master), b (first IDE controller slave), c (second IDE controller master), d (second IDE controller slave). If you cannot start the install process and you are using an LCD display, you should enter **nofb** at the boot prompt (no frame buffer).

```
Boot: linux nofb
```

If you are installing on file systems other than ext3, such as Reiser (**reiserfs**), JFS (**jfs**), or XFS (**xfs**), be sure to indicate them at the boot prompt. Also, JFS and Reiser do not support SELinux currently. Use the parameter **selinux=0** to disable SELinux. The parameters for Reiser file system are shown here.

```
Boot: linux selinux=0 resierfs
```

NOTE *As each screen appears in the installation, default entries will be already selected, usually by the autoprobing capability of the installation program. Selected entries will appear highlighted. If these entries are correct, you can simply click Next to accept them and go on to the next screen.*

Initial Setup: Upgrade or Install

If your basic device and hardware configuration was appropriately detected, a Welcome screen will be displayed, with a Next button on the lower-right corner. Fedora Core install screens will normally show two panels, one to the left with a detailed explanation of the current step, and the selection and configuration panel to the right where you make your entries. Once finished with a step, you click Next to move on. In some cases you will be able to click a Back button to return to a previous step.

The first screen will welcome you to the Fedora Core installation, with a brief description of the install screens. Press Next to start the install process.

You will then be asked to select your language, and then a keyboard configuration. A default language will already be selected, usually English.

You will then be asked to select a keyboard—the default is already selected, such as U.S. English.

You are then given the option to either Upgrade an older installed version or Install an entirely new system. For upgrading, the root partition of the installed system will be shown.

If you select Install, then you will be given four install options:

- **Personal Desktop**   Home or desktop systems.
- **Workstation**   Includes software development and system administration tools.
- **Server**   Includes the Internet and network servers, such as the Apache Web server, FTP servers, Samba and NFS file servers, and the DNS server.
- **Custom**   Select from all software packages and directly control partitioning.

The first three provide a quick install process, using a standard selection of software packages. The Custom option will let you select the packages you want, including all packages, as well as give you more control over configuring your partitions.

Partitions, RAID, and Logical Volumes

Then you will be asked to designate the Linux partitions and hard disk configurations you want to use on your hard drives. Red Hat provides automatic partitioning options if you just want to use an entire single hard drive for your Linux system. To manually configure your hard disks, Red Hat provides a very detailed and graphic-oriented partitioning tool called Disk Druid. With Disk Druid, you can create specific partitions, or configure RAID devices, or set up logical volumes (see Chapter 33).

No partitions will be changed or formatted until you select your packages later in the install process. You can opt out of the installation any time until that point, and your original partitions will remain untouched.

You will first be asked whether to use either automatic or manual partitioning.

Automatic Partitioning

If you choose automatic partitioning, an Automatic Partitioning screen will be displayed. Automatic partitioning provides three options. Be warned that if you chose the Server install option, then the Remove All Partitions options (2) will be selected for you by default. For Personal Desktop, Workstation, and Custom install, the Remove All Linux Partitions option (1) is selected by default.

- **Remove all Linux partitions on this system**   This removes just Linux partitions that are already on your disks. Any Windows or other OS partitions will remain untouched. Two Linux partitions will be set up for you: a boot partition of type ext3 (Linux native), and a LVM partition that will hold all your system files.

- **Remove all partitions on this system**   This removes all the partitions on the disk, effectively erasing it. You will lose any existing partitions, including Windows partitions.

- **Keep all partitions and use existing free space**   This is for disks that might be partially used, such as a partition for Windows that uses only part of the hard disk. This assumes that there is a significant amount of free space already on the disk.

In a pane below the options is a list of all the hard drives on your system. You can select the one you want Linux installed on. If you have only one, it will be selected for you.

An option at the bottom of the screen lets you review all your partitions in Disk Druid, letting you modify them if you need to. This will not be checked by default. Check this to see exactly how Disk Druid will be partitioning your system. You can also make changes if needed.

- **Review (and modify if needed) the partitions created**   This allows you to make changes manually to the partitions as well as see exactly what partitions will be created on your drives.

NOTE *If you want to organize your data using several partitions, such as /home, /, and /var, as well as boot, you will have to manually configure them. Automatic partitioning will set up a boot partition and an LVM Linux partition only.*

Manual and Review Partitioning

If you choose the Manual partition or checked the Review option in the Automatic Partitioning screen, the Disk Setup screen is displayed, placing you into the Disk Druid partition configurator. Here, you can manually create Linux partitions or select the one where you want to install Fedora Core. The top pane lists the hard drives on your computer (many computers will have only one hard drive), and the lower pane lists the partitions. Selecting a hard drive will list its partitions. The button above the partitions pane enables you to create, edit, and delete partitions. The Partitions screen is actually an interactive interface where you configure partitions as well as create new ones.

If you are reviewing after automatic partitioning, then the hard disk partitions set up for you will be displayed. The panel will show the specific partitions that will be created for your system.

If you are formatting any old Linux partitions that still have data on them, a dialog box will appear listing them and asking you to confirm that you want to format them (new Linux partitions that you created will automatically be formatted). If you already have a Linux system, you will most likely have several Linux partitions already. Some of these may be used for just the system software, such as the boot and root partitions. These should be formatted. Others may have extensive user files, such as a **/home** partition that normally holds user home directories and all the files they have created. You should *not* format such partitions.

Recommended Partitions

If you are manually creating your partitions, you are required to set up at least two Linux partitions: a swap partition and a root partition. The *root partition* is where the Linux system and application files are installed. In addition, it is recommended that you also set up a boot partition that would contain just your Linux kernel, and a **/home** partition that would hold all user files. Separating system files on the root and boot partitions from the user files on the home partition allows you to replace the system files should they ever become corrupt without touching the user files. Similarly, if just your kernel becomes corrupt, you would have to replace only the kernel files on your boot partition, leaving the system files on the root partition untouched. This strategy of separating system directories into different partitions can be carried further to ensure a more robust system. For example, the **/var** directory, which now holds Web and FTP server files, can be assigned its own partition, physically separating the servers from the rest of your system. The **/usr** directory, which holds most user applications, can be placed in its own partition and then be shared and mounted by other systems. One drawback to this strategy is that you would need to know ahead of time the maximum space you would want to use for each partition. For system and kernel files, this can be easily determined, but for directories whose disk usage can change dramatically, like **/home**, **/var**, and even **/usr**, this can be difficult to determine. As an alternative to creating separate physical partitions for each directory, you could use logical volumes (described later). A basic partition configuration is shown here:

- **Swap partition**   No mount point
- **/**   Root partition for system files (and all other files if no other partition is defined)
- **/boot**   Boot partition holding the Linux kernel (approximately 200MB)
- **/home**   User home directories and files

Except for the swap partition, when setting up a Linux partition, you must specify a mountpoint. A *mountpoint* is a directory where the files on that partition are connected to the overall Linux file structure for your system. The mountpoint for your root partition is the root directory, represented by a single slash (/). The mountpoint for your boot partition is the path **/boot**. For a user's partition, it would be **/home**.

The size of the swap partition should be the same size as your RAM memory, with a recommended minimum size of 64MB. With 512MB of RAM, you could use a 512MB swap partition. If your disk space is limited, you should make your swap size at least 64MB.

Creating Partitions

To create the new partition, click the Add button to display a dialog box where you can enter the mountpoint, the size (in megabytes), the partition type, and the hard disk on which you want to create the partition. For the size, you can select a "Grow to fill disk" option to have the partition automatically expand to the size of the remaining free space on the disk. You can have this option selected for more than one partition. In that case, the partition size will be taken as a required minimum and the remaining free space will be shared equally among the partitions. For partition type, select Linux native for standard Linux partitions and select the Linux swap type for your swap partition. You can even use Disk Druid to create Windows partitions. To make any changes later, you can edit a partition by selecting it and clicking the Edit button.

TIP *Currently, the Reiser and JFS file systems currently do not support SELinux. If you want to use Reiser or JFS file systems, be sure to disable SELinux on the network configuration panel.*

RAID Disks

You also have the option of creating software RAID disks. First create partitions and select as their type Software RAID (see Chapter 33 for more details on RAID). Once you have created your partitions, you can create a RAID disk. Click the RAID button and then select the partitions you previously created that you want to make up the RAID disk, choosing also the type of RAID disk. See the Red Hat Customization Guide for detailed information on creating RAID disks.

Logical Volumes

Fedora Core 4 also supports Logical Volume Management (LVM), letting you create *logical volumes*, which you can use instead of using hard disk partitions directly (see Chapter 33). Logical volumes are implemented by Logical Volume Management (LVM). They provide a more flexible and powerful way of dealing with disk storage, organizing physical partitions into logical volumes in which memory can be managed easily. Disk storage for a logical volume is treated as one pool of memory, though the volume may in fact contain several hard disk partitions spread across different hard disks. There is one restriction. The boot partition cannot be a logical volume. You still have to create a separate hard disk partition as your boot partition with the **/boot** mountpoint in which your kernel will be installed. If you selected automatic partitioning, the **/boot** partition will have already been set up for you, along with an LVM volume partition for the rest of the system.

Creating logical volumes involves several steps. First you create physical LVM partitions, then the volume groups you place these partitions in, and then from the volume groups you create the logical volumes, for which you then specify mountpoints and file system types. To create your physical LVM partitions, click New and select Physical Volume (LVM) for the File System Type. Create an LVM physical partition for each partition you want on your hard disks. Once you have created LVM physical partitions, you click the LVM button to create your logical volumes. You first need to assign the LVM physical partitions to volume groups. Volume groups are essentially logical hard drives. You could assign LVM physical partitions from different hard disks to the same volume group, letting the volume group span different hard drives. Once the volume groups are created, you are ready to create your logical volumes. You can create several logical volumes within each group. The logical volumes function like partitions. You will have to specify a file system type and a mountpoint for each logical volume you create.

Boot Loaders

Once your partitions are prepared, you install a boot loader. Fedora Core uses the Grand Unified Bootloader (GRUB). You use a boot loader to start Linux from your hard drive. The screen will display the partition to boot by default, listing all partitions with different operating systems installed on them, for instance, one with Windows along with the one for your Linux system. Your Windows system will simply be labeled as Other. Clicking the Advanced options lets you refine your boot procedure, enabling you to choose where to install the boot loader or determine the drive boot order. You have two choices for where to install the boot loader: the Master Boot Record (MBR) or the root partition. The recommended place is the MBR.

You can also set a boot loader password. When any user boots with GRUB, they can change the boot loader options (the Force LBA option is used for old hard drives and motherboards). A password will prevent other users on your system from changing the boot loader options.

Network Configuration

The Network Configuration screen displays tabbed panes in the top half for the different network devices on your computer. The screen displays segments for your network devices, hostname, and miscellaneous settings. If you use DHCP to automatically configure your network connection, as most networks do, you will most likely not need to do anything on this screen.

The Network devices segment will list your network connection devices, such as your Ethernet device. For computers already connected to a network with an Ethernet card, the first entry is usually labeled eth0. If you need to manually configure your device, entering an IP address for it, you can click Edit to display the device's configuration panel. Here you can choose to either manually configure the device or use DHCP to automatically configure it. For manual configuration, you can enter the device's IP address (usually your computer's IP address) and your network's netmask.

In the Hostname segment, you can choose either to manually provide your network information or to use DHCP to automatically obtain it. If you choose to manually provide your network information, you can enter a hostname and, in the Miscellaneous segment, enter your network's gateway and DNS servers' IP addresses.

Following network configuration, the Firewall Configuration screen then lets you create basic default levels of network security. You can also specify services you may be running that permit others to access to your system, such as Web or FTP services. The firewall configuration implements the newer IPtables firewall rules (see Chapter 20).

On this screen you will also be whether to enable Security-Enhanced Linux (SELinux). SELinux provides a very high level of security administration. You have three settings, Active to enable SELinux, Warn to provide warning messages only, and Disable to deactivate it.

The default will be Active, but a better selection may be Warn. The Active setting will enforce a security policy that will deny access by unauthorized users to files and applications. If your security policy is not accurately configured, access could be denied to valid users. At the Warn level you can see how SELinux performs and adjust its configuration appropriately. SELinux may not be fully compatible with older software.

System Configuration

On the Time Zone Configuration screen, you have the option of setting the time by using a map to specify your location or by using Universal Coordinated Time (UTC) entries.

On the next screen, you can set the root password for the root account on your system. This is the account used for system administration operations, such as installing software and managing users. After installation, a similar screen will let you also add an ordinary user account.

Software Installation

Depending on the kind of install you choose, Fedora Core will select a set of predetermined software collections tailored to personal desktops, workstations, or servers. You have the option to select the corresponding packages or choose a custom installation. The package groups selected by the tailored install will be listed.

If you choose custom install or choose to Customize your install packages, you will be placed in a Package Group Selection screen similar to the system-config-packages, discussed in Chapter 4. In this interface, you can select groups of packages, such as those for GNOME, KDE, different servers such as Web or FTP servers, games, editors, and development support, which includes compilers and debuggers. If you choose a tailored install, then the corresponding packages for them will already be selected. You can add or remove ones you want. To install all packages, select the Everything entry at the end of the list.

To select individual packages within a group, click the Details link to the right of a package category (this link appears on selected packages). This will list optional individual packages, which you can select or deselect by clicking their check boxes. There will normally be two segments, Base and Optional, though for many packages there will only be one or the other. For example, the Editors category has only an Optional segment listing Vi and Emacs editors. The Optional packages are those not considered essential to the category described, though commonly used packages will be already checked for you by default. The Editors category will have the Vi and Emacs editors already checked for you, even though they are optional. You can choose not to install one or the other by deselecting its entry. In the Web Server category, the Base segment contains the Apache Web server, and the Optional segment contains added modules and servers such as Squid and Tux. The Squid and Tux entries will already be checked, whereas specialize modules like those for MySQL database will not.

NOTE *Many software packages require that other software packages also be installed. This is called a* dependency. *If you don't have these already selected for installation, they will be selected for you.*

The Miscellaneous section at the end of the list gives you the option to install a Minimal selection or Everything, all packages. The Minimal selection is useful for just getting started, especially if you are having any difficulties with device detection or you have hard disk storage limitations. You can then use system-config-packages to install the packages you want.

- **Minimal configuration**   700MB
- **Everything**   7.5GB

Once selected, the About To Install screen lets you start the installation. This is your last chance to back out of the installation. You can press the Back button to reselect packages, or simply press your system's reset button to end the install process, leaving your original system untouched. Once you click the Next button, if you chose to format partitions, they will be formatted, erasing all data.

The packages are then installed, showing each package as it is installed and the progress of the installation. (For the Fedora Core 4 DVD-ROM, included with this book, the DVD-ROM will install in one continuous operation.) The install program detects all packages as residing on the single DVD-ROM. If you are using CD-ROMs instead (downloaded from the Internet), you will be prompted when to install the next CD-ROM. The current one will automatically be ejected for you. When the installation finishes, a postinstall process will complete. You are then usually given the option to create a boot disk. You can use this disk to access your Linux system should your hard disk boot somehow fail.

Finishing Installation

Once your installation is finished, you can click the Exit button to reboot. Be sure to remove the install or boot CD-ROM. If you booted from a CD, your CD will be ejected before rebooting. If you booted directly from the CD-ROM, you may want to change your boot sequence in your BIOS back to your original settings.

GRUB on Restart

When you reboot, a GRUB boot loader menu will be displayed listing Linux and other operating systems you specified, such as Windows. Use the arrow keys to move to the Linux entry, if it is not already highlighted, and press ENTER. The screen will appear for a few seconds and then run the default operating system. If you want to remain at the menu display until you specifically choose a system, you can press any key when GRUB starts up.

Setup

The first time you start up Red Hat Enterprise Linux or Fedora Core, the Setup Agent is run. This agent will help you perform basic configuration of your system, letting you set the date and time, configure your display (graphics card and monitor), and configure your sound card, as well as set up user accounts. The different steps will be listed on a side pane, with an arrow progressing through each one as you complete a task. For Fedora Core, you will be initially asked to approve the GNU General Public License for this distribution. The steps are listed here:

- License Agreement
- Date and Time
- Display
- System User
- Sound Card
- Additional CDs
- Finish Setup

Date and Time

The Date And Time Configuration panel will automatically probe for the date and time, displaying the date on a calendar and the time in hours, minutes, and seconds. You can easily change any entry with the click of a button. You can also choose to use the Network

Time Protocol, which will obtain the time automatically from a time server on the Internet, making sure your time is always correct. You can choose from servers listed, for instance, **clock.redhat.com**.

Display

The Display screen lets you further refine your display configuration. Your detected graphics card and monitor will be listed. Cards and monitors that could not be detected will be labeled as Unknown, as in Unknown Monitor. If the listed card or monitor could not be detected, you can manually make a selection by clicking on the Configure button. This will open a window with a listing of monitors, in the case of an Unknown monitor. This is an expandable list, showing vendor entries that will expand to a listing of all supported monitors for that vendor. You will need to know the vendor and model number for your monitor. For example, expanding Hitachi lists all the Hitachi monitors, from which the Hitachi CM828 could be selected. If your monitor does not appear on the list, select a Generic CRT or Generic LCD as appropriate and then select the supported resolution on your monitor.

The resolution and color depth entries let you select the resolution you want (default is usually 800 × 600) and the color depth (default 24 bit, millions of color) from pop-up menus. You can change them to other entries if you wish: 1024 × 768 for smaller monitors or 1280 × 1024 for larger ones.

Though this list is sufficient for most systems, you can further refine your display video card and monitor settings using system-config-display (the Display entry on the System Settings menu).

System User

The System User Accounts panel then lets you create a normal user account. You should have at least one, other than root. A dialog box is displayed with entries for the username, the user's full name, the password, and the password confirmation. Once you have entered in the information and clicked Next, the new user will be created.

You can also select LDAP, Windbind, Hesiod, or NIS to configure a user's network login process. Click the Use Network Login button. Here you can configure the servers. This starts up system-config-authentication. Use this also if your network supports the authentication server. On the Authentication panel, you can configure LDAP, Kerberos, Windbind, and SMB (Samba) authentication. You can enable and configure support for each, specifying NIS, LDAB, Kerberos, or SMB servers that your network may use.

Sound Configuration

On the Sound panel, your sound card will be automatically detected and configured. You can click a button to test the sound.

Red Hat Network (Enterprise Only)

The Red Hat Update Agent is then run to register you with the Red Hat Network so that you can automatically update the installed software on your system. Currently, access to the Red Hat Network is limited to subscribed customers. Free access is not provided. If you do not wish to register at this time, you can skip to the next panel. For Red Hat Enterprise Linux, you can activate access at this time. If you previously registered, you can log in using your current username and password. The Update Agent will detect your system's hardware configuration and generate a profile that you can register.

Installing Additional Software

You can then elect to install additional software from software discs like the Red Hat Documentation CD or Extras CD often included with Red Hat Enterprise Linux.

Login and Logout

The Setup Agent then concludes and your login screen is displayed. The login prompt or the login screen will appear. A graphical install will use the login screen. You can then log into your Linux system using a login name and a password for any of the users you have set up. If you log in as the root user, you can perform administrative operations, such as installing new software or creating more users. To log in as the root user, enter **root** at the login prompt and the root user password at the password prompt.

On the login screen, four pop-up menus are displayed in the lower-left corner: Language, Session, Reboot, and Shutdown. The Session menu lets you choose what desktop graphical interface to use, such as KDE or GNOME. You use the Shutdown menu to shut down, and the Reboot menu to reboot. The Language menu lets you select a language to use.

When you finish, you can shut down your system. If you are using a command line interface, use the command **halt**. From GNOME, you can elect to shut down the entire system. If you log out from either GNOME or KDE and return to the login screen, you can choose the shutdown entry from the Shutdown pop-up menu located at the bottom of the screen.

If the system should freeze on you for any reason, you can hold down the CTRL and ALT keys and press DEL (CTRL-ALT-DEL) to safely restart it. Never just turn it off. You can also use CTRL-ALT-F3 to shift to a command line prompt and login to check out your system, shutting down with the **halt** command.

Boot Disks

You can use **mkbootdisk** to create boot CD-ROM. Use the **--iso** option and the **--device** option with the name of an ISO image file to create. You then use CD-ROM-burning software to create the CD-ROM from the image file. The following example creates an CD-ROM image file called **mybootcd.iso** that can be used as a boot CD-ROM.

```
mkbootdisk --iso --device mybootcd.iso 2.6.11-1.1369_FC4
```

If for some reason you are not able to boot or access your system, it may be due to conflicting configuration, libraries, or applications. In this case, you can boot your Linux system in a rescue mode and then edit configuration files with a text editor such as Vi (see Chapter 11), remove the suspect libraries, or reinstall damaged software with RPM (see Chapter 31). To enter the rescue mode, boot from your floppy boot disk, your CD-ROM, or the DVD-ROM included with this book. At the boot prompt, enter

```
linux rescue
```

You will boot into the command line mode with your system's files mounted at **/mnt/sysimage**. Use the **cd** command to move between directories (see Chapter 10). Check **/mnt/sysimage/etc** and **/mnt/sysimage/etc/sysconfig** for your configuration files. You can use Vi to edit your files. To reinstall files, use the **rpm** command (see Chapter 4). When you are finished, enter the **exit** command.

Interface Basics: Login, Desktop, and Help

Using Linux has become an almost intuitive process, with easy-to-use interfaces, including graphical logins and graphical user interfaces (GUIs) like GNOME and KDE. Even the standard Linux command line interface has become more user-friendly with editable commands, history lists, and cursor-based tools. To start using Linux, you have to know how to access your Linux system and, once you are on the system, how to execute commands and run applications. Access is supported through either the default graphical login or a command line login. For the graphical login, a simple window appears with menus for selecting login options and text boxes for entering your username and password. Once you access your system, you can then interact with it using either a command line interface or a graphical user interface (GUI). With GUI interfaces like GNOME and KDE, you can use windows, menus, and icons to interact with your system. Red Hat has integrated the look and feel of both to provide one standard GUI interface called Bluecurve, making their use less confusing.

Linux is noted for providing easy access to extensive help documentation. It's easy to obtain information quickly about any Linux command and utility while logged in to the system. You can access an online manual that describes each command or obtain help that provides more detailed explanations of different Linux features. A complete set of manuals provided by the Linux Documentation Project is on your system and available for you to browse through or print. Both the GNOME and KDE desktops provide help systems that give you easy access to desktop, system, and application help files.

User Accounts

You never directly access a Linux system. Instead, Linux sets up an interface called a *shell* through which you can interact with it. Linux is a multiuser system that can support several user shells at once, accommodating several users simultaneously, each connected through their own terminal or from a remote system.

User access to the system is provided through *accounts*. Unix, which Linux is based on, was first used on large minicomputers and mainframes that could accommodate hundreds of users at the same time. Using one of many terminals connected to the computer, users could log in to the Unix system using their usernames and passwords. To gain access to the system, you need to have a user account set up for you. A system administrator creates the account, assigning a username and password for it. You then use your account to log in and use the system.

You can, in fact, create other new user accounts using special system administration tools like system-config-users as described in Chapter 4. These tools become available to you when you log in as the root user. The *root user* is a special user account reserved for system administration tasks, such as creating users and installing new software. Basic system administration operations are discussed briefly in Chapters 4 and 5, but they are discussed in detail in Chapters 29–41.

Accessing Your Linux System

To access and use your Linux system, you must carefully follow required startup and shutdown procedures. You do not simply turn off your computer. Fedora Core does, however, implement journaling, which allows you to automatically recover your system from situations where the computer suddenly loses power and is shut off.

If you have installed the boot loader GRUB, when you turn on or reset your computer, the boot loader first decides what operating system to load and run. GRUB will display a menu of operating systems to choose.

If, instead, you wait a moment or press the ENTER key, the boot loader loads the default operating system. If a Windows system is listed, you can choose to start that instead.

You can think of your Linux operating system as operating on two different levels, one running on top of the other. The first level is when you start your Linux system, and where the system loads and runs. It has control of your computer and all its peripherals. You still are not able to interact with it, however. After Linux starts, it displays a login screen, waiting for a user to log in to the system and start using it. You cannot gain access to Linux, unless you log in first.

You can think of logging in and using Linux as the next level. Now you can issue commands instructing Linux to perform tasks. You can use utilities and programs such as editors or compilers, or even games. Depending on a choice you made during installation, however, you may be interacting with the system either using a simple command line interface or using the desktop directly. There are both command line login prompts and graphical login windows. Fedora Core will use a graphical interface by default, presenting you with a graphical login window at which you enter your username and password. If you choose not to use the graphical interface, you are presented with a simple command line prompt to enter your username.

The Display Manager: GDM

With the graphical login, your GUI interface starts up immediately and displays a login window with boxes for a username and password. When you enter your username and password, and then press ENTER, your default GUI starts up. This is GNOME by default.

For Fedora Core, graphical logins are handled by the GNOME Display Manager (GDM). The GDM manages the login interface along with authenticating a user password and username, and then starting up a selected desktop. If problems ever occur using the GUI interface, you can force an exit of the GUI with the CTRL-ALT-BACKSPACE keys, returning to the Login screen (or the command line if you started your GUI from there). Also, from the GDM, you can shift to the command line interface with the CTRL-ALT-F1 keys, and then shift back to the GUI with the CTRL-ALT-F7 keys.

When the GDM starts up, it shows a login window with a box for login. Four pop-up menus are located at the bottom of the screen, labeled Session, Language, Reboot, and Shutdown. To log in, enter your username in the box labeled Username and press ENTER. You are prompted to enter your password. Do so, and press ENTER. By default, the GNOME desktop is then started up.

TIP *You can configure your GDM login window with different features like background images and user icons. The GDM even has its own selection of themes to choose from. Select Login Screen Setup entry on the Settings menu to configure your login window. See Chapter 4 for more details.*

When you log out from the desktop, you return to the GDM login window. To shut down your Linux system, click the Shutdown button. Alternatively, you can also shut down when you log out from GNOME. GNOME will display a logout screen with the options Logout, Shutdown, or Reboot. Logout is the default, but selecting Shutdown will also shut down your system. Selecting Reboot will shut down and restart your system. (You can also open a terminal window and enter the **shutdown**, **halt**, or **reboot** command as described in the next section; **halt** will log out and shut down your system.)

From the Session menu, you can select the desktop or window manager you want to start up. Here you can select KDE to start up the K Desktop, for example, instead of GNOME. Both KDE and GNOME will use an interface with a Bluecurve look and feel, appearing much the same. The Language menu lists a variety of different languages that Linux supports. Choose one to change the language interface.

Accessing Linux from the Command Line Interface

For the command line interface, you are initially given a login prompt. The system is now running and waiting for a user to log in and use it. You can enter your username and password to use the system. The login prompt is preceded by the hostname you gave your system. In this example, the hostname is **turtle**. When you finish using Linux, you first log out. Linux then displays exactly the same login prompt, waiting for you or another user to log in again. This is the equivalent of the login window provided by the GDM. You can then log into another account.

```
Fedora Core release 4.0
Kernel 2.6 on an i686

turtle login:
```

Logging In and Out

Once you log in to an account, you can enter and execute commands. Logging in to your Linux account involves two steps: entering your username and then entering your password. Type in the username for your user account. If you make a mistake, you can erase characters with the BACKSPACE key. In the next example, the user enters the username **richlp** and is then prompted to enter the password:

```
Fedora Core release 4.0
Kernel 2.6 on an i686

turtle login: richlp
Password:
```

When you type in your password, it does not appear on the screen. This is to protect your password from being seen by others. If you enter either the username or the password incorrectly, the system will respond with the error message "Login incorrect" and will ask for your username again, starting the login process over. You can then reenter your username and password.

Once you enter your username and password correctly, you are logged in to the system. Your command line prompt is displayed, waiting for you to enter a command. Notice the command line prompt is a dollar sign (**$**), not a number sign (**#**). The **$** is the prompt for regular users, whereas the **#** is the prompt solely for the root user. In this version of Fedora Core, your prompt is preceded by the hostname and the directory you are in. Both are bounded by a set of brackets.

```
[turtle /home/richlp]$
```

To end your session, issue the **logout** or **exit** command. This returns you to the login prompt, and Linux waits for another user to log in.

```
[turtle /home/richlp]$ logout
```

Shutting Down Linux

If you want to turn off your computer, you must first shut down Linux. If you don't shut down Linux, you could require Linux to perform a lengthy systems check when it starts up again. You shut down your system in either of two ways. First, log in to an account and then enter the **halt** command. This command will log you out and shut down the system.

```
$ halt
```

Alternatively, you can use the **shutdown** command with the **-h** option. With the **-r** option, it shuts down the system and then reboots it. In the next example, the system is shut down after five minutes. To shut down the system immediately, you can use **+0** or the word **now** (see Chapter 29 for more details).

```
# shutdown -h now
```

TIP *Shutting down involves a series of important actions, such as unmounting file systems and shutting down any servers. You should never simply turn off the computer, though it can normally recover.*

You can also force your system to reboot at the login prompt, by holding down the CTRL and ALT keys and then pressing the DEL key (CTRL-ALT-DEL). Your system will go through the standard shutdown procedure and then reboot your computer.

Starting a GUI from the Command Line

Once logged into the system, you have the option of starting an X Window System GUI, such as GNOME or KDE, and using it to interact with your Linux system. In Linux, the command **startx** starts the X Window System along with a GUI, which then enables you to interact with the system using windows, menus, and icons. The **startx** command starts the GUI desktop by default. Once you shut down the GUI interface, you will return to your command line interface, still logged in.

```
$ startx
```

On Fedora Core, you can use the Desktop Switcher while in your desktop to switch between GNOME or KDE. The Desktop Switcher is accessible from the System Settings | More System Settings menu as the Desktop Switching Tool, or with the `switchdesk` command. You make your selection and then quit the desktop to return to the command line interface. When you start up the GUI again, the desktop you selected is used.

Bluecurve and Clearlooks: The GNOME and KDE Desktops

Two alternative desktop GUI interfaces can be installed on Fedora Core: GNOME and KDE. Each has its own style and appearance. To provide a more consistent graphical interface, Red Hat has developed common look-and-feel default settings for both GNOME and KDE, which are called Bluecurve. GNOME now uses as its default Clearlooks, which uses the same elements as Bluecurve. With Bluecurve/Clearlooks, GNOME and KDE appear much the same, with similar menus, panel items, and window style. By default, Fedora Core installs GNOME, though you can choose to also install KDE. Both GNOME and KDE applications are accessible from either the Bluecurve GNOME or KDE menus. Red Hat provides a standard set of applications in its primary menus, such as OpenOffice, and other corresponding applications, such as Kontact and Evolution. Bluecurve and Clearlooks are essentially themes, which you can change with either GNOME or KDE configuration tools. This section describes the Bluecurve /Clearlooks interface for both the GNOME and KDE desktops.

It is important to keep in mind that though the GNOME and KDE Bluecurve interfaces appear similar, they are really two very different desktop interfaces with separate tools for selecting preferences. The Preferences menus on GNOME and KDE display a very different selection of desktop configuration tools. These are discussed in Chapters 6 and 7.

GNOME

The Bluecurve/Clearlooks GNOME desktop display, shown in Figure 3-1, initially displays two panels at the top and bottom of the screen, as well as any file manager folder icons for your home directory and for the system. The top panel is used for menus, application icons, and notification tasks like your clock. There are three menus:

- **Applications**   With category entries like Office and Internet, these submenus will list the applications installed on your system. Use this menu to start your applications.

- **Places**   This menu lets you easily access commonly used locations like your home directory, the desktop folder for any files on your desktop, and the Computer window through which you can access devices, shared file systems, and all the directories on your local system. It also has entries for searching for files (Search For Files), accessing recently used documents, and logging into remote servers, like NFS and FTP servers.

- **Desktop**   This includes Preferences and System Settings menus. The Preferences menu is used for configuring your GNOME settings, such as the theme you want to user and the behavior of your mouse. The System Settings menu holds all the Fedora Core system configuration tools used to perform administrative tasks like adding users, setting up printers, configuring network connections, and managing network services like a Web server or Samba Windows access. This menu also hold entries for locking the screen (Lock) and logging out of the system (Logout).

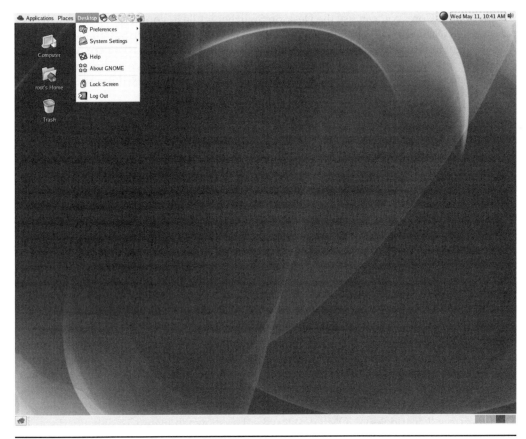

Figure 3-1 The Bluecurve/Clearlooks GNOME desktop

Next to the menus are application icons for commonly used applications. These include Firefox (the Mouse Fox and World logo), the Evolution mail utility, and several OpenOffice applications. Click one to start that application. You can also start applications using the Applications menu.

On the right you will see icons for the date/time, the sound volume control, and the Red Hat update notification. If updates are available, this icon will be flashing.

The bottom panel is used for interactive tasks like selecting workspaces and docking applications. The workspace switcher for virtual desktops appears as four squares in the lower-left corner. Clicking a square moves you to that area.

When you click the folder for your home directory on your desktop, a file manager window opens showing your home directory. The file manager uses a spatial design by default, opening a new window for each subdirectory you open. A directory window will show only the menus for managing files and the icons. The menu entries provide the full range of tasks involved in managing your files. On the lower-left bar of the window is a pop-up menu to access parent directories. The name of the currently displayed directory is shown.

The file manager also supports a browser view that has more displayed components, including a browser toolbar, location box, and sidebar commonly found on most traditional file managers. To use this format, right-click on the folder to display a pop-up menu, and select Browser View. This will open that folder with the enhanced format. Also, from within a special window, you can select a folder and then select Browser view from the File menu to open it. When you open a new directory from a Browser View window, the same window is used to display it, and you can use the forward and back arrows to move through previously opened directories. In the location window, you can enter the pathname for a directory to move directly to it. Figure 3-2 shows both the spatial and browser views for the file manager windows.

NOTE *For both GNOME and KDE, the file manager is Internet-aware. You can use it to display simple Web pages and access remote FTP directories and to display or download their files, though in KDE the file manager is also a fully functional Web browser.*

To move a window, left-click and drag its title bar. Each window supports Maximize, Minimize, and Close buttons. Double-clicking the title bar will maximize the window. Each window will have a corresponding button on the bottom panel. You can use this button to minimize and restore the window. The desktop supports full drag-and-drop capabilities. You can drag folders, icons, and applications to the desktop or other file manager windows open to other folders. The move operation is the default drag operation (you can also press the SHIFT key while dragging). To copy files, press the CTRL key and then click and drag before releasing the mouse button. To create a link, right-click the item and select Make Link from the pop-up menu. You can then drag the link wherever you wish.

To quit the GNOME desktop, select the Log Out entry from the Desktop menu. If you entered from a login window, you are then logged out of your account and returned to the login window. If you started GNOME from the command line, you are returned to the command line prompt, still logged into your account.

FIGURE 3-2 File manager spatial and browser views

FIGURE 3-3   GNOME applets

GNOME Applets

GNOME applets are small programs that operate off your panel. It is very easy to add applets. Right-click the panel and select the Add entry. This lists all available applets. Some helpful applets are dictionary lookup, the disk mounter for removable disks, the network monitor, which shows your CPU usage, and Find for searching your system for files, as well as Lock and Logout buttons. Some of these, including find, lock, and logout, are already on the Desktop menu. You could drag these directly from the menu to the panel to add the applet. Figure 3-3 shows some of the more common applets. Following the Web browser and e-mail icons, you have, from left to right: network server (FTP, NFS), dictionary lookup, eyes, lock screen, logout, network monitor, find, sticky notes, system monitor, trash, and weather.

KDE

The K Desktop Environment (KDE) looks like GNOME with Bluecurve as shown in Figure 3-1. It displays a panel at the bottom of the screen that is very similar to one displayed on the top of the GNOME desktop, though there is only one menu. The file manager appears slightly different but operates much the same way as the GNOME file manager. There is a Control Center entry in the main menu that opens the KDE control center, from which you can configure every aspect of the KDE environment, such as themes, panels, peripherals like printers and keyboards (already handled by Fedora Core system tools), even the KDE file manager's Web browsing capabilities.

NOTE   *Though GNOME and KDE are wholly integrated desktops, they in fact interact with the operating system through a window manager, Metacity in the case of GNOME and the KDE window manager for KDE. You can use a different GNOME- or KDE-compliant window manager if you wish, or simply use a window manager in place of either KDE or GNOME. You can find out detailed information about different window managers available for Linux from the X11 Web site at* **www.xwinman.org**.

Accessing File Systems, Devices, and Remote Hosts

Removable media will be displayed as icons on your desktop, like CD and DVD discs, USB storage disks, digital cameras, and floppy disks. These icons will not appear until you place the disks into their devices. To open a disk, double-click it to display a file manager window and the files on it.

The desktop will also display a Computer folder. Opening this folder will also list your removable devices, along with icons for your file system and network connections (see Figure 3-4). The file system icon can be used to access the entire file system on your computer, starting from the root directory. Regular users will have only read access to many of these directories, whereas the root user will have full read and write access.

Opening Network will list any hosts on your system with shared directories, like Windows systems accessible with Samba (see Chapters 5 and 41). GNOME uses DNS-based service discovery to automatically detect these hosts. Opening a host's icons will list the shared

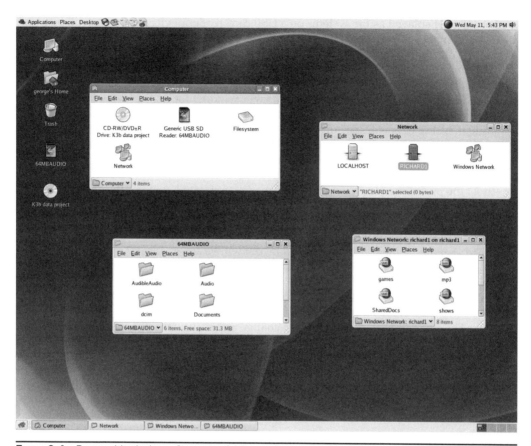

FIGURE 3-4   Removable devices, Computer folder, and shared network folders

directories available on that system. When opening a shared directory, you will be asked for a user and password, like the user and password for a directory owned by a Windows user. The first time you access a shared directory, you will also be asked to save this user and password in a keyring, which itself can be password protected. This allows repeated access without having to always enter the password.

TIP   *Fedora Core cannot play MP3, DVD, or DivX files as installed. You need to download and install supporting tools and libraries from either rpm.livna.org/fedora or freshrpms.net (see Chapter 4).*

Using Removable Devices and Media

Fedora Core 4 now supports removable devices and media like digital cameras, PDAs, card readers, and even USB printers. These devices are handled automatically with an appropriate device interface set up on the fly when needed. Such hotplugged devices are identified, and where appropriate, their icons will appear in the file manager window. For example, when you connect a USB card reader to your system, it will be detected and any cards in the reader will be displayed as file systems on a USB card reader device. The same will be true for digital cameras. Photo applications like gPhoto will be able to automatically access the photos on your digital camera.

DVD and CD discs are also treated like removable devices, with an icon for a disc automatically displayed when you put one in your CD/DVD drive. You can then double-click the CD/DVD disc icon to open a file manager window for it, displaying its contents.

For media discs, like music CD, your system is configured to play the appropriate application. Music CDs will start up the CD player, which will let you play the music. However, for DVD video discs, you will need to download and install supporting video codecs, libraries, and applications from **freshrpms.net** (see Chapters 4 and 12). DivX support must also be downloaded and installed separately.

To set the preferences for how removable media are treated, you use the Drives and Removable Media preferences tool, accessible with the Removable Media entry in the Preferences window. This displays the Removable Drives And Media Preferences window with two panels: one for storage devices and the other for media devices. Certain settings are already set. Removable and hotplugged media will be automatically mounted (see Figure 3-5). This includes floppy disks and data CD/DVDs. Blank CDs are opened for burning by Nautilus.

On the multimedia panel, there are settings for audio CDs and video DVDs, as well as digital cameras (see Figure 3-6). Audio CDs will be played by gnome-cd, and digital cameras will use gThumb to import photos. You can change any of the default applications used for these actions, as well as turn off default operations, such as automatically mounting or playing Audio CDs. DVD movies have no default set, because you should install a commercial DVD player to play DVDs on Linux, as you would on any other system (also check **freshrpms.net**). Once you have installed your DVD player, you can then use the Drives and Removable Media tool to have the DVD movie automatically start up in your selected player.

FIGURE 3-5
Storage media
preferences

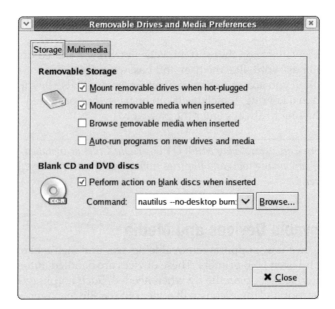

FIGURE 3-6
Multimedia media
preferences

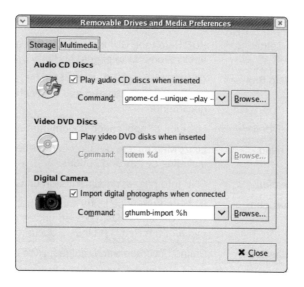

TIP *Fedora Core 4 now treats all devices as if they were hotplugged, automatically generating device interfaces even for fixed devices like hard disks (see Chapter 34).*

Command Line Interface

When using the command line interface, you are given a simple prompt at which you type in your command (see Chapter 8). Even with a GUI, you sometimes need to execute commands on a command line. Linux commands make extensive use of options and arguments. Be careful to place your arguments and options in their correct order on the command line. The format for a Linux command is the command name followed by options, and then by arguments, as shown here:

```
$ command-name options arguments
```

An *option* is a one-letter code preceded by one or two hyphens, which modifies the type of action the command takes. Options and arguments may or may not be optional, depending on the command. For example, the **ls** command can take an option, **-s**. The **ls** command displays a listing of files in your directory, and the **-s** option adds the size of each file in blocks. You enter the command and its option on the command line as follows:

```
$ ls -s
```

An *argument* is data the command may need to execute its task. In many cases, this is a filename. An argument is entered as a word on the command line after any options. For example, to display the contents of a file, you can use the **more** command with the file's name as its argument. The **less** or **more** command used with the filename **mydata** would be entered on the command line as follows:

```
$ less mydata
```

Resource	Description
KDE Help Center	KDE Help tool, GUI interface for documentation on KDE desktop and applications, Man pages, and info documents
GNOME Help Browser	GNOME Help tool, GUI interface for accessing documentation for the GNOME desktop and applications, Man pages, and info documents
/usr/share/doc	Location of application documentation
man *command*	Linux Man pages, detailed information on Linux commands, including syntax and options
info *application*	GNU info pages, documentation on GNU applications
www.redhat.com	Red Hat Enterprise Linux and Red Hat Linux 9 documentation, guides, HOWTOs, and FAQs. Located under "Support and Documentation," much of the Red Hat Linux 9 documentation may be helpful.
fedora.redhat.com	Online documentation, guides, HOWTOs, and FAQs for Fedora Core
fedoraforum.org	End-user discussion support forum, endorsed by the Fedora Project. Includes FAQs and news links.
www.fedorafaq.org	Unofficial FAQ with quick help topics

TABLE **3-1** Linux Help Resources

The command line is actually a buffer of text you can edit. Before you press ENTER, you can perform editing commands on the existing text. The editing capabilities provide a way to correct mistakes you may make when typing in a command and its options. The BACKSPACE and DEL keys let you erase the character you just typed in. With this character-erasing capability, you can BACKSPACE over the entire line if you want, erasing what you entered. CTRL-U erases the whole line and enables you to start over again at the prompt.

TIP You can use the UP ARROW *key to redisplay your last-executed command. You can then reexecute that command, or you can edit it and execute the modified command. This is helpful when you have to repeat certain operations over and over, such as editing the same file. This is also helpful when you've already executed a command you entered incorrectly.*

Help Resources

A great deal of support documentation is already installed on your system, as well as accessible from online sources. Table 3-1 lists Help tools and resources accessible on your Fedora Core system. Both the GNOME and KDE desktops feature Help systems that use a browser-like interface to display help files. To start the GNOME or KDE Help browser, select the Help entry in the main menu. You can then choose from the respective desktop user guides, including the KDE manual, Linux Man pages, and GNU info pages. The GNOME Help Browser also accesses documents for GNOME applications such as the File

Roller archive tool and Evolution mail client. The GNOME Help browser and the KDE Help Center also incorporate browser capabilities, including bookmarks and history lists for documents you view.

Context-Sensitive Help

Both GNOME and KDE, along with other applications, also provide context-sensitive help. Each KDE and GNOME application features detailed manuals that are displayed using their respective Help browsers. Also, system administrative tools feature detailed explanations for each task.

Application Documentation

On your system, the **/usr/share/doc** directory contains documentation files installed by each application. Within each directory, you can usually find HOW-TO, README, and INSTALL documents for that application.

The Man Pages

You can also access the Man pages, which are manuals for Linux commands available from the command line interface, using the **man** command. Enter **man** with the command on which you want information. The following example asks for information on the **ls** command:

```
$ man ls
```

Pressing the SPACEBAR key advances you to the next page. Pressing the B key moves you back a page. When you finish, press the Q key to quit the Man utility and return to the command line. You activate a search by pressing either the slash (/) or question mark (?). The / searches forward, and the ? searches backward. When you press the /, a line opens at the bottom of your screen, and you then enter a word to search for. Press ENTER to activate the search. You can repeat the same search by pressing the N key. You needn't reenter the pattern.

TIP *You can also use either the GNOME or KDE Help system to display Man pages.*

The Info Pages

Online documentation for GNU applications, such as the gcc compiler and the Emacs editor, also exist as *info* pages accessible from the GNOME and KDE Help Centers. You can also access this documentation by entering the command **info**. This brings up a special screen listing different GNU applications. The info interface has its own set of commands. You can learn more about it by entering **info info**. Typing **m** opens a line at the bottom of the screen where you can enter the first few letters of the application. Pressing ENTER brings up the info file on that application.

Web Resources

You can obtain documentation for Fedora Core at the Fedora Project and Red Hat Web sites (see Chapter 1, Table 1-8). Some of the Red Hat 9 documentation is still applicable to Fedora Core. Most Linux applications are covered by the Linux Documentation Project. The GNOME and KDE

Web sites also contain extensive documentation showing you how to use the desktop and taking you through a detailed explanation of Linux applications. Several dedicated Fedora Core support sites are also available.

- **fedoraforums.org**   Provides specific end-user support you can check the support forums on.
- **www.fedorafaq.org**   Lists quick answers to some common issues like enabling MP3 support.
- **fedoranews.org**   Provides the latest news and collection of recent articles as well as blog resources you can check.

System Configuration

To make effective use of your Linux system, you must know how to configure certain features and services. Administrative operations such as adding users and installing software can now be performed with user-friendly system tools. This chapter discusses basic system administration operations that you need to get your system up and running, as well as to perform basic maintenance such as adding new users or printers.

There are four basic system configuration tasks that you most likely will have to deal with: user management, printer setup, display configuration, and software management. You can manage users, adding new ones, removing others, and updating user properties. Different kinds of printers, remote and local, can be set up for your system. For your video card and monitor, you can select the resolutions and color depths you want. You can also install new software packages and update or remove current ones. You were asked to perform all of these tasks during installation. In addition, there are other tools you can use to configure devices such as your keyboard, sound card, and mouse, as well as perform tasks such as setting the system date and time or selecting a language to use. You can make changes or additions easily using the administrative tools described in this chapter.

Configuration operations can be performed from a GUI interface such as GNOME or KDE, or they can be performed using a simple shell command line at which you type configuration commands. You can manually access system configuration files, editing them and making entries yourself. For example, the domain name server entries are kept in the **/etc/resolv.conf** file. You can edit this file and type in the addresses for the servers.

NOTE *Configuration tools are accessible only to the root user. You will first need to log in using* ***root*** *as your username and providing the root password you specified during installation.*

Fedora Core Administrative Tools

Administration is handled by a set of separate specialized administrative tools developed and supported by Red Hat, such as those for user management and display configuration (see Table 4-1). To access the GUI-based Red Hat tools, you log in as the root user to the GNOME desktop and select the main menu. System administrative tools are listed on the

System Settings menu included in the main menu. Here you will find tools to set the time and date, manage users, configure printers, and update software. Users & Groups lets you create and modify users and groups. Printing lets you install and reconfigure printers. All tools provide very intuitive GUI interfaces that are easy to use. In the System Settings folder and menu, tools are identified by simple descriptive terms, whereas their actual names normally begin with the term system-config. For example, the printer configuration tool is listed as Printing, but its actual name is system-config-printer. You can separately invoke any tool by entering its name in a terminal window.

NOTE *Many configuration tasks can also be handled on a command line, invoking programs directly. To use the command line, open a terminal window by right-clicking on the desktop and selecting Open Terminal from the pop-up menu. This opens a terminal window with a command line prompt. Commands like* **rpm** *and* **make** *discussed later will require a terminal window.*

Editing Configuration Files Directly

Though the administrative tools will handle all configuration settings for you, there may be times when you will need to make changes by directly editing configuration files. These are usually text files in the **/etc** directory (see Chapter 29) or dot files in a user home directory, like **.bash_profile** (see Chapter 9). To change any of these files, you will need administrative access, requiring you to first log in as the **root** user.

You can use any standard editor such as Vi or Emacs (see Chapter 11) to edit these files, though one of the easiest ways to edit them is to use the Gedit editor on the GNOME desktop. Select Text Editor from the Accessories menu. This opens a Gedit window. Click Open to open a file browser where you can move through the file system to locate the file you want to edit.

CAUTION *Be careful when editing your configuration files. Editing mistakes can corrupt your configurations. It is advisable to make a backup of any configuration files you are working on first, before making major changes to the original.*

Gedit will let you edit several files at once, opening a tabbed pane for each. You can use Gedit to edit any text file, including ones you create yourself. In Figure 4-1 four configuration files are opened: **.bash_profile**, **/etc/fstab**, **/etc/sysconfig/rhn/sources**, and **/etc/grub.conf**. The **.bash_profile** configures your login shell (see Chapter 9), **/etc/fstab** lists all your file systems and how they are mounted (see Chapter 32), **/etc/sysconfig/rhn/sources** is where your Yum Fedora Core update repositories are listed (see "Updating Fedora Core with RHN, Yum, and APT" in this chapter and Chapter 31), and **/etc/grub.conf** is the configuration file for your GRUB boot loader (see Chapter 29).

Dot files like **.bash_profile** have to be chosen from the file manager window. First configure the file manager to display dot files by opening the Preferences dialog (select Preferences in the Edit menu of any file manager window) and then check the Show Hidden Files entry and close the dialog. Then choose Restore Default Settings in the View menu. This displays the dot files in your file manager window. Double-click to open one in Gedit.

Fedora Core Administration Tool	Description
System Settings	Fedora Core menu for accessing administrative tools
system-config-authentication	Sets authentication settings (see "Authentication Configuration" in this chapter and in Chapter 30)
system-config-boot	Sets operating system to boot default
system-config-date	Changes system time and date (see Chapter 29)
system-config-display	Fedora Core display configuration tool (video card and monitor)
system-config-httpd	Configures Apache Web server (see Chapter 23)
system-config-keyboard	Changes the keyboard configuration
system-config-kickstart	Configures Automatic install scripts (see Chapter 2)
system-config-language	Selects a language to use
system-config-logviewer	Views system log files (see Chapter 29)
system-config-lvm	Configures LVM file system volumes, Fedora Core 4 (see Chapter 33)
system-config-mouse	Configures your mouse
system-config-network	Configures your network interfaces (see Chapter 5)
system-config-network-tui	Configures your network interfaces using the command line; it is cursor based, with no GUI (see Chapter 5)
system-config-nfs	Configures your network interfaces (see Chapters 5 and 40)
system-config-packages	Software management (see Chapters 4 and 31)
system-config-printer	Printer configuration tool (see Chapters 4 and 26)
system-config-rootpassword	Changes the root user password (see Chapters 4 and 29)
system-config-samba	Configures your Samba server (see Chapters 5 and 41)
system-config-securitylevel	Configures your network firewall (see Chapters 5 and 20)
system-config-securitylevel-tui	Configures your network firewall on a command line interface (see Chapters 5 and 20)
system-config-services	Manages system and network services such as starting and stopping servers (see Chapters 4 and 21)
system-config-soundcard	Configures your sound card (see "Simple Administrative Tasks" later in this chapter)
system-config-switch-mail	Selects mail transport agent (server) (see Chapter 25)
system-config-users	User and Group configuration tool (see Chapter 30)

TABLE 4-1   Fedora Core 4 System Configuration Tools

FIGURE 4-1 Gedit text editor and configuration files

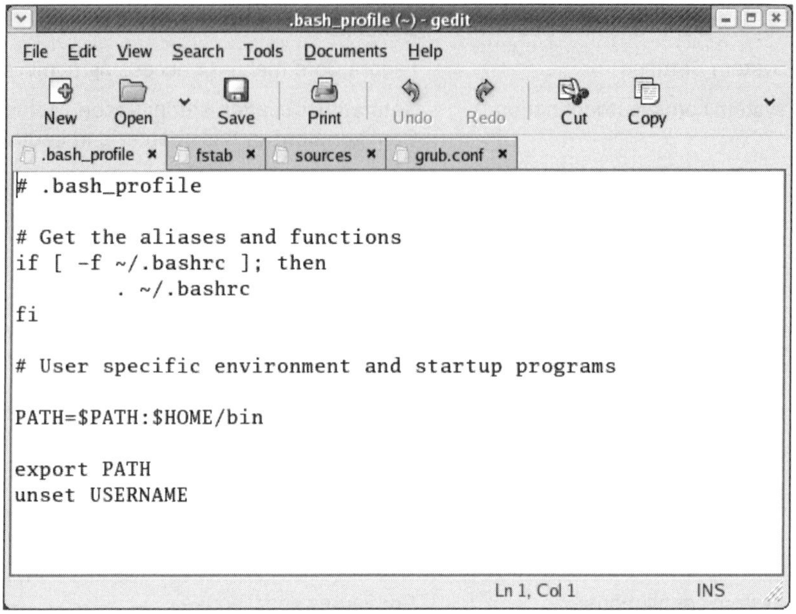
.bash_profile (~) - gedit
File Edit View Search Tools Documents Help
New Open Save Print Undo Redo Cut Copy
.bash_profile fstab sources grub.conf
# .bash_profile
# Get the aliases and functions
if [-f ~/.bashrc]; then
. ~/.bashrc
fi
# User specific environment and startup programs
PATH=$PATH:$HOME/bin
export PATH
unset USERNAME
Ln 1, Col 1
INS

Simple Administrative Tasks

Certain simple administrative tasks can be performed using some of the system-config tools. Most of these have obvious entries in the Settings menu. Others like Login Screen use their own configuration tools.

- **system-config-rootpassword (Root Password)** Use this tool to change your root password, something you may want to do regularly.
- **system-config-date (Date & Time)** Use this to set the date and time, as well as to select a time server for automatic time settings (see Chapter 29 for a detailed discussion).
- **system-config-boot (Bootloader)** Use this tool if you have set up a dual-boot system, with several operating systems on the same hard disks. This will list your operating systems and let you choose the default. Useful for selecting either Window or Linux on the same computer, or, say, a stable or test kernel. If you install a new kernel, it will become the default. Use system-config-boot to set the default back to the one you want.
- **system-config-mouse** Use this tool to configure a mouse, or check to see if it was configured correctly.
- **system-config-soundcard (Soundcard Detection)** This will detect and test a sound card.

Login Screen

If you want to change the login screen, you can use the Login Screen Setup window accessible from Login Screen entry in the Settings menu. This configures the GNOME Display Manager that runs your login process. Here you can set the background image, icons to be displayed, the theme to use, even the welcome message. You can choose between a Standard and a Graphical screen, and select which to use for local and remote logins. If you have only one user or a user that uses the system more than others, you can set up an automatic login, skipping the login screen on startup. You can even set a timed login, automatically logging in a specific user after displaying the login screen for a given amount of time.

The standard greeter is a simple version that will let you choose a background image and select a logo. The graphical greeter will let you choose from different GDM themes. The Red Hat Bluecurve theme is chosen by default, but you can select Happy Gnome with a browser to let you select users from an icon listing.

Basic security options can be set in the security panel, such as whether to allow root logins through the GNOME Display Manager. XDMCP is used to allow connected hosts to use applications on the system through the X server. Check the GNOME Display Manager Reference Manual, accessible with the Help button, for details.

Configuring Users

Currently, the easiest and most effective way to add new users on Fedora Core is to use system-config-users, also known as the Red Hat User Manager. You can access it from the GNOME Desktop's Start Here window's System Settings window. The system-config-users window will display panels for listing both users and groups (see Figure 4-2). A button bar will list various tasks you can perform, including creating new users or groups, editing current ones (Properties), or deleting a selected user or group.

To create a new user, click Add User. This opens a window with entries for the username, password, and login shell, along with options to create a home directory and a new group for that user. Once you have created a user, you can edit its properties to add or change features. Select the user's entry and click Properties. This displays a window with tabbed panels for User Data, Account Info, Password Info, and Groups. On the Groups panel, you can select the groups that the user belongs to, adding or removing group memberships.

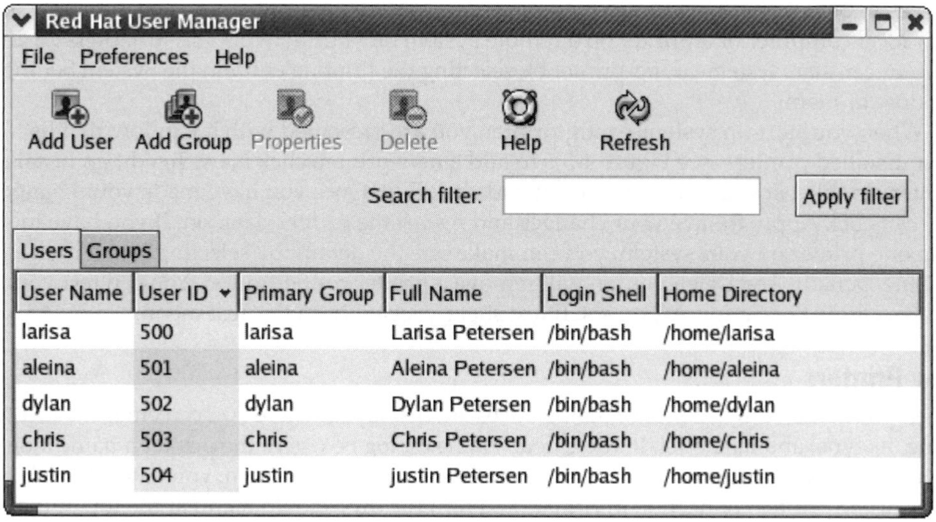

FIGURE 4-2   The Red Hat User Manager, system-config-users

Alternatively, you can use the **useradd** command in a terminal window or command line to add user accounts and the **userdel** command to remove them. The following example adds the user **dylan** to the system:

```
$ useradd dylan
```

One common operation performed from the command line is to change a password. Any user can change his or her own password with the **passwd** command. The command prompts you for your current password. After entering your current password and pressing ENTER, you are then prompted for your new password. After entering the new password, you are asked to reenter it. This is to make sure you actually entered the password you intended to enter.

```
$ passwd
Old password:
New password:
Retype new password:
$
```

TIP *You can use the system-config-rootpassword tool (Root Password on System Settings) to change the password for the root user.*

Printer Configuration

Whenever you first attach a local printer, like a USB printer, you will be asked to perform basic configuration such as confirming the make and model. Removable local printers are managed by udev and HAL, described in Chapter 34. To change your configuration or to add a remote printer, you can use the printer configuration tool, system-config-printer. This utility enables you to select the appropriate driver for your printer, as well as set print options such as paper size and print resolutions. You can configure a printer connected directly to your local computer or a printer on a remote system on your network (see Chapters 26 and 41). You can start system-config-printer by selecting the Printing entry in the System Settings window or menu.

When you start up system-config-printer, you are presented with a window that lists your installed printers (see Figure 4-3). To add a new printer, click New. To edit an installed printer, double-click its entry, or select it and click Edit. Once you have made your changes, you can click Apply to save your changes and restart the printer daemon. If you have more than one printer on your system, you can make one the default by selecting it and then clicking Default. The Delete button will remove a printer configuration. You can test your printer with a PostScript, A4, or ASCII test sheet selected from the Test menu.

New Printers

When you select New, a series of dialog boxes are displayed where you can enter the printer name, its type, and its model. In the Queue Name dialog box, give the printer a name along with any particular description. On the following Queue Type screen, you enter the appropriate printer connection information. From the drop-down menu at the top of the screen, you can select the kind of connection, the first choice being a locally connected

FIGURE 4-3
The system-
config-printer tool

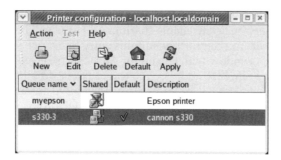

printer and the others, different kinds of remote printers. For a remote printer, you need to select the kind of network or system it is attached to, such as CUPS for Linux systems using the standard CUPS server, Novell for Novell networks, or Windows for printers attached to a Windows computer. For a local printer, you will need to determine the device the printer is connected to. The device is the port to which the printer is connected. This is usually determined by the device hotplug services udev and HAL, which now manage all devices. Click Rescan to have your printer automatically detected. If for some reason your device is not detected, you can use the Custom button to enter in the device name. For a remote printer, you will have to enter the appropriate server and remote queue information.

On the Printer Model screen, you select the manufacturer and model of your printer, which will determine the appropriate driver. Manufacturers are listed in a drop-down menu at the top of the screen. Click it and select your printer's manufacturer (if not listed, use Generic and select the printer type). A list of printer models for the selected manufacturer will be listed in the remainder of the window, automatically. For example, selecting Canon from the manufacturer list will then list all Canon printers in the Printer Model window. Click yours, and then the Forward button. You will be notified that the printer configuration is about to be created. Click Finish. You then see your printer listed in the system-config-printer window. You are now ready to print.

Editing Printers

You can also edit a printer to change any settings. For editing, a set of five tabbed panes are displayed for the printer name, queue type, queue options, driver, and driver options. For the queue type, you can specify entries for the printer device and spool directory. From a drop-down menu, you can also specify whether the printer is local or remotely accessed through a connection. Locally connected printers can be re-detected with the Rescan button, or have their driver automatically detected with the Autoselect Driver button. For the driver options selection, you can specify printer features such as paper size and resolution. When you finish, click OK to close the window. Choose the Quit item from the File menu to quit system-config-printer.

Sharing Local Printers

Shared printers will show a shared icon in their system-config-printers entry. A printer not shared will have this icon crossed out. In Figure 4-3, the Canon printer is shared, but the printer named myepson is not. To allow your local printer to be shared over a network, click the Sharing button at the bottom of the Edit window, or just click directly on the printer's Shared icon. This opens a Sharing Properties window with two panels: Queue and General.

The Queue panel will have a check box for a an entry labeled "This Queue is available to other computers." Click to enable sharing. All Hosts will be entered in the list of Allowed hosts by default. You can further edit this entry to restrict access. Click Edit to open an Edit Allowed Hosts window with entries for All Hosts (selected), network devices, Network Addresses, or a Single IP address. You can use the Add button to add more addresses.

On the General panel you can specify whether to automatically find remote shared queues, as well as whether to enable the older LDP protocol used on Unix systems still using LPRng print servers.

TIP *If you configure your printers with system-config-printer, this tool will use the CUPS print server for managing all your local printers.*

Remote Printers

You can also use system-config-printer to set up a remote printer on Linux, Unix, Microsoft, or Novell networks. When you add a new printer or edit one, the Queue Type pane is displayed with the following selections from a pop-up menu: Locally Connected, Networked Unix (LPD), Networked Windows (SMB), Networked CUPS (IPP), Networked Novell (NCP), or Network JetDirect. (If you edit an existing printer, the queue panel displays a drop-down menu where you can select a remote entry.) For a remote Linux or Unix printer, select Networked Unix (LPD). This displays a dialog box for configuring the remote printer with entries for the server and the queue. For the server, enter the hostname for the system that controls the printer. For the queue, enter the device name on that host for the printer. A Networked Novell (NCP) screen will add entries for the user and the password. A Networked Windows (SMB) screen will have entries for different connected printers. To add one, click Specify to open a window where you can enter the share name, host IP address, workgroup, user, and password. Networked CUPS (IPP) will have entries for the CUPS server and its directory.

A Windows (SMB share) printer is one located on a Windows network. When you click Specify, an authentication window will open in which you enter the Windows settings. You need to enter the Windows workgroup name, its server (host name or IP address), the name of the share, the name of the printer's workgroup, and the username and password. The share is the hostname and printer name in the format *hostname**printername*. The server is the computer where the printer is located. The username and password can be for the printer resource itself, or for access by a particular user. You can then use a print client like **lpr** to send a file to the Windows printer; **lpr** will invoke the Samba client **smbclient** to send the print job to the Windows printer.

To access an SMB shared remote printer, you need to install Samba and have the Server Message Block services enabled using the **smb** daemon. To do this, be sure to start Samba with the **smb** entry in system-config-services (System Settings | Servers | Services menu) and check its box to have it start each time you boot. Printer sharing must, in turn, be enabled on the Windows network.

X Window System Configuration: system-config-display

If you want to change your display settings, or if you are having trouble with your X Window System configuration, you can use system-config-display to change your configuration. You can run system-config-display by selecting Display on the System Settings window or menu.

FIGURE 4-4
The system-config-
display Display
Settings window

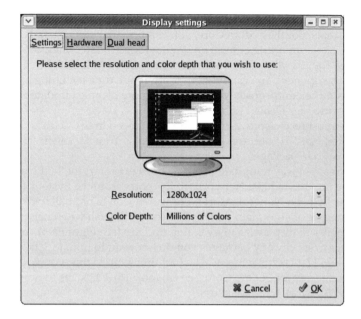

The system-config-display tool opens a Display Settings window with three panels: Settings, Hardware, and Dual Head (shown in Figure 4-4).

The Settings panel shows pop-up menus for selecting your resolution and color depth. Your current resolution and color depth will already be selected.

To change your monitor or video card settings, click the Hardware tab. This displays a panel with entries for Monitor and Video Card. Each will have a Configure button. Clicking the Video Card Configure button displays a list of supported video cards, with your current one selected. Clicking Monitor Configure lists supported monitors, with expandable vendor entries. A Reset default button will return to your default entries.

For video cards that support dual-head connections, you can use the Dual Head panel to configure your second monitor. First you enable dual head, and then you can configure the monitor connected to the second connection. For the Desktop Layout, you can have individual desktops or a spanning desktop over both monitors.

The system-config-display tool then generates an X Window System configuration file called **/etc/X11/xorg.conf**. This is the file the X Window System uses to start up. Fedora Core uses the X.org drivers for the X Window System. You can find out more about X.org at **www.x.org**.

Updating Fedora Core with RHN, Yum, and APT

New versions of Fedora Core are released every few months, and for Red Hat Enterprise, every year or so. In the meantime, new updates are continually being prepared for particular software packages. These are posted as updates you can download from software repositories and install on your system. These include new versions of applications, servers, and even the kernel. Such updates may range from single software packages to whole components—for instance, all the core, application, and development packages issued when a new release of GNOME, KDE, or XFree86 is made available.

Updating your Linux system has become a very simple procedure, using the automatic update tools. For the Fedora Core, you can update your system by accessing software repositories supporting either Yum (Yellowdog Update, Modified) or apt-rpm (Advanced Package Tool RPM) update methods. Yum uses RPM headers to determine which packages need to be updated. You can find out more about Yum, including a listing of Yum repositories, at **linux.duke.edu/projects/yum**. APT is a more complex update method originally implemented for Debian Linux.

The most recent software upgrades are placed in the Red Hat Rawhide directory, located at the Red Hat FTP site. You can access them as Yum packages, RPM packages, ISO images, or source code packages.

The easiest way to update Fedora Core 4 is to start the Red Hat Update Agent (up2date) by selecting the Red Hat Network (RHN) entry from the System Tools menu. You can also click the Red Hat Network Alert Notification icon (a red ball with an exclamation point on the right side of your main panel). This icon will flash when new updates are available. Clicking it will display list of available updates (see Figure 4-5). You can use the Ignored Packages to specify any packages you do not want to update. Click Launch Up2date to start up the Red Hat Up2date Agent. The first time you do this, you will be asked to download the GPG public key for Fedora Core (see Chapter 16). Click Yes to download the key. Then the Red Hat Network interface starts.

Though it is reserved for use by Red Hat Enterprise Linux, on the Fedora Core, you can use the Red Hat Update Agent to access the Yum Fedora Core Yum repository, letting you update quickly to the most recent software versions. The initial screen will list the available Fedora Core Yum repository link. Click Forward to continue. Channels are provided for the Fedora Core release, updates, and for Fedora Extras. You can add a testing channel for the newest releases (replaces Rawhide releases). Your packages will then be downloaded. Next, packages that are flagged to be skipped, like kernel packages, are listed. You can include these at this point. Then a list of packages that can be updated will be displayed, from which you can select the ones you want to update (see Figure 4-6). A Select All Packages check box lets you automatically select all downloaded updates.

To access other Yum repositories, you can configure the **/etc/sysconfig/rhn/sources** file to access them with the Red Hat Update Agent. You can also use the **yum** command, designating Yum repositories in the **/etc/yum.conf** file. A Yum entry in the **/etc/sysconfig/ rhn/sources** file consists of the type (yum), a channel label, and a URL referencing the site.

Figure 4-5
Red Hat network alert notification tool

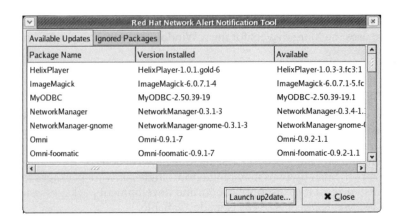

PART I

FIGURE 4-6
Up2date
installation

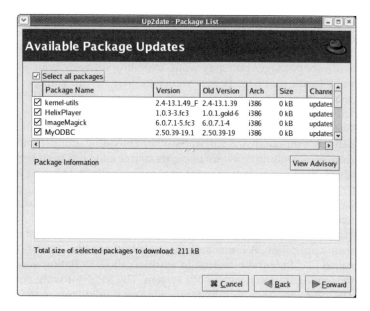

For updates Fedora Core often uses a mirror channel type to access updates from available mirrors. Mirror references are located at

```
http://fedora.redhat.com/download/up2date-mirrors/
```

A Yum entry for updating from mirrors for Fedora Core 4 would look like this, with the version number changing with each release:

```
yum-mirror updates-released-fc4 http://fedora.redhat.com/download/up2date-
mirrors/updates-released-fc4
```

To update particular advanced and test releases, you would use **updates-testing-fc4** or **fedora-core-rawhide** as the final item in the URL.

To update from a particular site, such as the Fedora Core release site at **download.fedora .redhat.com**, you would use a yum type and reference the particular directory where the packages are located. The ARCH variable holds the kind of platform you have, i386 or x86_64.

```
yum updates-released-fc4 http://download.fedora.redhat.com/pub/fedora/
linux/core/updates/4/$ARCH/
```

To update to a new Fedora Core release, you can download Fedora Core CD/DVD-ROM ISO images from **fedora.redhat.com/releases/fedora-core**, which you can burn and update from. ISO images can also be downloaded using the BitTorrent service (see Chapter 2). BitTorrent provides a very fast method for downloading ISO images.

For Red Hat Enterprise Linux, you can automatically update your system by registering as part of the Red Hat Network. The Red Hat Network service now only supports Red Hat Enterprise Linux, not Fedora Core Linux (though the RHN Up2date Agent is be configured to access Fedora repositories on Fedora systems). Registering with and configuring access to the Red Hat Network is a very simple procedure, using the Red Hat Network Registration client. The Red Hat Network is a subscription service included with your purchase of an enterprise package. Once registered with the Red Hat Network, you can use the Red Hat Update Agent to download and install Red Hat Enterprise updates almost automatically.

Installing Software Packages

Now that you know how to start Linux and access the root user account, you can install any other software packages you may want. Installing software is an administrative function performed by the root user. Unless you chose to install all your packages during your installation, only some of the many applications and utilities available for users on Linux were installed on your system. On Fedora Core, you can easily install or remove software from your system with either the system-config-packages tool, the **yum** tool, or the **rpm** command. Alternatively, you can install software by downloading and compiling its source code. The procedure for installing software using its source code has been simplified to just a few commands, though you have a great deal of flexibility in tailoring an application to your specific system.

Many distributions, including Fedora Core, Red Hat, Mandrake, and SuSE, use the Red Hat Package Manager (RPM) to organize Linux software into packages you can automatically install or remove. An RPM software package operates like its own installation program for a software application. A Linux software application often consists of several files that must be installed in different directories. In addition, the installation may require modification of certain configuration files on your system. The RPM software packages perform all these tasks for you. Also, if you later decide you don't want a specific application, you can uninstall packages to remove all the files and configuration information from your system (see Chapter 31 for more details).

The software packages on your CD-ROMs, as extensive as they are, represent only a small portion of the software packages available for Linux. Many Fedora-compliant RPM packages not included with the distribution can be found in the Fedora Extras repository, also at **download.fedora.org**. You can download additional software from online software sites such as **sourceforge.net**. The **sourceforge.net** site not only distributes software but also serves as the primary development site for a massive number of open source software projects. You can also locate many of the newest Linux applications from **freshmeat.net** or **rpmfind.net**. Many multimedia applications and support libraries can be found at **rpm .livna.org/fedora** and **freshrpms.net**. Here, you can link to the original development sites for these applications and download documentation and the recent versions. Table 4-2 lists several Fedora and Linux software sites. Downloading Fedora Extras software is a simple matter of entering the **yum** utility with the **install** option and the name of the package in a terminal window. **yum** will detect the software and any dependencies, and prompt you to download and install it. For example, the following command will install Abiword:

```
yum install abiword
```

Installing Packages with system-config-packages

The system-config-packages tool provides an effective and easy-to-use interface for managing the RPM packages provided by your Fedora Core distribution, whether you installed from CD-ROMs, DVD-ROM, hard disk, or network. It runs on any window manager, including GNOME and KDE. You can access system-config-packages using the Add/Remove Applications icon in the System Settings window. This opens an Add And Remove Software window that displays a left panel bar with icons for Install Software and Remove Software, and a panel that will display either software to be installed or software to be removed, depending on the icon selected. Initially, the Install Software icon will be displayed, showing

Internet Site	Description
ftp.redhat.com	Red Hat distribution RPM packages
download.fedora.redhat.com/pub/ fedora/linux/extras	Fedora Extras: Fedora-compliant software not included with the distribution
rpm.livna.org/fedora	Repository for multimedia and other RPM packages (Fedora Project extension)
rpmfind.net	RPM package repository
sourceforge.net	SourceForge open source software repository and development site
freshrpms.net	Multimedia Fedora–compliant RPM package repository
freshmeat.net	New Linux software
www.kde-apps.org	KDE software applications
www.gnome.org	GNOME software applications

TABLE 4-2   Fedora Core and Linux Software Sites

a list of software groups with packages you can install. The View menu will let you switch between group and individual package views. If you know the name of the individual package you want to install, you can use the Package view.

Groups with packages not yet been installed will have an Install link at the end (see Figure 4-7). Those with all packages installed will have no Install link. An uninstalled package group will be organized into required and optional packages. You can select the optional ones, and the required ones will always be installed. A partially installed group will be organized into installed and uninstalled packages. You can then select the uninstalled packages you want to add, by clicking their check boxes. Once you have made all your selections, click Install Packages; system-config-packages will prepare a list of packages to install, checking for dependent packages. Once the list is prepared, you can click Details to see which RPM packages will be installed, if you wish. Click Continue to perform the installation. You will be prompted to enter the appropriate CD-ROM or just the DVD-ROM.

You can also choose to list the uninstalled individual RPM packages provided with your distribution. You can then select the packages you want to install. From the View menu, select Package view to list all currently uninstalled RPM packages, and then click the check boxes for the ones you want. To switch back to the Group display, select Group from the View menu.

To uninstall a package, first click the Remove Software icon on the bar displayed to the left of the Package panel. In the Group view, installed groups will be displayed with a Remove link at the end. To uninstall packages from a group, click the Remove link. This displays a list of installed packages with a checked check box next to each one. Deselect the ones you want to remove and leave selected the ones you want to keep. When you have finished making your selections, click Remove Packages to queue the packages for removal. Click Continue to perform the removal. In the Package view, all installed packages are listed and you simply select the ones you want removed.

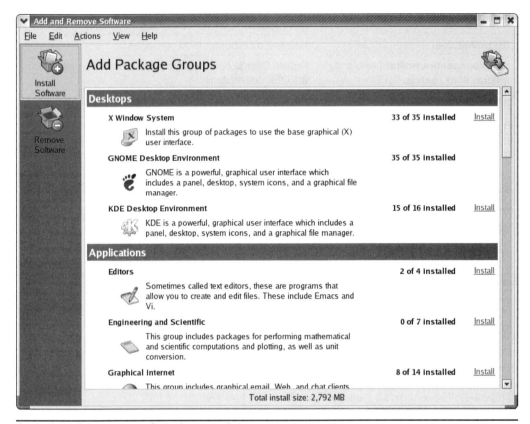

FIGURE 4-7 The system-config-packages tool

You can also install a particular RPM package directly. You can use this method to install RPM packages you have downloaded or individual packages on your distribution DVD/CD-ROM. First display it with the file manager, and then double-click the RPM package file. You can also right-click it and, on GNOME, select Open With and then Install Packages, or on KDE, select Install Package. This invokes the system-config-packages tool, which will install the package. It will also check for dependent packages and prompt you to install those. For packages that are part of your Fedora Core distribution, it will prompt you to insert any other CD-ROMs as needed (for the DVD-ROM included with this book, there will be no prompt, as it already holds all packages).

Installing Packages with the rpm Command

If you do not have access to the desktop or you prefer to work from the command line interface, you can use the **rpm** command to manage and install software packages (you can also open a terminal window by right-clicking on the desktop and selecting Open Terminal from the pop-up menu). The **rpm** command performs installation, removal, and verification of software packages. Each software package is actually an RPM package, consisting of an archive of software files and information about how to install those files.

Each archive resides as a single file with a name that ends with **.rpm**, indicating it is a software package that can be installed by the Red Hat Package Manager.

You can use the **rpm** command to either install or uninstall a package. The **rpm** command uses a set of options to determine what action to take. The **-i** option installs the specified software package, and the **-U** option updates a package. With an **-e** option, **rpm** uninstalls the package. A **q** placed before an **i** (**-qi**) queries the system to see if a software package is already installed and displays information about the software (**-qpi** queries an uninstalled package file). The **rpm** command with no options provides a complete list of **rpm** options. A set of commonly used options is shown here:

Option	Action
-U	Updates package
-I	Installs package
-e	Removes package
-qi	Displays information for an installed package
-ql	Displays file list for installed package
-qpi	Displays information from an RPM package file (used for uninstalled packages)
-qpl	Displays file list from an RPM package file (used for uninstalled packages)
-K	Authenticates and performs integrity check on a package

The software package name is usually quite lengthy, including information about the version and release date in its name. All end with **.rpm**. In the next example, the user installs the freeciv package using the **rpm** command. Notice that the full filename is entered. To list the full name, you can use the **ls** command with the first few characters and an asterisk. The following examples use the DivX xvidcore RPM packages downloaded from **rpm.livna .org**. (You can also download more recent versions of xvidcore from **freshrpms.net**.)

```
ls xvid*
```

You can also use the * to match the remainder of the name, as in the following:

```
ls xvidccore-1*.rpm
```

In most cases, you are installing packages with the **-U** option, for update. Even if the package is not already installed, **-U** still installs it.

```
$ rpm -Uvh xvidcore-1.0.3-0.lvn.1.3.i386.rpm
```

When RPM performs an installation, it first checks for any dependent packages. These are other software packages with programs the application you are installing needs to use. If other dependent packages must be installed first, RPM cancels the installation and lists those packages. You can install those packages and then repeat the installation of the application. To determine if a package is already installed, use the **-qi** option with **rpm**. The **-q** stands for query. To obtain a list of all the files the package has installed, as well as the directories it installed to, use the **-ql** option. To query package files, add the **p** option. The **-qpi** option displays information about a package, and **-qpl** lists the files in it. The following example lists all the files in the freeciv package:

```
$ rpm -qpl xvidcore-1.0.3-0.lvn.1.3.i386.rpm
```

To remove a software package from your system, first use **rpm -qi** to make sure it is actually installed, and then use the **-e** option to uninstall it. As with the **-qi** option, you needn't use the full name of the installed file. You only need the name of the application. In the next example, the user removes the DivX xvidcore from the system:

```
$ rpm -e xvidcore
```

Package Security Check

If you download an RPM package, you may want to check its integrity and authentication, making sure the package was not tampered with and that it was obtained from a valid source. To just check a package's integrity, you can use the **rpm** command with the **-K** and the **--nosignature** options. A value called the MD5 digest measures the contents of a package. If the value is incorrect, the package has been tampered with. (See Chapter 16 for more details on integrity checks and MD5 digests.) Some packages, like Webmin, provide just digest values, allowing only integrity checks. In the next example, the user checks whether the freeciv package has been tampered with. The **--nosignature** option says not to perform authentication, doing the integrity check only.

```
$ rpm -K --nosignaturexvidcore-1.0.3-0.lvn.1.3.i386.rpm
```

To authenticate a package, you check its digital signature. Packages are signed with encrypted digital keys that can be decrypted using the public key provided by the author of the package. This public key has to first be downloaded and installed on the encryption tool used on your system. Fedora Core, along with most Linux systems, use the GNU Privacy Guard (GPG) encryption tool. (GPG and authentication methods along with public keys are discussed in detail in Chapter 16.) To use a public key to authenticate an RPM package, you first have to download the public key and install it in the RPM key database. For all RPM packages that are part of the distribution, you can use the Red Hat public key, placed during installation in the **/usr/share/rhn/RPM-GPG-KEY** file. You need to manually import the key to the RPM database before you can check RPM packages, as shown here:

```
rpm --import /usr/share/rhn/RPM-GPG-KEY
```

If you have downloaded an RPM package from another site, you can also download and install its public key, with which you can authenticate that package.

Once the public key is installed, you can check the package's authentication using the **rpm** command with the **-K** option.

```
$ rpm -K xvidcore-1.0.3-0.lvn.1.3.i386.rpm
```

To see a list of all the keys you have imported, you can use the **-qa** option and match on the gpg-pubkey* pattern. Using **rpm** with the **-qi** option and the public key, you can display detailed information about the key. The following example shows the Red Hat public key:

```
$ rpm -qa gpg-pubkey*
gpg-pubkey-db42a60e-37ea5348
```

Installing Source Code Applications

Many programs are available for Linux in source code format. These programs are stored in a compressed archive that you need to decompress and then extract. The resulting source code can then be configured, compiled, and installed on your system. The process has been simplified to the extent that it involves not much more than installing an RPM package. The following example shows the common method to extract, compile, and install software, in this case the kat program, a desktop search and indexing tool. Always check the included README and INSTALL files that come with the source code to check the appropriate method for creating and installing that software.

TIP *Be sure that you have installed all development packages onto your system. Development packages contain the key components such as the compiler, GNOME and KDE headers and libraries, and preprocessors. You cannot compile source code software without them.*

First you locate the software—in this case, from **www.linuxgames.com**—and then you download it to your system. kat is downloaded in a file named - **freeciv-2.0.1.tar.bz2**. Then decompress and extract the file either with the Archive Manager on the desktop, or with the **tar** command in a terminal window.

Extracting the Archive

The easiest way to extract compressed archives is to use the Archive Manager (Applications | System Tools | Archive Manager) on GNOME (see Chapter 31). Either double-click the compressed archive file, or right-click and select Open With "Archive Manager". This displays the top-level contents of the archive, which you can browse if you wish, even reading text files like README and INSTALL files. You can also see what files will actually be installed. Use the button to navigate and double-click a directory to open it. Nothing is extracted at this point. To extract the archive, click Extract.

To use the **tar** command, first open a terminal window (right-click on the desktop and select Open Terminal). At the prompt, enter the **tar** command with the **xvjf** options (**j** for **bz2** and **z** for **gz**), as shown here:

```
tar xvjf freeciv-2.0.1.tar.bz2
```

Configure, Compile, and Install

Extracting the archive will create a directory with the name of the software, in this case **freeciv-2.0.1**. Once it is extracted, you have to configure, compile, and install the software. This usually needs to be done from a terminal window.

Change to the software directory with the **cd** command:

```
cd freeciv-2.0.1
```

Issue the command `./configure`. This generates a compiler configuration for your particular system.

```
./configure
```

Compile the software with the **make** command:

```
make
```

Then install the program with the **make install** command:

```
make install
```

Most KDE and GNOME software will also place an entry for the program in the appropriate menus—for example, a freeciv entry will be placed in the KDE Applications menu. You can then run freeciv from the menu entry. You could also open a terminal window and enter the program's name.

Security Configuration

Once you have installed your Linux system, you should carry out some basic security measures to protect your system from outside attacks. Systems connected to the Internet are open to attempts by outside users to gain unauthorized access. This usually takes the following forms:

- Trying to break into the system
- Having broken in, changing or replacing system files with hacked or corrupt versions
- Attempting to intercept communications from remote users
- Changing or replacing messages sent to or from users
- Pretending to be a valid user

Firewalls, intrusion protection, encryption, data integrity, and authentication are ways of protecting against such attacks.

- A firewall prevents any direct unauthorized attempts at access.
- Intrusion detection checks the state of your system files to see if they have been tampered with by someone who has broken in.
- Encryption protects transmissions by authorized remote users, providing privacy.
- Integrity checks such as modification digests guarantee that messages and data have not been intercepted and changed or substituted en route.
- Authentication methods such as digital signatures can verify that the user claiming to send a message or access your system is actually that person.

Security Services

Fedora Core includes several security services for protecting your system and your network transmissions (see Table 4-3). Using GNU Privacy Guard (GPG), you can encrypt your e-mail messages or files you want to send, as well as sign them with an encrypted digital signature authenticating that the message was sent by you (see Chapter 16). The digital signature also includes encrypted modification digest information that provides an integrity check, allowing the recipient to verify that the message received is the original and not one that has been changed or substituted.

With Security-Enhanced Linux a refined administrative approach is provided for greater security controls. User access to different parts of the operating system can be limited using roles and security contexts. Only qualified users can have access to certain objects like files and applications. Security-Enhanced Linux policy can be either strict or targeted. A targeted policy applies restrictions to daemons like Internet servers, restricting access for users that access those servers. You can choose which servers you want controlled. Use the system-config-securitylevel tool's SELinux panel to select the servers you want managed by SELinux (see Chapters 5 and 17).

A good foundation for your network security is to set up a Linux system to operate as a firewall for your network, protecting it from unauthorized access (see Chapter 20). You can use a firewall to implement either packet filtering or proxies. *Packet filtering* is simply the process of deciding whether a packet received by the firewall host should be passed on into the local system or network. The firewall package currently in use is Netfilter (iptables). Older releases use an earlier version called ipchains. To implement a firewall, you simply provide a series of rules to govern what kind of access you want to allow on your system. If that system is also a gateway for a private network, the system's firewall capability can effectively protect the network from outside attacks. You can provide a simple configuration for your own system using system-config-securitylevel as described in Chapter 5. Be sure to check the Fedora Core SELinux FAQ at **fedora.redhat.com** for implementation details and problems on using SELinux on Fedora Core.

Outside users may also try to gain unauthorized access through any Internet services you may be hosting, such as a Web site. In such a case, you can set up a proxy to protect your site from attack. For Linux systems, use Squid proxy software to set up a proxy to protect your Web server (see Chapter 20).

To further control access to your system, you can provide secure user authentication with encrypted passwords, a Lightweight Directory Access Protocol (LDAP) service, and Pluggable Authentication Modules (PAM) (see Chapter 30). User authentication can further be controlled for certain services by Kerberos servers (see Chapter 19). Kerberos authentication provides another level of security whereby individual services can be protected, allowing use of a service only to users who are cleared for access. LDAP and Kerberos are all enabled and configured with authconfig-gtk (Authentication in the System Settings menu or window).

To protect remote connections from hosts outside your network, transmissions can be encrypted. For Linux systems, you can use the Secure Shell (SSH) suite of programs to encrypt any transmissions, preventing them from being read by anyone else (see Chapter 19). The SSH programs are meant to replace the remote tools such as **rsh** and **rcp** (see Chapter 15), which perform no encryption.

The IPsec protocol also provides encryption of network transmissions, but integrated into the IP packet structure (see Chapter 18). With IPsec you can both encrypt and authenticate transmissions, ensuring that they were not intercepted and tampered with, and you can implement virtual private networks (VPNs), using encrypted transmissions to connect one local network to another using a larger network like the Internet.

You can find the latest news on security issues at the Red Hat Web site (**www.redhat .com**) along with other Linux sites such as Linux Security (**www.linuxsecurity.com**), Linux Weekly News (**lwn.net**), and Linux Today (**linuxtoday.com**).

Application	Description
GNU Privacy Guard (GPG)	Encryption and digital signatures (Chapter 16) **www.gnupg.org**
Netfilter (iptables)	Firewall packet filtering (Chapter 20) **www.netfilter.org**
Security-Enhanced Linux (SELinux)	Security-Enhanced Linux (Chapter 17) **www.nsa.gov/selinux**
Squid	Web proxy server (Chapter 24) **www.squid-chache.org**
OpenSSH	Secure Shell encryption and authentication for remote access (Chapter 19) **www.openssh.org**
Kerberos	User authentication for access to services (Chapter 19) **web.mit.edu/kerberos/www**
Pluggable Authorization Modules (PAM)	Authentication management and configuration (Chapter 30)
Shadow passwords	Password encryption (Chapter 30)
Lightweight Directory Access Protocol (LDAP)	User management and authorization (Chapter 30) **www.openldap.org**
system-config-authentication	Fedora Core tool to enable and configure authentication tools: Kerberos, LDAP, and shadow passwords
Internet Protocol Security (IPsec)	Protocol to implement Virtual Private Networks (Chapter 18)

TABLE 4-3 Security Applications

NOTE Numerous older security applications are also available for Linux such as COPS (Computer Oracle and Password System) to check password security; Tiger, which scans your system for unusual or unprotected files; and SATAN (Security Administration Tool for Analyzing Networks), which checks your system for security holes. Crack is a newer password auditing tool that you can use to check how well your password security performs under dictionary attacks.

Authentication Configuration

To confirm that user identities are valid, your network may provide several authentication services (see Chapter 30). These can be enabled on your system using system-config-authentication. You can invoke system-config-authentication by selecting Authentication from the System Settings menu. The system-config-authentication tool consists of two panels, User Information and Authentication. Configuration consists primarily of specifying the address of the service's server on your network. The User Information panel is used for services like NIS (see Chapter 40) and LDAP (see Chapter 30), which maintain configuration information about systems and users on your network. The Authentication panel lists services for authenticating users. The Shadow and MD5 Password options are normally selected by default and provide password protection (see Chapter 30).

If your network also maintains LDAP, Kerberos (see Chapter 19), and SMB (see Chapter 41) authentication servers, you can enable support for them here, specifying their servers and domains.

Unsupported Drivers

Drivers for most network devices are already included in your Fedora Core distribution. However, if you have a new device that is currently not supported, you should check with the provider's Web site for the appropriate Linux driver. A driver takes the form of a module that is loaded dynamically by the Linux kernel when your system starts up (see Chapters 34 and 35). Normally, compiled versions of a module are provided that you can download and then install on your system. To install a module, you use the **modprobe** command. Once installed, the module will be loaded automatically by the kernel each time you start your system. Should something go wrong with the install, you can always uninstall the module using the **modprobe** command with the **-r** option.

Many modules are provided as source code only. In this case, you will have to unpack and compile the module first, using the **tar** command as noted in the preceding section. Check the README or INSTALL files normally included with the source code for detailed instructions. If none are included, try the **./configure** and **make** commands. Usually a **make** command with the **install** option will install the module in your system's module library directory. The install option may also run the **depmod** command to updated the module dependencies, allowing **modprobe** to load it.

```
./configure
make
make install
```

If you are using a precompiled version, you need to follow any instruction for installing the module in the module library. This is located in **/lib/modules/**_version_ directory, which has several subdirectories for different kinds of modules. Here _version_ is the kernel version number, like **2.6.11-1.1286_FC4** on Fedora Core 4. Modules for network cards are kept in the **kernel/drivers/net** directory, as in **/lib/modules/2.6.11-1.1286_FC4/kernel/drivers/net**. You can copy a precompiled module for a network card to that directory.

Once you have created the module and installed it in the module library directory, the module needs to be checked for any dependent modules that may also need to be loaded with it to make it work. This is done by the **depmod** tool. If you installed from a source code version, **depmod** may have already been run. In this case, you can directly load the module with **modprobe**. If, however, you copied the precompiled version directly to the module library, or if your source code version did not run **depmod**, you should then restart your system. On restart, the **depmod** tool will run automatically and check for any module dependencies. You can then manually load the using the **modprobe** command and the module name.

You can add any parameters the module may require. To discover what parameters a module takes, you can use the **modinfo** command with the **-p** option. The **-v** option (verbose) lists all actions taken as they occur. In the next example, **modprobe** loads the **bcm4400.o** module for a Broadcom network device (do not use the **.o** suffix in the name):

```
# modprobe -v bcm4400
```

Options for the **modprobe** command are placed in the **/etc/modprobe.conf** file. Here, you can enter configuration options, such as default directories and aliases. An alias provides a simple name for a module. For example, the following entry enables you to reference the bcm4400.o Ethernet card module as **eth0** (Kmod, the Kernel module loader (see Chapter 32), automatically detects the Broadcom card and loads the bcm4400 module):

```
alias eth0 bcm4400
```

Once it is loaded, you need to restart your system. On restart, the new hardware will be detected and you will be asked you to configure it. You can configure it at this time, specifying any network information, or wait and use system-config-network after your system starts up. With system-config-network, you can create a new device for the hardware connection and provide configuration information such as whether to use DHCP for automatic configuration or manually supply network IP and DNS addresses.

Installing Access for Windows NTFS File Systems

If you have installed Fedora Core on a dual-boot system with Windows XP or otherwise need access NTFS partitions, you will not be able to access them until you install the Linux NTFS kernel module. Fedora Core does not include support for accessing Windows NTFS file systems (used on Windows XP, NT, and 2000), due to licensing issues. The Linux NTFS kernel is developed by the Linux NTFS Project. You can find detailed information and help at its Web site at **linux-ntfs.sourceforge.net**, though this site may not be up to date.

Installing and loading the module is a very simple process. RPM NTFS packages are already provided for the Fedora Core kernels at the Linux NTFS Project Web site as well as at **rpm.livna.org/fedora**. There is a different package for each kernel version, and you need to download the one for your installed kernel. If you have more than one installed kernel, download the packages for each.

Be sure to log in as the root user. You must first find out the version for your kernel. To do this, open a terminal window (right-click and select Open A Terminal Window) and enter the following command:

```
# uname -r
2.6.11-1.1286_FC4
```

To see all kernel versions installed, you can do this:

```
ls /lib/modules
```

You can download from either of these sites:

```
rpm.livna.org/fedora/4/i386/RPMS.stable
sourceforge.net/projects/linux-ntfs/
```

On the **rpm.livna.org/fedora** site, you will use the Fedora Core 4 packages. Be sure to select from the Fedora 4 packages on the NTFS SourceForge site.

You will see the different version packages for the NTFS kernel lists on the appropriate sites. Here are two packages for the FC4 smp and normal kernels with kernel version 2.6.11-1.1286.

```
kernel-module-ntfs-2.6.11-1.1286_FC4-2.1.22-0.lvn.1.3.i686.rpm
kernel-module-ntfs-2.6.11-1.1286_FC4smp-2.1.22-0.lvn.1.3.i686.rpm
```

When you download with Firefox, you can choose to immediately install the module. If you downloaded the file first, right-click the file icon and select Open With Install Packages. This will install the module in its appropriate module directory for use by the kernel. You then need to load the kernel with the **modprobe** command.

```
modprobe ntfs
```

Once the module is installed, you can then mount your NTFS file systems. First set up a directory where you want the Windows files system mounted. Usually this is in the **/mnt** directory under a subdirectory that could be named **windows**.

```
mkdir /mnt/windows
```

You will need to know your hard drive names for any NTFS partitions. You can find this out by entering the **fdisk -l** command. In the following example, the NTFS file system is located at **/dev/sda1**:

```
# fdisk -l
Disk /dev/sda: 250.0 GB, 250059350016 bytes
255 heads, 63 sectors/track, 30401 cylinders
Units = cylinders of 16065 * 512 = 8225280 bytes

   Device Boot      Start         End      Blocks   Id  System
/dev/sda1   *           1       15298   122881153+   7  HPFS/NTFS
/dev/sda2           15299       15426     1028160   82  Linux swap / Solaris
/dev/sda3           15427       16732    10490445   83  Linux
/dev/sda4           16733       30401   109796242+      Extended
/dev/sda5           16733       30401   109796211   83  Linux
```

To mount, use the **mount** command and specify the type with the **-t ntfs** option. List the directory first and then the file system name. Though the NTFS module supports limited write capability, it does not support full write operations. To be safe, you may want to limit it to just read capability. Do this with the **-o ro** option.

```
mount /dev/sda1  /mnt/windows  -t ntfs  -o ro
```

If you want the partition mounted automatically when you log in, you have to make an entry for it in the **/etc/fstab** file (see Chapter 32). You can use the text editor (Gedit) to edit the file. Be very careful editing this file. You may want to make a backup of it first. Using the previous example, the corresponding fstab entry would be

```
/dev/sda1    /mnt/windows     ntfs    ro     0 0
```

The Linux NTFS Project also provides an extensive set of tools for managing NTFS partitions from Linux, including **mktfs** to format NTFS partitions, **ntfsresize** to resize a partition, and **ntfsls** to list files in a partition. You can download these tools from the **sourceforge.net/projects/linux-ntfs** page.

```
ntfsprogs-1.9.4-1.i586.rpm
```

To enable the GNOME Virtual Filesystem to perform NTFS operations, you install **ntfsprogs-gnomevfs**.

```
ntfsprogs-gnomevfs-1.9.4-1.i586.rpm
```

Bluetooth

Fedora Core now provides Bluetooth support for both serial connections and BlueZ protocol–supported devices. Bluetooth is a wireless connection method for locally connected devices such as keyboards, mice, printers, and even PDAs and Bluetooth-capable cell phones. You can think of it as a small local network dedicated to your peripheral devices, eliminating the needs for wires. Bluetooth devices can be directly connected through your serial ports or through specialized Bluetooth cards connected to USB ports or inserted in a PCI slot. BlueZ is the official Linux Bluetooth protocol and has been integrated into the Linux kernel since version 2.4.6. The BlueZ protocol was developed originally by Qualcomm and is now an open source project, located at **bluez.sourceforge.net**. It is included with Fedora Core in the bluez-utils and bluez-libs packages, among others. Check the BlueZ site for a complete list of supported hardware, including adapters, PCMCIA cards, and serial connectors.

Both GNOME and KDE provide Bluetooth configuration and management tools. GNOME provides the GNOME Bluetooth subsystem, which features a device manager, a plug-in for Nautilus to let the GNOME file browser access Bluetooth devices, and a file server. For KDE, the KDE Bluetooth Utilities is currently under development, providing similar tools for accessing Bluetooth devices. To connect mobile phones to a system using Bluetooth, you can use the GNOME Phone Manager or KDE's K68 tool. Fedora Core also includes the Bluetooth File Sharing applet for receiving Bluetooth files.

NOTE *The Affix Frontend Environment (AFE) is an alternative to Bluez that provides an easy-to-use method for accessing Bluetooth devices (**affix.sourceforge.net**).*

NOTE *Currently under development, the GNOME Bluetooth subsystem provides a GNOME interface for administering and accessing your Bluetooth devices (gnome-bluetooth-admin). Check the gnome-bluetooth RPM package.*

Bluetooth Configuration

Configuration information is located in the **/etc/bluetooth** directory, along with the **/etc/pcmcia** directory for notebooks. Use the **hciconfig** command to configure Bluetooth devices, **hcitool** to configure Bluetooth connections. Use **hciattach** to attach serial devices to a serial port such as **/dev/ttyS1**, and **rfcomm** to configure and attach RFCOMM devices. The HCI information is saved in **/etc/bluetooth/hcid.conf**, and RFCOMM configuration information is in **/etc/bluetooth/rfcomm.conf**. With **l2ping**, you can detect a Bluetooth device.

You can start and stop the Bluetooth service using the **service** command and the Bluetooth service script, **/etc/rc.d/init.d/bluetooth**.

```
service bluetooth start
```

This script will start up the Bluetooth daemon for HCI devices, **hcid**, and run any detection and configuration tools, including **sdpd** for the Service Discovery Protocol, and **rfcomm**. It will also activate any serial Bluetooth devices, using **hciattach** to detect them.

BlueZ includes several modules and drivers, including the core Bluetooth protocols for HCI (Host Controller Interface) devices, HCI USB, UART, PCMCIA, and virtual HCI drivers, along with modules to support protocols for L2CAP (Logical Link Control and Adaptation

Protocol), serial port emulation (RFCOMM), Ethernet emulation (BNEP), SCO (Synchronous Connection-Oriented links for real-time voice), and the Service Discovery Protocol (SDP), which automatically detects services available for an application. In addition, extended services are supported such as PAN (personal area networking) and LAN (LAN access over PPP).

Personal Area Networks: PAN

PAN allows you to use Bluetooth to implement a personal area network supporting IP protocols, much like a wireless LAN for a small number of computers and devices. Bluetooth supports a much smaller bandwidth (1 to 2 megabits) than that used for a standard LAN, but it is sufficient for connecting and transferring data from handheld devices such as Palm Pilots. Several devices and computers can be configured as PAN users, connecting through a central Group Network (GN) computer. Alternatively, the PAN users could connect to a gateway system operating as a network access point connecting the Bluetooth personal network to a large LAN network. The PAN nodes run their own service daemon, **pand**. PAN user clients will also load the **bnep.o** module implementing a Bluetooth network device. The PAN server then needs to instructs its **pand** daemon to listen the address for that device (alternatively, you could use SDP). On both the server and user systems, a virtual network device is created called **bnep0**, which can be configured using local IP protocol addresses. You can create a **ifcfg-bnep0** file and have it configured to use either static or dynamic (DHCP) addressing (**/etc/sysconfig/network-scripts/**). Check the HOWTO-PAN file on the BlueZ site for more details (currently, there is no Red Hat Bluetooth networking tool).

Installing Multimedia Support: MP3, DVD, and DivX

Due to licensing and other restrictions, Fedora Core distribution disks do not include MP3, DVD, or DivX media support. You cannot play MP3 files, DVD discs, or DivX files after installing Fedora Core. However, as part of the Fedora Core project, an independent operation at **rpm.livna.org/fedora** does provide the needed libraries and support files for these media formats. Packages you cannot find at **rpm.livna.org** will usually be at **freshrpms.net**. All packages are RPM packages that you can install with the click of a button with Fedora Core's installation tool. The Firefox Web browser will let you run this tool when you download any RPM packages from a Web page.

Installing is a very simple process, though some files need to be installed before others. First you would use Firefox to display the **rpm.livna.org/fedora** RPM packages. This is the URL for Fedora Core 4:

```
rpm.livna.org/fedora/4/i386/RPMS.stable/
```

To install, just double-click a package, and Firefox will let you choose to open it with system-config-packages (first option). Select this and continue. The system-config-packages tool will then start up, checking the install configuration and automatically installing your packages. If supporting packages are missing, it will list the ones you will have to install first, and then you can reinstall the package later.

Many packages are not listed on the livna site. For those, you will have to use the **freshrpms.net** site. Click Packages to see a list of different releases. Click the release you want, such as the one for Fedora Core 4. This will list all current packages in the left-hand column. Click the entry for the one you want. It will be displayed on the right panel of the

Web page. Be sure to select the appropriate binary. There are both **i386** or **i686**, and **x86_64** versions for most packages.

```
www.freshrpms.net/packages
```

MP3 Support

To install MP3 support so that multimedia applications can run MP3 files, you need to download and install the **lame** package, which provides MP3 decoding, as well as the **libid3tag** and **libmad** packages.

```
libmad
libid3tag
lame
```

To allow GStreamer-supported applications like Rhythmbox to run MP3 files, you will also need the GStreamer MP3 plug-in.

```
gstreamer-plugins-mp3
```

TIP *To sync and import from your iPod, you can use iPod management software like GUI for iPod (gtkpod). Several scripts and tools are currently available for IPod operations, including syncpod, mypod, GUI for ipod (gtkpod), and iPod for Linux. Check **sourceforge.net** and search for ipod. Installation can be more complicated, as many are not in RPM package format (see "Installing Source Code Applications" earlier in this chapter).*

Video Support on Totem and Xine

For video support, you should install the full GStreamer and xine support. Download the following libraries from **freshrpms.net**. To install the GStreamer extras, you first have to install the sound libraries for MP3 support as noted in the previous section, and then install the gsm library. You then first install the gstreamer-audio, then gstreamer-video, and finally gstreamer-dvd extras. When using **freshrpms.net**, be sure to select the ix86 or 64bit versions as appropriate (not source code files). For DVD, you will also need the a52dec library.

```
gstreamer-ffmpeg
gsm
gstreamer-plugins-extras-audio
gstreamer-plugins-extras-video
a52dec
gstreamer-plugins-extras-dvd
```

DVD Support

For DVD support, you need to download several packages, including the MPEG2 library, the DVD navigation library that lets you navigate menus, as well as DVD play and read libraries to access DVD discs. (Commercial DVD software is available for PowerDVD and under development for InterVideo's LinDVD.) The libdvdcss needs to be installed first. You will have to install libdvdread next, before libdvdplay or libdvdnav.

```
libdvdcss
libdvdread
libdvdplay
libdvdnav
libdvdpsi
```

To actually play DVDs, you will need a DVD player. Both Mplayer and xine are available for Fedora Core. Be sure to install the DVD support packages listed previously first. For xine, you will first need the **aalib** and **libXvMCW** libraries from **freshrpms.net**.

```
mplayer-fonts
libXvMCW
xine-lib
xine
```

You can download Mplayer from **freshrpms.net** under the same name. You will need several support packages, including lirc, mplayer fonts, xvidcore, xmms, and lzo. Mplayer can play a variety of media formats, including DivX. By default, mplayer will normally select mcxv (motion compensation xv). If this does not work, open Preferences, select the video panel, and choose xv for the standard output.

```
lirc
mplayerfonts
xvidcore
xmms
lzo
mplayer
```

DivX Support

DivX support is a simple matter of installing the DivX codec. Then you can use a media player like xine to run them. Two packages are available: Divx4Linux and Xvid. Xvid is an OpenDivX implementation of DivX. The Xvid package is at the **rpm.livna.org/fedora** site under the name **xvidcore** with possibly more recent version at **freshrpms.net** (you may already have installed xvidcore for mplayer).

```
xvidcore
```

Divx4Linux can run DivX 5.05 versions. The Divix4Linux package can be obtained from the official DivX site at **www.divx.com/divx/linux/**.

Network Configuration

This chapter discusses the network configuration tools available for easily configuring network connections on Linux. Network configuration differs depending on whether you are connected to a local area network (LAN) with an Ethernet card or are using a DSL or ISDN modem, a wireless connection, or a dial-up modem connection. You had the opportunity to enter your LAN network settings during the installation process. For modifying your LAN settings and for configuring other kinds of interfaces such as DSL, wireless, or ISDN connections, you can configure your network connection using system-config-network. To add a new connection, you start up the Internet Configuration Wizard directly. Table 5-1 lists several different network configuration tools.

Network Configuration Tool	Description
Internet Configuration Wizard	Wizard to configure a new network connection such as Ethernet, modem, DSL, wireless, VPN, Token Ring, or ISDN. Invokes system-config-network.
system-config-network	Network configuration tool for all types of connections. Uses the Internet Configuration Wizard to add a new connection.
Network Device Control	Activates and deactivates network interfaces.
Network Manager	Automates wireless connection selection and notification.
Kwifimanager	Configures wireless connections.
system-config-services	Starts and stops servers, including network servers (smb for Samba, httpd for Web, bind for DNS, and nfs for NFS).
system-config-securitylevel	Sets up a network firewall.
system-config-bind	Configures a domain name server.
wvdial	PPP modem connection, enter on a command line.
pand	Implements the Bluetooth Personal Network.
system-config-samba	Configures Samba shares.
system-config-nfs	Configures NFS shares.
system-config-httpd	Configures an Apache Web server.
system-config-netboot	Configures diskless workstations and network installation.

TABLE 5-1   Red Hat Network Configuration Tools

Network Information: Dynamic and Static

If you are on a network, you may need to obtain certain information to configure your interface. Most networks now support dynamic configuration using either the older Dynamic Host Configuration Protocol (DHCP) or the new IPv6 Protocol and its automatic address configuration. In this case, you need only check the DHCP entry in most network configuration tools. For IPv6, you would check the Enable IPv6 configuration entry in the system-config-network device configuration window (see Figure 5-3 later in this chapter). However, if your network does not support DHCP or IPv6 automatic addressing, you will have to provide detailed information about your connection. Such connections are known as static connections, whereas DCHP and IPv6 connections are dynamic. In a static connection, you need to manually enter your connection information such as your IP address and DNS servers, whereas in a dynamic connection this information is automatically provided to your system by a DHCP server or generated by IPv6 when you connect to the network. For DHCP, a DHCP client on each host will obtain the information from a DHCP server serving that network. IPv6 generates its addresses directly from the device and router information such as the device hardware MAC address.

In addition, if you are using a DSL dynamic, ISDN, or modem connection, you will also have to supply provider, login, and password information, whether your system is dynamic or static. You may also need to supply specialized information such as DSL or modem compression methods, dial-up number, or wireless channels to select.

You can obtain most of your static network information from your network administrator or from your ISP (Internet service provider). You would need the following information:

- **The device name for your network interface**   For LAN and wireless connections, this is usually an Ethernet card with the name **eth0** or **eth1**. For a modem, DSL, or ISDN connection, this is a PPP device named **ppp0** (**ippp0** for ISDN). Virtual private network (VPN) connections are also supported with Crypto IP Encapsulation devices named **cipcb**.

- **Hostname**   Your computer will be identified by this name on the Internet. Do not use localhost; that name is reserved for special use by your system. The name of the host should be a simple word, which can include numbers, but not punctuation such as periods and backslashes. The hostname includes both the name of the host and its domain. For example, a hostname for a machine could be **turtle**, whose domain is **mytrek.com**, giving it a hostname of **turtle.mytrek.com**.

- **Domain name**   This is the name of your network.

- **The Internet Protocol (IP) address assigned to your machine**   This is needed only for static Internet connections. Dynamic connections use the DHCP protocol to automatically assign an IP address for you. Every host on the Internet is assigned an IP address. Traditionally, this address used an IPv4 format consisting of a set of four numbers, separated by periods, which uniquely identifies a single location on the Internet, allowing information from other locations to reach that computer. Networks are now converting to the new IP protocol version 6, IPv6, which uses a new format with a much more complex numbering sequence (see Chapter 38).

- **Your network IP address**   Static connections only. This address is usually similar to the IP address, but with one or more zeros at the end.

- **The netmask**   Static connections only. This is usually 255.255.255.0 for most networks. If, however, you are part of a large network, check with your network administrator or ISP.

- **The broadcast address for your network, if available (optional)**   Static connections only. Usually, your broadcast address is the same as your IP address with the number 255 added at the end.

- **The IP address of your network's gateway computer**   Static connections only. This is the computer that connects your local network to a larger one like the Internet.

- **Name servers**   Static connections only. The IP address of the name servers your network uses. These enable the use of URLs.

- **NIS domain and IP address for an NIS server**   Necessary if your network uses an NIS server (optional).

- **Login and password information**   Needed for dynamic DSL, ISDN, and modem connections.

Network Configuration with Network Tools

Fedora Core and Red Hat Enterprise Linux provide an easy-to-use network configuration and activation tool, which you can use to configure and control any kind of network connection, including Ethernet cards, modems, DSL and ISDN modems, and wireless connections (at this time, Bluetooth Personal Networks are not configured). All are supported with standard configuration panels like those for IP address settings, along with specialized panels used only for a particular kind of connection, such as Compression for modem connections or Wireless Settings for a wireless card. New connections are initially configured using the Internet Configuration Wizard, which will detect and prompt for basic configuration information and then place you in the system-config-network tool to let you refine your configuration, making or changing entries as you require. To control activation of your network connections, you use the Network Device Control tool. For more illustrations on how to configure network connections using the network tools, check the Official Red Hat Linux Customization Guide for Red Hat Linux.

system-config-network

You can access the system-config-network tool directly from the System Settings menu (Network entry). This tool opens a Network Configuration window that has five tabbed panels: Devices, Hardware, IPsec, DNS, and Hosts (see Figure 5-1). These panels are used for configuring the network settings for your entire system. The Devices panel lists all your network connections, and Hardware lists all the network components on your system, such as Ethernet cards and modems. The DNS panel is where you enter your own system's hostname and your network's name server addresses. The Hosts panel lists static host IP addresses and their domain names, including those for your own system. The IPsec panel is used to create secure encrypted and authenticated network connections, using the Internet Protocol. It is commonly used to create virtual private networks (VPNs), creating secure connections between hosts and local networks across a larger network such as the Internet.

FIGURE 5-1
The system-config-
network Network
Configuration
window

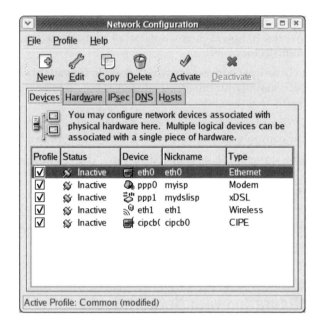

FIGURE 5-1
The system-config-
network Network
Configuration
window

DNS Settings

The DNS panel has a box at the top, labeled Hostname (see Figure 5-2). Here, you enter your system's fully qualified domain name. There are boxes for entering the IP addresses for your system's primary, secondary, and tertiary DNS servers, needed for static configurations. You can then list your search domain. Both the search domain and the name server addresses are saved in the **/etc/resolv.conf** file.

FIGURE 5-2
The system-config-
network DNS panel

Hosts

You use the Hosts panel to associate static IP addresses with certain hosts. The panel has a single pane with New, Edit, Copy, and Delete buttons. This panel lists entries that associate hostnames with static IP addresses. You can also add aliases (nicknames). The Hosts panel actually displays the contents of the **/etc/hosts** file and saves any entries you make to that file. To add an entry, click New. A window opens with boxes for the hostname, IP address, and nicknames. When you finish, the entry is added to the Hosts list. To edit an entry, click Edit and a similar window opens, enabling you to change any of the fields. To delete an entry, select it and click Delete.

NOTE   *If you are having trouble connecting with an Ethernet device using a static network connection, make sure that the Hosts panel lists your hostname and IP address, not just localhost. If your hostname is not there, add it.*

Device Configuration: Automatic or Static

The Devices panel will list the configured network devices on your system. An entry shows the device name and its type. Use the New, Edit, Copy, and Delete buttons to manage the device entries. To edit a device, you can just double-click its entry. For example, when you edit an Ethernet device, you open a tabbed panel for configuring it, enabling you to specify whether it is dynamic or static. There is an entry for automatically activating it when the system starts. You can choose to use IPv6 for automatic addressing. For DHCP you can automatically obtain DNS information. For a static connection you will be able to enter an IP address, netmask, and gateway (see Figure 5-3). A Hardware panel will let you choose the actual hardware device to use. The configuration panels will differ depending on the device you edit. For example, a modem device will add panels for provider, compression, and modem options, whereas a DSL connection will have panels for provider, route (gateway), and hardware device. An Ethernet connection will have only general, route, and hardware device panels. Making entries here performs the same function as **ifconfig**.

FIGURE 5-3
Device configuration in system-config-network

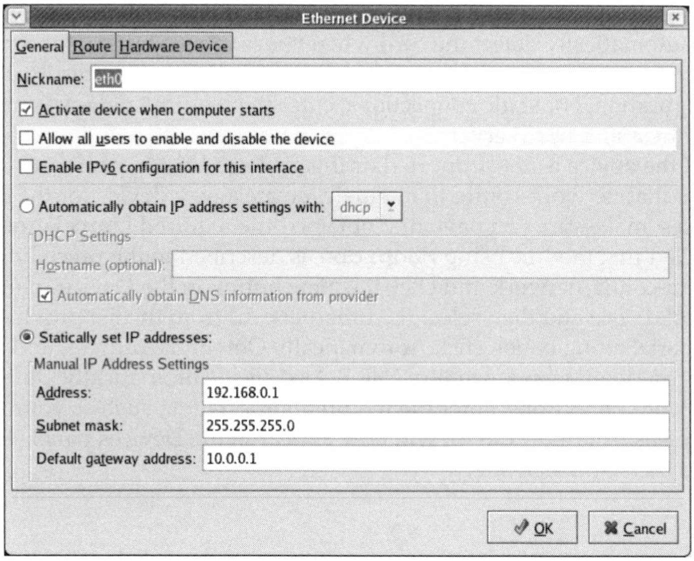

When you finish and are ready to save your configuration, select the Save entry from the File menu. If you want to abandon the changes you made, you can close without saving. You can run system-config-network at any time to make changes in your network configuration.

Profiles

The system-config-network tool also supports profiles. *Profiles* are commonly used for portable computers that may be moved from one environment to another. For example, at your office you could have an Office profile that uses an Ethernet card to connect to the office LAN. At home, you could use a Home profile that uses a modem to connect to the Internet. Profiles are integrated into the configuration process, with a Common profile functioning as the default configuration. The Common profile will be inherited by all other profiles, so make your basic configuration with that profile.

Profiles are accessed from the Profile menu. Select the profile you want, or select New to create a new profile. The name of the currently selected profile will be displayed at the bottom of the Network Configuration screen. The Delete entry in the Profile menu will delete the current profile. By default, the Common profile will be selected. To create a profile, click the New entry and enter the name of the profile. It will be added to the Profile menu. You can also remove or rename a profile. The new profile will inherit the setting of the common profile. Once you have selected a profile, you can then select devices or change DNS or host information. On the Devices panel of system-config-network, each device entry will have a check box. Selecting this check box selects the device for the current profiles. To select a device for a given profile, first be sure to select the profile you are configuring, and then click the device's check box. For other profiles, the device will be unchecked. Select the Save entry from the File menu when you are finished. The changes you make will be part of that profile, and not of any other.

Configuring Replaced or Unsupported Ethernet Cards

If you change your Ethernet card or if your card is not supported and you need to manually load a driver for it, you will have to manually configure the card. For supported cards, Kudzu will automatically detect the card when your system starts up and prompt you to configure it. For dynamic connections, simply select DHCP to automatically determine your network configuration. For static connections, enter the required network information, such as your IP address and DNS servers.

If the device is not supported or if you elected not to configure it with Kudzu, you can use redhat-network-config to manually create a new device for the card. For unsupported devices, make sure you have first obtained the required Linux kernel module for it and have installed that module using **modprobe** as described in the preceding chapter. Then, start up system-config-network and click the New button in the Devices panel. Select Ethernet as the type of device and then select the Ethernet card from the list provided. On the Configure Network Setting panel, click Automatically Obtain IP Address, and select the method from the drop-down menu, usually DHCP. Also click Automatically Obtain DNS Information. For static connections, enter the required information, such as your IP and DNS server addresses. Your new device will now appear in the Devices panel. To activate it, select it and then click Activate.

Network Device Control

With the Network Device Control tool, you can activate or deactivate configured network connections. A pop-up menu will also let you select available profiles, automatically activating network connections associated with each profile, and deactivating those that are not. The Network Device Control tool is accessible in the System Tools menu. Selecting a device and clicking Configure will open the system-config-network tool. You can then select and configure any network device, as well as add new ones.

The Internet Configuration Wizard

To configure a new network connection, you use the Internet Configuration Wizard, accessible from the System Tools menu. If you already have system-config-network open and want to add a new network connection, clicking New will also start the Internet Configuration Wizard. The wizard initially displays a list of all possible network connections (see Figure 5-4). When you select an entry, panels will prompt you to enter basic information about a connection; this will include phone number, username, and password for modem, DSL, and ISDN connections, whereas Ethernet connections will prompt only for IP addresses. The types of connections and devices currently supported are Ethernet (**eth**), ISDN (**ippp**), Modem (**ppp**), xDSL (**ppp**), Token Ring (**tr**), and wireless connections (**eth**). After completing your entries, the wizard will configure your connection setting and the new connection will be ready for use.

Modem Configuration

You can also use a modem with telephone lines to connect to a network. For a modem connection, the Internet Configuration Wizard will probe and detect your modem. A window will then display entries for the serial device, baud rate, hardware control, and modem volume, which you can modify. You are then prompted to enter the phone number, provider, username, and password for your ISP account. The system-config-network tool is then started up, listing your modem device as a **ppp** connection (**ppp** stands for the *Point-to-Point Protocol [PPP]* protocol that transmits IP communications across telephone lines). You can then edit the **ppp** device to modify your settings and enter any other settings; for instance, you can enter IP addresses for static connections, specify compression methods, or list your DNS servers.

Figure **5-4**
Internet
Configuration
Wizard

DSL and ISDN Configuration

To configure DSL, you will need to provide login and password information for DSL (Digital Subscriber Line) and ISDN. In other respects, DSL and ISDN connections operate much like a local area network (LAN), treating a host as an integrated part of a network. You can use the Internet Configuration Wizard to set up a DSL or ISDN connection. For DSL, the Internet Configuration Wizard will display a dialog box with entries for entering your login name, your password, and the Ethernet interface your DSL modem is attached to. You will also need to enter the IP addresses for the DNS servers provided by your ISP. You can elect to have the connection automatically made up when your system starts up (depending upon your selected network profile).

Wireless Configuration

A wireless connection operates much like a standard Ethernet connection, requiring only an IP address and DNS server information to connect to the Internet. In addition, you will have to specify wireless connection information such as the network name and channel used. To add a new wireless connection, you start the Internet Configuration Wizard (from the System Tools menu) and select the wireless connection. If system-config-network is open, you can click Add on the Devices panel to start the Internet Configuration Wizard. You are prompted to select your wireless card.

On the Configure Wireless Connection panel, you then configure your wireless connection, selecting the mode, network name, channel, transmit rate, and key information.

- **Mode**   Normally, you can leave this on Auto. For a simple network, one that does not require roaming, the mode is usually Ad Hoc. Managed networks allow roaming among different access points.

- **Network Name (SSID)**   Can be left on Auto for a simple network. The Network Name is used to identify a cell as part of a virtual network.

- **Channel**   Starting from 1, choose one with least interference.

- **Transmit Rate**   Usually set to Auto to adjust automatically to degraded transmissions. But you can set a specific rate such as 11M or 1M from the pop-up menu.

- **Key**   This is the encryption key for your wireless network. It must be the same for each cell on your network.

On the Configure Network Settings panel, you specify your IP address, whether it is obtained automatically with DHCP or one you enter yourself. For most company wireless networks, the IP address will be obtained automatically. Normally, the DNS servers are also provided. You can, if you wish, also specify a hostname.

If you are setting up a local or home network, you will most likely use static IP addresses you select yourself from the private IP pool, beginning with 192.168, such as 192.168.0.1. The static subnet mask for a small local network is usually 255.255.255.0. The Gateway is the IP address for the computer on your network that connects to the Internet, or to a larger network.

You can later edit a wireless connection, making changes. Wireless configuration has the same General and Hardware Device panels as an Ethernet or DSL connection, but instead of a Route panel, it has a Wireless Settings panel, where you can set your mode and network name along with channel, transmit, and key information.

Your configuration setting will be saved in an Ethernet configuration file in the **/etc/ sysconfig/network-scripts** directory. For example, if your wireless card is designated **eth1**, then its configuration information is saved in the **ifcfg-eth1** file. Here you will find the standard Ethernet connection parameters such as the IP address and gateway, as well as wireless parameters such as the channel used, the mode specified, and the encryption key. The standard setting can be modified using system-config-network on that device. You could also modify this file directly to enter additional parameters, like the frequency (FREQ) or sensitivity level (SENS). You can also specify any of the **iwconfig** parameters using the IWCONFIG option. Enter **IWCONFIG** followed by an assignment of an option with a value. For example, the following option sets the fragment threshold for packets:

```
IWCONFIG="frag 512"
```

Virtual Private Networks

A virtual private network lets you create your own private logical network on top of physical network connections, such as the Internet. Using encryption, your private network transmissions are kept secure from the physical network. Though a virtual private network (VPN) has no physical connections of its own and is not a actual network, the secure transmissions it sends have the effect of operating as if the network did exist as a separate entity. VPNs make use of tunneling, in which secure transmissions are sent directly through interconnecting systems on a large network like the Internet without being intercepted or, at any point, translated. To implement a VPN, each node has to use the same encryption support software. You can choose to use either the newer IPsec tools or the older third-party Crypto IP Encapsulation (CIPE) tool. To use IPsec to set up a VPN, you click the IPsec panel in system-config-network and create a new connection. This process is described in detail in Chapter 18.

Interface Configuration Scripts: /etc/sysconfig/network-scripts

Network configuration implemented by the Internet Configuration Wizard and system-config-network are saved in interface configuration scripts located in the **/etc/sysconfig/ network-scripts** directory (see Chapter 37). You can edit these scripts directly, changing specific parameters, as discussed previously for wireless connection. Interface configuration files bear the names of the network interfaces currently configured, such as **ifcfg-eth0** for the first Ethernet device, or **ifcfg-ppp0** for the first PPP modem device. These files define shell variables that hold information on the interface, such as whether to start them at boot time. For example, the **ifcfg-eth0** file holds definitions for NETWORK, BROADCAST, and IPADDR, which are assigned the network, broadcast, and IP addresses that the device uses. You can also manually edit these interface configuration files, making changes as noted previously for the wireless connection. A sample **ifcfg-eth0** file is shown here using a DHCP address.

/etc/sysconfig/network-scripts/ifcfg-eth0
```
DEVICE=eth0
BOOTPROTO=DHCP
HWDADDR=00:00:00:EF:AF:00
ONBOOT=yes
TYPE=Ethernet
```

Network Manager

With Fedora Core 4, Red Hat now provides the Network Manager tool for detecting and selecting network connections. With multiple wireless access points for Internet connections, a system could have several different network connections to choose from, instead of a single-line connection like DSL or Cable. This is particularly true for notebook computers that could access different wireless connections at different locations. Instead of manually configuring a new connection each time one is encountered, the Network Manager tool can automatically configure and select a connection to use.

By default, an Ethernet connection will be preferred if available. Direct lines that support Ethernet connections are normally considered faster than wireless ones. For wireless connections, you will need to choose the one you want.

Network Manager is designed to work in the background, providing status information for your connection and switching from one configured connection to another as needed. For initial configuration, it detects as much information as possible about the new connection. It operates as a GNOME Panel applet, monitoring your connection, and can work on any Linux distribution.

Network Manager operates as a daemon with the name NetworkManager. It is managed with the NetworkManager service script, which you can start and stop using the service command in a terminal window.

```
service NetworkManager start
```

To have it start up automatically, use **chkconfig**.

```
chkconfig NetworkManager on
```

The user interface for NetworkManager is NetworkManagerInfo. You can enter this at the terminal window to start it. The NetworkManager applet will appear in the panel.

```
NetworkManagerInfo
```

If no Ethernet connection is available, Network Manager will scan for a wireless connection, checking for Extended Service Set Identifiers (ESSIDs). If an ESSID identifies a previously used connection, then it is automatically selected. If several are found, then the most recently used one is chosen. If only a new connection is available, then Network Manager waits for the user to choose one. A connection is selected only if the user is logged in. If an Ethernet connection is later made, then Network Manager will switch to it from wireless.

Network Manager is user specific. When a user logs in, it selects the one preferred by that user. The first time a user runs NetworkManager, the notification applet will display a list of current possible connections. The user can then choose one.

Clicking the Network Manager icon in the panel will list available network connections. Password-protected access points will display a lock next to them. You will have to configure hidden access points yourself. Select Other Wireless Networks from the applets listing to open a dialog where you can enter the ESSID of the network, the key type, and the password.

Network Interface Connection (NIC cards) hardware is detected using HAL, as described in Chapter 34. Information provided by Network Manager is made available to other applications over D-Bus. Features currently under development include VPN and application notification. Network Manager uses the DHCPCD client to gather network information. For user interaction and notification, it uses NetworkManagerInfo.

18-261544-blue.

Command Line PPP Access: wvdial

If, for some reason, you have been unable to set up a modem connection on your X Window System, you may have to set it up from the command line interface instead of a desktop. For a dial-up PPP connection, you can use the wvdial dialer, which is an intelligent dialer that not only dials up an ISP service but also performs login operations, supplying your username and password. The wvdial program first loads its configuration from the **/etc/wvdial.conf** file. In here, you can place modem and account information, including modem speed and serial device, as well as ISP phone number, username, and password. The **wvdial.conf** file is organized into sections, beginning with a section label enclosed in brackets. A section holds variables for different parameters that are assigned values, such as **username = chris**. The default section holds default values inherited by other sections, so you needn't repeat them. Table 5-2 lists the wvdial variables.

Variable	Description
Inherits	Explicitly inherits from the specified section. By default, sections inherit from the [Dialer Defaults] section.
Modem	The device wvdial should use as your modem. The default is **/dev/modem**.
Baud	The speed at which wvdial communicates with your modem. The default is 57,600 baud.
Init1...Init9	Specifies the initialization strings to be used by your modem; wvdial can use up to 9. The default is "ATZ" for Init1.
Phone	The phone number you want wvdial to dial.
Area Code	Specifies the area code, if any.
Dial Prefix	Specifies any needed dialing prefix—for example, 70 to disable call waiting or 9 for an outside line.
Dial Command	Specifies the dial operation. The default is "ATDT".
Login	Specifies the username you use at your ISP.
Login Prompt	If your ISP has an unusual login prompt, you can specify it here.
Password	Specifies the password you use at your ISP.
Password Prompt	If your ISP has an unusual password prompt, you can specify it here.
Force Address	Specifies a static IP address to use (for ISPs that provide static IP addresses to users).
Stupid Mode	In Stupid Mode, wvdial does not attempt to interpret any prompts from the terminal server and starts pppd after the modem connects.
Auto Reconnect	If enabled, wvdial attempts to reestablish a connection automatically if you are randomly disconnected by the other side. This option is on by default.

TABLE 5-2   Variables for wvdial

You can use the wvdialconf utility to create a default **wvdial.conf** file for you automatically; wvdialconf will detect your modem and set default values for basic features. You can then edit the **wvdial.conf** file and modify the Phone, Username, and Password entries with your ISP dial-up information. Remove the preceding semicolon (;) to unquote the entry. Any line beginning with a semicolon is ignored as a comment.

```
$ wvdialconf
```

You can also create a named dialer, such as *myisp* in the following example. This is helpful if you have different ISPs you log in to. The following example shows the **/etc/wvdial.conf** file:

```
/etc/wvdial.conf [Modem0]
Modem = /dev/ttyS0
Baud = 57600
Init1 = ATZ
SetVolume = 0
Dial Command = ATDT

[Dialer Defaults]
Modem = /dev/ttyS0
Baud = 57600
Init1 = ATZ
SetVolume = 0
Dial Command = ATDT

[Dialer myisp]
Username = chris
Password = mypassword
Modem = /dev/ttyS0
Phone = 555-5555
Area Code = 555
Baud = 57600
Stupid mode = 0
```

To start wvdial, enter the command **wvdial**, which then reads the connection configuration information from the **/etc/wvdial.conf** file; wvdial dials the ISP and initiates the PPP connection, providing your username and password when requested.

```
$ wvdial
```

You can set up connection configurations for any number of connections in the **/etc/wvdial.conf** file. To select one, enter its label as an argument to the **wvdial** command, as shown here:

```
$ wvdial myisp
```

Wireless Tools

To avoid having different configuration options for each make of wireless device, most wireless devices currently support the Wireless Extensions. These extensions provide a standard format for configuring all wireless devices. With the same set of configuration options, you can configure any wireless device that supports Wireless Extensions. The

Wireless Tools package is a set of network configuration and reporting tools for wireless devices installed on a Linux system. They are currently supported and developed as part of the Linux Wireless Extension and Wireless Tools Project, an open source project maintained by Hewlett-Packard.

Wireless Tools consists of the configuration and report tools listed here:

Tool	Description
iwconfig	Sets the wireless configuration options basic to most wireless devices.
iwlist	Displays current status information of a device.
iwspy	Sets the list of IP addresses in a wireless network and checks the quality of their connections.
iwpriv	Accesses configuration options specific to a particular device.

The wireless LAN device will have an Ethernet name just like an Ethernet card. The appropriate modules will automatically be loaded, listing their aliases in the **/etc/modprobe .conf** file (see Chapter 34).

Kwifimanager

With Kwifimanager you can easily access a wireless connection. You can start Kwifimanager from its entry in the Internet submenu on the Applications menu. The main window shows the type, quality, and speed of the current wireless connection. The configuration for your wireless interface is also shown, including transmission frequency and channel, the IP address, encryption status, the network you are connected to, with its MAC address. Information about your current access point is displayed at the bottom of the window. Such information requires that MAC address of the access point be available. For private access points, check with your system administrator. Access points can be placed in .loc files in /**usr/share/apps/ kwifimanager/locations**.

Connection Tools and Applet

When you use Kwifimanager (Internet menu), an icon for it will appear in your GNOME or KDE panel. The applet will display yellow, orange, red if your signal quality degrades. You can click it to display the Kwifimanager main window showing your connection information.

The Statistics viewer, accessible from the Connection statistics entry in the File menu, displays graphs for your signal and noise levels for your current connection.

Clicking Scan For Networks will display a list of available networks. An Acoustic Scanning feature lets you find the strongest signal.

Configuration

The Configuration Editor, accessible from the Config menu, lets you configure up to four different connections. This is a KDE Control Center module, also accessible from the KDE Control Center but only to the root user. The Configuration Editor will display four tabbed panels labeled Config1–Config4. In the Network Name entry you enter the SSID for a particular network, or **ANY** to scan for available public networks. For the operation mode, you would use Infrastructure for access points (network nodes), and peer-to-peer when connecting directly to another computer. Normally you would set the signal speed to auto, letting the wireless interface set the speed, but you can select one manually. You can also specify any startup scripts to use.

For encrypted connections, click the Use Cryptography entry. This displays entries for Crypto mode and keys. The open mode will read unencrypted data, whereas restricted will read only encrypted ones. You can have up to four different keys. If you are using strings for your key, check the String box next to the key entry. Otherwise, you would use a Hex number for the key. The key you actually use is set in the Key To Use entry, which can take a value of 1–4.

If you are working from a notebook, you will probably want to set the power management options. Click Enable Power Management to display options for sleep and awaken durations to limit scanning, and set the Receive packet options to listen for either multicast or unicast packets (packets sent to you).

At the bottom of the Configuration panel are options for activating your interface and what configuration to use. You can autodetect your interface or specify one like eth0 or wlan0. You can also choose to have the selected configuration loaded automatically.

iwconfig

The `iwconfig` command works much like `ifconfig`, configuring a network connection. It is the tool used by the Internet Configuration Wizard and by system-config-network to configure a wireless card. Alternatively, you can run `iwconfig` directly on a command line, specifying certain parameters. Added parameters let you set wireless-specific features such as the network name (nwid), the frequency or channel the card uses (freq or channel), and the bit rate for transmissions (rate). See the `iwconfig` Man page for a complete listing of accepted parameters. Some of the commonly used parameters are listed in Table 5-3.

Parameter	Description
essid	A network name
freq	The frequency of the connection
channel	The channel used
nwid or domain	The network ID or domain
mode	The operating mode used for the device, such as Ad Hoc, Managed, or Auto. Ad Hoc = one cell with no access point, Managed = network with several access points and supports roaming, Master = the node is an access point, Repeater = node forwards packets to other nodes, Secondary = backup master or repeater, Monitor = only receives packets
sens	The sensitivity, the lowest signal level at which data can be received
key or enc	The encryption key used
frag	Cut packets into smaller fragments to increase better transmission
bit or rate	Speed at which bits are transmitted. The auto option automatically falls back to lower rates for noisy channels
ap	Specify a specific access point
power	Power management for wakeup and sleep operations

TABLE 5-3   Commonly Used Parameters

For example, to set the channel used for the wireless device installed as the first Ethernet device, you would use the following, setting the channel to 2:

```
iwconfig eth0 channel 2
```

You can also use **iwconfig** to display statistics for your wireless devices, just as **ifconfig** does. Enter the **iwconfig** command with no arguments or with the name of the device. Information such as the name, frequency, sensitivity, and bit rate is listed. Check also **/proc/net/wireless** for statistics.

Instead of using **iwconfig** directly to set parameters, you can specify them in the wireless device's configuration file. The wireless device configuration file will be located in the **/etc/sysconfig/network-scripts** directory and given a name like **ifcfg-eth1**, depending on the name of the device. This file will already contain many **iwconfig** settings. Any further setting can be set by assigning **iwconfig** values to the IWCONFIG parameter as shown here.

```
IWCONFIG="rate 11M"
```

iwpriv

The **iwpriv** command works in conjunction with **iwconfig**, allowing you set options specific to a particular kind of wireless device. With **iwpriv**, you can also turn on roaming or select the port to use. You use the *private-command* parameter to enter the device-specific options. The following example sets roaming on:

```
iwpriv eth0 roam on
```

iwspy

Your wireless device can check its connection to another wireless device it is receiving data from, reporting the quality, signal strength, and noise level of the transmissions. Your device can maintain a list of addresses for different devices it may receive data from. You use the **iwspy** tool to set or add the addresses that you want checked. You can list either IP addresses or the hardware versions. A + sign will add the address, instead of replacing the entire list:

```
iwspy eth0 +192.168.2.5
```

To display the quality, signal, and noise levels for your connections, you use the **iwspy** command with just the device name:

```
iwspy eth0
```

iwlist

To obtain more detailed information about your wireless device, such as all the frequencies or channels available, you use the **iwlist** tool. Using the device name with a particular parameter, you can obtain specific information about a device, including the frequency, access points, rate, power features, retry limits, and encryption keys used. You can use **iwlist** to obtain information about faulty connections. The following example will list the frequencies used on the **eth0** wireless device.

```
iwlist eth0 freq
```

linux-wlan

The linux-wlan project (**www.linux-wlan.org**) has developed a separate set of wireless drivers designed for Prism-based wireless cards supporting the new 802.11 wireless standard. The linux-wlan drivers are not currently included with Fedora Core 4; you will have to download the drivers. You can download RPM packages from **people.redhat.com** that include a base package, a modules packages, and packages for different kinds of hardware like PCMCIA or USB. You can also download RPM packages for specific kernels from **prism2.unixguru .raleigh.nc.us**.

The original source code package is available from the wlan-linux site at **www.linux-wlan.org**. The current package is linux-wlan-ng. You will have to unpack and compile the drivers as noted for source code software packages in the preceding chapter.

The drivers will install WLAN devices, with device configurations placed in the **/etc/ sysconfig/network-scripts** directory. For example, the configuration for the first WLAN device will be in the **ifcfg-wlan0** script. General wireless options are placed in the **/etc/wlan .conf** configuration file.

Setting Up Your Firewall and Security-Enhanced Linux: system-config-securitylevel

To set up your firewall and configure Security-Enhanced (SE) Linux, run system-config-securitylevel on your system (Security Level in the System Settings window and menu). You can enable or disable your firewall (see Figure 5-5). The Disable firewall option disables the firewall. You can run your firewall on a stand-alone system directly connected to the Internet, or on a gateway system that connects a local network to the Internet (as described in the previous sections). For a local network, be sure that the local hosts do not have any kind of firewall running. The firewall should run only on the gateway. Furthermore, the gateway will have at least two network connections, one for the local network and an Internet connection device for the Internet. Make sure that the firewall is applied to the

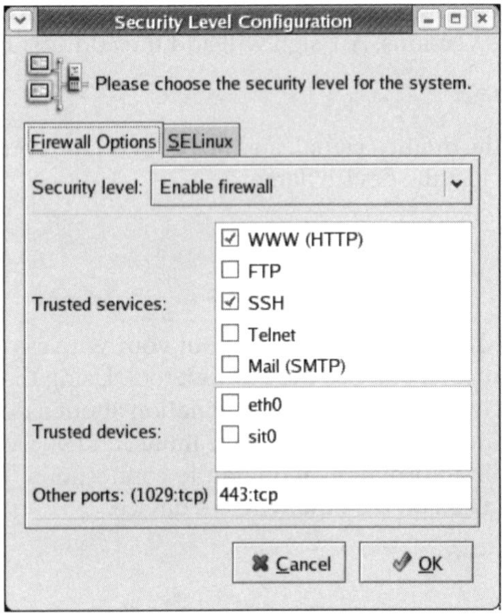

FIGURE 5-5
The system-config-securitylevel tool

Internet device, not to your local network. On system-config-securitylevel, you do this by making the local network device a trusted device. If you are creating a strong firewall but still want to run a service such as a Web server, allow users to perform FTP file transfers on the Internet, or allow remote encrypted connections such as SSH, you will have to specify them in the Trusted Services pane. Samba desktop browsing requires security level 1.5.9-1 or above (in development). In the network example used here, the firewall is run on the **eth0** network device, and the Web server and SSH encrypted access is allowed.

On the second panel you can set your SELinux settings. Here you can enable or disable SELinux and set the level of security you want, such as warning or targeted. You can further modify the control it implements for the Web server, DNS server, or NIS, as well as whether to disable it for particular servers such as DHCP or Squid. See Chapter 17 for more details on SELinux.

InfiniBand Support

Fedora Core 4, with the 2.6.10 kernel, now includes InfiniBand support. This is a new I/O architecture that is used to replace the older bus architectures used in current systems. Often InfiniBand is used as a replacement for local network connections. It is currently implemented in supercomputer and network server clusters. You can find more about InfiniBand at the Linux InfiniBand Project at **infiniband.sourceforge.net**. Support for InfiniBand is being carried out as an open source project by OpenIB Alliance, **www.openib.org**.

Systems today use the PCI bus or its enhanced versions, PCI X or PCI Express. This PCI I/O architecture uses a shared bus that can only reach about a half gigabits of throughput. Clustered servers are already reaching the limits of this I/O method. One alternative technology is the InfiniBand I/O architecture. InfiniBand uses serial channels instead of a shared bus. It has a 2.6 gigabits per second minimum and can go as high as 30 gigabits per second. Instead of having a bus processing transactions controlled by a single host, InfiniBand uses peer-to-peer channel architecture where multiple connections can be managed using different channels. This fabric switch architecture enables InfiniBand to switch among different nodes. PCI Express is limited to use as a local bus, connecting a CPU with peripherals. InfiniBand, by contrast, supports networking connections, letting you implement essentially a local high-speed intranet as well as shared high-speed connections to stand-alone storage devices like hard drives. Using an InfiniBand cable instead of an Ethernet cable, you can connection your hosts and shared devices (limited to 50 feet). The IPoIB (IP over InfiniBand) protocol lets you implement IP networking over InfiniBand connections, and the RDMA protocol can be used for remote storage devices. The higher speed of an InfiniBand connection is particularly important for servers needing high-bandwidth capability. In addition, the Sockets Direct Protocol can set up high-speed InfiniBand connections for streams, and the SCSI RDMA Protocol (SRP) manages connections to hard drives.

Machines with PCI Express can handle the greater bandwidth provided by a InfiniBand connection. A Host Channel Adapter (HCA) card placed in a PCI slot has InfiniBand connectors and will interface InfiniBand transmissions with the PCI Express bus. Drivers for several HCAs are already incorporated in the kernel, as are protocol drivers.

Configuring a Local Area Network

Creating a local network of your own involves just a few simple steps. You can set up a system to serve as the main server for your own local area network (LAN), providing such services as e-mail, a Web site, or shared printers. You can even connect different types of systems, such as those running Windows or the Mac OS. You can also configure your system to serve as a gateway to the Internet, through which all your other systems will connect. In fact, you could have one Internet connection on your gateway that each host on your network could use. A few security precautions allow your system to work as a firewall, protecting your local hosts from outside attacks. You could also set up a very simple configuration to provide Web access only. This section will cover the basic concepts for setting up such a network. Later chapters in this book will cover these topics in detail.

Your local area network consists of a collection of host systems connected to the main host running Linux. This main host will be referred to as the *gateway*. The steps for setting up a local network involve the following:

- Setting up and configuring the Ethernet cards on each system (connected or wireless). Your gateway should have two Ethernet cards (see Chapter 38)
- Setting up a proxy server to provide direct Web access (DNS is not required, see Chapter 24)
- Setting up your DNS server on the gateway (see Chapter 38)
- Configuring your DNS server to allow all other local hosts to access the Internet (see Chapter 20)
- Setting up firewall protection (see Chapter 20)
- Enabling e-mail services (see Chapter 25)
- Setting up local host access to the Internet through DNS (Chapter 38)
- Sharing printers with Windows hosts (see Chapter 41)
- Setting up a local Web site (see Chapter 23)

Along with setting up your connections, you will have to run at least one service on the main gateway computer you set up for your network. On Fedora Core, you can start and stop a service with the system-config-services tool (Services on the System Servers menu and window) or by using the **service** command. To have the service started automatically, you can use system-config-services. For a simple network, you should have the DNS and Network services running. If you have Windows systems on your network and you want to share printers with them, you will need the Samba service. The Network, Squid, Sendmail, Postfix, DNS, and Samba programs may have to be restarted as you configure them. You will have to know the names used for the DNS, Sendmail, Postfix, Squid, and Samba server programs to restart them with the service tool. They are shown here. In addition, you will have to add a firewall rule to enable your local hosts to access the Internet through your firewall.

Service Name	Service Program
Domain Name Service (DNS)	named
Samba	smb
Network connections	network
Firewall	iptables
Squid	squid
Sendmail	sendmail
Postfix	postfix

You use the **start**, **stop**, and **restart** arguments to start, stop, and restart a service. To restart the DNS service, you would use the following:

```
service named restart
```

Host Configuration

There are several ways to set up hosts for your network. On each host you could have direct Ethernet connections or wireless connections, each configured as noted previously with system-config-network.

Each host on your network will have to be assigned an address. There are several ways to do this:

- **DHCP** This method uses IPv4 addresses that are automatically assigned with a DHCP server. Most routers for home and small business networks also operate as DCHP servers and can automatically provide addresses from a pool of addresses. If you want a Linux system to run a DHCP server, you will need to configure it appropriately (see Chapter 39).

- **Static IPv4** This method is practical only for very small networks where you know the addresses will never change. It is sometimes used for special hosts whose address should not be changed for some reason. Each host is assigned an IPv4 address.

- **IPv6** This newer method, supported on many routers, automatically constructs an address from the host's hardware connection and the router's network address. This takes the least amount of administration.

IPv4 Addressing

Most networks, including the Internet, use a set of network protocols called TCP/IP, which stands for Transmission Control Protocol/Internet Protocol. On a TCP/IP network such as the Internet, each computer is given a unique address called an *IP address*. The IP address is used to identify and locate a particular host—a computer connected to the network. A small network still uses IPv4 addresses, though this will change as IPv6 automatic addressing becomes more prevalent. IPv4 addresses consist of a number, usually four sets of three digits separated by periods. An example of an IP address is 192.168.0.1.

To set up a local area network (LAN) whose hosts are not directly connected to the Internet, you would use a special set of IP numbers reserved for such non-Internet networks (also known as *private networks* or *intranets*). This is especially true if you are implementing IP masquerading, where only a gateway machine has an Internet address and the others make use of that one address to connect to the Internet. In IPv4 networks, these are numbers that have the special network number 192.168.0, as used in these examples (IPv6 networks use a special network address called site-local). If you are setting up a LAN, such as a small business or home network, you are free to use these numbers for your local machines. For a local network, assign IP addresses starting from 192.168.0.1. The host segment can range from 1 to 254, where 255 is used for the broadcast address. If you have three hosts on your home network, you can give them the addresses 192.168.0.1, 192.168.0.2, and 192.168.0.3.

NOTE *To allow local hosts in this example to connect to the Internet using the IP address of the gateway, you need to implement IP masquerading. In effect, the local hosts mask themselves by taking on the gateway's IP address, appearing to the Internet as the gateway system. IP masquerading is implemented as part of the Netfilter packet filtering program described in Chapter 20.*

The network address for such a network would be the first three segments of the IP address, 192.168.0. The network netmask would cover those first three segments, using the number 255.255.255.0. This mask is used to determine the host and network parts of an IP address. The broadcast address, 192.168.0.255 in this example, is used to allow an administrator to contact all hosts at once. You would then use these three IP addresses when configuring a host.

In the sample network used in these examples, there are three hosts, each with its own IP addresses and hostnames listed here. The network address, netmask, and broadcast address are the same as those just described:

```
192.168.0.1     turtle
192.168.0.2     rabbit
192.168.0.3     lizard
```

NOTE *See Chapters 37 and 38 for detailed information on IP addresses and DNS server setup.*

Firewall

If you are using a Linux system as a gateway, the firewall should run only on the gateway. Furthermore, the gateway will have two network connections, one for the local network and an Internet connection device for the Internet. Make sure that the firewall is applied to the device used as the Internet device, not to your local network. On system-config-securitylevel, you do this by making the local network device a trusted device. In the network example used here, the firewall is run on the **eth0** network device (the first Ethernet card), which functions as the gateway. The local network is connected through the **eth1** network device (the second Ethernet card).

Squid Proxy Server

If you only want to provide your hosts Internet Web access, you can do so by just running the Squid server on your gateway host. You will not have to set up and run a DNS server. Squid is a proxy server that can handle the Internet connection between a browser and Internet sites directly. You only have to configure the network connections for each host, providing their IP addresses. This you can do automatically with DHCP. Squid is included with the basic installation (see Chapter 24).

Each Web browser will have to be configured to reference the machine running the Squid server. On Mozilla, select Preferences from the Edit menu, and then select Proxies in the Advanced item. Here you can enter the IP address of the machine running the Squid server, normally the gateway.

You can start the Squid server by starting system-config-services (Services in the System Settings/Server Settings window), selecting squid, and then clicking Start. You can also manually start and stop Squid with the **service** command.

```
service squid start
```

The **chkconfig** command can automatically start Squid whenever your system boots.

```
chkconfig squid on
```

NOTE There are several ways to enable e-mail services on your network. You can either set up your network with a central server handling e-mail for all the users on your network, or have each host handle its own users independently. Internet mail setup also varies depending on whether you have a stand-alone system, a small network with one connection, or a larger network with its own official domain address (see Chapter 25).

DNS

For most small networks, you can just configure your router and connect your hosts. If, however, you want to provide services to your network, such as a mail server or a local Web site, you will need to set up your own DNS server. The DNS server resolves addresses with hostnames. This allow users to just use hostnames to access a service. If the network is small enough and your services are operating on one fixed host, you can bypass the DNS service by entering the server's hostname and IP address association in each host's **/etc/host** file. Still, this involves changing each host's configuration if the servers are moved to another computer.

If you need to set up a simple DNS server, you can use system-config-bind. This provides a graphical interface for creating DNS configuration files. You can access system-config-bind from the System Settings | Server Settings | Domain Name System menu entry. The system-config-bind tool provides a very detailed manual which you can display by clicking on the Help button. It also includes the BIND administrative manual. Key features are noted here.

To configure and run a Domain Name Service (DNS), which will allow all the hosts on your local network to identify each other using a hostname, involves several steps:

1. Decide on the IP addresses to assign to each local host. Use 192.168.0 as the network address.

2. Decide on the domain name for your local network.

3. Decide on the hostname for each host on your network.

4. Configure each host with its IP address and domain name address.

5. On the gateway/server, configure a DNS server listing each host's IP address and hostname.

6. Start the DNS service.

All hosts on the Internet are identified by their IP addresses. When you send a message to a host on the Internet, you must provide its IP address. Using a sequence of four numbers of an IP address, however, can be difficult. They are hard to remember, and it's easy to make mistakes when typing them. To make identifying a computer on the Internet easier, DNS was implemented. DNS establishes a fully qualified domain name address for each IP address. The fully qualified domain name consists of the name of the host and the network (domain) that it belongs to. Whenever you use that name, it is automatically converted to an IP address, which is then used to identify that Internet host. The fully qualified domain name is far easier to use than its corresponding IP address. For example, a DNS server will translate **www.linux.org** into its IP address, 198.182.196.56.

NOTE Instead of a Domain Name Service, you could have the /etc/hosts files in each machine contain the entire list of IP addresses and domain names for all the machines in your network. But for any changes, you would have to update each machine's /etc/hosts file.

Bind is the kind of DNS software used on most networks. You will need to create two zone configurations: a forward master zone and a reverse master zone. The main system-config-bind window will display all configured domains and their record entries. Buttons at the top let you create new domains, add new records, delete any domains or records, and save your configuration. Click a domain to select that domain. The Properties button will let you edit any selected entry.

To save your system-config-bind configuration, click the Save button to generate the DNS server configuration files. Files generated by system-config-bind are saved in the **/var/named** directory, under **chroot/var/named**.

Your forward master zone is where you enter your main DNS configuration entries for the host domain names and their IP addresses. Click New and select Zone from the pop-up menu. On a new zone window you will have entries for selecting the class, zone, and origin type. For the Class entry be sure Internet is selected and then click OK to enter the domain name you decided on for your local network, such as **mytrek.com**. Be sure to add a period at the end. You then enter configuration information like the refresh rates and the server name.

You will then return to the main system-config-bind window, which will now list the new domain, bearing the name you gave it. To add a record, select the domain entry and click New to display a pop-up window with all the types of records you can add. The standard host entries, A and A6, are the first two. There are others for the mail server (MX) and name server (NS).

You now need to add host entries for the different hosts on your system, providing both their hostnames and their IP addresses. To add host entries you import their hostname and IP address from a hosts file. Click the Import button and select the host file to import from. You can use either the **/etc/hosts** file or one you set up listing your local hosts and IP address information. For local networks you can filter just 192.168 entries. Once your hosts have been added you can add a record for them. Click New and select an A or A6 entry.

NOTE *If you want to set up a Web site on the gateway host, you should add an alias for it, where the alias uses the hostname **www**. When adding the alias, select the Alias panel in the Add Record window, enter the alias name, and select the host it will alias from the listed hosts.*

Make sure you have a nameserver entry to specify the host running the DNS server. The host running the DNS server is referred to as the *name server*.

You then have to create a reverse master zone. Click New and select Zone. Then in the Zone window select Reverse from the Origin Type pop-up menu. Then click OK on the Zone class item. Here you enter the network part of the zone's IP address. This is the first three sets of numbers for the IP addresses you are using for the hosts on your system. For example, the IP address for **turtle.mytrek.com** is 192.168.0.1, so the network part is 192.168.0 (IPv6 reverse addressing is also supported). The network part will be the same for all your hosts. You enter each segment of the address separately, clicking ADD to open a new box.

NOTE *To manually start your DNS service, you can use system-config-services (Services on the Server Settings menu).*

PART

II

Environments

GNOME

The GNU Network Object Model Environment, also known as *GNOME*, is a powerful and easy-to-use environment consisting primarily of a panel, a desktop, and a set of GUI tools with which program interfaces can be constructed. GNOME is designed to provide a flexible platform for the development of powerful applications. Currently, GNOME is supported by several distributions and is the primary interface for Red Hat Enterprise Linux and Fedora Core. GNOME is free and released under the GNU Public License. You can download the source code, as well as documentation and other GNOME software, directly from the GNOME Web site at **www.gnome.org**. Several companies have joined together to form the GNOME Foundation, an organization dedicated to coordinating the development of GNOME and GNOME software applications. These include such companies as Sun, IBM, and Hewlett-Packard as well as Linux distributors such as Mandrake, Red Hat, and TurboLinux. Modeled on the Apache Software Foundation, which developed the Apache Web server, the GNOME Foundation will provide direction to GNOME development as well as organization, financial, and legal support.

The core components of the GNOME desktop consist of a panel for starting programs and desktop functionality. Other components normally found in a desktop, such as a file manager, Web browser, and window manager, are provided by GNOME-compliant applications. GNOME provides libraries of GNOME GUI tools that developers can use to create GNOME applications. Programs that use buttons, menus, and windows that adhere to a GNOME standard can be said to be GNOME-compliant. The official file manager for the GNOME desktop is Nautilus. The GNOME desktop does not have its own window manager as KDE does. Instead, it uses any GNOME-compliant window manager. The Metacity window manager is the one bundled with the GNOME distribution.

Support for component model interfaces is integrated into GNOME, allowing software components to interconnect regardless of the computer language in which they are implemented or the kind of machine on which they are running. The standard used in GNOME for such interfaces is the Common Object Request Broker Architecture (CORBA), developed by the Object Model Group for use on Unix systems. GNOME uses the ORBit implementation of CORBA. With such a framework, GNOME applications and clients can directly communicate with each other, enabling you to use components of one application in another. With GNOME 2.0, GNOME officially adopted GConf and its libraries as the underlying method for configuring GNOME and its applications. GConf can configure independently coordinating programs such as those that make up the Nautilus file manager.

Web Site	Description
www.gnome.org	Official GNOME Web site
developer.gnome.org	GNOME developer Web site
art.gnome.org	Desktop themes and background art
www.gnomefiles.org	GNOME software applications, applets, and tools
www.gnome.org/gnome-office	GNOME Office applications

TABLE **6-1**   GNOME Resources

You can find out more about GNOME at its Web site, **www.gnome.org**. The Web site provides online documentation, such as the GNOME User's Guide and FAQs, and also maintains extensive mailing lists for GNOME projects to which you can subscribe. The **www.gnomefiles.org** site provides a detailed software listing of current GNOME applications and projects. If you want to develop GNOME programs, check the GNOME developer's Web site at **developer.gnome.org**. The site provides tutorials, programming guides, and development tools. Here you can find the complete API reference manual online, as well as extensive support tools such as tutorials and integrated development environments (IDEs). The site also includes detailed online documentation for the GTK+ library, GNOME widgets, and the GNOME desktop. Table 6-1 offers a listing of useful GNOME sites.

NOTE *Currently, new versions of GNOME are being released frequently, sometimes every few months. GNOME releases are designed to enable users to upgrade their older versions easily. For Red Hat Enterprise Linux and Fedora Core, you can use the update utility, the Red Hat Network, or download packages from the Red Hat and Fedora Core download site, and install with system-config-packages. Packages can also be downloaded from the GNOME FTP site at **ftp.gnome.org**.*

GNOME 2.x Features

Check **www.gnome.org** for a detailed description of GNOME features and enhancements, with screen shots and references. GNOME releases new revisions on a frequent schedule. Several versions since the 2.0 release have added many new capabilities. Fedora Core 4 uses GNOME 2.10.

GNOME 2.x Desktop Features

Some of GNOME desktop features added since version 2.0 are described here:

- Integrated theme management with several default themes is now provided.
- New font support tools let you more easily configure your fonts, enabling you to select and display fonts as they will appear for different components such as applications or windows.
- The Metacity window manager is based on the GTK+ elements and integrates closely with GNOME. You can, however, still use other GNOME-compliant window managers, like IceWM, Openbox, or sawfish. Unlike other window

managers, Metacity is hidden from direct user access. Configurations such as
themes are handled directly by GNOME.

- For archive management, File Roller provides integrated archive content display,
archive creation, and extraction. It is the simplest way to view either tar or RPM
package contents, letting you extract individual files and view text files directly.

- The Epiphany Web browser, the Evolution mail client, and the Totem video player
are now integrated parts of the GNOME desktop.

- The GNOME panel has been redesigned as a single panel type with different
possible features, instead of separate panel types. Panel applets now include
a network monitor and keyboard indicator. Panel applets selection has been
simplified. The clock applet now connects to the Evolution calendar, the network
monitor supports wireless connections, and the battery monitor for laptops has been
improved. Additional panel applets include a trash can, mounting removable media
like CD/DVD discs and card readers, sound mixer, and CPU frequency monitor
for notebooks.

- To support those with disabilities, GNOME provides the Gnopernicus magnifier
and reader, and the GOK dynamic onscreen keyboard.

- With the GNOME Volume Manager, a computer window is now included listing
your file system devices, including CD-ROMs as well as network file system devices.
The network device icon opens to a network window, where you can access your
remote systems, such as Samba Windows shares for NFS file systems.

- Multimedia key support is now included in the keyboard shortcut panel.

- A lockdown feature lets administrators restrict remote systems, preventing actions
like changing applets, entering certain kinds of URLs, editing bookmarks or toolbars,
and accessing the command line.

- GNOME also supports automatic mounting of removable devices. Connecting a
removable DVD or CD device as well as a Memory Stick will automatically display
the device icon in a file manager window. This feature relies on the hardware
abstraction layer developed by **freedesktop.org**.

- Like KDE, GNOME now includes a range of system administration tools for basic
administrative tasks such as setting the time, managing users, and configuring
network connections. See Chapters 4 and 5 for description of these tools. In
addition, GNOME also provides a network monitor tool, integrating tasks like
ping, netstat, and traceroute (see Chapter 15). GNOME also includes a virtual
networking computing client (VNC) to allow administrators to remotely control
a user's desktop.

- Default menus are improved, separating the main menu into Applications, Places,
and Desktop menus. The floppy formatter now supports USB floppy drives.

GNOME 2.x File Manager Features

Originally developed by Eazel, Nautilus is now the official file manager for the GNOME
desktop. You can find out more about Nautilus from the Nautilus user's manual that is
part of the GNOME User's Guide at **www.gnome.org**. The Nautilus file manager, as part
of GNOME, has also had several new features added.

- It is now more integrated into other applications such as File Roller for archives, the image viewer for pictures, and the GNOME media player for audio and video. You can now preview sound and video files within a Nautilus window.

- Nautilus can also now burn files to CD writers with drag-and-drop burning.

- Context-sensitive menus let you perform appropriate actions, such as extracting archive files. An Open With option lets you choose from a selection of appropriate applications. Multiple applications can now be registered for use with a file.

- With a spatial interface, only one window is used for each folder, remembering how that folder was displayed. A folder is always opened in a new window, instead of using the same file manager window for different folders. Using the SHIFT key when opening a folder lets you use the same window. In the lower corner of a folder window, a pop-up menu displays all the parent directories for that folder, allowing you to move to any of them quickly.

- The file manager can display network shares on local networks, using DNS-based service discovery (Rendezvous in Apple). The file manager also supports access to password-protected FTP sites.

GTK+

GTK+ is the widget set used for GNOME applications. Its look and feel was originally derived from Motif. The widget set is designed from the ground up for power and flexibility. For example, buttons can have labels, images, or any combination thereof. Objects can be dynamically queried and modified at runtime. It also includes a theme engine that enables users to change the look and feel of applications using these widgets. At the same time, the GTK+ widget set remains small and efficient.

The GTK+ widget set is entirely free under the Lesser General Public License (LGPL). The LGPL enables developers to use the widget set with proprietary software, as well as free software (the GPL would restrict it to just free software). The widget set also features an extensive set of programming language bindings, including C++, Perl, Python, Pascal, Objective C, Guile, and Ada. Internalization is fully supported, permitting GTK+-based applications to be used with other character sets, such as those in Asian languages. The drag-and-drop functionality supports both Xdnd and Motif protocols, allowing drag-and-drop operations with other widget sets that support these protocols, such as Qt and Motif.

The GNOME Interface

The GNOME interface consists of the panel and a desktop, as shown in Figure 6-1. The panel appears as a long bar across the bottom of the screen. It holds menus, programs, and applets. (An *applet* is a small program designed to be run within the panel.) On the top panel is a button with a large red hat on it. This is the GNOME Applications menu. The menu operates like the Start menu in Windows, listing entries for applications you can run on your desktop. You can display panels horizontally or vertically, and have them automatically hide to show you a full screen. The Applications menu is reserved for applications. Other tasks like opening a home directory window or logging out are located in the Places and Desktop menus. The Desktop menu holds the Preferences menu for configuring your GNOME interface, as well as the Settings menu for accessing the Fedora Core administrative tools.

FIGURE 6-1   GNOME with Preferences menu

NOTE   *The current Fedora Core 4 GNOME interface uses two panels, one on top for menus and notification tasks like your clock, and one on the bottom for interactive features for workspaces and docking applications. Three main menus are now used instead of one: an Applications menu, a Places menu, and the Desktop. The Desktop menu is used to log out of your session.*

The remainder of the screen is the desktop. Here, you can place directories, files, or programs. You can create them on the desktop directly or drag them from a file manager window. A click-and-drag operation will move a file from one window to another or to the desktop. A click and drag with the CTRL key held down will copy a file. A click-and-drag operation with the middle mouse button (two buttons at once on a two-button mouse) enables you to create links on the desktop to installed programs. Initially, the desktop holds only an icon for your home directory. Clicking it opens a file manager window to that directory. A right-click anywhere on the desktop displays a Desktop menu (see Table 6-2) with which you can open new windows, create new folders, and mount floppy disks and CD-ROMs.

TIP   *You can display your GNOME desktop using different themes that change the appearance of desktop objects such as windows, buttons, and scroll bars. GNOME functionality is not affected in any way. You can choose from a variety of themes. Many are posted on the Internet at **themes .freshmeat.net**. Technically referred to as GTK themes, these allow the GTK widget set to change its look and feel. To select a theme, select Theme in the Preferences menu. The default GNOME theme is Clearlooks.*

GNOME Components

From a user's point of view, you can think of the GNOME interface as having four components: the desktop, the panel, the main menus, and the file manager.

In its standard default configuration, the GNOME desktop displays a Folder icon for your home directory in the upper-left corner, along with a trash can to delete items. In addition, the desktop also displays a Computer window for accessing the entire file system, CD/DVD drives, and network shares. Double-clicking the home directory icon will open the file manager, displaying files in your home directory. On Fedora Core, you have two panels displayed, one used for menus, application icons, and running applets at the top of the screen, and one at the bottom of the screen used primarily for managing your windows and desktop spaces.

The top bar has several menus and application icons: the Applications menu (the red hat), the Places menu, the Desktop menu, the Mozilla Firefox Web browser (globe with fox), and the Evolution mail tool (envelope). See Chapter 3 for a detailed description of the menus. To the right are update and time and date icons. You can use the update icon to automatically update your system. The bottom bar holds icons for minimized windows as well as running applets. These include a Workspace Switcher (squares) placed to the right. An icon to the left lets you minimize all your open windows. When you open a window, a corresponding button for it will be displayed in the lower panel, which you can use to minimize and restore the window.

To start a program, you can select its entry in the Applications menu. You can also click its application icon in the panel (if there is one), drag a data file to its icon, or select the Run entry in the Desktop menu. This opens a small window where you can type in the program name.

Quitting GNOME

To quit GNOME, you select the Logout entry in the Actions menu. A Logout button then appears in the panel. When you log out, the Logout dialog box is displayed. You have three options. The first option, Logout, quits GNOME, returning you to the login window (or command line shell, still logged in to your Linux account, if you started GNOME with `startx`). The second option, Shut Down, not only quits GNOME but also shuts down your entire system. The third option, the Restart entry, shuts down and reboots your system. The Logout entry is selected by default. Shut Down and Restart are available only to the root user. If normal users execute them, they are prompted to enter the root user password to shut down. You can also elect to retain your desktop by clicking the Save Current Setup check box. This reopens any programs or directories left open when you logged out. GNOME-compliant window managers also quit when you log out of GNOME. You must separately quit a window manager that is not GNOME-compliant after logging out of GNOME.

GNOME Help

The GNOME Help system provides a browser-like interface for displaying the GNOME user's manual, Man pages, and info documents. You can select it from the Applications menu. It features a toolbar that enables you to move through the list of previously viewed documents. You can even bookmark specific items. A Web page interface enables you to use links to connect to different documents. You can easily move the manual or the list of Man pages and info documents. You can place entries in the location box to access specific documents directly. Special URL-like protocols are supported for the different types of documents: **ghelp**, for GNOME help; **man**, for Man pages; and **info**, for the info documents.

The GNOME Help Browser provides a detailed manual on every aspect of your GNOME interface. Initially it displays a set of GNOME categories, including Desktop, Applications, and Development. Consult the Desktop entry for a complete list of GNOME manuals and use guides. The Applications entry will provide detailed descriptions of all available GNOME applets, as well as applications developed as part of the GNOME project, like the Evolution mail client and the GNOME System Monitor.

The GNOME Desktop

The GNOME desktop provides you with all the capabilities of GUI-based operating systems (see Figure 6-1). You can drag files, applications, and directories to the desktop, and then back to GNOME-compliant applications. If the desktop stops functioning, you can restart it by starting the GNOME file manager (Nautilus). The desktop is actually a back-end process in the GNOME file manager. But you needn't have the file manager open to use the desktop.

NOTE *As an alternative to the desktop, you can drag any program, file, or directory to the panel.*

Drag and Drop Files to the Desktop

Any icon for an item that you drag from a file manager window to the desktop also appears on the desktop. However, the default drag-and-drop operation is a **move** operation. If you select a file in your file manager window and drag it to the desktop, you are actually moving the file from its current directory to the GNOME desktop directory, which is located in your home directory and holds all items on the desktop. For GNOME, the desktop directory is **DESKTOP**. In the case of dragging directory folders to the desktop, the entire directory and its subdirectories will be moved to the GNOME desktop directory. To remove an icon from the desktop, you move it to the trash.

You can also copy a file to your desktop by pressing the CTRL key and then clicking and dragging it from a file manager window to your desktop. You will see the small arrow in the upper-right corner of the copied icon change to a + symbol, indicating that you are creating a copy, instead of moving the original.

CAUTION *Be careful when removing icons from the desktop. If you have moved the file to the desktop, then its original is residing in the* **DESKTOP** *folder, and when you remove it you are erasing the original. If you have copied or linked the original, then you are simply deleting the copy. When you drag applications from the menu or panel to the desktop, you are just creating a copy of the application button in the* **DESKTOP** *directory. These you can safely remove.*

You can also create a link on the desktop to any file. This is useful if you want to keep a single version in a specified directory and just be able to access it from the desktop. You could also use links for customized programs that you may not want on the menu or panel. To create a link, first click and drag the file out of the window, and after moving the file but before lifting up the mouse button, press the ALT key. This will display a pop-up menu with selections for Cut, Copy, and Link. Select the Link option to create a link. A copy of the icon then appears with a small arrow in the right corner indicating it is a link. You can click this link to start the program, open the file, or open the directory, depending on what kind of file you linked to.

GNOME's drag-and-drop file operation works on virtual desktops provided by the GNOME Workspace Switcher. The GNOME Workspace Switcher on the bottom panel creates icons for each virtual desktop in the panel, along with task buttons for any applications open on them.

NOTE *Although the GNOME desktop supports drag-and-drop operations, these normally work only for applications that are GNOME-compliant. You can drag any items from a GNOME-compliant application to your desktop, and vice versa.*

Applications on the Desktop

In most cases, you only want to create on the desktop another way to access a file without moving it from its original directory. You can do this either by using a GNOME application launcher button or by creating a link to the original program. Application launcher buttons are the GNOME components used in menus and panels to display and access applications. The Open Office buttons on the top panel are application launcher buttons. To place an icon for the application on your desktop, you can simply drag the application button from the panel or from a menu. For example, to place an icon for the Firefox Web browser on your desktop, just drag the Web browser icon on the top panel to anywhere on your desktop space.

For applications that are not on the panel or in the menu, you can either create an application launcher button for it or create a direct link (see Chapter 10), as described in the preceding section. To create an application launcher, first right-click on the desktop background to display the Desktop menu. Then select the Create Launcher entry.

Desktop Menu

You can also right-click anywhere on the empty desktop to display the GNOME Desktop menu. This will list entries for common tasks, such as opening a new terminal window for entering shell commands, creating an application launcher, creating a new folder, or organizing the icon display. Keep in mind that the New Folder entry creates a new directory on your desktop, specifically in your GNOME desktop directory (**DESKTOP**), not your home directory. The entries for this menu are listed in Table 6-2.

Menu Item	Description
Open Terminal	Opens a new terminal window with a command line prompt.
Create Launcher	Creates a new desktop icon for an application.
Create Folder	Creates a new directory on your desktop, within your **DESKTOP** directory.
Create Document	Creates files using installed templates.
Clean Up by Name	Arranges your desktop icons.
Keep Aligned	Aligns your desktop icons.
Cut, Copy, Paste	Cuts, copies, or pastes files, letting you move or copy files between folders.
Change Desktop Background	Opens a Background Preferences dialog to let you select a new background for your desktop.

TABLE 6-2   The GNOME Desktop Menu

Window Manager

GNOME works with any window manager. However, desktop functionality, such as drag-and-drop capabilities and the GNOME workspace switcher (discussed later), works only with window managers that are GNOME-compliant. The current release of GNOME uses the Metacity window manager. It is completely GNOME-compliant and is designed to integrate with the GNOME desktop without any duplication of functionality. However, other window managers such as Enlightenment, IceWM, and Window Maker can also be used. Check a window manager's documentation to see if it is GNOME-compliant.

Metacity employs much the same window operations as used on other window managers. You can resize a window by clicking any of its sides or corners and dragging. You can move the window with a click-and-drag operation on its title bar. You can also right-click and drag any border to move the window, as well as ALT-click anywhere on the window. The upper-right corner shows the Maximize, Minimize, and Close buttons. Minimize creates a button for the window in the panel that you can click to restore it. You can right-click on the title bar of a window to display a window menu with entries for window operations. These include workspace entries to move the window to another workspace (virtual desktop) or to all workspaces, which display the window no matter to what workspace you move.

The GNOME Volume Manager

Managing CD-ROMs, card readers, floppy disks, digital cameras, and other removable media is the task of the GNOME Volume Manager. This is a lower-level utility that remains transparent to the user, though how you treat removable media can be configured with the Drives and Removable Media preferences tool, as noted in Chapter 3. The GNOME Volume Manager allows you not only to access removable media, but to access all your mounted file systems, remote and local, including any Windows shared directories accessible from Samba. You can browse all your file systems directly from GNOME, which implements this capability with the gnome virtual file system (gnome-vfs) mapping to your drives, storage devices, and removable media. The GNOME Volume Manager uses HAL and udev to access removable media (see Chapter 34), and Samba to provide Windows networking support (see Chapter 41).

You can access your file systems and removable media using the Computer icon on the desktop (see Figure 6-2). This opens a top-level window showing icons for all removable media (mounted CD-ROMs, floppies, etc.), your local file system, and your network shared resources. Double-click any icon to open a file manager window displaying its contents. The file system icon will open a window showing the root-level directory, the top directory for your file system. Access will be restricted for system directories, unless you log in as the root user. The network icon will open a window listing your connected network hosts. Opening these will display the shares, such as shared directories, that you can have access to. Drag-and-drop operations are supported for all shared directories, letting you copy files and folders between a shared directory on another host with a directory on your system.

Removable media will also appear automatically as icons directly on your desktop. A CD-ROM is automatically mounted when you insert it into your CD-ROM drive, displaying an icon for it with its label. To eject a CD-ROM, right-click its icon and select Eject from the pop-up menu. The same kind of access is also provided for card readers and digital cameras.

You can then access the disk in the CD-ROM drive either by double-clicking it or by right-clicking and selecting the Open entry. A file manager window opens to display the

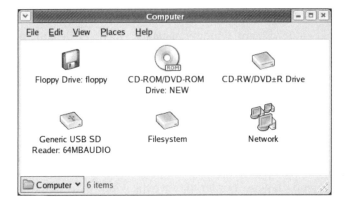

FIGURE 6-2
GNOME Computer
window (GNOME
Volume Manager)

contents of the CD-ROM disc. To unmount and eject a CD-ROM, right-click the CD-ROM icon and select the Eject entry. The same procedure works for floppy disks, using the Floppy Drive icon. Be sure you don't remove a mounted floppy disk until you have first unmounted it, selecting the Eject entry in the pop-up menu.

GNOME will display icons for any removable media and perform certain default actions on them. For example, Audio CDs will be automatically played in the CD player. DVD movies can be started up in a DVD player. To set the preferences for how removable media are treated, you use the Drives and Removable Media preferences tool, accessible with the Removable Media entry in the Preferences window (see Chapter 3). Certain settings are already set.

TIP If you have difficulty mounting a CD-ROM, you may need to configure user access with the HAL hotplug service. HAL manages all removable media (see Chapter 34).

The GNOME File Manager: Nautilus

Nautilus is the GNOME file manager, supporting the standard features for copying, removing, and deleting items as well as setting permissions and displaying items. It also provides enhancements such as zooming capabilities, user levels, and theme support. You can enlarge or reduce the size of your file icons, select from novice, intermediate, or expert levels of use, and customize the look and feel of Nautilus with different themes. Nautilus also lets you set up customized views of file listings, enabling you to display images for directory icons and run component applications within the file manager window.

Nautilus implements a spatial approach to file browsing. A new window is opened for each new folder.

Nautilus Window

Nautilus was designed as a desktop shell in which different components can be employed to add functionality. For example, within Nautilus, a Web browser can be executed to provide Web browser capabilities in a Nautilus file manager window. An image viewer can display images. The GNOME media player can run sound and video files. The GNOME File Roller tool can archive files, as well as extract them from archives. With the implementation of GStreamer, multimedia tools such as the GNOME audio recorder are now more easily integrated into Nautilus.

FIGURE 6-3
Default Nautilus window (spatial view)

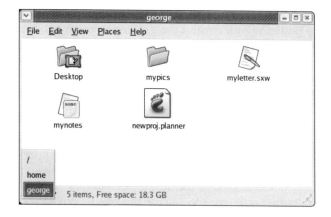

By default, the Nautilus window provides a streamlined display with no toolbars or sidebar (see Figure 6-3). Much of its functionality has been moved to menus and pop-up windows, leaving more space to display files and folders. You can, however, open a Nautilus window with the menu bar and location toolbars by right-clicking the folder icon and selecting Browse Folder from the pop-up menu.

The default Nautilus window displays a menu bar at the top with menus for managing your files. An information bar at the bottom displays information about the directory or selected files. To the lower left is a pop-up window displaying the parent directories for your current working directory. You can select any entry to open a window for that directory.

The alternate Nautilus window displays toolbars, including a menu bar of file manager commands and a Location box at the top (see Figure 6-4), along with a sidebar for file and directory information. The rest of the window is divided into two panes. The left pane is a side pane used to display information about the current working directory. The right pane is the main panel that displays the list of files and subdirectories in the current working directory. A status bar at the bottom of the window displays information about a selected file or directory. You can turn any of these elements on or off by selecting their entries in the View menu.

FIGURE 6-4
Alternate Nautilus file manager window with toolbars and sidebar (browser view)

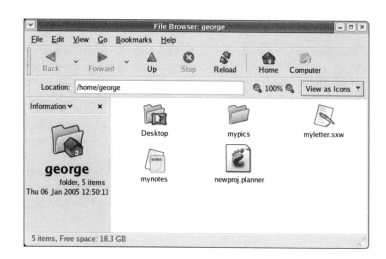

Next to the Location box is an element for zooming in and out of the view of the files. Click the + button to zoom in and the – button to zoom out. Next to the zoom element is a drop-down menu for selecting the different views for your files, such as icons, small icons, or details.

Nautilus Sidebar: Information, Tree, History, and Notes

The sidebar has several different views, selectable from a pop-up menu, for displaying additional information about files and directories: Information, Tree, History, and Notes. Information displays detailed information about the current directory or selected file. For example, if you double-click an image file, the Information pane will display detailed data on the image, while the window pane displays the full image. The Tree view will display a tree-based hierarchical view of the directories and files on your system, highlighting the one you have currently selected. You can use this tree to move to other directories and files. The tree maps all the directories on your system, starting from the root directory. You can expand or shrink any directory by clicking the + or – symbol before its name. Select a directory by clicking the directory name. The contents of that directory are then displayed in the main panel. The History view shows previous files or directories you have accessed, handy for moving back and forth between directories or files.

The Notes view will display notes you have entered about an item or directory. The Notes view opens an editable text window within the side pane. Just select the Notes view and type in your notes. To add a note for a particular item, such as an image or sound file, just double-click the item to display or run it, and then select the Note view to type in your note. You can also right-click the item, to display the item's pop-up menu and select preferences, from which you can click on a Notes panel. After you have added a note, you will see a note image added to the item's icon in the Nautilus window.

Displaying Files and Folders

You can view a directory's contents as icons or as a detailed list. In the default view, you select the different options from the View menu. On the Alternate view, you use the pop-up menu located on the right side of the Location bar. The List view provides the name, permissions, size, date, owner, and group. In the "View as List" view, buttons are displayed for each field across the top of the main panel. You can use these buttons to sort the lists according to that field. For example, to sort the files by date, click the Date button; to sort by size, click Size.

In the Icon view, you can sort icons and preview their contents without opening them. To sort items in the Icon view, select the Arrange Items entry in the View menu (default or alternate), and then select a layout option. Certain types of file icons will display previews of their contents—for example, the icons for image files will display a small version of the image. A text file will display in its icon the first few words of its text. The Zoom In entry enlarges your view of the window, making icons bigger, and Zoom Out reduces your view, making them smaller. Normal Size restores them to the standard size. You can also use the + and – buttons on the Location bar to change sizes.

In both the default and alternate views, you can also change the size of individual icons. Select the icon and then choose the Stretch entry from the Edit menu. Handles will appear on the icon image. Click and drag the handles to change its size. To restore the icon, select Restore Icon's Original Size in the Edit menu.

Nautilus Menu

You can click anywhere on the main panel to display a pop-up menu with entries for managing and arranging your file manager icons (see Table 6-3). The menu is the same for both default and alternate views. To create a new folder, select Create Folder. The Arrange Items entry displays a submenu with entries for sorting your icons by name, size, type, date, or even emblem. The Manually entry lets you move icons wherever you want on the main panel. You can also cut, copy, and paste files to more easily move or copy them between folders.

TIP *To change the background used on the File Manager window you now select Background & Emblems from the Edit menu, dragging the background you want to the file manager window.*

Navigating Directories

The default and alternate views use different tools for navigating directories. The default view relies more on direct window operations, whereas the alternate view works more like a browser. Recall that to open a directory with the alternate view, you need to right-click the directory icon and select Browse Folder.

Navigating in the Default View

By default, Nautilus will open a new window for each directory selected. To open a directory, either double-click it or right-click and select the Open entry. The parent directory pop-up menu at the bottom left lets to open a window for any parent directories, in effect, moving to a previous directory. To jump to a specific directory, select the Open Location entry from the File menu. This will, of course, open a new window for that directory. The Open Parent entry on the File menu lets you quickly open a new window for your parent. You will quickly find that moving to different directories entails opening many new windows.

Navigating in the Alternate View

The alternate view of the Nautilus file manager operates similarly to a Web browser, using the same window to display opened directories. It maintains a list of previously viewed directories, and you can move back and forth through that list using the toolbar buttons. The left arrow button moves you to the previously displayed directory, and the right arrow

Menu Item	Description
Create Folder	Creates a new subdirectory in the directory.
Create Document	Creates a new document using installed templates.
Arrange Items	Displays a submenu to arrange files by name, size, type, date, or emblem.
Cut, Copy, Paste	Cuts, copies, or pastes files, letting you move or copy files between folders.
Zoom In	Provides a close-up view of icons, making them appear larger.
Zoom Out	Provides a distant view of icons, making them appear smaller.
Normal Size	Restores view of icons to standard size.

TABLE 6-3 Nautilus File Manager Menu

button moves you to the next displayed directory. The up arrow button moves you to the parent directory, and the Home button moves you to your home directory. To use a pathname to go directly to a given directory, you can type the pathname in the Location box and press ENTER.

To open a subdirectory, you can double-click its icon or single-click the icon and select Open from the File menu. If you want to open a separate Nautilus alternate view window for that directory, right-click the directory's icon and select Open In A New Window.

Managing Files

As a GNOME-compliant file manager, Nautilus supports GUI drag-and-drop operations for copying and moving files. To move a file or directory, click and drag from one directory to another as you would on Windows or Mac interfaces. The move operation is the default drag-and-drop operation in GNOME. To copy a file, click and drag normally while pressing the CTRL key.

NOTE *If you move a file to a directory on another partition (file system), it will be copied instead of moved.*

NOTE *Nautilus now features built-in CD-burning support with the nautilus-cd-burner package. Just copy a file to Blank CD-burner disk.*

The File Menu

You can also perform remove, rename, and link creation operations on a file by right-clicking its icon and selecting the action you want from the pop-up menu that appears (see Table 6-4). For example, to remove an item, right-click it and select the Move To Trash entry from the pop-up menu. This places it in the Trash directory, where you can later delete it by selecting Empty Trash from the Nautilus File menu. To create a link, right-click the file and select Make Link from the pop-up menu. This creates a new link file that begins with the term "link."

Menu Item	Description
Open	Opens the file with its associated application. Directories are opened in the file manager. Associated applications will be listed.
Open In A New Window	Opens a file or directory in a separate window. Alternate view only.
Open With	Selects an application with which to open this file. A submenu of possible applications is displayed.
Cut, Copy, Paste files	Entries to cut, copy, paste files.
Make Link	Creates a link to that file in the same directory.
Rename	Renames the file.
Move To Trash	Moves a file to the Trash directory, where you can later delete it.
Create Archive	Archives a file using File Roller.
Send Via Bluetooth	Sends the file to a Bluetooth device.
Properties	Displays the Properties dialog box for this file. There are three panels: Statistics, Options, and Permissions.

TABLE 6-4 The Nautilus File Pop-Up Menu

Renaming Files

To rename a file, you can either right-click the file's icon and select the Rename entry from the pop-up menu or click the name of the file shown below its icon. The name of the icon will be highlighted in a black background, encased in a small text box. You can then click the name and delete the old name, typing a new one. You can also rename a file by entering a new name in its Properties dialog box. Use a right-click and select Properties from the pop-up menu to display the Properties dialog box. On the Basic tab, you can change the name of the file.

File Grouping

File operations can be performed on a selected group of files and directories. You can select a group of items in several ways. You can click the first item and then hold down the SHIFT key while clicking the last item. You can also click and drag the mouse across items you want to select. To select separated items, hold the CTRL key down as you click the individual icons. If you want to select all the items in the directory, choose the Select All entry in the Edit menu. You can then click and drag a set of items at once. This enables you to copy, move, or even delete several files at once.

Applications and Files: MIME Types

You can start any application in the file manager by double-clicking either the application itself or a data file used for that application. If you want to open the file with a specific application, you can right-click the file and select the Open With entry. A submenu displays a list of possible applications. If your application is not listed, you can select Other Application to open a Select An Application dialog box where you can choose the application with which you want to open this file. You can also use a text viewer to display the bare contents of a file within the file manager window. Drag-and-drop operations are also supported for applications. You can drag a data file to its associated application icon (say, one on the desktop); the application then starts up using that data file.

To associate a particular application with a certain type of file, you use the same Open With entry when you right-click the file. This displays an Open With box and a Browse button. If you already know the full pathname of the application, you can enter it directly. Normally you would click Browse to display a Select An Application box that will list applications you can choose. Initially, applications in the **/usr/bin** directory are listed, though you can browse to other directories. Once you select your application, you are then prompted whether to make the assignment permanent.

For example, to associate BitTorrent files (see Chapter 31), with the BitTorrent application, you would right-click any BitTorrent file (one with a **.torrent** extension) and select Open With. A list of installed applications will be displayed, but bittorrent will not be one of them. Click on Use Custom Application box and then its Browse button to open a list of all applications in the **/usr/bin** directory. Then select **btdownloadgui.py**, the BitTorrent client. It will appear in the Custom box. Click Open. You are then prompted as to whether to make this association permanent. This will associate **.torrent** files with the **btdownlaodgui.py** client. This creates the MIME type association in GNOME only, not in KDE or in applications like Firefox.

Default Applications

Different types of files will have default applications already associated with them. For example, double-clicking a text file will open the file in the Gedit text editor (also known simply as Text Editor). Double-clicking a Web page file will open the file in the Firefox Web browser. If you prefer to set a different default application, you can use the Preferred

FIGURE 6-5
Preferred
Applications tool

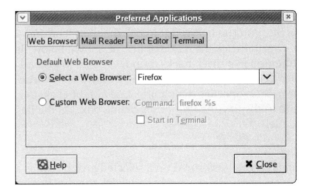

Applications tool (see Figure 6-5). This tool will let you set default applications for text files, Web pages, mail readers, and the Terminal window. You can even select from a list of installed applications to select a custom program. You access the Preferred Applications tool from the More Preferences submenu located in the Preferences menu.

File and Directory Properties

With the Properties dialog box, you can view detailed information on a file and set options and permissions (see Figure 6-6). A Properties box has five panels: Basic, Emblems, Permissions, Open With, and Notes. The Basic panel shows detailed information such as type, size, location, and date modified. The type is a MIME type, indicating the type of application associated with it. The file's icon is displayed at the top with a text box showing the file's name. You can edit the filename in this text box, changing that name. A button at the bottom labeled Select Custom Icon will open a dialog box showing available icons you can use. You can select the one you want from that window. The Remove Custom Icon button will restore the default icon image. The Emblems panel enables you to set the emblem you want displayed for this file, displaying all the emblems available. The Permissions panel shows the read, write, and execute permissions for user, group, and other, as set for this file. You can change any of the permissions here, provided the file belongs to you. The panel

FIGURE 6-6
File properties
on Nautilus

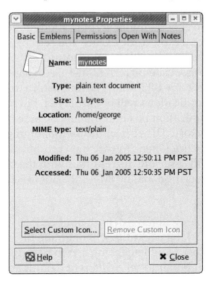

will also show the file's owner and its group. The group name expands to a pop-up menu listing different groups, allowing you to select one to change the file's group. The Open With panel lists all the applications associated with this kind of file. You can select which one you want as the default. This can be particularly useful for media files, where you may prefer a specific player for a certain file. The Notes panel will list any notes you want to make for the file or directory. It is an editable text window, so you can change or add to your notes, directly.

Certain kind of files will have added panels, providing information about the item. For example, an audio file will have an Audio panel listing the type of audio file and any other information like the song title or compressions method used. An image file will have an Image panel listing the resolution and type of image. A video file will contain a Video panel showing the type of video file along with compression and resolution information.

Nautilus Preferences

You can set preferences for your Nautilus file manager in the Preferences dialog box. Access this dialog box by selecting the Preferences item in the Edit menu. The Preferences dialog box shows a main panel with a sidebar with several configuration entries, including Views, Behavior, Display, List Columns, and Preview. You use these dialog boxes to set the default display properties for your Nautilus file manager.

- The Views panel allows you to select how files are displayed by default, such as the list or icon view.

- Behavior lets you choose how to select files, manage the trash, and handle scripts, as well as whether to use the Browse File alternate view as the default.

- Display lets you choose what added information you want displayed in a icon caption, like the size or date.

- List Columns lets you choose both the features to display in the detailed list and the order to display them in. In addition to the already-selected Name, Size, Date, and Type, you can add permissions, group, MIME type, and owner.

- Preview lets you choose whether you want small preview content displayed in the icons, like beginning text for text files.

Nautilus as a FTP Browser

Nautilus works as an operational FTP browser. You can use the Location box or the Open Location entry on the File menu to access any FTP site. Just enter the URL for the FTP site in the Location box and press ENTER (you do not need to specify **ftp://**). Folders on the FTP site will be displayed, and you can drag files to a local directory to download them. However, unlike KDE's Konqueror file manager, Nautilus is not a functional Web browser. When you access a Web page, it will display buttons in the sidebar to open the page using one of several Web browsers installed on your system, such as Mozilla Firefox and Epiphany. It is preferable that you use the Web browsers for access the Web.

The GNOME Panel

The *panel* is the center of the GNOME interface (see Figure 6-7). Through it you can start your applications, run applets, and access desktop areas. You can think of the GNOME panel as a type of tool you can use on your desktop. You can have several GNOME panels displayed on your desktop, each with applets and menus you have placed in them. In this respect, GNOME is flexible, enabling you to configure your panels any way you want. In fact, the default GNOME desktop that Red Hat Enterprise Linux and Fedora Core use features two panels, a menu panel at the top for your applications and actions, and a panel at the bottom used for minimized windows and the Workspace Switcher. You can customize a panel to fit your own needs, holding applets and menus of your own selection. You may add new panels, add applications to the panel, and add various applets.

Panel configuration tasks such as adding applications, selecting applets, setting up menus, and creating new panels are handled from the Panel pop-up menu. Just right-click anywhere on your panel to display a menu with entries for Properties, New Panel, Add To Panel, and Delete This Panel, along with Help and About entries. New Panel lets you create other panels; Add To Panel lets you add items to the panel such as application launchers, applets for simple tasks like the Workspace Switcher, and menus like the main applications menu. The Properties entry will display a dialog for configuring the features for that panel, like the position of the panel and its hiding capabilities.

To add a new panel, select the New Panel entry in the Panel pop-up menu. A new expanded panel is automatically created and displayed on the side of your screen. You can then use the panel's properties box to set different display and background features, as described in the following sections.

NOTE *What was formerly the Main Menu on Red Hat/Fedora Core versions prior to Fedora Core 4 is now split into three menus located in a panel at the top of your screen: Applications for all your applications and tools, Places for commonly used locations and searching for files, and Desktop, which holds the Preferences and Settings menus, as well as entries for locking your desktop and logging out.*

Panel Properties

To configure individual panels, you use the Panel Properties dialog box. To display this dialog box, you right-click the particular panel and select the Properties entry in the pop-up menu. For individual panels, you can set general configuration features and the background. The Panel Properties dialog box includes a tabbed pane, General and Background. With version 2.4, GNOME abandoned the different panel types in favor of just one kind of panel with different possible features that give it the same capabilities as the old panel types.

Displaying Panels

On the General pane of a panel's properties box, you determine how you want the panel displayed. Here you have options for orientation, size, and whether to expand, auto-hide, or display hide buttons. The Orientation entry lets you select which side of the screen you want the panel placed on. You can then choose whether you want a panel expanded or not. An expanded panel will fill the edges of the screen, whereas a nonexpanded panel is sized to the number of items in the panel and shows handles at each end. Expanded panels will remain fixed to the edge of screen, whereas unexpanded panels can be moved, provided the Show Hide Buttons feature is not selected.

FIGURE 6-7   The GNOME panel, at the top of Fedora Core desktop

Moving and Hiding Expanded Panels

Expanded panels can be positioned at any edge of your screen. You can move expanded panels from one edge of a screen to another by simply dragging the panel to another edge. If a panel is already there, the new one will stack on top of the current one. You cannot move unexpanded panels in this way. Bear in mind that if you place an expanded panel on the side edge, any menus will be displayed across at the top corner to allow proper pop-up display. The panel on the side edge will expand in size to accommodate its menus. If you have several menus or a menu with a lengthy name, you could end up with a very large panel.

You can hide expanded panels either automatically or manually. These are features specified in the panel properties General box as Auto Hide and Show Hide Buttons. To automatically hide panels, select the Auto Hide feature. To redisplay the panel, move your mouse to the edge where the panel is located. You can enable or disable the Hide buttons in the panel's properties window.

If you want to be able to hide a panel manually, select Show Hide Buttons. Two handles will be displayed at either end of the panel. You can further choose whether to have these handles display arrows or not. You can then hide the panel at any time by clicking either of the Hide buttons located on each end of the panel. The Hide buttons are thin buttons showing a small arrow. This is the direction in which the panel will hide.

Unexpanded Panels: Movable and Fixed

Whereas an expanded panel is always located at the edge of the screen, an unexpanded panel is movable. It can be located at the edge of a screen, working like a shrunken version of an expanded panel, or you can move it to any place on your desktop, just as you would an icon.

An unexpanded panel will shrink to the number of its components, showing handles at either end. You can then move the panel by dragging its handles. To access the panel menu with its properties entry, right-click either of its handles.

To fix an unexpanded panel at its current position, select the Show Hide Buttons feature on its properties box. This will replace the handles with Hide buttons and make the panel fixed. Clicking a Hide button will hide the panel to the edge of the screen, just as with expanded panels. If an expanded panel is already located on that edge, the button for a hidden unexpanded panel will be on top of it, just as with a hidden expanded panel. The Auto Hide feature will work for unexpanded panels placed at the edge of a screen.

If you want to fix an unexpanded panel to the edge of a screen, make sure it is placed at the edge you want, and then set its Show Hide Buttons feature.

Panel Background

With a panel's Background pane on its properties box, you can change the panel's background color or image. For a color background you click a color button to display a color selection window where you can choose a color from a color wheel or a list of color boxes, or else you can enter its number. Once your color is selected, you can use the Style slide bar to make it more transparent or opaque. To use an image instead of a color, select the image entry and use the Browse button to locate the image file you want. For an image, you can also drag and drop an image file from the file manager to the panel; that image then becomes the background image for the panel.

Panel Objects

A panel can contain several different types of objects. These include menus, launchers, applets, drawers, and special objects.

- **Menus**   The Applications menu is an example of a panel menu.
- **Launchers**   The Web browser icon is an example of a launcher button. You can select any application entry in the Applications menu and create a launcher for it on the panel. Launchers are buttons used to start an application or execute a command.
- **Applets**   An applet is a small application designed to run within the panel. The Workspace Switcher showing the different desktops is an example of a GNOME applet.
- **Drawers**   A drawer is an extension of the panel that can be open or closed. You can think of a drawer as a shrinkable part of the panel. You can add anything to it that you can to a regular panel, including applets, menus, and even other drawers.
- **Special objects**   These are used for special tasks not supported by other panel objects. For example, the Logout and Lock buttons are special objects.

Moving, Removing, and Locking Objects

To move any object within the panel, right-click it and choose Move Entry. You can move it either to a different place on the same panel or to a different panel. For launchers, you can just drag the object directly where you want it to be. To remove an object from the panel, right-click it to display a pop-up menu for it, and then choose the Remove From Panel entry. To prevent an object from being moved or removed, you set its lock feature (right-click the object and select the Lock entry). To later allow it to be moved, you first have to unlock the object (right-click it and select Unlock).

TIP   On the panel Add To list, common objects like the clock and the CD player are intermixed with object types like menus and applications. When adding a kind of object, like an application, you will have to search through the list to find the entry for that type; in the case of applications, it is the application launcher entry.

Adding Objects

To add an object to a panel, select the object from the panel's Add To box (see Figure 6-8). To display the Add To box, right-click on the panel and select the Add To Panel entry. This Add To box displays a lengthy list of common objects as well as object types. For example, it will display the Main menu as well as an entry for creating custom menus. You can choose to add an application that is already in the GNOME Application menu or to create an application launcher for one that is not. Launchers can be added to a panel by just dragging them directly. Launchers include applications, windows, and files.

Application Launchers

To add an application that already has an application launcher to a panel is easy. You just have to drag the application launcher to the panel. This will automatically create a copy of the launcher for use on that panel. Launchers can be menu items or desktop icons. All the entries in your Application menu are application launchers. To add an application from the menu, just select it and drag it to the panel. You can also drag any desktop application icon to a panel to add a copy of it to that panel.

FIGURE 6-8
Panel Add To
box listing panel
objects

For any menu item, you can also go to its entry and right-click it. Then select the Add This Launcher To Panel entry. An application launcher for that application is then automatically added to the panel. Suppose you use Gedit frequently and want to add its icon to the panel, instead of having to go through the Application menu all the time. Right-click the Text Editor menu entry in the Accessories menu, and select the Add This Launcher To Panel option. The Gedit icon now appears in your panel.

You can also select the Add To Panel entry from the panel menu and then choose the Application Launcher entry. This will display a box with a listing of all the Application menu entries along with Preferences and Settings menus, expandable to their items. Just find the application you want added and select it. This may be an easier approach if you are working with many different panels.

To add an application to a panel, it must have a launcher. You can create application launchers using the Create Launcher tool. This tool is accessible either from the Desktop menu as the Create Launcher item, or from the panel menu's Add To box as the Custom Application Launcher entry. When accessed from the desktop, the new launcher is placed on the desktop, and from the panel, it will be placed directly on the panel. As previously noted for creating a launcher on the desktop, the Create Launcher tool will prompt you for the application name, the command that invokes it, and its type. To select an icon for your launcher, click the Icon button. This opens the Icon Browser window, listing icons from which you can choose.

Keep in mind that for any launcher that you previously created on the desktop, you can just drag it to the panel, to have a copy of the launcher placed on the panel.

Folder and File Launchers
To add a folder to a panel, just drag it directly from the file manager window or from the desktop. To add a file, also drag it to directly to the panel, but you will then have to create a launcher for it. The Create Launcher window will be displayed, and you can give the file launcher a name and select an icon for it.

Adding Drawers

You can also group applications under a Drawer icon. Clicking the Drawer icon displays a list of the different application icons you can then select. To add a drawer to your panel, right-click the panel and select the Add To Panel entry to display the Add To list. From that list select the Drawer entry. This will create a drawer on your panel. You can then drag any items from desktop, menus, or windows to the drawer icon on the panel to have them listed in the drawer.

If you want to add, as a drawer, a whole menu of applications on the main menu to your panel, right-click any item in that menu, and then select Entire Menu from the pop-up menu, and then select the Add This As Drawer To Panel entry. The entire menu appears as a drawer on your panel, holding icons instead of menu entries. For example, suppose you want to place the Internet Applications menu on your panel. Right-click any entry item, selecting Entire Menu, and select Add This As Drawer To Panel. A drawer appears on your panel labeled Internet, and clicking it displays a pop-up list of icons for all the Internet applications.

Adding Menus

A menu differs from a drawer in that a *drawer* holds application icons instead of menu entries. You can add menus to your panel, much as you add drawers. To add a submenu from the Applications menu to your panel, right-click any item and select Entire Menu, and then select the Add This As Menu To Panel entry. The menu title appears in the panel; you can click it to display the menu entries.

You can also add a menu from the panel's Add To list, by selecting Custom menu.

Adding Folders

You can also add directory folders to a panel. Click and drag the Folder icon from the file manager window to your panel. Whenever you click this Folder button, a file manager window opens, displaying that directory. You already have a Folder button for your home directory. You can add directory folders to any drawer on your panel.

Special Panel Objects

Special panel objects perform operations not supported by other panel objects. Currently, these include the Lock, Logout, and Launcher buttons and the status dock. The Lock button, which displays a padlock, will lock your desktop, running the screensaver in its place. To access your desktop, click on it and then enter your user password at the password prompt. The Logout button shows a monitor with a half moon. Clicking it will display the Logout dialog box, and you can then log out. It is the same as selecting Logout from the Desktop menu. The Launcher button shows a launcher icon. It opens the Create Launcher dialog box, which allows you to enter or select an application to run.

The status dock is designed to hold status docklets. A status docklet provides current status information on an application. KDE applications that support status docklets can use the GNOME status dock, when run under GNOME.

GNOME Applets

Applets are small programs that perform tasks within the panel. To add an applet, right-click the panel and select Add To Panel from the pop-up menu. This displays the Add To box listing common applets along with other types of objects, such as launchers. Select the one you want. For example, to add the clock to your panel, select Clock from the panel's Add To box. Once added, the applet will show up in the panel. If you want to remove an applet, right-click it and select the Remove From Panel entry.

GNOME features a number of helpful applets. Some applets monitor your system, such as the Battery Charge Monitor, which checks the battery in laptops, and System Monitor, which shows a graph indicating your current CPU and memory use. The Volume Control applet displays a small scroll bar for adjusting sound levels. The CD player displays a small CD interface for playing music CDs.

For Internet tasks, there are Inbox Monitor, Modem Lights, and Wireless Link Monitor applets. Inbox Monitor checks for received mail. To configure Inbox Monitor, right-click it and select the Preferences entry. You can set the frequency of checks, as well as specify whether to check local mailboxes or remote POP3 and IMAP mailboxes. The Modem Lights feature monitors your modem connection. You can configure it to monitor a PPP connection to an ISP over a modem. Wireless Link enables you to monitor the quality of your wireless transmissions.

Several helpful utility applets provide added functionality to your desktop. The Clock applet can display time in a 12- or 24-hour format. Right-click the Clock applet and select the Preferences entry to change its setup. The Disk Mounter applet enables you to mount a drive using a single click. You can create a Disk Mounter applet for each device you have, such as a floppy drive and a CD-ROM. To mount a file system, all you have to do is click the appropriate Disk Mounter icon in the panel (helpful for mounting floppy drives quickly). To specify the file systems to mount, use the Disk Mounter Preferences dialog box.

Workspace Switcher

The *Workspace Switcher* appears in the panel and shows a view of your virtual desktops (see Figure 6-9). Virtual desktops are defined in the window manager. On the current Fedora Core configuration, the Workspace Switcher is located on the right side of the lower panel. The Workspace Switcher lets you easily move from one desktop to another with the click of a mouse. It is a panel applet that works only in the panel. You can add the Workspace Switcher to any panel by selecting it from that panel's Add To box.

The Workspace Switcher shows your entire virtual desktop as separate rectangles listed next to each other. Open windows show up as small colored rectangles in these squares. You can move any window from one virtual desktop to another by clicking and dragging its image in the Workspace Switcher. To configure the Workspace Switcher, right-click it and select Preferences to display the Preferences dialog box. Here, you can select the number of workspaces. The default is four.

GNOME Window List

The *Window List* shows currently opened windows (see Figure 6-9). The Window List arranges opened windows in a series of buttons, one for each window. A window can include applications such as a Web browser or a file manager window displaying a directory. You can move from one window to another by clicking its button. When you minimize a window, you can later restore it by clicking its entry in the Window List.

FIGURE 6-9 Panel with Workspace Switcher and Window List, at the bottom of Fedora Core desktop

Right-clicking a window's Window List button opens a menu that lets you Minimize or Unminimize, Roll Up, Move, Resize, Maximize, or Close the window. The Minimize operation will reduce the window to its Window List entry. Right-clicking the entry will display the menu with an Unminimize option instead of a Minimize one, which you can then use to redisplay the window. The Roll Up entry will reduce the window to its title bar. The Close entry will close the window, ending its application.

If there is not enough space on the Window List applet to display a separate button for each window, then common windows will be grouped under a button that will expand like a menu, listing each window in that group. For example, all open terminal windows would be grouped under a single button, which when clicked would pop up a list of their buttons.

The Window List applet is represented by a small serrated bar at the beginning of the window button list. To configure the Window List, right-click on this bar and select the Properties entry. Here, you can set features such as the size in pixels, whether to group windows, whether to show all open windows or those from just the current workspace, or which workspace to restore windows to.

GNOME Configuration

You can configure different parts of your GNOME interface using tools called *capplets.* Think of capplets as modules or plug-ins that can be added to enable you to configure various applications. Capplets exist for the core set of GNOME applications, as well as for other applications for which developers may have written capplets. On Fedora Core, you can access capplets from the Preferences menu in the Applications menu. This menu will display entries for the primary GNOME preferences, along with a submenu for more preferences listing task-specific capplets, like that for the Palm Pilot or Desktop Switcher. Selecting one will open a window labeled with the tool name, like mouse preferences.

NOTE *You can also open a window listing all the preferences as icons by entering the URL* ***preferences:*** *in the Nautilus file manager. Either select Open Location from the File menu and enter* ***preferences:*** *or open a Nautilus window in the Browse Folder mode and enter* ***preferences:*** *in the Location box. Be sure to include the trailing colon,* ***preferences:***.

Your GNOME system provides several desktop capplets you can use to configure your desktop, such as Desktop Background, Screensaver, and Theme. You use the Desktop Background capplet to select a background color or image, the Screensaver capplet to select the screen saver images and wait time, and the Theme capplet to choose a theme (see Figure 6-10).

The Removable Storage entry opens the Drives and Media preferences window where you can set what actions to perform on removable drives, CD and DVD discs, and digital cameras.

For the sound configuration, the Sound capplet lets you select sound files to play for events in different GNOME applications. For your keyboard, you can set the repeat sensitivity and click sound with the Keyboard capplet. You can configure mouse buttons for your right or left hand, and adjust the mouse motion.

The More Preferences menu will list configuration entries for specialized tasks like selecting a default printer, configuring a Palm Pilot interface, choosing default applications, and selecting a mail transport agent.

FIGURE **6-10**
Selecting GNOME
themes

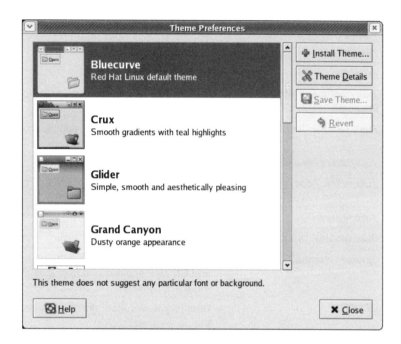

GNOME Directories and Files

Fedora Core installs GNOME binaries in the **/usr/bin** directory on your system. GNOME libraries are located in the **/usr/lib** directory. GNOME also has its own **include** directories with header files for use in compiling and developing GNOME applications, **/usr/include/ libgnome-2.0/libgnome** and **/usr/include/libgnomeui** (see Table 6-5). The directories located in **/usr/share/gnome** contain files used to configure your GNOME environment.

GNOME User Directories

GNOME sets up several configuration files and directories in your home directory. The **.gnome**, **.gnome2**, and **.gconf** directories hold configuration files for different desktop components, such as **nautilus** for the file manager and **panel** for the panels. The **DESKTOP** directory holds all the items you placed on your desktop. The **.gtckrc** file is the user configuration file for the GTK+ libraries, which contains current desktop configuration directives for resources such as key bindings, colors, and window styles.

The GConf Configuration Editor

With GNOME 2.0, GNOME officially implemented GConf to provide underlying configuration support. GConf corresponds to the Registry used on Windows system. It consists of a series of libraries used to implement a configuration database for a GNOME desktop. This standardized configuration database allows for consistent interactions between GNOME applications. GNOME applications that are built from a variety of other programs, as Nautilus is, can use GConf to configure all those programs according to a single standard, maintaining configurations in a single database. Currently the GConf database is implemented as XML files in the user's **.gconf** directory. Database interaction and access is carried out by the GConf daemon, **gconfd**.

System GNOME Directory	Contents
/usr/bin	GNOME programs
/usr/lib	GNOME libraries
/usr/include/libgnome-2.0/ libgnome	Header files for use in compiling and developing GNOME applications
/usr/include/libgnomeui	Header files for use in compiling and developing GNOME user interface components
/usr/share/gnome	Files used by GNOME applications
/usr/share/doc/gnome*	Documentation for various GNOME packages, including libraries
/etc/gconf	GConf configuration files
User GNOME Directory	**Contents**
.gnome, .gnome2	Holds configuration files for the user's GNOME desktop and GNOME applications. Includes configuration files for the panel, background, MIME types, and sessions
DESKTOP	Directory where files, directories, and links you place on the desktop will reside
.gnome2_private	The user's private GNOME directory
.gtkrc	GTK+ configuration file
.gconf	GConf configuration database
.gconfd	GConf **gconfd** daemon management files
.gstreamer	GNOME GStreamer multimedia configuration files
.nautilus	Configuration files for the Nautilus file manager

TABLE 6-5 GNOME Configuration Directories

You can use the GConf editor to configure different GNOME applications and desktop functions. To start the GConf editor, enter `gconf-editor` in a terminal window, or select Configuration Editor from the System Tools menu (Applications menu).

```
$ gconf-editor
```

Configuration elements are specified keys that are organized by application and program. You can edit the keys, changing their values. Figure 6-11 shows the GConf editor settings for the dialog display features used for the Epiphany Web browser.

The GConf editor has three panes (see Figure 6-11):

- **Tree**   A tree pane for navigating keys, with expandable trees for each application, is located on the left. Application entries expand to subentries, grouping keys into different parts or functions for the application. For example, the Epiphany entry expands to dialog, general, Web, and directories entries.

Figure **6-11**
GConf editor

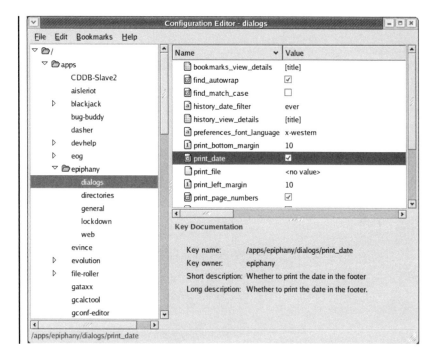

- **Modification**   A modification pane to the top right will display the keys for a selected entry. The name field will include an icon indicating its type, and the Value field is an editable field showing the current value. You can directly change this value.

- **Documentation**   The documentation field at the bottom right displays information about the selected key, showing the key name, the application that owns it, and a short and detailed description.

- **Results**   The results pane, displayed at the bottom, only appears when you do a search for a key.

A key has a specific type such as numeric or string, and you will only be able to make changes using the appropriate type. Each key entry has an icon specifying its type, such as a check mark for the Boolean values, a number 1 for numeric values, and a letter *a* for string values. Some keys have pop-up menus with limited selections to choose from, represented by an icon with a row of lines. To change the value of a key, click its value field. You can then edit the value. For pop-up menus, you right-click the value field to display the menu.

There are many keys distributed over several applications and groups. To locate one, you can use the search function. Select Find from the Edit menu and enter a pattern. The results are displayed in a Results pane, which you can use to scroll through matching keys, selecting the one you want.

Changes can be made either by users or by administrators. Administrators can set default or mandatory values for keys. Mandatory values will prevent users from making changes. For user changes, you can open a Settings window by selecting Settings from the File menu. This opens an identical GConf Editor window. For administrative changes, you first log in as the root user. For default changes, you select the Default entry from the File menu, and for mandatory changes, select the Mandatory entry.

The K Desktop Environment and the XFce4 Desktop: KDE

The *K Desktop Environment (KDE)* is a network-transparent desktop that includes the standard desktop features, such as a window manager and a file manager, as well as an extensive set of applications that cover most Linux tasks. KDE is an Internet-aware system that includes a full set of integrated network/Internet applications, including a mailer, a newsreader, and a Web browser. The file manager doubles as a Web and FTP client, enabling you to access Internet sites directly from your desktop. KDE aims to provide a level of desktop functionality and ease of use found in Macintosh and Windows systems, combined with the power and flexibility of the Unix operating system.

The KDE desktop is developed and distributed by the KDE Project, which is a large open group of hundreds of programmers around the world. KDE is entirely free and open software provided under a GNU Public License and is available free of charge along with its source code. KDE development is managed by a core group: the KDE Core Team. Anyone can apply, though membership is based on merit.

NOTE *KDE applications are developed using several supporting KDE technologies. These include KIO, which offers seamless and modular access of files and directories across a network. For interprocess communication, KDE uses the Desktop Communications Protocol (DCOP). KParts is the KDE component object model used to embed an application within another, such as a spreadsheet within a word processor. The XML GUI uses XML to generate and place GUI objects such as menus and toolbars. KHTML is an HTML rendering and drawing engine.*

Numerous applications written specifically for KDE are easily accessible from the desktop. These include editors, photo and paint image applications, spreadsheets, and office applications. Such applications usually have the letter *K* as part of their name—for example, KWord or KMail. A variety of tools are provided with the KDE desktop. These include calculators, console windows, notepads, and even software package managers. On a system administration level, KDE provides several tools for configuring your system. With KUser, you can manage user accounts, adding new ones or removing old ones.

Practically all your Linux tasks can be performed from the KDE desktop. KDE applications also feature a built-in Help application. Choosing the Contents entry in the Help menu starts the KDE Help viewer, which provides a Web page–like interface with links for navigating through the Help documents. KDE version 3.0 includes support for the office application suite KOffice, based on KDE's KParts technology. KOffice includes a presentation application, a spreadsheet, an illustrator, and a word processor, among other components (see Chapter 11 for more details). In addition, an integrated development environment (IDE), called KDevelop, is available to help programmers create KDE-based software.

NOTE   *On Fedora Core, KDE uses a Bluecurve theme to make it appear much the same as the GNOME desktop. However, on KDE, menus will show more KDE applications, including access to the KDE Control Center on the main menu.*

KDE, initiated by Matthias Ettrich in October 1996, has an extensive list of sponsors, including SuSE, Red Hat, Mandrake, O'Reilly, and others. KDE is designed to run on any Unix implementation, including Linux, Solaris, HP-UX, and FreeBSD. The official KDE Web site is **www.kde.org**, which provides news updates, download links, and documentation. KDE software packages can be downloaded from the KDE FTP site at **ftp.kde.org** and its mirror sites. Several KDE mailing lists are available for users and developers, including announcements, administration, and other topics. See the KDE Web site to subscribe. A great many software applications are currently available for KDE at **www.kde-apps.org**. Development support and documentation can be obtained at **developer.kde.org**. Various KDE Web sites are listed in Table 7-1. KOffice is now in Fedora Extras.

NOTE   *Currently, new versions of KDE are being released frequently, sometimes every few months. KDE releases are designed to enable users to upgrade their older versions easily. Normally, you can use the Red Hat Network update utility to automatically update KDE as updates become available. Alternatively, you can download new KDE packages from your distribution's FTP site and install them manually. Packages tailored for various distributions can be also downloaded through the KDE Web site at **www.kde.org** or directly from the KDE FTP site at **ftp.kde.org** and its mirror sites in the **stable** directory.*

TABLE 7-1
KDE Web Sites

Web Site	Description
www.kde.org	KDE Web site
ftp.kde.org	KDE FTP site
www.kde-apps.org	KDE software repository
developer.kde.org	KDE developer site
www.trolltech.com	Site for Qt libraries
www.koffice.org	KOffice office suite (Fedora RPMs at Fedora Extras)
www.kde-look.org	KDE desktop themes, select KDE entry
lists.kde.org	KDE mailing lists

The Qt Library

KDE uses as its library of GUI tools the Qt library, developed and supported by Trolltech (**www.trolltech.com**). Qt is considered one of the best GUI libraries available for Unix/ Linux systems. Using Qt has the advantage of relying on a commercially developed and supported GUI library. Also, using the Qt libraries drastically reduces the development time for KDE. Trolltech provides the Qt libraries as Open Source software that is freely distributable. Certain restrictions exist, however: Qt-based (KDE) applications must be free and open-sourced, with no modifications made to the Qt libraries. If you develop an application with the Qt libraries and want to sell it, then you have to buy a license from Trolltech. In other words, the Qt library is free for free and Open Source applications, but not for commercial ones.

The KDE Desktop

One of KDE's aims is to provide users with a consistent integrated desktop, where all applications use GUI interfaces (see Figure 7-1). To this end, KDE provides its own window manager (KWM), file manager (Konqueror), program manager, and desktop panel (Kicker).

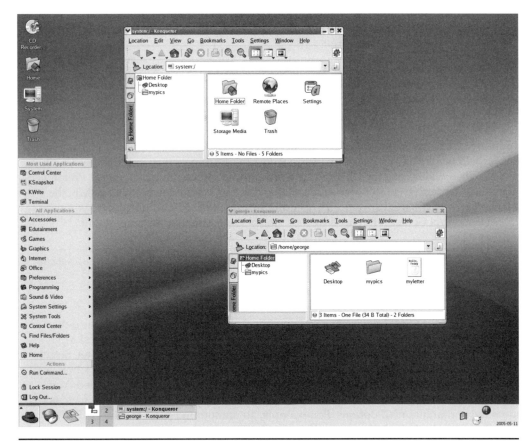

FIGURE 7-1   The KDE desktop

You can run any other X Window System–compliant application, such as Firefox, in KDE, as well as any GNOME application. In turn, you can also run any KDE application, including the Konqueror file manager. You can even run KDE applications in GNOME.

KDE Menus

When you start KDE, the KDE panel is displayed at the bottom of the screen. Located on the panel are icons for menus and programs, as well as buttons for different desktop screens. For the Bluecurve interface, the KDE panel is made to look similar to the GNOME panel. On Fedora Core 4, the button for the main menu shows a red fedora, just as the GNOME interface does (normally this is a K on a gear image with a small arrow at the top indicating it is a menu).

This is the button for the KDE main menu. Click this button to display the menu of applications you run (you can also open the main menu by pressing ALT-F1). From the KDE menu, you can access numerous submenus for different kinds of applications. The menu also includes certain key items such as Logout, to log out of KDE; Lock Screen, to lock your desktop; Control Center, to configure your KDE desktop; Run Command, to run programs from a command line; your Home directory, to quickly browse your home directory; and Help, which starts the KDE help tool.

TIP   *You can run the Desktop Settings Wizard on the More Preferences submenu within Preferences menu, to easily change your desktop settings.*

The standard KDE applications installed with KDE can be accessed through this menu. On Bluecurve, the main menu has most of the same entries as those found on GNOME. The entries have been standardized for both interfaces. You can find entries for categories such as Internet, System Settings, Graphics, and Office. On Fedora Core, these menus list both GNOME and KDE applications you can use. However, some of the KDE menus contain entries for a few more alternate KDE applications, like KMail on the Internet menu. Some entries will invoke the KDE version of a tool, like the Terminal entry in the System Tools menu, which will invoke the KDE terminal window, KConsole. In addition, the Preferences menu is nearly empty, with only the same More Preferences submenu. In GNOME, the Preferences menu is used specifically to configure GNOME. To configure KDE, you use the KDE Control Center referenced by the Control Center item in the main menu.

TIP   *In KDE you use the Control Center to configure the KDE desktop, not the Preferences menu.*

Displaying Device Icons

If your CD or DVD-ROM device icons are not displayed, you will need to enable device icon display on your desktop. Right-click on the desktop and choose Config-Desktop from the pop-up menu. This shows the desktop entries only of the Control Center. Select Behavior, and then on the Device Icons pane, select the Show Device Icons check box. A long list of connectable devices is displayed, with default devices already selected. You select and de-select the ones you want shown or hidden. For most devices, you have both mounted and unmounted options. For example, an unmounted entry for the DVD-ROM will display an DVD-ROM icon even if the DVD-ROM device is empty.

Quitting KDE

To quit KDE, you can select the Logout entry in the main menu, or you can right-click anywhere on the desktop and select the Logout entry from the pop-up menu. If you leave any KDE or X11 applications or windows open when you quit, they are automatically restored when you start up again. If you just want to lock your desktop, you can select the Lock Screen entry on the main menu and your screen saver will appear. To access a locked desktop, click on the screen and a box appears prompting you for your login password. When you enter the password, your desktop reappears.

NOTE *You can use the Create New menus to create new folders or files on the desktop, as well as links for applications and devices.*

KDE Desktop Operations

A row of icons are displayed along the left side. These include a home directory folder icon labeled Trash, and floppy and CD-ROM icons. The Trash icon operates like the Recycle Bin in Windows or the trash can on the Mac. Drag items to it to hold them for deletion. You can use the floppy and CD-ROM icons to mount, unmount, and display the contents of CD-ROMs and floppy disks. The System icon opens a window to allow access to different system resources like storage devices, network shares, and configuration tools.

The KDE panel displayed across the bottom of the screen initially shows small buttons for the KDE main menu, the Web browser, office tools, a clock, and buttons for virtual desktops, among others. The desktop supports drag-and-drop operations. For example, to print a document, drag it to the Printer icon. You can place any directories on the desktop by simply dragging them from a file manager window to the desktop. The desktop also supports copy-and-paste operations, holding text you copied from one application in a desktop clipboard that you can then use to paste to another application. You can even copy and paste from a Konsole window. For example, you can copy a Web address from a Web page and then paste it into an e-mail message or a word processing document. This feature is supported by the Klipper utility located on the panel.

You can create new directories on the desktop by right-clicking anywhere on the desktop and selecting Create New and then Directory from the pop-up menu. All items that appear on the desktop are located in the **Desktop** directory in your home directory. There you can find the **Trash** directory, along with any others you place on the desktop. You can also create simple text files and HTML files using the same menu.

Accessing System Resources from the Desktop

The System icon opens a file manager window with icons you can use to access various system resources such as storage media, remote hosts, Samba network shares, and your trash folder, and the KDE control center configuration tools. You will see icons labeled Home Folder, Remote Places, Settings, Storage Media, and Trash. The Settings icon opens a folder listing icons for all the KDE configuration categories as discussed in "KDE Configuration: KDE Control Center" later in this chapter. Under Remote Places you will find icons for your local network, network services, Samba shares, and a tool to add network folders. Through the Samba Shares icon you can access your shared Windows folders and printers. The Storage Media icon lists your storage media such as your CD-ROMs. You can open these to access their contents. Certain resources have their own URLs that you can enter into a file manager location box to directly access them. Remote Places has the URL **remote:/** and Samba uses **smb:/**. KDE configuration uses **settings:/** and Storage Media uses **media:/**.

Configuring Your Desktop

To configure your desktop, right-click the desktop and select the Configure Desktop entry. This displays a window with entries for Display, Behavior, Multiple Desktops, Background, and Screensaver. All these features can be configured also using the KDE Control Center's Appearance & Themes panels.

- Display lets you set the display resolution and orientation.
- Behavior lets you enable the display of certain features, such as displaying a desktop menu across the top of the screen, or showing icons on the desktop. You can also select the operations for a mouse click on the desktop. The right-click currently displays the desktop menu. You can also specify which devices to display on the desktop. The File and Device panes let you choose what kinds of file and device icons you will allow to be displayed, such as the CD-ROM mount icon for mounted CD-ROMs.
- The Multiple Desktops panel lets you select the number of virtual desktops to display.
- Background lets you choose a background color or image for each virtual desktop.
- Screensaver lets you select a screen saver along with its timing. Numerous screen savers are already configured.

For your desktop, you can also select a variety of different themes. A *theme* changes the look and feel of your desktop, affecting the appearance of GUI elements, such as scroll bars, buttons, and icons. For example, you use the Mac OS theme to make your K Desktop look like a Macintosh. You can use the Theme Manager in the KDE Control Center (Appearance & Themes) to select a theme and install new ones. Several may be installed for you, including Bluecurve (the current theme) or the Default (the KDE theme). Additional themes for the K Desktop can be downloaded from the **www.kde-look.org** Web site. This site displays themes for all window managers. You can also use **themes.freshmeat.net**; be sure to select the KDE entry for KDE themes.

Desktop Link Files and URL Locations

On the KDE desktop, special files called *link* files are used to access a variety of elements, including Web sites, application programs, and even devices. You create a link file by right-clicking the desktop and then selecting Create New. From this menu, you choose the type of link file you want to create.

The Link To Application entry is for launching applications. The Link To Location (URL) entry holds a URL address that you can use to access a Web or FTP site. The Link To Device submenu lets you create links to different kinds of devices, including CD-ROMs, hard disks, and cameras. Bear in mind that these are links only. You would rarely need to use them. Device icons that display on your desktop are now automatically generate directly by udev and HAL as needed (see Chapter 34).

To create a URL desktop file, right-click the desktop and select the Create New menu, and then the File submenu. Then select the Link To Location (URL) entry. A window appears that displays a box that prompts you to enter a name for the file and the URL address. Be sure to precede the URL with the appropriate protocol, like **http://** for Web pages. Alternatively, you can simply drag and drop a URL directly from the Location box on a Web browser such as Firefox. You can later edit the desktop file by right-clicking it and selecting Properties. A desktop dialog box for URL access is then displayed. This dialog box has three tabbed panels: General, Permissions, and URL (see Figure 7-2). On the General panel is the name of your desktop file. It will have as its name the name that you entered. An Icon button on this panel shows the icon that will be displayed for this desktop file on your desktop. You can select an icon by clicking the Icon button to open a window that lists icons you can choose from. Click OK when you are finished. The desktop file then appears on your desktop with that icon. On the URL panel, you will see a box labeled URL with a URL you entered already in it. You can change it if you want. For example, for online themes, the URL would be **http://www.kde-look.org**. Be sure to include the protocol, such as **http://** or **ftp://**.

On your desktop, you can click the URL icon anytime to access that Web site. An alternative and easier way to create a URL desktop file is simply to drag a URL for a Web page displayed on the file manager to your desktop. A pop-up window will let you select Copy or Link. Choose Link to create a URL desktop file (Copy will create local copy of that page). A desktop file is automatically generated with that URL. To change the default icon used, you can right-click the file and choose Properties to display the desktop dialog box.

KDE Windows

A KDE window has the same functionality you find in other window managers and desktops. You can resize the window by clicking and dragging any of its corners or sides. A click-and-drag operation on a side extends the window in that dimension, whereas a corner extends both height and width at the same time. Notice that the corners are slightly enhanced. The

FIGURE 7-2
The desktop
dialog box

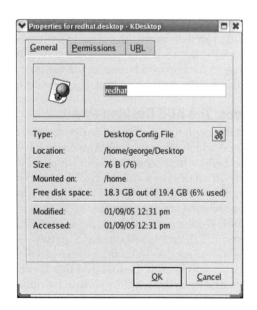

top of the window has a title bar showing the name of the window, the program name in the case of applications, and the current directory name for the file manager windows. The active window has the title bar highlighted. To move the window, click this title bar and drag it where you want. Right-clicking the window title bar displays a drop-down menu with entries for window operations, such as closing or resizing the window. Within the window, menus, icons, and toolbars for the particular application are displayed.

You can configure the appearance and operation of a window by selecting the Configure Window Behavior entry from the Window menu (right-click the title bar). Here you can set appearance (Window Decorations), button and key operations (Actions), the focus policy such as a mouse click on the window or just passing the mouse over it (Focus), how the window is displayed when moving it (Moving), and advanced features like moving a window directly to another virtual desktop, Active Desktop Borders. All these features can be configured also using the KDE Control Center's Appearance & Themes panels.

Opened windows are also shown as buttons on the KDE taskbar located on the panel. The taskbar shows the different programs you are running or windows you have open. This is essentially a docking mechanism that lets you change to a window or application just by clicking its button. When you minimize (iconify) a window, it is reduced to its taskbar button. You can then restore the window by clicking its taskbar button.

To the right of the title bar are three small buttons for minimizing, maximizing, or closing the window. You can switch to a window at any time by clicking its taskbar button. From the keyboard, you can use the ALT-TAB key combination to display a list of current applications. Holding down the ALT key and sequentially pressing TAB moves you through the list.

TIP *KDE supports numerous different themes, of which one is Red Hat's Bluecurve, each displaying window elements in different ways. The Red Hat Bluecurve window theme for KDE is shown in these examples.*

Application windows may display a Help Notes button, shown next to the iconify button and displaying a question mark. Clicking this button changes your cursor to a question mark. You can then move the cursor to an item such as an icon on a toolbar, and then click it to display a small help note explaining what the item does. For example, moving the mouse to the Forward button in the file manager taskbar will show a note explaining that this button performs a browser forward operation.

Virtual Desktops: The KDE Desktop Pager

KDE, like most Linux window managers, supports virtual desktops. In effect, this extends the desktop area on which you can work. You could have Mozilla running on one desktop and be using a text editor in another. KDE can support up to 16 virtual desktops, though the default is 4. Your virtual desktops can be displayed and accessed using the KDE Desktop Pager located on the panel. The KDE Desktop Pager represents your virtual desktops as miniature screens showing small squares for each desktop. It is made to look similar to the Bluecurve GNOME Workspace Switcher described in Chapter 6. By default, there are 4 squares, numbered 1, 2, 3, and 4. You can have up to 16. To move from one desktop to another, click the square for the destination desktop. Clicking 3 displays the third desktop, and clicking 1 moves you back to the first desktop. If you want to move a window to a different desktop, first open the window's menu by right-clicking the window's title bar. Then select the To Desktop entry, which lists the available desktops. Choose the one you want.

You can also configure KDE so that if you move the mouse over the edge of a desktop screen, it automatically moves to the adjoining desktop. You need to imagine the desktops arranged in a four-square configuration, with two top desktops next to each other and two desktops below them. You enable this feature by enabling the Active Desktop Borders feature in the Desktop | Window Behavior | Advanced panel in the KDE Control Center.

To change the number of virtual desktops, you use the KDE Control Center's Desktop entry. Either select the Configure Desktop entry in the Desktop pop-up menu (right-click anywhere on the desktop background) and choose Multiple Desktops, or select Control Center from the main menu and open the Desktop heading to select the Multiple Desktops entry. The visible bar controls the number of desktops. Slide this to the right to add more and to the left to reduce the number. You can change any of the desktop names by clicking a name and entering a new one. In the Appearance & Themes' Background entry, you can change the appearance for particular desktops such as color background and wallpaper (deselect Common background first).

KDE Panel: Kicker

The KDE panel (Kicker), located at the bottom of the screen, provides access to most KDE functions (see Figure 7-3). The panel includes icons for menus, directory windows, specific programs, and virtual desktops. At the left end of the panel is an button for the main menu (also know as the K menu), a red hat icon on Fedora Core.

To add an application to the panel, right-click anywhere on the panel and select Add from the pop-up menu. The Add menu displays the kind of objects you can add, including applets, applications, panels extensions, and special buttons. For KDE applications, select the applications entry. This lists all installed KDE applications on your main menu. Click the application entry to add an application button to the panel. You can also drag applications from a file manager window or from the main menu to the panel directly and have them automatically placed in the panel. The panel displays only desktop files. When you drag and drop a file to the panel, a desktop file for it is automatically generated.

Kicker also support numerous applets and several panel extensions, as well as special buttons.

- Applets are designed to run as icons in the panel. These include a clock, a pager, and a system monitor.

- Panel extensions add components to your desktop (select Panel from the Add menu). For example, the Kasbar extension sets up its own panel and list icons for each window you open. You can easily move from one window to another by clicking their corresponding icon in the Kasbar extension panel.

- Special buttons include buttons for KDE-specific operations like the KDE Window list, a Kterm terminal window, the KDE print manager, and KDE preferences.

To configure the panel position and behavior, right-click the panel and select the Configure Panel entry. This displays a customized control module window that collects the Panel configuration entries from the KDE Control Center. There are two configuration

FIGURE 7-3   KDE panel

windows, Layout and Taskbar. The Layout window lets you determine how the panel is displayed, and Taskbar configures how windows are shown on the taskbar. These conform to the KDE Control Center's Desktop | Panels and Desktop | Taskbar entries.

The Layout tool has four tabbed panes: Arrangement, Hiding, Menus, and Appearance. The Arrangement pane enables you to specify the edges of the screen where you want your panel and taskbar displayed. You can also enlarge or reduce it in size. The Hiding pane lets you set the hiding mode, whether to enable auto-hiding or to manually hide and display the taskbar. The Menus pane lets you control the size of your menus as well as whether to display recently opened documents as menu items. You can also select certain default entries like Preferences and Bookmarks, as well as edit the K menu directly, adding or removing items. The Appearance pane lets you set button colors for buttons and background image for the taskbar. With the Taskbar tool, you can control windows and tasks displayed on the taskbar, as well as set the button actions.

The KDE Help Center

The KDE Help Center provides a browser-like interface for accessing and displaying both KDE Help files and Linux Man and info files. You can start the Help Center by selecting its entry in the main menu (the life preserver), or by right-clicking the desktop and selecting the Help entry. The Help window is divided into two frames. The left frame of the Help screen holds two tabbed panels, one listing contents and the other providing a glossary. The right frame displays currently selected documents. A help tree on the contents panel lets you choose the kind of Help documents you want to access. Here you can choose manuals, Man pages, or info documents, even application manuals. The Help Center includes a detailed user manual, a FAQ, and KDE Web site access.

A navigation toolbar enables you to move through previously viewed documents. KDE Help documents use an HTML format with links you can click to access other documents. The Back and Forward commands move you through the list of previously viewed documents. The KDE Help system provides an effective search tool for searching for patterns in Help documents, including Man and info pages. Select the Find entry from the Edit menu to display a page where you can enter your pattern.

Applications

You can start an application in KDE in several ways. If an entry for it is in the main menu, you can select that entry to start the application. Some applications also have buttons on the KDE panel you can click to start them. On Fedora Core, the panel already holds the same applications as shown on the GNOME panel, including the Evolution mail client, Firefox Web browser, and several Office.org applications. You can also use the file manager to locate a file using that application or the application program itself. Clicking its icon starts the application. Or you can open a shell window and enter the name of the application at the shell prompt and press ENTER to start an application. You can also select Run Command from the main menu (or press ALT-F2) to open a small window consisting of a box to enter a single command. Previous commands can be accessed from a pop-up menu. An Options button will list options for running the program, such as priority or within a terminal window.

NOTE *You can create a desktop file on your desktop for any application already on your KDE menu by simply clicking and dragging its menu entry to the desktop. Select Copy and a desktop file for that application is created for you on your desktop, showing its icon.*

Application Standard Links

You can also access applications directly from your desktop. To access an application from the desktop, create either a desktop file or a standard link file that can link to the original application program. With a desktop file, you can choose your own icon and specify a ToolTip comment. You can also use a desktop file to start a shell-based application running in its own terminal window. A standard link, on the other hand, is a simple reference to the original program file. Using a link starts the program up directly with no arguments. To create a standard link file, either select and drag the application in the main menu to the desktop or locate the application on your file system, usually in the **/bin**, **/usr/bin**, or **/usr/sbin** directory, and then click and drag the application icon to your desktop. In the pop-up menu, select Link. The link has the same icon as the original application. Whenever you then double-click that icon, the application will start. You can also use this method to run a application program you have created yourself, locating it in your own directory and creating a link for it on your desktop.

Application Desktop Links

To create a new desktop file for an application, right-click anywhere on the empty desktop, select Create New from the pop-up menu, and then within the File submenu, choose Link To Application. Enter the name for the program and a desktop file for it appears on the desktop with that name. A Properties dialog box then opens with three panels: General, Permissions, and Application. The General panel displays the name of the link. To select an icon image for the desktop file, click the icon. The Select Icon window is displayed, listing icons from which you can choose.

On the Permissions panel, be sure to set execute permissions so that the program can be run. You can set permissions for yourself, for your group, or for any user on the system. The Meta Info panel will list the type of file system used.

To specify the application the desktop file runs, go to the Application panel and either enter the application's program name in the Command box or click Browse to select it. On this panel, you also specify the description and comment. For the description, enter the application name. This is the name used for the link, if you use the file manager to display it. The comment is the Help note that appears when you pass your mouse over the icon.

In the Application panel, you can also specify the type of documents to be associated with this application. The bottom of the panel shows Add and Remove buttons. To specify a MIME type, click Add. This displays a list of file types and their descriptions. Select the one you want associated with this program. Desktop files needn't reside on the desktop. You can place them in any directory and access them through the file manager. You can later make changes to a desktop file by right-clicking its icon and selecting Properties from the pop-up menu. This again displays the dialog box for this file. You can change its icon and even the application it runs.

The Advanced Options button contains execute options for the application, such as running it in a shell window, or as a certain user. To run a shell-based program such as Vi, select the Run In Terminal check box and specify any terminal options. Startup options let you list the program in the system tray.

Mounting Devices from the Desktop

Desktop icons were created for your installed devices like CD-ROMs and floppies when Fedora Core installed KDE. To access a CD-ROM disk, place the CD-ROM disk in your CD-ROM drive and double-click the CD-ROM icon. The file manager window then opens, displaying the contents of the CD-ROM's top-level directory. To eject the CD, right-click the CD-ROM's icon and select Eject from the pop-up menu (you can also elect to just unmount the CD-ROM). To access a floppy disk, you can perform a similar operation using the Floppy Disk icon. Place the floppy disk in the disk drive and double-click the Floppy Disk icon. This displays a file manager window with the contents of the floppy disk. Be careful not to remove the disk unless you first unmount it. To unmount the disk, right-click its icon and select Unmount from the icon's pop-up menu. You can perform one added operation with floppy disks. If you put in a blank disk, you can format it. You can choose from several file system formats, including MS-DOS. To format a standard Linux file system, select the ext3 entry.

A desktop file you use for your CD-ROM is a special kind of desktop file designed for devices. If you add a new CD-ROM or floppy drive, it will be automatically detected for you by udev and HAL, and a new desktop device file created for it to enable you to access the drive from your desktop. To edit this device file, right-click on its icon and select Properties. This opens a Properties window with tabs for General, Permissions, Device, and Meta Info. In the General tab, you can set the name for the device icon that will appear on the desktop as well as choose the icon you want to show for a mounted CD-ROM or floppy disk (a default is already provided). You can also choose the icon used to indicate when it is unmounted. On the Permissions panel, you can also indicate the permissions that have been set to allow access to the device. See the chapter on file administration, Chapter 32, for a discussion on devices and file systems.

An entry in the **/etc/fstab** file for the CD-ROM or floppy drive will be managed by HAL for you.

KDE File Manager and Internet Client: Konqueror

The KDE file manager, known as Konqueror, is a multifunctional utility with which you can manage files, start programs, browse the Web, and download files from remote sites (see Figure 7-4). Traditionally, the term "file manager" was used to refer to managing files on a local hard disk. The KDE file manager extends its functionality well beyond this traditional function because it is Internet capable, seamlessly displaying remote file systems as if they were your own, as well as viewing Web pages with browser capabilities. It is capable of displaying a multitude of different kinds of files, including image, PostScript, and text files. KOffice applications can be run within the Konqueror window. You can even open a separate pane within a file manager window to run a terminal window where you can enter shell commands (Window menu).

FIGURE **7-4**
The KDE file
manager

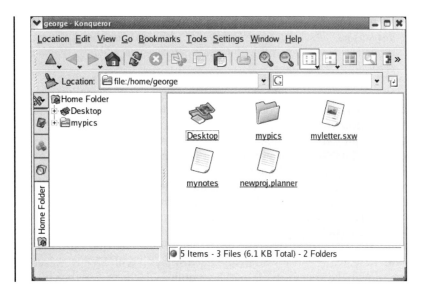

Konqueror Window

A KDE file manager window consists of a menu bar, a navigation toolbar, a location field, a status bar, and a sidebar that provides different views of user resources such as a tree view of file and directory icons for your home directory. When you first display the file manager window, it displays the file and subdirectory icons for your home directory. Files and directories are automatically refreshed. Thus if you add or remove directories, you do not have to manually refresh the file manager window. It automatically updates for your listing, showing added files or eliminating deleted ones. The files listed in a directory can be viewed in several different ways such as icons, multicolumn (small icons), expandable trees, file information, or in a detailed listing. The different views are listed in the View Mode submenu within the View menu, and the commonly used ones are listed as icons at the end of the icon bar. The Tree mode lists your subdirectories as expandable trees whose contents you can display by clicking their plus signs. The Info mode lists file information like the number of lines and characters in the file. The detailed listing provides permissions, owner, group, and size information. Permissions are the permissions controlling access to this file (see Chapter 30). The Text view does the same but does not display an icon next to the filename.

Konqueror also supports tabbed displays. Instead of opening a folder in the same file manager window or a new one, you can open a new tab for it using the same file manager window. One tab can display the initial folder opened, and other tabs can be used for folders opened later. You can then move from viewing one folder to another by simply clicking on their tab. This way you can view multiple folders with just one file manager window. To open a folder as a tab, right-click on its icon and select Open in New Tab. To later close the folder, right-click on its tab label and select Close tab. You can also detach a tab, opening it up in its own file manager window.

TIP Configuration files, known as hidden files, are not usually displayed. To have the file manager display these files, select Show Hidden Files from the View menu. Konqueror also supports split views, letting you view different directories in the same window (Windows menu). You can split vertically or horizontally.

You can open a file either by clicking it or by selecting it and then choosing the Open entry in the File menu. If you want to select the file or directory, you need to hold down the CTRL key while you click it, or single-click. A double-click opens the file. If the file is a program, that program starts up. If it is a data file, such as a text file, the associated application is run using that data file. For example, if you double-click a text file, the Kate application starts displaying that file. If Konqueror cannot determine the application to use, it opens a dialog box prompting you to enter the application name. You can click the Browse button on this box to use a directory tree to locate the application program you want.

The file manager can also extract tar archives and install RPM packages. An *archive* is a file ending in **.tar.gz**, **.tar**, or **.tgz**. Clicking the archive lists the files in it. You can extract a particular file simply by dragging it out the window. Clicking a text file in the archive displays it with Kate, while clicking an image file displays it with KView. Selecting an RPM package opens it with the system-config-packages utility, which you can then use to install the package.

If the folder is a CVS folder, used for managing different versions of a project, you can use the Cervisia tool listed in the View Mode submenu to display and examine CVS archives.

Navigation Panel

The Navigation panel is a sidebar that lists different resources that a user can access with Konqueror. You can turn the Navigation panel on or off by selecting its entry in the Windows menu. The sidebar is configured with the Navigation Panel Configuration tool, accessible as the first button on the Navigation panel's button bar.

TIP Konqueror also provides a sidebar media player for running selected media files within your file manager window.

The Navigation panel features a vertical button bar for displaying items such as your bookmarks, devices, home directory, services, and network resources. Dragging the mouse over the resource icon displays its full name. When you click an item, its icon will expand to the name of that resource. Resources such as bookmarks, devices, and your home directory are listed in an expandable tree. Click an entry to expand it. Double-click it to access it with Konqueror. For example, to move to a subdirectory, expand your home directory entry and then double-click the subdirectory you want. Konqueror will now display that subdirectory. To go to a previously bookmarked directory or Web page, find its entry in the Bookmarks listing and select it. The network button lists network resources you have access to, such as FTP and Web sites. The root folder button displays your system's root directory and its subdirectories.

To configure the Navigation panel, click its configure button in the sidebar button bar. Select the Multiple Views entry to allow the display of several resource listings at once, each in its separate subsidebar. You can also add a new resource listing, choosing from a bookmark, history, or directory type. A button will appear for the new listing. You can right-click the button to select a new icon for it or select a URL, either a directory pathname or a network address. To remove a button and its listing, right-click it and select the Remove entry.

Tip *If multiple views is enabled in the Navigation Panel Configuration, you can display several of these resources at once, just by clicking the ones you want. If the Multiple Views feature is not enabled, the previous listing is replaced by the selected one. Turn off a display by clicking its button again.*

Search

To search for files, select the Find entry in the Tools menu. This opens a pane within the file manager window in which you can search for filenames using wildcard matching symbols, such as *. Click Find to run the search and Stop to stop it. The search results are displayed in a pane in the lower half of the file manager window. You can click a file and have it open with its appropriate application. Text files are displayed by the Kate text editor. Images are displayed by KView, and PostScript files by KGhostView. Applications are run. The search program also enables you to save your search results for later reference. You can even select files from the search and add them to an archive.

Navigating Directories

Within a file manager window, a double-click on a directory icon moves to that directory and displays its file and subdirectory icons. To move back up to the parent directory, you click the up arrow button located on the left end of the navigation toolbar. A double-click on a directory icon moves you down the directory tree, one directory at a time. By clicking the up arrow button, you move up the tree. To move directly to a specific directory, you can enter its pathname in the Location box located just above the pane that displays the file and directory icons. Like a Web browser, the file manager remembers the previous directories it has displayed. You can use the back and forward arrow buttons to move through this list of prior directories. You can also use several keyboard shortcuts to perform such operations, as listed in Table 7-2.

Keys	Description
ALT-LEFT ARROW, ALT-RIGHT ARROW	Backward and forward in history
ALT-UP ARROW	One directory up
ENTER	Open a file/directory
ESC	Open a pop-up menu for the current file
LEFT/RIGHT/UP/DOWN ARROWS	Move among the icons
SPACEBAR	Select/unselect file
PAGE UP, PAGE DOWN	Scroll up fast
CTRL-C	Copy selected file to clipboard
CTRL-V	Paste files from clipboard to current directory
CTRL-S	Select files by pattern
CTRL-L	Open new location
CTRL-F	Find files
CTRL-W	Close window

TABLE 7-2   KDE File Manager Keyboard Shortcuts

If you know you want to access particular directories again, you can bookmark them, much as you do a Web page. Just open the directory and select the Add Bookmarks entry in the Bookmark menu. An entry for that directory is then placed in the file manager's Bookmark menu. To move to the directory again, select its entry in the Bookmark menu. To navigate from one directory to another, you can use the Location field or the directory tree. In the Location field, you can enter the pathname of a directory, if you know it, and press ENTER. The directory tree provides a tree listing all directories on your system and in your home directory. To display the directory tree, select the Tree View from the View menu's View Mode submenu, or click the Tree View icon in the icon bar. To see the Tree View for your home or root directory directly, you can use the Navigation panel's Home or Root Folder resources.

Copy, Move, Delete, Rename, and Link Operations

To perform an operation on a file or directory, you first have to select it. To select a file or directory, you click the file's icon or listing. To select more than one file, continue to hold the CTRL key down while you click the files you want. You can also use the keyboard arrow keys to move from one file icon to another and then use the ENTER key to select the file you want.

To copy and move files, you can use the standard drag-and-drop method with your mouse. To copy a file, you locate it by using the file manager. Open another file manager window to the directory to which you want the file copied. Then click and drag the File icon to that window. A pop-up menu appears with selections for Move, Copy, or Link. Choose Copy. To move a file to another directory, follow the same procedure, but select Move from the pop-up menu. To copy or move a directory, use the same procedure as for files. All the directory's files and subdirectories are also copied or moved.

To rename a file, click its icon and press F2, or right-click the icon and select Rename from the pop-up menu. The name below the icon will become boxed, editable text that you can then change.

You delete a file by either removing it immediately or placing it in a Trash folder to delete later. To delete a file, select it and then choose the Delete entry in the Edit menu. You can also right-click the icon and select Delete. To place a file in the Trash folder, click and drag it to the Trash icon on your desktop or select Move To Trash from the Edit menu. You can later open the Trash folder and delete the files. To delete all the files in the Trash folder, right-click the Trash icon and select Empty Trash Bin from the pop-up menu. To restore any files in the Trash bin, open the Trash bin and drag them out of the Trash folder.

Each file or directory has properties associated with it that include permissions, the filename, and its directory. To display the Properties window for a given file, right-click the file's icon and select the Properties entry. On the General panel, you see the name of the file displayed. To change the file's name, replace the name there with a new one. Permissions are set on the Permissions panel. Here, you can set read, write, and execute permissions for user, group, or other access to the file. See Chapter 30 for a discussion of permissions. The Group entry enables you to change the group for a file. The Meta Info panel lists information specific to that kind of file, for example, the number of lines and characters in a text file. An image file will list features like resolution, bit depth, and color.

TIP *KDE automatically searches for and reads an existing **.directory** file located in a directory. A **.directory** file holds KDE configuration information used to determine how the directory is displayed. You can create such a file in a directory and place a setting in it to set display features, such as the icon to use to display the directory folder.*

Web and FTP Access

The KDE file manager also doubles as a full-featured Web browser and an FTP client. It includes a box for entering either a pathname for a local file or a URL for a Web page on the Internet or your intranet. A navigation toolbar can be used to display previous Web pages or previous directories. The Home button will always return you to your home directory. When accessing a Web page, the page is displayed as on any Web browser. With the navigation toolbar, you can move back and forth through the list of previously displayed pages in that session.

The KDE file manager also operates as an FTP client. When you access an FTP site, you navigate the remote directories as you would your own. The operations to download a file are the same as copying a file on your local system. Just select the file's icon or entry in the file manager window and drag it to a window showing the local directory to which you want it downloaded. Then, select the Copy entry from the pop-up menu that appears. Konqueror also includes KSSL, which provides full SSL support for secure connections, featuring a secure connection status display.

TIP *KDE features the KGet tool for Konqueror, which manages FTP downloads, letting you select, queue, suspend, and schedule downloads, while displaying status information on current downloads.*

Configuring Konqueror

As a file browser, Web and FTP browser, and integral part of the KDE desktop, Konqueror has numerous configuration options. To configure Konqueror, open the Configure Konqueror window by selecting Configure Konqueror from a Konqueror window Settings menu (see Figure 7-5). This window displays a category listing on a sidebar. The initial categories deal with basic file management options like appearance, behavior, previews, and file associations. In behavior, you specify such actions as displaying ToolTips and opening folders in new windows. Appearance lets you select the font and size. With previews you can set the size of previewed icons, as well as specify the kind of files to retrieve metadata on. File Associations lets you set default applications for different kinds of files (same as File Association in KDE Components in Control Center).

FIGURE 7-5
Configure
Konqueror window

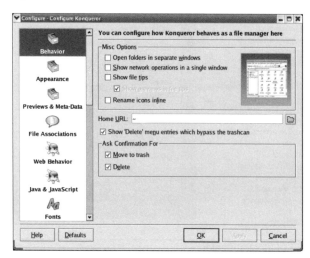

The remaining categories deal with Web browser configurations, including configuring proxies, and Web page displays, as well as such basic behavior as highlighting URLs, fonts to use, managing cookies, and selecting encryption methods. The History category lets you specify the number of history items and their expiration date. With the Plugins category you can see a listing of current browser plug-ins as well as scan for new ones.

KDE Configuration: KDE Control Center

With the KDE Control Center, you can configure your desktop and system, changing the way it is displayed and the features it supports (see Figure 7-6). The Control Center can be directly started by selecting Control Center from the main menu.

The Control Center window is divided into two panes. The left pane shows a tree view of all the components you can configure, and the right pane displays the dialog windows for a selected component. See the Help viewer for a current listing of K Desktop configuration modules.

On the left pane, components are arranged into categories whose titles you can expand or shrink. The Internet & Network heading holds entries for configuring the KDE file manager's network tools, including Web browser features as well as Samba (Windows) access and Wireless connectivity. Under Appearances & Themes, you can set different features for

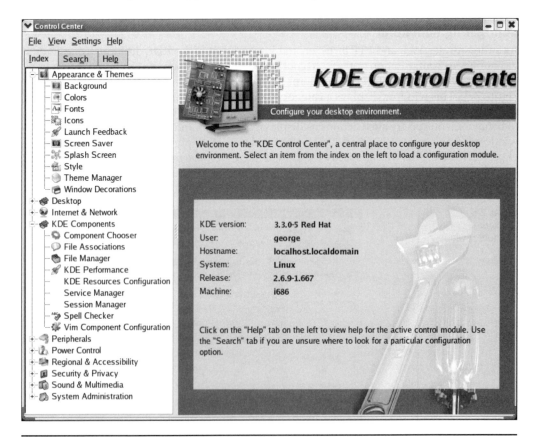

FIGURE 7-6 KDE Control Center

displaying and controlling your desktop. For example, the Background entry enables you to select a different background color or image for each one of your virtual desktops. Other entries enable you to configure components such as the screen saver, the language used, and the window style. The Peripherals heading holds entries that let you configure your mouse, keyboard, and printer. The Sound & Multimedia heading contains panels for configuring sound components. From the Control Center, you can also access a set of specialized KDE system configuration tools. Currently these include a login manager and a font manager.

The KDE Components category configures the behavior of your KDE interface. The Component Chooser lets you choose default components for applications, including the mail client to use, the default terminal tool, or Web browser. File Associations associates file MIME types with default applications. The File Manager entry lets you set file manager features such as the font used and the files to preview. With the Session Manager, you can configure session startup and shutdown actions, for instance, restoring previous sessions on startup or automatically shutting down the system when you exit KDE. The Service Manager will list KDE daemons, both those loaded on demand and those on startup. You can elect whether to have a daemon run at startup, as well as manually start and stop daemons. Currently, KDE file sharing and Internet daemons are started automatically. You could elect instead to have them turned off, letting you start them manually when you want that kind of connectivity.

.kde and Desktop User Directories

Your **.kde** directory holds files and directories used to maintain your KDE desktop. As with GNOME, the **Desktop** directory holds KDE desktop files whose icons are displayed on the desktop. Configuration files are located in the **.kde/share/config** directory. Here you can find the general configuration files for different KDE components: **kwinrc** holds configuration commands for the window manager, **kmailrc** for mail, and **kickerrc** for your panel, while **kdeglobals** holds keyboard shortcuts along with other global definitions. You can place configuration directives directly in any of these files; **.kde/share/mimelnk** holds the desktop files for the menu entries added by the user. The **.kde/share/apps** directory contains files and directories for configuring KDE applications, including **koffice**, **kmail**, and even **konqueror**.

MIME Types and Associated Applications

As you install new kinds of programs, they may use files of a certain type. In that case, you will need to register the type with KDE so that it can be associated with a given application or group of applications. For example, the MIME type for GIF images is **image/gif**, which is associated with image-viewing programs. You use the KDE Control Center to set up a new MIME type or to change MIME type associations with applications. Select the File Associations entry under KDE Components. This will list known MIME types and their associated filename extensions. Select an entry to edit it, where you can change the applications associated with it. KDE saves its MIME type information in a separate file called **mimelnk** in the KDE configuration directory.

KDE Directories and Files

When KDE is installed on your system, its system-wide application, configuration, and support files may be installed in the same system directories as other GUIs and user applications. On Fedora Core, KDE is installed in the standard system directories with some variations, such as **/usr/bin** for KDE program files, **/usr/lib/kde3**, which holds KDE libraries, and **/usr/include/kde**, which contains KDE header files used in application development.

The directories located in the **share** directory contain files used to configure system defaults for your KDE environment (the system **share** directory is located at **/usr/share**). The **share/mimelnk** directory maps its files to KDE icons and specifies MIME type definitions. Their contents consist of desktop files having the extension **.desktop**, one for each menu entry. The **share/apps** directory contains files and directories set up by KDE applications; **share/config** contains the configuration files for particular KDE applications. These are the system-wide defaults that can be overridden by users' own configurations in their own **.kde/share/config** directories. The **share/icons** directory holds the default icons used on your KDE desktop and by KDE applications as well as for the Bluecurve interface. As noted previously, in the user's home directory, the **.kde** directory holds a user's own KDE configuration for the desktop and its applications.

As noted previously, each user has a **Desktop** directory that holds KDE link files for all icons and folders on the user's desktop (see Table 7-3). These include the Trash folders and the CD-ROM and home directory links.

System KDE Directory	Description
/usr/bin	KDE programs
/usr/lib/kde3	KDE libraries
/usr/include/kde	Header files for use in compiling and developing KDE applications
/usr/share/config	KDE desktop and application configuration files
/usr/share/mimelnk	Desktop files used to build the main menu
/usr/share/apps	Files used by KDE applications
/usr/share/icons	Icons used in KDE desktop and applications
/usr/share/doc	KDE Help system
User KDE Directory	**Description**
.kde/AutoStart	Applications automatically started up with KDE
.kde/share/config	User KDE desktop and application configuration files for user-specified features
.kde/share/mimelnk	Desktop files used to build the user's menu entries on the KDE main menu
.kde/share/apps	Directories and files used by KDE applications
Desktop	Desktop files for icons and folders displayed on the user's KDE desktop
Desktop/Trash	Trash folder for files marked for deletion

TABLE 7-3   KDE Installation Directories

The XFce4 Desktop

The XFce4 desktop is a new lightweight desktop designed to run fast without the kind of overhead seen in full-featured desktops like KDE and GNOME. You can think of it as a window manager with desktop functionality. It includes its own file manager and panel, but the emphasis is on modularity and simplicity. Like GNOME, XFce is based on GTK+ GUI tools. The desktop consists of a collection of modules, including the xffm file manager, the xfce4-panel panel, and the xfwm4 window manager. Keeping with its focus on simplicity, XFce features only a few common applets on its panel. Its small scale makes it appropriate for laptops or dedicated systems that have no need for the complex overhead found in other desktops.

NOTE *XFce is not distributed with Fedora Core 4, but you can download it from Fedora Extras. Check **download.fedora.redhat.com/pub/fedora/linux/extras**.*

On Fedora Core, XFce will display a panel at the bottom of the screen and a taskbar at the top (see Figure 7-7). The panel will show icons for different applications and applets, including a virtual desktop switcher, a clock, a Web browser icon, and a folder for your

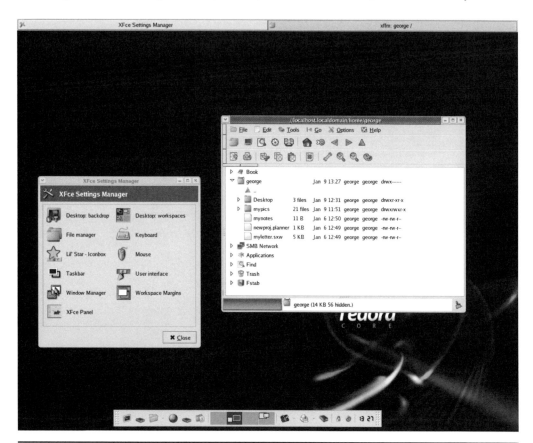

Figure 7-7   XFce desktop with settings and file manager

home directory. A settings icon opens the XFce Settings Manager, where you can configure your desktop components, including the keyboard, background image, panel display, and file manager options.

Opening the file manager lists entries not just for the home directory, but for bookmarks, search results, network shares, basic applications, and trash contents. From the Tools menu, you can search for items and manage deleted items. The File menu lets you perform file operations like renaming files or creating new directories.

From the desktop pop-up menu, you can quickly open a terminal window, the Web browser, the file manager, or the settings manager. You can also run a specific program. The manual can be accessed also from the desktop menu, as well as from the panel.

To add a new item to your panel, right-click on the panel and select the item you want added, including a program launcher.

To exit, click the Exit button next to the clock.

The Shell

The *shell* is a command interpreter that provides a line-oriented interactive and noninteractive interface between the user and the operating system. You enter commands on a command line; they are interpreted by the shell and then sent as instructions to the operating system. You can also place commands in a script file to be consecutively executed much like a program. This interpretive capability of the shell provides for many sophisticated features. For example, the shell has a set of file expansion characters that can generate filenames. The shell can redirect input and output, as well as run operations in the background, freeing you to perform other tasks.

Several different types of shells have been developed for Linux: the Bourne Again shell (BASH), the Public Domain Korn shell (PDKSH), the TCSH shell, and the Z shell. All shells are available for your use, although the BASH shell is the default. You only need one type of shell to do your work. Red Hat Enterprise Linux and Fedora Core include all the major shells, although they install and use the BASH shell as the default. If you use the Fedora Core command line shell, you will be using the BASH shell unless you specify another. This chapter discusses the BASH shell, which shares many of the same features as other shells.

You can find out more about shells at their respective Web sites as listed in Table 8-1. Also, a detailed online manual is available for each installed shell. Use the **man** command and the shells keyword to access them, **bash** for the BASH shell, **zsh** for the Z shell, and **tsch** for the TSCH shell. For example, the command **man bash** will access the BASH shell online manual.

Shell	Web Site
www.gnu.org/software/bash	BASH Web site with online manual, FAQ, and current releases
www.gnu.org/manual/bash	BASH online manual
www.zsh.org	Z shell Web site with referrals to FAQs and current downloads
www.tsch.org	TCSH Web site with detailed support including manual, tips, FAQ, and recent releases
web.cs.mun.ca/~michael/pdksh/	PDKSH site with manual and download

TABLE 8-1   Linux Shells

NOTE *You can find out more about the BASH shell at **www.gnu.org/software/bash**. A detailed online manual is available on your Linux system using the **man** command with the **bash** keyword.*

The Command Line

The Linux command line interface consists of a single line into which you enter commands with any of their options and arguments. From GNOME or KDE, you can access the command line interface by opening a terminal window. Should you start Linux with the command line interface, you will be presented with a BASH shell command line when you log in.

By default, the BASH shell has a dollar sign (**$**) prompt, but Linux has several other types of shells, each with its own prompt (like % for the C shell). The root user will have a different prompt, the **#**. A shell *prompt*, such as the one shown here, marks the beginning of the command line:

```
$
```

You can enter a command along with options and arguments at the prompt. For example, with an **-l** option, the **ls** command will display a line of information about each file, listing such data as its size and the date and time it was last modified. In the next example, the user enters the **ls** command followed by a **-l** option. The dash before the **-l** option is required. Linux uses it to distinguish an option from an argument.

```
$ ls -l
```

If you wanted only the information displayed for a particular file, you could add that file's name as the argument, following the **-l** option:

```
$ ls -l mydata
-rw-r--r-- 1 chris weather 207 Feb 20 11:55 mydata
```

TIP *Some commands can be complex and take some time to execute. When you mistakenly execute the wrong command, you can interrupt and stop such commands with the interrupt key—CTRL-C.*

You can enter a command on several lines by typing a backslash just before you press ENTER. The backslash "escapes" the ENTER key, effectively continuing the same command line to the next line. In the next example, the **cp** command is entered on three lines. The first two lines end in a backslash, effectively making all three lines one command line.

```
$ cp -i \
mydata \
/home/george/myproject/newdata
```

You can also enter several commands on the same line by separating them with a semicolon (**;**). In effect the semicolon operates as an execute operation. Commands will be executed in the sequence they are entered. The following command executes an **ls** command followed by a **date** command.

```
$ ls ; date
```

You can also conditionally run several commands on the same line with the **&&** operator. The next one is executed only if the previous one is true. This is useful for running several dependent scripts on the same line. In the next example, the **ls** command is run only if the **date** command is successfully executed.

```
$ date && ls
```

Command Line Editing

The BASH shell, which is your default shell, has special command line editing capabilities that you may find helpful as you learn Linux (see Table 8-2). You can easily modify commands you have entered before executing them, moving anywhere on the command line and inserting or deleting characters. This is particularly helpful for complex commands. You can use the CTRL-F or RIGHT ARROW key to move forward a character, or the CTRL-B or LEFT ARROW key to move back a character. CTRL-D or DEL deletes the character the cursor is on, and CTRL-H or BACKSPACE deletes the character before the cursor. To add text, you use the arrow keys to move the cursor to where you want to insert text and type the new characters. You can even cut words with the CTRL-W or ALT-D key and then use the CTRL-Y key to paste them back in at a different position, effectively moving the words. As a rule, the CTRL version of the command operates on characters, and the ALT version works on words, such as CTRL-T to transpose characters and ALT-T to transpose words. At any time, you can press ENTER to execute the command. For example, if you make a spelling mistake when entering a command, rather than reentering the entire command, you can use the editing operations to correct the mistake. The actual associations of keys and their tasks, along with global settings, are specified in the **/etc/inputrc** file.

TIP *The editing capabilities of the BASH shell command line are provided by Readline. Readline supports numerous editing operations. You can even bind a key to a selected editing operation. Readline uses the /etc/inputrc file to configure key bindings. This file is read automatically by your /etc/profile shell configuration file when you log in (see Chapter 9). You can find out more about Readline in the BASH shell reference manual at* ***www.gnu.org/manual/bash***.

Command and Filename Completion

The BASH command line has a built-in feature that performs command line and filename completion. Automatic completions can be effected using the TAB key. If you enter an incomplete pattern as a command or filename argument, you can then press the TAB key to activate the command and filename completion feature, which completes the pattern. Directories will have a / attached to their name. If more than one command or file has the same prefix, the shell simply beeps and waits for you to enter the TAB key again. It then displays a list of possible command completions and waits for you to add enough characters

Movement Command	Operation
CTRL-F, RIGHT-ARROW	Move forward a character
CTRL-B, LEFT-ARROW	Move backward a character
CTRL-A	Move to beginning of line
CTRL-E	Move to end of line
ALT-F	Move forward a word
ALT-B	Move backward a word
CTRL-L	Clear screen and place line at top
Editing Command	**Operation**
CTRL-D, DEL	Delete character cursor is on
CTRL-H, BACKSPACE	Delete character before the cursor
CTRL-K	Cut remainder of line from cursor position
CTRL-U	Cut from cursor position to beginning of line
CTRL-W	Cut previous word
CTRL-C	Cut entire line
ALT-D	Cut the remainder of a word
ALT-DEL	Cut from the cursor to the beginning of a word
CTRL-Y	Paste previous cut text
ALT-Y	Paste from set of previously cut text
CTRL-T	Transpose current and previous character
ALT-T	Transpose current and previous word
ALT-L	Lowercase current word
ALT-U	Uppercase current word
ALT-C	Capitalize current word
CTRL-SHIFT-_	Undo previous change

to select a unique command or filename. For situations where you know there are likely multiple possibilities, you can just press the ESC key instead of two TABS. In the next example, the user issues a **cat** command with an incomplete filename. When the user presses the TAB key, the system searches for a match and, when it finds one, fills in the filename. The user can then press ENTER to execute the command.

```
$ cat pre tab
$ cat preface
```

The automatic completions also work with the names of variables, users, and hosts. In this case, the partial text needs to be preceded by a special character, indicating the type of name. Variables begin with a $ sign, so any text beginning with a dollar sign is treated as a variable to be completed. Variables are selected from previously defined variables, like system shell variables (see Chapter 9). User names begin with a tilde (~). Hostnames begin with a @ sign, with possible names taken from the **/etc/hosts** file. A listing of possible automatic completions follows:

- Shell variable text begins with a $ sign.
- Username text begins with a ~ sign.
- Hostname text begins with a @.
- Commands, aliases, and text in files begin with normal text.

For example, to complete the variable HOME given just $HOM, simple enter a tab character.

```
$ echo $HOM <tab>
$ echo $HOME
```

If you entered just an H, then you could enter two tabs to see all possible variables beginning with H. The command line is redisplayed, letting you complete the name.

```
$ echo $H <tab> <tab>
$HISTCMD $HISTFILE $HOME $HOSTTYPE HISTFILE  $HISTSIZE $HISTNAME
$ echo $H
```

You can also specifically select the kind of text to complete, using corresponding command keys. In this case, it does not matter what kind of sign a name begins with. For example, ALT-~ will treat the current text as a username. ALT-@ will treat it as a hostname, and ALT-$, as a variable. ALT-! will treat it as a command. To display a list of possible completions, use the CTRL-X key with the appropriate completion key, as in CTRL-X-$ to list possible variable completions. See Table 8-3 for a complete listing.

TABLE 8-3 Command Line Text Completion Commands

Command (CTRL-R for listing possible completions)	Description
TAB	Automatic completion
TAB TAB or ESC	List possible completions
ALT-/, CTRL-R-/	Filename completion, normal text for automatic
ALT-$, CTRL-R-$	Shell variable completion, $ for automatic
ALT-~, CTRL-R-~	Username completion, ~ for automatic
ALT-@, CTRL-R-@	Hostname completion, @ for automatic
ALT-!, CTRL-R-!	Command name completion, normal text for automatic

History

The BASH shell keeps a list, called a *history list*, of your previously entered commands. You can display each command, in turn, on your command line by pressing the UP ARROW key. The DOWN ARROW key moves you down the list. You can modify and execute any of these previous commands when you display them on your command line.

TIP *The capability to redisplay a previous command is helpful when you've already executed a command you had entered incorrectly. In this case, you would be presented with an error message and a new, empty command line. By pressing the UP ARROW key, you can redisplay your previous command, make corrections to it, and then execute it again. This way, you would not have to enter the whole command again.*

History Events

In the BASH shell, the *history utility* keeps a record of the most recent commands you have executed. The commands are numbered starting at 1, and a limit exists to the number of commands remembered—the default is 500. The history utility is a kind of short-term memory, keeping track of the most recent commands you have executed. To see the set of your most recent commands, type **history** on the command line and press ENTER. A list of your most recent commands is then displayed, preceded by a number.

```
$ history
1 cp mydata today
2 vi mydata
3 mv mydata reports
4 cd reports
5 ls
```

Each of these commands is technically referred to as an event. An *event* describes an action that has been taken—a command that has been executed. The events are numbered according to their sequence of execution. The most recent event has the highest number. Each of these events can be identified by its number or beginning characters in the command.

The history utility enables you to reference a former event, placing it on your command line and enabling you to execute it. The easiest way to do this is to use the UP ARROW and DOWN ARROW keys to place history events on your command line, one at a time. You needn't display the list first with **history**. Pressing the UP ARROW key once places the last history event on your command line. Pressing it again places the next history event on your command. Pressing the DOWN ARROW key places the previous event on the command line.

You can use certain control and meta keys to perform other history operations like searching the history list. A meta key is the ALT key, and the ESC key on keyboards that have no ALT key. The ALT key is used here. ALT-< will move you to the beginning of the history list; ALT-N will search it. CTRL-S and CTRL-R will perform incremental searches, display matching commands as you type in a search string. Table 8-4 lists the different commands for referencing the history list.

TIP *If more than one history event matches what you have entered, you will hear a beep, and you can then enter more characters to help uniquely identify the event.*

TABLE **8-4** History Commands and History Event References

History Command	Description
CTRL-N or DOWN ARROW	Moves down to the next event in the history list
CTRL-P or UP ARROW	Moves up to the previous event in the history list
ALT-<	Moves to the beginning of the history event list
ALT->	Moves to the end of the history event list
ALT-N	Forward Search, next matching item
ALT-P	Backward Search, previous matching item
CTRL-S	Forward Search History, forward incremental search
CTRL-R	Reverse Search History, reverse incremental search
fc *event-reference*	Edits an event with the standard editor and then executes it **Options** **-l** List recent history events; same as **history** command **-e** *editor event-reference* Invokes a specified editor to edit a specific event

History Event Reference	Description
! *event num*	References an event with an event number
! !	References the previous command
! *characters*	References an event with beginning characters
! ? *pattern***?**	References an event with a pattern in the event
! *-event num*	References an event with an offset from the first event
! *num-num*	References a range of events

You can also reference and execute history events using the **!** history command. The **!** is followed by a reference that identifies the command. The reference can be either the number of the event or a beginning set of characters in the event. In the next example, the third command in the history list is referenced first by number and then by the beginning characters:

```
$ !3
mv mydata reports
$ !mv my
mv mydata reports
```

You can also reference an event using an offset from the end of the list. A negative number will offset from the end of the list to that event, thereby referencing it. In the next example, the fourth command, **cd mydata**, is referenced using a negative offset, and then executed. Remember that you are offsetting from the end of the list—in this case, event 5—

up toward the beginning of the list, event 1. An offset of 4 beginning from event 5 places you at event 2.

```
$ !-4
vi mydata
```

To reference the last event, you use a following !, as in **! !**. In the next example, the command **! !** executes the last command the user executed—in this case, **ls**:

```
$ !!
ls
mydata today reports
```

History Event Editing

You can also edit any event in the history list before you execute it. In the BASH shell, you can do this two ways. You can use the command line editor capability to reference and edit any event in the history list. You can also use a history **fc** command option to reference an event and edit it with the full Vi editor. Each approach involves two different editing capabilities. The first is limited to the commands in the command line editor, which edits only a single line with a subset of Emacs commands. At the same time, however, it enables you to reference events easily in the history list. The second approach invokes the standard Vi editor with all its features, but only for a specified history event.

With the command line editor, not only can you edit the current command, you can also move to a previous event in the history list to edit and execute it. The CTRL-P command then moves you up to the prior event in the list. The CTRL-N command moves you down the list. The ALT-< command moves you to the top of the list, and the ALT-> command moves you to the bottom. You can even use a pattern to search for a given event. The slash followed by a pattern searches backward in the list, and the question mark followed by a pattern searches forward in the list. The **n** command repeats the search.

Once you locate the event you want to edit, you use the Emacs command line editing commands to edit the line. CTRL-D deletes a character. CTRL-F or the RIGHT ARROW moves you forward a character, and CTRL-B or the LEFT ARROW moves you back a character. To add text, you position your cursor and type in the characters you want.

If you want to edit an event using a standard editor instead, you need to reference the event using the **fc** command and a specific event reference, such as an event number. The editor used is the one specified by the shell in the **EDITOR** variable. This serves as the default editor for the **fc** command. You can assign to the **EDITOR** variable a different editor if you wish, such as Emacs instead of Vi. The next example will edit the fourth event, **cd reports**, with the standard editor and then execute the edited event:

```
$ fc 4
```

You can select more than one command at a time to be edited and executed by referencing a range of commands. You select a range of commands by indicating an identifier for the first command followed by an identifier for the last command in the range. An identifier can be the command number or the beginning characters in the command. In the next example, the range of commands 2–4 is edited and executed, first using event numbers and then using beginning characters in those events:

```
$ fc 2 4
$ fc vi c
```

The **fc** command uses the default editor specified in the **FCEDIT** special variable. Usually, this is the Vi editor. If you want to use the Emacs editor instead, you use the **-e** option and the term **emacs** when you invoke **fc**. The next example will edit the fourth event, **cd reports**, with the Emacs editor and then execute the edited event:

```
$ fc -e emacs 4
```

Configuring History: HISTSIZE and HISTFILE

The number of events saved by your system is kept in a special system variable called **HISTSIZE**. By default, this is usually set to 500. You can change this to another number by simply assigning a new value to **HISTSIZE**. In the next example, the user changes the number of history events saved to 10 by resetting the **HISTSIZE** variable:

```
$ HISTSIZE=10
```

The actual history events are saved in a file whose name is held in a special variable called **HISTFILE**. By default, this file is the **.bash_history** file. You can change the file in which history events are saved, however, by assigning its name to the **HISTFILE** variable. In the next example, the value of **HISTFILE** is displayed. Then a new filename is assigned to it, **newhist**. History events are then saved in the **newhist** file.

```
$ echo $HISTFILE
.bash_history
$ HISTFILE="newhist"
$ echo $HISTFILE
newhist
```

Filename Expansion: *, ?, [ ]

Filenames are the most common arguments used in a command. Often you may know only part of the filename, or you may want to reference several filenames that have the same extension or begin with the same characters. The shell provides a set of special characters that search out, match, and generate a list of filenames. These are the asterisk, the question mark, and brackets (*, ?, []). Given a partial filename, the shell uses these matching operators to search for files and expand to a list of filenames found. The shell replaces the partial filename argument with the expanded list of matched filenames. This list of filenames can then become the arguments for commands such as **ls**, which can operate on many files. Table 8-5 lists the shell's file expansion characters.

Common Shell Symbol	Execution
ENTER	Execute a command line.
;	Separate commands on the same command line.
`command`	Execute a command.
$ (command)	Execute a command.
[ ]	Match on a class of possible characters in filenames.
\	Quote the following character. Used to quote special characters.
|	Pipe the standard output of one command as input for another command.
&	Execute a command in the background.
!	History command.
File Expansion Symbol	**Execution**
*	Match on any set of characters in filenames.
?	Match on any single character in filenames.
[ ]	Match on a class of characters in filenames.
Redirection Symbol	**Execution**
>	Redirect the standard output to a file or device, creating the file if it does not exist and overwriting the file if it does exist.
>!	The exclamation point forces the overwriting of a file if it already exists. This overrides the **noclobber** option.
<	Redirect the standard input from a file or device to a program.
>>	Redirect the standard output to a file or device, appending the output to the end of the file.
Standard Error Redirection Symbol	**Execution**
2>	Redirect the standard error to a file or device.
2>>	Redirect and append the standard error to a file or device.
2>&1	Redirect the standard error to the standard output.
>&	Redirect the standard error to a file or device.
|&	Pipe the standard error as input to another command.

TABLE 8-5   Shell Symbols

Matching Multiple Characters

The asterisk, *, references files beginning or ending with a specific set of characters. You place the asterisk before or after a set of characters that form a pattern to be searched for in filenames. If the asterisk is placed before the pattern, filenames that end in that pattern are searched for. If the asterisk is placed after the pattern, filenames that begin with that pattern are searched for. Any matching filename is copied into a list of filenames generated by this operation. In the next example, all filenames beginning with the pattern "doc" are searched for and a list generated. Then all filenames ending with the pattern "day" are searched for and a list is generated. The last example shows how the * can be used in any combination of characters.

```
$ ls
doc1 doc2 document docs mydoc monday tuesday
$ ls doc*
doc1 doc2 document docs
$ ls *day
monday tuesday
$ ls m*d*
monday
$
```

Filenames often include an extension specified with a period and followed by a string denoting the file type, such as **.c** for C files, **.cpp** for C++ files, or even **.jpg** for JPEG image files. The extension has no special status and is only part of the characters making up the filename. Using the asterisk makes it easy to select files with a given extension. In the next example, the asterisk is used to list only those files with a .c extension. The asterisk placed before the **.c** constitutes the argument for **ls**.

```
$ ls *.c
calc.c main.c
```

You can use * with the **rm** command to erase several files at once. The asterisk first selects a list of files with a given extension, or beginning or ending with a given set of characters, and then it presents this list of files to the **rm** command to be erased. In the next example, the **rm** command erases all files beginning with the pattern "doc":

```
$ rm doc*
```

TIP *Use the* ***** *file expansion character carefully and sparingly with the* **rm** *command. The combination can be dangerous. A misplaced* ***** *in an* **rm** *command without the* **-i** *option could easily erase all the files in your current directory. The* **-i** *option will first prompt the user to confirm whether the file should be deleted.*

Matching Single Characters

The question mark, **?**, matches only a single incomplete character in filenames. Suppose you want to match the files **doc1** and **docA**, but not the file **document**. Whereas the asterisk will match filenames of any length, the question mark limits the match to just one extra character. The next example matches files that begin with the word "doc" followed by a single differing letter:

```
$ ls
doc1 docA document
$ ls doc?
doc1 docA
```

Matching a Range of Characters

Whereas the * and ? file expansion characters specify incomplete portions of a filename, the brackets, [], enable you to specify a set of valid characters to search for. Any character placed within the brackets will be matched in the filename. Suppose you want to list files beginning with "doc", but only ending in *1* or *A*. You are not interested in filenames ending in *2* or *B*, or any other character. Here is how it's done:

```
$ ls
doc1 doc2 doc3 docA docB docD document
$ ls doc[1A]
doc1 docA
```

You can also specify a set of characters as a range, rather than listing them one by one. A dash placed between the upper and lower bounds of a set of characters selects all characters within that range. The range is usually determined by the character set in use. In an ASCII character set, the range "a-g" will select all lowercase alphabetic characters from *a* through *g*, inclusive. In the next example, files beginning with the pattern "doc" and ending in characters *1* through *3* are selected. Then, those ending in characters *B* through *E* are matched.

```
$ ls doc[1-3]
doc1 doc2 doc3
$ ls doc[B-E]
docB docD
```

You can combine the brackets with other file expansion characters to form flexible matching operators. Suppose you want to list only filenames ending in either a **.c** or **.o** extension, but no other extension. You can use a combination of the asterisk and brackets: ***[co]**. The asterisk matches all filenames, and the brackets match only filenames with extension **.c** or **.o**.

```
$ ls *.[co]
main.c  main.o  calc.c
```

Matching Shell Symbols

At times, a file expansion character is actually part of a filename. In these cases, you need to quote the character by preceding it with a backslash to reference the file. In the next example, the user needs to reference a file that ends with the ? character, **answers?**. The ? is, however, a file expansion character and would match any filename beginning with "answers" that has one or more characters. In this case, the user quotes the ? with a preceding backslash to reference the filename.

```
$ ls answers\?
answers?
```

Placing the filename in double quotes will also quote the character.

```
$ ls "answers?"
answers?
```

This is also true for filenames or directories that have white space characters like the space character. In this case you could either use the backslash to quote the space character in the file or directory name, or place the entire name in double quotes.

```
$ ls My\ Documents
My Documents
$ ls "My Documents"
My Documents
```

Generating Patterns

Though not a file expansion operation, { } is often useful for generating names that you can use to create or modify files and directories. The braces operation only generates a list of names. It does not match on existing filenames. Patterns are placed within the braces and separated with commas. Any pattern placed within the braces will be used to generate a version of the pattern, using either the preceding or following pattern, or both. Suppose you want to generate a list of names beginning with "doc", but only ending in the patterns "ument", "final", and "draft". Here is how it's done:

```
$ echo doc{ument,final,draft}
document docfinal docdraft
```

Since the names generated do not have to exist, you could use the { } operation in a command to create directories, as shown here:

```
$ mkdir {fall,winter,spring}report
$ ls
fallreport springreport winterreport
```

Standard Input/Output and Redirection

The data in input and output operations is organized like a file. Data input at the keyboard is placed in a data stream arranged as a continuous set of bytes. Data output from a command or program is also placed in a data stream and arranged as a continuous set of bytes. This input data stream is referred to in Linux as the *standard input*, while the output data stream is called the *standard output*. There is also a separate output data stream reserved solely for error messages, called the *standard error* (see the section "Redirecting and Piping the Standard Error: >&, 2>" later in this chapter).

Because the standard input and standard output have the same organization as that of a file, they can easily interact with files. Linux has a redirection capability that lets you easily move data in and out of files. You can redirect the standard output so that, instead of displaying the output on a screen, you can save it in a file. You can also redirect the standard input away from the keyboard to a file, so that input is read from a file instead of from your keyboard.

When a Linux command is executed that produces output, this output is placed in the standard output data stream. The default destination for the standard output data stream is a device—in this case, the screen. *Devices,* such as the keyboard and screen, are treated as files. They receive and send out streams of bytes with the same organization as that of a byte-stream file. The screen is a device that displays a continuous stream of bytes. By default, the standard output will send its data to the screen device, which will then display the data.

For example, the **ls** command generates a list of all filenames and outputs this list to the standard output. Next, this stream of bytes in the standard output is directed to the screen device. The list of filenames is then printed on the screen. The **cat** command also sends output to the standard output. The contents of a file are copied to the standard output, whose default destination is the screen. The contents of the file are then displayed on the screen.

Redirecting the Standard Output: > and >>

Suppose that instead of displaying a list of files on the screen, you would like to save this list in a file. In other words, you would like to direct the standard output to a file rather than the screen. To do this, you place the output redirection operator, **>** (greater-than sign), and the name of a file on the command line after the Linux command. Table 8-6 lists the different ways you can use the redirection operators. In the next example, the output of the **ls** command is redirected from the screen device to a file:

```
$ ls -l *.c > programlist
```

The redirection operation creates the new destination file. If the file already exists, it will be overwritten with the data in the standard output. You can set the **noclobber** feature to prevent overwriting an existing file with the redirection operation. In this case, the redirection operation on an existing file will fail. You can overcome the **noclobber** feature by placing an exclamation point after the redirection operator. You can place the **noclobber** command in a shell configuration file to make it an automatic default operation. The next example sets the **noclobber** feature for the BASH shell and then forces the overwriting of the **oldletter** file if it already exists:

```
$ set -o noclobber
$ cat myletter >! oldletter
```

Although the redirection operator and the filename are placed after the command, the redirection operation is not executed after the command. In fact, it is executed before the command. The redirection operation creates the file and sets up the redirection before it receives any data from the standard output. If the file already exists, it will be destroyed and replaced by a file of the same name. In effect, the command generating the output is executed only after the redirected file has been created.

In the next example, the output of the **ls** command is redirected from the screen device to a file. First the **ls** command lists files, and in the next command, **ls** redirects its file list to the **listf** file. Then the **cat** command displays the list of files saved in **listf**. Notice the list of files in **listf** includes the **listf** filename. The list of filenames generated by the **ls** command includes the name of the file created by the redirection operation—in this case, **listf**. The **listf** file is first created by the redirection operation, and then the **ls** command lists it along with other files. This file list output by **ls** is then redirected to the **listf** file, instead of being printed on the screen.

```
$ ls
mydata intro preface
$ ls > listf
$ cat listf
mydata intro listf preface
```

Command	Execution
ENTER	Execute a command line.
;	Separate commands on the same command line.
command\ opts args	Enter backslash before carriage return to continue entering a command on the next line.
`command`	Execute a command.
$ (command)	Execute a command.

Special Character for Filename Expansion	Execution
*	Match on any set of characters.
?	Match on any single character.
[]	Match on a class of possible characters.
\	Quote the following character. Used to quote special characters.

Redirection	Execution
command > filename	Redirect the standard output to a file or device, creating the file if it does not exist and overwriting the file if it does exist.
command < filename	Redirect the standard input from a file or device to a program.
command >> filename	Redirect the standard output to a file or device, appending the output to the end of the file.
command >! filename	In the C shell and the Korn shell, the exclamation point forces the overwriting of a file if it already exists. This overrides the **noclobber** option.
command 2> filename	Redirect the standard error to a file or device in the Bourne shell.
command 2>\> filename	Redirect and append the standard error to a file or device in the Bourne shell.
command 2>&1	Redirect the standard error to the standard output in the Bourne shell.
command >& filename	Redirect the standard error to a file or device in the C shell.

Pipe	Execution
command | command	Pipe the standard output of one command as input for another command.
command |& command	Pipe the standard error as input to another command in the C shell.

TABLE 8-6   The Shell Operations

TIP   *Errors occur when you try to use the same filename for both an input file for the command and the redirected destination file. In this case, because the redirection operation is executed first, the input file, because it exists, is destroyed and replaced by a file of the same name. When the command is executed, it finds an input file that is empty.*

You can also append the standard output to an existing file using the **>>** redirection operator. Instead of overwriting the file, the data in the standard output is added at the end of the file. In the next example, the **myletter** and **oldletter** files are appended to the **alletters** file. The **alletters** file will then contain the contents of both **myletter** and **oldletter**.

```
$ cat myletter >> alletters
$ cat oldletter >> alletters
```

The Standard Input

Many Linux commands can receive data from the standard input. The standard input itself receives data from a device or a file. The default device for the standard input is the keyboard. Characters typed on the keyboard are placed in the standard input, which is then directed to the Linux command. Just as with the standard output, you can also redirect the standard input, receiving input from a file rather than the keyboard. The operator for redirecting the standard input is the less-than sign (**<**). In the next example, the standard input is redirected to receive input from the **myletter** file, rather than the keyboard device (use CTRL-D to end the typed input). The contents of **myletter** are read into the standard input by the redirection operation. Then the **cat** command reads the standard input and displays the contents of **myletter**.

```
$ cat < myletter
hello Christopher
How are you today
$
```

You can combine the redirection operations for both standard input and standard output. In the next example, the **cat** command has no filename arguments. Without filename arguments, the **cat** command receives input from the standard input and sends output to the standard output. However, the standard input has been redirected to receive its data from a file, while the standard output has been redirected to place its data in a file.

```
$ cat < myletter > newletter
```

Pipes: |

You may find yourself in situations in which you need to send data from one command to another. In other words, you may want to send the standard output of a command to another command, not to a destination file. Suppose you want to send a list of your filenames to the printer to be printed. You need two commands to do this: the **ls** command to generate a list of filenames and the **lpr** command to send the list to the printer. In effect, you need to take the output of the **ls** command and use it as input for the **lpr** command. You can think of the data as flowing from one command to another. To form such a connection in Linux, you use what is called a *pipe*. The *pipe operator*, |, (vertical bar character) placed between two commands forms a connection between them. The standard output of one command becomes the standard input for the other. The pipe operation receives output from the command placed before the pipe and sends this data as input to the command placed after the pipe.

As shown in the next example, you can connect the **ls** command and the **lpr** command with a pipe. The list of filenames output by the **ls** command is piped into the **lpr** command.

```
$ ls | lpr
```

You can combine the **pipe** operation with other shell features, such as file expansion characters, to perform specialized operations. The next example prints only files with a **.c** extension. The **ls** command is used with the asterisk and ".c" to generate a list of filenames with the **.c** extension. Then this list is piped to the **lpr** command.

```
$ ls *.c | lpr
```

In the preceding example, a list of filenames was used as input, but what is important to note is pipes operate on the standard output of a command, whatever that might be. The contents of whole files or even several files can be piped from one command to another. In the next example, the **cat** command reads and outputs the contents of the **mydata** file, which are then piped to the **lpr** command:

```
$ cat mydata | lpr
```

Linux has many commands that generate modified output. For example, the **sort** command takes the contents of a file and generates a version with each line sorted in alphabetic order. The **sort** command works best with files that are lists of items. Commands such as **sort** that output a modified version of its input are referred to as *filters*. Filters are often used with pipes. In the next example, a sorted version of **mylist** is generated and piped into the **more** command for display on the screen. Note that the original file, **mylist**, has not been changed and is not itself sorted. Only the output of **sort** in the standard output is sorted.

```
$ sort mylist | more
```

The standard input piped into a command can be more carefully controlled with the standard input argument (–). When you use the dash as an argument for a command, it represents the standard input.

Redirecting and Piping the Standard Error: >&, 2>

When you execute commands, an error could possibly occur. You may give the wrong number of arguments, or some kind of system error could take place. When an error occurs, the system issues an error message. Usually such error messages are displayed on the screen, along with the standard output. Linux distinguishes between standard output and error messages, however. Error messages are placed in yet another standard byte stream, called the *standard error*. In the next example, the **cat** command is given as its argument the name of a file that does not exist, **myintro**. In this case, the **cat** command simply issues an error:

```
$ cat myintro
cat : myintro not found
$
```

Because error messages are in a separate data stream from the standard output, error messages still appear on the screen for you to see even if you have redirected the standard output to a file. In the next example, the standard output of the **cat** command is redirected to the file **mydata**. However, the standard error, containing the error messages, is still directed to the screen.

```
$ cat myintro > mydata
cat : myintro not found
$
```

You can redirect the standard error, as you can the standard output. This means you can save your error messages in a file for future reference. This is helpful if you need a record of the error messages. Like the standard output, the standard error has the screen device for its default destination. However, you can redirect the standard error to any file or device you choose using special redirection operators. In this case, the error messages will not be displayed on the screen.

Redirection of the standard error relies on a special feature of shell redirection. You can reference all the standard byte streams in redirection operations with numbers. The numbers 0, 1, and 2 reference the standard input, standard output, and standard error, respectively. By default, an output redirection, **>**, operates on the standard output, 1. You can modify the output redirection to operate on the standard error, however, by preceding the output redirection operator with the number 2. In the next example, the **cat** command again will generate an error. The error message is redirected to the standard byte stream represented by the number 2, the standard error.

```
$ cat nodata 2> myerrors
$ cat myerrors
cat : nodata not found
$
```

You can also append the standard error to a file by using the number 2 and the redirection append operator, **>>**. In the next example, the user appends the standard error to the **myerrors** file, which then functions as a log of errors:

```
$ cat nodata 2>> myerrors
```

Jobs: Background, Kills, and Interruptions

In Linux, you not only have control over a command's input and output, but also over its execution. You can run a job in the background while you execute other commands. You can also cancel commands before they have finished executing. You can even interrupt a command, starting it again later from where you left off. Background operations are particularly useful for long jobs. Instead of waiting at the terminal until a command has finished execution, you can place it in the background. You can then continue executing other Linux commands. You can, for example, edit a file while other files are printing. The background commands, as well as commands to cancel and interrupt jobs, are listed in Table 8-7.

Background Job	Execution
%*jobnum*	References job by job number, use **jobs** command to display job numbers.
%	References recent job.
%*string*	References job by an exact matching string.
%?*string*?	References job that contains unique string.
%--	References job before recent job.
&	Execute a command in the background.
fg %*jobnum*	Bring a command in the background to the foreground or resume an interrupted program.
bg	Place a command in the foreground into the background.
CTRL-Z	Interrupt and stop the currently running program. The program remains stopped and waiting in the background for you to resume it.
notify %*jobnum*	Notify you when a job ends.
kill %*jobnum* **kill** *processnum*	Cancel and end a job running in the background.
jobs	List all background jobs. The **jobs** command is not available in the Bourne shell, unless it is using the jsh shell.
ps -a	List all currently running processes, including background jobs.
at *time date*	Execute commands at a specified time and date. The time can be entered with hours and minutes and qualified as am or pm.

TABLE 8-7   *Job Management Operations*

Running Jobs in the Background

You execute a command in the background by placing an ampersand, **&**, on the command line at the end of the command. When you place a job in the background, a user job number and a system process number are displayed. The user job number, placed in brackets, is the number by which the user references the job. The system process number is the number by which the system identifies the job. In the next example, the command to print the file **mydata** is placed in the background:

```
$ lpr mydata &
[1]  534
$
```

You can place more than one command in the background. Each is classified as a job and given a name and a job number. The command **jobs** lists the jobs being run in the background. Each entry in the list consists of the job number in brackets, whether it is stopped or running, and the name of the job. The **+** sign indicates the job currently being processed, and the **-** sign indicates the next job to be executed. In the next example, two commands have been placed in the background. The **jobs** command then lists those jobs, showing which one is currently being executed.

```
$ lpr intro &
[1]   547
$ cat *.c > myprogs &
[2]   548
$ jobs
[1]   +   Running   lpr intro
[2]   -   Running   cat *.c > myprogs
$
```

Referencing Jobs

Normally jobs are referenced using the job number. You can obtain this number with the jobs command, which will list all background jobs, as shown in the previous example. In addition you can also reference a job using an identifying string (see Table 8-7). The string must be either an exact match or a partial unique match. If there is no exact or unique match, you will receive an error message. Also, the **%** symbol itself without any job number references the recent background job. Followed by a -- it references the second previous background job. The following example brings job 1 in the previous example to the foreground.

```
fg %lpr
```

Job Notification

After you execute any command in Linux, the system tells you what background jobs, if you have any running, have been completed so far. The system does not interrupt any operation, such as editing, to notify you about a completed job. If you want to be notified immediately when a certain job ends, no matter what you are doing on the system, you can use the **notify** command to instruct the system to tell you. The **notify** command takes a job number as its argument. When that job is finished, the system interrupts what you are doing to notify you the job has ended. The next example tells the system to notify the user when job 2 has finished:

```
$ notify %2
```

Bringing Jobs to the Foreground

You can bring a job out of the background with the foreground command, **fg**. If only one job is in the background, the **fg** command alone will bring it to the foreground. If more than one job is in the background, you must use the job's number with the command. You place the job number after the **fg** command, preceded with a percent sign. A **bg** command also places a job in the background. This command is usually used for interrupted jobs. In the next example, the second job is brought back into the foreground. You may not immediately receive a prompt again because the second command is now in the foreground and executing. When the command is finished executing, the prompt appears and you can execute another command.

```
$ fg %2
cat *.c > myprogs
$
```

Canceling Jobs

If you want to cancel a job running in the background, you can force it to end with the **kill** command. The **kill** command takes as its argument either the user job number or the system process number. The user job number must be preceded by a percent sign (%). You can find out the job number from the **jobs** command. In the next example, the **jobs** command lists the background jobs; then job 2 is canceled:

```
$ jobs
[1]  +  Running  lpr intro
[2]  -  Running  cat *.c > myprogs
$ kill %2
```

You can also cancel a job using the system process number, which you can obtain with the **ps** command. The **ps** command displays a great deal more information than the **jobs** command does. The next example lists the processes a user is running. The PID is the system process number, also known as the process ID. TTY is the terminal identifier. The time is how long the process has taken so far. COMMAND is the name of the process.

```
$ ps
PID      TTY        TIME       COMMAND
523      tty24      0:05       sh
567      tty24      0:01       lpr
570      tty24      0:00       ps
```

You can then reference the system process number in a **kill** command. Use the process number without any preceding percent sign. The next example kills process 567:

```
$ kill 567
```

Suspending and Stopping Jobs

You can suspend a job and stop it with the CTRL-Z key. This places the job to the side until it is restarted. The job is not ended; it merely remains suspended until you want to continue. When you're ready, you can continue with the job in either the foreground or the background using the **fg** or **bg** command. The **fg** command restarts a suspended job in the foreground. The **bg** command places the suspended job in the background.

At times, you may need to place a currently running job in the foreground into the background. However, you cannot move a currently running job directly into the background. You first need to suspend it with CTRL-Z and then place it in the background with the **bg** command. In the next example, the current command to list and redirect .c files is first suspended with CTRL-Z. Then that job is placed in the background.

```
$ cat *.c > myprogs
^Z
$ bg
```

NOTE *You can also use* CTRL-Z *to stop currently running jobs like Vi, suspending them in the background until you are ready to resume them. The Vi session remains a stopped job in the background until resumed with the* **bg** *command.*

Shell Variables

The BASH, Korn, and Z shells described previously are actually types of shells. A *shell*, by definition, is an interpretive environment within which you execute commands. You could have many environments running at the same time, either of the same type or of different types of shells. So you could have several shells running at the same time that are of the BASH shell type.

Within each shell, you could enter and execute commands. You can further enhance the capabilities of a shell using shell variables. With a shell variable, you can hold data that you could reference over and over again as you execute different commands within a given shell. For example, you could define a shell variable to hold the name of a complex filename. Instead of retyping the filename in different commands, you could reference it with the shell variable.

You define variables within a shell, and such variables are known as *shell variables.* Many different shells exist. Some utilities, such as the Mail utility, have their own shells with their own shell variables. You can also create your own shell using what are called *shell scripts.* You have a user shell that becomes active as soon as you log in. This is often referred to as the *login shell.* Special system-level parameter variables are defined within this login shell. Shell variables can also be used to define a shell's environment, as described in Chapter 9.

NOTE *Shell variables exist as long as your shell is active—that is, until you exit the shell. For example, logging out will exit the login shell. When you log in again, any variables you may need in your login shell must be defined again.*

Definition and Evaluation of Variables: =, $, set, unset

You define a variable in a shell when you first use the variable's name. A variable's name may be any set of alphabetic characters, including the underscore. The name may also include a number, but the number cannot be the first character in the name. A name may not have any other type of character, such as an exclamation point, an ampersand, or even a space. Such symbols are reserved by the shell for its own use. Also, a variable name may not include more than one word. The shell uses spaces on the command line to distinguish different components of a command such as options, arguments, and the name of the command.

You assign a value to a variable with the assignment operator (**=**). You type the variable name, the assignment operator, and then the value assigned. Do not place any spaces around the assignment operator. The assignment operation **poet = Virgil**, for example, will fail. (The C shell has a slightly different type of assignment operation.) You can assign any set of characters to a variable. In the next example, the variable **poet** is assigned the string **Virgil**:

```
$ poet=Virgil
```

Once you have assigned a value to a variable, you can then use the variable name to reference the value. Often you use the values of variables as arguments for a command. You can reference the value of a variable using the variable name preceded by the **$** operator. The dollar sign is a special operator that uses the variable name to reference a variable's value, in effect evaluating the variable. Evaluation retrieves a variable's value, usually a set of characters. This set of characters then replaces the variable name on the command line. Wherever a **$** is placed before the variable name, the variable name is replaced with the value of the variable. In the next example, the shell variable **poet** is evaluated and its contents, **Virgil**, are then used as the argument for an **echo** command. The **echo** command simply echoes or prints a set of characters to the screen.

```
$ echo $poet
Virgil
```

You must be careful to distinguish between the evaluation of a variable and its name alone. If you leave out the **$** operator before the variable name, all you have is the variable name itself. In the next example, the **$** operator is absent from the variable name. In this case, the **echo** command has as its argument the word "poet", and so prints out "poet":

```
$ echo poet
poet
```

The contents of a variable are often used as command arguments. A common command argument is a directory pathname. It can be tedious to retype a directory path that is being used over and over again. If you assign the directory pathname to a variable, you can simply use the evaluated variable in its place. The directory path you assign to the variable is retrieved when the variable is evaluated with the **$** operator. The next example assigns a directory pathname to a variable and then uses the evaluated variable in a copy command. The evaluation of **ldir** (which is **$ldir**) results in the pathname **/home/chris/letters**. The copy command evaluates to **cp myletter /home/chris/letters**.

```
$ ldir=/home/chris/letters
$ cp myletter $ldir
```

You can obtain a list of all the defined variables with the **set** command. If you decide you do not want a certain variable, you can remove it with the **unset** command. The **unset** command undefines a variable.

Shell Scripts: User-Defined Commands

You can place shell commands within a file and then have the shell read and execute the commands in the file. In this sense, the file functions as a shell program, executing shell commands as if they were statements in a program. A file that contains shell commands is called a *shell script*.

You enter shell commands into a script file using a standard text editor such as the Vi editor. The **sh** or **.** command used with the script's filename will read the script file and execute the commands. In the next example, the text file called **lsc** contains an **ls** command that displays only files with the extension **.c**:

lsc
```
ls *.c
```

A run of the **lsc** script is shown here:

```
$ sh lsc
main.c calc.c
$ . lsc
main.c calc.c
```

Executing Scripts

You can dispense with the **sh** and . commands by setting the executable permission of a script file. When the script file is first created by your text editor, it is given only read and write permission. The **chmod** command with the **+x** option will give the script file executable permission. (Permissions are discussed in Chapter 30.) Once it is executable, entering the name of the script file at the shell prompt and pressing ENTER will execute the script file and the shell commands in it. In effect, the script's filename becomes a new shell command. In this way, you can use shell scripts to design and create your own Linux commands. You need to set the permission only once. In the next example, the **lsc** file's executable permission for the owner is set to on. Then the **lsc** shell script is directly executed like any Linux command.

```
$ chmod u+x lsc
$ lsc
main.c calc.c
```

You may have to specify that the script you are using is in your current working directory. You do this by prefixing the script name with a period and slash combination, **./**, as in **./ lsc**. The period is a special character representing the name of your current working directory. The slash is a directory pathname separator, as explained more fully in Chapter 32 (you could also add the current directory to your PATH variable as discussed in Chapter 9). The following example would show how you would execute the **lsc** script:

```
$ ./lsc
main.c calc.c
```

Script Arguments

Just as any Linux command can take arguments, so also can a shell script. Arguments on the command line are referenced sequentially starting with 1. An argument is referenced using the **$** operator and the number of its position. The first argument is referenced with **$1**, the second, with **$2**, and so on. In the next example, the **lsext** script prints out files with a specified extension. The first argument is the extension. The script is then executed with the argument **c** (of course, the executable permission must have been set).

lsext
```
ls *.$1
```

A run of the **lsext** script with an argument is shown here:

```
$ lsext c
main.c calc.c
```

In the next example, the commands to print out a file with line numbers have been placed in an executable file called **lpnum**, which takes a filename as its argument. The **cat** command with the **–n** option first outputs the contents of the file with line numbers. Then this output is piped into the **lpr** command, which prints it. The command to print out the line numbers is executed in the background.

lpnum
```
cat -n $1 | lpr &
```

A run of the **lpnum** script with an argument is shown here:

```
$ lpnum mydata
```

You may need to reference more than one argument at a time. The number of arguments used may vary. In **lpnum,** you may want to print out three files at one time and five files at some other time. The **$** operator with the asterisk, **$***, references all the arguments on the command line. Using **$*** enables you to create scripts that take a varying number of arguments. In the next example, **lpnum** is rewritten using **$*** so that it can take a different number of arguments each time you use it:

lpnum
```
cat -n $* | lpr &
```

A run of the **lpnum** script with multiple arguments is shown here:

```
$ lpnum mydata preface
```

Control Structures

You can control the execution of Linux commands in a shell script with control structures. Control structures allow you to repeat commands and to select certain commands over others. A control structure consists of two major components: a test and commands. If the test is successful, then the commands are executed. In this way, you can use control structures to make decisions as to whether commands should be executed.

There are two different kinds of control structures: *loops* and *conditions.* A loop repeats commands, whereas a condition executes a command when certain conditions are met. The BASH shell has three loop control structures: **while**, **for**, and **for-in**. There are two condition structures: **if** and **case**. The control structures have as their test the execution of a Linux command. All Linux commands return an exit status after they have finished executing. If a command is successful, its exit status will be 0. If the command fails for any reason, its exit status will be a positive value referencing the type of failure that occurred. The control structures check to see if the exit status of a Linux command is 0 or some other value. In the case of the **if** and **while** structures, if the exit status is a zero value, then the command was successful and the structure continues.

Test Operations

With the **test** command, you can compare integers, compare strings, and even perform logical operations. The command consists of the keyword **test** followed by the values being compared, separated by an option that specifies what kind of comparison is taking place. The option can be thought of as the operator, but it is written, like other options, with a minus sign and letter codes. For example, **-eq** is the option that represents the equality comparison. However, there are two string operations that actually use an operator instead of an option. When you compare two strings for equality you use the equal sign (=). For inequality you use !=. Table 8-8 lists some of the commonly used options and operators used by **test**. The syntax for the **test** command is shown here:

```
test value -option value
test string = string
```

TABLE **8-8** BASH
Shell Test Operators

Integer Comparison	Function
`-gt`	greater-than
`-lt`	less-than
`-ge`	greater-than-or-equal-to
`-le`	less-than-or-equal-to
`-eq`	equal
`-ne`	not-equal
String Comparison	**Function**
`-z`	Tests for empty string
`=`	equal strings
`!=`	not-equal strings
Logical Operation	**Function**
`-a`	Logical AND
`-o`	Logical OR
`!`	Logical NOT
File Test	**Function**
`-f`	File exists and is a regular file
`-s`	File is not empty
`-r`	File is readable
`-w`	File can be written to, modified
`-x`	File is executable
`-d`	Filename is a directory name

In the next example, the user compares two integer values to see if they are equal. In this case, you need to use the equality option, **-eq**. The exit status of the **test** command is examined to find out the result of the test operation. The shell special variable **$?** holds the exit status of the most recently executed Linux command.

```
$ num=5
$ test $num -eq 10
$ echo $?
1
```

Instead of using the keyword **test** for the **test** command, you can use enclosing brackets. The command **test $greeting = "hi"** can be written as

```
$ [ $greeting = "hi" ]
```

Similarly, the test command **test $num -eq 10** can be written as

```
$ [ $num -eq 10 ]
```

The brackets themselves must be surrounded by white space: a space, TAB, or ENTER. Without the spaces, it would be invalid.

Conditional Control Structures

The BASH shell has a set of conditional control structures that allow you to choose what Linux commands to execute. Many of these are similar to conditional control structures found in programming languages, but there are some differences. The **if** condition tests the success of a Linux command, not an expression. Furthermore, the end of an **if-then** command must be indicated with the keyword **fi**, and the end of a **case** command is indicated with the keyword **esac**. The condition control structures are listed in Table 8-9.

The **if** structure places a condition on commands. That condition is the exit status of a specific Linux command. If a command is successful, returning an exit status of 0, then the commands within the **if** structure are executed. If the exit status is anything other than 0, then the command has failed and the commands within the **if** structure are not executed. The **if** command begins with the keyword **if** and is followed by a Linux command whose exit condition will be evaluated. The keyword **fi** ends the command. The **elsels** script in the next example executes the **ls** command to list files with two different possible options, either by size or with all file information. If the user enters an **s**, files are listed by size; otherwise, all file information is listed.

elsels
```
echo Enter s to list file sizes,
echo         otherwise all file information is listed.
echo -n "Please enter option: "
read choice
if [   "$choice" = s   ]
    then
          ls -s
    else
             ls -l
fi
echo Good-bye
```

A run of the program follows:

```
$ elsels
Enter s to list file sizes,
otherwise all file information is listed.
Please enter option: s
total 2
    1 monday     2 today
$
```

Loop Control Structures

The **while** loop repeats commands. A **while** loop begins with the keyword **while** and is followed by a Linux command. The keyword **do** follows on the next line. The end of the loop is specified by the keyword **done**. The Linux command used in **while** structures is often a test command indicated by enclosing brackets.

Condition Control Structures: if, else, elif, case	Function

`if` *command* `then`
  command
`fi`
	`if` executes an action if its test command is true.

`if` *command* `then`
  command
`else`
  command
`fi`
	`if-else` executes an action if the exit status of its test command is true; if false, then the `else` action is executed.

`if` *command* `then`
  command
`elif` *command* `then`
  command
`else`
  command
`fi`
	`elif` allows you to nest `if` structures, enabling selection among several alternatives; at the first true `if` structure, its commands are executed and control leaves the entire `elif` structure.

`case` *string* `in`
pattern`)`
  command`;;`
`esac`
	`case` matches the string value to any of several patterns; if a pattern is matched, its associated commands are executed.

command `&&` *command*	The logical AND condition returns a true 0 value if both commands return a true 0 value; if one returns a nonzero value, then the AND condition is false and also returns a nonzero value.
command `||` *command*	The logical OR condition returns a true 0 value if one or the other command returns a true 0 value; if both commands return a nonzero value, then the OR condition is false and also returns a nonzero value.
`!` *command*	The logical NOT condition inverts the return value of the command.
Loop Control Structures: while, until, for, for-in, select	**Function**

`while` *command*
`do`
  command
`done`
	`while` executes an action as long as its test command is true.

`until` *command*
`do`
  command
`done`
	`until` executes an action as long as its test command is false.

`for` *variable* `in` *list-values*
`do`
  command
`done`
	`for-in` is designed for use with lists of values; the variable operand is consecutively assigned the values in the list.

`for` *variable*
`do`
  command
`done`
	`for` is designed for reference script arguments; the variable operand is consecutively assigned each argument value.

`select` *string* `in` *item-list*
`do`
  command
`done`
	`select` creates a menu based on the items in the *item-list*; then it executes the command; the command is usually a `case`.

TABLE **8-9** BASH Shell Control Structures

The **for-in** structure is designed to reference a list of values sequentially. It takes two operands—a variable and a list of values. The values in the list are assigned one by one to the variable in the **for-in** structure. Like the **while** command, the **for-in** structure is a loop. Each time through the loop, the next value in the list is assigned to the variable. When the end of the list is reached, the loop stops. Like the **while** loop, the body of a **for-in** loop begins with the keyword **do** and ends with the keyword **done**. The **cbackup** script makes a backup of each file and places it in a directory called **sourcebak**. Notice the use of the * special character to generate a list of all filenames with a .c extension.

cbackup
```
for backfile in *.c
do
    cp $backfile sourcebak/$backfile
 echo $backfile
done
```

A run of the program follows:

```
$ cbackup
io.c
lib.c
main.c
$
```

The **for** structure without a specified list of values takes as its list of values the command line arguments. The arguments specified on the command line when the shell file is invoked become a list of values referenced by the **for** command. The variable used in the **for** command is set automatically to each argument value in sequence. The first time through the loop, the variable is set to the value of the first argument. The second time, it is set to the value of the second argument.

Filters and Regular Expressions

Filters are commands that read data, perform operations on that data, and then send the results to the standard output. Filters generate different kinds of output, depending on their task. Some filters generate information only about the input, other filters output selected parts of the input, and still other filters output an entire version of the input, but in a modified way. Some filters are limited to one of these, while others have options that specify one or the other. You can think of a filter as operating on a stream of data—receiving data and generating modified output. As data is passed through the filter, it is analyzed, screened, or modified.

The data stream input to a filter consists of a sequence of bytes that can be received from files, devices, or the output of other commands or filters. The filter operates on the data stream, but it does not modify the source of the data. If a filter receives input from a file, the file itself is not modified. Only its data is read and fed into the filter.

The output of a filter is usually sent to the standard output. It can then be redirected to another file or device, or piped as input to another utility or filter. All the features of redirection and pipes apply to filters. Often data is read by one filter and its modified output piped into another filter.

NOTE *Data could easily undergo several modifications as it is passed from one filter to another. However, it is always important to realize the original source of the data is never changed.*

Many utilities and filters use patterns to locate and select specific text in your file. Sometimes, you may need to use patterns in a more flexible and powerful way, searching for several different variations on a given pattern. You can include a set of special characters in your pattern to enable a flexible search. A pattern that contains such special characters is called a *regular expression*. Regular expressions can be used in most filters and utilities that employ pattern searches such as **sed**, **awk**, **grep**, and **egrep**.

TIP *Although many of the special characters used for regular expressions are similar to the shell file expansion characters, they are used in a different way. Shell file expansion characters operate on filenames. Regular expressions search text.*

You can save the output of a filter in a file or send it to a printer. To do so, you need to use redirection or pipes. To save the output of a filter to a file, you redirect it to a file using the redirection operation (**>**). To send output to the printer, you pipe the output to the **lpr** utility, which then prints it. In the next command, the **cat** command pipes its output to the **lpr** command, which then prints it.

```
$ cat complist | lpr
```

All filters accept input from the standard input. In fact, the output of one filter can be piped as the input for another filter. Many filters also accept input directly from files, however. Such filters can take filenames as their arguments and read data directly from those files.

Searching Files: grep

The **grep** and **fgrep** filters search the contents of files for a pattern. They then inform you of what file the pattern was found in and print the lines in which it occurred in each file. Preceding each line is the name of the file in which the line is located. The **grep** command can search for only one pattern, whereas **fgrep** can search for more than one pattern at a time.

The **grep** filter takes two types of arguments. The first argument is the pattern to be searched for; the second argument is a list of filenames, which are the files to be searched. You enter the filenames on the command line after the pattern. You can also use special characters, such as the asterisk, to generate a file list.

```
$ grep pattern filenames-list
```

If you want to include more than one word in the pattern search, you enclose the words within single quotation marks. This is to quote the spaces between the words in the pattern. Otherwise, the shell would interpret the space as a delimiter or argument on the command line, and **grep** would try to interpret words in the pattern as part of the file list. In the next example, **grep** searches for the pattern "text file":

```
$ grep 'text file' preface
A text file in Unix
text files, changing or
```

If you use more than one file in the file list, **grep** will output the name of the file before the matching line. In the next example, two files, **preface** and **intro**, are searched for the pattern "data". Before each occurrence, the filename is output.

```
$ grep data preface intro
preface: data in the file.
intro: new data
```

As mentioned earlier, you can also use shell file expansion characters to generate a list of files to be searched. In the next example, the asterisk file expansion character is used to generate a list of all files in your directory. This is a simple way of searching all of a directory's files for a pattern.

```
$ grep data *
```

The special characters are often useful for searching a selected set of files. For example, if you want to search all your C program source code files for a particular pattern, you can specify the set of source code files with ***.c**. Suppose you have an unintended infinite loop in your program and you need to locate all instances of iterations. The next example searches only those files with a .c extension for the pattern "while" and displays the lines of code that perform iterations:

```
$ grep while *.c
```

Regular Expressions

Regular expressions enable you to match possible variations on a pattern, as well as patterns located at different points in the text. You can search for patterns in your text that have different ending or beginning letters, or you can match text at the beginning or end of a line. The regular expression special characters are the circumflex, dollar sign, asterisk, period, and brackets: ^, $, *, ., [ ]. The circumflex and dollar sign match on the beginning and end of a line. The asterisk matches repeated characters, the period matches single characters, and the brackets match on classes of characters. See Table 8-10 for a listing of the regular expression special characters.

Character	Match	Operation
^	Start of a line	References the beginning of a line.
$	End of a line	References the end of a line.
.	Any character	Matches on any one possible character in a pattern.
*	Repeated characters	Matches on repeated characters in a pattern.
[]	Classes	Matches on classes of characters (a set of characters) in the pattern.

TABLE 8-10   Regular Expression Special Characters

NOTE *Regular expressions are used extensively in many Linux filters and applications to perform searches and matching operations. The Vi and Emacs editors and the* **sed***,* **diff***,* **grep***, and* **gawk** *filters all use regular expressions.*

Suppose you want to use the long-form output of **ls** to display just your directories. One way to do this is to generate a list of all directories in the long form and pipe this list to **grep**, which can then pick out the directory entries. You can do this by using the ^ special character to specify the beginning of a line. Remember, in the long-form output of **ls**, the first character indicates the file type. A **d** represents a directory, an **l** represents a symbolic link, and an **a** represents a regular file. Using the pattern '**^d**', **grep** will match only on those lines beginning with a *d*.

```
$ ls -l | grep '^d'
drwxr-x---  2  chris 512 Feb 10 04:30   reports
drwxr-x---  2  chris 512 Jan 6  01:20   letters
```

CHAPTER 9

Shell Configuration

Four different major shells are commonly used on Linux systems: the Bourne Again shell (BASH), the Public Domain Korn shell (PDKSH), the TCSH shell, and the Z shell. The BASH shell is an advanced version of the Bourne shell, which includes most of the advanced features developed for the Korn shell and the C shell. TCSH is an enhanced version of the C shell, originally developed for BSD versions of Unix. PDKSH is a subset of the Unix Korn shell, whereas the Z shell is an enhanced version of the Korn shell. Although their Unix counterparts differ greatly, the Linux shells share many of the same features. In Unix, the Bourne shell lacks many capabilities found in the other Unix shells. In Linux, however, the BASH shell incorporates all the advanced features of the Korn shell and C shell, as well as the TCSH shell. All four shells are available for your use, though the BASH shell is the default.

So far, all examples in this book have used the BASH shell, which is the default shell for Red Hat Enterprise Linux and Fedora Core. If you are logging into a command line interface, you will be placed in the default shell automatically and given a shell prompt at which to enter your commands. The shell prompt for the BASH shell is a dollar sign ($). In the GUI interface, like GNOME or KDE, you can open a terminal window that will display a command line interface with the prompt for the default shell (BASH). Though you log into your default shell or display

it automatically in a terminal window, you can change to another shell by entering its name. **tcsh** invokes the TCSH shell, **bash** the BASH shell, **ksh** the PDKSH shell, and **zsh** the Z shell. You can leave a shell with the CTRL-D or **exit** command. You only need one type of shell to do your work. This chapter describes common features of the BASH shell, such as aliases, as well as how to configure the shell to your own needs using shell variables and initialization files. The other shells share many of the same features and use similar variables and initialization files.

Though the basic shell features and configurations are shown here, you should consult the respective online manuals and FAQs for each shell for more detailed examples and explanations (see Table 8-1 in Chapter 8).

Aliases

You use the **alias** command to create another name for a command. The **alias** command operates like a macro that expands to the command it represents. The alias does not literally replace the name of the command; it simply gives another name to that command. An

alias command begins with the keyword **alias** and the new name for the command, followed by an equal sign and the command the alias will reference.

NOTE   *No spaces can be around the equal sign used in the* **alias** *command.*

In the next example, **list** becomes another name for the **ls** command:

```
$ alias list=ls
$ ls
mydata today
$ list
mydata today
$
```

Aliasing Commands and Options

You can also use an alias to substitute for a command and its option, but you need to enclose both the command and the option within single quotes. Any command you alias that contains spaces must be enclosed in single quotes. In the next example, the alias **lss** references the **ls** command with its **-s** option, and the alias **lsa** references the **ls** command with the **-F** option. The **ls** command with the **-s** option lists files and their sizes in blocks, and **ls** with the **-F** option places a slash after directory names. Notice how single quotes enclose the command and its option.

```
$ alias lss='ls -s'
$ lss
mydata 14   today  6    reports  1
$ alias lsa='ls -F'
$ lsa
mydata today reports/
$
```

Aliases are helpful for simplifying complex operations. In the next example, **listlong** becomes another name for the **ls** command with the **-l** option (the long format that lists all file information), as well as the **-h** option for using a human-readable format for file sizes. Be sure to encase the command and its arguments within single quotes so that they are taken as one argument and not parsed by the shell.

```
$ alias listlong='ls -lh'
$ listlong
-rw-r--r--   1 root    root    51K  Sep  18  2003 mydata
-rw-r--r--   1 root    root    16K  Sep  27  2003 today
```

Aliasing Commands and Arguments

You may often use an alias to include a command name with an argument. If you execute a command that has an argument with a complex combination of special characters on a regular basis, you may want to alias it. For example, suppose you often list just your source code and object code files—those files ending in either a **.c** or **.o**. You would need to use as an argument for **ls** a combination of special characters such as ***.[co]**. Instead, you could alias **ls** with the **.[co]** argument, giving it a simple name. In the next example, the user creates an alias called **lsc** for the command **ls.[co]**:

```
$ alias lsc='ls *.[co]'
$ lsc
main.c main.o lib.c lib.o
```

Aliasing Commands

You can also use the name of a command as an alias. This can be helpful in cases where you should use a command only with a specific option. In the case of the **rm**, **cp**, and **mv** commands, the **-i** option should always be used to ensure an existing file is not overwritten. Instead of constantly being careful to use the **-i** option each time you use one of these commands, you can alias the command name to include the option. In the next example, the **rm**, **cp**, and **mv** commands have been aliased to include the **-i** option:

```
$ alias rm='rm -i'
$ alias mv='mv -i'
$ alias cp='cp -i'
```

The **alias** command by itself provides a list of all aliases that have been defined, showing the commands they represent. You can remove an alias by using the **unalias** command. In the next example, the user lists the current aliases and then removes the **lsa** alias:

```
$ alias
lsa=ls -F
list=ls
rm=rm -i
$ unalias lsa
```

Controlling Shell Operations

The BASH shell has several features that enable you to control the way different shell operations work. For example, setting the **noclobber** feature prevents redirection from overwriting files. You can turn these features on and off like a toggle, using the **set** command. The **set** command takes two arguments: an option specifying on or off and the name of the feature. To set a feature on, you use the **-o** option, and to set it off, you use the **+o** option. Here is the basic form:

```
$ set -o feature      turn the feature on
$ set +o feature      turn the feature off
```

Three of the most common features are **ignoreeof**, **noclobber**, and **noglob**. Table 9-1 lists these different features, as well as the **set** command. Setting **ignoreeof** enables a feature that prevents you from logging out of the user shell with CTRL-D. CTRL-D is not only used to log out of the user shell, but also to end user input entered directly into the standard input. CTRL-D is used often for the Mail program or for utilities such as **cat**. You could easily enter an extra CTRL-D in such circumstances and accidentally log yourself out. The **ignoreeof** feature prevents such accidental logouts. In the next example, the **ignoreeof** feature is

TABLE **9-1** BASH Shell Special Features	Feature	Description
	`$ set -+o` *feature*	BASH shell features are turned on and off with the **set** command; **-o** sets a feature on and **+o** turns it off: `$ set -o noclobber` *set noclobber on* `$ set +o noclobber` *set noclobber off*
	`ignoreeof`	Disables ctrl-d logout
	`noclobber`	Does not overwrite files through redirection
	`noglob`	Disables special characters used for filename expansion: *****, **?**, **~**, and `[ ]`

turned on using the **set** command with the **-o** option. The user can now log out only by entering the **logout** command.

```
$ set -o ignoreeof
$ CTRL-D
Use exit to logout
$
```

Environment Variables and Subshells: export

When you log in to your account, Linux generates your user shell. Within this shell, you can issue commands and declare variables. You can also create and execute shell scripts. When you execute a shell script, however, the system generates a subshell. You then have two shells, the one you logged in to and the one generated for the script. Within the script shell, you could execute another shell script, which would have its own shell. When a script has finished execution, its shell terminates and you return to the shell from which it was executed. In this sense, you can have many shells, each nested within the other. Variables you define within a shell are local to it. If you define a variable in a shell script, then, when the script is run, the variable is defined with that script's shell and is local to it. No other shell can reference that variable. In a sense, the variable is hidden within its shell.

You can define environment variables in all types of shells, including the BASH shell, the Z shell, and the TCSH shell. The strategy used to implement environment variables in the BASH shell, however, is different from that of the TCSH shell. In the BASH shell, environment variables are exported. That is to say, a copy of an environment variable is made in each subshell. For example, if the **EDITOR** variable is exported, a copy is automatically defined in each subshell for you. In the TCSH shell, on the other hand, an environment variable is defined only once and can be directly referenced by any subshell.

In the BASH shell, an environment variable can be thought of as a regular variable with added capabilities. To make an environment variable, you apply the **export** command to a variable you have already defined. The **export** command instructs the system to define a copy of that variable for each new shell generated. Each new shell will have its own copy of the environment variable. This process is called *exporting variables.* To think of exported environment variables as global variables is a mistake. A new shell can never reference a variable outside of itself. Instead, a copy of the variable with its value is generated for the new shell.

NOTE *You can think of exported variables as exporting their values to a shell, not to themselves. If you are familiar with programming structures, think of exported variables as a form of "call by value."*

Configuring Your Shell with Shell Parameters

When you log in to your account, the system generates a shell for you. This shell is referred to as either your login shell or your user shell. When you execute scripts, you are generating subshells of your user shell. You can define variables within your user shell, and you can also define environment variables that can be referenced by any subshells you generate.

When you log in, Linux will set certain parameters for your login shell. These parameters can take the form of variables or features. See the earlier section "Controlling Shell Operations" for a description of how to set features. Linux reserves a predefined set of variables for shell and system use. These are assigned system values, in effect, setting parameters. Linux sets up parameter shell variables you can use to configure your user shell. Many of these parameter shell variables are defined by the system when you log in. Some parameter shell variables are set by the shell automatically, and others are set by initialization scripts, described later. Certain shell variables are set directly by the shell, and others are simply used by it. Many of these other variables are application specific, used for such tasks as mail, history, or editing. Functionally, it may be better to think of these as system-level variables, as they are used to configure your entire system, setting values such as the location of executable commands on your system, or the number of history commands allowable. See Table 9-2 for a list of those shell variables set by the shell for shell-specific tasks; Table 9-3 lists those used by the shell for supporting other applications.

A reserved set of keywords is used for the names of these system variables. You should not use these keywords as the names of any of your own variable names. The system shell variables are all specified in uppercase letters, making them easy to identify. Shell feature variables are in lowercase letters. For example, the keyword **HOME** is used by the system to define the **HOME** variable. **HOME** is a special environment variable that holds the pathname of the user's home directory. On the other hand, the keyword **noclobber** is used to set the **noclobber** feature on or off.

TABLE 9-2 Shell Variables, Set by the Shell

Shell Variable	Description
BASH	Holds full pathname of BASH command
BASH_VERSION	Displays the current BASH version number
GROUPS	Groups that the user belongs to
HISTCMD	Number of the current command in the history list
HOME	Pathname for user's home directory
HOSTNAME	The hostname
HOSTTYPE	Displays the type of machine the host runs on
OLDPWD	Previous working directory
OSTYPE	Operating system in use
PATH	List of pathnames for directories searched for executable commands
PPID	Process ID for shell's parent shell
PWD	User's working directory
RANDOM	Generates random number when referenced
SHLVL	Current shell level, number of shells invoked
UID	User ID of the current user

Shell Variable	Description
BASH_VERSION	Displays the current BASH version number
CDPATH	Search path for the **cd** command
EXINIT	Initialization commands for Ex/Vi editor
FCEDIT	Editor used by the history **fc** command
GROUPS	Groups that the user belongs to
HISTFILE	The pathname of the history file
HISTSIZE	Number of commands allowed for history
HISTFILESIZE	Size of the history file in lines
HISTCMD	Number of the current command in the history list
HOME	Pathname for user's home directory
HOSTFILE	Sets the name of the hosts file, if other than **/etc/hosts**
IFS	Interfield delimiter symbol
IGNOREEOF	If not set, EOF character will close the shell. Can be set to the number of EOF characters to ignore before accepting one to close the shell (default is 10)
INPUTRC	Sets the **inputrc** configuration file for Readline (command line). Default is current directory, **.inputrc**. Fedora Core sets this to **/etc/inputrc**
KDEDIR	The pathname location for the KDE desktop
LOGNAME	Login name
MAIL	Name of specific mail file checked by Mail utility for received messages, if MAILPATH is not set
MAILCHECK	Interval for checking for received mail
MAILPATH	List of mail files to be checked by Mail for received messages
PROMPT_COMMAND	Command to be executed before each prompt, integrating the result as part of the prompt
HISTFILE	The pathname of the history file
PS1	Primary shell prompt
PS2	Secondary shell prompt
QTDIR	Location of the Qt library (used for KDE)
SHELL	Pathname of program for type of shell you are using
TERM	Terminal type
TMOUT	Time that the shell remains active awaiting input
USER	User name

TABLE 9-3 System Environment Variables Used by the Shell

Shell Parameter Variables

Many of the shell parameter variables automatically defined and assigned initial values by the system when you log in can be changed, if you wish. Some parameter variables exist whose values should not be changed, however. For example, the **HOME** variable holds the pathname for your home directory. Commands such as **cd** reference the pathname in the **HOME** shell variable to locate your home directory. Some of the more common of these parameter variables are described in this section. Other parameter variables are defined by the system and given an initial value that you are free to change. To do this, you redefine them and assign a new value. For example, the **PATH** variable is defined by the system and given an initial value; it contains the pathnames of directories where commands are located. Whenever you execute a command, the shell searches for it in these directories. You can add a new directory to be searched by redefining the **PATH** variable yourself, so that it will include the new directory's pathname. Still other parameter variables exist that the system does not define. These are usually optional features, such as the **EXINIT** variable that enables you to set options for the Vi editor. Each time you log in, you must define and assign a value to such variables. Some of the more common parameter variables are **SHELL**, **PATH**, **PS1**, **PS2**, and **MAIL**. The **SHELL** variable holds the pathname of the program for the type of shell you log in to. The **PATH** variable lists the different directories to be searched for a Linux command. The **PS1** and **PS2** variables hold the prompt symbols. The **MAIL** variable holds the pathname of your mailbox file. You can modify the values for any of them to customize your shell.

NOTE *You can obtain a listing of the currently defined shell variables using the* **env** *command. The* **env** *command operates like the* **set** *command, but it lists only parameter variables.*

Using Initialization Files

You can automatically define parameter variables using special shell scripts called initialization files. An *initialization file* is a specially named shell script executed whenever you enter a certain shell. You can edit the initialization file and place in it definitions and assignments for parameter variables. When you enter the shell, the initialization file will execute these definitions and assignments, effectively initializing parameter variables with your own values. For example, the BASH shell's **.bash_profile** file is an initialization file executed every time you log in. It contains definitions and assignments of parameter variables. However, the **.bash_profile** file is basically only a shell script, which you can edit with any text editor such as the Vi editor; changing, if you wish, the values assigned to parameter variables.

In the BASH shell, all the parameter variables are designed to be environment variables. When you define or redefine a parameter variable, you also need to export it to make it an environment variable. This means any change you make to a parameter variable must be accompanied by an **export** command. You will see that at the end of the login initialization file, **.bash_profile**, there is usually an **export** command for all the parameter variables defined in it.

Your Home Directory: HOME

The **HOME** variable contains the pathname of your home directory. Your home directory is determined by the parameter administrator when your account is created. The pathname for your home directory is automatically read into your **HOME** variable when you log in. In the next example, the **echo** command displays the contents of the **HOME** variable:

```
$ echo $HOME
/home/chris
```

The **HOME** variable is often used when you need to specify the absolute pathname of your home directory. In the next example, the absolute pathname of **reports** is specified using **HOME** for the home directory's path:

```
$ ls $HOME/reports
```

Command Locations: PATH

The **PATH** variable contains a series of directory paths separated by colons. Each time a command is executed, the paths listed in the **PATH** variable are searched one by one for that command. For example, the **cp** command resides on the system in the directory **/usr/bin**. This directory path is one of the directories listed in the **PATH** variable. Each time you execute the **cp** command, this path is searched and the **cp** command located. The system defines and assigns **PATH** an initial set of pathnames. In Linux, the initial pathnames are **/usr/bin** and **usr/sbin**.

The shell can execute any executable file, including programs and scripts you have created. For this reason, the **PATH** variable can also reference your working directory; so if you want to execute one of your own scripts or programs in your working directory, the shell can locate it. No spaces are allowed between the pathnames in the string. A colon with no pathname specified references your working directory. Usually, a single colon is placed at the end of the pathnames as an empty entry specifying your working directory. For example, the pathname **/usr/bin:/usr/sbin:** references three directories: **/usr/bin**, **/usr/sbin**, and your current working directory.

```
$ echo $PATH
/usr/bin:/usr/sbin:
```

You can add any new directory path you want to the **PATH** variable. This can be useful if you have created several of your own Linux commands using shell scripts. You could place these new shell script commands in a directory you created and then add that directory to the **PATH** list. Then, no matter what directory you are in, you can execute one of your shell scripts. The **PATH** variable will contain the directory for that script, so that directory will be searched each time you issue a command.

You add a directory to the **PATH** variable with a variable assignment. You can execute this assignment directly in your shell. In the next example, the user **chris** adds a new directory, called **mybin,** to the **PATH**. Although you could carefully type in the complete pathnames listed in **PATH** for the assignment, you can also use an evaluation of **PATH**—**$PATH**—in their place. In this example, an evaluation of **HOME** is also used to designate the user's **home** directory in the new directory's pathname. Notice the empty entry between two colons, which specifies the working directory:

```
$ PATH=$PATH:$HOME/mybin:
$ export PATH
$ echo $PATH
/usr/bin:/usr/sbin::/home/chris/mybin
```

If you add a directory to **PATH** yourself while you are logged in, the directory would be added only for the duration of your login session. When you log back in, the login initialization file, **.bash_profile**, would again initialize your **PATH** with its original set of directories. The **.bash_profile** file is described in detail a bit later in this chapter. To add a new directory to your **PATH** permanently, you need to edit your **.bash_profile** file and find the assignment for the **PATH** variable. Then, you simply insert the directory, preceded by a colon, into the set of pathnames assigned to **PATH**.

Specifying the BASH Environment: BASH_ENV

The **BASH_ENV** variable holds the name of the BASH shell initialization file to be executed whenever a BASH shell is generated. For example, when a BASH shell script is executed, the **BASH_ENV** variable is checked and the name of the script that it holds is executed before the shell script. The **BASH_ENV** variable usually holds **$HOME/.bashrc**. This is the **.bashrc** file in the user's home directory. (The **.bashrc** file is discussed later in this chapter.) You could specify a different file if you wish, using that instead of the **.bashrc** file for BASH shell scripts.

Configuring the Shell Prompt

The **PS1** and **PS2** variables contain the primary and secondary prompt symbols, respectively. The primary prompt symbol for the BASH shell is a dollar sign (**$**). You can change the prompt symbol by assigning a new set of characters to the **PS1** variable. In the next example, the shell prompt is changed to the **->** symbol:

```
$ PS1= '->'
-> export PS1
->
```

You can change the prompt to be any set of characters, including a string, as shown in the next example:

```
$ PS1="Please enter a command: "
Please enter a command: export PS1
Please enter a command: ls
mydata /reports
Please enter a command:
```

The **PS2** variable holds the secondary prompt symbol, which is used for commands that take several lines to complete. The default secondary prompt is **>**. The added command lines begin with the secondary prompt instead of the primary prompt. You can change the secondary prompt just as easily as the primary prompt, as shown here:

```
$ PS2="@"
```

Like the TCSH shell, the BASH shell provides you with a predefined set of codes you can use to configure your prompt. With them you can make the time, your username, or your directory pathname a part of your prompt. You can even have your prompt display the history event number of the current command you are about to enter. Each code is preceded by a \ symbol: **\w** represents the current working directory, **\t** the time, and **\u** your username; **\!** will display the next history event number. In the next example, the user adds the current working directory to the prompt:

```
$ PS1="\w $"
/home/dylan $
```

The codes must be included within a quoted string. If no quotes exist, the code characters are not evaluated and are themselves used as the prompt. **PS1=\w** sets the prompt to the characters **\w**, not the working directory. The next example incorporates both the time and the history event number with a new prompt:

```
$ PS1="\t \! ->"
```

The following table lists the codes for configuring your prompt:

Prompt Code	Description
\!	Current history number
\$	Use $ as prompt for all users except the root user, which has the # as its prompt
\d	Current date
\#	History command number for just the current shell
\h	Hostname
\s	Shell type currently active
\t	Time of day
\u	Username
\v	Shell version
\w	Full pathname of the current working directory
\W	Name of the current working directory
\[\]	Allows entry of terminal display characters
\nnn	Character specified in octal format

The default BASH prompt is **\s-\v\$** to display the type of shell, the shell version, and the $ symbol as the prompt. Fedora Core and Red Hat Enterprise Linux have changed this to a more complex command consisting of the user, the hostname, and the name of the current working directory. The actual operation is carried out in the **/etc/bashrc** file discussed in the later section "The System /etc/bashrc BASH Script and the /etc/profile.d Directory." A sample configuration is shown here. The **/etc/bashrc** file uses USER, HOSTNAME, and PWD environment variables to set these values. A simple equivalent is show here with an @ sign in the hostname, and a $ for the final prompt symbol. The home directory is represented with a tilde (~).

```
$ PS1="\u@\h:\w$"
richard@turtle.com:~$
```

Specifying Your News Server

Several shell parameter variables are used to set values used by network applications, such as Web browsers or newsreaders. **NNTPSERVER** is used to set the value of a remote news server accessible on your network. If you are using an ISP, the ISP usually provides a news server you can access with your newsreader applications. However, you first have to provide your newsreaders with the Internet address of the news server. This is the role of the **NNTPSERVER** variable. News servers on the Internet usually use the NNTP protocol. **NNTPSERVER** should hold the address of such a news server. For many ISPs, the news server address is a domain name that begins with **nntp**. The following example assigns the news server address **nntp.myservice.com** to the **NNTPSERVER** shell variable. Newsreader applications automatically obtain the news server address from **NNTPSERVER**. Usually, this assignment is placed in the shell initialization file, **.bash_profile**, so that it is automatically set each time a user logs in.

```
NNTPSERVER=nntp.myservice.com
export NNTPSERVER
```

Configuring Your Login Shell: .bash_profile

The **.bash_profile** file is the BASH shell's login initialization file, which can also be named **.profile** (as in SuSE Linux). It is a script file that is automatically executed whenever a user logs in. The file contains shell commands that define system environment variables used to manage your shell. They may be either redefinitions of system-defined variables or definitions of user-defined variables. For example, when you log in, your user shell needs to know what directories hold Linux commands. It will reference the **PATH** variable to find the pathnames for these directories. However, first, the **PATH** variable must be assigned those pathnames. In the **.bash_profile** file, an assignment operation does just this. Because it is in the **.bash_profile** file, the assignment is executed automatically when the user logs in.

Exporting Variables

Parameter variables also need to be exported, using the **export** command, to make them accessible to any subshells you may enter. You can export several variables in one **export** command by listing them as arguments. Usually, the **.bash_profile** file ends with an **export** command with a list of all the variables defined in the file. If a variable is missing from this list, you may be unable to access it. Notice the **export** command at the end of the **.profile** file in the example described next. You can also combine the assignment and **export** command into one operation as shown here for **NNTPSERVER**:

```
export NNTPSERVER=nntp.myservice.com
```

Variable Assignments

A copy of the standard **.bash_profile** file provided for you when your account is created is listed in the next example. Notice how **PATH** is assigned, as is the value of **$HOME**. Both **PATH** and **HOME** are parameter variables the system has already defined. **PATH** holds the pathnames of directories searched for any command you enter, and **HOME** holds the pathname of your home directory. The assignment **PATH=$PATH:$HOME/bin** has the effect of redefining **PATH** to include your **bin** directory within your home directory so that your **bin** directory will also be searched for any commands, including ones you create yourself, such as scripts or programs. Notice **PATH** is then exported, so that it can be accessed by any subshells. Should you want to have your home directory searched also, you can use any text editor to modify this line in your **.bash_profile** file to **PATH=$PATH:$HOME/bin:$HOME**, adding **:$HOME** at the end. In fact, you can change this entry to add as many directories as you want searched.

.bash_profile
```
# .bash_profile

# Get the aliases and functions
if [ -f ~/.bashrc ]; then
      . ~/.bashrc
fi
```

```
# User specific environment and startup programs
PATH=$PATH:$HOME/bin
 unset USERNAME
export  PATH
```

Editing Your BASH Profile Script

Your **.bash_profile** initialization file is a text file that can be edited by a text editor, like any other text file. You can easily add new directories to your **PATH** by editing **.bash_profile** and using editing commands to insert a new directory pathname in the list of directory pathnames assigned to the **PATH** variable. You can even add new variable definitions. If you do so, however, be sure to include the new variable's name in the **export** command's argument list. For example, if your **.bash_profile** file does not have any definition of the **EXINIT** variable, you can edit the file and add a new line that assigns a value to **EXINIT**. The definition **EXINIT='set nu ai'** will configure the Vi editor with line numbering and indentation. You then need to add **EXINIT** to the **export** command's argument list. When the **.bash_profile** file executes again, the **EXINIT** variable will be set to the command **set nu ai**. When the Vi editor is invoked, the command in the **EXINIT** variable will be executed, setting the line number and auto-indent options automatically.

In the following example, the user's **.bash_profile** has been modified to include definitions of **EXINIT** and redefinitions of **PATH**, **PS1**, and **HISTSIZE**. The **PATH** variable has **$HOME**: added to its value. **$HOME** is a variable that evaluates to the user's home directory, and the ending colon specifies the current working directory, enabling you to execute commands that may be located in either the home directory or the working directory. The redefinition of **HISTSIZE** reduces the number of history events saved, from 1,000 defined in the system's **.profile** file, to 30. The redefinition of the **PS1** parameter variable changes the prompt to include the pathname of the current working directory. Any changes you make to parameter variables within your **.bash_profile** file override those made earlier by the system's **.profile** file. All these parameter variables are then exported with the **export** command.

.bash_profile
```
# .bash_profile
# Get the aliases and functions
if [ -f ~/.bashrc ];
  then
     . ~/.bashrc
fi
# User-specific environment and startup programs
PATH=$PATH:$HOME/bin:$HOME:
 unset USERNAME
HISTSIZE=30
NNTPSERVER=nntp.myserver.com
EXINIT='set nu ai'
PS1="\w \$"
export PATH HISTSIZE EXINIT PS1 NNTPSERVER
```

Manually Reexecuting the .bash_profile Script

Although **.bash_profile** is executed each time you log in, it is not automatically reexecuted after you make changes to it. The **.bash_profile** file is an initialization file that is executed *only* whenever you log in. If you want to take advantage of any changes you make to it without having to log out and log in again, you can reexecute **.bash_profile** with the dot (**.**)

command. The **.bash_profile** file is a shell script and, like any shell script, can be executed with the . command.

```
$ . .bash_profile
```

Alternatively, you can use the **source** command to execute the **.bash_profile** initialization file, or any initialization file such as **.login** used in the TCSH shell, or **.bashrc**.

```
$ source .bash_profile
```

System Shell Profile Script

Your Linux system also has its own profile file that it executes whenever any user logs in. This system initialization file is simply called **profile** and is found in the /etc directory, /etc/ **profile**. This file contains parameter variable definitions the system needs to provide for each user. A copy of the system's **.profile** file follows. Fedora Core uses a **pathmunge** function to generate a directory list for the **PATH** variable. Normal user paths will lack the system directories (those with sbin in the path) but include the name of their home directory, along with **/usr/kerberos/bin** for Kerberos tools. The path generated for the root user will include both system and user application directories, adding **/usr/kerberos/sbin**, **/sbin**, **/usr/sbin**, and **/usr/local/sbin**, as well as the root user local application directory, **/root/bin**.

```
# echo $PATH
/usr/kerberos/bin/usr/local/bin:usr/sbin:/bin:/usr/X11R6/bin:/home/richard/bin
```

HISTFILE is also redefined to include a larger number of history events. An entry has been added here for the **NNTPSERVER** variable. Normally, a news server address is a value that needs to be set for all users. Such assignments should be made in the system's **/etc/profile** file by the system administrator, rather than in each individual user's own **.bash_profile** file.

NOTE   *The /etc/profile file also executes any scripts in the directory /etc/profile.d. This design allows for a more modular structure. Rather than make entries by editing the /etc/profile file, you can just add a script to the **profile.d** directory.*

The **/etc/profile** file also runs the **/etc/inputrc** file, which configures your command line editor. Here you will find key assignments for different tasks, such as moving to the end of a line or deleting characters. Global options are set as well. Keys are represented in hexadecimal format.

The number of aliases and variable settings needed for different applications would make the **/etc/profile** file much too large to manage. Instead, application- and task-specific aliases and variables are placed in separate configuration files located in the **/etc/profile.d** directory. There are corresponding scripts for both the BASH and C shells. The BASH shell scripts are run by **/etc/profile**. The scripts are named for the kinds of tasks and applications they configure. For example, **colorls.sh** sets the file type color coding when the **ls** command displays files and directories. The **vim.sh** file sets the alias for the **vi** command, executing **vim** whenever the user enters just **vi**. The **kde.sh** file sets the global environment variable **KDEDIR**, specifying the KDE Desktop applications directory, in this case **/usr**. The

krb5.sh file adds the pathnames for Kerberos, **/usr/kerberos**, to the **PATH** variable. Files run by the BASH shell end in the extension **.sh**, and those run by the C shell have the extension **.csh**.

/etc/profile

```
# /etc/profile
# System wide environment and startup programs, for login setup
# Functions and aliases go in /etc/bashrc
pathmunge () {
      if ! echo $PATH | /bin/egrep -q "(^|:)$1($|:)" ; then
       if ["$2" = "after" ] ; then
          PATH=$PATH:$1
       else
          PATH=$1:$PATH
       fi
      fi
}

# Path manipulation
if [ `id -u` = 0 ]; then
      pathmunge /sbin
      pathmunge /usr/sbin
      pathmunge /usr/local/sbin
fi

pathmunge /usr/X11R6/bin after
unset pathmunge
# No core files by default
ulimit -S -c 0 > /dev/null 2>&1

USER="`id -un`"
LOGNAME=$USER
MAIL="/var/spool/mail/$USER"
HOSTNAME=`/bin/hostname`
HISTSIZE=1000
NNTPSERVER=nntp.myservice.com

if [ -z "$INPUTRC" -a ! -f "$HOME/.inputrc" ]; then
      INPUTRC=/etc/inputrc
fi

export PATH USER LOGNAME MAIL HOSTNAME HISTSIZE INPUTRC
export NNTPSERVER

for i in /etc/profile.d/*.sh ; do
   if [ -r "$i" ]; then
      . $i
   fi
done
unset i
unset pathmunge
```

Configuring the BASH Shell: .bashrc

The **.bashrc** file is a configuration file executed each time you enter the BASH shell or generate any subshells. If the BASH shell is your login shell, **.bashrc** is executed along with your **.bash_login** file when you log in. If you enter the BASH shell from another shell, the **.bashrc** file is automatically executed, and the variable and alias definitions it contains will be defined. If you enter a different type of shell, the configuration file for that shell will be executed instead. For example, if you were to enter the TCSH shell with the **tcsh** command, the **.tcshrc** configuration file would be executed instead of **.bashrc**.

The User .bashrc BASH Script

The **.bashrc** shell configuration file is actually executed each time you generate a BASH shell, such as when you run a shell script. In other words, each time a subshell is created, the **.bashrc** file is executed. This has the effect of exporting any local variables or aliases you have defined in the **.bashrc** shell initialization file. The **.bashrc** file usually contains the definition of aliases and any feature variables used to turn on shell features. Aliases and feature variables are locally defined within the shell. But the **.bashrc** file defines them in every shell. For this reason, the **.bashrc** file usually holds aliases and options you would want defined for each shell. In this example, the standard **.bashrc** installed by Fedora Core for users would included only the execution of the system **/etc/bashrc** file. As an example of how you can add your own aliases and options, aliases for the **rm**, **cp**, and **mv** commands and the shell **noclobber** and **ignoreeof** options have been added. For the root user **.bashrc**, the **rm**, **cp**, and **mv** aliases have already been set.

.bashrc
```
# Source global definitions
if [ -f /etc/bashrc ];
 then
    . /etc/bashrc
fi
set  -o ignoreeof
set  -o noclobber
alias rm='rm -i'
alias mv='mv -i'
alias cp='cp -i'
```

You can add any commands or definitions of your own to your **.bashrc** file. If you have made changes to **.bashrc** and you want them to take effect during your current login session, you need to reexecute the file with either the **.** or the **source** command.

```
$ . .bashrc
```

The System /etc/bashrc BASH Script and the /etc/profile.d Directory

Linux systems usually contain a system **bashrc** file executed for all users. The file contains certain global aliases and features needed by all users whenever they enter a BASH shell. This is located in the **/etc** directory, **/etc/bashrc**. A user's own **.bashrc** file, located in the home directory, contains commands to execute this system **bashrc** file. The **. /etc/bashrc** command in the previous example of **.bashrc** does just that. Currently the **/etc/bashrc** file sets the default shell prompt, one for a terminal window and another for a screen interface. Several other specialized aliases and variables are then set using configuration files located in the **/etc/profile.d** directory. These scripts are executed by **/etc/bashrc** if the shell is not the user login shell.

The BASH Shell Logout File: .bash_logout

The **.bash_logout** file is also a configuration file, but it is executed when the user logs out. It is designed to perform any operations you want done whenever you log out. Instead of variable definitions, the **.bash_logout** file usually contains shell commands that form a kind of shutdown procedure—actions you always want taken before you log out. One common logout command is to clear the screen and then issue a farewell message.

As with **.bash_profile**, you can add your own shell commands to **.bash_logout**. In fact, the **.bash_logout** file is not automatically set up for you when your account is first created. You need to create it yourself, using the Vi or Emacs editor. You could then add a farewell message or other operations. In the next example, the user has a **clear** command and an **echo** command in the **.bash_logout** file. When the user logs out, the **clear** command clears the screen, and then the **echo** command displays the message "Good-bye for now."

.bash_logout
```
# ~/.bash_logout
clear
echo "Good-bye for now"
```

Initialization and Configuration Files

Each type of shell has its own set of initialization and configuration files. The BASH shell configuration files were discussed previously. The TCSH shell uses **.login**, **.tcshrc**, and **.logout** files in place of **.bash_profile**, **.bashrc**, and **.bash_logout**. The Z shell has several initialization files: **.zshenv**, **.zlogin**, **.zprofile**, **.zschrc**, and **.zlogout**. See Table 9-4 for a listing. Check the Man pages for each shell to see how they are usually configured. When you install a shell, default versions of these files are automatically placed in the users' home directories. Except for the TCSH shell, all shells use much the same syntax for variable definitions and assigning values (TCSH uses a slightly different syntax, described in its Man pages).

Configuration Directories and Files

Applications often install configuration files in a user's home directory that contain specific configuration information, which tailors the application to the needs of that particular user. This may take the form of a single configuration file that begins with a period, or a directory that contains several configuration files. The directory name will also begin with a period. For example, Mozilla installs a directory called **.mozilla** in the user's home directory that contains configuration files. On the other hand, many mail application uses a single file called **.mailrc** to hold alias and feature settings set up by the user, though others like Evolution also have their own, **.evolution**. Most single configuration files end in the letters **rc**. **FTP** uses a file called **.netrc**. Most newsreaders use a file called **.newsrc**. Entries in configuration files

TABLE **9-4** Shell
Configuration Files

BASH Shell	Function
.bash_profile	Login initialization file
.bashrc	BASH shell configuration file
.bash_logout	Logout name
.bash_history	History file
/etc/profile	System login initialization file
/etc/bashrc	System BASH shell configuration file
/etc/profile.d	Directory for specialized BASH shell configuration files
TCSH Shell	**Function**
.login	Login initialization file
.tcshrc	TCSH shell configuration file
.logout	Logout file
Z Shell	**Function**
.zshenv	Shell login file (first read)
.zprofile	Login initialization file
.zlogin	Shell login file
.zshrc	Z shell configuration file
.zlogout	Logout file
PDKSH Shell	**Function**
.profile	Login initialization file
.kshrc	PDKSH shell configuration file

are usually set by the application, though you can usually make entries directly by editing the file. Applications have their own set of special variables to which you can define and assign values. You can list the configuration files in your home directory with the `ls -a` command.

Managing Linux Files and Directories: Directories, Archives, and Compression

In Linux, all files are organized into directories that, in turn, are hierarchically connected to each other in one overall file structure. A file is referenced not just according to its name, but also according to its place in this file structure. You can create as many new directories as you want, adding more directories to the file structure. The Linux file commands can perform sophisticated operations, such as moving or copying whole directories along with their subdirectories. You can use file operations such as **find**, **cp**, **mv**, and **ln** to locate files and copy, move, or link them from one directory to another. Desktop file managers, such as Konqueror and Nautilus used on the KDE and GNOME desktops, provide a graphical user interface to perform the same operations using icons, windows, and menus (see Chapters 6 and 7). This chapter will focus on the commands you use in the shell command line to manage files, such as **cp** and **mv**. However, whether you use the command line or a GUI file manager, the underlying file structure is the same.

The organization of the Linux file structure into its various system and network administration directories is discussed in detail in Chapter 32. Though not part of the Linux file structure, there are also special tools you can use to access Windows partitions and floppy disks. These follow much the same format as Linux file commands.

Archives are used to back up files or to combine them into a package, which can then be transferred as one file over the Internet or posted on an FTP site for easy downloading. The standard archive utility used on Linux and Unix systems is tar, for which several GUI front ends exist. You have several compression programs to choose from, including GNU zip (gzip), Zip, bzip, and compress.

NOTE *Linux also allows you to mount and access file systems used by other operating systems such as Unix or Windows. Linux itself supports a variety of different file systems such as ext2, ext3, and ReiserFS. File systems are discussed in Chapter 32. Access to remote file systems is discussed in Chapter 40.*

Linux Files

You can name a file using any letters, underscores, and numbers. You can also include periods and commas. Except in certain special cases, you should never begin a filename with a period. Other characters, such as slashes, question marks, or asterisks, are reserved for use as special characters by the system and should not be part of a filename. Filenames can be as long as 256 characters. Filenames can also include spaces, though to reference such filenames from the command line, be sure to encase them in quotes. On a desktop like GNOME or KDE you do not need quotes.

You can include an extension as part of a filename. A period is used to distinguish the filename proper from the extension. Extensions can be useful for categorizing your files. You are probably familiar with certain standard extensions that have been adopted by convention. For example, C source code files always have an extension of **.c**. Files that contain compiled object code have a **.o** extension. You can, of course, make up your own file extensions. The following examples are all valid Linux filenames. Keep in mind that to reference the last of these names on the command line, you would have to encase it in quotes as "New book review":

```
preface
chapter2
9700info
New_Revisions
calc.c
intro.bk1
New book review
```

Special initialization files are also used to hold shell configuration commands. These are the hidden, or dot, files, which begin with a period. Dot files used by commands and applications have predetermined names, such as the **.mozilla** directory used to hold your Mozilla data and configuration files. Recall that when you use **ls** to display your filenames, the dot files will not be displayed. To include the dot files, you need to use **ls** with the **-a** option. Dot files are discussed in more detail in the chapter on shell configuration, Chapter 9.

As shown in Figure 10-1, the **ls -l** command displays detailed information about a file. First the permissions are displayed, followed by the number of links, the owner of the file, the name of the group the user belongs to, the file size in bytes, the date and time the file was last modified, and the name of the file. Permissions indicate who can access the file: the user, members of a group, or all other users. Permissions are discussed in detail later in this chapter. The group name indicates the group permitted to access the file object. In Figure 10-1, the file type for **mydata** is that of an ordinary file. Only one link exists, indicating the file has no other names and no other links. The owner's name is **chris**, the same as the login name, and the group name is **weather**. Other users probably also belong to the **weather** group. The size of the file is 207 bytes and it was last modified on February 20, at 11:55 A.M. The name of the file is **mydata**.

If you want to display this detailed information for all the files in a directory, simply use the **ls -l** command without an argument.

```
$ ls -l
-rw-r--r-- 1 chris weather 207 Feb 20 11:55 mydata
-rw-rw-r-- 1 chris weather 568 Feb 14 10:30 today
-rw-rw-r-- 1 chris weather 308 Feb 17 12:40 monday
```

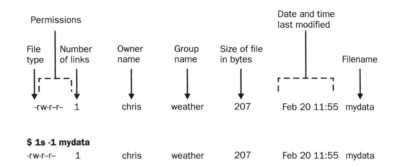

FIGURE **10-1**
File information displayed using the **-1** option for the **ls** command

All files in Linux have one physical format—a byte stream. A *byte stream* is just a sequence of bytes. This allows Linux to apply the file concept to every data component in the system. Directories are classified as files, as are devices. Treating everything as a file allows Linux to organize and exchange data more easily. The data in a file can be sent directly to a device such as a screen because a device interfaces with the system using the same byte-stream file format as regular files.

This same file format is used to implement other operating system components. The interface to a device, such as the screen or keyboard, is designated as a file. Other components, such as directories, are themselves byte-stream files, but they have a special internal organization. A directory file contains information about a directory, organized in a special directory format. Because these different components are treated as files, they can be said to constitute different *file types.* A character device is one file type. A directory is another file type. The number of these file types may vary according to your specific implementation of Linux. Five common types of files exist, however: ordinary files, directory files, first-in first-out pipes, character device files, and block device files. Although you may rarely reference a file's type, it can be useful when searching for directories or devices. Later in the chapter, you will see how to use the file type in a search criterion with the **find** command to search specifically for directory or device names.

Although all ordinary files have a byte-stream format, they may be used in different ways. The most significant difference is between binary and text files. Compiled programs are examples of binary files. However, even text files can be classified according to their different uses. You can have files that contain C programming source code or shell commands, or even a file that is empty. The file could be an executable program or a directory file. The Linux **file** command helps you determine what a file is used for. It examines the first few lines of a file and tries to determine a classification for it. The **file** command looks for special keywords or special numbers in those first few lines, but it is not always accurate. In the next example, the **file** command examines the contents of two files and determines a classification for them:

```
$ file monday reports
monday: text
reports: directory
```

If you need to examine the entire file byte by byte, you can do so with the **od** (octal dump) command. The **od** command performs a dump of a file. By default, it prints every byte in its octal representation. However, you can also specify a character, decimal, or hexadecimal representation. The **od** command is helpful when you need to detect any special character in your file or if you want to display a binary file.

The File Structure

Linux organizes files into a hierarchically connected set of directories. Each directory may contain either files or other directories. In this respect, directories perform two important functions. A *directory* holds files, much like files held in a file drawer, and a directory connects to other directories, much as a branch in a tree is connected to other branches. With respect to files, directories appear to operate like file drawers, with each drawer holding several files. To access files, you open a file drawer. Unlike file drawers, however, directories can contain not only files, but other directories as well. In this way, a directory can connect to another directory.

Because of the similarities to a tree, such a structure is often referred to as a *tree structure.* This structure could more accurately be thought of as an upside-down bush rather than a tree, however, because no trunk exists. The tree is represented upside down, with the root at the top. Extending down from the root are the branches. Each branch grows out of only one branch, but it can have many lower branches. In this respect, it can be said to have a *parent/child structure.* In the same way, each directory is itself a subdirectory of one other directory. Each directory may contain many subdirectories but is itself the child of only one parent directory.

The Linux file structure branches into several directories beginning with a root directory, */*. Within the root directory several system, directories contain files and programs that are features of the Linux system. The root directory also contains a directory called **home** that contains the home directories of all the users in the system. Each user's home directory, in turn, contains the directories the user has made for their own use. Each of these could also contain directories. Such nested directories would branch out from the user's home directory, as shown in Figure 10-2.

NOTE *The user's home directory can be any directory, though it is usually the directory that bears the user's login name. This directory is located in the directory named* **/home** *on your Linux system. For example, a user named* **dylan** *will have a home directory called* **dylan** *located in the system's* **/home** *directory. The user's home directory is a subdirectory of the directory called* **/home** *on your system.*

Home Directories

When you log in to the system, you are placed within your home directory. The name given to this directory by the system is the same as your login name. Any files you create when you first log in are organized within your home directory. Within your home directory, however, you can create more directories. You can then change to these directories and store files in them.

FIGURE 10-2
The Linux file structure beginning at the root directory

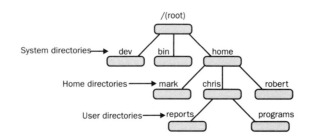

The same is true for other users on the system. Each user has his or her own home directory, identified by the appropriate login name. Users, in turn, can create their own directories.

You can access a directory either through its name or by making it the default directory. Each directory is given a name when it is created. You can use this name in file operations to access files in that directory. You can also make the directory your default directory. If you do not use any directory names in a file operation, the default directory will be accessed. The default directory is referred to as the *working directory*. In this sense, the working directory is the one from which you are currently working.

When you log in, the working directory is your home directory, usually having the same name as your login name. You can change the working directory by using the **cd** command to designate another directory as the working directory. As the working directory is changed, you can move from one directory to another. Another way to think of a directory is as a corridor. In such a corridor, there are doors with names on them. Some doors lead to rooms; others lead to other corridors. The doors that open to rooms are like files in a directory. The doors that lead to other corridors are like other directories. Moving from one corridor to the next corridor is like changing the working directory. Moving through several corridors is like moving through several directories.

Pathnames

The name you give to a directory or file when you create it is not its full name. The full name of a directory is its *pathname*. The hierarchically nested relationship among directories forms paths, and these paths can be used to identify and reference any directory or file unambiguously. In Figure 10-3, a path exists from the root directory, **/**, through the **home** directory to the **robert** directory. Another path exists from the root directory through the **home** and **chris** directories to the **reports** directory. Although parts of each path may at first be shared, at some point they differ. Both the directories **robert** and **reports** share the two directories **root** and **home**. Then they differ. In the **home** directory, **robert** ends with **robert**, but the directory **chris** then leads to **reports**. In this way, each directory in the file structure can be said to have its own unique path. The actual name by which the system identifies a directory always begins with the root directory and consists of all directories nested below that directory.

In Linux, you write a pathname by listing each directory in the path separated from the last by a forward slash. A slash preceding the first directory in the path represents the root. The pathname for the **robert** directory is **/home/robert**. The pathname for the **reports** directory is **/home/chris/reports**. Pathnames also apply to files. When you create a file within a

Figure 10-3
Directory
pathnames

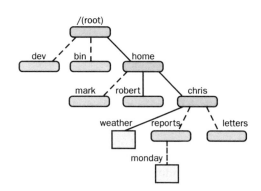

directory, you give the file a name. The actual name by which the system identifies the file, however, is the filename combined with the path of directories from the root to the file's directory. In Figure 10-3, the path for the **weather** file consists of the root, **home**, and **chris** directories and the filename **weather**. The pathname for **weather** is **/home/chris/weather** (the root directory is represented by the first slash).

Pathnames may be absolute or relative. An *absolute pathname* is the complete pathname of a file or directory beginning with the root directory. A *relative pathname* begins from your working directory; it is the path of a file relative to your working directory. The working directory is the one you are currently operating in. Using the directory structure described in Figure 10-3, if **chris** is your working directory, the relative pathname for the file **monday** is **reports/monday**. The absolute pathname for **monday** is **/home/chris/reports/monday**.

The absolute pathname from the root to your home directory could be especially complex and, at times, even subject to change by the system administrator. To make it easier to reference, you can use a special character, the tilde (**~**), which represents the absolute pathname of your home directory. In the next example, from the **thankyou** directory, the user references the **weather** file in the home directory by placing a tilde and slash before **weather**:

```
$ pwd
/home/chris/letters/thankyou
$ cat ~/weather
raining and warm
$
```

You must specify the rest of the path from your home directory. In the next example, the user references the **monday** file in the **reports** directory. The tilde represents the path to the user's home directory, **/home/chris**, and then the rest of the path to the **monday** file is specified.

```
$ cat ~/reports/monday
```

System Directories

The root directory that begins the Linux file structure contains several system directories. The system directories contain files and programs used to run and maintain the system. Many contain other subdirectories with programs for executing specific features of Linux. For example, the directory **/usr/bin** contains the various Linux commands that users execute, such as **cp** and **mv**. The directory **/bin** holds interfaces with different system devices, such as the printer or the terminal. Table 10-1 lists the basic system directories.

NOTE   *The overall organization of the Linux file structure for system directories and other useful directories such as those used for the kernel are discussed in detail in Chapter 32.*

Listing, Displaying, and Printing Files: ls, cat, more, less, and lpr

One of the primary functions of an operating system is the management of files. You may need to perform certain basic output operations on your files, such as displaying them on your screen or printing them. The Linux system provides a set of commands that perform basic file-management operations, such as listing, displaying, and printing files, as well as

Directory	Function
/	Begins the file system structure, called the root.
/home	Contains users' home directories.
/bin	Holds all the standard commands and utility programs.
/usr	Holds those files and commands used by the system; this directory breaks down into several subdirectories.
/usr/bin	Holds user-oriented commands and utility programs.
/usr/sbin	Holds system administration commands.
/usr/lib	Holds libraries for programming languages.
/usr/share/doc	Holds Linux documentation.
/usr/share/man	Holds the online manual Man files.
/var/spool	Holds spooled files, such as those generated for printing jobs and network transfers.
/sbin	Holds system administration commands for booting the system.
/var	Holds files that vary, such as mailbox files.
/dev	Holds file interfaces for devices such as the terminals and printers (dynamically generated by udev, do not edit, see Chapter 34).
/etc	Holds system configuration files and any other system files.

TABLE 10-1   Standard System Directories in Linux

copying, renaming, and erasing files. These commands are usually made up of abbreviated versions of words. For example, the **ls** command is a shortened form of "list" and lists the files in your directory. The **lpr** command is an abbreviated form of "line print" and will print a file. The **cat**, **less**, and **more** commands display the contents of a file on the screen. Table 10-2 lists these commands with their different options. When you log in to your Linux system, you may want a list of the files in your home directory. The **ls** command, which outputs a list of your file and directory names, is useful for this. The **ls** command has many possible options for displaying filenames according to specific features.

Displaying Files: cat, less, and more
You may also need to look at the contents of a file. The **cat** and **more** commands display the contents of a file on the screen. The name **cat** stands for *concatenate*.

```
$ cat mydata
computers
```

The **cat** command outputs the entire text of a file to the screen at once. This presents a problem when the file is large because its text quickly speeds past on the screen. The **more** and **less** commands are designed to overcome this limitation by displaying one screen of text at a time. You can then move forward or backward in the text at your leisure. You invoke

Command or Option	Execution
`ls`	This command lists file and directory names.
`cat` *filenames*	This filter can be used to display a file. It can take filenames for its arguments. It outputs the contents of those files directly to the standard output, which, by default, is directed to the screen.
`more` *filenames*	This utility displays a file screen by screen. Press the SPACEBAR to continue to the next screen and **q** to quit.
`less` *filenames*	This utility also displays a file screen by screen. Press the SPACEBAR to continue to the next screen and **q** to quit.
`lpr` *filenames*	Sends a file to the line printer to be printed; a list of files may be used as arguments. Use the **-P** option to specify a printer.
`lpq`	Lists the print queue for printing jobs.
`lprm`	Removes a printing job from the print queue.

TABLE 10-2   Listing, Displaying, and Printing Files

the **more** or **less** command by entering the command name followed by the name of the file you want to view (**less** is a more powerful and configurable display utility).

```
$ less mydata
```

When **more** or **less** invoke a file, the first screen of text is displayed. To continue to the next screen, you press the F key or the SPACEBAR. To move back in the text, you press the B key. You can quit at any time by pressing the Q key.

Printing Files: lpr, lpq, and lprm

With the printer commands such as **lpr** and **lprm**, you can perform printing operations such as printing files or canceling print jobs (see Table 10-2). When you need to print files, use the **lpr** command to send files to the printer connected to your system. See Chapter 26 to learn more about printing. In the next example, the user prints the **mydata** file:

```
$ lpr mydata
```

If you want to print several files at once, you can specify more than one file on the command line after the **lpr** command. In the next example, the user prints out both the **mydata** and **preface** files:

```
$ lpr mydata preface
```

Printing jobs are placed in a queue and printed one at a time in the background. You can continue with other work as your files print. You can see the position of a particular printing job at any given time with the **lpq** command, which gives the owner of the printing job (the login name of the user who sent the job), the print job ID, the size in bytes, and the temporary file in which it is currently held.

If you need to cancel an unwanted printing job, you can do so with the **lprm** command, which takes as its argument either the ID number of the printing job or the owner's name. It then removes the print job from the print queue. For this task, **lpq** is helpful, for it provides you with the ID number and owner of the printing job you need to use with **lprm**.

Managing Directories: mkdir, rmdir, ls, cd, and pwd

You can create and remove your own directories, as well as change your working directory, with the **mkdir**, **rmdir**, and **cd** commands. Each of these commands can take as its argument the pathname for a directory. The **pwd** command displays the absolute pathname of your working directory. In addition to these commands, the special characters represented by a single dot, a double dot, and a tilde can be used to reference the working directory, the parent of the working directory, and the home directory, respectively. Taken together, these commands enable you to manage your directories. You can create nested directories, move from one directory to another, and use pathnames to reference any of your directories. Those commands commonly used to manage directories are listed in Table 10-3.

Command	Execution
mkdir *directory*	Creates a directory.
rmdir *directory*	Erases a directory.
ls -F	Lists directory name with a preceding slash.
ls -R	Lists working directory as well as all subdirectories.
cd *directory name*	Changes to the specified directory, making it the working directory. **cd** without a directory name changes back to the home directory: `$ cd reports`
pwd	Displays the pathname of the working directory.
directory name/filename	A slash is used in pathnames to separate each directory name. In the case of pathnames for files, a slash separates the preceding directory names from the filename.

..	References the parent directory. You can use it as an argument or as part of a pathname:
	`$ cd ..`
	`$ mv ../larisa oldletters`

.	References the working directory. You can use it as an argument or as part of a pathname: `$ ls .`
~/*pathname*	The tilde is a special character that represents the pathname for the home directory. It is useful when you need to use an absolute pathname for a file or directory: `$ cp monday ~/today`

TABLE 10-3 Directory Commands

Creating and Deleting Directories

You create and remove directories with the **mkdir** and **rmdir** commands. In either case, you can also use pathnames for the directories. In the next example, the user creates the directory **reports**. Then the user creates the directory **letters** using a pathname:

```
$ mkdir reports
$ mkdir /home/chris/letters
```

You can remove a directory with the **rmdir** command followed by the directory name. In the next example, the user removes the directory **reports** with the **rmdir** command:

```
$ rmdir reports
```

To remove a directory and all its subdirectories, you use the **rm** command with the **-r** option. This is a very powerful command and could easily be used to erase all your files. You will be prompted for each file. To simply remove all files and subdirectories without prompts, add the **-f** option. The following example deletes the **reports** directory and all its subdirectories:

```
rm -rf reports
```

Displaying Directory Contents

You have seen how to use the **ls** command to list the files and directories within your working directory. To distinguish between file and directory names, however, you need to use the **ls** command with the **-F** option. A slash is then placed after each directory name in the list.

```
$ ls
weather reports letters
$ ls -F
weather reports/ letters/
```

The **ls** command also takes as an argument any directory name or directory pathname. This enables you to list the files in any directory without first having to change to that directory. In the next example, the **ls** command takes as its argument the name of a directory, **reports**. Then the **ls** command is executed again, only this time the absolute pathname of **reports** is used.

```
$ ls reports
monday tuesday
$ ls /home/chris/reports
monday tuesday
$
```

Moving Through Directories

The **cd** command takes as its argument the name of the directory to which you want to change. The name of the directory can be the name of a subdirectory in your working directory or the full pathname of any directory on the system. If you want to change back to your home directory, you only need to enter the **cd** command by itself, without a filename argument.

```
$ cd props
$ pwd
/home/dylan/props
```

Referencing the Parent Directory

A directory always has a parent (except, of course, for the root). For example, in the preceding listing, the parent for **props** is the **dylan** directory. When a directory is created, two entries are made: one represented with a dot (.), and the other represented by double dots (. .). The dot represents the pathnames of the directory, and the double dots represent the pathname of its parent directory. Double dots, used as an argument in a command, reference a parent directory. The single dot references the directory itself.

You can use the single dot to reference your working directory, instead of using its pathname. For example, to copy a file to the working directory retaining the same name, the dot can be used in place of the working directory's pathname. In this sense, the dot is another name for the working directory. In the next example, the user copies the **weather** file from the **chris** directory to the **reports** directory. The **reports** directory is the working directory and can be represented with the single dot.

```
$ cd reports
$ cp /home/chris/weather  .
```

The . . symbol is often used to reference files in the parent directory. In the next example, the **cat** command displays the **weather** file in the parent directory. The pathname for the file is the . . symbol followed by a slash and the filename.

```
$ cat ../weather
raining and warm
```

*TIP   You can use the **cd** command with the . . symbol to step back through successive parent directories of the directory tree from a lower directory.*

File and Directory Operations: find, cp, mv, rm, and ln

As you create more and more files, you may want to back them up, change their names, erase some of them, or even give them added names. Linux provides you with several file commands that enable you to search for files, copy files, rename files, or remove files (see Table 10-5 later in this chapter). If you have a large number of files, you can also search them to locate a specific one. The commands are shortened forms of full words, consisting of only two characters. The **cp** command stands for "copy" and copies a file, **mv** stands for "move" and renames or moves a file, **rm** stands for "remove" and erases a file, and **ln** stands for "link" and adds another name for a file, often used as a shortcut to the original. One exception to the two-character rule is the **find** command, which performs searches of your filenames to find a file. All these operations can be handled by the GUI desktops, like GNOME and KDE (see Chapters 6 and 7).

Searching Directories: find

Once you have a large number of files in many different directories, you may need to search them to locate a specific file, or files, of a certain type. The **find** command enables you to perform such a search from the command line. The **find** command takes as its arguments directory names followed by several possible options that specify the type of search and the criteria for the search; it then searches within the directories listed and their subdirectories for files that meet these criteria. The **find** command can search for a file by name, type, owner, and even the time of the last update.

```
$ find directory-list -option criteria
```

TIP   *From the GNOME desktop you can use the Search for Files tool in the Places menu to search for files. From the KDE desktop you can use the find tool in the file manager. Select find from the file manager (Konqueror) tools menu.*

The **-name** option has as its criterion a pattern and instructs **find** to search for the filename that matches that pattern. To search for a file by name, you use the **find** command with the directory name followed by the **-name** option and the name of the file.

```
$ find directory-list -name filename
```

The **find** command also has options that merely perform actions, such as outputting the results of a search. If you want **find** to display the filenames it has found, you simply include the **-print** option on the command line along with any other options. The **-print** option is an action that instructs **find** to write to the standard output the names of all the files it locates (you can also use the **-ls** option instead to list files in the long format). In the next example, the user searches for all the files in the **reports** directory with the name **monday**. Once located, the file, with its relative pathname, is printed.

```
$ find reports -name monday -print
reports/monday
```

The **find** command prints out the filenames using the directory name specified in the directory list. If you specify an absolute pathname, the absolute path of the found directories will be output. If you specify a relative pathname, only the relative pathname is output. In the preceding example, the user specified a relative pathname, **reports**, in the directory list. Located filenames were output beginning with this relative pathname. In the next example, the user specifies an absolute pathname in the directory list. Located filenames are then output using this absolute pathname.

```
$ find /home/chris -name monday -print
/home/chris/reports/monday
```

TIP   *Should you need to find the location of a specific program or configuration file, you could use **find** to search for the file from the root directory. Log in as the root user and use / as the directory. This command searched for the location of the **more** command and files on the entire file system: **find / -name more -print**.*

Searching the Working Directory

If you want to search your working directory, you can use the dot in the directory pathname to represent your working directory. The double dots would represent the parent directory. The next example searches all files and subdirectories in the working directory, using the dot to represent the working directory. If you are located in your home directory, this is a convenient way to search through all your own directories. Notice the located filenames are output beginning with a dot.

```
$ find . -name weather -print
./weather
```

You can use shell wildcard characters as part of the pattern criteria for searching files. The special character must be quoted, however, to avoid evaluation by the shell. In the next example, all files with the **.c** extension in the **programs** directory are searched for and then displayed in the long format using the **–ls** action:

```
$ find programs -name '*.c' -ls
```

Locating Directories

You can also use the **find** command to locate other directories. In Linux, a directory is officially classified as a special type of file. Although all files have a byte-stream format, some files, such as directories, are used in special ways. In this sense, a file can be said to have a file type. The **find** command has an option called **–type** that searches for a file of a given type. The **–type** option takes a one-character modifier that represents the file type. The modifier that represents a directory is a **d**. In the next example, both the directory name and the directory file type are used to search for the directory called **thankyou**:

```
$ find /home/chris -name thankyou -type d -print
/home/chris/letters/thankyou
$
```

File types are not so much different types of files as they are the file format applied to other components of the operating system, such as devices. In this sense, a device is treated as a type of file, and you can use **find** to search for devices and directories, as well as ordinary files. Table 10-4 lists the different types available for the **find** command's **–type** option.

You can also use the find operation to search for files by ownership or security criteria, like those belonging to a specific user or those with a certain security context. The user option lets you locate all files belonging to a certain user. The following example lists all files that the user **chris** has created or owns on the entire system. To list those just in the users' home directories, you would use **/home** for the starting search directory. This would find all those in a user's home directory as well as any owned by that user in other user directories.

```
$ find / -user chris -print
```

Copying Files

To make a copy of a file, you simply give **cp** two filenames as its arguments (see Table 10-5 later in this chapter). The first filename is the name of the file to be copied—the one that

Command or Option	Execution
find	Searches directories for files according to search criteria. This command has several options that specify the type of criteria and actions to be taken.
-name *pattern*	Searches for files with the *pattern* in the name.
-lname *pattern*	Searches for symbolic link files.
-group *name*	Searches for files belonging to the group *name*.
-gid *name*	Searches for files belonging to a group according to group ID.
-user *name*	Searches for files belonging to a user.
-uid *name*	Searches for files belonging to a user according to user ID.
-size *numc*	Searches for files with the size *num* in blocks. If **c** is added after *num*, the size in bytes (characters) is searched for.
-mtime *num*	Searches for files last modified *num* days ago.
-newer *pattern*	Searches for files modified after the one matched by *pattern*.
-context *scontext*	Searches for files according to security context (SELinux).
-print	Outputs the result of the search to the standard output. The result is usually a list of filenames, including their full pathnames.
-type *filetype*	Searches for files with the specified file type. File type can be *b* for block device, *c* for character device, *d* for directory, *f* for file, or *l* for symbolic link.
-perm *permission*	Searches for files with certain permissions set. Use octal or symbolic format for permissions (see Chapter 29).
-ls	Provides a detailed listing of each file, with owner, permission, size, and date information.
-exec *command*	Executes command when files found.

TABLE 10-4 The **find** Command

already exists. This is often referred to as the *source file*. The second filename is the name you want for the copy. This will be a new file containing a copy of all the data in the source file. This second argument is often referred to as the *destination file*. The syntax for the **cp** command follows:

```
$ cp source-file destination-file
```

In the next example, the user copies a file called **proposal** to a new file called **oldprop**:

```
$ cp proposal oldprop
```

You could unintentionally destroy another file with the **cp** command. The **cp** command generates a copy by first creating a file and then copying data into it. If another file has the same name as the destination file, that file is destroyed and a new file with that name is created. By default Fedora Core configures your system to check for an existing copy by the same name (**cp** is aliased with the **-i** option, see Chapter 9). To copy a file from your working directory to another directory, you only need to use that directory name as the second argument in the **cp** command. In the next example, the **proposal** file is overwritten by the **newprop** file. The **proposal** file already exists.

```
$ cp newprop proposal
```

You can use any of the wildcard characters to generate a list of filenames to use with **cp** or **mv**. For example, suppose you need to copy all your C source code files to a given directory. Instead of listing each one individually on the command line, you could use an ***** character with the **.c** extension to match on and generate a list of C source code files (all files with a **.c** extension). In the next example, the user copies all source code files in the current directory to the **sourcebks** directory:

```
$ cp *.c sourcebks
```

If you want to copy all the files in a given directory to another directory, you could use ***** to match on and generate a list of all those files in a **cp** command. In the next example, the user copies all the files in the **props** directory to the **oldprop** directory. Notice the use of a **props** pathname preceding the ***** special characters. In this context, **props** is a pathname that will be appended before each file in the list that ***** generates.

```
$ cp props/* oldprop
```

You can, of course, use any of the other special characters, such as **.**, **?**, or **[]**. In the next example, the user copies both source code and object code files (**.c** and **.o**) to the **projbk** directory:

```
$ cp *.[oc] projbk
```

When you copy a file, you may want to give the copy a different name than the original. To do so, place the new filename after the directory name, separated by a slash.

```
$ cp filename directory-name/new-filename
```

Moving Files

You can use the **mv** command either to rename a file or to move a file from one directory to another. When using **mv** to rename a file, you simply use the new filename as the second argument. The first argument is the current name of the file you are renaming. If you want to rename a file when you move it, you can specify the new name of the file after the directory name. In the next example, the **proposal** file is renamed with the name **version1**:

```
$ mv proposal version1
```

As with **cp**, it is easy for **mv** to erase a file accidentally. When renaming a file, you might accidentally choose a filename already used by another file. In this case, that other file will be erased. The **mv** command also has an **-i** option that checks first to see if a file by that name already exists.

You can also use any of the special characters described in Chapter 8 to generate a list of filenames to use with **mv**. In the next example, the user moves all source code files in the current directory to the **newproj** directory:

```
$ mv *.c newproj
```

If you want to move all the files in a given directory to another directory, you can use ***** to match on and generate a list of all those files. In the next example, the user moves all the files in the **reports** directory to the **repbks** directory:

```
$ mv reports/* repbks
```

NOTE *To copy files to a CD-R/RW or DVD-R/RW disc, you can use any number or CD/DVD burning tools. Many of these are interfaces to the cdrecord utility, along with mkisofs and cdda2wav. On KDE, you can use KOnCD, CD-Rchive, and KreateCD, and on GNOME, you can use the Nautilus file manager directly, as well as other tools like GNOME CD Master and CD-rec. With cdrecord, you can copy files to a CD-R/RW directly. The mkisofs utility is used to create CD images, and cdda2wav records tracks from music CDs. For DVD+RW/+R drives, you use the dvd+rw tools such as growisofs and dvd+rw-format (see Chapter 32).*

Copying and Moving Directories

You can also copy or move whole directories at once. Both **cp** and **mv** can take as their first argument a directory name, enabling you to copy or move subdirectories from one directory into another (see Table 10-5). The first argument is the name of the directory to be moved or copied, while the second argument is the name of the directory within which it is to be placed. The same pathname structure used for files applies to moving or copying directories.

You can just as easily copy subdirectories from one directory to another. To copy a directory, the **cp** command requires you to use the **-r** option. The **-r** option stands for "recursive." It directs the **cp** command to copy a directory, as well as any subdirectories it may contain. In other words, the entire directory subtree, from that directory on, will be copied. In the next example, the **thankyou** directory is copied to the **oldletters** directory. Now two **thankyou** subdirectories exist, one in **letters** and one in **oldletters**.

```
$ cp -r letters/thankyou oldletters
$ ls -F letters
/thankyou
$ ls -F oldletters
/thankyou
```

Erasing Files and Directories: rm

As you use Linux, you will find the number of files you use increases rapidly. Generating files in Linux is easy. Applications such as editors, and commands such as **cp**, easily create files. Eventually, many of these files may become outdated and useless. You can then remove them with the **rm** command. The **rm** command can take any number of arguments, enabling you to list several filenames and erase them all at the same time. In the next example, the user erases the file **oldprop**:

```
$ rm oldprop
```

Command	Execution
cp *filename filename*	Copies a file. **cp** takes two arguments: the original file and the name of the new copy. You can use pathnames for the files to copy across directories: `$ cp today reports/Monday`
cp -r *dirname dirname*	Copies a subdirectory from one directory to another. The copied directory includes all its own subdirectories: `$ cp -r letters/thankyou oldletters`
mv *filename filename*	Moves (renames) a file. The **mv** command takes two arguments: the first is the file to be moved. The second argument can be the new filename or the pathname of a directory. If it is the name of a directory, then the file is literally moved to that directory, changing the file's pathname: `$ mv today /home/chris/reports`
mv *dirname dirname*	Moves directories. In this case, the first and last arguments are directories: `$ mv letters/thankyou oldletters`
ln *filename filename*	Creates added names for files referred to as links. A link can be created in one directory that references a file in another directory: `$ ln today reports/Monday`
rm *filenames*	Removes (erases) a file. Can take any number of filenames as its arguments. Literally removes links to a file. If a file has more than one link, you need to remove all of them to erase a file: `$rm today weather weekend`

TABLE 10-5   File Operations

Be careful when using the **rm** command, because it is irrevocable. Once a file is removed, it cannot be restored (there is no undo). With the **-i** option, you are prompted separately for each file and asked whether to remove it. If you enter **y**, the file will be removed. If you enter anything else, the file is not removed. In the next example, the **rm** command is instructed to erase the files **proposal** and **oldprop**. The **rm** command then asks for confirmation for each file. The user decides to remove **oldprop**, but not **proposal**.

```
$ rm -i proposal oldprop
Remove proposal? n
Remove oldprop? y
$
```

Links: ln

You can give a file more than one name using the **ln** command. You might want to reference a file using different filenames to access it from different directories. The added names are often referred to as *links*. Linux supports two different types of links, hard and symbolic.

Hard links are literally another name for the same file, whereas symbolic links function like shortcuts referencing another file. Symbolic links are much more flexible and can work over many different file systems, whereas hard links are limited to your local file system. Furthermore, hard links introduce security concerns, as they allow direct access from a link that may have public access to an original file that you may want protected. Links are usually implemented as symbolic links.

Symbolic Links

To set up a symbolic link, you use the **ln** command with the **-s** option and two arguments: the name of the original file and the new, added filename. The **ls** operation lists both filenames, but only one physical file will exist.

```
$ ln -s original-file-name added-file-name
```

In the next example, the **today** file is given the additional name **weather**. It is just another name for the **today** file.

```
$ ls
today
$ ln -s today weather
$ ls
today weather
```

You can give the same file several names by using the **ln** command on the same file many times. In the next example, the file **today** is given both the names **weather** and **weekend**:

```
$ ln -s today weather
$ ln -s today weekend
$ ls
today weather weekend
```

If you list the full information about a symbolic link and its file, you will find the information displayed is different. In the next example, the user lists the full information for both **lunch** and **/home/george/veglist** using the **ls** command with the **-l** option. The first character in the line specifies the file type. Symbolic links have their own file type, represented by an l. The file type for **lunch** is l, indicating it is a symbolic link, not an ordinary file. The number after the term "group" is the size of the file. Notice the sizes differ. The size of the **lunch** file is only four bytes. This is because **lunch** is only a symbolic link—a file that holds the pathname of another file—and a pathname takes up only a few bytes. It is not a direct hard link to the **veglist** file.

```
$ ls -l lunch /home/george/veglist
lrw-rw-r-- 1 chris group 4 Feb 14 10:30 lunch
-rw-rw-r-- 1 george group 793 Feb 14 10:30 veglist
```

To erase a file, you need to remove only its original name (and any hard links to it). If any symbolic links are left over, they will be unable to access the file. In this case, a symbolic link would hold the pathname of a file that no longer exists.

Hard Links

You can give the same file several names by using the **ln** command on the same file many times. To set up a hard link, you use the **ln** command with no **-s** option and two arguments: the name of the original file and the new, added filename. The **ls** operation lists both filenames, but only one physical file will exist.

```
$ ln original-file-name added-file-name
```

In the next example, the **monday** file is given the additional name **storm**. It is just another name for the **monday** file.

```
$ ls
today
$ ln monday storm
$ ls
monday storm
```

To erase a file that has hard links, you need to remove all its hard links. The name of a file is actually considered a link to that file—hence the command **rm** that removes the link to the file. If you have several links to the file and remove only one of them, the others stay in place and you can reference the file through them. The same is true even if you remove the original link—the original name of the file. Any added links will work just as well. In the next example, the **today** file is removed with the **rm** command. However, a link to that same file exists, called **weather**. The file can then be referenced under the name **weather**.

```
$ ln today weather
$ rm today
$ cat weather
The storm broke today
and the sun came out.
$
```

> **NOTE** *Each file and directory in Linux contains a set of permissions that determine who can access them and how. You set these permissions to limit access in one of three ways: You can restrict access to yourself alone, you can allow users in a predesignated group to have access, or you can permit anyone on your system to have access. You can also control how a given file or directory is accessed. A file and directory may have read, write, and execute permissions. When a file is created, it is automatically given read and write permissions for the owner, enabling you to display and modify the file. You may change these permissions to any combination you want. (See Chapter 30 for more details.)*

The mtools Utilities: msdos

Your Linux system provides a set of utilities, known as *mtools,* that enable you to access floppy and hard disks formatted for MS-DOS easily. They work only with the old MS-DOS or FAT32 file systems, and not with Windows XP, NT, or 2000, which use the NTFS file system. The **mcopy** command enables you to copy files to and from an MS-DOS floppy disk in your floppy drive or a Windows partition on your hard drive. No special operations, such as mounting, are required. With mtools, you needn't mount an MS-DOS partition to access it. For an MS-DOS floppy disk, place the disk in your floppy drive, and you can then use mtool commands to access those files. For example, to copy a file from an MS-DOS floppy disk to your Linux system, use the **mcopy** command. You specify the MS-DOS disk with **a:** for the A drive. Unlike normal DOS pathnames, pathnames used with mtool commands use forward slashes instead of backslashes. The directory **docs** on the A drive would be referenced by the pathname **a:/docs**, not **a:\docs**. Unlike MS-DOS, which defaults the second argument to the current directory, you always need to supply the second argument for **mcopy**. The next example copies the file **mydata** to the MS-DOS disk and then copies the **preface** file from the disk to the current Linux directory.

```
$ mcopy mydata a:
$ mcopy a:/preface   .
```

TIP *You can use mtools to copy data to Windows-formatted floppy disks, which can also be read or written to by Windows XP, but you cannot access Windows XP, NT, or 2000 hard disk file systems (NTFS).*

You can use the **mdir** command to list files on your MS-DOS disk, and you can use the **mcd** command to change directories on it. The next example lists the files on the MS-DOS disk in your floppy drive and then changes to the **docs** directory on that drive:

```
$ mdir a:
$ mcd a:/docs
```

Most of the standard MS-DOS commands are available as mtool operations. You can create MS-DOS directories with **mmd** and erase MS-DOS files with **mdel**. For example, to display a file on drive B on an MS-DOS disk in the second floppy drive, use **mtype** and the name of the file preceded by **b:/**.

```
$ mtype b:/readme
```

Access to MS-DOS or Windows 95, 98, or ME partitions by mtools is configured by the **/etc/mtools.conf** file. This file lists several different default MS-DOS or Windows partitions and disk drives. Each drive or partition is identified with a particular device name. Entries for your floppy drives are already entered, using the device names **/dev/fd0** and **/dev/fd1** for the first and second floppy drives. An entry in the **/etc/mtools.conf** file takes the form of the drive label followed by the term **file** and the equal sign, and then the device name of the drive or partition you want identified with this label. The device name is encased in quotes. For example, assuming the first hard disk partition is an MS-DOS partition and has the device name of **/dev/hda1**, the following entry would identify this as the C drive on an MS-DOS system:

```
drive c: file="/dev/hda1"
```

You must have the correct device name for your partition. These device names are listed in the **/etc/fstab** file. Once the DOS hard disk partitions are referenced, you can then use their drive letters to copy files to and from them to your Linux partitions. The following command copies the file **mydoc.html** to the **c:** partition in the directory **webstuff** and renames it **mydoc .htm**. Notice the use of forward slashes instead of backward slashes.

```
$ mcopy mydoc.html c:/webstuff/mydoc.htm
```

Because of the differences in the way DOS and Linux handle newlines in text files, you should use the **-t** option whenever copying a DOS text file to a Linux partition. The following command copies the **mydoc.txt** file from the **c:/project** directory to the **/newdocs** directory:

```
$ mcopy -t c:/project/mydoc.txt /newdocs
```

Archiving and Compressing Files

Archives are used to back up files or to combine them into a package, which can then be transferred as one file over the Internet or posted on an FTP site for easy downloading. The standard archive utility used on Linux and Unix systems is tar, for which several GUI front ends exist. You have several compression programs to choose from, including GNU zip (gzip), Zip, bzip, and compress.

Archiving and Compressing Files with File Roller

Red Hat Enterprise Linux and Fedora Core provide the File Roller tool (accessible from the System Tools menu, labeled Archive Manager) that operates as a GUI front end to archive and compress files, letting you perform Zip, gzip, tar, and bzip2 operation using a GUI interface (see Figure 10-4). You can examine the contents of archives, extract the files you want, and create new compressed archives. When you create an archive, you determine its compression method by specifying its filename extension, such as **.gz** for gzip or **.bz2** for bzip2. You can select the different extensions from the File Type menu or enter the extension yourself. To both archive and compress files, you can choose a combined extension like .tar. bz2, which both archives with tar and compresses with bzip2. Click Add to add files to your archive. To extract files from an archive, open the archive to display the list of archive files. You can then click Extract to extract particular files or the entire archive. Other GUI tools available are guiTAR, LnxZip, Ark, KArchive, and Xtar.

FIGURE 10-4
File Roller archiving and compression tool

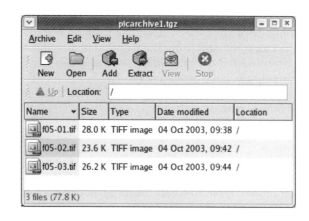

TIP *File Roller can also be use to examine the contents of an archive file easily. From the file manager, right-click the archive and select Open With "Archive Manager." The list of files and directories in that archive will be displayed. For subdirectories, double-click their entries. This method also works for RPM software files, letting you browse all the files that make up a software package.*

Archive Files and Devices: tar

The tar utility creates archives for files and directories. With tar, you can archive specific files, update them in the archive, and add new files as you want to that archive. You can even archive entire directories with all their files and subdirectories, all of which can be restored from the archive. The tar utility was originally designed to create archives on tapes. (The term "tar" stands for tape archive. You can create archives on any device, such as a floppy disk, or you can create an archive file to hold the archive.) The tar utility is ideal for making backups of your files or combining several files into a single file for transmission across a network (File Roller is a GUI interface for tar).

NOTE *As an alternative to tar, you can use pax, which is designed to work with different kinds of Unix archive formats such as cpio, bcpio, and tar. You can extract, list, and create archives. The pax utility is helpful if you are handling archives created on Unix systems that are using different archive formats.*

Displaying Archive Contents

Both file managers in GNOME and the K Desktop have the capability to display the contents of a tar archive file automatically. The contents are displayed as though they were files in a directory. You can list the files as icons or with details, sorting them by name, type, or other fields. You can even display the contents of files. Clicking a text file opens it with a text editor, and an image is displayed with an image viewer. If the file manager cannot determine what program to use to display the file, it prompts you to select an application. Both file managers can perform the same kinds of operations on archives residing on remote file systems, such as tar archives on FTP sites. You can obtain a listing of their contents and even read their readme files. The Nautilus file manager (GNOME) can also extract an archive. Right-click the Archive icon and select Extract.

Creating Archives

On Linux, tar is often used to create archives on devices or files. You can direct tar to archive files to a specific device or a file by using the **f** option with the name of the device or file. The syntax for the **tar** command using the **f** option is shown in the next example. The device or filename is often referred to as the archive name. When creating a file for a tar archive, the filename is usually given the extension **.tar**. This is a convention only and is not required. You can list as many filenames as you want. If a directory name is specified, all its subdirectories are included in the archive.

```
$ tar optionsf archive-name.tar directory-and-file-names
```

To create an archive, use the **c** option. Combined with the **f** option, **c** creates an archive on a file or device. You enter this option before and right next to the **f** option. Notice no dash precedes a tar option. Table 10-6 lists the different options you can use with tar. In the next

Commands	Execution
`tar` *options files*	Backs up files to tape, device, or archive file.
`tar` *options*`f` *archive_name filelist*	Backs up files to a specific file or device specified as *archive_name*. *filelist* can be filenames or directories.
Options	**Execution**
`c`	Creates a new archive.
`t`	Lists the names of files in an archive.
`r`	Appends files to an archive.
`U`	Updates an archive with new and changed files; adds only those files modified since they were archived or files not already present in the archive.
`--delete`	Removes a file from the archive.
`w`	Waits for a confirmation from the user before archiving each file; enables you to update an archive selectively.
`x`	Extracts files from an archive.
`m`	When extracting a file from an archive, no new timestamp is assigned.
`M`	Creates a multiple-volume archive that may be stored on several floppy disks.
`f` *archive-name*	Saves the tape archive to the file archive name, instead of to the default tape device. When given an archive name, the `f` option saves the tar archive in a file of that name.
`f` *device-name*	Saves a tar archive to a device such as a floppy disk or tape. **/dev/fd0** is the device name for your floppy disk; the default device is held in **/etc/default/tar-file**.
`v`	Displays each filename as it is archived.
`z`	Compresses or decompresses archived files using gzip.
`j`	Compresses or decompresses archived files using bzip2.

TABLE 10-6   File Archives: `tar`

example, the directory **mydir** and all its subdirectories are saved in the file **myarch.tar**. In this example, the **mydir** directory holds two files, **mymeeting** and **party**, as well as a directory called **reports** that has three files: **weather**, **monday**, and **friday**.

```
$ tar cvf myarch.tar mydir
mydir/
mydir/reports/
mydir/reports/weather
mydir/reports/monday
mydir/reports/friday
mydir/mymeeting
mydir/party
```

Extracting Archives

The user can later extract the directories from the tape using the **x** option. The **xf** option extracts files from an archive file or device. The tar extraction operation generates all subdirectories. In the next example, the **xf** option directs **tar** to extract all the files and subdirectories from the tar file **myarch.tar**:

```
$ tar xvf myarch.tar
mydir/
mydir/reports/
mydir/reports/weather
mydir/reports/monday
mydir/reports/friday
mydir/mymeeting
mydir/party
```

You use the **r** option to add files to an already-created archive. The **r** option appends the files to the archive. In the next example, the user appends the files in the **letters** directory to the **myarch.tar** archive. Here, the directory **mydocs** and its files are added to the **myarch .tar** archive:

```
$ tar rvf myarch.tar mydocs
mydocs/
mydocs/doc1
```

Updating Archives

If you change any of the files in your directories you previously archived, you can use the **u** option to instruct tar to update the archive with any modified files. The **tar** command compares the time of the last update for each archived file with those in the user's directory and copies into the archive any files that have been changed since they were last archived. Any newly created files in these directories are also added to the archive. In the next example, the user updates the **myarch.tar** file with any recently modified or newly created files in the **mydir** directory. In this case, the **gifts** file was added to the **mydir** directory.

```
tar uvf myarch.tar mydir
mydir/
mydir/gifts
```

If you need to see what files are stored in an archive, you can use the **tar** command with the **t** option. The next example lists all the files stored in the **myarch.tar** archive:

```
tar tvf myarch.tar
drwxr-xr-x root/root 0 2000-10-24 21:38:18 mydir/
drwxr-xr-x root/root 0 2000-10-24 21:38:51 mydir/reports/
-rw-r--r-- root/root 22 2000-10-24 21:38:40 mydir/reports/weather
-rw-r--r-- root/root 22 2000-10-24 21:38:45 mydir/reports/monday
-rw-r--r-- root/root 22 2000-10-24 21:38:51 mydir/reports/friday
-rw-r--r-- root/root 22 2000-10-24 21:38:18 mydir/mymeeting
-rw-r--r-- root/root 22 2000-10-24 21:36:42 mydir/party
```

```
drwxr-xr-x root/root 0 2000-10-24 21:48:45 mydocs/
-rw-r--r-- root/root 22 2000-10-24 21:48:45 mydocs/doc1
drwxr-xr-x root/root 0 2000-10-24 21:54:03 mydir/
-rw-r--r-- root/root 22 2000-10-24 21:54:03 mydir/gifts
```

Archiving to Floppies

To back up the files to a specific device, specify the device as the archive. For a floppy disk, you can specify the floppy drive. Be sure to use a blank floppy disk. Any data previously placed on it will be erased by this operation. In the next example, the user creates an archive on the floppy disk in the **/dev/fd0** device and copies into it all the files in the **mydir** directory:

```
$ tar cf /dev/fd0 mydir
```

To extract the backed-up files on the disk in the device, use the **xf** option:

```
$ tar xf /dev/fd0
```

If the files you are archiving take up more space than would be available on a device such as a floppy disk, you can create a tar archive that uses multiple labels. The **M** option instructs tar to prompt you for a new storage component when the current one is filled. When archiving to a floppy drive with the **M** option, tar prompts you to put in a new floppy disk when one becomes full. You can then save your tar archive on several floppy disks.

```
$ tar cMf /dev/fd0 mydir
```

To unpack the multiple-disk archive, place the first one in the floppy drive and then issue the following **tar** command using both the **x** and **M** options. You are then prompted to put in the other floppy disks as they are needed.

```
$ tar xMf /dev/fd0
```

Compressing Archives

The **tar** operation does not perform compression on archived files. If you want to compress the archived files, you can instruct tar to invoke the gzip utility to compress them. With the lowercase **z** option, tar first uses gzip to compress files before archiving them. The same **z** option invokes gzip to decompress them when extracting files.

```
$ tar czf myarch.tar.gz mydir
```

To use bzip instead of gzip to compress files before archiving them, you use the **j** option. The same **j** option invokes bzip to decompress them when extracting files.

```
$ tar cjf myarch.tar.bz2 mydir
```

Remember, a difference exists between compressing individual files in an archive and compressing the entire archive as a whole. Often, an archive is created for transferring several files at once as one tar file. To shorten transmission time, the archive should be as small as possible. You can use the compression utility gzip on the archive tar file to compress it, reducing its size, and then send the compressed version. The person receiving it can decompress it, restoring the tar file. Using gzip on a tar file often results in a file with the extension **.tar.gz**. The extension **.gz** is added to a compressed gzip file. The next example creates a compressed version of **myarch.tar** using the same name with the extension **.gz**:

```
$ gzip myarch.tar
$ ls
$ myarch.tar.gz
```

Instead of retyping the **tar** command for different files, you could place the command in a script and pass the files to it. Be sure to make the script executable. In the following example, a simple **myarchprog** script is created that will archive filenames listed as its arguments.

myarchprog
```
tar   cvf   myarch.tar   $*
```

A run of the **myarchprog** script with multiple arguments is shown here:

```
$ myarchprog mydata preface
mydata
preface
```

Archiving to Tape

If you have a default device specified, such as a tape, and you want to create an archive on it, you can simply use **tar** without the **f** option and a device or filename. This can be helpful for making backups of your files. The name of the default device is held in a file called **/etc/default/tar**. The syntax for the **tar** command using the default tape device is shown in the following example. If a directory name is specified, all its subdirectories are included in the archive.

```
$ tar option directory-and-file-names
```

In the next example, the directory **mydir** and all its subdirectories are saved on a tape in the default tape device:

```
$ tar c mydir
```

In this example, the **mydir** directory and all its files and subdirectories are extracted from the default tape device and placed in the user's working directory:

```
$ tar x mydir
```

NOTE *There are other archive programs you can use such as cpio, pax, and shar. However, tar is the one most commonly used for archiving application software.*

File Compression: gzip, bzip2, and Zip

Several reasons exist for reducing the size of a file. The two most common are to save space or, if you are transferring the file across a network, to save transmission time. You can effectively reduce a file size by creating a compressed copy of it. Anytime you need the file again, you decompress it. Compression is used in combination with archiving to enable you to compress whole directories and their files at once. Decompression generates a copy of the archive file, which can then be extracted, generating a copy of those files and directories. File Roller provides a GUI interface for these tasks.

Compression with gzip

Several compression utilities are available for use on Linux and Unix systems. Most software for Linux systems uses the GNU gzip and gunzip utilities. The gzip utility compresses files, and gunzip decompresses them. To compress a file, enter the command **gzip** and the filename. This replaces the file with a compressed version of it, with the extension **.gz**.

```
$ gzip mydata
$ ls
mydata.gz
```

To decompress a gzip file, use either **gzip** with the **-d** option or the command **gunzip**. These commands decompress a compressed file with the **.gz** extension and replace it with a decompressed version with the same root name, but without the **.gz** extension. When you use gunzip, you needn't even type in the **.gz** extension; **gunzip** and **gzip -d** assume it. Table 10-7 lists the different **gzip** options.

```
$ gunzip mydata.gz
$ ls
mydata
```

TIP *On your desktop, you can extract the contents of an archive by locating it with the file manager and double-clicking it. This will start the File Roller application, which will open the archive, listing its contents. You can then choose to extract the archive. File Roller will use the appropriate tools to decompress the archive (bzip2, Zip, or gzip) if compressed, and then extract the archive (tar) (see Chapter 4).*

You can also compress archived tar files. This results in files with the extensions **.tar.gz**. Compressed archived files are often used for transmitting extremely large files across networks.

```
$ gzip myarch.tar
$ ls
myarch.tar.gz
```

You can compress tar file members individually using the **tar z** option that invokes gzip. With the **z** option, tar invokes gzip to compress a file before placing it in an archive. Archives with members compressed with the **z** option, however, cannot be updated, nor is it possible to add to them. All members must be compressed, and all must be added at the same time.

The compress and uncompress Commands

You can also use the **compress** and **uncompress** commands to create compressed files. They generate a file that has a **.Z** extension and use a different compression format than gzip. The

Option	Execution
`-c`	Sends compressed version of file to standard output; each file listed is separately compressed: `gzip -c mydata preface > myfiles.gz`

`-d`	Decompresses a compressed file; or you can use gunzip:
	`gzip -d myfiles.gz`
	`gunzip myfiles.gz`

`-h`	Displays help listing.
`-l` *file-list*	Displays compressed and uncompressed size of each file listed: `gzip -l myfiles.gz`
`-r` *directory-name*	Recursively searches for specified directories and compresses all the files in them; the search begins from the current working directory. When used with **gunzip**, compressed files of a specified directory are uncompressed.
`-v` *file-list*	For each compressed or decompressed file, displays its name and the percentage of its reduction in size.
`-num`	Determines the speed and size of the compression; the range is from –1 to –9. A lower number gives greater speed but less compression, resulting in a larger file that compresses and decompresses quickly. Thus –1 gives the quickest compression, but with the largest size; –9 results in a very small file that takes longer to compress and decompress. The default is –6.

TABLE 10-7 The `gzip` Options

compress and **uncompress** commands are not that widely used, but you may run across .Z files occasionally. You can use the **uncompress** command to decompress a .Z file. The gzip utility is the standard GNU compression utility and should be used instead of **compress**.

Compressing with bzip2

Another popular compression utility is **bzip2**. It compresses files using the Burrows-Wheeler block-sorting text compression algorithm and Huffman coding. The command line options are similar to gzip by design, but they are not exactly the same. (See the bzip2 Man page for a complete listing.) You compress files using the **bzip2** command and decompress with **bunzip2**. The **bzip2** command creates files with the extension .bz2. You can use **bzcat** to output compressed data to the standard output. The **bzip2** command compresses files in blocks and enables you to specify their size (larger blocks give you greater compression). As when using gzip, you can use bzip2 to compress tar archive files. The following example compresses the **mydata** file into a bzip compressed file with the extension **.bz2**:

```
$ bzip2 mydata
$ ls
mydata.bz2
```

To decompress, use the **bunzip2** command on a bzip file.

```
$ bunzip2 mydata.bz2
```

Using Zip

Zip is a compression and archive utility modeled on PKZIP, which was used originally on DOS systems. Zip is a cross-platform utility used on Windows, Mac, MS-DOS, OS/2, Unix, and Linux systems. Zip commands can work with archives created by PKZIP and can use Zip archives. You compress a file using the **zip** command. This creates a Zip file with the **.zip** extension. If no files are listed, **zip** outputs the compressed data to the standard output. You can also use the – argument to have **zip** read from the standard input. To compress a directory, you include the **-r** option. The first example archives and compresses a file:

```
$ zip mydata
$ ls
mydata.zip
```

The next example archives and compresses the **reports** directory:

```
$ zip -r reports
```

A full set of archive operations is supported. With the **-f** option, you can update a particular file in the Zip archive with a newer version. The **-u** option replaces or adds files, and the **-d** option deletes files from the Zip archive. Options also exist for encrypting files, making DOS-to-Unix end-of-line translations, and including hidden files.

To decompress and extract the Zip file, you use the **unzip** command.

```
$ unzip mydata.zip
```

PART

Applications

11

Office and Database Applications

A variety of office suites are now available for Linux (see Table 11-1). These include professional-level word processors, presentation managers, drawing tools, and spreadsheets. The freely available versions are described in this chapter. Sun has initiated development of an open source Office suite using StarOffice code. The applications, known as OpenOffice, provide Office applications integrated with GNOME. OpenOffice is currently the primary office application supported by Red Hat. KOffice is an entirely free office suite designed for use with KDE. The GNOME Office suite integrates GNOME applications into a productivity suite that is freely available. CodeWeavers CrossOver Office provides support for running MS Office Windows applications directly on Linux, integrating them with KDE and GNOME. You can also purchase commercial office suites such as StarOffice from Sun.

A variety of database management systems are also available for Linux. These include high-powered, commercial-level database management systems, such as Oracle, IBM's DB2, and Sybase. Most of the database management systems available for Linux are designed to support large relational databases. Fedora Core 4 includes both MySQL and PostgreSQL databases in its distribution. For small personal databases, you can use the desktop database management systems being developed for KDE and GNOME. In addition, some software is available for databases accessed with the Xbase database programming language. These are smaller databases using formats originally developed for dBase on the PC. Various database management systems available to run under Linux are listed in Table 11-6 later in this chapter.

Red Hat Enterprise Linux and Fedora Core also provide several text editors that range from simple text editors for simple notes to editors with more complex features such as spell-checkers, buffers, or pattern matching. All generate character text files and can be used to edit any Linux text files. Text editors are often used in system administration tasks to change or add entries in Linux configuration files found in the **/etc** directory or a user's initialization or application dot files located in a user's home directory. You can use any text editor to work on source code files for any of the programming languages or shell program scripts.

TABLE 11-1 Linux
Office Suites

Web Site	Description
www.openoffice.org	OpenOffice open source office suite based on StarOffice
www.koffice.org	KOffice Suite, for KDE
www.gnome.org/gnome-office	GNOME Office, for GNOME
www.sun.com	StarOffice Suite
www.codeweavers.com	CrossOver Office (MS Office support)

Running Microsoft Office on Linux: CrossOver

One of the primary concerns for new Linux users is what kind of access they will have to their Microsoft Office files, particularly Word files. The Linux operating system and many applications for it are designed to provide seamless access to MS Office files. The major Linux Office suites, including KOffice, OpenOffice, and StarOffice, all read and manage any Microsoft Office files. In addition, these office suites are fast approaching the same level of features and support for office tasks as found in Microsoft Office.

If you want to use any Windows application on Linux, three important alternatives are the Wine virtual windows API support, VMware virtual platform technology, and CrossOver Office by CodeWeavers. VMware and CrossOver are commercial packages. Wine allows you to run many Windows applications directly, using a supporting virtual windows API. See the Wine Web site for a list of supported applications, **www.winehq.com**.

CrossOver Office also lets you install and run most Microsoft Office applications. CrossOver Office was developed by CodeWeavers, which also supports Windows Web browser plug-ins as well as several popular Windows applications like Adobe Photoshop. CrossOver features both standard and professional versions, providing reliable application support. You can find out more about CrossOver Office at **www.codeweavers.com**.

CrossOver can be installed either for private multiuser mode or managed multiuser mode. In private multiuser mode, each user installs his or her own Windows software, such as full versions of Office. In managed multiuser mode, the Windows software is installed once and all users share it. When you install new software, you first open the CrossOver startup tool, and then on the Add/Remove panel you will see a list of supported software. This will include Office applications as well as some Adobe applications, including earlier versions of Photoshop. An Install Software panel will then let you select whether to install from a CD-ROM or an .exe file. For Office on a CD-ROM, select CD-ROM, place the Windows CD-ROM in your CD-ROM drive, and then click Next. The Windows Office installer will start up in a Linux window and will proceed as if you were on a Windows system. When the install requires a restart of the system, CrossOver will simulate it for you. Once the software is installed, you will see a Windows Applications menu on the main menu, from which you can start your installed Windows software. The applications will run within a Linux window, just as if they were running in Windows.

You can also try CrossOver for unsupported applications. They may or may not run.

With VMware, you can run Windows under Linux, allowing you to run Windows applications, including Microsoft Office, on your Linux system. For more information, check the VMware Web site at **www.vmware.com**.

Note   *Though Linux allows users to directly mount and access any of the old DOS or FAT32 partitions used for Windows 95, 98, and ME, it can mount NTFS partitions (Windows XP, 2000, and NT) only as read only, with partial write support. The latest versions of Fedora Core ship with NTFS support disabled. You would have to generate and install the NTFS module for the kernel, to obtain NTFS support.*

OpenOffice

OpenOffice (OO) is a fully integrated suite of office applications developed as an open source project and freely distributed to all. It is included as the primary office suite for Fedora Core, accessible from the Office menu. It includes word processing, spreadsheet, presentation, and drawing applications (see Table 11-2). Versions of OpenOffice exist for Linux, Windows, and Mac OS. You can obtain information such as online manuals and FAQs as well as current versions from the OpenOffice Web site at **www.openoffice.org**.

Note   *Development for OpenOffice is being carried out as an open source project called openoffice .org. The core code is based on the original StarOffice. The code developed in the openoffice.org project will then be incorporated into future releases of StarOffice.*

OpenOffice is an integrated suite of applications. You can open the writer, spreadsheet, or presentation application directly. Also, in most OpenOffice applications, you can select New from the File menu and select a different application if you wish. The OpenWriter word processor supports standard word processing features, such as cut and paste, spell-checker, and text formatting, as well as paragraph styles (see Figure 11-1). You can embed objects within documents, such as using OpenDraw to create figures that you can then drag and drop to the OpenWriter document.

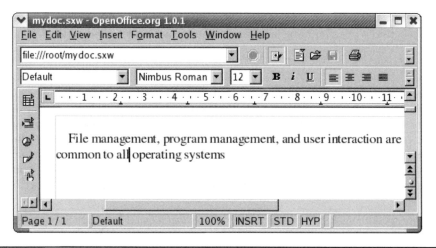

FIGURE 11-1   OpenOffice's OpenWriter word processor

Application	Description
OpenCalc	OpenOffice spreadsheet
OpenDraw	OpenOffice drawing application
OpenWriter	OpenOffice word processor
OpenMath	OpenOffice mathematical formula composer
OpenImpress	OpenOffice presentation manager

TABLE 11-2 GNOME OpenOffice

OpenCalc is a professional-level spreadsheet. With OpenMath, you can create formulas that you can then embed in a text document. With the presentation manager (OpenImpress), you can create images for presentations, such as circles, rectangles, and connecting elements like arrows, as well as vector-based illustrations. OpenImpress supports advanced features such as morphing objects, grouping objects, and defining gradients. OpenDraw is a sophisticated drawing tool that includes 3-D modeling tools. You can create simple or complex images, including animation text aligned on curves. OpenOffice also includes a printer setup tool with which you can select printers, fonts, paper sizes, and page formats.

NOTE *StarOffice is a fully integrated and Microsoft Office–compatible suite of office applications developed and supported by Sun Microsystems, www.sun.com/staroffice. Sun provides StarOffice as a commercial product, though educational use is free.*

OpenOffice also provides access to many database files. File types supported include ODBC 3.0 (Open Database Connectivity), JDBC (Java), ADO, MySQL, dBase, and CSV. Under development are drivers to access PostgresSQL and MDB (Microsoft Access) database files. Check the OpenOffice–Database Access Project for detailed information on drivers and supported databases.

OpenOffice features an underlying component model that can be programmed to develop customized applications. The OpenOffice Software Development Kit (SDK) provides support for using OpenOffice components in applications written in C++ or Java. The Unified Network Objects (UNO) model is the component model for OpenOffice, providing interaction between programming languages, other object models, and network connections.

KOffice

KOffice is an integrated office suite for the KDE (K Desktop Environment) consisting of several office applications, including a word processor, a spreadsheet, and graphic applications. KOffice is not part of the Fedora Core distribution. You will have to download it separately. All applications are written for the KOM component model, which allows components from any one application to be used in another. This means you can embed a spreadsheet from KSpread or a drawing from Kontour in a KWord document. You can obtain more information about KOffice from the KOffice Web site at **www.koffice.org**.

TIP *KOffice applications have import and export filters that allow them to import or export files from popular applications like Abiword, openoffice.org applications, MS Word, and even Palm documents. The reliability of these filters varies and you should check the KOffice Filters Web page for a listing of the different files and their stability.*

KOffice Applications

Currently, KOffice includes KSpread, KPresenter, Kontour, Karbon14, KWord, KFormula, KChart, Kugar, Krita, and Kivio (see Table 11-3). The contact application, Kontact, has been spun off as a separate project. Kontact is an integrated contact application including Kmail, Korganizer, Kaddressbook, and Knotes. KSpread is a spreadsheet, KPresenter is a presentation application, Kontour is a vector drawing program, Karbon14 is a vector graphics program, KWord is a Publisher-like word processor, KFormula is a formula editor, and KChart generates charts and diagrams. Kugar is a report generator, Krita is a bitmap image editor, and Kivio creates flow charts.

KSpread is the spreadsheet application, which incorporates the basic operations found in most spreadsheets, with formulas similar to those used in Excel. You can also embed charts, pictures, or formulas using KChart, Krita, Kontour, or KFormula.

With KChart, you can create different kinds of charts, such as bar graphs, pie charts, and line graphs, as well as create diagrams. To generate a chart, you can use data in KSpread to enter your data. With KPresenter, you can create presentations consisting of text and graphics modeled using different fonts, orientations, and attributes such as colors. You can add such elements as speech bubbles, arrows, and clip art, as well as embed any KOffice component. Kontour is a vector-based graphics program, much like Adobe Illustrator, OpenDraw, and Corel Draw. It supports the standard graphic operations such as rotating, scaling, and aligning objects.

KWord can best be described as a desktop publisher, with many of the features found in publishing applications like Microsoft Publisher and FrameMaker. Although it is also a fully functional word processor, KWord is not page-based like Word or WordPerfect. Instead, text is set up in frames that are placed on the page like objects. Frames, like objects in a drawing program, can be moved, resized, and even reoriented. You can organize frames into a frame

TABLE 11-3 KOffice Applications

Application	Description
KSpread	Spreadsheet
KPresenter	Presentation program
Kontour	Vector drawing program
Karbon14	Vector graphics program
KWord	Word processor (desktop publisher)
KFormula	Mathematical formula editor
KChart	Tool for drawing charts and diagrams
Kugar	Report generator
Krita	Paint and Image manipulation program
Kivio	Flow chart generator and editor (similar to Vivio)
Kexi	Database integration
KPlato	Project management and planning.
Kontact (separate project)	Contact application including mail, address book, and organizer

PART III

set, having text flow from one to the other. Formatting can be applied to a frame set, changing features in all the frames belonging to it at once. The default frame set up for you when you first create a document is the same size as the page. This gives you the effect of a page-based word processor, enabling you to work as if you were using a standard word processor. You can, of course, change the size of your frame and add new ones, if you want.

KFormula is a formula editor used to generate mathematical formulas. Kivio is a flow chart application similar to Visio. Kivio has the ability to generate flow charts using scriptable objects. Given a network, Kivio can generate a flow chart for it. With Java header files, it can generate a flow chart of Java objects. Krita (formerly KImageShop) is an image editor, much like Photoshop. Kexi provides database integration with KOffice applications, currently supporting PostgreSQL and MySQL.

KParts

Embedded components support real-time updates. For example, if you use KChart to generate a chart in a KWord document using data in a KSpread spreadsheet and then change the selected data in the spreadsheet, KChart automatically updates the chart in the KWord document. In effect, you are creating a compound document—one made up of several applications. This capability is implemented by the KDE component model known as KParts. KParts provides communication between distributed objects. In this respect, you can think of an application working also as a server, providing other applications with the services it specializes in. A word processor, specializing in services such as paragraph formatting or spell-checking, could provide these services to all KOffice applications. In that way, other applications do not need to have their own text formatting functions written into them.

KParts is implemented with DCOP, the Desktop Communications Protocol. This is a very simple, small, and fast IPC/RPC mechanism for interprocess communication (IPC) that is based on the X Window System's ICE (Inter-Client Exchange) Protocol. KDE applications now use DCOP libraries to manage their communications with each other. DCOP makes development of KOffice applications much easier and more stable.

With KOffice, you create one kind of document rather than separate ones for different applications. The different applications become views of this document, adding their components to it. KWord sets up the publishing and word processing components, Kontour adds drawing components, while KSpread adds spreadsheet components. You use the appropriate application to view the different components in the single document. This means you can have separate windows open at the same time for different components of the document.

GNOME Office

Office applications for GNOME have been developed independently, such as the Gnumeric spreadsheet and Novell Evolution e-mail client. Some are accessible from the Office and Internet menus. Certain applications like AbiWord and Gnumeric are now part of Fedora Extras. Use the `yum install` command to download and install them, as in `yum install gnumeric`. The GNOME Office project supports a few independent office applications such as Gnumeric and AbiWord. You can find out more from the GNOME Office site at **www.gnome.org/gnome-office**. Sun Microsystems has also integrated OpenOffice into GNOME. Novell, which acquired Ximian, provides and supports Novell Evolution, an e-mail, contact, and calendaring application (see Chapter 13).

A current listing for common GNOME office applications is shown in Table 11-4. All implement the CORBA model for embedding components, ensuring drag-and-drop capability throughout the GNOME interface. All are based on a set of GNOME technologies, including Bonobo, GNOME-Print, and XML. Bonobo is the GNOME architecture for supporting compound documents and reusable software components. GNOME-Print is the GNOME printing architecture designed to support graphics applications as well as work easily with any printing resource. XML is used as the native file format to support the easy exchange of data between GNOME applications.

Currently, GNOME Office includes AbiWord, Gnumeric, and GNOME-DB. AbiWord is a word processor, Gnumeric is a spreadsheet, and GNOME-DB provides database connectivity. Gnumeric is a GNOME spreadsheet, a professional-level program meant to replace commercial spreadsheets. Like GNOME, Gnumeric is freely available under the GNU Public License. Gnumeric is included with the GNOME release, and you will find it installed with GNOME on any distribution that supports GNOME. You can download current versions from **www .gnome.org/projects/gnumeric**. Gnumeric supports standard GUI spreadsheet features, including autofilling and cell formatting, and it provides an extensive number of formats. It supports drag-and-drop operations, enabling you to select and then move or copy cells to another location. Gnumeric also supports plug-ins, making it possible to extend and customize its capabilities easily.

AbiWord is an open source word processor that aims to be a complete cross-platform solution, running on Mac, Unix, and Windows, as well as Linux. It is part of a set of desktop productivity applications being developed by the AbiSource project (**www.abisource.com**).

The GNOME-DB project provides a GNOME Data Access (GDA) library supporting several kinds of databases like PostgreSQL, MySQL, Microsoft Access, and unixODBC. It provides an API to which databases can plug in. These back-end connections are based on CORBA. Through this API, GNOME applications can then access a database. You can find out more about GNOME-DB at **www.gnome-db.org.**.

TABLE 11-4
GNOME Office

Application	Description
AbiWord	Cross-platform word processor
Balsa	E-mail client
Gfax	Send and receive faxes
Gnumeric	Spreadsheet
GnuCash	Personal finance manager
Dia	Diagram and flow chart editor
GNOME-DB	Database connectivity
Evolution	Integrated e-mail, calendar, and personal organizer (Novell)
Guppi	Plotting and graphing program
Sketch	Vector drawing package
Planner	Project manager
OpenOffice	OpenOffice office suite

Dia is a drawing program designed to create diagrams. You can select different kinds of diagrams to create, such as database, circuit object, flow chart, and network diagrams. You can easily create elements along with lines and arcs with different types of endpoints such as arrows or diamonds. Data can be saved in XML format, making it easily transportable to other applications.

GnuCash (**www.gnucash.org**) is a personal finance application for managing accounts, stocks, and expenses. It includes support for home banking with the OpenHBCI interface. OpenHBCI is the open source home banking computer interface (**openhbci.sourceforge.net**).

Document Viewers (PostScript, PDF, and DVI)

Though located under Graphic headings in both the main menu and the Start Here window, PostScript, PDF, and DVI viewers are more commonly used with Office applications (see Table 11-5). Linux features a tool called Evince that can display any PDF and PostScript files. Several applications are available that can view both Adobe PDF and PostScript files. PostScript (.ps) and PDF (.pdf) files can be displayed using Evince or KGhostView. Another application, xpdf, displays only PDF files. Alternatively, you can download Acrobat reader for Linux from Adobe to display PDF and PostScript files. All these viewers also have the ability to print PDF and PostScript documents.

Linux also features a professional-level typesetting tool, called TeX, commonly used to compose complex mathematical formulas. TeX generates a DVI document that can then be viewed by DVI viewers, of which there are several for Linux. DVI files generated by the TeX document application can be viewed by KDVI, which is a plug-in to the KViewShell tool. KViewShell can display and print any kind of document for which it has a plug-in. You can access KDVI as the DVI viewer in the Graphics menu.

These applications are available under the Graphics submenu. The xpdf application bears the name PDF viewer, GVV uses the name Postscript viewer, KGhostView is named PS/PDF viewer (More Graphic Applications), and KDVI is called DVI viewer.

PDA Access

For many PDAs you can use the pilot tools to access your handheld, transferring information between it and your system. The pilot-link package holds the tools you use to access your PDA. Check **www.pilot-link.org** for detailed documentation and useful links. The tool usually begin with the term pilot, like **pilot-addresses**, to read addresses from an address

	Viewer	Description
TABLE 11-5 PostScript, PDF, and DVI Viewers	Evince	Document viewer for PostScript and PDF files
	KGhostView	KDE interface for displaying PostScript and PDF files
	xpdf	X Window System tool for displaying PDF files only
	KDVI	KDE tool for displaying TeX DVI files (plug-in to KViewShell)
	Acrobat Reader	Adobe PDF and PostScript display application

book. Other tools beginning with the term read allow you to convert Palm data for access by other applications like **read-expenses** that outputs expense data as standard text. One of the more useful tools is **pilot-xfer**, which backs up your Palm.

Instead of using command line commands directly, you can use the J-Pilot and KPilot application to access your Palm PDA. With J-Pilot you can perform most tasks such as synchronizing address books and memo pad. J-Pilot is accessible from the Office menu. KPilot is included with the kpim package installed as part of the KDE Desktop. On Fedora Core you need to open a terminal window and enter the kpilot command to run it. It will first let you automatically sync with your PDA. You then have the option to use either Evolution or KContact with your PDA, or just perform backups. You can then perform operations like hotsyncs, viewing addresses, and installing files. To use your PDA on GNOME, you can use the GNOME-pilot applet for your GNOME panel to specify the port to use and test the connection.

For text and Palm format conversions, you can use KPalmDoc on the Accessories menu. This tool will convert text files to Palm files, and Palm files to text files.

The device name used for your PDA is **/dev/pilot** which is managed by **udev**. You may need to specify the port to use for your PDA device. In that case you may need to add a new **udev** rule in the **/etc/udev/rules.d/10-local.rules** file (see Chapter 34). If the 10-local.rules file does not exist, you may have to create it. The following rule would set up a symbolic link for the **/dev/pilot** device to the first USB port.

```
KERNEL="ttyUSB1", SYMLINK=="pilot"
```

Database Management Systems

Database software can be generally organized into three categories: SQL, Xbase, and desktop databases. *SQL-based databases* are professional-level relational databases whose files are managed by a central database server program. Applications that use the database do not access the files directly. Instead, they send requests to the database server, which then performs the actual access. *SQL* is the query language used on these industrial-strength databases. Fedora Core includes both MySQL and PostgreSQL databases. Both are open source projects freely available for your use. Table 11-6 lists DBMSs currently available for Linux.

System	Site
PostgreSQL	The PostgreSQL database: **www.postgresql.org**
MySQL	MySQL database: **www.mysql.com**
Oracle	Oracle database: **www.oracle.com**
Sybase	Sybase database: **www.sybase.com**
DB2	IBM database: **www.software.ibm.com/data/db2/linux**
Informix	Informix database: **www.informix.com/linux**
MaxDB	SAP database now supported by MySQL: **www.mysql.com**
GNU SQL	The GNU SQL database: **www.ispras.ru/~kml/gss**
Flagship	Interface for Xbase database files: **www.fship.com/free.html**

TABLE 11-6 Database Management Systems for Linux

The *Xbase language* is an enhanced version of the dBase programming language used to access database files whose formats were originally developed for dBase on the PC. With Xbase, database management systems can directly access the database files. Xbase is used mainly for smaller personal databases, with database files often located on a user's own system.

SQL Databases (RDMS)

SQL databases are relational database management systems (RDMSs) designed for extensive database management tasks. Many of the major SQL databases now have Linux versions, including Oracle, Informix, Sybase, and IBM (but not, of course, Microsoft). These are commercial and professional database management systems of the highest order. Linux has proved itself capable of supporting complex and demanding database management tasks. In addition, many free SQL databases are available for Linux that offer much the same functionality. Most commercial databases also provide free personal versions, as do Oracle, Adabas D, and MySQL.

PostgreSQL

PostgreSQL, included with Fedora Core, is based on the POSTGRES database management system, though it uses SQL as its query language. POSTGRES is a next-generation research prototype developed at the University of California, Berkeley. Linux versions of PostgreSQL are included in most distributions, including the Fedora Core, Debian, and Mandrake distributions. You can find more information on it from the PostgreSQL Web site at **www .postgresql.org**. PostgreSQL is an open source project, developed under the GPL license. See Chapter 28 for a detailed discussion.

The Red Hat edition of PostgreSQL also includes the Red Hat Database Graphical tools used to easily manage and access PostgreSQL databases. With the administrator tool you can browse and manage databases, the Visual Explain tool analyzes query processes, and Control Center lets you manage databases on servers.

MySQL

MySQL, included with Fedora Core, is a true multiuser, multithreaded SQL database server, supported by MySQL AB. MySQL is an open source product available free under the GPL license. You can obtain current information on it from its Web site, **www.mysql.com**. The site includes detailed documentation, including manuals and FAQs. See Chapter 28 for a detailed discussion.

Oracle

Oracle offers a fully functional version of its Oracle9*i* database management system for Linux, as well as the Oracle Application Server. You can download trial versions from the Oracle Web site at **www.oracle.com**. Oracle is a professional database for large databases specifically designed for Internet e-business tasks. The Oracle Application Server provides support for real-time and commerce applications on the Web. As Linux is a fully functional version of Unix, Oracle is particularly effective on it. Oracle was originally designed to operate on Unix, and Linux is a far better platform for it than other PC operating systems. Oracle offers extensive documentation for its Linux version that you can download from its Documentation page, to which you can link from the Support pages on its Web site. The documentation available includes an installation guide, an administrator's reference, and release notes, as well as the generic documentation. You can find specific information on installing and configuring Oracle for Linux in the Oracle Database HOW-TO.

Informix

Informix (now controlled by IBM) offers an integrated platform of Internet-based applications called Informix Internet Foundation.2000 on Linux. These include the Informix Dynamic Server, their database server. Informix Dynamic Server features Dynamic Scalable Architecture, making it capable of effectively using any hardware setup. Informix provides only commercial products. No free versions exist, though the company currently provides special promotions for Linux products. You can find out more about Informix at **www-4.ibm.com/software/data/informix**. Informix strongly supports Linux development of its Informix line. You can find out more about Informix for Linux at **www-306.ibm.com/software/data/informix/linux**.

Sybase

For Linux, Sybase offers the Sybase Adaptive Server Enterprise server (see **www.sybase.com**). You can currently download the Adaptive Server Enterprise server from the Web site. The Sybase Enterprise database features data integration that coordinates all information resources on a network. SQL Anywhere is a database system designed for smaller databases, though with the same level of complexity found in larger databases.

DB2

IBM provides a Linux version of its DB2 Universal Database software. You can download it free from the IBM DB2 Web page for Linux, **www.software.ibm.com/data/db2/linux**. DB2 Universal Database for Linux includes Internet functionality along with support for Java and Perl. With the Web Control Center, administrators can maintain databases from a Web browser. DB2 features scalability to expand the database easily, support for Binary Large Objects, and cost-based optimization for fast access. DB2 is still very much a mainframe database, though IBM is currently working on refining its Unix/Linux version.

Max DB

Max DB is a SAP-certified database, originally developed by SAP. It provides capabilities comparable to many of the professional-level databases. Max DB is now developed by MySQL AB project, **www.mysql.com**. Recently, MySQL AB project also added MAX DB, formerly SAP DB.

GNU SQL

GNU SQL is the GNU relational database developed by a group at the Institute for System Programming of the Russian Academy of Sciences and supported by the GNU organization. It is a portable multiuser database management system with a client/server structure that supports SQL. The server process requests and performs basic administrative operations, such as unloading parts of the database used infrequently. The clients can reside on any computer of a local network. GNU SQL uses a dialect of SQL based on the SQL-89 standard and is designed for use on a Unix-like environment. You can download the database software from the GNU FTP site at **ftp.gnu.org**. For more information, contact the GNU SQL Web site at **www.ispras.ru/~kml/gss**.

Xbase Databases

Databases accessed with Xbase are smaller in scale, designed for small networks or for personal use. Many are originally PC database programs, such as dBase III, Clipper, FoxPro, and Quicksilver. Currently, only Flagship provides an interface for accessing Xbase database files.

Flagship is a compiler with which you can create interfaces for querying Xbase database files. The interfaces support menus and dialog boxes, and they have function calls that execute certain database queries. Flagship can compile dBase III+ code and up. It is compatible with dBase and Clipper and can access most Xbase file formats, such as **.dbf**, **.dbt**, **.fmt**, and **.frm**. One of Flagship's key features is that its interfaces can be attached to a Web page, enabling users to update databases. Flagship is commercial software, though you can download a free personal version from its Web site at **www.fship.com/free.html**.

Editors

Traditionally, most Linux distributions, including Fedora Core, install the cursor-based editors Vim and Emacs. *Vim* is an enhanced version of the Vi text editor used on the Unix system. These editors use simple, cursor-based operations to give you a full-screen format. You can start these editors from the shell command line without any kind of X Window System support. In this mode, their cursor-based operations do not have the ease of use normally found in window-based editors. There are no menus, scroll bars, or mouse-click features. However, the K Desktop and GNOME do support powerful GUI text editors with all these features. These editors operate much more like those found on Macintosh and Windows systems. They have full mouse support, scroll bars, and menus. You may find them much easier to use than the Vim and Emacs editors. These editors operate from their respective desktops, requiring you first have either KDE or GNOME installed, though the editors can run on either desktop. Vim and Emacs have powerful editing features that have been refined over the years. Emacs, in particular, is extensible to a full-development environment for programming new applications. Newer versions of Emacs, such as GNU Emacs and XEmacs, provide X Window System support with mouse, menu, and window operations. They can run on any window manager or desktop. In addition, the gvim version of the Vim editor also provides basic window operations. You can access it on both GNOME and KDE desktops. Table 11-7 lists several GUI-based editors for Linux.

NOTE *Fedora Core includes a fully functional word processor, OpenWriter (OpenOffice). AbiWord is now part of Fedora Extras. You can find out more on AbiWord at* ***www.abiword.com***. *For KWord, you have to download KOffice.*

GNOME Editor: Gedit

The Gedit editor is a basic text editor for the GNOME desktop (see Chapter 4). It provides full mouse support, implementing standard GUI operations, such as cut and paste to move text, and click and drag to select text. It supports standard text editing operations such as Find and Replace. You can use Gedit to create and modify your text files, including

The K Desktop	Description
KEdit	Text editor
Kate	Text and program editor
KJots	Notebook editor
KWord	Desktop publisher, part of KOffice
GNOME	
Gedit	Text editor
AbiWord	Word processor (Fedora Extras)
X Window System	**Description**
GNU Emacs	Emacs editor with X Window System support
XEmacs	X Window System version of Emacs editor
gvim	Vim version with X Window System support
OpenWriter	OpenOffice word processor that can edit text files

TABLE 11-7   Desktop Editors

configuration files. Gedit also provides more advanced features such as print preview and configurable levels of undo/redo operations, and it can read data from pipes. It features a plug-in menu that provides added functionality, and it includes plug-ins for spell-checking, encryption, e-mail, and text-based Web page display.

K Desktop Editors: Kate, KEdit, and KJot

All the K Desktop editors provide full mouse support, implementing standard GUI operations, such as cut and paste to move text, and click and drag to select text. Kate is an advanced editor, with such features as spell-checking, font selection, and highlighting. Most commands can be selected using menus. A sidebar displays panels for a file selector and a file list. With the file selector, you can navigate through the file system selecting files to work on. Kate also supports multiple views of a document, letting you display segments in their own windows, vertically or horizontally. You can also open several documents at the same time, moving between them with the file list. The KDE editors are only accessible on the KDE Desktop, under Accessories.

Kate is designed to be a program editor for editing software programming/development-related source code files. Although Kate does not have all the features of Emacs or Vi, it can handle most major tasks. Kate can format the syntax for different programming languages, such as C, Perl, Java, and XML. In addition, Kate has the capability to access and edit files on an FTP or Web site.

KEdit is an older simple text editor meant for editing simple text files such as configuration files. A toolbar of buttons at the top of the KEdit window enables you to execute common editing commands easily using just a mouse click. With KEdit, you can also mail files you are editing over a network. The entry for KEdit in the K menu is listed simply as Text Editor. You can start up KEdit by entering the **kedit** command in a terminal window. The KOffice Office Suite also includes a word processor called KWord, which is a high-powered word processor you can also use as a simple editor.

The editor KJots is designed to enable you to jot down notes in a notebook. It organizes notes you write into notebooks, called simply *books.* You can select the one you want to view or add to from the Books menu. To start KJots, select its entry in the Utilities menu or enter the `kjots` command in a terminal window.

The Emacs Editor

Emacs can best be described as a working environment featuring an editor, a mailer, a newsreader, and a Lisp interpreter. The editor is tailored for program development, enabling you to format source code according to the programming language you use. Many versions of Emacs are currently available for use on Unix and Linux systems. The versions usually included with Linux distributions are either GNU Emacs or XEmacs. The current version for GNU Emacs is 20.*x*; it is X Window System–capable, enabling GUI features such as menus, scroll bars, and mouse-based editing operations. (See Chapter 13 for a discussion of the GNU Emacs mailer and its newsreader.) Check the update FTP sites for your distribution for new versions as they come out, and also check the GNU Web site at **www.gnu.org** and the Emacs Web site at **www.emacs.org**. You can find out more information about XEmacs at its Web site, **www.xemacs.org**.

Emacs derives much of its power and flexibility from its capability to manipulate buffers. Emacs can be described as a buffer-oriented editor. Whenever you edit a file in any editor, the file is copied into a work buffer, and editing operations are made on the work buffer. Emacs can manage many work buffers at once, enabling you to edit several files at the same time. You can edit buffers that hold deleted or copied text. You can even create buffers of your own, fill them with text, and later save them to a file. Emacs extends the concept of buffers to cover any task. When you compose mail, you open a mail buffer; when you read news, you open a news buffer. Switching from one task to another is simply a matter of switching to another buffer.

The Emacs editor operates much like a standard word processor. The keys on your keyboard represent input characters. Commands are implemented with special keys, such as control (CTRL) keys and alternate (ALT) keys. There is no special input mode, as in Vi or Ed. You type in your text, and if you need to execute an editing command, such as moving the cursor or saving text, you use a CTRL key. Such an organization makes the Emacs editor easy to use. However, Emacs is anything but simple—it is a sophisticated and flexible editor with several hundred commands. Emacs also has special features, such as multiple windows. You can display two windows for text at the same time. You can also open and work on more than one file at a time, displaying each on the screen in its own window. You invoke the Emacs editor with the command **emacs**. You can enter the name of the file you want to edit, and if the file does not exist, it is created. In the next example, the user prepares to edit the file **mydata** with Emacs:

```
$ emacs mydata
```

The GNU Emacs editor now supports an X Window System graphical user interface. To enable X support, start Emacs within an X Window System environment, such as a KDE, GNOME, or XFce desktop. The basic GUI editing operations are supported: selection of text with click-and-drag mouse operations; cut, copy, and paste; and a scroll bar for moving through text. The Mode line and Echo areas are displayed at the bottom of the window, where you can enter keyboard commands. The scroll bar is located on the left side. To move the scroll bar down, click it with the left mouse button. To move the scroll bar up, click it with the right mouse button.

***

NOTE *XEmacs is the complete Emacs editor with a graphical user interface and Internet applications, including a Web browser, a mail utility, and a newsreader. XEmacs is available on Fedora Extras.*

The Vi Editor: Vim and gvim

The Vim editor included with most Linux distributions is an enhanced version of the Vi editor. It includes all the commands and features of the Vi editor. Vi, which stands for *visual*, remains one of the most widely used editors in Linux. Keyboard-based editors like Vim and Emacs use a keyboard for two different operations: to specify editing commands and to receive character input. Used for editing commands, certain keys perform deletions, some execute changes, and others perform cursor movement. Used for character input, keys represent characters that can be entered into the file being edited. Usually, these two different functions are divided among different keys on the keyboard. Alphabetic keys are reserved for character input, while function keys and control keys specify editing commands, such as deleting text or moving the cursor. Such editors can rely on the existence of an extended keyboard that includes function and control keys. Editors in Unix, however, were designed to assume a minimal keyboard with alphanumeric characters and some control characters, as well as the ESC and ENTER keys. Instead of dividing the command and input functions among different keys, the Vi editor has three separate modes of operation for the keyboard: command and input modes, and a line editing mode. In *command* mode, all the keys on the keyboard become editing commands; in the *input* mode, the keys on the keyboard become input characters. Some of the editing commands, such as **a** or **i**, enter the input mode. On typing **i**, you leave the command mode and enter the input mode. Each key now represents a character to be input to the text. Pressing ESC automatically returns you to the command mode, and the keys once again become editor commands. As you edit text, you are constantly moving from the command mode to the input mode and back again. With Vim, you can use the CTRL-O command to jump quickly to the command mode and enter a command, and then automatically return to the input mode. Table 11-8 lists a very basic set of Vi commands to get you started.

Although the Vi command mode handles most editing operations, it cannot perform some, such as file saving and global substitutions. For such operations, you need to execute line editing commands. You enter the line editing mode using the Vi colon command. The colon is a special command that enables you to perform a one-line editing operation. When you type the colon, a line opens up at the bottom of the screen with the cursor placed at the beginning of the line. You are now in the line editing mode. In this mode, you enter an editing command on a line, press ENTER, and the command is executed. Entry into this mode is usually only temporary. Upon pressing ENTER, you are automatically returned to the Vi command mode, and the cursor returns to its previous position on the screen.

Although you can create, save, close, and quit files with the Vi editor, the commands for each are not all that similar. Saving and quitting a file involves the use of special line editing commands, whereas closing a file is a Vi editing command. Creation of a file is usually specified on the same shell command line that invokes the Vi editor. To edit a file, type **vi** or **vim** and the name of a file on the shell command line. If a file by that name does not exist, the system creates it. In effect, giving the name of a file that does not yet exist instructs the Vi editor to create that file. The following command invokes the Vi editor, working on the file **booklist**. If **booklist** does not yet exist, the Vi editor creates it.

```
$ vim booklist
```

Command	Cursor Movement
h	Moves the cursor left one character.
l	Moves the cursor right one character.
k	Moves the cursor up one line.
j	Moves the cursor down one line.
CTRL-F	Moves forward by a screen of text; the next screen of text is displayed.
CTRL-B	Moves backward by a screen of text; the previous screen of text is displayed.
Input	*(All input commands place the user in input; the user leaves input with <ISA>esc.)*
a	Enters input after the cursor.
i	Enters input before the cursor.
o	Enters input below the line the cursor is on; inserts a new empty line below the one the cursor is currently on.
Text Selection (Vim)	**Cursor Movement**
v	Visual mode; move the cursor to expand selected text by character. Once selected, press key to execute action: c change, d delete, y copy, : line editing command, J join lines, U uppercase, u lowercase.
V	Visual mode; move cursor to expand selected text by line.
Delete	**Effect**
x	Deletes the character the cursor is on.
dd	Deletes the line the cursor is on.
Change	*(Except for the replace command, r, all change commands place the user into input after deleting text.)*
cw	Deletes the word the cursor is on and places the user into the input mode.
r	Replaces the character the cursor is on. After pressing r, the user enters the replacement character. The change is made without entering input; the user remains in the Vi command mode.
R	First places into input mode, and then overwrites character by character. Appears as an overwrite mode on the screen but actually is in input mode.
Move	Moves text by first deleting it, moving the cursor to desired place of insertion, and then pressing the p command. (When text is deleted, it is automatically held in a special buffer.)
p	Inserts deleted or copied text after the character or line the cursor is on.
P	Inserts deleted or copied text before the character or line the cursor is on.
dw p	Deletes a word, and then moves it to the place you indicate with the cursor (press p to insert the word *after* the word the cursor is on).
yy or Y p	Copies the line the cursor is on.
Search	The two search commands open up a line at the bottom of the screen and enable the user to enter a pattern to be searched for; press ENTER after typing in the pattern.
/pattern	Searches forward in the text for a pattern.
?pattern	Searches backward in the text for a pattern.
n	Repeats the previous search, whether it was forward or backward.
Line Editing Commands	**Effect**
w	Saves file.
q	Quits editor; q! quits without saving.

TABLE 11-8 Vi Editor Commands

After executing the **vim** command, you enter Vi's command mode. Each key becomes a Vi editing command, and the screen becomes a window onto the text file. Text is displayed screen by screen. The first screen of text is displayed, and the cursor is positioned in the upper-left corner. With a newly created file, there is no text to display. This fact is indicated by a column of tildes at the left side of the screen. The tildes represent the part of a screen that is not part of the file.

Remember, when you first enter the Vi editor, you are in the command mode. To enter text, you need to enter the input mode. In the command mode, **a** is the editor command for appending text. Pressing this key places you in the input mode. Now the keyboard operates like a typewriter and you can input text to the file. If you press ENTER, you merely start a new line of text. With Vim, you can use the arrow keys to move from one part of the entered text to another and work on different parts of the text. After entering text, you can leave the input mode and return to the command mode by pressing ESC. Once finished with the editing session, you exit Vi by typing two capital Z's, **ZZ**. Hold down the SHIFT key and press **Z** twice. This sequence first saves the file and then exits the Vi editor, returning you to the Linux shell. To save a file while editing, you use the line editing command **w**, which writes a file to the disk; **w** is equivalent to the Save command found in other word processors. You first type a colon to access the line editing mode, and then type **w** and press ENTER.

You can use the **:q** command to quit an editing session. Unlike the **ZZ** command, the **:q** command does not perform any save operation before it quits. In this respect, it has one major constraint. If any modifications have been made to your file since the last save operation, the **:q** command will fail and you will not leave the editor. However, you can override this restriction by placing a **!** qualifier after the **:q** command. The command **:q!** will quit the Vi editor without saving any modifications made to the file in that session since the last save (the combination **:wq** is the same as **ZZ**).

To obtain online help, enter the **:help** command. This is a line editing command. Type a colon, enter the word **help** on the line that opens at the bottom of the screen, and then press ENTER. You can add the name of a specific command after the word **help**. The F1 key also brings up online help.

As an alternative to using Vim in a command line interface, you can use gvim, which provides X Window System–based menus for basic file, editing, and window operations. To use gvim, enter the **gvim** command at an X Window System terminal prompt or select it from a window manager menu. The standard Vi interface is displayed, but with several menu buttons displayed across the top. All the standard Vi commands work just as described previously. However, you can use your mouse to select items on these menus. You can open and close a file, or open several files using split windows or different windows. The editing menu enables you to cut, copy, and paste text as well as undo or redo operations. In the editing mode, you can select text with your mouse with a click-and-drag operation, or use the Editing menu to cut or copy and then paste the selected text. Text entry, however, is still performed using the **a**, **i**, or **o** command to enter the input mode.

Graphics Tools and Multimedia

R ed Hat Enterprise Linux and Fedora Core include a wide range of both graphic and multimedia applications and tools, such as simple image viewers like KView, sophisticated image manipulation programs like GIMP, music and CD players like Rhythmbox, and TV viewers like Totem. Graphics tools available for use under Linux are listed later in Table 12-2. Additionally, there is strong support for multimedia tasks from video and DVD to sound and music editing (see Table 12-3 later). Thousands of multimedia and graphic projects, as well as standard projects, are under development or currently available from **www.sourceforge.net**, **rpm.livna.org**, and **freshrpms.net**. Be sure to check the SourceForge site for any kind of application you may need.

Support for many popular multimedia operations, specifically MP3, DVD, and DivX, are not included with the Fedora Core 4 distribution, due to licensing and other restrictions. To play MP3, DVD, or DivX files, you will have to download and install support packages manually. Precompiled RPM binary packages for many popular media applications and libraries, such as Mplayer and XviD, are available at **rpm.livna.org** and **freshrpms.net**. These include many that are not part of the Fedora Core distribution. The **rpm.livna.org** site is an official Fedora Core repository that provides RPM Fedora-compatible packages for many multimedia and other applications that cannot be included with the Fedora Core distribution. These include MP3 support, DVD and DivX codecs, and even NTFS file system support. The **freshrpms.net** site contains more packages, though the **rpm.livna.org** site packages may be compatible. If you cannot find a package at **rpm.livna.org**, you should check **freshrpms.net**. Current multimedia sites are listed in Table 12-1.

Projects and Sites	Description
SourceForge	This site holds a massive amount of multimedia software for Linux, much under development: **sourceforge.net**
KDE multimedia applications	KDE supports an extensive set of multimedia software applications: **www.kde-apps.org**
GNOME multimedia applications	Many multimedia applications have been developed for GNOME: **www.gnomefiles.org**
Sound & MIDI Software for Linux	Lists a wide range of multimedia and sound software: **linux-sound.org**
Advanced Linux Sound Architecture (ALSA)	The Advanced Linux Sound Architecture (ALSA) project is under development on Linux under the GPL: **www.alsa-project.org**
Open Sound System	Open Sound System, with a wide range of supporting multimedia applications: **www.opensound.com**
rpm.livna.org	Repository for RPM binary packages for popular applications and libraries, including ones for media that are not included with Fedora Core. This is an official extension of the Fedora Project and contains RPM file specifically designed for Fedora Core.
freshrpms.net	Repository for RPM binary packages for popular media applications and libraries, many of which are not included with Fedora Core. Holds a wide variety of current applications and libraries, Fedora Core compatible.

TABLE 12-1   Linux Multimedia Sites

Graphics Tools

GNOME, KDE, and the X Window System support an impressive number of graphics tools, including image viewers, window grabbers, image editors, and paint tools. On the KDE and GNOME desktops, these tools can be found under either a Graphics submenu or the Utilities menu.

KDE Graphics Tools

KView is a simple image viewer for GIF and JPEG image files. The KSnapshot program is a simple screen grabber for KDE, which currently supports only a few image formats. KFourier is an image-processing tool that uses the Fourier transform to apply several filters to an image at once. KuickShow is an easy-to-use, comfortable image browser and viewer supporting slide shows and numerous image formats, based on imlib. KolourPaint is a simple paint program with brushes, shapes, and color effects; it supports numerous image formats. Krita is the KOffice professional image paint and editing application, with a wide range of features, such as creating Web images and modifying photographs (formerly known as Krayon and KImageShop).

GNOME Graphics Tools

GNOME features several powerful and easy-to-use graphic tools. Some are installed with Fedora Core 4, whereas you can download others, such as GView and gtKam, from **www .gnomefiles.org**. Also, many of the KDE tools work just as effectively in GNOME and are accessible from the GNOME desktop.

The gThumb application is a thumbnail image viewer that lets you browse images using thumbnails, display them, and organize them into catalogs or easy reference. See **sourceforge .net** for more information.

GIMP is the GNU Image Manipulation Program, a sophisticated image application much like Adobe Photoshop. You can use GIMP for such tasks as photo retouching, image composition, and image authoring. It supports features such as layers, channels, blends, and gradients. GIMP makes particular use of the GTK+ widget set. You can find out more about GIMP and download the newest versions from its Web site at **www.gimp.org**. GIMP is freely distributed under the GNU Public License.

The gPhoto project provides software for accessing digital cameras (**www.gphoto.org**). Several front-end interfaces are provided for a core library, called libgphoto2, consisting of drivers and tools that can access numerous digital cameras. The gtKam application is a GNOME digital camera tool that can load, select, and edit photos from a digital camera connected to your system (although Fedora Core now uses gThumb). It operates as a GNOME interface for the libgphoto2 libraries. With gtKam, you can generate thumbnail images to select and organize your photos. You can also process photos, changing their orientation. The gPhoto2 program provides the command line interface for the libgphoto2 library, performing operations similar to gtKam.

X Window System Graphics Programs

X Window System–based applications run directly on the underlying X Window System, which supports the more complex desktops like GNOME and KDE. These applications tend to be simpler, lacking the desktop functionality found in GNOME or KDE applications. Xpaint is a paint program, much like MacPaint. You can load graphics or photographs, and then create shapes, add text, and add colors. You can use brush tools with various sizes and colors. Xfig is a drawing program, and Xmorph enables you to morph images, changing their shapes. ImageMagick lets you convert images from one format to another; you can, for instance, change a TIFF image to a JPEG image. Table 12-2 lists some popular graphics tools for Linux.

PART III

TABLE 12-2 Graphics Tools for Linux

Tool	Description
KDE	
KView	Simple image viewer for GIF and JPEG image files
KSnapshot	Screen grabber
KFourier	Image processing tool that uses the Fourier transform
KuickShow	Image browser and viewer
KolourPaint	Paint program
Krita	Image editor
GNOME	
gThumb	Image browser, viewer, and cataloger
GIMP	GNU Image Manipulation Program
gtKam	GNOME digital camera application, front end to libgphoto2 library
X Window System	
Xpaint	Paint program
Xfig	Drawing program
Xmorph	Tool that morphs images
Xfractals	Fractal image generator
ImageMagick	Image format conversion and editing tool

Multimedia

Many applications are available for both video and sound, including sound editors, MP3 players, and video players (see Table 12-3). Linux sound applications include mixers, digital audio tools, CD audio writers, MP3 players, and network audio support. There are literally thousands of projects currently under development at **www.sourceforge.net**. If you are looking for a specific kind of application, odds are you will find it there. Current projects include a full-featured video player, a digital video recorder, and a digital audio mixer. Many applications designed specifically for the GNOME or KDE user interface can be found at their respective software sites (**www.gnomefiles.org** and **www.kde-apps.org**). Precompiled binary RPM packages can be easily downloaded and installed from **freshrpms.net**.

GStreamer: Multimedia System Selector

Many of the GNOME-based applications make use of GStreamer. GStreamer is a streaming media framework based on graphs and filters. Using a plug-in structure, GStreamer applications can accommodate a wide variety of media types. You can download modules and plug-ins from **gstreamer.freedesktop.org**. Fedora Core includes several GStreamer applications:

- The Totem video player uses GStreamer to play DVDs, VCDs, and MPEG media.

- Rhythmbox provides integrated music management; it is similar to the Apple iTunes music player.

- Sound Juicer is an audio CD ripper.
- A CD player, a sound recorder, and a volume control are all provided as part of the GStreamer GNOME media package.

Multimedia System Selector

GStreamer can be configured to use different input and output sound and video drivers and servers. You can make these selections using the GStreamer properties tool (see Figure 12-1). To open this tool from the Desktop menu, first select Preferences, then More Preferences, and then the Multimedia Systems Selector entry. You can also enter `gstreamer-properties` in a terminal window. The properties window displays two tabbed panels, one for sound and the other for video. The output drivers and servers are labeled Default Sink, and the input

TABLE 12-3
Multimedia and
Sound Applications

Application	Description
Xine	Multimedia player for video, DVD, and audio
Rhythmbox	Music management (GStreamer)
Sound Juicer	GNOME CD audio ripper (GStreamer)
Grip	CD audio ripper
aKtion	KDE video player
Kscd	Music CD player
Krec	KDE sound recorder
Kaboodle	A media player
GNOME CD Player	CD Player
GNOME Sound Recorder	Sound recorder
XMMS	CD Player
Xplaycd	Music CD player
Noatun	KDE multimedia player
Xanim	Animation and video player
RealPlayer	RealMedia and RealAudio streaming media (**www.real.com**)
HelixPlayer	Open source version of Real Player (**www.real.com**)
K3b	KDE CD writing interface for cdrecord, mkisofs, and cdda2wav
KAudioCreator	KDE CD burner and ripper
dvdauthor	Tools for creating DVDs (**dvdauthor.sourceforge.net**). Download RPM from **rpm.livna.org**.
Qauthor	KDE front end for dvdauthor (**www.kde-apps.org**)
DVDStyler	DVD authoring application for Gnome (**dvdstyler.sourceforge.net**)

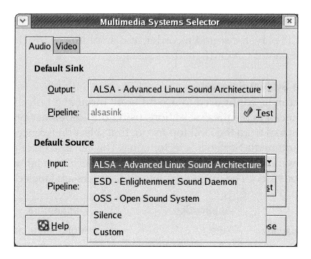

FIGURE 12-1
GStreamer driver
and server selection

divers are labeled Default Source. There are pop-up menus for each, listing the available sound or video drivers or servers. For example, the sound server used is ALSA, but you can change that to OSS.

GStreamer MP3 Compatibility: iPod

For your iPod and other MP3 devices to work with GNOME applications like Rhythmbox, you will need to install MP3 support for GStreamer. MP3 support is not included with Fedora Core distributions due to licensing issues. You can, however, download and install the GStreamer MP3 support package from **rpm.livna.org/fedora**, which maintains most multimedia support packages for Fedora Core that are not included with the distribution. These are all RPM packages configured to work on Fedora Core (also available at **freshrpms.net**).

You will need four packages, two of which are supporting libraries. The lame package provides MP3 decoding, and the gstreamer-plugins-mp3 package sets up MP3 accessibility for GStreamer-supported applications such as Rhythmbox. You will also need the id3tag and libmad libraries. Installation is very easy. See Chapter 4 for more detailed instructions on what libraries and packages to install.

To sync and import from your iPod, you can use iPod management software such as GUI for iPod (gtkpod). Several scripts and tools are currently available for IPod operations; they include SyncPOD, myPod, gtkpod (a GUI for iPod), and iPod for Linux. Check **sourceforge.net** and search for ipod.

Sound Applications

Sound devices on Linux are supported by drivers forming a sound system. With the current Fedora Core 4 kernel, sound support is implemented by the Advanced Linux Sound Architecture (ALSA) system. ALSA replaces the free version of the Open Sound System used in previous releases, as well as the original built-in sound drivers (see Chapter 34). You can find more about ALSA at **www.alsa-project.org**.

Due to licensing and patent issues, Red Hat has removed support for MP3 files. MP3 playback capability has been removed from multimedia players like XMMS and Noatun. As an alternative to MP3, you can use Ogg Vorbis compression for music files (**www.vorbis.com**).

NOTE Linux has become a platform of choice for many professional-level multimedia tasks such as generating computer-generated images (CGI) and animation for movie special effects, using such demanding software as Maya and Softimage. Linux graphic libraries include those for OpenGL, MESA, and SGI.

Many sound applications are currently available for GNOME, including sound editors, MP3 players, and audio players. You can use the GNOME CD Player to play music CDs and the GNOME Sound Recorder to record sound sources. Check the software map at **www .gnomefiles.org** for current releases. A variety of applications are also available for KDE, including two media players (Kaiman and Kaboodle), a mixer (KMix), and a CD player (Kscd). Check **www.kde-apps.org** for recent additions. Several X Window System–based multimedia applications are installed with most distributions. These include XMMS and Xplaycd, CD music players, and Xanim, an animation and video player. Currently a software repository for sound samples, open source applications, and articles is available at **www.opensound.com**.

Red Hat features the XMMS multimedia player, the GNOME CD Player, the GNOME Sound Recorder, and the GNOME Volume Control in the Sound And Video menu. The Extra Sound And Video menus list several KDE applications, including KMidi, Kaboodle, and Noatun. Fedora Core 4 also includes HelixPlayer, the open source project used for RealPlayer. HelixPlayer runs only open source media like Ogg Vorbis files (though you can obtain RealPlayer audio and video codecs for the player). See **helixcommunity.org** for more information. You can also download a copy of RealPlayer, the Internet streaming media player, from **www.real.com**. Be sure to choose RealPlayer for Unix, and as your OS.

The Open Sound System (OSS) site provides an extensive listing of available multimedia software at **www.opensound.com/ossapps.html**. Here you can find digital audio players, mixers, MP3 and MPEG players, and even speech tools. The Sound & Midi Software for Linux site currently at **linux-sound.org** hold links to Web and FTP sites for many sound applications.

CD Burners and Rippers

Several CD writer programs that can be used for CD music and MP3 writing (burners and rippers) are available from **www.kde-apps.org**. These include K3b, CD-Rchive, and KAudioCreator (CD ripper). For GNOME, you can use CD-REC and the Nautilus CD burner, which is integrated into the Nautilus file manager, the default file manager for the GNOME desktop. All use mkisofs, cdrecord, and cdda2wav CD writing programs, which are installed as part of the Fedora Core distribution. GNOME also features two CD audio rippers installed with Fedora Core, Grip and Sound Juicer.

TIP If your CD or DVD application has difficulty finding your CD/DVD player or burner, you may need to check whether HAL is creating an appropriate link to your CD/DVD device using /dev/cdrom or /dev/dvdrom. These links should be generated automatically. (See Chapter 34.)

Video Applications

Several projects are under way to provide TV, video, DivX, DVD, and DTV support for Linux (see Table 12-4). Many of these applications are not included with Fedora Core. In most cases, the most recent versions will be in source code format on the original site. For these you will have to download the source code, which you will then need to compile and install. Many applications, though, are already available in binary RPM packages at **rpm**

.livna.org and **freshrpms.net**. Be sure to select the version of Fedora Core you are using and to install any needed library packages. The **freshrpms.net site** will have a larger and more recent collection of packages, though **rpm.livna.org** may be more compatible with Fedora Core. In effect, Firefox provides near seamless install or extraction operations with downloads. For RPM packages, Firefox will give you the option to automatically install the RPM with system-install-packages. For compressed archives such as **.tar.bz** files, Firefox will automatically invoke File Roller, letting you immediately decompress and extract source code files to a selected directory.

Video and DVD Players

Access to current DVD and media players is provided at **dvd.sourceforge.net**. Here you will find links for players like VideoLAN, MPlayer, and Xine.

- The VideoLAN project (**www.videolan.org**) offers network streaming support for most media formats, including MPEG-4 and MPEG-2. It includes a multimedia player, VLC, that can work on any kind of system.

- MPlayer is one of the most popular and capable multimedia/DVD players in use. It is a cross-platform open source alternative to RealPlayer and Windows Media Player. MPlayer includes support for DivX. You can download MPlayer from **www.mplayerhq.hu**. If you download and install RPM binaries from **freshrpm.net**, be sure to first install needed libraries and supporting applications like **lirc**, **lame**, **lzo**, and **aalib**, which are also on the site. If you have trouble displaying video, be sure to check the preferences for different video devices, selecting one that works best.

- Xine is a multipurpose video player for Linux/Unix systems that can play video, DVD, and audio discs. See **xinehq.de** for more information. Xine is available in source code form, which you will have to compile and install, though you can download an RPM binary from **freshrpm.net**.

- Totem, installed with Fedora Core, is a GNOME movie player based on Xine that uses GStreamer. To expand Totem capabilities, you need to install added GStreamer plug-ins, such as the DivX plug-in to display DivX files.

- PowerDVD provides a commercial version of its PowerDVD DVD player for Linux (**gocyberlink.com**).

- LinDVD is the Linux version for Intervideo's WinDVD player, currently under development (**www.intervideo.com**).

- For DVD transcoding and DivX support, check the DVD::rip project (**www.exit1 .org/dvdrip**).

None of the open source software hosted at SourceForge performs CSS decryption of commercial DVDs. You could, however, download and install the **libdvdcss** library, which works around CSS decryption by treating the DVD as a block device, allowing you to use any of the DVD players to run commercial DVDs. It is also provides region-free access. Bear in mind that this may be not be legal in certain countries that require CSS licenses for DVD players.

NOTE *See Chapter 4 for information on what packages you will need to download and install to enable you to play DVD and DivX media on Fedora Core.*

Originally, many of these players did not support DVD menus. With the **libdvdnav** library, these player now feature full DVD menu support. The **libdvdread** library provides basic DVD interface support such as reading IFO files. You can download RPM binaries for these packages from **freshrpms.net**. See Chapter 4 for more details on packages you need to install.

DVD development efforts were initially supported by the Linux Video and DVD Project (LiViD). The development of an open source DVD player has been hampered by the concerns and restrictions of the MPAA and their control over the DVD decoding software (an officially licensed player is under development). Information about efforts to develop Linux DVD software can be found by doing a search for "**opendvd.org**".

TV Players

The site **linuxtv.org** provides detailed links to DVD, digital video broadcasting (DVB), and multicasting. The site also provides downloads of many Linux video applications.

The primary TV player on Fedora Core is tvtime, which works with many common video capture cards, relying on drivers developed for TV tuner chips on those cards like the Conexant chips. It can only display a TV image. It has no recording or file playback capabilities. Check **tvtime.sourceforge.net** for more information.

For KDE, several video applications are available or currently under development, including video players (aKtion and Noatun). Check **www.kde-apps.org** for downloads. Currently available or under development for GNOME are TV tuners (GnomeVision and GnomeTV), a video player (Gnome-Video), and a video editor (Trinity). Check **www .gnomefiles.org**.

DivX on Linux

DivX is a commercial video compression technology (free for personal use) for providing DVD-quality video with relatively small file sizes. You can compress 60 minutes of DVD video into about 400MB, while maintaining very good quality. DivX is based on the MPEG-4 compression format, whereas DVD is MPEG-2. You can download the Linux version of DivX for free from **www.divx.com/divx/linux**. If you download with Firefox, you can choose to extract the archive directly. Within the **divx** folder, you can then run **install.sh**, which will automatically install DivX libraries.

Often DivX files use the open source version of DivX known as XviD. XviD is an entirely independent open source project. Binary RPM versions can be obtained for Fedora from **rpm.livna.org** and **freshrpms.net**. The RPM package from **rpm.livna.org** was developed as part of the Fedora Core 4 project, though not included with the distribution.

You can also download the XviD source code from **www.xvid.org**. If you use Firefox to download, you will automatically have the option to download the original compressed **.tar.bz** file or to open File Roller and immediately extract the compressed archive. Once it is extracted, you can compile the source code and install the codec. The Linux version is built in the **build/generic** subdirectory, using the `./configure`, `make`, and `make install` commands (see Chapter 4). Open a terminal window and use the `cd` command to change to that directory, then run the commands.

To run DivX in GNOME GStreamer applications like Totem, you will need to download and install the GStreamer DivX plug-in. The simplest way to add DivX support on Fedora Core is to install the **freshrpms.net** packages for GStreamer video extra plug-ins. Be sure to install supporting libraries and applications. If you need to install them, system-install-packages will list them when you install the GStreamer extra plug-ins RPMs (see Chapter 4).

	Projects and Players	Site
TABLE 12-4 Video and DVD Projects and Applications	LinuxTV.org	Links to video, TV, and DVD sites: **linuxtv.org**
	DVD players list	**dvd.sourceforge.net**
	Xine	Xine video player: **xinehq.de**
	Totem	Totem video and DVD player for GNOME based on Xine and using GStreamer: **xinehq.de**
	VideoLAN	Network multimedia streaming: **www.videolan.org**
	MPlayer	MPlayer DVD/multimedia player: **www.mplayerhq.hu**
	PowerDVD	Cyberlink PowerDVD for Linux: **gocyberlink.com**
	WinDVD	Intervideo WinDVD player for Linux (under development): **www.intervideo.com**
	DVD::rip	DVD transcoding and DivX software: **www.exit1.org/dvdrip**
	GTV	GNOME MPEG video player
	tvtime	TV viewer: **tvtime.sourceforge.net**
	Linux 4 DivX	**www.divx.com/divx/linux**
	XviD	Open Source DivX: **www.xvid.org**

13
CHAPTER

Mail and News Clients

Y our Linux system supports a wide range of both electronic mail and news clients. Mail clients enable you to send and receive messages with other users on your system or accessible from your network. News clients let you read articles and messages posted in a newsgroups, which are open to access by all users. This chapter reviews mail and news clients installed with Red Hat Enterprise Linux and Fedora Core.

Mail Clients

You can send and receive e-mail messages in a variety of ways, depending on the type of mail client you use. Although all electronic mail utilities perform the same basic tasks of receiving and sending messages, they tend to have different interfaces. Some mail clients operate on a desktop, such as KDE or GNOME. Others run on any X Window System managers. Several popular mail clients were designed to use a screen-based interface and can be started only from the command line. Other traditional mail clients were developed for just the command line interface, which requires you to type your commands on a single command line. Most mail clients described here are included in standard Linux distributions and come in a standard RPM package for easy installation. For Web-based Internet mail services, such as Hotmail, Google, and Yahoo, you use a Web browser instead of a mail client to access mail accounts provided by those services. Table 13-1 lists several popular Linux mail clients. Mail is transported to and from destinations using mail transport agents. Sendmail, Exim, and Smail send and receive mail from destinations on the Internet or at other sites on a network (see Chapter 25). To send mail over the Internet, they use the Simple Mail Transport Protocol (SMTP). Most Linux distributions, including Fedora Core, automatically install and locally configure Sendmail for you. On starting up your system, having configured your network connections, you can send and receive messages over the Internet.

Mail Client	Description
Kontact (KMail, KAddressbook, KOrganizer)	Includes the K Desktop mail client, KMail; integrated mail, address book, and scheduler
Evolution	Primary mail client for Fedora Core
Balsa	GNOME mail client (see Table 13-2)
Thunderbird	Mozilla group stand-alone mail client and newsreader
Mozilla Mail	Web browser–based mail client
Netscape	Web browser–based mail client
GNUEmacs and XEmacs	Emacs mail clients
Mutt	Screen-based mail client
Sylpheed	Gtk mail and news client
Mail	Original Unix-based command line mail client
SquirrelMail	Web-based mail client

TABLE **13-1**   Linux Mail Clients

You can sign your e-mail message with the same standard signature information, such as your name, Internet address or addresses, or farewell phrase. Having your signature information automatically added to your messages is helpful. To do so, you need to create a signature file in your home directory and enter your signature information in it. A *signature file* is a standard text file you can edit using any text editor. Mail clients such as KMail enable you to specify a file to function as your signature file. Others, such as Mail, expect the signature file to be named **.signature**.

MIME

MIME (the term stands for *Multipurpose Internet Mail Extensions*) is used to enable mail clients to send and receive multimedia files and files using different character sets such as those for different languages. Multimedia files can be images, sound clips, or even video. Mail clients that support MIME can send binary files automatically as attachments to messages. MIME-capable mail clients maintain a file called **mailcap** that maps different types of MIME messages to applications on your system that can view or display them. For example, an image file will be mapped to an application that can display images. Your mail clients can then run that program to display the image message. A sound file will be mapped to an application that can play sound files on your speakers. Most mail clients have MIME capabilities built in and use their own version of the **mailcap** file. Others use a program called metamail that adds MIME support. MIME is not only used in mail clients. As noted in Chapters 6 and 7, both the KDE and GNOME file managers use MIME to map a file to a particular application so that you can launch the application directly from the file.

The mime.types File

Applications are associated with binary files by means of the **mailcap** and **mime.types** files. The **mime.types** file defines different MIME types, associating a MIME type with a certain application. The **mailcap** file then associates each MIME type with a specified application. Your system maintains its own MIME types file, usually **/etc/mime.types**.

Entries in the MIME types file associate a MIME type and possible subtype of an application with a set of possible file extensions used for files that run on a given kind of application. The MIME type is usually further qualified by a subtype, separated from the major type by a slash. For example, a MIME type image can have several subtypes such as jpeg, gif, or tiff. A sample MIME type entry defining a MIME type for JPEG files is shown here. The MIME type is image/jpeg, and the list of possible file extensions is "jpeg jpg jpe":

```
image/jpeg jpeg jpg jpe
```

The applications specified will depend on those available on your particular system. The MIME type is separated from the application with a semicolon. In many cases, X Window System–based programs are specified. Comments are indicated with a **#**. A ***** used in a MIME subtype references all subtypes. The entry **image/*** would be used for an application that can run all types of image files. A formatting code, **%s**, is used to reference the attachment file that will be run on this application. Sample **mailcap** entries are shown here. The first entry associates all **image** files with the xv image viewer. The next two associate video and video MPEG files with the XAnim application.

```
image/*; xv %s
video/*; xanim %s
video/mpeg; xanim %s
```

MIME Associations on GNOME and KDE

You can also create and edit MIME types on the GNOME and KDE desktops. For GNOME, use the GNOME Control Center's MIME types capplet. This capplet will list the MIME types defined for your system along with their associated filename extensions. Edit an entry to change the application and icon associated with that MIME type. On KDE, use the KDE Control Center's File Association entry under KDE Components. This will list MIME types and their associated filename extensions. Select an entry to edit it and change the applications associated with it. KDE saves its MIME type information in a separate file called **mimelnk** in the KDE configuration directory.

MIME Standard Associations

Though you can create your own MIME types, a standard set already is in use. The types text, image, audio, video, application, multipart, and message, along with their subtypes, have already been defined for your system. You will find that commonly used file extensions such as .**tif** and .**jpg** for TIFF and JPEG image files are already associated with a MIME type and an application. Though you can easily change the associated application, it is best to keep the MIME types already installed. The current official MIME types are listed at the IANA Web site (**www.iana.org**) under the name Media Types, provided as part of their Assignment Services. You can access the media types file directly on their site.

S/MIME and OpenPGP/MIME Authentication and Encryption Protocols

S/MIME and OpenPGP/MIME are authentication protocols for signing and encrypting mail messages. S/MIME was originally developed by the RSA Data Security. OpenPGP is an open standard based on the PGP/MIME protocol developed by the PGP (Pretty Good Privacy) group. Clients like KMail and Evolution can use OpenPGP/MIME to authenticate messages. Check the Internet Mail Consortium for more information, **www.imc.org**.

Evolution

Evolution is the primary mail client for Fedora Core. It is installed by default along with OpenOffice. Though designed for GNOME, it will work equally well on KDE. Evolution is an integrated mail client, calendar, and address book, currently being developed by Novell and now known as the Novell Evolution. The Evolution mailer is a powerful tool with support for numerous protocols (SMTP, POP, and IMAP), multiple mail accounts, and encryption. With Evolution, you can create multiple mail accounts on different servers, including those that use different protocols such as POP or IMAP. You can also decrypt PGP- or GPG-encrypted messages.

   The Evolution mailer provides a simple GUI interface, with a toolbar for commonly used commands and a sidebar for shortcuts. A menu of Evolution commands allows access to other operations. The main panel is divided into two panes, one for listing the mail headers and the other for displaying the currently selected message. You can click any header title to sort your headers by that category. Evolution also supports the use of virtual folders. These are folders created by the user to hold mail that meets specified criteria. Incoming mail can be automatically distributed to their particular virtual folder.

Thunderbird

Thunderbird is a full-featured stand-alone e-mail client provided by the Mozilla project (**www.mozilla.org**). It is designed to be easy to use, highly customized, and heavily secure. It features advanced intelligent spam filtering, as well as security features like encryption, digital signatures, and S/MIME. To protect against viruses, e-mail attachments can be examined without being run. Thunderbird supports both IMAP and POP, as well as functioning as a newsreader. It also features a built-in RSS reader. Thunderbird also supports the use of LDAP address books. Thunderbird is an extensible application, allowing customized modules to be added to enhance its capabilities. You can download extensions such as dictionary search and contact sidebars from its Web site. GPG encryption can be supported with the enigmail extension (see Chapter 16).

   The interface uses a standard three-pane format, with a side pane for listing mail accounts and their boxes. The top pane lists main entries, and the bottom pane shows text. Command can be run using the toolbar, menus, or keyboard shortcuts. You can even change the appearance using different themes. Thunderbird also support HTML mail, displaying Web components like URLs in mail messages.

   The message list pane will show several fields by which you can sort your messages. Some use just symbols like the Threads, Attachments, and Read icons. Clicking Threads will gather the messages into respective threads with replies grouped together. The last icon in the message list fields is a pop-up menu letting you choose which fields to display. Thunderbird provides a variety of customizable display filters, such as People I Know, which displays only messages from those in your address book, and Attachments, which displays messages with attached files. You can even create your own display filters. Search and sorting capabilities also include filters that can match selected patterns in any field, including subject, date, or the message body.

   When you first start up Thunderbird, you will be prompted to create an e-mail account. You can add more e-mail accounts or modify your current ones by selecting Account Settings from the Edit menu. Then click Add Account to open a dialog with four options, one of which is an e-mail account. Upon selecting the e-mail option, you are prompted to enter your e-mail address and name. In the next panel you specify either the POP or IMAP protocols, and enter the name of the incoming e-mail server, like **smtp.myemailserver.com**.

You then specify an incoming username, the username given you by your e-mail service. Then you enter an account name label to identify the account on Thunderbird. A final verification screen lets you confirm your entries. In the Account Settings window you will see an entry for your news server, with panels for Server Settings, Copies & Folders, Composition & Addressing, Offline & Disk Space, Return Receipt, and Security. The Server Settings panel has entries for your server name, port, username, and connection and task configurations like automatically downloading new messages. The Security panel opens the Certificate manager to let you select security certificates to use to digitally sign or encrypt messages.

Thunderbird provides an address book where you can enter complete contact information including e-mail addresses, street addresses, phone numbers, and notes. Select Address book from the tools menu to open the Address Book window. There are three panes, one for the available address books, one listing the address entries with field entries like name, e-mail, and organization. You can sort the entries by these fields. Clicking on an entry will display the address information, including e-mail address, street addresses, and phone. Only fields with values are displayed. To create an new entry in an address book, click New Card to open a window with panels for contact and address information. To create mailing lists from the address book entries, click the New List button and specify the name of the list and enter the e-mail addresses.

Once you have your address book set up, you can use its addresses when creating mail messages easily. On the Compose window, click the Contacts button to open a Contacts pane. Your address book entries will be listed using the contact's name. Just click on the name to add it to the address box of your e-mail message. Alternatively you can open the address book and drag-and-drop addresses to an address box on your message window.

A user's e-mail messages, addresses, and configuration information are kept in files located in the **.thunderbird** directory within the user's home directory. Backing up this information is as simple as making a copy of that directory. Messages for the different mail boxes are kept in a **Mail** subdirectory. If you are migrating to a new system, you can just copy the directory from the older system. To back up the mail for any given mail account, just copy the **Mail** subdirectory for that account. Though the default address books, **abook .mab** and **history.mab**, can be interchangeably copied, non-default address books need to be exported to an LDIF format and then imported to the new Thunderbird application. It is advisable to regularly export your address books to LDIF files as backups.

NOTE *Thunderbird is the next-generation mail client from the Mozilla project, Mozilla Mail being the first. In the second generation, the integrated approach used for Mozilla and Netscape was abandoned in favor of separate stand-alone tools, Firefox (browser), Thunderbird (mail), and Sunbird (calendar).*

Mozilla Mail

Mozilla Mail is an integrated tool that is part of the Mozilla Web browser. It is an open source product based on the source code used for Netscape. It is considered an older version of Thunderbird. To use the Mozilla mail client, you simply select it in the Tasks menu of the Mozilla Web browser or from the Internet menu on the GNOME program menu. When you first start Mozilla, you are prompted to enter new account information. You can add and edit accounts later by selecting the Mail/News Account Settings entry in the Edit menu. This opens a dialog box with a button for adding new accounts if you wish.

NOTE   *Netscape Communicator includes a mail client called Messenger. Account information, such as your mail server, username, and password, must be entered in the Mail panel in the Preferences window, accessible from the Edit menu. Fedora Core no longer includes Netscape in its distribution, though you can download and install it if you wish.*

GNOME Mail Clients: Evolution, Balsa, and Others

Several GNOME-based mail clients are now available (see Table 13-2). These include Evolution, Balsa, Pyne, and Sylpheed (Evolution is included with Fedora Core). Check **www.gnomefiles.org** for more mail clients as they come out. Many are based on the GNOME mail client libraries (camel), which provides support for standard mail operations. Balsa is a GNOME mail client with extensive features, though it can operate under any window manager, including KDE, as long as GNOME is installed on your system. As noted previously, Evolution is an integrated mail client, calendar, and contact manager from Novell. Pyne is a simple GNOME mail client written in the Python programming language that supports POP3 and IMAP as well as newsreading. Sylpheed is a mail and news client with an interface similar to Windows mail clients. Several support tools are also available like gnubiff, wmgmail, and mail notification mail checkers and notifiers.

Balsa

Balsa provides a full-featured GUI interface for composing, sending, and receiving mail messages. The Balsa window displays three panes for folders, headers, and messages. The left pane displays your mail folders. You initially have three folders: an inbox folder for received mail, an outbox folder for mail you have composed but have not sent yet, and a trash folder for messages you have deleted. You can also create your own mail folders in which you can store particular messages. To place a message in a folder you have created, click and drag the message header for that message to the folder.

Gmail

GNOME also provides clients for accessing and checking Google Gmail. On GNOME, both Mail Notification and wmgmail will check for and notify you of any Gmail messages. Gmail Todo will set up a to-do list using Gmail.

Application	Description
Balsa	E-mail client for GNOME that supports POP3, IMAP, local folders, and multithreading
Evolution	Ximian integrated mail client, calendar, and contact manager
Sylpheed	Mail and news client similar to Windows clients
Pyne	GNOME mail client and newsreader with support for POP3 and IMAP
gnubiff	E-mail checker and notification tool
Mail Notification	E-mail checker and notification that works with numerous mail clients including MH, Sylpheed, Gmail, and Mail
wmgmail	GNOME Gmail notification applet

TABLE 13-2   GNOME Mail Clients

The K Desktop Mail Client: KMail

The K Desktop mail client, KMail, provides a full-featured GUI interface for composing, sending, and receiving mail messages. KMail is now part of the KDE Personal Information Management suite, KDE-PIM, which also includes an address book (KAddressBook), an organizer and scheduler (KOrganizer), and a note writer (KNotes). All these components are also directly integrated on the desktop into Kontact. To start up KMail, you start the Kontact application. The KMail window displays three panes for folders, headers, and messages. The upper-left pane displays your mail folders. You have an inbox folder for received mail, an outbox folder for mail you have composed but have not sent yet, and a sent-mail folder for messages you have previously sent. You can create your own mail folders and save selected messages in them, if you wish. The top-right pane displays mail headers for the currently selected mail folder. To display a message, click its header. The message is then displayed in the large pane below the header list. You can also send and receive attachments, including binary files. Pictures and movies that are received are displayed using the appropriate K Desktop utility. If you right-click the message, a pop-up menu displays options for actions you may want to perform on it. KMail, along with Kontact, KOrganizer, and KAddressBook, is accessible from the KDE Desktop, Office, and Internet menus.

To set up KMail for use with your mail accounts, you must enter account information. Select the Configure entry in the Settings menu. Several panels are available on the Settings window, which you can display by clicking their icons in the left column. For accounts, you select the Network panel. You may have more than one mail account on mail servers maintained by your ISP or LAN. A configure window is displayed where you can enter login, password, and host information. For secure access, KMail now supports SSL, provided OpenSSL is installed. Messages can now be encrypted and decoded by users. It also supports IMAP in addition to POP and SMTP protocols.

SquirrelMail Web Mail Client

You can use the SquirrelMail Web mail tool to access mail on a Linux system using your Web browser. It will display a login screen for mail users. It features an inbox list and message reader, support for editing and sending new messages, and a plug-in structure for adding new features. You can find out more about SquirrelMail at **www.squirrelmail.org**. The Apache configuration file is **/etc/httpd/conf.d/squirrelmail.conf**, and SquirrelMail is installed in **/usr/share/squirrelmail**. Be sure that the IMAP mail server is also installed.

To configure SquirrelMail, you use the **config.pl** script in the **/usr/share/squirrelmail/config** directory. This displays a simple text-based menu where you can configure settings like the server to use, folder defaults, general options, and organization preferences.

```
./config.pl
```

To access SquirrelMail, use the Web server address with the **/squirrelmail** extension, as in **locahost/squirrelmail** for users on the local system, or **www.mytrek.com/squirrelmail** for remote users.

Emacs

The Emacs mail clients are integrated into the Emacs environment, of which the Emacs editor is the primary application. They are, however, fully functional mail clients. The GNU version of Emacs includes a mail client along with other components, such as a newsreader and editor. GNU Emacs is included on Fedora Core distributions. Check the Emacs Web site at **www.gnu.org/software/emacs** for more information. When you start up GNU Emacs, menu buttons are displayed across the top of the screen. If you are running Emacs in an X Window System environment, you have full GUI capabilities and can select menus using your mouse. To access the Emacs mail client, select from the mail entries in the Tools menu. To compose and send messages, just select the Send Mail item in the Tools menu. This opens a screen with prompts for To and Subject header entries. You then type the message below them, using any of the Emacs editing capabilities. GNU Emacs is a working environment within which you can perform a variety of tasks, with each task having its own buffer. When you read mail, a buffer is opened to hold the header list, and when you read a message, another buffer will hold the contents. When you compose a message, yet another buffer holds the text you wrote. The buffers you have opened for mail, news, or editing notes or files are listed in the Buffers menu. You can use this menu to switch among them.

XEmacs is another version of Emacs, designed to operate solely with a GUI interface. The Internet applications, which you can easily access from the main XEmacs button bar, include a Web browser, a mail utility, and a newsreader. When composing a message, you have full use of the Emacs editor with all its features, including the spell-checker and search/replace.

Command Line Mail Clients

Several mail clients use a simple command line interface. They can be run without any other kind of support, such as the X Window System, desktops, or cursor support. They are simple and easy to use but include an extensive set of features and options. Two of the more widely used mail clients of this type are Mail and Mutt. Mail is the mailx mail client that was developed for the Unix system. It is considered a kind of default mail client that can be found on all Unix and Linux systems. Mutt is a cursor-based client that can be run from the command line.

NOTE *You can also use the Emacs mail client from the command line, as described in the previous section.*

Mutt

Mutt has an easy-to-use screen-based interface. Mutt has an extensive set of features, such as MIME support. You can find more information about Mutt from the Mutt Web site, **www .mutt.org**. Here you can download recent versions of Mutt and access online manuals and help resources. On most distributions, the Mutt manual is located in the **/usr/doc** directory under Mutt. The Mutt newsgroup is **comp.mail.mutt**, where you can post queries and discuss recent Mutt developments.

Mail

What is known now as the Mail utility was originally created for BSD Unix and called, simply, mail. Later versions of Unix System V adopted the BSD mail utility and renamed it mailx. Now, it is simply referred to as Mail. Mail functions as a de facto default mail client on Unix and Linux systems. All systems have the mail client called Mail, whereas they may not have other mail clients.

To send a message with Mail, type **mail** along with the address of the person to whom you are sending the message. Press enter and you are prompted for a subject. Enter the subject of the message and press enter again. At this point, you are placed in input mode. Anything typed in is taken as the contents of the message. Pressing enter adds a new line to the text. When you finish typing your message, press ctrl-d on a line of its own to end the message. You will then be prompted to enter a user to whom to send a carbon copy of the message (Cc). If you do not want to sent a carbon copy, just press enter. You will then see *EOT (end-of-transmission)* displayed after you press ctrl-d

You can send a message to several users at the same time by listing those users' addresses as arguments on the command line following the **mail** command. In the next example, the user sends the same message to both **chris** and **aleina**.

```
$ mail chris aleina
```

To receive mail, you enter only the **mail** command and press enter. This invokes a Mail shell with its own prompt and mail commands. A list of message headers is displayed. Header information is arranged into fields beginning with the status of the message and the message number. The status of a message is indicated by a single uppercase letter, usually **N** for *new* or **U** for *unread*. A message number, used for easy reference to your messages, follows the status field. The next field is the address of the sender, followed by the date and time the message was received, and then the number of lines and characters in the message. The last field contains the subject the sender gave for the message. After the headers, the Mail shell displays its prompt, an ampersand, **&**. At the Mail prompt, you enter commands that operate on the messages. The commonly used Mail commands are listed in Table 13-3 later in this chapter. An example of a Mail header and prompt follows:

```
$ mail
Mail version 8.1 6/6/93. Type ? for help.
"/var/spool/mail/larisa": 3 messages 2 unread
 1 chris@turtle.mytrek. Thu Jun 7 14:17 22/554 "trip"
>U 2 aleina@turtle.mytrek Thu Jun 7 14:18 22/525 "party"
 U 3 dylan@turtle.mytrek. Thu Jun 7 14:18 22/528 "newsletter"
& q
```

Mail references messages either through a message list or through the current message marker (**>**). The greater-than sign (**>**) is placed before a message considered the current message. The current message is referenced by default when no message number is included with a Mail command. You can also reference messages using a message list consisting of several message numbers. Given the messages in the preceding example, you can reference all three messages with **1-3**.

You use the **R** and **r** commands to reply to a message you have received. The **R** command entered with a message number generates a header for sending a message and then places you into the input mode to type in the message. The **q** command quits Mail. When you quit, messages you have already read are placed in a file called **mbox** in your home directory. Instead of saving messages in the **mbox** file, you can use the **s** command to save a message explicitly to a file of your choice. Mail has its own initialization file, called **.mailrc**, that is executed each time Mail is invoked, for either sending or receiving messages. Within it, you can define Mail options and create Mail aliases. You can set options that add different features to mail, such as changing the prompt or saving copies of messages you send. To define an alias, you enter the keyword **alias**, followed by the alias you have chosen and then the list of addresses it represents. In the next example, the alias **myclass** is defined in the **.mailrc** file.

.mailrc

```
alias myclass chris dylan aleina justin larisa
```

In the next example, the contents of the file **homework** are sent to all the users whose addresses are aliased by **myclass**.

```
$ mail myclass < homework
```

Notifications of Received Mail

As your mail messages are received, they are automatically placed in your mailbox file, but you are not automatically notified when you receive a message. To find out if you have any messages waiting, you can use a mail client to retrieve messages or you can use a mail monitor tool to tell you if you have any mail waiting. There are also a number of mail monitors available for use on GNOME. Several operate as applets on the GNOME panel. On the GNOME desktop, there are two mail monitors you can choose from: the Mail Check and Clock and Mail Notify monitors. Both are applets that run inside a GNOME panel. The Mail Check applet will display a mail envelope when mail arrives, and the Clock and Mail Notify applet displays a small envelope and the number of messages received below the time. Other applets like gnubiff will notify you of any POP3 or IMAP mail arrivals. The wmgmail and Mail Notification tools will also notify you of any Gmail messages.

The KDE Desktop has a mail monitor utility called Korn that works in much the same way. Korn shows an empty inbox tray when there is no mail and a tray with slanted letters in it when mail arrives. If old mail is still in your mailbox, letters are displayed in a neat square. You can set these icons as any image you want. You can also specify the mail client to use and the polling interval for checking for new mail. If you have several mail accounts, you can set up a Korn profile for each one. Different icons can appear for each account telling you when mail arrives in one of them.

For command line interfaces, you can use the biff utility. The biff utility notifies you immediately when a message is received. This is helpful when you are expecting a message and want to know as soon as it arrives. Then biff automatically displays the header and beginning lines of messages as they are received. To turn on biff, you enter **biff y** on the command line. To turn it off, you enter **biff n**. To find out if biff is turned on, enter **biff** alone.

You can temporarily block biff by using the **mesg n** command to prevent any message displays on your screen. The **mesg n** command not only stops any Write and Talk messages, it also stops biff and Notify messages. Later, you can unblock biff with a **mesg y** command. A **mesg n** command comes in handy if you don't want to be disturbed while working on some project.

Accessing Mail on Remote POP Mail Servers

Most newer mail clients are equipped to access mail accounts on remote servers. For such mail clients, you can specify a separate mail account with its own mailbox. For example, if you are using an ISP, most likely you will use that ISP's mail server to receive mail. You will have set up a mail account with a username and password for accessing your mail.

Your e-mail address is usually your username and the ISP's domain name. For example, a username of **larisa** for an ISP domain named **mynet.com** would have the address **larisa@mynet.com**. The username would be **larisa**. The address of the actual mail server could be something like **mail.mynet.com**. The user **larisa** would log in to the **mail.mynet .com** server using the username **larisa** and password to access mail sent to the address **larisa@mynet.com**. Mail clients, such as Evolution, KMail, Balsa, and Mozilla, enable you to set up a mailbox for such an account and access your ISP's mail server to check for and download received mail. You must specify what protocol a mail server uses. This is usually either the Post Office Protocol (POP) or the IMAP protocol (IMAP). This procedure is used for any remote mail server. Using a mail server address, you can access your account with your username and password.

Should you have several remote e-mail accounts, instead of creating separate mailboxes for each in a mail client, you can arrange to have mail from those accounts sent directly to the inbox maintained by your Linux system for your Linux account. All your mail, whether from other users on your Linux system or from remote mail accounts, will appear in your local inbox. Such a feature is helpful if you are using a mail client, such as Mail, that does not have the capability to access mail on your ISP's mail server. You can implement such a feature with Fetchmail. Fetchmail checks for mail on remote mail servers and downloads it to your local inbox, where it appears as newly received mail (you will have to be connected to the Internet or the remote mail server's network).

To use Fetchmail, you have to know a remote mail server's Internet address and mail protocol. Most remote mail servers use the POP3 protocol, but others may use the IMAP or POP2 protocols. Enter **fetchmail** on the command line with the mail server address and any needed options. The mail protocol is indicated with the **-p** option and the mail server type, usually POP3. If your e-mail username is different from your Linux login name, you use the **-u** option and the e-mail name. Once you execute the **fetchmail** command, you are prompted for a password. The syntax for the **fetchmail** command for a POP3 mail server follows:

```
fetchmail -p POP3 -u username mail-server
```

To use Fetchmail, connect to your ISP and then enter the **fetchmail** command with the options and the POP server name on the command line. You will see messages telling you if mail is there and, if so, how many messages are being downloaded. You can then use a mail client to read the messages from your inbox. You can run Fetchmail in daemon mode to have it automatically check for mail. You have to include an option specifying the interval in seconds for checking mail.

```
fetchmail -d 1200
```

You can specify options such as the server type, username, and password in a **.fetchmailrc** file in your home directory. You can also have entries for other mail servers and accounts you may have. Instead of entering options directly into the **.fetchmailrc** file, you can use the **fetchmailconf** program, which provides a GUI interface for selecting Fetchmail options and entering mail account information. The **fetchmailconf** command runs only under X and requires that Python and Tk be installed. It displays windows for adding news servers, configuring a mail server, and configuring a user account on a particular mail server. The expert version displays the same kind of windows, but with many more options.

Once it is configured, you can enter `fetchmail` with no arguments; it will read entries from your **.fetchmailrc** file. You can also make entries directly in the **.fetchmailrc** file. An entry in the **.fetchmailrc** file for a particular mail account consists of several fields and their values: poll, protocol, username, and password. *Poll* is used to specify the mail server name, and *protocol*, the type of protocol used. Notice you can also specify your password, instead of having to enter it each time Fetchmail accesses the mail server.

Usenet News

Usenet is an open mail system on which users post messages that include news, discussions, and opinions. It operates like a mailbox that any user on your Linux system can read or send messages to. Users' messages are incorporated into Usenet files, which are distributed to any system signed up to receive them. Each system that receives Usenet files is referred to as a *site*. Certain sites perform organizational and distribution operations for Usenet, receiving messages from other sites and organizing them into Usenet files, which are then broadcast to many other sites. Such sites are called *backbone sites,* and they operate like publishers, receiving articles and organizing them into different groups.

To access Usenet news, you need access to a news server. A news server receives the daily Usenet newsfeeds and makes them accessible to other systems. Your network may have a system that operates as a news server. If you are using an Internet service provider (ISP), a news server is probably maintained by your ISP for your use. To read Usenet articles, you use a *newsreader*—a client program that connects to a news server and accesses the articles. On the Internet and in TCP/IP networks, news servers communicate with newsreaders using the Network News Transfer Protocol (NNTP) and are often referred to as NNTP news servers. Or you could also create your own news server on your Linux system to run a local Usenet news service or to download and maintain the full set of Usenet articles. Several Linux programs, called *news transport agents,* can be used to create such a server. This chapter focuses on the variety of newsreaders available for the Linux platform. The configuration administration and architecture of the NNTP server are covered in Chapter 27.

Usenet files were originally designed to function like journals. Messages contained in the files are referred to as *articles.* A user could write an article, post it in Usenet, and have it immediately distributed to other systems around the world. Someone could then read the article on Usenet, instead of waiting for a journal publication. Usenet files themselves were organized as journal publications. Because journals are designed to address specific groups, Usenet files were organized according to groups called *newsgroups.* When a user posts an article, it is assigned to a specific newsgroup. If another user wants to read that article, he or she looks at the articles in that newsgroup. You can think of each newsgroup as a constantly updated magazine. For example, to read articles on the Linux operating system, you would access the Usenet newsgroup on Linux. Usenet files are also used as bulletin boards on which people carry on debates. Again, such files are classified into newsgroups, though their articles read more like conversations than journal articles. You can also create articles of your own, which you can then add to a newsgroup for others to read. Adding an article to a newsgroup is called *posting* the article.

NOTE *The Google Web site maintains online access to Usenet newsgroups. It has the added capability of letting you search extensive newsgroup archives. You can easily locate articles on similar topics that may reside in different newsgroups. Other sites such as Yahoo maintain their own groups that operate much like Usenet newsgroups, but with more supervision.*

Linux has newsgroups on various topics. Some are for discussion, and others are sources of information about recent developments. On some, you can ask for help for specific problems. A selection of some of the popular Linux newsgroups is provided here:

Newsgroup	Topic
comp.os.linux.announce	Announcements of Linux developments
comp.os.linux.admin	System administration questions
comp.os.linux.misc	Special questions and issues
comp.os.linux.setup	Installation problems
comp.os.linux.help	Questions and answers for particular problems
linux.help	Obtain help for Linux problems

You read Usenet articles with a newsreader, such as KNode, Pan, Mozilla, trn, or tin, which enables you to first select a specific newsgroup and then read the articles in it. A newsreader operates like a user interface, enabling you to browse through and select available articles for reading, saving, or printing. Most newsreaders employ a sophisticated retrieval feature called *threads* that pulls together articles on the same discussion or topic. Newsreaders are designed to operate using certain kinds of interfaces. For example, KNode is a KDE newsreader that has a KDE interface and is designed for the KDE desktop. Pan has a GNOME interface and is designed to operate on the GNOME desktop. Pine is a cursor-based newsreader, meaning that it provides a full-screen interface that you can work with using a simple screen-based cursor that you can move with arrow keys. It does not support a mouse or any other GUI feature. The **trn** program uses a simple command line interface with limited cursor support. Most commands you type in and press enter to execute. Several popular newsreaders are listed in Table 13-3.

NOTE *Numerous newsreaders currently are under development for both GNOME and KDE. You can check for KDE newsreaders on the software list on the K Desktop Web site at **www.kde-apps.org**. For GNOME newsreaders, check Internet tools on the software map on the GNOME Web site at **www.gnome.org**. The Mozilla newsreader is integrated into the Mozilla Web browser and is available from **www.mozilla.org**.*

Most newsreaders can read Usenet news provided on remote news servers that use the NNTP. Many such remote news servers are available through the Internet. Desktop newsreaders, such as KNode and Pan, have you specify the Internet address for the remote news server in their own configuration settings. Several shell-based newsreaders, however, such as trn and tin, obtain the news server's Internet address from the **NNTPSERVER** shell variable. Before you can connect to a remote news server with such newsreaders, you first have to assign the Internet address of the news server to the **NNTPSERVER** shell variable, and then export that variable. You can place the assignment and export of **NNTPSERVER** in a login initialization file, such as **.bash_profile**, so that it is performed automatically whenever you log in. Administrators could place this entry in the **/etc/profile** file for a news server available to all users on the system.

```
$ NNTPSERVER=news.domain.com
$ export NNTPSERVER
```

TABLE 13-3 Linux Newsreaders

Newsreader	Description
Pan	GNOME desktop newsreader
KNode	KDE desktop newsreader
Mozilla	Web utility with newsreader capabilities (X based)
Thunderbird	Mail client with newsreader capabilities (X based)
Sylpheed	GNOME Windows-like Newsreader
Slrn	Newsreader (cursor based)
Emacs	Emacs editor, mail client, and newsreader (cursor based)
trn	Newsreader (command line interface)
tin	Newsreader (command line interface)

News Transport Agents

Usenet news is provided over the Internet as a daily newsfeed of articles and postings for thousands of newsgroups. This newsfeed is sent to sites that can then provide access to the news for other systems through newsreaders. These sites operate as news servers; the newsreaders used to access them are their clients. The news server software, called *news transport agents,* is what provides newsreaders with news, enabling you to read newsgroups and post articles. For Linux, three of the popular news transport agents are INN, Leafnode, and Cnews. Both Cnews and Leafnode are small and simple, and useful for small networks. INN is more powerful and complex, designed with large systems in mind (see **www.isc.org** for more details).

Daily newsfeeds on Usenet are often large and consume much of a news server's resources in both time and memory. For this reason, you may not want to set up your own Linux system to receive such newsfeeds. If you are operating in a network of Linux systems, you can designate one of them as the news server and install the news transport agent on it to receive and manage the Usenet newsfeeds. Users on other systems on your network can then access that news server with their own newsreaders.

If your network already has a news server, you needn't install a news transport agent at all. You only have to use your newsreaders to remotely access that server (see **NNTPSERVER** in the preceding section). In the case of an ISP, such providers often operate their own news servers, which you can also remotely access using your own newsreaders, such as KNode and Pan. Remember, though, that newsreaders must take the time to download the articles for selected newsgroups, as well as updated information on all the newsgroups.

You can also use news transport agents to run local versions of news for only the users on your system or your local network. To do this, install INN, Leafnode, slrnpull, or Cnews and configure them just to manage local newsgroups. Users on your system could then post articles and read local news.

Mailing Lists

As an alternative to newsgroups, you can subscribe to mailing lists. Users on mailing lists automatically receive messages and articles sent to the lists. Mailing lists work much like a mail alias, broadcasting messages to all users on the list. Mailing lists were designed to serve small, specialized groups of people. Instead of posting articles for anyone to see, only those who subscribe receive them. Numerous mailing lists, as well as other subjects, are available for Linux. For example, at the **www.gnome.org** site, you can subscribe to any of several mailing lists on GNOME topics, such as **gnome-themes-list@gnome.org**, which deals with GNOME desktop themes. You can do the same at **lists.kde.org** for KDE topics. At **www .liszt.com**, you can search for mailing lists on various topics. By convention, to subscribe to a list, you send a request to the mailing list address with a **–request** term added to its username. For example, to subscribe to **gnome-themes-list@gnome.org**, you send a request to **gnome-themes-list-request@gnome.org**. At **www.linux.org**, you can link to sites that support Linux-oriented mailing lists, such as the Red Hat mailing lists page and the Linux Mailing Lists Web site. Lists exist for such topics as the Linux kernel, administration, security, and different distributions. For example, **linux-admin** covers administration topics, and **linux-apps** discusses software applications; **vger.kernel.org** provides mailing list services for Linux kernel developers.

NOTE   *You can use the Mailman and Majordomo programs to automatically manage your mailing lists. Mailman is the GNU mailing list manager. You can find out more about Majordomo at www.greatcircle.com/majordomo, and about Mailman at sourceforge.net.*

Newsreaders

A variety of newsreaders are available for use on Fedora Core, including several specialized tools. Like the mail clients, there are newsreaders based on GNOME, KDE, Web interfaces, and the command line interface. All will work on any desktop, though those for the command line will use a terminal window to operate. GNOME newsreaders include Pan and Sylpheed, KDE provides KNode, Mozilla supports newsreader capabilities, and slrn uses a command line interface. In addition, specialized tools like inews are available to post news articles. If you just want to download and decode binaries attached to articles, you can use Glitter to detect, download, combine, and decode binary applications posted as several encoded news articles. Check the GNOME and KDE software sites for the latest GNOME and KDE newsreader applications, **www.gnomefiles.org** and **www.kde-apps.org**.

Pan is a powerful newsreader that lets you sort articles, decode binaries, and set up rules for selecting articles. Pan features both pane and notebook displays. Initially, newsgroups, article headers, and article contents are displayed in three panes. You can switch to a notebook display that will show each pane as a tabbed panel covering the entire window. In the newsgroup pane, a drop-down menu lets you choose whether to display all newsgroups or only subscribed ones. You can also search for particular newsgroups. For the article headers, an icon bar lets you display read or unread articles, as well as save and search articles. A selected article is displayed in the pane below the headers.

KNode is currently the standard newsreader distributed with KDE on Fedora Core. The KNode newsreader includes standard features such as follow-ups, saving and printing articles, article and newsgroup searches, and thread displays. It also supports more powerful features such as binary encoding and decoding, displaying attached image files, and separate window displays for articles. In addition, it supports multiple accounts, and customized configuration for features such as colors, fonts, window displays, and article search filters. You can find out more about KNode at **knode.sourceforge.net**. Other KDE newsreaders such as krn and kng are also available. You can download them from **www.kde-apps.org**.

The Mozilla newsreader is part of the Mozilla Web browser, and the Thunderbird newsreader is part of the Thunderbird e-mail client. For Mozilla Mail, you can set up and configure news accounts by selecting the Mail/News Account Settings from the Edit menu.

This displays a sidebar that will include any news server you have already set up. To create a new news account, click the New Account button. This opens a series of dialog boxes where you enter in information such as your news server address and e-mail address. An initial screen asks you to choose whether you are setting up a newsgroup or a mail account. Once you have created your news account, you can then click it to display panes where you can set other options, such as the number of articles to display at a time.

For Thunderbird, select Account Settings from the Edit menu. Then click Add Account to open a dialog with four options, one of which is a Newsgroup account. Upon selecting the Newsgroup option, you are prompted to enter your e-mail address and name, then the newsgroup server, like news.mynewserver.com. Then you enter an account name label to identify the account on Thunderbird. A final verification screen lets you confirm your entries. In the Account Settings window you will see an entry for your news server, with panels for Server Settings, Copies & Folders, Composition & Addressing, and Offline & Disk Space. The Server Settings panel has entries for your server name, port, and connection configurations as well as your newsrc file and download directory. On the Offline & Disk Space panel you can select newsgroups to be automatically downloaded and accessed offline.

The **slrn** newsreader is screen-based. Commands are displayed across the top of the screen and can be executed using the listed keys. Different types of screens exist for the newsgroup list, article list, and article content, each with its own set of commands. An initial screen lists your subscribed newsgroups with commands for posting, listing, and subscribing to your newsgroups.

NOTE   *When you start slrn for the first time, you may will have to create a .jnewsrc file in your home directory. Use the following command: **slrn -f .jnewsrc -create**. Also, you will have to set the **NNTPSERVER** variable and make sure it is exported (see Chapter 9).*

The slrn newsreader features a new utility called slrnpull that you can use to automatically download articles in specified newsgroups. This allows you to view your selected newsgroups offline. The slrnpull utility was designed as a simple single-user version of Leafnode; it will access a news server and download its designated newsgroups, making them available through slrn whenever the user chooses to examine them. Newsgroup articles are downloaded to the **SLRNPULL_ROOT** directory. On Fedora Core, this is **/var/spool/srlnpull**. The selected newsgroups to be downloaded are entered in the **slrnpull.conf** configuration file placed in the **SLRNPULL_ROOT** directory. In this file, you can specify how many articles to download for each group and when they should expire. To use slrn with slrnpull, you will have to further configure the **.slrnrc** file to reference the slrnpull directories where newsgroup files are kept.

NOTE   *Two other popular command line–based newsreaders are trn and tin. Though they are not distributed with all distributions, you can download versions from **www.gnu.org**.*

NOTE   *The GNU version of Emacs also includes a newsreader along with other components, such as a mailer and an editor. Check the Emacs Web site at **www.emacs.org** for more information. When you start up GNU Emacs, menu buttons are displayed across the top of the screen. If you are running Emacs in an X Window System environment, you have full GUI capabilities and can select menus using your mouse. Be sure the **NNTPSERVER** variable is set to your news server address in your .bash_profile file and it is exported.*

Web, FTP, and Java Clients

M ost Linux distributions will provide powerful Web and FTP clients for accessing the Internet. Many are installed automatically and are ready to use when you first start up your Linux system. Linux also includes full Java development support, letting you run and construct Java applets. This chapter will cover some of the more popular Web, Java, and FTP clients available on Linux.

Web and FTP clients connect to sites that run servers, using Web pages and FTP files to provide services to users. Sites are accessed using their Internet addresses. Local networks use the same addressing format. Though the topic is discussed in more detail in Chapter 38, a quick review is provided here. The Internet uses a set of network protocols called TCP/IP, which stands for Transmission Control Protocol/Internet Protocol. In a TCP/IP network, messages are broken into small components called *datagrams*, which are then transmitted through various interlocking routes and delivered to their destination computers. Once received, the datagrams are reassembled into the original message. Datagrams are also referred to as *packets*. Sending messages as small components has proved far more reliable and faster than sending them as one large, bulky transmission. With small components, if one is lost or damaged, only that component has to be resent, whereas if any part of a large transmission is corrupted or lost, the entire message must be resent.

On a TCP/IP network such as the Internet, each computer is given a unique address called an *IP address*. The IP address is used to identify and locate a particular host—a computer connected to the network. To make identifying a computer on the Internet easier, the Domain Name Service (DNS) was implemented. The DNS establishes a domain name address for each IP address. The domain name address is a series of names separated by periods. Whenever you use a domain name address, it is automatically converted to an IP address, which is then used to identify that Internet host. The domain name address is far easier to use than its corresponding IP address.

A domain name address needs to be registered with an Internet domain name registry such as the American Registry for Internet Numbers (ARIN) so that each computer on the Internet can have a unique name (see **www.iana.org** for more information). Creating a name follows specified naming conventions. The domain name address consists of the hostname, the name you gave to your computer; a domain name, the name that identifies your network; and an extension that identifies the type of network you are on. Here is the syntax for domain addresses:

```
host-name.domain-name.extension
```

For Web and FTP sites, the hostname is usually www and ftp respectively. For example:

```
www.ibiblio.org
```

More and more site names are now using more definitive descriptions for the hostname, such as the following for the Fedora Core Web site.

```
fedora.redhat.com
```

With the **whois** command, you can obtain information for domain name servers about different networks and hosts connected to the Internet. Enter **whois** and the domain name address of the host or network, and **whois** displays information about the host, such as the street address and phone number, as well as contact persons.

```
$ whois domain-address
```

Web Clients

The World Wide Web (WWW, or the Web) is a hypertext database of different types of information, distributed across many different sites on the Internet. A *hypertext database* consists of items linked to other items, which, in turn, may be linked to yet other items, and so on. Upon retrieving an item, you can use that item to retrieve any related items. For example, you could retrieve an article on the Amazon rain forest and then use it to retrieve a map or a picture of the rain forest. In this respect, a hypertext database is like a web of interconnected data you can trace from one data item to another. Information is displayed in pages known as *Web pages*. On a Web page, certain keywords or graphics are highlighted that form links to other Web pages or to items, such as pictures, articles, or files.

To access the Web, you use a Web *browser*. You can choose from many different Web browsers. On your Linux system, you can choose from several Web browsers, including Firefox, Konqueror, Epiphany, and Lynx. Firefox, Konqueror, and Epiphany are X Window System–based browsers that provide full picture, sound, and video display capabilities. Most distributions also include the Lynx browser, a line-mode browser that displays only lines of text. The K Desktop incorporates Web browser capabilities into its file manager, letting a directory window operate as a Web browser. GNOME-based browsers, such as Express and Mnemonic, are also designed to be easily enhanced.

Web browsers and FTP clients are commonly used to conduct secure transactions such as logging in to remote sites, ordering items, or transferring files. Such operations are currently secured by encryption methods provided by the Secure Sockets Layer (SSL). See Chapters 19 and 23 for more information about SSL and its counterpart, SSH, the Secure Shell. If you use a browser for secure transactions, it should be SSL enabled. Most browsers such as Mozilla and ELinks include SSL support. For FTP operations, you can use the SSH version of ftp, sftp, or the Kerberos 5 version (see Chapter 19). Linux distributions include SSL as part of a standard installation.

URL Addresses

An Internet resource is accessed using a Universal Resource Locator (URL). A URL is composed of three elements: the transfer protocol, the hostname, and the pathname. The transfer protocol and the hostname are separated by a colon and two slashes, *://*. The *pathname* always begins with a single slash:

```
transfer-protocol://host-name/path-name
```

The *transfer protocol* is usually HTTP (Hypertext Transfer Protocol), indicating a Web page. Other possible values for transfer protocols are **gopher**, **ftp**, and **file**. As their names suggest, **gopher** and **ftp** initiate Gopher and FTP sessions, whereas **file** displays a local file on your own system, such as a text or HTML file. Table 14-1 lists the various transfer protocols.

The *hostname* is the computer on which a particular Web site is located. You can think of this as the address of the Web site. By convention, most hostnames begin with **www**. In the next example, the URL locates a Web page called **guides.html** on the **www.kernel.org** Web site in the LDP directory:

```
http://www.kernel.org/LDP/guides.html
```

If you do not want to access a particular Web page, you can leave the file reference out, and then you automatically access the Web site's home page. To access a Web site directly, use its hostname. If no home page is specified for a Web site, the file **index.html** in the top directory is often used as the home page. In the next example, the user brings up the Red Hat home page:

```
http://www.redhat.com/
```

The pathname specifies the directory where the resource can be found on the host system, as well as the name of the resource's file. For example, **/pub/Linux/newdat.html** references an HTML document called **newdat** located in the **/pub/Linux** directory.

The resource file's extension indicates the type of action to be taken on it. A picture has a **.gif** or **.jpeg** extension and is converted for display. A sound file has an **.au** or **.wav** extension and is played. The following URL references a **.gif** file. Instead of displaying a Web page, your browser invokes a graphics viewer to display the picture. Table 14-2 provides a list of the different file extensions.

```
http://www.train.com/engine/engine1.gif
```

Protocol	Description
http	Uses Hypertext Transfer Protocol for Web site access.
gopher	Accesses Gopher site.
ftp	Uses File Transfer Protocol for anonymous FTP connections.
telnet	Makes a Telnet connection.
news	Reads Usenet news; uses Network News Transfer Protocol (NNTP).

TABLE 14-1 Web Protocols

File Type	Description
.html	Web page document formatted using HTML, the Hypertext Markup Language
Graphics File	
.gif	Graphics, using GIF compression
.jpeg	Graphics, using JPEG compression
Sound File	
.au	Sun (Unix) sound file
.wav	Microsoft Windows sound file
.aiff	Macintosh sound file
Video File	
.QT	QuickTime video file, multiplatform
.mpeg	Video file
.avi	Microsoft Windows video file

TABLE 14-2   Web File Types

Web Browsers

Most Web browsers are designed to access several different kinds of information. Web browsers can access a Web page on a remote Web site or a file on your own system. Some browsers can also access a remote news server or an FTP site. The type of information for a site is specified by the keyword **http** for Web sites, **nntp** for news servers, **ftp** for FTP sites, or **file** for files on your own system. As noted previously, several popular browsers are available for Linux. Three distinctive ones are described here: Mozilla, Konqueror, and Lynx. Mozilla is an X Window System–based Web browser capable of displaying graphics, video, and sound, as well as operating as a newsreader and mailer. Konqueror is the K Desktop file manager. KDE has integrated full Web-browsing capability into the Konqueror file manager, letting you seamlessly access the Web and your file system with the same application. Lynx and ELinks are command line–based browsers with no graphics capabilities, but in every other respect they are fully functional Web browsers.

To search for files on FTP sites, you can use search engines provided by Web sites, such as Yahoo!, Google, or Lycos. These usually search for both Web pages and FTP files. To find a particular Web page you want on the Internet, you can use any of these search engines or perform searches from any number of Web portals. Web searches have become a standard service of most Web sites. Searches carried out on documents within a Web site may use local search indexes set up and maintained by indexing programs like ht:/Dig. Sites using ht:/Dig use a standard Web page search interface. Hypertext databases are designed to access any kind of data, whether it is text, graphics, sound, or even video. Whether you can actually access such data depends to a large extent on the type of browser you use.

The Mozilla Framework

The Mozilla project is an open source project based on the original Netscape browser code that provides a development framework for Web-based applications, primarily the Web browser and e-mail client. Originally, the aim of the Mozilla project was to provide an end-user Web browser called Mozilla. Its purpose has since changed to providing a development framework that anyone can use to create Web applications, though the project also provides its own. Table 14-3 lists some Mozilla resources.

Currently the framework is used for Mozilla products like Firefox Web browser and Thunderbird mail client, as well as non-Mozilla products like the Netscape, Epiphany, and Galeon Web browsers. In addition, the framework is easily extensible, supporting numerous add-ons in the form of plug-ins and extensions. The Mozilla project site is **www.mozilla.org**, and the site commonly used for plug-in and extension development is **www.mozdev.org**.

The first-generation product of the Mozilla project was the Mozilla Web browser, which is still available. Like the original Netscape, it included a mail client and newsreader, all in one integrated interface. The second-generation products have split this integrated package into separate stand-alone applications, the Firefox Web browser and the Thunderbird e-mail/newsreader client. Also under development is the Camino Web browser for Mac OS X and the Sunbird calendar application.

In 1998, Netscape made its source code freely available under the Netscape Public License (NPL). Mozilla is developed on an open source model much like Linux, KDE, and GNOME. Developers can submit modifications and additions over the Internet to the Mozilla Web site. Mozilla releases are referred to as Milestones. Mozilla products are currently released under both the NPL license for modifications of mozilla code and the MPL license (Mozilla Public License) for new additions.

The Firefox Web Browser

Firefox is the next generation of browsers based on the Netscape core source code known as mozilla. In current releases, Red Hat Enterprise Linux and Fedora Core use Firefox as its primary browser, in place of Netscape. Firefox is a streamlined browser featuring fast Web access and secure protection from invasive spyware.

Firefox is an X Window System application you can operate from any desktop, including GNOME, KDE, and XFce. On Fedora Core, Firefox is installed by default with both a menu entry in the Main menu's Internet menu and an icon on the different desktop panels. When opened, Firefox displays an area at the top of the screen for entering a URL address and a series of buttons for various Web page operations like page navigation. Drop-down menus on the top menu bar provide access to such Firefox features as Tools, View, and Bookmarks (see Figure 14-1).

Web Site	Description
www.mozilla.org	The Mozilla project
www.mozdev.org	Mozilla plug-in and extensions
www.oreillynet.com/mozilla	Mozilla documentation and news
www.mozillazine.org	Mozilla news and articles
www.mozillanews.org	Mozilla news and articles
www.bugzilla.org	Mozilla bug reporting and tracking system

TABLE 14-3   Mozilla Resources

To the right of the URL box is a search box where you can use different search engines for searching the Web, selected sites, or particular items. A pop-up menu lets you select a search engine. Currently included are Google, Yahoo!, Amazon, and eBay, along with Dictionary.com for looking up word definitions. Firefox also features button links and tabbed pages. You can drag the URL from the URL box to the button link bar to create a button with which to quickly access the site. Use this for frequently accessed sites.

For easy browsing, Firefox features tabbed panels for displaying Web pages. To open an empty tabbed panel, enter CTRL-T or select New Tab from the File menu. To display a page in that panel, drag its URL from the URL box or from the bookmark list to the panel. You can have several panels open at once, moving from one page to the next by clicking their tabs. You can elect to open all your link buttons as tabbed panels by right-clicking the link bar and selecting Open in Tabs.

Firefox refers to the URLs of Web pages you want to keep as *bookmarks*, marking pages you want to access directly. The Bookmarks menu enables you add your favorite Web pages. You can then view your bookmarks and select one to view. You can also edit your list of bookmarks, adding new ones or removing old ones. History is a list of previous URLs you have accessed. The URL box also features a pop-up menu listing your previous history sites. Bookmarks and History can be viewed as sidebars, selectable from the View menu.

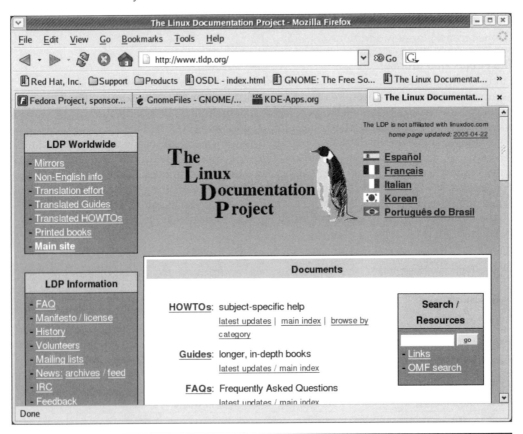

FIGURE 14-1   Firefox Web browser

When you download a file using Firefox, the download is managed by the Download Manager. You can download several files at once. Progress can be displayed in the Download Manager window, accessible from the Tools menu. You can cancel a download at any time, or just pause a download, resuming it later. Right-clicking a download entry will display the site it was downloaded from as well as the directory you saved it in. To remove an entry, click Remove. To clear out the entire list, click Clean Up.

The Preferences menu (Edit | Preferences) in Firefox enables you to set several different options. Firefox also supports such advanced features as cookie, form, image, and password management. You can elect to suppress cookies from sites, automatically fill in forms, not display site images, and set up login information such as usernames and passwords for selected sites. You can set preferences for general features, privacy, Web, and download management, as well as advanced features. In General preferences, you can determine your home page, page fonts and colors, as well as connection settings such as proxy information. For Privacy you can control information saved (such as the number of history sites to remember and the download history), set policy for saving cookies, and set the size of your cache. All of these you can manually clear. Under Web Features you can control pop-ups, allow software installs, and enable JavaScript. The Download Manager panel lets you configure your downloading operations, letting you specify a default download directory, whether to automatically prompt for one, and what plug-ins you may want run automatically on certain kinds of files, such as Adobe Acrobat for Adobe PDF files. The Advanced panel lets you control more complex features of browsing such as scrolling, security levels, and certificate management.

If you are on a network that connects to the Internet through a firewall, you must use the Proxies screen to enter the address of your network's firewall gateway computer. A *firewall* is a computer that operates as a controlled gateway to the Internet for your network. Several types of firewalls exist. One of the most restrictive uses programs called *proxies*, which receive Internet requests from users and then make those requests on their behalf. There is no direct connection to the Internet.

NOTE *The Privoxy Web proxy filters Web content to protect user privacy, intercepting unwanted advertising or blocking invasive cookies. Privoxy will execute rules listed in its action files, such as action.default, located in the **/etc/privoxy** directory. You can start Privoxy with the Services tool or the* **service** *command. To have your browser use Privoxy, configure it to use the host running Privoxy as a proxy.*

The K Desktop File Manager: Konqueror

If you are using the K Desktop, you can use a file manager window as a Web browser. The K Desktop's file manager is automatically configured to act as a Web browser. It can display Web pages, including graphics and links. The K Desktop's file manager supports standard Web page operation, such as moving forward and backward through accessed pages. Clicking a link accesses and displays the Web page referenced. In this respect, the Web becomes seamlessly integrated into the K Desktop.

GNOME Web Browsers: Nautilus, Galeon, and Epiphany

The new GNOME file manager, Nautilus, provides some basic Web browser capabilities. In the Nautilus location box, you can enter a Web address and Nautilus will access and display that Web page. The file manager Forward and Backward buttons, as well as bookmarks, help you navigate through previously viewed pages. However, it is not a fully functional Web browser. Nautilus will display icons in its sidebar for dedicated Web browsers installed on your system. Click one to start using that Web browser instead of Nautilus.

Several other GNOME-based Web browsers are also available. Epiphany, Galeon, and Kazehakase support standard Web operations. Epiphany is a GNOME Web browser designed to be fast with a simple interface. You can find out more about Epiphany at **epiphany .mozdev.org**. Epiphany is included with Fedora Core. Galeon is a fast, light browser also based on the Mozilla browser engine (Gecko). Kazehakase emphasizes a customizable interface with download boxes and RSS bookmarks.

For GNOME, you can also download numerous support tools, such as the RSSOwl to display news feeds and the GNOME Download Manager (Gwget) for controlling Web-based downloads. The Downloader for X client is useful for both FTP and Web file downloads. It has numerous features, letting you control download speeds, as well as downloading subdirectories. Though it is not part of the Fedora Core distribution, you can download it from **rpmfind.net**.

NOTE *Epiphany has replaced Galeon in Fedora Core, but you can download current versions of Galeon from **www.gnomefiles.org**.*

Lynx and ELinks: Line-Mode Browsers

Lynx is a line-mode browser you can use without the X Window System. A Web page is displayed as text only. A text page can contain links to other Internet resources but does not display any graphics, video, or sound. Except for the display limitations, Lynx is a fully functional Web browser. You can use Lynx to download files or to make Telnet connections. All information on the Web is still accessible to you. Because it does not require much of the overhead that graphics-based browsers need, Lynx can operate much faster, quickly displaying Web page text. To start the Lynx browser, you enter **lynx** on the command line and press ENTER.

Another useful text-based browser shipped with most distributions is ELinks. ELinks is a powerful screen-based browser that includes features such as frame, form, and table support. It also supports SSL secure encryption. To start ELinks, enter the **elinks** command in a terminal window.

Creating Your Own Web Site

To create your own Web site, you need access to a Web server. Fedora Core automatically installs the Apache Web server on its Linux systems. You can also rent Web page space on a remote server—a service many ISPs provide, some for free. On Fedora Core systems, the directory set up by your Apache Web server for your Web site pages is **/var/httpd/html**. Other servers provide you with a directory for your home page. Place the Web pages you create in that directory. You place your home page here. You can make other subdirectories with their own Web pages to which these can link. Web pages are not difficult to create. Links from one page to another move users through your Web site. You can even create links to Web pages or resources on other sites. Many excellent texts are available on Web page creation and management.

Web pages are created using either HTML, the Hypertext Markup Language, or the newer extended version, XML, the Extended Markup Language. They are a subset of Standard

Generalized Markup Language (SGML). Creating an HTML or XML document is a matter of inserting HTML or XML tags in a text file. In this respect, creating a Web page is as simple as using a tag-based word processor. You use the HTML tags to format text for display as a Web page. XML tags can include more detailed information about a particular connection such as object data or transaction characteristics. The Web page itself is a text file you can create using any text editor, such as Vi. If you are familiar with tag-based word processing on Unix systems, you will find it conceptually similar to nroff. Some HTML tags indicate headings, lists, and paragraphs, as well as links to reference Web resources.

Instead of manually entering HTML or XML code, you can use Web page composers. A Web page composer provides a graphical interface for constructing Web pages. Special Web page creation programs can easily help you create complex Web pages without ever having to type any HTML tags explicitly. Remember, though, no matter what tool you use to create your Web page, the Web page itself will be an HTML document. As part of the KDE project, KDE Web Dev (**www.kdewebdev.org**) provides several Web development applications, like the Quanta Plus Web editor and the Kommander dialog builder.

NOTE *Many of the standard editors for the K Desktop and GNOME include Web page construction features. Many enable you to insert links or format headings. For example, the KEdit program supports basic text-based Web page components. You can add headings, links, or lines, but not graphics.*

Java for Linux

To develop Java applications, use Java tools, and run many Java products, you must install the Java 2 Software Development Kit (SDK) and the Java 2 Runtime Environment (JRE) on your system. Together, they make up the Java 2 Platform, Standard Edition (J2SE). Sun currently supports and distributes Linux versions of these products. You can download them from Sun at **java.sun.com/j2se** and install them on your system. The current version of the J2SE is known as Java version 5.0 (though its internal version is 1.5).

Blackdown

Though Sun supports Linux versions of Java, more thorough and effective Linux ports of Java can be obtained from the Blackdown project at **www.blackdown.org**. The Blackdown project has ported the J2SE, including versions 1.4 of the SDK and the JRE. J2SE 5.0 (1.5) is currently under development. They have also ported previous versions of Java, including 1.1, 1.2, and 1.3. More information and documentation is also available at this Blackdown Web site. Blackdown Java packages and applications are listed in Table 14-4.

NOTE *See java.sun.com/products for an extensive listing of Java applications.*

Installing the Java Runtime Environment: JRE

Many Web sites will run applications that require the Java Runtime Environment (JRE). Fedora Core does not come with the Java Runtime Environment already installed. You will have to download and install the JRE on your Linux system. You can obtain a copy from

Application	Description
Java 2 Software Development Kit (SDK)	A Java development environment with a compiler, interpreters, debugger, and more, **java.sun.com/j2se**. Part of the Java 2 Platform. Download the Linux port from **www.blackdown.org**.
Java 2 Runtime Environment 1.4 (J2RE)	A Java Runtime Environment used to run Java applets, **www.java.com**. Part of the Java 2 Platform. Download the Linux port from **www.java.com** on the Java Software Download page, or **www.blackdown.org**.
Java 3D for Linux	Sun's 3D Application Program Interface for 3D Java programs. Download the Linux port from **www.blackdown.org**.
Java Media Framework (JMF) for Linux	Enable audio and video to be added to Java. Download the Linux port from **www.blackdown.org**.
Java Advanced Imaging (JAI) for Linux	Java Advanced Imaging API. Download the Linux port from **www.blackdown.org**.
Java 1.1 Development Kit (JDK) and Java 1.1 Runtime Environment (JRE) for Linux	The older Java 1.1 development environment with a compiler, interpreters, debugger, and more. Download the Linux port for your distribution's update through **www.blackdown.org**.
Java System Web Server	A Web server implemented with Java. Available at the Java Web site at **java.sun.com**.
GNU Java Compiler	GNU Public Licensed Java Compiler (GJC) to compile Java programs, **gcc.gnu.org/java**.
Jakarta Project	Apache Software Foundation project for open source Java applications, **jakarta.apache.org**. RPM packages at **jpackage.org**.

TABLE 14-4   Blackdown Java Packages and Java Web Applications

the Sun Java site (**www.java.com**), Blackdown, or **jpackage.org**. The SDK and JRE are available in the form of self-extracting compressed archives, **.bin**. These files are actually a shell script with an embedded compressed archive. (Separate install instructions are available.) Because of filename conflicts, you should not use the Sun RPM package (**.bin .rpm**). Instead you should download the **.bin** package and extract it in the **/opt** directory. Alternatively you can use the RPM package from **jpackage.org**. You will have to make the self-extracting bin file executable with the **chmod** command. The following command will change the JRE file, **jre-1_5_0_02-linux-i586.bin**, to an executable and then run it to extract the JRE. You will be prompted first to accept the license agreement.

```
chmod a+x jre-1_5_0_02-linux-i586.bin
./ jre-1_5_0_02-linux-i586.bin
```

The JRE would be installed in the **/opt** directory, in this case under **/opt/jre1.5.0_02**.

Enabling the Java Runtime Environment for Mozilla/Firefox

To allow either the Mozilla or Firefox Web browser to use the JRE, you need to create a link from the Mozilla plug-in directory to the Java plug-in libraries. Be sure you have first installed the JRE. Within the **/usr/lib/mozilla/plugins** directory, you will have to create a link to the **libjavaplugin_oji.so** library in the JRE's **/plugin/i386/ns7** subdirectory, where "ns7" indicates Netscape 7.

```
# cd /usr/lib/mozilla/plugins
# ln -s /opt/jre1.5.0_02/plugin/i386/ns7/libjavaplugin_oji.so libjavaplugin_oji.so
```

NOTE   *On Firefox and Mozilla, be sure Java support is enabled.*

The Java Applications

Numerous additional Java-based products and tools are currently adaptable for Linux. Tools include Java 3D, Java Media Framework (JMF), and Java Advanced Imaging (JAI), all Blackdown projects (see Table 14-4). Many of the products run directly as provided by Sun such as the Java Web server. You can download several directly from the Sun Java Web site at **java.sun.com**. The Jakarta project (**jakarta.apache.org**), part of the Apache Software Foundation, provides open source Java tools and applications, including libraries, server applications, and engines (see Chapter 23). Jakarta RPM packages are available at **jpackage.org**.

The Java 2 Software Development Kit: SDK

The Java Software Development Kit (SDK) provides tools for creating and debugging your own Java applets and provides support for Java applications. The kit includes demonstration applets with source code. You can obtain detailed documentation about the SDK from the Sun Web site at **java.sun.com**. Four major releases of the SDK are currently available—1.2, 1.3, 1.4.*x*, and 1.5 (also known as 5.0)—with corresponding versions for the Java 2 Runtime Environment (J2RE) for 1.2, 1.3, 1.4, and 1.5(5.0). The Java SDK adds capabilities for security, GUI support with JFC (also know as Swing), and running Java enhancements, such as Java 3D and Java Sound.

The SDK includes standard features found in the JDK features for internationalization, signed applets, the JAR file format, AWT (window toolkit) enhancements, the JavaBeans component model, networking enhancements, a math package for large numbers, database connectivity (JDBC), object serialization, and inner classes. Java applications include a Java compiler (javac), a Java debugger (jdb), and an applet viewer (appletviewer). In addition, the SDK offers the Java Naming and Directory Interface (JNDI), integrated Swing, Java 2D, network and security enhancements, and CORBA. With SDK, you can run the Blackdown port of Java 3D, Java Advanced Imaging, and the Java Media Framework. Detailed descriptions of these features can be found in the SDK documentation.

You create a Java applet much as you would create a program using a standard programming language. You first use a text editor to create the source code, which is saved in a file with a **.java** extension. Then you can use the **javac** compiler to compile the source code file, generating a Java applet. Numerous integrated development environment (IDE) applications are available for composing Java applets and applications. Although most are commercial, some provide free shareware versions. An IDE provides a GUI interface for constructing Java applets. You can link to and download several IDE applications through the Blackdown Web page.

PART III

FTP Clients

With FTP clients, you can connect to a corresponding FTP site and download files from it. FTP clients are commonly used to download software from public FTP sites that operate as software repositories. Most Linux software applications can be downloaded to your Linux system from such sites. These sites feature anonymous logins that let any user access their files. A distribution site like **ftp.redhat.com** is an example of one such FTP site, holding an extensive set of packaged Linux applications you can download using an FTP client and then easily install on your system. Basic FTP client capabilities are incorporated into the Konqueror (KDE) and Nautilus (GNOME) file managers. You can use a file manager window to access an FTP site and drag files to local directories to download them. Effective FTP clients are also now incorporated into most Web browsers, making Web browsers a primary downloading tool. Firefox in particular has strong FTP download capabilities.

Though file managers and Web browsers provide effective access to public (anonymous login) sites, to access private sites you may need a stand-alone FTP client like gFTP or **ftp**. These clients let you enter usernames and passwords with which you can access a private FTP site. The stand-alone clients are also useful for large downloads from public FTP sites, especially those with little or no Web display support. Popular Linux FTP clients are listed in Table 14-5.

Network File Transfer: FTP

With File Transfer Protocol (FTP) clients you can transfer extremely large files directly from one site to another. FTP can handle both text and binary files. This is one of the TCP/IP protocols, and it operates on systems connected to networks that use the TCP/IP protocols, such as the Internet. FTP performs a remote login to another account on another system connected to you on a network. Once logged in to that other system, you can transfer files to and from it. To log in, you need to know the login name and password for the account on the remote system. For example, if you have accounts at two different sites on the Internet, you can use FTP to transfer files from one to the other. Many sites on the Internet allow public access using FTP, however. Such sites serve as depositories for large files anyone can access

FTP Client	Description
Firefox	Mozilla Web and FTP browser
Konqueror	K Desktop file manager
Nautilus	GNOME file manager
gFTP	GNOME FTP client
ftp	Command line FTP client
lftp	Command line FTP client capable of multiple connections
NcFTP	Screen-based FTP client (Fedora extras)

TABLE 14-5   Linux FTP Clients

and download. These sites are often referred to as *FTP sites*, and in many cases, their Internet addresses begin with the word *ftp*, such as **ftp.gnome.org** or **ftp.redhat.com**. Others begin with other names, such as **metalab.unc.edu**. These public sites allow anonymous FTP login from any user. For the login name, you use the word "anonymous," and for the password, you use your Internet address. You can then transfer files from that site to your own system.

You can perform FTP operations using any one of a number of FTP client programs. For Linux systems, you can choose from several FTP clients. Many now operate using GUI interfaces such as GNOME. Some, such as Firefox, have limited capabilities, whereas others, such as NcFTP, include an extensive set of enhancements. The original FTP client is just as effective, though not as easy to use. It operates using a simple command line interface and requires no GUI or cursor support, as do other clients.

The Internet has a great many sites open to public access. They contain files anyone can obtain using file transfer programs. Unless you already know where a file is located, however, finding it can be difficult. To search for files on FTP sites, you can use search engines provided by Web sites, such as Yahoo!, Google, or Lycos. For Linux software, you can check sites such as **freshmeat.net**, **sourceforge.net**, **rpmfind.net**, **freshrpms.net**, **apps.kde.com**, and **www .gnome.org**. These sites usually search for both Web pages and FTP files.

Web Browser–Based FTP: Firefox

You access an FTP site and download files from it with any Web browser. A Web browser is effective for checking out an FTP site to see what files are listed there. When you access an FTP site with a Web browser, the entire list of files in a directory is listed as a Web page. You can move to a subdirectory by clicking its entry. With Firefox, you can easily browse through an FTP site to download files. To download a file with Firefox, click the download link. This will start the transfer operation, opening a box for selecting your local directory and the name for the file. The default name is the same as on the remote system. You can manage your downloads with the download manager, which will let you cancel a download operation in progress or remove other downloads requested. The manager will show the time remaining, speed, and the amount transferred for the current download. Browsers are useful for locating individual files, though not for downloading a large set of files, as is usually required for a system update.

The K Desktop File Manager: Konqueror

On the K Desktop, the desktop file manager (Konqueror) has a built-in FTP capability. The FTP operation has been seamlessly integrated into standard desktop file operations. Downloading files from an FTP site is as simple as copying files by dragging them from one directory window to another, but one of the directories happens to be located on a remote FTP site. On the K Desktop, you can use a file manager window to access a remote FTP site. Files in the remote directory are listed just as your local files are. To download files from an FTP site, you open a window to access that site, entering the URL for the FTP site in the window's location box. Open the directory you want, and then open another window for the local directory to which you want the remote files copied. In the window showing the FTP files, select the ones you want to download. Then simply click and drag those files to the window for the local directory. A pop-up menu appears with choices for Copy, Link, or Move. Select Copy. The selected files are then downloaded. Another window then opens, showing the download progress and displaying the name of each file in turn, along with a bar indicating the percentage downloaded so far.

PART III

GNOME Desktop FTP: Nautilus

The easiest way to download files is to use the built-in FTP capabilities of the GNOME file manager, Nautilus. On GNOME, the desktop file manager—Nautilus—has a built-in FTP capability much like the KDE file manager. The FTP operation has been seamlessly integrated into standard desktop file operations. Downloading files from an FTP site is as simple as dragging files from one directory window to another, where one of the directories happens to be located on a remote FTP site. Use the GNOME file manager to access a remote FTP site, listing files in the remote directory, just as local files are. Just enter the FTP URL following the prefix **ftp://** and press ENTER. The top directory of the remote FTP site will be displayed. Simply use the file manager to progress through the remote FTP site's directory tree until you find the file you want. Then open another window for the local directory to which you want the remote files copied. In the window showing the FTP files, select those you want to download. Then CTRL-click and drag those files to the window for the local directory. CTRL-clicking performs a copy operation, not a move. As files are downloaded, a dialog window appears showing the progress.

gFTP

The gFTP program is a simpler GNOME FTP client designed to let you make standard FTP file transfers. The gFTP window consists of several panes. The top-left pane lists files in your local directory, and the top-right pane lists your remote directory. Subdirectories have folder icons preceding their names. The parent directory can be referenced by the double period entry (..) with an up arrow at the top of each list. Double-click a directory entry to access it. The pathnames for all directories are displayed in boxes above each pane. You can enter a new pathname for a different directory to change to it, if you want.

Two buttons between the panes are used for transferring files. The left arrow button, <-, downloads selected files in the remote directory, and the right arrow button, ->, uploads files from the local directory. To download a file, click it in the right-side pane and then click the left arrow button, <-. When the file is downloaded, its name appears in the left pane, your local directory. Menus across the top of the window can be used to manage your transfers. A connection manager enables you to enter login information about a specific site. You can specify whether to perform an anonymous login or to provide a username and password. Click Connect to connect to that site. A drop-down menu for sites enables you to choose the site you want. Interrupted downloads can be restarted easily.

ftp

The name ftp designates the original FTP client used on Unix and Linux systems. The ftp client uses a command line interface, and it has an extensive set of commands and options you can use to manage your FTP transfers. You start the ftp client by entering the command **ftp** at a shell prompt. If you have a specific site you want to connect to, you can include the name of that site on the command line after the ftp keyword. Otherwise, you need to connect to the remote system with the ftp command **open**. You are then prompted for the name of the remote system with the prompt "(to)". Upon entering the remote system name, ftp connects you to the system and then prompts you for a login name. The prompt for the login name consists of the word "Name" and, in parentheses, the system name and your local login name. Sometimes the login name on the remote system is the same as the login name on your own system. If the names are the same, press ENTER at the prompt. If they are different, enter the remote system's login name. After entering the login name, you are prompted for the password. In the next example, the user connects to the remote system **garnet** and logs in to the **robert** account:

```
$ ftp
ftp> open
(to) garnet
Connected to garnet.berkeley.edu.
220 garnet.berkeley.edu FTP server ready.
Name (garnet.berkeley.edu:root): robert
password required
Password:
user robert logged in
ftp>
```

Once logged in, you can execute Linux commands on either the remote system or your local system. You execute a command on your local system in ftp by preceding the command with an exclamation point. Any Linux commands without an exclamation point are executed on the remote system. One exception exists to this rule. Whereas you can change directories on the remote system with the **cd** command, to change directories on your local system, you need to use a special ftp command called **lcd** (local **cd**). In the next example, the first command lists files in the remote system, while the second command lists files in the local system:

```
ftp> ls
ftp> !ls
```

The ftp program provides a basic set of commands for managing files and directories on your remote site, provided you have the permission to do so (see Table 14-6). You can use **mkdir** to create a remote directory, and **rmdir** to remove one. Use the **delete** command to erase a remote file. With the **rename** command, you can change the names of files. You close your connection to a system with the **close** command. You can then open another connection if you want. To end the ftp session, use the **quit** or **bye** command.

```
ftp> close
ftp> bye
Good-bye
$
```

To transfer files to and from the remote system, use the **get** and **put** commands. The **get** command receives files from the remote system to your local system, and the **put** command sends files from your local system to the remote system. In a sense, your local system gets files *from* the remote and puts files *to* the remote. In the next example, the file **weather** is sent from the local system to the remote system using the **put** command:

```
ftp> put weather
PORT command successful.
ASCII data connection
ASCII Transfer complete.
ftp>
```

Command	Effect
`ftp`	Invokes the ftp program.
open *site-address*	Opens a connection to another system.
`close`	Closes a connection to a system.
quit or **bye**	Ends ftp session.
`ls`	Lists the contents of a directory.
`dir`	Lists the contents of a directory in long form.
get *filename*	Sends file from remote system to local system.
put *filename*	Sends file from local system to remote system.
mget *regular-expression*	Enables you to download several files at once from a remote system. You can use special characters to specify the files; you are prompted to transfer each file in turn.
mput *regular-expression*	Enables you to send several files at once to a remote system. You can use special characters to specify the files; you are prompted for each file to be transferred.
`runique`	Toggles storing of files with unique filenames. If a file already exists with the same filename on the local system, a new filename is generated.
reget *filename*	Resumes transfer of an interrupted file from where you left off.
`binary`	Transfers files in binary mode.
`ascii`	Transfers files in ASCII mode.
cd *directory*	Changes directories on the remote system.
lcd *directory*	Changes directories on the local system.
help or **?**	Lists ftp commands.
mkdir *directory*	Creates a directory on the remote system.
`rmdir`	Deletes a remote directory.
delete *filename*	Deletes a file on the remote system.
mdelete *file-list*	Deletes several remote files at once.
`rename`	Renames a file on a remote system.
`hash`	Displays progressive hash signs during download.
`status`	Displays current status of ftp.

TABLE 14-6 The `ftp` Client Commands

If a download is ever interrupted, you can resume the download with **reget**. This is helpful for an extremely large file. The download resumes from where it left off, so the whole file needn't be downloaded again. Also, be sure to download binary files in binary mode. For most FTP sites, the binary mode is the default, but some sites might have ASCII (text) as the default. The command **ascii** sets the character mode, and the command **binary** sets the binary mode. Most software packages available at Internet sites are archived and compressed files, which are binary files. In the next example, the transfer mode is set to binary, and the archived software package **mydata.tar.gz** is sent from the remote system to your local system using the **get** command:

```
ftp> binary
ftp> get mydata.tar.gz
PORT command successful.
Binary data connection
Binary Transfer complete.
ftp>
```

You may often want to send several files, specifying their names with wildcard characters. The **put** and **get** commands, however, operate only on a single file and do not work with special characters. To transfer several files at a time, you have to use two other commands, **mput** and **mget**. When you use **mput** or **mget**, you are prompted for a file list. You can then enter either the list of files or a file-list specification using special characters. For example, ***.c** specifies all the files with a **.c** extension, and ***** specifies all files in the current directory. In the case of **mget**, files are sent one by one from the remote system to your local system. Each time, you are prompted with the name of the file being sent. You can type **y** to send the file or **n** to cancel the transmission. You are then prompted for the next file. The **mput** command works in the same way, but it sends files from your local system to the remote system. In the next example, all files with a **.c** extension are sent to your local system using **mget**:

```
ftp> mget
(remote-files) *.c
mget calc.c? y
PORT command successful
ASCII data connection
ASCII transfer complete
mget main.c? y
PORT command successful
ASCII data connection
ASCII transfer complete
ftp>
```

Answering the prompt for each file can be a tedious prospect if you plan to download a large number of files, such as those for a system update. In this case, you can turn off the prompt with the **prompt** command, which toggles the interactive mode on and off. The **mget** operation then downloads all files it matches, one after the other.

```
ftp> prompt
Interactive mode off.
ftp> mget
(remote-files) *.c
 PORT command successful
ASCII data connection
ASCII transfer complete
PORT command successful
ASCII data connection
ASCII transfer complete
ftp>
```

NOTE *To access a public FTP site, you have to perform an anonymous login. Instead of a login name, you enter the keyword **anonymous** (or **ftp**). Then, for the password, you enter your Internet address. Once the ftp prompt is displayed, you are ready to transfer files. You may need to change to the appropriate directory first or set the transfer mode to binary.*

Automatic Login and Macros: .netrc

The ftp client has an automatic login capability and support for macros. Both are entered in a user's ftp configuration file called **.netrc**. Each time you connect to a site, the **.netrc** file is checked for connection information, such as a login name and password. In this way, you needn't enter a login name and password each time you connect to a site. This feature is particularly useful for anonymous logins. Instead of your having to enter the username "anonymous" and your e-mail address as your password, they can be automatically read from the **.netrc** file. You can even make anonymous login information your default so that, unless otherwise specified, an anonymous login is attempted for any FTP site to which you try to connect. If you have sites you must log in to, you can specify them in the **.netrc** file and, when you connect, either automatically log in with your username and password for that site or be prompted for them.

Entries in the **.netrc** file have the following syntax. An entry for a site begins with the term "machine," followed by the network or Internet address, and then the login and password information.

```
machine system-address login remote-login-name password password
```

The following example shows an entry for logging in to the **dylan** account on the **turtle .trek.com** system:

```
machine golf.mygames.com login dylan password legogolf
```

For a site you would anonymously log in to, you enter the word "anonymous" for the login name and your e-mail address for the password.

```
machine ftp.redhat.com login anonymous password dylan@turtle.trek.com
```

In most cases, you are using ftp to access anonymous FTP sites. Instead of trying to make an entry for each one, you can make a default entry for anonymous FTP login. When you connect to a site, ftp looks for a machine entry for it in the **.netrc** file. If none exists, ftp looks for a default entry and uses that. A default entry begins with the word "default" with no network address. To make anonymous logins your default, enter **anonymous** and your e-mail address as your login and password.

```
default login anonymous password dylan@turtle.trek.com
```

A sample **.netrc** file with a machine definition and a default entry is shown here.

.netrc
```
machine golf.mygames.com login dylan password legogolf
default login anonymous password dylan@turtle.trek.com
```

You can also define macros in your **.netrc** file. With a macro, you can execute several ftp operations at once using only the macro name. Macros remain in effect during a connection. When you close a connection, the macros are undefined. Although a macro can be defined on your ftp command line, defining them in **.netrc** entries makes more sense. This way, you needn't redefine them again. They are read automatically from the **.netrc** file and defined for you. You can place macro definitions within a particular machine entry in the **.netrc** file or in the default entry. Macros defined in machine entries are defined only when you connect to that site. Macros in the default entry are defined whenever you make a connection to any site.

The syntax for a macro definition follows. It begins with the keyword **macdef**, followed by the macro name you want to give it, and ends with an empty line. An ftp macro can take arguments, referenced within the macro with **$n**, where **$1** references the first argument, and **$2** the second, and so on. If you need to use a **$** character in a macro, you have to quote it using the backslash, **\$**.

```
macdef macro-name
ftp commands
empty-line
```

The **redupd** macro, defined next, changes to a directory where it then downloads Red Hat updates for the current release. It also changes to a local directory where the update files are to be placed. The **prompt** command turns off the download prompts for each file. The **mget** command then downloads the files. The macro assumes you are connected to the Red Hat FTP site.

```
defmac redupd
cd pub/redhat/current
lcd /root/redupdate
prompt
mget *
```

A sample **.netrc** file follows with macros defined for both specific and default entries. An empty line is placed after each macro definition. You can define several macros for a machine or the default entry. The macro definitions following a machine entry up to the next machine entry are automatically defined for that machine connection.

```
machine updates.redhat.com login anonymous password dylan@turtle.trek.com
# define a macro for downloading updated from the Red Hat site
defmac redupd
 cd pub/redhat/current
 lcd /root/redupdate
 prompt
 mget *

default login anonymous password dylan@turtle.trek.com
defmac lls
!ls
```

lftp

The lftp program is an enhanced FTP client with advanced features such as the capabilities to download mirror sites and to run several FTP operations in the background at the same time. It uses a command set similar to that for the ftp client. You use **get** and **mget** commands to download files, with the **-o** option to specify local locations for them. Use **lcd** and **cd** to change local and remote directories.

To manage background commands, you use many of the same commands as for the shell (see Chapter 8). The **&** placed at the end of a command puts it into the background. Use CTRL-Z to put a job already running into the background. Commands can be grouped with parentheses and placed together into the background. Use the **jobs** command to list your background jobs and the **wait** or **fg** command to move jobs from the background to the foreground. When you exit lftp, the program will continue to run any background jobs. In effect, lftp becomes a background job itself.

When you connect to a site, you can queue commands with the **queue** command, setting up a list of FTP operations to perform. With this feature, you could queue several download operations to a site. The queue can be reordered and entries deleted if you wish. You can also connect to several sites and set up a queue for each one. The **mirror** command lets you maintain a local version of a mirror site. You can download an entire site or just update newer files, as well as removing files no longer present on the mirror.

You can tailor lftp with options set in the **.lftprc** file. System-wide settings are placed in the **/etc/lftp.conf** file. Here, you can set features like the prompt to use and your anonymous password. The **.lftp** directory holds support files for command history, logs, bookmarks, and startup commands. The lftp program also supports the **.netrc** file, checking it for login information.

NcFTP

The NcFTP program has a screen-based interface that can be run from any shell command line. It does not use a desktop interface. Though no longer part of the Fedora Core, it can be found in Fedora Extras, currently in the development branch. To start up NcFTP, you enter the **ncftp** command on the command line. If you are working in a window manager, such as KDE, GNOME, or XFce, open a shell terminal window and enter the command at its prompt. The main NcFTP screen consists of an input line at the bottom of the screen with a status line above it. The remainder of the screen is used to display commands and responses from remote systems. For example, when you download files, a message specifying the files to be downloaded is displayed in the status line. NcFTP lets you set preferences for different features, such as anonymous login, progress meters, or a download directory. Enter the **pref** command to open the preferences screen. From there, you can select and modify the listed preferences.

To connect to an FTP site, you enter the **open** command on the input line, followed by the site's address. The address can be either an IP address or a domain name, such as **ftp .gnome.org**. If you don't supply an address, a list of your bookmarked sites is displayed, and you can choose one from there. By default, NcFTP attempts an anonymous login, using the term "anonymous" as your username and your e-mail address as the password. When you successfully connect, the status bar displays the remote site's name on the left and the remote directory name.

If you want to log in to a specific account on a remote site, have yourself prompted for the username and password by using the **-u** option with the **open** command. The **open** command remembers the last kind of login you performed for a specific site and repeats it.

If you want to change back to an anonymous login from a user login, you use the **-a** option with the **open** command.

Once connected, you enter commands on the input line to perform FTP operations such as displaying file lists, changing directories, or downloading files. With the **ls** command, you can list the contents of the current remote directory. Use the **cd** command to change to another remote directory. The **dir** command displays a detailed listing of files. With the **page** command, you view the contents of a remote file, a screen at a time. To download files, you use the **get** command, and to upload files, you use the **put** command. During a download, a progress meter above the status bar displays how much of the file has been downloaded so far. The **get** command has several features described in more detail in the following section. When you finish, you can disconnect from the site with the **close** command. You can then use **open** to connect to another site, or quit the NcFTP program with the **quit** command. The **help** command lists all NcFTP commands. You can use the **help** command followed by the name of a command to display specific information on it.

The NcFTP **get** command differs significantly from the original FTP client's **get** command. Whereas the original FTP client uses two commands, **get** and **mget**, to perform download operations, NcFTP uses only the **get** command. However, the NcFTP **get** command combines the capabilities of both **mget** and **get** into the **get** command, as well as adding several new features. By default, the NcFTP **get** command performs wildcard matching for filenames. If you enter only part of a filename, the **get** command tries to download all files beginning with that name. You can turn off wildcard matching with the **-G** option, in which case you must enter the full names of the files you want.

Network Tools

Y ou can use a variety of network tools to perform tasks such as obtaining information about other systems on your network, accessing other systems, and communicating directly with other users. Network information can be obtained using utilities such as **ping**, **finger**, **traceroute**, and **host**. Talk, ICQ, and IRC clients enable you to communicate directly with other users on your network. Telnet performs a remote login to an account you may have on another system connected on your network. Some tools have a corresponding K Desktop or GNOME version. In addition, your network may make use of network remote access commands. These are useful for smaller networks and enable you to access remote systems directly to copy files or execute commands.

Network Information: ping, finger, traceroute, and host

You can use the **ping**, **finger**, **traceroute**, and **host** commands to find out status information about systems and users on your network. The **ping** command is used to check if a remote system is up and running. You use **finger** to find out information about other users on your network, seeing if they are logged in or if they have received mail; **host** displays address information about a system on your network, giving you a system's IP and domain name addresses; and **traceroute** can be used to track the sequence of computer networks and systems your message passed through on its way to you. Table 15-1 lists various network information tools.

GNOME Network Tools: gnome-nettool

For the GNOME desktop, the gnome-nettool utility (see Figure 15-1) provides a GNOME interface for entering the **ping**, **traceroute**, and **host** commands, among other features, including Finger, Whois, and Lookup for querying users and hosts on the network. You can access gnome-nettool with the Network Tools entry in the System Tools menu. It also includes network status tools such as netstat and Ethereal, which are described in more detail in Chapter 37. The first panel, Devices, describes your connected network devices, including configuration and transmission information about each device such as the hardware address and bytes transmitted. Both IPv4 and IPv6 host IP addresses will be listed (see Chapter 37 for more information on addresses).

Network Information Tool	Description
ping	Detects whether a system is connected to the network.
finger	Obtains information about users on the network.
who	Checks what users are currently online.
host	Obtains network address information about a remote host.
traceroute	Tracks the sequence of computer networks and hosts your message passes through.
ethereal	Protocol analyzer to examine network traffic.
gnome-nettool	GNOME interface for various network tools including ping, finger, and traceroute.
mtr and xmtr	My traceroute combines both ping and traceroute operations (Traceroute on System Tools menu).

TABLE 15-1   Network Tools

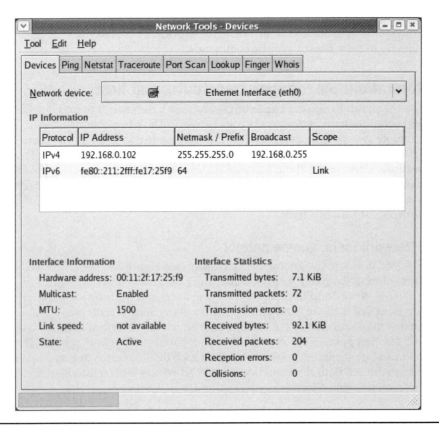

FIGURE 15-1   gnome-nettool

ping

The **ping** command detects whether a system is up and running. **ping** takes as its argument
the name of the system you want to check. If the system you want to check is down, **ping**
issues a timeout message indicating a connection could not be made. The next example
checks to see if **www.redhat.com** is up and connected to the network:

```
$ ping www.redhat.com
PING www.portal.redhat.com (206.132.41.231): 56 data bytes
64 bytes from 206.132.41.231: icmp_seq=0 ttl=248 time=24.0 ms
64 bytes from 206.132.41.231: icmp_seq=1 ttl=248 time=124.5 ms
64 bytes from 206.132.41.231: icmp_seq=2 ttl=248 time=77.9 ms
64 bytes from 206.132.41.231: icmp_seq=3 ttl=248 time=220.1 ms
64 bytes from 206.132.41.231: icmp_seq=4 ttl=248 time=14.9 ms

--- www.portal.redhat.com ping statistics ---
6 packets transmitted, 5 packets received, 16% packet loss
round-trip min/avg/max = 14.9/92.2/220.1 ms
```

You can also use **ping** with an IP address instead of a domain name. With an IP address,
ping can try to detect the remote system directly without having to go through a domain
name server to translate the domain name to an IP address. This can be helpful for situations
where your network's domain name server may be temporarily down and you want to
check if a particular remote host on your network is connected. In the next example, the
user checks the Red Hat site using its IP address:

```
$ ping 206.132.41.231
PING 206.132.41.231 (206.132.41.231): 56 data bytes
64 bytes from 206.132.41.231: icmp_seq=0 ttl=248 time=16.6 ms
64 bytes from 206.132.41.231: icmp_seq=1 ttl=248 time=65.1 ms
64 bytes from 206.132.41.231: icmp_seq=2 ttl=248 time=70.1 ms
64 bytes from 206.132.41.231: icmp_seq=3 ttl=248 time=336.6 ms
64 bytes from 206.132.41.231: icmp_seq=4 ttl=248 time=53.6 ms
64 bytes from 206.132.41.231: icmp_seq=5 ttl=248 time=42.1 ms

--- 206.132.41.231 ping statistics ---
6 packets transmitted, 6 packets received, 0% packet loss
round-trip min/avg/max = 16.6/97.3/336.6 ms
```

NOTE *A **ping** operation could also fail if **ping** access is denied by a network's firewall. See
Chapter 20 for more details.*

finger and who

You can use the **finger** command to obtain information about other users on your network
and the **who** command to see what users are currently online on your system. The **who** and
w commands list all users currently connected, along with when, how long, and where they
logged in. The **w** command provides more detailed information. It has several options for
specifying the level of detail. The **who** command is meant to operate on a local system or
network; **finger** can operate on large networks, including the Internet, though most systems
block it for security reasons.

NOTE *Ethereal is a protocol analyzer that can capture network packets and display detailed information about them. You can detect what kind of information is being transmitted on your network as well as its source and destination. Ethereal is used primarily for network and server administration. Ethereal is discussed in detail in Chapter 37.*

host

With the **host** command, you can find network address information about a remote system connected to your network. This information usually consists of a system's IP address, domain name address, domain name nicknames, and mail server. This information is obtained from your network's domain name server. For the Internet, this includes all systems you can connect to over the Internet.

The **host** command is an effective way to determine a remote site's IP address or URL. If you have only the IP address of a site, you can use **host** to find out its domain name. For network administration, an IP address can be helpful for making your own domain name entries in your **/etc/host** file. That way, you needn't rely on a remote domain name server (DNS) for locating a site.

```
$ host www.gnome.org
www.gnome.org is a nickname for gnome.labs.redhat.com
gnome.labs.redhat.com has address 199.183.24.235
gnome.labs.redhat.com mail is handled (pri=10) by mail.redhat.com

$ host 199.183.24.235
235.24.183.199.IN-ADDR.ARPA domain name pointer
gnome.labs.redhat.com
```

traceroute

Internet connections are made through various routes, traveling through a series of interconnected gateway hosts. The path from one system to another could take different routes, some of which may be faster than others. For a slow connection, you can use **traceroute** to check the route through which you are connected to a host, monitoring the speed and the number of intervening gateway connections a route takes. The **traceroute** command takes as its argument the hostname or IP addresses for the system whose route you want to check. Options are available for specifying parameters like the type of service (**-t**) or the source host (**-s**). The **traceroute** command will return a list of hosts the route traverses, along with the times for three probes sent to each gateway. Times greater than five seconds are displayed with a asterisk, *.

```
traceroute rabbit.mytrek.com
```

You can also use the mtr or xmtr tools to perform both ping and traces (Traceroute on the System Tools menu).

Network Talk and Messenger Clients: ICQ, IRC, AIM, and Talk

You may, at times, want to communicate directly with other users on your network. You can do so with Talk, ICQ, instant messenger, and IRC utilities, provided the other user is also logged in to a connected system at the same time (see Table 15-2). The Talk utility operates like a telephone, enabling you to have a direct two-way conversation with another user. Talk is designed for users on the same system or connected on a local network. ICQ (I Seek

You) is an Internet tool that notifies you when other users are online and enables you to communicate with them. ICQ works much like an instant messenger. With an Internet Relay Chat utility (IRC), you can connect to a remote server where other users are also connected and talk with them. Instant messenger (IM) clients operate much the same way, allowing users on the same IM system to communicate anywhere across the Internet. Currently the major IM systems are AOL, Microsoft Network (MSN), Yahoo!, ICQ, and Jabber. Unlike the others, Jabber is an Open Source instant messenger service (**www.jabber.org**).

ICQ

The ICQ protocol enables you to communicate directly with other users online, like an instant messenger utility. Using an ICQ client, you can send users messages, chat with them, or send files. You can set up a contact list of users you may want to contact when they are online. You are then notified in real time when they connect, and you can communicate with them if you wish. Several modes of communication are supported. These include chat, message, e-mail, file transfer, and games. To use ICQ, you register with an ICQ server that provides you with an ICQ number, also known as a Universal Internet Number (UIN). You can find out more about the ICQ protocol at **www.icq.com**.

Several GNOME-based ICQ clients are available for your use. Check the GNOME software map at **www.gnome.org** for new versions and recent updates. GnomeICU is an ICQ client that can communicate with other ICQ users on any platform, whether Linux, Windows, or Macintosh. GnomeICU features include message history for individual users, chat, messages, and sound events. Kicq and KXicq2 are K Desktop ICQ clients currently under development. They will support instant messaging, client lists, and other ICQ features.

Internet Relay Chat (IRC) operates like a chat room, where you can enter channels and talk to other users already there. First, you select an IRC server to connect to. Various servers are available for different locales and topics. Once connected to a server, you can choose from a list of channels to enter. The interface works much like a chat room. When you connect to the server, you can choose a nickname by which you will be known. Several Internet Relay Chat clients are available for use on Linux systems. Most operate on either the X Window System, KDE, or GNOME platforms. LostIRC and X-Chat are GNOME IRC clients, though there are versions for other platforms. Both have support for multiple concurrent server connections, multiple windows, Direct Client Communication (DCC) to bypass intermediate servers, and Perl scripts. X-Chat has a plug-in interface for adding new features (see **xchat.linuxpower.org** for more details). KVIrc is a K Desktop IRC client. KVIrc features an alias and events editor, DCC, and scripting.

TABLE 15-2 Talk and Messenger Clients	**Client**	**Description**
	Kicq, KXicq2	KDE ICQ clients
	GnomeICU	GNOME ICQ client
	X-Chat	Internet Relay Chat (IRC) client
	Kit	KDE AOL Instant Messenger (AIM) client
	Kaim	KDE AIM client
	Gabber	Jabber client
	Gaim	GNOME AIM client
	GNU Talk	Talk client and server

Instant Messenger

AOL Instant Messenger (AIM) is a free service provided by AOL for anyone who registers for it, as well as those who are already members of AOL. With AIM, you can send messages to members instantly, play games with them, and receive stock alerts. You can even share images, sounds, and photographs. AOL already provides clients for Windows and Macintosh. A new version called AIM Express is designed to run on any Web browser and will run on systems with JDK 1.1 or greater. You can find out more about AIM at **www.aim.com**.

Kit is the KDE desktop AOL Instant Messenger (AIM) client, providing support for panel docking and session management. Kit is included as a standard part of KDE 2.*x*. When you first start Kit, you are asked to create an initial profile, providing a screen name and password. Once they are selected, the main window will display your buddy list, organizing them by group. From the Settings menu you can open a configuration window where you can enter your buddy list as well as set permissions and edit your user information. If a buddy is also logged in, you can click his or her entry and open an instant messenger window to send and receive messages. You can find out more about Kit at **www.hakubi.us/kit**. Other AIM clients also available are Kaim and Gaim.

Several GNOME instant messaging clients are designed to work with all instant messaging systems, including AIM, Yahoo!, MSN, and ICQ. Gaim has plug-ins that let you connect to ICQ, Yahoo!, MSN, IRC, Jabber, and Zephyr. Gabber, a Jabber client, is an open source instant messaging system that allows communication with all other systems, including AIM, Yahoo!, MSN, and ICQ.

NOTE *Talk is the original Unix talk utility designed to set up an interactive two-way communication between you and another user using a command line interface. It works much like instant messenger. Due to security concerns, you should use Talk only on a locally secure system. A K Desktop version of Talk called KTalk displays user screens as panes in a K Desktop window. GNU Talk is a GNOME version of Talk that supports multiple clients, file transfers, encryption, shared applications, auto-answer, and call forwarding.*

Telnet

You use the **telnet** command to log in remotely to another system on your network. The system can be on your local area network or available through an Internet connection. Telnet operates as if you were logging in to another system from a remote terminal. You will be asked for a login name and, in some cases, a password. In effect, you are logging in to another account on another system. In fact, if you have an account on another system, you could use Telnet to log in to it.

CAUTION *The original version of Telnet is noted for being very insecure. For secure connections over a network or the Internet, you should use the SSH or Kerberos versions of Telnet (see Chapter 19). They operate in the same way as the original but use authentication and encryption to secure the Telnet connection. Even so, it is advisable never to use Telnet to log in to your root account.*

You invoke the Telnet utility with the keyword **telnet**. If you know the name of the site you want to connect with, you can enter **telnet** and the name of the site on the Linux command line. As an alternative, you can use the K Desktop KTelnet utility. This provides a GUI interface for connecting and logging in to remote systems.

```
$ telnet garnet.berkeley.edu
Connected to garnet
login:
```

The Telnet program also has a command mode with a series of commands you can use to configure your connection. You can enter the **telnet** command mode either by invoking Telnet with the keyword **telnet** or by pressing CTRL-] during a session. The Telnet **help** command lists all the Telnet commands you can use. A comprehensive list is available on the Man pages (**man telnet**). In the next example, the user first invokes the Telnet utility. A prompt is displayed next, indicating the command mode, **telnet>**. The Telnet command **open** then connects to another system.

```
$ telnet
telnet> open garnet.berkeley.edu
Connected to garnet.berkeley.edu
login:
```

Once connected, you follow the login procedure for that system. If you are logging in to a regular system, you must provide a login name and password. Once logged in, you are provided with the operating system prompt; in the case of Linux or Unix, this will be either **$** or **%**. You are then directly connected to an account on that system and can issue any commands you want. When you finish your work, you log out. This breaks the connection and returns you to the Telnet prompt on your own system. You can then quit Telnet with the **quit** command.

```
telnet> quit
```

When using Telnet to connect to a site that provides public access, you needn't provide a login name or password. Access is usually controlled by a series of menus that restrict what you can do on that system. If you are logging in to a specific account on another system, you can use the **-l** option to specify the login name of that account.

RSH, Kerberos, and SSH Remote Access Commands

The remote access commands were designed for smaller networks, such as intranets. They enable you to log in remotely to another account on another system and to copy files from one system to another. You can also obtain information about another system, such as who is logged on currently (see Table 15-3). Many of the remote commands have comparable network communication utilities used for the Internet. For example, **rlogin**, which remotely logs in to a system, is similar to **telnet**. The **rcp** command, which remotely copies files, performs much the same function as **ftp**.

There are security risks with the use of remote operations like rcp, rlogin, and rsh (RSH package). Such commands allow easy unencrypted remote access to a Linux system. These commands should be used only within a local secure network. For Internet operations like these, you should use the secure versions of these commands provided by Kerberos and the Secure Shell (SSH), such as ssh, slogin, or scp (see Chapter 19). SSH commands are encrypted,

Remote Command	Effect
`rwho`	Displays all users logged in to systems in your network.
`ruptime`	Displays information about each system on your network.
`rlogin` *system-name*	Allows you to log in remotely to an account on another system. The `-l` option allows you to specify the login name of the account.
`slogin` *system-name*	Secure login to an account on another system.
`rcp` *sys-name:file1* *sys-name:file2*	Allows you to copy a file from an account on one system to an account on another system. With the `-p` option, preserves the modification times and modes of source files.
`scp` *sys-name:file1* *sys-name:file2*	Secure copy of a file from an account on one system to an account on another system.
`rsh` *sys-name Linux-command*	Allows you to remotely execute a command on another system. The `-l` option allows you to specify the login name; `-n` redirects input from the null special device, **/dev/null**.
`ssh` *sys-name Linux-command*	Secure remote execution of a command on another system.

TABLE **15-3** Remote Access Commands

providing a much higher level of security. Kerberos provides versions for Telnet, rlogin, rcp, rsh, and ftp, which provide authentication and encryption. The Kerberos versions operate using the same commands and options as the originals, making their use transparent to the user. If you install Kerberos on your system, Fedora Core configures the user **PATH** variable to access the Kerberos versions of the remote commands, located at **/usr/kerberos/bin**, instead of **/usr/bin**.

You can use several commands to obtain information about different systems on your network. You can find out who is logged in, get information about a user on another system, or find out if a system is up and running. For example, the **rwho** command functions in the same way as the **who** command. It displays all the users currently logged in to each system in your network.

```
$ rwho
violet robert:tty1 Sept 10 10:34
garnet chris:tty2 Sept 10 09:22
```

The **ruptime** command displays information about each system on your network. The information shows how each system has been performing: **ruptime** shows whether a system is up or down, how long it has been up or down, the number of users on the system, and the average load on the system for the last five, ten, and fifteen minutes.

```
$ ruptime
violet up 11+04:10, 8 users, load 1.20 1.10 1.00
garnet up 11+04:10, 20 users, load 1.50 1.40 1.30
```

Remote Access Permission: .rhosts and .k5login

You use the **.rhosts** and **.k5login** (Kerberos) files to control access to your account by users using remote commands. Users create these files on their own accounts using a standard editor. They must be located in the user's home directory. In the next example, the user displays the contents of an **.rhosts** file:

```
$ cat .rhosts
garnet chris
violet robert
```

The **.rhosts** and **.k5login** files are a simple way to allow other people access to your account without giving out your password. To deny access to a user, simply delete the system's name and the user's login name from your **.rhosts** file. If a user's login name and system are in an **.rhosts** file, that user can directly access that account without knowing the password (in place of using **.rhosts**, you could use a password). The **.k5login** file will contain Kerberos names for users, including usernames and realms. Such a user will undergo Kerberos authentication to gain access. **.rhosts** or **.k5login** files are required for other remote commands, such as remotely copying files or remotely executing Linux commands.

The type of access **.rhosts** and **.k5login** provide enables you to use remote commands to access accounts directly that you might have on other systems. You do not have to log in to them first. In effect, you can treat your accounts on other systems as extensions of the one you are currently logged in to. Using the **rcp** command, you can copy any files from one directory to another no matter what account they are on. With the **rsh** command, you can execute any Linux command you want on any of your other accounts.

rlogin, slogin, rcp, scp, rsh, and ssh

You may have accounts on different systems in your network, or you may be permitted to access someone else's account on another system. You could access an account on another system by first logging in to your own and then remotely logging in across your network to the account on the other system. You can perform such a remote login using the **rlogin** command, which takes as its argument a system name. The command connects you to the other system and begins login procedures. Bear in mind that if you are using an SSH-enabled network connection, you would use **slogin** instead of **rlogin**. Either **slogin** or Kerberos **rlogin** will provide secure encrypted login access.

You can use the **rcp** command to copy files to and from remote and local systems. For SSH-enabled network connections, you would use **scp** instead of **rcp**. The **rcp** and **scp** commands are file transfer tools that operate like the **cp** command, but across a network connection to a remote system. The **rcp** command requires the remote system to have your local system and login name in its **.rhosts** file. The **rcp** command begins with the keyword **rcp** and has as its arguments the names of the source file and the copy file. To specify the file on the remote system, you need to place the remote system name before the filename, separated from it by a colon. When you are copying a file on the remote system to your own, the source file is a remote file and requires the remote system's name. The copy file is a file on your own system and does not require a system name:

```
$ rcp remote-system-name:source-file copy-file
```

In the next example, the user copies the file **wednesday** from the remote system **violet** to her own system and renames the file **today**:

```
$ rcp violet:wednesday today
```

You can also use **scp** or **rcp** to copy whole directories to or from a remote system. The **scp** command with the **-r** option copies a directory and all its subdirectories from one system to another. Like the **cp** command, these commands require source and destination directories. The directory on the remote system requires that the system name and colon be placed before the directory name. When you copy a directory from your own system to a remote system, the copy directory is on the remote system and requires the remote system's name. In the next example, the user uses the **scp** command to copy the directory **letters** to the directory **oldnotes** on the remote system **violet**:

```
$ scp -r letters violet:oldnotes
```

At times, you may need to execute a single command on a remote system. The **rsh** command executes a Linux command on another system and displays the results on your own. Your system name and login name must, of course, be in the remote system's **.rhosts** file. For SSH-enabled network connections, you would use **ssh** instead of **rsh**. The **ssh** and **rsh** commands take two general arguments: a system name and a Linux command. The syntax is as follows:

```
$ rsh remote-system-name Linux-command
```

In the next example, the **rsh** command executes an **ls** command on the remote system **violet** to list the files in the **/home/robert** directory on **violet**:

```
$ rsh violet ls /home/robert
```

Special characters are evaluated by the local system unless quoted. If you quote a special character, it becomes part of the Linux command evaluated on the remote system. Quoting redirection operators enables you to perform redirection operations on the remote system. In the next example, the redirection operator is quoted. It becomes part of the Linux command, including its argument, the filename **myfiles**. The **ls** command then generates a list of filenames that is redirected on the remote system to a file called **myfiles**, also located on the remote system.

```
$ ssh violet ls /home/robert '>' myfiles
```

The same is true for pipes. The first command (shown next) prints the list of files on the local system's printer. The standard output is piped to your own line printer. In the second command, the list of files is printed on the remote system's printer. The pipe is quoted and evaluated by the remote system, piping the standard output to the printer on the remote system.

```
$ ssh violet ls /home/robert | lpr
$ ssh violet ls /home/robert '|' lpr
```

NOTE *The Kerberos version of the remote commands also lets you specify Kerberos realms and credentials.*

IV PART

Security

Encryption, Integrity Checks, and Signatures: GNU Privacy Guard

Y ou can use encryption, integrity checks, and digital signatures to protect data transmitted over a network. For example, the GNU Privacy Guard encryption package lets you encrypt your e-mail messages or files you want to send, as well as letting you sign them with an encrypted digital signature authenticating that the message was sent by you. The digital signature also includes encrypted modification digest information that provides an integrity check, allowing the recipient to verify that the message received is the original and not one that has been changed or substituted.

Encryption was originally implemented with Pretty Good Privacy (PGP). Originally a privately controlled methodology, it was handed over to the Internet Engineering Task Force (IETF) to support an open standard for PGP called OpenPGP (see Table 16-1). Any project can use OpenPGP to create encryption applications, such as GnuPGP. Commercial products for PGP are still developed by the PGP corporation, which also uses the OpenPGP standard.

NOTE *An intrusion detection system is not included with Fedora Core, but you can use the Linux Intrusion Detection System (LIDS) at www.lids.org to implement one. Be sure to use the RPM for the kernel version you are using.*

TABLE 16-1
PGP Sites

Web Site	Description
www.gnupg.org	GnuPGP, Gnu Privacy Guard
www.opengpg.org	IETF open standard for Pretty Good Privacy (PGP)
www.pgp.com	PGP Corporation, Pretty Good Privacy commercial products

Public-Key Encryption, Digital Signatures, and Integrity Checks

Encrypting data is the only sure way to secure data transmitted over a network. Encrypt data with a key, and the receiver or receivers can later decrypt it. To fully protect data transmitted over a network, you should not only encrypt it but also check that it has not been modified, as well as confirm that it was actually created by the claimed author. An encrypted message could still be intercepted and modified, and then reencrypted. Integrity checks such as modification digests make sure that the data was not altered. Though encryption and integrity checks protect the data, they do not authenticate it. You also need to know that the person who claimed to send a message actually is the one who sent it, rather than an imposter. To authenticate a message, the author can sign it using a digital signature. This signature can also be encrypted, allowing the receiver to validate it. Digital signatures ensure that the message you receive is authentic.

Public-Key Encryption

Encryption uses a key to encrypt data in such a way that a corresponding key can decrypt it. In the past, older forms of encryption used the same key to both encrypt and decrypt a message. This, however, involved providing the receiver with the key, opening up the possibility that anyone who obtained the key could decrypt the data. Public-key encryption uses two keys to encrypt and decrypt a message, a private key and a public key. The *private* key you always keep and use to decrypt messages you have received. The *public* key you make available to those you send messages to. They then use your public key to encrypt any message they want to send to you. The private key decrypts messages, and the public key encrypts them. Each user has a set of private and public keys. Reciprocally, if you want to send messages to another user, you would first obtain the user's public key and use it to encrypt the message you want to send to the user. The user then decrypts the messages with their own private key. In other words, your public key is used by others to encrypt the messages you receive, and you use other users' public keys to encrypt messages you send to them. Each user on your Linux system can have their own public and private keys. They will use the **gpg** program to generate them and keep their private key in their own directory.

Digital Signatures

A *digital signature* is used to both authenticate a message and provide a integrity check. Authentication guarantees that the message has not been modified—that it is the original message sent by you—and the integrity check verifies that it has not been changed. Though usually combined with encrypted messages to provide a greater level of security, digital signatures can also be used for messages that can be sent in the clear. For example, you would want to know if a public notice of upgrades of a Red Hat release was actually sent by Red Hat, and not by someone trying to spread confusion. Such a message still needs to be authenticated, checked to see if it was actually sent by the sender or, if sent by the original sender, was not somehow changed en route. Verification like this protects against modification or substitution of the message by someone pretending to be the sender.

Integrity Checks

Digitally signing a message involves generating a checksum value from the contents of the message using an encryption hash algorithm such as the SHA2 modification digest algorithm. This is a unique value that accurately represents the size and contents of your message. Any changes to the message of any kind would generate a different value. Such a value provides a way to check the integrity of the data. The value is commonly known as the MD5 value, reflective of the MD5 hash algorithm that was used to encrypt the value. The MD5 algorithm has since been replaced by the more secure SHA2 algorithms.

The MD5 value is then itself encrypted with your private key. When the user receives your message, they decrypt your digital signature with your public key. The user then generates an MD5 value of the message received and compares it with the MD5 value you sent. If they are the same, the message is authenticated—it is the original message sent by you, not a false one sent by a user pretending to be you. The user can use GnuPG (described in the next section) to decrypt and check digital signatures.

Combining Encryption and Signatures

Normally, digital signatures are combined with encryption to provide a more secure level of transmission. The message would be encrypted with the recipient's public key, and the digital signature encrypted with your private key. The user would decrypt both the message (with their own private key) and then the signature (with your public key). They would then compare the signature with one the user generates from the message to authenticate it. When GnuPG decodes a message, it will also decode and check a digital signature automatically. Figure 16-1 shows the process for encrypting and digitally signing a message.

GNU Privacy Guard

To protect messages that you send by e-mail, most Linux distributions provide GNU Privacy Guard (GnuPG) encryption and authentication (**www.gnupg.org**). GnuPG is GNU open source software that works much like Pretty Good Privacy (PGP) encryption. It is based on

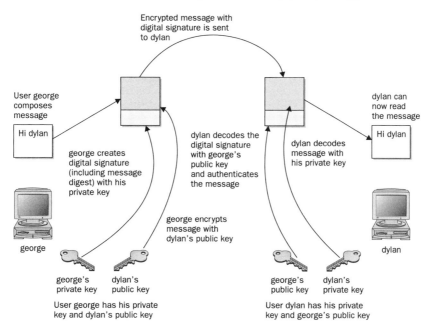

FIGURE 16-1   Public-key encryption and digital signatures

OpenPGP, the open source version of PGP. With GnuPG, you can both encrypt your messages and digitally sign them—protecting the message and authenticating that it is from you. Currently, Evolution and KMail both support GnuPG encryption and authentication, along with Thunderbird with added GPG extensions. On Evolution, you can select PGP encryption and signatures from the Security menu to use GnuPG (the PGP options use GnuPG on Fedora Core Linux). On KMail, you can select the encryption to use on the Security panel in the Options window. For Thunderbird you can use the enigmail extension to support GPG and PGP encryption (**enigmail.mozdev.org**).

GNU Privacy Guard (GnuPG) operations are carried out with the **gpg** command, which uses both commands and options to perform tasks. Commonly used commands and options are listed in Table 16-2. Some commands and options have a short form that uses only one hyphen. Normally, two hyphens are used. The first time you use **gpg**, a **.gnugpg** directory is created in your home directory with a file named **options**. The **.gnugpg/options** file contains commented default options for GPG operations (changed to **.gnupg/gpg.conf** for next release, 1.2). You can edit this file and uncomment or change any default options you want implemented for GPG. You can use a different options file and specify it with the **--options** parameter when invoking **gpg**. Helpful options include keyserver entries. The **.gnugpg** directory will also hold encryption files such as **secring.gpg** for your secret keys (secret keyring), **pubring.gpg** for your public keys (public keyring), and **trustdb.gpg**, which is a database for trusted keys.

TIP *You can use Gnome Keyring Manager (**gnome-keyring**) to manage your PGP secret keys.*

GnuPG Setup: gpg

Before you can use GnuPG, you will have to generate your private and public keys. On the command line (terminal window), enter the **gpg** command with the **--gen-key** command. The **gpg** program will then prompt with different options for creating your private and public keys. You can check the **gpg** Man page for information on using the **gpg** program.

```
gpg --gen-key
```

Creating Your Key

You are first asked to select the kind of key you want. Normally, you would just select the default entry, which you can do by pressing the ENTER key. Then you choose the key size, usually the default 1024. You then specify how long the key is to be valid—usually, there is no expiration. You will be asked to enter a user ID, a comment, and an e-mail address. Press ENTER to be prompted for each in turn. These elements, any of which can be used as the key's name, identify the key. You use the key name when performing certain GPG tasks such as signing a key or creating a revocation certificate. For example, the following elements create a key for the user richlp with the comment "author" and the e-mail address richlp@turtle .mytrek.com:

```
Richard Petersen (author) <richlp@turtle.mytrek.com>
```

GPG Command	Description
`-s, --sign`	Signs a document, creating a signature. May be combined with `--encrypt`.
`--clearsign`	Creates a clear-text signature.
`-b, --detach-sign`	Creates a detached signature.
`-e, --encrypt`	Encrypts data. May be combined with `--sign`.
`--decrypt<>` [*file*]	Decrypts file (or stdin if no file is specified) and writes it to stdout (or the file specified with `--output`). If the decrypted file is signed, the signature is verified.
`--verify` [[*sigfile*] [*signed-files*]]	Verifies a signed file. The signature can either be contained with the file or be a separate detached signature file.
`--list-keys` [*names*]	Lists all keys from the keyrings or those specified.
`--list-public-keys` [*names*]	Lists all keys from the public keyrings or those specified.
`--list-secret-keys` [*names*]	Lists your private (secret) keys.
`--list-sigs` [*names*]	Lists your keys along with any signatures they have.
`--check-sigs` [*names*]	Lists keys and their signatures and verifies the signatures.
`--fingerprint` [*names*]	Lists fingerprints for specified keys.
`--gen-key`	Generates a new set of private and public keys.
`--edit-key` *name*	Edits your keys. Use commands to perform most key operations such as **sign** to sign a key or **passwd** to change your passphrase.
`--sign-key` *name*	Signs a public key with your private key. Same as **sign in --edit-key**.
`--delete-key` *name*	Removes a public key from the public keyring.
`--delete-secret-key` *name*	Removes private and public keys from both the secret and public keyrings.
`--gen-revoke`	Generates a revocation certificate for your own key.
`--export` [*names*]	Exports a specified key from your keyring. With no arguments, exports all keys.
`--send-keys` [*names*]	Exports and sends specified keys to a keyserver. The option `--keyserver` must be used to give the name of this keyserver.
`--import` [*files*]	Imports keys contained in files into your public keyring.
GPG Option	**Description**
`-a, --armor`	Creates ASCII armored output, ASCII version of encrypted data.
`-o, --output` *file*	Writes output to a specified file.
`--default-key` *name*	Specifies the default private key to use for signatures.
`--keyserver` *site*	The keyserver to look up public keys not on your keyring. Can also specify the site to send your public key to. **host -l pgp.net	grep www.keys** will list the keyservers.
`-r, --recipient` *names*	Encrypts data for the specified user, using that user's public key.
`--default-recipient` *names*	Specifies the default recipient to use for encrypting data.

TABLE 16-2   GPG Commands and Options

PART IV

You can use any unique part of a key's identity to reference that key. For example, the string "Richard" would reference the preceding key, provided there are no other keys that have the string "Richard" in them. The string "richlp" would also reference the key, as would "author". Where a string matches more than one key, all the matched ones would be referenced.

Protecting Your Key

The **gpg** program will then ask you to enter a passphrase, used to protect your private key. Be sure to use a real phrase, including spaces, not just a password. **gpg** then generates your public and private keys and places them in the **.gnupg** directory. The private keys are kept in a file called **secring.gpg** in your **.gnupg** directory. The public key is placed in the **pubring.gpg** file, to which you can add the public keys of other users. You can list these keys with the **--list-keys** command.

In case you later need to change your keys, you can create a revocation certificate to notify others that the public key is no longer valid. For example, if you forget your password or someone else discovers it, you can use the revocation certificate to tell others that your public key should no longer be used. In the next example, the user creates a revocation certificate for the key richlp and places it in the file **myrevoke.asc**:

```
gpg --output myrevoke.asc --gen-revoke richlp
```

Making Your Public Key Available

For other users to decrypt your messages, you have to make your public key available to them. They, in turn, have to send you their public keys so that you can decrypt any messages you receive from them. In effect, enabling encrypted communications between users involves all of them exchanging their public keys. The public keys then have to be verified and signed by each user that receives them. The public keys can then be trusted to safely decrypt messages.

If you are sending messages to just a few users, you can manually e-mail them your public key. For general public use, you can post your public key on a keyserver, which anyone can then download and use to decrypt any message they receive from you. The OpenPGP Public Keyserver is located at **www.keyserver.net**, which is listed in your **.gnupg/options** file. You can send directly to the keyserver with the **-keyserver** option and **--send-key** command. The **--send-key** command takes as its argument your e-mail address. You need to send to only one keyserver, as it will share your key with other keyservers automatically.

```
gpg --keyserver search.keyserver.net --send-key chris@turtle.mytrek.com
```

If you want to send your key directly to another user, you should generate an armored text version of the key that you can then e-mail. You do this with the **--armor** and **--export** options, using the **--output** option to specify a file to place the key in. The **--armor** option will generate an ASCII text version of the encrypted file so that it can be e-mailed directly, instead of as an attached binary. Files that hold an ASCII encoded version of the encryption normally have the extension **.asc**, by convention. Binary encrypted files normally use the extension **.gpg**. You can then e-mail the file to users you want to send encrypted messages.

```
# gpg --armor --export richlp@turtle.mytrek.com --output richlp.asc
# mail -s 'mypubkey' george@rabbit.mytrek.com < richlp.asc
```

Many companies and institutions post their public key files on their Web sites, where they can be downloaded and used to verify encrypted software downloads or official announcements.

NOTE *Some commands and options for GPG have both long and short forms. For example, the* **--armor** *command can be written as* **-a**, **--output** *as* **-o**, **--sign** *as* **-s**, *and* **--encrypt** *as* **-e**. *Most others, like* **--export**, *have no short form.*

Obtaining Public Keys

To decode messages from other users, you will need to have their public keys. They can either send them to you or you can download them from a keyserver. Save the message or Web page containing the public key to a file. You will then need to import, verify, and sign the key. Use the file you received to import the public key to your **pubring** file. In the following example, the user imports George's public key, which he has received as the file **georgekey.asc**.

```
gpg --import georgekey.asc
```

All Linux distribution sites have their own public keys available for download. You should, for example, download the Red Hat public key, which can be accessed from the Red Hat site on its security resources page (**www.redhat.com**). Click the Public Encryption Key link. From there, you can access a page that displays just the public key. You can save this page as a file and use that file to import the Red Hat public key to your keyring. (Your Red Hat distribution also places the Red Hat public key in the **/usr/share/doc/rpm4-1** directory with versions for both GPG and PGP encryption, **RPM-GPG-KEY** and **RPM-PGP-KEY** files.) In the following example, the user saved the page showing just the Red Hat public key as **myredhat.asc**, and then imported that file:

```
gpg --import myredhat.asc
```

NOTE *You can remove any key, including your own private key, with the* **--delete-key** *and* **--delete-secret-key** *commands.*

Validating Keys

To manually check that a public key file was not modified in transit, you can check its fingerprint. This is a hash value generated from the contents of the key, much like a modification digest. Using the **--fingerprint** option, you can generate a hash value from the key you installed, and then contact the sender and ask them what the hash value should really be. If they are not the same, you know the key was tampered with in transit.

```
gpg --fingerprint george@rabbit
```

You do not have to check the fingerprint to have **gpg** operate. This is just an advisable precaution you can perform on your own. The point is that you need to be confident that the key you received is valid. Normally you can accept most keys from public servers or known sites as valid, though it is easy to check their posted fingerprints. Once assured of the key's validity, you can then sign it with your private key. Signing a key notifies **gpg** that you officially accept the key.

To sign a key, you use the **gpg** command with the **--sign-key** command and the key's name.

```
gpg --sign-key george@rabbit
```

Alternatively, you can edit the key with the **--edit-key** command to start an interactive session in which you can enter the command **sign** to sign the key and **save** to save the change. Signing a key involves accessing your private key, so you will be prompted for your passphrase. When you are finished, leave the interactive session with the **quit** command.

Normally, you would want to post a version of your public key that has been signed by one or more users. You can do the same for other users. Signing a public key provides a way to vouch for the validity of a key. It indicates that someone has already checked it out. Many different users could sign the same public key. For a key that you have received from another user, and that you have verified, you can sign and return the signed version to that user. Once you have signed the key, you can generate a file containing the signed public version. You can then send this file to the user. This process builds a Web of Trust, where many users vouch for the validity of public keys.

```
gpg -a --export george@rabbit --output  georgesig.asc
```

The user would then import the signed key and export it to a keyserver.

TIP *If you want to start over from scratch, you can just erase your .gnupg directory, though this is a drastic measure, as you will lose any keys you have collected.*

Using GnuPG

GnuPG encryption is currently supported by most mail clients, including Kmail, Thunderbird, and Evolution. You can also use the GNU Privacy Assistant (GPA), a GUI front end, to manage GPG tasks, or you can use the **gpg** command to manually encode and decode messages, including digital signatures, if you wish. As you perform GPG tasks, you will need to reference the keys you have using their key names. Bear in mind that you only need a unique identifying substring to select the key you want. GPG performs a pattern search on the string you specify as the key name in any given command. If the string matches more than one key, all those matching will be selected. In the following example, the "Sendmail" string selects matches on the identities of two keys.

```
# gpg --list-keys "Sendmail"
pub   1024R/CC374F2D 2000-12-14
              Sendmail Signing Key/2001 <sendmail@Sendmail.ORG>
pub   1024R/E35C5635 1999-12-13
              Sendmail Signing Key/2000 <sendmail@Sendmail.ORG>
```

Encrypting Messages

The **gpg** command provides several options for managing secure messages. The **e** option encrypts messages, the **a** option generates an armored text version, and the **s** option adds a digital signature. You will need to specify the recipient's public key, which you should already have imported into your **pubring** file. It is this key that is used to encrypt the message. The recipient will then be able to decode the message with their private key. Use the **--recipient** or **-r** option to specify the name of the recipient key. You can use any unique substring in the user's public key name. The e-mail address usually suffices. You use the **d** option to decode received messages. In the following example, the user encrypts (**e**) and signs (**s**) a file generated in armored text format (**a**). The **-r** option indicates the recipient for the message (whose public key is used to encrypt the message).

```
gpg e -s -a -o myfile.asc -r george@rabbit.mytrek.com myfile
# mail george@rabbit.mytrek.com < myrile.asc
```

You can leave out the ASCII armor option if you want to send or transfer the file as a binary attachment. Without **--armor** or **-a** options, **gpg** generates an encoded binary file, not an encoded text file. A binary file can be transmitted through e-mail only as an attachment. As noted previously, ASCII armored versions usually have an extension of **.asc**, whereas binary versions use **.gpg**.

Decrypting Messages
When the other user receives the file, they can save it to a file named something like **myfile .asc** and then decode the file with the **-d** option. The **-o** option will specify a file to save the decoded version in. GPG will automatically determine if it is a binary file or an ASCII armored version.

```
gpg -d -o myfile.txt myfile.asc
```

To check the digital signature of the file, you use the **gpg** command with the **--verify** option. This assumes that the sender has signed the file.

```
gpg --verify myfile.asc
```

Decrypting a Digital Signature
You will need to have the signer's public key to decode and check the digital signature. If you do not, you will receive a message saying that the public key was not found. In this case, you will first have to obtain the signer's public key. You could access a keyserver that you think may have the public key, or request the public key directly from a Web site or from the signer. Then import the key as described previously.

Signing Messages
You do not have to encrypt a file to sign it. A digital signature is a separate component. You can either combine the signature with a given file or generate one separately. To combine a signature with a file, you generate a new version that incorporates both. Use the **--sign** or **-s** option to generated a version of the document that includes the digital signature. In the following example, the **mydoc** file is digitally signed with the **mydoc.gpg** file containing both the original file and the signature.

```
gpg  -o mydoc.gpg  --sign mydoc
```

If, instead, you want to just generate a separate signature file, you use the **--detach- sig** command. This has the advantage of not having to generate a complete copy of the original file. That file remains untouched. The signature file usually has an extension like **.sig**. In the following example, the user creates a signature file called **mydoc2.sig** for the **mydoc2** file.

```
gpg -o mydoc2.sig --detach-sig mydoc2
```

To verify the file using a detached signature, the recipient user specifies both the signature file and the original file.

```
gpg --verify mydoc2.sig  mydoc2
```

You could also generate a clear sign signature to be used in text files. A *clear sign* signature is a text version of the signature that can be attached to a text file. The text file can be further edited by any text editor. Use the **--clearsign** option to create a clear sign signature. The following example creates a clear signed version of a text file called **mynotice.txt**.

```
gpg -o mysignotice.txt --clearsign mynotice.txt
```

NOTE *Numerous GUI front ends and filters are available for GnuPG at **www.gnupg.org**. GPA (GNU Privacy Assistant) provides a GNOME-based front end to easily encrypt and decrypt files. You can select files to encode, choose the recipients (public keys to use), and add a digital signature if you wish. You can also use GPA to decode encoded files you receive. You can manage your collection of public keys, the keys in your keyring file.*

TIP *Steganography is a form of encryption that hides data in other kinds of objects, such as images. You can use JPEG Hide and Seek software (JPHS) to encode and retrieve data in a JPEG image (jphide and jpseek). See **linux01.gwdg.de/~alatham/stego.html** for more details.*

Checking Software Package Digital Signatures

One very effective use for digital signatures is to verify that a software package has not been tampered with. It is possible that a software package could be intercepted in transmission and some of its system-level files changed or substituted. Software packages from your distribution, as well as those by reputable GNU and Linux projects, are digitally signed. The signature provides modification digest information with which to check the integrity of the package. The digital signature may be included with the package file or posted as a separate file. You use the **gpg** command with the **--verify** option to check the digital signature for a file.

TIP *Fedora Core will install the Red Hat public key in the RPM documentation directory in a file called **RPM-GPG-KEY**, **/usr/share/doc/rpm-4.3.2**. Fedora Core uses this key to check RPM packages during installation.*

Importing Public Keys

First, however, you will need to make sure that you have the signer's public key. The digital signature was encrypted with the software distributor's private key. That distributor is the signer. Once you have that signer's public key, you can check any data you receive from them. In the case of a software distributor, once you have their public key, you can check any software they distribute. To obtain the public key, you can check a keyserver or, more likely, check their Web site. As noted previously, you can download the Red Hat public key from the Red Hat Web site security resources page or use the version installed in the RPM documentation directory. Once you have obtained the public key, you can add to your keyring with the **-import** option, specifying the name you gave to the downloaded key file (in this case, **myredhat.asc**):

```
# gpg --import myredhat.asc
gpg: key CBA29BF9: public key imported
gpg: Total number processed: 1
gpg: imported: 1 (RSA: 1)
```

To download from a keyserver instead, you use the **--keyserver** option and the keyserver name.

To import the Red Hat public key from the RPM directory, you would specify the RPM-GPG-KEY file. This is the key provided by the Fedora Core 4 distribution on your DVD-ROM or CD-ROMs. Though used during installation, the key has to be imported to verify packages again after they have been installed.

```
rpm --import /usr/share/doc/rpm-4.1/RPM-GPG-KEY
```

Validating Public Keys

You can use the **--fingerprint** option to check a key's validity if you wish. If you are confident that the key is valid, you can then sign it with the **--sign-key** command. In the following example, the user signs the Red Hat key, using the string "Red Hat" in the key's name to reference it. The user is also asked to enter his passphrase to allow use of his private key to sign the Red Hat public key.

```
# gpg --sign-key "Red Hat"
pub  1024R/CBA29BF9  created: 1996-02-20 expires: never  trust: -/q
(1). Red Hat Software, Inc. <redhat@redhat.com>
pub  1024R/CBA29BF9  created: 1996-02-20 expires: never  trust: -/q
 Fingerprint: 6D 9C BA DF D9 60 52 06  23 46 75 4E 73 4C FB 50
 Red Hat Software, Inc. <redhat@redhat.com>

Are you really sure that you want to sign this key
with your key: "Richard Petersen (author) <richlp@turtle.mytrek.com>"
Really sign? yes>
You need a passphrase to unlock the secret key for
user: "Richard Petersen (author) <richlp@turtle.mytrek.com>"
1024-bit DSA key, ID 73F0A73C, created 2001-09-26
Enter passphrase:
#
```

PART IV

Checking RPM Packages

Once you have the public key, you can check any RPM software packages for Fedora Core with the **rpm** command and **-K** option. The following example checks the validity of the xcdroast and balsa software packages:

```
# >rpm -K xcdroast-0.98alpha9-1.i386.rpm
xcdroast-0.98alpha9-1.i386.rpm: md5 OK
# rpm -K balsa-1.1.7-1.i386.rpm
balsa-1.1.7-1.i386.rpm: md5 OK
```

Many software packages in the form of compressed archives, **.tar.gz** or **tar.bz2**, will provide signatures in separate files that end with either the **.asc** or **.sig** extension. To check these, you use the **gpg** command with the **--verify** option. For example, the most recent Sendmail package is distributed in the form of a compressed archive, **.tar.gz**. Its digital signature is provided in a separate **.sig** file. First you would download and install the public key for Sendmail software obtained from the Sendmail Web site.

```
# gpg --import sendmail.asc
```

You should then sign the Sendmail public key that you just imported. In this example, the e-mail address was used for the key name.

```
gpg --sign-key sendmail@Sendmail.ORG
```

You could also check the fingerprint of the key for added verification.
You would then download both the compressed archive and the digital signature files. Decompress the **.gz** file to the **.tar** file with **gunzip**. Then, with the **gpg** command and the **--verify** option, use the digital signature in the **.sig** file to check the authenticity and integrity of the software compressed archive.

```
# gpg --verify sendmail.8.12.0.tar.sig sendmail.8.12.0.tar
gpg: Signature made Fri 07 Sep 2001 07:21:30 PM PDT using RSA key ID CC374F2D
gpg: Good signature from "Sendmail Signing Key/2001 <sendmail@Sendmail.ORG>"
```

You could also just specify the signature file and **gpg** will automatically search for and select a file of the same name, but without the **.sig** or **.asc** extension.

```
# gpg --verify sendmail.8.12.0.tar.sig
```

In the future, when you download any software from the Sendmail site that uses this key, you just have to perform the **--verify** operation. Bear in mind, though, that different software packages from the same site may use different keys. You would have to make sure that you have imported and signed the appropriate key for the software you are checking.

Intrusion Detection: Tripwire and AIDE

When someone breaks into a system, they will usually try to gain control by making their own changes to system administration files, such as password files. They could create their own user and password information, allowing them access at any time, or simply change the root user password. They could also replace entire programs, such as the login program, with their own version. One method of detecting such actions is to use an integrity checking tool such as Tripwire or AIDE to detect any changes to system administration files. AIDE (Advanced Intrusion Detection Environment) is an alternative to Tripwire. It provides easy configuration and detailed reporting. Neither is included with Fedora Core.

An integrity checking tool works by first creating a database of unique identifiers for each file or program to be checked. These can include features such as permissions and file size, but also, more importantly, checksum numbers generated by encryption algorithms from the file's contents. For example, in Tripwire, the default identifiers are checksum numbers created by algorithms like the SHA2 modification digest algorithm and Snefru (Xerox secure hash algorithm). An encrypted value that provides such a unique identification of a file is known as a signature. In effect, a signature provides an accurate snapshot of the contents of a file. Files and programs are then periodically checked by generating their identifiers again and matching them with those in the database. Tripwire will generate signatures of the current files and programs and match them against the values previously generated for its database. Any differences are noted as changes to the file, and Tripwire then notifies you of the changes.

NOTE *You can also check your log files for any suspicious activity. See Chapter 29 for a discussion on system logs. The **/var/log/messages** file in particular is helpful for checking for critical events such as user logins, FTP connections, and superuser logins.*

PART IV

17

CHAPTER

Security Enhanced Linux: SELinux

Though numerous security tools exist for protecting specific services, as well as user information and data, no tool has been available for protecting the entire system at the administrative level. Security-Enhanced Linux is an project to provide built-in administrative protection for aspects of your Linux system. Instead of relying on users to protect their files or on a specific network program to control access, security measures would be built into the basic file management system and the network access methods. All controls can be managed directly by an administrator as part of Linux system administration.

Security-Enhanced Linux (SELinux) is a project developed and maintained by the National Security Agency (NSA), which chose Linux as its platform for implementing a secure operating system. Fedora Core has embraced SELinux and has incorporated it as a standard feature of its distribution. Detailed documentation is available from resources listed in Table 17-1, including sites provided by the NSA, SourceForge, and Fedora Core. A very detailed

Resource	Location
Red Hat Enterprise SELinux Guide	**www.redhat.com/docs/manuals/enterprise/RHEL-4-Manual/selinux-guide/**
Fedora SELinux FAQ	**fedora.redhat.com/docs/selinux-faq**
NSA SELinux	**www.nsa.gov/selinux**
NSA SELinux FAQ	**www.nsa.gov/selinux/info/faq.cfm**
SELinux at sourceforge.net	**selinux.sourceforge.net**
Writing SELinux Policy HOWTO	Accessible from "SELinux resources at sourceforge" link at **selinux.sourceforge.net**
NSA SELinux Documentation	**www.nsa.gov/selinux/info/docs.cfm**
Configuring SELinux Policy	Accessible from NSA SELinux Documentation

TABLE 17-1 SELinux Resources

manual for SELinux on Red Hat Enterprise Linux and Fedora Core is provided by the Red Hat Enterprise Linux SELinux Guide, located on the Documentation Web page for Red Hat Enterprise Linux Documentation at the Red Hat site, **www.redhat.com**. It is advised that you read this guide. Its content is also applicable to Fedora Core.

Linux and Unix systems normally use a discretionary access control (DAC) method for restricting access. In this approach users and the objects they own, such as files, determine permissions. The user has complete discretion over the objects it owns. The weak point in many Linux/Unix systems has been the user administrative accounts. If an attacker managed to gain access to an administrative account, they would have complete control over the service the account managed. Access to the root user would give control over the entire system, all its users, and any network services it was running. To counter this weakness, the NSA set up a mandatory access control (MAC) structure. Instead of an all-or-nothing set of privileges based on accounts, services and administrative tasks are compartmentalized and separately controlled with policies detailing what can and cannot be done. Access is granted not just because one is an authenticated user, but when specific security criteria are met. Users, applications, processes, files, and devices can be given just the access they need to do their job, and nothing more.

Flask Architecture

The Flask architecture organizes operating system components and data into subjects and objects. Subjects are processes: applications, drivers, system tasks that are currently running. Objects are fixed components such as files, directories, sockets, network interfaces, and devices. For each subject and object, a security context is defined. A *security context* is a set of security attributes that determine how a subject or object can be used. This approach provides a very fine-grained control over every element in the operating system as well as all data on your computer.

The attributes designated for the security contexts and the degree to which they are enforced are determined by an overall security policy. The policies are enforced by a security server.

SELinux uses a combination of the Type Enforcement (TE) and Role Based Access Control (RBAC) security models. Type Enforcement focuses on objects and processes like directories and applications, whereas Role Based Access Enforcement controls user access. For the Type Enforcement model, the security attributes assigned to an object are known as either domains or types. Types are used for fixed objects such as files, and domains are used for processes such as running applications. For user access to processes and objects, SELinux makes use of the Role Based Access Control model. When new processes or objects are created, transition rules specify the type or domain they belong to in their security contexts.

With the RBAC model, users are assigned roles for which permissions are defined. The roles restrict what objects and processes a user can access. The security context for processes will include a role attribute, controlling what objects it can assess. Objects will have a generic object_r role, which does nothing.

Users are given separate SELinux user identities. Normally these correspond to the user IDs set up under the standard Linux user creation operations. Though they may have the same name, they are not the same identifiers. Standard Linux identities can be easily changed with commands like **setuid** and **su**. Changes to the Linux user ID will not affect the SELinux ID. This means that even if a user changes its ID, SELinux will still be able to track it, maintaining control over that user.

System Administration Access

It is critically important that you make sure you have system administrative access under SELinux before you enforce its policies. This is especially true if you are using a strict policy, which imposes restrictions on administrative access. You should always use SELinux in permissive mode first and check for any messages denying access. With SELinux enforced, it may no longer matter whether you can access the root user or not. What matters is whether your user, even the root user, has sysadm_r role and sysadm_t object access. You may not be able to just use the **su** command to access the root user and expect to have root user administrative access. Recall that SELinux keeps its own security identities that are not the same as Linux user IDs. Though you might change your user ID with **su**, you still have not changed your security ID.

The targeted policy will set up rules that allow standard system administrator access using normal Linux procedures. The root user will be able to access the root user account normally. In the strict policy, however, the root user needs to access its account using the appropriate security ID. If you want administrative access through the **su** command (from another user), you would first use the **su** command to log in as the root user. You then have to change your role to that of the sysadm_r role, as well as already be configured by SELinux policy rules to be allowed to take on the sysadm_r role. A user can have several allowed possible roles it could assume.

To change the role, you use the **newrole** command with the **-r** option.

```
newrole -r sysadm_r
```

Terminology

SELinux uses several terms that have different meanings in other contexts. The terminology can be confusing because some of the terms, such as domain, have different meanings in other, related areas. For example, a domain in SELinux is a process as opposed to an object, whereas in networking the term refers to network DNS addresses.

Identity

SELinux creates identities with which to control access. Identities are not the same as traditional user IDs. At the same time, each user normally has an SELinux identity, though the two are not linked. Affecting a user does not affect the corresponding SELinux identity. SELinux can set up a separate corresponding identity for each user, though on the less secure policies, like targeted policies, general identities are used. A general user identity is used for all normal users, restricting users to user-level access, whereas administrators are given administrative identities. You can further define security identities for particular users.

The identity makes up part of a security context that determines what a user can or cannot do. Should a user change user IDs, their security identity will not change. A user will always have the same security identity. In traditional Linux systems, a user could use commands like **su** to change their user ID, becoming a different user. On SELinux, even though a user could still change their Linux user ID, they retain their original security ID. You always know what a particular person is doing on your system, no matter what user ID they may assume.

The security identity can have limited access. So even though a user may use the Linux **su** command to become the root user, their security identity could prevent them from performing any root user administrative commands. As noted previously, to gain an administrative access, the role for their security identity would have to change as well.

Use **id -Z** to see what the security context for your security identity is, what roles you have, and what kind of object you can access. This will list the user security context that starts with the security ID, followed by a colon, and then the roles a user has and the objects they can control. Security identities can have roles that control what they can do. A user role is user_r, and a system administration role is system_r. The general security identity is user_u, whereas a particular security identity will normally use the user name. The following example shows a standard user with the general security identity:

```
$ id -Z
context=user_u:user_r:user_t
```

In this example the user has a security identity called george:

```
$ id -Z
context=george:user_r:user_t
```

As noted previously, you can use the **newrole** command to change the role a user is allowed. Changing to a system administrative role, the user can then have equivalent root access.

```
$ id -Z
context=george:sysadm_r:sysadm_t
```

Domains

Domains are used to identify and control processes. Each process is assigned a domain within which it can run. A domain sets restrictions on what a process can do. Traditionally, a process was given a user ID to determine what it could do, and many had to have root user ID to gain access to the full file system. This also could be used to gain full administrative access over the entire system. A domain, on the other hand, can be tailored to access some areas but not others. Attempts to break into another domain, say the administrative domain, would be blocked. For example, the administrative domain is sysadm_t, whereas the DNS server uses only named_t and users have a user_t domain.

Types

Whereas domains control processes, *types* control objects like files and directories. Files and directories are grouped into types that can be used to control who can have access to them. The type names have the same format as the domain names, ending with a _t suffix. Unlike domains, types reference objects, including files, devices, and network interfaces.

Roles

Types and domains are assigned to roles. Users (security identities) with a given role can access types and domains assigned to that role. For example, most users can access user_t type objects, but not sysadm_t objects. The types and domains a user can access are set by the role entry in configuration files. The following example allows users to access objects with the user password type:

```
role user_r types user_passwd_t
```

Security Context

Each object has a security context that sets its security attributes. These include identity, role, domain, or type. A file will have a security context listing the kind of identity that can assess it, the role under which it can be accessed, and the security type it belongs to. Each component adds its own refined level of security. Passive objects are usually assigned a generic role, **object_r**, which has no effect, as such objects cannot initiate actions.

For a normal file created by users in their own directories, you would have the following identity, role, and type. The identity is a user and the role is that of an object. The type is the user's home directory. This type is used for all subdirectories and their files created within a user's home directory.

```
user_u:object_r:user_home_t
```

A file or directory created by that same user in a different part of the file system will have a different type. For example, the type for files created in the **/tmp** directory will be tmp_t.

```
user_u:object_r:tmp_t
```

Transition: Labeling

A *transition*, also known as labeling, assigns a security context to a process or file. For a file, the security context is assigned when it is created, whereas for a process the security context is determined when the process is run.

Making sure every file has an appropriate security context is called *labeling*. Adding a another file system would require that you label (add security contexts) to the directories and files on it. Labeling varies, depending on the policy you use. Each policy may have different security contexts for objects and processes. Relabeling is carried out using the **make** command in the policy source directory, such as **/etc/selinux/targeted/src/policy**.

```
make relabel
```

Policies

A *policy* is a set of rules to determine the relationships among users, roles, and types or domains. These rules state what types a role can access and what roles a user can have.

SELinux Tools

SELinux provides a number of tools to let you manage your SELinux configuration and policy implementation. The command line user management tools (see Chapter 30), useradd, usermod, and userdel, all have SELinux options that can be applied when SELinux is installed.

PART IV

Command	Description
seinfo	Display policy statistics
sestatus	Check status of SELinux on your system, including the contexts of processes and files
sesearch	Search for type enforcement rules in policies
seuser	Display and set users and roles for policies
seaudit	Examine SELinux log files
apol	SELinux Policy Analysis
system-config-securitylevel	SELinux GUI configuration to enable and select policies
checkpolicy	The SELinux policy compiler
fixfiles	Check file systems and set security contexts
restorecon	Set security features for particular files
newrole	New role
setfiles	Set security context for files
chcon	Change context
chsid	Change security ID

In the current version of SELinux on Fedora Core, special scripts are used for corresponding user management programs, such as **seuserad** for **useradd** and **seusermod** for **usermod**. In future versions, you will be able to use the user commands like **useradd** directly. These scripts check the user role submitted and then use **seuser** to add, delete, or change the user entries for the SELinux policy.

Command	Description
seuseradd	SELinux-enhanced **useradd** to add users along with SELinux features such as roles (invokes **useradd** to create user accounts)
seusermod	Modify user accounts, including SELinux features (invokes **usermod**)
seuserdel	Remove users, along with SELinux features they may have (invokes **userdel**)

Management Operations for SELinux

Certain basic operations such as checking the SELinux status, checking a user's or file's security context, or disabling SELinux at boot can be very useful.

Turning Off SELinux

Check the Fedora Core SELinux FAQ for details on how to turn off Fedora. Should you want to turn off SELinux before you even start up your system, you can turn it off at the boot prompt. Just add the following parameter to the end of your GRUB boot line.

```
selinux=0
```

To turn off SELinux permanently, you can use the system-config-securitylevel SELinux tab to disable SELinux or set the **SELINUX** variable in the **/etc/selinux/config** file to **disabled**.

```
SELINUX=disabled
```

To turn off SELinux temporarily without rebooting, use the **setenforce** command with the 0 option; use 1 to turn it back on. You must first have the sysadm_r role, which you can obtain by logging in as the root user.

```
setenforce 1
```

If you are using the targeted policy, you can turn off SELinux for specific daemons with system-config-securitylevel's SELinux panel.

Checking Status and Statistics

To check the current status of your SELinux system, you can use **sestatus**. Adding the **–v** option will also display process and file contexts, as listed in **/etc/sestatus.conf**. The contexts will specify the roles and types assigned to a particular process, file, or directory.

```
sestatus -v
```

Use the **seinfo** command to display your current SELinux statistics.

```
# seinfo
Statistics for policy file: /etc/selinux/targeted/policy/policy.18
Policy Version: v.18
Policy Type: binary
   Classes:            54    Permissions:        200
   Types:             583    Attributes:           0
   Users:               3    Roles:                5
   Booleans:           60    Cond. Expr.:         66
   Allow:           82757    Neverallow:           0
   Auditallow:          9    Dontaudit:         5192
   Type_trans:        378    Type_change:          0
   Role allow:          5    Role trans:           0
   Initial SIDs:        0
```

Basic Configuration with SecurityLevel

You can use system-config-securitylevel to configure basic settings for SELinux (see Figure 17-1). Here you can choose whether to enable SELinux, and if so, whether to enforce it or not. No enforcement will issue warnings only. You can also select the policy to use: targeted or strict. Changing policies will relabel the file system. Enablement and policy selections will be saved to the **/etc/sysconfig/selinux** file. You can wait for a reboot to relabel.

For the targeted policy, you can further modify how each service is controlled. There are expandable menus for the Apache (the Apache Web server), Name Service (BIND DNS server), NIS, and Transition, which lists several other servers and daemons. For example,

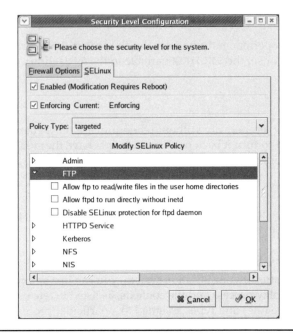

Figure 17-1 The system-config-securitylevel SELinux panel

the FTP entry lets you choose whether to allow access to home directories or to let FTP run as a stand-alone server.

Checking Security Context

The **-Z** option used with the **ls**, **id**, and **ps** commands can be used to check the security context for files, users, and processes respectively. The security context tells you the roles that users must have to access given processes or objects.

```
ls -lZ
id -Z
ps -eZ
```

SELinux Policy Customization and Editing Tool (sepcut)

Instead of manually editing configuration files to change policy rules as well as compiling and installing new policy configurations, you can use sepcut. The sepcut tool provides an easy-to-use GUI interface for configuring your SELinux policy. Detailed explanations of configuration files and rules are presented in later sections. Enter the **sepcut** command at the terminal window to start sepcut.

From the Policy menu, select Choose Policy and select the policy directory, for instance, **/etc/selinux/targeted/src/policy**. The tabbed panels are displayed: browse policy directories to display and edit configuration files; enable policy modules; and test, install, and load policies (see Figure 17-2). Use the Policy Directory and Directory Contents to locate and select a file you want to view or edit. Use the File menu save entry to save your changes to the file.

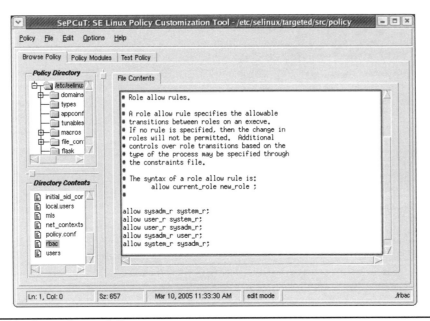

Figure 17-2   Sepcut Browse Policy

Click on Policy Modules to see different policy rules for applications or services such as for Apache or Dovecot. These correspond to the configuration files in the **src/policy/domains** directory. You can choose to disable a module, no longer including its configuration file in the policy. Use the File menu save entry to save your changes to the file.

Use the Test Policy panel to compile and install your policy. Test will run the makefile for the given policy, generating a **policy.conf** file and running `checkpolicy` to compile the policy to text its validity. Once you are satisfied with your configuration, you can choose Install, which will compile the policy and also install it for use. The Load button will also compile the policy but then load it into the kernel (see Figure 17-3). An open policy.conf option lets you view the **policy.conf** generated by any of the compile operations.

Checking SELinux Messages: seaudit

SELinux AVC messages are now saved in the **/var/log/audit/audit.log** file. These are particularly important if you are using the permissive mode to test a policy you want to later enforce. You need to find out if you are being denied access where appropriate and afforded control when needed. To see just the SELinux messages, you can use the seaudit tool. Check the Red Hat Enterprise Linux SELinux Guide for a detailed description on using seaudit. Startup messages for the SE Linux service are still logged in **/var/log/messages**.

NOTE   *The SELinux Policy Analysis tool,* **apol***, provides a complex and detailed analysis of a selected policy. Check the Red Hat Enterprise Linux SELinux Guide for a detailed description. Enter the* **apol** *command in a terminal window to start it.*

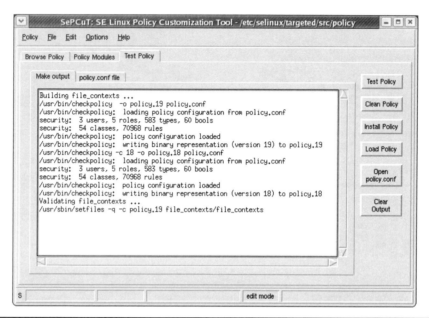

FIGURE 17-3   Sepcut Test Policy

Policy Implementation

A system is secured using a policy. For Fedora Core 4, there are currently two policies provided: targeted and strict. The *targeted* policy is used to control specific services, like network and Internet servers such as Web, DNS, and FTP servers. It also can control local services with network connections like hotplug. The policy will not affect just the daemon itself, but all the resources it uses on your system. Fedora Core 4 has added a large number of daemons that are now controlled by the targeted policy. See the Fedora Core 4 Release Notes and the Fedora SELinux FAQ at **fedora.redhat.com** for a complete listing.

The strict policy provides complete control over your system. It is under this kind of policy that your users and even administrators can be inadvertently locked out of the system. A strict policy needs to be carefully tested to make sure access is denied and granted where appropriate.

Policy Methods

Operating system services and components are categorized in SELinux by their type and their role. Rules controlling these objects can be type based or role based. Policies are implemented using two different kinds of rules, type enforcement (TE) and role-based access control (RBAC).

Type Enforcement

With a type structure, the operating system resources are partitioned off into types, with each object assigned a type. Processes are assigned to domains. Users are restricted to certain domains, allowed to use only objects accessible in those domains.

Role-Based Access Control

A role-based approach focuses on controlling users. Users are assigned roles, which define what resources they can use. In a standard system, file permissions, such as those for groups, can control user access to files and directories. With roles, permissions become more flexible and refined. Certain users can have more access to services than others.

SELinux Users

Users will retain the permissions available on a standard system. In addition, SELinux can set up its own controls for a given user, defining a role for that user. General security identities created by SELinux include:

- **system_u**   The user for system processes
- **user_u**   To allow normal users to use a service
- **root**   For the root user

Policy Files

Policies are implemented in policy files. These are binary files compiled from source files. On Fedora Core you have both strict and targeted policy files, each with corresponding source files. The policy binary and source files are in policy subdirectories in the **/etc/selinux** configuration directory, **/etc/selinux/targeted** and **/etc/selinux/strict**. For example, the policy file for the targeted policy is

```
/etc/selinux/targeted/policy/policy.18
```

The targeted source that holds the configuration files is

```
/etc/selinux/targeted/src
```

You use the SELinux policy compiler, **checkpolicy**, to create policy binaries for source files.

SELinux Configuration

Configuration for general SELinux server settings is carried out in the **/etc/selinux/config** directory. Currently there are only two settings to make: the state and the policy. You set the SELINUX variable to the state, such as enforcing or permissive, and the SELINUXTYPE variable to the kind of policy you want. These correspond to the securitylevel-config SELinux settings for disabled and enforcing, as well as the policy to use, such as targeted. A sample config file is shown here:

```
# This file controls the state of SELinux on the system.
# SELINUX= can take one of these three values:
#     enforcing - SELinux security policy is enforced.
#     permissive - SELinux prints warnings instead of enforcing.
#     disabled - SELinux is fully disabled.
SELINUX=permissive
# SELINUXTYPE= type of policy in use. Possible values are:
#     targeted - Only targeted network daemons are protected.
#     strict - Full SELinux protection.
SELINUXTYPE=targeted
```

PART IV

SELinux Policy Rules

Policy rules can be made up of either type (Type Enforcement) or rbac (Role Based Access Control) statements. A type statement can be a type or attribute declaration, or a transition, change, or assertion rule. The rbac statements can be role declarations or dominance or allow roles. Policy configuration can be difficult, using extensive and complicated rules. For this reason, many rules are implemented using M4 macros that will in turn generate the appropriate rules (Sendmail uses M4 macros in a similar way).

Type and Role Declarations

A type declaration starts with the keyword **type**, followed by the type name (identifier) and any optional attributes or aliases. The type name will have a _t suffix. Standard type definitions are included for objects such as files. The following is a default type for any file, with attributes file_type and sysadmfile:

```
type file_t, file_type, sysadmfile;
```

The root will have its own type declaration.

```
type root_t, file_type, sysadmfile;
```

Specialized directories such as the boot directory will also have their own type.

```
type boot_t, file_type, sysadmfile;
```

More specialized rules are set up for specific targets like the Amanda server. The following example is the general type definition for amanda_t objects, those objects used by the Amanda backup server, as listed in the targeted policy's **src/program/amanda.te** file.

```
type amanda_t, domain, privlog, auth, nscd_client_domain ;
```

A role declaration determines the roles that can access objects of a certain type. These rules begin with the keyword **role** followed by the role and the objects associated with that role. In this example, the amanda objects (amanda_t) can be accessed by a user or process with the system role (system_r).

```
role system_r types amanda_t;
```

A more specific type declaration is provided for executables, such as the following for the Amanda server (amanda_exec_t). This defines the Amanda executable as a system administration–controlled executable file.

```
type amanda_exec_t, file_type, sysadmfile, exec_type;
```

Associated configuration files often have their own rules.

```
type amanda_config_t, file_type, sysadmfile;
```

In the targeted policy a general unconfined type is created that user and system roles can access, giving complete unrestricted access to the system. More specific rules will restrict access to certain targets like the Web server.

```
type unconfined_t, domain, privuser, privhome, privrole, privowner, admin,
auth_write, fs_domain, privmem;
role system_r types unconfined_t;
role user_r types unconfined_t;
role sysadm_r types unconfined_t;
```

Types are also set up for the files created in the user home directory.

```
type user_home_t, file_type, sysadmfile, home_type;
type user_home_dir_t, file_type, sysadmfile, home_dir_type;
```

File Contexts

File contexts associate specific files with security contexts. The file or files are listed first, with multiple files represented with regular expressions. The following creates a security context for all files in the **/etc** directory (configuration files). These are accessible from the system user (system_u) and are objects of the etc type.

```
/etc(/.*)?                system_u:object_r:etc_t
```

Certain files can belong to other types; for instance, the **resolve.conf** configuration file belongs to the net_conf type.

```
/etc/resolv\.conf.*     --     system_u:object_r:net_conf_t
```

Certain services will have their own security contexts for their configuration files.

```
/etc/amanda(/.*)?            system_u:object_r:amanda_config_t
```

User Roles

User roles define what roles a user can take on. Such a role begins with the keyword **user** followed by the username, then the keyword **roles**, and finally the roles it can use. The following example is a definition of the system_u user:

```
user system_u roles system_r;
```

If a user can have several roles, then they are listed in brackets. The following is the definition of the standard user role in the targeted policy, which allows users to take on system administrative roles.

```
user user_u roles { user_r sysadm_r system_r };
```

The strict policy lists only the user_r role.

```
user user_u roles { user_r };
```

Access Vector Rules: allow

Access vector rules are used to define permissions for objects and processes. The **allow** keyword is followed by the object or process type, and then the types it can access or be accessed by and the permissions used. The following allows processes in the amanda_t domain to search the Amanda configuration directories (any directories of type amanda_config_t).

```
allow amanda_t amanda_config_t:dir search;
```

The following example allows Amanda to read the files in a user home directory:

```
allow amanda_t user_home_type:file { getattr read };
```

The next example allows Amanda to read, search, and write files in the Amanda data directories:

```
allow amanda_t amanda_data_t:dir { read search write };
```

Role Allow Rules

Roles can also have allow rules. Though they can be used for domains and objects, they are usually used to control role transitions, specifying whether a role can transition to another role. These rules are listed in the rbac configuration file. The following entry allows the user to transition to a system administrator role:

```
allow user_r sysadm_r;
```

Transition and Vector Rule Macros

The type transition rules set the type used for rules to create objects. Transition rules also require corresponding access vector rules to enable permissions for the objects or processes. Instead of creating separate rules, macros are used that will generate the needed rules. The following example sets the transition and access rules for user files in the home directory using the file_type_auto_trans macro:

```
file_type_auto_trans(privhome, user_home_dir_t, user_home_t)
```

The next example sets the Amanda process transition and access rules for creating processes:

```
domain_auto_trans(inetd_t, amanda_inetd_exec_t, amanda_t)
```

Constraint Rules

Restrictions can be further placed on processes such as transitions to ensure greater security. These are implemented with constraint definitions in the constraints file. Constraint rules are often applied to transition operations, such as requiring that, in a process transition, user identities remain the same, or that process 1 be in a domain that has the privuser attribute and process 2 be in a domain with the userdomain attribute. The characters **u**, **t**, and **r** refer to user, type, and role.

```
constrain process transition
    ( u1 == u2 or ( t1 == privuser and t2 == userdomain ))
```

SELinux Policy Configuration Files

The rules are held in configuration files located in various subdirectories in a policy's **src** directory. For example, you will find the configuration files for the targeted policy in the **/etc/selinux/targeted/policy/src** directory. You will have configuration files for both type enforcement and security contexts. Type enforcement files have the extension **.te**, whereas security contexts have an **.sc** extension.

Reflecting the fine-grained control that SELinux provides, you have numerous configuration files for the many kinds of objects and processes on your system. The primary configuration files and directories are listed in Table 17-2, but several expand to the listing of detailed subdirectories and files.

Directories and Files	Description
assert.te	Access vector assertions
attrib.te	Type attribute definitions
macros	Macros directory with M4 macros files
macros/program	Macro files for specific programs
types	Type configuration files
domains	Domain configuration files
domains/program	Domain files for specific programs
domains/user.te	Strict policy general user domains
domains/admin.te	Strict policy administrative domains
domains/unrestriced.te	Target policy general unrestricted domains
appconfig	Application-specific rules
rbac	Role-based access control (RBAC) configuration
users	General users definition
local.users	Define your own SELinux users
constraints	Additional constraints for role transition and object access
initial_sid_contexts	Security contexts for initial general security identities
fs_use	Security contexts for file systems
genfs_contexts	Security contexts for files in nonpersistent file systems such as removable or network devices
net_contexts	Security contexts of network objects such as ports and interfaces
file_contexts	Directory for security contexts for files and directories
file_contexts/program	Directory for security contexts for files and directories belonging to particular applications and services
tunables	Defines policy tunables for customization
mls	Multilevel security (MLS) configuration

TABLE 17-2 SELinux Policy Configuration Files

Macro Files

Macros are placed in their own directory, **macros**. These files will include a **_macros** suffix as part of their name. The main directory holds general configuration files for different scopes such as **admin_macros.te** for administration and **network_macros.te** for networking. A program subdirectory has macro files for specific applications and commands, such as **apache_macros.te** for the Apache Web server, **samba_macros.te** for the Samba server, **inetd_ macros.te** for the **xinetd** service, and even **lpr_macros.te** and **su_macros.te** for the **lpr** and **su** commands. The strict policy will have many more program macros than the targeted policy, reflecting its greater level of control.

Types Files

In the targeted policy, the types directory that defines types holds a range of files, including **nfs.te** and **network.te** configuration files. Here you will find type declarations for the different kinds of objects on your system.

Domain Files

The configuration files for your domains (process groups) are held in the **domains** directory. General domain configuration is managed by files within the **domains** directory, and specific configuration is performed in the **program** subdirectory. A **misc** subdirectory handles special cases. The targeted and strict policies have different general domain configuration files reflecting their different levels of control. The targeted policy has only one general file, **unrestricted**, which basically makes all domains other than the targeted ones fully accessible. In the **program** subdirectory you find an extensive list of service-based configuration files, including **apache**, **sendmail**, **squid**, **ssh**, and even **rsync**. In contrast, the strict policy has two general configuration files, **admin** and **user**, providing control over administrative tasks and general user access. Its **program** subdirectory lists more configuration files, such as **passwd**, **anaconda**, **bluetooth**, and even **sound**.

The **unused** subdirectory, located within the **misc** subdirectory, holds configuration files that can be added to provide even more control. In the targeted policies **unused** holds files like **screensaver**, **startx**, and **kernel**. In the strict policy, the **unused** directory is empty, its files moved up the **misc** directory and already in use.

Security Context Files

Security contexts for different files are detailed in security context files. In the **policy** directory, several general configuration files are used to set standard contexts for file systems and devices. For file systems and devices, the **fs_use** file sets preferred security context for standard file systems such as ext3. In **genfs_contexts**, you find the security contexts for removable devices like CD-ROM discs, network file systems, and virtual file systems like sysfs. The **net_contexts** file covers network devices. The **initial_sid_contexts** file sets up initial security contexts for general and system identities such as kernel, file, and port.

The **file_contexts** directory holds security context configurations for different groups, directories, and files. Each configuration file has an **.fc** extension. The **types.fc** file holds security contexts for various system files and directories, particularly access to configuration files in the **/etc** directory. The **distros.fc** file defines distribution-dependent configurations,

including security contexts for all the Fedora Core system configuration tools. The
homedir_template file defines security contexts for dot files that may be set up in a
user's home directory, such as **.mozilla**, **.gconf**, and **.java**.

A program subdirectory has file context files for particular applications and services.
For example, **apache.fc** has the security contexts for all the files and directories used by the
Apache Web server, such as **/var/www** and **/etc/httpd**. An **unconfined.fc** file is used to list
files and applications not to be controlled by SELinux.

User Configuration: Roles

Global user configuration is defined in the policy directory's **users** file. Here you find the
user definitions and the roles they have for standard users (user_u) and administrators
(admin_u). To add your own users, you use the **local.users** file. Here you will find examples
for entering your own SELinux users. Both the strict and targeted policies use the general
user_u SELinux identity for users. To set up a separate SELinux identity for a user, you
would define that user in the **local.users** file.

The **rbac** file defines the allowed roles one role can transition to. For example, can the
user role transition to an system administration role? The targeted policy has several entries
allowing a user to freely transition to an administrator, and vice versa. The strict policy has
no such definitions.

Role transitions are further restricted by rules in the **constraints** file. Here the change to
other users is controlled, and changing object security contexts (labeling) is restricted.

Vector Assertions: assert.te

Vector assertions can be listed in the **assert.te** file to have the policy compiler check to see if
certain vector access rules are being implemented correctly. These rules specify domains or
types that should not be allowed access. Each rule begins with the keyword **noallow** and
is followed by the domain or type and then by the domains and types that should not be
allowed to access it. Often exclusiveness is denoted with a ~ representing 'not', as in ~domain
for any process not a domain. The following example allows a domain to transition only to
another domain, not to a process that does not belong to any domain:

```
neverallow domain ~domain:process { transition dyntransition };
```

Application Configuration: appconfig

Certain services and applications are security aware and will request default security
contexts and types from SELinux (see also the "Runtime Security Contexts" section). These
application configurations are kept file located in the **src/policy/appconfig** directory. The
default_types file holds type defaults; **default_contexts** holds default security contexts.
The **initrc_context** file has the default security context for running **/etc/rc.d** scripts. A special
root_default_contexts file details how the root user can be accessed. The **removable_context**
file holds the security context for removable devices, and **media** lists media devices, such as
cdrom for CD-ROMs. Runtime values can also be entered in corresponding files in the policy
contexts directory, such as **/etc/selinux/targeted/contexts**.

PART IV

Creating an SELinux Policy: make and checkpolicy

Once you have configured your policy you can create it with the **make policy** and **checkpolicy** commands. The **make policy** command generates a **policy.conf** file for your configuration files, which **checkpolicy** can then use to generate a policy binary file. A policy binary file will be created in the **policy** subdirectory with a numeric extension for the policy version, such as **policy.18**. Recall that you can also use **sepcut** to create your policy; **sepcut** will invoke **make** with the policy option and run **checkpolicy** to compile your policy.

To generate a **policy.conf** file, you enter the following command in the policy **src** directory, which may be **/etc/selinux/targeted/src/policy**.

```
make policy
```

The policy configuration files, all those in the **src** directory with a **.te** extension, are merged into one long file. The m4 macros are then processed using the m4 macro processor, generating a **policy.conf** file in the **policy** subdirectory. This will be **/etc/selinux/targeted/src/policy/policy.conf** for the targeted policy.

To compile the policy, you run the **checkpolicy** command on the **policy.conf** file. This will generate a policy binary, with a version number as its extension. Use the **-o** option to specify a policy file. To specify a particular version number, you use the **-C** option.

```
checkpolicy policy.conf
```

You then need to install the policy in the **/etc/security/selinux** directory using the **make** command with the **install** option in the policy **src** directory.

```
make install
```

Once you have installed the policy, you need to relabel your file system with the corresponding security contexts. For this you use either the **make** command or the **fixfiles** tool. With the **make** command, you use the **relabel** argument.

```
make relabel
```

For **fixfiles**, you use

```
fixfiles relabel
```

SELinux Administrative Operations

There are several tasks you can perform on your SELinux system without having to recompile your entire configuration. Security contexts for certain files and directories can be changed as needed. For example, when you add a new file system, you will need to label it with the appropriate security contexts. Also, when you add users, you may need to have a user given special attention by the system.

Using Security Contexts: fixfiles, setfiles, restorecon, and chcon

Several tools are available for changing your objects' security contexts. The **fixfiles** command can set the security context for file systems. You use the **relabel** option to set security contexts, and the **check** option to see what should be changed. The **fixfiles** tool is a script that uses **setfiles** and **restorecon** to make actual changes.

The **restorecon** command will let you restore the security context for files and directories, but **setfiles** is the basic tool for setting security contexts. It can be applied to individual files or directories. It is used to label the file when a policy is first installed.

With **chcon**, you can change the permissions of individual files and directories, much as **chmod** does for general permissions.

Adding New Users

If a new user needs no special access, you can generally just use the generic SELinux user_u identity. If, however, you need to allow the user to take on roles that would otherwise be restricted, such as a system administrator role in the strict policy, you need to configure the user accordingly. To do this, you add the user to the **local.users** file in the policy users directory, as in **/etc/selinux/targeted/policy/users/local.users**. Note that this is different from the **local.users** file in the **src** directory which compiled directly into the policy. The user rules have the syntax

```
user username roles { rolelist };
```

The following example adds the sysadm role to the **george** user:

```
user george roles { user_r sysadm_r };
```

Once the role is added, you have to reload the policy.

```
make reload
```

You can also manage users with the **seuser** command. To see what users are currently active, you can list them with the **seuser** command and the **show users** option.

```
# seuser show users
system_u: system_r
user_u: user_r sysadm_r system_r
root: user_r sysadm_r system_r
```

The **seuser** command has **add**, **delete**, **change**, and **rename** options for managing users. The **add** and **change** options let you specify roles to add to a user, whereas the **delete** option will remove the user.

Runtime Security Contexts and Types: contexts

Several applications and services are security aware and will need default security configuration information such as security contexts. Runtime configurations for default security contexts and types are kept in files located in the policy context directory, such as **/etc/selinux/targeted/policy/contexts**. Types files will have the suffix **_types**, and security context files will use **_context**. For example, the default security context for removable files is located in the **removable_context** file. The contents of that file are shown here:

```
system_u:object_r:removable_t
```

The **default_context** file is used to assign a default security context for applications. In the strict policy it is used to control system admin access, providing it where needed, for instance, during the login process.

The following example sets the default roles for users in the login process:

```
system_r:local_login_t user_r:user_t
```

This would allows users to log in either as administrators or as regular users.

```
system_r:local_login_t sysadm_r:sysadm_t user_r:user_t
```

This next example is for remote user logins, where system administration is not included:

```
system_r:remote_login_t user_r:user_t staff_r:staff_t
```

The **default_types** file defines default types for roles. This file has role/type entries, and when a transition takes place to a new role, the default type specified here is used. For example, the default type for the sysadm_r role is sysadm_t.

```
sysadm_r:sysadm_t
user_r:user_t
```

Of particular interest is the **initrc_context** file, which sets the context for running the system scripts in the **/etc/rc.d** directory. In the targeted policy these are open to all users.

```
user_u:system_r:unconfined_t
```

In the strict policy these are limited to the system user.

```
system_u:system_r:initrc_t
```

users

Default security contexts may also need to be set up for particular users such as the root user. In the **contexts/users** directory you will find a root file that lists roles and types the root user can take on, such as the following example for the **su** operation:

```
sysadm_r:sysadm_su_t     sysadm_r:sysadm_t staff_r:staff_t user_r:user_t
```

context/files

Default security contexts for your files and directories are located in the **contexts/files** directory. The **file_contexts** directory lists the default security contexts for all your files and directories as set up by your policy. The **file_context.homedirs** directory sets the file contexts for user home directory files as well as the root directory, including dot configuration files like **.mozilla** and **.gconf**. The media file sets the default context for media devices such as CD-ROMs and disks.

```
cdrom system_u:object_r:removable_device_t
floppy system_u:object_r:removable_device_t
disk system_u:object_r:fixed_disk_device_t
```

Internet Protocol Security: IPsec

The Internet Security Protocol, IPsec, incorporates security for network transmission into the Internet Protocol (IP) directly. IPsec is integrated into the new IPv6 protocol (Internet Protocol version 6). It can also be used with the older IPv4 protocol (see Chapter 37). IPsec provides methods for both encrypting data and authenticating the host or network it is sent to. The process can be handled manually or automated using the IPsec **racoon** key exchange tool. With IPsec, the kernel can automatically detect and decrypt incoming transmissions, as well as encrypt outgoing ones. You can also use IPsec to implement virtual private networks, encrypting data sent over the Internet from one local network to another. Though IPsec is a relatively new security method, its integration into the Internet Protocol will eventually provide it wide acceptance. Check the IPsec Howto for a detailed explanation of IPsec implementation on Linux, **www.ipsec-howto.org**. The Red Hat Linux Enterprise Security Guide provides a helpful description on using IPsec on the Fedora Core system in its Virtual Private Network section. The Guide can be found at the Red Hat Linux Enterprise Documentation page on the Red Hat site, **www.redhat.com**.

Several projects currently provide development and implementation of IPsec tools (see Table 18-1). The original IPsec tools are provided by the KAME project at **www.kame.net** and IPsec-Tools (2.6 kernel) at **ipsec-tools.sourceforge.net**. Current versions can be obtained from **sourceforge.net/projects/ipsec-tools**. RPM packages are included with Fedora Core and can also be obtained from **rpmfind.net**. Also included with Fedora Core is Openswan, based on FreeS/WAN at **www.openswan.org**, which provides opportunistic encryption for greater security in large VPNs.

NOTE *Openswan uses its own implementation of **Ipsec** (KLIPS, Kernel Layer IPsec) and of IKE authentication (Pluto). The service script ipsec starts Openswan, and **ipsec.conf** holds configuration. See **/usr/share/doc/openswan-doc** for detailed documentation.*

Web Site	Project
www.kame.net	KAME project for IPsec tools
www.openswan.org	Openswan project supported by Xeleance
www.vpnc.org	VPN Consortium
www.ipsec-howto.org	IPsec Howto documentation
ipsec-tools.sourceforge.net	IPsec tools resources
www.redhat.com/docs/manuals/ enterprise/RHEL-4-Manual/security-guide	Red Hat Enterprise Linux Security Guide, Virtual Private Networks section

TABLE 18-1   IPsec Resources

IPsec Protocols

IPsec is made up of several protocols that provide authentication (AH), encryption (ESP), and the secure exchange of encryption keys (IKE). The Authentication Header protocol (AH) confirms that the packet was sent by the sender, and not by someone else. IPsec also includes an integrity check to detect any tampering in transit. Packets are encrypted using the Encapsulating Security Payload (ESP). Encryption and decryption are performed using secret keys shared by the sender and the receiver. These keys are themselves transmitted using the IPsec Internet Key Exchange protocol, which provides a secure exchange. ESP encryption can degrade certain compression transmission methods like PPP for dial-up Internet connections. To accommodate these compression methods, IPsec provides the IP Payload Compression Protocol (IPComp), with which packets can be compressed before being sent.

Encrypted authentication and integrity checks are incorporated using Hash Methods Authentication Codes (HMAC) generated from hash security methods like SHA2 using a secret key. The HMAC is the included in the IPsec header, which the receiver can then check with the secret key. Encryption of transmitted data is performed by symmetric encryption methods like 3DES, Blowfish, and DES.

The AH, ESP, and IPComp protocols are incorporated into the Linux kernel. The IKE protocol is implemented as a separate daemon. It simply provides a way to share secret keys, and can be replaced by other sharing methods.

IPsec Modes

You can use IPsec capabilities for either normal transport or packet tunneling. With normal transport, packets are encrypted and sent to the next destination. The normal transport mode is used to implement direct host-to-host encryption, where each host handles the IPsec encryption process. Packet tunneling is used to encrypt transmissions between gateways, letting the gateways handle the IPsec encryption process for traffic directed to or from an entire network, rather than having to configure IPsec encryption for each host. With packet tunneling, the packets are encapsulated with new headers for a specific destination, enabling you to implement virtual private networks (VPNs). Packets are directed to VPN gateways, which encrypt and send on local network packets.

NOTE *You can choose to encrypt packets for certain hosts or for those passing through specific ports.*

Tools	Description
`libipsec`	Build PFkey.
`setkey`	Manage policy (SPD) and association (SAD) databases.
`racoon`	Configure and implement secure key exchanges using IPsec Internet Key Exchange (IKE).
`setkey-D`	Examine security associations in SAD database.
`setkey-DP`	Examine security policies in SPD database.

TABLE 18-2   IPsec Tools

IPsec Security Databases

The packets you choose to encrypt are designated by the IPsec Security Policy Database (SPD). The method you use to encrypt them is determined by the IPsec Security Association Database (SAD). The SAD associates an encryption method and key with a particular connection or kind of connection. The connections to be encrypted are designated in the Security Policy Database.

IPsec Tools

Several IPsec tools are provided with which you can manage your IPsec connections (see Table 18-2). All are included in the Fedora Core ipsec-tools RPM package. The **libipsec** tool lets you build a key library. With **setkey**, you can manage both the policy and association databases. The **racoon** tool configures the key exchange process to implement secure decryption key exchanges across connections. To see what your current security policies are in the SPD database, you can use **setkey-DP**. For security associations in SAD, you can use **setkey-D**.

NOTE *To enable IPsec in the kernel, be sure to enable the PF_KEY, AH, and ESP options in Cryptographic Options.*

Configuring IPsec with system-config-network

The system-config-network tool now provides support for implementing IPsec connections. On the system-config-network tool, select the IPsec panel (see Figure 18-1) and click New to start the IPsec settings wizard for creating an IPsec connection. You are first asked to enter a nickname for the connection and to specify if you want it started automatically. You then choose the connection type. This can be either a direct host-to-host connection or a connection between two networks. A network connection implements a virtual private network (VPN) and runs IPsec in tunnel mode. (Both the host and VPN connections are described in detail in the following sections.) You then select the kind of encryption you want to use. This can either be manual or use IKE, letting **racoon** automatically manage the encryption and authentication process.

FIGURE 18-1   IPsec on system-config-network

You then will configure both your local and remote connections, starting with the local settings. For a host-to-host connection, you need only enter the IP address for the remote host. For a VPN, you will have to enter corresponding addresses for the local and remote networks. For the local network, you will need to enter the IP addresses for the local network, the local network's gateway computer, and the local network's netmask. For the remote VPN connection, you will need the remote IP address, the remote network's address, its netmask, and its gateway address. Finally, you enter the authentication key. Click the Generate button to create one.

A final screen will display your entries. Click Apply to save them. Your connection will appear in the IPsec panel, showing its type, destination, and nickname. To establish a connection, select the IPsec connection and click Activate. This will run the **ifup-ipsec** script in the **/etc/sysconfig/network-scripts** directory, which will execute IPsec tools such as **setkey** and **racoon** to establish your connection. Configuration data will be kept in the /etc/sysconfig/networking/devices directory, using the name of the IPsec connections. For example, configuration information on the myipsec IPsec connection is kept in the **ifcfg-myipsec** file. Corresponding keys for each connection are kept in the keys files, including **keys-myipsec**. A sample ifcfg configuration file for a VPN is shown here. The IKE method is a private shared key (PSK). The destination (remote) gateway is 10.0.0.1, and the source (local) gateway is 192.168.0.1. The destination (remote) network address is 10.0.0.0/24, and the source (local) address is 192.168.0.0/24. The destination host is 10.0.0.2.

```
ONBOOT=no
IKE_METHOD=PSK
DSTGW=10.0.0.1
SRCGW=192.168.0.1
DSTNET=10.0.0.0/24
SRCNET=192.168.0.0/24
DST=10.0.0.2
TYPE=IPSEC
```

The corresponding keys file would specify the key used.

```
IKE_PSK=myvpnkey
```

Configuring Connections with setkey

To configure your IPsec connections, you can use the **setkey** tool. This tool contains several instructions for managing rules in the IPsec policy and security databases. You use the **add** instruction to add a security association to the security database (SAD), and the **spdadd** instruction to add a policy to the policy database (SPD). The **ah** term designates that the instruction is being applied to the authentication header (AH), and **esp** indicates the encryption is to be implemented by the encryption security payload (ESP). To implement **setkey** operations, it is best to use a script invoking **setkey** with the **-f** option and listing the **setkey** instructions. The following example creates a simple script to add authentication and encryption instructions for a particular connection, as well as create a security policy for it:

```
#!/sbin/setkey -f
add 192.168.0.2 192.168.0.5 ah 15700 -A hmac-md5 "secret key";
add 192.168.0.2 192.168.0.5 esp 15701 -E 3des-cbc "secret key ";
spdadd 192.168.0.2 192.168.0.5 any -P out ipsec
   esp/transport//require
   ah/transport//require;
```

Security Associations: SA

You use security associations to indicate you want the authentication header (AH) and encryption payload (ESP) encrypted. A particular connection, such as that between two hosts, can have those hosts' authentication headers encrypted using specified encryption methods and designated secret keys. The same can be done for the encryption payload, the main content of transmissions. A secret key can be determined manually or automatically using key exchanges. The following example specifies that for the connection between 192.168.0.2 and 192.168.0.5, the **hmac-md5** authentication method and a secret key (here designated by the placeholder **secret key**) will be used for the authentication header, **ah**.

```
add 192.168.0.2 192.168.0.5 ah 15700 -A hmac-md5 "secret key";
```

The security association for the encryption payload uses the 3des-cbc encryption method and a different secret key.

```
add 192.168.0.2 192.168.0.5 esp 15701 -E 3des-cbc "secret key";
```

Each instruction is identified with a security parameter index (SPI), in this case, 15700 and 15701. In fact, identical instructions with different SPIs are considered different instructions.

Bear in mind that the security associations only specify possible encryption procedures. They do not implement them. For that, you need to set security policies.

Security Policy: SP

A security policy will implement an IPsec security procedure for a connection. You can designate a host or port connection. Once a policy is set for a connection, the kernel will determine what security associations to apply, using the SAD database. A security policy is added with the **spdadd** instruction. Either encryption or authentication, or both, can be required.

The following example will encrypt and authenticate transmissions between hosts 192.168.0.2 and 192.168.0.5. Any outgoing transmissions between these hosts will be both encrypted and authenticated:

```
spdadd 192.168.0.2 192.168.0.5 any -P out ipsec esp/transport//require
ah/transport/require;
```

In the **spdadd** instruction, you will need to specify the connection, such as one between two hosts or two networks. For two hosts, you would use their IP addresses, in this example, 192.168.0.2 and 192.168.0.5. You then specify the kind of packet and its direction, in this case any outgoing packet, **any -P out**. Then you can specify the **ipsec** directives for either the ESP or AH protocol, or both. For each entry, you specify the mode (transport or tunnel), the hosts involved (this can be different in tunnel mode), and the policy for the encryption, usually **require**. This example shows that the ESP protocol will use the transport mode for connections between 192.168.0.2 and 192.168.0.5, and it will be required:

```
esp/transport/192.168.02-192.168.0.5/require
```

You can leave out the host information if it is the same, as in the prior example.

```
esp/transport//require
```

Receiving Hosts

For a host to receive an encrypted IPsec transmission, it must have corresponding security association instructions in its own SAD database that tell it how to authenticate and decrypt the received instructions. The security association instructions would mirror those of the sender's instructions, using the same encryption method, secret keys, and security indexes. A corresponding policy, though, is not required.

```
#!/sbin/setkey -f
add 192.168.0.2 192.168.0.5 ah 15700 -A hmac-md5 "secret key";
add 192.168.0.2 192.168.0.5 esp 15701 -E 3des-cbc "secret key";
```

Receiving hosts may want to set up policies to screen incoming packets on secure connections, discarding those not encrypted. The following policy will accept only incoming IPsec encrypted and authenticated transmissions from 192.168.0.2.

```
spdadd 192.168.0.2 192.168.0.5 any -P in ipsec esp/transport//require
ah/transport//require;
```

Two-way Transmissions

The preceding example set up a secure connection between two hosts going only one way, from 192.168.0.2 to 192.168.0.5, not the other way, from 192.168.0.5 to 192.168.0.2.

To implement two-way secure transmissions between two hosts, both need to be configured as the sender and the receiver, with corresponding security associations to match. The following scripts are based on common examples of a simple two-way IPsec connection between two hosts. They set up a secure two-way IPsec connection between hosts 192.168.0.2 and 192.168.0.5. Corresponding incoming policies are also included, but not required.

First is the configuration for host 192.168.0.2:

```
#!/sbin/setkey -f
add 192.168.0.2 192.168.0.5 ah 15700 -A hmac-md5 "secret key";
add 192.168.0.5 192.168.0.2 ah 24500 -A hmac-md5 "secret key";

add 192.168.0.2 192.168.0.5 esp 15701 -E 3des-cbc "secret key";
add 192.168.0.5 192.168.0.2 esp 24501 -E 3des-cbc "secret key";

spdadd 192.168.0.2 192.168.0.5 any -P out ipsec esp/transport//require
ah/transport//require;
spdadd 192.168.0.5 192.168.0.2 any -P in ipsec esp/transport//require
ah/transport//require;
```

The corresponding host, 192.168.0.5, would uses the same instructions, but with the IP connections reversed. Notice that the security indexes for instructions for the sender and receiver at each end correspond:

```
#!/sbin/setkey -f
add 192.168.0.5 192.168.0.2 ah 15700 -A hmac-md5 "secret key";
add 192.168.0.2 192.168.0.5 ah 24500 -A hmac-md5 "secret key";

add 192.168.0.5 192.168.0.2 esp 15701 -E 3des-cbc "secret key";
add 192.168.0.2 192.168.0.5 esp 24501 -E 3des-cbc "secret key";

spdadd 192.168.0.5 192.168.0.2 any -P out ipsec esp/transport//require
ah/transport//require;
spdadd 192.168.0.2 192.168.0.5 any -P in ipsec esp/transport//require
ah/transport//require;
```

Configuring IPsec with racoon: IKE

IPsec keys can be implemented as manual keys, as shared keys, or with certificates. Manual keys are explicitly exchanged and are prone to security problems. Both shared keys and certificates are managed using the IPsec Internet Key Exchange protocol, which will automatically exchange keys, changing them randomly to avoid detection.

One of the advantages of using IKE is that it will automatically generate any needed security associations, if none are provided. This means that to configure secure connections, with IKE you would need to specify only a security policy, not the security associations.

The **racoon** tool is the key exchange daemon for the IPsec IKE protocol. In the case of shared keys, hosts are authenticated dynamically by **racoon** using preshared secret keys. With the certificate method, hosts are authenticated using certificate files. The **racoon** configuration file is located at **/etc/racoon/racoon.conf**. Here you can set general parameters. You can use the default **racoon.conf** file for most connections.

The **racoon** configuration consists of stanzas containing parameters for possible connections. A very simple configuration is shown in the following example, which uses a simple shared secret key. The location is specified by the **path pre_shared_key** option, in this case **/etc/racoon/psk.txt**. Certificate keys, a more secure method using public and private keys, are discussed later.

```
path pre_shared_key "/etc/racoon/psk.txt";

remote anonymous
{
      exchange_mode aggressive,main;
      doi ipsec_doi;
      situation identity_only;

      my_identifier address;

      lifetime time 2 min;    # sec,min,hour
      initial_contact on;
      proposal_check obey;     # obey, strict or claim

      proposal {
            encryption_algorithm 3des;
            hash_algorithm sha1;
            authentication_method pre_shared_key;
            dh_group 2 ;
      }
}
sainfo anonymous
{
      pfs_group 1;
      lifetime time 2 min;
      encryption_algorithm 3des, blowfish, des, cast128, rijndael ;
      authentication_algorithm hmac_sha1, hmac_md5;
            compression_algorithm deflate ;
}
```

This configuration defines stanzas for default (anonymous) connections. The **remote anonymous** stanza defines parameters for connecting to remote systems, and the **sainfo anonymous** section provides information for security association instructions, such as the encryption and authentication methods to use.

Certificates

To use certificates instead of shared keys, you first have to create certificates using OpenSSL. Then instruct **racoon** to use them. Specify the path for the certificates.

```
path certificate "/usr/local/etc/racoon/certs";
```

You can now configure **racoon** to use the public and private keys generated by the certificates. In the appropriate stanza in the **/etc/racoon/racoon.conf** file, the **certificate_ type** directive specifies the public and private keys for this system. The **peers_certfile** directive specifies the location of the remote system's public key. The **authentication_**

method directive is now set to **rsasig**, the RSA public/private keys. Make sure each system has its corresponding public and private keys.

```
certificate_type x509 "192.168.0.2.public" "192.168.0.2.private";
peers_certfile "192.168.0.5.public";
authentication_method rsasig;
```

Connection Configuration with racoon

With **racoon**, you will only need to specify the security policy for the connection configuration, as shown here for the sender. The receiver will have corresponding policies:

```
spdadd 192.168.0.5 192.168.0.2 any -P out ipsec
        esp/transport//require
        ah/transport//require;
spdadd 192.168.0.2 192.168.0.5 any -P in ipsec
        esp/transport//require
        ah/transport//require;
```

IPsec and IPtables: Net Traversal

IPtables netfiltering will stop many IPsec packets. To enable IPtables to pass IPsec packets, use the following IPtables commands. The number for the AH protocol is 51, and for the ESP protocol, it is 50. To allow IPsec packets, you should set Policy rules such as the following:

```
iptables -A INPUT -p 50 -j ACCEPT
iptables -A OUTPUT -p 51 -j ACCEPT
```

For netfiltering that implements IP masquerading, you will need to add a **net_traversal** option to your racoon IPsec configuration. With Net Traversal, the IPsec connection will bypass the IP address substitution performed by IPtables when masquerading IP addresses. In addition, the **nat_keepalive** option will maintain the connection, and with the **iskamp_natt** option you specify the IP address and port to connect to.

IPsec Tunnel Mode: Virtual Private Networks

Instead of encrypting two hosts directly, you could use IPsec to just encrypt the gateways between the networks those hosts belong to, assuming that communication within those networks can be trusted. This would significantly reduce the encryption configuration setup, letting hosts from an entire network reach those of another network, using an intermediate secure IPsec connection between their gateways. For connections between gateways, transmissions sent through intervening routers can be tunneled. This is known as the tunnel mode for IPsec, which is used to implement virtual private networks (VPNs). Encrypted transmissions between gateways effectively implements a VPN, securing transmissions across a larger network from one local net to another.

To tunnel transmissions from a host through a gateway to a network, you would use the **-m tunnel** option. The IPsec connection would be between the two gateways. The following example is the security association on gateway 10.0.0.1 that encrypts transmissions from gateway 10.0.0.1 to gateway 10.0.23.5. The examples used here are for a gateway-to-gateway connection, set up as a direct connection between two hosts using manual keys.

```
add 10.0.0.1 10.0.23.5 esp 34501 -m tunnel -E 3des-cbc "secretkey";
```

The security policy on 10.0.0.1 then implements encryption for communication from one network to another using their respective gateways. The two networks are 192.168.0.0 and 192.168.1.0. Transmissions from hosts on the 192.168.0.0 network are encrypted by their gateway, 10.0.0.1, and are then sent to the gateway for the 192.168.1.0 network, 10.0.23.5, which then decrypts them.

```
spdadd 192.168.0.0/24 192.168.1.0/24 any -P out ipsec esp/tunnel/10.0.0.1-
10.0.23.5/require;
```

Notice that the gateway IP addresses are specified in the **spdadd** instruction's **ipsec** directive. The mode specified is the tunnel mode, rather than the transport mode.

```
ipsec esp/tunnel/10.0.0.1-10.0.23.5/require
```

The receiving gateway, 10.0.23.5, will have a corresponding security association and policy, as shown here. The policy is set for incoming transmissions. In both gateway configurations, other than specifying the tunnel option and using network addresses in the security policy, the security associations and policies are the same as those used for host-to-host connections.

```
add 10.0.0.1 10.0.23.5 esp 34501 -m tunnel -E 3des-cbc "secretkey";

spdadd 192.168.0.0/24 192.168.1.0/16 any -P in ipsec esp/tunnel/10.0.0.1-
10.0.23.5/require;
```

To set up full two-way communication, the two gateways would have corresponding security associations and policies to handle traffic in both directions. The following example is for the configuration on gateway 10.0.0.1 and handles two-way traffic to and from gateway 10.0.23.5. Gateway 10.0.23.5 would have a similar configuration:

```
add 10.0.0.1 10.0.23.5 esp 34501 -m tunnel -E 3des-cbc "secretkey";
add 10.0.23.5 10.0.03.1 esp 34501 -m tunnel -E 3des-cbc "secretkey";

spdadd 192.168.0.0/24 192.168.1.0/24 any -P out ipsec esp/tunnel/10.0.0.1-
10.0.23.5/require;
spdadd 192.168.1.0/16 192.168.0.0/24 any -P in ipsec esp/tunnel/10.0.23.5-
10.0.0.1/require;
```

If you use **racoon** to configure gateway connections, you would only have to set the security policies on each gateway, letting the **racoon** server generate the needed security associations.

NOTE *Fedora Core no longer includes Crypto IP Encapsulation (CIPE), an alternative to IPsec for implementing Virtual Private Networks. It is currently not supported in the 2.6 kernel.*

Secure Shell and Kerberos

To protect remote connections from hosts outside your network, transmissions can be encrypted (see Table 19-1). For Linux systems, you can use the Secure Shell (SSH) suite of programs to encrypt and authenticate transmissions, preventing them from being read or modified by anyone else, as well as confirming the identity of the sender. The SSH programs are meant to replace the remote tools such as rsh and rcp (see Chapter 15), which perform no encryption and include security risks such as transmitting passwords in clear text. User authentication can be controlled for certain services by Kerberos servers. Kerberos authentication provides another level of security whereby individual services can be protected, allowing use of a service only to users who are cleared for access.

The Secure Shell: OpenSSH

Although a firewall can protect a network from attempts to break into it from the outside, the problem of securing legitimate communications to the network from outside sources still exists. A particular problem is one of users who want to connect to your network remotely. Such connections could be monitored, and information such as passwords and user IDs used when the user logs into your network could be copied and used later to break in. One solution is to use SSH for remote logins and other kinds of remote connections such as FTP transfers. SSH encrypts any communications between the remote user and a system on your network.

Two different implementations of SSH currently use what are, in effect, two different and incompatible protocols. The first version of SSH, known as SSH1, uses the original SSH protocol. Version 2.0, known as SSH2, uses a completely rewritten version of the SSH protocol. Encryption is performed in different ways, encrypting different parts of a packet.

Web Site	Description
www.openssh.org	OpenSSH open source version of SSH
www.ssh.com	SSH Communications Security, commercial SSH version
web.mit.edu/kerberos	Kerberos authentication

TABLE 19-1   SSH and Kerberos Resources

SSH1 uses server and host keys to authenticate systems, whereas SSH2 uses only host keys. Furthermore, certain functions, such as sftp, are supported only by SSH2.

NOTE *A commercial version of SSH is available from SSH Communications Security, whose Web site is **www.ssh.com**. SSH Communications Security provides a commercial version called SSH Tectia, designed for enterprise and government use. The older noncommercial SSH package is still freely available, which you can download and use.*

The SSH protocol has become an official Internet Engineering Task Force (IETF) standard. A free and open source version is developed and maintained by the OpenSSH project, currently supported by the OpenBSD project. OpenSSH is the version supplied with most Linux distributions, including Fedora Core, Mandrake, Novell, and Debian. You can find out more about OpenSSH at **www.openssh.org**, where you can download the most recent version, though your distribution will provide current RPM versions.

SSH Encryption and Authentication

SSH secures connections by both authenticating users and encrypting their transmissions. The authentication process is handled with public-key encryption (see Chapter 16). Once authenticated, transmissions are encrypted by a cipher agreed upon by the SSH server and client for use in a particular session. SSH supports multiple ciphers. Authentication is applied to both hosts and users. SSH first authenticates a particular host, verifying that it is a valid SSH host that can be securely communicated with. Then the user is authenticated, verifying that the user is who they say they are.

SSH uses strong encryption methods, and their export from the United States may be restricted. Currently, SSH can deal with the following kinds of attacks:

- IP spoofing, where a remote host sends out packets that pretend to come from another, trusted host
- IP source routing, where a host can pretend an IP packet comes from another, trusted host
- DNS spoofing, where an attacker forges name server records
- Interception of clear-text passwords and other data by intermediate hosts
- Manipulation of data by people in control of intermediate hosts
- Attacks based on listening to X authentication data and spoofed connections to the X11 server

Encryption

The public-key encryption used in SSH authentication makes use of two keys: a public key and a private key. The *public key* is used to encrypt data, while the *private key* decrypts it. Each host or user has its own public and private keys. The public key is distributed to other hosts, who can then use it to encrypt authentication data that only the host's private key can decrypt. For example, when a host sends data to a user on another system, the host encrypts the authentication data with a public key, which it previously received from that user. The data can be decrypted only by the user's corresponding private key. The public key can safely be sent in the open from one host to another, allowing it to be installed safely on different hosts. You can think of the process as taking place between a client and a server. When the client sends data to the server, it first encrypts the data using the server's public key. The server can then decrypt the data using its own private key.

It is recommended that SSH transmissions be authenticated with public-private keys controlled by passphrases. Unlike PGP, SSH uses public-key encryption for the authentication process only. Once authenticated, participants agree on a common cipher to use to encrypt transmission. Authentication will verify the identity of the participants. Each user who intends to use SSH to access a remote account first needs to create the public and private keys along with a passphrase to use for the authentication process. A user then sends their public key to the remote account they want to access and installs the public key on that account. When the user attempts to access the remote account, that account can then use the user's public key to authenticate that the user is who they claim to be. The process assumes that the remote account has set up its own SSH private and public key. For the user to access the remote account, they will have know the remote account's SSH passphrase. SSH is often used in situations where a user has two or more accounts located on different systems and wants to be able to securely access them from each other. In that case, the user already has access to each account and can install SSH on each, giving each its own private and public keys along with their passphrases.

Authentication

The mechanics of authentication in SSH version 1 and version 2 differ slightly. However, the procedure on the part of users is the same. Essentially, a user creates both public and private keys. For this you use the **ssh-keygen** command. The user's public key then has to be distributed to those users that the original user wants access to. Often this is an account a user has on another host. A passphrase further protects access. The original user will need to know the other user's passphrase to access it.

SSH version 1 uses RSA authentication. When a remote user tries to log in to an account, that account is checked to see if it has the remote user's public key. That public key is then used to encrypt a challenge (usually a random number) that can be decrypted only by the remote user's private key. When the remote user receives the encrypted challenge, that user decrypts the challenge with its private key. SSH version 2 can use either RSA or DSA authentication. The remote user will first encrypt a session identifier using its private key, signing it. The encrypted session identifier is then decrypted by the account using the remote user's public key. The session identifier has been previously set up by SSH for that session.

SSH authentication is first carried out with the host, and then with users. Each host has its own host keys, public and private keys used for authentication. Once the host is authenticated, the user is queried. Each user has their own public and private keys. Users on an SSH server who want to receive connections from remote users will have to keep a list of those remote users' public keys. Similarly, an SSH host will maintain a list of public keys for other SSH hosts.

SSH Tools

SSH is implemented on Linux systems with OpenSSH. The full set of OpenSSH packages includes the general OpenSSH package (openssh), the OpenSSH server (openssh-server), and the OpenSSH clients (openssh-clients). These packages also require OpenSSL (openssl), which installs the cryptographic libraries that SSH uses. You can easily update them from distribution FTP.

The SSH tools are listed in Table 19-2. They include several client programs like scp and ssh, as well as the ssh server. The ssh server (sshd) provides secure connections to anyone from the outside using the ssh client to connect. Several configuration utilities are also included, such as ssh-add, which adds valid hosts to the authentication agent, and ssh-keygen, which generates the keys used for encryption.

On Fedora Core, you can start, restart, and stop the sshd server with the **service** command or redhat-config-services (Services on Server Settings window and menu):

```
service sshd restart
```

For version 2, names of the actual tools have a 2 suffix. Version 1 tools have a 1 as their suffix. During installation, however, links are set for each tool to use only the name with the suffix. For example, if you have installed version 2, there is a link called scp to the scp2 application. You can then use the link to invoke the tool. Using scp starts scp2. Table 19-2 specifies only the link names, as these are the same for each version. Remember, though, some applications, such as sftp, are available only with version 2.

SSH Setup

Using SSH involves creating your own public and private keys and then distributing your public key to other users you want to access. These can be different users or simply user

Application	Description
ssh	SSH client
sshd	SSH server (daemon)
sftp	SSH FTP client, Secure File Transfer Program. Version 2 only. Use help to list sftp commands (SFTP protocol)
sftp-server	SSH FTP server. Version 2 only (SFTP protocol)
scp	SSH copy command client
ssh-keygen	Utility for generating keys. -h for help
ssh-keyscan	Tool to automatically gather public host keys to generate ssh_known_hosts files
ssh-add	Adds RSA and DSA identities to the authentication agent
ssh-agent	SSH authentication agent that holds private keys for public-key authentication (RSA, DSA)
ssh-askpass	X Window System utility for querying passwords, invoked by ssh-add (openssh-askpass)
ssh-askpass-gnome	GNOME utility for querying passwords, invoked by ssh-add
ssh-signer	Signs host-based authentication packets. Version 2 only. Must be suid root (performed by installation)
slogin	Remote login (version 1)

TABLE 19-2 SSH Tools

accounts of your own that you have on remote systems. Often people remotely log in from a local client to an account on a remote server, perhaps from a home computer to a company computer. Your home computer would be your client account, and the account on your company computer would be your server account. On your client account, you would need to generate your public and private keys. Then you would have to place a copy of your public key in the server account. You can do this by simply e-mailing the key file or copying the file from a floppy disk. Once the account on your server has a copy of your client user's public key, you can access the server account from your client account. You will be also prompted for the server account's passphrase. You will have to know this to access that account. Figure 19-1 illustrates the SSH setup that allows a user **george** to access the account **cecelia**.

The following steps are needed to allow you to use SSH to access other accounts:

- Create public and private keys on your account along with a passphrase. You will need to use this passphrase to access your account from another account.

- Distribute your public key to other accounts you want to access, placing them in the **.ssh/authorized_keys** file.

- Other accounts also have to set up public and private keys along with a passphrase.

- You will need to also know the other account's passphrase to access it.

Creating SSH Keys with ssh-keygen

You create your public and private keys using the **ssh-keygen** command. You need to specify the kind of encryption you want to use. You can use either DSA or RSA encryption. Specify the type using the **-t** option and the encryption name in lowercase (**dsa** or **rsa**). In the following example, the user creates a key with the RSA encryption:

```
ssh-keygen -t rsa
```

The **ssh-keygen** command prompts you for a passphrase, which it will use as a kind of password to protect your private key. The passphrase should be several words long. You

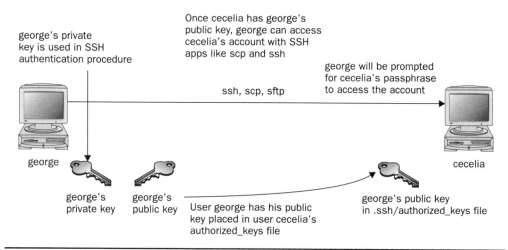

FIGURE 19-1   SSH setup and access

are also prompted to enter a filename for the keys. If you do not enter one, SSH will use its defaults. The public key will be given the extension **.pub**. The **ssh-keygen** command generates the public key and places it in your **.ssh/id_dsa.pub** or **.ssh/id_dsa.pub** file depending on the type of key you specified; it places the private key in the corresponding **.ssh/id_dsa** or **.ssh/id_rsa.pub** file.

If you need to change your passphrase, you can do so with the **ssh-keygen** command and the **-p** option. Each user will have their own SSH configuration directory, called **.ssh**, located in their own home directory. The public and private keys, as well as SSH configuration files, are placed here. If you build from the source code, the **make install** operation will automatically run **ssh-keygen**. Table 19-3 lists the SSH configuration files.

File	Description
$HOME/.ssh/known_ hosts	Records host keys for all hosts the user has logged in to (that are not in **/etc/ssh/ssh_known_hosts)**.
$HOME/.ssh/random_ seed	Used for seeding the random number generator.
$HOME/.ssh/id_rsa	Contains the RSA authentication identity of the user.
$HOME/.ssh/ id_dsa	Contains the DSA authentication identity of the user.
$HOME/.ssh/id_rsa. pub	Contains the RSA public key for authentication. The contents of this file should be added to **$HOME/.ssh/authorized_keys** on all machines where you want to log in using RSA authentication.
$HOME/.ssh/id_dsa. pub	Contains the DSA public key for authentication. The contents of this file should be added to **$HOME/.ssh/authorized_keys** on all machines where you want to log in using DSA authentication.
$HOME/.ssh/config	The per-user configuration file. SSH performs strict ownership checks on this file and permissions should be set to 600 (owner r/w only).
$HOME/.ssh/ authorized_keys	Lists the RSA or DSA keys that can be used for logging in as this user.
/etc/ssh/ssh_known_ hosts	System-wide list of known host keys.
/etc/ssh/ssh_config	System-wide configuration file. This file provides defaults for those values not specified in the user's configuration file.
/etc/ssh/sshd_config	SSH server configuration file.
/etc/ssh/sshrc	System default. Commands in this file are executed by ssh when the user logs in just before the user's shell (or command) is started.
$HOME/.ssh/rc	Commands in this file are executed by ssh when the user logs in just before the user's shell (or command) is started.

TABLE 19-3   SSH Configuration Files

Authorized Keys

A public key is used to authenticate a user and its host. You use the public key on a remote system to allow that user access. The public key is placed in the remote user account's **.ssh/ authorized_keys** file. Recall that the public key is held in the **.ssh/id_dsa.pub** file. If a user wants to log in remotely from a local account to an account on a remote system, they would first place their public key in the **.ssh/authorized_keys** file in the account on the remote system they want to access. If the user **larisa** on **turtle.mytrek.com** wants to access the **aleina** account on **rabbit.mytrek.com**, **larisa**'s public key from **/home/larisa/.ssh/id_dsa .pub** first must be placed in **aleina**'s **authorized_keys** file, **/home/aleina/.ssh/authorized_ keys**. User **larisa** could send the key or have it copied over. A simple cat operation can append a key to the authorized key file. In the next example, the user adds the public key for **aleina** in the **larisa.pub** file to the authorized key file. The **larisa.pub** file is a copy of the **/home/larisa/.ssh/id_dsa.pub** file that the user received earlier.

```
cat larisa.pub >>  .ssh/authorized_keys
```

Loading Keys

If you regularly make connections to a variety of remote hosts, you can use the **ssh-agent** command to place private keys in memory where they can be accessed quickly to decrypt received transmissions. The **ssh-agent** command is intended for use at the beginning of a login session. For GNOME, you can use the openssh-askpass-gnome utility, invoked by **ssh-add**, which allows you to enter a password when you log in to GNOME. GNOME will automatically supply that password whenever you use an SSH client.

Although the **ssh-agent** command enables you to use private keys in memory, you also must specifically load your private keys into memory using the **ssh-add** command. **ssh-add** with no arguments loads your private key from your **.ssh/id_dsa** or **.ssh/id_rsa .pub** file. You are prompted for your passphrase for this private key. To remove the key from memory, use **ssh-add** with the **-d** option. If you have several private keys, you can load them all into memory. **ssh-add** with the **-l** option lists those currently loaded.

SSH Clients

SSH was originally designed to replace remote access operations, such as rlogin, rcp, and Telnet (see Chapter 15), which perform no encryption and introduce security risks such as transmitting passwords in clear text. You can also use SSH to encode X server sessions as well as FTP transmissions (sftp). The ssh-clients package contains corresponding SSH clients to replace these applications. With slogin or ssh, you can log in from a remote host to execute commands and run applications, much as you can with rlogin and rsh. With scp, you can copy files between the remote host and a network host, just as with rcp. With sftp, you can transfer FTP files secured by encryption.

ssh

With ssh, you can remotely log in from a local client to a remote system on your network operating as the SSH server. The term *local client* here refers to one outside the network, such as your home computer, and the term *remote* refers to a host system on the network to which you are connecting. In effect, you connect from your local system to the remote network host. It is designed to replace rlogin, which performs remote logins, and rsh, which executes remote commands. With ssh, you can log in from a local site to a remote host on your network and then send commands to be executed on that host. The ssh command is also capable of supporting X Window System connections. This feature is automatically enabled if you make an ssh connection from an X Window System environment, such as GNOME or KDE. A connection is set up for you between the local X server and the remote X server. The remote host sets up a dummy X server and sends any X Window System data through it to your local system to be processed by your own local X server.

The ssh login operation function is much like the **rlogin** command. You enter the **ssh** command with the address of the remote host, followed by a **-l** option and the login name (username) of the remote account you are logging into. The following example logs into the **aleina** user account on the **rabbit.mytrek.com** host:

```
ssh rabbit.mytrek.com -l aleina
```

You can also use the username in an address format with ssh, as in

```
ssh aleina@rabbit.mytrek.com
```

The following listing shows how the user **george** accesses the **cecelia** account on **turtle .mytrek.com**:

```
[george@turtle george]$ ssh turtle.mytrek.com -l cecelia
cecelia@turtle.mytrek.com's password:
Last login: Fri Sep 19 15:13:05 2003 from turtle.mytrek.com
[cecelia@turtle cecelia]$
```

A variety of options are available to enable you to configure your connection. Most have corresponding configuration options that can be set in the configuration file. For example, with the **-c** option, you can designate which encryption method you want to use, for instance, **idea**, **des**, **blowfish**, or **arcfour**. With the **-i** option, you can select a particular private key to use. The **-C** option enables you to have transmissions compressed at specified levels (see the **ssh** Man page for a complete list of options).

scp

You use scp to copy files from one host to another on a network. Designed to replace rcp, scp actually uses ssh to transfer data and employs the same authentication and encryption methods. If authentication requires it, scp requests a password or passphrase. The scp program operates much like rcp. Directories and files on remote hosts are specified using the username and the host address before the filename or directory. The username specifies the remote user account that scp is accessing, and the host is the remote system where that account is located. You separate the user from the host address with an @, and you separate the host address from the file or directory name with a colon. The following example copies the file **party** from a user's current directory to the user **aleina**'s **birthday** directory, located on the **rabbit.mytrek.com** host:

```
scp party aleina@rabbit.mytrek.com:/birthday/party
```

Of particular interest is the **-r** option (recursive) option, which enables you to copy whole directories. See the **scp** Man page for a complete list of options. In the next example, the user copies the entire **reports** directory to the user **justin**'s **projects** directory:

```
scp -r reports justin@rabbit.mytrek.com:/projects
```

In the next example, the user **george** copies the **mydoc1** file from the user **cecelia**'s home directory:

```
[george@turtle george]$ scp cecelia@turtle.mytrek.com:mydoc1  .
cecelia@turtle.mytrek.com's password:
mydoc1     0% |                                 |    0 --:--
ETA
mydoc1   100% |*****************************|  17 00:00
[george@turtle george]$
```

From a Windows system, you can also use **scp** clients such as **winscp**, which will interact with Linux scp-enabled systems.

sftp and sftp-server

With **sftp**, you can transfer FTP files secured by encryption. The **sftp** program uses the same commands as **ftp** (see Chapter 14). This client, which works only with SSH version 2, operates much like **ftp**, with many of the same commands. Use **sftp** instead of **ftp** to invoke the **sftp** client.

```
sftp ftp.redhat.com
```

To use the **sftp** client to connect to an FTP server, that server needs to be operating the sftp-server application. The ssh server invokes sftp-server to provide encrypted FTP transmissions to those using the **sftp** client. The sftp server and client use the SSH File Transfer Protocol (SFTP) to perform FTP operations securely.

Port Forwarding (Tunneling)

If, for some reason, you can connect to a secure host only by going through an insecure host, ssh provides a feature called port forwarding. With *port forwarding,* you can secure the insecure segment of your connection. This involves simply specifying the port at which the insecure host is to connect to the secure one. This sets up a direct connection between the local host and the remote host, through the intermediary insecure host. Encrypted data is passed through directly. This process is referred to as tunneling, creating a secure tunnel of encrypted data through connected servers.

You can set up port forwarding to a port on the remote system or to one on your local system. To forward a port on the remote system to a port on your local system, use **ssh** with the **-R** option, followed by an argument holding the local port, the remote host address, and the remote port to be forwarded, each separated from the next by a colon. This works by allocating a socket to listen to the port on the remote side. Whenever a connection is made to this port, the connection is forwarded over the secure channel, and a connection is made to a remote port from the local machine. In the following example, port 22 on the local system is connected to port 23 on the **rabbit.mytrek.com** remote system:

```
ssh -R 22:rabbit.mytrek.com:23
```

To forward a port on your local system to a port on a remote system, use the **ssh -L** option, followed by an argument holding the local port, the remote host address, and the remote port to be forwarded, each two arguments separated by a colon. A socket is allocated to listen to the port on the local side. Whenever a connection is made to this port, the connection is forwarded over the secure channel and a connection is made to the remote port on the remote machine. In the following example, port 22 on the local system is connected to port 23 on the **rabbit.mytrek.com** remote system:

```
ssh -L 22:rabbit.mytrek.com:23
```

You can use the LocalForward and RemoteForward options in your **.ssh/config** file to set up port forwarding for particular hosts or to specify a default for all hosts you connect to.

SSH Configuration

The SSH configuration file for each user is in their **.ssh/config** file. The **/etc/ssh/sys_config** file is used to set site-wide defaults. In the configuration file, you can set various options, as listed in the **ssh_config** Man document. The configuration file is designed to specify options for different remote hosts to which you might connect. It is organized into segments, where each segment begins with the keyword **HOST**, followed by the IP address of the host. The following lines hold the options you have set for that host. A segment ends at the next **HOST** entry. Of particular interest are the **User** and **Cipher** options. Use the **User** option to specify the names of users on the remote system who are allowed access. With the **Cipher** option, you can select which encryption method to use for a particular host. Encryption methods include IDEA, DES (standard), triple-DES (3DES), Blowfish (128 bit), Arcfour (RSA's RC4), and Twofish. The following example allows access from **larisa** at **turtle .mytrek.com** and uses Blowfish encryption for transmissions:

```
Host turtle.mytrek.com
     User larisa
     Compression no
     Cipher blowfish
```

To specify global options that apply to any host you connect to, create a **HOST** entry with the asterisk as its host, **HOST ***. This entry must be placed at the end of the configuration file because an option is changed only the first time it is set. Any subsequent entries for an option are ignored. Because a host matches on both its own entry and the global one, its specific entry should come before the global entry. The asterisk (*) and the question mark (?) are both wildcard matching operators that enable you to specify a group of hosts with the same suffix or prefix.

```
Host *
  FallBackToRsh yes
  KeepAlive no
  Cipher idea
```

Kerberos

User authentication can further be controlled for certain services by Kerberos servers, discussed in this chapter. Kerberos authentication provides another level of security whereby individual services can be protected, allowing use of a service only to users who are cleared for access. Kerberos servers are all enabled and configured with **authconfig-gtk** (Authentication in the System Settings menu).

Kerberos is a network authentication protocol that provides encrypted authentication to connections between a client and a server. As an authentication protocol, Kerberos requires a client to prove its identity using encryption methods before it can access a server. Once authenticated, the client and server can conduct all communications using encryption. Whereas firewalls protect only from outside attacks, Kerberos is designed to also protect against attacks from those inside the network. Users already within a network could try to break into local servers. Kerberos places protection around the servers themselves, rather than an entire network or computer. A free version is available from the Massachusetts Institute of Technology at **web.mit.edu/kerberos** under the MIT Public License, which is similar to the GNU Public License. The name *Kerberos* comes from Greek mythology and is the name of the three-headed watchdog for Hades. Be sure to check the **web.mit.edu/kerberos** site for recent upgrades and detailed documentation, including FAQs, manuals, and tutorials.

TIP *The Kerberos V5 package includes its own versions of network tools such as Telnet, RCP, FTP, and RSH. These provide secure authenticated access by remote users. The tools operate in the same way as their original counterparts described in Chapter 15. The package also contains a Kerberos version of the **su** administrative login command, **ksu**.*

Kerberos Servers

The key to Kerberos is a Kerberos server through which all requests for any server services are channeled. The Kerberos server then authenticates a client, identifying the client and validating the client's right to use a particular server. The server maintains a database of authorized users. Kerberos then issues the client an encrypted ticket that the client can use to gain access to the server. For example, if a user needs to check their mail, a request for use of the mail server is sent to the Kerberos server, which then authenticates the user and issues a ticket that is then used to access the mail server. Without a Kerberos-issued ticket, no one can access any of the servers. Originally, this process required that users undergo a separate authentication procedure for each server they wanted to access. However, users now only need to perform an initial authentication that is valid for all servers.

TIP *On Fedora Core, you can use the Kerberos Ticket Manager (Extras Accessories menu) to manage Kerberos tickets, and the authconfig-gtk tool (Authentication in System Settings window or menu) to specify and enable Kerberos realms.*

This process actually involves the use of two servers, an authentication server (AS) and a ticket-granting server (TGS). Together they make up what is known as the key distribution center (KDC). In effect, they distribute keys used to unlock access to services. The authentication server first validates a user's identity. The AS issues a ticket called the ticket-granting ticket (TGT) that allows the user to access the ticket-granting server. The TGS then issues the user another ticket to actually access a service. This way, the user never has any direct access of any kind to a server during the authentication process. The process is somewhat more complex than described. An authenticator using information such as the current time, a checksum, and an optional encryption key is sent along with the ticket and is decrypted with the session key. This authenticator is used by a service to verify your identity.

NOTE *You can view your list of current tickets with the* **klist** *command.*

Authentication Process

The authentication server validates a user using information in its user database. Each user needs to be registered in the authentication server's database. The database will include a user password and other user information. To access the authentication server, the user provides the username and the password. The password is used to generate a user key with which communication between the AS and the user is encrypted. The user will have their own copy of the user key with which to decrypt communications. The authentication process is illustrated in Figure 19-2.

Accessing a service with Kerberos involves the following steps:

1. The user has to be validated by the authentication server and granted access to the ticket-granting server with a ticket access key. You do this by issuing the **kinit** command, which will ask you enter your Kerberos username and then send it on to the authentication server (the Kerberos username is usually the same as your username).

```
kinit
```

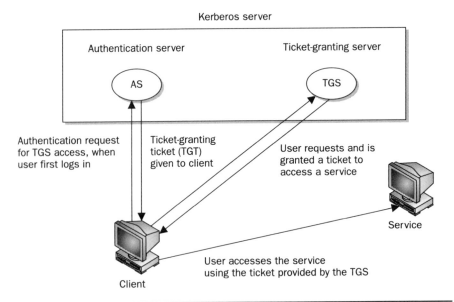

FIGURE 19-2 Kerberos authentication

2. The AS generates a ticket-granting ticket with which to access the ticket-granting server. This ticket will include a session key that will be used to let you access the TGS. The TGT is sent back to you encrypted with your user key (password).

3. The **kinit** program then prompts you to enter your Kerberos password, which it then uses to decrypt the TGT. You can manage your Kerberos password with the **kpasswd** command.

4. Now you can use a client program such as a mail client program to access the mail server, for instance. When you do so, the TGT is used to access the TGS, which then will generate a ticket for accessing the mail server. The TGS will generate a new session key for use with just the mail server. This will be provided in the ticket sent to you for accessing the mail server. In effect, there is a TGT session key used for accessing the TGS, and a mail session key used for accessing the mail server. The ticket for the mail server is sent to you encrypted with the TGS session key.

5. The client then uses the mail ticket received from the TGS to access the mail server.

6. If you want to use another service such as FTP, when your FTP client sends a request to the TGS for a ticket, the TGS will automatically obtain authorization from the authentication server and issue an FTP ticket with an FTP session key. This kind of support remains in effect for a limited period of time, usually several hours, after which you again have to use **kinit** to undergo the authentication process and access the TGS. You can manually destroy any tickets you have with the **kdestroy** command.

NOTE *With Kerberos V5 (version 5), a Kerberos login utility is provided whereby users are automatically granted ticket-granting tickets when they log in normally. This avoids the need to use* **kinit** *to manually obtain a TGT.*

Kerberized Services

Setting up a particular service to use Kerberos (known as Kerberizing) can be a complicated process. A Kerberized service needs to check the user's identity and credentials, check for a ticket for the service, and if one is not present, obtain one. Once they are set up, use of Kerberized services is nearly transparent to the user. Tickets are automatically issued and authentication carried out without any extra effort by the user. The **/etc/services** file should contain a listing of specific Kerberized services. These are services such as **kpasswd**, **ksu**, and **klogin** that provide Kerberos password, superuser access, and login services.

Kerberos also provides its own kerberized network tools for ftp, rsh, rcp, and rlogin (see Chapter 15). These are located at **/usr/kerberos/bin**, and most have the same name as the original network tools. In the Fedora Core installation, the PATH variable, which contains the directories for all your commands, will list **/usr/kerberos/bin** before **/usr/bin**. This means that when you invoke ftp, you are actually using the Kerberos version of ftp in **/usr/kerberos/bin**, instead of the original ftp which is still located in **/usr/bin**. The same is true for rlogin and rcp. The original name for the Kerberized network tools had a **k** prefix, and there are still links with some of these original names, such as krlogin, which links to the kerberos rlogin.

Configuring Kerberos Servers

Installing and configuring a Kerberos server is also a complex process. Carefully check the documentation for installing the current versions. Some of the key areas are listed here. In the Kerberos configuration file, **krb5.conf**, you can set such features as the encryption method used and the database name. When installing Kerberos, be sure to carefully follow the instructions for providing administrative access. To run Kerberos, you start the Kerberos server with **service** command and the **krb5kdc**, **kadmin**, and **krb524** scripts.

TIP   Check the Red Hat Linux Reference Manual for more detailed instructions on setting up Kerberos servers and clients on your system.

Consult the Red Hat Linux Reference Guide for detailed instructions on how to install and configure Kerberos on Fedora Core. You will need to configure the server for your network, along with clients for each host. To configure your server, you first specify your Kerberos realm and domain by manually replacing the lowercase **example.com** and the uppercase **EXAMPLE.COM** entries in the **/etc/krb5.conf** and **/var/kerberos/krb5kdc/kdc.conf** files with your own domain name. Maintain the same case for each entry. Realms are specified in uppercase, and simple host and domain names are in lowercase. You then create a database with the **kdb5_util** command and the **create** option. You will be prompted to enter a master key.

```
kdb5_util create -s
```

Full administrative access to the server is controlled by user entries in the **var/kerberos/krb5kdc/kadm5.acl** file. Replace the **EXAMPLE.COM** text with your Kerberos realm (usually your domain name in uppercase). You then need to add a local principal, a local user with full administrative access from the host the server runs on. Start the kadmin.local tool and use the **addprinc** command to add the local principal. You can then start your **krb5kdc**, **kadmin**, and **krb524** servers.

On each client host, use the kadmin tool with the **addprincipal** command to add a principal for the host. Also add a host principal for each host on your network with **host/** qualifier, as in **host/rabbit.mytrek.com**. You can use the **-randkey** option to specify a random key. Then save local copies of the host keys, using the **ktadd** command to save them in its **/etc/krb5.keytab** file. Each host needs to also have the same **/etc/krb5.conf** configuration file on its system, specifying the Kerberos server and the kdc host.

NOTE   When you configure Kerberos with the Authentication tool, you will be able to enter the realm, kdc server, and Kerberos server. Default entries will be displayed using the domain "example.com." Be sure to specify the realm in uppercase. A new entry for your realm will be made in the realms segment of the /etc/krb5.conf, listing the kdc and server entries you made.

20
CHAPTER

Network Firewalls: Netfilter

M ost systems currently connected to the Internet are open to attempts by outside users to gain unauthorized access. Outside users can try to gain access directly by setting up an illegal connection, by intercepting valid communications from users remotely connected to the system, or by pretending to be a valid user. Firewalls, encryption, and authentication procedures are ways of protecting against such attacks. A *firewall* prevents any direct unauthorized attempts at access, *encryption* protects transmissions from authorized remote users, and *authentication* verifies that a user requesting access has the right to do so. The current Linux kernel incorporates support for firewalls using the Netfilter (IPtables) packet filtering package (the previous version, IP Chains, is used on older kernel versions). To implement a firewall, you simply provide a series of rules to govern what kind of access you want to allow on your system. If that system is also a gateway for a private network, the system's firewall capability can effectively help protect the network from outside attacks.

NOTE *You can set up basic Netfilter firewall protection with the system-config-securitylevel tool (Security Level on the System Settings menu or window). This tool will generate a basic set of IPtables rules to protect your system and network (see Chapter 5).*

To provide protection for remote communications, transmission can be simply encrypted. For Linux systems, you can use the Secure Shell (SSH) suite of programs to encrypt any transmissions, preventing them from being read by anyone else (see Chapter 19). Kerberos authentication provides another level of security whereby individual services can be protected, allowing use of a service only to users who are cleared for access (see Chapter 19). Outside users may also try to gain unauthorized access through any Internet services you may be hosting, such as a Web site. In such a case, you can set up a proxy to protect your site from attack. For Linux systems, use Squid proxy software to set up a proxy to protect your Web server (see Chapter 24). Table 20-1 lists several network security applications commonly used on Linux.

Web Site	Security Application
www.netfilter.org	Netfilter Project, IPtables and NAT
www.netfilter.org/ipchains	IP Chains firewall
www.openssh.org	Secure Shell encryption
www.squid-cache.org	Squid Web Proxy server
web.mit.edu/Kerberos	Kerberos network authentication

TABLE 20-1 Network Security Applications

Firewalls: IPtables, NAT, and ip6tables

A good foundation for your network's security is to set up a Linux system to operate as a firewall for your network, protecting it from unauthorized access. You can use a firewall to implement either packet filtering or proxies. *Packet filtering* is simply the process of deciding whether a packet received by the firewall host should be passed on into the local network. The packet-filtering software checks the source and destination addresses of the packet and sends the packet on, if it's allowed. Even if your system is not part of a network but connects directly to the Internet, you can still use the firewall feature to control access to your system. Of course, this also provides you with much more security.

With proxies, you can control access to specific services, such as Web or FTP servers. You need a proxy for each service you want to control. The Web server has its own Web proxy, while an FTP server has an FTP proxy. Proxies can also be used to cache commonly used data, such as Web pages, so that users needn't constantly access the originating site. The proxy software commonly used on Linux systems is Squid, discussed in Chapter 24.

An additional task performed by firewalls is network address translation (NAT). Network address translation redirects packets to appropriate destinations. It performs tasks such as redirecting packets to certain hosts, forwarding packets to other networks, and changing the host source of packets to implement IP masquerading.

NOTE *The IP Chains package is the precursor to IPtables that was used on Linux systems running the 2.2 kernel. It is still in use on many Linux systems. The Linux Web site for IP Chains, which is the successor to ipfwadm used on older versions of Linux, is currently www.netfilter.org/ipchains. IP Chains in no longer included with Fedora Core.*

The Netfilter software package implements both packet-filtering and NAT tasks for the Linux 2.4 kernel and above. The Netfilter software is developed by the Netfilter Project, which you can find out more about at **www.netfilter.org**. The Red Hat Enterprise Linux Security Guide provides a helpful description on using Netfilter (**www.redhat.com**, Red Hat Enterprise Linux Documentation page).

IPtables

The command used to execute packet filtering and NAT tasks is **iptables**, and the software is commonly referred to as simply IPtables. However, Netfilter implements packet filtering and NAT tasks separately using different tables and commands. A table will hold the set of commands for its application. This approach streamlines the packet-filtering task, letting

IPtables perform packet-filtering checks without the overhead of also having to address translations. NAT operations are also freed from being mixed in with packet-filtering checks. You use the `iptables` command for both packet-filtering and NAT tasks, but for NAT you add the `-nat` option. The IPtables software can be built directly into the 2.4 kernel or loaded as a kernel module, **iptable_filter.o**.

ip6tables

The ip6tables package provides support for IPv6 addressing. It is identical to IPtables except that it allows the use of IPv6 addresses instead of IPv4 addresses (see Chapter 37). Both filter and mangle tables are supported in ip6tables, but not NAT tables. The filter tables support the same options and commands as in IPtables. The mangle tables will allow specialized packet changes like those for IPtables, using PREROUTING, INPUT, OUTPUT, FORWARD, and POSTROUTING rules. Some extensions have ipv6 labels for their names, such as ipv6-icmp, which corresponds to the IPtables icmp extension. The ipv6headers extension is used to select IPv6 headers.

Modules

Unlike its predecessor, IP Chains, Netfilter is designed to be modularized and extensible. Capabilities can be added in the form of modules such as the state module, which adds connection tracking. Most modules are loaded as part of the IPtables service. Others are optional; you can elect to load them before installing rules. The IPtables modules on your Fedora Core system are located at /usr/lib/*kernel-version*/kernel/net/ipv4/netfilter, where *kernel-version* is your kernel number, such as **2.6.9-1.667**. For IPv6 modules, check the **ipv6/netfilter** directory. Modules that load automatically will have an **ipt_** prefix, and optional ones have just an **ip_** prefix.

Optional modules can be specified as a list assigned to the IPTABLES_MODULES parameters located in the **/etc/sysconfig/iptables-config** file, which is used by the iptables service script. Whenever you start IPtables with the iptables service script, they will be automatically loaded.

```
# service iptables start
```

If you are writing you own iptables script, instead of using the Fedora Core service iptables script, you would have to add **modpobe** commands to load optional modules directly.

NOTE *The IPtables package includes backward-compatible modules for both ipfwadm and IP Chains. In fact, IPtables is very similar to IP Chains. You can still use IP Chains and the earlier* ***ipfwadm*** *commands by loading the* ***ipchains.o*** *or* ***ipfwadm.o*** *modules provided with the Netfilter software. These provide full backward compatibility.*

Packet Filtering

Netfilter is essentially a framework for packet management that can check packets for particular network protocols and notify parts of the kernel listening for them. Built on the Netfilter framework is the packet selection system implemented by IPtables. With IPtables, different tables of rules can be set up to select packets according to differing criteria. Netfilter currently supports three tables: filter, nat, and mangle. Packet filtering is implemented using a filter table that holds rules for dropping or accepting packets. Network address translation operations such as IP masquerading are implemented using the NAT table that holds IP masquerading rules. The mangle table is used for specialized packet changes. Changes can be made to packets before they are sent out, when they are received, or as they are being forwarded. This structure is extensible in that new modules can define their own tables with their own rules. It also greatly improves efficiency. Instead of all packets checking one large table, they access only the table of rules they need to.

IP table rules are managed using the **iptables** command. For this command, you will need to specify the table you want to manage. The default is the filter table, which need not be specified. You can list the rules you have added at any time with the **-L** and **-n** options, as shown here. The **-n** option says to use only numeric output for both IP addresses and ports, avoiding a DNS lookup for hostnames. You could, however, just use the **-L** option to see the port labels and hostnames:

```
iptables -L -n
```

NOTE *In IPtables commands, chain names have to be entered in uppercase, as with the chain names INPUT, OUTPUT, and FORWARD.*

Chains

Rules are combined into different chains. The kernel uses chains to manage packets it receives and sends out. A *chain* is simply a checklist of rules. These rules specify what action to take for packets containing certain headers. The rules operate with an if-then-else structure. If a packet does not match the first rule, the next rule is then checked, and so on. If the packet does not match any rules, the kernel consults chain policy. Usually, at this point the packet is rejected. If the packet does match a rule, it is passed to its target, which determines what to do with the packet. The standard targets are listed in Table 20-2. If a packet does not match any of the rules, it is passed to the chain's default target.

Targets

A *target* could, in turn, be another chain of rules, even a chain of user-defined rules. A packet could be passed through several chains before finally reaching a target. In the case of user-

TABLE 20-2
IPtables Targets

Target	Function
ACCEPT	Allow packet to pass through the firewall.
DROP	Deny access by the packet.
REJECT	Deny access and notify the sender.
QUEUE	Send packets to user space.
RETURN	Jump to the end of the chain and let the default target process it.

defined chains, the default target is always the next rule in the chains from which it was called. This sets up a procedure or function call–like flow of control found in programming languages. When a rule has a user-defined chain as its target, when activated, that user-defined chain is executed. If no rules are matched, execution returns to the next rule in the originating chain.

TIP Specialized targets and options can be added by means of kernel patches provided by the Netfilter site. For example, the SAME patch returns the same address for all connections. A patch-o-matic option for the Netfilter make file will patch your kernel source code, adding support for the new target and options. You can then rebuild and install your kernel.

Firewall and NAT Chains

The kernel uses three firewall chains: INPUT, OUTPUT, and FORWARD. When a packet is received through an interface, the INPUT chain is used to determine what to do with it. The kernel then uses its routing information to decide where to send it. If the kernel sends the packet to another host, the FORWARD chain is checked. Before the packet is actually sent, the OUTPUT chain is also checked. In addition, two NAT table chains, POSTROUTING and PREROUTING, are implemented to handle masquerading and packet address modifications. The built-in Netfilter chains are listed in Table 20-3.

Adding and Changing Rules

You add and modify chain rules using the **iptables** commands. An **iptables** command consists of the keyword **iptables**, followed by an argument denoting the command to execute. For example, **iptables -A** is the command to add a new rule, whereas **iptables -D** is the command to delete a rule. The **iptables** commands are listed in Table 20-4. The following command simply lists the chains along with their rules currently defined for your system. The output shows the default values created by **iptables** commands.

```
iptables -L -n
Chain input (policy ACCEPT):
Chain forward (policy ACCEPT):
Chain output (policy ACCEPT):
```

TABLE **20-3** Netfilter
Built-in Chains

Chain	Description
INPUT	Rules for incoming packets
OUTPUT	Rules for outgoing packets
FORWARD	Rules for forwarded packets
PREROUTING	Rules for redirecting or modifying incoming packets, NAT table only
POSTROUTING	Rules for redirecting or modifying outgoing packets, NAT table only

PART IV

Table 20-4
IPtables Commands

Command	Function
-A chain	Appends a rule to a chain.
-D chain [rulenum]	Deletes matching rules from a chain. Deletes rule rulenum (1 = first) from chain.
-I chain [rulenum]	Inserts in chain as rulenum (default 1 = first).
-R chain rulenum	Replaces rule rulenum (1 = first) in chain.
-L [chain]	Lists the rules in chain or all chains.
-E [chain]	Renames a chain.
-F [chain]	Deletes (flushes) all rules in chain or all chains.
-R chain	Replaces a rule; rules are numbered from 1.
-Z [chain]	Zero counters in chain or all chains.
-N chain	Creates a new user-defined chain.
-X chain	Deletes a user-defined chain.
-P chain target	Changes policy on chain to target.

To add a new rule to a chain, you use **-A**. Use **-D** to remove it, and **-R** to replace it. Following the command, list the chain to which the rule applies, such as the INPUT, OUTPUT, or FORWARD chain, or a user-defined chain. Next, you list different options that specify the actions you want taken (most are the same as those used for IP Chains, with a few exceptions). The **-s** option specifies the source address attached to the packet, **-d** specifies the destination address, and the **-j** option specifies the target of the rule. The ACCEPT target will allow a packet to pass. The **-i** option now indicates the input device and can be used only with the INPUT and FORWARD chains. The **-o** option indicates the output device and can be used only for OUTPUT and FORWARD chains. Table 20-5 lists several basic options.

IPtables Options

The IPtables package is designed to be extensible, and there are a number of options with selection criteria that can be included with IPtables. For example, the TCP extension includes the **--syn** option that checks for SYN packets. The ICMP extension provides the **--icmp-type** option for specifying ICMP packets as those used in ping operations. The limit extension includes the **--limit** option with which you can limit the maximum number of matching packets in a specified time period, such as a second.

In the following example, the user adds a rule to the INPUT chain to accept all packets originating from the address 192.168.0.55. Any packets that are received (**INPUT**) whose source address (**-s**) matches 192.168.0.55 are accepted and passed through (**-j ACCEPT**):

```
iptables -A INPUT -s 192.168.0.55 -j ACCEPT
```

Option	Function
-p [!] *proto*	Specifies a protocol, such as TCP, UDP, ICMP, or ALL.
-s [!] *address*[/*mask*] [!] [*port*[:*port*]]	Source address to match. With the *port* argument, you can specify the port.
--sport [!] [*port*[:*port*]]	Source port specification. You can specify a range of ports using the colon, *port:port*.
-d [!] *address*[/*mask*] [!] [*port*[:*port*]]	Destination address to match. With the *port* argument, you can specify the port.
--dport [!] [*port*[:*port*]]	Destination port specification.
--icmp-type [!] *typename*	Specifies ICMP type.
-I [!] *name*[+]	Specifies an input network interface using its name (for example, **eth0**). The + symbol functions as a wildcard. The + attached to the end of the name matches all interfaces with that prefix (**eth+** matches all Ethernet interfaces). Can be used only with the INPUT chain.
-j *target* [**port**]	Specifies the target for a rule (specify [**port**] for REDIRECT target).
--to-source < *ipaddr*> [-< *ipaddr*>] [: *port- port*]	Used with the SNAT target, rewrites packets with new source IP address.
--to-destination < *ipaddr*>[-< *ipaddr*>] [: *port- port*]	Used with the DNAT target, rewrites packets with new destination IP address.
-n	Numeric output of addresses and ports, used with **-L**.
-o [!] *name*[+]	Specifies an output network interface using its name (for example, **eth0**). Can be used only with FORWARD and OUTPUT chains.
-t *table*	Specifies a table to use, as in **-t nat** for the NAT table.
-v	Verbose mode, shows rule details, used with **-L**.
-x	Expands numbers (displays exact values), used with **-L**.
[!] **-f**	Matches second through last fragments of a fragmented packet.
[!] **-V**	Prints package version.
!	Negates an option or address.
-m	Specifies a module to use, such as state.
--state	Specifies options for the state module such as NEW, INVALID, RELATED, and ESTABLISHED. Used to detect packet's state. NEW references SYN packets (new connections).
--syn	SYN packets, new connections.
--tcp-flags	TCP flags: SYN, ACK, FIN, RST, URG, PS, and ALL for all flags.
--limit	Option for the limit module (**-m limit**). Used to control the rate of matches, matching a given number of times per second.
--limit-burst	Option for the limit module (**-m limit**). Specifies maximum burst before the limit kicks in. Used to control denial-of-service attacks.

TABLE 20-5   IPtables Options

Accepting and Denying Packets: DROP and ACCEPT

There are two built-in targets, DROP and ACCEPT. Other targets can be either user-defined chains or extensions added on, such as REJECT. Two special targets are used to manage chains, RETURN and QUEUE. RETURN indicates the end of a chain and returns to the chain it started from. QUEUE is used to send packets to user space.

```
iptables -A INPUT -s www.myjunk.com -j DROP
```

You can turn a rule into its inverse with an **!** symbol. For example, to accept all incoming packets except those from a specific address, place an **!** symbol before the **-s** option and that address. The following example will accept all packets except those from the IP address 192.168.0.45:

```
iptables -A INPUT -j ACCEPT ! -s 192.168.0.45
```

You can specify an individual address using its domain name or its IP number. For a range of addresses, you can use the IP number of their network and the network IP mask. The IP mask can be an IP number or simply the number of bits making up the mask. For example, all of the addresses in network 192.168.0 can be represented by 192.168.0.0/225.255.255.0 or by 192.168.0.0/24. To specify any address, you can use 0.0.0.0/0.0.0.0 or simply 0/0. By default, rules reference any address if no **-s** or **-d** specification exists. The following example accepts messages coming in that are from (source) any host in the 192.168.0.0 network and that are going (destination) anywhere at all (the **-d** option is left out or could be written as **-d 0/0**):

```
iptables -A INPUT -s 192.168.0.0/24  -j ACCEPT
```

The IPtables rules are usually applied to a specific network interface such as the Ethernet interface used to connect to the Internet. For a single system connected to the Internet, you will have two interfaces, one that is your Internet connection and a localhost interface (**lo**) for internal connections between users on your system. The network interface for the Internet is referenced using the device name for the interface. For example, an Ethernet card with the device name **/dev/eth0** would be referenced by the name **eth0**. A modem using PPP protocols with the device name **/dev/ppp0** would have the name **ppp0**. In IPtables rules, you use the **-i** option to indicate the input device; it can be used only with the INPUT and FORWARD chains. The **-o** option indicates the output device and can be used only for OUTPUT and FORWARD chains. Rules can then be applied to packets arriving and leaving on particular network devices. In the following examples, the first rule references the Ethernet device **eth0**, and the second, the localhost:

```
iptables -A INPUT -j DROP -i eth0 -s 192.168.0.45
iptables -A INPUT -j ACCEPT  -i lo
```

User-Defined Chains

With IPtables, the FORWARD and INPUT chains are evaluated separately. One does not feed into the other. This means that if you want to completely block certain addresses from passing through your system, you will need to add both a FORWARD rule and an INPUT rule for them.

```
iptables -A INPUT -j DROP -i eth0 -s 192.168.0.45
iptables -A FORWARD -j DROP -i eth0 -s 192.168.0.45
```

A common method for reducing repeated INPUT and FORWARD rules is to create a user chain that both the INPUT and FORWARD chains feed into. You define a user chain with the **-N** option. The next example shows the basic format for this arrangement. A new chain is created called incoming (it can be any name you choose). The rules you would define for your FORWARD and INPUT chains are now defined for the incoming chain. The INPUT and FORWARD chains then use the incoming chain as a target, jumping directly to it and using its rules to process any packets they receive.

```
iptables -N incoming

iptables -A incoming -j DROP -i eth0 -s 192.168.0.45
iptables -A incoming -j ACCEPT  -i lo

iptables -A FORWARD -j incoming
iptables -A INPUT -j incoming
```

ICMP Packets

Firewalls often block certain Internet Control Message Protocol (ICMP) messages. ICMP redirect messages, in particular, can take control of your routing tasks. You need to enable some ICMP messages, however, such as those needed for ping, traceroute, and particularly destination-unreachable operations. In most cases, you always need to make sure destination-unreachable packets are allowed; otherwise, domain name queries could hang. Some of the more common ICMP packet types are listed in Table 20-6. You can enable an ICMP type of packet with the **--icmp-type** option, which takes as its argument a number or a name representing the message. The following examples enable the use of echo-reply, echo-request, and destination-unreachable messages, which have the numbers 0, 8, and 3 respectively:

```
iptables -A INPUT -j ACCEPT  -p icmp -i eth0 --icmp -type  echo-reply -d 10.0.0.1
iptables -A INPUT -j ACCEPT  -p icmp -i eth0 --icmp-type  echo-request -d 10.0.0.1
iptables -A INPUT -j ACCEPT -p icmp -i eth0 --icmp-type  destination-unreachable -d
10.0.0.1
```

Their rule listing will look like this:

```
ACCEPT     icmp -- 0.0.0.0/0            10.0.0.1           icmp type 0
ACCEPT     icmp -- 0.0.0.0/0            10.0.0.1           icmp type 8
ACCEPT     icmp -- 0.0.0.0/0            10.0.0.1           icmp type 3
```

Ping operations need to be further controlled to avoid the ping-of-death security threat. You can do this several ways. One way is to deny any ping fragments. Ping packets are normally very small. You can block ping-of-death attacks by denying any ICMP packet that is a fragment. Use the **-f** option to indicate fragments.

```
iptables -A INPUT -p icmp -j DROP -f
```

Another way is to limit the number of matches received for ping packets. You use the limit module to control the number of matches on the ICMP ping operation. Use **-m limit** to use the limit module, and **--limit** to specify the number of allowed matches. **1/s** will allow one match per second.

```
iptables -A FORWARD -p icmp --icmp-type echo-request -m limit --limit 1/s -j ACCEPT
```

Number	Name	Required By
0	echo-reply	ping
3	destination-unreachable	Any TCP/UDP traffic
5	redirect	Routing if not running routing daemon
8	echo-request	ping
11	time-exceeded	traceroute

TABLE 20-6   Common ICMP Packets

Controlling Port Access

If your system is hosting an Internet service, such as a Web or FTP server, you can use IPtables to control access to it. You can specify a particular service by using the source port (**--sport**) or destination port (**--dport**) options with the port that the service uses. IPtables lets you use names for ports such as **www** for the Web server port. The names of services and the ports they use are listed in the **/etc/services** file, which maps ports to particular services. For a domain name server, the port would be **domain**. You can also use the port number if you want, preceding the number with a colon. The following example accepts all messages to the Web server located at 192.168.0.43:

```
iptables -A INPUT -d 192.168.0.43 --dport www -j ACCEPT
```

You can also use port references to protect certain services and deny others. This approach is often used if you are designing a firewall that is much more open to the Internet, letting users make freer use of Internet connections. Certain services you know can be harmful, such as Telnet and NTP, can be denied selectively. For example, to deny any kind of Telnet operation on your firewall, you can drop all packets coming in on the Telnet port, 23. To protect NFS operations, you can deny access to the port used for the portmapper, 111. You can use either the port number or the port name.

```
# deny outside access to portmapper port on firewall.
iptables -A arriving  -j DROP -p tcp -i eth0  --dport 111
# deny outside access to telnet port on firewall.
iptables -A arriving  -j DROP -p tcp -i eth0  --dport telnet
```

The rule listing will look like this:

```
DROP      tcp  --  0.0.0.0/0    0.0.0.0/0     tcp dpt:111
DROP      tcp  --  0.0.0.0/0    0.0.0.0/0     tcp dpt:23
```

One port-related security problem is access to your X server on the XFree86 ports that range from 6000 to 6009. On a relatively open firewall, these ports could be used to illegally access your system through your X server. A range of ports can be specified with a colon, as in 6000:6009. You can also use x11 for the first port, x11:6009. Sessions on the X server can be secured by using SSH, which normally accesses the X server on port 6010.

```
iptables -A arriving  -j DROP -p tcp -i eth0  --dport 6000:6009
```

Common ports checked and their labels are shown here:

Service	Port Number	Port Label
Auth	113	auth
Finger	79	finger
FTP	21	ftp
NTP	123	ntp
Portmapper	111	sunrpc
Telnet	23	telnet
Web server	80	www
XFree86	6000:6009	x11:6009

Packet States: Connection Tracking

One of the more useful extensions is the state extension, which can easily detect tracking information for a packet. Connection tracking maintains information about a connection such as its source, destination, and port. It provides an effective means for determining which packets belong to an established or related connection. To use connection tracking, you specify the state module first with **-m state**. Then you can use the **--state** option. Here you can specify any of the following states:

State	Description
NEW	A packet that creates a new connection
ESTABLISHED	A packet that belongs to an existing connection
RELATED	A packet that is related to, but not part of, an existing connection, such as an ICMP error or a packet establishing an FTP data connection
INVALID	A packet that could not be identified for some reason
RELATED+REPLY	A packet that is related to an established connection, but not part of one directly

If you are designing a firewall that is meant to protect your local network from any attempts to penetrate it from an outside network, you may want to restrict packets coming in. Simply denying access by all packets is unfeasible because users connected to outside servers—say, on the Internet—must receive information from them. You can, instead, deny access by a particular kind of packet used to initiate a connection. The idea is that an attacker must initiate a connection from the outside. The headers of these kinds of packets have their SYN bit set on and their FIN and ACK bits empty. The state module's NEW state matches on any such SYN packet. By specifying a DROP target for such packets, you deny access by any packet that is part of an attempt to make a connection with your system. Anyone trying to connect to your system from the outside is unable to do so. Users on your local system who have initiated connections with outside hosts can still communicate with them. The following example will drop any packets trying to create a new connection on the **eth0** interface, though they will be accepted on any other interface:

```
iptables -A INPUT -m state --state NEW -i eth0 -j DROP
```

You can use the **!** operator on the **eth0** device combined with an ACCEPT target to compose a rule that will accept any new packets except those on the **eth0** device. If the **eth0** device is the only one that connects to the Internet, this still effectively blocks outside access. At the same time, input operation for other devices such as your localhost are free to make new connections. This kind of conditional INPUT rule is used to allow access overall with exceptions. It usually assumes that a later rule such as a chain policy will drop remaining packets.

```
iptables -A INPUT -m state --state NEW ! -i eth0 -j ACCEPT
```

The next example will accept any packets that are part of an established connection or related to such a connection on the **eth0** interface:

```
iptables -A INPUT -m state --state ESTABLISHED,RELATED -j ACCEPT
```

TIP *You can use the iptstate tool to display the current state table.*

Specialized Connection Tracking: ftp, irc, Amanda, tftp

To track certain kinds of packets, IPtables uses specialized connection tracking modules. These are optional modules that you have to have loaded manually. To track passive FTP connections, you would have to load the ip_conntrack_ftp module. To add NAT table support, you would also load the ip_nat_ftp module. For IRC connections, you use ip_conntrack_irc and ip_nat_irc. There are corresponding modules for Amanda (the backup server) and TFTP (Trivial FTP).

To have these modules loaded automatically by the Fedora Core iptables service script, you have to list them in the IPTABLES_MODULE parameter in the **/etc/sysconfig/iptables-config** file. For example, the following assignment adds support for both FTP and Amanda.

```
IPTABLES_MODULES="ip_conntrack, ip_conntrack_ftp, ip_nat_ftp, ip_conntrack_amanda,
ip_nat_amanda"
```

If you were writing your own iptables script, instead of using the service iptables script, you would have to add **modprobe** commands to load the modules.

```
modprobe ip_conntrack ip_conntrack_ftp ip_nat_ftp
modprobe ip_conntrack_amanda ip_nat_amanda
```

Network Address Translation (NAT)

Network address translation (NAT) is the process whereby a system will change the destination or source of packets as they pass through the system. A packet will traverse several linked systems on a network before it reaches its final destination. Normally, they will simply pass the packet on. However, if one of these systems performs a NAT on a packet, it can change the source or destination. A packet sent to a particular destination could have its destination address changed. To make this work, the system also needs to remember such changes so that the source and destination for any reply packets are altered back to the original addresses of the packet being replied to.

NAT is often used to provide access to systems that may be connected to the Internet through only one IP address. Such is the case with networking features such as IP masquerading, support for multiple servers, and transparent proxying. With IP masquerading, NAT operations will change the destination and source of a packet moving through a firewall/ gateway linking the Internet to computers on a local network. The gateway has a single IP address that the other local computers can use through NAT operations. If you have multiple servers but only one IP address, you can use NAT operations to send packets to the alternate servers. You can also use NAT operations to have your IP address reference a particular server application such as a Web server (transparent proxy). NAT tables are not implemented for ip6tables.

Adding NAT Rules

Packet selection rules for NAT operations are added to the NAT table managed by the **iptables** command. To add rules to the NAT table, you have to specify the NAT table with the **-t** option. Thus to add a rule to the NAT table, you would have to specify the NAT table with the **-t nat** option as shown here:

```
iptables -t nat
```

With the **-L** option, you can list the rules you have added to the NAT table:

```
iptables -t nat -L -n
```

Adding the **-n** option will list IP addresses and ports in numeric form. This will speed up the listing, as iptables will not attempt to do a DNS lookup to determine the hostname for the IP address.

NAT Targets and Chains

In addition, there are two types of NAT operations: source NAT, specified as SNAT target, and destination NAT, specified as DNAT target. SNAT target is used for rules that alter source addresses, and DNAT target, for those that alter destination addresses.

Three chains in the NAT table are used by the kernel for NAT operations. These are PREROUTING, POSTROUTING, and OUTPUT. PREROUTING is used for destination NAT (DNAT) rules. These are packets that are arriving. POSTROUTING is used for source NAT (SNAT) rules. These are for packets leaving. OUTPUT is used for destination NAT rules for locally generated packets.

As with packet filtering, you can specify source (**-s**) and destination (**-d**) addresses, as well as the input (**-i**) and output (**-o**) devices. The **-j** option will specify a target such as MASQUERADE. You would implement IP masquerading by adding a MASQUERADE rule to the POSTROUTING chain:

```
# iptables -t nat -A POSTROUTING -o eth0 -j MASQUERADE
```

To change the source address of a packet leaving your system, you would use the POSTROUTING rule with the SNAT target. For the SNAT target, you use the **--to-source** option to specify the source address:

```
# iptables -t nat -A POSTROUTING -o eth0 -j SNAT --to-source 192.168.0.4
```

To change the destination address of packets arriving on your system, you would use the PREROUTING rule with the DNAT target and the **`--to-destination`** option:

```
# iptables -t nat -A PRETROUTING -i eth0 \
         -j DNAT --to-destination 192.168.0.3
```

Specifying a port lets you change destinations for packets arriving on a particular port. In effect, this lets you implement port forwarding. In the next example, every packet arriving on port 80 (the Web service port) is redirected to 10.0.0.3, which in this case would be a system running a Web server.

```
# iptables -t nat -A PRETROUTING -i eth0 -dport 80 \
         -j DNAT --to-destination 10.0.0.3
```

With the TOS and MARK targets, you can mangle the packet to control its routing or priority. A TOS target sets the type of service for a packet, which can set the priority using criteria such as normal-service, minimize-cost, and maximize-throughput, among others.

The targets valid only for the NAT table are shown here:

Target	Description
SNAT	Modify source address, use **`--to-source`** option to specify new source address.
DNAT	Modify destination address, use **`--to-destination`** option to specify new destination address.
REDIRECT	Redirect a packet.
MASQUERADE	IP masquerading.
MIRROR	Reverse source and destination and send back to sender.
MARK	Modify the Mark field to control message routing.

NAT Redirection: Transparent Proxies

NAT tables can be used to implement any kind of packet redirection, a process transparent to the user. Redirection is commonly used to implement a transparent proxy. Redirection of packets is carried out with the REDIRECT target. With transparent proxies, packets received can be automatically redirected to a proxy server. For example, packets arriving on the Web service port, 80, can be redirected to the Squid Proxy service port, usually 3128. This involves a command to redirect a packet, using the REDIRECT target on the PREROUTING chain:

```
# iptables -t nat -A PRETROUTING -i eth1 --dport 80 -j REDIRECT --to-port 3128
```

Packet Mangling: the Mangle Table

The *packet mangling* table is used to actually modify packet information. Rules applied specifically to this table are often designed to control the mundane behavior of packets, like routing, connection size, and priority. Rules that actually modify a packet, rather than simply redirecting or stopping it, can be used only in the mangle table. For example, the TOS target can be used directly in the mangle table to change the Type of Service field to modifying a packet's priority. A TCPMSS target could be set to control the size of a connection. The ECN target lets you work around ECN black holes, and the DSCP target will let you change DSCP bits. Several extensions such as the ROUTE extension will change a packet, in this case, rewriting its destination, rather than just redirecting it.

The mangle table is indicated with the **-t mangle** option. Use the following command to see what chains are listed in your mangle table:

```
iptables -t mangle  -L
```

Several mangle table targets are shown here:

Target	Description
TOS	Modify the Type of Service field to manage the priority of the packet.
TCPMSS	Modify the allowed size of packets for a connection, enabling larger transmissions.
ECN	Remove ECN black hole information.
DSCP	Change DSCP bits.
ROUTE	Extension TARGET to modify destination information in the packet.

NOTE   *The IPtables package is designed to be extensible, allowing customized targets to be added easily. This involves applying patches to the kernel and rebuilding it. See **www.netfilter.org** for more details, along with a listing of extended targets.*

IPtables Scripts

Though you can enter IPtables rules from the shell command line, when you shut down your system, these commands will be lost. On Fedora Core, you can make use of the built-in support for saving and reading IPtables rules using the iptables service script. Alternatively, you can manage the process yourself, saving to files of your own choosing. In either event, you will most likely need to place your IPtables rules in a script that can then be executed directly. This way you can edit and manage a complex set of rules, adding comments and maintaining their ordering.

NOTE   *IPtables support in the kernel is enabled by default. If you recompile the kernel, make sure that support for packet filtering is turned on, check Networking Options in the 2.4 kernel, and Networking Support/Networking Options under Device Drivers in the 2.6 kernel.*

Fedora Core IPtables Support

Fedora Core provides support for IPtables as part of their system configuration using various scripts and configuration files (see Table 20-7). When you install the RPM package for IPtables, an iptables service script is installed that will read and save IPtables commands using the **/etc/sysconfig/iptables** file. If you have set IPtables to be started up automatically when you boot your system, this file will be checked to see if it exists and is not empty. If so, IPtables will automatically read the IPtables commands that it holds. This helps to integrate IPtables more smoothly into the system setup process.

Script and Tool	Description
`/etc/sysconfig/iptables`	IPtables script to create IPtables rules.
`/etc/sysconfig/iptables.save`	IPtables backup script to create IPtables rules. This is a copy made of original IPtables, when a new IPtables file is generated with the save option.
`/etc/sysconfig/iptables-config`	Configuration file for **/etc/rc.d/init.d/iptables** service script, containing shell variable definitions.
`/etc/rc.d/init.d/iptables`	IPtables service script to manage IPtables rules in **/etc/sysconfig/iptables**.
`system-config-securitylevel`	Tool for creating basic IPtables firewall rules for **/etc/syscofig/iptables**.

TABLE 20-7 Fedora Core IPtables Scripts and Tools

IPtables Rules: /etc/sysconfig/iptables and system-config-security-level

The **/etc/sysconfig/iptables** script is automatically generated by **system-config-securitylevel**, which is run during the installation process. When you first start up your system, the **/etc/sysconfig/iptables** file will contain the IPtables rules for the configuration you selected when you ran **system-config-securitylevel**. If you run **system-config-securitylevel** again, changing your configuration, the **/etc/sysconfig/iptables** file will be overwritten with the new IPtables rules. You can access **system-config-securitylevel** as the Security Level entry on the System Settings menu.

You can sidestep this automatic IPtables setup by simply deleting the **/etc/sysconfig/iptables** file. (Running **system-config-securitylevel** and choosing No Firewall will do the same.) Be sure you back it up first in case it has important commands. It is possible to edit the **/etc/sysconfig/iptables** file directly and enter IPtables commands, but it is not recommended. Instead, you should think of this file as holding a final installation of your IPtables commands.

The iptables Service Script: /etc/rc.d/init.d/iptables and /etc/sysconfig/iptables-config

You should think of the iptables service script that Fedora Core provides as a versatile management tool, not as a service startup script. The use of the **service** command for this script can be confusing. The iptables script only manages IPtables rules, flushing, adding, or reporting them. It does not start and stop the IPtables service. If Netfilter is not running, you will need to specify that it be started up when your system boots. For this, you can use **system-config-service** (Services in the Server Settings window) and then select IPtables from the list of services.

The iptables service script makes use of several predefined shell parameters for specifying modules along with start and stop options. Default definitions are placed within the iptables service script, whereas corresponding custom definitions are located in a special file called **/etc/sysconfig/iptables-config**. Here the system administrator can set options like what modules to load or whether to save rules whenever IPtables is stopped, without having to edit the iptables service script directly. Table 20-8 lists the current IPtables parameters. Each time the iptables service script is used to start IPtables, it will load the modules specified in IPTABLES_MODULES as listed in **iptables-config**.

Parameter	Description
IPTABLES_MODULES	List of IPtables modules to load. Empty by default.
IPTABLES_MODULES_UNLOAD	Default is yes, if set to yes to unload modules at service script start and stop operations.
IPTABLES_SAVE_ON_STOP	Default is no, if set to yes, will save all rules when service script stops firewall.
IPTABLES_ SAVE_ON_RESTART	Default is no, if set to yes, will save all rules when service script restarts firewall.
IPTABLES_SAVE_COUNTERS	Default is no, if set to yes, will save counters if save for stopping or restarting is enabled.
IPTABLES_STATUS_NUMERIC	Default is yes, if set to yes, will display addresses and ports numerically.

TABLE 20-8   Configuration Parameters for iptables-config

The service script **/etc/rc.d/init.d/iptables** supports several options with which to manage your rules. The **status** option displays a listing of all your current rules. The **stop** option will flush your current rules. Unlike **stop** and **status**, the **start** and **save** options are tied directly to the **/etc/sysconfig/iptables** file. The **start** option will flush your current IPtables rules and add those in the **/etc/sysconfig/iptables** file. The **save** option will save your current rules to the **/etc/sysconfig/iptables** file. Keep in mind that the **stop** and **status** operations work on the current IPtables rules, no matter if they were added manually on the command line, added by your own script, or added by the **start** option from **/etc/sysconfig/iptables**. The following command will list your current rules:

```
service iptables status
```

Perhaps the most effective way to think of the iptables service script is as an IPtables development tool. When creating complex firewall rules (beyond the simple set generated by **system-config-securitylevel**), you should first create a script and place your rules in them, as described later in the IPtables script example. Make the script executable. Any changes you need to make as you debug your firewall, you make to this script. Before you run it, run the iptables service script with the **stop** option to clear out any previous rules:

```
service iptables stop
```

Then run your script, as shown here for the **myfilters** script:

```
./myfilters
```

To see how the commands have been interpreted by IPtables, use the service script with the **status** option:

```
service iptables status
```

For any changes, edit your iptables script. Then run the service script again to clear out the old rules. Run the iptables script again, and use the **status** option with the service script to see how they were implemented:

```
service iptables stop
./myfilters
service iptables status
```

Saving IPtables Rules

Once you are satisfied that your IPtables rules are working correctly, you can save your rules to the **/etc/sysconfig/iptables** file. Use the iptables service script with the **save** option. Now your rules will be read automatically when your system starts up. You can think of the save operation as installing your IPtables rules on your system, making them part of your system setup whenever you start your system.

```
service iptables save
```

To make changes, modify your iptables script, run the service script with **stop** to clear out the old rules, run the iptables script, and then use the service script with the **save** option to generate a new **/etc/sysconfig/iptables** file. A backup of the original is saved in **/etc/sysconfig/iptables.save**, in case you need to restore the older rules.

Instead of using the service script, you can save your rules using the **iptables-save** script. The recommended file to use is **/etc/iptables.rules**. The service script actually used **iptables-save** with the **-c** option to save rules to the **/etc/sysconfig/iptables** file. The **-c** option for **iptables-save** includes counters in the output (the iptables service script is designed to parse counter information along with the commands). The **iptables-save** command outputs rules to the standard output. To save them in a file, you must redirect the output to a file with the redirection operator, **>**, as shown here:

```
iptables-save -c > /etc/sysconfig/iptables
```

You can also save your rules to a file of your choosing, such as **/etc/iptables.rules**. The **/etc/rc.d/init.d/iptables** service script defines the IPTABLES_CONFIG variable, which holds the name of the IPtables configuration file, **/etc/sysconfig/iptables**.

```
iptables-save > /etc/iptables.rules
```

Then, to restore the rules, use the **iptables-restore** script to read the IPtables commands from that saved file:

```
iptables-restore < /etc/iptables.rules
```

Fedora Core ip6tables Support

For ip6tables, Fedora Core uses a different, corresponding set of supporting scripts and configuration files. ip6tables has its own service script, **ip6tables**, as well as its own restore and save scripts, **ip6tables-save** and **ip6tables-restore**. In their names, they have the number 6, as in **/etc/sysconfig/ip6tables**. The ip6tables configuration scripts and files are shown in Table 20-9.

Script and Tool	Description
`/etc/sysconfig/ip6tables`	Ip6tables script to create IPv6 IPtables rules.
`/etc/sysconfig/ip6tables-config`	Configuration file for `/etc/rc.d/init.d/ip6tables` service script, containing shell variable definitions.
`/etc/rc.d/init.d/ip6tables`	Ip6tables service script to manage ip6tables rules in **/etc/sysconfig/ip6tables**.
`ip6tables-save`	Ip6tables save script, operates like **iptables-save** (see previous section).
`ip6tables-restore`	Ip6tables restore script, operates like **iptables-restore** (see previous section).

TABLE 20-9   Configuration File and Support Scripts for ip6tables

An IPtables Script Example: IPv4

You now have enough information to create a simple IPtables script that will provide basic protection for a single system connected to the Internet. The following script, **myfilter**, provides an IPtables filtering process to protect a local network and a Web site from outside attacks. This example uses IPtables and IPv4 addressing (see Chapter 37). For IPv6 addressing you would use ip6tables, which has corresponding commands, except for the NAT rules, which would be implemented as mangle rules.

The script configures a simple firewall for a private network (check the IPtables HOWTO for a more complex example). If you have a local network, you could adapt this script to it. In this configuration, all remote access initiated from the outside is blocked, but two-way communication is allowed for connections that users in the network make with outside systems. In this example, the firewall system functions as a gateway for a private network whose network address is 192.168.0 (see Figure 20-1). The Internet address is, for the sake

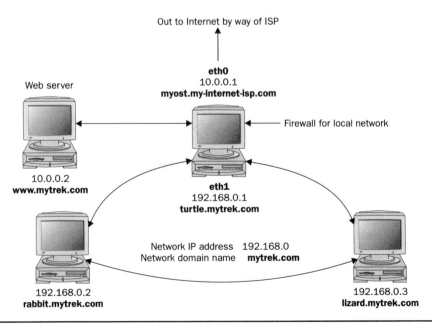

FIGURE 20-1   A network with a firewall

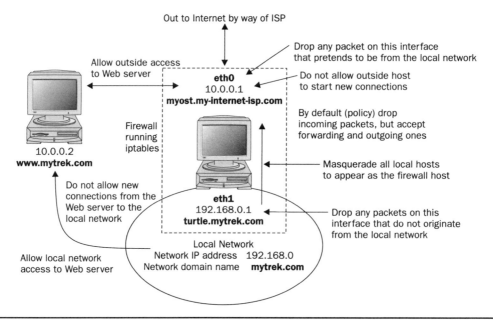

FIGURE 20-2   Firewall rules applied to a local network example

of this example, 10.0.0.1. The system has two Ethernet devices: one for the private network
(**eth1**) and one for the Internet (**eth0**). The gateway firewall system also supports a Web
server at address 10.0.0.2. Entries in this example that are too large to fit on one line are
continued on a second line.

The basic rules as they apply to different parts of the network are illustrated in Figure 20-2.

myfilter
```
Firewall Gateway system IP address is 10.0.0.1 using Ethernet device eth0
# Private network address is 192.168.0.0 using Ethernet device eth1
# Web site address is 10.0.0.2
# turn off IP forwarding
echo 0 > /proc/sys/net/ipv4/ip_forward
# Flush chain rules
iptables -F INPUT
iptables -F OUTPUT
iptables -F FORWARD
# set default (policy) rules
iptables -P INPUT DROP
iptables -P OUTPUT ACCEPT
iptables -P FORWARD ACCEPT

# IP spoofing, deny any packets on the internal network that have an
external source address.
iptables -A INPUT -j LOG  -i eth1 \! -s 192.168.0.0/24
iptables -A INPUT -j DROP  -i eth1 \! -s 192.168.0.0/24
```

```
iptables -A FORWARD -j DROP  -i eth1 \! -s 192.168.0.0/24
# IP spoofing, deny any outside packets (any not on eth1) that have the
source address of the internal network
iptables -A INPUT -j DROP \! -i eth1 -s 192.168.0.0/24
iptables -A FORWARD -j DROP \! -i eth1 -s 192.168.0.0/24
# IP spoofing, deny any outside packets with localhost address
# (packets not on the lo interface (any on eth0 or eth1) that have the
source address of localhost)
iptables -A INPUT -j DROP  -i \! lo  -s  127.0.0.0/255.0.0.0
iptables -A FORWARD -j DROP  -i \! lo  -s  127.0.0.0/255.0.0.0

# allow all incoming messages for users on your firewall system
iptables -A INPUT -j ACCEPT  -i lo

# allow  communication to the Web server (address 10.0.0.2), port www
iptables -A INPUT  -j ACCEPT -p tcp -i eth0  --dport www -s 10.0.0.2
# Allow  established connections from Web servers to internal network
iptables -A INPUT -m state --state ESTABLISHED,RELATED -i eth0 -p tcp  --
sport www -s 10.0.0.2 -d 192.168.0.0/24  -j ACCEPT
# Prevent new  connections from Web servers to internal network
iptables -A OUTPUT -m state --state  NEW -o eth0 -p tcp  --sport www -d
192.168.0.0/24  -j DROP

# allow established and related outside communication to your system
# allow outside communication to the firewall, except for ICMP packets
iptables -A INPUT -m state --state ESTABLISHED,RELATED -i eth0 -p \!
icmp -j ACCEPT
# prevent outside initiated connections
iptables -A INPUT -m state --state NEW -i eth0 -j DROP
iptables -A FORWARD -m state --state NEW -i eth0 -j DROP
# allow all local communication to and from the firewall on eth1  from
the local network
iptables -A INPUT -j ACCEPT -p all -i eth1 -s 192.168.0.0/24
# Set up masquerading to allow internal machines access to outside
network
iptables -t nat -A POSTROUTING -o eth0 -j MASQUERADE
# Accept ICMP Ping and Destination unreachable messages
# Others will be rejected by INPUT and OUTPUT DROP policy
iptables -A INPUT -j ACCEPT  -p icmp -i eth0 --icmp-type  echo-reply -d
10.0.0.1
iptables -A INPUT -j ACCEPT  -p icmp -i eth0 --icmp-type  echo-request
-d 10.0.0.1
iptables -A INPUT -j ACCEPT -p icmp -i eth0 --icmp-type  destination-
unreachable -d 10.0.0.1
# Turn on IP Forwarding
echo 1 > /proc/sys/net/ipv4/ip_forward
```

Initially, in the script you would clear your current IPtables with the flush option (**-F**), and then set the policies (default targets) for the non-user-defined rules. IP forwarding should also be turned off while the chain rules are being set:

```
echo 0 > /proc/sys/net/ipv4/ip_forward
```

DROP Policy

First, a DROP policy is set up for INPUT and FORWARD built-in IP chains. This means that if a packet does not meet a criterion in any of the rules to let it pass, it will be dropped. Then both IP spoofing attacks and any attempts from the outside to initiate connections (SYN packets) are rejected. Outside connection attempts are also logged. This is a very basic configuration that can easily be refined to your own needs by adding IPtables rules.

```
iptables -P INPUT DROP
iptables -P OUTPUT ACCEPT
iptables -P FORWARD ACCEPT
```

IP Spoofing

One way to protect the private network from IP spoofing any packets is to check for any outside addresses on the Ethernet device dedicated to the private network. In this example, any packet on device **eth1** (dedicated to the private network) whose source address is not that of the private network (**! -s 192.168.0.0**) is denied. Also, check to see if any packets coming from the outside are designating the private network as their source. In this example, any packets with the source address of the private network on any Ethernet device other than for the private network (**eth1**) are denied. The same strategy can be applied to the local host.

```
# IP spoofing, deny any packets on the internal network
# that have an external source address.
iptables -A INPUT -j LOG  -i eth1 \! -s 192.168.0.0/24
iptables -A INPUT -j DROP  -i eth1 \! -s 192.168.0.0/24
iptables -A FORWARD -j DROP  -i eth1 \! -s 192.168.0.0/24
# IP spoofing, deny any outside packets (any not on eth1)
# that have the source address of the internal network
iptables -A INPUT -j DROP \! -i eth1 -s 192.168.0.0/24
iptables -A FORWARD -j DROP \! -i eth1 -s 192.168.0.0/24
# P spoofing, deny any outside packets with localhost address
# (packets not on the lo interface (any on eth0 or eth1)
# that have the source address of localhost)
iptables -A INPUT -j DROP  -i \! lo  -s  127.0.0.0/255.0.0.0
iptables -A FORWARD -j DROP  -i \! lo  -s  127.0.0.0/255.0.0.0
```

Then, you would set up rules to allow all packets sent and received within your system (localhost) to pass.

```
iptables -A INPUT -j ACCEPT  -i lo
```

Server Access

For the Web server, you want to allow access by outside users but block access by anyone attempting to initiate a connection from the Web server into the private network. In the next example, all messages are accepted to the Web server, but the Web server cannot initiate contact with the private network. This prevents anyone from breaking into the local network through the Web server, which is open to outside access. Established connections are allowed, permitting the private network to use the Web server.

```
# allow  communication to the Web server (address 10.0.0.2), port www
iptables -A INPUT  -j ACCEPT -p tcp -i eth0  --dport www -s 10.0.0.2
# Allow  established connections from Web servers to internal network
iptables -A INPUT -m state --state ESTABLISHED,RELATED -i eth0 \
  -p tcp  --sport www -s 10.0.0.2 -d 192.168.0.0/24  -j ACCEPT
# Prevent new  connections from Web servers to internal network
iptables -A OUTPUT -m state --state  NEW -o eth0 -p tcp \
  --sport www -d 192.168.0.1.0/24  -j DROP
```

Firewall Outside Access

To allow access by the firewall to outside networks, you allow input by all packets except for ICMP packets. These are handled later. The firewall is specified by the firewall device, **eth0**. First your firewall should allow established and related connections to proceed, as shown here. Then you would block outside access as described later.

```
# allow outside communication to the firewall,
# except for ICMP packets
iptables -A INPUT -m state --state ESTABLISHED,RELATED \
        -i eth0 -p \! icmp -j ACCEPT
```

Blocking Outside Initiated Access

To prevent outsiders from initiating any access to your system, create a rule to block access by SYN packets from the outside using the **state** option with NEW. Drop any new connections on the **eth0** connection (assumes only **eth0** is connected to the Internet or outside network).

```
# prevent outside initiated connections
iptables -A INPUT -m state --state NEW -i eth0 -j DROP
iptables -A FORWARD -m state --state NEW -i eth0 -j DROP
```

Local Network Access

To allow interaction by the internal network with the firewall, you allow input by all packets on the internal Ethernet connection, **eth1**. The valid internal network addresses are designated as the input source.

```
iptables -A INPUT -j ACCEPT -p all -i eth1 -s 192.168.0.0/24
```

Masquerading Local Networks

To implement masquerading, where systems on the private network can use the gateway's Internet address to connect to Internet hosts, you create a NAT table (**-t nat**) POSTROUTING rule with a MASQUERADE target.

```
iptables -t nat -A POSTROUTING -o eth0 -j MASQUERADE
```

Controlling ICMP Packets

In addition, to allow ping and destination-reachable ICMP packets, you enter INPUT rules with the firewall as the destination. To enable ping operations, you use both echo-reply and echo-request ICMP types, and for destination unreachable, you use the destination-unreachable type.

```
iptables -A INPUT -j ACCEPT  -p icmp -i eth0 --icmp-type \
   echo-reply -d 10.0.0.1
iptables -A INPUT -j ACCEPT  -p icmp -i eth0 --icmp-type \
   echo-request -d 10.0.0.1
iptables -A INPUT -j ACCEPT -p icmp -i eth0 --icmp-type \
   destination-unreachable -d 10.0.0.1
```

At the end, IP forwarding is turned on again.

```
echo 1 > /proc/sys/net/ipv4/ip_forward
```

Listing Rules

A listing of these **iptables** options shows the different rules for each option, as shown here:

```
# iptables -L
Chain INPUT (policy DROP)
target   prot opt source            destination
LOG      all  -- !192.168.0.0/24    anywhere       LOG level warning
DROP     all  -- !192.168.0.0/24    anywhere
DROP     all  -- 192.168.0.0/24     anywhere
DROP     all  -- 127.0.0.0/8        anywhere
ACCEPT   all  -- anywhere           anywhere
ACCEPT   tcp  -- 10.0.0.2           anywhere       tcp dpt:http
ACCEPT   tcp  -- 10.0.0.2           192.168.0.0/24 state RELATED,ESTABLISHED
                                                         tcp spt:http

ACCEPT  !icmp -- anywhere           anywhere       state RELATED,ESTABLISHED
DROP     all  -- anywhere           anywhere       state NEW
ACCEPT   all  -- 192.168.0.0/24     anywhere
ACCEPT   icmp -- anywhere           10.0.0.1       icmp echo-reply
ACCEPT   icmp -- anywhere           10.0.0.1       icmp echo-request
ACCEPT   icmp -- anywhere           10.0.0.1       icmp destination-unreachable
Chain FORWARD (policy ACCEPT)
target   prot opt source            destination
DROP     all  -- !192.68.0.0/24     anywhere
DROP     all  -- 192.168.0.0/24     anywhere
DROP     all  -- 127.0.0.0/8        anywhere
DROP     all  -- anywhere           anywhere       state NEW

Chain OUTPUT (policy ACCEPT)
target   prot opt source            destination
DROP        tcp  -- anywhere        192.168.0.0/24 state NEW tcp spt:http


# iptables -t nat -L
Chain PREROUTING (policy ACCEPT)
target      prot opt source         destination
Chain POSTROUTING (policy ACCEPT)
target      prot opt source         destination
MASQUERADE  all  -- anywhere         anywhere
Chain OUTPUT (policy ACCEPT)
target      prot opt source         destination
```

User-Defined Rules

For more complex rules, you may want to create your own chain to reduce repetition. A common method is to define a user chain for both INPUT and FORWARD chains, so that you do not have to repeat DROP operations for each. Instead, you would have only one user chain that both FORWARD and INPUT chains would feed into for DROP operations. Keep in mind that both FORWARD and INPUT operations may have separate rules in addition to the ones they share. In the next example, a user-defined chain called arriving is created. The chain is defined with the **-N** option at the top of the script:

```
iptables -N arriving
```

A user chain has to be defined before it can be used as a target in other rules. So you have to first define and add all the rules for that chain, and then use it as a target. The arriving chain is first defined and its rules added. Then, at the end of the file, it is used as a target for both the INPUT and FORWARD chains. The INPUT chain lists rules for accepting packets, whereas the FORWARD chain has an ACCEPT policy that will accept them by default.

```
iptables -N arriving
iptables -F arriving
# IP spoofing, deny any packets on the internal network
# that has an external source address.
iptables -A arriving -j LOG  -i eth1 \! -s 192.168.0.0/24
iptables -A arriving -j DROP  -i eth1 \! -s 192.168.0.0/24
iptables -A arriving -j DROP \! -i eth1 -s 192.168.0.0/24
...........................
# entries at end of script
iptables -A INPUT -j arriving
iptables -A FORWARD -j arriving
```

A listing of the corresponding rules is shown here:

```
Chain INPUT (policy DROP)
target     prot opt source            destination
arriving   all  --  0.0.0.0/0          0.0.0.0/0
Chain FORWARD (policy ACCEPT)
target     prot opt source            destination
arriving   all  --  0.0.0.0/0          0.0.0.0/0
Chain arriving (2 references)
target     prot opt source            destination
LOG        all  -- !192.168.0.0/24    0.0.0.0/0      LOG flags 0 level 4
DROP       all  -- !192.168.0.0/24    0.0.0.0/0
DROP       all  --  192.168.0.0/24    0.0.0.0/0
```

For rules where chains may differ, you will still need to enter separate rules. In the **myfilter** script, the FORWARD chain has an ACCEPT policy, allowing all forwarded packets to the local network to pass through the firewall. If the FORWARD chain had a DROP policy, like the INPUT chain, then you may need to define separate rules under which the FORWARD chain could accept packets. In this example, the FORWARD and INPUT chains have different rules for accepting packets on the **eth1** device. The INPUT rule is more restrictive. To enable the local network to receive forwarded packets through the firewall, you could enable forwarding on its device using a separate FORWARD rule, as shown here:

```
iptables -A FORWARD -j ACCEPT -p all -i eth1
```

The INPUT chain would accept packets only from the local network.

```
iptables -A INPUT -j ACCEPT -p all -i eth1 -s 192.168.0.0/24
```

Simple LAN Configuration

To create a script to support a simple LAN without any Internet services like Web servers, you would just not include rules for supporting those services. You would still need FORWARD and POSTROUTING rules for connecting your local hosts to the Internet, as well as rules governing interaction between the hosts and the firewall. To modify the example script to support a simple LAN without the Web server, just remove the three rules governing the Web server. Leave everything else the same.

LAN Configuration with Internet Services on the Firewall System

Often, the same system that functions as a firewall is also used to run Internet servers, like Web and FTP servers. In this case the firewall rules are applied to the ports used for those services. The example script dealt with a Web server running on a separate host system. If the Web server were instead running on the firewall system, you would apply the Web server firewall rules to the port that the Web server uses. Normally the port used for a Web server is 80. In the following example, the IPtables rules for the Web server have been applied to port www, port 80, on the firewall system. The modification simply requires removing the old Web server host address references, 10.0.0.2.

```
# allow  communication to the Web server, port www (port 80)
iptables -A INPUT  -j ACCEPT -p tcp -i eth0  --dport www
# Allow  established connections from Web servers to internal network
iptables -A INPUT -m state --state ESTABLISHED,RELATED -i eth0 \
   -p tcp  --sport www -d 192.168.0.0/24  -j ACCEPT
# Prevent new  connections from Web servers to internal network
iptables -A OUTPUT -m state --state  NEW -o eth0 -p tcp \
  --sport www -d 192.168.0.1.0/24 -j DROP
```

Similar entries could be set up for an FTP server. Should you run several Internet services, you could use a user-defined rule to run the same rules on each service, rather than repeating three separate rules per service. Working from the example script, you would use two defined rules, one for INPUT and one for OUTPUT, controlling incoming and outgoing packets for the services.

```
iptables -N inputservice
iptables -N outputservice
iptables -F inputservice
iptables -F outputservice
# allow  communication to the service
iptables -A inputservice  -j ACCEPT -p tcp -i eth0
# Allow  established connections from the service to internal network
iptables -A inputservice -m state --state ESTABLISHED,RELATED -i eth0 \
   -p tcp  -d 192.168.0.0/24  -j ACCEPT
# Prevent new  connections from service to internal network
iptables -A outputservice -m state --state  NEW -o eth0 -p tcp \
  -d 192.168.0.1.0/24 -j DROP
..........................
# Run rules for the Web server, port www (port 80)
iptables -A INPUT  --dport www -j inputservice
iptables -A INPUT  --dport www -j outputservice
# Run rules for the FTP server, port ftp (port 21)
iptables -A OUTPUT  --dport ftp -j inputservice
iptables -A OUTPUT  --dport ftp -j outputservice
```

IP Masquerading

On Linux systems, you can set up a network in which you can have one connection to the Internet, which several systems on your network can use. This way, using only one IP address, several different systems can connect to the Internet. This method is called *IP masquerading*, where a system masquerades as another system, using that system's IP address. In such a network, one system is connected to the Internet with its own IP address, while the other systems are connected on a local area network (LAN) to this system. When a local system wants to access the network, it masquerades as the Internet-connected system, borrowing its IP address.

IP masquerading is implemented on Linux using the IPtables firewalling tool. In effect, you set up a firewall, which you then configure to do IP masquerading. Currently, IP masquerading supports all the common network services—as does IPtables firewalling— such as Web browsing, Telnet, and ping. Other services, such as IRC, FTP, and RealAudio, require the use of certain modules. Any services you want local systems to access must also be on the firewall system because request and response actually are handled by services on that system.

You can find out more information on IP masquerading at the IP Masquerade Resource Web site at **ipmasq.webhop.net**. In particular, the Linux IP Masquerade mini-HOWTO provides a detailed, step-by-step guide to setting up IP masquerading on your system. IP masquerading must be supported by the kernel before you can use it. If your kernel does not support it, you may have to rebuild the kernel, including IP masquerade support, or use loadable modules to add it. See the IP Masquerade mini-HOWTO for more information.

With IP masquerading, as implemented on Linux systems, the machine with the Internet address is also the firewall and gateway for the LAN of machines that use the firewall's Internet address to connect to the Internet. Firewalls that also implement IP masquerading are sometimes referred to as *MASQ gates.* With IP masquerading, the Internet-connected system (the firewall) listens for Internet requests from hosts on its LAN. When it receives one, it replaces the requesting local host's IP address with the Internet IP address of the firewall and then passes the request out to the Internet, as if the request were its own. Replies from the Internet are then sent to the firewall system. The replies the firewall receives are addressed to the firewall using its Internet address. The firewall then determines the local system to whose request the reply is responding. It then strips off its IP address and sends the response on to the local host across the LAN. The connection is transparent from the perspective of the local machines. They appear to be connected directly to the Internet.

Masquerading Local Networks

IP masquerading is often used to allow machines on a private network to access the Internet. These could be machines in a home network or a small LAN, such as for a small business. Such a network might have only one machine with Internet access, and as such, only the one Internet address. The local private network would have IP addresses chosen from the private network allocations (10., 172.16., or 192.168.). Ideally, the firewall has two Ethernet cards: one for an interface to the LAN (for example, **eth1**) and one for an interface to the Internet, such as **eth0** (for dial-up ISPs, this would be **ppp0** for the modem). The card for the Internet connection (**eth0**) would be assigned the Internet IP address. The Ethernet interface for the local network (**eth1**, in this example) is the firewall Ethernet interface. Your private LAN would have a network address like 192.168.0. Its Ethernet firewall interface (**eth1**) would be assigned the IP address 192.168.0.1. In effect, the firewall interface lets the firewall operate as the local network's gateway. The firewall is then configured to masquerade any packets coming from the private network. Your LAN needs to have its own domain name server, identifying the machines on your network, including your firewall. Each local machine needs to have the firewall specified as its gateway. Try not to use IP aliasing to assign both the firewall and Internet IP addresses to the same physical interface. Use separate interfaces for them, such as two Ethernet cards, or an Ethernet card and a modem (**ppp0**).

Masquerading NAT Rule

In Netfilter, IP masquerading is a NAT operation and is not integrated with packet filtering as in IP Chains. IP masquerading commands are placed on the NAT table and treated separately from the packet-filtering commands. Use IPtables to place a masquerade rule on the NAT table. First reference the NAT table with the **-t nat** option. Then add a rule to the POSTROUTING chain with the **-o** option specifying the output device and the **-j** option with the MASQUERADE command.

```
iptables -t nat -A POSTROUTING -o eth0 -j MASQUERADE
```

IP Forwarding

The next step is to turn on IP forwarding, either manually or by setting the **net.ipv4.ip_ forward** variable in the **/etc/sysctl.conf** file and running **sysctl** with the **-p** option. IP forwarding will be turned off by default. For IPv6, use **net.ipv6.conf.all.forwarding**. The **/etc/sysctl.conf** entries are shown here:

```
net.ipv4.ip_forward = 1
net.ipv6.conf.all.forwarding = 1
```

You then run **sysctl** with the **-p** option.

```
sysctl -p
```

You can directly change the respective forwarding files with an **echo** command as shown here:

```
echo 1 > /proc/sys/net/ipv4/ip_forward
```

For IPv6, you would to use the forwarding file in the corresponding **/proc/sys/net/ipv6** directory, **conf/all/forwarding**.

```
echo 1 > /proc/sys/net/ipv6/conf/all/forwarding
```

Masquerading Selected Hosts

Instead of masquerading all local hosts as the single IP address of the firewall/gateway host, you could use the NAT table to rewrite addresses for a few selected hosts. Such an approach is often applied to setups where you want several local hosts to appear as Internet servers. Using the DNAT and SNAT targets, you can direct packets to specific local hosts. You would use rules on the PREROUTING and POSTROUTING chains to direct input and output packets.

For example, the Web server described in the previous example could have been configured as a local host to which a DNAT target could redirect any packets originally received for 10.0.0.2. Say the Web server was set up on 192.168.0.5. It could appear as having the address 10.0.0.2 on the Internet. Packets sent to 10.0.0.2 would be rewritten and directed to 192.168.0.5 by the NAT table. You would use the PREROUTING chain with the **-d** option to handle incoming packets and POSTROUTING with the **-s** option for outgoing packets.

```
iptables -t nat -A PREROUTING -d 10.0.0.2  \
        --to-destination 192.168.0.5 -j DNAT
iptables -t nat -A POSTROUTING -s 192.168.0.5 \
        --to-source 10.0.0.2 -j SNAT
```

TIP *Bear in mind that with IPtables, masquerading is no longer combined with the FORWARD chain, as it is with IP Chains. So, if you specify a DROP policy for the FORWARD chain, you will also have to specifically enable FORWARD operation for the network that is being masqueraded. You will need both a POSTROUTING rule and FORWARD rule.*

Network Servers

PART

V

Managing Services

A single Linux system can provide several different kinds of services, ranging from security to administration, and including more obvious Internet services like Web and FTP sites, e-mail, and printing. Security tools such as SSH and Kerberos run as services, along with administrative network tools such as DHCP and LDAP. The network connection interface is itself a service that you can restart at will. Each service operates as a continually running daemon looking for requests for its particular services. In the case of a Web service, the requests will come from remote users. You can turn services on or off by starting or shutting down their daemons.

The process of starting up or shutting down a service is handled by service scripts, described in detail in this chapter. It applies to all services including those discussed in the Security, Administration, and Network Administration sections, as well as the Servers section. It is covered at this point since you will most likely use them to start and stop Internet services like Web and mail servers.

System Startup Files: /etc/rc.d

Each time you start your system, it reads a series of startup commands from system initialization files located in your **/etc/rc.d** directory. These initialization files are organized according to different tasks. Some are located in the **/etc/rc.d** directory itself, while others are located in a subdirectory called **init.d**. You should not have to change any of these files. The organization of system initialization files varies among Linux distributions. The Fedora Core organization is described here. Some of the files you find in **/etc/rc.d** are listed in Table 21-1.

/etc/rc.d/rc.sysinit

The **/etc/rc.d/rc.sysinit** file holds the commands for initializing your system, including the mounting and unmounting of your file systems. Kernel modules for specialized features or devices can be loaded in an **rc.modules** file. The **/etc/rc.d/rc.local** file is the last initialization file executed. You can place commands of your own here. When you shut down your system, the system calls the **halt** file, which contains shutdown commands. The files in **init.d** are then called to shut down daemons, and the file systems are unmounted. In the current distribution of Fedora Core, **halt** is located in the **init.d** directory.

File	Description
/etc/sysconfig	Directory that holds system configuration files and directories.
/etc/rc.d	Directory that holds system startup and shutdown files.
/etc/rc.d/rc.sysinit	Initialization file for your system.
/etc/rc.d/rc.local	Initialization file for your own commands; you can freely edit this file to add your own startup commands; this is the last startup file executed.
/etc/rc.d/init.d	Directory that holds network scripts to start up network connections.
/etc/rc.d/rcnum**.d**	Directories for different runlevels, where *num* is the runlevel. The directories hold links to scripts in the **/etc/rc.d/init.d** directory.
/etc/rc.d/init.d	Directory that holds system service scripts. See Table 21-2.
/etc/rc.d/init.d/halt	Operations performed each time you shut down the system, such as unmounting file systems; called **rc.halt** in other distributions.

TABLE 21-1   System Startup Files and Directories

/etc/rc.d/init.d

The **/etc/rc.d/init.d** directory is designed primarily to hold scripts that start up and shut down different specialized daemons, such as network and printer daemons and those for font and Web servers. These files perform double duty, starting a daemon when the system starts up and shutting down the daemon when the system shuts down. The files in **init.d** are designed in a way to make it easy to write scripts for starting up and shutting down specialized applications. They use functions defined in the **functions** file. Many of these files are set up for you automatically. You shouldn't need to change them. If you do change them, be sure you know how these files work first.

When your system starts up, several programs are automatically started and run continuously to provide services, such as a Web site or print servers. Depending on what kind of services you want your system to provide, you can add or remove items in a list of services to be started automatically. For example, the Web server is run automatically when your system starts up. If you are not hosting a Web site, you would have no need for the Web server. You could prevent the service from starting, removing an extra task the system does not need to perform, freeing up resources and possibly reduce potential security holes. Several of the servers and daemons perform necessary tasks. The **sendmail** server enables you to send messages across networks, and the **cupsd** server performs printing operations.

To configure a service to start up automatically at boot, you can use the system-config-services tool available on the desktop or the **chkconfig** tool, which is run at a command line. The system-config-services tool displays a list of available services, letting you choose the ones you want to start or prevent from starting. The **chkconfig** command uses the **on** and **off** options to select and deselect services for startup at boot (see the section on **chkconfig** later in this chapter).

```
chkconfig httpd on
```

To start and stop services manually at any time, you can use either system-config-services or the **service** command. With the **service** command, you list the service with the **stop** argument to stop it, the **start** argument to start it, and the **restart** argument to restart it.

```
service httpd start
```

TIP *When your system starts up, it uses links in special runlevel directories in the /etc/rc.d/ directory to run the service scripts in the /etc/rc.d/init.d directory. A runlevel directory bears the number of its runlevel, as in /etc/rc.d/rc3.d for runlevel 3, and /etc/rc.d/rc5.d for runlevel 5. To prevent a service from starting up, remove its link from that runlevel directory, or change the first letter in the name of the link from S to K.*

SysV Init: init.d Scripts

You can manage the startup and shutdown of server daemons with special service scripts located in the **/etc/rc.d/init.d** directory. These scripts often have the same name as the service's program. For example, for the **/usr/sbin/httpd** Web server program, the corresponding script is called **/etc/rc.d/init.d/httpd**. This script starts and stops the Web server. This method of using **init.d** service scripts to start servers is called *SysV Init*, after the method used in Unix System V. Some of the more commonly used service scripts are listed in Table 21-2.

TIP *If you change the configuration of a server, you may need to start and stop it several times as you refine the configuration. Several servers provide special management tools that enable you to perform this task easily. The **apachectl** utility enables you to start and stop the Apache Web server easily. It is functionally equivalent to using the **/etc/rc.d/init.d/httpd** script to start and stop the server. For the domain name server, the **ndc** utility enables you to start and stop the **named** server, the DNS server discussed in Chapter 38. However, it is not advisable to mix the use of **init.d** scripts and the management tools.*

The service scripts in the **/etc/rc.d/init.d** directory can be executed automatically whenever you boot your system. Be careful when accessing these scripts, however. These start essential programs, such as your network interface and your printer daemon. These init scripts are accessed from links in subdirectories set up for each possible runlevel. The **/etc/rc.d** directory holds a set of subdirectories whose names have the format **rc***n***.d**, where *n* is a number referring to a runlevel. The **rc** script detects the runlevel in which the system was started, and then executes only the service scripts specified in the subdirectory for that runlevel. When you start your system, the **rc** script executes the service scripts specified in the **rc3.d** directory, if you are performing a command line login, or the **rc5.d** directory, if you are using a graphical login. The **rc3.d** and **rc5.d** directories hold symbolic links to certain service scripts in the **/etc/rc.d/init.d** directory. Thus, the **httpd** script in the **/etc/rc.d/init.d** directory is actually called through a symbolic link in the **rc3.d** or the **rc5.d** directory. The symbolic link for the **/etc/rc.d/httpd** script in the **rc3.d** directory is **S85httpd**. The *S* prefixing the link stands for "startup"; thus, the link calls the corresponding **init.d** script with the **start**

Service Script	Description
network	Operations to start up or shut down your network connections
xinetd	Operations to start up or shut down the **xinetd** daemon
autofs	Automatic file system mounting (see Chapter 32)
cups	CUPS printer daemon (see Chapter 26)
cyrus-imapd	Cyrus IMAP mail service (see Chapter 25)
dhcpd	Dynamic Host Configuration Protocol daemon (see Chapter 40)
httpd	Apache Web server (see Chapter 23)
innd	Internet News service (see Chapter 27)
ipsec	IPsec secure VPN service (see Chapter 18)
iptables	Controls IPtables daemon
ip6tables	IPtables for IP protocol version 6 (see Chapter 20)
krb5kdc	Kerberos kdc server (see Chapter 19)
kudzu	Detects new hardware
ldap	LDAP service (see Chapter 29)
nfs	Network Filesystem (see Chapter 40)
postfix	Postfix mail server (see Chapter 25)
sendmail	Sendmail MTA daemon (see Chapter 25)
smb	Samba for Windows hosts (see Chapter 41)
squid	Squid proxy-cache server (see Chapter 24)
sshd	Secure Shell daemon (see Chapter 19)
syslog	System logging daemon (see Chapter 29)
vsftpd	Very Secure FTP server (see Chapter 22)
xfs	X Window System font server
ypbind	Network Information Service (NFS) (see Chapter 40)

TABLE 21-2   Selection of Service Scripts in **/etc/rc.d/init.d**

option. The number indicates the order in which service scripts are run; lower numbers run first. **S85httpd** invokes **/etc/rc.d/init.d/httpd** with the option **start**. If you change the name of the link to start with a *K*, the script is invoked with the **stop** option, stopping it. Such links are used in the runlevels 0 and 6 directories, **rc0.d** and **rc6.d**. Runlevel 0 halts the system, and runlevel 6 reboots it. You can use the **runlevel** command to find out what runlevel you are currently operating at (see Chapter 29 for more details on runlevels). A listing of runlevels is shown in Table 21-3.

Runlevel	rc.d Directory	Description
0	**rc0.d**	Halt (shut down) the system
1	**rc1.d**	Single-user mode (no networking, limited capabilities)
2	**rc2.d**	Multiuser mode with no NFS support (limited capabilities)
3	**rc3.d**	Multiuser mode (full operational mode)
4	**rc4.d**	User-defined, implemented by default the same as runlevel 3, multiuser mode
5	**rc5.d**	Multiuser mode with graphical login (full operation mode with graphical login added)
6	**rc6.d**	Reboot system

TABLE 21-3   System Runlevels

Starting Services: Stand-Alone and xinetd

A *service* is a daemon that runs concurrently with your other programs, continually looking for a request for its services, either from other users on your system or from remote users connecting to your system through a network. When a server receives a request from a user, it starts up a *session* to provide its services. For example, if users want to download a file from your system, they can use their own FTP client to connect to your FTP server and start up a session. In the session, they can access and download files from your system. Your server needs to be running for a user to access its services. For example, if you set up a Web site on your system with HTML files, you must have the **httpd** Web server program running before users can access your Web site and display those files.

Starting Services Directly

You can start a server in several ways. One way is to do it manually from the command line by entering the name of the server program and its arguments. When you press ENTER, the server starts, although your command line prompt reappears. The server runs concurrently as you perform other tasks. To see if your server is running, you can use the **service** command with the **status** option.

```
# service httpd status
```

Alternatively, you can use the **ps** command with the **-aux** option to list all currently running processes. You should see a process for the server program you started. To refine the list, you can add a **grep** operation with a pattern for the server name you want. The second command lists the process for the Web server.

```
# ps -aux
# ps -aux | grep 'httpd'
```

PART V

Starting and Stopping Services with Service Scripts

On Red Hat Enterprise Linux and Fedora Core systems, you use service scripts to start and stop your server manually. These scripts are located in the **/etc/rc.d/init.d** directory and have the same names as the server programs. For example, the **/etc/rc.d/init.d/ httpd** script with the **start** option starts the Web server. Using this script with the **stop** option stops it. Instead of using the complete pathname for the script, you can use the **service** command and the script name. The following commands are equivalent:

```
/etc/rc.d/init.d/httpd stop
service httpd stop
```

Starting Services Automatically

Instead of manually executing all the server programs each time you boot your system, you can have your system automatically start the servers for you. You can do this in two ways, depending on how you want to use a server. You can have a server running continuously from the time you start your system until you shut it down, or you can have the server start only when it receives a request from a user for its services. If a server is being used frequently, you may want to have it running all the time. If it is used rarely, you may want the server to start only when it receives a request. For example, if you are hosting a Web site, your Web server is receiving requests all the time from remote users on the Internet. For an FTP site, however, you may receive requests infrequently, in which case you may want to have the FTP server start only when it receives a request. Of course, certain FTP sites receive frequent requests, which would warrant a continuously running FTP server.

Stand-Alone Servers

A server that starts automatically and runs continuously is referred to as a *stand-alone* server. Red Hat uses the SysV Init procedure to start servers automatically whenever your system boots. This procedure uses service scripts for the servers located in the **/etc/rc.d/init.d** directory. Most Linux systems configure the Web server to start automatically and to run continuously by default. A script for it called **httpd** is in the **/etc/rc.d/init.d** directory.

xinetd Servers

To start the server only when a request for its services is received, you configure it using the **xinetd** daemon. If you add, change, or delete server entries in the **/etc/xinetd** files, you will have to restart the **xinetd** daemon for these changes to take effect. On Fedora Core, you can restart the **xinetd** daemon using the **/etc/rc.d/init.d/xinetd** script with the **restart** argument, as shown here:

```
# service xinetd restart
```

You can also use the **xinetd** script to start and stop the **xinetd** daemon. Stopping effectively shuts down all the servers that the **xinetd** daemon manages (those listed in the **/etc/xinetd.conf** file or the **xinetd.d** directory).

```
# service xinetd stop
# service xinetd start
```

You can also directly restart **xinetd** by stopping its process directly. To do this, you use the **killall** command with the **-HUP** signal and the name **xinetd**.

```
# killall -HUP xinetd
```

TIP *Versions prior to Red Hat 7.0 used the **inetd** daemon (the term stands for the Internet Services Daemon) instead of **xinetd**, which is meant to be the enhanced replacement for **inetd**. If you are upgrading from **inetd**, you can use the **inetdconvert** command to convert **inetd** entries into **xinetd** configurations.*

Service Management Tools: chkconfig and system-config-services

On Fedora Core, system-config-services and the **chkconfig** command provide simple interfaces you can use to choose what servers you want started up and how you want them to run. You use these tools to control any daemon you want started up, including system services such as **cron**, the print server, remote file servers for Samba and NFS, authentication servers for Kerberos, and, of course, Internet servers for FTP or HTTP. Such daemons are referred to as *services,* and you should think of these tools as managing these services. Any of these services can be set up to start or stop at different runlevels.

These tools manage services that are started up by scripts in the **/etc/rc.d/init.d** directory. If you add a new service, either **chkconfig** or system-config-services can manage it. As described in the following section, services are started up at specific runlevels using service links in various runlevel directories. These links are connected to the service scripts in the **init.d** directory. Runlevel directories are numbered from 0 to 6 in the **/etc/rc.d** directory, such as **/etc/rc.d/rc3.d** for runlevel 3 and **/etc/rc.d/rc5.d** for runlevel 5. Removing a service from a runlevel only changes its link in the corresponding runlevel **rc.d** directory. It does not touch the service script in the **init.d** directory.

system-config-services

With the system-config-services utilities, you can simply select from a list of commonly used services those that you want to run when your system boots up. You can access system-config-services from the Services icon in the Server Settings window or menu, located under System Settings. The system-config-services tool lets you start, stop, and restart a server, much like the **service** command (see Figure 21-1), providing a GNOME GUI interface for easy use. It displays a list of your installed servers, with checked check boxes for those currently chosen to start up. You can start, stop, or restart any particular service by selecting it and choosing either Start Service, Stop Service, or Restart Service from the Action menu.

You can also set startup runlevels for services, just as you can with **chkconfig**, though you are limited to levels 3, 4, and 5. The list of checked entries differs depending on the runlevel you choose from the Edit Runlevel menu. In effect, you are choosing which services to start at a given runlevel. The default is runlevel 5, the GUI startup level. You may want a different set of services started or stopped for runlevel 3, the command line startup level. In that case, you would select Runlevel 3 from the Edit Runlevel menu to display the services with selected check boxes for runlevel 3.

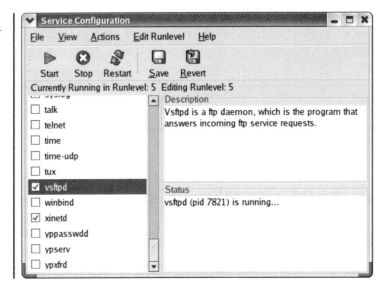

FIGURE **21-1**
The system-config-
services tool

chkconfig

You can specify the service you want to start and the level you want to start it at with the **chkconfig** command. Unlike other service management tools, **chkconfig** works equally well on stand-alone and **xinetd** services. Though stand-alone services can be run at any runlevel, you can also turn **xinetd** services on or off for the runlevels that **xinetd** runs in. Table 21-4 lists the different **chkconfig** options.

Option	Description
--level *runlevel*	Specifies a runlevel to turn on, turn off, or reset a service.
--list *service*	Lists startup information for services at different runlevels. **xinetd** services are just **on** or **off**. With no argument, all services are listed, including **xinetd** services.
--add *service*	Adds a service, creating links in the default-specified runlevels (or all runlevels, if none are specified).
--del *service*	Deletes all links for the service (startup and shutdown) in all runlevel directories.
service **on**	Turns a service on, creating a service link in the specified or default runlevel directories.
service **off**	Turns a service off, creating shutdown links in specified or default directories.
service **reset**	Resets service startup information, creating default links as specified in the **chkconfig** entry in the service's **init.d** service script.

TABLE **21-4**   Options for **chkconfig**

Listing Services with chkconfig

To see a list of services, use the `--list` option. A sampling of services managed by `chkconfig` are shown here. The on or off status of the service is shown at each runlevel, as are **xinetd** services and their statuses:

```
chkconfig -list
dhcpd  0:off 1:off 2:off 3:off 4:off 5:off 6:off
httpd  0:off 1:off 2:off 3:off 4:off 5:off 6:off
named  0:off 1:off 2:off 3:off 4:off 5:off 6:off
lpd    0:off 1:off 2:on  3:on  4:on  5:on  6:off
nfs    0:off 1:off 2:off 3:off 4:off 5:off 6:off
crond  0:off 1:off 2:on  3:on  4:on  5:on  6:off
xinetd 0:off 1:off 2:off 3:on  4:on  5:on  6:off
xinetd based services:
      time:      off
      finger:    off
      pop3s:     off
      swat:      on
```

Starting and Stopping Services with chkconfig

You use the **on** option to have a service started at specified runlevels, and the **off** option to disable it. You can specify the runlevel with the `--level` option. If no level is specified, `chkconfig` will use any `chkconfig` default information in a service's `init.d` service script. Fedora Core installs its services with `chkconfig` default information already entered (if this is missing, `chkconfig` will use runlevels 3, 4, and 5). The following example has the Web server (**httpd**) started at runlevel 5:

```
chkconfig --level 5 httpd on
```

The **off** option configures a service to shut down if the system enters a specified runlevel. The next example shuts down the Web server if runlevel 3 is entered. If the service is not running, it remains shut down:

```
chkconfig --level 3 httpd off
```

The **reset** option restores a service to its `chkconfig` default options as specified in the service's `init.d` service script:

```
chkconfig httpd reset
```

To see just the startup information for a service, you use just the service name with the `--list` option:

```
chkconfig --list httpd
httpd   0:off  1:off 2:off 3:on 4:off 5:on 6:off
```

Enabling and Disabling xinetd Services with chkconfig

Unlike system-config-services, `chkconfig` can also enable or disable **xinetd** services. Simply enter the **xinetd** service with either an **on** or **off** option. The service will be started up or shut down, and the disable line in its **xinetd** configuration script in the **/etc/xinetd.d** directory will be edited accordingly. For example, to start swat, the Samba configuration server, which runs on **xinetd**, you simply enter:

```
chkconfig swat on
chkconfig --list swat
     swat            on
```

The **swat** configuration file for **xinetd**, */etc/xinetd.d/swat*, will have its disable line edited to no, as shown here:

```
disable=no
```

If you want to shut down the swat server, you can use the **off** option. This will change the disable line in **/etc/xinetd.d/swat** to read "disable=yes".

```
chkconfig swat off
```

The same procedure works for other **xinetd** services such as the POP3 server and **finger**.

Removing and Adding Services with chkconfig
If you want a service removed entirely from the entire startup and shutdown process in all runlevels, you can use the **--del** option. This removes all startup and shutdown links in all the runlevel directories.

```
chkconfig --del httpd
```

You can also add services to **chkconfig** management with the **--add** option; **chkconfig** will create startup links for the new service in the appropriate startup directories, **/etc/rc.d/ rc***n***.d**. If you have previously removed all links for a service, you can restore them with the **add** option.

```
chkconfig --add httpd
```

Configuring xinetd Services for Use by chkconfig
Default runlevel information should be placed in the service scripts that are to be managed by **chkconfig**. Fedora Core has already placed this information in the service scripts for the services that are installed with its distribution. You can edit these scripts to change the default information if you wish. This information is entered as a line beginning with a **#** sign and followed by the **chkconfig** keyword and a colon. Then you list the default runlevels that the service should start up on, along with the start and stop priorities. The following entry lists runlevels 3 and 5 with a start priority of 85 and a stop of 15. See the section "Service Script Tags" later in this chapter for more information:

```
# chkconfig: 35 85 15
```

So when a user turns on the **httpd** service with no level option specified, **chkconfig** will start up **httpd** at runlevels 3 and 5.

```
chkconfig httpd on
```

How chkconfig Works

The **chkconfig** tool works by creating startup and shutdown links in the appropriate runlevel directories in the **/etc/rc.d** directory. For example, when **chkconfig** adds the **httpd** service at runlevel 5, it creates a link in the **/etc/rc.d/rc5.d** directory to the service script **httpd** in the **/etc/rc.d/init.d** directory. When it turns off the Web service from runlevel 3, it creates a shutdown link in the **/etc/rc.d/rc3.d** directory to use the script **httpd** in the **/etc/ rc.d/initd** directory to make sure the Web service is not started. In the following example, the user turns on the Web service (**httpd**) on runlevel 3, creating the startup link in **rc5.d**, **S85httpd**, and then turns off the Web service on runlevel 3, creating a shutdown link in **rc3.d**, **K15httpd**.

```
chkconfig --level 5 httpd on
ls /etc/rc.d/rc5.d/*httpd
   /etc/rc.d/rc5.d/S85httpd
chkconfig -level 3 httpd off
ls /etc/rc.d/rc3.d/*httpd
   /etc/rc.d/rc3.d/K15httpd
```

Service Scripts: /etc/init.d

Most software using RPM packages will automatically install any appropriate service scripts and create the needed links in the appropriate **rc*n*.d** directories, where *n* is the runlevel number. Service scripts, though, can be used for any program you may want run when your system starts up. To have such a program start automatically, you first create a service script for it in the **/etc/rc.d/init.d** directory and then create symbolic links to that script in the **/etc/rc.d/rc3.d** and **/etc/rc.d/rc5.d** directories. A shutdown link (*K*) should also be placed in the **rc6.d** directory used for runlevel 6 (reboot).

Service Script Functions

A simplified version of the service script **httpd** uses on Fedora Core systems is shown in a later section. You can see the different options, listed in the **/etc/rc.d/init.d/httpd** example, under the **case** statement: **start**, **stop**, **status**, **restart**, and **reload**. If no option is provided (*****), the script use syntax is displayed. The **httpd** script first executes a script to define functions used in these service scripts. The **daemon** function with **httpd** actually executes the **/usr/sbin/httpd** server program.

```
echo -n "Starting httpd: "
 daemon httpd
 echo
touch /var/lock/subsys/httpd
```

The **killproc** function shuts down the daemon. The lock file and the process ID file (**httpd.pid**) are then deleted:

```
killproc httpd
echo
rm -f /var/lock/subsys/httpd
rm -f /var/run/httpd.pid
```

Init Script Function	Description
`daemon` [+/−*nicelevel*] *program* [*arguments*] [&]	Starts a daemon, if it is not already running.
`killproc` *program* [*signal*]	Sends a signal to the program; by default it sends a **SIGTERM**, and if the process doesn't stop, it sends a **SIGKILL**. It will also remove any PID files, if it can.
`pidofproc` *program*	Used by another function, it determines the PID of a program.
`status` *program*	Displays status information.

TABLE **21-5**   Init Script Functions

The **daemon**, **killproc**, and **status** functions are shell scripts defined in the **functions** script, also located in the **inet.d** directory. The **functions** script is executed at the beginning of each service script to activate these functions. A list of these functions is provided in Table 21-5.

```
. /etc/rc.d/init.d/functions
```

Service Script Tags

The beginning of the service script holds tags used to configure the server. These tags, which begin with an initial **#** symbol, are used to provide runtime information about the service to your system. The tags are listed in Table 21-6, along with the service functions. You enter a tag with a preceding **#** symbol, the tag name with a colon, and then the tag arguments. For example, the **processname** tag specifies the name of the program being executed, in this example **httpd**:

```
# processname: httpd
```

If your script starts more than one daemon, you should have a **processname** entry for each. For example, the Samba service starts up both the **smdb** and **nmdb** daemons.

```
# processname: smdb
# processname: nmdb
```

The end of the tag section is indicated by an empty line. After this line, any lines beginning with a **#** are treated as comments. The **chkconfig** line lists the default runlevels that the service should start up on, along with the start and stop priorities. The following entry lists runlevels 3, 4, and 5 with a start priority of 85 and a stop of 15:

```
# chkconfig: 345 85 15
```

For the description, you enter a short explanation of the service, using the \ symbol before a newline to use more than one line.

```
# description: Apache Web server
```

Init Script Tags	Description
# `chkconfig`: *startlevellist startpriority endpriority*	Required. Specifies the default start levels for this service as well as start and end priorities.
# `description` [*ln*] : *description of service*	Required. The description of the service, continued with \ characters. Use an initial # for any added lines. With the *ln* option, you can specify the language the description is written in.
# `autoreload`: `true`	Optional. If this line exists, the daemon checks its configuration files and reloads them automatically when they change.
# `processname`: *program*	Optional, multiple entries allowed. The name of the program or daemon started in the script.
# `config`: *configuration-file*	Optional, multiple entries allowed. Specifies a configuration file used by the server.
# `pidfile`: *pid-file*	Optional, multiple entries allowed. Specifies the PID file.
# `probe`: `true`	Optional, used *in place* of `autoreload`, `processname`, `config`, and `pidfile` entries to automatically probe and start the service.

TABLE 21-6 System V init Script Tags

With `config` tags, you specify the configuration files the server may use. In the case of the Apache Web server, there may be three configuration files:

```
# config: /etc/httpd/conf/access.conf
# config: /etc/httpd/conf/httpd.conf
# config: /etc/httpd/conf/srm.conf
```

The **pidfile** entry indicates the file where the server's process ID is held.

Service Script Example

As an example, a simplified version of the Web server service script, **/etc.rc.d/init.d/httpd**, is shown here. Most scripts are much more complicated, particularly when determining any arguments or variables a server may need to specify when it starts up. This script has the same name as the Web server daemon, **httpd**:

```
#!/bin/sh
#
# Service script for the Apache Web Server
#
# chkconfig: 35 85 15
# description: Apache is a World Wide Web server. \
# It is used to serve HTML files and CGI.
```

```
# processname: httpd
# pidfile: /var/run/httpd.pid
# config: /etc/httpd/conf/access.conf
# config: /etc/httpd/conf/httpd.conf
# config: /etc/httpd/conf/srm.conf
# Source function library.
. /etc/rc.d/init.d/functions

# See how we were called.
case "$1" in
 start)
   echo -n "Starting httpd: "
     daemon httpd
     echo
     touch /var/lock/subsys/httpd
     ;;
   stop)
     killproc httpd
     echo
     rm -f /var/lock/subsys/httpd
     rm -f /var/run/httpd.pid
     ;;
 status)
     status httpd
     ;;
 restart)
     $0 stop
     $0 start
     ;;
 reload)
     echo -n "Reloading httpd: "
     killproc httpd -HUP
     echo
     ;;
 *)
     echo "Usage: $0 {start|stop|restart}"
     exit 1
 esac
exit 0
```

Installing Service Scripts

The RPM-packaged version for a service includes a service script. For example, an Internet server package includes the service script for that server. Installing the RPM package installs the script in the **/etc/rc.d/init.d** directory and creates its appropriate links in the runlevel directories, such as **/etc/rc.h/rc3.d**. If you decide, instead, to create the server using its source code files, you can then manually install the service script. If no service script exists, you first make a copy of the **httpd** script—renaming it—and then edit the copy to replace all references to **httpd** with the name of the server daemon program. Then place the copy of the script in the **/etc/rc.d/init.d** directory and make a symbolic link to it in the **/etc/rc.d/ rc3.d** directory. Or you could use system-config-services to create the link in the **/etc/rc.d/rc3.d** directory. Select File | Refresh Services. When you start your system now, the new server is automatically started up, running concurrently and waiting for requests.

Extended Internet Services Daemon (xinetd)

If your system averages only a few requests for a specific service, you don't need the server for that service running all the time. You need it only when a remote user is accessing its service. The Extended Internet Services Daemon (**xinetd**) manages Internet servers, invoking them only when your system receives a request for their services. **xinetd** checks continuously for any requests by remote users for a particular Internet service; when it receives a request, it then starts the appropriate server daemon.

The **xinetd** program is designed to be a replacement for **inetd**, providing security enhancements, logging support, and even user notifications. For example, with **xinetd** you can send banner notices to users when they are not able to access a service, telling them why. **xinetd** security capabilities can be used to prevent denial-of-service attacks, limiting remote hosts' simultaneous connections or restricting the rate of incoming connections. **xinetd** also incorporates TCP, providing TCP security without the need to invoke the **tcpd** daemon. Furthermore, you do not have to have a service listed in the **/etc/services** file. **xinetd** can be set up to start any kind of special-purpose server. The Red Hat Linux versions 7.0 and up use **xinetd**.

Starting and Stopping xinetd Services

You can start, stop, and restart **xinetd** using its service script in the **/etc/rc.d/init.d** directory, as shown here:

```
# service xinetd start
# service xinetd stop
# service xinetd restart
```

On Red Hat, you can also turn on and off particular **xinetd** services with **chkconfig**, as described earlier. Use the **on** and **off** options to enable or disable a service; **chkconfig** will edit the disable option for the service, changing its value to "yes" for off and "no" for on. For example, to enable the swat server, you could enter:

```
chkconfig swat on
```

xinetd Configuration: xinetd.conf

The **xinetd.conf** file is the configuration file for **xinetd**. Entries in it define different servers to be activated when requested along with any options and security precautions. An entry consists of a block of attributes defined for different features, such as the name of the server program, the protocol used, and security restrictions. Each block for an Internet service such as a server is preceded by the keyword **service** and the name by which you want to identify the service. A pair of braces encloses the block of attributes. Each attribute entry begins with the attribute name, followed by an assignment operator, such as **=**, and then the value or values assigned. A special block specified by the keyword **default** contains default attributes for services. The syntax is shown here:

```
service <service_name>
{
<attribute> <assign_op> <value> <value> ...
 ...
}
```

xinetd Attributes

Most attributes take a single value for which you use the standard assignment operator, **=**. Some attributes can take a list of values. You can assign values with the = operator, but you can also add or remove items from these lists with the **=+** and **=-** operators. Use **=+** to add values and **=-** to remove values. You often use the **=+** and **=-** operators to add values to attributes that may have an initial value assigned in the default block.

Attributes are listed in Table 21-7. Certain attributes are required for a service. These include **socket_type** and **wait**. For a standard Internet service, you also need to provide the **user** (user ID for the service), the **server** (name of the server program), and the **protocol** (protocol used by the server). With **server_args**, you can also list any arguments you want passed to the server program (this does not include the server name as with **tcpd**). If **protocol** is not defined, the default protocol for the service is used.

```
service tftp
    {
      socket_type = dgram
      wait = no
      user = root
      protocol = udp
      server = /usr/sbin/in.tftpd
      server_args = -s /tfpdboot
      disable = yes
    }
```

Attribute	Description
ids	Identifies a service. By default, the service ID is the same as the service name.
type	Type of service: **RPC**, **INTERNAL** (provided by **xinetd**), or **UNLISTED** (not listed in a standard system file).
flags	Possible flags include **REUSE**, **INTERCEPT**, **NORETRY**, **IDONLY**, **NAMEINARGS** (allows use of **tcpd**), **NODELAY**, and **DISABLE** (disable the service). See the **xinetd.conf** Man page for more details.
disable	Specify **yes** to disable the service.
socket_type	Specify **stream** for a stream-based service, **dgram** for a datagram-based service, **raw** for a service that requires direct access to IP, and **seqpacket** for reliable sequential datagram transmission.
protocol	Specifies a protocol for the service. The protocol must exist in **/etc/protocols**. If this attribute is not defined, the default protocol employed by the service will be used.
wait	Specifies whether the service is single-threaded or multithreaded (**yes** or **no**). If **yes**, the service is single-threaded, which means that **xinetd** will start the server and then stop handling requests for the service until the server stops. If **no**, the service is multithreaded and **xinetd** will continue to handle new requests for it.
user	Specifies the user ID (UID) for the server process. The username must exist in **/etc/passwd**.
group	Specifies the GID for the server process. The group name must exist in **/etc/group**.
instances	Specifies the number of server processes that can be simultaneously active for a service.
nice	Specifies the server priority.

TABLE 21-7 Attributes for **xinetd**

Attribute	Description
`server`	Specifies the program to execute for this service.
`server_args`	Lists the arguments passed to the server. This does not include the server name.
`only_from`	Controls the remote hosts to which the particular service is available. Its value is a list of IP addresses. With no value, service is denied to all remote hosts.
`no_access`	Controls the remote hosts to which the particular service is unavailable.
`access_times`	Specifies the time intervals when the service is available. An interval has the form hour: min-hour:min.
`log_type`	Specifies where the output of the service log is sent, either the syslog facility (**SYSLOG**) or a file (**FILE**).
`log_on_success`	Specifies the information that is logged when a server starts and stops. Information you can specify includes **PID** (server process ID), **HOST** (the remote host address), **USERID** (the remote user), **EXIT** (exit status and termination signal), and **DURATION** (duration of a service session).
`log_on_failure`	Specifies the information that is logged when a server cannot be started. Information you can specify includes **HOST** (the remote host address), **USERID** (user ID of the remote user), **ATTEMPT** (logs a failed attempt), and **RECORD** (records information from the remote host to allow monitoring of attempts to access the server).
`rpc_version`	Specifies the RPC version for an RPC service.
`rpc_number`	Specifies the number for an UNLISTED RPC service.
`env`	Defines environment variables for a service.
`passenv`	The list of environment variables from **xinetd**'s environment that will be passed to the server.
`port`	Specifies the service port.
`redirect`	Allows a TCP service to be redirected to another host.
`bind`	Allows a service to be bound to a specific interface on the machine.
`interface`	Synonym for **bind**.
`banner`	The name of a file to be displayed for a remote host when a connection to that service is established.
`banner_success`	The name of a file to be displayed at the remote host when a connection to that service is granted.
`banner_fail`	The name of a file to be displayed at the remote host when a connection to that service is denied.
`groups`	Allows access to groups the service has access to (**yes** or **no**).
`enabled`	Specifies the list of service names to enable.
`include`	Inserts the contents of a specified file as part of the configuration file.
`includedir`	Takes a directory name in the form of `includedir /etc/xinetd.d`. Every file inside that directory will be read sequentially as an **xinetd** configuration file, combining to form the **xinetd** configuration.

TABLE 21-7 Attributes for **xinetd** *(continued)*

Disabling and Enabling xinetd Services

Services can be turned on and off with the `disable` attribute. To enable a service, you set the `disable` attribute to **no**, as shown here:

```
disable = no
```

You then have to restart **xinetd** to start the service.

```
# /etc/rc.d/init.d/xinetd restart
```

TIP *Fedora Core currently disables all the services it initially set up when it installs **xinetd**. To enable a particular service, you will have to set its disable attribute to **no**.*

To enable management by **chkconfig**, a commented default and description entry needs to be placed before each service segment. Where separate files are used, the entry is placed at the head of each file. Fedora Core already provides these for the services it installs with its distribution, such as POP3 and SWAT. A default entry can be either on or off. For example, the **chkconfig** default and description entries for the FTP service are shown here:

```
# default: off
# description: The POP3 service allows users\
#     to access their mail using a POP3 client \
#     such as Netscape Communicator, or fetchmail.
```

Fedora Core indicates whether a service is set on or off by default. If you want to turn on a service that is off by default, you have to set its **disable** attribute to **no** and restart **xinetd**. The Fedora Core entry for the POP3 mail server, **ipop3d**, is shown here. An initial comment tells you that it is off by default, but then the **disable** attribute turns it on:

```
# default: off
# description: The POP3 service allows users\
#     to access their mail using a POP3 client \
#     such as Netscape Communicator, or fetchmail.
service pop3
{
    socket_type      = stream
    wait             = no
    user          = root
    server           = /usr/sbin/ipop3d
    log_on_success += HOST_DURATION
    log_on_failure += HOST
    disable          = no
}
```

Logging xinetd Services

You can further add a variety of other attributes such as logging information about connections and server priority (**nice**). In the following example, the **log_on_success** attribute logs the duration (**DURATION**) and the user ID (**USERID**) for connections to a service, **log_on_failure** logs the users that failed to connect, and **nice** sets the priority of the service to 10.

```
log_on_success += DURATION USERID
log_on_failure += USERID
nice = 10
```

The default attributes defined in the defaults block often set global attributes such as default logging activity and security restrictions: **log_type** specifies where logging information is to be sent, such as to a specific file (**FILE**) or to the system logger (**SYSLOG**),

`log_on_success` specifies information to be logged when connections are made, and `log_on_failure` specifies information to be logged when they fail.

```
log_type = SYSLOG authpriv
log_on_success = HOST PID
log_on_failure = HOST RECORD
```

xinetd Network Security

For security restrictions, you can use `only_from` to restrict access by certain remote hosts. The `no_access` attribute denies access from the listed hosts, but no others. These controls take IP addresses as their values. You can list individual IP addresses, a range of IP addresses, or a network, using the network address. The **instances** attribute limits the number of server processes that can be active at once for a particular service. The following examples restrict access to a local network 192.168.1.0 and the localhost, deny access from 192.168.1.15, and use the **instances** attribute to limit the number of server processes at one time to 60.

```
only_from = 192.168.1.0
only_from = localhost
no_access = 192.168.1.15
instances = 60
```

xinetd Defaults and Internal Services

A sample default block is shown here:

```
defaults
{
 instances = 60
 log_type = FILE /var/log/servicelog
 log_on_success = HOST PID
 log_on_failure = HOST RECORD
 only_from = 192.168.1.0
 only_from = localhost
 no_access = 192.168.1.15
}
```

The **xinetd** program also provides several internal services, including **time**, **services**, and **servers**, and **xadmin**: **services** provides a list of currently active services, and **servers** provides information about servers; **xadmin** provides **xinetd** administrative support.

Service Files in xinetd.d Directory

Instead of having one large **xinetd.conf** file, you can split it into several configuration files, one for each service. You do this by creating an **xinetd.conf** file with an **includedir** attribute that specifies a directory to hold the different service configuration files. In the following example, the **xinetd.d** directory holds **xinetd** configuration files for services like swat. Fedora Core uses just such an implementation. This approach has the advantage of letting you add services by just creating a new configuration file for them. Modifying a service involves editing only its configuration file, not an entire **xinetd.conf** file.

```
includedir /etc/xinetd.d
```

The following example shows the **xinetd.conf** file used for Fedora Core Linux:

```
#
# Simple configuration file for xinetd
# Some defaults, and include /etc/xinetd.d/

defaults
{
    instances                = 60
    log_type                  = SYSLOG authpriv
    log_on_success     = HOST PID
    log_on_failure      = HOST
    cps                          =  25 30
}
includedir /etc/xinetd.d
```

As an example, the **swat** file in the **xinetd.d** directory is shown here. Notice that it is disabled by default:

```
# default: off
# description: SWAT is the Samba Web Admin Tool.\
# Use swat to configure your Samba server. \
# To use SWAT, connect to port 901 with your \
# favorite web browser.
service swat
{
    port                     = 901
    socket_type      = stream
    wait                     = no
    only_from        = localhost
    user                     = root
    server                   = /usr/sbin/swat
    log_on_failure    += USERID
    disable                = yes
}
```

TCP Wrappers

TCP wrappers add another level of security to **xinetd**-managed servers. In effect, the server is wrapped with an intervening level of security, monitoring connections and controlling access. A server connection made through **xinetd** is monitored, verifying remote user identities and checking to make sure they are making valid requests. Connections are logged with the **syslogd** daemon (see Chapter 29) and may be found in **syslogd** files such as **/var/log/secure**. With TCP wrappers, you can also restrict access to your system by remote hosts. Lists of hosts are kept in the **hosts.allow** and **hosts.deny** files. Entries in these files have the format `service:hostname:domain`. The domain is optional. For the service, you can specify a particular service, such as FTP, or you can enter **ALL** for all services. For the hostname, you can specify a particular host or use a wildcard to match several hosts. For example, **ALL** will match on all hosts. Table 21-8 lists the available wildcards. In the following example, the first entry allows access by all hosts to the Web service, **http**. The second entry allows access to all services by the **pango1.train.com** host. The third and fourth entries allow FTP access to **rabbit.trek.com** and **sparrow.com**:

```
http:ALL
ALL:pango1.train.com
ftp:rabbit.trek.com
ftp:sparrow.com
```

The **hosts.allow** file holds hosts to which you allow access. If you want to allow access to all but a few specific hosts, you can specify **ALL** for a service in the **hosts.allow** file but list the ones you are denying access to in the **hosts.deny** file. Using IP addresses instead of hostnames is more secure because hostnames can be compromised through the DNS records by spoofing attacks where an attacker pretends to be another host.

When **xinetd** receives a request for an FTP service, a TCP wrapper monitors the connection and starts up the **in.ftpd** server program. By default, all requests are allowed. To allow all requests specifically for the FTP service, you would enter the following in your **/etc/hosts.allow** file. The entry **ALL:ALL** opens your system to all hosts for all services:

```
ftp:ALL
```

TIP   *Originally, TCP wrappers were managed by the **tcpd** daemon. However, **xinetd** has since integrated support for TCP wrappers into its own program. You can explicitly invoke the **tcpd** daemon to handle services if you wish. The **tcpd** Man pages (**man tcpd**) provide more detailed information about **tcpd**.*

Wildcard	Description
ALL	Matches all hosts or services.
LOCAL	Matches any host specified with just a hostname without a domain name. Used to match on hosts in the local domain.
UNKNOWN	Matches any user or host whose name or address is unknown.
KNOWN	Matches any user or host whose name or address is known.
PARANOID	Matches any host whose hostname does not match its IP address.
EXCEPT	An operator that lets you provide exceptions to matches. It takes the form of *list1* **EXCEPT** *list2* where those hosts matched in *list1* that are also matched in *list2* are excluded.

TABLE 21-8   TCP Wrapper Wildcards

PART V

FTP Servers

The File Transfer Protocol (FTP) is designed to transfer large files across a network from one system to another. Like most Internet operations, FTP works on a client/server model. FTP client programs can enable users to transfer files to and from a remote system running an FTP server program. Chapter 14 discusses FTP clients. Any Linux system can operate as an FTP server. It only has to run the server software—an FTP daemon with the appropriate configuration. Transfers are made between user accounts on client and server systems. A user on the remote system has to log in to an account on a server and can then transfer files to and from that account's directories only. A special kind of user account, named *ftp*, allows any user to log in to it with the username "anonymous." This account has its own set of directories and files that are considered public, available to anyone on the network who wants to download them. The numerous FTP sites on the Internet are FTP servers supporting FTP user accounts with anonymous login. Any Linux system can be configured to support anonymous FTP access, turning such a system into a network FTP site. Such sites can work on an intranet or on the Internet.

NOTE *On Fedora Core, the configuration files for anonymous FTP are now included with the vsftpd package. Installing this package sets up your FTP directories and configures the FTP account.*

FTP Servers

FTP server software consists of an FTP daemon and configuration files. The *daemon* is a program that continuously checks for FTP requests from remote users. When a request is received, it manages a login, sets up the connection to the requested user account, and executes any FTP commands the remote user sends. For anonymous FTP access, the FTP daemon allows the remote user to log in to the FTP account using anonymous or ftp as the username. The user then has access to the directories and files set up for the FTP account. As a further security measure, however, the daemon changes the root directory for that session to be the FTP home directory. This hides the rest of the system from the remote user. Normally, any user on a system can move around to any directories open to him or her. A user logging in with anonymous FTP can see only the FTP home directory and its subdirectories. The remainder of the system is hidden from that user. This effect is achieved by the **chroot** operation (discussed later) that literally changes the system root directory for that user to that of the FTP directory. By default, the FTP server also requires a user be using a valid shell. It checks for a list of valid shells in the **/etc/shells** file. Most daemons have options for turning off this feature.

Available Servers

Several FTP servers are available for use on Fedora Core systems (see Table 22-1). Fedora Core comes with the Very Secure FTP Server, vsftpd. You can download RPM package updates for particular distributions from their FTP sites, such as **ftp.redhat.com**. The software package contains the term *ftpd*. The Very Secure FTP Server provides a simple and more secure alternative to WU-FTPD, though it lacks the security options and configurability of ProFTPD.

ProFTPD is a popular FTP daemon based on an Apache Web server design. It features simplified configuration and support for virtual FTP hosts. Although it is not currently included with most distributions, you can download RPM packages from the ProFTPD site and from **freshrpms.net**. The package begins with the term *proftpd*. The compressed archive of the most up-to-date version, along with documentation, is available at the ProFTPD Web site at **www.proftpd.org**. Another FTP daemon, NcFTPd, is a commercial product produced by the same programmers who did the NcFTP FTP client. NcFTPd is free for academic use and features a reduced fee for small networks. Check **www.ncftpd.org** for more information.

Several security-based FTP servers are also available, including SSLFTP and SSH **sftpd**, along with **gssftpd**. SSLFTP uses SSL (Secure Sockets Layer) to encrypt and authenticate transmissions, as well as MD5 digests to check the integrity of transmitted files. SSH **sftpd** is an FTP server that is now part of the OpenSSH package, using SSH encryption and authentication to establish secure FTP connections. The **gssftpd** server is part of the Kerberos 5 package and provides Kerberos-level security for FTP operations.

Fedora Core FTP Server Directories

Fedora Core currently installs the **vsftpd** server package along with anonymous FTP support during installation. At that time, an **ftp** directory is created along with several subdirectories where you can place files for FTP access. The directories have already been configured to control access by remote users, restricting use to only the **ftp** directories and any subdirectories. The **ftp** directory is placed in different directories by different distributions. The **ftp** directory is placed in the **/var** directory, **/var/ftp**. Place the files you want to allow access to in the **/var/ftp/pub** directory. For example, on Fedora Core this would be at **/var/ftp/pub**.

TABLE 22-1
FTP Servers

FTP Server	Site
Very Secure FTP Server (vsftpd)	**vsftpd.beasts.org**
ProFTPD	**www.proftpd.org (freshrpms.net)**
NcFTPd	**www.ncftpd.org**
SSH sftp-server	**www.openssh.org**
Washington University Web server (WU-FTPD)	**www.wu-ftpd.org**
Tux	Web server with FTP capabilities
gssftpd	Kerberos FTP server

You can also create subdirectories and place files there. Once you are connected to a network, a remote user can connect to your system and download files you placed in **/var/ftp/pub** or any of its subdirectories. The **vsftpd** FTP package implements a default configuration for those directories and their files. You can change these if you want. If you are installing an FTP server yourself, you need to know the procedures detailed in the following sections to install an FTP server and create its data directories.

The **vsftpd** FTP package does not create a directory where users can upload files to the FTP site. Such a directory is usually named the incoming directory, located at **ftp/pub/upload**. If you want such a directory, you will have to create it, make it part of the **ftp** group, and then set its permissions to allow users write access.

```
chgrp ftp /var/ftp/pub/upload
chmod g+w /var/ftp/pub/upload
```

FTP Users

Normal users with accounts on an FTP server can gain full FTP access simply by logging into their accounts. Such users can access and transfer files directly from their own accounts or any directories they may have access to. You can also create users, known as guest users, that have restricted access to the FTP publicly accessible directories. This involves setting standard user restrictions, with the FTP public directory as their home directory. Users can also log in as anonymous users, allowing anyone on the network or Internet to access files on an FTP server.

Anonymous FTP: vsftpd

An anonymous FTP site is essentially a special kind of user on your system with publicly accessible directories and files in its home directory. Anyone can log in to this account and access its files. Because anyone can log in to an anonymous FTP account, you must be careful to restrict a remote FTP user to only the files on that anonymous FTP directory. Normally, a user's files are interconnected to the entire file structure of your system. Normal users have write access that lets them create or delete files and directories. The anonymous FTP files and directories can be configured in such a way that the rest of the file system is hidden from them and remote users are given only read access. In ProFTPD, this is achieved through configuration directives placed in its configuration file. An older approach involves having copies of certain system configuration, command, and library files placed within subdirectories of the FTP home directory. Restrictions placed on those subdirectories then control access by other users. Within the FTP home directory, you then have a publicly accessible directory that holds the files you want to make available to remote users. This directory usually has the name **pub**, for public.

An FTP site is made up of an FTP user account, an FTP home directory, and certain copies of system directories containing selected configuration and support files. Newer FTP daemons, such as ProFTPD, do not need the system directories and support files. Most distributions have already set up an FTP user account when you installed your system.

*****

NOTE *On Fedora Core, the **vsftpd** RPM package will set up the home directory and the copies of the system directories when it is installed. If, for some reason, you do not want to use the **vsftpd** RPM package (like recompiling the source code), you may have to create these system directories yourself.*

The FTP User Account: anonymous

To allow anonymous FTP access by other users to your system, you must have a user account named *FTP*. Most distributions already create this account for you. If your system does not have such an account, you will have to create one. You can then place restrictions on the FTP account to keep any remote FTP users from accessing any other part of your system. You must also modify the entry for this account in your **/etc/passwd** file to prevent normal user access to it. The following is the entry you find in your **/etc/passwd** file on Fedora Core systems that sets up an FTP login as an anonymous user:

```
ftp:x:14:50:FTP User:/var/ftp:
```

The **x** in the password field blocks the account, which prevents any other users from gaining access to it, thereby gaining control over its files or access to other parts of your system. The user ID, 14, is a unique ID. The comment field is FTP User. The login directory is **/var/ftp**. When FTP users log in to your system, they are placed in this directory. If a home directory has not been set up, create one and then change its ownership to the FTP user with the **chown** command.

FTP Group

The group ID is the ID of the **ftp** group, which is set up only for anonymous FTP users. You can set up restrictions on the **ftp** group, thereby restricting any anonymous FTP users. Here is the entry for the **ftp** group you find in the **/etc/group** file. If your system does not have one, you should add it:

```
ftp::50:
```

Creating New FTP Users

If you are creating virtual FTP hosts, you will need to create an FTP user for each one, along with its directories. For example, to create an FTP server for a host1-ftp host, you would create a host1-ftp user with its own directory.

```
useradd -d /var/host1-ftp host1-ftp
```

This would create a user such as that described here:

```
host1-ftp:x:14:50:FTP User:/var/host1-ftp:
```

You would also need to create the corresponding home directory, **/var/host1-ftp** in this example, and set its permissions to give users restricted access.

```
mkdir /var/host1-ftp
chmod 755 /var/host1-ftp
```

You also need to make sure that the root user owns the directory, not the new FTP users. This gives control of the directory only to the root user, not to any user that logs in.

```
chown root.root /var/host1-ftp
```

Anonymous FTP Server Directories

As previously noted, the FTP home directory is named **ftp** and is placed in the **/var** directory. When users log in anonymously, they are placed in this directory. An important part of protecting your system is preventing remote users from using any commands or programs not in the restricted directories. For example, you would not let a user use your **ls** command to list filenames, because **ls** is located in your **/bin** directory. At the same time, you want to let the FTP user list filenames using an **ls** command. Newer FTP daemons like vsftpd and ProFTPD solve this problem by creating secure access to needed system commands and files, while restricting remote users to only the FTP site's directories. In any event, make sure that the FTP home directory is owned by the root user, not by the FTP user. Use the **ls -d** command to check on the ownership of the FTP directory.

```
ls -d /var/ftp
```

To change a directory's ownership, you use the **chown** command, as shown in this example:

```
chown  root.root /var/ftp
```

Another, more traditional, solution is to create copies of certain system directories and files needed by remote users and to place them in the **ftp** directory where users can access them. A **bin** directory is placed in the **ftp** directory and remote users are restricted to it, instead of the system's **bin** directory. Whenever they use the **ls** command, remote users are using the one in **ftp/bin**, not the one you use in **/bin**. If, for some reason, you set up the anonymous FTP directories yourself, you must use the **chmod** command to change the access permissions for the directories so that remote users cannot access the rest of your system. Create an **ftp** directory and use the **chmod** command with the permission 555 to turn off write access: **chmod 555 ftp**. Next, make a new **bin** directory in the **ftp** directory, and then make a copy of the **ls** command and place it in **ftp/bin**. Do this for any commands you want to make available to FTP users. Then create an **ftp/etc** directory to hold a copy of your **passwd** and **group** files. Again, the idea is to prevent any access to the original files in the **/etc** directory by FTP users. The **ftp/etc/passwd** file should be edited to remove any entries for regular users on your system. All other entries should have their passwords set to **x** to block access. For the **group** file, remove all user groups and set all passwords to **x**. Create an **ftp/lib** directory, and then make copies of the libraries you need to run the commands you placed in the **bin** directory.

Anonymous FTP Files

A directory named **pub**, located in the FTP home directory, usually holds the files you are making available for downloading by remote FTP users. When FTP users log in, they are placed in the FTP home directory (**/var/ftp** on Fedora Core), and they can then change to the **pub** directory to start accessing those files (**/var/ftp/pub** on Fedora Core). Within the **pub** directory, you can add as many files and directories as you want. You can even designate some directories as upload directories, enabling FTP users to transfer files to your system.

In each subdirectory set up under the **pub** directory to hold FTP files, you should create a **README** file and an **INDEX** file as a courtesy to FTP users. The **README** file contains a brief description of the kind of files held in this directory. The **INDEX** file contains a listing of the files and a description of what each one holds.

Using FTP with rsync

Many FTP servers also support rsync operations using **rsync** as a daemon. This allows intelligent incremental updates of files from an FTP server. You can update multiple files in a directory or a single file such as a large ISO image.

Accessing FTP Sites with rsync

To access the FTP server running an rsync server, you enter the **rsync** command, and following the hostname, you enter a double colon and then either the path of the directory you want to access or one of the FTP server's modules. In the following example, the user updates a local **myproject** directory from the one on the **mytrek.com** FTP site:

```
rsync ftp.mytrek.com::/var/ftp/pub/myproject  /home/myproject
```

To find out what directories are supported by rsync, you check for rsync modules on that site. These are defined by the site's **/etc/rsyncd.conf** configuration file. A *module* is just a directory with all its subdirectories. To find available modules, you enter the FTP site with a double colon only.

```
rsync ftp.mytrek.com::
ftp
```

This tell me that the **ftp.mytrek.com** site has an FTP module. To list the files and directories on the module, you can use the **rsync** command with the **-r** option.

```
rsync -r ftp.mytrek.com::ftp
```

Many sites that run the rsync server will have an rsync protocol that will already be set to access the available rsync module (directory). For example, the following URL can be used with rsync to access the ibiblio location for the Fedora Core distribution. The module is named fedora-linux-core, which follows the hostname.

```
rsync://distro.ibiblio.org/fedora-linux-core/
```

You can even use rsync to update just a single file, such as an ISO image that may have been changed. The following example updates the Fedora Core 4 ISO disk 1 image. The **--progress** option will show the download progress.

```
rsync -a --progress rsync://distro.ibiblio.org/fedora-linux-core/3/i386/iso/
FC3-i386-disc1.iso
```

Configuring an rsync Server

To configure your FTP server to let clients use rsync on your site, you need to first run rsync as server. Use system-config-services or **chkconfig** to turn on the rsync daemon, commonly known as **rsyncd**. This will run the rsync daemon through **xinetd**, using an **rsync** script in **/etc/xinetd.d** to turn it on and set parameters.

```
chkconfig rsync on
```

When run as a daemon, rsync will read the **/etc/rsyncd.conf** file for its configuration options. Here you can specify FTP options such as the location for the FTP site files. The configuration file is segmented into modules, each with its own options. A module is a symbolic representation of an exported tree (a directory and its subdirectories). The module name is enclosed in brackets, for instance, **[ftp]** for an FTP module. You can then enter options for that module, as by using the path option to specify the location of your FTP site directories and files. The user and group IDs can be specified with the **uid** and **gid** options. The default is nobody. A sample FTP module for anonymous access is shown here:

```
[ftp]
        path = /var/ftp/pub
        comment = ftp site
```

For more restricted access, you could add an **auth users** option to specify authorized users; rsync will allow anonymous access to all users by default. The hosts allow or deny to control access from specific hosts. Access to areas on the FTP site by rsync can be further controlled using a secrets file, like **/etc/rsyncd.secrets**. This is a colon-separated list of usernames and passwords.

```
aleina:mypass3
larisa:yourp5
```

A corresponding module to the controlled area would look like this:

```
[specialftp]
        path = /var/projects/special
        command = restricted access
        auth users = aleina,larisa
        secrets file = /etc/rsyncd.secrets
```

If you are on your FTP server and want to see what modules will be made available, you can run **rsync** with the **localhost** option and nothing following the double colon.

```
$ rsync localhost::
ftp
specialftp
```

Remote users can find out what modules you have by entering your hostname and double colon only.

```
rsync ftp.mytrek.com::
```

rsync Mirroring

Some sites will allow you to use rsync to perform mirroring operations. With rsync you would not have to copy the entire site, just those files that have been changed. The following example will mirror the mytrek FTP site to the **/var/ftp/mirror/mytrek** directory on a local system:

```
rsync -a --delete ftp.mytrek.com::ftp /var/ftp/mirror/mytrek
```

The options uses are as follows: the **-a** option is archive mode, which includes several other options, such as **-r** (recursive) to include all subdirectories, **-t** to preserves file times and dates, **-l** recreate symbolic links, and **-p** to preserve all permissions. In addition, the **--delete** option is added to delete files that don't exist on the sending side, removing obsolete files.

The Very Secure FTP Server

The Very Secure FTP Server (vsftpd) is small, fast, easy, and secure. It is designed to avoid the overhead of large FTP server applications like ProFTPD, while maintaining a very high level of security. It can also handle a very large workload, managing high traffic levels on an FTP site. It is perhaps best for sites where many anonymous and guest users will be downloading the same files. Beginning with Red Hat 9, it replaced the Washington University FTP server, WU-FTPD.

The Very Secure FTP Server is inherently designed to provide as much security as possible, taking full advantage of Unix and Linux operating system features. The server is separated into privileged and unprivileged processes. The unprivileged process receives all FTP requests, interpreting them and then sending them over a socket to the privileged process, which then securely filters all requests. Even the privileged process does not run with full root capabilities, using only those that are necessary to perform its tasks. In addition, the Very Secure FTP Server uses its own version of directory commands like **ls**, instead of the system's versions.

Running vsftpd

The Very Secure FTP Server's daemon is named **vsftpd**. On Fedora Core, it is now designed to be run as a stand-alone server, which can be started and stopped using the **/etc/rc.d/init.d/vsftpd** server script. To start, stop, and restart **vsftpd**, you can use the **service** command.

```
service vsftpd start
```

To have the server start automatically, you can turn it on with the **chkconfig** command and the **on** argument, as shown here. Use the **off** argument to disable the server. If you previously enabled another FTP server such as ProFTPD, be sure to disable it first.

```
chkconfig vsftpd on
```

You can also use system-config-services to start and stop **vsftpd**, or to have it started automatically.

Alternatively, you can implement **vsftpd** to be run by **xinetd**, running the server only when a request is made by a user. The use of **xinetd** for the servers is described in detail in Chapter 21. The **xinetd** daemon will run an **xinetd** script file called **vsftpd** located in the **/etc/xinetd.d** directory. A copy of the xinetd vsftpd script is in **/usr/share/doc/vsftpd**-*version*.

Initially, the server will be turned off. You can turn it on in **xinetd** with the **chkconfig** command and the **on** argument, as shown here. Use the **off** argument to disable the server.

```
chkconfig vsftpd on
```

Restart **xinetd** with the **service** command (or system-config-services) to restart the **vsftpd** server, should you make configuration changes.

```
service xinetd restart
```

Configuring vsftpd

You configure **vsftpd** using one configuration file, **/etc/vsftpd/vsftpd.conf**, with several supporting files, all now located at **/etc/vsftpd** (see Table 22-2). (Use **vsftpd_conf_migrate.sh** to move old configuration files.) The **vsftpd.conf** file contains a set of directives where an option is assigned a value (there are no spaces around the = sign). Options can be on and off flags assigned a YES or NO value, features that take a numeric value, or ones that are assigned a string. Fedora Core installs a default **vsftpd.conf** file in the **/etc/vsftpd** directory. This file lists some of the commonly used options available with detailed explanations for each. Those not used are commented out with a preceding # character. Option names are very understandable. For example, **anon_upload_enable** allows anonymous users to upload files, whereas **anon_mkdir_write_enable** lets anonymous users create directories. The Man page for **vsftpd.conf** lists all options, providing a detailed explanation for each.

Option	Description
`listen`	Set stand-alone mode.
`listen_port`	Specify port for stand-alone mode.
`anonymous_enable`	Enable anonymous user access.
`local_enable`	Enable access by local users.
`no_anon_password`	Specify whether anonymous users must submit a password.
`anon_upload_enable`	Enable uploading by anonymous users.
`anon_mkdir_write_enable`	Allow anonymous users to create directories.
`anon_world_readable_only`	Make uploaded files read only to all users.
`idle_session_timeout`	Time limit in seconds for idle sessions.
`data_connection_timeouts`	Time limit in seconds for failed connections.
`dirmessage_enable`	Display directory messages.
`ftpd_banner`	Display FTP login message.
`xferlog_enable`	Enable logging of transmission transactions.
`xferlog_file`	Specify log file.
`deny_email_enable`	Enable denying anonymous users, whose e-mail addresses are specified in **/etc/vsftpd/banned_emails**.
`userlist_enable`	Deny access to users specified in the **/etc/vsftpd/user_list** file.
`userlist_file`	Deny or allow users access depending on setting of **userlist_deny**.
`userlist_deny`	When set to YES, **userlist_file** list users are denied access. When set to NO, **userlist_file** list users, and only those users, are allowed access.
`chroot_list_enable`	Restrict users to their home directories.
`chroot_list_file`	Allow users access to home directories. Unless **chroot_local_user** is set to YES, this file contains a list of users not allowed access to their home directories.
`chroot_local_user`	Allow access by all users to their home directories.
`pam_service_name`	Specify PAM script.
`ls_recurse_enable`	Enable recursive listing.

TABLE 22-2 Configuration Options for **vsftpd.conf**

PART V

Enabling Stand-Alone Access

To run **vsftpd** as a stand-alone server, you set the **listen** option to YES. This instructs **vsftpd** to continually listen on its assigned port for requests. You can specify the port it listens on with the **listen_port** option.

```
listen=YES
```

Enabling Login Access

In the following example taken from the **vsftpd.conf** file, anonymous FTP is enabled by assigning the YES value to the **anonymous_enable** option. The **local_enable** option allows local users on your system to use the FTP server.

```
# Allow anonymous FTP?
anonymous_enable=YES
#
# Uncomment this to allow local users to log in.
local_enable=YES
```

Should you want to let anonymous users log in without providing a password, you can set **no_anon_password** to YES.

Local User Permissions

A variety of user permissions control how local users can access files on the server. If you want to allow local users to create, rename, and delete files and directories on their account, you have to enable write access with the **write_enable** option. This way, any files they upload, they can also delete. Literally, the **write_enable** option activates a range of commands for changing the file system, including creating, renaming, and deleting both files and directories.

```
write_enable=YES
```

You can further specify the permissions for uploaded files using the **local_umask** option (022 is the default set by Fedora Core in **vsftpd.conf**, read and write for the owner and read only for all other users, 644).

```
local_umask=022
```

Though ASCII uploads are disabled by default, you can also enable this feature. ASCII uploads entail certain security risks and are turned off by default. But if you are uploading large text files, you may want to enable them in special cases. Use **ascii_upload_enable** to allow ASCII uploads.

Anonymous User Permissions

You can also allow anonymous users to upload and delete files, as well as create or remove directories. Uploading by anonymous users is enabled with the **anon_upload_enable** option. To let anonymous users also rename or delete their files, you set the **anon_other_write_enable** option. To also let them create directories, you set the **anon_mkdir_write_enable** option.

```
anon_upload_enable=YES
anon_other_write_enable=YES
anon_mkdir_write_enable=YES
```

The **anon_world_readable_only** option will make uploaded files read only (downloadable), restricting write access to the user that created them. Only the user that uploaded a file could delete it.

All uploaded files are owned by the anonymous FTP user. You can have the files owned by another user, adding greater possible security. In effect, the actual user owning the uploaded files becomes hidden from anonymous users. To enable this option, you use **chown_uploads** and specify the new user with **chown_username**. Never make the user an administrative user like root.

```
chown_uploads=YES
chown_username=myftpfiles
```

The upload directory itself should be given write permission by other users.

```
chmod 777 /var/ftp/pub/upload
```

You can control the kind of access that users have to files with the **anon_mask** option, setting default read/write permissions for uploaded files. The default is 077, which gives read/write permission to the owner only (600). To allow all users read access, you would set the umask to 022, where the 2 turns off write permission but sets read permission (644). The value 000 would allow both read and write for all users.

Connection Time Limits
To more efficiently control the workload on a server, you can set time limits on idle users and failed transmissions. The **idle_session_timeout** option will cut off idle users after a specified time, and **data_connection_timeout** will cut off failed data connections. The defaults are shown here:

```
idle_session_timeout=600
data_connection_timeout=120
```

Messages
The **dirmessage_enable** option will allow a message held in a directory's **.message** file to be displayed whenever a user accesses that directory. The **ftpd_banner** option lets you set up your own FTP login message. The default is shown here:

```
ftpd_banner=Welcome to blah FTP service.
```

Logging
A set of **xferlog** options control logging. You can enable logging, as well as specify the format and the location of the file.

```
xferlog_enable=YES
```

Use the **xferlog_file** option to specify the log file you want to use. The default is shown here:

```
xferlog_file=/var/log/vsftpd.log
```

vsftpd Access Controls

Certain options control access to the FTP site. As previously noted, the **anonymous_enable** option allows anonymous users access, and **local_enable** permits local users to log in to their accounts.

Denying Access

The **deny_email_enable** option lets you deny access by anonymous users, and the **banned_email** file option designates the file (usually **/etc/vstfpd/banned_emails**) that holds the e-mail addresses of those users. The **/etc/vsftpd/ftpusers** file lists those users that can never be accessed. These are usually system users like root, mail, and nobody. See Table 22-3 for a list of vsftpd files.

User Access

The **userlist_enable** option controls access by users, denying access to those listed in the file designated by the **userlist_file** option (usually **/etc/vsftpd/user_list**). If, instead, you want to restrict access to just certain select users, you can change the meaning and usage of the **vsftpd/user_list** file to indicate only those users allowed access, instead of those denied access. To do this, you set the **userlist_deny** option to NO (its default is YES). Only users listed in the **user_list** file will be granted access to the FTP site.

User Restrictions

The **chroot_list_enable** option controls access by local users, letting them access only their home directories, while restricting system access. The **chroot_list_file** option designates the file (usually **/etc/vstfpd/chroot_list**) that lists those users allowed access. You can allow access by all local users with the **chroot_local_user** option. If this option is set, then the file designated by **chroot_list_file** will have an inverse meaning, listing those users not allowed access. In the following example, access by local users is limited to those listed in **/etc/vsftpd/chroot_list**:

```
chroot_list_enable=YES
chroot_list_file=/etc/vsftpd/chroot_list
```

TABLE 22-3
Files for vsftpd

File	Description
/etc/vsftpd/ftpusers	Users always denied access
/etc/vsftpd/user_list	Specified users denied access (allowed access if **userlist_deny** is NO)
/etc/vsftpd/chroot_list	Local users allowed access (denied access if **chroot_local_user** is on)
/etc/vsftpd/vsftpd.conf	vsftpd configuration file
/etc/pam.d/vsftpd	PAM vsftpd script
/etc/rc.d/init.d/vsftpd	Service vsftpd server script, stand-alone (Fedora Core default)
/etc/xinetd.d/vsftpd	xinetd vsftpd server script (not installed on Fedora Core)

User Authentication

The **vsftpd** server makes use of the PAM service to authenticate local users that are remotely accessing their accounts through FTP. In the **vsftpd.conf** file, the PAM script used for the server is specified with the **pam_service_name** option.

```
pam_service_name=vsftpd
```

In the **etc/pam.d** directory, you will find a PAM file named **vsftpd** with entries for controlling access to the **vsftpd** server. PAM is currently set up to authenticate users with valid accounts, as well as deny access to users in the **/etc/vsftpd.ftpusers** file. The default **/etc/pam.d/vsftpd** file is shown here:

```
#%PAM-1.0
auth required pam_listfile.so item=user sense=deny
              file=/etc/vsftpd.ftpusers onerr=succeed
auth    required  pam_stack.so service=system-auth
auth    required  pam_shells.so
account required  pam_stack.so service=system-auth
session required  pam_stack.so service=system-auth
```

Command Access

Command usage is highly restricted by **vsftpd**. Most options for the **ls** command that lists files are not allowed. Only the asterisk file-matching operation is supported (see Chapter 8). To enable recursive listing of files in subdirectories, you have to enable the use of the **-R** option by setting the **ls_recurse_enable** option to YES. Some clients, such as **ncftp** (see Chapter 14), will assume that the recursive option is enabled.

vsftpd Virtual Hosts

Though the capability is not inherently built in to **vsftpd**, you can configure and set up the **vsftpd** server to support virtual hosts. *Virtual hosting* is where a single FTP server operates as if it has two or more IP addresses. Several IP addresses can then be used to access the same server. The server will then use a separate FTP user directory and files for each host. With **vsftpd**, this involves manually creating separate FTP users and directories for each virtual host, along with separate **vsftpd** configuration files for each virtual host in the **/etc/ vsftpd** directory. On Fedora Core, **vsftpd** is configured to run as a stand-alone service. Its **/etc/rc.d/init.d/vsftpd** startup script will automatically search for and read any configuration files listed in the **/etc/vsftpd** directory.

If, on the other hand, you wish to run **vsftpd** as a **xinetd** service, you would have to create a separate **xinetd** service script for each host in the **/etc/xinetd.d** directory. In effect, you have several **vsftpd** services running in parallel for each separate virtual host. The following example uses two IP addresses for an FTP server:

- First, create an FTP user for each host. Create directories for each host (you could use the one already set up for one of the users). For example, for the first virtual host you could use **FTP-host1**. Be sure to set root ownership and the appropriate permissions.

```
useradd -d /var/ftp-host1 FTP-host1
chown root.root /var/ftp-host1
chmod a+rx /var/ftp-host1
umask 022
mkdir /var/ftp-host1/pub
```

- Set up two corresponding **vsftpd** service scripts in the **/etc/xinetd.d** directory. On Fedora Core, the **vsftpd** directory in **/usr/share/doc** has an **xinetd** example script, **vsftpd.xinetd**. Within each, enter a **bind** command to specify the IP address the server will respond to.

  ```
  bind  192.168.0.34
  ```

- Within the same scripts, enter a **server_args** entry specifying the name of the configuration file to use.

  ```
  server_args = vsftpd-host1.conf
  ```

- Within the **/etc/vsftpd** directory, create separate configuration files for each virtual host. Within each, specify the FTP user you created for each, using the **ftp_username** entry.

  ```
  ftp_username = FTP-host1
  ```

vsftpd Virtual Users

Virtual users can be implemented by making use of PAM to authenticate authorized users. In effect, you are allowing access to certain users, while not having to actually set up accounts for them on the FTP server system. First create a PAM login database file to use along with a PAM file in the **/etc/pam.d** directory that will access the database. Then create a virtual FTP user along with corresponding directories that the virtual users will access (see the vsftpd documentation at **vsftpd.beasts.org** for more detailed information). Then in the **vsftpd.conf** file, you can disable anonymous FTP:

```
anonymous_enable=NO
local_enable=YES
```

and then enable guest access:

```
guest_enable=YES
guest_username=virtual
```

Professional FTP Daemon: ProFTPD

ProFTPD is based on the same design as the Apache Web server, implementing a similar simplified configuration structure and supporting such flexible features as virtual hosting. ProFTPD is an open source project made available under a GPL license. You can download the current version from its Web site at **www.proftpd.org**. There you will also find detailed documentation including FAQs, user manuals, and sample configurations. Check the site for new releases and updates.

RPM packages are available for many distributions, and from **freshrpms.net** and **www.proftpd.org**. Unlike when installing other FTP daemons, you do not need to set up special subdirectories of system files in the FTP home directory. No special **bin** or **etc** files are needed. You can also set up ProFTPD to alternate automatically between **xinetd** startups or as a stand-alone server constantly running, depending on the system load.

Web Servers: Apache

L inux distributions provide several Web servers for use on your system. The primary Web server is normally Apache, which has almost become the standard Web server for Red Hat Enterprise Linux and Fedora Core. It is a very powerful, stable, and fairly easy-to-configure system. Other Web servers are also available, such as Tux. Tux is smaller, but very fast, and is very efficient at handling Web data that does not change. Red Hat Enterprise Linux and Fedora Core provide default configurations for the Web servers, making them usable as soon as they are installed.

Apache freely supports full secure shell encryption using OpenSSL. There are also private cryptographic products available only with licensing fees. Instead of obtaining the licensing directly, you can simply buy a commercial version of Apache that includes such licensing such as Stronghold and Raven (**www.covalent.net**). Formerly, this kind of restriction applied to the use of RSA technology only in the United States, where it was once patented. The RSA patent has since expired and is now available for use in freely distributed products like OpenSSL.

Tux

Tux, the Red Hat Content Accelerator, is a static-content Web server designed to be run very fast from within the Linux kernel. In effect, it runs in kernel space, making response times much faster than standard user-space Web servers like Apache. As a kernel-space server, Tux can handle static content such as images very efficiently. At the same time, it can coordinate with a user-space Web server, like Apache, to provide the dynamic content, like CGI programs. Tux can even make use of a cache to hold previously generated dynamic content, using it as if it were static. The ability to coordinate with a user-space Web server lets you use Tux as your primary Web server. Anything that Tux cannot handle, it will pass off to the user-space Web server.

NOTE *Tux is freely distributed under the GNU Public License and is included with many distributions.*

The Tux configuration file is located in **/proc/sys/net/tux**. Here you enter parameters such as `serverport`, `max_doc_size`, and `logfile` (check the Tux reference manual at **www.redhat.com/docs/manuals/tux** for a detailed listing). Defaults are already entered; `serverport`, `clientport`, and `documentroot` are required parameters that must be set.

serverport is the port Tux will use—80 if it is the primary Web server. **clientport** is the port used by the user-space Web server Tux coordinates with, like Apache. **documentroot** specifies the root directory for your Web documents (**/var/www/html** on Fedora Core).

Ideally, Tux is run as the primary Web server and Apache as the secondary Web server. To configure Apache to run with Tux, the port entry in the Apache **httpd.conf** file needs to be changed from 80 to 8080.

```
Port 8080
```

You can start, stop, and restart the server with the **service** command and the **/etc/rd.d/ init.d/tux** script. Several parameters like **DOCROOT** can be specified as arguments to this Tux command. You can enter them in the **/etc/sysconfig/tux** file.

NOTE   *You can also run Tux as an FTP server. In the **/proc/sys/net/tux** directory, you change the contents of the file **serverport** to 21, **application_protocol** to 1, and **nonagle** to 0, and then restart Tux. Use the **generatetuxlist** command in the document root directory to generate FTP directory listings.*

Alternate Web Servers

Other Web servers available for Linux include the Stronghold Enterprise Server and the Apache-SSL server. A listing is provided here.

- Apache-SSL (**www.apache-ssl.org**) is an encrypting Web server based on Apache and OpenSSL (**www.openssl.org**).

- Sun Java System Web server (**www.sun.com**) features Java development support and security.

- Zope application server (**www.zope.org**) is an open source Web server with integrated security, Web-based administration and development, and database interface features. It was developed by the Zope Corporation, which also developed the Python programming language.

- Stronghold Enterprise Server (**www.redhat.com/software/stronghold**) is a commercial version of the Apache Web server featuring improved security and administration tools.

- Netscape Enterprise Server (**enterprise.netscape.com**), part of Netscape security solutions, features open standards with high performance.

- You can also use the original NCSA Web server, though it is no longer under development and is not supported (**hoohoo.ncsa.uiuc.edu**).

- AOLserver is America Online's Web server that is now available under the GPL license (**www.aolserver.com**).

Apache Web Server

The Apache Web server is a full-featured free HTTP (Web) server developed and maintained by the Apache Server Project. The aim of the project is to provide a reliable, efficient, and easily extensible Web server, with free open source code made available under its own

Apache Software License. The server software includes the server daemon, configuration files, management tools, and documentation. The Apache Server Project is maintained by a core group of volunteer programmers and supported by a great many contributors worldwide. The Apache Server Project is one of several projects currently supported by the Apache Software Foundation (formerly known as the Apache Group). This nonprofit organization provides financial, legal, and organizational support for various Apache Open Source software projects, including the Apache HTTPD Server, Java Apache, Jakarta, and XML-Apache. The Web site for the Apache Software Foundation is at **www.apache.org**. Table 23-1 lists various Apache-related Web sites.

Apache was originally based on the NCSA Web server developed at the National Center for Supercomputing Applications, University of Illinois, Urbana-Champaign. Apache has since emerged as a server in its own right and has become one of the most popular Web servers in use. Although originally developed for Linux and Unix systems, Apache has become a cross-platform application with Windows and OS/2 versions. Apache provides online support and documentation for its Web server at **httpd.apache.org**. An HTML-based manual is also provided with the server installation. You can use the Apache Configuration Tool to help configure your Apache server easily. It operates on any X Window System window manager, including GNOME and KDE. In addition, you can use the Comanche configuration tool. Webmin conf also provides Apache configuration support.

Java: Apache Jakarta Project

The Apache Jarkarta Project supports the development of Open Source Java software; its Web site is located at **jakarta.apache.org**. Currently, Jakarta supports numerous projects, including libraries, tools, frameworks, engines, and server applications. Tomcat is an open source implementation of the Java Servlet and JavaServer Pages specifications. Tomcat is designed for use in Apache servers, and is included with Fedora Core 4. JMeter is a Java desktop tool to test performance of server resources, such as servlets and CGI scripts. Velocity is a template engine that provides easy access to Java objects. Watchdog is a tool that checks the compatibility of servlet containers. Struts, Cactus, and Tapestry are Java frameworks, established methods for developing Java Web applications.

Web Site	Description
www.apache.org	Apache Software Foundation
httpd.apache.org	Apache HTTP Server Project
jakarta.apache.org	Apache Jakarta Project (Tomcat)
www.comanche.org	Comanche (Configuration Manager for Apache)
www.apache-ssl.org	Apache-SSL server
www.openssl.org	OpenSSL project (Secure Socket Layer)
www.modssl.org	The SSL module (mod_ssl) project to add SSL encryption to an Apache Web server
www.php.net	PHP Hypertext Preprocessor, embedded Web page programming language

TABLE 23-1 Apache-Related Web Sites

Linux Apache Installations

Your Linux distribution will normally provide you with the option of installing the Apache Web server during your initial installation of your Linux system. All the necessary directories and configuration files are automatically generated for you. Then, whenever you run Linux, your system is already a fully functional Web site. Every time you start your system, the Web server will also start up, running continuously. On most distributions, the directory reserved for your Web site data files is **/var/www/html**. Place your Web pages in this directory or in any subdirectories. Your system is already configured to operate as a Web server. All you need to do is perform any needed network server configurations, and then designate the files and directories open to remote users. You needn't do anything else. Once your Web site is connected to a network, remote users can access it.

The Web server normally sets up your Web site in the **/var/www** directory. It also sets up several directories for managing the site. The **/var/www/cgi-bin** directory holds the CGI scripts, and **/var/www/html/manual** holds the Apache manual in HTML format. You can use your browser to examine it. Your Web pages are to be placed in the **/var/www/html** directory. Place your Web site home page there. Your configuration files are located in a different directory, **/etc/httpd/conf**. Table 23-2 lists the various Apache Web server directories and configuration files.

To upgrade your Apache server, either use the Red Hat Network (RHN, the Red Hat upgrade tool) or look for recent Apache update files at the Red Hat and Fedora Core FTP site. For binary versions of an RPM-supported distribution Red Hat, you can download RPM packages containing the latest version of the Apache Web server, specially configured for your Fedora Core distribution. The RPM packages for the Apache Web server are now named *httpd* instead of *apache*.

Alternatively, you can download the source code version for the latest Apache Web server directly from Apache and compile it on your system. You must decompress the file and extract the archive. Many of the same directories are created, with added ones for the source code. The server package includes installation instructions for creating your server directories and compiling your software. Make sure the configuration files are set up and installed.

NOTE *If you are installing Apache from the source code, notice that versions of the configuration files ending with the extension **.conf-dist** are provided. You have to make copies of these configuration files with the same prefix, but only with the extension **.conf** to set up a default configuration. The Web server reads configuration information only from files with a **.conf** extension.*

NOTE *Fedora Core now uses Apache version 2.0 and up, which replaces the older 1.3 (see the* Red Hat Linux Reference Guide *for conversion instructions). Most directives and features for Apache 1.3 still work on Apache 2.0.*

Apache Multiprocessing Modules: MPM

Apache now uses a new architecture that uses multiprocessing modules (MPMs), which are designed to customize Apache to different operating systems, as well as handle certain multiprocessing operations. For the main MPM, a Linux system would use either the

Web Site Directory	Description
/var/www/html	Web site Web files
/var/www/cgi-bin	CGI program files
/var/www/html/manual	Apache Web server manual
Configuration File	**Description**
.htaccess	Directory-based configuration files; an **.htaccess** file holds directives to control access to files within the directory in which it is located
/etc/httpd/conf	Directory for Apache Web server configuration files
/etc/httpd/conf/httpd.conf	Apache Web server configuration file
/etc/httpd/conf.d	Directory holding module configuration files like **ssl.conf** for SSL and **php.conf** for PHP
Service Script	**Description**
/etc/rc.d/init.d/httpd	Service script for Web server daemon
/etc/sysconfig/httpd	Fedora Core configuration options for Web server daemon, as used by the httpd service script
Application and Module File	**Description**
/usr/sbin	Location of the Apache Web server program file and utilities
/usr/share/doc/	Apache Web server documentation
/var/log/http	Location of Apache log files
/etc/httpd/modules	Directory holding Apache modules
/etc/httpd/run	Directory holding Apache process IDs

TABLE 23-2   Apache Web Server Files and Directories (RPM Installation)

prefork or worker MPM, whereas Windows would use the mpm_winnt MPM. The prefork is a standard MPM module designed to be compatible for older Unix and Linux systems, particularly those that do not support threading. It is the module loaded by default by Fedora Core. The worker MPM implements threading for Apache server processes, a feature supported by the Native POSIX Thread Libraries (NPTL) that are part of Fedora Core. You can configure the workload parameters for both in the Apache configuration file, **/etc/httpd/ conf/httpd.conf**.

Apache Web Server Modules

Apache 2.0 has adopted a much more modular architecture than 1.3. Many directives that once resided in the Apache core are now placed in respective modules and MPMs (see Table 23-3). With this modular design, several directives have been dropped, such as ServerType. Configuration files for these modules are located in the **/etc/httpd/conf.d** directory.

NOTE *A selected MPM is usually integrated into Apache when it is compiled. Future Linux distributions of Apache should use the Linux/Unix default MPM, which is named "threaded."*

Starting and Stopping the Web Server

On most systems, Apache is installed as a stand-alone server, continually running. As noted in Chapter 21, in the discussion of init scripts, your system automatically starts up the Web server daemon, invoking it whenever you start your system. On Fedora Core, a service script for the Web server called **httpd** is in the **/etc/rc.d/init.d** directory. Symbolic links through which this script is run are located in corresponding runlevel directories. You will usually find the **S85httpd** link to **/etc/rc.d/init.d/httpd** in the runlevel 3 and 5 directories, **/etc/rc.d/rc3.d** and **/etc/rc.d/rc5.d**. You can use the **chkconfig** command or the System V Init Editor to set the runlevels at which the httpd server will start, creating links in appropriate runlevel directories. The following command will set up the Web server (httpd) to start up at runlevels 3 and 5 (see Chapters 21 and 29 for more details on runlevels):

```
chkconfig --level 35 httpd on
```

On Fedora Core, you can also use the **service** command to start and stop the httpd server manually. This may be helpful when you are testing or modifying your server. The **httpd** script with the **start** option starts the server, the **stop** option stops it, and **restart** will restart it. Simply killing the Web process directly is not advisable.

```
service httpd restart
```

The **service** command uses Red Hat's own **/etc/sysconfig/httpd** configuration file to set options for the **httpd** service script. Here you can specify such options as whether to use the worker or prefork Apache MPM modules.

Apache also provides a control tool called **apachectl** (Apache control) for managing your Web server. With **apachectl**, you can start, stop, and restart the server from the command line. The **apachectl** command takes several arguments: **start** to start the server, **stop** to stop it, **restart** to shut down and restart the server, and **graceful** to shut down and restart gracefully. In addition, you can use **apachectl** to check the syntax of your configuration files with the **config** argument. You can also use **apachectl** as a system service file for your server in the **/etc/rc.d** directory.

Remember, **httpd** is a script that calls the actual **httpd** daemon. You could call the daemon directly using its full pathname. This daemon has several options. The **-d** option enables you to specify a directory for the httpd program if it is different from the default directory. With the **-f** option, you can specify a configuration file different from **httpd.conf**. The **-v** option displays the version.

```
/usr/sbin/httpd -v
```

To check your Web server, start your Web browser and enter the Internet domain name address of your system. For the system **turtle.mytrek.com**, the user enters **http://turtle.mytrek.com**. This should display the home page you placed in your Web root directory. A simple way to do this is to use Lynx, the command line Web browser. Start Lynx, and type **g** to open a line where you can enter a URL for your own system. Lynx displays your Web site's home page. Be sure to place an **index.html** file in the **/var/www/html** directory first.

Once you have your server running, you can check its performance with the **ab** benchmarking tool, also provided by Apache: **ab** shows you how many requests at a time your server can handle. Options include **-v**, which enables you to control the level of detail displayed, **-n**, which specifies the number of requests to handle (default is 1), and **-t**, which specifies a time limit.

NOTE *Currently there is no support for running Apache under **xinetd**. In Apache 2.0, such support is determined by choosing an MPM module designed to run on **xinetd**.*

Apache Configuration Files

Configuration directives are placed in the **httpd.conf** configuration file. A documented version of the **httpd.conf** configuration file is installed automatically in **/etc/httpd/conf**. It is strongly recommended that you consult this file on your system. It contains detailed descriptions and default entries for Apache directives.

Any of the directives in the main configuration files can be overridden on a per-directory basis using an **.htaccess** file located within a directory. Although originally designed only for access directives, the **.htaccess** file can also hold any resource directives, enabling you to tailor how Web pages are displayed in a particular directory. You can configure access to .htaccess files in the **httpd.conf** file.

In addition, many of the modules provided for Apache have their own configurations files. These are places in the **/etc/httpd/conf.d** directory.

NOTE *With Apache versions 1.3.4 and 2.0, all configuration directives are placed in one file, the **httpd.conf** file. Older versions used two other files, the **srm.conf** and **access.conf** files.*

Apache Configuration and Directives

Apache configuration operations take the form of directives entered into the Apache configuration files. With these directives, you can enter basic configuration information, such as your server name, or perform more complex operations, such as implementing virtual hosts. The design is flexible enough to enable you to define configuration features for particular directories and different virtual hosts. Apache has a variety of different directives performing operations as diverse as controlling directory access, assigning file icon formats, and creating log files. Most directives set values such as **DirectoryRoot**, which holds the root directory for the server's Web pages, or **Port**, which holds the port on the system that the server listens on for requests. Table 23-4 provides a listing of the more commonly used Apache directives. The syntax for a simple directive is shown here:

```
directive option option ...
```

Certain directives create blocks able to hold directives that apply to specific server components (also referred to as sectional directives). For example, the **Directory** directive is used to define a block within which you place directives that apply only to a particular directory. Block directives are entered in pairs: a beginning directive and a terminating directive. The terminating directive defines the end of the block and consists of the same name beginning with a slash. Block directives take an argument that specifies the particular object to which the directives apply. For the **Directory** block directive, you must specify a

Module	Description
mod_access	Access control based on client hostname or IP address
mod_actions	Executes CGI scripts based on media type or request method
mod_alias	Maps different parts of the host file system in the document tree; performs URL redirection
mod_asis	Sends files that contain their own HTTP headers
mod_auth	User authentication using text files
mod_auth_anon	Anonymous user access to authenticated areas
mod_auth_dbm	User authentication using DBM files
mod_auth_digest	MD5 authentication
mod_auth_ldap	Authentication using LDAP directory
mod_autoindex	Automatic directory listings
mod_cache	Cache Web content
mod_cern_meta	Support for CERN HTTP header metafiles
mod_cgi	Invokes CGI scripts
mod_cgid	Invokes CGI scripts using an external daemon
mod_charset_lite	Configures character set translation
mod_dav	Distributed Authoring and Versioning, WebDAV HTTP extensions
mod_dav_fs	File system support for mod_dav
mod_deflate	Compresses date before sending to client
mod_dir	Basic directory handling
mod_disk_cache	Storage manager for cache content, used with mod_proxy
mod_env	Manages environment parameters sent to CGI scripts
mod_example	Demonstrates Apache API
mod_expires	Applies Expires: headers to resources
mod_ext_filter	Filters output with external programs
mod_file_cache	Caches files in memory for faster serving
mod_headers	Generates custom HTTP headers
mod_imap	Image-map file handler
mod_include	Support and processing of server-side includes (server-parsed HTML documents)
mod_info	Server configuration information
mod_isapi	Windows ISAPI Extension support
mod_ldap	Support for Web sites using LDAP servers, providing connection pools and caches
mod_log_config	User-configurable logging

TABLE 23-3 Apache Modules

Module	Description
mod_mem_cache	Memory-based storage manager, used for mod_cache
mod_mime	Associates meta information with a document using MIME types and file extensions
mod_mime_magic	Determines document type by examining first few bytes of document content
mod_negotiation	Content negotiation to select from alternative content that best matches client capabilities, using type-maps or multiviews
mod_proxy	Provides cache proxy abilities
mod_proxy_connect	Connection request extension for mod_proxy
mod_proxy_ftp	FTP support for mod_proxy
mod_proxy_http	HTTP request support for mod_proxy
mod_rewrite	Powerful URI-to-filename mapping using regular expressions
mod_setenvif	Sets environment variables according to client information
mod_so	Support for loading modules at runtime
mod_speling	Automatically corrects minor typos in URLs
mod_ssl	Interface for SSL encryption supported by OpenSSL
mod_status	Server status display
mod_suexec	Runs CGI scripts as specified user or group
mod_userdir	Allows user directories to be used for Web page content
mod_unique_id	Generates unique request identifier for every request
mod_usertrack	User tracking using cookies
mod_vhost_alias	Support for dynamically configured mass virtual hosting

TABLE 23-3   Apache Modules *(continued)*

directory name to which it will apply. The **<Directory** `mydir`**>** block directive creates a block whose directives within it apply to the *mydir* directory. The block is terminated by a **</Directory>** directive. The **<VirtualHost** *hostaddress***>** block directive is used to configure a specific virtual Web server and must include the IP or domain name address used for that server. **</VirtualHost>** is its terminating directive. Any directives you place within this block are applied to that virtual Web server. The **<Limit** *method***>** directive specifies the kind of access method you want to limit, such as GET or POST. The access control directives located within the block list the controls you are placing on those methods. The syntax for a block directive is as follows:

```
<block-directive option ... >
 directive option ...
 directive option ...
</block-directive>
```

PART V

Usually, directives are placed in one of the main configuration files. Directory directives in those files can be used to configure a particular directory. However, Apache also makes use of directory-based configuration files. Any directory may have its own **.htaccess** file that holds directives to configure only that directory. If your site has many directories, or if any directories have special configuration needs, you can place their configuration directives in their **.htaccess** files, instead of filling the main configuration file with specific **Directory** directives for each one. You can control what directives in an **.htaccess** file take precedence over those in the main configuration files. If your site allows user- or client-controlled directories, you may want to carefully monitor or disable the use of **.htaccess** files in them. (It is possible for directives in an **.htaccess** file to override those in the standard configuration files unless disabled with AllowOverride directives.)

Global Configuration

The standard Apache configuration has three sections: Global Settings, Server Settings, and Virtual Hosts. The Global Settings control the basic operation and performance of the Web server. Here you set configuration locations, process ID files, timing, settings for the MPM module used, and what Apache modules to load (see Table 23-4).

The **ServerTokens** directive prevents disclosure of any optional modules your server is using. The **ServerRoot** directive specifies where your Web server configuration, error, and log files are kept. This is **/etc/httpd** on Fedora Core, which will also include your error and log files, as well as the server modules. This server root directory is then used as a prefix to other directory entries.

```
ServerRoot /etc/httpd
```

The server's process ID (PID) file is usually **/etc/httpd/run/httpd.pid**, as set by **PidFile**.

```
PidFile run/httpd.pid
```

Connection and request timing is handled by **Timeout**, **KeepAlive**, **MaxKeepAliveRequests**, and **KeepAliveTimeout** directives. **Timeout** is the time in seconds that the Web server times out a send or receive request. **KeepAlive** allows persistent connections, several requests from a client on the same connection. This is turned off by default. **MaxKeepAliveRequests** sets the maximum number of requests on a persistent connection. **KeepAliveTimeout** is the time that a given connection to a client is kept open to receive more requests from that client.

The **Listen** directive will bind the server to a specific port or IP address. By default this is port 80.

```
Listen 80
```

Modules

Much of the power and flexibility of the Apache Web server comes from its use of modules to extend its capabilities. Apache is implemented with a core set of directives. Modules can be created that hold definitions of other directives. They can be loaded into Apache, enabling you to use those directives for your server. A standard set of modules is included with the Apache distribution, though you can download others and even create your own. For example, the mod_autoindex module holds the directives for automatically indexing directories (as described in the following section). The mod_mime module holds the MIME type and handler directives. Modules are loaded with the **LoadModule** directive. You can find **LoadModule** directives in the **httpd.conf** configuration file for most of the standard modules.

```
LoadModule mime_module modules/mod_mime.so
```

Directive	Description
ServerToken *url-path directory-filename*	Enables access to documents stored in the local file system, other than under the document root.
BindAddress *saddr*	Binds the server to a specified IP address. For more control over the address and ports listened to, use the **Listen** directive. (Replaced in Apache 2.0 with the **Listen** directive.)
<IfDefine [!]*parameter-name*> ... **</IfDefine>**	The **<IfDefine test>** ... **</IfDefine>** section specifies conditional directives. Directives within an **IfDefine** section are processed if the test is true and are ignored otherwise. The test consists of a parameter name, which is true if the parameter is defined, and false if undefined. An **!** placed before the parameter makes the test true if the parameter is undefined (not).
<IfModule [!]*module-name*> ... **</IfModule>**	The **<IfModule test>** ... **</IfModule>** section specifies conditional directives. The test checks to see if a module is compiled in Apache. It is true if present, and false if not. An **!***module-name* is true if the module is not present.
Include *filename*	Inclusion of other configuration files.
KeepAlive *on/off*	Enables persistent connections, "Off" to disable.
KeepAliveTimeout *seconds*	The number of seconds Apache waits for another request before closing the connection.
MaxKeepAliveRequests *seconds*	Maximum number of request per connection.
Listen [*IP address:*]*port number*	Listens to more than one IP address or port. By default, it responds to requests on all IP interfaces, but only on the port given by the **Port** directive. Context: server config
ListenBacklog *backlog*	The maximum length of the queue of pending connections.
LoadFile *filename filename* ...	Links in the named object files or libraries when the server is started or restarted. Used to load additional code required for some module to work.
LoadModule *module filename*	Links in the object file or library filename and adds the module structure named *module* to the list of active modules.
LockFile *filename*	Path to the lockfile used when Apache is compiled.
PidFile *filename*	File holding server process ID.
ServerRoot *directory-filename*	Sets the directory in which the server configuration, module, log, and error files reside.
TimeOut *number*	Sets the timeout in seconds for receiving GET requests, receipt of POST and PUT requests, and TCP packet transmissions acknowledgments.

TABLE 23-4 Global Directives

LoadModule takes as its arguments the name of the module and its location. The modules are stored in the **/etc/httpd/modules** directory, referenced here by the **modules/** prefix.

Configuration files for different modules are located in **/etc/httpd/conf.d** directory. These are also loaded using the **Include** directive. The following inserts all configuration files (those with a **.conf** extension) in the **/etc/httpd/conf.d** directory.

```
Include conf.d/*.conf
```

The apxs application provided with the Apache package can be used to build Apache extension modules. With the apxs application, you can compile Apache module source code in C and create dynamically shared objects that can be loaded with the **LoadModule** directive. The apxs application requires that the mod_so module be part of your Apache application. It includes extensive options such as **-n** to specify the module name, **-a** to add an entry for it in the **httpd.conf** file, and **-i** to install the module on your Web server.

You can find a complete listing of Apache Web configuration directives at the Apache Web site, **httpd.apache.org**, and in the Apache manual located in your site's Web site root directory. On many systems, this is located in the manual subdirectory in the Web site default directory set up by the distribution (on Fedora Core, this is **/var/www/manual**).

MPM Configuration

Configuration settings for MPM prefork and worker modules let you tailor your Apache Web server to your workload demands. Default entries will already be set for a standard Web server operating under a light load. You can modify these settings for different demands. Several common prefork and worker directives are listed in Table 23-5.

Fedora Core conditionally configures two MPM modules commonly available to Unix and Linux systems, prefork and worker. The prefork module supports one thread per process,

TABLE 23-5 MPM Prefork and Worker Directives

MPM Prefork Directive	Description
StartServers	Number of server processes to start
MinSpareServers	Minimum spare servers
MaxSpareServers	Maximum spare servers
ServerLimit	Maximum servers allowed
MaxClients	Maximum servers started
MaxRequestsPerChild	Maximum requests allowed per server
MPM Worker Directive	**Description**
StartServers	Number of server processes to start
MaxClients	Maximum number of clients
MinSpareThreads	Minimum spare threads
MaxSpareThreads	Maximum spare threads
ThreadsPerChild	Number of threads per server process
MaxRequestsPerChild	Maximum number of requests for server

which maintains compatibility with older systems and modules. The worker module supports multiple threads for each process, placing a much lower load on system resources. They share several of the same directives, such as **StartServers** and **MaxRequestsPerChild**. You can decide which module to load with the `httpd` service script by setting the HTTPD option in the **/etc/sysconfig/httpd** file. The prefork module is loaded by default.

Apache runs a single parent process with as many child processes as are needed to handle requests. Configuration for MPM modules focuses on the number of processes that should be available. The prefork module will list server numbers, as a process is started for each server; worker will control threads, since it uses threads for each process. The **StartServers** directive lists the number of server processes to start for both modules. This will normally be larger for prefork than for worker.

In the prefork module you need to set minimum and maximum settings for spare servers. **MaxClients** sets the maximum number of servers that can be started, and **ServerLimit** sets the number of servers allowed. The **MaxRequestsPerChild** sets the maximum number of requests allowed for a server.

In the worker module, **MaxClients** also sets the maximum number of client threads, and **ThreadsPerChild** sets the number of threads for each server. **MaxRequestsPerChild** limits the maximum number of requests for a server. Spare thread limits are also configured.

The directives serve as a kind of throttle on the Web server access, controlling processes to keep available and limiting the resources that can be used. In the prefork configuration, Fedora Core sets the **StartServers** number to 8, and the spare minimum to 5, with the maximum spare as 20. This means that initially 8 server processes will be started up, waiting for requests, along with 5 spare processes. When server processes are no longer being used, they will be terminated until the number of these spare processes is less than 20. The maximum number of server processes that can be started is 256. The maximum number of connections per server process is set at 4000.

In the worker MPM, only 2 server processes are initially started. Spare threads are set at 25 and 75. The maximum number of threads is set at 150, with the threads per child at 25.

Server Configuration

Certain directives are used to configure your server's overall operations. These directives are placed midway in the **httpd.conf** configuration file, directly under the section labeled Server Settings. Some directives require pathnames, whereas others only need to be turned on or off with the keywords **on** and **off**. The default **httpd.conf** file already contains these directives. Some are commented out with a preceding **#** symbol. You can activate a directive by removing its **#** sign. Many of the entries are preceded by comments explaining their purpose.

Several of the commonly used server-level directives are listed in Table 23-6. The following is an example of the **ServerAdmin** directive used to set the address where users can send mail for administrative issues. You replace the **you@your.address** entry with the address you want to use to receive system administration mail. By default, this is set to **root@localhost**.

```
# ServerAdmin: Your address, where problems should be e-mailed.
ServerAdmin you@your.address
```

Directive	Description
`AddModule` *module module ...*	Apache 1.3: Enables use of modules compiled, but not in use (dropped in Apache 2.0). Context: server config
`Alias` *url-path directory-filename*	Enables access to documents stored in the local file system, other than under the document root.
`BindAddress` *saddr*	Binds the server to a specified IP address. For more control over the address and ports listened to, use the **Listen** directive. (Replaced in Apache 2.0 with the **Listen** directive.)
`DefaultLanguage` *MIME-lang*	Specifies *MIME-lang* as the default file language. Context: server config, virtual host, directory, **.htaccess**
`DefaultType` *MIME-type*	Default type for documents whose type cannot be determined by their MIME types mappings.
`DocumentRoot` *directory-filename*	The directory from which httpd serves files. Default: DocumentRoot /usr/**local/apache/htdocs** (/**var/www/html** on Fedora Core systems)
`Group` *unix-group*	Sets the group for the server. The stand-alone server must be run initially as root. The recommendation is for you to set up a new group specifically for running the server.
`HostNameLookups` on | off | double	Enables DNS lookups so that hostnames can be logged. "Double" refers to double-reverse DNS.
`LoadFile` *filename filename ...*	Links in the named object files or libraries when the server is started or restarted. Used to load additional code required for some module to work.
`Port` *number*	If no **Listen** or **BindAddress** directives exist, a **port** directive sets the network port on which the server listens. Ports for a virtual host are set by the **VirtualHost** directive.
`ServerAdmin` *e-mail-address*	The e-mail address for the server administrator.
`ServerAlias` *host1 host2 ...*	Sets the alternate names for a host, for use with name-based virtual hosts.
`ServerName` *fully qualified domain name*	Sets the hostname of the server. This is used only when creating redirection URLs. If it is not specified, the server attempts to deduce it from its own IP address.
`ServerPath` *pathname*	Sets the legacy URL pathname for a host, for use with name-based virtual hosts.
`ServerSignature` Off | On | EMail	Configures a trailing footer line under server-generated documents, such as error messages.
`SetHandler` *handler-name*	Forces all matching files to be parsed through the handler given by *handler-name*.
`User` *unix-userid*	Specifies the user ID for the server. The stand-alone server must be run as root initially. You can use a username or a user ID number. The user should have no access to system files. The recommendation is for you to set up a new user and group specifically for running the server.
`UserDir` *directory/filename*	Sets the real directory in a user's home directory to use when a request for a document for a user is received.
`Redirect` [*status*] *url-path url*	Maps an old URL into a new one.
`ScoreBoardFile` *filename*	Specifies the **ScoreBoardFile** file.

TABLE 23-6   Server Directives

Apache can run with its own specific user and group, rather than as the root user. On Fedora Core this is set as the **apache** user and group. These are restricted users.

```
User apache
Group apache
```

A Web server usually uses port 80, which is the Apache default. If you want to use a different port, specify it with the **Port** directive.

```
Port 80
```

The **ServerName** directive holds the hostname for your Web server. Specifying a hostname is important to avoid unnecessary DNS lookup failures that can hang your server. Notice the entry is commented with a preceding **#**. Simply remove the **#** and type your Web server's hostname in place of *new.host.name*. If you are using a different port than 80, be sure to specify it attached to the hostname, as in **turtle.mytrek.com:80**. Here is the original default entry:

```
# ServerName allows you to set a hostname which is sent
# back to clients for your server if it's different than the
# one the program would get (i.e. use
# "www" instead of the host's real name).

#ServerName new.host.name:80
```

A modified **ServerName** entry would look like this:

```
ServerName turtle.mytrek.com
```

When receiving URL requests for the server system, like those for local files on the system, the **UseCanonicalName** directive will use the **ServerName** and **Port** directives to generate the host URL server name. When off, it will just use the name supplied by the client request. This can be confusing if the Web server is referenced by one name but uses another, like www.mytrek.com used to reference turtle.mytrek.com. **UseCanonicalName** set to on will overcome this problem, generating the correct local URL.

On Fedora Core systems, entries have already been made for the standard Web server installation using **/var/www** as your Web site directory. You can tailor your Web site to your own needs by changing the appropriate directives. The **DocumentRoot** directive determines the home directory for your Web pages.

```
DocumentRoot /var/www/html
```

NOTE *You can also configure Apache to operate as just a proxy and/or cache server. Default proxy and cache server directives are already included in the **httpd.conf** file. The **ProxyRequests** directive turns proxy activity on. Caching can be configured with directives like **CacheRoot** to specify the cache directory, **CacheSize** for the cache size (500KB default), and **CacheMaxExpire** to set a time limit on unmodified documents.*

PART V

Directory-Level Configuration: .htaccess and <Directory>

One of the most flexible aspects of Apache is its ability to configure individual directories. With the **Directory** directive, you can define a block of directives that apply only to a particular directory. **Directory** directives are listed in Table 23-7. Such a directive can be placed in the **httpd.conf** or **access.conf** configuration file. You can also use an **.htaccess** file within a particular directory to hold configuration directives. Those directives are then applied only to that directory. The name ".htaccess" is actually set with the **AccessFileName** directive. You can change this if you want.

```
AccessFileName .htaccess
```

Directive	Description
AccessFileName *filename filename*	Default directory configuration filenames located within directories.
<Directory *directory>* ... **</Directory>**	**<Directory>** and **</Directory>** directives operate as tags that enclose a group of directives applying only to the named directory and subdirectories of that directory.
<DirectoryMatch *regex>* ... **</DirectoryMatch>**	**<DirectoryMatch>** and **</DirectoryMatch>** enclose a group of directives that apply only to the named directory. It operates the same as **<Directory>**, but takes a regular expression as an argument.
DirectoryIndex *local-url local-url* ...	Specifies the list of resources to look for when the client requests an index of the directory by specifying a **/** at the end of a directory name (usually **index.html**).
Options [+|-]*option* [+|-]*option* ...	Controls the server features available in a particular directory. OPTIONS **None** If set to None, none of the extra features are enabled. **All** All options except for MultiViews. This is the default setting. **ExecCGI** Execution of CGI scripts is permitted. **FollowSymLinks** The server follows symbolic links in this directory. **Includes** Server-side includes are permitted. **IncludesNOEXEC** Server-side includes are permitted, but the **#exec** command and **#include** of CGI scripts are disabled. **Indexes** Returns a formatted listing of the directory for directories with no DirectoryIndex. **MultiViews** Content-negotiated MultiViews are allowed. **SymLinksIfOwnerMatch** The server follows only symbolic links for which the target file or directory is owned by the same user ID as the link.
AllowOverride *override override* ...	Directives that can be overridden by entries in an **.htaccess** file. All allows overrides, and None denies them. Default: AllowOverride All Context: directory

TABLE 23-7 **Directory** Directives

A Directory block begins with a **<Directory** *pathname***>** directive, where *pathname* is the directory to be configured. The ending directive uses the same **<>** symbols, but with a slash preceding the word "Directory": **</Directory>**. Directives placed within this block apply only to the specified directory. The following example denies access to only the **mypics** directory by requests from **www.myvids.com**.

```
<Directory /var/www/html/mypics>
 Order Deny,Allow
 Deny from www.myvids.com
</Directory>
```

With the **Options** directive, you can enable certain features in a directory, such as the use of symbolic links, automatic indexing, execution of CGI scripts, and content negotiation. The default is the **All** option, which turns on all features except content negotiation (**MultiViews**). The following example enables automatic indexing (**Indexes**), symbolic links (**FollowSymLinks**), and content negotiation (**Multiviews**).

```
Options Indexes FollowSymLinks Multiviews
```

Configurations made by directives in main configuration files or in upper-level directories are inherited by lower-level directories. Directives for a particular directory held in **.htaccess** files and Directory blocks can be allowed to override those configurations. This capability can be controlled by the **AllowOverride** directive. With the **all** argument, **.htaccess** files can override any previous configurations. The **none** argument disallows overrides, effectively disabling the **.htaccess** file. You can further control the override of specific groups of directives. **AuthConfig** enables use of authorization directives, **FileInfo** is for type directives, Indexes is for indexing directives, Limit is for access control directives, and **Options** is for the options directive.

```
AllowOverride all
```

Access Control

With access control directives, such as **allow** and **deny**, you can control access to your Web site by remote users and hosts. Access control directives are listed in Table 23-8. The **allow** directive followed by a list of hostnames restricts access to only those hosts. The **deny** directive with a list of hostnames denies access by those systems. The argument **all** applies the directive to all hosts. The **order** directive specifies in what order the access control directives are to be applied. Other access control directives, such as **require**, can establish authentication controls, requiring users to log in. The access control directives can be used globally to control access to the entire site or placed within **Directory** directives to control access to individual directives. In the following example, all users are allowed access:

```
order allow,deny
allow from all
```

You can further qualify access control directives by limiting them to certain HTML access methods. HTML access methods are ways a browser interacts with your Web site. For example, a browser could get information from a page (GET) or send information through it (POST). You can control such access methods using the **<Limit>** directive. **Limit** takes as its argument

Directive	Description
deny *from host host ...*	Determines hosts that can access a given directory: all, partial, or full domain name, or IP address.
allow *from host host ...*	Determines which hosts can access a given directory: all, partial, or full domain name, or IP address.
<Files *filename>* ... **</Files>**	Provides for access control by filename. Similar to the **<Directory>** directive and **<Location>** directive. **<Files>** sections are processed in the order they appear in the configuration file, after the **<Directory>** sections and **.htaccess** files are read, but before **<Location>** sections. **<Files>** can be nested inside **<Directory>** sections to restrict the portion of the file system to which they apply.
<FilesMatch *regex>* ... **</FilesMatch>**	Provides for access control by filename like the **<Files>** directive, but uses a regular expression.
<Limit *method method ... >* ... **</Limit>**	**<Limit>** and **</Limit>** specify a group of access control directives that apply only to the specified access methods, any valid HTTP method. Access control directives appearing outside a **<Limit>** directive apply to all access methods. Method names are GET, POST, PUT, DELETE, CONNECT, and OPTIONS.
<LimitExcept *method method ... >* ... **</LimitExcept>**	**<LimitExcept>** and **</LimitExcept>** specify a group of access control directives, which then apply to any HTTP access method *not* listed in the arguments.
<Location *URL>* ... **</Location>**	The **<Location>** directive provides for access control by URL. Similar to the **<Directory>** directive.
<LocationMatch *regex>* ... **</LocationMatch>**	Provides access control by URL, in an identical manner to **<Location>**, using a regular expression as an argument.
order *ordering*	Controls the order in which **allow** and **deny** directives are evaluated.
Satisfy *directive*	Access policy if both **allow** and **require** are used. The parameter can be either all or any.
LimitRequestBody number	Limits the size of an HTTP request message body.

TABLE 23-8   Access Control Directives

a list of access methods to be controlled. The directive then pairs with a **</Limit>** directive to define a **Limit** block within which you can place access control directives. These directives apply only to the specified access methods. You can place such **Limit** blocks with a **Directory** block to set up controls of access methods for a specific directory. The following **Directory** block in the **/etc/config/httpd.conf** file controls access methods for your Web site's home directory, **/var/www/html**.

```
# This should be changed to whatever you set DocumentRoot to.
<Directory /var/www/html>
    Options Indexes FollowSymLinks
    AllowOverride All
    <Limit GET>
        order allow,deny
        allow from all
    </Limit>
</Directory>
```

Controls are inherited from upper-level directories to lower-level ones. If you want to control access strictly on a per-directory basis to your entire Web site, you can use the following entry to deny access to all users. Then, in individual directories, you can allow access to certain users, groups, or hosts.

```
<Directory /var/www/html>
    Order Deny,Allow
    Deny from All
</Directory>
```

URL Pathnames

Certain directives can modify or complete pathname segments of a URL used to access your site. The pathname segment of the URL specifies a particular directory or Web page on your site. Directives enable you to alias or redirect pathnames, as well as to select a default Web page. With the **Alias** directive, you can let users access resources located in other parts of your system, on other file systems, or on other Web sites. An alias can use a URL for sites on the Internet, instead of a pathname for a directory on your system. With the **Redirect** directive, you can redirect a user to another site.

```
Alias /mytrain /home/dylan/trainproj
Redirect /mycars http://www.myautos.com/mycars
```

If Apache is given only a directory to access, rather than a specific Web page, it looks for an index Web page located in that directory and displays it. The possible names for a default Web page are listed by the **DirectoryIndex** directive. The name usually used is **index.html**, but you can add others. The standard names are shown here. When Apache is given only a Web directory to access, it looks for and displays the **index.html** Web page located in it.

```
DirectoryIndex index.html index.shtml index.cgi
```

Apache also lets a user maintain Web pages located in a special subdirectory in the user's home directory, rather than in the main Web site directory. Using a ~ followed by the username accesses this directory. The name of this directory is specified with the **UserDir** directive. The default name is **public_html**, as shown here. The site **turtle.mytrek .com/~dylan** accesses the directory **turtle.mytrek.com/home/dylan/public_html** on the host **turtle.mytrek.com**.

```
UserDir public_html
```

If you want, instead, to allow people to use a full pathname, then use a pathname reference. For example, for the user **dylan**, **/usr/www** would translate to a URL reference of **/usr/www/dylan**, where the HTML files would be located; **/home/*/www** would translate to **/home/dylan/www**, a www directory in the user **dylan**'s home directory.

```
UserDir /usr/www
UserDir /home/*/www
```

UserDir access is commented out by default in the standard configuration file. Usually there are users like **root** that you want access denied to. With the disable and enable options, you can open access to certain users, while disabling access to others, as shown here:

```
UserDir disable root
UserDir disabled
UserDir enabled dylan chris justin
```

MIME Types

When a browser accesses Web pages on a Web site, it is often accessing many different kinds of objects, including HTML files, picture or sound files, and script files. To display these objects correctly, the browser must have some indication of what kind of objects they are. A JPEG picture file is handled differently from a simple text file. The server provides this type of information in the form of MIME types (see Chapter 13). MIME types are the same types used for sending attached files through Internet mailers, such as Pine. Each kind of object is associated with a given MIME type. Provided with the MIME type, the browser can correctly handle and display the object.

The MIME protocol associates a certain type with files of a given extension. For example, files with a **.jpg** extension would have the MIME type image/jpeg. The **TypesConfig** directive holds the location of the **mime.types** file, which lists all the MIME types and their associated file extensions. **DefaultType** is the default MIME type for any file whose type cannot be determined. **AddType** enables you to modify the **mime.type** types list without editing the MIME file.

```
TypesConfig /etc/mime.types
DefaultType text/plain
```

Other type directives are used to specify actions to be taken on certain documents. **AddEncoding** lets browsers decompress compressed files on the fly. **AddHandler** maps file extensions to actions, and **AddLanguage** enables you to specify the language for a document. The following example marks filenames with the **.gz** extension as gzip-encoded files and files with the **.fr** extension as French language files:

```
AddEncoding x-gzip gz
AddLanguage fr .fr
```

A Web server can display and execute many different types of files and programs. Not all Web browsers are able to display all those files, though. Older browsers are the most limited. Some browsers, such as Lynx, are not designed to display even simple graphics. To allow a Web browser to display a page, the server negotiates with it to determine the type of files it can handle. To enable such negotiation, you need to enable the **MultiViews** option.

```
Option multiviews
```

CGI Files

Common Gateway Interface (CGI) files are programs that can be executed by Web browsers accessing your site. CGI files are usually initiated by Web pages that execute the program as part of the content they display. Traditionally, CGI programs were placed in a directory called **cgi-bin** and could be executed only if they resided in such a special directory. Usually, only one **cgi-bin** directory exists per Web site. Distributions will normally set up a **cgi-bin** directory in the default Web server directory (**/var/www/cgi-bin** on Fedora Core). Here, you place any CGI programs that can be executed on your Web site. The **ScriptAlias** directive specifies an alias for your **cgi-bin** directory. Any Web pages or browsers can use the alias to reference this directory.

```
ScriptAlias /cgi-bin/ /var/www/cgi-bin/
```

If you want to execute CGI programs that reside anywhere on your Web site, you can specify that files with a **.cgi** extension are treated as executable CGI programs. You do this with the **AddHandler** directive (see Table 23-9). This directive applies certain handlers to files of a given type. The handler directive to do this is included in the default **httpd.conf** file, provided with the Apache source code files, though commented out. You can remove the comment symbol (#) to enable it.

```
AddHandler cgi-script cgi
```

Directive	Description
Action *action-type cgi-script*	Adds an action, which activates *cgi-script* when *action-type* is triggered by the request.
AddHandler *handler-name extension extension ...*	Maps the filename extensions *extension* to the handler *handler-name*.
RemoveHandler *extension extension ...*	Removes handler associations for files with the given extensions. This allows **.htaccess** files in subdirectories to undo any associations inherited from parent directories or the server configuration files.
Script *method cgi-script*	Adds an action, which activates *cgi-script* when a file is requested using the method of *method,* which can be one of GET, POST, PUT, or DELETE.
ScriptAlias *url-path directory-filename*	Marks the target directory as containing CGI scripts.
ScriptInterpreterSource 'registry' or 'script'	Finds the interpreter used to run CGI scripts. The default method is to use the interpreter pointed to by the **#!** line in the script.

TABLE 23-9 *CGI Directives*

Automatic Directory Indexing

When given a URL for a directory instead of an HTML file, and when no default Web page is in the directory, Apache creates a page on the fly and displays it. This is usually only a listing of the different files in the directory. In effect, Apache indexes the items in the directory for you. You can set several options for generating and displaying such an index. Indexing directives are listed in Table 23-10. If **FancyIndexing** is turned on, Web page items are displayed with icons and column headers that can be used to sort the listing.

```
FancyIndexing on
```

Icon directives tell Apache what icon to display for a certain type of file. The **AddIconByType** and **AddIconByEncoding** directives use MIME-type information to determine the file's type and then associate the specified image with it. **AddIcon** uses the file's extension to determine its type.

With the **IndexOptions** directive, you can set different options for displaying a generated index. Options exist for setting the heights and widths of icons and filenames. The **IconsAreLinks** option makes icons part of filename anchors. The **ScanHTMLTitles** option reads the titles in HTML documents and uses those to display entries in the index listing instead of filenames. Various options exist for suppressing different index display features such as sorting, descriptions, and header/readme inserts.

Directive	Description
AddDescription *string file file* ...	Sets the description to display for a file. Can be a file extension, partial filename, wildcard expression, or full filename. String is enclosed in double quotes (").
IndexOptions [+l-]*option* [+l-]*option* ...	Set options for directory indexing: FancyIndexing, IconHeight, IconsAreLinks, IconWidth, NameWidth, ScanHTMLTitles, SuppressDescription.
ReadmeName *filename*	Specifies the name of the file to be appended to the end of the index listing.
AddIcon *icon name name* ...	Specifies the icon to display next to a file ending in *name*.
AddIconByEncoding *icon MIME-encoding MIME-encoding* ...	Specifies the icon to display next to files with *MIME-encoding* (FancyIndexing).
AddLanguage *MIME-lang extension extension* ...	Maps the given filename extensions to the specified content language.
FancyIndexing *Boolean*	Sets the FancyIndexing option for a directory. Boolean can be on or off.
DefaultIcon *url*	Specifies the icon to display for files when no specific icon is known (FancyIndexing).
HeaderName *filename*	Specifies the name of the file to be inserted at the top of the index listing (FancyIndexing).

TABLE 23-10 Indexing Directives

Authentication

Your Web server can also control access on a per-user or per-group basis to particular directories on your Web site. You can require various levels for authentication. Access can be limited to particular users and require passwords, or expanded to allow members of a group access. You can dispense with passwords altogether or set up an anonymous type of access, as used with FTP. Authentication directives are shown in Table 23-11.

To apply authentication directives to a certain directory, you place those directives within either a **Directory** block or the directory's **.htaccess** file. You use the **require** directive to determine what users can access the directory. You can list particular users or groups. The **AuthName** directive provides the authentication realm to the user, the name used to identify the particular set of resources accessed by this authentication process. The **AuthType** directive specifies the type of authentication, such as basic or digest. A **require** directive requires also **AuthType**, **AuthName**, and directives specifying the locations of group and

Directive	Description
allow *from host host* ...	Determines which hosts can access a given directory: all, partial, or full domain name, or IP address.
AllowOverride *override override* ...	Directives that can be overridden by entries in an **.htaccess** file. **All** allows overrides, and **none** denies them.
Anonymous *user user* ...	Users who are allowed access without password verification. *User* is usually anonymous (case-sensitive).
Anonymous_Authoritative on | off	When on, there is no fall-through to other authorization methods.
AuthDBMUserFile *filename*	DBM file containing the list of users and passwords for user authentication.
AuthName *auth-domain*	The authorization realm for a directory. A realm is given to the client so that the user knows which username and password to send.
AuthType *type*	Type of user authentication for a directory. Only Basic and Digest are currently implemented.
require *entity-name entity entity* ...	Selects the authenticated users that can access a directory. *entity-name* is either the user or group, followed by a list of users or groups. **require user** *userid userid* ... **require** *group group-name group-name* ...
AuthUserFile *filename*	Sets the name of the file with the list of users and passwords for user authentication.

Table 23-11   Authentication Directives

PART V

user authentication files. In the following example, only the users **george**, **robert**, and **mark** are allowed access to the **newpics** directory:

```
<Directory /var/www/html/newpics
    AuthType Basic
    AuthName Newpics
    AuthUserFile /web/users
    AuthGroupFile /web/groups
    <Limit GET POST>
        require users george robert mark
    </Limit>
</Directory>
```

The next example allows group access by administrators to the CGI directory:

```
<Directory /var/www/html/cgi-bin
    AuthType Basic
    AuthName CGI
    AuthGroupFile /web/groups
    <Limit GET POST>
        require groups admin
    </Limit>
s</Directory>
```

To set up anonymous access for a directory, place the **Anonymous** directive with the user anonymous as its argument in the directory's Directory block or **.htaccess** file. You can also use the **Anonymous** directive to provide access to particular users without requiring passwords from them.

Apache maintains its own user and group authentication files specifying what users and groups are allowed to which directories. These files are normally simple flat files, such as your system's password and group files. They can become large, however, possibly slowing down authentication lookups. As an alternative, many sites have used database management files in place of these flat files. Database methods are then used to access the files, providing a faster response time. Apache has directives for specifying the authentication files, depending on the type of file you are using. The **AuthUserfile** and **AuthGroupFile** directives are used to specify the location of authentication files that have a standard flat file format. The **AuthDBUserFile** and **AuthDBGroupFile** directives are used for DB database files, and the **AuthDBMGUserFile** and **AuthDBMGGroupFile** are used for DBMG database files.

The programs htdigest, htpasswd, and dbmmanage are tools provided with the Apache software package for creating and maintaining *user authentication files,* which are user password files listing users who have access to specific directories or resources on your Web site. The htdigest and htpasswd programs manage a simple flat file of user authentication records, whereas dbmmanage uses a more complex database management format. If your user list is extensive, you may want to use a database file for fast lookups. htdigest takes as its arguments the authentication file, the realm, and the username, creating or updating the user entry. htpasswd can also employ encryption on the password. dbmmanage has an extensive set of options to add, delete, and update user entries. A variety of different database formats are used to set up such files. Three common ones are Berkeley DB2, NDBM, and GNU GBDM. dbmmanage looks for the system libraries for these formats in that order. Be careful to be consistent in using the same format for your authentication files.

Log Files

Apache maintains logs of all requests by users to your Web site. By default, these logs include records using the Common Log Format (CLF). The record for each request takes up a line composed of several fields: host, identity check, authenticated user (for logins), the date, the request line submitted by the client, the status sent to the client, and the size of the object sent in bytes. Log file directives are listed in Table 23-12.

Webalizer

Reports on Web logs can be generated using the Webalizer tool. Webalizer will display information on your Web site usage. When you run the **webalizer** command, usage reports will be placed in the **/var/www/html/usage** directory. Access the index page to display a page with links to monthly reports, **file:/var/www/html/usage/index.html**. Report configuration is specified in the **/etc/webalizer.conf** file. Previous summaries are kept in the **/etc/webalizer.history** file.

Customizing Logs

Using the **LogFormat** and **CustomLog** directives, you can customize your log record to add more fields with varying levels of detail. These directives use a format string consisting of field specifiers to determine the fields to record in a log record. You add whatever fields you want and in any order. A field specifier consists of a percent (**%**) symbol followed by an identifying character. For example, **%h** is the field specifier for a remote host, **%b** for the size in bytes, and **%s** for the status. See the documentation for the mod_log_config module for a complete listing. Table 23-13 lists several of the commonly used ones. You should quote fields whose contents may take up more than one word. The quotes themselves must be quoted with a backslash to be included in the format string. The following example is the Common Log Format implemented as a **FormatLog** directive:

```
FormatLog "%h %l %u %t \"%r\" %s %b"
```

Directive	Description
CustomLog *file-pipe format-or-nickname*	Creates a new log file with the specified format.
ErrorDocument *error-code document*	Redirects to a local or external URL to handle the problem/error.
ErrorLog *filename|syslog[:facility]*	The file on which the server logs errors.
LogFormat *format [nickname]*	Sets the format of the default log file named by the **TransferLog** directive. Default: **LogFormat "%h %l %u %t \"%r\"** **%s %b"**
TransferLog *file-pipe*	Adds a log file in the format defined by the most recent **LogFormat** directive or Common Log Format if default is specified.
LogLevel *level*	Adjusts the verbosity of the messages recorded in the error logs.

TABLE **23-12**   Logging Directives

TABLE 23-13   Apache
Log Field Specifiers

Field Specifier	Description
%a	Remote IP address
%A	Local IP address
%b	Bytes sent, excluding HTTP headers
%{variable}e:	The contents of the environment variable
%f	Filename
%h	Remote host
%l	Remote logname (from identd, if supplied)
%m	The request method
%P	The process ID of the child that serviced the request
%r	First line of request
%s	Status
%t	Time, in Common Log Format time format (standard English format)
%u	Remote user (from auth; may be bogus if return status [%s] is 401)
%U	The URL path requested
%v	The canonical **ServerName** of the server serving the request

Certain field specifiers in the log format can be qualified to record specific information (see Table 23-13). The %i specifier records header lines in requests the server receives. The reference for the specific header line to record is placed within braces between the % and the field specifier. For example, **User-agent** is the header line that indicates the browser software used in the request. To record User-agent header information, use the conversion specifier %{User-agent}i.

To maintain compatibility with NCSA servers, Apache originally implemented **AgentLog** and **RefererLog** directives to record User-agent and Referer headers. These have since been replaced by qualified %i field specifiers used for the **LogFormat** and **CustomLog** directives. A Referer header records link information from clients, detecting who may have links to your site. The following is an NCSA-compliant log format:

```
"%h %l %u %t \"%r\" %s %b\"%{Referer}i\" \"%{User-agent}i\"".
```

Generating and Managing Log Files

Instead of maintaining one large log file, you can create several log files using the **CustomLog** or **TransferLog** directive. This is helpful for virtual hosts where you may want to maintain a separate log file for each host. You use the **FormatLog** directive to define a default format for log records. **TransferLog** then uses this default as its format when creating a new log file. **CustomLog** combines both operations, enabling you to create a new file and to define a format for it.

```
FormatLog "%h %l %u %t \"%r\" %s %b"
# Create a new log file called myprojlog using the FormatLog format
TransferLog myprojlog
# Create a new log file called mypicslog using its own format
CustomLog mypicslog "%h %l %u %t \"%r\" %s %b"
```

Apache provides two utilities for processing and managing log files: **logresolve** resolves IP addresses in your log file to hostnames; **rotatelogs** rotates log files without having to kill the server. You can specify the rotation time.

NOTE *The Apache Web server can also provide detailed reports on server activity and configuration, letting you display this information to remote servers. The Location directive server-info will display the configuration details of your Web server, and the server-status directive will show Web processes. The pages server-info and server-status will display the reports, as in **http://localhost/server-info**. Use the ExtendedStatus directive to enable detailed reports.*

Virtual Hosting on Apache

Virtual hosting allows the Apache Web server to host multiple Web sites as part of its own. In effect, the server can act as several servers, each hosted Web site appearing separate to outside users. Apache supports both IP address–based and name-based virtual hosting. IP address–based virtual hosts use valid registered IP addresses, whereas name-based virtual hosts use fully qualified domain addresses. These domain addresses are provided by the host header from the requesting browser. The server can then determine the correct virtual host to use on the basis of the domain name alone. Note that SSL servers require IP virtual hosting. See **httpd.apache.org** for more information.

IP Address–Based Virtual Hosts

In the IP address–based virtual hosting method, your server must have a different IP address for each virtual host. The IP address you use is already set up to reference your system. Network system administration operations can set up your machine to support several IP addresses. Your machine could have separate physical network connections for each one, or a particular connection could be configured to listen for several IP addresses at once. In effect, any of the IP addresses can access your system.

You can configure Apache to run a separate daemon for each virtual host, separately listening for each IP address, or you can have a single daemon running that listens for requests for all the virtual hosts. To set up a single daemon to manage all virtual hosts, use **VirtualHost** directives. To set up a separate daemon for each host, also use the **Listen** directive.

A **VirtualHost** directive block must be set up for each virtual host. Within each **VirtualHost** block, you place the appropriate directives for accessing a host. You should have **ServerAdmin**, **ServerName**, **DocumentRoot**, and **TransferLog** directives specifying the particular values for that host. You can use any directive within a **VirtualHost** block, except for **ServerType (1.3)**, **StartServers**, **MaxSpareServers**, **MinSpareServers**, **MaxRequestsPerChild**, **Listen**, **PidFile**, **TypesConfig**, **ServerRoot**, and **NameVirtualHost**.

Although you can use domain names for the address in the **VirtualHost** directive, using the actual IP address is preferable. This way, you are not dependent on your domain name service to make the correct domain name associations. Be sure to leave an IP address for your main server. If you use all the available IP addresses for your machine for virtual hosts, you can no longer access your main server. You could, of course, reconfigure your main server as a virtual host. The following example shows two IP-based virtual hosts blocks: one using an IP address, and the other a domain name that associates with an IP address:

```
<VirtualHost 192.168.1.23>
 ServerAdmin webmaster@mail.mypics.com
 DocumentRoot /groups/mypics/html
 ServerName www.mypics.com
 ErrorLog /groups/mypics/logs/error_log
 .....
</VirtualHost>

<VirtualHost www.myproj.org>
 ServerAdmin webmaster@mail.myproj.org
 DocumentRoot /groups/myproj/html
 ServerName www.myproj.org
 ErrorLog /groups/myproj/logs/error_log
 ....
</VirtualHost>
```

Name-Based Virtual Hosts

With IP-based virtual hosting, you are limited to the number of IP addresses your system supports. With name-based virtual hosting, you can support any number of virtual hosts using no additional IP addresses. With only a single IP address for your machine, you can still support an unlimited number of virtual hosts. Such a capability is made possible by the HTTP/1.1 protocol, which lets a server identify the name by which it is being accessed. This method requires the client, the remote user, to use a browser that supports the HTTP/1.1 protocol, as current browsers do (though older ones may not). A browser using such a protocol can send a host header specifying the particular host to use on a machine.

To implement name-based virtual hosting, use a **VirtualHost** directive for each host and a **NameVirtualHost** directive to specify the IP address you want to use for the virtual hosts. If your system has only one IP address, you need to use that address. Within the **VirtualHost** directives, you use the **ServerName** directive to specify the domain name you want to use for that host. Using **ServerName** to specify the domain name is important to avoid a DNS lookup. A DNS lookup failure disables the virtual host. The **VirtualHost** directives each take the same IP address specified in the **NameVirtualHost** directive as their argument. You use Apache directives within the **VirtualHost** blocks to configure each host separately. Name-based virtual hosting uses the domain name address specified in a host header to determine the virtual host to use. If no such information exists, the first host is used as the default. The following example implements two name-based virtual hosts. Here, **www.mypics.com** and **www.myproj.org** are implemented as name-based virtual hosts instead of IP-based hosts:

```
ServerName turtle.mytrek.com

NameVirtualHost 192.168.1.5

<VirtualHost 192.168.1.5>
 ServerName www.mypics.com
 ServerAdmin webmaster@mail.mypics.com
 DocumentRoot /var/www/mypics/html
```

```
ErrorLog /var/www/mypics/logs/error_log
 ...
</VirtualHost>

<VirtualHost 192.168.1.5>
 ServerName www.myproj.org
 ServerAdmin webmaster@mail.myproj.org
 DocumentRoot /var/www/myproj/html
 ErrorLog /var/www/myproj/logs/error_log
 ....
</VirtualHost>
```

If your system has only one IP address, implementing virtual hosts prevents access to your main server with that address. You could no longer use your main server as a Web server directly; you could use it only indirectly to manage your virtual host. You could configure a virtual host to manage your main server's Web pages. You would then use your main server to support a set of virtual hosts that would function as Web sites, rather than the main server operating as one site directly. If your machine has two or more IP addresses, you can use one for the main server and the other for your virtual hosts. You can even mix IP-based virtual hosts and name-based virtual hosts on your server. You can also use separate IP addresses to support different sets of virtual hosts. You can further have several domain addresses access the same virtual host. To do so, place a **ServerAlias** directive listing the domain names within the selected **VirtualHost** block.

```
ServerAlias www.mypics.com www.greatpics.com
```

Requests sent to the IP address used for your virtual hosts have to match one of the configured virtual domain names. To catch requests that do not match one of these virtual hosts, you can set up a default virtual host using _default_:*. Unmatched requests are then handled by this virtual host.

```
<VirtualHost _default_:*>
```

Dynamic Virtual Hosting

If you have implemented many virtual hosts on your server that have the same configuration, you can use a technique called *dynamic virtual hosting* to have these virtual hosts generated dynamically. The code for implementing your virtual hosts becomes much smaller, and as a result, your server accesses them faster. Adding yet more virtual hosts becomes a simple matter of creating appropriate directories and adding entries for them in the DNS server.

To make dynamic virtual hosting work, the server uses commands in the mod_vhost_alias module (supported in Apache version 1.3.6 and up) to rewrite both the server name and the document root to those of the appropriate virtual server (for older Apache versions before 1.3.6, you use the mod_rewrite module). Dynamic virtual hosting can be either name-based or IP-based. In either case, you have to set the **UseCanonicalName** directive in such a way as to allow the server to use the virtual hostname instead of the server's own name. For name-based hosting, you simply turn off **UseCanonicalName**. This allows your server to obtain the hostname from the host header of the user request. For IP-based hosting, you set the **UseCanonicalName** directive to DNS. This allows the server to look up the host in the DNS server.

```
UseCanonicalName Off
UseCanonicalName DNS
```

You then have to enable the server to locate the different document root directories and CGI bin directories for your various virtual hosts. You use the **VirtualDocumentRoot** directive to specify the template for virtual hosts' directories. For example, if you place the different host directories in the **/var/www/hosts** directory, then you could set the **VirtualDocumentRoot** directive accordingly.

```
VirtualDocumentRoot /var/www/hosts/%0/html
```

The %0 will be replaced with the virtual host's name when that virtual host is accessed. It is important that you create the dynamic virtual host's directory using that host's name. For example, for a dynamic virtual host called **www.mygolf.org**, you would create a directory named **/var/www/hosts/www.mygolf.org**. Then create subdirectories for the document root and CGI programs as in **/var/www/hosts/www.mygolf.org/html**. For the CGI directory, use the **VirtualScriptAlias** directive to specify the CGI subdirectory you use.

```
VirtualScriptAlias /var/www/hosts/%0/cgi-bin
```

A simple example of name-based dynamic virtual hosting directives follows:

```
UseCanonicalName Off
VirtualDocumentRoot /var/www/hosts/%0/html
VirtualScriptAlias /var/www/hosts/%0/cgi-bin
```

If a request was made for **www.mygolf.com/html/mypage**, that would evaluate to

```
/var/www/hosts/www.mygolf.com/html/mypage
```

A simple example of dynamic virtual hosting is shown here:

```
UseCanonicalName Off

NameVirtualHost 192.168.1.5

<VirtualHost 192.168.1.5>
 ServerName www.mygolf.com
 ServerAdmin webmaster@mail.mygolf.com
 VirtualDocumentRoot /var/www/hosts/%0/html
 VirtualScriptAlias /var/www/hosts/%0/cgi-bin
 ...
</VirtualHost>
```

To implement IP-based dynamic virtual hosting instead, set **UseCanonicalName** to DNS instead of Off.

```
UseCanonicalName DNS
VirtualDocumentRoot /var/www/hosts/%0/html
VirtualScriptAlias /var/www/hosts/%0/cgi-bin
```

Interpolated Strings
The mod_vhots_alias module supports various interpolated strings, each beginning with a % symbol and followed by a number. As you have seen, %0 references the entire Web address. %1 references only the first segment, %2 references the second, %-1 references the last part,

and **%2+** references from the second part on. For example, if you want to use only the second part of a Web address for the directory name, you would use the following directives:

```
VirtualDocumentRoot /var/www/hosts/%2/html
VirtualScriptAlias /var/www/hosts/%2/cgi-bin
```

In this case, a request made for **www.mygolf.com/html/mypage** would use only the second part of the Web address. This would be "mygolf" in **www.mygolf.com**, and would evaluate to

```
/var/www/hosts/mygolf/html/mypage
```

If you used **%2+** instead, as in **/var/www/hosts/%2/html**, the request for **www.mygolf.com/html/mypage** would evaluate to

```
/var/www/hosts/mygolf.com/html/mypage
```

The same method works for IP addresses, where **%1** references the first IP address segment, **%2** references the second, and so on.

Logs for Virtual Hosts
One drawback of dynamic virtual hosting is that you can set up only one log for all your hosts. However, you can create your own shell program to simply cut out the entries for the different hosts in that log.

```
LogFormat "%V %h %l %u %t \"%r\" %s %b" vcommon
CustomLog logs/access_log vcommon
```

IP Addressing
Implementing dynamic virtual hosting in the standard way as shown previously will slow down the process, as your server will have to perform a DNS lookup to discover the name of your server using its IP address. You can avoid this step by simply using the IP address for your virtual host's directory. So, for IP virtual host 192.198.1.6, you would create a directory **/var/www/hosts/192.198.1.6**, with an **html** subdirectory for that host's document root. You would use the **VirtualDocumentRootIP** and **VirtualScriptAliasIP** directives to use IP addresses as directory names. Now the IP address can be mapped directly to the document root directory name, no longer requiring a DNS lookup. Also be sure to include the IP address in your log, **%A**.

```
UseCanonicalName DNS
LogFormat "%A %h %l %u %t \"%r\" %s %b" vcommon
CustomLog logs/access_log vcommon
VirtualDocumentRootIP /var/www/hosts/%0/html
VirtualScriptAliasIP /var/www/hosts/%0/cgi-bin
```

You can mix these commands in with other virtual host entries as you need them. For example, to specify the document root directory for a nondynamic name-based virtual host, you could simply use the **VirtualDocumentRoot** directive. In other words, you can simply use the same directories for both dynamic and nondynamic virtual hosts. You could still specify other directories for different nondynamic virtual hosts as you wish. In the following example, the **www.mypics.com** name-based virtual host uses the dynamic virtual host directive **VirtualDocumentRoot** to set its document root directory. It now uses **/var/www/ www.mypics.com/html** as its document root directory. The CGI directory, however, is set as a nondynamic directory, **/var/www/mypics/cgi-bin**.

```
UseCanonicalName Off

NameVirtualHost 192.168.1.5

<VirtualHost 192.168.1.5>
 ServerName www.mypics.com
 ServerAdmin webmaster@mail.mypics.com
 VirtualDocumentRoot /var/www/%0/html
 ScriptAlias /var/www/mypics/cgi-bin
 ...
</VirtualHost>
```

Server-Side Includes

Server-side includes (SSIs) are designed to provide a much more refined control of your Web site content, namely the Web pages themselves. Server-side includes are Apache directives placed within particular Web pages as part of the page's HTML code. You can configure your Apache Web server to look for SSI directives in particular Web pages and execute them. First, you have to use the **Options** directive with the **include** option to allow SSI directives,

```
Options Includes
```

You need to instruct the server to parse particular Web pages. The easiest way to enable parsing is to instruct Apache to parse HTML files with specified extensions. Usually, the extension **.shtml** is used for Web pages that have SSI directories. In fact, in the default Apache configuration files, you can find the following entry to enable parsing for SSI directives in HTML files. The **AddType** directive here adds the **.shtml** type as an HTML type of file, and the **AddHandler** directive specifies that **.shtml** files are to be parsed (server-parsed):

```
# To use server-parsed HTML files
AddType text/html .shtml
AddHandler server-parsed .shtml
```

Instead of creating a separate type of file, you can use the **XBitHack** directive to have Apache parse any executable file for SSI directives. In other words, any file with execute permission (see Chapter 30) will be parsed for SSI directives.

SSI directives operate much like statements in a programming language. You can define variables, create loops, and use tests to select alternate directives. An SSI directive consists of an element followed by attributes that can be assigned values. The syntax for a SSI directive is shown here:

```
<!--#element attribute=value ... -->
```

You can think of an element as operating much like a command in a programming language and attributes as its arguments. For example, to assign a value to a variable, you use the **set** element with the variable assignment as its attribute. The **if** directive displays any following text on the given Web page. The **if** directive takes as its attribute **expr**, which is assigned the expression to test. The test is able to compare two strings using standard comparison operators such as **<=**, **!=**, or **=**. Variables used in the test are evaluated with the **$** operator.

```
<!--#set myvar="Goodbye" -->
<!--#if expr="$myvar = Hello" -->
```

Other helpful SSI elements are **exec**, which executes CGI programs, or shell commands, which read the contents of a file into the Web page and also execute CGI files. The **echo** element displays values such as the date, the document's name, and the page's URL. With the **config** element, you can configure certain values, such as the date or file size.

PHP

PHP (PHP: Hypertext Preprocessor) is a scripting language designed for use in Web pages. PHP-enabled pages allow you to create dynamic Web pages that can perform tasks instead of just displaying data. PHP is an official project of the Apache Software Foundation. You can find out more about PHP at **www.php.net**.

Unlike CGI programs, which are executed separately from a Web page, PHP commands are embedded as tags within the page itself, much as SSI commands are. PHP support to interpret and execute these commands is provided directly by the Web server. This embedded support is enabled in Apache with the mod_php module (**/etc/httpd/conf.d/php.conf** configuration file). Instead of having to separately construct programs to be invoked and run outside the Web server, with PHP, such commands are embedded within a Web page and run by the Web server. The Web server maintains complete control at all times whenever tasks are being performed. It is possible, however, to implement PHP in a CGI mode, where PHP pages are constructed as separate programs, invoked by a Web page much as a Perl-based CGP program is.

PHP has flexible and powerful programming capabilities on the same level as C and Perl. As in those languages, you can create control structures such as if statements and loops. In addition, PHP has capabilities specifically suited to Web page tasks. PHP can interact directly with databases such as Oracle, MySQL, and IBM DB2. It can easily interact with all the standard protocols, such as IMAP, LDAP, HTTP, and POP3. It even has text processing abilities such as interpreting regular expressions and displaying XML documents. There are also extensions for searches, compression tools like gzip, and language translations. PHP supports a massive collection of possible operations. Check its Web site for a complete listing, as well as online manuals and tutorials.

Apache GUI Configuration Tools

Fedora Core provides a GUI configuration tool called the Apache Configuration Tool, accessible from the GNOME and KDE desktops. On GNOME, from the System Settings menu, select Server Settings submenu, and then HTTP. Also available is Comanche, a popular Apache configuration tool that you download from the Internet. The Apache GUI Project (**gui.apache.org**) provides a set of GUI tools for configuring and managing your Apache Web server. Its currently active projects are Comanche and TkApache. In the Linuxconf utility, you can also configure your Apache Web server. Webmin provides a very complete Apache Web server module.

The Apache Configuration Tool opens with a window displaying panels for Main, Virtual Hosts, Server, and Performance Tuning. In each of these you will see buttons to open dialog boxes where you can enter default settings. You will also be able to enter settings for particular items such as virtual hosts and directories. For example, in the Virtual Hosts panel you can enter default settings for all virtual hosts, as well as add and edit particular virtual hosts. Click the Help button to display a Web page–based reference manual that details how to use each panel.

- On the Main panel, you enter your Web server address, the Webmaster's e-mail address, and the ports the Web server will be listening on (see Figure 23-1).

- On the Virtual Hosts panel, be sure to select Default Virtual Host and click Edit to set the default settings for server options, pages searches, SSL support, log files, CGI environment support, and directories (Performance). To add a virtual host, click Add to open a window where you can enter host information such as the virtual hostname and IP address. You can select different configuration panels for the virtual host, such as log files and directory controls.

- On the server panel, you set administrative settings such as the Apache server's user ID and the process ID file, along with the user and group.

- The Performance Tuning panel lets you set different usage limits such as the maximum number of requests and the number of requests per connection.

When the Apache Configuration Tool saves its settings, it will overwrite the Apache configuration file, **/etc/httpd/conf/httpd.conf**. It is advisable that you first make a backup copy of your **httpd.conf** file in case you want to restore the original settings created by your distribution for Apache. If you have already manually edited this file, you will receive a warning, and the Apache Configuration Tool will make a backup copy in **/etc/httpd/conf/ httpd.conf.bak**.

FIGURE 23-1
Apache
Configuration Tool

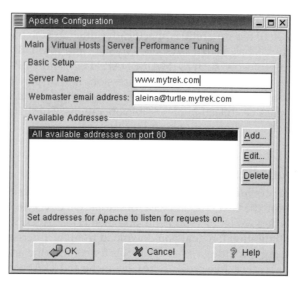

Web Server Security: SSL

Web server security deals with two different tasks: protecting your Web server from unauthorized access, and providing security for transactions carried out between a Web browser client and your Web server. To protect your server from unauthorized access, you use a proxy server such as Squid. Squid is a GNU proxy server often used with Apache on Linux systems. (See Chapter 24 for a detailed explanation of the Squid server.) Apache itself has several modules that provide security capabilities. These include mod_access for mandatory controls; mod_auth, mod_auth_db, mod_auth_digest, and mod_auth_dbm, which provide authentication support; and mod_auth_anon for anonymous FTP-like logging (see previous sections on access control and authentication).

To secure transmissions, you need to perform three tasks. You have to verify identities, check the integrity of the data, and ensure the privacy of the transmission. To verify the identities of the hosts participating in the transmission, you perform authentication procedures. To check the integrity of the data, you add digital signatures containing a digest value for the data. The digest value is a value that uniquely represents the data. Finally, to secure the privacy of the transmission, you encrypt it. Transactions between a browser and your server can then be encrypted, with the browser and your server alone able to decrypt the transmissions. The protocol most often used to implement secure transmissions with Linux Apache Web servers is the Secure Sockets Layer (SSL) protocol, which was originally developed by Netscape for secure transactions on the Web.

Like the Secure Shell (SSH) described in Chapter 19 and the GNU Privacy Guard discussed in Chapter 16, SSL uses a form of public- and private-key encryption for authentication. Data is encrypted with the public key but can be decrypted only with the private key. Once the data is authenticated, an agreed-upon cipher is used to encrypt it. Digital signatures encrypt an MD5 digest value for data to ensure integrity. Authentication is carried out with the use of certificates of authority. Certificates identify the different parties in a secure transmission, verifying that they are who they say they are. A Web server will have a certificate verifying its identity, verifying that it is the server it claims to be. The browser contacting the server will also have a certificate identifying who it is. These certificates are, in turn, both signed by a certificate authority, verifying that they are valid certificates. A certificate authority is an independent entity that both parties trust.

A certificate contains the public key of the particular server or browser it is given to, along with the digital signature of the certificate authority and identity information such as the name of the user or company running the server or browser. The effectiveness of a certificate depends directly on the reliability of the certificate authority issuing it. To run a secure Web server on the Internet, you should obtain a certificate from a noted certificate authority such as VeriSign. A commercial vendor such as Stronghold can do this for you. Many established companies already maintain their own certificate authority, securing transmissions within their company networks. An SSL session is set up using a handshake sequence in which the server and browser are authenticated by exchanging certificates, a cipher is agreed upon to encrypt the transmissions, and the kind of digest integrity check is chosen. There is also a choice in the kind of public-key encryption used for authentication, either RSA or DSA. For each session, a unique session key is set up that the browser and server use.

A free open source version of SSL called OpenSSL is available for use with Apache (see **www.openssl.org**). It is based on SSLeay from Eric A. Young and Tim J. Hudson. However, U.S. government restrictions prevent the Apache Web server from being freely distributed with SSL capabilities built in. You have to separately obtain SSL and update your Apache server to incorporate this capability.

The U.S. government maintains export restrictions on encryption technology over 40 bits. SSL, however, supports a number of ciphers using 168-, 128-, and 40-bit keys (128 is considered secure, and so by comparison the exportable 40-bit versions are useless). This means that if Apache included SSL, it could not be distributed outside the United States. Outside the United States, however, there are projects that do distribute SSL for Apache using OpenSSL. These are free for noncommercial use in the United States, though export restrictions apply. The Apache-SSL project freely distributes Apache with SSL built in, apache+ssl. You can download this from their Web site at **www.apache-ssl.org** (though there are restrictions on exporting encryption technology, there are none on importing it). In addition, the mod_ssl project provides an SSL module with patches you can use to update your Apache Web server to incorporate SSL (**www.modssl.org**). mod_ssl is free for both commercial and noncommercial use under an Apache-style license. Fedora Core includes the mod_ssl module with its distribution in the mod_ssl package (**/etc/httpd/conf.d/ssl.conf** configuration file).

The mod_ssl implementation of SSL provides an alternate access to your Web server using a different port (443) and a different protocol, https. In effect, you have both an SSL server and a nonsecure version. To access the secure SSL version, you use the protocol https instead of http for the Web server's URL address. For example, to access the SSL version for the Web server running at **www.mytrek.com**, you would use the protocol https in its URL, as shown here:

```
https://www.mytrek.com
```

You can configure mod_ssl using a number of configuration directives in the Apache configuration file, **smb.conf**. On Fedora Core, the default configuration file installed with Apache contains a section for the SSL directives along with detailed comments. Check the online documentation for mod_ssl at **www.modssl.org** for a detailed reference listing all the directives. There are global, server-based, and directory-based directives available.

In the **smb.conf** file, the inclusion of SSL directives is controlled by IfDefine blocks enabled by the HAVE_SSL flag. For example, the following code will load the SSL module:

```
<IfDefine HAVE_SSL>
LoadModule ssl_module      modules/libssl.so
</IfDefine>
```

The SSL version for your Apache Web server is set up in the **smb.conf** file as a virtual host. The SSL directives are enabled by an ifDefine block using the HAVE_SSL flag. Several default directives are implemented such as the location of SSL key directories and the port that the SSL version of the server will listen on (443). Others are commented out. You can enable them by removing the preceding # symbol, setting your own options. Several of the directives are shown here:

```
<IfDefine HAVE_SSL>
## SSL Virtual Host Context
```

```
#  Server Certificate:
SSLCertificateFile /etc/httpd/conf/ssl.crt/server.crt

#  Server Private Key:
SSLCertificateKeyFile /etc/httpd/conf/ssl.key/server.key

#  Certificate Authority (CA):
#SSLCACertificatePath /etc/httpd/conf/ssl.crt
#SSLCACertificateFile /etc/httpd/conf/ssl.crt/ca-bundle.crt
```

In the **/etc/httpd/conf** directory, mod_ssl will set up several SSL directories that will contain SSL authentication and encryption keys and data. The **ssl.crt** directory will hold certificates for the server. The **ssl.key** directory holds the public and private keys used in authentication encryption. Revocation lists for revoking expired certificates are kept in **ssl.crl**. The **ssl.csr** directory holds the certificate signing request used to request an official certificate from a certificate authority. **ssl.prm** holds parameter files used by the DSA key encryption method. Check the README files in each directory for details on the SSL files they contain.

The mod_ssl installation will provide you with a demonstration certificate called snakeoil that you can use to test your SSL configuration. When you have an official certificate, you can install it with the **make certificate** command within the **ssl.crt** directory. This will overwrite the **server.crt** server certificate file.

24

Proxy Server: Squid

Proxy servers operate as an intermediary between a local network and services available on a larger one such as the Internet. Requests from local clients for Web services can be handled by the proxy server, speeding transactions as well as controlling access. Proxy servers maintain current copies of commonly accessed Web pages, speeding Web access times by eliminating the need to access the original site constantly. They also perform security functions, protecting servers from unauthorized access. *Squid* is a free, open source, proxy-caching server for Web clients, designed to speed Internet access and provide security controls for Web servers. It implements a proxy-caching service for Web clients that caches Web pages as users make requests. Copies of Web pages accessed by users are kept in the Squid cache, and as requests are made, Squid checks to see if it has a current copy. If Squid does have a current copy, it returns the copy from its cache instead of querying the original site. If it does not have a current copy, it will retrieve one from the original site. Replacement algorithms periodically replace old objects in the cache. In this way, Web browsers can then use the local Squid cache as a proxy HTTP server. Squid currently handles Web pages supporting the HTTP, FTP, and SSL protocols, each with an associated default port (see Table 24-1). It also supports ICP (Internet Cache Protocol), HTCP (Hypertext Caching Protocol) for Web caching, and SNMP (Simple Network Management Protocol) for providing status information. You can find out more about Squid at **www.squid-cache.org**.

TABLE 24-1
Protocols
Supported
by Squid

Protocol	Description and Port
HTTP	Web pages, port 3128
FTP	FTP transfers through Web sites, port 3128
ICP	Internet Caching Protocol, port 3130
HTCP	Hypertext Caching Protocol, port 4827
CARP	Cache Array Routing Protocol
SNMP	Simple Network Management Protocol, port 3401
SSL	Secure Socket Layer
Gopher	Deprecated

As a proxy, Squid does more that just cache Web objects. It operates as an intermediary between the Web browsers (clients) and the servers they access. Instead of connections being made directly to the server, a client connects to the proxy server. The proxy then relays requests to the Web server. This is useful for situations where a Web server is placed behind a firewall server, protecting it from outside access. The proxy is accessible on the firewall, which can then transfer requests and responses back and forth between the client and the Web server. The design is often used to allow Web servers to operate on protected local networks and still be accessible on the Internet. You can also use a Squid proxy to provide Web access to the Internet by local hosts. Instead of using a gateway providing complete access to the Internet, local hosts can use a proxy to allow them just Web access (see Chapter 5). You can also combine the two, allowing gateway access, but using the proxy server to provide more control for Web access. In addition, the caching capabilities of Squid can provide local hosts with faster Web access.

Technically, you could use a proxy server to simply manage traffic between a Web server and the clients that want to communicate with it, without doing caching at all. Squid combines both capabilities as a proxy-caching server.

Squid also provides security capabilities that let you exercise control over hosts accessing your Web server. You can deny access by certain hosts and allow access by others. Squid also supports the use of encrypted protocols such as SSL (see Chapter 23). Encrypted communications are tunneled (passed through without reading) through the Squid server directly to the Web server.

Squid is supported and distributed under a GNU Public License by the National Laboratory for Applied Network Research (NLANR) at the University of California, San Diego. The work is based on the Harvest Project to create a Web indexing system that included a high-performance cache daemon called **cached**. You can obtain current source code versions and online documentation from the Squid home page at **www.squid-cache .org**. The Squid software package consists of the Squid server, a domain name lookup program called dnsserver, an FTP client called ftpget, and a cache manager script called **cachemgr.cgi**. The dnsserver resolves IP addresses from domain names, and the ftpget program is an FTP client Squid uses to retrieve files from FTP servers; **cachemgr.cgi** lets you view statistics for the Squid server as it runs.

On Red Hat, you can start, stop, and restart the Squid server using the **squid** script, as shown here:

```
service squid restart
```

You can also set the Squid server to start up automatically using the system-config-services tool or **chkconfig**.

Configuring Client Browsers

Squid supports both standard proxy caches and transparent caches. With a standard proxy cache, users will need to configure their browsers to specifically access the Squid server. A transparent cache, on the other hand, requires no browser configuration by users. The cache is transparent, allowing access as if it were a normal Web site. Transparent caches are implemented by IPtables using net filtering to intercept requests and direct them to the proxy cache (see Chapter 20).

With a standard proxy cache, users need to specify their proxy server in their Web browser configuration. For this they will need the IP address of the host running the Squid proxy server as well as the port it is using. Proxies usually make use of port 3128. To configure use of a proxy server running on the local sample network described in Chapter 5, you would enter the following. The proxy server is running on **turtle.mytrek.com** (192.168.0.1) and using port 3128.

```
192.168.0.1 3128
```

On Firefox, Mozilla, and Netscape, the user on the sample local network would first select the Proxy panel located in Preferences under the Edit menu. Then, in the Manual proxy configuration's View panel, enter the previous information. The user will see entries for FTP, Gopher, HTTP, and Security proxies. For standard Web access, enter the IP address in the FTP, Gopher, and Web boxes. For their port boxes, enter 3128.

For GNOME, select Network Proxy in the Preferences menu, and for Konqueror on the KDE Desktop, select the Proxies panel on the Preferences | Web Browsing menu. Here, you can enter the proxy server address and port numbers. If your local host is using Internet Explorer (such as a Windows system does), you set the proxy entries in the Local Area Network settings accessible from the Internet Options window.

On Linux or Unix systems, local hosts can set the **http_proxy**, **gopher_proxy**, and **ftp_proxy** shell variables to configure access by Linux-supported Web browsers such as Lynx. You can place these definitions in your **.bash_profile** or **/etc/profile** file to have them automatically defined whenever you log in.

```
http_proxy=192.168.0.1:3128
ftp_proxy=192.168.0.1:3128
gopher_proxy=192.168.0.1:3128
export http_proxy ftp_proxy gopher_proxy
```

Alternatively, you can use the proxy's URL.

```
http_proxy=http://turtle.mytrek.com:3128
```

For the Elinks browser, you can specify a proxy in its configuration file, **/etc/elinks.conf**. Set both FTP and Web proxy host options, as in:

```
protocol.http.proxy.host  turtle.mytrek.com:3128
protocol.ftp.proxy.host   turtle.mytrek.com:3128
```

Before a client on a local host could use the proxy server, access permission would have to be given to it in the server's **squid.conf** file, described in the later section "Security." Access can easily be provided to an entire network. For the sample network used here, you would have to place the following entries in the **squid.conf** file. These are explained in detail in the following sections:

```
acl mylan src 192.168.0.0/255.255.255.0
http_access allow mylan
```

TIP *Web clients that need to access your Squid server as a standard proxy cache will need to know the server's address and the port for Squid's HTTP services, by default 3128.*

PART V

The squid.conf File

The Squid configuration file is **squid.conf**, located in the **/etc/squid** directory. In the **/etc/squid/squid.conf** file, you set general options such as ports used, security options controlling access to the server, and cache options for configuring caching operations. You can use a backup version called **/etc/squid/squid.conf.default** to restore your original defaults. The default version of **squid.conf** provided with Squid software includes detailed explanations of all standard entries, along with commented default entries. Entries consist of tags that specify different attributes. For example, **maximum_object_size** and **maximum_object** set limits on objects transferred.

```
maximum_object_size 4096 KB
```

As a proxy, Squid will use certain ports for specific services, such as port 3128 for HTTP services like Web browsers. Default port numbers are already set for Squid. Should you need to use other ports, you can set them in the **/etc/squid/squid.conf** file. The following entry shows how you would set the Web browser port:

```
http_port 3128
```

> **NOTE**   *Squid uses the Simple Network Management Protocol (SNMP) to provide status information and statistics to SNMP agents managing your network. You can control SNMP with the **snmp access** and **port** configurations in the **squid.conf** file.*

Security

Squid can use its role as an intermediary between Web clients and a Web server to implement access controls, determining who can access the Web server and how. Squid does this by checking access control lists (ACLs) of hosts and domains that have had controls placed on them. When it finds a Web client from one of those hosts attempting to connect to the Web server, it executes the control. Squid supports a number of controls with which it can deny or allow access to the Web server by the remote host's Web client (see Table 24-2). In effect, Squid sets up a firewall just for the Web server.

The first step in configuring Squid security is to create ACLs. These are lists of hosts and domains for which you want to set up controls. You define ACLs using the **acl** command, in which you create a label for the systems on which you are setting controls. You then use commands such as **http_access** to define these controls. You can define a system, or a group of systems, by use of several **acl** options, such as the source IP address, the domain name, or even the time and date. For example, the **src** option is used to define a system or group of systems with a certain source address. To define a **mylan acl** entry for systems in a local network with the addresses 192.168.0.0 through 192.168.0.255, use the following ACL definition:

```
acl mylan src 192.168.0.0/255.255.255.0
```

Once it is defined, you can use an ACL definition in a Squid option to specify a control you want to place on those systems. For example, to allow access by the mylan group of

Option	Description
src *ip-address/netmask*	Client's IP address
src *addr1-addr2/netmask*	Range of addresses
dst *ip-address/netmask*	Destination IP address
myip *ip-address/netmask*	Local socket IP address
srcdomain *domain*	Reverse lookup, client IP
dstdomain *domain*	Destination server from URL; for **dstdomain** and **dstdom_regex**, a reverse lookup is tried if an IP-based URL is used
srcdom_regex **[-i]** *expression*	Regular expression matching client name
dstdom_regex **[-i]** *expression*	Regular expression matching destination
time *[day-abbrevs] [h1:m1-h2:m2]*	Time as specified by day, hour, and minutes. Day abbreviations: S = Sunday, M = Monday, T = Tuesday, W = Wednesday, H = Thursday, F = Friday, A = Saturday
url_regex **[-i]** *expression*	Regular expression matching on whole URL
urlpath_regex **[-i]** *expression*	Regular expression matching on URL path
port *ports*	Specify a port or range of ports
proto *protocol*	Specify a protocol, such as HTTP or FTP
method *method*	Specify methods, such as GET and POST
browser **[-i]** *regexp*	Pattern match on user-agent header
ident *username*	String match on **ident** output
src_as *number*	Source Autonomous System number (cache routing)
dst_as *number*	Destination Autonomous System number (cache routing)
proxy_auth *username*	List of valid usernames
snmp_community *string*	A community string to limit access to your SNMP agent

TABLE 24-2   Squid ACL Options

local systems to the Web through the proxy, use an **http_access** option with the **allow** action specifying **mylan** as the **acl** definition to use, as shown here:

```
http_access allow mylan
```

By defining ACLs and using them in Squid options, you can tailor your Web site with the kind of security you want. The following example allows access to the Web through the proxy by only the **mylan** group of local systems, denying access to all others. Two **acl** entries are set up: one for the local system and one for all others; **http_access** options first allow access to the local system and then deny access to all others.

```
acl mylan src 192.168.0.0/255.255.255.0
acl all src 0.0.0.0/0.0.0.0
```

```
http_access allow mylan
http_access deny all
```

The default entries that you will find in your **squid.conf** file, along with an entry for the mylan sample network, are shown here. You will find these entries in the ACCESS CONTROLS section of the **squid.conf** file.

```
acl all src 0.0.0.0/0.0.0.0
acl manager proto cache_object
acl localhost src 127.0.0.1/255.255.255.255
acl mylan src 192.168.0.0/255.255.255.0
acl SSL_ports port 443 563
```

The order of the **http_access** options is important. Squid starts from the first and works its way down, stopping at the first **http_access** option with an ACL entry that matches. In the preceding example, local systems that match the first **http_access** command are allowed, whereas others fall through to the second **http_access** command and are denied.

For systems using the proxy, you can also control what sites they can access. For a destination address, you create an **acl** entry with the **dst** qualifier. The **dst** qualifier takes as its argument the site address. Then you can create an **http_access** option to control access to that address. The following example denies access by anyone using the proxy to the destination site **rabbit.mytrek.com**. If you have a local network accessing the Web through the proxy, you can use such commands to restrict access to certain sites.

```
acl myrabbit dst rabbit.mytrek.com
http_access deny myrabbit
```

The **http_access** entries already defined in the **squid.conf** file, along with an entry for the mylan network, are shown here. Access to outside users is denied, whereas access by hosts on the local network and the local host (Squid server host) is allowed.

```
http_access allow localhost
http_access allow mylan
http_access deny all
```

You can also qualify addresses by domain. Often, Web sites can be referenced using only the domain. For example, a site called **www.mybeach.com** can be referenced using just the domain **mybeach.com**. To create an **acl** entry to reference a domain, use the **dstdomain** or **srcdomain** option for destination and source domains, respectively. Remember, such a reference refers to all hosts in that domain. An **acl** entry with the **dstdomain** option for **mybeach.com** restricts access to **www.mybeach.com**, **ftp.mybeach.com**, **surf.mybeach.com**, and so on. The following example restricts access to the **www.mybeach.com** site along with all other **.mybeach.com** sites and any hosts in the **mybeach.com** domain:

```
acl thebeach dstdomain .mybeach.com
http_access deny thebeach
```

You can list several domains or addresses in an **acl** entry to reference them as a group, but you cannot have one domain that is a subdomain of another. For example, if

mybeachblanket.com is a subdomain of **mybeach.com**, you cannot list both in the same **acl** list. The following example restricts access to both **mybeach.com** and **mysurf.com**:

```
acl beaches dstdomain .mybeach.com .mysurf.com
http_access deny beaches
```

An **acl** entry can also use a pattern to specify certain addresses and domains. In the following example, access is denied to any URL with the pattern "chocolate" but allowed to all others:

```
acl Choc1 url_regex chocolate
http_access deny Choc1
http_access allow all
```

Squid also supports ident and proxy authentication methods to control user access. The following example allows only the users **dylan** and **chris** to use the Squid cache:

```
ident_lookup on
acl goodusers user chris dylan
http_access allow goodusers
http_access deny all
```

Caches

Squid primarily uses the Internet Cache Protocol (ICP) to communicate with other Web caches. It also provides support for the more experimental Hypertext Cache Protocol (HTCP) and the Cache Array Routing Protocol (CARP).

Using the ICP protocols, your Squid cache can connect to other Squid caches or other cache servers, such as Microsoft proxy server, Netscape proxy server, and Novell BorderManager. This way, if your network's Squid cache does not have a copy of a requested Web page, it can contact another cache to see if it is there instead of accessing the original site. You can configure Squid to connect to other Squid caches by connecting it to a cache hierarchy. Squid supports a hierarchy of caches denoted by the terms *child, sibling,* and *parent.* Sibling and child caches are accessible on the same level and are automatically queried whenever a request cannot be located in your own Squid's cache. If these queries fail, a parent cache is queried, which then searches its own child and sibling caches—or its own parent cache, if needed—and so on.

You can set up a cache hierarchy to connect to the main NLANR server by registering your cache using the following entries in your **squid.conf** file:

```
cache_announce 24
announce_to sd.cache.nlanr.net:3131
```

Connecting to Caches

Use **cache_peer** to set up parent, sibling, and child connections to other caches. This option has five fields. The first two consist of the hostname or IP address of the queried cache and the cache type (parent, child, or sibling). The third and fourth are the HTTP and the ICP ports of that cache, usually 3128 and 3130. The last is used for cache_peer options such as proxy-only to not save fetched objects locally, no-query for those caches that do not support ICP, and weight, which assigns priority to a parent cache. The following example sets up a connection to a parent cache:

```
cache_peer sd.cache.nlanr.net parent 3128 3130
```

Memory and Disk Configuration

Squid provides several options for configuring cache memory. The **cache_mem** option sets the memory allocated primarily for objects currently in use (objects in transit). If available, the space can also be use for frequently accessed objects (hot objects) and failed requests (negative-cache objects). The default is 8MB. The following example sets it to 256MB:

```
cache_mem 256 MB
```

You can further specify the minimum and maximum sizes of objects saved either in disk or in memory. On disk, you use **maximum_object_size** and **minimum_object_size**. The default maximum is 4KB. The default minimum is set to 0, indicating no minimum. For memory, you use **maximum_object_size_in_memory** and **minimum_object_size_in_memory**.

The **cache_swap_high** and **cache_swap_low** options let you set bars for replacing objects in your cache.

To designate where cache objects are to be located, you use the **cache _dir** option. Here you specify what directories to use for your cache.

Administrative Settings

The e-mail address for the administrator for your Squid cache is specified in the **cache_mgr** option.

If you run Squid as the root user, then Squid will change its user and group ID from **root** to **nobody**. The group ID will be changed to **nogroup**. This is to protect root user access. Should you run Squid as a user other than root, Squid will retain that original user as its user ID. If, when running Squid from the root user, you want to designate another user other than nobody, you can use **cache_effective_user** to change user IDs, and **cache_effective_group** to change the group.

You can also specify an special hostname to be displayed in error messages. Use **visible_hostname** to set the name.

Logs

Squid keeps several logs detailing access, cache performance, and error messages.

- **access.log** holds requests sent to your proxy.
- **cache.log** holds Squid server messages such as errors and startup messages.
- **store.log** holds information about the Squid cache such as objects added or removed.

You can use the cache manager (**cachemgr.cgi**) to manage the cache and view statistics on the cache manager as it runs. To run the cache manager, use your browser to execute the **cachemgr.cgi** script (this script should be placed in your Web server's **cgi-bin** directory).

Web Server Acceleration: Reverse Proxy Cache

Though Squid caches can enhance access by clients to a Web server, Squid can also reduce the load on a Web server. Web servers that become overwhelmed by requests can move their cachable pages to a Squid proxy server that can serve as a kind of alternate site, handling requests for those pages. In effect, the Web server becomes accelerated. Such a cache is known as a reverse proxy cache, focusing on the server instead of the client. A reverse proxy cache will intercept requests to a server, processing any for its cached pages. Only requests for noncached pages are forwarded to the original Web server.

To configure a reverse proxy cache, you use the **httpd_accel** directives: **httpd_accel_host** specifies the address of the original Web server, and **httpd_accel_port** is the port it uses. If the proxy supports only one Web server, you set **httpd_accel_single_host** to on, whereas if the proxy is supporting several Web servers, set it to off. If you want to use the proxy server both as a proxy for clients and as a reverse proxy for the Web server, you set the **httpd_accel_with_proxy** option to on. However, clients would then need to configure their browsers to access the Web server, as they would to access any standard proxy server. The **httpd_accel_uses_host_header** directive is used to implement transparent caches; it should be turned off for reverse proxy caches.

```
http_port 80 # Port of Squid proxy
httpd_accel_host 172.16.1.115 # IP address of web server
httpd_accel_port 80 # Port of web server
httpd_accel_single_host on # Forward uncached requests to host
httpd_accel_with_proxy on #
httpd_accel_uses_host_header off
```

If your Squid proxy server and the Web server are operating on the same host, you need to specify the port that the Web server is using. This cannot be the same port as Squid is using. In the following example, the Web server is using port 81, whereas Squid is using port 80:

```
http_port 80 # Port of Squid proxy
httpd_accel_host localhost # IP address of web server
httpd_accel_port 81 # Port of web server
```

In addition, DNS entries for the external network would use the IP address of the proxy server for the Web server hostname, directing all the Web server requests to the proxy server. DNS entries for the internal network would use the Web server's IP address for the Web server hostname, allowing the proxy to redirect noncached requests onto the Web server. If your network uses only one DNS server, you can set up a Split DNS server to specify internal and external addresses (see Chapter 38).

Proxy Authentication

You can control access to Squid by users either through ident lookups or authentication services. The ident lookups require the use of an ident server. For these you set up a simple acl entry and deny or allow access.

Squid now uses independent services to perform authentication, such as ldap, pam, smb, msnt (NT servers), winbind, or ncsa. You specify an authentication service with an **acl proxy_auth** rule. The corresponding Squid authentication will then be loaded. Several are available such as pam_auth, squid_ldap_auth, and squid_ldap_group, which support PAM and LDAP authentication. Needed configuration files for authenticators can be found in the **/etc/squid** directory, such as the **msntauth.conf** configuration file used for NT authentication (msnt).

Mail Servers: SMTP, POP, and IMAP

Mail servers provide Internet users with electronic mail services. They have their own TCP/IP protocols such as the Simple Mail Transfer Protocol (SMTP), the Post Office Protocol (POP), and the Internet Mail Access Protocol (IMAP). Messages are sent across the Internet through mail servers that service local domains. A *domain* can be seen as a subnet of the larger Internet, with its own server to handle mail messages sent from or received for users on that subnet. When a user mails a message, it is first sent from their host system to the mail server. The mail server then sends the message to another mail server on the Internet, the one servicing the subnet on which the recipient user is located. The receiving mail server then sends the message to the recipient's host system.

At each stage, a different type of operation takes place using different agents (programs). A mail user agent (MUA) is a mail client program, such as mail or Elm. With an MUA, a user composes a mail message and sends it. Then a mail transfer agent (MTA) transports the message over the Internet. MTAs are mail servers that use SMTP to send messages across the Internet from one mail server to another, transporting them among subnets. On Linux and Unix systems, the commonly used MTA is Sendmail, a mail server daemon that constantly checks for incoming messages from other mail servers and sends outgoing messages to appropriate servers. Other MTAs becoming more popular are Postfix, Exim, Courier, and Qmail (see Table 25-1). Incoming messages received by a mail server are distributed to a user with mail delivery agents (MDAs). Most Linux systems use procmail as their MDA, taking messages received by the mail server and delivering them to user accounts (see **www .procmail.org** for more information).

Mail Transport Agents

Fedora Core automatically installs and configures both Sendmail and Postfix for you. On starting your system, you can send and receive messages between local users using Sendmail or Postfix. Fedora Core includes a special tool called the Mail Transport Agent Switcher, accessible from the System Settings menu or window, to let you switch between the two. You can also set up your Linux system to run a POP server. POP servers hold users'

Agent	Description
Sendmail	Sendmail mail transfer agent, supported by the Sendmail consortium **www.sendmail.org**
Postfix	Fast, easy to configure, and secure mail transfer agent compatible with Sendmail and designed to replace it **www.postfix.org**
Qmail	Fast, flexible, and secure MTA with its own implementation and competitive with Postfix **www.qmail.org**
Exim	MTA based on smail3 **www.exim.org**
Courier	Courier MTA **www.courier-mta.org**
Mail Transport Agent Switcher	Tool to let you switch between using Sendmail and Postfix (Mail Transport Agent Switcher in System Settings menu and window)

TABLE 25-1   Mail Transfer Agents

mail until they log in to access their messages, instead of having mail sent to their hosts directly. Both Postfix and Sendmail will be discussed in this chapter.

Courier is a fast, small, and secure MTA that maintains some compatibility with Sendmail. The Courier software package also includes POP, IMAP, and webmail servers along with mailing list services. It supports extensive authentication methods including shadow passwords, PAM, and LDAP.

Exim is a fast and flexible MTA similar to Smail. Developed at the University of Cambridge, it has a very different implementation than Sendmailc.

Qmail is also a fast and secure MTA, but it has little compatibility with Sendmail. It has its own configuration and maintenance files. Like Postfix, it has a modular design, using a different program for each mail task. It also focuses on security, speed, and easy configuration.

NOTE *Messages sent within a single stand-alone system require a loopback interface. Most Linux distributions do this automatically for you during the installation process. A* loopback interface *enables your system to address itself, allowing it to send and receive mail to and from itself. A loopback interface uses the hostname **localhost** and a special IP address reserved for use by local systems, 127.0.0.1. You can examine your* **/etc/hosts** *file to see if your loopback interface has been configured as the local host. You should see **127.0.0.1 localhost** listed as the first entry.*

Received Mail: MX Records

A mail address consists of a username and a host address. The host address takes the form of a fully qualified domain name, listing the hostname and the domain name, separated by periods. Most uses of a hostname, such as FTP connections, translate the hostname into an IP address and use the IP address to locate the host system. Mail messages operate nearly the same way. However, they make use of the Domain Name Service to determine which host to actually send a message to. The host specified in the mail address may not be the host to which delivery should actually be made. Different networks will often specify a mail server to which mail for the hosts in a network should be delivered. For example, mail addressed to the **rabbit.mytrek.com** host may actually be delivered to the **turtle.mytrek.com** host. **turtle.mytrek.com** may be running a POP mail server that users on **rabbit.mytrek.com** can access to read their mail.

Such mail servers are associated with different hosts by mail exchange records, known as MX records, in a network's DNS configuration (see Chapter 38). When mail is received in a network, the network's DNS configuration is first checked for MX records to determine if the mail is to be delivered to a host different from that in the mail message address. For example, the following MX record says that any mail for the **rabbit.mytrek.com** host is to be delivered to the **turtle.mytrek.com** host; **turtle.mytrek.com** is the mail exchanger for **rabbit.mytrek.com**:

```
rabbit.mytrek.com. IN   MX    0   turtle.mytrek.com.
```

A host could have several mail exchangers, each with a different priority. If one is down, the one with next highest priority will be accessed. Such a design provides for more robust mail delivery, letting a few well-maintained servers handle received mail, instead of each host on its own.

Mail exchange records are also used for mail addresses for which there are no hosts. For example, you could designate virtual hosts or use the domain name as an address. To use a domain name, you would have an MX record with the domain name mapped to a mail server on the network. Mail addressed to the domain name would be sent to the mail server. For example, with the following MX record, mail sent to **mytrek.com** would be delivered to **turtle.mytrek.com**, which would be running a mail server like Sendmail:

```
mytrek.com. IN   MX    0   turtle.mytrek.com.
```

Mail addressed to george@mytrek.com would be sent to george@turtle.mytrek.com.

NOTE *MX records are used not only for incoming mail, but also for outgoing mail. An MX record can specify a mail server to use for relaying mail from a given host out to a larger network.*

MX records come into play with certain mail configurations such as masquerading or centralized mail services. MX records are not required. If you have a stand-alone system or a small network with only a few hosts, you may want mail received directly by different hosts.

Postfix

Postfix is a fast, secure, and flexible MTA designed to replace Sendmail while maintaining as much compatibility as possible. Written by Wietse Venema and originally released as the IBM Secure Mailer, it is now available under the GNU license (**www.postfix.org**). Postfix is included as part of the Fedora Core distribution. Postfix was created with security in mind, treating all incoming mail as potential security risks. Postfix uses many of the same Sendmail directories and files and makes use of Sendmail wrappers, letting Sendmail clients interact seamlessly with Postfix servers. Postfix is also easier to configure, using its own configuration file. Fedora Core now provides Postfix along with Sendmail.

Instead of one large program, Postfix is implemented as a collection of smaller programs, each designed to perform a specific mail-related task. A Postfix master daemon runs continuously and manages the use of the other Postfix daemons, running them only as needed. A **bounce** daemon handles undeliverable mail, a **trivial-rewrite** daemon redirects messages, and the **showq** daemon provides information on the print queues.

Postfix Commands

Several Postfix commands allow you to manage your server tasks. The **sendmail** command sends messages. You use **mailq** to display the status of your mail queues. The **newaliases** command takes mail aliases listed in the aliases files and stores them in a database file that can be used by Postfix. The **postmap** command is used to maintain various database files used by Postfix, such as the alias file for mail aliases and the access file that restricts messages received by the server. In addition, Postfix provides lower-level tools, all beginning with the term **post**, such as the **postalias** command, which maintains the alias database, and **postcat**, which displays print queue files.

Postfix Configuration: main.cf

Postfix configuration is handled by setting parameters in its configuration file, **main.cf**. Fedora Core installs a default **/etc/postfix/main.cf** file with Postfix, with most of the essential configuration values already set. Parameter names tend to be user friendly. For example, directory locations are specified by parameters ending in the term **directory**, such as **queue_directory** for the location of Postfix queues and **daemon_directory** for the location of the Postfix daemons. Defaults are already implemented for most parameters. For example, defaults are set for particular resource controls, such as message size, time limits, and the number of allowed messages per queue. You can edit the **main.cf** file to change the parameter values to meet your own needs. After making any changes, you only need to reload the configuration using the **postfix reload** command:

```
postfix reload
```

Network Parameters

You will most likely need to set several network parameters. To ease this process, Postfix defines parameters that hold key network information, such as **myhostname**, which holds the hostname of your system, and **mydomain**, which holds the domain name of your network. For example, **myhostname** would be set to the host **turtle.mytrek.com**, whereas **mydomain** would be just **mytrek.com**. Parameters like **myhostname** and **mydomain** are themselves used as values assigned to other parameters. In the next example, **myhostname** and **mydomain** are set to the host the mail server is running on and its network domain:

```
myhostname=turtle.mytrek.com
mydomain=mytrek.com
```

The **myorigin** parameter specifies the origin address for e-mail sent by the server. By default, this is set to the value of the parameter **myhostname**, as shown here. Note that a **$** precedes the **myhostname** variable to evaluate it.

```
myorigin=$myhostname
```

If you are using a single system directly attached to the Internet, you may want to keep this configuration, labeling mail as being sent by your host. However, if your system is operating as a gateway for a network, your mail server is sending out mail from different hosts on that network. You may wish to change the origin address to the domain name, so that mail is perceived as sent from the domain.

```
myorigin=$mydomain
```

Local Networks

The **mydestination** parameter holds the list of domains that your mail server will receive mail for. By default, these include **localhost** and your system's hostname.

```
mydestination = $myhostname localhost.$mydomain
```

If you want the mail server to receive mail for an entire local network, you need to also specify its domain name. That way, the server can receive mail addressed just to the domain, instead of your specific host.

```
mydestination = $myhostname localhost.$mydomain $mydomain
```

Also, if your host goes by other hostnames and there are DNS records identifying your host by those names, you need to specify those names also. For example, your host could also be a Web server to which mail could be directed. A host **turtle.mytrek.com** may also be identified as the Web site **www.mytrek.com**. Both names would have to be listed in the **mydestination** parameter.

```
mydestination = $myhostname localhost.$mydomain $mydomain www.$mydomain
```

If your system is a gateway for one or more local networks, you can specify them with the **mynetworks** parameter. This allows your mail server to relay mail addressed to those networks. Networks are specified using their IP addresses. The **relay_domains** parameter lets you specify domain addresses of networks for which you can relay messages. By default, this is set to **mydestination**:

```
mynetworks=192.168.0.0
relay_domains=$mydestination
```

Hosts within the local network connected to the Internet by a gateway need to know the identity of the relay host, the mail server. You set this with the **relay_host** parameter. Also, **myorigin** should be set to just **mydomain**. If there is a DNS server identifying the gateway as the mail server, you can just set **relay_host** to the value of **mydomain**. If not, then **relay_host** should be set to the specific hostname of the gateway/mail server. If your local network is not running a DNS server, be sure to set **disable_dns_lookups** to **yes**.

```
relay_host=$mydomain
```

Direct Connections

If your system is directly connected to the Internet and you use an ISP for receiving mail, you can configure Postfix as a null client to just send mail. Set the **relay_host** parameter to just your own domain name. Also, in the **master.cf** file, comment out the SMTP server and local delivery agent entries.

```
relay_host = $mydomain
```

Masquerading
If your mail server is operating on a gateway for a local network and you want to hide the hosts in that network, you can opt to masquerade the local hosts, letting it appear that all mail is coming from the domain in general, instead of a particular host. To set this option, you use the **masquerade_domains** parameter. In the following example, all mail sent by a local host such as **rabbit.mytrek.com** will be addressed as just coming from **mytrek.com**. Thus a message sent by the user **chris@rabbit.mytrek.com** is sent out as coming from **chris@mytrek.com**:

```
masquerade_domains = $mydomain
```

Received mail is not masqueraded by default. This allows Postfix to still deliver received mail to particular hosts. If you want received mail to also be masqueraded, you have to add the **envelope_recipients** parameter to the list of values assigned to the **masquerade_class** parameter. In that case, Postfix will no longer be able to deliver received mail.

Virtual Domains
If your network has implemented virtual domains, you will need to set up a virtual domain table and then specify that table with the **virtual_maps** option. Setting up a table is a simple matter of listing virtual names and their real addresses in a text file such as **/etc/postfix/virtual**. Then use the **postmap** command to create a Postfix table:

```
postmap /etc/postfix/virtual
```

In the **main.cf** file, specify the table with the **virtual_maps** parameter. Postfix will then use this table to look up virtual domains.

```
virtual_maps = hash:/etc/postfix/virtual
```

NOTE *See the Postfix FAQ at **www.postfix.org** for detailed information on how to set up Postfix for a gateway, a local workstation, or a host directly connected to the Internet (null server).*

Security: UCM
Postfix parameters let you configure methods for controlling what it politely refers to as unsolicited commercial mail (UCM). These include controlling user access, blocking hosts, and checking header content.

Controlling User and Host Access
With an access file, you can control access by certain users, hosts, and domains. The access file works much like the one used for Sendmail. Entries are made in a text file beginning with the user, host, or domain name or address, followed by an action to be take. A user,

host, or domain can be accepted, rejected, or rejected with a message. Once entries are made, they can be installed in a Postfix database file with the **postmap** command:

```
postmap /etc/postfix/access
```

You can then use the access file in various Postfix operations to control clients, recipients, and senders.

Blocking Access

Access can also be controlled by use of the Mail Abuse Prevention System (MAPS), which provides the RBL+ service, a collection of mail address DNS-based databases (**mail-abuse .com**). These databases, like the Realtime Blackhole List (RBL), list mail addresses that are known to be used by mail abusers. A domain or host is matched against a list maintained by the service, which can be accessed on a local server or directly from an online site. Various Postfix operations let you use MAPS databases to control access by clients, recipients, or senders.

Header and Body Checks

With the **header_checks** parameter, you can specify a Postfix table where you can list criteria for rejecting messages. The criteria are patterns that can match message headers. You can have matching messages rejected, rejected with a reply, simply deleted, or logged with a warning. You have the option of taking several actions, including REJECT, DISCARD, WARN, HOLD, and IGNORE.

```
header_checks = regexp:/etc/postfix/header_checks
```

The database, in this case **/etc/postfix/header_checks**, will have lines, each with a regular expression and a corresponding action. The regular expression can either be a standard regular expression as denoted by **regexp** in the **header_checks** parameter (see Chapter 8) or conform to a Perl Compatible Regular Expression, **prece**.

The **body_checks** parameter lets you check the body of text messages, line by line, using regular expressions and actions like those used for **header_checks**.

Controlling Client, Senders, and Recipients

With the **smtpd_client_restrictions** parameter, you can restrict access to the mail server by certain clients. Restrictions you can apply include **reject_unknown_client**, which will reject any clients with unresolved addresses, **permit_mynetworks**, which allows access by any clients defined by **mynetworks**, and **check_client_access**, which will check an access database to see if a client should be accepted or rejected. The **reject_ rbl_ client** and **reject_rhsbl_client** parameters will reject clients from specified domains.

```
smtpd_client_restrictions = permit_mynetworks, \
            reject_unknown_client, check_client_access, reject_maps_rbl
```

The **reject_rbl_client** restriction rejects domain addresses according to a specified MAPS service. The site can be an online site or a local one set up to provide the service. The **reject_rhsbl_client** restriction rejects host addresses.

```
smtpd_client_restrictions = reject_rbl_client relays.mail-abuse.org
```

To implement restrictions from a access file, you can use the **hash** directive and the name of the file.

```
smtpd_client_restrictions = hash:/etc/postfix/access
```

The corresponding **smtpd_sender_restrictions** parameter works much the same way as its client counterpart but controls access from specific senders. It has many of the same restrictions but adds **reject_non_fqdn_sender**, which will reject any mail header without a fully qualified domain name, and **reject_sender_login_mismatch**, which will require sender verification. The **reject_rhsbl_sender** restriction rejects domain addresses according to a specified MAPS service.

The **smtpd_recipient_restrictions** parameter will restrict the recipients the server will accept mail for. Restrictions include **permit_auth_destination**, which allows authorized messages, and **reject_auth_destination**, which rejects unauthorized messages. The **check_recipient_address** restriction will check local networks for a recipient address, and **check_recipient_maps** will reject an address not verified in recipient tables listing local, relay, and virtual recipients along with aliases. The **reject_unknown_recipient_domain** restriction rejects recipient addresses with no DNS entry. The **reject_rhsbl_recipient** restriction rejects domain addresses according to a specified MAPS service.

You can further refine restrictions with parameters like **smtpd_helo_restrictions**, which requires a HELO command from a client. Restriction parameters include **reject_invalid_hostname**, which checks for faulty syntax, **reject_unknown_hostname**, for hosts with no DNS entry, and **reject_non_fqdn_hostname**, for hosts whose names are not fully qualified. The **strict_rfc821_envelopes** parameter will implement strict envelope protocol compliance.

Sendmail

Sendmail operates as a server to both receive and send mail messages. Sendmail listens for any mail messages received from other hosts and addressed to users on the network hosts it serves. At the same time, Sendmail handles messages users are sending out to remote users, determining what hosts to send them to. You can learn more about Sendmail at **www.sendmail.org**, including online documentation and current software packages. The Sendmail newsgroup is **comp.mail.sendmail**. You can also obtain a commercial version from **www.sendmail.com**.

The domain name server for your network designates the host that runs the Sendmail server. This is your mail host. Messages are sent to this host, whose Sendmail server then sends the message to the appropriate user and its host. In your domain name server configuration file, the mail host entry is specified with an MX entry. To print the mail queue of messages for future delivery, you can use **mailq** (or **sendmail -v -q**). This runs Sendmail with instructions to print the mail queue.

The Sendmail software package contains several utilities for managing your Sendmail server. These include mailq, which displays the queue of outgoing messages; mailstats, which shows statistics on mail server use; hoststat, which provides the stats of remote hosts that have connected with the mail server; and praliases, which prints out the mail aliases listed in the **/etc/aliases** file. Some, like mailq and hoststat, simply invoke Sendmail with certain options. Others, like mailstats and praliases, are separate programs.

Sendmail now maintains all configuration and database files in the **/etc/mail** directory. Here you will find the Sendmail macro configuration file, **sendmail.mc**, as well as several database files (see Table 25-2). Many have changed their names with the release of Sendmail 8.10. For example, the help file is now **/etc/mail/helpfile** instead of **/etc/sendmail.ht**. Specialized files provide support for certain features such as **access**, which lets you control access by different hosts and networks to your mail server, and **virtusertable**, which lets you designate virtual

File	Description
/etc/mail/sendmail.cf	Sendmail configuration file
/etc/mail/sendmail.mc	Sendmail M4 macro configuration file
/etc/aliases	Sendmail aliases file for mailing lists
/etc/aliases.db	Sendmail aliases database file generated by the **newaliases** command using the aliases file
/etc/mail/access	Sendmail access text file. Access control for screening or relaying messages from different hosts, networks, or users. Used to generate the **access.db** file
/etc/mail/access.db	Sendmail access database file. Generated from the access text file
/etc/mail/local-host-names	Sendmail local hosts file for multiple hosts using the same mail server (formerly **sendmail.cw**)
/etc/mail/trusted-users	Sendmail trusted users file (formerly **sendmail.ct**)
/etc/mail/error-header	Sendmail error header file (formerly **sendmail.oE**)
/etc/mail/helpfile	Sendmail help file (formerly **sendmail.ht**)
/etc/mail/statistics	Sendmail statistics file (formerly **sendmail.st**)
/etc/mail/virtusertable	Sendmail virtual user table text file. Maps user virtual domain addresses, allowing virtual domains to be hosted on one system. Make entries in this file and then use it to generate the **virtusertable.db** file
/etc/mail/virtusertable.db	Sendmail virtual user table database generated from the **virtusertable** file
/etc/mail/mailertable	Sendmail mailer table text file, used to override routing for your domains
/etc/mail/mailertable.db	Sendmail mailer table database file, generated from the **mailertable** file
/etc/mail/userdb	Sendmail user database file
/etc/mail/domaintable	Sendmail **domaintable** file, maps a domain name to another domain name
/etc/mail/domaintable.db	Sendmail **domaintable** database file, generated from the **domaintable** file
/var/spool/mail	Incoming mail
/var/spool/mqueue	Outgoing mail
/var/spool/maillog	Mail log file

TABLE 25-2   Sendmail Files and Directories

hosts. These files have both text and database versions. The database version ends with the extension **.db** and is the file actually used by Sendmail. You would make your entries in the text version and then effect the changes by generating a corresponding database version. Database versions are generated using the **makemap** command with the **hash** option and a redirection operation for the text and database file. For example, to deny access to a particular host, you would place the appropriate entry for it in the **/etc/mail/access** file, editing the file using any text word processor. Then, to generate the **/etc/mail/access.db** version of the access file, you would change to the **/etc/mail** directory and use the following command:

```
cd /etc/mail
makemap hash access < access
```

To regenerate all the database files, just use the **make** command in the **/etc/mail** directory:

```
make
```

Certain files and directories are used to manage the mail received and sent. Incoming mail is usually kept in the **/var/spool/mail** directory, and outgoing messages are held in the **/var/spool/mqueue** directory, with subdirectories for different users. Monitoring and error messages are logged in the **/var/log/maillog** file.

NOTE *Fedora Core now places the Sendmail configuration file, **sendmail.cf**, in the /etc/mail directory instead of the /etc directory as it did in previous versions (7.3 and earlier).*

NOTE *If your mail server services several hosts, you will need to enter them in the /etc/mail/local-host-names file.*

Aliases and LDAP

Sendmail can now support the Lightweight Directory Access Protocol (LDAP). LDAP enables the use of a separate server to manage Sendmail queries about user mail addresses. Instead of maintaining aliases and **virtusertable** files on different servers, Sendmail uses LDAP support to simply use one centralized LDAP server to locate recipients. Mail addresses are looked up in the LDAP server, instead of having to search several aliases and **virtusertable** files on different servers. LDAP also provides secure authentication of users, allowing controlled access to mail accounts. The following example enables LDAP support on Sendmail in the **sendmail.mc** file:

```
FEATURE('ldap_routing')dnl
LDAPROUTE_DOMAIN('mytrek.com')dnl
```

Alternatively, Sendmail still supports the use of aliases, for either sent or received mail. It checks an aliases database file called **aliases.db** that holds alias names and their associated e-mail addresses. This is often used for administrator mail, where mail may be sent to the system's root user and then redirected to the mail address of the actual system administrator. You can also alias host addresses, enabling you to address hosts on your network using only their aliases. Alias entries are kept in the **/etc/aliases** file. This file consists of one-line alias records associating aliases with user addresses. You can edit this file to add new entries or to change old ones. They are then stored for lookup in the **aliases.db** file using the command **newaliases**, which runs Sendmail with instructions to update the **aliases.db** file.

Aliases allow you to give different names for an e-mail address or collection of e-mail addresses. One of its most useful features is to create a mailing list of users. Mail addresses to an alias will be sent to the user or list of users associated with the alias. An alias entry consists of an alias name terminated by a colon and followed by a username or a comma-separated list of users. For example, to alias **filmcritic** with the user **george@rabbit.mytrek.com**, you would use the following entry:

```
filmcritic:    george@rabbit.mytrek.com
```

To alias **singers** with the local users **aleina** and **larisa**, you would use

```
singers:    aleina, larisa
```

You can also use aliases as the target addresses, in which case they will expand to their respective user addresses. For example, the **performers** alias will expand through the **filmcritic** and **singers** aliases to the users **george@rabbit.mytrek.com**, **aleina**, and **larisa**:

```
performers:    filmcritic, singers
```

Once you have made your entries in the **/etc/mail/aliases** file, you need to generate a database version using the **newaliases** command:

```
newaliases
```

Sendmail Configuration

The main Sendmail configuration file is **sendmail.cf**, located in the **/etc** directory. This file consists of a sometimes lengthy list of mail definitions that set general options, designate MTAs, and define the address rewrite rules. A series of options set features, such as the maximum size of mail messages or the name of host files. The MTAs are those mailers through which Sendmail routes messages. The rewrite rules "rewrite" a mail address to route through the appropriate Internet connections to its destination (these rules can be complex). Check the Sendmail HOW-TO and the online documentation for a detailed explanation.

The **sendmail.cf** definitions can be complex and confusing. To simplify the configuration process, Sendmail supports the use of macros you can use to generate the **sendmail.cf** file using the M4 preprocessor (this requires installation of the sendmail-cf package). Macros are placed in the **/etc/mail/sendmail.mc** file. Here, you can use macros to designate the definitions and features you want for Sendmail, and then the macros are used to generate the appropriate definitions and rewrite rules in the **sendmail.cf** file. As part of the Sendmail package, several specialized versions of the **sendmail.mc** file are made available in the **/usr/share/sendmail-cf** directory. These begin with a system name and have the suffix **.mc**. On many distributions, a specialized version tailored to your distribution is already installed as your **/etc/mail/ sendmail.mc** file.

Once you configure your **sendmail.mc** file, you use the following command to generate a **sendmail.cf** file (be sure first to back up your original **sendmail.cf** file). You can rename the **sendmail.mc** file to reflect the specific configuration. You can have as many different **.mc** files as you want and use them to implement different configurations. On Fedora Core you can use the following command in the **/etc/mail** directory:

```
make -C /etc/mail
```

Alternatively, you can use the original **m4** macro command:

```
m4 sendmail.mc > /etc/mail/sendmail.cf
```

You will then need to restart the Sendmail server to make the configuration effective:

```
service sendmail restart
```

In the **sendmail.mc** file, you configure different aspects of Sendmail using either a **define** command to set the value of Sendmail variables or a Sendmail macro that has already been defined to set a particular Sendmail feature. For example, to assign the **PROCMAIL_MAILER_ PATH** variable to the directory **/usr/bin/procmail**, you would use the following:

```
define('PROCMAIL_MAILER_PATH','/usr/bin/procmail')
```

Similarly, if there are variables that you do not want defined, you can remove them with the **undefine** command:

```
undefine('UUCP_RELAY')
```

To specify the type of operating system that your Sendmail server is running on, you would use the **OSTYPE** Sendmail macro. The following example specifies the Linux operating system:

```
OSTYPE('linux')
```

The **MAILER** macro specifies the mail delivery agents (MDAs) to be used. You may have more than one. Usually, you will need a mail delivery agent such as procmail for delivering mail to hosts on your network. In addition, Sendmail in effect operates as an MDA to receive messages from hosts in its local network, which it will then send out to the larger network.

```
MAILER(procmail)
MAILER(smtp)
```

Sendmail also supports an extensive number of features that you need to explicitly turn on. You can do this with the Sendmail **FEATURE** macro. See Table 25-3 for a list of commonly used Sendmail features. The following example turns on the **redirect** feature, which is used to inform a sender that a recipient is now at a different address:

```
FEATURE(redirect)
```

In addition, you can set certain configuration options. These are variables beginning with the prefix **conf** that you can set and assign values to using the **define** command. There are an extensive number of configuration options, most of which you will not need to change.

Feature	Description
`use_cw_file`	Checks for hosts served by the mail server **/etc/mail/ local-host-names** file.
`use_ct_file`	Reads a list of users from the **/etc/trusted-users** file. These are trusted users that can change the sender name for their messages.
`redirect`	Rejects all mail addressed to "address.REDIRECT", providing a forwarding address is placed in the **/etc/ aliases** file.
`mailertable`	Uses a mailer table file, **/etc/mail/mailertable**, to override routing for particular domains.
`domaintable`	Uses a domain table file, **/etc/mail/domaintable**, to map one domain to another. Useful if you change your domain name.
`allmasquerade`	Causes recipient addresses to also masquerade as being from the masquerade host.
`masquerade_entire_domain`	Masquerades all hosts within the domain specified in **MASQUERADE_AS**.
`masquerade_envelope`	Masquerades envelope sender and recipient along with headers.
`virtusertable`	For virtual hosts, maps virtual addresses to real addresses.
`nullclient`	Turns a Sendmail server into a null client, which simply forwards mail messages to a central mail server for processing.
`local_procmail`	Uses procmail as the local mailer.
`smrsh`	Uses the Sendmail Restricted Shell (smrsh) for mailing.
`promiscuous_relay`	Allows you to relay mail, allowing mail to be received from outside your domain and sent on to hosts outside your domain.
`relay_entire_domain`	Allows any host in your domain to relay mail (default limits this to hosts in the access database).
`relay_hosts_only`	Checks for relay permission for particular hosts instead of domains.
`accept_unqualified_senders`	Allows sender e-mail addresses to be single usernames instead of just fully qualified names that include domain names.
`accept_unresolvable_domains`	Allows Sendmail to accept unresolvable domain names. Useful for those users in a local network blocked by a firewall from the full DNS namespace. By default, Sendmail requires domains in addresses to be resolvable with DNS.

TABLE 25-3 Sendmail Features

PART V

Feature	Description
`access_db`	Accepts or rejects mail from domains and hosts in the access database.
`blacklist_recipients`	Blocks mail to certain users, such as those that should never receive mail—like the users **nobody** and **host**.
`dnsbl`	Rejects hosts in the Realtime Blackhole List. Managed by MAPS (Mail Abuse Prevention System LLC) and designed to limit transport of unwanted mass e-mail (**mail-abuse.org**).
`ldap_routing`	Enables LDAP use.

TABLE 25-3 Sendmail Features *(continued)*

The following example defines the **confAUTO_REBUILD** configuration option, which will automatically rebuild the aliases database if needed:

```
define('confAUTO_REBUILD')
```

Certain macros and types of macros need to be placed in the **sendmail.mc** file in a particular sequence as shown here. Notice that **MAILER** is toward the end and **OSTYPE** at the beginning. Local macro definitions (**define**) and **FEATURE** entries follow the **OSTYPE** and **DOMAIN** entries:

```
VERSIONID
OSTYPE
DOMAIN
define
FEATURE
local macro definitions
MAILER
LOCAL_RULE_*
LOCAL_RULESETS
```

The local macro and configuration option definitions that affect a particular feature need to be entered before the **FEATURE** entry. For example, the **redirect** feature uses the aliases file. Any local definition of the aliases file needs to be entered before the **redirect** feature.

```
define('ALIAS_FILE','/etc/aliases')
FEATURE(redirect)
```

You need to be careful how you enter comments into a **sendmail.mc** file. This file is read as a stream of macros, ignoring all white spaces, including newlines. No special comment characters are looked for. Instead, you have to simulate comment indicators using the **dnl** or **divert** commands. The **dnl** command instructs that all characters following that **dnl** command up to and including the next newline are to be ignored. If you place a **dnl** command at the beginning of a text line in the **sendmain.mc** file, it has the effect of turning that line into a comment, ignoring everything on that line—including its newline. Even empty lines will require a **dnl** entry to ignore the newline character:

```
dnl you will have to /etc/mail/sendmail.cf by running this the m4
dnl macro config through preprocessor:
dnl
```

Alternatively, you can use the **divert** command. The **divert** command will ignore all data until another **divert** command is reached:

```
divert(-1)
 This is the macro config file used to generate
 the /etc/mail/sendmail.cf file. If you modify the file regenerate
 you will have to regenerate /etc/mail/sendmail.cf by running the m4
 macro
divert(0)
```

For Sendmail to work at all, it requires only that the **OSTYPE** and **MAILERS** macros be defined, along with any needed features and options. A very simple Sendmail file is shown here:

mysendmail.mc
```
dnl My sendmail.mc file
OSTYPE('linux')
define('PROCMAIL_MAILER_PATH','/usr/bin/procmail')
FEATURE(redirect)
MAILER(procmail)
MAILER(smtp)
```

A **sendmail.mc** file usually contains many more entries, particularly for parameters and features. Check the **/etc/mail/sendmail.mc** file on your Fedora Core system to see the standard default entries for Sendmail.

Sendmail Masquerading

For a mail server that is relaying messages from local hosts to the Internet, you may want to masquerade the source of the messages. In large networks that have their own mail servers connected to the Internet, Sendmail masquerading can make messages sent by local hosts appear to be sent by the mail server. Their host address will be replaced by the mail server's address. Returned mail can then be sent to the mail server and held in POP or IMAP server mailboxes that can be later accessed by users on the local hosts. Also, entries in the server's virtual user table could forward mail to corresponding users in local hosts.

Masquerading is often used to mask local hosts with a domain name. Any subdomains can also be masqueraded. This method can be applied to situations where an ISP or your network administrator has assigned your network its own domain name. You can then mask all mail messages as coming from your domain name instead of from particular hosts or from any subdomains you may have. For example, if a network's official domain name is **mytrek.com**, all messages from the hosts in the **mytrek.com** network, such as **rabbit.mytrek.com** and **turtle.mytrek.com**, could be masqueraded to appear as just coming from **mytrek.com**. Should the **mytrek.com** network have a subnetwork whose domain is **mybeach.com**, any messages from **mybeach.com** could also be masqueraded as coming from **mytrek.com**.

Masquerading is turned on with the **MASQUERADE_AS** command. This takes as its argument the name you want to masquerade your mail as. Normally, the name used is just the domain name, without the mail host. In the following example, the mail is masqueraded as simply

mytrek.com. Mail sent from a local host like **turtle.mytrek.com** will appear to be sent by just **mytrek.com**:

```
MASQUERADE_AS('mytrek.com')dnl
```

You will also have to specify the hosts and domains on your local network that your Sendmail server should masquerade. If you have decided to masquerade all the hosts in your local network, you just need to set the **masquerade_entire_domain** feature, as in

```
FEATURE('masquerade_entire_domain')dnl
```

If, instead, you want to masquerade particular hosts or your domain has several subdomains that you want masqueraded, you list them in the **MASQUERADE_DOMAIN** entry. You can list either particular hosts or entire domains. For example, given a local network with the local hosts **turtle.mytrek.com** and **rabbit.mytrek.com**, you can list them with the **MASQUERADE_DOMAIN** to have them masqueraded. The domain they are masqueraded as is specified in the **MASQUERADE_AS** entry.

```
MASQUERADE_DOMAIN('turtle.mytrek.com rabbit.mytrek.com')dnl
```

If you want to masquerade all the hosts in your local network, you can simply list your local network's domain name. If your local network also supports several subdomains, you can list those as well to masquerade them. For example, to masquerade all the hosts in the **mybeach.com** domain, you would use the following entry:

```
MASQUERADE_DOMAIN('mytrek.com mybeach.com')dnl
```

If you have a long list of domains or hosts, or if you want to be able to easily change those that should be masqueraded, you can place them in a file to be read by Sendmail. Specify the file with the **MASQUERADE_DOMAIN_FILE** command:

```
MASQUERADE_DOMAIN_FILE('mydomains')dnl
```

If you just want to masquerade all the hosts in your local domain, you use the **masquerade_entire_domain** feature:

```
FEATURE(masquerade_entire_domain)dnl
```

A common configuration for a local network would specify the domain name in the **MASQUERADE_AS** entry and in the **MASQUERADE_DOMAIN** entry. Using the example **myisp.com** for the domain, the entries would look like this:

```
MASQUERADE_AS('mytrek.com')dnl
FEATURE(masquerade_entire_domain)dnl
```

If you wanted to masquerade as an ISP's mail domain, you would use the ISP's domain in the **MASQUERADE_AS** entry as shown here:

```
MASQUERADE_AS('myisp.com')dnl
MASQUERADE_DOMAIN('mytrek.com')dnl
```

When mail is received from the outside bearing just the address **mytrek.com**, your network needs to know what host to send it to. This is the host designated as the mail server for the **mytrek.com** network. This information is provided by a mail exchange record (MX) in your DNS configuration that will specify that mail sent to **mytrek.com** will be handled by the mail server—in this case, **turtle.mytrek.com**:

```
mytrek.com.   IN   MX   0   turtle.mytrek.com.
```

You further have to be sure that MX relaying is enabled with the `relay_based_on_MX` feature:

```
FEATURE(relay_based_on_MX)dnl
```

All messages will appear to originate from the mail server's host. For example, if your Sendmail mail server is running on **turtle.mytrek.com**, mail sent from a local host called **rabbit.mytrek.com** will appear to have been sent from **turtle.mytrek.com**.

You can also masquerade recipient addresses, so that mail sent to users on your local host will be sent instead to the masqueraded address. Use the `allmasquerade` feature to enable recipient masquerading:

```
FEATURE(allmasquerade)dnl
```

Configuring Mail Servers and Mail Clients

Sendmail can be used either as a mail server, handling mail for various hosts on a network, or as a mail client, managing mail for local users on a particular host. In a simple network configuration, you would have each host running Sendmail in a client configuration, and one host operating as a mail server, relaying mail for the network hosts. For a local network connected to the Internet, your local hosts would run Sendmail in a client configuration, and your gateway would run Sendmail in a server configuration (though the mail server would not have to necessarily run on the gateway). The mail server would relay messages from the local network hosts out to the Internet. The mail server could also be used to block unwanted access from outside hosts, such as those sending spam mail. A basic client or server Sendmail configuration involves just a few features in the **/etc/mail/sendamail.mc** file. The default Fedora Core configuration installed on your system allows use on a single host, managing messages between users on that host. To enable client and server use, you will need to make changes to the **/etc/mail/sendmail.mc** file.

Configuring Sendmail for a Simple Network Configuration

Fedora Core initially configures Sendmail to work only on the system it is running on, **localhost**. To use Sendmail to send messages to other hosts on a local network, you need to change and add settings in the **sendmail.mc** and **/etc/mail/access** files. A simple network configuration would have Sendmail running on each host, handling both mail sent between users on that host and mail to and from users on other hosts. For each Sendmail server configuration, you would make the changes described in the following section on simple local network configuration.

For messages sent between hosts on your network, you only need to run the Sendmail server on each, making a few changes to their Sendmail configurations. The Sendmail server on one of your hosts can be configured to handle the task of relaying messages between hosts. Using the network example described earlier, the hosts **turtle**, **rabbit**, and **lizard** will be running their own Sendmail servers. The Sendmail server on the **turtle** host will be configured to relay messages between all the hosts, itself included.

On each host on your network, edit the **/etc/mail/sendmail.mc** file and make the following changes. On Fedora Core systems, comment out the **DAEMON_OPTIONS** line in the default **sendmail.mc** file by placing a **dnl** word in front of it, as shown here. Removing this feature will allow you to receive messages over your local network. This entry is restricting Sendmail to the **localhost** (127.0.0.1):

```
dnl DAEMON_OPTIONS('Port=smtp,Addr=127.0.0.1, Name=MTA')dnl
```

In the **sendmail.mc** file located on the host that you want to have handle the relaying of messages, you need to also add the following line:

```
FEATURE(relay_entire_domain)dnl
```

Run the **m4** operation to install the changed configuration and then restart the server with the service operation, as described earlier.

You can now e-mail messages from one user to another across your network. For example, **george@turtle.mytrek.com** can now e-mail a message to **larisa@rabbit.mytrek.com**. The local Sendmail servers will take care of sending and delivering mail both to users within their hosts and those located on other network hosts.

Configuring Sendmail for a Centralized Mail Server

Alternatively, you could set up a central mail server to handle all the mail on your network. Mail clients on various hosts could send their messages to the central mail server, which would then relay them out to the larger network or Internet. Mail could then be received at the central mail server, where clients could later retrieve it. There are several ways to set up a central mail server. One of the simplest is to run a central mail server on your gateway host, and then have null client versions of the Sendmail server running on local hosts. Any mail sent from local hosts would be automatically forwarded to the central mail server. Received mail could only be delivered to the central server, usually to a POP or IMAP server also running on the central server's host. Users could then access the POP server to retrieve their mail.

For a centralized configuration, it would make sense to treat users as having their network domain as their address, rather than separate hosts in their network. Thus the user **cece** on **rabbit.mytrek.com** would use the mail address **cece@mytrek.com**, not **cece@rabbit.mytrek .com**. Users could have the same name as those on their respective hosts, but corresponding users would be set up on the gateway host to handle received mail managed by the POP or IMAP servers.

An effective simple mail server would involve several components:

- A central mail server running on the gateway host
- Each client running Sendmail as a null client
- Masquerading all mail to use the domain address only, not host addresses
- A POP or IMAP server running on the gateway host to handle received mail

Configuring a Workstation with Direct ISP Connection

If you are running a Linux system that is not part of a network but does have a direct connection to the Internet through an ISP (Internet service provider), you could simply use the ISP mail servers for sending and receiving mail. Normally, you would have an SMTP mail server for outgoing mail and a POP server for incoming mail. However, you can also configure Sendmail to interface with your ISP.

Be sure to first comment out the **DAEMON_OPTIONS** option as shown in the previous sections.

Normally, your ISP will provide a mail server that will handle mail for its hosts. To make use of the ISP mail server, you can define it with the **SMART_HOST** option. Mail will be sent through the ISP mail server. **SMART_HOST** has the format *type:hostname,* where *type* is the kind of mail server used, usually SMTP. The default is relay. Define the **SMART_HOST** option to use your ISP to send and receive mail:

```
define ('SMART_HOST', 'smtp:mail.my-isp.com')dnl
```

The **SMART_HOST** option is used to indicate a specific remote mail server that you want to have handle the relaying of your network messages. It can be an ISP mail server, as well as any mail server in a larger network.

For a dial-up connection over a modem, you can use various configuration options to control your connection. The **confMESSAGE_TIMEOUT** option lets you control how long mail can remain on the output queue, letting you keep mail until you are ready to dial in and send it. Setting the **confDELIVERY_MODE** option to **queueonly** lets you send mail only when you are ready.

The Mailer Table

The mailer table lets you route messages addressed to a specified host or domain to a particular mail server. You can use the mailer table to have mail addressed to a virtual domain routed to the mail server for your network. To reference an entire domain, prefix the domain name with a period. The host to which the mail is routed is prefixed by the mailer used, usually **smtp** for Sendmail. The following entry will route mail addressed to **.mybeach.com** to the mail server **turtle.mytrek.com**:

```
.mybeach.com        smtp:turtle.mytrek.com
```

Entries are placed in the **/etc/mail/mailertable** file. Once you have made your entries, generate the **mailertable.db** database file with the **make** command:

```
make mailertable
```

Virtual Domains: virtusertable

As you will see in Chapter 38, you can define virtual domains for your network. These virtual domains are mapped to one or more real domains by your DNS server. However, you can receive messages with mail addresses for users on your virtual domains. In this case, you need to map these addresses to users on your real domain so that the mail can be delivered to an existing location. This mapping is carried out by the virtual user table called **/etc/mail/ virtusertable**. The virtual user table lets you map mail addresses for virtual domains to users on real domains. Once you have made your entries, generate the **virtusertable.db** database file with the **make** command:

```
make virtusertable
```

Security

For security, Sendmail lets you screen specific messages as well as provide authentication and encryption for Sendmail transmissions. With version 8.11, Sendmail incorporated support for the Secure Sockets Layer (SSL) and the Simple Authentication and Security Layer (SASL). Support for SSL goes by the Sendmail command **STARTTLS**, which stands for "start transport layer security." SSL provides authentication, encryption, and integrity checks for Sendmail operations (see Chapters 19 and 23). OpenSSL must first be installed to allow use of SSL encryption and authentication methods.

The SASL is implemented by the **AUTH** command and is referred to as SMTP AUTH. SASL provides authentication for mail users and servers. It can make use of already-installed Kerberos services to provide authentication.

Sendmail also provides you with the capability of screening out messages from specific domain, host, IP, and user addresses. Rules to perform such screening are kept in the **/etc/mail/access** file. You can edit this file and add your own rules. A rule consists of an address followed by an action to take. (The actions supported are listed in Table 25-4.) For example, to remove all messages from the **myannoyingad.com** domain, you would enter

```
myannoyingad.com DISCARD
```

The next example rejects any message from **larisa@turtle.mycar.com** and sends a notice of the rejection:

```
larisa@turtle.mycar.com REJECT
```

You can also specify an error message to return, as shown here:

```
cecelia@rabbit.mytrek.com    ERROR:"Retired yesterday"
```

To send an error message to spammers, you could include a message as shown here. The first number is an error code:

```
cyberspammer.com    ERROR:"550 We don't accept mail from spammers"
```

Action	Description
OK	Accepts message even if other rules would reject (exception to the rules).
DISCARD	Discards the message completely.
REJECT	Rejects the message, sending a rejection notice to the sender.
RELAY	Relays messages for specified domain.
SMTP-code message	Code and message to be sent to sender.

TABLE 25-4 Access Actions

An **/etc/mail/access** file with the previous entries would look like the following:

```
myannoyingad.com              DISCARD
larisa@turtle.mycar.com       REJECT
cecelia@rabbit.mytrek.com     ERROR:"Retired yesterday"
cyberspammer.com              ERROR:"550 We don't accept mail from spammers"
```

Sendmail actually reads the access rules from a database file called **access.db**, also located in the **/etc/mail** directory. To implement your rules, you have to regenerate the **access.db** file using the access file. You can do this with the **make** command using **access** as the argument, as shown here:

```
make access
```

Sendmail then has to be restarted to read the new **access.db** file.

The use of the access file is enabled in the **sendmail.mc** file with the **access_db** feature:

```
FEATURE('access_db')dnl
```

The access file will deny mail received from the listed addresses. However, you can also reject any mail sent to them. Additionally, you can also receive mail for certain hosts on your network. You do this by enabling the **blacklist_recipients** option in the **sendmail.mc** file. This option governs recipients, whereas **access** normally governs senders. Those addresses listed will not be able to receive any mail. This feature is also used for certain administrative users that should never receive mail, such as **nobody** (the guest user) or **ftp** (the FTP user):

```
FEATURE('blacklist_recipients')dnl
```

The following example will not allow mail to be sent to **cyberspammer.com** (a recipient), nor can mail be received for **justin@lizard.mytrek.com**, **secretproject@rabbit.mytrek.com**, or **mysurfboard.com**:

```
mysurfboard.com               ERROR:"Domain does not exist"
justin@lizard.mytrek.com       "Moved to Hawaii"
secretproject@rabbit.mytrek.com  REJECT
cyberspammer.com              REJECT
```

Your distribution version of **smb.conf** may configure Sendmail to use **access_db**. Access is granted only to users on the local host. If your system is being used as a mail server for a network and you have not enabled the **relay_entire_domain** feature, you will need to allow access by other hosts on your network. In the access file, you can place a **RELAY** rule for your network. The **RELAY** rule will let other hosts use your mail server to send messages out to other hosts. This is normally done for a gateway host that needs to relay messages from a local network out to the Internet. The following example allows access from the **mytrek.com** network:

```
mytrek.com      RELAY
```

For a specific host, place an entry for it in the access file as shown here:

```
rabbit.mytrek.com    RELAY
```

To further secure Sendmail, you should disable the use of **VRFY**. This option allows remote users to try to verify the existence of a user address. This can be used to guess valid users on your system. This option is disabled with the **noverify** feature:

```
FEATURE('noverify')dnl
```

Another potential security breach is the **EXPN** option, which expands mailing lists and aliases to their actual addresses. Use the **noexpn** feature to turn it off:

```
FEATURE('noexpn')dnl
```

By default, Sendmail will refuse mail from any domain that cannot be resolved. You can override this restriction with the **accept_unresolvable_domains** feature. Sendmail will also reject mail whose addresses do not have fully qualified domain names. You can override this feature with **accept_unqualified_senders**.

POP and IMAP Servers: Dovecot

The protocols Internet Mail Access Protocol (IMAP) and Post Office Protocol (POP) allow a remote server to hold mail for users who can then fetch their mail from it when they are ready. Unlike procmail, which delivers mail messages directly to a user account on a Linux system, the IMAP and POP protocols hold mail until a user accesses an account on the IMAP or POP server. The server then transfers any received messages to the user's local mailbox. Such servers are often used by ISPs to provide Internet mail services for users. Instead of being sent directly to a user's machine, the mail resides in the IMAP or POP server until it's retrieved. Fedora Core installs Dovecot as both its IMAP and POP servers, and it also includes the Cyrus IMAP server. Other popular IMAP and POP servers available are Qpopper, the Qmail POP server, the Washington University POP and IMAP servers, and the Courier POP and IMAP servers.

You can access the POP server from different hosts; however, when you do, all the messages are transferred to that host. They are not kept on the POP server (though you can set an option to keep them). The POP server simply forwards your messages on the requesting host. When you access your messages from a certain computer, they will be transferred to that computer and erased from the POP server. If you access your POP server again from a different computer, those previous messages will be gone.

The Internet Mail Access Protocol (IMAP) allows a remote server to hold mail for users who can then log in to access their mail. Unlike the POP servers, IMAP servers retain user mail messages. Users can even save their mail on the IMAP mail server. This has the advantage of keeping a user's mail in one centralized location accessible anywhere on the network. Users can log in to the mail server from any host on the network and read, send, and save their mail.

Unlike POP, IMAP allows users to set up multiple folders on their mail server in which they can organize their mail. IMAP also supports the use of shared folders to which several users can access mail on a given topic.

Dovecot

Dovecot is a combination IMAP and POP server. Using its own indexing methods, Dovecot is able to handle a great deal of e-mail traffic. It features support for SSL, along with numerous authentication methods. Password database support includes shadow passwords, LDAP, PAM, and MySQL. On Fedora Core, the **/etc/dovecot.conf** file is configured to use plain password authentication with PAM, using the **passwd** file.

Dovecot is a service that is managed with a service script: **/etc/rc.d/init.d/dovecot**. You can start, stop, or restart with either the **service** command or system-config-services.

```
service dovecot start
```

Configuration options are placed in **/etc/dovecot.conf**. This file contains commented default settings with detail explanations for each. These are some basic settings to configure:

- **protocols**   This can be set to imap and pop as well as imaps and pops for SSL-encrypted connections.

- **imap_listen** and **pop_listen**   These can be set to IPv4 or IPv4 protocols; IPv6 is set by default. **imaps_listen** and **pops_listen** are for SSL connections.

- **auth_mechanism**   This is plain by default. digest-MD5 and cran-MD5 are supported, but they are not needed if you are using SSL.

- **auth_userdb**   The user database. This is set to passwd, but options include LDAP and pgsql (PostgreSQL).

- **auth_passwd**   The password database. This is set to pam, but options include passwd, shadow, LDAP, and pgsql.

- **auth_root**   The authentication user, set to root by default, since pam requires it (passwd also requires root).

- **default_mail_env**   The default mail storage method and location.

Dovecot supports either mailbox or Maildir (IMAP) storage formats. The mailbox format uses single large mailbox files to hold several mail messages. Updates can be time consuming. The Maildir format uses a separate file for each message, making updates much more efficient. Dovecot will automatically detect the kind of storage use, referencing the MAIL environment variable. On Fedora Core, this will be the user's mbox file at **/var/mail**. You can configure Dovecot to use a Maildir format by setting the **default_mail_env** option to use a Maildir setting, specifying the directory to use. The **%u** symbol can be used to represent the username, **%h** for the home directory. Messages will be stored in a user's Maildir directory instead of an mbox file. Be sure to create the Maildir directory and give it read, write, execute access.

```
default_mail_env=maildir:/var/mail/%1u/%u/maildir
```

Other POP and IMAP Servers

Fedora Core also includes the Cyrus IMAP server, which you can install and use instead of Dovecot. In addition, several other IMAP and POP servers are available for use on Linux:

- The University of Washington POP and IMAP servers (**ftp.cac.washington.edu/imap**) are part of the University of Washington's **imap** RPM package. The POP server daemons are called **ipop2d** and **ipop3d**. Your Linux system then runs as a POP2 and POP3 server for your network. These servers are run through **xinetd**. The POP3 server uses the **ipop3** file in the **/etc/xinetd.d**, and the IMAP server uses **imap**.

- The Cyrus IMAP server (**asg.web.cmu.edu/cyrus**) is included with Fedora Extras (**download.fedora.redhat.com/pub/fedora/linux/extras**). Cyrus IMAP servers feature security controls and authentication, using a private mailbox structure that is easily scalable. Designed to be run on dedicated mail servers, it is supported and maintained by Carnegie Mellon. The name of the Cyrus IMAP server daemon is **imapd**. On Fedora Core, there will be a file called **imap** in the **/etc/xinetd.d** directory. You turn it on or off with the `chkconfig` command.

- The Courier-IMAP server (**www.courier-mta.org**) is a small, fast IMAP server that provides extensive authentication support including LDAP and PAM.

- Qpopper is the Berkeley POP server (popper). Qpopper is unsupported software, currently available from Qualcomm, makers of Eudora e-mail software. The Qpopper Web page is located at the Eudora site archives (**www.eudora.com**).

NOTE *The IMAP and POP servers included with Fedora Core provide SSL encryption for secure e-mail transmissions. You can also run IMAP and POP servers using Stunnel to provide similar security. Stunnel is an SSL wrapper for daemons like **imapd, popd**, and even **pppd** (modem connections). In the service's **xinetd** script, you can invoke the server with the* `stunnel` *command instead of running the server directly.*

Spam: SpamAssassin

With SpamAssassin, you can filter sent and received e-mail for spam. The filter examines both headers and content, drawing on rules designed to detect common spam messages. When they are detected, it then tags the message as spam, so that a mail client can then discard it. SpamAssassin will also report spam messages to spam detection databases. The version of SpamAssassin distributed for Linux is the open source version developed by the Apache project, located at **spamassassin.apache.org**. There you can find detailed documentation, FAQs, mailing lists, and even a listing of the tests that SpamAssasin performs.

On Fedora Core, SpamAssassin rule files are located at **/usr/share/spamassassin**. The files contain rules for running tests such as detecting the fake hello in the header. Configuration files for SpamAssassin are located at **/etc/mail/spamassassin**. The **local.cf** file lists system-wide SpamAssassin options such as how to rewrite headers. The **init.pre** file holds spam system configurations. The **spamassassin-spamc.rc** file will redirect all mail to the **spamc** client.

Users can set their own SpamAssassin option in their **.spamassasin/user_prefs** file. Common options include `required_score`, which sets a threshold for classifying a message as SPAM, numerous whitelist and blacklist options that accept and reject messages from certain users and domains, and tagging options that either rewrite or just add SPAM labels. Check the Mail::SpamAssassin::Conf Man page for details.

SpamAssassin is run as a service using the `/etc/init.d/spamassassin` service script. This runs the **spamd** server, which in turn is accessed by the **spamc** client. Using the server/

client structure greatly enhances SpamAssassin's efficiency. Options for **spamd** can be set in the **/etc/sysconfig/spamassassin** file.

```
service spamassassin start
```

To configure procmail to use SpamAssassin, you need to have procmail run the **/etc/mail/ spamassassin/spamassassin-spamc.rc** file. This will filter all mail through SpamAssassin. The **spamassassin-spamc.rc** file uses the **spamd** daemon, which means you have to have the SpamAssassin service running. The **spamassassin-default.rc** file runs a less efficient script to use SpamAssassin, instead of the daemon. If you want system-wide procmail filtering, you use the **/etc/procmailrc** file, whereas to implement filtering on a per-user basis, use a **.procmail** file in the user's home directory. Within the respective procmail files add the following at the top:

```
INCLUDERC=/etc/mail/spamassassin/spamassassin-spamc.rc
```

Configuring Postfix for use with SpamAssassin can be complicated. A helpful tool for this task would be **amavisd-new**, an interface between a mail transport agent like Sendmail or Postfix, and content checkers like SpamAssassin and virus checkers. Check **www.ijs.si/ software/amavisd** for more details. Though this tool is currently not part of the Fedora Core distribution, you can download Fedora Core RPM packages for it.

26

CHAPTER

Print Server: CUPS

Once treated as devices attached to a system directly, printers are now treated as network resources managed by print servers. In the case of a single printer attached directly to a system, the networking features become transparent and the printer appears as just one more device. On the other hand, you could easily make use of a print server's networking capability to let several systems use the same printer. Although printer installation is almost automatic on most Linux distributions, it helps to understand the underlying process. You can find out more information about printing in Linux at **www .linuxprinting.org**. Printing sites and resources are listed in Table 26-1.

The Common Unix Printing System (CUPS) provides printing services. It is freely available under the GNU Public License. Though it is now included with most distributions, you can also download the most recent source-code version of CUPS from **www.cups.org**. The site also provides detailed documentation on installing and managing printers. CUPS is based on the Internet Printing Protocol (IPP), which is designed to establish a printing standard for the Internet (for more information, see **www.pwg.org/ipp**). Whereas the older LPD-based printing systems focused primarily on line printers, an IPP-based system provides networking, PostScript, and Web support. CUPS works like an Internet server and employs a configuration setup much like that of the Apache Web server. Its network support lets clients directly access printers on remote servers, without having to configure the printers themselves. Configuration needs to be maintained only on the print servers.

The Common Unix Printing System (CUPS) is the primary print server for Red Hat since version 9, and it has always been the primary server for Fedora Core. CUPS is the print server supported by system-config-printer. With libgnomecups, GNOME now provides integrated support for CUPS, allowing GNOME-based applications to directly access CUPS printers.

Resource	Description
www.cups.org	Common Unix Printing System
www.linuxprinting.org	Print drivers and information for Linux
www.pwg.org/ipp	Internet Printing Protocol
sourceforge.net/projects/lprng	LPRng print server

TABLE 26-1   Print Resources

Once you have installed your printers and configured your print server, you can print and manage your print queue using print clients. There are a variety of printer clients available for the CUPS server, including system-config-printer, GNOME print manager, the CUPS configuration tool, and various line printing tools like **lpq** and **lpc**. These are described in further detail later in this chapter. The CUPS configuration tool is a Web-based configuration tool that can also manage printers and print jobs (open your browser and enter the URL **http://127.0.0.1:631**). A Web page is displayed with entries for managing jobs, managing printers, and administrative tasks. Select the Manage Jobs entry to remove or reorder jobs you have submitted.

NOTE *Line Printer, Next Generation (LPRng) was the traditional print server for Linux and Unix systems, but it has since been dropped from the Fedora Core distributions. You can find out more about LPRng at **sourceforge.net/projects/lprng**.*

Printer Devices and Configuration

Before you can use any printer, you first have to install it on a Linux system on your network. A local printer is installed directly on your own system. This involves creating an entry for the printer in a printer configuration file that defines the kind of printer it is, along with other features such as the device file and spool directory it uses. On CUPS, the printer configuration file is **/etc/cups/printers.conf**. Installing a printer is fairly simple: determine which device file to use for the printer and the configuration entries for it. On Fedora Core, you can use the system-config-printer configuration tool to set up and configure your printer easily. Depending on the interface you are using, system-config-printer will invoke either system-config-printer-gui, a GUI GNOME printer configuration tool, or system-config-printer-tui, the same tool with a screen-based cursor driven interface.

TIP *If you cannot find the drivers for your printer, you may be able to download them from **www .linuxprinting.org**. The site maintains an extensive listing of drivers.*

Printer Device Files

Linux dynamically creates the device names for printers that are installed (see Chapter 34). For parallel printers, the device names will be **lp0**, **lp1**, and **lp2**, depending on how many parallel printers are connected. The number used in these names corresponds to a parallel port on your PC; **lp0** references the LPT1 parallel port and **lp1** references the LPT2 parallel port. Serial printers will use serial ports, referenced by the device files like **ttyS0**, **ttyS1**, **ttyS2**, and so on. A USB-connected printer will have a device like **/dev/usb/lp1** which will be dynamically generated by udev and HAL. With HAL removable devices can easily be attached to other connections and still be recognized.

Spool Directories

When your system prints a file, it makes use of special directories called *spool directories*. A *print job* is a file to be printed. When you send a file to a printer, a copy of it is made and placed in a spool directory set up for that printer. The location of the spool directory is obtained from the printer's entry in its configuration file. On Linux, the spool directory is located at **/var/spool/cups** under a directory with the name of the printer. For example, the spool directory for the **myepson** printer would be located at **/var/spool/cups/myepson**. The spool directory contains several files for managing print jobs. Some files use the name of the printer as their extension. For example, the **myepson** printer has the files **control.myepson**, which provides printer queue control, and **active.myepson** for the active print job, as well as **log.myepson**, which is the log file.

Starting the CUPS Server

With the RPM version used by Fedora Core, a **cups** startup script is installed in the **/etc/rc.d/init.d** directory. You can start, stop, and restart CUPS using the `service` command and the **cups** script. When you make changes or install printers, be sure to restart CUPS to have your changes take effect. On Fedora Core, you can use the following command:

```
service cups restart
```

Installing Printers with CUPS

The easiest way to configure and install printers with CUPS is to use system-config printer, as described in Chapter 4, or use the CUPS configuration tool, which is a Web browser–based configuration tool. To ensure browser access, be sure to first select CUPS with the Printer System Switcher, or if you are using **xinetd** for CUPS, turn on **cups** with the `chkconfig` command.

```
chkconfig cups on
```

To start the Web interface, enter the following URL into your Web browser:

```
http://localhost:631
```

This opens an administration screen where you can manage and add printers. You will first be asked to enter the administrator's username (usually **root**) and password (usually the root user's password).

With the CUPS configuration tool, you install a printer on CUPS through a series of Web pages, each of which requests different information. To install a printer, click the Add Printer button to display a page where you enter the printer name and location (see Figure 26-1). The location is the host to which the printer is connected.

Subsequent pages will prompt you to enter the model of the printer and driver, which you select from available listings. Once you have added the printer, you can configure it. Clicking the Manage Printers entry in the Administration page lists your installed printers. You can then click a printer to display a page that lets you control the printer. You can stop the printer, configure its printing, modify its installation, and even delete the printer. Clicking the Configure Printer button displays a page where you can configure how your printer prints, by specifying the resolution or paper size.

Configured information for a printer will be stored in the **/etc/cups/printers.conf** file. You can examine this file directly, even making changes. Here is an example of a printer configuration entry. Notice that it was created using system-config-printer. The `DeviceURI`

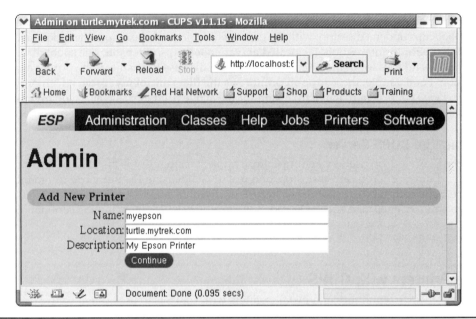

FIGURE 26-1 CUPS Add Printer page

entry specifies the device used, in this case the **lp0**, a parallel device. It is currently idle, with nothing in its queue:

```
<DefaultPrinter myepson>
Info Created by system-config-printer  0.6.x
DeviceURI parallel:/dev/lp0
Location
State Idle
Accepting Yes
JobSheets none none
QuotaLimit 0
PageLimit 0
Klimit 0
</Printer>
```

NOTE *You can perform all administrative tasks from the command line using the* **lpadmin** *command. See the CUPS documentation for more details.*

Configuring Remote Printers on CUPS

To install a remote printer that is attached to a Windows system or another Linux system running CUPS, you specify its location using special URL protocols. For another CUPS printer on a remote host, the protocol used is **ipp**, for Internet Printing Protocol, whereas for a Windows printer it would be **smb**. Older Unix or Linux systems using LPRng would use the **lpd** protocol.

As shown in Chapter 4, you can use system-config-printer to configure a remote printer with CUPS. Create a new print queue and select a network type. The entries displayed are

different for some types. A CUPS or LPD remote server will just need the IP address and
queue name, whereas the Windows server will need a Samba share name. You can also use
the CUPS configuration tool to configure a remote Windows printer. Select the Windows
Printer Via Samba entry and then enter the appropriate SMB URL.

In the **cupsd.conf** file, for a remote printer, the DeviceURI entry, instead of listing the
device, will have an Internet address, along with its protocol. For example, a remote printer
on a CUPS server (**ipp**) would be indicated as shown here (a Windows printer would use an
smb protocol):

```
DeviceURI ipp://mytsuff.com/printers/queue1
```

For a Windows printer, you first need to install, configure, and run Samba. (CUPS uses
Samba to access Windows printers.) When you install the Windows printer on CUPS, you
specify its location using the URL protocol **smb**. The user allowed to log in to the printer is
entered before the hostname and separated from it by a @ sign. On most configurations, this
is the **guest** user. The location entry for a Windows printer called **myhp** attached to a Windows
host named **lizard** is shown here. Its Samba share reference would be **//lizard/myhp**:

```
DeviceURI smb://guest@lizard/myhp
```

To enable CUPS on Samba, you also have to set the printing option in the **/etc/samba/smb
.conf** file to **cups**, as shown here:

```
printing = cups
printcap name = cups
```

To enable CUPS to work with Samba, you have to link the **smbspool** to the CUPS **smb** spool
directory:

```
ln -s /usr/bin/smbspool   /usr/cups/backend/smb
```

Configuring a Shared CUPS Printer

To allow a printer to be accessed by the hosts on your local network, you can simply enable
printer sharing for that printer. On the host to which the printer is directly connected, use
system-config-printer to select its print queue entry. Then choose Sharing from the Action
menu. In the Sharing properties window that then displays, select the entry labeled "This
queue is available to other printers."

An All Hosts entry will be automatically generated, providing access to all hosts on the
network. You can further limit access to hosts, by specifying either the device they are
connected to, a network address, or an IP address. Select the entry and click Edit to list the
options.

The General tab lists options to automatically detect remote hosts configured for this
printer, which is already selected by default, and whether any of those hosts still use the
older LPD Unix (LPRng) interface. You also need to turn on the **cups-lpd** daemon.

```
chkconfig cups-lpd on
```

NOTE *To configure a shared Linux printer for access by Windows hosts, you need to configure it as*
a SMB shared printer. You do this with Samba (see Chapter 41).

CUPS Printer Classes

CUPS features a way to let you select a group of printers to print a job instead of selecting just one. That way, if one printer is busy or down, another printer can be automatically selected to perform the job. Such groupings of printers are called *classes.* Once you have installed your printers, you can then group them into different classes. For example, you may want to group all inkjet printers into one class and laser printers into another, or you may want to group printers connected to one specific printer server in their own class. To create a class, select Classes on the Administration page and enter the name of the class. You can then add printers to it.

CUPS Configuration

CUPS configuration files are placed in the **/etc/cups** directory. These files are listed in Table 26-2. The **classes.conf**, **printers.conf**, and **client.conf** files can be managed by the Web interface. The **printers.conf** file contains the configuration information for the different printers you have installed. Any of these files can be edited manually, if you wish.

cupsd.conf

The CUPS server is configured with the **cupsd.conf** file located in **/etc/cups**. You must edit configuration options manually; the server is not configured with the Web interface. Your installation of CUPS installs a commented version of the **cupsd.conf** file with each option listed, though most options will be commented out. Commented lines are preceded with a **#** symbol. Each option is documented in detail. The server configuration uses an Apache Web server syntax consisting of a set of directives. As with Apache, several of these directives can group other directives into blocks.

CUPS Directives

Certain directives allow you to place access controls on specific locations. These can be printers or resources, such as the administrative tool or the spool directories. Location controls are implemented with the **Location** directive. **Allow From** and **Deny From** directives can permit or deny access from specific hosts. CUPS supports both Basic and Digest forms of authentication, specified in the **AuthType** directive. Basic authentication uses a user and password. For example, to use the Web interface, you are prompted to enter the root user and the root user password. Digest authentication makes use of user and password information kept in the CUPS **/etc/cups/passwd.md5** file, using MD5 versions of a user and password for authentication. The **AuthClass** directive specifies the class allowed access. The **System**

Filename	Description
classes.conf	Configurations for different local printer classes
client.conf	Lists specific options for specified clients
cupsd.conf	Configures the CUPS server, **cupsd**
printers.conf	Printer configurations for available local printers

TABLE 26-2 CUPS Configuration Files

class includes the **root**, **sys**, and **system** users. The following example shows the **Location** directive for the **/admin** resource, the administrative tool:

```
<Location /admin>

AuthType Basic
AuthClass System

## Restrict access to local domain
Order Deny,Allow
Deny From All
Allow From 127.0.0.1

</Location>
```

CUPS Command Line Print Clients

Once a print job is placed on a print queue, you can use any of several print clients to manage the printing jobs on your printer or printers, such as Klpq, the GNOME Print Manager, and the CUPS Printer Configuration tool for CUPS. You can also use several command line print CUPS clients. These include the **lpr**, **lpc**, **lpq**, and **lprm** commands (see Chapter 10). The Printer System Switcher moves you from one set to the other. With these clients, you can print documents, list a print queue, reorder it, and remove print jobs, effectively canceling them. For network connections, CUPS features an encryption option for its commands, **-E**, to encrypt print jobs and print information sent over a network. Table 26-3 shows various printer commands.

NOTE   *The command line clients have the same name, and much the same syntax, as the older LPR and LPRng command line clients used in Unix and older Linux systems.*

Printer Management	Description
GNOME Print Manager	GNOME print queue management tool (CUPS).
CUPS Configuration Tool	Print, manage, and configure CUPS.
lpr *options file-list*	Prints a file, copies the file to the printer's spool directory, and places it on the print queue to be printed in turn. **-P** *printer* prints the file on the specified printer.
lpq *options*	Displays the print jobs in the print queue. **-P** *printer* prints the queue for the specified printer. **-l** prints a detailed listing.
lpstat *options*	Displays printer status.
lprm *options printjob-id* **or** *printer*	Removes a print job from the print queue. You identify a particular print job by its number as listed by **lpq**. **-P** *printer* removes all print jobs for the specified printer.
lpc	Manages your printers. At the **lpc>** prompt, you can enter commands to check the status of your printers and take other actions.

TABLE 26-3   CUPS Print Clients

PART V

lpr

The **lpr** client submits a job, and **lpd** then takes it in turn and places it on the appropriate print queue; **lpr** takes as its argument the name of a file. If no printer is specified, then the default printer is used. The **-P** option enables you to specify a particular printer. In the next example, the user first prints the file **preface** and then prints the file **report** to the printer with the name **myepson**:

```
$ lpr preface
$ lpr -P myepson report
```

lpc

You can use **lpc** to enable or disable printers, reorder their print queues, and reexecute configuration files. To use **lpc**, enter the command **lpc** at the shell prompt. You are then given an **lpc>** prompt at which you can enter **lpc** commands to manage your printers and reorder their jobs. The **status** command with the name of the printer displays whether the printer is ready, how many print jobs it has, and so on. The **stop** and **start** commands can stop a printer and start it back up. The printers shown depend on the printers configured for a particular print server. A printer configured on CUPS will only show if you have switched to CUPS.

```
# lpc
lpc> status myepson
myepson:
 printer is on device 'parallel'
 queuing is enabled
 printing is enabled
 1 entry in spool area
```

lpq and lpstat

You can manage the print queue using the **lpq** and **lprm** commands. The **lpq** command lists the printing jobs currently on the print queue. With the **-P** option and the printer name, you can list the jobs for a particular printer. If you specify a username, you can list the print jobs for that user. With the **-l** option, **lpq** displays detailed information about each job. If you want information on a specific job, simply use that job's ID number with **lpq**. To check the status of a printer, use **lpstat**.

```
# lpq
myepson is ready and printing
Rank    Owner   Jobs  File(s)         Total Size
active  chris    1    report          1024
```

lprm

The **lprm** command enables you to remove a print job from the queue, erasing the job before it can be printed. The **lprm** command takes many of the same options as **lpq**. To remove a specific job, use **lprm** with the job number. To remove all printing jobs for a particular printer, use the **-P** option with the printer name. **lprm** with no options removes the job printing currently. The following command removes the first print job in the queue (use **lpq** to obtain the job number):

```
# lprm 1
```

CUPS Command Line Administrative Tools

CUPS provides command line administrative tools like **lpadmin**, **lpoptions**, **lpinfo**, **enable**, **disable**, **accept**, and **reject**. The **enable** and **disable** commands start and stop print queues directly, whereas the **accept** and **reject** commands start and stop particular jobs. The **lpinfo** command provides information about printers, and **lpoptions** lets you set printing options. The **lpadmin** command lets you perform administrative tasks like adding printers and changing configurations. CUPS administrative tools are listed in Table 26-4.

lpadmin

You can use the **lpadmin** command to either set the default printer or configure various options for a printer. You can use the **-d** option to specify a particular printer as the default destination (you can also do this in system-config-printer). Here **myepson** is made the default printer:

```
lpadmin -d myepson
```

The **-p** option lets you designate a printer for which to set various options. The following example sets printer description information:

```
lpadmin -p myepson  -D  Epson550
```

Certain options let you control per-user quotas for print jobs. The **job-k-limit** option sets the size of a job allowed per user, **job-page-limit** sets the page limit for a job, and **job-quota-period** limits the number of jobs with a specified time frame. The following command set a page limit of 100 for each user:

```
lpadmin -p myepson  -o job-page-limit=100
```

User access control is determined with the **-u** option with an **allow** or **deny** list. Users allowed access are listed following the **allow**: entry, and those denied access are listed with a **deny**: entry. Here access is granted to **chris** but denied to **aleina** and **larisa**.

```
lpadmin -p myepson -u allow:chris  deny:aleina,larisa
```

Administration Tool	Description
`lpadmin`	CUPS printer configuration
`lpoptions`	Set printing options
`enable`	Activate a printer
`disable`	Stop a printer
`accept`	Allow a printer to accept new jobs
`reject`	Prevent a printer from accepting print jobs
`lpinfo`	List CUPS devices available

TABLE 26-4   CUPS Administrative Tools

Use **all** or **none** to permit or deny access to all or no users. You can create exceptions by using **all** or **none** in combination with user-specific access. The following example allows access to all users except **justin**:

```
lpadmin -p myepson  -u allow:all   deny:justin
```

lpoptions

The **lpoptions** command lets you set printing options and defaults that mostly govern how your print jobs will be printed. For example, you can set the color or page format to be used with a particular printer. Default settings for all users are maintained by the root user in the **/etc/cups/lpoptions** file, and each user can create their own configurations, which are saved in their **.lpoptions** files. The **-l** option lists current options for a printer, and the **-p** option designates a printer (you can also set the default printer to use with the **-d** option).

```
lpoptions -p myepson -l
```

Printer options are set using the **-o** option along with the option name and value, **-o** *option=value*. You can remove a printer option with the **-r** option. For example, to print on both sides of your sheets, you can set the **sides** option to **two-sided**:

```
lpoptions -p myepson -o sides=two-sided
```

To remove the option, use **-r**.

```
lpoptions -p myepson -r sides
```

To display a listing of available options, check the standard printing options in the CUPS Software Manual at **www.cups.org**.

enable and disable

The **enable** command starts a printer, and the **disable** command stops it. With the **-c** option, you can also cancel all jobs on the printer's queue, and with the **-r** option, you broadcast a message explaining the shutdown.

```
disable myepson
```

accept and reject

The **accept** and **reject** commands let you control access to the printer queues for specific printers. The **reject** command prevents a printer from accepting jobs, whereas **accept** allows new print jobs.

```
reject myepson
```

lpinfo

The **lpinfo** command is a handy tool for letting you know what CUPS devices and drivers are available on your system. Use the **-v** option for devices, and the **-m** option for drivers.

```
lpinfo -m
```

CHAPTER 27

News and Search Servers

News servers provide Internet users with Usenet news services. They have their own TCP/IP protocol, the Network News Transfer Protocol (NNTP). On most Linux systems, including Fedora Core, the InterNetNews (INN) news server provides news services (**www.isc.org**). In addition, servers exist that provide better access to Internet resources. The search and indexing server ht://Dig enables document searches of Web and FTP sites (**www.htdig.org**). With it, you can index documents and carry out complex search requests.

News Servers: INN

The InterNetNews (INN) news server accesses Usenet newsfeeds, providing news clients on your network with the full range of newsgroups and their articles. Newsgroup articles are transferred using NNTP, and servers that support this protocol are known as *NNTP servers*. INN was written by Rich Salz and is currently maintained and supported by the Internet Software Consortium (ISC). You can download current versions from its Web site at **www .isc.org**. INN is also included with most Linux distributions. The documentation directory for INN in **/usr/share/doc** contains extensive samples. The primary program for INN is the **innd** daemon.

INN Configuration Files

Various INN configuration files can be found in **/etc/news**, including **inn.conf**, **storage.conf**, **readers.conf**, and **incoming.conf** (see Table 27-1); **inn.conf** sets options for INN, and **incoming.conf** holds the hosts from which you receive newsfeeds. Place entries for remote hosts in the **readers.conf** file to allow them access to your news server. Actual newsfeeds are managed in directories in the **/var/spool/news** directory. Here you will find directories such as **article**, which holds newsgroup articles, **outgoing** for articles being posted by your users to newsgroups, and **overview**, which holds summary information about articles. Correct configuration of INN can be a complex and time-consuming process, so be sure to consult references and online resources, such as the documents. When you change configurations, be sure to restart the INN server. An **innd** script is in the **/etc/rc.d/init.d** directory, which has similar arguments to the Web **httpd** script. You can use **start**, **restart**, and **stop** arguments with the **innd** script to start, restart, and stop the INN server.

531

File	Description
inn.conf	General INN configuration file.
incoming.conf	Specifies hosts from which newsfeeds are received.
cycbuff.conf	Configures buffers used in cnfs storage format.
storage.conf	Defines storage classes. These consist of a storage method and the newsgroups that use it. Storage methods are the storage formats: tradspool, timehash, timecaf, and cnfs. An additional method, trash, throws out the articles.
expire.ctl	Sets the expiration policy for articles on the news server.
readers.conf	Designates hosts whose users can access the news server with newsreaders.
ovdb.conf	Configures ovdb storage method for overviews.
newsfeeds	Defines how your news server feeds articles to other news servers.
moderated	Moderated newsgroups.
active	Supported newsgroups.
history	Record of posted articles.
innfeed.conf	Configures newsfeed processes for innfeed.
innreport.conf	Configures innreport utility for generating log-based reports.
buffindexed.conf	Configures overview buffer for buffindexed method.

TABLE 27-1   INN Configuration Files

TIP   There is a Man page for each configuration file in INN, providing detailed information on how to configure their features.

inn.conf

On many distributions, a basic **inn.conf** file is already set up for you with default settings. Several of the initial parameters you will have to set yourself, such as **domain**, which holds the domain name for your server; **pathhost**, in which you specify the name for your newsreader as you want it to appear in the Path header field for news articles you post; and **server**, in which you specify your newsreader's IP or fully qualified domain name address, as in **mynews.mytrek.com**. Different Path options have already been set up for you defining the location of different INN directories, such as **patharticles**, set to **/var/spool/ news/articles** that holds your newsgroup articles, and **pathetc**, set to **/etc/news** for your configuration files.

Storage Formats

Storage formats for the vast number of news articles that are often downloaded and accessed are a central concern for a full-scale news server like INN. INN lets you choose among four possible storage formats: tradspool, timehash, timecaf, and cnfs. The tradspool format is the traditional method whereby articles are arranged in a simple directory structure according to their newsgroups. This is known to be very time-consuming to access and store. timehash stores articles in directories organized by the time they were received, making it easier to remove outdated articles. timecaf is similar to timehash, but articles received at a given time are placed in the same file, making access much faster. cnfs stores articles into buffer files that have already been set up. When a buffer file becomes full, the older articles are overwritten by new ones as they come in. This is an extremely fast method, since no new files are created. There is no need to set maximum article limits, but there is also no control on how long an article is retained. In the **storage.conf** file, storage formats are assigned as storage methods to different newsgroups.

Newsreader Access

Users access your news server using newsreaders, as described in Chapter 13. You can place controls on users with options in the **readers.conf** file. Control is specified in two components: authentication and access definitions. The authentication definition creates a user category and the hosts and their authentication tools for users. The access definition applies restrictions to a user category, such as what newsgroups can be accessed and whether posting articles is allowed.

Overviews

INN also supports overviews. These are summaries of articles that readers can check, instead of having to download the entire article to see what it is. Overviews have their own storage methods: tradindexed, buffindexed, and ovdb. You specify the one you want to use in the ovmethod feature in **inn.conf**. tradindexed is fast for readers but difficult for the server to generate. buffindexed is fast for news servers but slow for readers. ovdb uses Berkeley DB database files and is very fast for both but uses more disk space. If you choose ovdb, you can set configuration parameters for it in **ovdb.conf**.

INN Implementation

On many distributions, a **news** user is already created with a newsgroup for use by your INN daemon and sets up the news directories in **/var/spool/news**. INN software also installs **cron** scripts, which are used to update your news server, removing old articles and fetching new ones. These are usually placed in the **/etc/cron.daily** directory, though they may reside anywhere. `inn-cron-expire` removes old articles, and `inn-cron-rnews` retrieves new ones. `inn-cron-nntpsend` sends articles posted from your system to other news servers.

INN also includes several support programs to provide maintenance and crash recovery, and to perform statistical analysis on server performance and usage. cleanfeed implements spam protection, and innreport generates INN reports based on logs. INN also features a very strong filter system for screening unwanted articles.

NOTE *Leafnode is an NNTP news server designed for small networks that may have slow connections to the Internet. You can obtain the Leafnode software package along with documentation from its Web site at* ***www.leafnode.org***. *Along with the Leafnode NNTP server, the software package includes several utilities such as Fetchnews, Texpire, and Newsq that send, delete, and display news articles. slrnpull is a simple single-user version of Leafnode that can be used only with the slrn newsreader.*

Dig Server

Dig, known officially as ht://Dig, is a Web indexing and search system designed for small networks or intranets. Dig is not considered a replacement for full-scale Internet search systems, such as Lycos, Infoseek, or AltaVista. Unlike Web server–based search engines, Dig can span several Web servers at a site. Dig was developed at San Diego State University and is distributed free under the GNU Public License. You can obtain information and documentation at **www.htdig.org**. ht://Dig is part of the Fedora Core distribution which includes two RPM packages, the ht://Dig software and the Web page interface scripts and elements (htdig-web).

Dig Searches

Dig supports simple and complex searches, including complex Boolean and fuzzy search methods. *Fuzzy searching* supports a number of search algorithms, including exact, soundex, and synonyms. Searches can be carried out on both text and HTML documents. HTML documents can have keywords placed in them for more accurate retrieval, and you can also use HTML templates to control how results are displayed.

Searches can be constrained by authentication requirements, location, and search depth. To protect documents in restricted directories, Dig can be informed to request a specific username and password. You can also restrict a search to retrieve documents in a certain URL, to search subsections of the database, or to retrieve only documents that are a specified number of links away.

Dig Configuration

All the ht://Dig programs use the same configuration file, **htdig.conf**, located in the **/etc/htdig** directory. The configuration file consists of attribute entries, each beginning with the attribute line and followed by the value after a colon. Each program takes only the attributes it needs:

```
max_head_length: 10000
```

You can specify attributes such as **allow_virtual_hosts**, which indexes virtual hosts as separate servers, and **search_algorithm**, which specifies the search algorithms to use for searches.

Dig Tools

Dig consist of five programs: htdig, htmerge, htfuzzy, htnotify, and htsearch. htdig, htmerge, and htfuzzy generate the index, while htsearch performs the actual searches. First, htdig gathers information on your database, searching all URL connections in your domain and associating Web pages with terms. The htmerge program uses this information to create a searchable database, merging the information from any previously generated database. htfuzzy creates indexes to allow searches using fuzzy algorithms, such as soundex and synonyms. Once the database is created, users can use Web pages that invoke htsearch to search this index. Results are listed on a Web page. You can use META tags in your HTML documents to enter specific htdig keywords, exclude a document from indexing, or provide notification information such as an e-mail address and an expiration date. htnotify uses the e-mail address and expiration date to notify Web page authors when their pages are out of date.

The htsearch program is a CGI script that expects to be invoked by an HTML form, and it accepts both the GET and POST methods of passing data. The htsearch program can accept a search request from any form containing the required configuration values. Values include search features such as config (configuration file), method (search method), and sort (sort criteria). For the Web page form that invokes htsearch, you can use the default page provided by htdig or create your own. Output is formatted using templates you can modify. Several sample files are included with the htdig software: **rundig** is a sample script for creating a database, **searchform.html** is a sample HTML document that contains a search form for submitting htdig searches, **header.html** is a sample header for search headers, and **footer .html** is for search footers.

Database Servers: MySQL and PostgreSQL

A s noted in Chapter 11, Fedora Core includes two fully functional database servers in its distribution, MySQL and PostgreSQL. MySQL is by far the more popular of the two, though PostgreSQL is noted for providing more features. Recently, the MySQL AB project added MaxDB, formerly SAP DB, which provides capabilities comparable to many professional-level database management systems. This chapter will cover how to set up and manage a MySQL database and will offer a brief introduction to PostgreSQL. You can learn more about these products through the sites listed in Table 28-1.

Relational Database Structure

Both MySQL and PostgreSQL use a relational database structure. Essentially, this means data is placed in tables, with identifier fields used to relate the data to entries in other tables. Each row in the table is a record, each with a unique identifier, like a record number. The connections between records in different tables are implemented by special tables that associate the unique identifiers from records in one table with those of another. Relational database theory and implementation are subjects beyond the scope of this chapter.

A simple, single-table database would have no need for a unique identifier. A simple address book listing names and addresses is an example of a single-table database. However, most databases access complex information of different types, related in various ways. Instead of having large records with repeated information, you would divide the data in different tables, each holding the unique instance of the data. This way, data is not repeated. You would have only one table that held a single record for a person's name, rather than repeating that person's name each time the data references him or her. The relational organization then takes on the task of relating one piece of data to another. This way, you can store a great deal of information using relatively small database files.

TABLE 28-1
Database Resources

Database	Resource
MySQL	**www.mysql.com**
PostgreSQL	**www.postgresql.org**
MaxDB	**www.mysql.com**

Though there are many ways to implement a relational database, a simple rule of thumb is to organize data into tables where you have a unique instance of each item of data. Each record is given a unique identifier, usually a number. To associate the records in one table with another, you create tables that associate their identifiers.

SQL

The SQL query language is the language used by most relational database management systems (RD-MSs), including both MySQL and PostgreSQL. Though many RDBMSs use administrative tools to manage databases, on Linux MySQL and PostgreSQLs you still have to use the SQL commands directly. Common SQL commands that you may use are listed in Table 28-2. The commands are often written in uppercase by convention, though they can be in lowercase.

Using the previously described relational database, the following command will create the database:

```
CREATE DATABASE myphotos
```

Before performing any operations on a database, you first access it with the USE command.

```
USE myphotos
```

The tables are created using the CREATE TABLE command; the fields for each table are listed within parentheses following the table name. For each field, you need to specify a name, data type, and other options, such as whether it can have a null value or not.

```
CREATE TABLE names (
    personid INT(5) UNSIGNED NOT NULL,
    name VARCHAR(20) NOT NULL,
    street VARCHAR(30) NOT NULL,
    phone CHAR(8)
    );
```

To insert a record into a table, you can use the INSERT INTO command, though many databases support using data files that can be read all at once. To add records, you use the

Command	Description
CREATE DATABASE *name*	Create a database.
CREATE TABLE *name* {*fields*, ..}	Create a table within a database, specifying fields.
INSERT INTO *table-name* VALUES (*value list*)	Create and insert a record into a table.
INSERT INTO *table-name* VALUES (*value list*), (*value list*), ...	Insert multiple records at once.
SELECT *field* FROM *table-name* WHERE *value*	Search operation, selecting certain records in a table based on a value in a specified field.
USE *database*	Use a particular database; following commands will operate on it.

TABLE 28-2 SQL Commands

INSERT INTO command with the table name followed by the VALUES option, which is followed in turn by a comma-delimited list of values, one for each field. Character values are quoted with single quotes. The list is enclosed in parentheses. If you have not done so previously, you access the database with the USE command.

```
INSERT INTO names VALUES (1, 'justin','111 mordor','555-7543');
```

Once values are added to the tables, you can search them with the SELECT command, specifying field, table name, and the value to be searched.

```
SELECT phone FROM names WHERE phone='555-7543';
```

MySQL

MySQL is structured on a client/server model with a server daemon (**mysqld**) filling requests from client programs. MySQL is designed for speed, reliability, and ease of use. It is meant to be a fast database management system for large databases and, at the same time, a reliable one, suitable for intensive use.

To create databases, you use the standard SQL language. User access can be controlled by assigning privileges.

MySQL Configuration

MySQL supports three different configuration files, one for global settings, another for server-specific settings, and an optional one for user-customized settings.

- The **/etc/my.cnf** configuration file is used for global settings applied to both clients and servers. The **/etc/my.cnf** file provides information such as the data directory (**/var/lib/mysql**) and log file (**/var/log/mysql.log**) locations, as well as the server base directory (**/var/lib**).

- The **/var/lib/mysql/my.cnf** file is used for server settings only.

- The **.my.cnf** file allows users to customize their access to MySQL. It is located in a user's home directory. Note that this is a dot file.

Sample configuration **.my.cnf** files can be found in the **mysql-server** directory in **/usr/share/doc**. The **mysql-server** directory lists configurations for small, medium, large, and huge implementations. The administrative manual is located in the mysql directory for **/usr/share/doc**. It is in the info format. Use **info mysql** to start it, and the arrow and ENTER keys to move through the menus. Here you can find more information about different options.

Global Configuration:/etc/my.cnf

MySQL specifies options according to different groups, usually the names of server tools. The options are arranged in group segments. The group name is placed within brackets, and options applied to it follow. The default **/etc/my.cnf** file is shown here:

```
[mysqld]
datadir=/var/lib/mysql
socket=/var/lib/mysql/mysql.sock

[mysql.server]
user=mysql
basedir=/var/lib
```

```
[safe_mysqld]
err-log=/var/log/mysqld.log
pid-file=/var/run/mysqld/mysqld.pid
```

Mysql global options are listed in the **/etc/my.cnf** file. Options are set up according to groups that control different behaviors of the MySQL server: **mysqld** for the daemon, **mysql .server** for server options, and **safe_mysqld** for MySQL startup script. The **datadir** directory, **/var/lib/mysql**, is where your database files will be placed. Server tools and daemons are located in the **basedir** directory, **/var/lib**, and the user that MySQL will run as has the name **mysql**, as specified in the **user** option.

A client group will set up options to be sent to clients, such as the port and socket to use to access the MySQL database.

```
[client]
port=3306
socket=/var/lib/mysql/mysql.sock
```

To see what options are currently set for both client and server, you run **mysqladmin** directly with the **variables** option.

```
mysqladmin variables
```

User Configuration: .my.cnf
Users who access the database server will have their own configuration file in their home directory: **.my.cnf**. Here the user can specify connection options such as the password used to access the database and the connection timeouts.

```
[client]
password=mypassword

[mysql]
no-auto-rehash
set-variable = connect_timeout=2

[mysql-hotcopy]
interactive-timeout
```

Starting and Stopping the MySQL Server
The MySQL server, **mysqld**, can be managed with the **service** command or the services tool.

```
service mysqld start
```

The **mysqld** script invokes **safe_mysqld**, which is designed to run MySQL on Unix systems, making sure that data directories are set and log files are running. The **safe_mysqld** script in turn will start up the **mysqld** daemon.

MySQL Tools
MySQL provides a variety of tools (as shown in Table 28-3), including server, client, and administrative tools. Backups can be handled with the **mysqldump** command. The **mysqlshow** command will display a database, just as issuing the SQL command SELECT *.* does, and **mysqlimport** can import text files, just like LOAD INFILE.

TABLE **28-3**
MySQL Commands

Command	Description
`mysqld`	MySQL server
`mysql`	MySQL client
`mysqladmin`	Create and administer databases
`mysqldump`	Database backup
`mysqlimport`	Import text files
`mysqlshow`	Display databases

MySQL Management with mysql

To manage your MySQL database, you use the mysql as the root user. The **mysql** client starts up the MySQL monitor. As the root user, you can enter administrative commands to create databases and database tables, add or remove entries, as well as carry out standard client tasks such as displaying data.

Log in as the root user and open a terminal window. Then enter the **mysql** command. This will start a MySQL monitor shell with a **mysql>** prompt. Be sure to end your commands with a semicolon; otherwise, the monitor will provide an indented arrow prompt waiting for added arguments. In the monitor, the semicolon, not the ENTER key, ends commands.

```
 # mysql -u root -p
mysql>
```

If you have set up a MySQL root user, you can use the **-u root** with the **-p** option. You will be prompted for a password.

```
# mysql -u root -p
```

Once the mysql client has started, you can use the **status** command to check the status of your server, and **show databases** to list current databases.

```
mysql> status;
mysql> show databases;
```

Initially two databases set up by MySQL for its own management are displayed: mysql and test. The mysql database holds MySQL user information, and the test database is used to test the server.

PostgreSQL

PostgreSQL, included with Fedora Core, is based on the POSTGRES database management system, though it uses SQL as its query language. POSTGRES is a next-generation research prototype developed at the University of California, Berkeley. Linux versions of PostgreSQL are included in most distributions, including Fedora Core, Debian, and Mandrake distributions. You can find more information on it from the PostgreSQL Web site at **www.postgresql.org**. PostgreSQL is an open source project, developed under the GPL license.

PostgreSQL is often used to provide database support for Internet servers with heavy demands, such as Web servers. With a few simple commands, you can create relational database tables. Use the **createuser** command to create a PostgreSQL user that you can then log into the server with. You can then create a database with the **createdb** command and construct relational tables using the **create table** directive. With an **insert** command, you can add records and then view them with the **select** command. Access to the server by remote users is controlled by entries in the **pg_hba.conf** file located in PostgreSQL directory, usually **/var/lib/pgsql**.

The Red Hat edition of PostgreSQL also includes the Red Hat Database Graphical tools used to easily manage and access PostgreSQL databases. With the administrator tool, you can browse and manage databases, the Visual Explain tool analyzes query processes, and the Control Center lets you manage databases on servers.

PART

VI

System Administration

Basic System Administration

L inux is designed to serve many users at the same time, providing an interface between the users and the system with its resources, services, and devices. Users have their own shells through which they interact with the operating system, but you may need to configure the operating system itself in different ways. You may need to add new users, devices like printers and scanners, and even file systems. Such operations come under the heading of system administration. The person who performs such actions is referred to as either a *system administrator* or a *superuser.* In this sense, there are two types of interaction with Linux: regular users' interactions, and those of the superuser, who performs system administration tasks. The chapters in this book cover operations such as changing system runlevels, managing users, configuring printers, adding file systems, and compiling the kernel. You perform most of these tasks only rarely, such as adding a new printer or mounting a file system. Other tasks, such as adding or removing users, you perform on a regular basis. Basic system administration covers topics such as system access by superusers, selecting the runlevel to start, system configuration files, and performance monitoring.

With Linux, you have the ability to load different versions of the Linux kernel as well as other operating systems that you have installed on your system. The task of selecting and starting up an operating system or kernel is managed by a boot management utility, the Grand Unified Bootloader (GRUB). This is a versatile tool, letting you load operating systems that share the same disk drive, as well as letting you choose from different Linux kernels that may be installed on the same Linux system.

Superuser Control: the Root User

To perform system administration operations, you must first have access rights such as the correct password that enables you to log in as the root user, making you the superuser. Because a superuser has the power to change almost anything on the system, such a password is usually a carefully guarded secret, changed very frequently, and given only to those whose job is to manage the system. With the correct password, you can log in to the system as a system administrator and configure the system in different ways. You can start up and shut down the system, as well as change to a different operating mode, such as a single-user mode. You can also add or remove users, add or remove whole file systems, back up and restore files, and even designate the system's name and address.

NOTE *If SELinux is enabled, superuser access will be controlled by SELinux rules. See Chapter 17.*

To become a superuser, you log in to the *root user account.* This is a special account reserved for system management operations with unrestricted access to all components of your Linux operating system. You can log in as the root user from either the GUI (graphical user interface) login screen or the command line login prompt. You then have access to all administrative tools. Using a GUI interface like GNOME, the root user has access to a number of Fedora Core GUI administrative tools such as system-config-packages for installing software or system-config-users for managing users. If you log in from the command line interface, you can run corresponding administrative commands like **rpm** to install packages or **useradd** to add a new user. From your GUI desktop, you can also run command line administrative tools using a terminal window. The command line interface for the root user uses a special prompt, the sharp sign, **#**. In the next example, the user logs in to the system as the root user and receives the **#** prompt.

```
login: root
password:
#
```

Root User Password

As the root user, you can use the **passwd** command to change the password for the root login, as well as for any other user on the system. The **passwd** command will check your password with Pluggable Authentication Modules (PAM), as discussed in Chapter 30, to see if you've selected one that can be easily cracked. To more easily change your root password from a GUI interface, you can use the system-config-rootpassword tool.

```
# passwd root
New password:
Re-enter new password:
#
```

You must take precautions to protect your root password. Anyone who gains access as the root user will have complete control over your system. The online manual for the **passwd** command provides detailed recommendations for handling and choosing your password. For example, never store your password in a file on your system, and never choose one based on any accessible information, such as your phone number or date of birth. A basic guideline is to make your password as complex as possible, using a phrase of several words with numbers and upper- and lowercase, yet something you can still remember easily so that you never have to write it down. You can access the **passwd** online manual page with the command

```
# man passwd
```

Root User Access: su

While you are logged in to a regular user account, it may be necessary for you to log in as the root and become a superuser. Ordinarily, you would have to log out of your user account first, and then log in to the root. Instead, you can use the **su** command (switch user) to log in directly to the root while remaining logged in to your user account. If you are using a GUI desktop like GNOME, you can enter the **su** command from a terminal window, or use ALT-CTRL-F1 to switch to a command line interface (ALT-CTRL-F10 returns you to the GUI interface). A CTRL-D or **exit** command returns you to your own user login. When you are logged in as the root, you can use **su** to log in as any user, without providing the password. In the next example, the user is logged in already. The **su** command then logs in as the root user, making the user a superuser. Some basic superuser commands are shown in Table 29-1.

```
$ pwd
/home/chris
$su
 password:
# cd
# pwd
/root
# exit
$
```

CAUTION   *For security reasons, Linux distributions do not allow the use of **su** in a telnet session to access the root user. For SSH- or Kerberos-enabled systems, Fedora Core provides secure login access using slogin (SSH) and rlogin (Kerberos version).*

Command	Description
`su root`	Logs a superuser into the root from a user login; the superuser returns to the original login with a CTRL-D.
`sudo` command	Restricted administrative access for specified users.
`passwd` login-name	Sets a new password for the login name.
`crontab` options filename	With *filename* as an argument, installs `crontab` entries in the file to a **crontab** file; these entries are operations executed at specified times (see later section): `-e` Edits the **crontab** file `-l` Lists the contents of the **crontab** file `-r` Deletes the **crontab** file
`telinit` runlevel	Changes the system runlevels.
`shutdown` options time	Shuts down the system.
`date`	Sets the date and time for the system.
system-config-date	GUI tool to set system time and date (System Settings | Date & Time).
Kcron	KDE GUI interface **cron** management tool (System Tools | Task Scheduler).
system-config-rootpassword	GUI tool to change the root user (administrator) password (System Settings | Root Password).

TABLE 29-1   Basic System Administration Tools

Controlled Administrative Access: sudo

With the sudo tool you can allow ordinary users to have limited root user–level administrative access for certain tasks. This allows other users to perform specific superuser operations without having full root level control. You can find more about sudo at **www.sudo.ws**. To use sudo to run an administrative command, the user precedes the command with the **sudo** command. The user is issued a time-sensitive ticket to allow access.

```
sudo date
```

Access is controlled by the **/etc/sudoers** file. This file lists users and the commands they can run, along with the password for access. If the NOPASSWD option is set, then users will not need a password. ALL, depending on the context, can refer to all hosts on your network, all root-level commands, or all users.

To make changes or add entries, you have to edit the file with the special sudo editing command **visudo**. This invokes the Vi editor to edit the **/etc/sudoers** file. Unlike a standard editor, **visudo** will lock the **/etc/sodoers** file and check the syntax of your entries. You are not allowed to save changes unless the syntax is correct. If you want to use a different editor, you can assign it to the EDITOR shell variable.

A **sudoers** entry has the following syntax:

```
user   host=command
```

The host is a host on your network. You can specify all hosts with the ALL term. The command can be a list of commands, some or all qualified by options such as whether a password is required. To specify all commands, you can also use the ALL term. The following gives the user **george** full root-level access to all commands on all hosts:

```
george  ALL = ALL
```

In addition, you can let a user run as another user on a given host. Such alternate users are placed within parentheses before the commands. For example, if you want to give **george** access to the **beach** host as the user **mydns**, you use the following:

```
george beach = (mydns) ALL
```

By default sudo will deny access to all users, including the root. For this reason, the default **/etc/sudoers** file sets full access for the root user to all commands. The ALL=(ALL) ALL entry allows access by the root to all hosts as all users to all commands.

```
root   ALL=(ALL)   ALL
```

To specify a group name, you prefix the group with a % sign, as in **%mygroup**. This way, you can give the same access to a group of users. The **/etc/sudoers** file contains samples for a **%wheel** group.

To give **robert** access on all hosts to the **date** command, you would use

```
robert ALL=/usr/bin/system-config-date
```

If a user wants to see what commands he or she can run, that user would use the **sudo** command with the **-l** option.

```
sudo -l
```

System Time and Date

You can set the system time and date using the shell **date** command or the Fedora Core GUI tool system-config-date. You probably set the time and date when you first installed your system. You should not need to do so again. If you entered the time incorrectly or moved to a different time zone, though, you could use this utility to change your time.

Using the system-config-date Utility

The preferred way to set the system time and date is to use the Fedora Core Date and Time Properties utility (system-config-date). Select it on the System Settings window accessible from the Start Here window. There are three panels, one for the date and time, one for the Network Time Protocol, and one for the time zone (see Figure 29-1). Use the calendar to select the year, month, and date. Then use the Time box to set the hour, minute, and second. The Time Zone panel shows a map with locations. Select the one nearest you to set your time zone.

The Network Time Protocol (NTP) allows a remote server to set the date and time, instead of using local settings. NTP allows for the most accurate synchronization of your system's clock. It is often used to manage the time and date for networked systems, freeing the administrator from having to synchronize clocks manually. You can download current documentation and NTP software from the **www.ntp.org** site.

On the Network Time Protocol panel you can choose to enable NTP and select the server to use. Two are already available for your use from the drop-down menu: **clock.redhat.com** and **clock2.redhat.com**. NTP servers operate through pools which will randomly select an available server to increase efficiency. You can choose from a set of pools beginning with **0.pool.ntp.org**. If access with one pool is slow, you can change to another. The **pool.ntp.org** pool serves North America. Pools for other locations can be found at the NTP Public Services Project site (Time Servers link), **ntp.isc.org**. Here you can also find the list of primary and secondary time servers which you can access directly.

Using the date Command

You can also use the **date** command on your root user command line to set the date and time for the system. As an argument to **date**, you list (with no delimiters) the month, day, time, and year. In the next example, the date is set to 2:59 P.M., June 21, 2005 (06 for June, 21 for the day, 1459 for the time, and 05 for the year 2005):

```
# date 0621145905
Tue Jun 21 02:59:27 PDT 2005
```

NOTE *You can also set the time and date with the Date & Time tool in the KDE Control Center.*

PART VI

FIGURE **29-1**
system-config-date

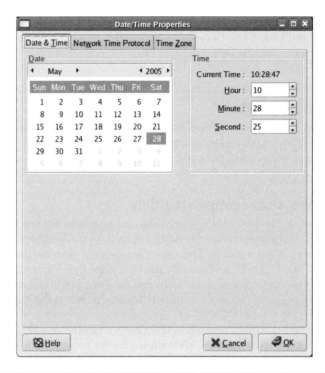

Scheduling Tasks: cron

Scheduling regular maintenance tasks, such as backups, is managed by the **cron** service on Linux, implemented by a **cron** daemon. A daemon is a continually running server that constantly checks for certain actions to take. These tasks are listed in the **crontab** file. The **cron** daemon constantly checks the user's **crontab** file to see if it is time to take these actions. Any user can set up a **crontab** file of his or her own. The root user can set up a **crontab** file to take system administrative actions, such as backing up files at a certain time each week or month.

The crond Service

The name of the **cron** daemon is **crond**. Normally it is started automatically when your system starts up. You can set this feature using system-config-services or **chkconfig**, as described in Chapter 21. The following example starts the **crond** service automatically whenever you boot the system.

```
chkconfig crond on
```

You can also start and stop the **crond** service manually, which you may want to do for emergency maintenance or during upgrades. Use the **service** command and the **stop** option to shut down the service, and the **start** option to run it again:

```
service crond stop
```

crontab Entries

A **crontab** entry has six fields: the first five are used to specify the time for an action, while the last field is the action itself. The first field specifies minutes (0–59), the second field specifies the hour (0–23), the third field specifies the day of the month (1–31), the fourth field specifies the month of the year (1–12, or month prefixes like *Jan* and *Sep*), and the fifth field specifies the day of the week (0–6, or day prefixes like *Wed* and *Fri*), starting with 0 as Sunday. In each of the time fields, you can specify a range, a set of values, or use the asterisk to indicate all values. For example, **1-5** for the day-of-week field specifies Monday through Friday. In the hour field, **8, 12, 17** would specify 8 A.M., 12 noon, and 5 P.M. An ***** in the month-of-year field indicates every month. The format of a **crontab** field follows:

```
minute  hour  day-month  month  day(s)-week  task
```

The following example backs up the **projects** directory at 2:00 A.M. every weekday:

```
0 2 * * 1-5   tar cf /home/backp /home/projects
```

The same entry is listed here again using prefixes for the month and weekday:

```
0 2 * * Mon-Fri tar cf /home/backp /home/projects
```

To specify particular months, days, weeks, or hours, you can list them individually, separated by commas. For example, to perform the previous task on Sunday, Wednesday, and Friday, you could use **0,3,5** in the day-of-week field, or their prefix equivalents, **Sun,Wed,Fri**.

```
0 2 * * 0,3,5   tar cf /home/backp /home/projects
```

cron also supports comments. A comment is any line beginning with a **#** sign.

```
# Weekly backup for Chris's projects
0 2 * * Mon-Fri  tar cf /home/backp /home/projects
```

Environment Variables for cron

The **cron** service also lets you define environment variables for use with tasks performed. Fedora Core defines variables for **SHELL**, **PATH**, **MAILTO**, and **HOME**. **SHELL** designates the shell to use tasks, in this case the BASH shell. **PATH** lists the directories where programs and scripts can be found. This example lists the standard directories, **/usr/bin** and **/bin**, as well as the system directories reserved for system applications, **/usr/sbin** and **/sbin**. **MAILTO** designates to whom the results of a task are to be mailed. By default, these are mailed to the user who schedules it, but you can have the results sent to a specific user, such as the administrator's e-mail address, or an account on another system in a network. **HOME** is the home directory for a task, in this case the top directory.

```
SHELL=/bin/bash
PATH=/sbin:/bin:/usr/sbin:/usr/bin
MAILTO=root
HOME=/
```

The cron.d Directory

On a heavily used system, the **/etc/crontab** file can become crowded easily. There may also be instances where certain entries require different variables. For example, you may need to run some task under a different shell. To help better organize your `crontab` tasks, you can place `crontab` entries in files within the **cron.d** directory. The files in the **cron.d** directory all contain `crontab` entries of the same format as **/etc/crontab**. They may be given any name. They are treated as added `crontab` files, with **cron** checking them for tasks to run. For example, Fedora Core installs a **sysstat** file in **cron.d** that contains `crontab` entries to run tools to gather system statistics.

The crontab Command

You use the `crontab` command to install your entries into a **crontab** file. To do this, first create a text file and type your `crontab` entries. Save this file with any name you want, such as **mycronfile**. Then, to install these entries, enter **crontab** and the name of the text file. The `crontab` command takes the contents of the text file and creates a **crontab** file in the **/var/spool/cron** directory, adding the name of the user who issued the command. In the following example, the root user installs the contents of **mycronfile** as the root's **crontab** file. This creates a file called **/var/spool/cron/root**. If a user named justin installed a **crontab** file, it would create a file called **/var/spool/cron/justin**. You can control use of the `crontab` command by regular users with the **/etc/cron.allow** file. Only users with their names in this file can create **crontab** files of their own. Conversely, the **/etc/cron.deny** file lists those users denied use of the **cron** tool, preventing them from scheduling tasks. If neither file exists, access is denied to all users. If a user is not in an **/etc/cron.allow** file, access is denied. However, if the **/etc/cron.allow** file does not exist, and the **/etc/cron.deny** file does, then all users not listed in **/etc/cron.deny** are automatically allowed access.

```
# crontab mycronfile
```

Editing in cron

Never try to edit your **crontab** file directly. Instead, use the `crontab` command with the `-e` option. This opens your **crontab** file in the **/var/spool/cron** directory with the standard text editor, such as Vi—`crontab` uses the default editor as specified by the **EDITOR** shell environment variable. To use a different editor for `crontab`, change the default editor by assigning the editor's program name to the **EDITOR** variable and exporting that variable. Normally, the editor variable is set in the **/etc/profile** script. Running `crontab` with the `-l` option displays the contents of your **crontab** file, and the `-r` option deletes the entire file. Invoking `crontab` with another text file of `crontab` entries overwrites your current **crontab** file, replacing it with the contents of the text file.

Organizing Scheduled Tasks

You can organize administrative **cron** tasks into two general groups: common administrative tasks that can be run at regular intervals, or specialized tasks that need to be run at a unique time. Unique tasks can be run as entries in the **/etc/crontab** file, as described in the next section. Common administrative tasks, though they can be run from the **/etc/crontab** file, are better organized into specialized **cron** directories. Within such directories, each task is placed in its own shell script that will invoke the task when run. For example, there may be several administrative tasks that all need to be run each week on the same day, say if maintenance for a system is scheduled on a Sunday morning. For these kinds of tasks, **cron** provides several specialized directories for automatic daily, weekly, monthly, and yearly tasks. Each contains a **cron** prefix and a suffix for the time interval. The **/etc/cron.daily** directory is used for tasks that need to be performed every day, whereas weekly tasks can be placed in the **/etc/cron.weekly** directory. The **cron** directories are listed in Table 29-2.

Running cron Directory Scripts

Each directory contains scripts that are all run at the same time. The scheduling for each group is determined by an entry in the **/etc/crontab** file. The actual execution of the scripts is performed by the **/usr/bin/run-parts** script, which runs all the scripts and programs in a given directory. Scheduling for all the tasks in a given directory is handled by an entry in the **/etc/crontab** file. Fedora Core provides entries with designated times, which you may change for your own needs. The default Fedora Core **crontab** file is shown here, with times for running scripts in the different **cron** directories. Here you can see that most scripts are run at about 4 A.M. either daily (4:02), Sunday (4:22), or the first day of each month (4:42). Hourly ones are run one minute after the hour.

```
SHELL=/bin/bash
PATH=/sbin:/bin:/usr/sbin:/usr/bin
MAILTO=root
HOME=/
# run-parts
01 * * * * root run-parts /etc/cron.hourly
02 4 * * * root run-parts /etc/cron.daily
22 4 * * 0 root run-parts /etc/cron.weekly
42 4 1 * * root run-parts /etc/cron.monthly
```

*TIP   Scripts within a **cron** directory are run alphabetically. If you need a certain script to run before any others, you may have to alter its name. One method is to prefix the name with a numeral. For example, in the /cron.weekly directory, the **anacron** script is named **0anacron** so that it will run before any others.*

cron Files and Directories	Description
/etc/crontab	System `crontab` file, accessible only by the root user
/etc/cron.d	Directory containing multiple `crontab` files, accessible only by the root user
/etc/cron.hourly	Directory for tasks performed hourly
/etc/cron.daily	Directory for tasks performed daily
/etc/cron.weekly	Directory for tasks performed weekly
/etc/cron.monthly	Directory for tasks performed monthly
/etc/cron.yearly	Directory for tasks performed yearly
/etc/cron.allow	Users allowed to submit **cron** tasks
/etc/cron.deny	Users denied access to **cron**

TABLE 29-2   **cron** Files and Directories

Keep in mind though that these are simply directories that contain executable files. The actual scheduling is performed by the entries in the **/etc/crontab** file. For example, if the weekly field in the **cron.weekly crontab** entry is entry is changed to * instead of **0**, and the monthly field to **1** (**22 4 1 * *** instead of **22 4 * * 0**), tasks in the **cron.weekly** file would end up running monthly instead of weekly.

cron Directory Names

The names used for these directories are merely conventions. They have no special meaning to the **cron** daemon. You could, in fact, create your own directory, place scripts within it, and schedule run-parts to run those scripts at a given time. In the next example, scripts placed in the **/etc/cron.mydocs** directory will run at 12 noon every Wednesday.

```
* 12 * * 3 root run-parts /etc/cron.mydocs
```

anacron

For a system that may normally be shut down during times that **cron** is likely to run, you may want to supplement **cron** with **anacron**. **anacron** activates only when scheduled tasks need to be executed. For example, if a system is shut down on a weekend when **cron** jobs are scheduled, then the jobs will not be performed; **anacron**, however, checks to see what jobs need to be performed when the system is turned on again, and then runs them. It is designed only for jobs that run daily or weekly.

For **anacron** jobs, you place **crontab** entries in the **/etc/anacrontab** file. For each scheduled task, you specify the number of intervening days when it is executed (7 is weekly, 30 is monthly), the time of day it is run (numbered in minutes), a description of the task, and the command to be executed. For backups, the command used would be **tar** operation. You can use system-config-services to turn on the **anacron** service or have it start up automatically at boot time.

System Runlevels: telinit, initab, and shutdown

A Linux system can run in different levels, depending on the capabilities you want to give it. For example, you can run your system at an administrative level, locking out user access. Normal full operations are activated by simply running your system at a certain level of operational capability such as supporting multiuser access or graphical interfaces. These levels (also known as states or modes) are referred to as *runlevels*, the level of support that you are running your system at.

Runlevels

A Linux system has several runlevels, numbered from 0 to 6. When you power up your system, you enter the default runlevel. Runlevels 0, 1, and 6 are special runlevels that perform specific functions. Runlevel 0 is the power-down state and is invoked by the **halt** command to shut down the system. Runlevel 6 is the reboot state—it shuts down the system and reboots. Runlevel 1 is the single-user state, which allows access only to the superuser and does not run any network services. This enables you, as the administrator, to perform administrative actions without interference from others.

Other runlevels reflect how you want the system to be used. Runlevel 2 is a partial multiuser state, allowing access by multiple users, but without network services like NFS or **xinetd** (eXtended InterNET services daemon). This level is useful for a system that is not part of a network. Both runlevel 3 and runlevel 5 run a fully operational Linux system, with multiuser support and remote file sharing access. They differ in terms of the interface they use. Runlevel 3 starts up your system with the command line interface (also known as the text mode interface). Runlevel 5 starts up your system with an X session, running the X Window System server and invoking a graphical login, using display managers, such as gdm or xdm. If you choose to use graphical logins during installation, runlevel 5 will be your default runlevel. Linux provides two keyboard sequences to let you switch between the two during a login session: CTRL-ALT-F1 changes from the graphical interface (runlevel 5) to the command line interface (runlevel 3), and CTRL-ALT-F7 changes from the command line interface to the graphical interface. The runlevels are listed in Table 29-3.

Changing runlevels can be helpful if you have problems at a particular runlevel. For example, if your video card is not installed properly, then any attempt to start up in runlevel 5 will likely fail, as this level immediately starts your graphical interface. Instead, you should use the command line interface, runlevel 3, to fix your video card installation.

System Runlevels (states)	Description
0	Halt (do *not* set the default to this level); shuts down the system completely.
1	Administrative single-user mode; denies other users access to the system, but allows root access to the entire multiuser file system. Startup scripts are not run. (Use **s** or **S** to enter single-user mode with startup scripts run.)
2	Multiuser, without network services like NFS, **xinetd**, and NIS (the same as 3, but you do not have networking).
3	Full multiuser mode with login to command line interface; allows remote file sharing with other systems on your network. Also referred to as the *text mode state*.
4	Unused.
5	Full multiuser mode that starts up in an X session, initiating a graphical login; allows remote file sharing with other systems on your network (same as 3, but with graphical login).
6	Reboots; shuts down and restarts the system (do *not* set the default to this).

TABLE **29-3**   System Runlevels (States)

TIP *You can use the single-user runlevel (1) as a recovery mode state, allowing you to start up your system without running startup scripts for services like DNS. This is helpful if your system hangs when you try to start such services. Networking is disabled, as well as any multiuser access. You can also use **linux -s** at the boot prompt to enter runlevel 1. If you want to enter the single-user state and also run the startup scripts, you can use the special **s** or **S** runlevels.*

Runlevels in initab

When your system starts up, it uses the default runlevel as specified in the default **init** entry in the **/etc/inittab** file. For example, if your default init runlevel is 5 (the graphical login), the default **init** entry in the **/etc/inittab** file would be

```
id:5:initdefault:
```

You can change the default runlevel by editing the **/etc/inittab** file and changing the **init** default entry. Editing the **/etc/inittab** file can be dangerous. You should do this with great care. As an example, if the default runlevel is 3 (command line), the entry for your default runlevel in the **/etc/inittab** file should look like the following:

```
id:3:initdefault:
```

You can change the 3 to a 5, to change your default runlevel from the command line interface (3) to the graphical login (5). Change only this number and nothing else.

```
id:5:initdefault:
```

TIP *If your /etc/inittab file becomes corrupted, you can reboot and enter **linux single** at the boot prompt to start up your system, bypassing the **inittab** file. You can then edit the file to fix it.*

Changing Runlevels with telinit

No matter what runlevel you start in, you can change from one runlevel to another with the **telinit** command. If your default runlevel is 3, you power up in runlevel 3, but you can change to, say, runlevel 5 with **telinit 5**. The command **telinit 0** shuts down your system. In the next example, the **telinit** command changes to runlevel 1, the administrative state:

```
# telinit 1
```

The **telinit** command is really a symbolic link (another name for a command) to the **init** command. The **init** command performs the actual startup operations and is automatically invoked when your system starts up. Though you could use **init** to change runlevels, it is best to use **telinit**. When invoked as **telinit**, **init** merely changes runlevels.

The runlevel Command

Use the **runlevel** command to see what state you are currently running in. It lists the previous state followed by the current one. If you have not changed states, the previous state will be listed as N, indicating no previous state. This is the case for the state you boot up in. In the next example, the system is running in state 3, with no previous state change:

```
# runlevel
N 3
```

Shutdown

Although you can power down the system with the **telinit** command and the 0 state, you can also use the **shutdown** command. The **shutdown** command has a time argument that gives users on the system a warning before you power down. You can specify an exact time to shut down, or a period of minutes from the current time. The exact time is specified by *hh:mm* for the hour and minutes. The period of time is indicated by a **+** and the number of minutes. The **shutdown** command takes several options with which you can specify how you want your system shut down. The **–h** option, which stands for halt, simply shuts down the system, whereas the **–r** option shuts down the system and then reboots it. In the next example, the system is shut down after ten minutes:

```
# shutdown -h +10
```

To shut down the system immediately, you can use **+0** or the word **now**. The following example shuts down the system immediately and then reboots:

```
# shutdown -r now
```

With the **shutdown** command, you can include a warning message to be sent to all users currently logged in, giving them time to finish what they are doing before you shut them down.

```
# shutdown -h +5 "System needs a rest"
```

If you do not specify either the **–h** or the **–r** option, the **shutdown** command shuts down the multiuser mode and shifts you to an administrative single-user mode. In effect, your system state changes from 3 (multiuser state) to 1 (administrative single-user state). Only the root user is active, allowing the root user to perform any necessary system administrative operations with which other users might interfere.

TIP   *You can also shut down your system from the GNOME desktop.*

The shutdown options are listed in Table 29-4.

Command	Description
`shutdown [-rkhncft]` *time* [*warning-message*]	Shuts the system down after the specified time period, issuing warnings to users; you can specify a warning message of your own after the time argument; if neither `-h` nor `-r` is specified to shut down the system, the system sets to the administrative mode, runlevel state 1.
Argument	**Description**
Time	Has two possible formats: it can be an absolute time in the format *hh:mm*, with *hh* as the hour (one or two digits) and *mm* as the minute (in two digits); it can also be in the format +*m*, with *m* as the number of minutes to wait; the word **now** is an alias for **+0**.
Option	**Description**
`-t` *sec*	Tells `init` to wait *sec* seconds before sending processes the warning and the kill signals, before changing to another runlevel.
`-k`	Doesn't actually shut down; only sends the warning messages to everybody.
`-r`	Reboots after shutdown, runlevel state 6.
`-h`	Halts after shutdown, runlevel state 0.
`-n`	Doesn't call `init` to do the shutdown; you do it yourself.
`-f`	Skips file system checking (fsck) on reboot.
`-c`	Cancels an already running shutdown; no time argument.

TABLE 29-4 System Shutdown Options

Managing Services

As noted previously for the **crond** service, you can select certain services to run and the runlevel at which to run them. Most services are servers like a Web server or proxy server. Other services provide security, such as SSH or Kerberos. You can decide which services to use with the **chkconfig**, service, or system-config-services tools. These are described here briefly, and in more detail in Chapter 21.

chkconfig

To configure a service to start up automatically, you can use the system-config-services tool available on the desktop or the **chkconfig** tool, which is run on a command line. The system-config-services tool will display a list of available services, letting you choose the ones you want to start and deselect. The **chkconfig** command uses the **on** and **off** options to select and deselect services for startup (see Chapter 21 for more details).

```
chkconfig httpd on
```

The service Command

To start and stop services manually, you can use either system-config-services or the **service** command. With the **service** command, you list the service with the **stop** argument to stop it, the **start** argument to start it, and the **restart** argument to restart it.

```
service httpd start
```

system-config-services

Most administration tools provide interfaces displaying a simple list of services from which you can select the ones you want to start up. On the system-config-services tool, the main panel lists different daemons and servers that you can have start by just clicking a check box.

Fedora Core Administration Tools

On Fedora Core, most administration tasks can be handled by a set of separate specialized administrative tools developed and supported by Red Hat, such as those for user management and display configuration. Many of these are GUI-based and will work on any X Window System environment, such as GNOME or KDE. To access the GUI-based tools, you log in as the root user to the GNOME desktop and open the Start Here window or select the main menu. System administration tools are listed in the System Settings folder, and on the System Settings menu listed in the main menu. Here you will find tools to set the time and date, manage users, configure printers, and update software. Users & Groups lets you create and edit users. Printing lets you install and reconfigure printers. All tools provide very intuitive GUI interfaces that are easy to use. In the System Settings folder and menu, tools are identified by simple descriptive terms, whereas their actual name normally begins with the term system-config. For example, the printer configuration tool is listed as Printing, but its actual name is system-config-printer. You can separately invoke any tool by entering its name in a terminal window. Table 29-5 provides a complete listing of administration tools.

Administration Tool	Description
System Settings	Menu for accessing administration tools
system-config-users	User and Group configuration tool
system-config-printer	Printer configuration tool
system-config-display	Display configuration tool (video card and monitor)
system-config-packages	Software management
system-config-rootpassword	Changes the root user password
system-config-keyboard	Changes the keyboard configuration
system-config-date	Changes system time and date
system-config-mouse	Configures your mouse
system-config-language	Selects a language to use
system-config-soundcard	Configures your sound card

TABLE 29-5   Administration Tools

System Directories

Your Linux file system is organized into directories whose files are used for different system functions (see Table 29-6). For basic system administration, you should be familiar with the system program directories where applications are kept, the system configuration directory (**/etc**) where most configuration files are placed, and the system log directory (**/var/log**) that holds the system logs, recording activity on your system. Other system directories are covered in their respective chapters, with many discussed in Chapter 32.

Program Directories

Directories with "bin" in the name are used to hold programs. The **/bin** directory holds basic user programs, such as login shells (BASH, TCSH, and ZSH) and file commands (**cp**, **mv**, **rm**, **ln**, and so on). The **/sbin** directory holds specialized system programs for such tasks as file system management (**fsck**, **fdisk**, **mkfs**) and system operations like shutdown and startup (**init**). The **/usr/bin** directory holds program files designed for user tasks. The **/usr/**

Directory	Description
/bin	System-related programs
/sbin	System programs for specialized tasks
/lib	System and application libraries
/etc	Configuration files for system and network services and applications
/home	The location of user home directories and server data directories, such as Web and FTP site files
/mnt	The location where CD-ROM and floppy disk file systems are mounted (Chapter 32)
/var	The location of system directories whose files continually change, such as logs, printer spool files, and lock files (Chapter 32)
/usr	User-related programs and files. Includes several key subdirectories, such as **/usr/bin, /usr/X11**, and **/usr/doc**
/usr/bin	Programs for users
/dev	Dynamically generated directory for device files (Chapter 34)
/usr/X11	X Window System configuration files
/usr/share	Shared files
/usr/share/doc	Documentation for applications
/tmp	Directory for system temporary files
/var/log	Logging directory
/var/log/	System logs generated by **syslogd**
/var/log/audit	Audit logs generated by **auditd**

TABLE 29-6 System Directories

sbin directory holds user-related system operations, such as **useradd** to add new users. The **/lib** directory holds all the libraries your system makes use of, including the main Linux library, **libc**, and subdirectories such as **modules**, which holds all the current kernel modules.

Configuration Directories and Files

When you configure different elements of your system, like users, applications, servers, or network connections, you make use of configuration files kept in certain system directories. On Fedora Core, configuration files are placed in the **/etc** directory, with more specific device and service configuration located in the **/etc/sysconfig** directory.

Configuration Files: /etc

The **/etc** directory holds your system, network, server, and application configuration files. Here you can find the **fstab** file listing your file systems, the **hosts** file with IP addresses for hosts on your system, and **grub.conf** (a link to **/boot/grub/grub.conf**) for the boot systems supported by the GRUB boot loader. This directory includes various subdirectories, such as **/etc/apache** for the Apache Web server configuration files, **/etc/X11** for the X Window System and window manager configuration files, and **/etc/udev** for rules to generate device files in **/dev**. You can configure many applications and services by directly editing their configuration files, though it is best to use a corresponding administration tool. Table 29-7 lists several commonly used configuration files found in the **/etc** directory.

/etc/sysconfig

On Fedora Core systems, configuration and startup information is also kept in the **/etc/sysconfig** directory. Here you will find files containing definitions of system variables used to configure devices such as your keyboard and mouse, along with settings for network connections, as well as options for service scripts, covering services such as the Web server or the IPtables firewall. These entries were defined for you when you configured your devices during installation or installed your service software.

A sample of the keyboard file, **/etc/sysconfig/keyboard**, is shown here.

```
KEYBOARDTYPE="pc"
KEYTABLE="us"
```

Several of these files are generated by administration tools such as system-config-mouse, system-config-keyboard, or system-config-network. Table 29-8 lists several commonly used tools and the sysconfig files they control. For example, system-config-mouse generates configuration variables for the mouse device name, type, and certain features, placing them in the **/etc/sysconfig/mouse** file, shown here:

```
FULLNAME="Generic - 3 Button Mouse (PS/2)"
MOUSETYPE="PS/2"
XMOUSETYPE="PS/2"
XEMU3="no"
DEVICE=/dev/mouse
```

File	Description
/etc/bashrc	Default shell configuration file for BASH shell
/etc/group	Contains a list of groups with configurations for each
/etc/fstab	Automatically mounts file systems when you start your system
/boot/grub/grub.conf	The GRUB configuration file for the GRUB boot loader, linked to by /etc/grub.conf
/etc/inittab	Sets the default state, as well as terminal connections
/etc/profile	Default shell configuration file for users
/etc/modprobe.conf	Modules on your system to be automatically loaded
/etc/motd	System administrator's message of the day
/etc/mtab	Currently mounted file systems
/etc/passwd	Contains user password and login configurations
/etc/services	Services run on the system and the ports they use
/etc/shadow	Contains user-encrypted passwords
/etc/shells	Shells installed on the system that users can use
/etc/sudoers	Sudo configuration to control administrative access
/etc/termcap	Contains a list of terminal type specifications for terminals that could be connected to the system
/etc/xinetd.conf	Xinetd server configuration
Directory	**Description**
/etc/cron	Cron scripts
/etc/cups	CUPS printer configuration files
/etc/init.d	Service scripts
/etc/mail	Sendmail configuration files
/etc/openldap	Configuration for Open LDAP server
/etc/rc.d	Startup scripts for different runlevels
/etc/skel	Directory that holds the versions of initialization files, such as .bash_profile, which are copied to new users' home directories
/etc/sysconfig	Device and service configuration environments and support
/etc/X11	X Window System configuration files
/etc/xinetd.d	Configuration scripts for services managed by Xinetd server
/etc/udev	Rules for generating removable and fixed devices (Chapter 34)
/etc/hal	Rules for information about removable devices (Chapter 34)

TABLE 29-7 Configuration Files and Directories

Tool	Configuration File	Description
system-config-authentication	**/etc/sysconfig/authconfig** **/etc/sysconfig/network**	Authentication options, such as enabling NIS, shadow passwords, Kerberos, and LDAP.
system-config-securitylevel	**/etc/sysconfig/iptables**	Selects the level of firewall protection: High, Medium, and None.
system-config-keyboard	**/etc/sysconfig/keyboard**	Selects the keyboard type.
system-config-mouse	**/etc/sysconfig/mouse**	Selects the mouse type.
system-config-network	**/etc/sysconfig/network** **/etc/sysconfig/network-scripts/ifcfg-eth**N	Sets your network settings.
system-config-date	**/etc/sysconfig/clock**	Sets the time and date.
system-config-users	**/etc/sysconfig/system-config-users**	Settings for system-config-users.
system-config-samba	**/etc/sysconfig/samba**	Settings for Samba service.
system-config-httpd	**/etc/sysconfig/httpd**	Settings for Apache Web server.
system-config-securitylevel	**/etc/sysconfig/system-config-securitylevel**	Settings for system-config-securitylevel.

TABLE 29-8   Sysconfig Files with Corresponding System Administration Tools

Other files, like **hwconf**, list all your hardware devices, defining configuration variables such as its class (video, CD-ROM, hard drive), the bus it uses (PCI, IDE), its device name (such as **hdd** or **st0**), the drivers it uses, and a description of the device. A CD-ROM entry is shown here:

```
class: CDROM
bus: IDE
detached: 0
device: hdd
driver: ignore
desc: "TOSHIBA DVD-ROM SD-M1402"
```

Some files provide global or system configuration support for service scripts, like **iptables**, **samba**, **httpd** (Apache), or **spamassassin**. Other files provide configuration settings for corresponding tools like system-config-users.

Several directories are included, such as **network-scripts**, which lists several startup scripts for network connections—an example is **ifup-ppp**, which starts up PPP connections.

Some administration tools use more than one **sysconfig** file; for example, system-config-network places its network configuration information such as the hostname and gateway in the **/etc/sysconfig/network** file. Specific Ethernet device configurations, which would include your IP address and netmask, are placed in the appropriate Ethernet device configuration file in the **/etc/sysconfig/network-scripts** directory. For example, the IP address and netmask used for the **eth0** Ethernet device can be found in **/etc/sysconfig/network-scripts/ifcfg-eth0**. Local host settings are in **/etc/sysconfig/network-scripts/ifcfg-lo**.

PART VI

TIP Some administration tools, like system-config-authentication, will further configure configuration files for the services selected. The system-config-authentication tool configures /etc/sysconfig/ authconfig, as well as /etc/krb5.conf for Kerberos authentication, /etc/yp.conf for NIS support, and /etc/openldap/ldap.conf for LDAP authentication.

System Logs: /var/log and syslogd

Various system logs for tasks performed on your system are stored in the **/var/log** directory. Here you can find logs for mail, news, and all other system operations, such as Web server logs. The **/var/log/messages** file is a log of all system tasks not covered by other logs. This usually includes startup tasks, such as loading drivers and mounting file systems. If a driver for a card failed to load at startup, you find an error message for it here. Logins are also recorded in this file, showing you who attempted to log in to what account. The **/var/log/ maillog** file logs mail message transmissions and news transfers.

NOTE The Log Viewer, system-logviewer, has been moved out of Fedora Core. The Log Viewer displays a list of all current system logs and lets you search them.

syslogd and syslog.conf

The **syslogd** daemon manages all the logs on your system, as well as coordinating with any of the logging operations of other systems on your network. Configuration information for **syslogd** is held in the **/etc/syslog.conf** file, which contains the names and locations for your system log files. Here you find entries for **/var/log/messages** and **/var/log/maillog**, among others. Whenever you make changes to the **syslog.conf** file, you need to restart the **syslogd** daemon using the following command (or use system-config-services, Server Settings | Services):

```
service syslog restart
```

Entries in syslogd.conf

An entry in **syslog.conf** consists of two fields: a *selector* and an *action*. The selector is the kind of service to be logged, such as mail or news, and the action is the location where messages are to be placed. The action is usually a log file, but it can also be a remote host or a pipe to another program. The kind of service is referred to as a *facility*. The **syslogd** daemon has several terms it uses to specify certain kinds of service (see Table 29-9). A facility can be further qualified by a priority. A *priority* specifies the kind of message generated by the facility; **syslogd** uses several designated terms to indicate different priorities. A *sector* is constructed from both the facility and the priority, separated by a period. For example, to save error messages generated by mail systems, you use a sector consisting of the **mail** facility and the **err** priority, as shown here:

```
mail.err
```

To save these messages to the **/var/log/maillog** file, you specify that file as the action, giving you the following entry:

```
mail.err /var/log/maillog
```

The **syslogd** daemon also supports the use of * as a matching character to match either all the facilities or all the priorities in a sector: **cron.*** would match on all **cron** messages

Facility	Description
`authpriv`	Security/authorization messages (private)
`cron`	Clock daemon (cron and at) messages
`daemon`	Other system daemon messages
`kern`	Kernel messages
`lpr`	Line printer subsystem messages
`mail`	Mail subsystem messages
`mark`	Internal use only
`news`	Usenet news subsystem messages
`syslog`	Syslog internal messages
`user`	Generic user-level messages
`uucp`	UUCP subsystem messages
`local0` through `local7`	Reserved for local use
Priority	**Description**
`debug`	7, Debugging messages, lowest priority
`info`	6, Informational messages
`notice`	5, Notifications, normal, but significant, condition
`warning`	4, Warnings
`err`	3, Error messages
`crit`	2, Critical conditions
`alert`	1, Alerts, action must be taken immediately
`emerg`	0, Emergency messages, system is unusable, highest priority
Operator	**Description**
`*`	Matches all facilities or priorities in a sector
`=`	Restrict to a specified priority
`!`	Exclude specified priority and higher ones
`/`	A file to save messages to
`@`	A host to send messages to
`|`	A FIFO pipe to send messages to

TABLE 29-9 **syslogd** Facilities, Priorities, and Operators

no matter what the priority, `*.err` would match on error messages from all the facilities, and `*.*` would match on all messages. The following example saves all mail messages to the **/var/log/maillog** file and all critical messages to the **/var/log/mycritical** file:

```
mail.* /var/log/maillog
*.crit /var/log/mycritical
```

Priorities

When you specify a priority for a facility, all messages with a higher priority are also included. Thus the **err** priority also includes the **crit**, **alert**, and **emerg** priorities. If you just want to select the message for a specific priority, you qualify the priority with the = operator. For example, **mail.=err** will select only error messages, not **crit**, **alert**, or **emerg** messages. You can also restrict priorities with the ! operator. This will eliminate messages with the specified priority and higher. For example, **mail.!crit** will exclude **crit** messages, as well as the higher **alert** and **emerg** messages. To specifically exclude all the messages for an entire facility, you use the **none** priority; for instance, **mail.none** excludes all mail messages. This is usually used when you're defining several sectors in the same entry.

You can list several priorities or facilities in a given sector by separating them with commas. You can also have several sectors in the same entry by separating them with semicolons. The first example saves to the **/var/log/messages** file all messages with **info** priority, excluding all mail and authentication messages (**authpriv**). The second saves all **crit** messages and higher for the **uucp** and **news** facilities to the **/var/log/spooler** file:

```
*.info;mail.none;news.none;authpriv.none /var/log/messages
uucp,news.crit /var/log/spooler
```

Actions and Users

In the action field, you can specify files, remote systems, users, or pipes. An action entry for a file must always begin with a / and specify its full pathname, such as **/var/log/messages**. To log messages to a remote host, you simply specify the hostname preceded by an @ sign. The following example saves all kernel messages on **rabbit.trek.com**:

```
kern.* @rabbit.trek.com
```

To send messages to users, you list their login names. The following example will send critical news messages to the consoles for the users **chris** and **aleina**:

```
news.=crit chris,aleina
```

You can also output messages to a named pipe (FIFO). The pipe entry for the action field begins with a |. The following example pipes kernel debug messages to the named pipe |**/usr/adm/debug**:

```
kern.=debug |/usr/adm/debug
```

The Linux Auditing System: auditd

The Linux Auditing System provides system call auditing. The auditing is performed by a server called **auditd**, with logs saved to the **/var/log/audit** directory. It is designed to compliment SELinux, which saves its messages to the **auditd** log in the **/var/log/audit/audit .log** file. The audit logging service provides specialize logging for services like SELinux. Logs are located at **/var/log/audit**. To refine the auditing, you can create audit rules to check certain system calls like those generated by a specific user or group. You can turn auditing on (1) or off (0) using the audit parameter when you boot, **audit=1**, or the **auditctl -e 1** command in a terminal window.

You can use the **/etc/init.d/auditd** service script to start up and shut down the **auditd** server. Use system-config-services or the **service** command to start and stop the server.

```
service auditd start
```

Configuration for **auditd** is located in both the **/etc/auditd.conf** and the **/etd/sysconfig/auditd** files. Primary configuration is handled with **/etc/auditd.conf** where options like the log filename, log format, the maximum size of log files, and actions to take when disk space diminishes. See the **auditd.conf** Man page for a detailed description of all options. The **/etc/sysconfig/auditd** file sets server startup options and locale location like **en_US**.

The audit package includes the **auditd** server and three commands: **autrace**, **ausearch**, and **auditctl**. You use **ausearch** to query the audit logs. You can search by various ids, process, user, group, or event, as well as by filename or even time or date. Check the **ausearch** Man page for a complete listing. **autrace** is a specialized tool that lets you trace a specific process. It operates similar to strace, recording the system calls and actions of a particular process.

You can control the behavior of the **auditd** server with the **auditctl** tool. With **auditctl** you can turn auditing on and off, check the status, and add audit rules for specific events. Check the **auditctl** Man page for a detailed description.

Audit rules are organized into predetermined lists with a specific set of actions for system calls. Currently there are three lists: task, entry, and exit; and three actions: never, always, and possible. When adding a rule, the list and action are paired, separated by a comma, as in:

```
exit,always
```

To add a rule you use the **-a** option. With the **-S** option you can specify a particular system call, and with the **-F** option specify a field. There are several possible fields you can use such as loginuid (user login id), pid (process id), and exit (system call exit value). For a field you specify a value, such as **longinuid=510** for the user with a user login id of 510. The following rule, as described in the documentation, checks all files opened by a particular user.

```
auditctl -a exit,always  -S open -F loginuid=510
```

Place rules you want loaded automatically in the **/etc/auditd.rules**. The **sample.rules** file in the **/usr/share/doc/auditd*** directory lists rule examples. You can also create a specific file of audit rules and use **auditctl** with the **-R** option to read the rules from it.

Performance Analysis Tools and Processes

Linux treats each task performed on your system as a process, which is assigned a number and a name. You can examine these processes and even stop them. Fedora Core provides several tools for examining processes as well as your system performance. Easy monitoring is provided by the GNOME System Monitor. Other tools are also available, such as GKrellM and KSysguard.

A number of utilities on your system provide detailed information on your processes, as well as other system information such as CPU and disk use (see Table 29-10). Although these tools were designed to be used on a shell command line, displaying output in text lines, several now have KDE and GNOME versions that provide a GUI interface for displaying results and managing processes.

Performance Tool	Description
`vmstat`	Performance of system components
`top`	Listing of most CPU-intensive processes
`free`	Listing of free RAM memory
`sar`	System activity information
`iostat`	Disk usage
GNOME System Monitor	System monitor for processes and usage monitoring (System Monitor on System Tools menu)
GKrellM	Stackable, flexible, and extensible monitoring tool that displays information on a wide variety of system, network, and storage operations, as well as services, easily configurable with themes
KDE Task Manager and Performance Monitor	KDE system monitor for processes and usage monitoring

TABLE **29-10**   Performance Tools

The ps Command

From the command line, you can use the **ps** command to list processes. With the **-aux** option, you can list all processes. Piping the output to a **grep** command with a pattern enables you to search for a particular process. A pipe funnels the output of a preceding command as input to a following command. The following command lists all X Window System processes:

```
ps -aux | grep 'X'
```

vmstat, top, free, Xload, iostat, and sar

The **vmstat** command outputs a detailed listing indicating the performance of different system components, including CPU, memory, I/O, and swap operations. A report is issued as a line with fields for the different components. If you provide a time period as an argument, it repeats at the specified interval—usually a few seconds. The **top** command provides a listing of the processes on your system that are the most CPU intensive, showing what processes are using most of your resources. The listing is in real time and updated every few seconds. Commands are provided for changing a process's status, such as its priority.

The **free** command lists the amount of free RAM memory on your system, showing how much is used and how much is free, as well as what is used for buffers and swap memory. **Xload** is an X Window System tool showing the load, CPU, and memory, **iostat** displays your disk usage, and **sar** shows system activity information.

GNOME System Manager

The current version of Fedora Core provides the GNOME System Manager for displaying system information and managing system processes, accessible from System Tools | System Monitor. There are two panels, one for processes and one for system information. The System Monitor panel displays graphs for CPU, Memory, and Swap memory usage (see

Figure 29-2). Your disk devices are also listed, showing the amount of disk space used and how much is free. The Process Listing panel lists your processes, letting you sort or search for processes. You can use field buttons to sort by name, process ID, user, and memory. The View pop-up menu lets you select all processes, just your own, or active processes. You can easily stop any process by selecting it and then clicking the End Process button. Right-clicking an item displays actions you can take on the process such as stopping or hiding it. The Memory Maps display, selected from the View menu, shows information on virtual memory, inodes, and flags.

GKrellM

GKrellM is a GTK-based set of small stackable monitors for various system, network, and device operations. A title bar at the top of the stack will display the hostname of your system. By default, GKrellM will display the hostname, system time, CPU load, process chart, disk access, network devices like **eth0**, memory use, and a mail check. You can change the chart display of a monitor, like its height, by right-clicking it to show a display options panel.

Each monitor will have a title bar, showing, for instance, CPU for CPU load, Disk for disk access, and Mem for memory. To configure the monitor, right-click its title bar. This will display the configuration panels for that task. For example, the Disk configuration will let you choose particular hard disks and partitions to monitor. The full configuration window will be displayed, showing a sidebar with configuration menus, with the built-in menu expanded to the selected monitor.

Figure 29-2
System Manager

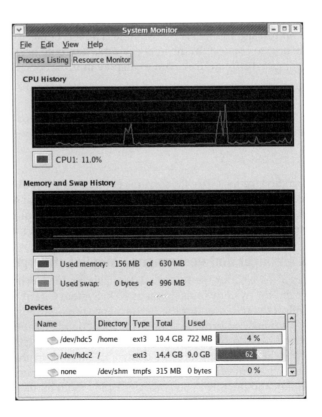

See the **gkrellm** Man page for a detailed description of all monitor configuration options. The GKrellM site, **www.gkrellm.net**, offers resources for documentation, program support, and themes. Fedora Core comes with GKrellM installed with the built-in plug-ins and with the WiFi plug-in. For added plug-ins and themes, you can download and install the RPM packages for Fedora Core provided by **freshrpms.net**. These will provide an extensive set of plug-ins and themes for your use, including radio controls, a keyboard LED monitor, and a large list of themes such as marble, Gotham city, and shiny metal blue. Plug-ins can also be downloaded directly from **www.gkrellm.net** and themes from **www.muhri.net**. User themes can be placed in a user's **.gkrellm2/themes** directory.

GKrellM Configuration

You can open the configuration window directly by clicking any monitor and pressing F1. Alternatively, you can open the main menu and select the Configuration entry. To open the main menu, either press F2 or right-click the top monitor. You can use this same menu to move through themes or to quit GKrellM. The configuration window shows a sidebar of configuration entries such as General, Builtins, Plugins, and Themes. Panels to the right let you set the configuration options. The General panel shows global options such as displaying the hostname, the overall window size, and window priority.

GKrellM Server

You can use GKrellM to monitor hosts remotely using the GKrellM server, **gkrellmd**. You run the server on the system you wish to monitor, letting it allow remote systems to use **gkrellm** clients to gather and display its monitoring statistics. To run **gkrellm** as a client to gather and display information from another system running a **gkrellmd** server, you use the **-s** option and the server's hostname. The server has to be configured to allow that remote host to connect. In the next example, a remote host connects to a **gkrellmd** server running on **turtle.mytrek.com** to display information about the turtle host:

```
gkrellm -s turtle.mytrek.com
```

On Fedora Core, GKrellM is a service managed by the **/etc/init.d/gkrellmd** script. You can start and stop it with system-config-services or with the **service** command.

```
service gkrellmd start
```

Configuration for the GKrellM server is handled by the **/etd/gkrellmd.conf** configuration file. Here you can specify the hosts to monitor as well as global options such as the frequency of updates, the port to listen on, and the maximum number of simultaneous clients. Options are documented in detail. Check the Man page for **gkrellmd** for a complete listing.

KDE Task Manager and Performance Monitor (KSysguard)

Fedora Core also provides the KDE Task Manager and Performance Monitor, KSysguard, accessible from the System Tools menu as KDE System Guard only on the KDE desktop. This tools allows you to monitor the performance of your own system as well as remote systems. KSysguard can provide simple values or detailed tables for various parameters. A System Load panel provides graphical information about CPU and memory usage, and a Process Table lists current processes using a tree format to show dependencies. You can design your own monitoring panels with worksheets, showing different types of values you want to display and the form you want to display them in, like a bar graph or digital meter.

The Sensor Browser pane is an expandable tree of sensors for information like CPU System Load or Memory's Used Memory. There is a top entry for each host you are connected to, including your own, localhost. To design your own monitor, create a worksheet and drag and drop a sensor onto it.

Grand Unified Bootloader (GRUB)

The Grand Unified Bootloader (GRUB) is a multiboot boot loader used for Fedora Core systems. With GRUB, users can select operating systems to run from a menu interface displayed when a system boots up. Use arrow keys to move to an entry and press ENTER. Type **e** to edit a command, letting you change kernel arguments or specify a different kernel. The **c** command places you in a command line interface. Provided your system BIOS supports very large drives, GRUB can boot from anywhere on them. Linux and Unix operating systems are known as multiboot operating systems and take arguments passed to them at boot time. Check the grub Man page for GRUB options. You can use the Boot Configuration tool to select your default system or kernel as well as set the timeout limit (accessible from System Settings menu as Boot Loader).

GRUB configuration is held in the **/boot/grub/grub.conf** file. (You can also access this file as **/etc/grub.conf**, which links to **/boot/grub/grub.conf**.) You only need to make your entries and GRUB will automatically read them when you reboot. There are several options you can set, such as the timeout period and the background image to use. Check the GRUB info documentation for a detailed description, **info grub**. You can specify a system to boot by creating a title entry for it, beginning with the term **title**. You then have to specify where the operating system kernel or program is located, which hard drive and what partition on that hard drive. This information is listed in parentheses following the **root** option. Numbering starts from 0, not 1, and hard drives are indicated with an **hd** prefix, whether they are IDE or SCSI hard drives. So **root(hd0,2)** references the first hard drive (**hda**) and the third partition on that hard drive (**hda3**). For Linux systems, you will also have to use the **kernel** option to indicate the kernel program to run, using the full pathname and any options the kernel may need. The RAM disk is indicated by the **initrd** option.

```
title Red Hat Linux (2.6.11-1.1369)
     root (hd0,2)
     kernel /boot/vmlinuz-2.6.11-1.1369_FC4 ro root=/dev/hda3 rhgb quiet
     initrd /boot/initrd-2.6.11-1.1369_FC4.img
```

The kernel option specifies the kernel to run. The kernel is located in the **/boot** directory and has the name **vmlinuz** with the kernel version number. You can have several kernels in the **/boot** directory and use GRUB to choose the one to use. After the kernel program, you specify any options you want for the kernel. This includes a **ro** option, which initially starts the kernel as read only. The root option is used to specify the device on which your system was installed, your root directory. In the previous example the system was installed on device **/dev/hda3**. The **rhgb quiet** options uses the Red Hat Graphical Boot interface to start your system, instead of listing all the startup messages on a text display.

NOTE *If you are having startup problems with your graphic card driver, you may need to remove* **rhgb quiet** *from your kernel option in* **grub.conf**.

If you installed the standard Workstation configuration, your root directory will be installed on a logical volume. Your root option would reference the logical volume, specifying the volume group and the logical volume, as shown here.

```
kernel /vmlinuz-2.6.11-1.1369_FC4 ro root=/dev/VolGroup00/LogVol00 rhgb quiet
```

For another operating system such as Windows, you would use the **rootnoverify** option to specify where Windows is installed. This option instructs GRUB not to try to mount the partition. Use the **chainloader+1** options to allow GRUB to access it. The **chainloader** option tells GRUB to use another boot program for that operating system. The number indicates the sector on the partition where the boot program is located—for example, **+1** indicates the first sector.

```
title Windows XP
      rootnoverify (hd0,0)
      chainloader +1
```

Windows systems will all want to boot from the first partition on the first disk. This becomes a problem if you want to install several versions of Windows on different partitions or install Windows on a partition other than the first one. GRUB lets you work around this by letting you hide other partitions in line, and then unhiding the one you want, making it appear to be the first partition. In this example, the first partition is hidden, and the second is unhidden. This assumes there is a Windows system on the second partition on the first hard drive (**hd0,1**). Now that the first partition is hidden, the second one appears as the first partition:

```
hide (hd0,0)
unhide (hd0,1)
rootnoverify (hd0,1)
```

A sample **grub.conf** file follows with entries for both Linux and Windows. Notice that kernel parameters are listed in the **kernel** option as arguments to the kernel.

/boot/grub/grub.conf
```
grub.conf generated by anaconda
#
#boot=/dev/hda
default=0
timeout=30
splashimage=(hd0,2)/boot/grub/splash.xpm.gz
title Red Hat Linux (2.6.11-1.1369_FC4)
      root (hd0,2)
      kernel /boot/vmlinuz-2.6.11-1.1369_FC4 ro root=/dev/hda3 rhgb quiet
      initrd /boot/initrd-2.6.11-1.1369_FC4.img
title Windows
      rootnoverify (hd0,0)
      chainloader +1
```

NOTE *Older Red Hat versions provide the older Linux Loader (LILO) as their boot manager. It performs the same kind of tasks as GRUB. You can modify your LILO configuration either by using an administration tool like Boot Manager (LILO-config) or by editing the **/etc/lilo.conf** configuration file directly. You can also configure LILO with the KDE Klilo2 tool.*

Managing Users

A s a system administrator, you must manage the users of your system. You can add or remove users, as well as add and remove groups, and you can modify access rights and permissions for both users and groups. You also have access to system initialization files you can use to configure all user shells. And you have control over the default initialization files copied into a user account when it is first created. You can decide how new user accounts should be configured initially by configuring these files.

TIP *Every file is owned by a user who can control access to it. System files are owned by the root user and accessible by the root only. Services like FTP are an exception to this rule. Though accessible by the root, a service's files are owned by their own special user. For example, FTP files are owned by an **ftp** user. This provides users with access to a service's files without also having root user access.*

User Configuration Files

Any utility to manage a user, such as the system-config-users, makes use of certain default files, called *configuration files*, and directories to set up the new account. A set of pathnames is used to locate these default files or to indicate where to create certain user directories. For example, **/etc/skel** holds initialization files for a new user. A new user's home directory is created in the **/home** directory. Table 30-1 has a list of the pathnames.

TIP *You can find out which users are currently logged in with the **w** or **who** command. The **w** command displays detailed information about each connected user, such as from where they logged in and how long they have been inactive, and the date and time of login. The **who** command provides less detailed data.*

Directory and Files	Description
/home	Location of the user's own home directory.
/etc/skel	Holds the default initialization files for the login shell, such as **.bash_profile**, **.bashrc**, and **.bash_logout**. Includes many user setup directories and files such as **.kde** for KDE and **Desktop** for GNOME.
/etc/shells	Holds the login shells, such as BASH or TCSH.
/etc/passwd	Holds the password for a user.
/etc/group	Holds the group to which the user belongs.
/etc/shadow	Encrypted password file.
/etc/gshadow	Encrypted password file for groups.
/etc/login.defs	Default login definitions for users.

TABLE 30-1 Paths for User Configuration Files

The Password Files

A user gains access to an account by providing a correct login and password. The system maintains passwords in password files, along with login information like the username and ID. Tools like the **passwd** command let users change their passwords by modifying these files; **/etc/passwd** is the file that traditionally held user passwords, though in encrypted form. However, all users are allowed to read the **/etc/passwd** file, which would have allowed access by users to the encrypted passwords. For better security, password entries are kept in the **/etc/shadow** file, which is restricted to the root user.

/etc/passwd

When you add a user, an entry for that user is made in the **/etc/passwd** file, commonly known as the *password file*. Each entry takes up one line that has several fields separated by colons. The fields are as follows:

- **Username**   Login name of the user
- **Password**   Encrypted password for the user's account
- **User ID**   Unique number assigned by the system
- **Group ID**   Number used to identify the group to which the user belongs
- **Comment**   Any user information, such as the user's full name
- **Home directory**   The user's home directory
- **Login shell**   Shell to run when the user logs in; this is the default shell, usually /bin/bash

Depending on whether or not you are using shadow passwords, the password field (the second field) will be either an **x** or an encrypted form of the user's password. Fedora Core implements shadow passwords by default, so these entries should have an **x** for their passwords. The following is an example of an **/etc/passwd** entry. For such entries, you must use the **passwd** command to create a password. Notice also that user IDs in this particular system start at 500 and increment by one. With Fedora Core, the group given is not the generic User, but a group consisting uniquely of that user. For example, the **dylan** user belongs to a group named **Dylan**, not to the generic **User** group.

```
dylan:x:500:500:Dylan:/home/dylan:/bin/bash
chris:x:501:501:Chris:/home/chris:/bin/bash
```

TIP *If you turn off shadow password support, entries in your passwd file will display encrypted passwords. Because any user can read the /etc/passwd file, intruders can access and possibly crack the encrypted passwords.*

TIP *Although it is technically possible to edit entries in the /etc/passwd file directly, it is not recommended. In particular, deleting an entry does not remove any other information, permissions, and data associated with a user, which opens a possible security breach whereby an intruder could take over the deleted user's ID or disk space.*

/etc/shadow and /etc/gshadow

The **/etc/passwd** file is a simple text file and is vulnerable to security breaches. If anyone gains access to the **/etc/password** file, they might be able to decipher or crack the encrypted passwords through a brute-force crack. The shadow suite of applications implements a greater level of security. These include versions of **useradd**, **groupadd**, and their corresponding update and delete programs. Most other user configuration tools, including system-config-users, support shadow security measures. With shadow security, passwords are no longer kept in the **/etc/password** file. Instead, passwords are kept in a separate file called **/etc/shadow**. Access is restricted to the root user.

The following example shows the **/etc/shadow** entries for two users, listing their encrypted passwords. The entry for **chris** has an **x** in its Password field, indicating that a password has not yet been created for this user:

```
dylan:YOTPd3Pyy9hAc:500:500:Dylan:/home/dylan:/bin/bash
chris:x:501:501:Chris:/home/chris:/bin/bash
```

A corresponding password file, called **/etc/gshadow**, is also maintained for groups that require passwords. Red Hat supports shadow passwords by default. You can manually specify whether you want to use shadow passwords with the authentication tool.

Password Tools

To change any particular field for a given user, you should use the user management tools provided, such as the **passwd** command, system-config-users, **adduser**, **usermod**, **useradd**, and **chage**, discussed in this chapter. The **passwd** command lets you change the password only. Other tools, such as system-config-users, not only make entries in the **/etc/passwd** file but also create the home directory for the user and install initialization files in the user's home directory.

These tools also let you control users' access to their accounts. You can set expiration dates for users or lock them out of their accounts. Users locked out of their accounts will have their password in the **/etc/shadow** file prefixed by the invalid string, **!!**. Unlocking the account removes this prefix.

PART VI

TIP *With the Authentication tool (system-config-authentication, see Chapter 4), you can enable and configure various authentication tools such as NIS and LDAP servers, as well as enabling shadow passwords, LDAP, and Kerberos authentication (accessible as Authentication on the System Settings menu and windows).*

Managing User Environments

Each time a user logs in, two profile scripts are executed, a system profile script that is the same for every user, and a user login profile script that can be customized to each user's needs. When the user logs out, a user logout script is run. In addition, each time a shell is generated, including the login shell, a user shell script is run. There are different kinds of scripts used for different shells. On Fedora Core, the default shell commonly used is the BASH shell. As an alternative, users could use different shells such as TCSH or the Z shell, both installed with Fedora Core.

Profile Scripts

For the BASH shell, each user has his or her own BASH login profile script named **.bash_ profile** in the user's home directory. The system profile script is located in the **/etc** directory and named **profile** with no preceding period. The BASH shell user shell script is called **.bashrc**. The **.bashrc** file also runs the **/etc/bashrc** file to implement any global definitions such as the **PS1** and **TERM** variables. The **/etc/bashrc** file also executes any specialized initialization file in the **/etc/profile.d** directory, such as those used for KDE and GNOME. The **.bash_profile** file runs the **.bashrc** file, and through it, the **/etc/bashrc** file, implementing global definitions.

As a superuser, you can edit any of these profile or shell scripts and put in any commands you want executed for each user when that user logs in. For example, you may want to define a default path for commands, in case the user has not done so. Or you may want to notify the user of recent system news or account changes.

/etc/skel

When you first add a user to the system, you must provide the user with skeleton versions of their login, shell, and logout initialization files. For the BASH shell, these would be the **.bash_profile, .bashrc,** and **.bash_logout** files. The **useradd** command and other user management tools such as system-config-users add these files automatically, copying any files in the directory **/etc/skel** to the user's new home directory. The **/etc/skel** directory contains a skeleton initialization file for the **.bash_profile, .bashrc,** and **.bash_logout** files or, if you are using the TCSH shell as your login shell, the **.login, .tcshrc,** and **.logout** files. The **/etc/skel** directory also contains default files and directories for your desktops. These include a **.screenrc** file for the X Window System, a **.kde** directory for the KDE desktop, and a **Desktop** directory that contains default configuration files for the GNOME desktop.

As a superuser, you can configure the **.bash_profile** or **.bashrc** file in the **/etc/skel** directory any way you want. Usually, basic system variable assignments are included that define pathnames for commands and command aliases. The **PATH** and **BASH_ENV** variables are defined in **.bash_profile**. Once users have their own **.bash_profile** or **.bashrc** file, they can redefine variables or add new commands as they choose.

/etc/login.defs

System-wide values used by user and group creation utilities such as **useradd** and **usergroup** are kept in the **/etc/login.defs** file. Here you will find the range of possible user and group IDs listed. **UID_MIN** holds the minimum number for user IDs, and **UID_MAX** the maximum number. Various password options control password controls—such as **PASS_MIN_LEN**, which determines the minimum number of characters allowable in a password. Options such as **CREATE_HOME** can be set to tell user tools like **useradd** to create home directories for new accounts by default. Samples of these entries are shown here:

```
MAIL_DIR /var/spool/mail
PASS_MIN_LEN        5
CREATE_HOME yes
```

/etc/security/access.conf

You can control user login access by remote users to your system with the **/etc/security/access.conf** file, part of Linux-PAM which is now used for login authentication (replaces **login.access**). The file consists of entries listing users, whether they are allowed access, and from where they can access the system. A record in this file consists of three colon-delimited fields: a plus (**+**) or minus (**–**) sign indicating whether users are allowed access, user login names allowed access, and the remote system (host) or terminal (tty device) from which they are trying to log in. The following enables the user **chris** to access the system from the **rabbit.mytrek.com** remote system:

```
+:chris:rabbit.mytrek.com
```

You can list more than one user or location, or use the **ALL** option in place of either users or locations to allow access by all users and locations. The **ALL** option can be qualified with the **EXCEPT** option to allow access by all users except certain specified ones. The following entry allows any valid user to log in to the system using the console, except for the users **larisa** and **aleina**:

```
+:ALL EXCEPT larisa aleina:console
```

Other access control files are used to control access for specific services, such as the **hosts.deny** and **hosts.allows** files used with the **tcpd** daemon for **xinetd**-supported servers.

Controlling User Passwords

Once you have created a user account, you can control the user's access to it. Both the system-config-users and the **passwd** tool let you lock and unlock a user's account. You use the **passwd** command with the **–l** option to lock an account, invalidating its password, and you use the **–u** option to unlock it.

You can also force a user to change his or her password at given intervals by setting an expiration date for that password. Both system-config-users and the **chage** command let you specify an expiration limit for a user's password. A user could be required to change his or her password every month, every week, or at a given date. Once the password expires, the user will be prompted to enter a new one. You can issue a warning beforehand, telling the user how much time is left before the password expires. For an account that you want to close, you can permanently expire a password. You can even shut down accounts that are inactive too long. In the next example, the password for the **chris** account will stay valid for only seven days. The **–M** option with the number of days sets the maximum time that a password can be valid.

```
chage -M 7  chris
```

To set a particular date for the account to expire, use the **-E** option with the date specified mm/dd/yyyy.

```
chage -E 07/30/2003  chris
```

To find out what the current expiration settings are for a given account, use the **-l** option.

```
chage -l chris
```

You can also combine your options into one command,

```
chage -M 7 -E 07/30/2003  chris
```

A listing of the **chage** options appears in Table 30-2.

Adding and Removing Users with useradd, usermod, and userdel

Linux also provides the **useradd**, **usermod**, and **userdel** commands to manage user accounts. All these commands take in all their information as options on the command line. If an option is not specified, they use predetermined default values. These are command line operations. To use them on your desktop you first need to open a terminal window (right-click on desktop and select Open Terminal), and then enter the commands at the shell prompt.

If you are using a desktop interface with Red Hat Enterprise Linux and Fedora Core distributions, you should use the system-config-users to manage user accounts (see Chapter 4). You can access system-config-users from the System Settings menu under the Desktop menu. It is labeled simply as Users and Groups.

useradd

With the **useradd** command, you enter values as options on the command line, such as the name of a user, to create a user account. It then creates a new login and directory for that name using all the default features for a new account.

```
# useradd chris
```

TABLE 30-2 Options for the **chage** Command

Option	Description
-m	Minimum number of days a user must go before being able to change his password
-M	Maximum number of days a user can go without changing his password
-d	The last day the password was changed
-E	Specific expiration date for a password, date in format in yyyy-mm-dd or in commonly used format like mm/dd/yyyy
-I	Allowable account inactivity period (in days), after which password will expire
-W	Warning period, number of days before expiration when the user will be sent a warning message
-l	Display current password expiration controls

The **useradd** utility first checks the **/etc/login.defs** file for default values for creating a new account. For those defaults not defined in the **/etc/login.defs** file, **useradd** supplies its own. You can display these defaults using the **useradd** command with the **-D** option. The default values include the group name, the user ID, the home directory, the **skel** directory, and the login shell. Values the user enters on the command line will override corresponding defaults. The group name is the name of the group in which the new account is placed. By default, this is **other**, which means the new account belongs to no group. The user ID is a number identifying the user account. The **skel** directory is the system directory that holds copies of initialization files. These initialization files are copied into the user's new home directory when it is created. The login shell is the pathname for the particular shell the user plans to use.

The **useradd** command has options that correspond to each default value. Table 30-3 holds a list of all the options you can use with the **useradd** command. You can use specific values in place of any of these defaults when creating a particular account. The login is inaccessible until you do. In the next example, the group name for the **chris** account is set to **intro1** and the user ID is set to 578:

```
# useradd chris -g intro1 -u 578
```

Option	Description
-d *dir*	Sets the home directory of the new user.
-D	Displays defaults for all settings. Can also be used to reset default settings for the home directory (**-b**), group (**-g**), shell (**-s**), expiration date (**-e**), and password expirations (**-f**).
-e *mm/dd/yy*	Sets an expiration date for the account (none, by default). Specified as month/day/year.
-f *days*	Sets the number of days an account remains active after its password expires.
-g *group*	Sets a group.
-m	Creates user's home directory, if it does not exist.
-m **-k** *skl-dir*	Sets the skeleton directory that holds skeleton files, such as **.profile** files, which are copied to the user's home directory automatically when it is created; the default is **/etc/skel**.
-M	Does not create user's home directory.
-p *password*	Supplies an encrypted password (crypt or MD5). With no argument, the account is immediately disabled.
-r	A Fedora Core–specific option that creates a system account (one whose user ID is lower than the minimum set in **logon.defs**). No home directory is created unless specified by **-m**.
-s *shell*	Sets the login shell of the new user. This is **/bin/bash** by default, the BASH shell.
-u *userid*	Sets the user ID of the new user. The default is the increment of the highest number used so far.

TABLE 30-3   Options for **useradd** and **usermod**

Once you add a new user login, you need to give the new login a password. Password entries are placed in the **/etc/passwd** and **/etc/shadow** files. Use the **passwd** command to create a new password for the user, as shown here. The password you enter will not appear on your screen. You will be prompted to repeat the password. A message will then be issued indicating that the password was successfully changed.

```
# passwd chris
Changing password for user chris
New UNIX password:
Retype new UNIX password:
passwd: all authentication tokens updated successfully
#
```

usermod

The **usermod** command enables you to change the values for any of these features. You can change the home directory or the user ID. You can even change the username for the account. The **usermod** command takes the same options as **useradd**, listed in Table 30-3.

userdel

When you want to remove a user from the system, you can use the **userdel** command to delete the user's login. With the **-r** option, the user's home directory will also be removed. In the next example, the user **chris** is removed from the system:

```
# userdel -r chris
```

Managing Groups

You can manage groups using either shell commands or window utilities like system-config-users. Groups are an effective way to manage access and permissions, letting you control several users with just their group name.

/etc/group and /etc/gshadow

The system file that holds group entries is called **/etc/group**. The file consists of group records, with one record per line and its fields separated by colons. A group record has four fields: a group name, a password, its ID, and the users who are part of this group. The Password field can be left blank. The fields for a group record are as follows:

- **Group name**   The name of the group, which must be unique.
- **Password**   With shadow security implemented, this field is an **x**, with the password indicated in the **/etc/gshadow** file.
- **Group ID**   The number assigned by the system to identify this group.
- **Users**   The list of users that belong to the group, separated by commas.

Here is an example of an entry in an **/etc/group** file. The group is called **engines**, the password is managed by shadow security, the group ID is 100, and the users who are part of this group are **chris**, **robert**, **valerie**, and **aleina**:

```
engines:x:100:chris,robert,valerie,aleina
```

As in the case of the **/etc/passwd** file, it is best to change group entries using a group management utility like **groupmod**, **groupadd**, or system-config-users. All users have read access to the **/etc/group** file. With shadow security, secure group data such as passwords are kept in the **/etc/gshadow** file, to which only the root user has access.

User Private Groups

A new user can be assigned to a special group set up for just that user and given the user's name. Thus the new user **dylan** is given a default group also called **dylan**. The group **dylan** will also show up in the listing of groups. This method of assigning default user groups is called the User Private Group (UPG) scheme. UPG is currently used on Fedora Core systems. The supplementary groups are additional groups that the user may want to belong to. Traditionally, users were all assigned to one group named **users** that would subject all users to the group permission controls for the **users** group. With UPG, each user has its own group, with its own group permissions.

Group Directories

As with users, you can create a home directory for a group. To do so, you simply create a directory for the group in the **/home** directory and change its group to that of the group, along with allowing access by any member of the group. The following example creates a directory called **engines** and changes its group to that of the **engines** group:

```
mkdir /home/engines
chgrp engines /home/engines
```

Then the read, write, and execute permissions for the group level should be set with the **chmod** command, discussed later in this chapter:

```
chmod g+rwx /home/engines
```

Any member of the **engines** group can now access the **/home/engines** directory and any shared files placed therein. This directory becomes a shared directory for the group. You can, in fact, use the same procedure to make other shared directories at any location on the file system.

Files within the shared directory should also have their permissions set to allow access by other users in the group. When a user places a file in a shared directory, the user needs to set the permissions on that file to allow other members of the group to access it. A read permission will let others display it, write lets them change it, and execute lets them run it (used for scripts and programs). The following example first changes the group for the **mymodel** file to **engines**. Then it copies the **mymodel** file to the **/home/engines** directory and sets the group read and write permission for the **engines** group:

```
$ chgrp engines mymodel
$ cp mymodel /home/engines
$ chmod g+rw /home/engines/mymodel
```

Managing Groups with system-config-users

You can add, remove, and modify any groups easily with system-config-users. First, access system-config-users by clicking the Users and Groups entry in the System Settings menu, listed in the Desktop menu. Then click the tabbed panel labeled Groups in the User Manager window. This will list all your current groups. There will be three fields for each entry: Group Name, Group ID, and Group Members.

To add a group, just click the Add Group button. This opens a small window where you can enter the group name. The new group will be listed in the Groups listing. To add users as members of the group, select the group's entry and click the Properties button. This opens a window with tabbed panels for Group Data and Group Users. The Group Users panel lists all current users with check boxes. Click the check boxes for the users you want to be members of this group. If you want to remove a user as member, click the check box to remove its check. Click OK to effect your changes. If you want to remove a group, just select its entry in the Groups panel and then click the Delete button.

Managing Groups Using groupadd, groupmod, and groupdel

You can also manage groups with the **groupadd**, **groupmod**, and **groupdel** commands. These command line operations let you quickly manage a group from a terminal window.

groupadd and groupdel

With the **groupadd** command, you can create new groups. When you add a group to the system, the system places the group's name in the **/etc/group** file and gives it a group ID number. If shadow security is in place, changes are made to the **/etc/gshadow** file. The **groupadd** command only creates the group category. You need to add users to the group individually. In the following example, the **groupadd** command creates the **engines** group:

```
# groupadd engines
```

You can delete a group with the **groupdel** command. In the next example, the **engines** group is deleted:

```
# groupdel engines
```

groupmod

You can change the name of a group or its ID using the **groupmod** command. Enter **groupmod -g** with the new ID number and the group name. To change the name of a group, you use the **-n** option. Enter **groupmod -n** with the new name of the group, followed by the current name. In the next example, the **engines** group has its name changed to **trains**:

```
# groupmod -n trains engines
```

Controlling Access to Directories and Files: chmod

Each file and directory in Linux contains a set of permissions that determine who can access them and how. You set these permissions to limit access in one of three ways: You can restrict access to yourself alone, you can allow users in a predesignated group to have access, or you can permit anyone on your system to have access. You can also control how a given file or directory is accessed.

NOTE   *See Chapter 17 to learn how to use SELinux to set permissions on users and files.*

Permissions

A file or directory may have read, write, and execute permissions. When a file is created, it is automatically given read and write permissions for the owner, enabling you to display and modify the file. You may change these permissions to any combination you want. A file could also have read-only permission, preventing any modifications.

Permission Categories

Three different categories of users can have access to a file or directory: the owner, the group, and all others not belonging to that group. The owner is the user who created the file. Any file you create, you own. You can also permit a group to have access to a file. Often, users are collected into groups. For example, all the users for a given class or project could be formed into a group by the system administrator. A user can grant access to a file to the members of a designated group. Finally, you can also open up access to a file to all other users on the system. In this case, every user not part of the file's group could have access to that file. In this sense, every other user on the system makes up the "others" category. If you want to give the same access to all users on your system, you set the same permissions for both the group and the others. That way, you include both members of the group (group permission) and all those users who are not members (others permission).

Read, Write, Execute Permissions

Each category has its own set of read, write, and execute permissions. The first set controls the user's own access to his or her files—the owner access. The second set controls the access of the group to a user's files. The third set controls the access of all other users to the user's files. The three sets of read, write, and execute permissions for the three categories—owner, group, and other—make a total of nine types of permissions.

The **ls** command with the **-l** option displays detailed information about the file, including the permissions. In the following example, the first set of characters on the left is a list of the permissions set for the **mydata** file:

```
$ ls -l mydata
-rw-r--r-- 1 chris weather 207 Feb 20 11:55 mydata
```

An empty permission is represented by a dash, **-**. The read permission is represented by **r**, write by **w**, and execute by **x**. Notice there are ten positions. The first character indicates the file type. In a general sense, a directory can be considered a type of file. If the first character is a dash, a file is being listed. If the first character is **d**, information about a directory is being displayed.

The next nine characters are arranged according to the different user categories. The first set of three characters is the owner's set of permissions for the file. The second set of three characters is the group's set of permissions for the file. The last set of three characters is the other users' set of permissions for the file.

Permissions on GNOME

On GNOME, you can set a directory or file permission using the Permissions panel in its Properties window. Right-click the file or directory entry in the file manager window and select Properties. Then select the Permissions panel. Here you will find a table of boxes with columns for Read, Write, and Execute along with rows for Owner, Group, and Other. Check the appropriate box for the permission you want. Normally, the Read and Write boxes for owner permission will already be set. You can specify the group you want access provided to from the Group drop-down menu. This displays the groups a user belongs to.

chmod

You use the **chmod** command to change different permission configurations. **chmod** takes two lists as its arguments: permission changes and filenames. You can specify the list of permissions in two different ways. One way uses permission symbols and is referred to as the *symbolic method*. The other uses what is known as a "binary mask" and is referred to as either the absolute or the relative method. Table 30-4 lists options for the **chmod** command.

NOTE   *When a program is owned by the root, setting the user ID permission will give the user the ability to execute the program with root permissions. This can be a serious security risk for any program that could effect changes—such as* **rm***, which removes files.*

Ownership

Files and directories belong to both an owner and a group. A group usually consists of a collection of users, all belonging to the same group. In the following example, the **mydata** file is owned by the user **robert** and belongs to the group **weather**:

```
-rw-r--r-- 1 robert weather 207 Feb 20 11:55 mydata
```

A group can also consist of one user, though normally it is the same as the user who created the file. Each user on the system, including the root user, is assigned their own group, of which they are the only member, ensuring access only by that user. In the next example, the report file is owned by the **robert** user and belongs to that user's single user group, **robert**:

```
-rw-r--r-- 1 robert robert 305 Mar 17 12:01 report
```

The root user, the system administrator, owns most of the system files that also belong to the root group, of which only the root user is a member. Most administration files, like configuration files in the **/etc** directory, are owned by the root user and belong to the root group. Only the root user has permission to modify them, whereas normal users can read and, in the case of programs, also execute them. In the next example, the root user owns the **fstab** file in the **/etc** directory, which also belongs to the root user group.

```
-rw-r--r-- 1 root root 621 Apr 22 11:03 fstab
```

Certain directories and files located in the system directories are owned by a service, rather than the root user, because the services need to change those files directly. This is particularly true for services that interact with remote users, such as Internet servers. Most of these files are located in the **/var** directory. Here you will find files and directories managed by services like the Squid proxy server and the Domain Name Server (named). In this example, the Squid proxy server directory is owned by the **squid** user and belongs to the **squid** group:

```
drwxr-x--- 2 squid squid 4096 Jan 24 16:29 squid
```

Command	Execution
`chmod`	Changes the permission of a file or directory.
Option	**Execution**
`+`	Adds a permission.
`-`	Removes a permission.
`=`	Assigns entire set of permissions.
`r`	Sets read permission for a file or directory. A file can be displayed or printed. A directory can have the list of its files displayed.
`w`	Sets write permission for a file or directory. A file can be edited or erased. A directory can be removed.
`x`	Sets execute permission for a file or directory. If the file is a shell script, it can be executed as a program. A directory can be changed to and entered.
`u`	Sets permissions for the user who created and owns the file or directory.
`g`	Sets permissions for group access to a file or directory.
`o`	Sets permissions for access to a file or directory by all other users on the system.
`a`	Sets permissions for access by the owner, group, and all other users.
`s`	Sets User ID and Group ID permission; program owned by owner and group.
`t`	Sets sticky bit permission; program remains in memory.
`chgrp` *groupname filenames*	Changes the group for a file or files.
`chown` *user-name filenames*	Changes the owner of a file or files.
`ls -l` *filename*	Lists a filename with its permissions displayed.
`ls -ld` *directory*	Lists a directory name with its permissions displayed.
`ls -l`	Lists all files in a directory with its permissions displayed.

TABLE 30-4   File and Directory Permission Operations

Changing a File's Owner or Group: chown and chgrp

Although other users may be able to access a file, only the owner can change its permissions. If, however, you want to give some other user control over one of your file's permissions, you can change the owner of the file from yourself to the other user. The **chown** command transfers control over a file to another user. This command takes as its first argument the name of the other user. Following the username, you list the files you are transferring. In the next example, the user gives control of the **mydata** file to user **robert**:

```
$ chown robert mydata
$ ls -l mydata
-rw-r--r-- 1 robert weather 207 Feb 20 11:55 mydata
```

You can also, if you wish, change the group for a file, using the **chgrp** command. **chgrp** takes as its first argument the name of the new group for a file or files. Following the new group name, you list the files you want changed to that group. In the next example, the user changes the group name for **today** and **weekend** to the **forecast** group. The **ls -l** command then reflects the group change.

```
$ chgrp forecast today weekend
$ ls -l
-rw-rw-r-- 1 chris forecast 568 Feb 14 10:30 today
-rw-rw-r-- 1 chris forecast 308 Feb 17 12:40 weekend
```

You can combine the **chgrp** operation in the **chown** command by attaching a group to the new owner with a colon.

```
$ chown george:forecast tomorrow
-rw-rw-r-- 1 george forecast 568 Feb 14 10:30 tomorrow
```

Setting Permissions: Permission Symbols

The symbolic method of setting permissions uses the characters **r**, **w**, and **x** for read, write, and execute, respectively. Any of these permissions can be added or removed. The symbol to add a permission is the plus sign, **+**. The symbol to remove a permission is the minus sign, **-**. In the next example, the **chmod** command adds the execute permission and removes the write permission for the **mydata** file for all categories. The read permission is not changed.

```
$ chmod +x-w mydata
```

Permission symbols also specify each user category. The owner, group, and others categories are represented by the **u**, **g**, and **o** characters, respectively. Notice the owner category is represented by a **u**, and can be thought of as the user. The symbol for a category is placed before plus and minus signs preceding the read, write, and execute permissions. If no category symbol is used, all categories are assumed, and the permissions specified are set for the user, group, and others. In the next example, the first **chmod** command sets the permissions for the group to read and write. The second **chmod** command sets permissions for other users to read. Notice no spaces are between the permission specifications and the category. The permissions list is simply one long phrase, with no spaces.

```
$ chmod g+rw mydata
$ chmod o+r mydata
```

A user may remove permissions as well as add them. In the next example, the read permission is set for other users, but the write and execute permissions are removed:

```
$ chmod o+r-wx mydata
```

Another permission character exists, **a**, which represents all the categories. The **a** character is the default. In the next example, the two commands are equivalent. The read permission is explicitly set with the **a** character denoting all types of users: other, group, and user.

```
$ chmod a+r mydata
$ chmod +r mydata
```

One of the most common permission operations is setting a file's executable permission. This is often done in the case of shell program files. The executable permission indicates a file contains executable instructions and can be directly run by the system. In the next example, the file **lsc** has its executable permission set and then executed:

```
$ chmod u+x lsc
$ lsc
main.c lib.c
$
```

Absolute Permissions: Binary Masks

Instead of the permission symbols in Table 30-4, many users find it more convenient to use the absolute method. The *absolute method* changes all the permissions at once, instead of specifying one or the other. It uses a *binary mask* that references all the permissions in each category. The three categories, each with three permissions, conform to an octal binary format. Octal numbers have a base 8 structure. When translated into a binary number, each octal digit becomes three binary digits. A binary number is a set of 1 and 0 digits. Three octal digits in a number translate into three sets of three binary digits, which is nine altogether— and the exact number of permissions for a file.

You can use the octal digits as a mask to set the different file permissions. Each octal digit applies to one of the user categories. You can think of the digits matching up with the permission categories from left to right, beginning with the owner category. The first octal digit applies to the owner category, the second to the group, and the third to the others category. The actual octal digit you choose determines the read, write, and execute permissions for each category. At this point, you need to know how octal digits translate into their binary equivalents.

Calculating Octal Numbers

A simple way to calculate the octal number makes use of the fact that any number used for permissions will be a combination derived from adding in decimal terms the numbers 4, 2, and 1. Use 4 for read permission, 2 for write, and 1 for execute. The read, write, execute permission is simply the addition of 4 + 2 + 1 to get 7. The read and execute permission adds 4 and 1, to get 5. You can use this method to calculate the octal number for each category. To get 755, you would add 4 + 2 + 1 for the owner read, write, and execute permission, 4 + 1 for the group read and execute permission, and 4 + 1 again for the other read and execute permission.

Binary Masks

When dealing with a binary mask, you need to specify three digits for all three categories, as well as their permissions. This makes a binary mask less versatile than the permission symbols. To set the owner execute permission on and the write permission off for the **mydata** file and retain the read permission, you need to use the octal digit 5 (101). At the same time, you need to specify the digits for group and other users access. If these categories are to retain read access, you need the octal number 4 for each (100). This gives you three octal digits, 544, which translate into the binary digits 101 100 100.

```
$ chmod 544 mydata
```

Execute Permissions

One of the most common uses of the binary mask is to set the execute permission. You can create files that contain Linux commands, called *shell scripts.* To execute the commands in a shell script, you must first indicate the file is executable—that it contains commands the system can execute. You can do this in several ways, one of which is to set the executable permission on the shell script file. Suppose you just completed a shell script file and you need to give it executable permission to run it. You also want to retain read and write permission but deny any access by the group or other users. The octal digit 7 (111) will set all three permissions, including execute (you can also add 4-read, 2-write, and 1-execute to get 7). Using 0 for the group and other users denies them access. This gives you the digits 700, which are equivalent to the binary digits 111 000 000. In this example, the owner permission for the **myprog** file is set to include execute permission:

```
$ chmod 700 myprog
```

If you want others to be able to execute and read the file, but not change it, you can set the read and execute permissions and turn off the write permission with the digit 5 (101). In this case, you would use the octal digits 755, having the binary equivalent of 111 101 101.

```
$ chmod 755 myprog
```

Directory Permissions

You can also set permissions on directories. The read permission set on a directory allows the list of files in a directory to be displayed. The execute permission enables a user to change to that directory. The write permission enables a user to create and remove his or her files in that directory. If you allow other users to have write permission on a directory, they can add their own files to it. When you create a directory, it is automatically given read, write, and execute permission for the owner. You may list the files in that directory, change to it, and create files in it.

Like files, directories have sets of permissions for the owner, the group, and all other users. Often, you may want to allow other users to change to and list the files in one of your directories, but not let them add their own files to it. In this case, you would set read and execute permissions on the directory, but not write permission. This would allow other users to change to the directory and list the files in it, but not to create new files or to copy any of their files into it. The next example sets read and execute permission for the group for the **thankyou** directory, but removes the write permission. Members of the group may enter the **thankyou** directory and list the files there, but they may not create new ones.

```
$ chmod g+rx-w letters/thankyou
```

Just as with files, you can also use octal digits to set a directory permission. To set the same permissions as in the preceding example, you would use the octal digits 750, which have the binary equivalents of 111 101 000.

```
$ chmod 750 letters/thankyou
```

Displaying Directory Permissions

The **ls** command with the **-l** option lists all files in a directory. To list only the information about the directory itself, add a **d** modifier. In the next example, **ls -ld** displays information about the **thankyou** directory. Notice the first character in the permissions list is **d**, indicating it is a directory:

```
$ ls -ld thankyou
drwxr-x--- 2 chris 512 Feb 10 04:30 thankyou
```

Parent Directory Permissions

If you have a file you want other users to have access to, you not only need to set permissions for that file, you also must make sure the permissions are set for the directory in which the file is located. To access your file, a user must first access the file's directory. The same applies to parents of directories. Although a directory may give permission to others to access it, if its parent directory denies access, the directory cannot be reached. Therefore, you must pay close attention to your directory tree. To provide access to a directory, all other directories above it in the directory tree must also be accessible to other users.

Ownership Permissions

In addition to the read/write/execute permissions, you can also set ownership permissions for executable programs. Normally, the user who runs a program owns it while it is running, even though the program file itself may be owned by another user. The Set User ID permission allows the original owner of the program to own it always, even while another user is running the program. For example, most software on the system is owned by the root user but is run by ordinary users. Some such software may have to modify files owned by the root. In this case, the ordinary user would need to run that program with the root retaining ownership so that the program could have the permissions to change those root-owned files. The Group ID permission works the same way, except for groups. Programs owned by a group retain ownership, even when run by users from another group. The program can then change the owner group's files. There is a potential security risk involved in that you are essentially giving a user some limited root-level access.

Ownership Permissions Using Symbols

To add both the User ID and Group ID permissions to a file, you use the **s** option. The following example adds the User ID permission to the **pppd** program, which is owned by the root user. When an ordinary user runs **pppd**, the root user retains ownership, allowing the **pppd** program to change root-owned files.

```
# chmod +s /usr/sbin/pppd
```

The Set User ID and Set Group ID permissions show up as an **s** in the execute position of the owner and group segments. Set User ID and Group ID are essentially variations of the execute permission, **x**. Read, write, and User ID permission would be **rws** instead of just **rwx**.

```
# ls -l /usr/sbin/pppd
-rwsr-sr-x 1 root root 184412 Jan 24 22:48 /usr/sbin/pppd
```

Ownership Permissions Using the Binary Method

For the ownership permissions, you add another octal number to the beginning of the octal digits. The octal digit for User ID permission is 4 (100) and for Group ID, it is 2 (010) (use 6 to set both—110). The following example sets the User ID permission to the **pppd** program, along with read and execute permissions for the owner, group, and others:

```
# chmod 4555 /usr/sbin/pppd
```

Sticky Bit Permissions

One other special permission provides for greater security on directories, the *sticky bit*. Originally the sticky bit was used to keep a program in memory after it finished execution to increase efficiency. Current Linux systems ignore this feature. Instead, it is used for directories to protect files within them. Files in a directory with the sticky bit set can only be deleted or renamed by the root user or the owner of the directory.

Sticky Bit Permission Using Symbols

The sticky bit permission symbol is **t**. The sticky bit shows up as a **t** in the execute position of the other permissions. A program with read and execute permission with the sticky bit would have its permissions displayed as **r-t**.

```
# chmod +t /home/dylan/myreports
# ls -l /home/dylan/myreports
-rwxr-xr-t 1 root root 4096 /home/dylan/myreports
```

Sticky Bit Permission Using the Binary Method

As with ownership, for sticky bit permissions, you add another octal number to the beginning of the octal digits. The octal digit for the sticky bit is 1 (001). The following example sets the sticky bit for the **myreports** directory:

```
# chmod 1755 /home/dylan/myreports
```

The next example sets both the sticky bit and the User ID permission on the **newprogs** directory. The permission 5755 has the binary equivalent of 101 111 101 101:

```
# chmod 5755 /usr/bin/newprogs
# ls -l /usr/bin/newprogs
drwsr-xr-t 1 root root 4096  /usr/bin/newprogs
```

Permission Defaults: umask

Whenever you create a file or directory, it is given default permissions. You can display the current defaults or change them with the **umask** command. The permissions are displayed in binary or symbolic format as described in the following sections. The default permissions include any execute permissions that would be applied to a directory. Execute permission for a file is turned off by default when you create it. This is because standard data files do not use the executable permissions (for a file that you want to be executable like a script, you will have to manually set its execute permission).To display the current default permissions, use the **umask** command with no arguments. The **-S** option uses the symbolic format.

```
$ umask -S
u=rwx,g=rx,o=rx
```

This default umask provides **rw-r--r--** permission for standard files and adds execute permission for directories, **rwxr-xr-x**.

You can set a new default by specifying permissions in either symbolic or binary format. To specify the new permissions, use the **-S** option. The following example denies others read permission, while allowing user and group read access, which results in permissions of **rwxr-x---**:

```
$ umask -S  u=rwx,g=rx,o=
```

When you use the binary format, the mask is the inverse of the permissions you want to set. So to set both the read and execute permission on and the write permission off, you would use the octal number 2, a binary 010. To set all permissions on, you would use an octal 0, a binary 000. The following example shows the mask for the permission defaults **rwx**, **rx**, and **rx** (**rw**, **r**, and **r** for files):

```
$ umask
0022
```

To set the default to only deny all permissions for others, you would use 0027, using the binary mask 0111 for the other permissions.

```
$ umask 0027
```

Disk Quotas

You can use disk quotas to control how much disk space a particular user makes use of on your system. On your Linux system, unused disk space is held as a common resource that each user can access as they need it. As users create more files, they take the space they need from the pool of available disk space. In this sense, all the users are sharing a single resource of unused disk space. However, if one user were to use up all the remaining disk space, none of the other users would be able to create files or even run programs. To counter this problem, you can create disk quotas on particular users, limiting the amount of available disk space they can use.

Quota Tools

Quota checks can be implemented on the file system of a hard disk partition mounted on your system. The quotas are enabled using the **quotacheck** and **quotaon** programs. On Fedora Core, they are executed in the **/etc/rc.d/rc.sysinit** script, which is run whenever you start up your system. Each partition needs to be mounted with the quota options, **usrquota** or **grpquota**. **usrquota** enables quota controls for users, and **grpquota** works for groups. These options are usually placed in the mount entry in the **/etc/fstab** file for a particular partition (see Chapter 32). For example, to mount the **/dev/hda6** hard disk partition mounted to the **/home** directory with support for user and group quotas, you would require a mount entry like the following:

```
/dev/hda6 /home ext2 defaults,usrquota,grpquota 1 1
```

You also need to create **quota.user** and **quota.group** files for each partition for which you enable quotas. These are the quota databases used to hold the quota information for each user and group. You can create these files by running the **quotacheck** command with the **-a** option or the device name of the file system where you want to enable quotas. The following example creates the quota database on the **hda1** hard disk partition:

```
quotacheck -a  /dev/hda1
```

edquota

You can set disk quotas using the **edquota** command. With it, you can access the quota record for a particular user and group, which is maintained in the disk quota database. You can also set default quotas that will be applied to any user or group on the file system for which quotas have not been set. **edquota** will open the record in your default editor, and you can use your editor to make any changes. To open the record for a particular user, use the **-u** option and the username as an argument for **edquota** (see Table 30-5). The following example opens the disk quota record for the user **larisa**:

```
edquota -u larisa
```

The limit you set for a quota can be hard or soft. A hard limit will deny a user the ability to exceed his or her quota, whereas a soft limit will just issue a warning. For the soft limit, you can designate a grace period during which time the user has the chance to reduce their disk space below the limit. If the disk space still exceeds the limit after the grace period expires, the user can be denied access to their account. For example, a soft limit is typically 75 megabytes, whereas the hard limit could be 100 megabytes. Users who exceed their soft limit could have a 48-hour grace period.

The quota record begins with the hard disk device name and the blocks of memory and inodes in use. The Limits segments have parameters for soft and hard limits. If these entries are 0, there are no limits in place. You can set both hard and soft limits, using the hard limit as a firm restriction. Blocks in Linux are currently about 1,000 bytes. The inodes are used by files to hold information about the memory blocks making up a file. To set the time limit for a soft limit, use the **edquota** command with the **-t** option. The following example displays the quota record for **larisa**:

```
Quotas for user larisa:
/dev/hda3: blocks in use: 9000, limits (soft = 40000, hard = 60000)
  inodes in use: 321, limits (soft = 0, hard = 0)
```

quotacheck, quotaon, and quotaoff

The quota records are maintained in the quota database for that partition. Each partition that has quotas enabled has its own quota database. You can check the validity of your quota database with the **quotacheck** command. You can turn quotas on and off using the **quotaon** and **quotaoff** commands. When you start up your system, **quotacheck** is run to check the quota databases, and then **quotaon** is run to turn on quotas.

repquota and quota

As the system administrator, you can use the **repquota** command to generate a summary of disk usage for a specified file system, checking to see what users are approaching or exceeding quota limits. **repquota** takes as its argument the file system to check; the **-a** option checks all file systems.

```
repquota /dev/hda1
```

	edquota Option	Description
TABLE 30-5 Options for **edquota**	-u	Edits the user quota. This is the default.
	-g	Edits the group quota.
	-p	Duplicates the quotas of the typical user specified. This is the normal mechanism used to initialize quotas for groups of users.
	-t	Edits the soft time limits for each file system.

quota Option	Description
-g	Prints group quotas for the group of which the user is a member.
-u	Prints the user's quota.
-v	Displays quotas on file systems where no storage is allocated.
-q	Prints information on file systems where usage is over quota.

TABLE 30-6
Options for `quota`

Individual users can use the **quota** command to check their memory use and how much disk space they have left in their quota (see Table 30-6).

Lightweight Directory Access Protocol

The Lightweight Directory Access Protocol (LDAP) is designed to implement network-accessible directories of information. In this context, the term *directory* is defined as a database of primarily read-only, simple, small, widely accessible, and quickly distributable information. It is not designed for transactions or updates. It is primarily used to provide information about users on a network, such as their e-mail address or phone number. Such directories can also be used for authentication purposes, identifying that a certain user belongs to a specified network. You can find out more information on LDAP at **www .ldapman.org**. You can think of an LDAP directory for users as an Internet-accessible phone book, where anyone can look you up to find your e-mail address or other information. In fact, it may be more accurate to refer to such directories as databases. They are databases of user information, accessible over networks like the Internet. Normally, the users on a local network are spread across several different systems, and to obtain information about a user, you would have to know what system the user is on, and then query that system. With LDAP, user information for all users on a network is kept in the LDAP server. You only have to query the network's LDAP server to obtain information about a user. For example, Sendmail can use LDAP to look up user addresses. You can also use Firefox or Netscape to query LDAP.

NOTE *LDAP is a directory access protocol to an X.500 directory service, the OSI directory service.*

LDAP Clients and Servers

LDAP directories are implemented as clients and servers, where you use an LDAP client to access an LDAP server that manages the LDAP database. Most Linux distributions, including Fedora Core, use OpenLDAP, an open-source version of LDAP (you can find out more about OpenLDAP at **www.openldap.org**). This package includes an LDAP server (**slapd**), an LDAP replication server (**slurpd**), an LDAP client, and tools. **slurpd** is used to update other LDAP servers on your network, should you have more than one. Once the LDAP server is installed, you can start, stop, and restart the LDAP server (**slapd**) with the **ldap** startup script or system-config-services:

```
service ldap restart
```

594 **Part VI:** **S y s t e m   A d m i n i s t r a t i o n**

TIP   *Fedora Core clients can enable LDAP services and select an LDAP server using the Fedora Authentication tool (system-config-authentication) accessible as the Authentication entry in the System Settings menu and window (see Chapter 4).*

LDAP Configuration Files

All LDAP configuration files are kept in the **/etc/openldap** directory. These include **slapd .conf**, the LDAP server configuration file, and **ldap.conf**, the LDAP clients and tools configuration file. To enable the LDAP server, you have to manually edit the **slapd.conf** file, and change the domain value (dc) for the suffix and rootdn entries to your own network's domain address. This is the network that will be serviced by the LDAP server.

To enable LDAP clients and their tools, you have to specify the correct domain address in the **ldap.conf** file in the BASE option, along with the server's address in the HOST option (domain name or IP address). For clients, you can either edit the **ldap.conf** file directly or use the System Settings Authentication tool, clicking the Configure LDAP button on either the User Information or Authentication panel. Here you can enter the domain name and the LDAP server's address. See the **ldap.conf** Man entry for detailed descriptions of LDAP options.

TIP   *Keep in mind that the /etc/ldap.conf and /etc/openldap/ldap.conf files are not the same: /etc/ldap.conf is used to configure LDAP for the Nameservice Switch and PAM support, whereas /etc/openldap/ldap.conf is used for all LDAP clients.*

Configuring the LDAP Server: /etc/slapd.conf

You configure the LDAP server with the **/etc/slapd.conf** file. Here you will find entries for loading schemas and for specifying access controls, the database directory, and passwords. The file is commented in detail, with default settings for most options, although you will have to enter settings for several. First you need to specify your domain suffix and root domain manager. The default settings are shown here:

```
suffix              "dc=my-domain,dc=com"
rootdn              "cn=Manager,dc=my-domain,dc=com"
```

In this example, **suffix** is changed to **mytrek**, for **mytrek.com**. **rootdn** remains the same.

```
suffix              "dc=mytrek,dc=com"
rootdn              "cn=Manager,dc=mytrek,dc=com"
```

Next you will have to specify a password with **rootpw**. There are entries for both plain text and encrypted versions. Both are commented. Remove the comment for one. In the following example the plain text password option is used, "secret":

```
rootpw              secret
# rootpw            {crypt}ijFYNcSNctBYg
```

For an encrypted password, you can first create the encrypted version with **slappasswd**. This will generate a text encryption string for the password. Then copy the generated encrypted string to the **rootpw** entry. On GNOME you can simply cut and paste from a terminal window to the **/etc/slapd.conf** file in Text Editor (Accessories). You can also redirect the encrypted string to a file and read it in later. SSHA encryption will be used by default.

```
# slappasswd
New password:
Re-enter new password:
{SSHA}0a+szaAwElK57Y8AoD5uMULSvLfCUfg5
```

The **rootpw** root password entry should then look like this:

```
rootpw          {SSHA}0a+szaAwElK57Y8AoD5uMULSvLfCUfg5
```

Use the password you entered at the **slappasswd** prompt to access your LDAP directory.

The configuration file also lists the schemas to be used. Schemas are included with the **include** directive.

```
include             /etc/openldap/schema/core.schema
include             /etc/openldap/schema/cosine.schema
include             /etc/openldap/schema/inetorgperson.schema
include             /etc/openldap/schema/nis.schema
```

NOTE *LDAP supports the Simple Authentication and Security Layer (SASL) for secure authentication with methods like MD5 and Kerberos.*

LDAP Directory Database: ldif

A record (also known as entry) in an LDAP database begins with a name, known as a *distinguishing name*, followed by a set of attributes and their values. The distinguishing name uniquely identifies the record. For example, a name could be a username and the attribute would be the user's e-mail address, the address being the attribute's value. Allowable attributes are determined by schemas defined in the **/etc/openldap/schema** directory. This directory will hold various schema definition files, each with a **schema** extension. Some will be dependent on others, enhancing their supported classes and attributes. The basic core set of attributes are defined in the **core.schema** file. Here you will find definitions for attributes like country name and street address. Other schemas, like **inetorgperson.schema**, specify **core.schema** as a dependent schema, making its attributes available to the inetOrgPerson classes. The inetOrgPerson schema will also define its own attributes such as jpegPhoto for a person's photograph.

Schema Attributes and Classes

Attributes and classes are defined officially by RFC specifications that are listed with each attribute and class entry in the schema files. These are standardized definitions and should not be changed. Attributes are defined by an **attributetype** definition. Each is given a unique identifying number followed by a name by which it can be referenced. Fields include the attribute description (DESC), search features such as EQUALITY and SUBSTR, and the object identifier (SYNTAX). See the OpenLDAP administrative guide for a detailed description.

```
attributetype ( 2.5.4.9 NAME ( 'street' 'streetAddress' )
      DESC 'RFC2256: street address of this object'
      EQUALITY caseIgnoreMatch
      SUBSTR caseIgnoreSubstringsMatch
      SYNTAX 1.3.6.1.4.1.1466.115.121.1.15{128} )
```

A class defines the kind of database (directory) you can create. This will specify the kinds of attributes you can include in your records. Classes can be dependent, where one class becomes an extension of another. The class most often used for LDAP databases is inetOrgPerson, defined in the **inetOrgPerson.schema** file. The term *inetOrgPerson* stands for Internet Organization Person, as many LDAP directories perform Internet tasks. The class is derived from the organizationalPerson class defined in **core.schema**, which includes the original attributes for commonly used fields like street address and name.

```
# inetOrgPerson
# The inetOrgPerson represents people who are associated with an
# organization in some way.  It is a structural class and is derived
# from the organizationalPerson which is defined in X.521 [X521].
objectclass ( 2.16.840.1.113730.3.2.2
    NAME 'inetOrgPerson'
      DESC 'RFC2798: Internet Organizational Person'
    SUP organizationalPerson
    STRUCTURAL
      MAY (
            audio $ businessCategory $ carLicense $ departmentNumber $
            displayName $ employeeNumber $ employeeType $ givenName $
            homePhone $ homePostalAddress $ initials $ jpegPhoto $
            labeledURI $ mail $ manager $ mobile $ o $ pager $
            photo $ roomNumber $ secretary $ uid $ userCertificate $
            x500uniqueIdentifier $ preferredLanguage $
            userSMIMECertificate $ userPKCS12 )
      )
```

You can create your own classes, building on the standard ones already defined. You can also create your own attributes. But each attribute will require a unique object identifier (OID).

Distinguishing Names

Data in an LDAP directory is organized hierarchically, from general categories to specific data. An LDAP directory could be organized starting with countries, narrowing to states, then organizations and their subunits, and finally individuals. Commonly, LDAP directories are organized along the lines of Internet domains. In this format, the top category would be the domain name extension, for instance .com or .ca. The directory would then break down to the network (organization), units, and finally users.

This organization is used to help define distinguishing names that will identify the LDAP records. In a network-based organization, the top-level organization is defined by a domain component specified by the dcObject class, which includes the domainComponent (dc) attribute. Usually you define the network and extension as domain components to make up the top-level organization that becomes the distinguishing name for the database itself.

```
dc=mytrek, dc=com
```

Under the organization name is an organizational unit, such as users. These are defined as an organizationalUnitName (ou), which is part of the organizationalUnit class. The distinguishing name for the user's organizational unit would be

```
ou=users, dc=mytrek, dc=com
```

Under the organizational unit you could then have individual users. Here the username is defined with the commonName (cn) attribute, which is used in various classes, including Person, which is part of organizationalPerson, which in turn is part of inetOrgPerson. The distinguishing name for the user **dylan** would then be

```
cn=dylan,ou=users,dc=mytrek,dc=com
```

LDIF Entries

Database entries are placed in an LDAP Interchange Format (LDIF) file. This format provides a global standard that allows a database to be accessed by any LDAP-compliant client. An LDIF file is a simple text file with an **.ldif** extension, placed in the **/etc/openldap** directory. The entries for an LDIF record consist of a distinguishing name or attribute, followed by a colon, and its list of values. Each record begins with a distinguishing name to uniquely identify the record. Attributes then follow. You can think of the name as a record and the attributes as fields in that record. You end the record with an empty line.

Initially you create an LDIF file using any text editor. Then enter the records. In the following example, the **mytrek.ldif** LDIF file contains records for users on the network.

First you create records defining your organization and organization units. These distinguishing names will be used in user-level records. You will also have to specify a manager for the database, in this case simply Manager. Be sure to include the appropriate object classes. The organization uses both the dcObject (domain component object) and organization objects. The Manager uses organizationalRole, and users use the organizationalUnit. Within each record you can have attribute definitions, like the organization attribute, o, in the first record, which is set to MyTrek.

```
dn: dc=mytrek,dc=com
objectclass: dcobject
objectclass: organization
dc: mytrek
o: MyTrek

dn: cn=Manager,dc=mytrek,dc=com
cn: Manager
objectclass: organizationalRole

dn: ou=users,dc=mytrek,dc=com
objectclass: organizationalUnit
ou: users
```

Individual records then follow, such as the following for **dylan**. Here the object classes are organizationalPerson and inetOrgPerson. Attributes then follow, like common name (cn), user ID (uid), organization (o), surname (sn), and street.

```
dn: cn=dylan,ou=users,dc=mytrek,dc=com
objectclass: organizationalPerson
objectclass: inetOrgPerson
cn: dylan
uid: dylan
o: MyTrek
sn: shark
street: 77777 saturn ave
```

An example of an LDIF file is shown here. The organization is mytrek.com. There are two records, one for **dylan** and the other for **chris**:

mytrek.ldif

```
dn: dc=mytrek,dc=com
objectclass: dcobject
objectclass: organization
dc: mytrek
o: MyTrek

dn: cn=Manager,dc=mytrek,dc=com
cn: Manager
objectclass: organizationalRole

dn: ou=users,dc=mytrek,dc=com
objectclass: organizationalUnit
ou: users

dn: cn=dylan,ou=users,dc=mytrek,dc=com
objectclass: organizationalPerson
objectclass: inetOrgPerson
cn: dylan
uid: dylan
o: MyTrek
sn: shark
street: 77777 saturn ave

dn: cn=chris,ou=users,dc=mytrek,dc=com
objectclass: organizationalPerson
objectclass: inetOrgPerson
cn: chris
uid: chris
o: MyTrek
sn: dolphin
street: 99999 neptune way
```

Adding the Records

Once you have created your LDIF file, you can then use the **ldapadd** command to add the records to your LDAP directory. Use the **-D** option to specify the directory to add the records to, and the **-f** option to specify the LDIF file to read from. You could use **ldapadd** to enter fields directly. The **-x** option says to use simple password access, the **-W** will prompt for the password, and the **-D** option specifies the directory manager.

```
# ldapadd -x -D "cn=Manager,dc=mytrek,dc=com" -W -f mytrek.ldif

Enter LDAP Password:

adding new entry "dc=mytrek,dc=com"

adding new entry "cn=Manager,dc=mytrek,dc=com"

adding new entry "ou=users,dc=mytrek,dc=com"

adding new entry "cn=dylan,ou=users,dc=mytrek,dc=com"
```

```
adding new entry "cn=chris,ou=users,dc=mytrek,dc=com"
```

Be sure to restart the LDAP server to have your changes take effect.

Searching LDAP

Once you have added your records, you can use the **ldapsearch** command to search your LDAP directory. The **-x** and **-W** options provide simple password access, and the **-b** option will specify the LDAP database to use. Following the options are the attributes to search for, in this case the street attribute.

```
# ldapsearch -x -W -D 'cn=Manager,dc=mytrek,dc=com' -b 'dc=mytrek,dc=com' street
```

LDAP Tools

To actually make or change entries in the LDAP database, you use the **ldapadd** and **ldapmodify** utilities. With **ldapdelete**, you can remove entries. Once you have created an LDAP database, you can then query it, through the LDAP server, with **ldapsearch**. For the LDAP server, you can create a text file of LDAP entries using the LDAP Data Interchange Format (LDIF). Such text files can then be read in all at once to the LDAP database using the **slapadd** tool. The **slapcat** tool extracts entries from the LDAP database and saves them in an LDIF file. To reindex additions and changes, you use the **slapindex** utility. See the LDAP Howto at the Linux documentation project for details on using and setting up LDAP databases such as address books (**www.tldp.org**).

TIP *You can enable and designate LDAP servers with the system-config-authentication tool (Authentication in the System Settings window and menu, see Chapter 4). You can also use the LDAP Browser/Editor or the GNOME Directory Administrator to manage and edit LDAP directories.*

LDAP and PAM

With LDAP, you can also more carefully control the kind of information given out and to whom. Using a PAM module (**pam_ldap**), LDAP can perform user authentication tasks, providing centralized authentication for users. Login operations that users perform for different services such as POP mail server logins, system logins, and Samba logins can all be carried out through LDAP using a single PAM-secured user ID and password. To configure PAM to use LDAP, use the System Settings Authentication tool (system-config-authentication), and select Enable LDAP Support on the Authentication panel (see Chapter 4). You should also make sure that the LDAP server is correctly specified. To use LDAP for authentication, you need to configure PAM to use it, as well as migrate authentication files to the LDAP format. The **/usr/share/openldap/migration** directory holds scripts you can use to translate the old files into LDAP versions.

LDAP and the Nameservice Switch Service

With the **libnss_ldap** module, LDAP can also be used in the Nameservice Switch (NSS) service along with NIS and system files for system database services like passwords and groups. Clients can easily enable LDAP for NSS by using the System Settings Authentication tool and selecting Enable LDAP Support in the User Information panel. You also need to make sure that the LDAP server is specified. You could also manually add **ldap** for entries in the **/etc/nsswitch.conf** file.

> **TIP**   *To better secure access to the LDAP server, you should encrypt your LDAP administrator's password. The LDAP administrator is specified in the* **rootdn** *entry, and its password in the* **rootpw** *entry. To create an encrypted password, use the* **slappasswd** *command. This prompts you for a password and displays its encrypted version. Copy that encrypted version in the* **rootpw** *entry.*

> **NOTE**   *In Thunderbird, open the address book, then select File | New, and choose the LDAPD directory. Here you can enter the LDAP server. This displays a panel where you can enter the address book name, the hostname of the LDAP server, the Base DN to search, and the port number, 389 on Fedora Core.*

Pluggable Authentication Modules (Linux-PAM)

Pluggable Authentication Modules (PAM) is an authentication service that lets a system determine the method of authentication to be performed for users. In a Linux system, authentication has traditionally been performed by looking up passwords. When a user logs in, the login process looks up their password in the password file. With PAM, users' requests for authentication are directed to PAM, which in turn uses a specified method to authenticate the user. This could be a simple password lookup or a request to an LDAP server, but it is PAM that provides authentication, not a direct password lookup by the user or application. In this respect, authentication becomes centralized and controlled by a specific service, PAM. The actual authentication procedures can be dynamically configured by the system administrator. Authentication is carried out by modules that can vary according to the kind of authentication needed. An administrator can add or replace modules by simply changing the PAM configuration files. PAM is provided by the Linux-PAM Project. See the Linux-PAM Web site at **www.kernel.org/pub/linux/libs/pam** for more information and a listing of PAM modules. PAM modules are located in the **/lib/security** directory. Security configuration files are in **/etc/security**.

PAM Configuration Files

On Fedora Core, PAM uses different configuration files for different services that request authentication. Such configuration files are kept in the **/etc/pam.d** directory. For example, you have a configuration file for logging into your system (**/etc/pam.d/login**), one for the graphical login (**/etc/pam.d/gdm**), and one for accessing your Samba server (**/etc/pam.d/samba**). A default PAM configuration file, called **/etc/pam.d/other**, is invoked if no services file is present. On Fedora Core, the **system-auth** file contains standard authentication modules for system services generated by system-config-authentication and is invoked in many of the other configuration files. In addition, Fedora Core sets up PAM authentication for its configuration tools, such as system-config-services and system-config-network.

PAM Modules

A PAM configuration file contains a list of modules to be used for authentication. They have the following format:

```
module-type control-flag module-path module-args
```

The *module-path* is the module to be run, and *module-args* are the parameters you want passed to that module. Though there are a few generic arguments, most modules have their own. The *module-type* refers to different groups of authentication management: account, authentication, session, and password. The account management performs account verification, checking such account aspects as whether the user has access, or whether the password has expired. Authentication (**auth**) verifies who the user is, usually through a password confirmation. Password management performs authentication updates such as password changes. Session management refers to tasks performed before a service is accessed and before it is shut down. These include tasks like initiating a log of a user's activity or mounting and unmounting home directories.

TIP *As an alternative to the /etc/pam.d directory, you could create one configuration file called the /etc/pam.conf file. Entries in this file have a service field, which refers to the application that the module is used for. If the /etc/pam.d directory exists, /etc/pam.conf is automatically ignored.*

The *control-flag* field indicates how PAM is to respond if the module fails. The control can be a simple directive or a more complicated response that can specify return codes like **open_err** with actions to take. The simple directives are **requisite**, **required**, **sufficient**, and **optional**. The **requisite** directive ends the authentication process immediately if the module fails to authenticate. The **required** directive only ends the authentication after the remaining modules are run. The **sufficient** directive indicates that success of this module is enough to provide authentication unless a previous required module has failed. The **optional** directive indicates the module's success is not needed unless it is the only authentication module for its service. If you specify return codes, you can refine the conditions for authentication failure or success. Return codes can be given values such as **die** or **ok**. The **open_err** return code could be given the action **die**, which would stop all authentication and return failure. The **/etc/pam.d/vsftpd** configuration file for the FTP server is shown here:

```
#%PAM-1.0
auth required pam_listfile.so item=user sense=deny
                file=/etc/vsftpd.ftpusers onerr=succeed
auth     required  pam_stack.so service=system-auth
auth     required  pam_shells.so
account  required  pam_stack.so service=system-auth
session  required  pam_stack.so service=system-auth
```

Corresponding user configuration files for several PAM modules are located in the **/etc/security** directory. The **access.conf** file controls login access by users, **limits.conf** sets usage limits, **time.conf** can set time limits, **groups.conf** controls group usage, and **chroot .conf** specifies chroot directories for users.

Software Management

Installing, uninstalling, or updating software packages has always been a simple process in Red Hat Enterprise Linux and Fedora Core due to the widespread use of the Red Hat Package Manager (RPM). Instead of using a standard TAR archive, software is packaged in a special archive for use with RPM. An RPM archive contains all the program files, configuration files, data files, and even documentation that constitute a software application. With one simple operation, the Red Hat Package Manager installs all these for you. It also checks for any other software packages that the program may need to run correctly. You can even create your own RPM packages. Red Hat provides an RPM window-based tool called system-config-packages to manage your RPM packages, installing new ones and updating or uninstalling ones you already have. Many Fedora packages are now in the Fedora Extras repository. You can use the Yum tool to download and install Fedora Extras packages directly.

TIP *You can update Fedora Core 4 using Yum and APT repositories, accessible with the Red Hat Update Agent, RHN (see Chapter 4). You can also use Yum tools like* **yum** *to download from different Fedora software repositories (**linux.duke.edu/projects/yum**). New Fedora Core releases can be downloaded with BitTorrent from* **torrent.linux.duke.edu**.

You can also download source code versions of applications and then compile and install them on your system. Where this process once was complex, it has been significantly streamlined with the addition of *configure scripts*. Most current source code, including GNU software, is distributed with a configure script. The configure script automatically detects your system configuration and generates a *Makefile*, which is used to compile the application and create a binary file that is compatible with your system. In most cases, with a few Makefile operations, you can compile and install complex source code on any system.

Software Repositories

You can download Linux software from many online sources. You can find sites for particular kinds of applications, such as GNOME and KDE, as well as for particular distributions, such as Fedora Core. The Red Hat Network can automatically download and update

FTP or Web Site	Application
download.fedora.redhat.com	Software packaged in RPM packages for Fedora Core and Fedora Core Extras
freshmeat.net	Linux software, including RPMs
rpmfind.net	RPM package repository
freshrpms.net	Customized RPM packages featuring multimedia apps
sourceforge.net	Linux Open Source software projects
www.gnomefiles.org	GNOME software
www.kde-apps.org	KDE software
rpmseek.com	Linux software search site
www.gnu.org	GNU archive
torrent.linux.duke.edu	Fedora BitTorrent files for ISO and DVD disks

TABLE 31-1   Linux Software Sites

software installed from RPM packages that make up the Fedora Core distribution. You can also download Fedora Core packages directly from **download.fedora.redhat.com** for both Fedora Core and Extras collections. Some sites are repositories for RPM packages, such as **rpmfind.net**, and others like **freshmeat.net** refer you to original sites. A great many of the Open Source Linux projects can be found at **sourceforge.net**. Here you will find detailed documentation and recent versions of software packages. For applications designed for the GNOME desktop, you can check **www.gnomefiles.org**, and you can find KDE applications at **www.kde-apps.org**. For particular database and office applications, you can download software packages directly from the company's Web site, such as **www.oracle.com** for the Oracle database. Table 31-1 lists several popular Linux software sites.

Software Package Types

The software packages on RPM sites like **freshrpms.net** and **rpmfind.net** will have the file extension **.rpm**. RPM packages that contain source code have an extension **.src.rpm**. Other packages, such as those in the form of source code that you need to compile, come in a variety of compressed archives. These commonly have the extensions **.tar.gz**, **.tgz**, or **.tar.bz2**. They are explained in detail later in the chapter. Table 31-2 lists several common file extensions that you will find for the great variety of Linux software packages available to you.

Downloading ISO and DVD Distribution Images with BitTorrent

Very large files like distribution ISO images can be downloaded using BitTorrent. BitTorrent is a distributed download operation, where many users on the Internet participate in the same download, each uploading parts that others can in turn download. The file is cut into small IP packets, and each packet is individually uploaded and downloaded as if it were a separate

Extension	File
.rpm	A software package created with the Red Hat Software Package Manager, used on Red Hat Enterprise Linux, Fedora Core, Mandrake, and SuSE distributions
.src.rpm	Software packages that are source code versions of applications, created with the Red Hat Software Package Manager
.gz	A `gzip`-compressed file (use `gunzip` to decompress)
.bz2	A `bzip2`-compressed file (use `bunzip2` to decompress, also use the `j` option with `tar`, as in `xvjf`)
.tar	A `tar` archive file, use `tar` with `xvf` to extract
.tar.gz	A `gzip`-compressed `tar` archive file. Use `gunzip` to decompress and `tar` to extract. Use the `z` option with `tar`, as in `xvzf` to both decompress and extract in one step
.tar.bz2	A `bzip2`-compressed `tar` archive file. Extract with `tar -xvzj`
.tz	A `tar` archive file compressed with the `compress` command
.Z	A file compressed with the `compress` command (use the `decompress` command to decompress)
.deb	A Debian Linux package
.bin	A self-extracting software file
.torrent	A BitTorrent file for performing BitTorrent-distributed downloads (torrent information only)

TABLE 31-2   Linux Software Package File Extensions

file. Your BitTorrent client will automatically combine the packets into the complete file. There is no shared disk space like what you have in file sharing methods. No access is granted to other uses. A user simply requests that others send him or her a packet. It is strictly a transmission operation, as if many users were participating in the same transmission instead of just one.

NOTE   *The Fedora Core download site supports FTP downloading of DVD images directly with fairly fast speeds when not busy:* **download.fedora.redhat.com.**

You will first need to download and install the BitTorrent client. An RPM package version is available from Fedora Extras at **download.fedora.com**. Be sure to select the RPM for Fedora Core 4. There are two packages, **bittorrent** and **bittorrent-gui**, which provide a GNOME interface. You can also obtain a copy from **torrent.linux.duke.edu**, the primary Fedora Core BitTorrent site which also includes Fedora Core torrents for Fedora Core 4 ISO and DVD image files. You can download the original RPM package from **www.bittorrent.com**, but that version may not be compatible with Fedora Core 4. You will need to associate **.torrent** files with the **/usr/bin/btdownloadgui.py** application. You can do this at download by choosing the Open With option.

To start a torrent, just click the torrent entry for a file on your Web browser. Firefox will prompt you whether to start up the application directly or download the file. If you run the application, the BitTorrent client will be started and your download will begin. You can stop at any time and restart the torrent later. It will automatically start up where you left off, keeping what you have downloaded so far. For example, to start the Fedora Core 4 DVD torrent to download the DVD image, click the **stenz-DVD-i386.torrent** entry in the **torrent .linux.duke.edu** Web page. The BitTorrent client will automatically adjust to the appropriate download/upload scale, but you can adjust this as you wish. There are buttons for pausing and stopping the download, as well as for obtaining detailed information about the torrent. An icon bar shows the progress and the estimated time remaining, though this may shorten as the download progresses. The client will show all torrents you have in process, showing how much is downloaded for each and letting you choose which you want active. The Settings entry in the View menu lets you adjust such behavior as what port to use, the default download directory, and whether to allow torrents to run in parallel.

The file that Firefox will prompt you to download is not the ISO or DVD image. That will be downloaded by BitTorrent. Instead this is a simple, small BitTorrent file that holds information on how to access and start this particular torrent. You can download the torrent file and later start it to start up the torrent download. You can have a collection of torrent files that you can start and stop as you want. For example, if you download the **stentz-binary-i386.torrent** torrent file from **torrent.linux.duke.edu**, you will have a small torrent file of type **.torrent** on your disk. Double-click it to start the BitTorrent client and the download torrent for the Fedora Core 4 binary ISO images (Fedora 4 is also known as stentz).

NOTE *The BitTorrent package also provides the tools for creating your own torrent to distribute a file. Two distribution methods are now available: tracker and trackerless. A trackerless method requires no server support. The **btmaketorrent.py** command is used to make a torrent file, and **btmaketorrent-gui** provides a GNOME interface.*

Downloading and Updating Using Yum and APT

As described in Chapter 4, you can update software using the up2date tool. This tool accesses either Yum (Yellowdog Update, Modified) or apt-rpm (Advanced Package Tool RPM) repositories that hold Fedora Core software. Yum uses RPM headers to determine which packages need to be updated. You can find out more about Yum, including a listing of Yum repositories, at **linux.duke.edu/projects/yum**. APT is an older, more complex update method originally implemented for Debian Linux.

up2date

As noted, the easiest way to update Fedora Core 4 is to start the Red Hat Update Agent (up2date) by selecting the Red Hat Network (RHN) entry from the System Tools menu. You can use the Red Hat Update Agent to access the Fedora Core Yum repository, letting you update quickly to the most recent software versions. A list of packages that can be updated will be displayed, from which you can select the ones you want to update. The Red Hat Network, which also uses the Red Hat Update Agent, is reserved for use by Red Hat Enterprise Linux.

To access other repositories with the Red Hat Update Agent, you would list them in the **/etc/sysconfig/rhn/sources** file. A repository entry can be for either a Yum or APT repository. Each has a different set of fields, beginning with the repository type, yum or apt. The entry will include a URL specifying the repository location.

Yum

You can also use the **yum** command to access Yum repositories directly, downloading new software. Yum options are configured in the **/etc/yum.conf** file, and the **/etc/yum.repos.d** directory holds repository (repo) files that list accessible Yum repositories. The repository files have the extension **.repo**. Check the **yum.conf** Man page for a listing of the different Yum options along with entry formats. The **yum.conf** file consists of different segments separated by bracket-encased headers, the first of which is always the main segment. Segments for different Yum server repositories can follow, beginning with the repository label encased in brackets. However, these are currently placed in separate repository files in the **/etc/yum .repos.d** directory. The **yum.conf** file will just have the main segment with settings for Yum options. These include options like **logfile**, which lists the location of Yum logs, **distroverpkg**, which is used to determine which release to use, and **gpgcheck**, which checks for GPG software signatures.

Downloading and Installing Fedora Extras and Fedora Core Packages with Yum

The Fedora Extras and Fedora Core repositories are already configured for use by Yum. To download any Fedora Extras package, enter the **yum** command with the install option on a command line (on your desktop open a terminal window (right-click on desktop) first). The package will be detected, along with any dependent software, and you will be asked to confirm installation. The download and installation will be automatic. Check **fedoraproject .org/extras/4/** to find the list of available Fedora Extras. The following install gnumeric which is now a Fedora Extras package.

```
yum install gnumeric
```

Should you not have your Fedora Core 4 DVD-ROM available, you can use the same **yum** command to download and install any additional Fedora Core packages you want. For example, if you needed to install gnucash, you could just enter the following:

```
yum install gnucash
```

Yum Repositories

The repository entries in the repos files begin with a bracket-enclosed server ID, a single-word unique name. The **name** option provides a name for the repository. The URL reference is then assigned to the **baseurl** option. There should be only one **baseurl** option, but you can list several URLs for it, each on its own line. With the **mirrorlist** option you can just list a URL for a list of mirrors, instead of listing each mirror separately in the **baseurl** option. The URL entries often make use of special variables, **releaserver** and **basearch**. The **releaserver** obtains the release information from the **distroverpkg** option set in the main segment. The **basearch** variable specifies the architecture you are using as determined by Yum, such as i386. The entry for the **freshrpms.net** repository is listed here.

In this example, **mirrorlist** is used instead of **baseurl**, which is commented out. **releaserver** and **basearch** are used to determine the release and architecture names:

```
[freshrpms]
name=Red Hat Linux $releasever - $basearch - freshrpms
#baseurl=http://ayo.freshrpms.net/fedora/linux/$releasever/$basearch/freshrpms
mirrorlist=http://ayo.freshrpms.net/fedora/linux/$releasever/mirrors-freshrpms
gpgcheck=1
```

Some software projects are electing to distribute updates through Yum and APT, instead of providing RPMs directly. The K3b KDE burner does this, providing the following entry for Yum:

```
[xcyb-stable]
name=Fedora Core 4 ( xcyborg / stable
baseurl=http://rpms.xcyb.org/fedora/4/stable/
```

Using Yum

Once you have configured Yum, you can use the **yum** command to download and update packages. Enter the **yum** command on a command line with options to install or update packages. Check the **yum** Man page for options. Basic operations include **install** to install new packages, **update** to update currently installed packages, and **check-update** to see what packages need to be updated. The following example installs the Xine video player:

```
yum install xine
```

You can also remove packages, as well as search for packages and list packages by different criteria, such as those for update, those on the repository not yet installed, and those already installed. The following example lists all installed packages:

```
yum list installed
```

If you do not specify a file, it will operate on all. The following will update all files that needed updates.

```
yum update
```

> **TIP** *Many multimedia add-on packages not included with Fedora Core 4 are accessible from freshrpms .net. This site provides Yum-supported RPM configuration files that you can download and install to let you use up2date as well as Yum to download the add-on packages. A freshrpms .repo file will be installed at /etc/yum.repos.d.*

Automatic Yum Update

Yum also installs a **yum.cron** file in the **/etc/cron.daily** directory, which will automatically update your system. The cron entry will first update the Yum software if needed and then proceed to download and install any updates for your installed packages. It runs **yum** with the **update** option.

The automatic update will run only if it detects a Yum lock file in the **/var/lock/subsys** directory. By default, this is missing. You can add it using the **yum** service script. The **start** option creates the lock file, enabling the cron-supported updates, and the **stop** option removes the file, disabling the automatic update.

```
service yum start
```

APT

The Advanced Package Tool is an older installation tool based originally on the Debian version. The current one is modified for use with RPMS packages. You can download APT from Fedora Extras or **freshrpms.net**. APT places configuration files in the **/etc/apt** directory. The **apt.conf** file contains setting for options, using a more complex format similar to that used for DNS configuration.

Repositories are listed in the **sources.list** file. Each entry consists of type, URL, and pathname, along with components identifying the software. The last component is the name of the repository. The following example is the **sources.list** entry for freshrpms:

```
rpm http://ayo.freshrpms.net fedora/linux/4/i386 core updates freshrpms
```

You use the **apt-get** command to install and manage software packages. The **apt-get** tool takes two arguments, the command to perform and the name of the package. The command is a term such as **install** for installing packages or **remove** to uninstall a package. To install a package, you would use:

```
apt-get install xine
```

Upgrading is a simple matter of using the **upgrade** command. With no package specified, **apt-get** with the **update** option will upgrade your entire system, downloading from an FTP site or copying from a CD-ROM, and installing packages as needed. Add the **-u** option to list packages as they are upgraded.

```
apt-get -u update
```

Red Hat Package Manager (RPM)

Several Linux distributions, including Fedora Core, Red Hat, and Mandrake, use RPM to organize Linux software into packages you can automatically install, update, or remove. RPM is a command line–driven package management system that is capable of installing, uninstalling, querying, verifying, and updating software packages installed on Linux systems. An RPM software package operates as its own installation program for a software application. A Linux software application often consists of several files that need to be installed in different directories. The program itself is most likely placed in a directory called **/usr/bin**, online manual files like Man pages go in other directories, and library files in yet another directory. In addition, the installation may require modification of certain configuration files on your system. The RPM software package performs all these tasks for you. Also, if you later decide you don't want a specific application, you can uninstall packages to remove all the files and configuration information from your system. RPM works similarly to the Windows Install Wizard, automatically installing software, including configuration, documentation, image, sample, and program files, along with any other files an application may use. All are installed in their appropriate directories on your system. RPM maintains a database of installed software, keeping track of all the files installed. This enables you to use RPM also to uninstall software, automatically removing all files that are part of the application.

RPM Tools

To install and uninstall RPM packages, you can use the **rpm** command directly from a shell prompt, or the software management tool, system-config-packages. The system-config-packages tools is a GUI front end for the **rpm** command. Although you should download RPM packages for your particular distribution, numerous RPM software packages are designed to run on any Linux system. You can learn more about RPM at its Web site at **www.rpm.org**. The site contains up-to-date versions for RPM, documentation, and RPM support programs, such as **rpm2html** and **rpm2cpio**. The **rpm2html** program takes a directory containing RPM packages and generates Web pages listing those packages as links that can be used to download them; **rpm2cpio** is a Perl script to extract RPMs. Also, the Red Hat Linux Customization Guide provides an excellent tutorial for both RPM and system-config-packages.

RPM Packages

The naming conventions for RPM packages vary from one distribution to another. The package name includes the package version along with its platform (**i386** for Intel PCs) and the **.rpm** extension. An example of the Emacs editor's RPM package for Intel systems is shown here:

```
emacs-21.4-3.i386.rpm
```

The RPM packages on your DVD-ROM or distribution CD-ROM represent only a small portion of the software packages available for Linux. An extensive repository for RPM packages is also located at **rpmfind.net**. Packages here are indexed according to distribution, group, and name. The site includes packages for every distribution.

> **TIP** *RPM packages with the term* **noarch** *are used for architecture-independent packages. This means that they are designed to install on any Linux system. Packages without* **noarch** *may be distribution- or architecture-dependent, designed to install on a particular type of machine.*

You could place these packages in a directory on your system, and then use either **rpm** or a GUI RPM utility such as the system-config-packages tool to install it.

> **TIP** *Normally, you should always try to use the version of the RPM package set up for your Red Hat Enterprise Linux or Fedora Core distribution; for instance, if you run Fedora Core 4, it is best to download the software package designated for Fedora Core 4 instead of downloading the same package for Red Hat 7.3. Packages for specific releases will be kept in the release directories. In many cases, attempting to install an RPM package meant for a different distribution may fail.*

Installing from the Desktop: system-config-packages

The system-config-packages tool provides an effective and easy-to-use interface for managing the RPM packages provided by your Red Hat Enterprise Linux or Fedora Core distribution, whether you installed from CD-ROMs, DVD-ROM, hard disk, or network. It runs on any window manager, including GNOME and KDE. You can access system-config-packages using the Packages icon in the System Settings window. This opens a Package Management window that initially displays a listing of package categories from which you can install packages. See Chapter 4 for more details.

> **TIP** *You can also install a particular RPM package directly. First display it with the file manager, and then double-click it. This invokes the system-config-packages tool, which installs the package. It also checks for dependent packages and installs those also. If you are using CD-ROMs instead of the DVD-ROM, you will be prompted to insert any other CD-ROMs as needed.*

Installing with Download Using a Web Browser: system-config-packages

As noted in Chapter 4, if you are downloading an RPM package using a Web browser like Firefox or Epiphany, you can choose to have the package automatically installed. This is the easiest way to both download and install a software package. Downloading and installation become one seamless and simple process. Upon initiating a download, Firefox will prompt you to either install or save the package. If you choose install, the Firefox will invoke system-config-packages to install your software, first checking for any needed dependent packages. If all dependent packages are present, you are then provided with a Continue prompt. Upon clicking the Continue button, the package is installed. If dependent packages are needed, a window listing those packages is displayed. You will need to locate, download, and install these packages first. You can use the same simple Web-based download/install procedure.

Updating Software

You can update your Linux system automatically using a distribution update agent like the Red Hat Network. You can also manually download packages using an FTP client, Web browser, or the GNOME or KDE file managers, and then use the **rpm** command or the system-config-packages tool to install the software.

For system-config-packages, you can use your file manager to locate the RPM file and double-click the RPM package file. You can also, on GNOME, right-click it, and select Open With | Install Packages, or on KDE, select Install Package; system-config-packages starts up and checks for any dependent packages you may need. It then installs the RPM package for you.

If you are using the **rpm** command, you use the **–U** option to upgrade packages. In the following example, the **rpm** command with the **–Uvh** option installs an upgrade for Emacs:

```
# rpm –Uvh emacs-21.4-3.i386.rpm
```

Command Line Installation: rpm

If you do not have access to the desktop, or you prefer to work from the command line interface, you can use the **rpm** command to manage and install software packages; **rpm** is the command that actually performs installation, removal, and queries of software packages. In fact, system-config-packages uses the **rpm** command to install and remove packages. An RPM package is an archive of software files that includes information about how to install those files. The filenames for RPM packages end with **.rpm**, indicating software packages that can be installed by the Red Hat Package Manager.

The rpm Command

With the **rpm** command, you can maintain packages, query them, build your own, and verify the ones you have. Maintaining packages involves installing new ones, upgrading to new versions, and uninstalling packages. The **rpm** command uses a set of options to determine what action to take. In addition, certain tasks, such as installing or querying packages, have their own options that further qualify the kind of action they take. For example, the **–q** option queries a package, but when combined with the **–l** option, it lists all the files in that package. Table 31-3 lists the set of **rpm** options. The syntax for the **rpm** command is as follows (*rpm-package-name* is the name of the software package you want to install):

```
rpm options rpm-package-name
```

A complete description of **rpm** and its capabilities is provided in the online manual:

```
# man rpm
```

Mode of Operation	Effect
`rpm -i`*options* *package-file*	Installs a package; the complete name of the package file is required.
`rpm -e`*options* *package-name*	Uninstalls (erases) a package; you only need the name of the package, often one word.
`rpm -q`*options* *package-name*	Queries a package. An option can be a package name, a further option and package name, or an option applied to all packages.
`rpm -U`*options* *package-name*	Upgrades; same as install, but any previous version is removed.
`rpm -F`*options* *package-name*	Upgrades, but only if package is currently installed.
`rpm -verify`*options*	Verifies a package is correctly installed; uses same options as query. You can use `-V` or `-y` in place of `-verify`.
`--percent`	Displays percentage of package during installation.
`--replacepks`	Installs an already-installed package.
`--replacefiles`	Replaces files installed by other packages.
`--redhatprovides` *dependent-files*	Searches for dependent packages.
`--oldfiles`	Installs an older version of a package already installed.
`--test`	Tests installation; does not install, only checks for conflicts.
`-h`	Displays # symbols as package is installed.
`--excludedocs`	Excludes documentation files.
`--nodeps`	Installs without doing any dependency checks (dangerous).
`--force`	Forces installation despite conflicts (dangerous).
Uninstall Option (to be used with -e)	
`--test`	Tests uninstall. Does not remove, only checks for what is to be removed.
`--nodeps`	Uninstalls without checking for dependencies.
`--allmatches`	Removes all versions of package.
Query Option (to be used with -q)	
package-name	Queries package.
`-qa`	Queries all packages.
`-qf` *filename*	Queries package that owns *filename*.
`-qR`	List packages on which this package depends.
`-qp` *package-name*	Queries an uninstalled package.
`-qi`	Displays all package information.
`-ql`	Lists files in package.
`-qd`	Lists only documentation files in package.
`-qc`	Lists only configuration files in package.
`-q --dump`	Lists only files with complete details.

TABLE 31-3   Red Hat Package Manager (RPM) Options

Mode of Operation	Effect
General Option (to be used with any option)	
-vv	Debugs; displays descriptions of all actions taken.
--quit	Displays only error messages.
--version	Displays RPM version number.
--help	Displays detailed use message.
--root*directory*	Uses directory as top-level directory for all operations (instead of root).
--dbpath*directory*	Uses RPM database in the specified directory.
--dbpath *cmd*	Pipes output of RPM to the command **cmd**.
--rebuilddb	Rebuilds the RPM database; can be used with the **-root** and **-dbpath** options.
--initdb	Builds a new RPM database; can be used with the **-root** and **-dbpath** options.
Other Sources of Information	**Description**
www.rpm.org	The RPM Web site with detailed documentation.
RPM Man page (**man rpm**)	Detailed list of options.

TABLE 31-3 Red Hat Package Manager (RPM) Options *(continued)*

Querying Information from RPM Packages and Installed Software

The **-q** option tells you if a package is already installed, and the **-qa** option displays a list of all installed packages. Piping this output to a pager utility, such as **more**, is best.

```
# rpm -qa | more
```

In the next example, the user checks to see if Mozilla is already installed on the system. Notice the full filename of the RPM archive is unnecessary. If the package is installed, your system has already registered its name and where it is located.

```
# rpm -q mozilla
mozilla-1.7.7-3
```

You can combine the **q** option with the **i** or **l** option to display information about the package. The option **-qi** displays information about the software, such as the version number or author (**-qpi** queries an uninstalled package file). The option **-ql** displays a listing of all the files in the software package. The **--h** option provides a complete list of **rpm** options. Common query options are shown in Table 31-4.

TIP *Keep in mind the distinction between the installed software package name and the package filename. The filename ends in a* **.rpm** *extension and can only be queried with a* **p** *option.*

TABLE 31-4 Query
Options for Installed
Software

Option	Meaning
-q *application*	Checks to see if an application is installed.
-qa *application*	Lists all installed RPM applications.
-qf *filename*	Queries applications that own *filename*.
-qR *application*	Lists applications on which this application depends.
-qi *application*	Displays all application information.
-ql *application*	Lists files in the application.
-qd *application*	Lists only documentation files in the application.
-qc *application*	Lists only configuration files in the application.

To display information taken directly from an RPM package, you add the **p** qualifier to the **q** options as shown in Table 31-5. The **-qpi** combination displays information about a specific package, and **-qpl** displays a listing of the files a given RPM package contains. In this case, you must specify the entire filename of the RPM package. You can avoid having to enter the entire name simply by entering a unique part of the name and using the * filename-matching character to generate the rest.

TIP *The easiest way to examine the contents of an RPM file is to open the RPM file with File Roller from the GNOME Desktop. Right-click the RPM file icon in the file manager window and select Open With Archive Manager. This displays a File Roller window listing the top install directories for files in the packages. Double-click these entries to see the files or subdirectories. You can double-click text files like README files and have them directly displayed in your text editor.*

If your RPM query outputs a long list of data, like an extensive list of files, you can pipe the output to the **more** command to look at it screen by screen, or even redirect the output to a file.

```
# rpm -ql mozilla | more
# rpm -qpl emacs-21.4-3.i386.rpm  > mytemp
```

Installing and Updating Packages with rpm

You use the **-i** option to install new packages and the **-U** option to update currently installed packages with new versions. With an **-e** option, **rpm** uninstalls the package. If you try to use the **-i** option to install a newer version of an installed package, you will receive an error saying the package is already installed. When a package is installed, RPM checks its signature, using imported public keys from the software vendor. If the signature check fails, an error

TABLE 31-5 Query
Options for RPM
Packages

Option	Meaning
-qpi *RPM-file*	Displays all package information in the RPM package.
-qpl *RPM-file*	Lists files in the RPM package.
-qpd *RPM-file*	Lists only documentation files in the RPM package.
-qpc *RPM-file*	Lists only configuration files in the RPM package.
-qpR *RPM-file*	Lists packages on which this RPM package depends.

message is displayed, specifying NOKEY if you do not have the appropriate public key. If you want to install over an already-installed package, you can force installation with the **--replacepks** option. Sometimes a package will include a file, such as a library, that is also installed by another package. To allow a package to overwrite the file installed by another package, you use the **--replacefiles** option. Many packages depend on the libraries installed by other packages. If these dependent packages are not already installed, you will first have to install them. RPM informs you of the missing dependent files and suggests packages to install. If no packages are suggested, you can use the **--redhatprovides** option with the missing files to search for needed packages.

The **-U** option also installs a package if it is not already installed, whereas the **-F** option will only update installed packages. If the package includes configuration files that will overwrite currently installed configuration files, it will save a copy of each current configuration file in a file ending with **.rpmsave**, such as **/etc/mtools.conf.rpmsave**. This preserves any customized configuration changes you may have made to the file. Be sure to also check for configuration compatibilities between the previous and updated versions. If you are trying to install a package that is older than the one already installed, then you need to use the **--oldpackages** option.

```
# rpm -Uvh mozilla-1.7.7-3.i386.rpm
```

If you are installing from a DVD-ROM, you can change to the DVD-ROM's **RPMS** directory, which holds the RPM packages (the **RPMS** directory may be located within a directory like **RedHat** or **Fedora** on the DVD-ROM). An **ls** command lists all the software packages. If you know how the name of a package begins, you should include that with the **ls** command and an attached *****. The list of packages is extensive and does not all fit on one screen. This is helpful for displaying the detailed name of the package. The following example lists most X Window System packages:

```
# ls x*
```

Verifying an RPM Installation

You can use the verify option (**-V**) to see if any problems occurred with the installation. RPM compares the current attributes of installed files with information about them placed in the RPM database when the package was installed. If no discrepancies exist, RPM outputs nothing. Otherwise, RPM outputs a sequence of eight characters, one for each attribute, for each file in the package that fails. Those that do not differ have a period. Those that do differ have a corresponding character code, as shown in Table 31-6.

TABLE **31-6** RPM Discrepancy Codes

Attribute	Explanation
5	MD5 checksum
S	File size
L	Symbolic link
T	File modification time
D	Device
U	User
G	Group
M	Mode (includes permissions and file types)

The following example verifies the ProFTPD package:

```
[root@turtle mypackages]# rpm -V proftpd
```

To compare the installed files directly with the files in an RPM package file, you use the **-Vp** option, much like the **-qp** option. To check all packages, use the **-Va** option as shown here:

```
# rpm -Va
```

If you want to verify a package, but you only know the name of a file in it, you can combine verify with the **-f** option. The following example verifies the RPM package containing the **ftp** command:

```
# rpm -Vf  /bin/ftp
```

Rebuilding the RPM Database

RPM maintains a record of the packages it has installed in its **RPM** database. You may, at times, have to rebuild this database to ensure RPM has current information on what is installed and what is not. Use the **--rebuilddb** option to rebuild your database file:

```
#  rpm --rebuilddb
```

To create a new RPM database, use the **--initdb** option. This option can be combined with **--dbpath** to specify a location for the new database.

Installing Software from RPM Source Code Files: SRPMs

Fedora Core and several other distributors also make available source code versions of their binary RPM-packaged software. The source code is packaged into RPM packages that will be automatically installed into designated directories where you can easily compile and install the software. Source code packages are called SRPMs. The names for these packages end in the extension **.src.rpm**. Source code versions for packages in the Fedora Core distribution are located in the **SRPMS** directory. Many online sites like **rpmfind.net** also list SRPM packages. Source code versions have the advantage of letting you make your own modifications to the source code, allowing you to generate your own customized versions of RPM-packaged software. You still use the **rpm** command with the **-i** option to install source code packages. In the following example, you install the source code for Freeciv:

```
# rpm -i freeciv-1.14.2-1.src.rpm
```

Source Code RPM Directories

The SRPM files are installed in various subdirectories in the **/usr/src/redhat** directory. When SRPMs are installed, a spec file is placed in the **/usr/src/redhat/SPECS** directory, and the compressed archive of the source code files is placed in the **/usr/src/redhat/SOURCES** directory. For Freeciv, a spec file called **freeciv.spec** is placed in **/usr/src/redhat/SPECS**, and a compressed archive called **freeciv-1.14.2-1.tar.gz** is placed in the **/usr/src/redhat/SOURCES** directory.

Building the Source Code

To build the source code files, you need to extract them and run any patches on them that may be included with the package. You do this by changing to the **/usr/src/redhat/SPECS** directory and using the **rpm** command, this time with the **–bp** option, to generate the source code files:

```
# cd /usr/src/redhat/SPECS
# rpm -bp freeciv.spec
```

The resulting source code files are placed in their own subdirectory with the package's name in the **/usr/src/redhat/BUILD** directory. For Freeciv, the Freeciv source code is placed in the **/usr/src/redhat/BUILD/freeciv-1.14.2-1** directory. In this subdirectory, you can then modify the source code, as well as compile and install the application. Check the software's **README** and **INSTALL** files for details.

Installing Software from Compressed Archives: .tar.gz

Linux software applications in the form of source code are available at different sites on the Internet. You can download any of this software and install it on your system. Recent releases are often available in the form of compressed archive files. Applications will always be downloadable as compressed archives, if they don't have an RPM version. This is particularly true for the recent versions of GNOME or KDE packages. RPM packages are only intermittently generated.

Decompressing and Extracting Software in One Step

Though you can decompress and extract software in separate operations, you will find that the more common approach is to perform both actions with a single command. The **tar** utility provides decompression options you can use to have **tar** first decompress a file for you, invoking the specified decompression utility. The **z** option automatically invokes **gunzip** to unpack a **.gz** file, and the **j** option unpacks a **.bz2** file. Use the **Z** option for **.Z** files. For example, to combine the decompressing and unpacking operation for a **tar.gz** file into one **tar** command, insert a **z** option to the option list, **xzvf** (see the later section "Extracting Software" for a discussion of these options). The next example shows how you can combine decompression and extraction in one step:

```
# tar xvzf htdig-3.1.6.tar.gz
```

For a **.bz2**-compressed archive, you would use the **j** option instead of the **z** option.

```
# tar xvjf htdig-3.1.6.tar.bz2
```

Decompressing Software

Many software packages under development or designed for cross-platform implementation may not be in an RPM format. Instead, they may be archived and compressed. The filenames for these files end with the extension **.tar.gz**, **.tar.bz2**, or **.tar.Z**. The different extensions indicate different decompression methods using different commands: **gunzip** for **.gz**, **bunzip2** for **.bz2**, and **decompress** for **.Z**. In fact, most software with an RPM format also has a corresponding **.tar.gz** format. After you download such a package, you must first decompress it, and then unpack it with the **tar** command. The compressed archives could hold either source code that you then need to compile or, as is the case with Java packages, binaries that are ready to run.

A *compressed archive* is an archive file created with **tar**, and then compressed with a compression tool like **gzip**. To install such a file, you must first decompress it with a decompression utility like **gunzip** utility, and then use **tar** to extract the files and directories making up the software package. Instead of the **gunzip** utility, you could also use **gzip -d**. The next example decompresses the **htdig-3.2.6.tar.gz** file, replacing it with a decompressed version called **htdig-3.2.6.tar**:

```
# ls
 htdig-3.2.6.tar.gz
# gunzip htdig-3.2.6.tar.gz
# ls
htdig-3.2.6.tar
```

You can download compressed archives from many different sites, including those mentioned previously. Downloads can be accomplished with FTP clients such as ncftp and Gftp, or with any Web browser, such as Mozilla. Once downloaded, any file that ends with **.Z**, **.bz2**, **.zip**, or **.gz** is a compressed file that must be decompressed.

For files ending with **.bz2**, you would use the **bunzip2** command. The following example decompresses a **bz2** version:

```
# ls
 htdig-3.2.6.tar.bz2
# bunzip2 htdig-3.2.6.tar.bz2
# ls
htdig-3.2.6.tar
```

Files ending with **.bin** are self-extracting archives. Run the bin file as if it were a command. You may have to use **chmod** to make it executable. The blackdown j2sdk software package is currently distributed as a self-extracting bin file.

```
# j2sdk-1.4.2-FCS-linux-i386.tar.bin
# ls
j2sdk-1.3.0-FCS-linux-i386.tar
```

Selecting an Install Directory

Before you unpack the archive, move it to the directory where you want it. Source code packages are often placed in a directory like **/usr/local/src**, and binary packages go in designated directories. When source code files are unpacked, they generate their own subdirectories from which you can compile and install the software. Once the package is installed, you can delete this directory, keeping the original source code package file (**.tar.gz**).

Packages that hold binary programs ready to run, like Java, are meant to be extracted in certain directories. Usually this is the **/usr/local** directory. Most archives, when they unpack, create a subdirectory named with the application name and its release, placing all those files or directories making up the software package into that subdirectory. For example, the file **htdig-3.2.6.tar** unpacks to a subdirectory called **htdig-3.2.6**. In certain cases, the software package that contains precompiled binaries is designed to unpack directly into the system subdirectory where it will be used. For example, it is recommended that **j2sdk-1.4.2-FCS-linux-i386.tar** be unpacked in the **/usr/local** directory, where it will create a subdirectory called **j2sdk-1.4.2**. The **/usr/local/j2sdk-1.4.2/bin** directory holds the Java binary programs.

Extracting Software

First, use **tar** with the **t** option to check the contents of the archive. If the first entry is a directory, then when you extract the archive, that directory is created and the extracted files are placed in it. If the first entry is not a directory, you should first create one and then copy the archive file to it. Then extract the archive within that directory. If no directory exists as the first entry, files are extracted to the current directory. You must create a directory yourself to hold these files.

```
# tar tvf htdig-3.1.6.tar
```

Now you are ready to extract the files from the tar archive. You use **tar** with the **x** option to extract files, the **v** option to display the pathnames of files as they are extracted, and the **f** option, followed by the name of the archive file:

```
# tar xvf htdig-3.2.6.tar
```

The extraction process creates a subdirectory consisting of the name and release of the software. In the preceding example, the extraction created a subdirectory called **htdig-3.2.6**. You can change to this subdirectory and examine its files, such as the **README** and **INSTALL** files.

```
# cd htdig-3.2.6
```

Installation of your software may differ for each package. Instructions are usually provided along with an installation program. Be sure to consult the **README** and **INSTALL** files, if included. See the following section on compiling software for information on how to create and install the application on your system.

Compiling Software

Some software may be in the form of source code that you need to compile before you can install it. This is particularly true of programs designed for cross-platform implementations. Programs designed to run on various Unix systems, such as Sun, as well as on Linux, may be distributed as source code that is downloaded and compiled in those different systems. Compiling such software has been greatly simplified in recent years by the use of configuration scripts that automatically detect a given system's hardware and software configuration and then allow you to compile the program accordingly. For example, the name of the C compiler on a system could be **gcc** or **cc**. Configuration scripts detect which is present and select it for use in the program compilation.

A configure script works by generating a customized Makefile, designed for that particular system. A Makefile contains detailed commands to compile a program, including any preprocessing, links to required libraries, and the compilation of program components in their proper order. Many Makefiles for complex applications may have to access several software subdirectories, each with separate components to compile. The use of configure and Makefile scripts vastly automates the compile process, reducing the procedure to a few simple steps.

First change to the directory where the software's source code has been extracted:

```
# cd /usr/local/src/htdig-3.2.6
```

Before you compile software, read the **README** or **INSTALL** files included with it. These give you detailed instructions on how to compile and install this particular program.

Most software can be compiled and installed in three simple steps. Their first step is the `./configure` command, which generates your customized Makefile. The second step is the **make** command, which uses a Makefile in your working directory (in this case the Makefile you just generated with the `./configure` command) to compile your software. The final step also uses the **make** command, but this time with the **install** option. The Makefile generated by the `./configure` command also contains instructions for installing the software on your system. Using the **install** option runs just those installation commands. To perform the installation, you have to be logged in as the root user, giving you the ability to add software files to system directories as needed. If the software uses configuration scripts, compiling and installing usually involves only the following three simple commands:

```
# ./configure
# make
# make install
```

In the preceding example, the `./configure` command performs configuration detection. The **make** command performs the actual compiling, using a Makefile script generated by the `./configure` operation. The **make install** command installs the program on your system, placing the executable program in a directory, such as **/usr/local/bin**, and any configuration files in **/etc**. Any shared libraries it created may go into **/usr/local/lib**.

Once you have compiled and installed your application, and you have checked that it is working properly, you can remove the source code directory that was created when you extracted the software. You can keep the archive file (**tar**) in case you need to extract the software again. Use **rm** with the **-rf** options so that all subdirectories will be deleted and you do not have to confirm each deletion.

TIP   *Be sure to remember to place the period and slash before the* **configure** *command. The* `./` *references a command in the current working directory, rather than another Linux command.*

Configure Command Options
Certain software may have specific options set up for the `./configure` operation. To find out what these are, you use the `./configure` command with the **--help** option:

```
#   ./configure --help
```

A useful common option is the **-prefix** option, which lets you specify the install directory:

```
#   ./configure -prefix=/usr/bin
```

TIP   *Some older X applications use* **xmkmf** *directly instead of a configure script to generate the needed Makefile. In this case, enter the command* **xmkmf** *in place of* `./configure`. *Be sure to consult the* **INSTALL** *and* **README** *files for the software.*

Development Libraries

If you are compiling an X-, GNOME-, or KDE-based program, be sure their development libraries have been installed. For X applications, be sure the **xmkmf** program is also installed. If you chose a standard install when you installed your distribution system, these most likely were not installed. For distributions using RPM packages, these come in the form of a set of development RPM packages, usually with the word "development" or "develop" in their names. You need to install them using either **rpm** or system-config-packages. GNOME, in particular, has an extensive set of RPM packages for development libraries. Many X applications need special shared libraries. For example, some applications may need the **xforms** library or the **qt** library. Some of these you may need to obtain from online sites.

Makefile File

If no configure script exists and the program does not use **xmkmf**, you may have to edit the software's Makefile directly. Be sure to check the documentation for such software to see if any changes must be made to the Makefile. Only a few changes may be necessary, but more detailed changes require an understanding of C programming and how **make** works with it. If you successfully configure the Makefile, you may only have to enter the **make** and **make install** commands. One possible problem is locating the development libraries for C and the X Window System. X libraries are in the **/usr/X11R6/lib** directory. Standard C libraries are located in the **/usr/lib** directory.

Command and Program Directories: PATH

Programs and commands are usually installed in several standard system directories, such as **/bin**, **/usr/bin**, **/usr/X11R6/bin**, or **/usr/local/bin**. Some packages place their commands in subdirectories, however, which they create within one of these standard directories or in an entirely separate directory. In such cases, you may be unable to run those commands because your system may be unable to locate them in the new subdirectory. Your system maintains a set of directories that search for commands each time you execute one. This set of directories is kept in a system variable called **PATH** that is created when you start your system. If a command is in a directory that is not in this list, your system will be unable to locate and run it. To use such commands, you first need to add the new directory to the set of directories in the **PATH** variable. Installation tools like RPM will automatically update the **PATH** with the appropriate directories for you.

The **PATH** variable is originally assigned in the **/etc/rc.d/rc.sysinit** file and further added to by different services that start up when the system boots. You could edit the **/etc/rc.d/rc.sysinit** file directly, but you would have to be very careful not to change anything else. A safer approach is to add a **PATH** definition in the **/etc/profile** file.

/etc/profile

To make an application available to all users, you can add the software's directory to the path entry in the **/etc/profile** script. The **/etc/profile** script is a system script executed for each user when the user logs in. Carefully edit the **/etc/profile** file using a text editor, such as KEdit, Gedit, Emacs, or Vi (you may want to make a backup copy first with the **cp** command). You add a line that begins with **PATH**, followed by an = sign, and the term **$PATH**, followed by a colon, and then the directory to be added. The **$** before **PATH** extracts the pathname from the **PATH** variable. If you add more than one directory, be sure a colon separates them. You should also have a colon at the end. For example, if you install the Java 2 SDK, the Java commands are installed in a subdirectory called **j2sdk-1.4.2/bin** in the **/usr/**

local directory. The full pathname for this directory is **/usr/local/j2sdk-1.4.2/bin**. You need to add this directory to the list of directories assigned to **PATH** in the **/etc/profile** file. The following example shows the **PATH** variable with its list of directories and the **/usr/local/ j2sdk-1.4.2/bin** directory added. Notice the **$** before **PATH** after the **=** sign, **PATH=$PATH**.

```
PATH=$PATH:/usr/local/j2sdk-1.4.2/bin
```

After making your changes, you can execute the profile file to have the changes take effect.

```
$  . /etc/profile
```

.bash_profile

Individual users can customize their **PATH** variables by placing a **PATH** assignment in either their **.bashrc** or **.bash_profile** file. In this way, users can access commands and programs they create or install for their own use in their own user directories (see Chapter 9 for more details). The user **.bash_profile** files already contain the following **PATH** definition. Notice the use of **$PATH**, which keeps all the directories already added to the **PATH** in previous startup scripts like **/etc/profile** and **/etc/rc.d/rc.sysinit**.

```
PATH=$PATH:$HOME/bin
```

The following entry in the **.bash_profile** file adds a user's **newbin** directory to the **PATH** variable. Notice both the colon placed before the new directory and the use of the **$HOME** variable to specify the pathname for the user's home directory.

```
PATH=$PATH:$HOME/bin/:$HOME/newbin
```

For the **root** user, the **PATH** definition also includes **sbin** directories. The **sbin** directories hold system administration programs that the **root** user would need to have access to. The **root** user **PATH** is shown here:

```
PATH=/usr/local/sbin:/usr/sbin:/sbin:$PATH:$HOME/bin
```

Subversion and CVS

Subversion and the Concurrent Versions System (CVS) are software development methods that allow developers from remote locations to work on software stored on a central server. Subversion is an enhanced version of CVS, designed to eventually replace it. Like CVS, Subversion works with CVS repositories, letting you access software in much the same way. Subversion adds features such as better directory and file access as well as support for metadata information.

CVS sites allow several developers to work on a file at the same time. This means that they support parallel development, so programmers around the world can work on the same task at the same time through a simple Internet connection. It has become popular among Linux developers as a means of creating software using the Internet. CVS sites are also the source for the most up-to-date versions for different software. Ongoing projects like KDE and GNOME use Subversion or CVS servers to post the most recent versions of their desktop applications, primarily because it is easy to use for program development over the Internet. The **sourceforge.net** site provides a CVS repository for many ongoing Linux projects.

The Fedora Project maintains a CVS repository of software under development, **cvs.fedora .redhat.com**. Many CVS sites now support ViewCVS (an enhanced version of WebCVS), a Web browser front end to a CVS repository that lets you browse and select software versions easily. You can find out more about CVS from **www.cvshome.org**, and about Subversion from **subversion.tigris.org**.

TIP *You can also use CVS GUI clients on GNOME and KDE, along with ViewCVS, to manage to your CVS repositories or access those on the Internet. For GNOME, you can use Pharmacy, and for KDE, you can use Cervisia or LinCVS.*

Using a CVS repository for software development involves procedures for accessing a software version, making your changes locally on your system, and then uploading your changed version back to the CVS repository. In effect, you check out software, make your changes in such a way that they are carefully recorded, and then check your version back in to the repository. CVS was originally developed as a front end to the older Revision Control System (RCS) and shares many of the same commands.

Packaging Your Software with RPM

Many research and corporate environments develop their own customized software for distribution within their organization. Sometimes software packages are downloaded and then customized for use in a particular organization. To more easily install such customized software, administrators pack the programs into their own RPM packages. In such packages, you can include your own versions of configuration files, documentation, and modified source and binaries. RPM automatically installs software on a system in the designated directories, along with any documentation, libraries, or support programs.

The package creation process is designed to take the program through several stages, starting with unpacking it from an archive, then compiling its source code, and finally, generating the RPM package. You can skip any of these stages, up to the last one. If your software is already unpacked, you can start with compiling it. If your software is compiled, you can start with installation. If it is already installed, you can go directly to creating the RPM package.

The build processes for RPM used to be included with the **rpm** command. They are now incorporated into a separate tool called **rpmb**. This tool along with supporting libraries and documentation is located in the rpm-build package. Be sure this package is installed before you try to build RPM packages. You can still run the **rpm** command with the build options, but these are simply aliases for corresponding **rpmb** commands.

32
CHAPTER

File System Management

Files reside on physical storage devices such as hard drives, CD-ROMs, or floppy disks. The files on each storage device are organized into a file system. The storage devices on your Linux system are presented as a collection of file systems that you can manage. When you want to add a new storage device, you need to format it as a file system and then attach it to your Linux file structure. Hard drives can be divided into separate storage devices called *partitions,* each of which has its own file system. You can perform administrative tasks on your file systems, such as backing them up, attaching or detaching them from your file structure, formatting new devices or erasing old ones, and checking a file system for problems.

To access files on a device, you attach its file system to a specified directory. This is called *mounting* the file system. For example, to access files on a floppy disk, you first mount its file system to a particular directory. With Linux, you can mount a number of different types of file systems. You can even access a Windows hard drive partition or tape drive, as well as file systems on a remote server. Fedora Core 4 also configures CD-ROM and floppy media to be mounted automatically from GNOME or KDE.

Recently developed file systems for Linux now support *journaling,* which allows your system to recover from a crash or interruption easily. The ext3, ReiserFS, and JFS (IBM) file systems maintain a record of file and directory changes, called a *journal,* which can be used to recover files and directories in use when a system suddenly crashes due to unforeseen events such as power interruptions. Most distributions currently use the ext3 file system as their default, though you also have the option of using ReiserFS or JFS, an independently developed journaling system.

Your Linux system is capable of handling any number of storage devices that may be connected to it. You can configure your system to access multiple hard drives, partitions on a hard drive, CD-ROM discs, DVDs, floppy disks, and even tapes. You can elect to attach these storage components manually or have them automatically mount when you boot. Automatic mounts are handled by configuring the **/etc/fstab** file. For example, the main partitions holding your Linux system programs are automatically mounted whenever you boot, whereas a floppy disk can be manually mounted when you put one in your floppy drive, though even these can also be automatically mounted. Removable storage devices like CD-ROMs, as well as removable devices like USB cameras and printers, are now handled by udev and the Hardware Abstract Layer (HAL), as described in Chapter 34 and partially discussed here.

File Systems

Although all the files in your Linux system are connected into one overall directory tree, parts of that tree may reside on different storage devices such as hard drives or CD-ROMs. Files on a particular storage device are organized into what is referred to as a *file system*. A file system is a formatted device, with its own tree of directories and files. Your Linux directory tree may encompass several file systems, each on different storage devices. On a hard drive with several partitions, you would have a file system for each partition. The files themselves are organized into one seamless tree of directories, beginning from the root directory. For example, if you attach a CD-ROM to your system, a pathname will lead directly from the root directory on your hard disk partition's file system to the files in the CD-ROM file system.

TIP *With Linux you can mount file systems of different types, including those created by other operating systems, including Windows, IBM OS, Unix, and SGI. Within Linux a variety of file systems are supported, including several journaling systems like ReiserFS and ext3.*

A file system has its files organized into its own directory tree. You can think of this as a *subtree* that must be attached to the main directory tree. The tree remains separate from your system's directory tree until you specifically connect it. For example, a floppy disk with Linux files has its own tree of directories. You need to attach this subtree to the main tree on your hard drive partition. Until they are attached, you cannot access the files on your floppy disk.

Filesystem Hierarchy Standard

Linux organizes its files and directories into one overall interconnected tree, beginning from the root directory and extending down to system and user directories. The organization and layout for the system directories are determined by the Filesystem Hierarchy Standard (FHS). The FHS provides a standardized layout that all Linux distributions should follow in setting up their system directories. For example, there must be an **/etc** directory to hold configuration files and a **/dev** directory for device files. You can find out more about FHS, including the official documentation, at **www.pathname.com/fhs**. Linux distributions, developers, and administrators all follow the FHS to provide a consistent organization to the Linux file system.

Linux uses a number of specifically named directories for specialized administration tasks. All these directories are at the very top level of your main Linux file system, the file system root directory, represented by a single slash, **/**. For example, the **/dev** directory holds device files, and the **/home** directory holds the user home directories and all their user files. You have access to these directories and files only as the system administrator (though users normally have read-only access). You need to log in as the root user, placing yourself in a special root user administrative directory called **/root**. From here, you can access any directory on the Linux file system, both administrative and user.

Root Directory: /

The subdirectories held in the root directory, **/**, are listed in Table 32-1, along with other useful subdirectories. Directories that you may commonly access as an administrator are the **/etc** directory, which holds configuration files; the **/dev** directory, which holds dynamically generated device files; and the **/var** directory, which holds server data files for DNS, Web, mail, and FTP servers, along with system logs and scheduled tasks. For managing different

Directory	Function
/	Begins the file system structure—called the root.
/boot	Holds the kernel image files and associated boot information and files.
/home	Contains users' home directories.
/sbin	Holds administration-level commands and any commands used by the root user.
/dev	Holds dynamically generated file interfaces for devices such as the terminal and the printer (see "udev: Device Files" in Chapter 34).
/etc	Holds system configuration files and any other system files.
/etc/opt	Holds system configuration files for applications in **/opt**.
/etc/X11	Holds system configuration files for the X Window System and its applications.
/bin	Holds the essential user commands and utility programs.
/lib	Holds essential shared libraries and kernel modules.
/lib/modules	Holds the kernel modules.
/media	Holds directories for mounting media-based removable file systems, like CD-ROMs, floppy disks, USB card readers, and digital cameras.
/mnt	Holds directories for additional file systems such as hard disks.
/opt	Holds added software applications (for example, KDE on some distributions).
/proc	Process directory, a memory-resident directory containing files used to provide information about the system.
/sys	The **sysfs** file system for kernel objects, listing supported kernel devices and modules.
/tmp	Holds temporary files.
/usr	Holds those files and commands used by the system; this directory breaks down into several subdirectories.
/var	Holds files that vary, such as mailbox, Web, and FTP files.

TABLE 32-1 Linux File System Directories

versions of the kernel, you may need to access the **/boot** and **/lib/modules** directories as well as **/usr/src/linux**. The **/boot** directory holds the kernel image files for any new kernels you install, and the **/lib/modules** directory holds modules for your different kernels.

System Directories

Your Linux directory tree contains certain directories whose files are used for different system functions. For basic system administration, you should be familiar with the system program directories where applications are kept, the system configuration directory (**/etc**) where most configuration files are placed, and the system log directory (**/var/log**) that holds the system logs, recording activity on your system. Both are covered in detail in Chapter 29. Table 32-2 lists the system directories.

Program Directories

Directories with **bin** in the name are used to hold programs. The **/bin** directory holds basic user programs, such as login, shells (BASH, TCSH, and zsh), and file commands (**cp**, **mv**, **rm**, **ln**, and so on). The **/sbin** directory holds specialized system programs for such tasks as file system management (**fsck**, **fdisk**, **mkfs**) and system operations like shutdown and startup (**init**). The **/usr/bin** directory holds program files designed for user tasks. The **/usr/sbin** directory holds user-related system operation, such as **useradd** for adding new users. The **/lib** directory holds all the libraries your system makes use of, including the main Linux library, **libc**, and subdirectories such as **modules**, which holds all the current kernel modules.

Configuration Directories and Files

When you configure different elements of your system, such as user accounts, applications, servers, or network connections, you make use of configuration files kept in certain system

Directory	Description
/bin	System-related programs
/sbin	System programs for specialized tasks
/lib	System libraries
/etc	Configuration files for system and network services and applications
/home	The location of user home directories and server data directories, such as Web and FTP site files
/media	The location where removable media file systems like CD-ROMs and floppy disks are mounted
/var	The location of system directories whose files continually change, such as logs, printer spool files, and lock files
/usr	User-related programs and files. Includes several key subdirectories, such as **/usr/bin**, **/usr/X11**, and **/usr/share/doc**
/usr/bin	Programs for users
/dev	Device files
/sys	The **sysfs** file system with device information for kernel-supported devices on your system
/usr/X11	X Window System configuration files
/usr/share	Shared files
/usr/share/doc	Documentation for applications
/usr/share/hal	Configuration for HAL removable device information
/etc/udev	Configuration for device files
/tmp	Directory for system temporary files

TABLE 32-2   System Directories

directories. On Red Hat Enterprise Linux and Fedora Core, configuration files are placed in the **/etc** directory, with more specific device and service configurations located in the **/etc/sysconfig** directory (see Chapter 34 for more details).

The /usr Directory

The **/usr** directory contains a multitude of important subdirectories used to support users, providing applications, libraries, and documentation. The **/usr/bin** directory holds numerous user-accessible applications and utilities; **/usr/sbin** hold user-accessible administrative utilities. The **/usr/share** directory holds architecture-independent data that includes an extensive number of subdirectories, including those for documentation, such as **man**, **info**, and **doc** files. Table 32-3 lists the subdirectories of the **/usr** directory.

The /media Directory

The **/media** directory is used for mountpoints for removable media like CD-ROM, DVD, floppy, or Zip drives, as well as for other media-based file systems such as USB card readers, cameras, and MP3 players. These are file systems you may be changing frequently, unlike partitions on fixed disks. Red Hat Enterprise Linux and Fedora Core use the Hardware Abstraction Layer (HAL) to invoke a callout tool of its own named **fstab-sync** to dynamically manage the creation, mounting, and device assignment of these devices. As instructed by HAL, this tool will create floppy, CD-ROM, storage card, camera, and MP3 player subdirectories in **/media** as needed, though floppy and CD-ROM directories are persistent. The default floppy and CD-ROM subdirectories for mounting floppies and CD-ROMs are **/media/floppy** and **/media/cdrom**. Additional drives have a number attached to their name, as in **/media/cdrom1** for a second CD-ROM drive. CD-RWs will be mounted at **/media/cdrecorder**. Card readers will bear the label of the card installed.

The /mnt Directory

The **/mnt** directory is usually used for mountpoints for other mounted file systems such as Windows partitions. You can create directories for any partitions you want to mount, such as **/mnt/windows** for a Windows partition.

	Directory	Description
TABLE 32-3 **/usr** Directories	**/usr/bin**	Holds most user commands and utility programs.
	/usr/sbin	Holds administrative applications.
	/usr/lib	Holds libraries for applications, programming languages, desktops, and so on.
	/usr/games	Holds games and educational programs.
	/usr/include	Holds C programming language header files (**.h**).
	/usr/doc	Holds Linux documentation.
	/usr/local	Holds locally installed software.
	/usr/share	Holds architecture-independent data such as documentation: **man**, **info**, and **doc** subdirectories.
	/usr/src	Holds source code, including the kernel source code.
	/usr/X11R6	Holds X Window System–based applications and libraries.

The /home Directory

The **/home** directory holds user home directories. When a user account is set up, a home directory is set up here for that account, usually with the same name as the user. As the system administrator, you can access any user's home directory, and so you have control over their files.

The /var Directory

The **/var** directory holds subdirectories for tasks whose files change frequently, such as lock files, log files, Web server files, or printer spool files. For example, the **/var** directory holds server data directories, such as **/var/www** for the Apache Web server Web site files or **/var/ftp** for your FTP site files, as well as **/var/named** for the DNS server. The **/tmp** directory is simply a directory to hold any temporary files programs may need to perform a particular task.

The **/var** directories are designed to hold data that changes with the normal operation of the Linux system. For example, spool files for documents that you are printing are kept here. A spool file is created as a temporary printing file and is removed after printing. Other files, such as system log files, are changed constantly. Table 32-4 lists the subdirectories of the **/var** directory.

Directory	Description
/var/account	Processes accounting logs.
/var/cache	Holds application cache data for Man pages, Web proxy data, fonts, or application-specific data.
/var/crash	Holds system crash dumps.
/var/games	Holds varying games data.
/var/lib	Holds state information for particular applications.
/var/local	Used for data that changes for programs installed in **/usr/local**.
/var/lock	Holds lock files that indicate when a particular program or file is in use.
/var/log	Holds log files such as **/var/log/messages** that contain all kernel and system program messages.
/var/mail	Holds user mailbox files.
/var/opt	Holds variable data for applications installed in **/opt**.
/var/run	Holds information about system's running processes.
/var/spool	Holds applications' spool data such as that for mail, news, and printer queues, as well as **cron** and **at** jobs.
/var/tmp	Holds temporary files that should be preserved between system reboots.
/var/YP	Holds Network Information Service (NIS) data files.
/var/www	Holds Web server Web site files.
/var/ftp	Holds FTP server FTP files.
/var/named	Holds DNS server domain configuration files.

TABLE 32-4   /var Subdirectories

The /proc File System

The **/proc** file system is a special file system that is generated in system memory. It does not exist on any disk. **/proc** contains files that provide important information about the state of your system. For example, **/proc/cpuinfo** holds information about your computer's CPU processor. **/proc/devices** lists those devices currently configured to run with your kernel. **/proc/filesystems** lists the file systems. **/proc** files are really interfaces to the kernel, obtaining information from the kernel about your system. Table 32-5 lists the **/proc** subdirectories and files.

Like any file system, **/proc** has to be mounted. The **/etc/fstab** file will have a special entry for **/proc** with a file system type of proc and no device specified.

```
none     /proc      proc      defaults   0     0
```

> **TIP** *You can use **sysctl**, the Kernel Tuning tool, to set proc file values you are allowed to change, like the maximum number of files, or turning on IP forwarding.*

The sysfs File System: /sys

The **sysfs** file system is a virtual file system that provides a hierarchical map of your kernel-supported devices such as PCI devices, buses, and block devices, as well as supporting kernel modules. The **classes** subdirectory will list all your supported devices by category,

File	Description
/proc/num	There is a directory for each process labeled by its number. **/proc/1** is the directory for process 1.
/proc/cpuinfo	Contains information about the CPU, such as its type, make, model, and performance.
/proc/devices	Lists the device drivers configured for the currently running kernel.
/proc/dma	Displays the DMA channels currently used.
/proc/filesystems	Lists file systems configured into the kernel.
/proc/interrupts	Displays the interrupts in use.
/proc/ioports	Shows the I/O ports in use.
/proc/kcore	Holds an image of the physical memory of the system.
/proc/kmsg	Contains messages generated by the kernel.
/proc/loadavg	Lists the system load average.
/proc/meminfo	Displays memory usage.
/proc/modules	Lists the kernel modules currently loaded.
/proc/net	Lists status information about network protocols.
/proc/stat	Contains system operating statistics, such as page fault occurrences.
/proc/uptime	Displays the time the system has been up.
/proc/version	Displays the kernel version.

TABLE 32-5   **/proc** Subdirectories and Files

such as net and sound devices. With **sysfs** your system can easily determine the device file a particular device is associated with. This is very helpful for managing removable devices as well as dynamically configuring and managing devices as HAL and udev do. The **sysfs** file system is used by udev to dynamically generate needed device files in the **/dev** directory, as well as by HAL to manage removable device files and support as needed (HAL technically provides information only about devices, though it can use tools to dynamically change configurations as needed). The **/sys** file system type is **sysfs**. The **/sys** subdirectories organize your devices into different categories. The file system is used by **systool** to display a listing of your installed devices. The following example will list all your system devices.

```
systool
```

Like **/proc**, the **/sys** directory resides only in memory, but you still need to mount it in the the **/etc/fstab** file. Fedora Core 4 will include such an entry for you.

```
none    /sys       sysfs      defaults   0       0
```

Device Files: /dev, udev, and HAL

To mount a file system, you have to specify its device name. The interfaces to devices that may be attached to your system are provided by special files known as *device files*. The names of these device files are the device names. Device files are located in the **/dev** directories and usually have abbreviated names ending with the number of the device. For example, **fd0** may reference the first floppy drive attached to your system. The prefix **sd** references SCSI hard drives, so **sda2** would reference the second partition on the first SCSI hard drive. In most cases, you can use the **man** command with a prefix to obtain more detailed information about this kind of device. For example, **man sd** displays the Man pages for SCSI devices. An official listing of all device prefixes can be found in the **devices** file located in the **linux/doc/device-list** directory at the **www.kernel.org** Web site, and in the **devices.txt** file in the **/usr/share/doc/kernel-doc-2.6.11/Documentation** directory on your Red Hat system. Table 32-6 lists several of the commonly used device names.

udev and HAL

With Fedora Core 3, device files were no longer handled in a static way. Instead they are now dynamically generated as needed. Previously a device file was created for each possible device, leading to a very large number of device files in the **/etc/dev** directory. Now, your system will detect only those devices it uses and create device files for those only, giving you a much smaller listing of device files. The tool used to detect and generate device files is udev, user devices. Each time your system is booted, udev will automatically detect your devices and generate device files for them in the **/etc/dev** directory. This means that the **/etc/dev** directory and its files are re-created each time you boot. It is a dynamic directory, no longer static. To manage these device files, you need to use udev configuration files located in the **/etc/udev** directory. This means that udev is able to also dynamically manage all removable devices; udev will generate and configure devices files for removable devices as they are attached, and then remove these files when the devices are removed. In this sense, all devices are now considered hotplugged, with fixed devices simply being hotplugged devices that are never removed.

As **/etc/dev** is now dynamic, any changes you would make manually to the **/etc/dev** directory will be lost when you reboot. This includes the creation of any symbolic links like

Device Name	Description
hd	IDE hard drives; 1–4 are primary partitions; 5 and up are logical partitions
sd	SCSI hard drives
scd	SCSI CD-ROM drives
fd	Floppy disks
st	SCSI tape drives
nst	SCSI tape drives, no rewind
ht	IDE tape drives
tty	Terminals
lp	Printer ports
pty	Pseudoterminals (used for remote logins)
js	Analog joysticks
usb	Directory that holds USB devices like printers
ttyS	Serial ports
md	RAID devices
rd/cn**d**n	The directory that holds RAID devices is **rd**; **c**n is the RAID controller and **d**n is the RAID disk for that controller
cdrom	Link to your CD-ROM device file, set in **/etc/udev/rules.d**
cdrecorder	Link to your CD-R or CD-RW device file, set in **/etc/udev/rules.d**
modem	Link to your modem device file, set in **/etc/udev/rules.d**
floppy	Link to your floppy device file, set in **/etc/udev/rules.d**
tape	Link to your tape device file, set in **/etc/udev/rules.d**
scanner	Link to your scanner device file, set in **/etc/udev/rules.d**

TABLE 32-6   Device Name Prefixes

/dev/cdrom that many software applications use. Instead, such symbolic links have to be configured using udev rules listed in configuration files located in the **/etc/udev/rules.d** directory. Default rules are already in place for symbolic links, but you can create rules of your own. See Chapter 34 for more details.

In addition to udev, information about removable devices like CD-ROMs and floppy disks, along with cameras and USB printers, used by applications like the desktop to dynamically interface with them, is managed by a separate utility called the Hardware Abstract Layer (HAL). HAL allows a removable device like a USB printer to be recognized no matter what particular connections it may be using. For example, you can attach a USB printer in one USB port at one time and then switch it to another later. The **fstab** file is edited using the **fstab-sync** tool, which is invoked by HAL rules in configuration files in the **/usr/share/hal/fdi** directory. See Chapter 34 for more details.

The use of HAL has a major impact on the **/etc/fstab** file used to manage file systems. HAL entries in the **/etc/fstab** file are denoted by the **managed** command. These entries are not static. Instead they are automatically generated by HAL using the **fstab-sync** tool when your system reboots, restarting the **haldaemon** service, which detects removable devices. Any changes you make to these entries manually will not be kept. Instead you now have to use the HAL configuration files to manage your **/etc/fstab** entries for your removable file systems (see Chapter 34).

Floppy and Hard Disk Devices

The device name for your floppy drive is **fd0**; it is located in the directory **/dev**. **/dev/fd0** references your floppy drive. Notice the numeral **0** after **fd**. If you have more than one floppy drive, additional drives are represented by **fd1**, **fd2**, and so on.

IDE hard drives use the prefix **hd**, whereas SCSI hard drives use the prefix **sd**. RAID devices, on the other hand, use the prefix **md**. The prefix for a hard disk is followed by a letter that labels the hard drive and a number for the partition. For example, **hda2** references the second partition on the first IDE hard drive, where the first hard drive is referenced with the letter **a**, as in **hda**. The device **sdb3** refers to the third partition on the second SCSI hard drive (**sdb**). RAID devices, however, are numbered from 0, like floppy drives. Device **md0** references the first RAID device, and **md1** references the second. On an IDE hard disk device, Linux supports up to four primary IDE hard disk partitions, numbered 1 through 4. You are allowed any number of logical partitions. To find the device name, you can use **df** to display your hard partitions or examine the **/etc/fstab** file.

CD-ROM Devices

The device name for your CD-ROM drive varies depending on the type of CD-ROM you have. The device name for an IDE CD-ROM has the same prefix as an IDE hard disk partition, **hd**, and is identified by a following letter that distinguishes it from other IDE devices. For example, an IDE CD-ROM connected to your secondary IDE port may have the name **hdc**. An IDE CD-ROM connected as a slave to the secondary port may have the name **hdd**. The actual name is determined when the CD-ROM is installed, as happened when you installed your Linux system. SCSI CD-ROM drives use a different nomenclature for their device names. They begin with **scd** for SCSI drive and are followed by a distinguishing number. For example, the name of a SCSI CD-ROM could be **scd0** or **scd1**. The name of your CD-ROM was determined when you installed your system. You can find out what it is by examining the **/etc/fstab** file.

As noted previously, CD-ROM devices are now configured by HAL. HAL does this in a device information file in its policy configuration directory. To configure a CD-ROM device, as by adding user mount capability, you need to configure its entry in the **storage-policy.fdi** configuration file (see Chapter 34 for details). Editing the **/etc/fstab** file directly no longer works. If you do not want HAL to manage your CD-ROMs, you would remove the **managed** option in its **/etc/fstab** entry. You can then manually add options to that entry.

Mounting File Systems

Attaching a file system on a storage device to your main directory tree is called *mounting* the device. The file system is mounted to an empty directory on the main directory tree. You can then change to that directory and access those files. If the directory does not yet exist, you have to create it. The directory in the file structure to which the new file system is attached is referred to as the *mountpoint.* For example, to access files on a CD-ROM, first you have to mount the CD-ROM.

Mounting file systems can normally be done only as the root user. This is a system administration task and should not usually be performed by a regular user. As the root user, you can, however, make a particular device, like a CD-ROM, user-mountable. In this way, any user could mount a CD-ROM. You could do the same for a floppy drive.

TIP *On GNOME, you can use the Disk Management tool on the System Settings window and menu to mount and unmount file systems, including floppy disks and CD-ROMs. On KDE, you can use the KDiskFree utility (More System Tools menu), which also lists your mountable file systems as well as their disk usage.*

Even the file systems on your hard disk partition must be explicitly mounted. When you install your Linux system and create the Linux partition on your hard drive, however, your system is automatically configured to mount your main file system whenever it starts. When your system shuts down, they are automatically unmounted. You have the option of unmounting any file system, removing it from the directory tree, and possibly replacing it with another, as is the case when you replace a CD-ROM.

Once a file system it actually mounted, an entry for it is made by the operating system in the **/etc/mstab** file. Here you will find listed all file systems currently mounted.

File System Information

The file systems on each storage device are formatted to take up a specified amount of space. For example, you may have formatted your hard drive partition to take up 3GB. Files installed or created on that file system take up part of the space, while the remainder is available for new files and directories. To find out how much space you have free on a file system, you can use the **df** command or, on GNOME, either the System Monitor or the KDE KDiskFree utility. For the System Monitor (System Tools menu), click the Resources tab to display a list of the free space on your file systems. KDiskFree displays a list of devices, showing how much space is free on each partition, and the percentage used.

df

The **df** command reports file system disk space usage. It lists all your file systems by their device names, how much disk space they take up, and the percentage of the disk space used, as well as where they are mounted. With the **-h** option, it displays information in a more readable format; such as measuring disk space in megabytes instead of memory blocks. The **df** command is also a safe way to obtain a listing of all your partitions, instead of using **fdisk** (with **fdisk** you could erase partitions). **df** shows only mounted partitions, however, whereas **fdisk** shows all partitions.

```
$ df -h
Filesystem Size Used Avail Use% Mounted on
/dev/hda3  9.7G 2.8G 6.4G  31%   /
/dev/hda2  99M  6.3M 88M   7%    /boot
/dev/hda2  22G  36M  21G   1%    /home
/dev/hdc   525M 525M 0     100%  /media/cdrom
```

You can also use **df** to tell you to what file system a given directory belongs. Enter **df** with the directory name or **df** . for the current directory.

```
$ df .
Filesystem 1024-blocks Used Available Capacity Mounted on
/dev/hda3 297635 169499 112764 60% /
```

e2fsck and fsck

To check the consistency of the file system and repair it if it is damaged, you can use file system checking tools. **fsck** checks and repairs a Linux file system. **e2fsck** is designed to support ext2 and ext3 file systems, whereas the more generic **fsck** also works on any other file systems. The ext2 and ext3 file systems are the file systems normally used for Linux hard disk partitions and floppy disks. Linux file systems for Red Hat Enterprise Linux and Fedora Core are normally ext3, which you would use **e2fsck** to check. **fsck** and **e2fsck** take as their argument the device name of the hard disk partition that the file system uses.

```
fsck     device-name
```

Before you check a file system, be sure that the file system is unmounted. **e2fsck** should not be used on a mounted file system. To use **e2fsck**, enter **e2fsck** and the device name that references the file system. The **-p** option automatically repairs a file system without first requesting approval from the user for each repair task. The following examples check the disk in the floppy drive and the primary hard drive:

```
# e2fsck /dev/fd0
# e2fsck /dev/hda1
```

With **fsck**, the **-t** option lets you specify the type of file system to check, and the **-a** option automatically repairs systems, whereas the **-r** option first asks for confirmation. The **-A** option checks all systems in the **/etc/fstab** file.

TIP *In earlier distribution versions, **fsck** and **e2fsck** were also used to recover file systems after disk crashes or reset-button reboots. With recent releases, journaling capabilities were introduced with file systems like ext3 and ReiserFS. Journaling provides for fast and effective recovery in case of disk crashes, so recovering with **fsck** or **e2fsck** is no longer necessary.*

Journaling

The ext3 and ReiserFS file systems introduced journaling capabilities to Linux systems. Journaling provides for fast and effective recovery in case of disk crashes, instead of using **e2fsck** or **fsck**. With journaling, a log is kept of all file system actions, which are placed in a journal file. In the event of a crash, Linux only needs to read the journal file and replay it to restore the system to its previous (stable) state. Files that were in the process of writing to the disk can be restored to their original state. Journaling also avoids lengthy **fsck** checks on reboots that occur when your system suddenly loses power or freezes and has to be restarted physically. Instead of using **fsck** to manually check each file and directory, your system just reads its journal files to restore the fil5e system.

Keeping a journal entails more work for a file system than a nonjournal method. Though all journaling systems maintain a file system's directory structure (what is known as the *metadata*), they offer various levels of file data recovery. Maintaining file data recovery information can be time-consuming, slowing down the file system's response time. At the same time, journaling systems make more efficient use of the file system, providing a faster response time than the nonjournal ext2 file system.

There are other kind of journaling file systems you can use on Linux. These include ReiserFS, JFS, and XFS. ReiserFS, named after Hans Reiser, provides a completely reworked file system structure based on journaling (**www.namesys.com**). Most distributions also provide support for ReiserFS file systems. JFS is the IBM version of a journaling file system, designed for use on servers providing high throughput such as e-business enterprise servers (**http://jfs.sourceforge.net**). It is freely distributed under the GNU public license. XFS is another high-performance journaling system developed by Silicon Graphics (**oss.sgi.com/ projects/xfs**). XFS is compatible with RAID and NFS file systems.

ext3 Journaling

Journaling is supported in the Linux kernel with ext3. The ext3 file system is also fully compatible with the earlier ext2 version it replaces. To create an ext3 file system, you use the **mkfs.ext3** command. You can even upgrade ext2 file systems to ext3 versions automatically, with no loss of data or change in partitions. This upgrade just adds a journal file to an ext2 file system and enables journaling on it, using the **tune2fs** command. Be sure to change the ext2 file type to ext3 in any corresponding **/etc/fstab** entries. The following example converts the ext2 file system on **/dev/hda3** to an ext3 file system by adding a journal file (**-j**).

```
tune2fs -j /dev/hda3
```

Though the ext3 file system maintains full metadata recovery support (directory tree recovery), it offers various levels of file data recovery. In effect, you are trading off less file data recovery for more speed. The ext3 file system supports three options: **writeback**, **ordered**, and **journal**. The default is **writeback**. The **writeback** option provides only metadata recovery, no file data recovery. The **ordered** option supports limited file data recovery, and the **journal** option provides for full file data recovery. Any files in the process of being changed during a crash will be recovered. To specify a ext3 option, use the **data** option in the **mount** command.

```
data=ordered
```

ReiserFS

Though journaling is often used to recover from disk crashes, a journal-based file system can do much more. The ext3, JFS, and XFS file systems only provide the logging operations used in recovery, whereas ReiserFS uses journaling techniques to completely rework file system operations. In ReiserFS, journaling is used to read and write data, abandoning the block structure used in traditional Unix and Linux systems. This gives it the capability to access a large number of small files very quickly, as well as use only the amount of disk space they need. However, efficiency is not that much better with larger files.

Mounting File Systems Automatically: /etc/fstab

File systems are mounted using the **mount** command, described in the next section. Although you can mount a file system directly with only a **mount** command, you can simplify the process by placing mount information in the **/etc/fstab** configuration file. Using entries in this file, you can have certain file systems automatically mounted whenever your system boots. For others, you can specify configuration information, such as mountpoints and access permissions, which can be automatically used whenever you mount a file system. You needn't enter this information as arguments to a **mount** command as you otherwise must. This feature is what allows mount utilities on GNOME or KDE to enable you to mount a file system simply by clicking a window icon. All the mount information is already in the **/etc/fstab** file. For example, when you add a new hard disk partition to your Linux system, you most likely want to have it automatically mounted on startup, and then unmounted when you shut down. Otherwise, you must mount and unmount the partition explicitly each time you boot up and shut down your system.

HAL and fstab

To have Linux automatically mount the file system on your new hard disk partition, you only need to add its name to the **fstab** file, except in the case of removable devices like CD-ROMs and USB printers. Removable devices are managed by HAL, using the storage policy files located in **/usr/share/hal/fdi** and **/etc/hal/fdi** directories. The devices are automatically detected by the **haldaemon** service, which will invoke the **fstab-sync** tool to write the appropriate default entry in the **/etc/fstab** file, including specified default options. If you want different options set for the device, you should create your own **storage-policy.fdi** file in the **30user** directory. The configuration is implemented using XML language. Check the default storage file in **10osvendors/10-storage-policy.fdi** as well as samples in the **/usr/share/doc/hal**version**/conf** directory. See Chapter 34 for examples of using HAL to set device options.

If you do not want HAL to manage an **fstab** entry, you can disable access by removing the **managed** option.

fstab Fields

An entry in an **fstab** file contains several fields, each separated from the next by a space or tab. These are described as the device, mountpoint, file system type, options, dump, and **fsck** fields, arranged in the sequence shown here:

```
<device> <mountpoint> <filesystemtype> <options> <dump> <fsck>
```

The first field is the name of the file system to be mounted. This entry can be either a device name or an ext2 or ext3 file system label. A device name usually begins with **/dev**, such as **/dev/hda3** for the third hard disk partition. A label is specified by assigning the label name to the tag **LABEL**, as in **LABEL=/** for an ext2 root partition. The next field is the directory in your file structure where you want the file system on this device to be attached. These are empty directories to be used for file systems, such as **/dev/floppy**. The third field is the type of file system being mounted. Table 32-7 provides a list of all the different types you can mount. The type for a standard Linux hard disk partition is ext3. The next example shows an entry for the main Linux hard disk partition. This entry is mounted at the root directory, /, and has a file type of ext3:

```
/dev/hda3    /     ext3    defaults    0    1
```

Type	Description
`auto`	Attempts to detect the file system type automatically.
`minux`	Minux file systems (filenames are limited to 30 characters).
`ext`	Earlier version of Linux file system, no longer in use.
`ext3`	Standard Linux file system supporting long filenames and large file sizes. Includes journaling.
`ext2`	Older standard Linux file system supporting long filenames and large file sizes. Does not have journaling.
`xiaf`	Xiaf file system.
`msdos`	File system for MS-DOS partitions (16-bit).
`vfat`	File system for Windows 95, 98, and Millennium partitions (32-bit).
`reiserfs`	A ReiserFS journaling file system.
`xfs`	A Silicon Graphics (SGI) file system.
`ntfs`	Windows NT, Windows XP, and Windows 2000 file systems. (It affords read access with limited write capability. Install the current version from **rpm-livna.org/fedora**.)
`smbfs`	Samba remote file systems, such as NFS.
`hpfs`	File system for OS/2 high-performance partitions.
`nfs`	NFS file system for mounting partitions from remote systems.
`nfs4`	NFSv4 file system for mounting partitions from remote systems.
`umsdos`	UMS-DOS file system.
`swap`	Linux swap partition or swap file.
`sysv`	Unix System V file systems.
`iso9660`	File system for mounting CD-ROM.
`proc`	Used by operating system for processes (kernel support file system).
`sysfs`	Used by operating system for devices (kernel support file system).
`usbfs`	Used by operating system for USB devices (kernel support file system).
`devpts`	Unix 98 Pseudo Terminals (ttys, kernel interface file system).
`shmfs` and `tmpfs`	Linux Virtual Memory, POSIX shared memory maintenance access (kernel interface file system).
`adfs`	Apple DOS file systems.
`affs`	Amiga fast file systems.
`ramfs`	RAM-based file systems.
`udf`	Universal Disk Format used on CD/DVD-ROMs.
`ufs`	Unix File System, found on Unix system (older format).

TABLE 32-7   File System Types

The following example shows a **LABEL** entry for the hard disk partition, where the label name is /:

```
LABEL=/     /      ext3    defaults   0    1
```

Auto Mounts

The file system type for a floppy may differ depending on the disk you are trying to mount. For example, you may want to read a Windows-formatted floppy disk at one time and a Linux-formatted floppy disk at another time. For this reason, the file system type specified for the floppy device is **auto**. With this option, the type of file system formatted on the floppy disk is detected automatically, and the appropriate file system type is used.

```
/dev/fd0  /media/floppy  auto   defaults,noauto   0 0
```

mount Options

The field after the file system type lists the different options for mounting the file system. The default set of options is specified by **defaults**, and specific options are listed next to each other separated by a comma (no spaces). The **defaults** option specifies that a device is read/write (**rw**), that it is asynchronous (**async**), that it is a block device (**dev**), that it cannot be mounted by ordinary users (**nouser**), and that programs can be executed on it (**exec**).

Removable devices like your CD-ROMs and floppy disks are now managed by HAL, the Hardware Abstraction Layer. These entries will have the **managed** option, indicating that the device is dynamically controlled by HAL. HAL uses its own configuration files to set the options for these devices. You cannot directly edit the **/etc/fstab** file to add or remove these options, unless you first remove the **managed** option. This will, however, no longer let your CD-ROMs and DVD-ROMs be automatically detected.

A CD-ROM entry will include **ro** and **noauto** options. **ro** specifies that the device is read-only, and **noauto** specifies it is not automatically mounted. The **noauto** option is used with both CD-ROMs and floppy drives, so they won't automatically mount, because you don't know if you have anything in them when you start up. At the same time, the entries for both the CD-ROM and the floppy drive specify where they are to be mounted when you decide to mount them. The **pamconsole** option is a more secure option used in place of the user option. The **pamconsole** option will only allow users logged in directly to the system to mount the device, instead of remote users, as the user option does. The **managed** option indicates that the device is managed by HAL. The **fscontext** option is use by SELinux as discussed in Chapter 17. Table 32-8 lists the options for mounting a file system. An example of CD-ROM and floppy drive entries follows. The code listing is to be read as two lines, not four, with each line starting with **/dev**.

```
/dev/hdc   /media/cdrom    auto
 pamconsole,fscontext=system_u:object_r:removable_t,ro,exec,noauto,managed  0 0
/dev/fd0   /media/floppy   auto
 pamconsole,fscontext=system_u:object_r:removable_t,exec,noauto,managed   0 0
```

Boot and Disk Check

The last two fields of an **fstab** entry consist of integer values. The first one is used by the **dump** command to determine if a file system needs to be dumped, backing up the file system. The second value is used by **fsck** to see if a file system should be checked at reboot, and in

Option	Description
`async`	Indicates that all I/O to the file system should be done asynchronously.
`auto`	Indicates that the file system can be mounted with the **-a** option. A **mount -a** command executed when the system boots, in effect, mounts file systems automatically.
`defaults`	Uses default options: **rw**, **suid**, **dev**, **exec**, **auto**, **nouser**, and **async**.
`dev`	Interprets character or block special devices on the file system.
`kudzu`	Checks that the device is installed and accessible.
`noauto`	Indicates that the file system can only be mounted explicitly. The **-a** option does not cause the file system to be mounted.
`exec`	Permits execution of binaries.
`managed`	Removable device that is managed by HAL. Options for this device have to be specified in the HAL configuration files.
`nouser`	Forbids an ordinary (that is, nonroot) user to mount the file system.
`pamconsole`	Allows any user to mount the device if directly logged, denies access to remote users (adds more security in place of the user option).
`remount`	Attempts to remount an already-mounted file system. This is commonly used to change the mount flags for a file system, especially to make a read-only file system writable.
`ro`	Mounts the file system as read-only.
`rw`	Mounts the file system as read/write.
`suid`	Allows set-user-identifier or set-group-identifier bits to take effect.
`sync`	Indicates that all I/O to the file system should be done synchronously.
`user`	Enables an ordinary user to mount the file system. Ordinary users always have the following options activated: **noexec**, **nosuid**, and **nodev**.
`nodev`	Does not interpret character or block special devices on the file system.
`noexec`	Does not allow execution of binaries on the mounted file systems.
`nosuid`	Does not allow set-user-identifier or set-group-identifier bits to take effect.

TABLE 32-8   Mount Options for File Systems

what order with other file systems. If the field has a value of 1, it indicates a boot partition, and 2 indicates other partitions. The 0 value means **fsck** needn't check the file system.

fstab Sample

A copy of an **/etc/fstab** file is shown here. Notice the first line is a comment. All comment lines begin with a **#**. The entries for the **/proc** and **/sys** file systems are special entries used by your Linux operating system for managing its processes and devices; they are not actual devices. To make an entry in the **/etc/fstab** file, you can edit the **/etc/fstab** file directly. You can use the example **/etc/fstab** file shown here as a guide to show how your entries should look. The **/proc** and **swap** partition entries are particularly critical. The third and fourth lines from the last line is really one line, beginning with **/dev/hdc**.

/etc/fstab

# <device>	<mountpoint>	<filesystemtype>	<options>	<dump>	<fsck>
/dev/hda3	/	ext3	defaults	0	1
none	/proc	proc	defaults	0	0
none	/sys	sysfs	defaults	0	0
none	/dev/pts	devpts	gid=5,mode=620	0	0
none	/dev/shm	tmpfs	defaults	0	0
/dev/hda2	swap	swap	defaults	0	0
/dev/hdc	/media/cdrom	auto			

pamconsole,fscontext=system_u:object_r:removable_t,ro,exec,noauto,managed 0 0

| /dev/fd0 | /media/floppy | auto | pamconsole,rw,exec,noauto,managed | 0 | 0 |
| /dev/hda1 | /mnt/windows | vfat | defaults | 0 | 0 |

Removable Media Defaults: CD-ROM, Floppy, Card Readers, Cameras, Etc.

Using the Hardware Abstraction Layer, HAL, with its fstab-sync tool, your system will create entries in the **fstab** file for any removable media. You will find entries already placed for any CD-ROM and floppy devices you may have. It also creates directories where these drives can be mounted. These are **/media/cdrom** for your CD-ROM, **/media/cdrecorder** for a CD-RW, and **/media/floppy** for your floppy disk. If you have several CD-ROMs or floppy drives, directories are created for them with sequential numbers. So a second CD-ROM drive will use a directory named **/media/cdrom1**.

USB card readers will use the label of the storage cards, generating a subdirectory for a card on the fly in **/media**, as well as corresponding **/etc/fstab** entry. A device name is also assigned, usually a SCSI device like **sda1** (if not already in use). All are automatically removed when you remove the card. USB and FireWire cameras and MP3 devices will also have corresponding **/media** directories and **/etc/fstab** entries. All these directories and entries, as well as device assignments, are automatically managed for you by HAL.

Partition Labels: e2label

Red Hat uses file system labels for ext2 and ext3 file systems on hard disk partitions. Thus in the **/etc/fstab** file previously shown, the first entry would use a label for its device name, as shown here. In this case, the label is the slash, **/**, indicating the root partition. You could change this device's label with **e2label**, but be sure to also change the **/etc/fstab** entry for it.

```
LABEL=/     /     ext3    defaults    0    1
```

For ext2 and ext3 partitions, you can change or add a label with the **e2label** tool or **tune2fs** with the **-L** option. Specify the device and the label name. If you change a label, be sure to change corresponding entries in the **/etc/fstab** file. Just use **e2label** with the device name to find out what the current label is. In the next example, the user changes the label of the **/dev/hda3** device to **TURTLE**:

```
e2label /dev/hda3  TURTLE
```

Windows Partitions

You can mount MS-DOS; Windows 95/98/ME; or Windows XP, NT, and 2000 partitions used by your Windows operating system onto your Linux file structure, just as you would mount any Linux file system. You have to specify the file type of **vfat** for Windows 95/98/ ME, and **msdos** for MS-DOS. Windows XP, NT, and 2000 use the **ntfs** file type. You may find it convenient to have your Windows partitions automatically mounted when you start up your Linux system. To do this, you need to put an entry for your Windows partitions in your **/etc/fstab** file and give it the **defaults** option, or be sure to include an **auto** option. You make an entry for each Windows partition you want to mount, and then specify the device name for that partition, followed by the directory in which you want to mount it. The **/mnt/windows** directory would be a logical choice (be sure the **windows** directory has already been created in **/mnt**). The next example shows a standard Windows partition entry for an **/etc/fstab** file. Notice the last entry in the **/etc/fstab** file example is an entry for mounting a Windows partition.

```
/dev/hda1 /mnt/windows vfat defaults 0 0
```

For Windows XP, NT, and 2000, you would specify the **ntfs** type. Be sure to have already downloaded and installed the NTFS kernel module (see Chapter 4).

```
/dev/hda2 /mnt/windows ntfs defaults 0 0
```

TIP *Linux kernel systems currently can only reliably mount **ntfs** file systems (Windows NT, Windows 2000, and Windows XP) as read-only. They have limited write capability for these partitions. Support is provided using the ntfs kernel module. This module is not included with the Fedora Core 4 kernel distribution. To obtain NTFS support, you will have to compile the module and load it (download from either **rpm.livna.org/fedora** or the Linux-NTFS Project at **linux-ntfs.sourceforge.net**).*

Linux Kernel Interfaces

Your **/etc/fstab** file may also have entries for two special kernel interface file systems, **devpts** and **tmpfs**. Both provide kernel interfaces that are not supported by standard devices. The **/dev/pts** entry mounts a **devpts** file system for pseudoterminals. The **/dev/shm** entry mounts the **tmpfs** file system (also known as **shmfs**) to implement Linux Virtual Memory, POSIX shared memory maintenance access. This is designed to overcome the 4GB memory limitation on current systems, extending usable memory to 64GB.

If your **/etc/fstab** file ever becomes corrupt—say, if a line gets deleted accidentally or changed—your system will boot into a maintenance mode, giving you read-only access to your partitions. To gain read/write access so that you can fix your **/etc/fstab** file, you have to remount your main partition. The following command performs such an operation:

```
# mount -n -o remount,rw /
```

noauto

File systems listed in the **/etc/fstab** file are automatically mounted whenever you boot, unless this feature is explicitly turned off with the **noauto** option. Notice that the CD-ROM and floppy disks in the sample **fstab** file earlier in this chapter have a **noauto** option. Also, if you issue a **mount -a** command, all the file systems without a **noauto** option are mounted. If you want to make the CD-ROM user-mountable, add the **user** option.

```
/dev/hdc /media/cdrom iso9660 ro,noauto,user 0 0
```

TIP *The "automatic" mounting of file systems from /etc/fstab is actually implemented by executing a* **mount** *-a command in the /etc/rc.d/rc.sysinit file that is run whenever you boot. The* **mount** *-a command mounts any file system listed in your /etc/fstab file that does not have a* **noauto** *option. The* **umount** *-a command (which is executed when you shut down your system) unmounts the file systems in /etc/fstab.*

Mounting File Systems Directly: mount and umount

You can also mount or unmount any file system using the **mount** and **umount** commands directly (notice that **umount** lacks an *n*). The mount operations discussed in the previous sections use the **mount** command to mount a file system. Normally, file systems can be mounted on hard disk partitions only by the root user, whereas CD-ROMs and floppies can be mounted by any user. Table 32-9 lists the different options for the **mount** command.

The mount Command

The **mount** command takes two arguments: the storage device through which Linux accesses the file system, and the directory in the file structure to which the new file system is attached. The *mountpoint* is the directory on your main directory tree where you want the files on the storage device attached. The *device* is a special device file that connects your system to the hardware device. The syntax for the **mount** command is as follows:

```
# mount device mountpoint
```

As noted previously, device files are located in the **/dev** directories and usually have abbreviated names ending with the number of the device. For example, **fd0** may refer to the first floppy drive attached to your system. The following example mounts a floppy disk in the first floppy drive device (**fd0**) to the **/media/floppy** directory. The mountpoint directory needs to be empty. If you already have a file system mounted there, you will receive a message that another file system is already mounted there and that the directory is busy. If you mount a file system to a directory that already has files and subdirectories in it, those will be bypassed,

Mount Option	**Description**
-f	Fakes the mounting of a file system. Use it to check if a file system can be mounted.
-v	Verbose mode. **mount** displays descriptions of the actions it is taking. Use with -f to check for any problems mounting a file system, -fv.
-w	Mounts the file system with read/write permission.
-r	Mounts the file system with read-only permission.
-n	Mounts the file system without placing an entry for it in the **mstab** file.
-t type	Specifies the type of file system to be mounted. See Table 32-7 for valid file system types.
-a	Mounts all file systems listed in **/etc/fstab**.
-o option-list	Mounts the file system using a list of options. This is a comma-separated list of options following -o. See Table 32-8 for a list of the options.

TABLE **32-9**   The mount Command

giving you access only to the files in the mounted file system. Unmounting the file system, of course, restores access to the original directory files.

```
# mount /dev/fd0 /media/floppy
```

For any partition with an entry in the **/etc/fstab** file, you can mount the partition using only the mount directory specified in its **fstab** entry; you needn't enter the device filename. The **mount** command looks up the entry for the partition in the **fstab** file, using the directory to identify the entry and, in that way, find the device name. For example, to mount the **/dev/hda1** Windows partition in the preceding example, the **mount** command only needs to know the directory it is mounted to—in this case, **/mnt/windows**.

```
# mount /mnt/windows
```

If you are unsure as to the type of file system that the floppy disk holds, you can mount it specifying the **auto** file system type with the **-t** option. Given the **auto** file system type, **mount** attempts to detect the type of file system on the floppy disk automatically.

```
# mount -t auto /dev/fd0 /media/floppy
```

The umount Command

If you want to replace one mounted file system with another, you must first explicitly unmount the one already mounted. Say you have mounted a floppy disk, and now you want to take it out and put in a new one. You must unmount that floppy disk before you can put in and mount the new one. You unmount a file system with the **umount** command. The **umount** command can take as its argument either a device name or the directory where it was mounted. Here is the syntax:

```
# umount device-or-mountpoint
```

The following example unmounts the floppy disk wherever it is mounted:

```
# umount /dev/fd0
```

Using the example where the device was mounted on the **/mydir** directory, you could use that directory to unmount the file system:

```
# umount /mydir
```

One important constraint applies to the **umount** command. You can never unmount a file system in which you are currently working. If you change to a directory within a file system that you then try to unmount, you receive an error message stating that the file system is busy. For example, suppose you mount a CD-ROM on the **/media/cdrom** directory and then change to that **/media/cdrom** directory. If you decide to change CD-ROMs, you first have to unmount the current one with the **umount** command. This will fail because you are currently in the directory in which it is mounted. You have to leave that directory before you can unmount the CD-ROM.

```
# mount /dev/hdc /media/cdrom
# cd /media/cdrom
# umount /media/cdrom
umount: /dev/hdd: device is busy
# cd /root
# umount /media/cdrom
```

---

*TIP   If other users are using a file system you are trying to unmount, you can use the **lsof** or **fuser** command to find out who they are.*

Mounting Floppy Disks

As noted previously, to access a file on a floppy disk, the disk first has to be mounted on your Linux system. The device name for your floppy drive is **fd0**, and it is located in the directory **/dev**. Entering **/dev/fd0** references your floppy drive. Notice the number **0** after **fd**. If you have more than one floppy drive, the additional drives are represented by **fd1**, **fd2**, and so on. You can mount to any directory you want. Your system creates a convenient directory to use for floppy disks, **/media/floppy**. The following example mounts the floppy disk in your floppy drive to the **/media/floppy** directory:

```
# mount /dev/fd0 /media/floppy
```

TIP   On GNOME, you can mount a floppy drive by right-clicking the desktop background to display the desktop menu and then selecting Floppy in the Disk entry. To unmount, right-click the Floppy icon and select Eject from the pop-up menu.

Remember, you are mounting a particular floppy disk, not the floppy drive. You cannot simply remove the floppy disk and put in another one. The **mount** command has attached those files to your main directory tree, and your system expects to find those files on a floppy disk in your floppy drive. If you take out the disk and put another one in, you get an error message when you try to access it.

To change disks, you must first unmount the floppy disk already in your disk drive. Then, after putting in the new disk, you must explicitly mount that new disk. To do this, use the **umount** command.

```
# umount /dev/fd0
```

For the **umount** or **mount** operations, you can specify either the directory it is mounted on or the **/dev/fd0** device.

```
# umount /media/floppy
```

You can now remove the floppy disk, put in the new one, and then mount it:

```
# mount /media/floppy
```

When you shut down your system, any disk you have mounted is automatically unmounted. You do not have to unmount it explicitly.

Mounting CD-ROMs

Remember, when you mount a CD-ROM or floppy disk, you cannot then simply remove it to put another one in the drive. You first have to unmount it, detaching the file system from the overall directory tree. In fact, the CD-ROM drive remains locked until you unmount it. Once you unmount a CD-ROM, you can then take it out and put in another one, which you then must mount before you can access it. When changing several CD-ROMs or floppy disks, you are continually mounting and unmounting them. For a CD-ROM, instead of using the

umount command, you can use the **eject** command with the device name or mountpoint, which will unmount and then eject the CD-ROM from the drive.

You can also mount CD-ROM disks to your Linux system using the **mount** command. On many distributions, the directory **/media/cdrom** has been reserved for CD-ROM file systems. You can see an entry for this in the **/etc/fstab** file presented earlier in the chapter. With such an entry, to mount a CD-ROM, all you have to do is enter the command **mount** and the directory **/media/cdrom**. You needn't specify the device name. Once it is mounted, you can access the CD-ROM through the **/media/cdrom** directory.

```
# mount /media/cdrom
```

TIP *On GNOME, CD-ROMs are automatically mounted, though you can manually mount them by right-clicking the desktop background to display the desktop menu and then selecting CD-ROM in the Disk entry. To unmount, right-click the CD-ROM icon and select Eject from the pop-up menu.*

```
# umount /media/cdrom
```

If you want to mount a CD-ROM to another directory, you have to include the device name in the **mount** command. The following example mounts the disc in your CD-ROM drive to the **/mydir** directory. The particular device name for the CD-ROM in this example is **/dev/hdc**.

```
# mount /dev/hdc /mydir
```

When you burn a CD, you may need to create a CD image file. You could access such an image file from your hard drive, mounting it as if it were another file system (even ripped images could be mounted in this way). For this, you use the **loop** option, specifying an open loop device such as **/dev/loop0**. If no loop device is indicated, **mount** will try to find an open one. The file system type is **iso9660**, a CD-ROM ISO image file type.

```
# mount -t iso9660 -o loop=/dev/loop0 image-file mount-directory
```

To mount the image file **mymusic.cdimage** to the **/mnt/mystuff** directory and make it read-only, you would use

```
# mount -t iso9660 -o ro,loop=/dev/loop0 mymusic.cdimage /mnt/mystuff
```

Once it is mounted, you can access files on the CD-ROM as you would in any directory.

TIP *You use **mkisofs** to create a CD-ROM image made up from your files or another CD-ROM.*

Mounting Hard Drive Partitions: Linux and Windows

You can mount either Linux or Windows hard drive partitions with the **mount** command. However, it is much more practical to have them mounted automatically using the **/etc/fstab** file as described previously. The Linux hard disk partitions you created during installation are already automatically mounted for you. As noted previously, to mount a Linux hard disk partition, enter the **mount** command with the device name of the partition and the directory to which you want to mount it. IDE hard drives use the prefix **hd**, and

SCSI hard drives use the prefix **sd**. The next example mounts the Linux hard disk partition on **/dev/hda4** to the directory **/mnt/mydata**:

```
# mount -t ext3 /dev/hda4 /mnt/mydata
```

You can also mount a Windows partition and directly access the files on it. As with a Linux partition, you use the **mount** command, but you also have to specify the file system type as Windows. For that, use the **-t** option, and then type **vfat** for Windows 95/98/ME (**msdos** for MS-DOS). For Windows XP, 2000, and NT, you would use **ntfs** (full read-only access with limited write access). In the next example, the user mounts the Windows hard disk partition **/dev/hda1** to the Linux file structure at directory **/mnt/windows**. The **/mnt/windows** directory is a common designation for Windows file systems, though you can mount it in any directory (such as **/mnt/dos** for MS-DOS). If you have several Windows partitions, you could create a Windows directory and then a subdirectory for each drive using the drive's label or letter, such as **/mnt/windows/a** or **/mnt/windows/mystuff**. Be sure you have already created the directory before mounting the file system.

```
# mount -t vfat /dev/hda1 /mnt/windows
```

Installing IDE CD-R/RW and DVD-R/RW Devices

With the current 2.6 kernel, which now includes SG_IO support, Linux CD-burning applications will treat CD-R/RW and DVD-R/RW drives as appropriate IDE or SCSI drives. This means that IDE CD-R/RW drives no longer have to emulate SCSI drives for them to be recognized and used by CD- or DVD-writing software. If you want to use an IDE CD-ROM or DVD-ROM in a CD-writing application—say, as just the reader to copy a CD disc—that IDE CD-ROM drive can be referenced as an IDE device, such as **/dev/hdc**. A SCSI drive would be referenced by its device name, such as **/dev/scd0**.

NOTE *Starting with Fedora Core 2, improved I/O support using SG_IO eliminates the need to have IDE CD-R and DVD-R drives emulate SCSI devices. Support is implemented directly by the kernel.*

To check that your IDE CD/DVD drives are being recognized, run **cdrecord** with the **-scanbus** option.

Creating File Systems: mkfs, mke2fs, mkswap, parted, and fdisk

Linux provides a variety of tools for creating and managing file systems, letting you add new hard disk partitions, create CD images, and format floppies. To use a new hard drive, you will have to first partition it and then create a file system on it. You can use either **parted** or **fdisk** to partition your hard drive. To create the file system on the partitions, you use the **mkfs** command, which is a front end for various file system builders. For swap partitions, you use a special tool, **mkswap**, and to create file systems on a CD-ROM, you use the **mkisofs** tool. Linux partition and file system tools are listed in Table 32-10.

fdisk

To start **fdisk**, enter **fdisk** on the command line with the device name of the hard disk you are partitioning. This brings up an interactive program you can use to create your Linux partition. Be careful using Linux **fdisk**. It can literally erase entire hard disk partitions and

Tool	Description
`fdisk`	Menu-driven program to create and delete partitions.
`cfdisk`	Screen-based interface for `fdisk`.
`parted`	GNU partition management tool.
`mkfs`	Creates a file system on a partition or floppy disk using the specified file system type. Front end to formatting utilities.
`mke2fs`	Creates an ext2 file system on a Linux partition; use the `-j` option to create an ext3 file system.
`mkfs.ext3`	Creates an ext3 file system on a Linux partition.
`mkfs.ext2`	Creates an ext2 file system on a Linux partition.
`mkfs.reiserfs`	Creates a Reiser journaling file system on a Linux partition (links to `mkreiserfs`).
`mkfs.jfs`	Creates a JFS journaling file system on a Linux partition.
`mkfs.xfs`	Creates an XFS journaling file system on a Linux partition.
`mkfs.dos`	Creates a DOS file system on a given partition.
`mkfs.vfat`	Creates a Windows 16-bit file system on a given partition (Windows 95, 98, and ME).
`mkfs.cramfs`	Creates a CRAMFS compressed flash memory file system, read-only (used for embedded devices).
`mkswap`	Tool to set up a Linux swap area on a device or in a file.
`mkdosfs`	Creates an MS-DOS file system under Linux.
`mkisofs`	Creates an ISO CD-ROM disk image.
`dumpe2fs`	Displays lower-level block information for a file system.
`gfloppy`	GNOME tool to format a floppy disk (Floppy Formatter entry on the System Tools menu).
`ext2online`	Tool to extend the size of a partition, using unused space currently available on a disk.
`hdparm`	IDE hard disk tuner, to set IDE hard disk features.
`tune2fs`	Tunes a file system, setting features such as the label, journaling, and reserved block space.

TABLE 32-10   Linux Partition and File System Creation Tools

all the data on those partitions if you are not careful. The following command invokes **fdisk** for creating partitions on the **hdb** hard drive.

```
fdisk    /dev/hdb
```

The partitions have different types that you need to specify. Linux **fdisk** is a line-oriented program. It has a set of one-character commands that you simply press. Then you may be prompted to type in certain information and press ENTER. If you run into trouble during the **fdisk** procedure, you can press Q at any time, and you will return to the previous screen without any changes having been made. No changes are actually made to your hard disk until you press W. This should be your very last command; it makes the actual changes to your hard disk and then quits **fdisk**, returning you to the installation program. Table 32-11 lists the commonly used **fdisk** commands. Perform the following steps to create a Linux partition.

When you press N to define a new partition, you will be asked if it is a primary partition. Press P to indicate that it is a primary partition. Linux supports up to four primary partitions. Enter the partition number for the partition you are creating. Enter the beginning cylinder for the partition. This is the first number in parentheses at the end of the prompt. You are then prompted to enter the last cylinder number. You can either enter the last cylinder you want for this partition or enter a size. You can enter the size as **+1000M** for 1GB, preceding the amount with a + sign. Bear in mind that the size cannot exceed your free space. You then specify the partition type. The default type for a Linux partition is 83. If you are creating a different type of partition, such as a swap partition, press T to indicate that the type you want. Enter the partition number, such as 82 for a swap partition. When you are finished, press W to write out the changes to the hard disk, and then press ENTER to continue.

parted

As an alternative to **fdisk**, you can use **parted** (**www.gnu.org/software/parted**). **parted** lets you manage hard disk partitions, create new ones, and delete old ones. Unlike **fdisk**, it also lets you resize partitions. For you to use **parted** on the partitions in a given hard drive, none of the partitions on that drive can be in use. This means that if you wish to use parted on partitions located on that same hard drive as your kernel, you have to boot your system in rescue mode and choose not to mount your system files. For any other hard drives, you only need to unmount their partitions and turn your swap space off with the **swapoff** command. You can then start **parted** with the **parted** command and the device name of the hard disk you want to work on. The following example starts **parted** for the hard disk **/dev/hda**.

```
parted /dev/hda
```

You use the **print** command to list all your partitions. The partition number for each partition will be listed in the first column under the Minor heading. The Start and End columns list the beginning and end positions that the partition uses on the hard drive. The

TABLE 32-11
Commonly Used
fdisk Commands

Command	Action
a	Toggles a bootable flag
l	Lists known partition types
m	Lists commands
n	Adds a new partition
p	Prints the partition table
q	Quits without saving changes
t	Changes a partition's system ID
w	Writes table to disk and exit

numbers are in megabytes, starting from the first megabyte to the total available. To create a new partition, use the **mkpart** command with either **primary** or **extended**, the file system type, and the beginning and end positions. You can create up to three primary partitions and one extended partition (or four primary partitions if there is no extended partition). The extended partition can, in turn, have several logical partitions. Once you have created the partition, you can later use **mkfs** to format it with a file system. To remove a partition, use the **rm** command and the partition number. To resize a partition, use the **resize** command with the partition number and the beginning and end positions. You can even move a partition using the **move** command. The **help** command lists all commands.

mkfs

Once you create your partition, you have to create a file system on it. To do this, use the **mkfs** command to build the Linux file system and pass the name of the hard disk partition as a parameter. You must specify its full pathname with the **mkfs** command. Table 32-12 lists the options for the **mkfs** command. For example, the second partition on the first hard drive has the device name **/dev/hdb1**. You can now mount your new hard disk partition, attaching it to your file structure. The next example formats that partition:

```
# mkfs -t ext3 /dev/hdb1
```

The **mkfs** command is really just a front end for several different file system builders. A *file system builder* performs the actual task of creating a file system. Fedora Core 4 supports various file system builders, including several journaling file systems and Windows file systems. The name of a file system builder has the prefix **mkfs** and a suffix for the name of the type of file system. For example, the file system builder for the ext3 file system is **mkfs .ext3**. For Reiser file systems, it is **mkfs.reiserfs**, and for Windows 16-bit file systems (95, 98, ME), it is **mkfs.vfat**. Some of these file builders are just other names for traditional file system creation tools. For example, the **mkfs.ext2** file builder it just another name for the **mke2fs** ext2 file system creation tool, and **mkfs.msdos** is the **mkdosfs** command. As

Option	Description
Blocks	Number of blocks for the file system. There are 1,440 blocks for a 1.44MB floppy disk.
-t *file-system-type*	Specifies the type of file system to format. The default is the standard Linux file system type, ext3.
file-system-options	Options for the type of file system specified. Listed before the device name, but after the file system type.
-V	Verbose mode. Displays description of each action **mkfs** takes.
-v	Instructs the file system builder program that **mkfs** invokes to show actions it takes.
-c	Checks a partition for bad blocks before formatting it (may take some time).
-l *filename*	Reads a list of bad blocks.

TABLE **32-12**   The **mkfs** Options

ext3 is an extension of ext2, **mkfs.ext3** simply invokes **mke2fs**, the tool for creating ext2 and ext3 file systems, and directs it to create an ext3 file system (using the **-j** option). Any of the file builders can be used directly to create a file system of that type. Options are listed before the device name. The next example is equivalent to the preceding one, creating an ext3 file system on the **hdb1** device.

```
mkfs.ext3 /dev/hdb1
```

The syntax for the **mkfs** command is as follows. You can add options for a particular file system after the type and before the device. The block size is used for file builders that do not detect the disk size.

```
mkfs options [-t type] file-sysoptions device size
```

---

*TIP Once you have formatted your disk, you can label it with the **e2label** command as described earlier in the chapter.*

The same procedure works for floppy disks. In this case, the **mkfs** command takes as its argument the device name. It uses the ext2 file system (the default for **mkfs**), because a floppy is too small to support a journaling file system.

```
# mkfs /dev/fd0
```

TIP On the desktop, you can use the Floppy Formatter tool listed in the System Tools menu to format your floppy disks. The formatter enables you to choose an MS-DOS or Linux file system type.

mkswap

If you want to create a swap partition, you first use **fdisk** or **parted** to create the partition, if it does not already exist, and then you use the **mkswap** command to format it as a swap partition. **mkswap** formats the entire partition unless otherwise instructed. It takes as its argument the device name for the swap partition.

```
mkswap /dev/hdb2
```

You then need to create an entry for it in the **/etc/fstab** file so that it will be automatically mounted when your system boots.

CD-ROM and DVD-ROM Recording

Recording data to CD-ROM discs on Linux involves creating a CD image file of the CD-ROM, and then writing that image file to a CD-R or CD-RW disc in your CD-R/RW drive. With the **mkisofs** command, you can create a CD image file, which you can then write to a CD-R/RW write device. Once you create your CD image file, you can write it to a CD-write device, using the **cdrecord** or **cdwrite** application. The **cdrecord** application is a more powerful application with many options. You can also use GNOME and KDE CD recording applications such as KOnCD and GNOME Toaster to create your CDs easily. Most are front ends to the **mkisofs** and **cdrecord** tools. To record DVD discs on DVD writers, you can use **cdrecord** for DVD-R/RW drives and the dvd+rw tools for DVD+RW/R drives. If you want to record CD-ROMs on a DVD writer, you can just use **cdrecord**.

The **cdrecord** application currently works only on DVD-R/RW drives; it is part of the dvdrtools package. If you want to use DVD+RW/R drives, you would use the dvd+rw tools such as **growisofs** and **dvd+rw-format**. Some dvd+rw tools are in the dvd+rw-tools package. Check the DVD+RW tools Web site for more information, **http://fy.chalmers. se/~appro/linux/DVD+RW**.

mkisofs

To create a CD image, you first select the files you want on your CD. Then you can use **mkisofs** to create an ISO CD image of them.

mkisofs Options

You may need to include several important options with **mkisofs** to create a data CD properly. The **-o** option is used to specify the name of the CD image file. This can be any name you want to give it. The **-R** option specifies RockRidge CD protocols, and the **-J** option provides for long Windows 95/98/ME or XP names. The **-r** option, in addition to the RockRidge protocols (**-R**), sets standard global permissions for your files, such as read access for all users and no write access because the CD-ROM is read-only. The **-T** option creates translation tables for filenames for use on systems that are not RockRidge compliant. The **-U** option provides for relaxed filenames that are not standard ISO compliant, such as long filenames, those with more than one period in their name, those that begin with a period such as shell configuration files, and ones that use lowercase characters (there are also separate options for each of these features if you just want to use a few of them). Most RPM and source code package names fall in this category. The **-iso-level** option lets you remove ISO restrictions such as the length of a filename. The **-V** option sets the volume label (name) for the CD. Finally, the **-v** option displays the progress of the image creation.

Disk Image Creation

The last argument is the directory that contains the files for which you want to make the CD image. For this, you can specify a directory. For example, if you are creating a CD-ROM to contain the data files in the **mydocs** directory, you would specify that directory. This top directory will not be included, just the files and subdirectories in it. You can also change to that directory and then use . to indicate the current directory.

If you were creating a simple CD to use on Linux, you would use **mkisofs** to first create the CD image. Here the verbose option will show the creation progress, and the **-V** option lets you specify the CD label. A CD image called **songs.iso** is created using the file located in the **newsongs** directory:

```
mkisofs -v -V "Goodsongs" -o moresongs.iso  newsongs
```

If you also wanted to use the CD on a Windows system, you would add the **-r** (RockRidge with standard global file access) and **-J** (Joliet) options:

```
mkisofs -v -r -J -V "Goodsongs" -o moresongs.iso  newsongs
```

You need to include certain options if you are using filenames that are not ISO compliant, such as ones with more than 31 characters or ones that use lowercase characters. The **-U** option lets you use completely unrestricted filenames, whereas certain options like **-L** for the unrestricted length will release specific restrictions only. The following example creates a CD image called **mydocuments.iso** using the files and subdirectories located in the **mydocs** directory and labels the CD image with the name "Greatdocs":

```
mkisofs -v -r -T -J -U -V "Greatdocs" -o mydocuments.iso   mydocs
```

Mounting Disk Images

Once you have created your CD image, you can check to see if it is correct by mounting it as a file system on your Linux system. In effect, to test the CD image, you mount it to a directory and then access it as if it were simply another file system. Mounting a CD image requires the use of a loop device. Specify the loop device with the **loop** option as shown in the next example. Here **mydocuments.iso** is mounted to the **/media/cdrom** directory as a file system of type **iso9660**. Be sure to unmount it when you finish.

```
mount -t iso9660 -o ro,loop=/dev/loop0 mydocuments.iso /media/cdrom
```

Bootable CD-ROMs

If you are creating a bootable CD-ROM, you need to indicate the boot image file to use and the boot catalog. With the **-c** option, you specify the boot catalog. With the **-b** option, you specify the boot image. The *boot image* is a boot disk image, like that used to start up an installation procedure. For example, on the Fedora Core CD-ROM, the boot image is **isolinux/ isolinux.bin**, and the boot catalog is **isolinux/boot.cat** (you can also use **images/boot.img** and **boot.cat**). Copy those files to your hard disk. The following example creates a bootable CD-ROM image using Fedora Core 4 distribution files located on the CD-ROM drive.

```
mkisofs -o rd8-0.iso -b isolinux/isolinux.bin -c isolinux/boot.cat \
  -no-emul-boot -boot-load-size 4 -boot-info-table \
  -v -r -R -T -J -V "Fed4"  /media/cdrom
```

cdrecord

Once **mkisofs** has created the CD image file, you can use **cdrecord** or **cdwrite** to write it to a CD write disc. If you have more than one CD-writer device, you should specify the CD-R/RW drive to use by indicating its device name. In this example, the device is an IDE CD-R located at **/dev/hdc**. The **dev=** option is used to indicate this drive. The final argument for **cdrecord** is the name of the CD image file. **cdrecord** works the same way on DVD-R/ RW writers.

```
cdrecord  dev=/dev/hdc  mydocuments.iso
```

In this example, a SCSI rewritable CD-RW device with the device **/dev/scd0** is used.

```
cdrecord  dev=/dev/scd0  mydocuments.iso
```

If you are creating an audio CD, use the **-audio** option, as shown here. This option uses the CD-DA audio format:

```
cdrecord  dev=/dev/hdc -audio moresongs.iso
```

TIP   *The **dummy** option for **cdrecord** lets you test the CD writing operation for a given image.*

dvd+rw Tools

The primary dvd+rw tool is **growisofs**, with which you create DVD+RW/R disks. Two other minor supporting tools are also included, a formatter, dvd+rw-format, and a compatibility tool, dvd+rw-booktype. See the dvd+rw-tools page in **/usr/share/doc** for detailed instructions.

The **growisofs** tool functions like the **mkisofs** tool, except that it writes directly to the DVD+RW/R disc, rather than to an image. It has the same options as **mkisofs**, with a few exceptions, and is actually a front end to the **mkisofs** command. There is, of course, no **-o** option for specifying a disk image. You specify the DVD device instead. For example, to write the contents of the **newsongs** directory to a DVD+RW disc, you would use **growisofs** directly.

```
growisofs -v -V "Goodsongs" -Z /dev/hdc  newsongs
```

The device is specified by its name, usually **/dev/scd0** for the first SCSII device or **/dev/hdc** for the first secondary IDE drive. Recall that IDE DVD writers are configured as SCSI devices when your system boots up. **growisofs** provides a special **-Z** option for burning an initial session. For multisessions (DVD-RW), you can use the **mkisofs -M** option. If you want to reuse a DVD-RW disc, just overwrite it. You do not have to reformat it.

To burn an ISO image file to the disc, use the **-Z** option and assign the ISO image to the device.

```
growisofs -v -V "Goodsongs" -Z /dev/hdc=moresongs.iso
```

Though **growisofs** will automatically format new DVD+RW discs, the dvd+rw tools also include the dvd+rw-format tool for explicitly performing formats only. You use the dvd+rw-format tool only to explicitly format new DVD+RW (read/write) discs, preparing them for writing. This is done only once, and only for DVD+RW discs that have never been used before. DVD+R discs do not need any formatting.

The dvd+rw-booktype tool sets the compatibility setting for older DVD-ROM readers that may not be able to read DVD+RW/R discs.

CHAPTER

RAID and LVM

With the onset of cheap, efficient, and very large hard drives, even the most professional systems employ several hard drives. The use of multiple hard drives opens up opportunities for ensuring storage reliability as well as more easily organizing access to your hard disks. Linux provides two methods for better managing your hard disks: Redundant Arrays of Independent Disks (RAID) and Logical Volume Management (LVM). RAID is a way of storing the same data in different places on multiple hard disks. These multiple hard drives are treated as a single hard drive. They include recovery information that allows you to restore your files should one of the drives fail. LVM is a method for organizing all your hard disks into logical volumes, letting you pool the storage capabilities of several hard disks into an single logical volume. Your system then sees one large storage device, and you do not have to micromanage each underlying hard disk and its partitions.

Enabling RAID and LVM in the Kernel

Fedora Core 4 provides methods for creating, installing, and configuring RAID and LVM devices during the Linux installation process. If, instead, you wish to add these devices later, you need to first enable support for RAID in the kernel. RAID is not enabled by default unless you installed RAID devices during installation. As discussed in Chapters 34 and 35, you need to configure kernel modules, in this case, modules for RAID and LVM devices. During kernel configuration, select Multi-Device Support (RAID and LVM) from the Linux Kernel Configuration window. You can then choose to enable support for RAID and LVM, either as modules or as a built-in kernel feature. (If you make them parts of the kernel, you will have to rebuild the entire kernel.) For RAID devices, you can choose the type of Linux software RAID devices you want to install.

Configuring RAID Devices

RAID is a method of storing data across several disks to provide greater performance and redundancy. In effect, you can have several hard disks treated as just one hard disk by your operating system. RAID then efficiently stores and retrieves data across all these disks, instead of having the operating system access each one as a separate file system. Lower-level details of storage and retrieval are no longer a concern of the operating system. This

657

allows greater flexibility in adding or removing hard disks, as well as implementing redundancy in the storage system to provide greater reliability. With RAID, you can have several hard disks that are treated as one virtual disk, where some of the disks are used as real-time mirrors, duplicating data. You can use RAID in several ways, depending upon the degree of reliability you need. When you place data on multiple disks, I/O operations can overlap in a balanced way, improving performance. Because having multiple disks increases the mean time between failures (MTBF), storing data redundantly also increases fault tolerance.

RAID can be implemented on a hardware or software level. On a hardware level, you can have hard disks connected to a RAID hardware controller, usually a special PC card. Your operating system then accesses storage through the RAID hardware controller. Alternatively, you can implement RAID as a software controller, letting a software RAID controller program manage access to hard disks treated as RAID devices. The software version lets you use IDE hard disks as RAID disks. Linux uses the MD driver, supported in the 2.6 kernel, to implement a software RAID controller. Linux software RAID supports six levels (linear, 0, 1, 4, 5, and 6), whereas hardware RAID supports many more. Hardware RAID levels, such as 7 through 10, provide combinations of greater performance and reliability.

TIP *Before you can use RAID on your system, make sure it is supported on your kernel, along with the RAID levels you want to use. If not, you will have to reconfigure and install a RAID module for the kernel. Check the Multi-Driver Support component in your kernel configuration. You can specify support for any or all of the RAID levels.*

Hardware RAID Support: dmraid

With kernel 2.6, hardware RAID devices are supported with the *dmraid* module. The dmraid module currently supports a wide range of hardware RAID devices. This module will map your system to hardware RAID devices such as those provided by Intel, Promise, and Silicon Magic, and often included on motherboards. You use your BIOS RAID configuration utility to set up your RAID devices as instructed by your hardware documentation. During a Linux installation, the RAID devices are automatically detected and the dmraid module is loaded, selecting the appropriate drivers.

With the **dmraid** command you can detect and activate RAID devices. The following command would display your RAID sets in column format, **c**.

```
dmraid -c
```

To list currently supported devices, use **dmraid** with the **-l** option.

```
dmraid -l
```

The dmraid tool is still being developed and may not work well with some RAID devices.

TIP *Keep in mind that many "hardware" RAID devices are, in effect, really software RAID (fakeraid). Though you configure them in the BIOS, the drivers operate as software, like any other drivers. In this respect they could be considered less flexible than a Linux software RAID solution, as well as depending directly on vendor support for any fixes or updates.*

Linux Software RAID Levels

Linux software RAID can be implemented at different levels, depending on whether you want organization, efficiency, redundancy, or reconstruction capability. Each capability corresponds to different RAID levels. For most levels, the size of the hard disk devices should be the same. For mirroring, RAID 1, disks of the same size are required, and for RAID 5 they are recommended. Linux software RAID supports five levels as shown in Table 33-1. (On Fedora Core, level 4 is implemented as part of level 5.)

Linear

The *linear* level lets you simply organize several hard disks into one logical hard disk, providing a pool of continuous storage. Instead of being forced to set up separate partitions on each hard drive, in effect you have only one hard drive. The storage is managed sequentially. When one hard disk fills up, the next one is used. In effect, you are *appending* one hard disk to the other. This level provides no recovery capability. If you had a hard disk RAID array containing two 80GB disks, after you used up the storage on one, you would automatically start on the next.

RAID 0: Striping

For efficiency, RAID stores data using disk *striping,* where data is organized into standardized stripes that can be stored across the RAID drives for faster access (level 0). RAID 0 also organizes your hard disks into common RAID devices but treats them like single hard disks, storing data randomly across all the disks. If you had a hard disk RAID array containing two 80GB disks, you could access them as one 160GB RAID device.

RAID 1: Mirroring

RAID level 1 implements redundancy through *mirroring.* In mirroring, the same data is written to each RAID drive. Each disk has a complete copy of all the data written, so that

RAID Level	Capability	Description
Linear	Appending	Simply treats RAID hard drives as one virtual drive with no striping, mirroring, or parity reconstruction.
0	Striping	Implements disk striping across drives with no redundancy.
1	Mirroring	Implements a high level of redundancy. Each drive is treated as a mirror for all data.
5	Distributed parity	Implements data reconstruction capability using parity information. Parity information is distributed across all drives, instead of using a separate drive as in RAID 4.
6	Distributed parity	Implements data reconstruction capability using dual distributed parity information. Dual sets of parity information are distributed across all drives. Can be considered an enhanced form of 5.
Multipath	Multiple access to devices	Supports multiple access to the same device.

TABLE 33-1 Linux Software RAID Levels

if one or more disks fail, the others still have your data. Though extremely safe, redundancy can be very inefficient and consumes a great deal of storage. For example, on a RAID array of two 80GB disk drives, one disk is used for standard storage and the other is a real-time backup. This leaves you with only 80GB for use on your system. Write operations also have to be duplicated across as many mirrored hard disks as are used by the RAID array, slowing down operations.

RAID 5 and 6: Distributed Parity

As an alternative to mirroring, data can be reconstructed using *parity information* in case of a hard drive crash. Parity information is saved instead of full duplication of the data. Parity information takes up the space equivalent of one drive, leaving most of the space on the RAID drives free for storage. RAID 5 combines both striping and parity (see RAID 4), where parity information is distributed across the hard drives, rather than in one drive dedicated to that purpose. This allows the use of the more efficient access method, striping. With both striping and parity, RAID 5 provides both fast access and recovery capability, making it the most popular RAID level used. For example, a RAID array of four 80GB hard drives would be treated as one 320GB hard drive with part of that storage (80GB) used to hold parity information, leaving 240GB free.

RAID 6 operates the same as RAID 5, but it uses dual sets of parity information for the data, providing even greater restoration capability.

RAID 4: Parity

Though it is not supported in Fedora Core due to overhead costs, RAID 4, like RAID 5, supports a more compressed form of recovery using parity information instead of mirrored data. With RAID 4, parity information is kept on a separate disk, while the others are used for data storage, much like in a linear model.

TIP *Fedora Core also allows you to create and format RAID drives during installation. At that time, you can create your RAID partitions and devices.*

Multipath

Though not actually a RAID level, Multipath allows for multiple access to the same device. Should one controller fail, another can be used to access the device. In effect, you have controller-level redundancy. Support is implemented on Fedora Core using the **mdadmd** daemon. This is started with the **mdadmd** service script.

```
start mdadmd start
```

RAID Devices and Partitions: md and fd

A RAID device is named an **md** and uses the MD driver. These devices are already defined on your Linux system in the **/etc/dev** directory, starting with **md0**: **/dev/md0** is the first RAID device, **/dev/md1** is the second, and so on. Each RAID device, in turn, uses hard disk partitions, where each partition contains an entire hard disk. These partitions are usually referred to as RAID disks, whereas a RAID device is an array of the RAID disks it uses.

When creating a RAID partition, you should set the partition type to be **fd**, instead of 83 for the standard Linux partition. The **fd** type is that used by RAID for automatic detection.

Corresponding Hard Disk Partitions

The term *device* can be confusing, because it is also used to refer to the particular hard disk partitions that make up a RAID device. In fact, a software RAID device is an array of hard disk partitions, where each partition could, but not necessarily does, take up an entire hard disk. In that case, you can think of a RAID device as consisting of a set (array) of hard disks (devices). In practice, the hard disks in your RAID configuration would normally contain several corresponding hard disk partitions, each set having the same size. Each set of corresponding partitions would make up a RAID device. So you could have several RAID devices using the same set of hard disks. This is particularly true for Linux partition configurations, where different system directories are placed in their own partitions. For example, **/boot** could be in one partition, **/home** in another, and **/** (the root) in yet another partition. To set up RAID devices so that you have separate partitions for **/boot**, **/home**, and **/** (root), you need to create three different RAID devices, say **md0** for **/boot**, **md1** for **/root**, and **md2** for the **/home**. If you have two hard disks, for example **hda** and **hdc**, each would have three partitions, **/boot**, **/home**, and **/**. The first RAID device, **md0**, would consist of the two **/boot** partitions, the one on **hda** and the one on **hdb**. Similarly, the second RAID device, **md1**, would be made up of the two root partitions, **/**, the one on **hda** and the other on **hdc**. **md3** would consist of the **/home** partitions on **hda** and **hdc** (see Figure 33-1).

When you create the partitions for a particular RAID device, it is important to make sure that each partition has the same size. For example, the **/** partition used for the **md0** device on the **hda** disk must have the same size as the corresponding **md0** partition on the **hdc** disk. So if the **md1** partition on **hda** is 20GB, then its corresponding partition on **hdc** must also be 20GB. If **md2** is 100GB on one drive, its corresponding partitions on all other drives must also be 100GB.

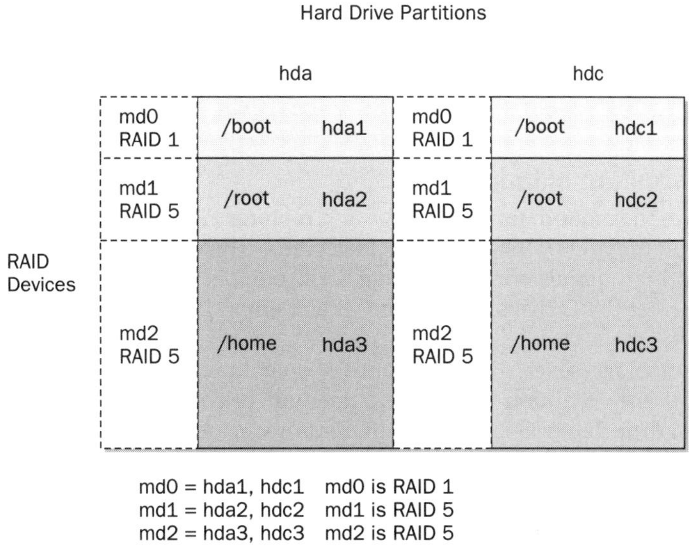

FIGURE 33-1   RAID devices

TIP *During installation, Disk Druid supports the Clone tool that lets you automatically create the corresponding partitions on other hard disks based on one already set up. In effect, you set up the RAID partitions for each RAID device on one hard disk, and then use the Clone tool to create their corresponding partitions on your other hard disks.*

Booting from a RAID Device

As part of the installation process, Fedora Core lets you create RAID devices from which you can also boot your system. Your Linux system will be configured to load RAID kernel support and automatically detect your RAID devices. The boot loader will be installed on your RAID device, meaning on all the hard disks making up that device.

Fedora Core does not support booting from RAID 5, only RAID 1. This means that if you want to use RAID 5 and still boot from RAID disks, you will need to create at least two (or more if you want) RAID devices using corresponding partitions for each device across your hard disks. One device would hold your **/boot** partition and be installed as a RAID 1 device. This RAID 1 device would be the first RAID device, **md0**, consisting of the first partition on each hard disk. The second RAID device, **md1**, could then be a RAID 5 device. It would consist of corresponding partitions on the other hard disks. Your system could then boot from the RAID 1 device but use the RAID 5 device.

If you do not create RAID disks during installation, but create them later and want to boot from them, you will have to make sure your system is configured correctly. The RAID devices need to be created with persistent superblocks. Support for the RAID devices has to be enabled in the kernel. On Fedora Core, this support is enabled as a module. Difficulties occur if you are using RAID 5 for your **/** (root) partition. This partition contains the RAID 5 module, but to access the partition, you have to already load the RAID 5 module. To work around this limitation, you can create a RAM disk in the **/boot** partition that contains the RAID 5 module. Use the `mkinitrd` command to create the RAM disk and the `--with` option to specify the module to include.

```
mkinitrd --preload raid5 --with=raid5 raid-ramdisk 2.6.9-1
```

RAID Administration: mdadm

Fedora Core uses the mdadm tool to manage and monitor RAID devices. It replaces the older raidtools used on previous versions of Red Hat Linux. The mdadm is an all-purpose tool for creating, monitoring, administering, and fixing RAID devices. You can run commands directly to create and format RAID disks. It also runs as a daemon to monitor and detect problems with the devices.

The mdadm tool has seven different modes of operation, each with its own set of options, like monitor with the `-f` option to run it as a daemon, or create with the `-l` option to set a RAID level for a disk. Table 33-2 lists the different modes of operation. Check the mdadm Man page for a detailed listing of the options for each mode.

Mode	Description
assemble	Assemble RAID array from devices.
build	Build array without per-device superblocks.
create	Build array with per-device superblocks.
grow	Change array size, as when replacing smaller devices with larger ones.
manage	Manage array devices, adding or removing disks.
misc	Specify operations on a device, such as making it read only.
monitor	Monitor arrays for changes and act on them (used for RAID 1, 4, 5, 6).

TABLE 33-2   mdadm Modes

Creating and Installing RAID Devices

If you created your RAID devices and their partitions during the installation process, you should already have working RAID devices. Your RAID devices will be configured in the **/etc/mdadm.conf** file, and the status of your RAID devices will be listed in the **/proc/mdstat** file. You can manually start or stop your RAID devices with the **raidstart** and **mdadm** commands. The **-a** option operates on all of them, though you can specify particular devices if you want.

To create a new RAID device manually for an already-installed system, follow these steps:

- Make sure that your kernel supports the RAID level you want for the device you are creating.

- If you have not already done so, create the RAID disks (partitions) you will use for your RAID device.

- Create your RAID device with the **mdadm** command in the build or create mode. The array will also be activated.

- Alternatively, you can configure your RAID device (**/dev/md**n) in the **/etc/mdadm .conf** file, specifying the RAID disks to use, and then use the **mdadm** command specifying the RAID device to create.

- Create a file system on the RAID device (**mkfs**) and then mount it.

Creating Hard Disk Partitions: fd

To add new RAID devices or to create them in the first place, you need to manually create the hard disk partitions they will use, and then configure RAID devices to use those partitions. To create a hard disk partition for use in a RAID array, use **fdisk** or **parted** and specify **fd** as the file system type. You invoke **fdisk** or **parted** with the device name of the hard disk you want to create the partition on. Be sure to specify **fd** as the partition type. The following example invokes **fdisk** for the hard disk **/dev/hdc** (the first hard disk on the secondary IDE connection):

```
fdisk /dev/hdc
```

Though technically partitions, these hard disk devices are referred to as disks in RAID configuration documentation and files.

Configuring RAID: /etc/mdadm.conf

Once you have your disks, you then need to configure them as RAID devices. RAID devices are configured in the **/etc/mdadm.conf** file, with options as shown in Table 33-3. This file will be used by the **mdadm** command in the create mode to create the RAID device. In the **/etc/mdadm.conf** file, you create both DEVICE and ARRAY entries. The DEVICE entries list the RAID devices. The ARRAY entries list the RAID arrays and their options.

```
DEVICE  /dev/hda1 /dev/hda2 /dev/hdc1
```

You can list more than one device for a DEVICE entry, as well as have separate DEVICE entries. You can also specify multiple devices using file matching symbols, like *, ?, or []. The following would specify all the partitions on the **hda** drive as RAID devices:

```
DEVICE  /dev/dha*  /dev/hdc1
```

For an **ARRAY** entry, you specify the name of the RAID device you are configuring, such as **/dev/md0** for the first RAID device. You then add configuration options such as **devices** to list the partitions that make up the array, **level** for the RAID level, and **num-devices** for the number of devices.

```
ARRAY /dev/md0   devices=/dev/hdb1,/dev/hdc1   level=5 num-devices=3
```

The preceding example configures the RAID array **/dev/md0** as a RAID 5 (**level=5**) device. Two disks (partitions) make up this RAID array, **/dev/hdb1** and **/dev/hdc1**.

Directive or Option	Description
DEVICE *devices-list*	Partitions and drives used for RAID devices.
ARRAY	ARRAY configuration section for a particular RAID device.
level=*num*	The RAID level for the RAID device, such as 0, 1, 4, 5, and –1 (linear).
devices=*disk-device-list*	The disk devices (partitions) that make up the RAID array.
num-devices=*count*	Number of RAID devices in an array. Each RAID device section must have this directive. The maximum is 12.
spare-group=*name*	Text name for a spare group, whose devices can be used for other arrays.
auto=*option*	Automatically create specified devices if they do not exist. You can create traditional nonpartitioned (**yes** or **md** option) or the newer partitionable arrays (**mdp** or **part** option). For partitionable arrays the default is 4, which you can change.
super-minor	Minor number of the array superblock, same as md device number.
uuid=*UUID-number*	UUID identifier stored in array superblock, used to identify the RAID array. Can be used to reference an array in commands.
MAILADDR	Monitor mode, mail address where alerts are sent.
PROGRAM	Monitor mode, program to run when events occur.

TABLE 33-3   mdadm.conf Options

Creating a RAID Array

You can create a RAID array either using options specified with the **mdadm** command or using configurations listed in the **/etc/mdadm.conf** file. Use of the **/etc/mdadm.conf** file is not required, though it does make RAID creation more manageable, especially for large or complex arrays. Once you have created your RAID devices, your RAID devices will be automatically activated. The following command creates a RAID array, **/dev/md0**, using two devices, **/dev/hda1** and **/dev/hdc1**, at level 5.

```
mdadm --create /dev/md0 --raid-devices=2 /dev/hda1 /dev/hdc1 --level=5
```

Each option has a corresponding short version, as shown in Table 33-4. The same command is shown here with single-letter options.

```
mdadm -C /dev/md0 -n2 /dev/hda1 /dev/hdc1 -l5
```

If you have configured your RAID devices in the **/etc/mdadm.conf** file, you then use the **mdadm** command in the create mode to create your RAID devices. **mdadm** takes as its argument the name of the RAID device, such as **/dev/md0** for the first RAID device. It then locates the entry for that device in the **/etc/mdadm.conf** file and uses that configuration information to create the RAID file system on that device. You can specify an alternative configuration file with the **-c** option, if you wish. **mdadm** operates as a kind of **mkfs** command for RAID devices, initializing the partitions and creating the RAID file systems. Any data on the partitions making up the RAID array will be erased.

```
mdadm /dev/md0
```

Creating Spare Groups

Linux Software RAID now allows RAID arrays to share their spare devices. This means that if arrays belong to the same spare group, then, should a device in one array fail, it can automatically use the spare in another array. Spare devices from any array can be used in another as needed. You set the spare group that an array belongs to with the **--spare-group** option. The mdadm monitoring mode will detect a failed device in an array and automatically replace it with a spare device from arrays in the same spare group. The first command in the next example creates a spare drive called **/dev/hdd1** for the **/dev/md0** array and labels it mygroup. In the second command, array **/dev/md1** has no spare drive but belongs to the same

mdadm --create Option	Description
-n --raid-devices	Number of RAID devices
-l --level	RAID level
-C --create	Create mode
-c --chunk	Specify chunk (stripe) size in powers of 2, default is 64KB
-x --spare-devices	Number of spare devices in the array
-z --size	Size of blocks used in devices, by default set to the smallest device if not the same size
-p --parity	Specify the parity algorithm; left-symmetric is used by default

TABLE 33-4 The **mdadm --create** Options

PART VI

spare group as array **/dev/md0**. Should a drive in **/dev/md1** fail, it can automatically use the spare device, **/dev/hdd1**, from **/dev/md0**. The following code lines are really two single lines, each beginning with **mdadm**.

```
mdadm --create /dev/md0 --raid-devices=3 /dev/hda1 /dev/hdc1 -x
     /dev/hdd1 --level=5 --spare-group=mygroup
mdadm --create /dev/md1 --raid-devices=2 /dev/hda2 /dev/hdc2 --level=5
     --spare-group=mygroup
```

Creating a File System

Once the RAID devices are activated, you can then create file systems on the RAID devices and mount those file systems. The following example creates a standard Linux file system on the **/dev/md0** device:

```
mkfs.ext3 /dev/md0
```

In the following example, the user then creates a directory called **/myraid** and mounts the RAID device there:

```
mkdir /myraid
mount /dev/md0 /myraid
```

If you plan to use your RAID device for maintaining your user directories and files, you would mount the RAID device as your **/home** partition. Such a mounting point might normally be used if you created your RAID devices when installing your system. To transfer your current home directories to a RAID device, first back them up on another partition, and then mount your RAID device, copying your home directories to it.

Managing RAID Arrays

You can manage RAID arrays with the **mdadm** manage mode operations. In this mode you can add or remove devices in arrays, as well as mark ones as failed. The **--add** option lets you add a device to an active array, essentially a hot swap operation.

```
mdadm /dev/md0 --add /dev/hdd1
```

To remove a device from an active array, you first have to mark it as failed with the **--fail** option and then remove it with **--remove**.

```
mdadm /dev/md0 --fail /dev/hdc1 --remove /dev/hdc1
```

Starting and Stopping RAID Arrays

To start an already existing RAID array, you use **mdadm** with the assemble mode (newly created arrays are automatically started). To do so directly on the command line requires that you also know what devices make up the array, listing them after the RAID array.

```
mdadm -A /dev/md0 /dev/hda1  /dev/hdc1
```

It is easier to configure your RAID arrays in the **/etc/mdadm.conf** file. With the scan option, **-s**, **mdadm** will then read array information from the **/etc/mdadm.conf** file. If you do not specify a RAID array, all arrays will be started.

```
mdadm -As /dev/md0
```

To stop a RAID array, you use the **-S** option.

```
mdadm -S /dev/md0
```

Monitoring RAID Arrays

As a daemon, **mdadm** is started and stopped using the **mdmonitor** service script in **/etc/init.d**. This will invoke **mdadm** in the monitor mode, detecting any problems that arise and logging reports as well as taking appropriate action.

```
service mdadm start
```

You can monitor devices directly by invoking **mdadm** with the monitor mode.

```
mdadm --monitor /dev/md0
```

Monitor-related options can be set in the **/etc/mdadm.conf** file. MAILADDR sets the mail address where notification of RAID events are sent. PROGRAM sets the program to use if events occur.

If you decide to change your RAID configuration or add new devices, you first have to deactivate your currently active RAID devices. To deactivate a RAID device, you use the **mdadm** command in the misc mode. Be sure to close any open files and unmount any file systems on the device first.

```
umount /dev/md0
mdadm -S /dev/md0
```

RAID Example

Figure 33-1 shows a simple RAID configuration with three RAID devices using corresponding partitions on two hard disks for **/boot**, **/** (root), and **/home** partitions. The boot partition is configured as a RAID 1 device because systems can be booted only from a RAID 1 device, not RAID 5. The other partitions are RAID 5 devices, a more commonly used RAID access method.

You could set up such a system during installation, selecting and formatting your RAID devices and their partitions using Disk Druid. The steps described here assume you have your system installed already on a standard IDE drive and are setting up RAID devices on two other IDE disk drives. You can then copy your file from your standard drive to your RAID devices.

First you create the hard disk partitions using a partition tool like **parted** or **fdisk**. Then configure the three RAID devices in the **/etc/mdadm.conf** file.

```
DEVICE  /dev/hda1 /dev/hda2 /dev/hda3 /dev/hdc1 /dev/hdc2 /dev/hdc3

ARRAY /dev/md0    devices=/dev/hda1,/dev/hdc1   level=5 num-devices=2
ARRAY /dev/md1    devices=/dev/hda2,/dev/hdc2   level=5 num-devices=2
ARRAY /dev/md2    devices=/dev/hda3,/dev/hdc3   level=5 num-devices=2
```

Then create your RAID devices with **mdadm**, which will then be automatically activated.

```
mdadm --create /dev/md0 /dev/md1 /dev/md2
```

Create your file systems on the RAID devices.

```
mkfs.ext3 md0 md1 md2
```

You can then migrate the **/boot**, **/**, and **/home** files from your current hard disk to your RAID devices. Install your boot loader on the first RAID device, **md0**, and load the root file system from the second RAID device, **md1**.

Alternatively, you can first create the arrays with the **mdadm** command and then generate the ARRAY entries for an **/etc/mdadm.conf** file from the created RAID information to later manage your arrays, adding or removing components. The following commands would create the three RAID devices in the previous example:

```
mdadm --create /dev/md0 --raid-devices=2 /dev/hda1 /dev/hdc1 --level=5
mdadm -C /dev/md2 -n3 /dev/hda2 /dev/hdc2 -l5
mdadm -C /dev/md2 -n3 /dev/hda3 /dev/hdc3 -l5
```

You can then generate the ARRAY entries for the **/etc/mdadm.conf** file directly using the following command. You will still have to edit **mdadm.conf** and add the DEVICE entries as well as the monitoring entries, like MAILADDR.

```
mdadm --detail --scan > /etc/mdadm.conf
```

Logical Volume Manager

For easier hard disk storage management, you can set up your system to use the Logical Volume Manager (LVM), creating LVM partitions that are organized into logical volumes to which free space is automatically allocated. Logical volumes provide a more flexible and powerful way of dealing with disk storage, organizing physical partitions into logical volumes in which you can easily manage disk space. Disk storage for a logical volume is treated as one pool of memory, though the volume may in fact contain several hard disk partitions spread across different hard disks. Adding a new LVM partition merely increases the pool of storage accessible to the entire system. The original LVM package was developed for kernel 2.4. The current LVM2 package is used for kernel 2.6. Check the LVM HOWTO at **tldp.org** for detailed examples.

LVM Structure

In an LVM structure, LVM physical partitions, also known as *extents*, are organized into logical groups, which are in turn used by logical volumes. In effect, you are dealing with three different levels of organization. At the lowest level, you have physical volumes. These are physical hard disk partitions that you create with partition creation tools such as **parted** or **fdisk**. The partition type can be any standard Linux partition type, such as **ext3** or **ext2**. These physical volumes are organized into logical groups, known as volume groups, that operate much like logical hard disks. You assign collections of physical volumes to different logical groups. For example, if you have physical volumes consisting of the hard disk partitions **hda2**, **hda3**, **hdb1**, **hdb2**, and **hdb3** on two hard disks, **hda** and **hdb**, you could assign some of them to one logical group and others to another logical group. The partitions making up the different logical groups can be from different physical hard drives.

For example, **hda2** and **hdb3** could belong to the logical group **turtle**, and **hda3**, **hdb2**, and **hdb3** could make up a different logical group, say **rabbit**. The logical group name could be any name you want to give it. It is much like naming a hard drive.

Once you have your logical groups, you can then create logical volumes. Logical volumes function much like hard disk partitions on a standard setup. For example, on the **turtle** group volume, you could create a **/var** logical volume, and on the **rabbit** logical group, you could create **/home** and **/projects** logical volumes. You can have several logical volumes on one logical group, just as you can have several partitions on one hard disk.

You treat the logical volumes as you would any ordinary hard disk partition. You create a file system on it with the **mkfs** command, and then you can mount the file system to use it with the **mount** command.

Storage on logical volumes is managed using what are known as extents. A logical group defines a standard size for an extent, say 4MB, and then divides each physical volume in its group into extents of that size. Logical volumes are, in turn, divided into extents of the same size, which are then mapped to those on the physical volumes.

There is one restriction and recommendation for logical volumes. The boot partition cannot be part of a logical volume. You still have to create a separate hard disk partition as your boot partition with the **/boot** mountpoint in which your kernel and all needed boot files are installed. In addition, it is recommended that you not place your root partition on a logical volume. Doing so can complicate any needed data recovery.

Creating LVMs with Disk Druid

Creating logical volumes involves several steps. First, you create physical LVM partitions, then the volume groups you place these partitions in, and then from the volume groups you create the logical volumes for which you then specify mountpoints and file system types. On Fedora Core, you can create LVM partitions during the installation process using Disk Druid. In Disk Druid, click New and select "physical volume (LVM)" for the File System Type. Create an LVM physical partition for each partition you want on your hard disks. Once you have created LVM physical partitions, you click the LVM button to create your logical volumes. You first need to assign the LVM physical partitions to volume groups. Volume groups are essentially logical hard drives. You could assign LVM physical partitions from different hard disks to the same volume group, letting the volume group span different hard drives. Once the volume groups are created, you are ready to create your logical volumes. You can create several logical volumes within each group. The logical volumes function like partitions. You will have to specify a file system type and mountpoint for each logical volume you create.

system-config-lvm

The system-config-lvm tool provides a GUI interface for managing your Logical Volume Manager. With it you can obtain information about your logical and physical volumes, as well as perform simple tasks such as deleting and extending logical volumes, or migrating and removing physical volumes. You can invoke it with the Logical Volume Management entry in the Desktop System Settings menu. You can also enter **system-config-lvm** in a terminal window. system-config-lvm will display a window with three panes: one listing all your logical and physical volumes, one showing a graphical representation of a selected volume or volume group, and one that displays information about the selected volumes.

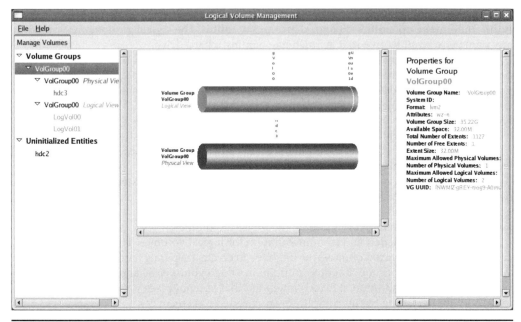

FIGURE 33-2 GUI Logical Volume Manager administration (system-config-lvm)

Figure 33-2 shows a volume group generated by the Workstation install option selected during installation. There is one Volume Group, VolGroup00 with one physical volume and two logical volumes. Selecting a physical volume displays buttons with the options to remove or migrate the volume. Selecting a logical volume shows options to remove or expand the volume.

The uninitialized entries are partitions that do not belong to any volume. The entry listed in Figure 33-2 is actually for the boot partition. Recall that the boot partition cannot belong to a volume group, it cannot be a logical volume. Be sure to leave it alone. For other uninitialized partitions, you can select their entries and initialize them to add them to a volume group.

LVM Tools

On Fedora Core, you can either create logical volumes during the installation process or later use a collection of LVM tools to manage your LVM volumes, adding new LVM physical partitions and removing current ones. You can either use LVM tools directly or use the **lvm** command to generate an interactive shell from which you can run LVM commands. There are Man pages for all the LVM commands. LVM maintains configuration information in the **/etc/lvm/lvm.conf** directory, where you can configure LVM options such as the log file or the directory for LVM devices (see the **lvm.conf** Man page for more details).

Displaying LVM Information

You can use the **pvdisplay**, **vgdisplay**, and **lvdisplay** commands to show detailed information about a physical partition, volume groups, and logical volumes. **pvscan**, **vgscan**, and **lvscan** list your physical, group, and logical volumes.

Managing LVM Physical Volumes

A physical volume can be any hard disk partition or RAID device. A RAID device is seen as a single physical volume. You can create physical volumes either from a single hard disk or from partitions on a hard disk. On very large systems with many hard disks, you would more likely use an entire hard disk for each physical volume.

To create a new physical volume, you initialize it with the **pvcreate** command with the partition's device name, as shown here:

```
pvcreate /dev/hda3
```

To initialize a physical volume on an entire hard disk, you use the hard disk device name, as shown here:

```
pvcreate /dev/hdc
```

Then use the **vgextend** command to add the partition to a logical group, in this case, **rabbit**. In effect, you are extending the size of the logical group by adding a new physical partition.

```
vgextend  rabbit  /dev/hda3
```

To remove a physical partition, first remove it from its logical volume. You may have to use the **pmove** command to move any data off the physical partition. Then use the **vgreduce** command to remove it from its logical group.

Managing LVM Groups

You can manually create a volume group using the **vgcreate** command and the name of the group along with a list of physical partitions you want in the group. The following example creates a group called **rabbit** consisting of three physical partitions, **/dev/hda3**, **/dev/hdb2**, and **/dev/hdb4**:

```
vgcreate rabbit  /dev/hda3 /dev/hdb2 /dev/hdb4
```

You can remove a volume group by first deactivating it with **vgchange -a n** and then using the **vgremove** command.

Activating Volume Groups

Whereas in a standard file system structure, you mount and unmount hard disk partitions, with an LVM structure, you activate and deactivate entire volume groups. The group volumes are accessible until you activate them with the **vgchange** command with the **-a** option. To activate a group, first reboot your system, and then enter the **vgchange** command with the **-a** option and the **y** argument to activate the logical group (an **n** argument will deactivate the group).

```
vgchange -a  y  rabbit
```

Managing LVM Logical Volumes

To create logical volumes, you use the **lvcreate** command. With the **-n** option you specify the volume's name, which functions like a hard disk partition's label. You use the **-L** option to specify the size of the volume. The following example creates a logical volume named **projects** on the **rabbit** logical group with a size of 20GB.

```
lvcreate -n projects  -L 20000M rabbit
```

You can remove a logical volume with the **lvremove** command. With **lvextend**, you can increase the size of the logical volume, and **lvreduce** will reduce its size.

LVM Example

Using the example in Figure 33-3, the steps involved in creating and accessing logical volumes are described in the following commands. First use a partition creation tool like **fdisk** or **parted** to create the physical partitions on the hard disks **hda** and **hdb**. In this example, you create the partitions **hda1**, **hda2**, **hda3**, **hdb1**, **hdb2**, **hdb3**, and **hdb4**.

Then you initialize the physical volumes with the **pvcreate** command. The **hda1** and **hda2** partitions are reserved for the boot and root partitions and are not initialized.

```
pvcreate /dev/hda3 /dev/hdb1 /dev/hdb2
pvcreate /dev/hdb3 /dev/hdb4
```

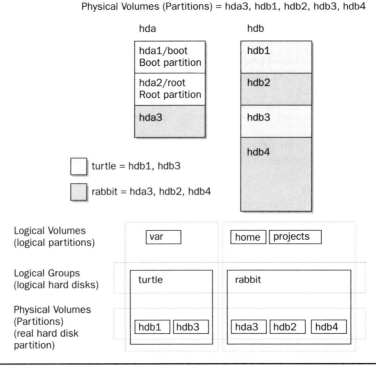

FIGURE 33-3 Logical Volume Management

You then create the logical groups you want using the **vgcreate** command. In this case there are two logical groups, **turtle** and **rabbit**. The **turtle** group uses **hdb1** and **hdb3**, and **rabbit** uses **hda3**, **hdb2**, and **hdb4**. If you create a physical volume later and want to add it to a volume group, you would use the **vgextend** command.

```
vgcreate turtle  /dev/hdb1 /dev/hdb3
vgcreate rabbit  /dev/hda3  /dev/hdb2 /dev/hdb4
```

You can now create the logical volumes in each volume group, using the **lvcreate** command.

```
lvcreate  -n var       -l 2000M     turtle
lvcreate  -n home      -l 50000M    rabbit
lvcreate  -n projects  -l 20000M    rabbit
```

Then you can activate the logical volumes. Reboot and use **vgchange** with the **-a y** option to active the logical volumes.

```
vgchange -a y turtle rabbit
```

You can now make file systems for each logical volume.

```
mkfs.ext3 var
mkfs.ext3 home
mkfs.ext3 projects
```

Then you can mount the logical volumes.

```
mount var  /var
mount home /home
mount projects /mnt/myprojects
```

Devices and Modules

All devices, such as printers, terminals, and CD-ROMs, are connected to your Linux operating system through special files called *device files*. Such a file contains all the information your operating system needs to control the specified device. This design introduces great flexibility. The operating system is independent of the specific details for managing a particular device; the specifics are all handled by the device file. The operating system simply informs the device what task it is to perform, and the device file tells it how. If you change devices, you have to change only the device file, not the whole system.

To install a device on your Linux system, you need a device file for it, software configuration such as that provided by a configuration tool, and kernel support—usually supplied by a module or support that is already compiled and built into the kernel. As noted in Chapter 32, starting with Fedora Core 3, device files are no longer handled in a static way. Instead they are now dynamically generated as needed by udev and managed by HAL. Previously a device file was created for each possible device, leading to a very large number of device files in the **/etc/dev** directory. Now, your system will detect only those devices it uses and create device files for those only, giving you a much smaller listing of device files. Both udev and HAL are hotplug systems, with udev used for creating devices and HAL designed for providing information about them, as well as managing the configuration for removable devices such as those with file systems like USB card readers and CD-ROMs.

When you add new hardware devices, Kudzu, the Red Hat Enterprise Linux and Fedora Core hardware probing tool, checks for the new hardware when your system boots. The Kudzu tool automatically detects a new device and lets you configure it. For more specialized kernel support, you may have to load a kernel module or recompile the kernel, both simple procedures (see Chapter 35). In most cases, support is already built into the kernel. Keep in mind that the directory for kernel headers used in module compilation has changed since Fedora Core 3.

Managing devices is at the same time easier but much more complex. You now have to use udev and HAL to configure devices, though much of this is now automatic. Device information is maintained in a special device file system called sysfs located at **/sys**. This is a virtual file system like **/proc** and is used to keep track of all devices supported by the kernel. Several of the resources you may need to consult and directories you may have to use are listed in Table 34-1.

Resource	Description
/etc/sysconfig/hwconf	Hardware configuration and listing for your system
/sys	The sysfs file system listing configuration information for all the devices on your system
/proc	An older process file system listing kernel information, including device information
www.kernel.org/pub/linux/docs/device-list/devices.txt	Linux device names
www.kernel.org/pub/linux/utils/kernel/hotplug/udev.html	The udev Web site
fedora.redhat.com/docs/udev	Fedora-specific udev information
/etc/udev	The udev configuration directory
www.freedesktop.org	The HAL Web site
/etc/hal	The HAL configuration directory
/usr/share/hal/fdi	The HAL device information files, for configuring HAL information support and policies

TABLE 34-1   Device Resource

Hardware Device Installation: Kudzu

Hardware devices are automatically detected by the hardware probing tool known as Kudzu, a tool that detects and configures new or changed hardware on a system. Kudzu is run when you boot to configure new hardware devices and detect removed ones. You can also run Kudzu manually. When you start Kudzu, it detects the current hardware and checks it against a database stored in **/etc/sysconfig/hwconf**. It then determines if any hardware has been added to or removed from the system. When it detects new or added hardware, Kudzu will, if needed, invoke the appropriate configuration tool for the device, such as system-config-display for video cards, or system-config-keyboard for keyboards. For simple hardware configurations like CD-ROMs, Kudzu just links the **cdrom** device symbolic link to the new device, **/dev/cdrom**.

Kudzu then updates its database in **/etc/sysconfig/hwconf**. If a removed device is detected, the **hwconf** file is updated accordingly. If the device was installed simply with a device link such as **/dev/cdrom** or **/dev/mouse**, that link is removed. In the case of network cards, alias entries like that for **eth0** will be removed.

Device Information: /sys, /proc, and /etc/sysconfig/hwconf

Kudzu maintains a complete profile of all your installed hardware devices in the **/etc/sysconfig/hwconf** file (**/etc/sysconfig** is discussed in Chapter 29). As noted previously, this file is updated by Kudzu (**kudzu**); your new hardware is added and old devices removed.

Entries define configuration variables such as a device's class (video, CD-ROM, hard drive, and so on), the bus it uses (PCI, IDE, and so on), its device name (such as **hdd** or **st0**), the drivers it uses, and a description of the device. A mouse entry is shown here:

```
class: MOUSE
bus: PSAUX
detached: 0
device: psaux
driver: generic3ps/2
desc: "Generic 3 Button Mouse (PS/2)"
```

The sysfs File System: /sys

The system file system is designed to hold detailed information about system devices. This information can be used by hotplug tools like udev to create device interfaces as they are needed. Instead of having a static and complete manual configuration for a device, the sysfs system is used to maintain configuration information about the device, which is then used as needed by the hotplugging system to created device interfaces when a device is attached to the system. More and more devices are now removable, and many are meant to be attached temporarily (cameras, for example). Instead of maintaining separate static and dynamic methods for configuring devices, Red Hat Enterprise Linux and Fedora Core make all devices structurally hotplugged.

The sysfs file system is a virtual file system that provides a hierarchical map of your kernel-supported devices such as PCI devices, buses, and block devices, as well as supporting kernel modules. The **classes** subdirectory will list all your supported devices by category, such as net and sound devices. With sysfs your system can easily determine the device file a particular device is associated with. This is very helpful for managing removable devices as well as dynamically managing and configuring devices as HAL and udev do. The sysfs file system is used by udev to dynamically generate needed device files in the **/dev** directory, as well as by HAL to manage removable device files as needed. The **/sys** file system type is sysfs. The **/sys** subdirectories organize your devices into different categories. The file system is used by **systool** to display a listing of your installed devices. The following example will list all your system devices.

```
systool
```

Like **/proc**, the **/sys** directory resides only in memory, but it is still mounted in the **/etc/ fstab** file. Fedora Core 4 will include such an entry for you.

```
none    /sys      sysfs     defaults  0       0
```

The proc File System: /proc

The **/proc** file system (see Chapter 32) is an older file system that was used to maintain information about kernel processes, including devices. It maintains special information files for your devices, though many of these are now supported by the sysfs file system. The **/proc/devices** file lists your installed character and block devices along with their major numbers. IRQs, DMAs, and I/O ports currently used for devices are listed in the **interrupts**, **dma**, and **ioports** files, respectively. Certain files list information covering several devices, such as **pci**, which lists all your PCI devices, and **sound**, which lists all your sound devices. The **sound** file lists detailed information about your sound card. Several subdirectories, such as **net**, **ide**, and **scsi**, contain information files for different devices. Certain files hold configuration information that can be changed dynamically, such as the IP packet forwarding capability and the maximum number of files. You can change these values with the sysctl tool (Kernel Tuning in the System Tools menu) or by manually editing certain files. Table 34-2 lists several device-related **/proc** files (see Chapter 32 for other entries).

udev: Device Files

Devices are now treated as *hotplugged,* meaning they can be easily attached and removed. Their configuration is dynamically detected and does not rely on manual administrative settings. The hotplug tool used to detect device files is udev, user devices. Each time your system is booted, udev will automatically detect your devices and generate device files for them in the **/etc/dev** directory. This means that the **/etc/dev** directory and its files are recreated each time you boot. It is a dynamic directory, no longer static. udev uses a set of rules to direct how device files are to be generated, including any corresponding symbolic links. These are located in the **/etc/udev/rules.d** file. You can find out more about udev at **www.kernel.org/pub/linux/utils/kernel/hotplug/udev.html** and **fedora .redhat.com/docs/udev**.

As part of the hotplug system, udev will automatically detect kernel devices that are added or removed from the system. When the device interface is first created, its corresponding sysfs file is located and read, determining any additional attributes such as serial numbers and device major and minor numbers that can be used to uniquely identify the device. These can be used as keys in udev rules to create the device interface. Once the device is created, it is listed in the udev database, which keeps track of currently installed devices.

If a device is added, udev is called by hotplug. It checks the sysfs file for that device for the major and minor numbers, if provided. It then uses the rules in its rules file to create the device file and any symbolic links to create the device file in **/dev**, with permissions specified for the device in the udev permissions files (**/etc/udev/permissions.d**). Once the device file is created, udev runs the programs in **/etc/dev.d**.

File	Description
/proc/devices	Lists the device drivers configured for the currently running kernel
/proc/dma	Displays the DMA channels currently used
/proc/interrupts	Displays the IRQs (interrupts) in use
/proc/ioports	Shows the I/O ports in use
/proc/pci	Lists PCI devices
/proc/asound	Lists sound devices
/proc/ide	Directory for IDE devices
/proc/net	Directory for network devices

TABLE 34-2   **proc** Device Information Files

NOTE *On Fedora Core 4, when the system starts, it invokes /sbin/udevstart, which runs udev and creates all the kernel devices making device files in the /dev directory. udevstart is first run by initrd and then again by rc.sysinit to simulate a hotplug process on system startup.*

As **/etc/dev** is now dynamic, any changes you would make manually to the **/etc/dev** directory will be lost when you reboot. This includes the creation of any symbolic links such as **/dev/cdrom** that many software applications use. Instead, such symbolic links have to be configured udev rules files located in the **/etc/udev/rules.d** directory. Default rules are already in place for symbolic links, but you can create rules to add your own.

udev Configuration

The configuration file for udev is **/etc/udev/udev.conf**. Here are set global udev options such as the location of the udev database; the defaults for device permissions, owner, and group; and the location of udev rules files. The udev tool uses the udev **rules.d** file to dynamically create your device files. Be very careful in making any changes, particularly to rules file locations. Support for all devices on your system relies on these rules. The default **udev.conf** file is shown here:

```
# udev.conf
# The main config file for udev
#
# This file can be used to override some of udev's default values
# for where it looks for files, and where it places device nodes.
#
# WARNING: changing any value can cause serious system breakage!
#

# udev_root - where in the filesystem to place the device nodes
udev_root="/dev/"

# udev_db - The name and location of the udev database
udev_db="/dev/.udev.tdb"

# udev_rules - The name and location of the udev rules file
udev_rules="/etc/udev/rules.d/"

# udev_permissions - The name and location of the udev permission file
udev_permissions="/etc/udev/permissions.d/"

# default_mode - set the default mode for all nodes that have no
#                explicit match in the permissions file
default_mode="0600"

# default_owner - set the default owner for all nodes that have no
#                 explicit match in the permissions file
default_owner="root"

# default_group - set the default group for all nodes that have no
#                 explicit match in the permissions file
default_group="root"

# udev_log - set to "yes" if you want logging, else "no"
udev_log="no"
```

The location of the device files directory is set by **udev_root** to **/dev**. This is the official device directory on Linux systems and should never be changed. The **udev_rules** file specifies where the rules files that udev uses to generate the device files are located. The **dev_log** option lets you turn logging on and off, useful for detecting errors. The **udev_permissions** option specifies the location of the permission files that hold the permissions to be applied to certain devices. Default permissions are already listed for you. In the case where a device has no permission listed in a permission file, then the defaults set by **default_mode**, **default_owner**, and **default_group** are used. These function more like fail-safes. A device permission should be set in a udev permission file.

Device Names:/etc/udev/rules.d

The name of a device file is designed to reflect the task of the device. Printer device files begin with **lp** for "line print." Because you could have more than one printer connected to your system, the particular printer device files are distinguished by two or more numbers or letters following the prefix **lp**, such as **lp0, lp1, lp2**. The same is true for terminal device files. They begin with the prefix **tty**, for "teletype," and are further distinguished by numbers or letters such as **tty0, tty1, ttyS0**, and so on. You can obtain a complete listing of the current device filenames and the devices for which they are used from the kernel.org Web site at **www.kernel.org/pub/linux/docs/device-list/devices.txt**.

With udev, device names are determined dynamically by rules listed in the udev rules files. These are located in **/etc/udev/rules.d**. The rules files that you will find in this directory are generated by your system during installation. You should never edit them. If you need to add rules of your own, you should create your own rules file. The rules files are named, beginning with a number to establish priority. They are read sequentially, with the first rules overriding any conflicting later ones. All rules files have a **.rules** extension. The primary rules file is **50-udev.rules**. Here you will find the rules for most of your system devices. Other rules files may be set up for more specialized devices like **10-rules.wacom**.

The rules files already present in the **rules.d** directory have been provided for your Fedora Core 4 distribution and are designed specifically for it. You should never modify these rules. To customize your setup, create your own separate rules files in **/etc/udev/ruled.d**. In your rules file you would normally define only symlinks, using SYMLINK fields alone, as described in the following sections. These set up symbolic links to devices, letting you access them with other device names. NAME fields are used to create the original device interface, a task usually left to udev itself.

Each line maps a device attribute to a device name, as well as specifying any symbolic names (links). Attributes are specified using keys, of which there may be more than one. If all the keys match a device, then the associated name is used for it and a device file of that name will be generated. Instead of listing a device name, a program or script may be specified instead to generate the name. This is often the case for CD-ROM devices, where the device name could be a cdrecorder, cdrom, or dvdrom.

The rules consists of a comma-separated list of fields. A field consists of a field name and its assigned valued. The udev fields are listed in Table 34-3. Check the udev Man page for detailed descriptions.

The key fields such as KERNEL support pattern matching to specify collections of devices. See the section "Filename Expansion: *, ?, [ ]" in Chapter 8 to see how these pattern matching operators work. For example, mouse* will match all devices beginning with the

Field	Description
BUS	Match the bus type of the device. (The sysfs device bus must be able to be determined by a "device" symlink.)
KERNEL	Match the kernel device name.
ID	Match the device number on the bus, for instance, the PCI bus ID.
PLACE	Match the location on the bus, such as the physical port of a USB device.
SYSFS{{filename}}	Match the sysfs device attribute, for instance, a label, vendor, USB serial number, SCSI UUID, or file system label.
PROGRAM	Use an external program to determine the device. This key is valid if the program returns successful. The string returned by the program may be additionally matched with the RESULT key.
RESULT	Match the returned string of the last PROGRAM call. This key may be used in any following rule after a PROGRAM call.
NAME	The name of the node to be created, or the name the network interface should be renamed to.
SYMLINK	The name of the symbolic link (symlink) for the device.
OWNER, GROUP, MODE	The permissions for the device. Takes priority over permissions in the udev permissions file.

TABLE 34-3 udev Rule Fields

pattern "mouse". The following field uses the KERNEL key to match on all mouse devices as listed by the kernel:

```
KERNEL="mouse*"
```

The next key will match on all printer devices numbered **lp0** through **lp9**. It uses brackets to specify a range of numbers or characters, in this case 0 through 9, **[0-9]**:

```
KERNEL="lp[0-9]*"
```

The NAME, SYMLINK, and PROGRAM fields support string substitution codes similar to the way printf codes work. Such a code is preceded by a % symbol,. The code allows several possible devices and names to be referenced in the same rule. Table 34-4 lists the supported codes.

The udev Man page provides many examples of udev rules using various fields. The **50-udev.rules** file holds rules that primarily use KERNEL keys to designate devices. The KERNEL key is followed by either a NAME field to specify the device filename or a SYMLINK field to set up a symbolic link for a device file. The following rule uses the KERNEL key to match on all mouse devices as listed by the kernel. Corresponding device names are placed in the **/dev/input** directory, and the name used is the kernel name for the device (**%k**):

```
KERNEL="mouse*",  NAME="input/%k"
```

Substitution Code	Description
%n	The kernel number of the device
%k	The kernel name for the device
%M	The kernel major number
%m	The kernel minor number
%b	The bus ID
%c	The string returned by a PROGRAM field (can't be used in a PROGRAM field)
%s {*filename*}	Content of sysfs attribute
%e	Used to generate sequentially numbered devices of the same type, such as cdrom1 or cdrom2. The %e adds the next smallest number to the device name, as in 1 or 2.
%%	Quotes the % character in case it is needed in the device name.

TABLE 34-4   udev Substitution Codes

This rule uses both a BUS key and a KERNEL key to set up device files for USB printers, whose kernel names will be used to create device files in **/dev/usb**:

```
BUS="usb", KERNEL="lp[0-9]*", NAME="usb/%k"
```

Symbolic Links

Certain device files are really symbolic links bearing common device names that are often linked to the actual device file used. A *symbolic link* is another name for a file that is used like a shortcut, referencing that file. Common devices like printer, CD-ROM, hard drive, SCSI, and sound devices, along with many others, will have corresponding symbolic links. For example, a **/dev/cdrom** symbolic link links to the actual device file used for your CD-ROM. If your CD-ROM is an IDE device, it may use the device file **hdc**. In this case, **/dev/cdrom** would be a link to **/dev/hdc**. In effect, **/dev/cdrom** is another name for **/dev/hdc**. A **/dev/modem** link file also exists for your modem. If your modem is connected to the second serial port, its device file would be **/dev/ttyS1**. In this case, **/dev/modem** would be a link to that device file. Applications can then use **/dev/modem** to access your modem, instead of having to know the actual device file used. Table 34-5 lists commonly used device links.

Symbolic links are created by udev using the SYMLINK field. The symbolic links for a device can be listed either with the same rule creating a device file or in a separate rule that will specify only a symbolic link. Rules that specify a symbolic link only will have just a SYMLINK field with no NAME field. In this case the symbolic link is kept on a list awaiting the creation of its device. This allows you to add other symbolic links for a device in other rules files. For example, you could create your own rules file with symbolic links for devices. Such a file would have rules that used just SYMLINK fields for devices. Rules with NAME fields would be still be handled by udev.

This situation can be confusing because symbolic links can be created for devices that are not yet generated. The symbolic links will be defined and held until needed, when the device is generated. This is why you have many more SYMLINK rules than NAME rules in

Link	Description
cdrom	Link to your CD-ROM device file, set in **/etc/udev/rules.d**
cdrecorder	Link to your CD-R or CD-RW device file, set in **/etc/udev/rules.d**
modem	Link to your modem device file, set in **/etc/udev/rules.d**
floppy	Link to your floppy device file, set in **/etc/udev/rules.d**
tape	Link to your tape device file, set in **/etc/udev/rules.d**
scanner	Link to your scanner device file, set in **/etc/udev/rules.d**
mouse	Link to your mouse device file, set in **/etc/udev/rules.d**
tape	Link to your tape device file, set in **/etc/udev/rules.d**

TABLE 34-5   Device Symbolic Links

udev that actually set up device files. In the case of removable devices, they will not have a device name generated until they are connected.

In the **50-rules.udev** file you will find numerous SYMLINK rules for optical devices as shown here:

```
KERNEL="scd[0-9]*",         SYMLINK="cdrom%e"
```

Program Fields and /etc/udev/scripts

Several kinds of devices use special scripts to determine the name to be used for the device. This is particularly true of CD/DVD readers or writers, for which there can be multiple devices of very different types, such as CD-ROMs, DVD-RWs, or CD-RWs. The symbolic link used can be **cdrecorder** for a CD-RW, **cdrom** for a CD-ROM, or even **dvdrom** for a DVD-ROM. To determine the correct symbolic link the **50-udev.rules** use a **PROGRAM** field to invoke a script to determine the device. Many of these programs are specialized scripts kept in the **/etc/ udev/scripts** directory, such as **check-cdrom.sh**, which determines the cdrom type. In this rule the check-cdrom script is used to see if an IDE device (hd) is DVD. The script is passed the kernel name and the DVD parameter and will return a positive value if the device is a DVD-ROM. It is then assigned a **dvd**_n_ symbolic link, as in **dvd1**. Two other keys are used in this example. The BUS key checks to see if the device is an IDE CD-ROM, and SYSFS{removable} confirms whether it is removable. The following lines are really one line:

```
KERNEL="hd[a-z]", BUS="ide", SYSFS{removable}="1",
    PROGRAM="/etc/udev/scripts/check-cdrom.sh %k DVD", SYMLINK="dvd%e"
```

You may want to test the results for some keys with the RESULT field. The following rule is used for simple CD-ROMs. The PROGRAM field invokes the **cat** command to list the name of the IDE device in the **/proc** file system. The output is tested in the RESULT field to see if it is a CD-ROM. Then a symbolic link is assigned, as in **cdrom1**. The following lines are one line:

```
KERNEL="hd[a-z]", PROGRAM="/bin/cat /proc/ide/%k/media",
    RESULT="cdrom", SYMLINK="cdrom%e"
```

The following rule is also used for simple CD-ROMs. The SYSFS field will return the name of the IDE device in the **sys** filesystem. The output is tested in the RESULT field to see if it is a CD-ROM. Then a symbolic link is assigned, as in **cdrom1**. The following lines are one line:

```
KERNEL="hd[a-z]", BUS="ide", SYSFS{removable}="1",
    RESULT="cdrom", SYMLINK="cdrom%e"
```

Writing udev Rules

Default rules for your devices are placed by udev in the **/etc/udev/rules.d/50-udev.rules** file. You should never edit this file, though you can check it to see how device naming is handled. This file will create the device files using the official kernel names. These names are often referenced directly by applications that expect to find devices with these particular names, such as **lp0** for a printer device.

If you want to create rules of your own, you should place them in a separate rules file. The NAME rules that name devices are read lexically, where the first NAME rule will take precedence over any later ones. Only the first NAME rule for a device will be used. Later NAME rules for that same device will be ignored.

Since rules are being created that are meant to replace the default rules, they would have to be run first. To do this, you would place them in a rules file that begins with a very low number, say 10. Such a rules file would be executed before the **50-udev.rules** file, which holds the default rules. Rules files are read in lexical order, with the lower numbers read first. You could create a file called **10-user.rules** in the **/etc/udev/rules.d** directory. Here you would place your own rules. Conversely, if you wanted rules that would run only if the defaults failed for some reason, you would use a rules file numbered after 50, like **90-mydefaults.rules**.

The next section describe how to create a canon-pr rule to replace the default printer rule for that printer. The new user canon-pr rule would be placed in a **10-user.rules** file to be executed before the printer rules in the **50-udev.rules** file, thereby taking precedence. The default printer rule in the **50-udev.rules** file (shown here) would not be applied to the Canon printer.

```
BUS="usb", KERNEL="lp[0-9]*", NAME="usb/%k"
```

SYMLINK Rules

In most cases, you will only need to create symbolic links for devices, using the official name. You can also create rules that just create symbolic links. However, these need to be placed before the name rules that name the devices. These SYMLINK rules are read by udev and kept until a device is named. Then all the symbolic names will be used for that device. You can have as many symbolic links for the same device as you want, meaning that you could have several SYMLINK rules for the same device. When the NAME rule for the device is encountered, the previous SYMLINK keys are simply appended.

Most standard symbolic names are already defined in the **50-udev.rules** file, such as audio for the audio device. In the following example, the device is referenced by its KERNEL key and the symbolic link is applied with the SYMLINK key. There is no NAME key to name the device:

```
KERNEL="audio0", SYMLINK="audio"
```

If you always know the name for a device, you can easily add a SYMLINK rule. For example, if you know your DVD-ROM is attached to the first secondary IDE connection (**hdc**), you can create a symbolic name of your own choosing with a SYMLINK rule. In the next example a new symbolic link, **mydvdrom**, is created for the DVD-ROM on the **/dev/hdc** device.

```
KERNEL="hdc",    SYMLINK="mydvdrom"
```

For a SYMLINK rule to be used, it must occur before a NAME rule that names the device. You should place these rules in a file that will precede the **50-udev.rules** file, such as **10-user.rules**.

Persistent Names: udevinfo

The default udev rules will provide names for your devices using the official symbolic names reserved for them, for instance, lp*n* for printer, where *n* is the number of the printer. For fixed devices, such as fixed printers, this is normally adequate. However, for removable devices, such as USB printers, that may be attached in different sequences at different times to USB ports, the names used may not refer to the same printer. For example, if you have two USB printers, an Epson and Canon, and attach the Epson first and the Canon second, the Epson will be given the name **lp0** and the Canon will have the name **lp1**. If, however, you later detach them and reattach the Canon first and the Epson second, then the Canon will have the name **lp0** and the Epson will have **lp1**. If you want the Epson to always have the same name, say **epson-pr**, and likewise the Canon, as in **canon-pr**, you would have to create your own rule for detecting these printers and giving them your own symbolic names.

The key task in creating a persistent name is to use unique information to identify the device. You then create a rule that references the device with the unique information, identifying it, and then name it with an official name, but giving it a unique symbolic name. You can then use the unique symbolic name, like **canon-pr**, to always reference just that printer and no other, when it is plugged in. In this example, unique information such as the Canon printer serial number is used to identify the Canon printer. It is next named with the official name, **lp0** or **lp1**, depending on whether another printer was plugged in first, and then it is given a unique symbolic name, **canon-pr**, which will reference that official name, whatever it may be. Keeping the official name, like **lp0**, preserves standard access to the device as used by many applications.

You use **/sys** file system information about the device to detect the correct device to reference with the symbolic link. Unique **/sys** device information such as the vendor serial number or the vendor name can be used to uniquely reference the device. To obtain this information, you need to first query the **/sys** file system. You do this with the **udevinfo** command.

First you will need to know where the device is located in the **/sys** file system. You plug in your device, which will automatically configure and name it, using the official name. For example, plugging in the USB printer will create a **/dev/lp0** device name for it. You can use this device name to find out where the USP printer information is in **/sys**. Use the **udevinfo** command with the **-q** path option to query for the **/sys** pathname, and add the **-n** option with the device's full pathname to identify the device you are searching for. The following command will display the **/sys** path for the printer with the device name **lp0**. In this case, the device is in the **class** subdirectory under **usb**. The path will assume **/sys**.

```
udevinfo -q path -n  /dev//usb/lp0
  /class/usb/lp0
```

Once you have the device's **/sys** path, you can use that path to display information about it. Use the **udevinfo** command again with the **–a** option to display all information about the device and the **–p** option to specify its path in the **/sys** file system. The listing can be extensive, so you should pipe the output to **less** or redirect it to a file.

```
udevinfo -a  -p  /sys/class/usb/lp0 | less
```

Some of the key output to look for is the BUS used and information such as the serial number, product name, or manufacturer. Look for information that would uniquely identify the device, such as serial number. Some devices will support different buses, and the information may be different for each. Be sure to use the information for that bus when setting up your keys in the udev rule.

```
BUS="usb"
SYSFS{serial}="300HCR"
SYSFS{manufacturer}="Canon"
SYSFS{idproduct}="1074"
SYSFS{product}="S330"
```

You can use much of this information in a SYSFS key in a udev rule to identify the device. The SYSFS key is used to obtain **/sys** information about a device. You use the SYSFS key with the field you want referenced placed in braces. You can then match that field to a value to reference the particular device you want. Use the = sign and a valid field value to match against. Once you know the **/sys** serial number of a device, you can use it in SYSFS keys in udev rules to uniquely reference the device. The following key checks the serial number of the devices field for the Canon printer's serial number:

```
SYSFS{serial}="300HCR"
```

A user rule can now be created for the Canon printer.

In another rules file you can add your own symbolic link using **/sys** information to uniquely identify the printer, and name the device with its official kernel name. The first two keys, BUS and SYSFS, specify the particular printer. In this case the serial number of the printer is used to uniquely identify it. The NAME key will name the printer using the official kernel name, always referenced with the **%k** code. Since this is a USB printer, its device file would be placed in the **usb** subdirectory, **usb/%k**. Then the SYMLINK key defines the unique symbolic name to use, in this case **canon-pr** in the **/dev/usb** directory.

```
BUS="usb", SYSFS{serial}="300HCR", NAME="usb/%k", SYMLINK="usb/canon-pr"
```

The rules are applied dynamically in real time. To run a new rule, simple attach your USB printer (or detach and reattach). You will see the device files automatically generated.

Permission Files

Permissions that will be given to different device files are determined by rules in the udev permission files located in the **/etc/udev/permissions.d** directory. The standard udev permission file, **50-udev.permissions**, is already listed. You should not edit this file. Instead, to modify permissions, create your own permissions file. Using a filename without a preceding number, like **myrules.permissions**, will take precedence (you could copy the

50-udeb.permissions file and start editing from there, listing only the devices you want to change). Permission files will have a **.permissions** extension. An udev permissions rule consists of four fields: name, user, group, and mode. The mode is a octal bit permission setting, the same as used for file permissions (see Chapter 30). Usually this is set to 660, owner and group read/write permission. Pattern matching is supported with the *, ?, and [] operators, just as with the rules files. The following example sets all sound devices in the sound directory to the root owner and group with read/write owner and group permission:

```
snd/*:root:root:0660
```

Some devices may have a different group; DVDs and hard disks, for instance, use the disk group.

```
dvd:root:disk:0660
hd*:root:disk:0660
```

The udev tool also supports a **$local** option for the user field, which lets a local user own the device at the time it is activated. For example, the user who connects a camera would be the user of that device.

Manual Devices

Several devices still need to be created manually, printer parallel ports, for example. Most of these devices are already configured with MAKEDEV and the **/etc/makedev.d** files. To have these devices created by udev, their names are placed in configuration files in the **/etc/udev/makedev.d** directory. The **50-udev.nodes** file contains a list of device names that udev will use MAKEDEV to manually construct when udev generates the **/dev** device directory. Here you will find entries for parallel printers like **lp0** through **lp3** (these will be in the **/dev** directory, not in the **/dev/usb** directory, which is used for USB printers).

You can, if you wish, create device file interfaces manually yourself using the **MAKEDEV** or **mknod** commands. To have them added to the **/dev** directory by udev, place them in the **/etc/udev/devices** directory; udev will copy them for you to the **/dev** directory when it generates them. For some devices, such as ISDN devices, you may have to do this. The following example makes an ISDN device using **MAKEDEV** and places it in the **/etc/udev/devices** directory.

```
/sbin/MAKEDEV -d /etc/udev/devices isdn
```

Hardware Abstraction Layer: HAL

The purpose of the Hardware Abstraction Layer (HAL) is to abstract the process of applications accessing devices. Applications should not have to know anything about a device, even the device's symbolic name. It should just have to request a device of a certain type, and then a service, like HAL, should provide what is available. Device implementation becomes hidden from applications.

HAL is an information service for devices. The HAL daemon maintains a dynamic database of connected hardware devices. This information can be used by specialized callout programs to maintain certain device configuration files. This is the case with the **/etc/fstab** file used to configure and mount storage devices. HAL will invoke the **fstab-sync** callout program that will use HAL information to dynamically change managed entries in the **fstab** file. Removable devices like CD-ROM discs or USB card readers are managed by **fstab-sync** with HAL information, telling **fstab-sync** when such disks are attached. The situation can be confusing. Callout programs perform the actual tasks, but HAL provides the device information. For example, though **fstab-sync** changes the **fstab** file, the options and mountpoints used for CD-ROM entries are specified in HAL device information files that set policies for storage management.

As noted in Chapter 32, HAL has a major impact on the **/etc/fstab** file used to manage file systems. HAL entries in the **/etc/fstab** file are denoted by the **managed** command. These entries are not static. Instead they are automatically generated by HAL when your system reboots. Any changes you make to these entries manually will not be kept. Instead you now have to use the HAL device information files to manage your removable file systems.

HAL is a software project of freedesktop.org, which specializes in open source desktop tools. Check the latest HAL specification documentation at **www.freedesktop.org** for detailed explanations of how HAL works.

The HAL Daemon and hal-device-manager

The HAL daemon, **hald**, is run as the **haldaemon** process. You can start and stop it using the **haldaemon** service script, as well as with system-config-services.

```
service haldaemon start
```

Information provided by the HAL daemon for all your devices can be displayed using the HAL device manager. This is located at **/usr/share/hal/device-manager** and is named **hal-device-manager**. To run the device manager, enter its name in any terminal window.

```
# hal-device-manager
```

When you run the manager, it will display an expandable tree of your devices arranged by category, in the left panel. The right panel will display information about the selected device. A Device pane will list the basic device information such as the vendor and the bus type. The Advanced pane will list the HAL device properties defined for this device, as described in later sections, as well as **/sys** file system paths for this device. For example, a DVD writer could have an entry for the **storage.cdrom.cdr** property that says it can write CD-R discs. A typical entry would look like this. The **int** is the type of entry, namely integer:

```
storage.cdrom.cdr    int    1  (0x1)
```

Strings will use a **string** type. The following policy mountpoint property has a string value **"cdrecorder"**:

```
storage.policy.desired_mount_point    string    cdrecorder
```

The **/sys** file system path will also be a string. It will be preceded by a linux property category. This following locates the **/sys** file system path at **/sys/block/hdc**:

```
linuxy.sysfs_path    string    /sys/block/hdc
```

HAL Configuration: /etc/hal/hald.conf, /etc/hal/fdi, and /usr/share/hal/fdi

Basic configuration for HAL is performed in the configuration files in **/etc/hal**. Here the **hal .conf** file lets you set standard global options. Information about devices and policies to manage devices are held in device information files in the **/etc/hal/fdi** and **/usr/share/hal/fdi** directories. These directories are where you would set properties such as options that are to be used for CD-ROMs in **/etc/fstab**.

The **hald.conf** file contains haldconfig directives for managing **haldaemon**. These entries are meant to be set by the operating system vendor, in this case, the Fedora Core 4 distribution. Three directives are currently set for you: `storage_media_check_enabled` (true), which checks media by default, `storage_automount_enabled_hint` (true), which will always auto-mount media by default, and `persistent_device_list` (false), which will not save the device list.

Device Information Files: fdi

HAL properties for these devices are handled by device information files (fdi) in the **/usr/share/hal/fdi** and **/etc/hal/fdi** directories. The **/usr/share/hal/fdi** directory is used for configurations provided by the distribution, in this case, Fedora Core 4, whereas **/etc/hal/fdi** is used for setting user administrative configurations. In both are listed subdirectories for the different kinds of information that HAL manages, such as **policy**, whose subdirectories have files with policies for how to manage devices. The files, known as device information files, have rules for obtaining information about devices, as well as detecting and assigning options for removable devices. The device information files have the extension **.fdi**, as in **storage-policy.fdi**. For example, the **policy** directory has two subdirectories: **10osvendor** and **30thirdpary**. **10osvendor** holds the fdi files that have policy rules for managing removable devices (**10osvendor** replaces **90defaultpolicy** in Fedora Core 3). This directory holds the **10-storage-policy.fdi** policy file used for storage devices. Here you will find the properties that specify options for removable storage devices such as CD-ROMs. The directories begin with numbers; lower numbers are read first. Unlike with udev, the last property read will override any previous property settings, so priority is given to higher-numbered directories and the fdi files they hold. This is why the default policies are in **10osvendor**, whereas the user policies, which would override the defaults, would be in a higher-numbered directory like **30user**, as are third-party policies, **20thirdpolicy**.

There are currently three device information file directories set up in the device information file directories, each for different kinds of information: **information**, **policy**, and **preprobe**.

- **Information** The **information** directory is for information about devices.
- **Policy** The **policy** directory is for setting policies such as storage policies. The default policies for a storage device are in a **10-storage-policy.fdi** file in the **policy/ 10osvendor** directory.
- **Preprobe** The **preprobe** directory handles difficult devices such as unusual drives or drive configurations, for instance, those in **preprobe/10osvendor/10-ide-drives .fdi**. This contains information needed even before the device is probed.

Within these subdirectories are still other subdirectories indicating where the device information files come from, such as **vendor**, **thirdparty**, or **user**, and their priority. Certain critical files are listed here:

- **information/10freedesktop**   Information provided by freedesktop.org
- **policy/10osvendor**   Default policies (set by system administrator and OS distribution)
- **preprobe/10osvendor**   Preprobe policies for difficult devices

Properties

Information for a device is specified with a *property* entry. Such entries consist of a key/value pair, where the key specifies the device and its attribute and the value is the value for that attribute. There are many kinds of values, such as Boolean true/false, string values such as those use to specify directory mountpoints, or integer values.

Properties are classified according to metadata, physical connection, function, and policies. Metadata provides general information about a device, such as the bus it uses, its driver, or its HAL ID. Metadata properties begin with the key info, as in info.bus. Physical properties describe physical connections, namely the buses used. The IDE, PCI, and SCSI bus information is listed in ide, pci, and scsi keys. The usb_device properties are used for the USB bus; an example is usb_device.number.

The functional properties apply to specific kinds of devices. Here you will find properties for storage devices, such as the **storage.cdrom** keys that specify if an optical device has writable capabilities. For example, the **storage.cdrom.cdr** key set to true will specify that an optical drive can write to CD-R discs. If a storage drive has no partition table, such as a CD-ROM drive, setting the **storage.no_partitions_hint** property to true will allow **fstab-sync** to maintain an entry for it in the **fstab** file.

The policies are not properties as such. They indicate how devices are to be handled. They are, in effect, the directives that callout programs will use to carry out tasks. The **storage.policy** properties are used by **fstab-sync** to generate and manage entries in the **/etc/fstab** file. One of the most important of these is the policy for **mount_option** defaults, as shown here:

```
storage.policy.default.mount_option.
```

The **mount_option** policy can take any of the mount options you would use for an **fstab** file entry, such as **noauto** or **exec** (see Chapter 32). Its value is Boolean, true or false. The following is the key for the **noauto** option as a default option for storage devices:

```
storage.policy.default.mount_option.noauto
```

For particular storage devices, you can use the **storage.policy.mount_option** key.

```
storage.policy.mount_option.noauto
```

Several of the commonly used storage policy properties are listed in Table 34-6.

Property	Description
`storage.policy.should_mount` (bool)	Whether storage device should be mounted
`storage.policy.desired_mount_point` (string)	The preferred mountpoint for the storage device, uses **mount_root** value for full path
`storage.policy.mount_option.*` (bool)	Mount options to use for specific device, where * can be any mount option, such as **noauto** or **exec**
`storage.policy.mount_filesystem` (string)	File system to use when mounting the storage device
`storage.policy.default.mount_root` (string)	The default mount root to use for a storage device's mountpoint
`storage.policy.default.mount_option.*` (bool)	Default mount options for storage devices, where * can be any mount option, such as **noauto** or **exec**

TABLE 34-6   HAL Storage Policies

Device Information File Directives

Properties are defined in directives listed in device information files. As noted, device information files have **.fdi** extensions. A directive is encased in greater and less than symbols. There are three directives:

- The merge directive will merge a new property into a device's information database.
- The append directive will append or modify a property for that device already in the database.
- The match directive will test device information values.

A directive will include a type attribute designating the type of value to be stored such as string, bool, int, and double. The **copy_property** type will copy a property. The following discussion of the **storage.fdi** file shows several examples of merge and match directives.

storage.fdi

The **10storage-policy.fdi** file in the **/usr/share/hal/fdi/policy/10osvendor** directory lists the policies for your removable storage devices. Here is where your options for optical drive (e.g., CD-ROM) entries in the **/etc/fstab** file are actually specified. The file is organized in sections beginning with standard defaults and moving to particular types of devices, such as floppy disks and CD-ROMs. Keys are used to define options, such as the **storage.policy.mount_option**, which will specify a mount option for a storage device such as a CD-ROM. The keys are organized into subcategories, such as the mount policy for a storage device, **storage .policy.mount_option**, or the bus for a storage device, as in **storage.bus**.

The **storage-policy.fdi** file begins with default properties and then lists those for specific kinds of devices. Unless redefined in a later key, the default will remain in effect. The options you will see listed for a CD-ROM are mainly those used for the default storage devices. For example, the **noauto** option is set as a default. The following sets **noauto** as a default mount option for a storage device. There are also entries for **exec** and **pamconsole**. The merge operation sets the policy option.

```
<merge key="storage.policy.default.mount_option.noauto" type="bool">true</merge>
```

The default mountpoint root directory for storage devices is set by **storage.policy .default.mount_root** to the **/media** directory.

```
<merge key="storage.policy.default.mount_root" type="string">/media</merge>
```

In the optical storage section, the optical devices are checked for using the match operation, and then CD-ROMs are given the cdrom mountpoint, and all others the cdrecorder mountpoint, **/media/cdrecorder**. The **storage.policy.desired_mount_point** key is used to specify the mountpoint. The following example shows that a DVD+RW drive will be mounted at **/media/cdrecorder**:

```
<match key="storage.cdrom.dvdplusrw" bool="true">
  <merge key="storage.policy.desired_mount_point" type="string">cdrecorder</merge>
```

The file system type for optical, floppy, and Zip drives is set to auto using the **storage.policy.mount_filesystem** key.

```
<merge key="storage.policy.mount_filesystem" type="string">auto</merge>
```

Hotpluggable hard disk partitions are mounted according to their file system type using the **volume.policy.mount_filesystem** key, which uses the volume label and drive type. The following lines are one line.

```
<merge key="volume.policy.mount_filesystem"
            type="copy_property">volume.fstype</merge>
```

The **storage.policy.should_mount** key specifies whether a kind of device should be mounted or not. These keys are set according to the bus for different devices. The following specifies that all IDE devices should be mounted. This will include IDE CD-ROMs and floppy disks:

```
<match key="storage.bus" string="ide">
<merge key="storage.policy.should_mount" type="bool">true</merge>
```

This default **should_mount** policy can be overridden by a later entry that would set the **should_mount** policy to false. This is done for fixed, nonremovable hard disks.

```
<match key="storage.hotpluggable" bool="false">
  <match key="storage.removable" bool="false">
  <merge key="storage.policy.should_mount" type="bool">false</merge>
```

HAL Callouts

Callouts are programs invoked when the device object list is modified or when a device changes. As such, callouts can be used to maintain system-wide policy (that may be specific to the particular OS) such as changing permissions on device nodes, updating the system-wide **/etc/fstab** file, or configuring the networking subsystem. There are three different kinds of callouts for devices, capabilities, and properties. *Device* callouts are run when a device is added or removed. *Capability* callouts add or remove device capabilities, and *property* callouts add or remove a device's property. In the current release, callouts are implemented using info.callout property rules, such as those in the **90-fstab-sync.fdi** file in the **10osvendor** directory, which invokes the fstab-sync callout when CD/DVD-ROMs are inserted or removed. The add and remove callout properties rules for **fstab-sync** are shown here:

```
<append key="info.callouts.add" type="strlist">fstab-sync</append>
<append key="info.callouts.remove" type="strlist">fstab-sync</append>
```

Currently, callout rules are placed in their own fdi files, such as **90fstab-sync.fdi** and **10hal_lpadmin.fdi**.

In earlier versions of HAL, special callout files were placed each in their own directories in **/etc/hal**. Such files had the extension **.hal** and could be binary or shell scripts.

D-BUS: org.freedesktop.Hal.Manager

HAL makes devices easily available to desktops and applications using a D-BUS, device bus, structure. Devices are managed as objects that applications can easily access. The D-BUS service is provided by the HAL daemon, **haldaemon**. Interaction with the device object is provided by the org.freedesktop.HAL service, which is managed by **/org/freedesktop/HAL/ Manager**. The Manager references the device with a UDI, User Device Identifier.

Creating Device Files Manually

Although with udev, device files are now automatically generated, it is possible to create your own using either the **MAKEDEV** or **mknod** commands. Linux implements two types of devices: block and character. A *block device,* such as a hard disk, transmits data a block at a time. A *character device,* such as a printer or modem, transmits data one character at a time, or rather as a continuous stream of data, not as separate blocks. Device driver files for character devices have a *c* as the first character in the permissions segment displayed by the **ls** command. Device driver files for block devices have a *b*. In the next example, **lp0** (the printer) is a character device and **hda1** (the hard disk) is a block device:

```
# ls -l hda1 lp0
brw-rw---- 1 root disk 3, 1 Jan 30 02:04 hda1
crw-rw---- 1 root lp   6, 0 Jan 30 02:04 lp0
```

Device Types

The device type can be either *b, c, p,* or *u.* As already mentioned, the *b* indicates a block device, and *c* is for a character device. The *u* is for an unbuffered character device, and the *p* is for a FIFO (first in, first out) device. Devices of the same type often have the same name; for example, serial interfaces all have the name **ttyS**. Devices of the same type are then uniquely identified by a number attached to the name. This number has two components: the major number and the minor number. Devices may have the same major number, but if so, the minor number is always different. This major and minor structure is designed to deal with situations in which several devices may be dependent on one larger device, such as several modems connected to the same I/O card. All the modems would have the same major number that references the card, but each modem would have a unique minor number. Both the minor and major numbers are required for block and character devices (*b*, *c*, and *u*). They are not used for FIFO devices, however.

Valid device names along with their major and minor numbers are listed in the **devices .txt** file located in the **/Documentation** directory for the kernel source code, **/usr/src/linux-***ver*/**Documentation**. When you create a device, you use the major and minor numbers as well as the device name prefix for the particular kind of device you are creating. Most of these devices are already created for you and are listed in the **/etc/dev** directory.

MAKEDEV

You use **MAKEDEV** to create device files. **MAKEDEV** uses device configuration files located in the **/etc/makedev.d** directory to determine device options like the major or minor number of the device or any symbolic links that should be created for it. For example, the **/etc/ makedev.d/sound** file lists sound devices. A **MAKEDEV** configuration file can have three different kinds of records, each beginning with a different operator:

- **b or c**   Create a block (b) or character (c) device. These entries hold several options: mode (permissions), owner, group, major and minor numbers, inc, count (number of devices created), and fmt (the name of the device). The fmt option is technically a format string, which can include a format specifier for numerically incrementing names of the similar devices, such as **cdrom%d** for **cdrom0**, **cdrom1**, and so on. The inc option sets an increment.

- **l**   Creates a symbolic link for a device.

- **a**   An alias applies the commands used for one device for those of another. This lets you create a sound device, which in turn automatically creates audio, midi, and mixer devices, and so on.

In the **/etc/makedev.d/sound** file, there are numerous alias entries for sound, such as the following:

```
a   sound audio
```

A link entry will create a symbolic link called **audio0** for the audio device file.

```
l audio0 audio
```

The actual sound device file creation is configured in the **alsa** file. Sound devices use ALSA sound drivers. Here you will find numerous c entries with permission, owner, group values, etc.

With so much of the configuration handled in the **MAKEDEV** device configuration files, the command to create a device is very simple. However, bear in mind that with udev, device files cannot be created in **/dev**. This directory is automatically regenerated by udev. To have udev place your device file in **/dev** when it generates it, you place the device file you made in **/etc/udev/devices**. Use the **−d** option to specify the udev device directory. The following would create an ISDN device:

```
MAKEDEV −d /etc/udev/devices  isdn
```

mknod

Though the **MAKEDEV** command is preferable for creating device files, it can only create files for which it is configured. For devices not configured for use by **MAKEDEV**, you will have to use the **mknod** command. This is a lower-level command that requires manual configuration of all its settings. With the **mknod** command you can create a device file in the traditional manner without any of the configuration support that **MAKEDEV** provides.

The **mknod** command can create either a character- or block-type device. The **mknod** command has the following syntax:

```
mknod options device device-type major-num minor-num
```

As most devices are easily covered by **MAKEDEV** as well as automatically generated by udev, you will rarely if ever need to use **mknod**. As a simple example, creating a device file with **mknod** for a printer port is discussed here. Linux systems usually provide device files for printer ports (**lp0–2**). As an example, you can see how an additional port could be created manually with the **mknod** command. Printer devices are character devices and must be owned by the root and daemon. The permissions for printer devices are read and write for the owner and the group, 660 (see Chapter 30 for a discussion of file permissions). The major device number is set to 6, while the minor device number is set to the port number of the printer, such as 0 for LPT1 and 1 for LPT2. Once the device is created, you use **chown** to change its ownership to the **root** user, since only the administrator should control it. Change the group to **lp** with the **chgrp** command.

Most devices belong to their own groups, such as **disks** for hard disk partitions, **lp** for printers, **floppy** for floppy disks, and **tty** for terminals. In the next example, a printer device is made on a fourth parallel port, **lp3**. The **-m** option specifies the permissions—in this case, 660. The device is a character device, as indicated by the **c** argument following the device name. The major number is 6, and the minor number is 3. If you were making a device at **lp4**, the major number would still be 6, but the minor number would be 4. Once the device is made, the **chown** command then changes the ownership of the parallel printer device to **root**. For printers, be sure that a spool directory has been created for your device. If not, you need to make one. Spool directories contain files for data that varies according to the device output or input, like that for printers or scanners.

As with all manual devices, the device file has to be placed in the **/etc/udev/devices** directory; udev will later put it in **/dev**.

```
# mknod -m 660 /etc/udev/devices/lp3 c 6 3
# chown root /etc/udev/devices/lp3
# chgrp lp /etc/udev/devices/lp3
```

Installing and Managing Terminals and Modems

In Linux, several users may be logged in at the same time. Each user needs his or her own terminal through which to access the Linux system, of course. The monitor on your PC acts as a special terminal, called the *console*, but you can add other terminals through either the serial ports on your PC or a special multiport card installed on your PC. The other terminals can be stand-alone terminals or PCs using terminal emulation programs. For a detailed explanation of terminal installation, see the **Term-HOWTO** file in **/usr/share/doc/ HOWTO** or at the Linux Documentation Project site (**www.tldp.org**). A brief explanation is provided here.

Serial Ports

The serial ports on your PC are referred to as COM1, COM2, COM3, and COM4. These serial ports correspond to the terminal devices **/dev/ttyS0** through **/dev/ttyS3**. Note that several of these serial devices may already be used for other input devices such as your mouse, and for communications devices such as your modem. If you have a serial printer, one of these serial devices is already used for that. If you installed a multiport card, you have many more ports from which to choose. For each terminal you add, udev will create the appropriate character device on your Linux system. The permissions for a terminal device are normally 660. *Terminal devices* are character devices with a major number of 4 and minor numbers usually beginning at 64.

TIP   *The /dev/pts entry in the /etc/fstab file mount a **devpts** file system at /dev/pts for Unix98 Pseudo-TTYs. These pseudo-terminals are identified by devices named by number.*

mingetty, mgetty, and agetty

Terminal devices are managed by your system using the **getty** program and a set of configuration files. When your system starts, it reads a list of connected terminals in the **inittab** file and then executes an appropriate **getty** program for each one, either **mingetty**, **mgetty**, or **agetty**. Such **getty** programs set up the communication between your Linux system and a specified terminal. **mingetty** provides minimal support for virtual consoles, whereas **agetty** provides enhanced support for terminal connections. **agetty** also includes parameters for the baud rate and timeout. **mgetty** is designed for fax/modem connections, letting you configure dialing, login, and fax parameters. **mgetty** configuration files are held in the **/etc/mgetty+sendfax** directory. Modem connection information is held in the **/etc/mgetty+sendfax/mgetty.config** file. All **getty** programs can read an initial message placed in the **/etc/issue** file, which can contain special codes to provide the system name and current date and time.

termcap and inittab Files

The **/etc/inittab** file holds instructions for your system on how to manage terminal devices. A line in the **/etc/inittab** file has four basic components: an ID, a runlevel, an action, and a process. Terminal devices are identified by ID numbers, beginning with 1 for the first device. The runlevel at which the terminal operates is usually 1. The action is usually *respawn*, which means to run the process continually. The process is a call to **mingetty**, **mgetty**, or **agetty** with the terminal device name. The **/etc/termcap** file holds the specifications for different terminal types. These are the different types of terminals users could use to log in to your system. Your **/etc/termcap** file is already filled with specifications for most of the terminals currently produced. An entry in the **/etc/termcap** file consists of various names that can be used for a terminal separated by a pipe character (|) and then a series of parameter specifications, each ending in a colon. You find the name used for a specific terminal type here. You can use **more** to display your **/etc/termcap** file, and then use a search, **/**, to locate your terminal type. You can set many options for a terminal device. To change these options, use the **stty** command instead of changing configuration files directly. The **stty** command with no arguments lists the current setting of the terminal.

tset

When a user logs in, having the terminal device initialized using the **tset** command is helpful. Usually the **tset** command is placed in the user's **.bash_profile** file and is automatically executed whenever the user logs in to the system. You use the **tset** command to set the terminal type and any other options the terminal device requires. A common entry of **tset** for a **.bash_profile** file follows. The **-m dialup:** option prompts the user to enter a terminal type. The type specified here is a default type that is displayed in parentheses. The user presses ENTER to choose the default. The prompt looks like this: **TERM=(vt100)?**.

```
eval 'tset -s -Q -m dialup:?vt00'
```

Input Devices

Input devices, such as mice and keyboards, are displayed on several levels. Initial configuration is performed during installation where you select the mouse and keyboard types. You can change that configuration with your administration configuration tools, such as system-config-mouse and system-config-keyboard (Mouse and Keyboard in the System Settings menu and window). Special configurations also exist for mice and keyboard for the X Window System, and for the KDE and GNOME desktops. You select the keyboard layout and language, as well as configure the speed and display of the mouse.

PCMCIA Devices

PCMCIA devices are card readers commonly found on laptops to connect devices like modems or wireless cards, though they are becoming standard on many desktop systems as well. The same PCMCIA device can support many different kinds of devices, including network cards, modems, hard disks, and Bluetooth devices. In addition to configuring the PCMCIA card holder itself, you can also configure each particular device you may insert into it, such as a wireless card. The configurations will be similar to configurations for standard devices connected directly to your system. Check the PCMCIA-HOWTO at the **www.tldp.org** site for a detailed discussion of PCMCIA cards and their configuration.

Support for PCMCIA devices is managed like a service. Instead of being loaded directly like most device modules, support is loaded by the **pcmcia** service script, just as services like networks or servers are loaded by service scripts. Like other service scripts, the **pcmcia** script is located in the **/etc/rc.d/init.d** directory. You can manually enable or disable support using the script with the **service** command. As with any service, you can use the Service tool or **chkconfig** to configure **pcmcia** to run automatically, when your system starts, along with specifying runlevels.

```
service pcmcia start
```

Basic configuration is handled by a **pcmcia** script in the **/etc/sysconfig** directory, instead of in the **/etc** directory. Here you can set basic startup options such as PCMCIA to enable **pcmcia**, PCIC to specify the card interface controller (yenta_socket), and PCIC_OPTS to specify controller options. CORE_OPTS holds option for the pcmcia_core module, and CARDMGR_OPTS holds options for the **cardmgr** daemon. The SCHEME entry can be used to select a scheme to use.

Detailed configuration information for the different kinds of devices that you can attach to a PCMCIA device is kept in the **/etc/pcmcia** directory. Here you will find configuration files for PCMCIA wireless, ISDN, serial, SCSI and IDE hard disk, and Bluetooth devices. There are startup scripts for each, along with corresponding options files, such as **wireless** and **wireless.opts**, **ide** and **ide.opts**, and **bluetooth** and **bluetooth.conf**. Each script will hold the commands appropriate for configuring that device, like the **wfconfig** command for wireless devices, **hciattach** for Bluetooth, and **updfstab** to update partition entries for IDE and SCSI drives. The corresponding option files will hold configuration settings for the corresponding kinds of devices. The **bluetooth.opts** file holds parameters for different kinds of Bluetooth devices, whereas the **wireless.opts** file lists possible options for different wireless cards. The **shared** file holds functions used in the various startup scripts, such as **add_parts**, which will add block devices such as a partition on an IDE or SCSI hard disk PCMCIA device, invoking a **add_blkdev** function, which will check and mount the partition. Many scripts will run the **shared** script to enable these functions.

You can interchangeably add and remove PCMCIA cards as you wish. They will be recognized from a database of supported cards and configured using their appropriate startup scripts. This task is handled by the **cardmgr** daemon, which scans for insertion and removal events on the PCMCIA device, detecting an added device automatically and loading the appropriate kernel module. The **cardmgr** tool will generate a **/var/lib/pcmcia/stab** file, which will list the socket number, device class, driver, and a device number for devices that use the same driver. A **stab** entry can use the device class to determine which startup configuration script to use for that device. To determine the kernel module to use, **cardmgr** consults the **/etc/pcmcia/config** file, which holds the PCMCIA card database, listing supported cards and their associated kernel modules, driver, and resources such as IRQs to use. The corresponding **config.opts** file will specify local resources and list options for certain modules.

You can obtain information about a PCMCIA device with the **cardctl** command, as well as manually eject and insert a device. The **status**, **config**, and **ident** options will display the device's socket status and configuration, and the identification of the device. The **insert** and **eject** options will let you add and remove a device. The **cardinfo** command also provides device information.

It is not advisable to hot-swap IDE or SCSI devices. For these you should first manually shut down the device using the **cardctl** command.

```
cardctl eject
```

All PCMCIA configurations support the use of schemes that let you specify different sets of settings for your devices. For example, for an Ethernet device you could have one set of settings to use at the office and one to use at home. For the office settings, you could create an office scheme and for the home settings, a home scheme. When starting up the device, you can specify which scheme to use. You can find out the current scheme in use with the **cardctl** command and the **scheme** option with no argument. To change to a certain scheme, you supply the **scheme** option plus an argument.

```
cardctl scheme home
```

Installing Sound, Network, and Other Cards

For you to install a new card, your kernel must first be configured to support it. Support for most cards is provided in the form of modules that can be dynamically loaded into the kernel. Installing support for a card is usually a simple matter of loading a module that includes the drivers for it. For example, drivers for the Sound Blaster sound card are in the module **sb.o**. Loading this module makes your sound card accessible to Linux. Most distributions automatically detect the cards installed on your system and load the needed modules. If you change sound cards, the new card is automatically detected by Kudzu, invoking system-config-soundcard to configure it. For network cards, Kudzu invokes system-config-network to perform the configuration. You could also load modules you need manually, removing an older conflicting one. The section "Modules" later in this chapter describes this process.

Device files for most cards are already set up for you in the **/dev** directory by **udev**. For example, the device name for your sound card is **/dev/audio**. The device names for network cards are aliases for network modules instead of device files. For example, the device name for your Ethernet card begins with **eth,** with the numbering starting from **0,** as in **eth0** for the first Ethernet card on your system. An alias is used to reference the module used for that particular card; for example, a 3Com Etherlink card aliases the 3c59x network module, whose alias would be **eth0** if it is the first Ethernet card. The modules themselves are kept in the kernel's module directory located at **/lib/modules**, as described in the last section of this chapter.

Sound Devices

You can use the system-config-soundcard utility to install most sound cards on Linux. A listing of the different sound devices is provided in Table 34-7. Some sound cards may require more specialized support. For sound cards, you can tell what your current sound configuration is by listing the contents of the **/proc/asound/oss/sndstat** file. You can test your card by simply redirecting a sound file to it, as shown here:

```
cat sample.au > /dev/audio.
```

Device	Description
/dev/sndstat	Sound driver status
/dev/audio	Audio output device
/dev/dsp	Sound sampling device
/dev/mixer	Control mixer on sound card
/dev/music	High-level sequencer
/dev/sequencer	Low-level sequencer
/dev/midi	Direct MIDI port

TABLE 34-7   Sound Devices

PART VI

For the 2.4 kernel, most Linux sound drivers are developed as part of the Open Sound System (OSS) and freely distributed as OSS/Free. These are installed as part of Linux distributions. The OSS device drivers are intended to provide a uniform API for all Unix platforms, including Linux. They support Sound Blaster– and Windows Sound System–compatible sound cards (ISA and PCI). OSS is also available for a nominal fee and features configuration interfaces for device setup.

The Advanced Linux Sound Architecture (ALSA) replaces OSS in the 2.6 Linux kernel that aims to be a better alternative to OSS, while maintaining compatibility with it. ALSA provides a modular sound driver, an API, and a configuration manager. ALSA is a GNU project and is entirely free; its Web site at **www.alsa-project.org** contains extensive documentation, applications, and drivers. Currently available are the ALSA sound driver, the ALSA Kernel API, the ALSA library to support application development, and the ALSA manager to provide a configuration interface for the driver. ALSA evolved from the Linux Ultra Sound Project. The ALSA project currently supports most Creative sound cards.

The Linux Musical Instrument Digital Interface (MIDI) and Sound Pages, currently at **www.linux-sound.org**, includes links to sites for Linux MIDI and sound software.

Video and TV Devices

Device names used for TV, video, and DVD devices are listed in Table 34-8. Drivers for DVD and TV decoders have been developed. mga4linux (**marvel.sourceforge.net**) is developing video support for the Matrox Multimedia cards such as the Marvel G200. The General ATI TV and Overlay Software (GATOS) (**gatos.sourceforge.net**) has developed drivers for the currently unsupported features of ATI video cards, specifically TV features. The BTTV Driver Project has developed drivers for the Booktree video chip. Creative Labs sponsors Linux drivers for the Creative line of DVD DXR2 decoders (**opensource.creative.com**).

Device Name	Type of Device
/dev/video	Video capture interface
/dev/vfx	Video effects interface
/dev/codec	Video codec interface
/dev/vout	Video output interface
/dev/radio	AM/FM radio devices
/dev/vtx	Teletext interface chips
/dev/vbi	Data services interface

TABLE 34-8   Video Devices

Modules

The Linux kernel employs the use of modules to support different operating system features, including support for various devices such as sound and network cards. In many cases, you do have the option of implementing support for a device either as a module or by directly compiling it as a built-in kernel feature, which requires you to rebuild the kernel (see Chapter 35). A safer and more robust solution is to use modules. *Modules* are components of the Linux kernel that can be loaded as needed. To add support for a new device, you can now simply instruct a kernel to load the module for that device. In some cases, you may have to recompile only that module to provide support for your device. The use of modules has the added advantage of reducing the size of the kernel program as well as making your system more stable. The kernel can load modules in memory only as they are needed. Should a module fail, only the module stops running, and it will not affect the entire system. For example, the module for the PPP network interface used for a modem needs to be used only when you connect to an ISP.

Kernel Module Tools

The modules your system needs are usually determined during installation, according to the kind of configuration information you provided and the automatic detection performed by Kudzu. For example, if your system uses an Ethernet card whose type you specified during installation, the system loads the module for that card. You can, however, manually control what modules are to be loaded for your system. In effect, this enables you to customize your kernel whatever way you want. You can use several commands, configuration tools, and daemons to manage kernel modules. The 2.6 Linux kernel includes the Kernel Module Loader (Kmod), which has the capability to load modules automatically as they are needed. Kernel module loading support must also be enabled in the kernel, though this is usually considered part of a standard configuration. In addition, several tools enable you to load and unload modules manually, if you must. The Kernel Module Loader uses certain kernel commands to perform the task of loading or unloading modules. The **modprobe** command is a general-purpose command that calls **insmod** to load modules and **rmmod** to unload them. These commands are listed in Table 34-9. Options for particular modules, general configuration, and even specific module loading

Command	Description
`lsmod`	Lists modules currently loaded.
`insmod`	Loads a module into the kernel. Does not check for dependencies.
`rmmod`	Unloads a module currently loaded. Does not check for dependencies.
`modinfo`	Displays information about a module: **-a** (author), **-d** (description), **-p** (module parameters), **-f** (module filename), -v (module version).
`depmod`	Creates a dependency file listing all other modules on which the specified module may rely.
`modprobe`	Loads a module with any dependent modules it may also need. Uses the file of dependency listings generated by depmod: **-r** (unload a module), **-l** (list modules).

TABLE 34-9 Kernel Module Commands

can be specified in the **/etc/modprobe.conf** file. You can use this file to automatically load and configure modules. You can also specify modules to be loaded at the boot prompt or in **grub.conf** (see Chapter 29).

Module Files and Directories: /lib/modules

The filename for a module has the extension **.o**. Kernel modules reside in the **/lib/modules/** *version* directory, where *version* is the version number for your current kernel with the extension FC4. The directory for the 2.6.11.1-1369_FC4 kernel is **/lib/modules/2.6.11-1.1369_FC4**. As you install new kernels on your system, new module directories are generated for them. One method to access the directory for the current kernel is to use the **uname -r** command to generate the kernel version number. This command needs to have backquotes.

```
cd /lib/modules/`uname -r`
```

In this directory, modules for the kernel reside in the **/kernel** directory. Within the **/kernel** directory are several subdirectories, including the **/drivers** directory that holds subdirectories for modules like sound drivers or video drivers. These subdirectories serve to categorize your modules, making them easier to locate. For example, the **kernel/drivers/net** directory holds modules for your Ethernet cards, and the **kernel/drivers/sound** directory contains sound card modules.

TIP *You will notice that there are no entries for the Ethernet devices in the /dev file, such as eth0 or eth1. That is because these are really aliases for kernel modules defined in the /etc/modprobe .conf file, or devices handled by the kernel directly. They are not device files.*

Managing Modules with /etc/moprobe.conf

As noted previously, there are several commands you can use to manage modules. The **lsmod** command lists the modules currently loaded into your kernel, and **modinfo** provides information about particular modules. Though you can use the **insmod** and **rmmod** commands to load or unload modules directly, you should use only **modprobe** for these tasks. (See Table 34-9 for kernel module commands.) Often, however, a given module requires other modules to be loaded. For example, the module for the Sound Blaster sound card, **sb.o**, requires the **sound.o** module to be loaded also.

The depmod Command

Instead of manually trying to determine what modules a given module depends on, you use the **depmod** command to detect the dependencies for you. The **depmod** command generates a file that lists all the modules on which a given module depends. The **depmod** command generates a hierarchical listing, noting what modules should be loaded first and in what order. Then, to load the module, you use the **modprobe** command using that file. **modprobe** reads the file generated by **depmod** and loads any dependent modules in the correct order, along with the module you want. You need to execute **depmod** with the **-a** option once, before you ever use **modprobe**. Entering **depmod -a** creates a complete listing of all module dependencies. This command creates a file called **modules.dep** in the module directory for your current kernel version, **/lib/modules/***version*.

```
depmod -a
```

The modprobe Command

To install a module manually, you use the **modprobe** command and the module name. You can add any parameters the module may require. The following command installs the Sound Blaster sound module with the I/O, IRQ, and DMA values. **modprobe** also supports the use of the * character to enable you to use a pattern to select several modules. This example uses several values commonly used for sound cards. You would use the values recommended for your sound card on your system.

```
modprobe sb io=0x220 irq=5 dma=1
```

To discover what parameters a module takes, you can use the **modinfo** command with the **-p** option.

```
modinfo -p sb
```

You can use the **-l** option to list modules and the **-t** option to look for modules in a specified subdirectory. In the next example, the user lists all modules in the **sound** directory:

```
# modprobe -l -t sound
/lib/modules/2.6.11-1.1369_FC4/kernel/drivers/sound/sb.o
/lib/modules/2.6.11-1.1369_FC4/kernel/drivers/sound/sb_lib.o
/lib/modules/2.6.11-1.1369_FC4/kernel/drivers/sound/sound.o
/lib/modules/2.6.11-1.1369_FC4/kernel/drivers/sound/soundcore.o
```

Options for the **modprobe** command are placed in the **/etc/modprobe.conf** file. Here, you can enter configuration options, such as default directories and aliases. An alias provides a simple name for a module. For example, the following entry enables you to reference the **3c59x.o** Ethernet card module as **eth0** (Kmod automatically detects the 3Com Ethernet card and loads the 3c59x module):

```
alias eth0 3c59x
```

The insmod Command

The **insmod** command performs the actual loading of modules. Both **modprobe** and the Kernel Module Loader make use of this command to load modules. Though **modprobe** is preferred, because it checks for dependencies, you can load or unload particular modules individually with **insmod** and **rmmod** commands. The **insmod** command takes as its argument the name of the module, as does **rmmod**. The name can be the simple base name, like **sb** for the **sb.o** module. You can specify the complete module file name using the **-o** option. Other helpful options are the **-p** option, which lets you probe your system first to see if the module can be successfully loaded, and the **-n** option, which performs all tasks except actually loading the module (a dummy run). The **-v** option (verbose) lists all actions taken as they occur. In those rare cases where you may have to force a module to load, you can use the **-f** option. In the next example, **insmod** loads the **sb.o** module:

```
# insmod -v sb
```

The rmmod Command

The **rmmod** command performs the actual unloading of modules. It is the command used by **modprobe** and the Kernel Module Loader to unload modules. You can use the **rmmod** command to remove a particular module as long as it is not being used or required by other modules. You can remove a module and all its dependent modules by using the **-r** option. The **-a** option removes all unused modules. With the **-e** option, when **rmmod** unloads a module, it saves any persistent data (parameters) in the persistent data directory, usually **/var/lib/modules/persist**.

The /etc/modprobe.conf File

Module loading can require system renaming as well as specifying options to use when loading specific module. Even when removing or installing a module, certain additional programs may have to be run or other options specified. These parameters can be set in the **/etc/modprobe.conf** file. The **mobprobe.conf** file supports four actions: alias, options, install, and remove. You can also specify additional configuration files.

- **alias** *module name*   Provides another name for the module, used for network and sound devices.
- **options** *module options*   Specifies any options a particular module may need.
- **install** *module commands*   Uses the specified commands to install a module, letting you control module loading.
- **remove** *module commands*   Specifies commands to be run when a module is unloaded.
- **include** *config-file*   Additional configuration files.

Among the more common entries are aliases used for network cards. Notice that there is no device name for Ethernet devices in the **/dev** directory. This is because the device name is really an alias for a Ethernet network module that has been defined in the **modprobe.conf** file (this was called **modules.conf** in previous releases). If you were to add another Ethernet card of the same type, you would place an alias for it in the **modprobe.conf** file. For a second Ethernet card, you would use the device name **eth1** as the alias. This way, the second Ethernet device can be referenced with the name **eth1**. A **modprobe.conf** entry is shown here:

```
alias eth1 ne2k-pci
```

TIP *After making changes to /etc/ modprobe.conf, you should run **depmod** again to record any changes in module dependencies.*

If you had added a different model Ethernet card, you would have to specify the module used for that kind of card. In the following example, the second card is a standard PCI Realtek card. Kmod has already automatically detected the new card and loaded the **ne2k-pci** module for you. You only need to identify this as the **eth1** card in the **/etc/ modprobe.conf** file.

```
alias eth0 3c59x
alias eth1 ne2k-pci
```

NOTE   *Instead of a single **modprobe.conf** file, modprobe configuration can be implemented using separate files in an **/etc/modprobe.d** directory.*

A sample **modprobe.conf** file is shown here. Notice the aliases for the USB controller, the FireWire connection, and the sound card. The sound card is referenced by its alias, snd-atiixp, in later install and remove operations. Lines 5 through 8 are two lines, beginning with install and remove.

```
alias eth0 3c59x
alias eth1 ne2k-pci
alias snd-card-0 snd-atiixp
options snd-card-0 index=0
install snd-atiixp /sbin/modprobe --ignore-install snd-atiixp &&
   /usr/sbin/alsactl restore >/dev/null 2>&1 || :
remove snd-atiixp { /usr/sbin/alsactl store >/dev/null 2>&1
   || : ; }; /sbin/modprobe -r --ignore-remove snd-atiixp
 alias usb-controller ehci-hcd
alias usb-controller1 ohci-hcd
alias ieee1394-controller ohci1394
```

Configuration can become complicated, since you are usually using another modprobe operation in an install or remove operation to actually install or remove the module. In effect you then have nested modprobe operations, a second one that was invoked from an install or remove operation within the first. This is the case with the **install snd-atiixp** and **remove snd-atiixp** entries in the previous example. The problem here is that the second modprobe operation will also read the **modprobe.conf** file and try to reexecute the install and restore commands. This is remedied by using the **--ignore-install** option to ignore the install and remove operations the second time.

TIP   *In some cases, Kmod may not detect a device in the way you want, and thereby not load the kernel module you would like. In this case, kernel parameters were specified to the GRUB boot loader to load the correct modules.*

Installing New Modules from Vendors

Often you may find that your hardware device is not supported by current Linux modules. In this case you may have to download drivers from the hardware vendor or open source development group to create your own driver and install it for use by your kernel.

Driver Packages

The drivers could be in RPM or compressed archives. The process for installing drivers differs depending on how a vendor supports the driver. Different kinds of packages are listed here:

- **RPM packages**   Some support sites will provide drivers already packaged in RPM files for direct installation on Fedora. For these you can just run system-config-packages or **rpm** to install the module.

- **Drivers compiled in archives**   Some will provide drivers already compiled for Fedora, but packaged in compressed archives. In this case a simple install operation will place the supporting module in the **modules** directory and make it available for use by the kernel.

- **Source code**   Others provide just the source code, which, when compiled, will detect your system configuration and compile the module accordingly.

- **Scripts with source code**   Some will provide customized scripts that may prompt you for basic questions about your system and then both compile and install the module.

For drivers that come in the form of compressed archives (**tar.gz** or **tar.bz2**), the compile and install operations normally make use a Makefile script operated by the **make** command. A simple install would usually just require running the following command in the driver's software directory:

```
make install
```

In the case of sites that just supply the source code, you may have to perform both configure and compile operations as you would for any software.

```
./configure
make
make install
```

For packages that have no install option, compiled or source, you will have to manually move the module to the kernel module directory, **/lib/modules/***version*, and use **depmod** and **modprobe** to load it (see the previous section).

If a site gives you a customized script, you would just run that script. For example the Marvel gigabit LAN network interfaces found on many motherboards use the SysKonnect Linux drivers held in the sk98lin.o module. The standard kernel configuration will generate and install this module. But if you are using a newer motherboard, you may need to download and install the latest Linux driver. SysKonnect provides a script, **install.sh**, that you run to configure, compile, and install the module.

```
./install.sh
```

If you are only provided a source code file for the module, such as a **.c** file, you can use the kernel files in the **/lib/modules/***version***/build** directory to compile the module. See the Release Note on the DVD/CD-ROM for details on how to create a customized Makefile for creating modules. You will not have to download and install the source code.

Kernel Header Files: /lib/modules/*version*/build

If you need to compile modules, your module source code will make use of kernel headers. The location of these headers was changed with Fedora 3. Normally most module source expects to find the kernel headers along with the kernel source code in the **/usr/src/linux** directory. This usually required installing the entire kernel source code on your system, which seemed excessive just to compile a downloaded module.

With Fedora 4 the kernel headers were placed in the **/usr/src/kernels/***version* directory, where *version* is the kernel name. If your system has more than one kernel installed, you will find the header directories for each here. In the **modules** directory for an installed kernel there is a link to its headers, named **build**, **/lib/modules/***version***/build** (**/lib/modules/***version***/source** is a link to the **build** directory). This link can be used in the source code for kernel modules to reference the kernel headers. The headers are installed as part of the kernel binary packages, and the kernel source is now maintained solely as a source code package to be downloaded separately if needed. To compile modules, you just need to use the kernel headers in **/lib/modules/***version***/build**. The **/lib/modules/***version***/source** directory is actually a link to **/lib/modules/***version***/build**, which in turn links to **/usr/src/kernels/***version*.

Problems occur when module source code expects to find the kernel headers in **/usr/src/linux**. In this case you would receive missing kernel header errors when you tried to compile. To remedy the problem, you can just create **/usr/src/linux** as a link to the kernel header directory in **/usr/src/kernels/***version* or to the link **/lib/modules/***version***/build**. The following example creates **/usr/src/linux** as a symbolic link to **/usr/src/kernels/2.6.11-1.1369_FC4**.

```
ln -s  /usr/src/kernels/2.6.11-1.1369_FC4 /usr/src/linux
```

You can then compile your module or run your script.

If you have more than one kernel installed on your system, be sure to make the **/usr/src/linux** symbolic link reference the kernel for the one you want to create the module. Each kernel binary RPM package will include its own source subdirectory with its own kernel headers. These are used for creating modules for its kernel. You cannot mix module and headers for one kernel with another.

Installing New Modules from the Kernel

The source code for your Linux kernel contains an extensive set of modules, of which not all are actually used on your system. The kernel binaries provided by Fedora Core 4 come with a extensive set of modules already installed. If, however, you install a device for which kernel support is not already installed, you will have to configure and compile the kernel module that provides the drivers for it. This involves using the kernel source code to select the module you need from a list in a kernel configuration tool, and then regenerating your kernel modules with the new module included. Then the new module is copied into the module library, installing it on your system. You can also enter it in the **/etc/modprobe.conf** file with any options, or use **modprobe** to install it manually.

First, make sure you have installed the kernel source code in the **/usr/src/redhat/BUILD** directory (see Chapter 35). If not, simply use the **rpm** tool to install the kernel source RPM package for Fedora Core 4. This can be found with the SRPMS for your distribution. To generate the source code, you then use the **rpmbuild** command with the kernel spec file and specify the type of architecture you want. Change to the **/usr/src/redhat/SPECS** directory and run the **rpmbuild** command with the **-bp** option (build) and the **--target** option to specify the architecture. The following command will extract the i686 version of the kernel:

```
rpmbuild -bp --target=i686  kernel-2.6.spec
```

If instead you are using the original source code version of the kernel in the compressed archive from kernel.org, then unpack it in any directory (but do not use **/usr/src/linux**).

Now change to the kernel directory. For the RPM source package this will be in **/usr/src/redhat/BUILD/kernel-***version***/linux-***version**, where *version* is the kernel version. Then use the **make** command with the **xconfig** or **menuconfig** argument to display the kernel configuration menus, invoking them with the following commands. The **make xconfig** command starts an X Window System interface that needs to be run on your desktop from a terminal window.

```
make xconfig
```

Using the menus, as described in Chapter 35, select the modules you need. Make sure each is marked as a module, clicking the Module check box in **xconfig** or typing **m** for **menuconfig**. Once the kernel is configured, save it and exit from the configuration menus. Then you compile the modules, creating the module binary files with the following command:

```
make modules
```

This places the modules in the kernel source modules directory. You can copy the one you want to the kernel modules directory, **/lib/modules/***version***/kernel**, where *version* is the version number of your Linux kernel. A simpler approach is to reinstall all your modules, using the following command. This copies all the compiled modules to the **/lib/modules/***version***/kernel** directory:

```
make modules_install
```

For example, if you want to provide AppleTalk support, and your distribution did not create an AppleTalk module or incorporate the support into the kernel directly, you can use this method to create and install the AppleTalk modules. First, check to see if your distribution has the module already included. The AppleTalk modules should be in the **/lib/modules/***version***/kernel/net/appletalk** directory. If not, you can move to the kernel source directory, run **make xconfig**, and select AppleTalk as a module. Then generate the modules with the **make modules** command. You could then use the **make modules_install** command to install the new module, along with your other modules. Or you can copy the **appletalk** directory and the modules it holds to the module directory.

CHAPTER

Kernel Administration

The *kernel* is the operating system, performing core tasks such as managing memory and disk access, as well as interfacing with the hardware that makes up your system. For example, the kernel makes possible such standard Linux features as multitasking and multiuser support. It also handles communications with devices like your CD-ROM or hard disk. Users send requests for access to these devices through the kernel, which then handles the lower-level task of actually sending appropriate instructions to a device. Given the great variety of devices available, the kind of devices connected to a Linux system will vary. When Linux is installed, the kernel is appropriately configured for your connected devices. However, if you add a new device, you may have to enable support for it in the kernel. This involves reconfiguring the existing kernel to support the new device through a procedure that is often referred to as *building* or *compiling the kernel.* In addition, new versions of the kernel are continuously made available that provide improved support for your devices, as well as support for new features and increased reliability for a smoother-running system. You can download, compile, and install these new versions on your system.

Kernel Versions

The version number for a Linux kernel consists of three segments: the major, minor, and revision numbers. The *major number* increments with major changes in the kernel. The *minor number* indicates stability. *Even numbers* are used for stable releases, whereas *odd numbers* are reserved for development releases, which may be unstable. New features first appear in the development versions. If you're concerned about stability, you should wait for the stable version. The *revision number* refers to the corrected versions. As bugs are discovered and corrected, and as new features are introduced, new revisions of a kernel are released. A development kernel may have numerous revisions. For example, kernel 2.6.11 has a major number of 2 and a minor number of 6, with a revision number of 11. Distributions often add another number that refers to a specific set of patches applied to the kernel. For example, for Fedora Core 4, the kernel is 2.6.11-1.1369_FC4, where 1369 is the patch number. On distributions that support RPM packages, you can use an RPM query to learn what version is installed, as shown here:

```
rpm -q kernel
```

You could have more than one version of the kernel installed on your system. To see which one is running currently, you use the **uname** command with the **-r** option (the **-a** option provides more detailed information).

```
uname -r
```

New kernels are released on two different tracks, a stable track and a development track. Stable kernels have an even revision number, whereas development kernels use an odd number. The stable kernel would be 2.6, and its development kernel is 2.7. Often development kernels, though unstable, include support for the most recent hardware and software features. However, unless you are experimenting with kernel development, you should always install a stable version of the kernel.

The Linux kernel is being worked on constantly, and new versions are released when they are ready. Distributions may include different kernel versions. Fedora Core includes the most up-to-date stable kernel in its releases. Linux kernels are available at **kernel.org**. Also, RPM packages for a new kernel are often available at distribution update sites. One reason you may need to upgrade your kernel is to provide support for new hardware or for features not supported by your distribution's version. For example, you may need support for a new device not provided in your distribution's version of the kernel. Certain features may not be included in a distribution's version because they are considered experimental or a security risk.

NOTE *In many cases, you don't need to compile and install a new kernel just to add support for a new device. Kernels provide most device support in the form of loadable modules, of which only those needed are installed with the kernel. Most likely, your current kernel has the module you need; you simply have to compile it and install it. For this task, see the section "Installing New Modules from the Kernel" in Chapter 34.*

TIP *Many modules can be separately compiled using sources provided by vendors, such as updated network device drivers. For these you only need the Kernel headers, which are already installed in the /usr/lib/modules/version/source directory, where version is an installed kernel version. In these cases, you do not have to install the full kernel source to add or modify modules.*

You can learn more about the Linux kernel from **kernel.org**, the official repository for the current Linux kernels. The most current source code, as well as documentation, is there. Your distribution Web site will also provide online documentation for installing and compiling the kernel on its systems. Several Linux HOW-TOs also exist on the subject. The kernel source code software packages also include extensive documentation. Kernel source code files are always installed either directly in a local directory or in the Fedora Core **/usr/ src/redhat/BUILD** directory (the **/usr/src/linux** directory is reserved for library headers and no longer used for the kernel source). The source itself will be in a directory labeled **linux-***version*, where *version* is the kernel release, as in **linux-2.6.11**. In this directory, you can find a subdirectory named **/Documentation**, which contains an extensive set of files and directories documenting kernel features, modules, and commands. The following listing of kernel resources also contains more information:

- **kernel.org**   The official Linux kernel Web site. All new kernels originate from here.
- **www.linuxhq.com**   Linux headquarters, kernel sources, and patches

- **kernelnewbies.org**   Linux kernel sources and information
- **www.tldp.org**   Linux Documentation Project

Kernel Tuning: Kernel Runtime Parameters

Several kernel features, such as IP forwarding or the maximum number of files, can be turned on or off without compiling and installing a new kernel or module. These tunable parameters are controlled by the files in **/proc/sys** directory. The **/proc** file system is described in Chapter 32. Parameters that you set are made in the **/etc/sysctl.conf** file. Fedora Core 4 installs this file with basic configuration entries such as those for IP forwarding and debugging control. You use the **sysctl** command directly. The **-p** option causes **sysctl** to read parameters from the **/etc/sysctl.conf** file (you can specify a different file). You can use the **-w** option to change specific parameters. You reference a parameter with its key. A key is the parameter name prefixed with its **proc** system categories (directories), such as **net.ipv4 .ip_forward** for the **ip_forward** parameter located in **/proc/sys/net/ipv4/**. To display the value of a particular parameter, just use its key. The **-a** option lists all available changeable parameters. In the next example, the user changes the domain name parameter, referencing it with the **kernel.domainname** key (the **domainname** command also sets the **kernel .domainname** parameter):

```
# sysctl -w kernel.domainname="mytrek.com"
```

The following example turns on IP forwarding:

```
# sysctl -w net.ipv4.ip_forward=1
```

If you use just the key, you display the parameter's current value:

```
# sysctl net.ipv4.ip_forward
 net.ipv4.ip_forward = 1
```

Installing a New Kernel Version

To install a new kernel, you need to download the software packages for that kernel to your system. You can install a new kernel either by downloading a binary version from your distribution's Web site and installing it or by downloading the source code, compiling the kernel, and then installing the resulting binary file along with the modules. For Fedora Core, the binary version of the kernel is provided in an RPM package. You can install a new kernel, just as you would any other RPM software package.

The easiest way to install a new kernel on Fedora Core is to use the Red Hat Network update agent (for Red Hat Enterprise Linux, the Red Hat Network is a subscription service). The update agent automatically downloads, updates, and installs a new kernel. The Red Hat Network does not automatically select kernel files for download. Although they are listed, you have to explicitly select them to be downloaded and installed.

If you want to download kernel RPM packages manually, keep in mind that the complete kernel installation usually includes a series of RPM packages, all beginning with the word *kernel.* There are also other packages you may need, which contain updated system configuration files used by the new kernel. You can use the packages already installed on your system as a guide. Use the **rpm** command with the **-qa** option to list all packages and then pipe that list through the **grep** command with the **kernel** pattern to display only the kernel packages:

```
rpm -qa | grep kernel
```

The source code version is available for download from distribution FTP sites in the source directory and is included on the distribution source code CD-ROM. You can also download the latest source directly from **www.kernel.org**. Wherever you download a kernel version from, it is always the same. The source code downloaded for a particular kernel version from a distribution site is the same as the one from **www.kernel.org**. Patches for that version can be applied to any distribution. Specific kernel configuration may differ.

Fedora Core 4 Kernel Packages

As an example, the Fedora Core 4 x86 kernel packages are listed here. You should install only one of the **kernel-*version*-i*x*86** packages. This will suffice for standard single-processor computers. The SMP packages are for multiprocessor machines and Pentium 4s that support hyperthreading.

```
kernel-2.6.11-1.1369_FC4.i586.rpm
kernel-2.6.11-1.1369_FC4.i686.rpm
kernel-smp-2.6.11-1.1369_FC4.i586.rpm
kernel-smp-2.6.11-1.1369_FC4.i686.rpm
kernel-doc-2.6.11-1.1369_FC4.noarch.rpm
```

If you have a 64-bit system, you will use a set of 64-bit files, instead of the x86 ones.

```
kernel-2.6.11-1.1369_FC4.x86_64.rpm
kernel-smp-2.6.11-1.1369_FC4.x86_64.rpm
```

CPU Kernel Packages

Fedora Core provides different kernel packages optimized for various popular CPUs. Choose the appropriate one for your machine. The x86 distribution will include the x86 versions, and the 64-bit distribution will hold the x86_64 versions. Each package is named kernel, but each has a different qualifier. For the x86, Fedora Core includes two different kernel packages, one for the newer Pentium 2, 3, and 4 CPUs, and one for the older Pentiums, AMD K6 CPUs, and other older systems. Each package will have a CPU reference in its filename: 686 for Pentium 2, 3, and 4, 586 for Pentium, K6, and other systems.

```
kernel-2.6.11-1.1369_FC4.i586.rpm
kernel-2.6.11-1.1369_FC4.i686.rpm
```

For 64-bit systems, like the Athlon 64 series, the 64-bit distribution will include only a x86_64 package.

```
kernel-2.6.11-1.1369_FC4.x86_64.rpm
```

If your system supports multiple CPU processors, you will also need to install the SMP package instead of the standard CPU ones. For Pentium 4, which simulates multiple CPUs with hyperthreading, you have the option of using the SMP packages for greater speed.

```
kernel-smp-2.6.11-1.1369_FC4.i586.rpm
kernel-smp-2.6.11-1.1369_FC4.i686.rpm
```

The 64-bit distribution also includes an SMP version for multiple processors.

```
kernel-smp-2.6.11-1.1369_FC4.x86_64.rpm
```

There are also kernel packages for the Xen virtualization kernel, both for privileged (0) and unprivileged (U) versions. See the section "Xen Virtualization Kernel" later in this chapter.

```
kernel-xen0-2.6.11-1.1369_FC4.i686.rpm
kernel-xenU-2.6.11-1.1369_FC4.x86_64.rpm
```

For each kernel, there are also corresponding kernel header packages (also known as builds), denoted with the term **devel**, that contain only the kernel headers. These are used for compiling kernel modules or software applications that do not need the full kernel source code, just the headers. The headers for your current kernel are already installed. The kernel headers will be installed in the **/etc/src/kernels** directory with a **build** link to it in the kernel's **/lib/modules** directory. The Fedora Core 4 kernel header packages are listed here:

```
kernel-devel-2.6.11-1.1369_FC4.i586.rpm
kernel-devel-2.6.11-1.1369_FC4.i686.rpm
kernel-devel-2.6.11-1.1369_FC4.i586.rpm
kernel-devel-2.6.11-1.1369_FC4.i686.rpm
kernel-devel-2.6.11-1.1369_FC4.x86_64.rpm
kernel-devel-smp-2.6.11-1.1369_FC4.x86_64.rpm
kernel-xen0-devel-2.6.11-1.1369_FC4.x86_64.rpm
kernel-xenU-devel-2.6.11-1.1369_FC4.x86_64.rpm
```

Support Packages

In addition, the doc package provides updated documentation. Notice that it is architecture independent, noarch. The utils package contains various hardware monitoring tools like **smardctl** for hard drives, along with user-mode Linux (UML) tools.

```
kernel-utils-2.4-13.1.39.i386.rpm
kernel-doc-2.6.11-1.1369_FC4.noarch.rpm
```

Installing Kernel Packages: /boot

You will not need all of these packages. For example, for a simple kernel upgrade for a basic Pentium computer (Pentium 3 or 4 with less than 4GB memory, single processor, and no customization), you would need only the 686 package. For a more complete upgrade, you would include the pcmcia, source, doc, and utils packages. If your system supports multiple processors or hyperthreading, you would use the SMP packages.

To make sure a kernel RPM package was downloaded without any errors and to verify its authentication, you can use the **rpm** command with the **-K** option (to authenticate the package, you need the Red Hat public key):

```
rpm -K *rpm
```

You can now install the kernel. As a safety precaution, you should preserve your old kernel in case the new one does not work out for some reason. This involves installing with the install (**-i**) option instead of the update (**-U**) option, creating a separate RAM disk for the new kernel, and then modifying **grub.conf** to have GRUB start up using the new kernel.

```
# rpm -ivh kernel-2.6.11-1.1369_FC4.i686.rpm
```

If your system has a SCSI controller or any other specialized hardware, RPM will also create a RAM disk to hold appropriate support modules (you can create a RAM disk manually with the **mkinitrd** command). The RAM disk is named **initrd-**_kernel-version_**.img** and is located in the **/boot** directory, as in **/boot/initrd-2.6.1-11.1369_FC4.img**.

TIP   *The system-config-packages tool does not support kernel package installation. You have to install the kernel package manually using the **rpm** command in a terminal window.*

On most distributions, kernels are installed in the **/boot** directory. Performing an **ls -l** operation on this directory lists all the currently installed kernels. A file for your old kernel and a file for your new one now exist. If you took the precautions described in the preceding section, you may have already renamed the older kernel. If you are using a boot loader such as GRUB, you need not change its configuration file (**/boot/grub.conf**) to add the entry to invoke the new kernel. The kernel boots using the selected **/boot/vmlinuz**_version_ kernel file. In your **grub.conf** file, you need a kernel line to reference this kernel file. You also need to include a line for the RAM disk, **initrd**.

```
kernel /boot/vmlinuz-2.6.11-1.1369_FC4 ro root=/dev/hda3
initrd /boot/initrd-2.6.11-1.1369_FC4.img
```

TIP   *Although it is not included with Fedora Core, user-mode Linux (UML) is an optional version of the kernel designed to run as a stand-alone program separate from the kernel. In effect, it creates a virtual machine with disk storage implemented on a user file. UML is often used to test software or experiment with kernel configurations, without harming the real system. You can also use UML to implement virtual hosting, by running several virtual machines on one physical host. With a virtual machine, you can control the access to the host system, providing greater security. You can find out more about user-mode Linux at **user-mode-linux.sourceforge.net**.*

Precautionary Steps for Modifying a Kernel of the Same Version

If you want to modify your kernel configuration and build a new one, you should retain a copy of your current kernel. In case something goes wrong with your modified version, you can always boot from the copy you kept. You do not have to worry about this happening if you are installing a new version of the kernel. New kernels are given different names, so the older one is not overwritten.

To retain a copy of your current kernel, you can make a backup copy of it, letting the original be overwritten. An installed version of a kernel makes use of several files in the **/boot** directory. Each file ends with that kernel version's number. These include the **vmlinuz** file, which is the actual kernel image file, along with several support files, **System.map**, **config**, and **initrd**. This **System.map** file contains kernel symbols needed by modules to start kernel functions. For example, the kernel image file is called **vmlinuz-***version*, where *version* is the version number attached, as in **vmlinuz-2.6.11-1.1369_FC4**. The **System.map** file for this kernel is called **System.map-2.6.11-1.1369_FC4**. The config file holds kernel system settings. Here are the kernel files for version **2.6.11-1.1369_FC4**.

```
/boot/vmlinuz-2.6.11-1.1369_FC4
/boot/System.map-2.6.11-1.1369_FC4
/boot/initrd-2.6.11-1.1369_FC4.img
/boot/config-2.6.11-1.1369_FC4
```

If, on the other hand, you are creating a modified version of the same kernel, the kernel file, here called **vmlinuz-2.6.11-1.1369_FC4**, will be overwritten with the new kernel image file, along with the **System.map** and **config** files. To keep your current working version, you first have to make a copy of these files. You would make a copy of the **/boot/vmlinux-2.6.11-1.1369_FC4** file, giving it another name, as shown here:

```
cp /boot/vmlinuz-2.6.11-1.1369_FC4 /boot/vmlinuz-2.6.11-1.1369_FC4.old
```

You would also make backups of the **System.map** and **config** files. You should also back up your modules located in the **/lib/modules/***version* directory, where *version* is the version number of the kernel. Otherwise, you will lose the modules already set up to work with the original kernel. For version 2.6.11-1.1369_FC4, the libraries are located in **/lib/modules/2.6.11-1.1369_FC4**. If you are compiling a different version, those libraries are placed in a new directory named with the new version number.

Boot Loader

If you are using a boot loader, you should create a new entry for the old kernel in the boot loader configuration file. You can then make an entry for the new kernel. Leaving the entry for the old kernel is advisable in case something goes wrong with the new kernel. This way, you can always reboot and select the old kernel. For example, in **/boot/grub.conf**, add a new entry, similar to the one for the old kernel, which references the new kernel in its kernel statement. The **grub.conf** entry would look something like the following code. You could then select the entry with the title "Old Linux (2.6.9-1.667.old)" at the GRUB menu to launch the old kernel.

```
title Old Linux (2.6.9-1.667.old)
 root (hd0,2)
 kernel /boot/vmlinuz-2.6.9-1.667.old root=/dev/hda3
 initrd /boot/initrd-2.6.9-1.667.old.img
```

If you use a label for the boot partition, the **root** option for the **kernel** statement would look like this for a boot partition labeled **/**:

```
kernel /boot/vmlinuz-2.6.9-1.667.old ro root=LABEL=/
```

PART VI

Boot Disk

You should also have a boot CD-ROM ready, just in case something goes wrong with the installation (normally you created one during installation). With a boot CD-ROM, you can start your system without using the boot loader. You can create a boot CD-ROM using the **mkbootdisk** utility. To create a boot CD-ROM, you need to know the full version number for your kernel. You can, in fact, have several kernels installed, and create boot CD-ROMs for each one (your **grub.conf** file lists your kernel version number). If the kernel version is 2.6.11-1.1396_FC4, use it as the argument to the **mkbootdisk** command to create a boot CD-ROM for your system.

To make a boot CD-ROM, you can use the **--iso** option with the **--device** option to specify the CD image file. You can then burn the image file to a CD-ROM with a application like K3b. In the next example, the user creates a CD-ROM image file, called **myimage.iso**, for a boot CD-ROM of the 2.6.11-1.1396_FC4 kernel:

```
mkbootdisk --iso --device myimage.iso  2.6.11-1.1396_FC4
```

Compiling the Kernel from Source Code

Instead of installing already-compiled binary versions of the kernel, you can install the kernel source code on your system and use it to create the kernel binary files yourself. Kernel source code files are compiled with the **gcc** compiler just as any other source code files are. One advantage to compiling the kernel is that you can enhance its configuration, adding support for certain kinds of devices such as Bluetooth devices. The 2.6 kernel is described here.

Installing Kernel Sources with Fedora Core 4 SRPM

You can obtain a recent version of the kernel source code from the Fedora Core 4 distribution's **SRPMS** directory. It is no longer included with the binary RPMS files. It will have the name **kernel-source**. New versions of the Fedora Core 4 source can be downloaded by directly accessing the Fedora Core distribution's FTP site. You simply install them as you would any RPM package. You can also use Firefox to download the package; however, system-config-packages will not install source packages. You have to use the **rpm** command in a terminal window as shown here:

```
# rpm -ivh kernel- 2.6.11-1.1369_FC4.src.rpm
```

Building the Kernel Source

With Fedora Core 3, the management of Fedora Core kernel source RPM packages changed significantly. Fedora Core RPM sources are now managed through the Fedora Core RPM build directories, not in the traditional **/usr/src/linux** directory. When you install the Fedora Core kernel RPM, the RPM spec file, **kernel-2.6.spec**, is placed in the **/usr/src/redhat/SPECS** directory. Configuration information, patches, and the compressed archive for the kernel source are placed in the **/usr/src/redhat/SOURCES** directory.

To generate the source code, you then use the **rpmbuild** command with the kernel spec file and specify the type of architecture you want. Change to the **/usr/src/redhat/SPECS** directory and run **rpmbuild** with the **-bp** option (build) and the **--target** option to specify the architecture. The following command will extract the i686 version of the kernel:

```
rpmbuild -bp --target=i686  kernel-2.6.spec
```

The extracted kernel source will be placed in the **/usr/src/redhat/BUILD** directory under **kernel-2.6.11/linux-2.6.11**. You can then run commands like **make xconfig** to configure the kernel source.

Often, when compiling software using the kernel source, some software expects to find the kernel source in the **/etc/src/linux** directory. To accommodate this situation, you can first move the kernel source directory to **/etc/src**.

```
mv /usr/src/redhat/BUILD/kernel-2.6.11/linux-2.6.11  /usr/src
```

You can then create a link name **linux** to **linux-2.6.11** in the **/usr/src** directory.

```
ln -s /usr/src/linux-2.6.11  /usr/src/linux
```

Different Kernel System Configurations

Should you want to use a different configuration, say an SMP version instead of the plain i*x*86 one, you need to configure your kernel source for that particular system. To do this, you use the appropriate configuration file for your systems. These are located in the kernel source's **configs** directory. For the i386 RPM source you will find kernel configuration files for the x86 systems, i586 and i686, along with their SMP versions.

The **.config** file will already be the version you specified in the target option when you extracted the source with **rpmbuild**. For a different configuration, you copy the config file you want as the **.config** file in the top kernel source directory. The following example copies the i686-smp configuration file as the kernel source configuration file:

```
cp configs/kernel.2.6.9-i686-smp.config  .config
```

Then update your kernel source with the new configuration by issuing the following command:

```
make oldconfig
```

Installing Kernel Sources: Kernel Archives and Patches

You can also download the original kernel source from **www.kernel.org**. This version will not be optimized for Fedora Core 4 or Red Hat Enterprise Linux. It should be placed in directory of your choosing, but not in the **/usr/src/linux** directory.

These versions are normally much more recent than those available on your distribution site, but they may not have been thoroughly tested on the distribution platform. The kernel source is in the form of compressed archives (**.tar.gz**). They have the prefix **linux** with the version name as the suffix. You decompress and extract the archive with the following commands. You first change to the local directory you chose and then unpack the archive with either Fileroller or the **tar** command. It creates a directory with the prefix **linux** where the source files are placed. The following example extracts the 2.6.11.12 kernel:

```
cd mykernel
tar -xzvf linux-2.6.11.12.tar.gz
```

Be sure to unpack the archive for the kernel.org version in a directory you choose, like **mykernel** in a home directory. The source will reside within a subdirectory that has the prefix **linux** and a suffix consisting of the kernel version, as in **linux-2.6.11.12** for kernel 2.6, revision 11.12. The local directory in this example would be **mykernel/linux-2.6.11.12**.

TIP *If you are using the original kernel source, you should also check for any patches.*

Configuring the Kernel

Once the source is installed, you must configure the kernel. Configuration consists of determining the features for which you want to provide kernel-level support. These include drivers for different devices, such as sound cards and SCSI devices. You can configure features as directly included in the kernel itself or as modules the kernel can load as needed. You can also specifically exclude features. Features incorporated directly into the kernel make for a larger kernel program. Features set up as separate modules can also be easily updated. Documentation for many devices that provide sound, video, or network support can be found in the **/usr/share/doc** directory. Check the kernel-doc package to find a listing of the documentation provided.

```
rpm -ql kernel-doc
```

NOTE *If you configured your kernel previously and now want to start over from the default settings, you can use the **make mrproper** command to restore the default kernel configuration.*

Kernel Configuration Tools

You can configure the kernel using one of several available configuration tools: **config**, **menuconfig**, **xconfig** (qconf), and **gconfig** (gkc). You can also edit the configuration file directly. These tools perform the same configuration tasks but use different interfaces. The **config** tool is a simple configure script providing line-based prompts for different configuration options. The **menuconfig** tool provides a cursor-based menu, which you can still run from the command line. Menu entries exist for different configuration categories, and you can pick and choose the ones you want. To mark a feature for inclusion in the kernel, move to it and press the SPACEBAR. An asterisk appears in the empty parentheses to the left of the entry. If you want to make it a module, press M and an *M* appears in the parentheses. The **xconfig** option runs qconf, the QT (KDE)–based GUI kernel configuration tool, and requires that the QT libraries (KDE) be installed first. The **gconfig** option runs the gkc tool, which uses a GTK interface, requiring that GNOME be installed first. Both qconf and gkc provide expandable menu trees, selectable panels, and help windows. Selectable features include check buttons you can click. All these tools save their settings to the **.config** file in the kernel source's directory. If you want to remove a configuration entirely, you can use the **mrproper** option to remove the **.config** file and any binary files, starting over from scratch.

```
make mrproper
```

You start a configuration tool by preceding it with the **make** command. Be sure you are in the kernel directory (either **/usr/src/redhat/BUILD** for RPM kernel packages, or the local directory you used for the compressed archive, such as **tar.gz**). The process of starting a configuration tool is a **make** operation that uses the Linux kernel Makefile. The **xconfig** tool should be started from a terminal window on your window manager. The **menuconfig** and **config** tools are started on a shell command line. The following example lists commands to start **gconfig**, **xconfig**, **menuconfig**, and **config**:

```
make gconfig
make xconfig
make menuconfig
make config
```

NOTE *On the older 2.4 kernel, the **xconfig** tool opens an X Window System–based Linux Kernel Configuration window listing the different configuration categories. Buttons at the right of the screen are used to save the configuration or to copy it to a file, as well as to quit. Clicking an entry opens a window that lists different features you can include. Three check boxes to the left of each entry enable you to choose to have a feature compiled directly into the kernel, created as a separate module that can be loaded at runtime, or not included at all.*

gconfig (gkc)

The GTK kernel configuration tool (gkc) is invoked with the **gconfig** option. This uses a GNOME-based interface that is similar to qconf (**xconfig**). The gkc tool opens a Linux Kernel Configuration window with expandable submenus like those for qconf. Figure 33-1 shows the configuration categories. Many categories are organized into a few major headings, with many now included under the Device Drivers menu. The Load and Save buttons and File menu entries can be used to save the configuration or to copy it to a file. Single, Split, and Full view buttons let you display menus in one window, in a display panel with another panel containing an expandable tree to select entries, or as a single expandable tree of entries. The Expand button will expand all headings and subheadings, whereas Collapse will let you expand only those you want displayed. Use the down and side triangles for each entry to expand or collapse subentries.

Clicking an entry opens a window that lists different features you can include. Entries are arranged in columns listing the option, its actual name, its range (yes, module, or no), and its data (yes, no, or module status). Entries in the Options menu let you determine what columns to display: Name for the actual module name; Range for the selectable yes, no, and module entries; and Data for the option status, titled as Value.

The Range entries are titled N, M, and Y and are used to select whether not to include an option (N), to load it as a module (M), or to compile it directly into the kernel (Y). Entries that you can select will display a underscore. Clicking the underscore will change its entry to Y for module or direct kernel inclusion, and N for no inclusion. The Value column will show which is currently selected.

The Options column will include a status showing whether the option is included directly (check mark), included as a module (line mark), or not included at all (empty). To quickly select or deselect an entry, double-click the option name in the Options field. You will see its check box checked, lined (module), or empty. Corresponding N, M, and Y entries for no inclusion, module, or kernel inclusion are selected. The default preference for either module or direct kernel inclusion for that option is selected automatically. You can change it manually if you wish.

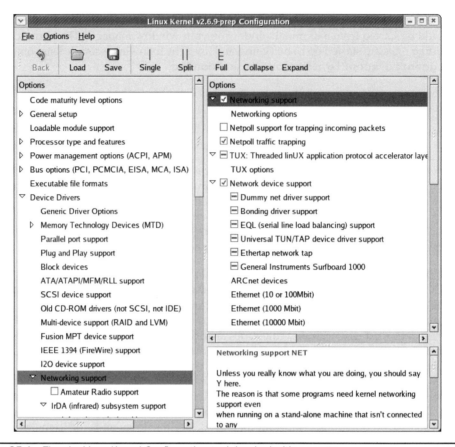

FIGURE 35-1   The gkc Linux Kernel Configuration tool, invoked with `gconfig`

xconfig (qconf)

The **xconfig** option invokes the qconf tool, which is based on KDE QT libraries. KDE has to first be installed. The qconf tool opens a Linux Kernel Configuration window listing the different configuration categories. It has a slightly simpler interface, without the expand or collapse buttons or the columns for module and source status.

Important Kernel Configuration Features

The **xconfig**, **menuconfig**, and **gconfig** tools provide excellent context-sensitive help for each entry. To the right of each entry is a Help button. Click it to display a detailed explanation of what that feature does and why you would include it either directly or as a module, or even exclude it. When you are in doubt about a feature, always use the Help button to learn exactly what it does and why you would want to use it. Many of the key features are described here. The primary category for a feature is listed in parentheses.

TIP *As a rule, features in continual use, such as network and file system support, should be compiled directly into the kernel. Features that could easily change, such as sound cards, or features used less frequently should be compiled as modules. Otherwise, your kernel image file may become too large and slower to run.*

- **Loadable Module Support**   In most cases, you should make sure your kernel can load modules. Click the Loadable Module Support button to display a listing of several module management options. Make sure Enable Loadable Module Support is marked Yes. This feature allows your kernel to load modules as they are needed. Kernel Module Loader should also be set to Yes, because this allows your daemons, such as your Web server, to load any modules they may need.

- **Processor Type And Features**   The Processor Type And Features window enables you to set up support for your particular system. Here, you select the type of processor you have (486, 586, 686, Pentium III, Pentium IV, and so forth), as well as the amount of maximum memory your system supports.

- **General Setup**   The General Setup window enables you to select general features, such as networking, PCI BIOS support, and power management, as well as support for ELF and **a.out** binaries. Also supported is `sysctl` for dynamically changing kernel parameters specified in the **/proc** files. You can use redhat-config-proc (the Kernel Tuning tool in the System Tools menu) to make these dynamic changes to the kernel. In the additional device driver support menu, you can enable specialized features like accelerated SSL.

- **Block Devices (Device Drivers)**   The Block Devices window lists entries that enable support for your IDE, floppy drive, and parallel port devices. Special features, such as RAM disk support and the loopback device for mounting CD-ROM image files, are also there.

- **Multi-Device Support (RAID and LVM) (Device Drivers)**   The Multi-Device Support window lists entries that enable the use of RAID devices. You can choose the level of RAID support you want. Here you can also enable Logical Volume Management support (LVM), which lets you combine partitions into logical volumes that can be managed dynamically.

- **Networking Options (Device Drivers/Networking Support)**   The Networking Options window lists an extensive set of networking capabilities. The TCP/IP Networking entry must be set to enable any kind of Internet networking. Here, you can specify features that enable your system to operate as a gateway, firewall, or router. Network Packet Filtering enables support for an IPtables firewall. Support also exists for other kinds of networks, including AppleTalk and IPX. AppleTalk must be enabled if you want to use NetTalk to connect to a Macintosh system on your network (Filesystems).

- **ATA/IDE/MFM/RLL Support (Device Drivers)**   In the ATA/IDE/MFM/RLL Support window, you can click on the "IDE, ATA, and ATAPI Block Device" button to open a window where you can select support for IDE hard drives and ATAPI CD-ROMs.

- **SCSI Support (Device Drivers)**   If you have any SCSI devices on your system, make sure the entries in the SCSI Support window are set to Yes. You enable support for SCSI disks, tape drives, and CD-ROMs here. The SCSI Low-Level Drivers window displays an extensive list of SCSI devices currently supported by Linux. Be sure the ones you have are selected.

- **Network Device Support (Device Drivers/Networking Support)**   The Network Device Support window lists several general features for network device support. There are entries here for windows that list support for particular types of network devices, including Ethernet (10 or 100Mb) devices, token ring devices, WAN interfaces, and AppleTalk devices. Many of these devices are created as modules you can load as needed. You can elect to rebuild your kernel with support for any of these devices built directly into the kernel.

- **Multimedia Devices (Device Drivers)**   Multimedia devices provide support for various multimedia cards as well as Video4Linux.

- **File Systems**   The File Systems window lists the different types of file systems Linux can support. These include Windows file systems such as DOS, VFAT (Windows 95/98), and NTFS, as well as CD-ROM file systems such as ISO and UDF. Network file systems such as NFS, SMB (Samba), and NCP (NetWare) are included, as well as miscellaneous file systems such as HFS (Macintosh).

- **Character Devices (Device Drivers)**   The Character Devices window lists features for devices such as your keyboard, mouse, and serial ports. Support exists for both serial and bus mice.

- **Sound (Device Drivers)**   For the 2.4 kernel, the Sound window lists different sound cards supported by the kernel. Select the one on your system. For older systems, you may have to provide the IRQ, DMA, and Base I/O your sound card uses. These are compiled as separate modules, some of which you could elect to include directly in the kernel if you want. For the 2.6 kernel, you can select the Advanced Linux Sound Architecture sound support, expanding it to the drivers for particular sound devices (the Open Sound System is also included, though deprecated).

- **Bluetooth Devices (Device Drivers/Networking Support)**   Support is here for Bluetooth-enabled peripherals, listing drivers for USB, serial, and PC card interfaces.

- **Kernel Hacking**   The Kernel Hacking window lists features of interest to developers who work at the kernel level and need to modify the kernel code. You can have the kernel include debugging information, and also provide some measure of control during crashes.

Once you set your options, save your configuration. Then select the Save entry on the File menu to overwrite your **.config** configuration file. The Save As option lets you save your configuration to a particular file.

TIP *Red Hat Enterprise Linux and Fedora Core incorporate support for the Native POSIX Thread Library (NPTL), an updated version of Linux POSIX threads, providing for more efficient use of high-end processors. Though this feature is designed to be backward compatible, some older modules may prove incompatible and may need to be recompiled with the new kernel.*

Compiling and Installing the Kernel

Now that the configuration is ready, you can compile your kernel. You first need to generate a dependency tree to determine what part of the source code to compile, given your configuration. Use the following command in the kernel source directory:

```
make dep
```

You also have to clean up any object and dependency files that may remain from a previous compilation. Use the following command to remove such files:

```
make clean
```

You can use several options to compile the kernel (see Table 33-1). The **bzImage** option simply generates a kernel file called **bzImage** and places it in the **arch** directory. For Intel and AMD systems, you find **bzImage** in the **i386/boot** subdirectory, **arch/i386/boot**. For a kernel source, this would be in **arch/i386/boot**.

```
make bzImage
```

The options in Table 33-1 create the kernel, but not the modules—those features of the kernel to be compiled into separate modules. To compile your modules, use the **make** command with the **modules** argument.

```
make modules
```

To install your modules, use the **make** command with the **modules_install** option. This installs the modules in the **/lib/modules/**_version-num_ directory, where _version-num_ is the version number of the kernel. You should make a backup copy of the old modules before you install the new ones.

```
make modules_install
```

The **install** option both generates the kernel files and installs them on your system as **vmlinuz**, incorporating the **make bzImage** step. This operation will place the kernel files

Option	Description
zImage	Creates the kernel file called **zImage** located in the **arch** or **arch/i386/boot** directory.
install	Creates the kernel and installs it on your system.
zdisk	Creates a kernel file and installs it on a floppy disk (creates a boot disk, 1.44MB).
bzImage	Creates the compressed kernel file and calls it **bzImage**.
bzdisk	Creates the kernel and installs it on a floppy disk (creates a boot disk). Useful only for smaller kernel builds, 1.44MB.
fdimage	Creates floppy disk image with the kernel, 1.44MB (bootable).
fdimage288	Creates floppy disk 2.88 image with the kernel (bootable).

TABLE 35-1   Compiling Options for Kernel **make** Command

such as **bzImage** in the **/boot** directory, giving them the appropriate names and kernel version number.

```
make install
```

If you are booting Linux from DOS using `loadlin`, you will need to copy the **bzImage** file to the **loadlin** directory on the DOS partition where you are starting Linux from.

The commands for a simple compilation and installation are shown here:

```
make dep
make clean
make bzImage
make modules
make modules_install
make install
```

If you want, you could enter these all on fewer lines, separating the commands with semicolons, as shown here:

```
make dep; make clean; make bzImage; make modules
make modules_install; make install
```

A safer way to perform these operations on single lines is to make them conditionally dependent on one another, using the **&&** command. In the preceding method, if one operation has a error, the next one will still be executed. By making the operations conditional, the next operation is run only if the preceding one is successful.

```
make dep && make clean && make bzImage
make modules
make modules_install &&  make install
```

Installing the Kernel Image Manually

To install a kernel **bzImage** file manually, copy the **bzImage** file to the directory where the kernel resides and give it the name used on your distribution, such as **vmlinuz-2.6.11-1.1369_FC4**. Remember to first back up the old kernel file, as noted in the precautionary steps. **vmlinuz** is a symbolic link to an actual kernel file that will have the term **vmlinuz** with the version name. So, to manually install a **bzImage** file, you copy it to the **/boot** directory with the attached version number such as **vmlinuz-2.6.11.12**.

```
make bzImage
cp arch/i386/boot/bzImage /boot/vmlinuz-2.6.11.12.
```

TIP *The `bzImage` option, and those options that begin with the letter b, create a compressed kernel image. This kernel image may not work on older systems. If not, try using the `zImage` option to create a kernel file called zImage. Then install the zImage file manually the same way as you would do with bzImage. Bear in mind that support for `zImage` will be phased out eventually.*

You will also have to make a copy of the **System.map** file, linking it to the **System.map** symbolic link.

```
cp arch/i386/boot/System.map  /boot/System.map-2.6.11.12_FC4
```

The following commands show a basic compilation and a manual installation. First, all previous binary files are removed with the **clean** option. Then the kernel is created using the **bzImage** option. This creates a kernel program called **bzImage** located in the **arch/i386/ boot** directory. This kernel file is copied to the **/boot** directory and given the name **vmlinuz-2.6.11.12**. Then a symbolic link called **/boot/vmlinuz** is created to the kernel **vmlinuz-2.6.11.12** file. Finally, the modules are created and installed:

```
make dep
make clean
make bzImage
make modules
make modules_install
cp arch/i386/boot/bzImage /boot/vmlinuz-2.6.11.12
cp System.map /boot/System.map-2.6.11.12
```

Kernel Boot Disks

Instead of installing the kernel on your system, you can simply place it on a boot disk or CD-ROM and boot your system from that disc. For a CD-ROM you can first create the kernel as a **bzImage,** install the kernel, and then use **mkbootdisk** to create a bootable CD-ROM (see Chapter 2). For a boot disk you have the option of creating either a floppy disk directly or a floppy disk image.

If you are using a stripped-down configured version of the kernel, which will fit on a 1.44MB floppy disk, you can use the **bzdisk** or **zdisk** options to compile the kernel and install directly on a floppy. You will be need a floppy disk placed in your floppy drive. A standard kernel 2.6 configuration is too large to fit on a floppy, though most older 2.4 versions will.

For a floppy disk image you can create either a 1.44 or 2.88 image (which will hold the 2.6 kernel). Use the **fdimage** option for a 1.44 image and **fdimage288** for the 2.88 image. Both fdimage and fdimage288 create corresponding floppy disk images in the **arch/i386/ boot** directory. They use their own **mtools.conf** configuration located in the directory to generate the letters for the floppy disk image, which **mcopy** can then use to create the images. The **fdimage288** image is often used for virtual users.

```
make bzdisk
make fdimage
make fdimage288
```

TIP *If you are experimenting with your kernel configurations, it may be safer to put a new kernel version on a boot CD-ROM, rather than installing it on your system. If something goes wrong, you can always boot up normally with your original kernel still on your system (though you can always configure your boot loader to access previous versions).*

Boot Loader Configurations

If you are using a boot loader such as GRUB or LILO, you can configure your system to enable you to start any of your installed kernels. As seen in the earlier section "Precautionary Steps

PART VI

for Modifying a Kernel of the Same Version," you can create an added entry in the boot loader configuration file for your old kernel. As you install new kernel versions, you could simply add more entries, enabling you to use any of the previous kernels. Whenever you boot, your boot loader will then present you with a list of kernels to choose from. For example, you could install a developmental version of the kernel, along with a current stable version, while keeping your old version. In the image line for each entry, you specify the filename of the kernel. You can create another boot loader entry for your older kernel.

GRUB Configurations

In the next example, the **/boot/grub.conf** file contains entries for two Linux kernels, one for the kernel installed earlier, **2.6.9-1.667**, and one for a more recent kernel, **2.6.11-1.1369_FC4**. With GRUB, you only have to add an new entry for the new kernel.

```
# grub.conf generated by anaconda
#
#boot=/dev/hda
default=0
timeout=30
splashimage=(hd0,2)/boot/grub/splash.xpm.gz
title New Linux (2.6.11-1)
    root (hd0,2)
    kernel /boot/vmlinuz-2.6.11-1.1369_FC4 ro root=/dev/hda3
    initrd /boot/initrd-2.6.11-1.1369_FC4.img
title  Old Linux (2.6.9-1.667)
    root (hd0,2)
    kernel /boot/vmlinuz-2.6.9-1.667 ro root=/dev/hda3
    initrd /boot/initrd-2.6.9-1.667.img
title Windows XP
    rootnoverify (hd0,0)
    chainloader +1
```

Pentium 4 systems that support hyperthreading will normally install both the standard and SMP versions of the kernel, letting you choose to use the **smp** kernel to take advantage of the Pentium hyperthreading multiprocessor simulation. A **grub.conf** configuration would look similar to this, including entries for both the **smp** and standard versions:

```
default=2
timeout=5
splashimage=(hd0,2)/boot/grub/splash.xpm.gz
hiddenmenu
title Fedora Core (2.6.11-1.1369_FC4-smp)
    root (hd0,2)
    kernel /boot/vmlinuz-2.6.11-1.1369_FC4-smp ro root=LABEL=/ rhgb quiet
    initrd /boot/initrd-2.6.11-1.1369_FC4-smp.img
title Fedora Core-up (2.6.11-1.1369_FC4)
    root (hd0,2)
    kernel /boot/vmlinuz-2.6.11-1.1369_FC4 ro root=LABEL=/ rhgb quiet
    initrd /boot/initrd-2.6.11-1.1369_FC4.img
title Windows
    rootnoverify (hd0,0)
    chainloader +1
```

Module RAM Disks

If your system uses certain block devices unsupported by the kernel, such as some SCSI, RAID, or IDE devices, you will need to load certain required modules when you boot. Such block device modules are kept on a RAM disk that is accessed when your system first starts up (RAM disks are also used for diskless systems). For example, if you have a SCSI hard drive or CD-ROMs, the SCSI drivers for them are often held in modules that are loaded whenever you start up your system. These modules are stored in a RAM disk from which the startup process reads. If you create a new kernel that needs to load modules to start up, you must create a new RAM disk for those modules. You need to create a new RAM disk only if your kernel has to load modules at startup. If, for example, you use a SCSI hard drive but you incorporated SCSI hard drive and CD-ROM support (including support for the specific model) directly into your kernel, you don't need to set up a RAM disk (support for most IDE hard drives and CD-ROMs is already incorporated directly into the kernel).

If you need to create a RAM disk, you can use the **mkinitrd** command to create a RAM disk image file. The **mkinitrd** command incorporates all the IDE, SCSI, and RAID modules that your system uses, including those listed in your **/etc/modules.conf** file. See the Man pages for **mkinitrd** and RAM disk documentation for more details. **mkinitrd** takes as its arguments the name of the RAM disk image file and the kernel that the modules are taken from. In the following example, a RAM disk image called **initrd-2.6.11.12.img** is created in the **/boot** directory, using modules from the 2.6.10 kernel. The 2.6.11.12 kernel must already be installed on your system and its modules created.

```
# mkinitrd /boot/initrd-2.6.11.12.img 2.6.11.12
```

You can select certain modules to loaded before or after any SCSI module. The **--preload** option loads before the SCSI modules, and **--with** loads after. For example, to load RAID5 support before the SCSI modules, use **--preload=raid5**:

```
mkinitrd --preload=raid5 raid-ramdisk 2. 6.11.12
```

In the **grub.conf** segment for the new kernel, place an **initrd** entry specifying the new RAM disk:

```
initrd /boot/initrd-2.6.11.12.img
```

Xen Virtualization Kernel

Fedora Core 4 now includes versions of the kernel that incorporate Xen Virtualization. Xen Virtualization technology allows you to run different operating systems on a Linux system, as well as running virtual versions of the kernel to test new applications. Xen is an open source project run by the University of Cambridge Computer Laboratory in coordination with the Open Source Development Labs and several Linux distributors, including Red Hat. You can find more about Xen at **www.cl.cam.ac.uk/Research/SRG/netos/xen**. Here you can find current documentation. Source code and support programs can be downloaded from **sf.net**. Fedora Core 4 provides its own Xen kernel versions in RPM packages. These are included with the distributions, and updated versions can be easily obtained from Fedora Core 4 update sites.

On a single Xen server you can run several virtual machines to run different operating systems at the same time. Commercial virtualization is currently provided by VMware. Xen is a para-virtualized system, meaning that the guest operation system has to be modified to run on Xen. It cannot run without modification as it could on a fully virtualized system like VMware. Xen uses a para-virtualization approach to increase efficiency, giving its virtual machines nearly the same level of efficiency as the native kernel. This makes virtualization practical for enterprise-level systems. These are some of the advantages cited for Xen:

- You can test and debug kernel modifications in a virtual machine on your system, instead of using a separate test system.

- You can test and debug applications on a separate kernel running in a virtual machine on your system, instead of using your native kernel (similar to the task user mode Linux performs).

- You can run multiple operating systems on the same system.

- You can isolate servers on the same system by placing them in separate virtual machines.

- You have better control of clustering systems.

- You can customize an operating system in a virtual machine, while still accessing hardware support provided by the native kernel.

For an operating system to work on Xen, it must be configured to access the Xen interface. Currently only Unix and Linux operating systems are configured to be Xen compatible, though work is progressing on Windows.

To use the Xen kernel, you first have to install the Xen kernel packages as well as the Xen server, tools, and documentation. There are two Xen kernel packages, one for running Xen in domain 0 (xen0) and one for unprivileged use (xenU). You would normally use the xen0 version. This is a privileged version that contains device drivers and can be used to boot the system. The xenU version has no drivers, though it is smaller and can be used for unprivileged domains (virtual machines). Detailed documentation will be in **/usr/share/xen-2**. Configuration files will be placed in the **/etc/xen** directory, and corresponding kernels in the **/boot** and **/lib/modules** directories. In the **/etc/xen** directory you will find the **xend-config** file for configuring the Xen **xend** server, as well as example Xen configuration files.

```
kernel-xen0-2.6.11-1.1369_FC4.686.rpm
kernel-xenU-2.6.11-1.1369_FC4.686.rpm
xen-2-2050403.i386.rpm
```

Xen sets up separate virtual machines called domains. When the Xen kernel starts up, it creates a primary domain, domain0, which manages your system and sets up virtual machines for other operating systems. Management of the virtual machines is handled by the **xend** server. Your native kernel is installed on domain0, which will handle most of the hardware devices for all the other virtual machines.

To create a virtual machine, you have to first create a configuration file for it in the **/etc/xen** directory. Here you will find sample configuration files you can use as a template. Here are settings you may want to change:

- **kernel** The path to the kernel image used by the virtual machine
- **memory** The amount of memory you will allow the domain to use
- **disk** The block devices (partitions) you want the domain to use
- **dhcp** Have the domain use DHCP to set networking. For manual configuration, you can set netmask and gateway parameters
- **hostname** The hostname for the virtual machine
- **vif** The MAC address to use (random ones will be generated if none is specified)
- **extra** Additional boot parameters
- **restart** Automatic restart options: always, never, onreboot

You will have to set the kernel and disk entries. This is the location of the kernel to use and the partition where it is located.

You control the domains with the **xend** servers. xend messages are placed in the **/var/log/xend.log** file. There is a xend service script on Fedora Core 4 letting you start the **xend** server with the following command, as well as managing xend from system-config-services:

```
service xend start
```

The **xm** tool creates and manages your domains (virtual machines). Check the xm Man page for a complete listing of operations. To create a virtual machine, use the **create** option and specify that domain's configuration file. If you want to connect directly to that virtual machine's console, you can use the **-c** option.

```
# xm create -c mynewvm
```

To start and stop your domains, you can use the **xendomains** service script. The **xendomains** script will use xm with the **create** option to create a domain configured in the **/etc/xen/auto** directory. Place Xen domain configuration files in this directory for **xendomains** to start. These domains will be started automatically when the kernel for domain0 is started. The following command manually starts your domains:

```
service xendomains start
```

To have your domains start automatically at boot, use **chkconfig** with the **xendomains** script to add the script.

```
chkconfig --add xendomains
```

To access domains, you use the **xm** command. The listing will include detailed information such as its domain ID, the CPU time used, memory used, and the domain state. The following lists your domains:

```
xm list
```

To access a particular domain, use the **console** option and the domain name.

```
xm console mynewvm
```

The **xm save** and **restore** options can be used to suspend and restart a domain.

Block devices such as partitions and CD-ROMs can be exported from the main domain to virtual domains. This allows a given virtual domain to use a particular partition. You can even share block devices between domains, though such shared devices should be read only.

NOTE *To more efficiently use block memory (hard disk partitions), you could implement dynamically allocated space using either file VBDs (virtual block devices implemented as files) or LVM VBDs.*

You can also manage your domains using the xensv web interface using port 8080. Start the xensv server with the following command:

```
xensv start
```

Backup Management: rsync, Amanda, and dump/restore

Backup operations have become an important part of administrative duties. Several backup tools are provided on Linux systems, including Anaconda and the traditional dump/restore tools, as well as the **rsync** command for making individual copies. Anaconda provides server-based backups, letting different systems on a network back up to a central server. The dump tools let you refine your backup process, detecting data changed since the last backup. Table 36-1 lists Web sites for Linux backup tools.

Individual Backups: archive and rsync

You can back up and restore particular files and directories with archive tools like **tar**, restoring the archives later. For backups, **tar** is usually used with a tape device. To automatically schedule backups, you can schedule appropriate **tar** commands with the **cron** utility. The archives can be also compressed for storage savings. You can then copy the compressed archives to any medium, such as a DVD disc, a floppy, or tape. On GNOME you can use File Roller to create archives easily (Archive Manager under System Tools). The Kdat tool on KDE will back up to tapes, a front end to **tar**. See Chapter 10 for a discussion of compressed archives.

If you want to remote-copy a directory or files from one host to another, making a particular backup, you can use **rsync**, which is designed for network backups of particular directories or files, intelligently copying only those files that have been changed, rather than the contents of an entire directory. In archive mode, it can preserve the original ownership and permissions, providing corresponding users exist on the host system. The following

Web Site	Tools
rsync.samba.org	rsync remote copy backup
www.amanda.org	Amanda network backup
dump.sourceforge.net	dump and restore tools

TABLE 36-1 Backup Resources

example copies the **/home/george/myproject** directory to the **/backup** directory on the host **rabbit**, creating a corresponding **myproject** subdirectory. The **-t** specifies that this is a transfer. The remote host is referenced with an attached colon, **rabbit:**.

```
rsync -t /home/george/myproject    rabbit:/backup
```

If, instead, you wanted to preserve the ownership and permissions of the files, you would use the **-a** (archive) option. Adding a **-z** option will compress the file. The **-v** option provides a verbose mode.

```
rsync -avz  /home/george/myproject    rabbit:/backup
```

A trailing slash on the source will copy the contents of the directory, rather than generating a subdirectory of that name. Here the contents of the **myproject** directory are copied to the **george-project** directory.

```
rsync -avz  /home/george/myproject/    rabbit:/backup/george-project
```

The **rsync** command is configured to use SSH remote shell by default. You can specify it or an alternate remote shell to use with the **-e** option. For secure transmission you can encrypt the copy operation with ssh. Either use the **-e ssh** option or set the **RSYNC_RSH** variable to ssh.

```
rsync -avz -e ssh  /home/george/myproject    rabbit:/backup/myproject
```

As when using **rcp**, you can copy from a remote host to the one you are on.

```
rsync -avz  lizard:/home/mark/mypics/  /pic-archice/markpics
```

You can also run **rsync** as a server daemon. This will allow remote users to sync copies of files on your system with versions on their own, transferring only changed files rather than entire directories. Many mirror and software FTP sites operate as **rsync** servers, letting you update files without have to download the full versions again. Configuration information for **rsync** as a server is kept in the **/etc/rsyncd.conf** file. On Fedora Core 4, **rsync** as a server is managed through **xinetd**, using the **/etc/xinetd.d/rsync** file, which starts **rsync** with the **--daemon** option. In the **/etc/services** file, it is listed to run on port 873. It is off by default, but you can enable it with system-config-services or **chkconfig**.

```
chkconfig rsync on
```

---

*TIP   Though it is designed for copying between hosts, you can also use **rsync** to make copies within your own system, usually to a directory in another partition or hard drive. In fact there are eight different ways of using **rsync**. Check the **rsync** Man page for detailed descriptions of each.*

Amanda

To back up hosts connected to a network, you can use the Advanced Maryland Automatic Network Disk Archiver (Amanda) to archive hosts. Amanda uses **tar** tools to back up all hosts to a single host operating as a backup server. Backup data is sent by each host to the host operating as the Amanda server, where they are written out to a backup medium such as tape. With an Amanda server, the backup operations for all hosts become centralized in one server, instead of each host having to perform its own backup. Any host that needs to restore data simply requests it from the Amanda server, specifying the file system, date, and filenames. Backup data are copied to the server's holding disk and from there to tapes. Detailed documentation and updates are provided at **www.amanda.org**.

Amanda is designed for automatic backups of hosts that may have very different configurations, as well as operating systems. You can back up any host that supports GNU tools, including Mac OS X and Windows systems connected through Samba.

Amanda Commands

Amanda has its own commands corresponding to the common backup tasks, beginning with "am," such as **amdump**, **amrestore**, and **amrecover**. The commands are listed in Table 36-2. The **amdump** command is the primary backup operation.

The **amdump** command performs requested backups; it is not designed for interactive use. For an interactive backup, you would use an archive tool like **tar** directly. **amdump** is placed within a cron instruction to be run at a specified time. If, for some reason, **amdump** cannot save all its data to the backup medium (tape or disk), it will retain the data on the holding disk. The data can then later be directly written with the **amflush** command.

You can restore particular files as well as complete systems with the **amrestore** command. With the **amrecover** tool, you can select from a list of backups.

Command	Description
amdump	Perform automatic backups for the file systems listed in the disklist configuration file.
amflush	Used to directly back up data from the holding disk to a tape.
amcleanup	Clean up if there is a system failure on the server.
amrecover	Select backups to restore using an interactive shell.
amrestore	Restore backups, either files or complete systems.
amlabel	Label the backup medium for Amanda.
amcheck	Check the backup systems and files as well as the backup tapes before backup operations.
amadmin	Back up administrative tasks.
amtape	Manage backup tapes, loading and removing them.
amverify	Check format of tapes.
amverifyrun	Check the tapes from the previous run, specify the configuration directory for the backup.
amrmtape	Remove a tape from the Amanda database, use for damaged tapes.
amstatus	Show the status of the current Amanda backup operation.

TABLE 36-2   Amanda Commands

Amanda Configuration

Configuration files are placed in **/etc/amanda**, and log and database files in **/var/lib/amanda**. These are created automatically when you install the Amanda RPM package. You will also need to create a directory to use as a holding disk where backups are kept before writing to the tape. This should be on a file system with very large available space, enough to hold the backup of your largest entire host.

/etc/amanda

Within the **/etc/amanda** directory are subdirectories for the different kind of backups you want to perform. Each directory will contain its own **amanda.conf** and **disklist** file. By default a daily backup directory is created called **DailySet1**, with a default **amanda.conf** and a sample **disklist** file. To use them, you will have to edit them to enter your system's own settings. For a different backup configuration, you can create a new directory and copy the **DailySet1 amanda.conf** and **dislist** files to it, editing them as appropriate. When you issue Amanda commands like **amdump** to perform backups, you will use the name of the **/etc/amanda** subdirectory to indicate the kind of backup you want performed.

```
amdump DailySet1
```

The **/etc/amanda** directory also contains a sample cron file, **crontab.sample**, that shows how a cron entry should look.

amanda.conf

The **amanda.conf** file contains basic configuration parameters such as the tape type and logfile as well as holding file locations. In most cases you can just use the defaults as listed in the **DailySet1/amanda.conf** file. The file is commented in detail, telling you what entries you will have to change. You will need to set the tapedev entries to the tape device you use, and the tape type entry for your tape drive type. In the holding disk segment, you will need to specify the partition and the directory for the holding disk you want to use. See the amanda Man page and documentation for detailed information on various options.

disklist

The **disklist** file is where you specify the file systems and partitions to be backed up. An entry lists the host, the partition, and the dump-type. The possible dump-types are defined in **amanda.conf**. The dump-types set certain parameters such as the priority of the backup and whether to use compression or not. The comp-root type will back up root partitions with compression and low priority, whereas the always-full type will back up an entire partition with no compression and the highest priority. You can define other dump-types in **amanda.conf** and use them for different partitions.

Backups will be performed in the order listed; be sure to list the more important ones first. The **disklist** file in **DailySet1** provides detailed examples.

Enabling Amanda on the Network

To use Amanda on the network, you need to run two servers on the Amanda server as well as an Amanda client on each network host. Access must be enabled for both the clients and the server.

Amanda Server

The Amanda server runs through **xinetd**, using **xinetd** service files located in **/etc/xinetd.d**. The two service files are **amidxtape** and **amandaidx**. You can turn these on with **chkconfig** or with system-config-services. You only need to do this once.

```
chkconfig amidxtape on
chkconfig amandaidx on
```

Then restart the **xinetd** daemon to have it take immediate effect.

```
service xinetd restart
```

For clients to be able to recover backups from the server, the clients' hostnames must be placed in the **.amandahosts** file in the server's Amanda users' directory. On Fedora Core 4, this is **/var/lib/amanda**. On the server, **/var/lib/amanda/.amandahosts** will list all the hosts that are backed up by Amanda.

Amanda Hosts

Each host needs to allow access by the Amanda server. To do this, you place the hostname of the Amanda server in each client's **.amandahosts** dot file. This file is located in the client's Amanda user home directory. On Fedora Core 4 systems, this is the **/var/lib/amanda** directory.

Each host needs to run the Amanda client daemon, **amanda**, which also runs under **xinetd**. Use either **chkconfig** or system-config-services to turn it on.

```
chkconfig amanda on
```

TIP   If your server and hosts have firewalls, you will need to allow access through the ports that Amanda uses, usually 10080, 10082, and 10083.

Using Amanda

Backups are performed by the **amdump** command.

```
amdump DailySet1
```

An **amdump** command for each backup is placed in the Amanda **crontab** file. It is helpful to run an **amcheck** operation to make sure that a tape is ready.

```
0 16 * * 1-5 /usr/sbin/amcheck -m DailySet1
45 0 * * 2-6 /usr/sbin/amdump DailySet1
```

Before you can use a tape, you will have to label it with **amlabel**. Amanda uses the label to determine what tape should be used for a backup. Log in as the Amanda user (not root) and label the tape so that it can be used.

```
amlabel DailySet DailySet1
```

A client can recover a backup using **amrecover**. This needs to be run as the root user, not as the Amanda user. The **amrecover** command works through an interactive shell much like **ftp**, letting you list available files and select them to restore. Within the **amrecover** shell the **ls** command will list available backups, the **add** command will select one, and the extract operation will restore it. The **lcd** command lets you change the client directory;

amrecover will use **DailySet1** as the default, but for other configurations you will need to specify their configuration directory with the **-C** option. Should you have more than one Amanda server, you can list the one you want with the **-t** option.

```
amrecover -C DailySet1
```

To restore full system backups, you use the **amrestore** command, specifying the tape device and the hostname.

```
amrestore /dev/rmt1 rabbit
```

To select certain files, you can pipe the output to a recovery command such as **restore** (discussed in the next section).

```
amrestore -p /dev/rmt1 rabbit mydir | restore -ibvf 2 -
```

Backups with dump and restore

You can back up and restore your system with the dump and restore utilities. dump can back up your entire system or perform incremental backups, saving only those files that have changed since the last backup. dump supports several options for managing the backup operation, such as specifying the size and length of storage media (see Table 36-3).

NOTE *Several disk dump tools are also available. The* **diskdumpfmt** *command can be used to format tapes for use by dump.* **diskdumpctl** *registers a dump partition with the system.* **savecore** *saves a* **vmcore** *file from the data in a dump partition. Dumped cores can be read by the* **crash** *tool. Check the* **crash** *Man page for details.*

The dump Levels

The dump utility uses *dump levels* to determine to what degree you want your system backed up. A dump level of 0 will copy file systems in their entirety. The remaining dump levels perform incremental backups, backing up only files and directories that have been created or modified since the last lower-level backup. A dump level of 1 will back up only files that have changed since the last level 0 backup. The dump level 2, in turn, will back up only files that have changed since the last level 1 backup (or 0 if there is no level 1), and so on up to dump level 9. You could run an initial complete backup at dump level 0 to back up your entire system, and then run incremental backups at certain later dates, having to back up only the changes since the full backup.

Using dump levels, you can devise certain strategies for backing up a file system. It is important to keep in mind that an incremental backup is run on changes from the last lower-level backup. For example, if the last backup was 6 and the next backup was 8, then level 8 would back up everything from the level 6 backup. The sequence of the backups is important. If there were three backups with levels 3, then 6, and then 5, the level 5 backup would take everything from the level 3 backup, not stopping at level 6. Level 3 is the next-*lower*-level backup for level 5, in this case. This can make for some complex incremental backup strategies. For example, if you want each succeeding incremental backup to include all the changes from the preceding incremental backups, you could run the backups in descending dump level order. Given a backup sequence of 7, 6, and 5, with 0 as the initial full backup, 6 would include all the changes to 7, because its next lower level is 0. Then 5 would include all the changes for 7 and 6, also because its next lower level is 0, making all the changes since the level 0 full backup. A simpler way to implement this is to make the incremental levels all the same. Given an initial level of 0, and then two backups both with level 1, the last level 1 would include all the changes from the backup with level 0, since level 0 is the next *lower* level—not the previous level 1 backup.

Option	Description
-0 through **-9**	Specifies the dump level. A dump level 0 is a full backup, copying the entire file system (see also the **-h** option). Dump level numbers above 0 perform incremental backups, copying all new or modified files in the file system since the last backup at a lower level. The default level is 9.
-B *records*	Lets you specify the number of blocks in a volume, overriding the end-of-media detection or length and density calculations that dump normally uses for multivolume dumps.
-a	Lets dump bypass any tape length calculations and write until an end-of-media indication is detected. Recommended for most modern tape drives and is the default.
-b *blocksize*	Lets you specify the number of kilobytes per dump record. With this option, you can create larger blocks, speeding up backups.
-d *density*	Specifies the density for a tape in bits per inch (default is 1,600 BPI).
-h *level*	Files that are tagged with a user's nodump flag will not be backed up at or above this specified level. The default is 1, which will not back up the tagged files in incremental backups.
-f *file/device*	Backs up the file system to the specified file or device. This can be a file or tape drive. You can specify multiple filenames, separated by commas. A remote device or file can be referenced with a preceding hostname, *hostname:file*.
-k	Uses Kerberos authentication to talk to remote tape servers.
-M *file/device*	Implements a multivolume backup, where the *file* written to is treated as a prefix and the suffix consisting of a numbered sequence from 001 is used for each succeeding file, *file*001, *file*002, etc. Useful when backup files need to be greater than the Linux **ext3** 2GB file size limit.
-n	Notifies operators if a backup needs operator attention.
-s *feet*	Specifies the length of a tape in feet. dump will prompt for a new tape when the length is reached.
-S	Estimates the amount of space needed to perform a backup.
-T *date*	Allows you to specify your own date instead of using the **/etc/dumpdates** file.
-u	Writes an entry for a successful update in the **/etc/dumpdates** file.
-W	Detects and displays the file systems that need to be backed up. This information is taken from the **/etc/dumpdates** and **/etc/fstab** files.
-w	Detects and displays the file systems that need to be backed up, drawing only on information in **/etc/fstab**.

TABLE 36-3   Options for dump

Recording Backups

Backups are recorded in the **/etc/dumpdates** file. This file will list all the previous backups, specifying the file system they were performed on, the dates they were performed, and the dump level used. You can use this information to restore files from a specified backup. Recall that the **/etc/fstab** file records the dump level as well as the recommended backup frequency for each file system. With the **–W** option, dump will analyze both the **/etc/dumpdates** and **/etc/fstab** files to determine which file systems need to be backed up. The **dump** command with the **–w** option just uses **/etc/fstab** to report the file systems ready for backup.

Operations with dump

The **dump** command takes as its arguments the dump level, the device it is storing the backup on, and the device name of the file system that is being backed up. If the storage medium (such as a tape) is too small to accommodate the backup, **dump** will pause and let you insert another. **dump** supports backups on multiple volumes. The **u** option will record the backup in the **/etc/dumpdates** file. In the following example, an entire backup (dump level 0) is performed on the file system on the **/dev/hda3** hard disk partition. The backup is stored on a tape device, **/dev/tape**.

```
dump -0u -f /dev/tape /dev/hda5
```

NOTE *You can use the **mt** command to control your tape device; **mt** has options to rewind, erase, and position the tape. The **rmt** command controls a remote tape device.*

The storage device can be another hard disk partition, but it is usually a tape device. When you installed your system, your system most likely detected the device and set up **/dev/tape** as a link to it (just as it did with your CD-ROMs). If the link was not set up, you have to create it yourself or use the device name directly. Tape devices can have different device names, depending on the model or interface. SCSI tape devices are labeled with the prefix **st**, with a number attached for the particular device: **st0** is the first SCSI tape device. To use it in the **dump** command, just specify its name.

```
dump -0u -f /dev/st0 /dev/hda5
```

Should you need to back up to a device located on another system on your network, you would have to specify that hostname for the system and the name of its device. The hostname is entered before the device name and delimited with a colon. In the following example, the user backs up file system **/dev/hda5** to the SCSI tape device with the name **/dev/st1** on the **rabbit.mytrek.com** system:

```
dump -0u -f rabbit.mytrek.com:/dev/st0 /dev/hda5
```

The **dump** command works on one file system at a time. If your system has more than one file system, you will need to issue a separate **dump** command for each.

TIP *You can use the system **cron** utility to schedule backups using dump at specified times.*

Recovering Backups

You use the **restore** command either to restore an entire file system or to just retrieve particular files. **restore** will extract files or directories from a backup archive and copy them to the current working directory. Make sure you are in the directory you want the files restored to when you run **restore**. **restore** will also generate any subdirectories as needed. **restore** has several options for managing the restore operation (see Table 36-4).

Operation	Description
-C	Lets you check a backup by comparing files on a file system with those in a backup.
-i	The interactive mode for restoring particular files and directories in a backup. A shell interface is generated where the user can use commands to specify file and directories to restore (see Table 36-5).
-R	Instructs **restore** to request a tape that is part of a multivolume backup, from which to continue the restore operation. Helpful when multivolume restore operations are interrupted.
-r	Restores a file system. Make sure that a newly formatted partition has been mounted and that you have changed to its top directory.
-t	Lists the contents of a backup or specified files in it.
-x	Extracts specified files or directories from a backup. A directory is restored with all its subdirectories. If no file or directory is specified, the entire file system is restored.
Additional Option	**Description**
–b *blocksize*	Uses a specific blocksize; otherwise, restore will dynamically determine it from the block device.
–f *file/device*	Restores the backup on the specified file or device. Specifies a hostname for remote devices.
–F *script*	Runs a script at the beginning of the restore.
–k	Uses Kerberos authentication for remote devices.
–h	Extracts only the specified directories, without their subdirectories.
–M *file/device*	Restores from multivolume backups, where the *file* is treated as a prefix and the suffix is a numbered sequence, *file*001, *file*002.
–N	Displays the names of files and directories, does not extract them.
–T *directory*	Specifies a directory to use for the storage of temporary files. The default value is **/tmp**.
–v	The verbose mode, where each file and its file type that **restore** operates on is displayed.
–y	By default, **restore** will query the operator to continue if an error occurs, such as bad blocks. This option suppresses that query, allowing **restore** to automatically continue.

TABLE **36-4**   Operations and Options for **restore**

To recover individual files and directories, you run **restore** in an interactive mode using the **-i** option. This will generate a shell with all the directories and files on the tape, letting you select the ones you want to restore. When you are finished, **restore** will then retrieve from a backup only those files you selected. This shell has its own set of commands that you can use to select and extract files and directories (see Table 36-5). The following command will generate an interactive interface listing all the directories and files backed up on the tape in the **/dev/tape** device:

```
restore -ivf /dev/tape
```

This command will generate a shell encompassing the entire directory structure of the backup. You are given a shell prompt and can use the **cd** command to move to different directories, and the **ls** command to list files and subdirectories. You use the **add** command to tag a file or directory for extraction. Should you later decide not to extract it, you can use the **delete** command to remove it from the tagged list. Once you have selected all the items you want, you enter the **extract** command to retrieve them from the backup archive. To quit the restore shell, you enter **quit**. The **help** command will list the restore shell commands.

If you need to restore an entire file system, you would use restore with the **-r** option. You can restore the file system to any blank formatted hard disk partition of adequate size, including the file system's original partition. If may be advisable, if possible, to restore the file system on another partition and check the results.

Command	Description
add [*arg*]	Adds files or directories to the list of files to be extracted. Such tagged files display an * before their names when listed with **ls**. All subdirectories of a tagged directory are also extracted.
cd [*arg*]	Changes the current working directory.
delete [*arg*]	Deletes a file or directory from the extraction list. All subdirectories for deleted directories will also be removed.
extract	Extracts files and directories on the extraction list.
help	Displays a list of available commands.
ls [*arg*]	Lists the contents of the current working directory or a specified directory.
pwd	Displays the full pathname of the current working directory.
quit	Exits the restore interactive mode shell. The **quit** command does not perform any extraction, even if the extraction list still has items in it.
setmodes	Sets the owner, modes, and times for all files and directories in the extraction list. Used to clean up an interrupted restore.
verbose	In the verbose mode, each file is listed as it is extracted. Also, the **ls** command lists the inode numbers for files and directories.

TABLE 36-5   Interactive Mode Shell Commands for **restore**

Restoring an entire file system involves setting up a formatted partition, mounting it to your system, and then changing to its top directory to run the **restore** command. First you should use **mkfs** to format the partition where you are restoring the file system, and then mount it onto your system. Then you use restore with the **-r** option and the **-f** option to specify the device holding the file system's backup. In the next example, the user formats and mounts the **/dev/hda5** partition and then restores on that partition the file system backup, currently on a tape in the **/dev/tape** device.

```
mkfs /dev/hda5
mount /dev/hda5 /mystuff
cd /mystuff
restore -rf /dev/tape
```

To restore from a backup device located on another system on your network, you would have to specify that hostname for the system and the name of its device. The hostname is entered before the device name and delimited with a colon. In the following example, the user restores a file system from the backup on the tape device with the name **/dev/tape** on the **rabbit.mytrek.com** system:

```
restore -rf rabbit.mytrek.com:/dev/tape
```

VII PART

Network Administration

37
CHAPTER

Administering TCP/IP Networks

L inux systems are configured to connect into networks that use the TCP/IP protocols. These are the same protocols that the Internet uses, as do many local area networks (LANs). TCP/IP is a robust set of protocols designed to provide communications among systems with different operating systems and hardware. The TCP/IP protocols were developed in the 1970s as a special DARPA project to enhance communications between universities and research centers. These protocols were originally developed on Unix systems, with much of the research carried out at the University of California, Berkeley. Linux, as a version of Unix, benefits from much of this original focus on Unix. Currently, the TCP/IP protocol development is managed by the Internet Engineering Task Force (IETF), which, in turn, is supervised by the Internet Society (ISOC). The ISOC oversees several groups responsible for different areas of Internet development, such as the Internet Assigned Numbers Authority (IANA), which is responsible for Internet addressing (see Table 37-1). Over the years, TCP/IP protocol standards and documentation have been issued in the form of Request for Comments (RFC) documents. Check the most recent ones for current developments at the IETF Web site at **www.ietf.org**.

TCP/IP Protocol Suite

The TCP/IP protocol suite actually consists of different protocols, each designed for a specific task in a TCP/IP network. The three basic protocols are the Transmission Control Protocol (TCP), which handles receiving and sending out communications, the Internet Protocol (IP), which handles the actual transmissions, and the User Datagram Protocol (UDP), which also handles receiving and sending packets. The IP protocol, which is the base protocol that all others use, handles the packets of data with sender and receiver information in each. The TCP protocol is designed to work with cohesive messages or data. This protocol checks received packets and sorts them into their designated order, forming the original message. For data sent out, the TCP protocol breaks the data into separate packets, designating their order. The UDP protocol, meant to work on a much more raw level, also breaks down data into packets but does not check their order. The TCP/IP protocol is designed to provide stable and reliable connections that ensure that all data

Group	Title	Description
ISOC	Internet Society	Professional membership organization of Internet experts that oversees boards and task forces dealing with network policy issues **www.isoc.org**
IESG	The Internet Engineering Steering Group	Responsible for technical management of IETF activities and the Internet standards process **www.ietf.org/iesg.html**
IANA	Internet Assigned Numbers Authority	Responsible for Internet Protocol (IP) addresses **www.iana.org**
IAB	Internet Architecture Board	Defines the overall architecture of the Internet, providing guidance and broad direction to the IETF **www.iab.org**
IETF	Internet Engineering Task Force	Protocol engineering and development arm of the Internet **www.ietf.org**

TABLE 37-1   TCP/IP Protocol Development Groups

is received and reorganized into its original order. UDP, on the other hand, is designed to simply send as much data as possible, with no guarantee that packets will all be received or placed in the proper order. UDP is often used for transmitting very large amounts of data of the type that can survive the loss of a few packets—for example, temporary images, video, and banners displayed on the Internet.

Other protocols provide various network and user services. The Domain Name Service (DNS) provides address resolution. The File Transfer Protocol (FTP) provides file transmission, and the Network File System (NFS) provides access to remote file systems. Table 37-2 lists the different protocols in the TCP/IP protocol suite. These protocols make use of either the TCP or UDP protocol to send and receive packets, which, in turn, uses the IP protocol for actually transmitting the packets.

In a TCP/IP network, messages are broken into small components, called *datagrams*, which are then transmitted through various interlocking routes and delivered to their destination computers. Once received, the datagrams are reassembled into the original message. Datagrams themselves can be broken down into smaller packets. The *packet* is the physical message unit actually transmitted among networks. Sending messages as small components has proved to be far more reliable and faster than sending them as one large, bulky transmission. With small components, if one is lost or damaged, only that component must be resent, whereas if any part of a large transmission is corrupted or lost, the entire message has to be resent.

The configuration of a TCP/IP network on your Linux system is implemented using a set of network configuration files (later in this chapter, Table 37-5 provides a complete listing). Many of these can be managed using administrative programs, such as system-config-network (see Chapter 5) as well as third-party tools like Webmin, on your root user desktop. You can also use the more specialized programs, such as netstat, ifconfig, Ethereal, and route. Some configuration files are easy to modify yourself using a text editor.

TCP/IP networks are configured and managed with a set of utilities: ifconfig, route, and netstat. The ifconfig utility operates from your root user desktop and enables you to configure

Transport	Description
TCP	Transmission Control Protocol; places systems in direct communication
UDP	User Datagram Protocol Description
IP	Internet Protocol; transmits data
ICMP	Internet Control Message Protocol; status messages for IP
Routing	**Description**
RIP	Routing Information Protocol; determines routing
OSPF	Open Shortest Path First; determines routing
Network Address	**Description**
ARP	Address Resolution Protocol; determines unique IP address of systems
DNS	Domain Name Service; translates hostnames into IP addresses
RARP	Reverse Address Resolution Protocol; determines addresses of systems
User Service	**Description**
FTP	File Transfer Protocol; transmits files from one system to another using TCP
TFTP	Trivial File Transfer Protocol; transfers files using UDP
Telnet	Remote login to another system on the network
SMTP	Simple Mail Transfer Protocol; transfers e-mail between systems
RPC	Remote Procedure Call; allows programs on remote systems to communicate
Gateway	**Description**
EGP	Exterior Gateway Protocol; provides routing for external networks
GGP	Gateway-to-Gateway Protocol; provides routing between Internet gateways
IGP	Interior Gateway Protocol; provides routing for internal networks
Network Service	**Description**
NFS	Network File System; allows mounting of file systems on remote machines
NIS	Network Information Service; maintains user accounts across a network
BOOTP	Boot Protocol; starts system using boot information on server for network
SNMP	Simple Network Management Protocol; provides status messages on TCP/IP configuration
DHCP	Dynamic Host Configuration Protocol; automatically provides network configuration information to host systems

TABLE 37-2 TCP/IP Protocol Suite

your network interfaces fully, adding new ones and modifying others. The ifconfig and route utilities are lower-level programs that require more specific knowledge of your network to use effectively. The netstat utility provides you with information about the status of your network connections. Ethereal is a network protocol analyzer that lets you capture packets as they are transmitted across your network, selecting those you want to check.

IPv4 and IPv6

Traditionally, a TCP/IP address is organized into four segments, consisting of numbers separated by periods. This is called the *IP address.* The IP address actually represents a 32-bit integer whose binary values identify the network and host. This form of IP addressing adheres to Internet Protocol, version 4, also known as IPv4. IPv4, the kind of IP addressing described here, is still in wide use.

Currently, a new version of the IP protocol called Internet Protocol, version 6 (IPv6) is gradually replacing the older IPv4 version. IPv6 expands the number of possible IP addresses by using 128 bits. It is fully compatible with systems still using IPv4. IPv6 addresses are represented differently, using a set of eight 16-bit segments, each separated from the next by a colon. Each segment is represented by a hexadecimal number. A sample address would be

```
FEC0:0:0:0:800:BA98:7654:3210
```

Advantages for IPv6 include the following:

- IPv6 features simplified headers that allow for faster processing.
- IPv6 provides support for encryption and authentication along with Virtual Private Networks (VPNs) using the integrated IPsec protocol.
- One of its most significant advantage lies in its extending the address space to cover 2 to the power of 128 possible hosts (billions of billions). This extends far beyond the 4.2 billion supported by IPv4.
- IPv6 supports stateless autoconfiguration of addresses for hosts, bypassing the need for DHCP to configure such addresses. Addresses can be generated directly using the MAC (Media Access Control) hardware address of an interface.
- IPv6 provides support for Quality of Service (QoS) operations, providing sufficient response times for services like multimedia and telecom tasks.
- Multicast capabilities are built into the protocol, providing direct support for multimedia tasks. Multicast addressing also provides that same function as IPv4 broadcast addressing.
- More robust transmissions can be ensured with anycast addressing, where packets can be directed to an anycast group of systems, only one of which needs to receive them. Multiple DNS servers supporting a given network could be designated as an anycast group, of which only one DNS server needs to receive the transmission, providing greater likelihood that the transmissions will go through.
- IPv6 provides better access for mobile nodes, like PDAs, notebooks, and cell phones.

TCP/IP Network Addresses

As noted previously, the traditional IPv4 TCP/IP address is organized into four segments, consisting of numbers separated by periods. This kind of address is still in widespread use and is what people commonly refer to as an *IP address.* Part of an IP address is used for the network address, and the other part is used to identify a particular interface on a host in that network. You should realize that IP addresses are assigned to interfaces—such as

Ethernet cards or modems—and not to the host computer. Usually a computer has only one interface and is accessed using only that interface's IP address. In that regard, an IP address can be thought of as identifying a particular host system on a network, and so the IP address is usually referred to as the *host address.*

In fact, though, a host system could have several interfaces, each with its own IP address. This is the case for computers that operate as gateways and firewalls from the local network to the Internet. One interface usually connects to the LAN and another to the Internet, as by two Ethernet cards. Each interface (such as an Ethernet card) has its own IP address. For example, when you use the Network Configuration tool to specify an IP address for an Ethernet card on your system, the Devices panel lists an entry for each Ethernet card installed on your computer, beginning with **eth0** for the first. Opening up a Device window, you can select the TCP protocol in the Protocols panel to open a TCP/IP setting window where you can enter the card's IP address. Other Ethernet cards have their own IP addresses. If you use a modem to connect to an ISP, you would set up a PPP interface that would also have its own IP address (usually dynamically assigned by the ISP). Remembering this distinction is important if you plan to use Linux to set up a local or home network, using Linux as your gateway machine to the Internet (see the section "IP Masquerading" in Chapter 20).

IPv4 Network Addresses

The IP address is divided into two parts: one part identifies the network, and the other part identifies a particular host. The network address identifies the network of which a particular interface on a host is a part. Two methods exist for implementing the network and host parts of an IP address: the original class-based IP addressing and the current Classless Interdomain Routing (CIDR) addressing. Class-based IP addressing designates officially predetermined parts of the address for the network and host addresses, whereas CIDR addressing allows the parts to be determined dynamically using a netmask.

Class-Based IP Addressing

Originally, IP addresses were organized according to classes. On the Internet, networks are organized into three classes depending on their size—classes A, B, and C. A class A network uses only the first segment for the network address and the remaining three for the host, allowing a great many computers to be connected to the same network. Most IP addresses reference smaller, class C networks. For a class C network, the first three segments are used to identify the network, and only the last segment identifies the host. Altogether, this forms a unique address with which to identify any network interface on computers in a TCP/IP network. For example, in the IP address 192.168.1.72, the network part is 192.168.1 and the interface/host part is 72. The interface/host is a part of a network whose own address is 192.168.1.0.

In a class C network, the first three numbers identify the network part of the IP address. This part is divided into three network numbers, each identifying a subnet. Networks on the Internet are organized into subnets, beginning with the largest and narrowing to small subnetworks. The last number is used to identify a particular computer, referred to as a *host.* You can think of the Internet as a series of networks with subnetworks; these subnetworks have their own subnetworks. The rightmost number identifies the host computer, and the number preceding it identifies the subnetwork of which the computer is a part. The number to the left of that identifies the network the subnetwork is part of, and so on. The Internet address 192.168.187.4 references the fourth computer connected to the network identified by the number 187. Network 187 is a subnet to a larger network identified as 168. This larger network is itself a subnet of the network identified as 192. Here's how it breaks down:

192.168.187.4	IPv4 address
192.168.187	Network identification
4	Host identification

Netmask

Systems derive the network address from the host address using the netmask. You can think of an IP address as a series of 32 binary bits, some of which are used for the network and the remainder for the host. The *netmask* has the network set of bits set to 1s, with the host bits set to 0s (see Figure 37-1). In a standard class-based IP address, all the numbers in the network part of your host address are set to 255, and the host part is set to 0. This has the effect of setting all the binary bits making up the network address to 1s. This, then, is your netmask. So, the netmask for the host address 192.168.1.72 is 255.255.255.0. The network part, 192.168.1, has been set to 255.255.255, and the host part, 72, has been set to 0. Systems can then use your netmask to derive your network address from your host address. They can determine what part of your host address makes up your network address and what those numbers are.

For those familiar with computer programming, a bitwise AND operation on the netmask and the host address results in zeroing the host part, leaving you with the network part of the host address. You can think of the address as being implemented as a four-byte integer, with each byte corresponding to a segment of the address. In a class C address, the three network segments correspond to the first three bytes and the host segment corresponds to the fourth byte. A netmask is designed to mask out the host part of the address, leaving the network segments alone. In the netmask for a standard class C network, the first three bytes are all 1s and the last byte consists of 0s. The 0s in the last byte mask out the host part of the address, and the 1s in the first three bytes leave the network part of the address alone. Figure 37-1 shows the bitwise operation of the netmask on the address 192.168.1.4. This is a class C address to the mask, which consists of twenty-four 1s making up the first three bytes and eight 0s making up the last byte. When it is applied to the address 192.168.1.4, the network address remains (192.168.1) and the host address is masked out (4), giving you 192.168.1.0 as the network address.

The netmask as used in Classless Interdomain Routing (CIDR) is much more flexible. Instead of having the size of the network address and its mask determined by the network class, it is determined by a number attached to the end of the IP address. This number simply specifies the size of the network address, how many bits in the address it takes up. For example, in an IP address whose network part takes up the first three bytes (segments), the number of bits used for that network part is 24—eight bits to a byte (segment). Instead of using a netmask to determine the network address, the number for the network size is attached to the end of the address with a slash, as shown here:

```
192.168.1.72/24
```

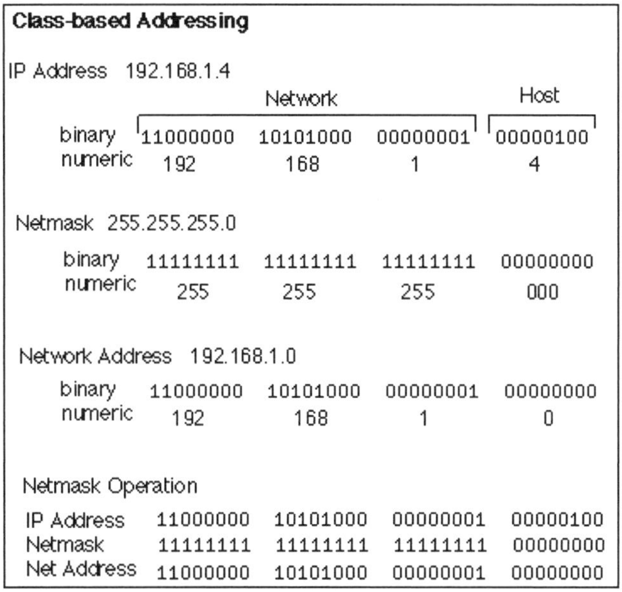

```
Class-based Addressing

IP Address   192.168.1.4
                           Network                        Host
      binary   11000000   10101000   00000001   00000100
      numeric    192        168         1          4


Netmask  255.255.255.0

      binary   11111111   11111111   11111111   00000000
      numeric    255        255        255         000


Network Address   192.168.1.0

      binary   11000000   10101000   00000001   00000000
      numeric    192        168         1           0


Netmask Operation

IP Address    11000000   10101000   00000001   00000100
Netmask       11111111   11111111   11111111   00000000
Net Address   11000000   10101000   00000001   00000000
```

FIGURE 37-1   Class-based netmask operations

CIDR gives you the advantage of specifying networks that are any size bits, instead of only three possible segments. You could have a network whose addresses take up 14 bits, 22 bits, or even 25 bits. The host address can use whatever bits are left over. An IP address with 21 bits for the network can cover host addresses using the remaining 11 bits, 0 to 2,047.

Classless Interdomain Routing (CIDR)

Currently, the class-based organization of IP addresses is being replaced by the CIDR format. CIDR was designed for midsized networks, those between a class C and classes with numbers of hosts greater than 256 and smaller than 65,534. A class C network–based IP address uses an 8-bit integer, with a maximum value of 256. A class B network–based IP address uses two segments, which make up a 16-bit integer whose maximum value is 65,534. You can think of an address as a 32-bit integer taking up four bytes, where each byte is 8 bits. Each segment conforms to one of the four bytes. A class C network uses three segments, or 24 bits, to make up its network address. A class B network, in turn, uses two segments, or 16 bits, for its address. With this scheme, allowable host and network addresses are changed an entire byte at a time, segment to segment. With CIDR addressing, you can define host and network addresses by bits, instead of whole segments. For example, you can use CIDR addressing to expand the host segment from 8 bits to 9, rather than having to jump it to a class B 16 bits (two segments).

CIDR addressing notation achieves this by incorporating netmask information in the IP address (the netmask is applied to an IP address to determine the network part of the address). In the CIDR notation, the number of bits making up the network address is placed after the

IP address, following a slash. For example, the CIDR form of the class C 192.168.187.4 IP address is

```
192.168.187.4/24
```

Figure 37-2 shows an example of a CIDR address and its network mask. The IP address is 192.168.1.6 with a network mask of 22 bits, 192.168.1.6/22. The network address takes up the first 22 bits of the IP address, and the remaining 10 bits are used for the host address. The host address is taking up the equivalent of a class-based IP address's fourth segment (8 bits) and 2 bits from the third segment.

Table 37-3 lists the different IPv4 CIDR network masks available along with the maximum number of hosts. Both the short forms and the full forms of the netmasks are listed.

IPv4 CIDR Addressing

The network address for any standard class C IPv4 IP address takes up the first three segments, 24 bits. If you want to create a network with a maximum of 512 hosts, you can give them IP addresses where the network address is 23 bits and the host address takes up 9 bits (0–511). The IP address notation remains the same, however, using the four 8-bit segments. This means a given segment's number could be used for both a network address and a host address. Segments are no longer wholly part of either the host address or the network address. Assigning a 23-bit network address and a 9-bit host address means that the number in the third segment is part of both the network address and the host address, the first 7 bits for the network and the last bit for the host. In this following example, the third number, 145, is used as the end of the network address and as the beginning of the host address:

```
192.168.145.67/23
```

This situation complicates CIDR addressing, and in some cases the only way to represent the address is to specify two or more network addresses. Check RFC 1520 at **www.ietf.org** for more details.

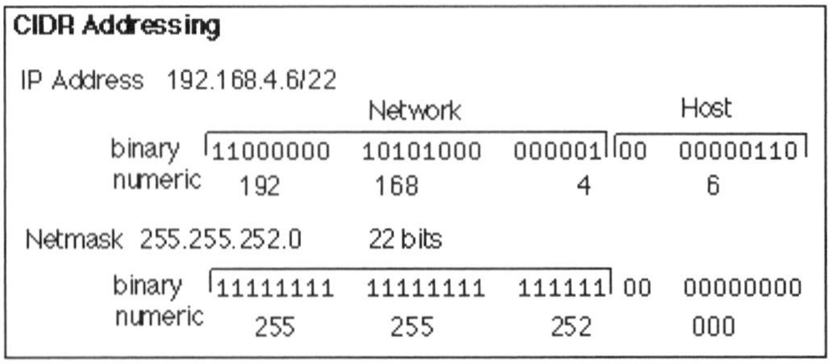

```
CIDR Addressing

IP Address   192.168.4.6/22
                                   Network                        Host
            binary   11000000    10101000   000001 00    00000110
            numeric    192          168         4            6

Netmask  255.255.252.0          22 bits

            binary   11111111    11111111   111111 00    00000000
            numeric    255          255        252          000
```

FIGURE 37-2   CIDR addressing

Short Form	Full Form	Maximum Number of Hosts
/8	/255.0.0.0	16,777,215 (A class)
/16	/255.255.0.0	65,535 (B class)
/17	/255.255.128.0	32,767
/18	/255.255.192.0	16,383
/19	/255.255.224.0	8,191
/20	/255.255.240.0	4,095
/21	/255.255.248.0	2,047
/22	/255.255.252.0	1,023
/23	/255.255.254.0	511
/24	/255.255.255.0	255 (C class)
/25	/255.255.255.128	127
/26	/255.255.255.192	63
/27	/255.255.255.224	31
/28	/255.255.255.240	15
/29	/255.255.255.248	7
/30	/255.255.255.252	3

TABLE 37-3   CIDR IPv4 Network Masks

NOTE *A simple way to calculate the number of hosts a network can address is to take the number of bits in its host segment as a power of 2, then subtract 2—that is, 2 to the number of host bits, minus 2. For example, an 8-bit host segment would be 2 to the power of 8, which equals 256. Subtract 2 (1 for the broadcast address, 255, and 1 for the zero value, 000) to leave you with 254 possible hosts.*

CIDR also allows a network administrator to take what is officially the host part of an IP address and break it up into subnetworks with fewer hosts. This is referred to as *subnetting*. A given network will have its official IP network address recognized on the Internet or by a larger network. The network administrator for that network could, in turn, create several smaller networks within it using CIDR network masking. A classic example is to take a standard class C network with 254 hosts and break it up into two smaller networks, each with 64 hosts. You do this by using a CIDR netmask to take a bit from the host part of the IP address and use it for the subnetworks. Numbers within the range of the original 254 addresses whose first bit would be set to 1 would represent one subnet, and the others, whose first bit would be set to 0, would constitute the remaining network. In the network whose network address is 192.168.187.0, where the last segment is used for the hostnames, that last host segment could be further split into two subnets, each with its own hosts. For two subnets, you would use the first bit in the last 8-bit segment for the network. The remaining 7 bits could then be used for host addresses, giving you a range of 127 hosts per network. The subnet whose bit is set to 0 would have a range of 1 to 127, with a CIDR netmask of 25. The 8-bit segment for the first host would be 00000001. So the host with the address of 1 in that network would have this IP address:

```
192.168.187.1/25
```

For the subnet where the first bit is 1, the first host would have an address of 129, with the CIDR netmask of 25, as shown here. The 8-bit sequence for the first host would be 10000001.

```
192.168.187.129/25
```

Each subnet would have a set of 126 addresses, the first from 1 to 126, and the second from 129 to 254; 127 is the broadcast address for the first subnet, and 128 is the network address for the second subnet. The possible subnets and their masks that you could use are shown here:

Subnetwork	CIDR Address	Binary Mask
First subnet network address	.0/25	00000000
Second subnet network address	.128/25	10000000
First subnet broadcast address	.127/25	01111111
Second subnet broadcast address	.255/25	11111111
First address in first subnet	.1/25	00000001
First address in second subnet	.129/25	10000001
Last address in first subnet	.126/25	01111110
Last address in second subnet	.254/25	11111110

IPv6 CIDR Addressing

IPv6 CIDR addressing works much the same as with the IPv4 method. The number of bits used for the network information is indicated by the number following the address. A host (interface) address could take up much more than the 64 bits that it usually does in an IPv6 address, making the network prefix (address) section smaller than 64 bits. How many bits that the network prefix uses is indicated by the following number. In the next example the network prefix (address) uses only the first 48 bits of the IPv6 address, and the host address uses the remaining 80 bits:

```
FEC0:0000:0000:0000:FEDC:BA98:7654:3210/48
```

You can also use a two-colon notation (::) for the compressed version:

```
FEC0::FEDC:BA98:7654:3210/48
```

Though you can use CIDR to subnet addresses, IPv6 also supports a subnet field that can be used for subnets.

Obtaining an IP Address

IP addresses are officially allocated by IANA, which manages all aspects of Internet addressing (**www.iana.org**). IANA oversees Internet Registries (IRs), which, in turn, maintain Internet addresses on regional and local levels. The Internet Registry for the Americas is the American Registry for Internet Numbers (ARIN), whose Web site is at **www.arin.net**. These addresses are provided to users by Internet service providers (ISPs). You can obtain your own Internet address from an ISP, or if you are on a network already connected to the Internet, your network administrator can assign you one. If you are using an ISP, the ISP may temporarily assign one from a pool it has on hand with each use.

IPv4 Reserved Addresses

Certain numbers are reserved. The numbers 127, 0, or 255 cannot be part of an official IP address. The number 127 is used to designate the network address for the loopback interface on your system. The loopback interface enables users on your system to communicate with each other within the system without having to route through a network connection. Its network address would be 127.0.0.0, and its IP address is 127.0.0.1. For class-based IP addressing, the number 255 is a special broadcast identifier you can use to broadcast messages to all sites on a network. Using 255 for any part of the IP address references all nodes connected at that level. For example, 192.168.255.255 broadcasts a message to all computers on network 192.168, all its subnetworks, and their hosts. The address 192.168.187.255 broadcasts to every computer on the local network. If you use 0 for the network part of the address, the host number references a computer within your local network. For example, 0.0.0.6 references the sixth computer in your local network. If you want to broadcast to all computers on your local network, you can use the number 0.0.0.255. For CIDR IP addressing, the broadcast address may appear much like a normal IP address. As indicated in the preceding section, CIDR addressing allows the use of any number of bits to make up the IP address for either the network or the host part. For a broadcast address, the host part must have all its bits set to 1 (see Figure 37-3).

A special set of numbers is reserved for use on non-Internet LANs (RFC 1918). These are numbers that begin with the special network number 192.168 (for class C networks), as used in these examples. If you are setting up a LAN, such as a small business or a home network, you are free to use these numbers for your local machines. You can set up an intranet using network cards, such as Ethernet cards and Ethernet hubs, and then configure your machines with IP addresses starting from 192.168.1.1. The host segment can go up to 256. If you have three machines on your home network, you could give them the addresses 192.168.1.1, 192.168.1.2, and 192.168.1.3. You can implement Internet services, such as FTP, Web, and mail services, on your local machines and use any of the Internet tools to make use of those services. They all use the same TCP/IP protocols used on the Internet. For example, with FTP tools, you can transfer files among the machines on your network. With mail tools, you can send messages from one machine to another, and with a Web browser, you can access local Web sites that may be installed on a machine running its own Web servers. If you want to have one of your machines connected to the Internet or some other network, you can set it up to be a gateway machine. By convention, the gateway machine is usually given the address 192.168.1.1. With a method called *IP masquerading*, you can have any of the non-Internet machines use a gateway to connect to the Internet.

IPv4 Private Network Address	Network Class
10.0.0.0	Class A network
172.16.0.0–172.31.255.255	Class B network
192.168.0.0	Class C network
127.0.0.0	Loopback network (for system self-communication)

TABLE 37-4 Non-Internet IPv4 Private Network IP Addresses

Numbers are also reserved for class A and class B non-Internet local networks. Table 37-4 lists these addresses. The possible addresses available span from 0 to 255 in the host segment of the address. For example, class B network addresses range from 172.16.0.0 to 172.31.255.255, giving you a total of 32,356 possible hosts. The class C network ranges from 192.168.0.0 to 192.168.255.255, giving you 256 possible subnetworks, each with 256 possible hosts. The network address 127.0.0.0 is reserved for a system's loopback interface, which allows it to communicate with itself, enabling users on the same system to send messages to each other.

Broadcast Addresses

The broadcast address allows a system to send the same message to all systems on your network at once. With IPv4 class-based IP addressing, you can easily determine the broadcast address using your host address: the broadcast address has the host part of your address set to 255. The network part remains untouched. So the broadcast address for the host address 192.168.1.72 is 192.168.1.255 (you combine the network part of the address with 255 in the host part). For CIDR IP addressing, you need to know the number of bits in the netmask. The remaining bits are set to 1 (see Figure 37-3). For example, an IP address of 192.168.4.6/22 has a broadcast address of 192.168.7.255/22. In this case, the first 22 bits are the network address and the last 10 bits are the host part set to the broadcast value (all 1s).

In fact, you can think of a class C broadcast address as merely a CIDR address using 24 bits (the first three segments) for the network address, and the last 8 bits (the fourth segment) as the broadcast address. The value 255 expressed in binary terms is simply 8 bits that are all 1s. 255 is the same as 11111111.

IP Address	Broadcast Address	IP Broadcast Number	Binary Equivalent
192.168.1.72	192.168.1.255	255	11111111
192.168.4.6/22	192.168.7.255/22	7.255 (last 2 bits in 7)	1111111111

Gateway Addresses

Some networks have a computer designated as the gateway to other networks. Every connection to and from a network to other networks passes through this gateway computer. Most local networks use gateways to establish a connection to the Internet. If you are on this type of network, you must provide the gateway address. If your network does not have a connection to the Internet, or a larger network, you may not need a gateway address. The gateway address is the address of the host system providing the gateway service to the network. On many networks, this host is given a host ID of 1: the gateway address for a

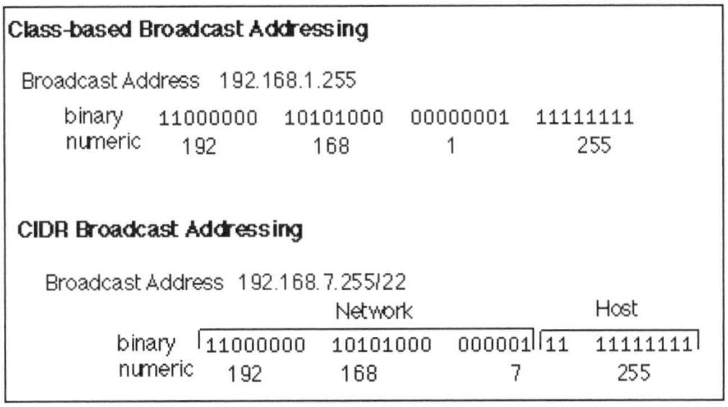

```
Class-based Broadcast Addressing

Broadcast Address   192.168.1.255
        binary    11000000   10101000   00000001   11111111
        numeric      192        168         1         255


CIDR Broadcast Addressing

Broadcast Address   192.168.7.255/22
                                    Network                Host
        binary    11000000   10101000   000001 11   11111111
        numeric      192        168         7          255
```

FIGURE 37-3   Class-based and CIDR broadcast addressing

network with the address 192.168.1 would be 192.168.1.1, but this is only a convention. To be sure of your gateway address, ask your network administrator.

Name Server Addresses

Many networks, including the Internet, have computers that provide a Domain Name Service (DNS) that translates the domain names of networks and hosts into IP addresses. These are known as the network's *domain name servers*. The DNS makes your computer identifiable on a network, using only your domain name, rather than your IP address. You can also use the domain names of other systems to reference them, so you needn't know their IP addresses. You must know the IP addresses of any domain name servers for your network, however. You can obtain the addresses from your system administrator (often more than one exists). Even if you are using an ISP, you must know the address of the domain name servers your ISP operates for the Internet.

IPv6 Addressing

IPv6 addresses introduces major changes into the format and method of addressing systems under the Internet Protocol (see RFC 3513 at **www.ietf.org/rfc** or **www.faqs.org** for more details). There are several different kinds of addressing with different fields for the network segment. The host segment has been expanded to a 64-bit address, allowing direct addressing for a far larger number of systems. Each address begins with a type field specifying the kind of address, which will then determine how its network segment is organized. These changes are designed not only to expand the address space but to also provide greater control over transmissions at the address level.

NOTE   *Red Hat Enterprise Linux and Fedora Core are distributed with IPv6 support already enabled in the kernel. Kernel support for IPv6 is provided by the IPv6 kernel module. Kernel configuration support can be found under Device Drivers | Networking Support | Networking Options | The IPv6 Protocol (see Chapter 35).*

IPv6 Address Format

An IPv6 address consists of 128 bits, up from the 32 bits used in IPv4 addresses. The first 64 bits are used for network addressing, of which the first few bits are reserved for indicating the address type. The last 64 bits are used for the interface address, known as the interface identifier field. The amount of bits used for subnetting can be adjusted with a CIDR mask, much like that in IPv4 CIDR addressing (see the preceding section).

An IPv6 address is written as eight segments representing 16 bits each (128 bits total). To more easily represent 16-bit binary numbers, hexadecimal numbers are used. Hexadecimal numbers use 16 unique numbers, instead of the 8 used in octal numbering. These are 0–9, continuing with the characters A–F.

In the following example the first four segments represent the network part of the IPv6 address, and the following four segments represent the interface (host) address:

```
FEC0:0000:0000:0000:0008:0800:200C:417A
```

You can cut any preceding zeros, but not trailing zeros, in any given segment. Segments with all zeros can be reduced to a single zero.

```
FEC0:0:0:0:8:800:200C:417A
```

The loopback address used for localhost addressing can be written with seven preceding zeros and a 1.

```
0:0:0:0:0:0:0:1
```

Many addresses will have sequences of zeros. IPv6 supports a shorthand symbol for representing a sequence of several zeros in adjacent fields. This consists of a double colon (::). There can be only one use of the :: symbol per address.

```
FEC0::8:800:200C:417A
```

The loopback address 0000000000000001 can be reduced to just the following:

```
::1
```

To ease the transition from IPv4 addressing to IPv6, a form of addressing incorporating IPv4 addresses is also supported. In this case, the IPv4 address (32 bits) can be used to represent the last two segments of an IPv6 address and can be written using IPv4 notation.

```
FEC0::192.168.0.3
```

IPv6 Interface Identifiers

The identifier part of the IPv6 address takes up the second 64 bits, consisting of four segments containing four hexadecimal numbers. The interface ID is an 64-bit (four-segment) Extended Unique Identifier (EUI-64) generated from a network device's Media Access Control (MAC) address.

IPv6 Address Types

There are three basic kinds of IPv6 addresses: unicast, multicast, and anycast. These, in turn, can have their own types of addresses.

- A *unicast* address is used for a packet that is sent to a single destination.
- An *anycast* address is used for a packet that can be sent to more than one destination.
- A *multicast* address is used to broadcast a packet to a range of destinations.

In IPv6, addressing is controlled by the format prefix that operates as a kind of address type. The format prefix is the first field of the IP address. The three major kinds of unicast network addresses are global, link-local, and site-local. Global, site-local, and link-local are indicated by their own format prefix (see Table 37-5).

- Global addresses begin with the address type 3, site-local with FEC, and link-local with FE8. Global addresses can be sent across the Internet.
- Link-local addresses are used for physically connected systems on a local network.
- Site-local can be used for any hosts on a local network. Site-local addresses operate similar to IPv4 private addresses; they are used only for local access and cannot be used to transmit over the Internet.

In addition, IPv6 has two special reserved addresses. The address 0000000000000001 is reserved for the loopback address used for a system's localhost address, and the address 0000000000000000 is the unspecified address.

IPv6 Unicast Global Addresses

IPv6 global addresses currently use four fields: the format prefix, a global routing prefix, the subnet identifier, and the interface identifier. The format prefix for a unicast global address is 3 (3 bits). The global routing prefix references the network address (45 bits), and the subnet ID references a subnet within the site (16 bits).

IPv6 Format Prefixes and Reserved Addresses	Description
3	Unicast global addresses
FE8	Unicast link-local addresses, used for physically connected hosts on a network
FEC	Unicast site-local addresses, comparable to IPv4 private addresses
0000000000000001	Unicast loopback address (for system self-communication, localhost)
0000000000000000	Unspecified address
FF	Multicast addresses

TABLE 37-5   IPv6 Format Prefixes and Reserved Addresses

IPv6 Unicast Local Use Addresses: Link-Local and Site-Local Addresses

For local use, IPv6 provides both link-local and site-local addresses. Link-local addressing is used for interfaces (hosts) that are physically connected to a network. This is usually a small local network. A link-local address uses only three fields, the format prefix FE8 (10 bits), an empty field (54 bits), and the interface identifier (host address) (64 bits). In effect, the network section is empty.

IPv6 site-local addresses have three fields: the format prefix (10 bits), the subnet identifier (54 bits), and the interface identifier (64 bits). Except for any local subnetting, there is no network address.

IPv6 Multicast Addresses

Multicast addresses have a format prefix of FF (8 bits) with flag and scope fields to indicate whether the multicast group is permanent or temporary and whether it is local or global in scope. A group identifier (112 bits) references the multicast group. For the scope, 2 is link-local, 5 is site-local, and E is global. In addition to their interface identifiers, hosts will also have a group ID that can be used as a broadcast address. You use this address to broadcast to the hosts. The following example will broadcast only to those hosts on the local network (5) with the group ID 101:

```
FF05:0:0:0:0:0:0:101
```

To broadcast to all the hosts in a link-local scope, you would use the broadcast address:

```
FF02:0:0:0:0:0:0:1
```

For a site-local scope, a local network, you would use

```
FF05:0:0:0:0:0:0:2
```

IPv6 and IPv4 Coexistence Methods

In the transition from IPv4 to IPv6, many networks will find the need to support both. Some will be connected to networks that use the contrary protocol, and others will have to connect through other network connections that use that protocol. There are several official IETF methods for providing IPv6 and IPv4 cooperation, which fall into three main categories:

- **Dual-stack**   Allows IPv4 and IPv6 to coexist on the same networks.
- **Translation**   Enables IPv6 devices to communicate with IPv4 devices.
- **Tunneling**   Allows transmission from one IPv6 network to another through IPv4 networks as well as allowing IPv6 hosts to operate on or through IPv4 networks.

In the dual-stack methods both IPv6 and IPv4 addresses are supported on the network. Applications and DNS servers can use either to transmit data.

Translation uses NAT tables (see Chapter 20) to translate IPv6 addresses to corresponding IPv4 addresses and vice versa as needed. IPv4 applications can then freely interact with IPv6 applications. IPv6-to-IPv6 transmissions are passed directly through, enabling full IPv6 functionality.

Tunneling is used when one IPv6 network needs to transmit to another through an IPv4 network that cannot handle IPv6 addresses. With tunneling, the IPv6 packet is encapsulated within an IPv4 packet, where the IPv4 network then uses the outer IPv4 addressing to pass on the packet. Several methods are used for tunneling, as shown here, as well as direct manual manipulation:

- **6-over-4**   Used within a network to use IPv4 multicasting to implement a virtual LAN to support IPv6 hosts, without an IPv6 router (RFC 2529)
- **6-to-4**   Used to allow IPv6 networks to connect to and through a larger IPv4 network (the Internet), using the IPv4 network address as an IPv6 network prefix (RFC 3056)
- **Tunnel brokers**   Web-based services that create tunnels (RFC 3053)

TCP/IP Configuration Files

A set of configuration files in the **/etc** directory, shown in Table 37-6, are used to set up and manage your TCP/IP network. These configuration files specify such network information as hostnames and domain names, IP addresses, and interface options. The IP addresses and domain names of other Internet hosts you want to access are entered in these files. If you configured your network during installation, you can already find that information in these files.

Identifying Hostnames: /etc/hosts

Without the unique IP address the TCP/IP network uses to identify computers, a particular computer cannot be located. Because IP addresses are difficult to use or remember, domain names are used instead. For each IP address, a domain name exists. When you use a domain name to reference a computer on the network, your system translates it into its associated IP address. This address can then be used by your network to locate that computer.

Originally, every computer on the network was responsible for maintaining a list of the hostnames and their IP addresses. This list is still kept in the **/etc/hosts** file. When you use a domain name, your system looks up its IP address in the **hosts** file. The system administrator is responsible for maintaining this list. Because of the explosive growth of the Internet and the development of more and more large networks, the responsibility for associating domain names and IP addresses has been taken over by domain name servers. The **hosts** file is still used to hold the domain names and IP addresses of frequently accessed hosts, however. Your system normally checks your **hosts** file for the IP address of a domain name before taking the added step of accessing a name server.

The format of a domain name entry in the **hosts** file is the IP address followed by the domain name, separated by a space. You can then add aliases for the hostname. After the entry, on the same line, you can enter a comment. A comment is always preceded by a **#** symbol. You can already find an entry in your **hosts** file for localhost with the IP address 127.0.0.1; localhost is a special identification used by your computer to enable users on your system to communicate locally with each other. The IP address 127.0.0.1 is a special reserved address used by every computer for this purpose. It identifies what is technically referred to as a *loopback device*. A sample **/etc/hosts** file is shown here:

```
/etc/hosts
127.0.0.1         turtle.mytrek.com localhost
192.168.0.1       turtle.mytrek.com
192.168.0.2       rabbit.mytrek.com
192.168.34.56     pango1.mytrain.com
```

Address	Description
Host address	IP address of your system; it has a network part to identify the network you are on and a host part to identify your own system
Network address	IP address of your network
Broadcast address	IP address for sending messages to all hosts on your network at once
Gateway address	IP address of your gateway system, if you have one (usually the network part of your host IP address with the host part set to 1)
Domain name server addresses	IP addresses of domain name servers your network uses
Netmask	Used to determine the network and host parts of your IP address
File	**Description**
/etc/hosts	Associates hostnames with IP addresses, lists domain names for remote hosts with their IP addresses
/etc/sysconfig/network-scripts	Network connection configurations
/etc/host.conf	Lists resolver options
/etc/nsswitch.conf	Name Switch Service configuration
/etc/resolv.conf	Lists domain name server names, IP addresses (nameserver), and domain names where remote hosts may be located (search)
/etc/protocols	Lists protocols available on your system
/etc/services	Lists available network services, such as FTP and Telnet, and the ports they use
/etc/sysconfig/networking	Holds network configuration files managed by system-config-network
/etc/sysconfig/network	Network configuration information

TABLE 37-6   TCP/IP Configuration Addresses and Files

/etc/resolv.conf

As noted in Chapter 38, the **/etc/resolv.conf** file holds the IP addresses for your DNS servers along with domains to search. A DNS entry will begin with the term nameserver followed by the name server's IP address. A search entry will list network domain addresses. Check this file to see if your network DNS servers have been correctly listed.

/etc/resolv.conf
```
search  mytrek.com   mytrain.com
nameserver  192.168.0.1
nameserver  192.168.0.3
```

/etc/sysconfig/network-scripts

The **/etc/sysconfig/network-scripts** directory holds configuration information for different network connection devices such the IP address and network address used. For a detailed discussion, see the section "Network Interfaces and Routes: ifconfig and route" later in this chapter.

/etc/sysconfig/networking

The **/etc/sysconfig/networking** directory holds configuration information set up with system-config-network (Network on the System Settings menu and window). These files should not be edited manually. The profiles directory holds configurations for the different profiles you set up. Different profiles directories will include the hosts file listing host domain names and IP addresses, the network file holding your system's hostname, and the **resolv.conf** file, which contains your domain name servers. The device configuration file for the connection you use for that profile will also be listed, such as **ifcfg-eth0** for the first Ethernet device. These are all configurations that may change depending on the profile you use. For example, at the office you may use an Ethernet connection on a company network with its own DNS servers, whereas at home you may use a modem connection to an ISP with its own Internet DNS servers. Your hostname and domain name may vary depending on the networks your different profiles connect to.

/etc/services

The **/etc/services** file lists network services available on your system, such as FTP and Telnet, and associates each with a particular port. Here, you can find out what port your Web server is checking or what port is used for your FTP server. You can give a service an alias, which you specify after the port number. You can then reference the service using the alias.

/etc/protocols

The **/etc/protocols** file lists the TCP/IP protocols currently supported by your system. Each entry shows the protocol number, its keyword identifier, and a brief description. See **www.iana.org/assignments/protocol-numbers** for a complete listing.

/etc/sysconfig/network

The **/etc/sysconfig/network** file contains system definitions for your network configuration. These include definitions for your domain name, hostname, and gateway, as shown here:

```
NETWORKING=yes
HOSTNAME=turtle.mytrek.com
GATEWAY=192.168.0.1
```

Domain Name System (DNS)

Each computer connected to a TCP/IP network, such as the Internet, is identified by its own IP address. IP addresses are difficult to remember, so a domain name version of each IP address is also used to identify a host. As described in Chapter 38, a domain name consists of two parts, the hostname and the domain. The hostname is the computer's specific name, and the domain identifies the network of which the computer is a part. The domains used for the United States usually have extensions that identify the type of host.

For example, **.edu** is used for educational institutions and **.com** is used for businesses. International domains usually have extensions that indicate the country they are located in, such as **.de** for Germany or **.au** for Australia. The combination of a hostname, domain, and extension forms a unique name by which a computer can be referenced. The domain can, in turn, be split into further subdomains.

As you know, a computer on a network can still be identified only by its IP address, even if it has a hostname. You can use a hostname to reference a computer on a network, but this involves using the hostname to look up the corresponding IP address in a database. The network then uses the IP address, not the hostname, to access the computer. Before the advent of large TCP/IP networks, such as the Internet, it was feasible for each computer on a network to maintain a file with a list of all the hostnames and IP addresses of the computers connected on its network. Whenever a hostname was used, it was looked up in this file and the corresponding IP address was located. You can still do this on your own system for remote systems you access frequently.

As networks became larger, it became impractical—and, in the case of the Internet, impossible—for each computer to maintain its own list of all the domain names and IP addresses. To provide the service of translating domain addresses to IP addresses, databases of domain names were developed and placed on their own servers. To find the IP address of a domain name, you send a query to a name server, which then looks up the IP address for you and sends it back. In a large network, several name servers can cover different parts of the network. If a name server cannot find a particular IP address, it sends the query on to another name server that is more likely to have it.

If you are administering a network and you need to set up a name server for it, you can configure a Linux system to operate as a name server. To do so, you must start up a name server daemon and then wait for domain name queries. A name server makes use of several configuration files that enable it to answer requests. The name server software used on Linux systems is the Berkeley Internet Name Domain (BIND) server distributed by the Internet Software Consortium (**www.isc.org**). Chapter 38 describes the process of setting up a domain name server in detail.

Name servers are queried by resolvers. These are programs specially designed to obtain addresses from name servers. To use domain names on your system, you must configure your own resolver. Your local resolver is configured with your **/etc/host.conf** and **/etc/resolv.conf** files. You can use **/etc/nsswitch** in place of **/etc/host.conf**.

host.conf

Your **host.conf** file lists resolver options (shown in Table 37-7). Each option can have several fields, separated by spaces or tabs. You can use a **#** at the beginning of a line to enter a comment. The options tell the resolver what services to use. The order of the list is important. The resolver begins with the first option listed and moves on to the next ones in turn. You can find the **host.conf** file in your **/etc** directory, along with other configuration files.

Option	Description
`order`	Specifies sequence of name resolution methods: **hosts** Checks for name in the local **/etc/host** file **bind** Queries a DNS name server for an address **nis** Uses Network Information Service protocol to obtain an address
`alert`	Checks addresses of remote sites attempting to access your system; you turn it on or off with the **on** and **off** options
`nospoof`	Confirms addresses of remote sites attempting to access your system
`trim`	Checks your local host's file; removes the domain name and checks only for the hostname; enables you to use only a hostname in your host file for an IP address
`multi`	Checks your local hosts file; allows a host to have several IP addresses; you turn it on or off with the **on** and **off** options

TABLE 37-7   Resolver Options, **host.conf**

In the next example of a **host.conf** file, the `order` option instructs your resolver first to look up names in your local **/etc/hosts** file, and then, if that fails, to query domain name servers. The system does not have multiple addresses.

/etc/host.conf
```
# host.conf file
# Lookup names in host file and then check DNS
order bind host
# There are no multiple addresses
multi off
```

/etc/nsswitch.conf: Name Service Switch

Different functions in the standard C Library must be configured to operate on your Linux system. Previously, database-like services, such as password support and name services like NIS or DNS, directly accessed these functions, using a fixed search order. For GNU C Library 2.*x*, used on current versions of Linux, this configuration is carried out by a scheme called the Name Service Switch (NSS), which is based on the method of the same name used by Sun Microsystems Solaris 2 OS. The database sources and their lookup order are listed in the **/etc/nsswitch.conf** file.

The **/etc/nsswitch.conf** file holds entries for the different configuration files that can be controlled by NSS. The system configuration files that NSS supports are listed in Table 37-8. An entry consists of two fields: the service and the configuration specification. The service consists of the configuration file followed by a colon. The second field is the configuration specification for that file, which holds instructions on how the lookup procedure will work. The configuration specification can contain service specifications and action items. Service specifications are the services to search. Currently, valid service specifications are nis, nisplus, files, db, dns, and compat (see Table 37-9). Not all are valid for each configuration file. For example, the dns service is valid only for the **hosts** file, whereas nis is valid for all files. The following example will first check the local **/etc/password** file and then NIS.

```
passwd:  files nisplus
```

File	Description
aliases	Mail aliases, used by Sendmail
ethers	Ethernet numbers
group	Groups of users
hosts	Hostnames and numbers
netgroup	Network-wide list of hosts and users, used for access rules; C libraries before glibc 2.1 only support netgroups over NIS
network	Network names and numbers
passwd	User passwords
protocols	Network protocols
publickey	Public and secret keys for SecureRPC used by NFS and NIS+
rpc	Remote procedure call names and numbers
services	Network services
shadow	Shadow user passwords

TABLE 37-8   NSS-Supported Files

An action item specifies the action to take for a specific service. An action item is placed within brackets after a service. A configuration specification can list several services, each with its own action item. In the following example, the entry for the network file has a configuration specification that says to check the NIS service and, if not found, to check the **/etc/protocols** file:

```
protocols: nisplus [NOTFOUND=return] files
```

An action item consists of a status and an action. The status holds a possible result of a service lookup, and the action is the action to take if the status is true. Currently, the possible status values are SUCCESS, NOTFOUND, UNAVAIL, and TRYAGAIN (service temporarily unavailable). The possible actions are return and continue: return stops the lookup process for the configuration file, whereas continue continues on to the next listed service. In the preceding example, if the record is not found in NIS, the lookup process ends.

Service	Description
files	Checks corresponding **/etc** file for the configuration (for example, **/etc/hosts** for hosts); this service is valid for all files
db	Checks corresponding **/var/db** databases for the configuration; valid for all files except **netgroup**
compat	Valid only for passwd, group, and shadow files
dns	Checks the DNS service; valid only for **hosts** file
nis	Checks the NIS service; valid for all files
nisplus	NIS version 3
hesiod	Uses Hesiod for lookup

TABLE 37-9   NSS Configuration Services

Shown here is a copy of the current **/etc/nsswitch.conf** file, which lists commonly used entries. Comments and commented-out entries begin with a **#** sign:

```
/etc/nsswitch.conf
#
# /etc/nsswitch.conf
#
# An example Name Service Switch config file.
passwd:             db files nisplus nis
shadow:             db files nisplus nis
group:              db files nisplus nis
hosts:              files nisplus dns
bootparams:         nisplus [NOTFOUND=return] files
ethers:             files
netmasks:           files
networks:           files
protocols:          files
rpc:                files
services:           files
netgroup:           nisplus
publickey:          nisplus
automount:          files
aliases:            files nisplus
```

Network Interfaces and Routes: ifconfig and route

Your connection to a network is made by your system through a particular hardware interface, such as an Ethernet card or a modem. Data passing through this interface is then routed to your network. The **ifconfig** command configures your network interfaces, and the **route** command sets up network connections accordingly. If you configure an interface with a network configuration tool, such as system-config-network, you needn't use **ifconfig** or **route**. However, you can directly configure interfaces using **ifconfig** and **route**, if you want. Every time you start your system, the network interfaces and their routes must be established. This is done automatically for you when you boot up by **ifconfig** and **route** commands executed for each interface by the **/etc/rc.d/init.d/ network** initialization file, which is executed whenever you start your system. If you are manually adding your own interfaces, you must set up the network script to perform the **ifconfig** and **route** operations for your new interfaces.

Network Startup Script: /etc/rc.d/init.d/network

On Fedora Core, your network interface is started up using the **network** script in the **/etc/ rc.d/init.d** directory. This script will activate your network interface cards (NICs) as well as implement configuration information such as gateway, host, and name server identities. You can manually shut down and start your network interface using this script and the **restart**, **start**, or **stop** options, as well as system-config-services. You can run the script on Fedora Core with the **service** command. The following commands shut down and then start up your network interface:

```
service network stop
service network start
```

If you are changing network configuration, you will have to restart your network interface for the changes to take effect:

```
service network restart
```

To test if your interface is working, use the **ping** command with an IP address of a system on your network, such as your gateway machine. The **ping** command continually repeats until you stop it with a CTRL-C.

```
ping 192.168.0.1
```

Interface Configuration Scripts: /etc/sysconfig/network-scripts

The **/etc/rc.d/init.d/network** file performs the startup operations by executing several specialized scripts located in the **/etc/sysconfig/network-scripts** directory. The **network** script uses a script in that directory called **ifup** to activate a network connection, and **ifdown** to shut it down; **ifup** and **ifdown** will invoke other scripts tailored to the kind of device being worked on, such as **ifup-ppp** for modems using the PPP protocol, or **ifup-ipv6** for network devices that use IP Protocol version 6 addressing.

NOTE *You can activate and deactivate network interfaces using the Network Device Control tool accessible from the System Tools menu.*

The **ifup** and **ifdown** scripts make use of interface configuration files that bear the names of the network interfaces currently configured, such as **ifcfg-eth0** for the first Ethernet device. These files define shell variables that hold information on the interface, such as whether to start them at boot time. For example, the **ifcfg-eth0** file holds definitions for NETWORK, BROADCAST, and IPADDR, which are assigned the network, broadcast, and IP addresses that the device uses.

The **ifdown** and **ifup** scripts, in turn, hold the **ifconfig** and **route** commands to activate scripts using these variables defined in the interface configuration files. If you want to manually start up an interface with **ifup**, you simply use the interface configuration file as its argument. The following command starts up the second Ethernet card:

```
cd /etc/sysconfig/network-scripts
ifup ifcfg-eth1
```

Interface configuration files are automatically generated when you configure your network connections, such as with a distribution's network administrative tool or third-party tools like rp3 or Webmin. You can also manually edit these interface configuration files, making changes such as whether to start up the interface at boot or not (though using a configuration tool such as system-config-network is easier). A sample **ifcfg-eth0** file is shown here using a static IP address:

/etc/sysconfig/network-scripts/ifcfg-eth0

```
DEVICE=eth0
BOOTPROTO=static
BROADCAST=192.168.0.255
IPADDR=192.168.0.1
NETMASK=255.255.255.0
NETWORK=192.168.0.0
ONBOOT=yes
```

A DHCP-based interface would look something like this, where BOOTPROTO is assigned dhcp:

/etc/sysconfig/network-scripts/ifcfg-eth0
```
DEVICE=eth0
BOOTPROTO=dhcp
HWADDR=00:00:00:00:00:01
TYPE=Ethernet
ONBOOT=yes
```

ifconfig

The `ifconfig` command takes as its arguments the name of an interface and an IP address, as well as options. The `ifconfig` command then assigns the IP address to the interface. Your system now knows that such an interface exists and that it references a particular IP address. In addition, you can specify whether the IP address is a host address or a network address. You can use a domain name for the IP address, provided the domain name is listed along with its IP address in the **/etc/hosts** file. The syntax for the `ifconfig` command is as follows:

```
# ifconfig interface -host_net_flag address options
```

The *host_net_flag* can be either **-host** or **-net** to indicate a host or network IP address. The **-host** flag is the default. The `ifconfig` command can have several options, which set different features of the interface, such as the maximum number of bytes it can transfer (**mtu**) or the broadcast address. The **up** and **down** options activate and deactivate the interface. In the next example, the `ifconfig` command configures an Ethernet interface:

```
# ifconfig eth0 192.168.0.1
```

For a simple configuration such as this, `ifconfig` automatically generates a standard broadcast address and netmask. The standard broadcast address is the network address with the number 255 for the host address. For a class C network, the standard netmask is 255.255.255.0, whereas for a class A network, the standard netmask is 255.0.0.0. If you are connected to a network with a particular netmask and broadcast address, however, you must specify them when you use `ifconfig`. The option for specifying the broadcast address is **broadcast**; for the network mask, it is **netmask**. Table 37-10 lists the different `ifconfig` options. In the next example, `ifconfig` includes the netmask and broadcast address:

```
# ifconfig eth0 192.168.0.1 broadcast 192.168.0.255 netmask 255.255.255.0
```

Once you configure your interface, you can use `ifconfig` with the **up** option to activate it and with the **down** option to deactivate it. If you specify an IP address in an `ifconfig` operation, as in the preceding example, the **up** option is implied.

```
# ifconfig eth0 up
```

Point-to-point interfaces such as Parallel IP (PLIP), Serial Line IP (SLIP), and Point-to-Point Protocol (PPP) require you to include the **pointopoint** option. A PLIP interface name is identified with the name **plip** with an attached number. For example, **plip0** is the first PLIP interface. SLIP interfaces use **slip0**. PPP interfaces start with **ppp0**. Point-to-point

Option	Description
Interface	Name of the network interface, such as **eth0** for the first Ethernet device or **ppp0** for the first PPP device (modem)
up	Activates an interface; implied if IP address is specified
down	Deactivates an interface
allmulti	Turns on or off the promiscuous mode; preceding hyphen (-) turns it off; this allows network monitoring
mtu *n*	Maximum number of bytes that can be sent on this interface per transmission
dstaddr *address*	Destination IP address on a point-to-point connection
netmask *address*	IP network mask; preceding hyphen (-) turns it off
broadcast *address*	Broadcast address; preceding hyphen (-) turns it off
point-to-point *address*	Point-to-point mode for interface; if address is included, it is assigned to remote system
hw	Sets hardware address of interface
Address	IP address assigned to interface

TABLE **37-10**   The **ifconfig** Options

interfaces are those that usually operate between only two hosts, such as two computers connected over a modem. When you specify the **pointopoint** option, you need to include the IP address of the host. In the next example, a PLIP interface is configured that connects the computer at IP address 192.168.1.72 with one at 204.166.254.14. If domain addresses were listed for these systems in **/etc/hosts**, those domain names could be used in place of the IP addresses.

```
# ifconfig plip0 192.168.1.72 pointopoint 204.166.254.14
```

If you need to, you can also use **ifconfig** to configure your loopback device. The name of the loopback device is **lo**, and its IP address is the special address 127.0.0.1. The following example shows the configuration:

```
# ifconfig lo 127.0.0.1
```

The **ifconfig** command is useful for checking on the status of an interface. If you enter the **ifconfig** command along with the name of the interface, information about that interface is displayed:

```
# ifconfig eth0
```

To see if your loopback interface is configured, you can use **ifconfig** with the loopback interface name, **lo**:

```
# ifconfig lo
lo        Link encap:Local Loopback
```

```
inet addr:127.0.0.1  Mask:255.0.0.0
inet6 addr: ::1/128 Scope:Host
UP LOOPBACK RUNNING  MTU:16436  Metric:1
RX packets:1975 errors:0 dropped:0 overruns:0 frame:0
TX packets:1975 errors:0 dropped:0 overruns:0 carrier:0
collisions:0 txqueuelen:0
RX bytes:2415146 (2.3 MiB)  TX bytes:2415146 (2.3 MiB)
```

Routing

A packet that is part of a transmission takes a certain *route* to reach its destination. On a large network, packets are transmitted from one computer to another until the destination computer is reached. The route determines where the process starts and to what computer your system needs to send the packet for it to reach its destination. On small networks, routing may be static—that is, the route from one system to another is fixed. One system knows how to reach another, moving through fixed paths. On larger networks and on the Internet, however, routing is dynamic. Your system knows the first computer to send its packet off to, and then that computer takes the packet from there, passing it on to another computer, which then determines where to pass it on. For dynamic routing, your system needs to know little. Static routing, however, can become complex because you have to keep track of all the network connections.

Your routes are listed in your routing table in the **/proc/net/route** file. To display the routing table, enter **route** with no arguments (the **netstat -r** command will also display the routing table):

```
# route
Kernel routing table
Destination Gateway       Genmask      Flags Metric Ref Use  Iface
192.168.0.0    *          255.255.255.0 U     0      0   0    etho
127.0.0.0      *          255.0.2055.0  U     0      0   0    lo
default     192.168.0.1   0.0.0.0       UG    0      0   0    eth0
```

Each entry in the routing table has several fields, providing information such as the route destination and the type of interface used. The different fields are listed in Table 37-11.

Field	Description
Destination	Destination IP address of the route
Gateway	IP address or hostname of the gateway the route uses; * indicates no gateway is used
Genmask	The netmask for the route
Flags	Type of route: U = up, H = host, G = gateway, D = dynamic, M = modified
Metric	Metric cost of route
Ref	Number of routes that depend on this one
Window	TCP window for AX.25 networks
Use	Number of times used
Iface	Type of interface this route uses

TABLE 37-11 Routing Table Entries

With the **add** argument, you can add routes either for networks with the **-net** option or with the **-host** option for IP interfaces (hosts). The **-host** option is the default. In addition, you can then specify several parameters for information, such as the netmask (**netmask**), the gateway (**gw**), the interface device (**dev**), and the default route (**default**). If you have more than one IP interface on your system, such as several Ethernet cards, you must specify the name of the interface using the **dev** parameter. If your network has a gateway host, you use the **gw** parameter to specify it. If your system is connected to a network, at least one entry should be in your routing table that specifies the default route. This is the route taken by a message packet when no other route entry leads to its destination. The following example is the routing of an Ethernet interface:

```
# route add 192.168.1.2 dev eth0
```

If your system has only the single Ethernet device as your IP interface, you could leave out the **dev eth0** parameter:

```
# route add 192.168.1.2
```

You can delete any route you establish by invoking **ifconfig** with the **del** argument and the IP address of that route, as in this example:

```
# route del 192.168.1.2
```

For a gateway, you first add a route to the gateway interface, and then add a route specifying that it is a gateway. The address of the gateway interface in this example is 192.168.1.1:

```
# route add 192.168.1.1
# route add default gw 192.168.1.1
```

If you are using the gateway to access a subnet, add the network address for that network (in this example, 192.168.23.0):

```
# route add -net 192.168.23.0 gw dev eth1
```

To add another IP address to a different network interface on your system, use the **ifconfig** and **route** commands with the new IP address. The following command configures a second Ethernet card (**eth1**) with the IP address 192.168.1.3:

```
ifconfig eth1 192.168.1.3
route add 192.168.1.3 dev eth1
```

Monitoring Your Network: ping, netstat, tcpdump, and Ethereal

With the ping program, you can check to see if you can actually access another host on your network. The ping program sends a request to the host for a reply. The host then sends a reply back, and it is displayed on your screen. The ping program continually sends such a request until you stop it with a **break** command, CTRL-C. You see one reply after another scroll by on your screen until you stop the program. If ping cannot access a host, it issues a message saying the host is unreachable. If ping fails, this may be an indication that your network connection is not working. It may be only the particular interface, a basic configuration problem, or a bad physical connection. The ping utility uses the Internet Control Message Protocol (ICMP), discussed in Chapter 20. Networks may block these protocols as a security measure, also preventing ping from working. A ping failure may simply indicate a security precaution on the part of the queried network.

To use ping, enter **ping** and the name of the host.

```
$ ping ftp.redhat.com
```

Ethereal

Ethereal is a network protocol analyzer that lets you capture packets transmitted across your network, selecting and examining those from protocols you want to check. You can examine packets from a particular transmission, displaying the data in readable formats. The Ethereal interface displays three panes: a listing of current packets, the protocol tree for the currently selected packet, and a display of the selected packets contents. The first pane categorizes entries by time, source, destination, and protocol. There are button headers for each. To sort a set of entries by a particular category, click its header. For example, for group entries by protocol, click the Protocol button; for destinations, use the Destination button.

Capture Options

To start Ethereal, you select the Start entry from the Capture menu. This opens an options window where you can select the network interface to watch. Here you can also select options such as the file to hold your captured information in and a size limit for the capture, along with a filter to screen packets. With the promiscuous mode selected, you can see all network traffic passing through that device, whereas with it off, you will see only those packets destined for that device.

- The Capture Files option lets you select a file to save your capture in. If no file is selected, then data is simply displayed in the Ethereal window. If you want to keep a continuous running snapshot of your network traffic, you can use ring buffers. These are a series of files that are used to save captured data. When they fill up, the capture begins saving again to the first file, and so on.

- Display options control whether packets are displayed in real time on the Ethereal window.

- Capture limits let you set a limit for the capture either by packets, size, or time.

- Name resolution enables the display of hostnames and domain names instead of IP addresses, if possible.

Ethereal Filters

A filter lets you select packets that match specified criteria, such as packets from a particular host. Criteria are specified using expressions supported by the Packet Capture Library and implemented by **tcpdump**. Ethereal filters use similar expressions as those used by the **tcpdump** command. Check the **tcpdump** Man page for detailed descriptions.

An expression consists of an ID, such as the name or number of host, and a qualifier. Qualifiers come in three types: type, direction, and protocol. The type can reference the host, network, or port. The type qualifiers are **host**, **net**, and **port**. Direction selects either source or destination packets, or both. The source qualifier is **src**, and the destination, **dst**. With no destination qualifier, both directions are selected. Protocol lets you specify packets for a certain protocol. Protocols are represented using their lowercase names, such as **icmp** for ICMP. For example, the expression to list all packets coming in from a particular host would be **src host** *hostname*, where *hostname* is the source host. The following example will display all packets from the 192.168.0.3 host.

```
src host 192.168.0.3
```

Using just **host** will check for all packets going out as well as coming in for that host. The **port** qualifier will check for packets passing through a particular port. To check for a particular protocol, you use the protocol name. For example, to check for all ICMP packets you would use the expression

```
icmp
```

There are also several special qualifiers that let you further control your selection. The **gateway** qualifier lets you detect packets passing through a gateway. The **broadcast** and **multi-cast** qualifiers detect packets broadcast to a network. The **greater** and **less** qualifiers can be applied to numbers such as ports or IP addresses.

You can combine expressions into a single complex Boolean expression using **and**, **or**, or **not**. This lets you create a more refined filter. For example, to capture only the ICMP packets coming in from host 192.168.0.2, you can use

```
src host 192.168.0.3 and icmp
```

To create or select filters, click the Filter button in the options window when you first start a capture. This opens a Capture Filter window with a listing of filters you have already created. Boxes for the filter name and filter string are displayed below. To create a new filter, enter the name you want to give it in the Filter Name box. Then in the Filter String box, enter the filter expression, like **icmp**. Then click New. Your new filter will appear in the list. To change a filter, select it and change its expression in the Filter String box, then click Change.

tcpdump

Like Ethereal, **tcpdump** will capture network packets, saving them in a file where you can examine them. **tcpdump** operates entirely from the command line. You will have to open a terminal window to run it. Using various options, you can refine your capture, specifying the kinds of packets you want. **tcpdump** uses a set of options to specify actions you want to take, which include limiting the size of the capture, deciding which file to save it to, and choosing any filter you want to apply to it. Check the **tcpdump** Man page for a complete listing.

- The **-i** option lets you specify an interface to listen to.
- With the **-c** option, you can limit the number of packets to capture.

- Packets will be output to the standard output by default. To save them to a file, you can use the **-w** option.

- You can later read a packet file using the **-r** option and apply a filter expression to it.

The **tcpdump** command takes as its argument a filter expression that you can use to refine your capture. Ethereal uses the same filter expressions as **tcpdump** (see the filters discussion in Ethereal).

netstat

The netstat program provides real-time information on the status of your network connections, as well as network statistics and the routing table. The **netstat** command has several options you can use to bring up different sorts of information about your network:

```
# netstat
Active Internet connections
Proto Recv-Q Send-Q Local Address Foreign Address (State) User
tcp 0 0 turtle.mytrek.com:01 pango1.mytrain.com.:ftp ESTABLISHED dylan
Active UNIX domain sockets
Proto RefCnt Flags Type State Path
unix 1 [ ACC ] SOCK_STREAM LISTENING /dev/printer
unix 2 [ ] SOCK_STREAM CONNECTED /dev/log
unix 1 [ ACC ] SOCK_STREAM LISTENING /dev/nwapi
unix 2 [ ] SOCK_STREAM CONNECTED /dev/log
unix 2 [ ] SOCK_STREAM CONNECTED
unix 1 [ ACC ] SOCK_STREAM LISTENING /dev/log
```

The **netstat** command with no options lists the network connections on your system. First, active TCP connections are listed, and then the active domain sockets are listed. The domain sockets contain processes used to set up communications among your system and other systems. You can use **netstat** with the **-r** option to display the routing table, and **netstat** with the **-i** option displays the uses of the different network interfaces.

38
CHAPTER

Domain Name System

The Domain Name System (DNS) is an Internet service that locates and translates domain names into their corresponding Internet Protocol (IP) addresses. As you may recall, all computers connected to the Internet are addressed using an IP address. As a normal user on a network might have to access many different hosts, keeping track of the IP addresses needed quickly became a problem. It was much easier to label hosts with names and use the names to access them. Names were associated with IP addresses. When a user used a name to access a host, the corresponding IP address was looked up first and then used to provide access.

With the changeover from IPv4 to IPv6 address, DNS servers will have some configuration differences. Both are covered here, though some topics will use IPv4 addressing for better clarity, as they are easier to represent. IPv4 and IPv6 addressing are discussed in detail in Chapter 37.

DNS Address Translations

The process of translating IP addresses into associated names is fairly straightforward. Small networks can be set up easily, with just the basic configuration. The task becomes much more complex when you deal with larger networks and with the Internet. The sheer size of the task can make DNS configuration a complex operation.

Fully Qualified Domain Names

IP addresses are associated with corresponding names, called fully qualified domain names. A *fully qualified domain name* is composed of three or more segments. The first segment is the name that identifies the host, and the remaining segments are for the network in which the host is located. The network segments of a fully qualified domain name are usually referred to simply as the domain name, while the host part is referred to as the hostname (though this is also used to refer to the complete fully qualified domain name). In effect, subnets are referred to as domains. The fully qualified domain name **www.linux.org** could have an IPv4 address 198.182.196.56, where 198.182.196 is the network address and 56 is the host ID. Computers can be accessed only with an IP address, so a fully qualified domain name must first be translated into its corresponding IP address to be of any use. The parts of the IP address that make up the domain name and the hosts can vary. See Chapter 37 for a detailed discussion of IP addresses, including network classes and Classless Interdomain Routing (CIDR).

IPv4 Addresses

The IP address may be implemented in either the newer IPv6 (Internet Protocol version 6) format or the older and more common IPv4 (Internet Protocol version 4) format. Since the IPv4 addressing is much easier to read, that format will be used in these examples. In the older IPv4 format, the IP address consists of a number composed of four segments separated by periods. Depending on the type of network, several of the first segments are used for the network address and one or more of the last segments are used for the host address. In a standard class C network used in smaller networks, the first three segments are the computer's network address and the last segment is the computer's host ID (as used in these examples). For example, in the address 192.168.0.2, 192.168.0 is the network address and 2 is the computer's host ID within that network. Together, they make up an IP address by which the computer can be addressed from anywhere on the Internet. IP addresses, though, are difficult to remember and easy to get wrong.

IPv6 Addressing

IPv6 addressing uses a very different approach designed to provide more flexibility and support for very large address spaces (see Chapter 37). There are three different types of IPv6 addresses, unicast, multicast, and anycast, of which unicast is the most commonly used. A unicast address is directed to a particular interface. There are several kinds of unicast addresses, depending on how the address is used. For example, you can have a global unicast address for access through the Internet or a site-level unicast address for private networks.

Though consisting of 128 bits in eight segments (16 bits, 2 bytes, per segment), an IPv6 address is made up of several fields that conform roughly to the segments and capabilities of an IPv4 address, networking information, subnet information, and the interface identifier (host ID). The network information includes a format prefix indicating the type of network connection. In addition, a subnet identifier can be used to specify a local subnet (see Chapter 37). The network information takes up the first several segments. The remainder are used for the interface ID. The interface ID is an 64-bit (four-segment) Extended Unique Identifier (EUI-64) generated from a network device's Media Access Control (MAC) address. IP addresses are written in hexadecimal numbers, making them difficult to use. Each segment is separated from the next by a colon, and a set of consecutive segments with zero values like the reserved segment can be left empty.

Manual Translations: /etc/hosts

Any computer on the Internet can maintain a file that manually associates IP addresses with domain names. On Linux and Unix systems, this file is called the **/etc/hosts** file. Here, you can enter the IP addresses and domain names of computers you commonly access. Using this method, however, each computer needs a complete listing of all other computers on the Internet, and that listing must be updated constantly. Early on, this became clearly impractical for the Internet, though it is still feasible for small, isolated networks as well as simple home networks.

DNS Servers

The Domain Name System has been implemented to deal with the task of translating the domain name of any computer on the Internet to its IP address. The task is carried out by interconnecting servers that manage the Domain Name System (also referred to as DNS servers or name servers). These DNS servers keep lists of fully qualified domain names and their IP addresses, matching one up with the other. This service that they provide to a network is referred to as the Domain Name System. The Internet is composed of many connected subnets called *domains,* each with its own Domain Name System (DNS) servers that keep track of all the fully qualified domain names and IP addresses for all the computers on its network. DNS servers are hierarchically linked to root servers, which, in turn, connect to other root servers and the DNS servers on their subnets throughout the Internet. The section of a network for which a given DNS server is responsible is called a *zone.* Although a zone may correspond to a domain, many zones may, in fact, be within a domain, each with its own name server. This is true for large domains where too many systems exist for one name server to manage.

DNS Operation

When a user enters a fully qualified domain name to access a remote host, a resolver program queries the local network's DNS server requesting the corresponding IP address for that remote host. With the IP address, the user can then access the remote host. In Figure 38-1, the user at **rabbit.mytrek.com** wants to connect to the remote host **lizard.mytrek.com**. **rabbit.mytrek.com** first sends a request to the network's DNS server—in this case, **turtle .mytrek.com**—to look up the name **lizard.mytrek.com** and find its IP address. **turtle.mytrek .com**, then returns the IP address for **lizard.mytrek.com**, 192.168.0.3, to the requesting host, **rabbit.mytrek.com**. With the IP address, the user at **rabbit.mytrek.com** can then connect to **lizard.mytrek.com**.

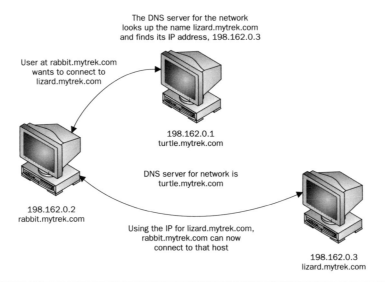

FIGURE 38-1 DNS server operation

DNS Clients: Resolvers

The names of the DNS servers that service a host's network are kept in the host's **/etc/resolv .conf** file (see Chapter 37). When setting up an Internet connection, the name servers provided by your Internet service provider (ISP) were placed in this file. These name servers resolve any fully qualified domain names that you use when you access different Internet sites. For example, when you enter a Web site name in your browser, the name is looked up by the name servers and the name's associated IP address is then used to access the site.

/etc/resolv.conf
```
search  mytrek.com    mytrain.com
nameserver  192.168.0.1
nameserver  192.168.0.3
```

Local Area Network Addressing

If you are setting up a DNS server for a local area network (LAN) that is not connected to the Internet, you should use a special set of IP numbers reserved for such local networks (also known as *private networks* or *intranets*). This is especially true if you are implementing IP masquerading, where only a gateway machine has an Internet address, and the others make use of that one address to connect to the Internet. Though structurally the same, IPv4 and IPv6 use different addressing formats for local addresses. Many local and home networks still use the IPv4 format, and this is the format used in the following local addressing example.

IPv4 Private Networks

IPv4 provides a range of private addresses for the three classes supported by IPv4. As you have seen, class C IPv4 network numbers have the special network number 192.168. Numbers are also reserved for class A and class B non-Internet local networks. Table 38-1 lists these addresses. The possible addresses available span from 0 to 255 in the host segment of the address. For example, class B network addresses range from 172.16.0.0 to 172.31.255.255, giving you a total of 65,534 possible hosts. The class C network ranges from 192.168.0.0 to 192.168.255.255, giving you 254 possible subnetworks, each with 254 possible hosts. The number 127.0.0.0 is reserved for a system's loopback interface, which allows it to communicate with itself, as it enables users on the same system to send messages to each other.

These numbers were originally designed for class-based addressing. However, they can just as easily be used for Classless Interdomain Routing (CIDR) addressing, where you can create subnetworks with a smaller number of hosts. For example, the 254 hosts addressed in a class C network could be split into two subnetworks, each with 125 hosts. See Chapter 37 for more details.

Address	Network
10.0.0.0	Class A network
172.16.0.0–172.31.255.255	Class B network
192.168.0.0	Class C network
127.0.0.0	Loopback network (for system self-communication)

TABLE 38-1   Non-Internet Private Network IP Addresses

IPv6 Private Networks

IPv6 supports private networks with site-local addresses that provide the same functionality of IPv4 private addresses. The site-local addresses have no public routing information. They cannot access the Internet. They are restricted to the site they are used on. The site-local addresses use only three fields: format prefix, subnet identifier, and interface identifier. A site-level address has the format prefix **fec0**. If you have no subnets, it will be set to 0. This will give you a network prefix of **fec0:0:0:0**. You can drop the set of empty zeros to give you **fec0::**. The interface ID field will hold the interface identification information, similar to the host ID information in IPv4.

```
fec0::           IPv6 site-local prefix
```

The loopback device will have the special address of **::1**, also known as localhost.

```
::1              IPv6 loopback network
```

Rather than using a special set of reserved addresses as IPv4 does, with IPv6 you only use the site-local prefix, **fec0**, and the special loopback address, **::1**.

TIP *Once your network is set up, you can use ping6 or ping to see if it is working. The ping6 tool is designed for Ipv6 addresses, whereas ping is used for IPv4.*

Local Network Address Example Using IPv4

If you are setting up a LAN, such as a small business or home network, you are free to use class C IPv4 network (254 hosts or less), that have the special network number 192.168, as used in these examples. These are numbers for your local machines. You can set up a private network, such as an intranet, using network cards such as Ethernet cards and Ethernet hubs, and then configure your machines with IP addresses starting from 192.168.0.1. The host segment can range from 1 to 254, where 255 is used for the broadcast address. If you have three machines on your home network, you can give them the addresses 192.168.0.1, 192.168.0.2, and 192.168.0.3. You can then set up domain name services for your network by running a DNS server on one of the machines. This machine becomes your network's DNS server. You can then give your machines fully qualified domain names and configure your DNS server to translate the names to their corresponding IP addresses. As shown in Figure 38-2, for example, you could give the machine 192.168.0.1 the name **turtle.mytrek.com** and the machine 192.168.0.2 the name **rabbit.mytrek.com**. You can also implement Internet services on your network such as FTP, Web, and mail services by setting up servers for them on your machines. You can then configure your DNS server to let users access those services using fully qualified domain names. For example, for the **mytrek.com** network, the Web server could be accessed using the name **www.mytrek.com**. Instead of a Domain Name Service, you could have the **/etc/hosts** files in each machine contain the entire list of IP addresses and domain names for all the machines in your network. But for any changes, you would have to update each machine's **/etc/hosts** file.

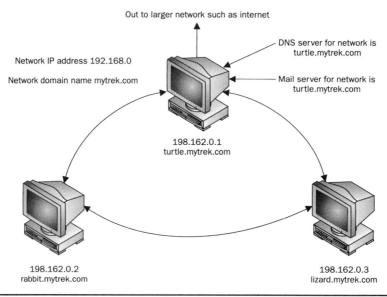

Out to larger network such as internet

Network IP address 192.168.0

Network domain name mytrek.com

DNS server for network is
turtle.mytrek.com

Mail server for network is
turtle.mytrek.com

198.162.0.1
turtle.mytrek.com

198.162.0.2
rabbit.mytrek.com

198.162.0.3
lizard.mytrek.com

Figure 38-2   DNS server and network

BIND

The DNS server software currently in use on Linux systems is Berkeley Internet Name Domain (BIND). BIND was originally developed at the University of California, Berkeley, and is currently maintained and supported by the Internet Software Consortium (ISC). You can obtain BIND information and current software releases from its Web site at **www.isc .org**. Web page documentation and manuals are included with the software package. RPM packages are available at distribution FTP sites. The BIND directory in **/usr/share/doc** contains extensive documentation, including Web page manuals and examples. The Linux HOW-TO for the Domain Name System, DNS-HOW-TO, provides detailed examples. Documentation, news, and DNS tools can be obtained from the DNS Resource Directory (DNSRD) at **www .dns.net/dnsrd**. The site includes extensive links and online documentation, including the *BIND Operations Guide (BOG)*. See Table 38-2 for a list of DNS resources.

Alternative DNS Servers

Several alternative DNS servers are now available. These include djbdns, noted for its security features, CustomDNS, a dynamic server implemented in Java (**customdns.sourceforge.net**), and Yaku-NS, an embedded server. The djbdns server (**cr.yp.to/djbdns.html**), written by D.J. Bernstein, is designed specifically with security in mind, providing a set of small server daemons, each performing specialized tasks. In particular, djbdns separates the name server, caching server, and zone transfer tasks into separate programs: tinydns (tinydns.org) implements the authoritative name server for a network, whereas dnscache implements a caching server that will resolve requests from DNS clients such as Web browsers. In effect, dnscache operates as the name server that your applications will use to resolve addresses. dnscache will then query tinydns to resolve addresses on your local network. Zone transfers are handled separately by axfrdns and asfget.

Web Site	Resource
www.isc.org	Internet Software Consortium
www.dns.net/dnsrd	DNS Resource Directory
www.nominum.com	Nominum, BIND support and consulting

TABLE 38-2 BIND Resources

DNS Documentation

Currently, ISC has contracted with two companies, Nominum and Mind, to provide BIND support. Nominum is an ISC support partner and has taken an active role in BIND development. At its Web site at **www.nominum.com**, you can find BIND documentation, including the BIND 9 Administrator's Reference. Nominum, like many commercial companies that support open source software, provides professional consultant and support services, while freely contributing to Open Source development. Mind provides consulting services for the European market.

BIND Servers and Tools

The BIND DNS server software consists of a name server daemon, several sample configuration files, and resolver libraries. As of 1998, a new version of BIND, beginning with the series number 8.*x*, implemented a new configuration file using a new syntax. Version 9.0 adds new security features and support for IPv6. Older versions, which begin with the number 4.*x*, use a different configuration file with an older syntax. Most distributions currently install the newer 9.*x* version of BIND.

The name of the BIND name server daemon is **named**. To operate your machine as a name server, simply run the **named** daemon with the appropriate configuration. The **named** daemon listens for resolution requests and provides the correct IP address for the requested hostname. You can use the Remote Name Daemon Controller utility, **rndc**, provided with BIND to start, stop, restart, and check the status of the server as you test its configuration. **rndc** with the **stop** command stops **named** and, with the **start** command, starts it again, reading your **named.conf** file. **rndc** with the **help** command provides a list of all **rndc** commands. Configuration is set in the **/etc/rndc.conf** file. See the Red Hat Reference Guide (Red Hat Enterprise Linux 4 documentation) for detailed information on configuring **rndc** access to your DNS server. Once your name server is running, you can test it using the **dig** or **nslookup** utility, which queries a name server, providing information about hosts and domains. If you start **dig** with no arguments, it enters an interactive mode where you can issue different **dig** commands to refine your queries.

To check the syntax of your DNS server configuration and zone files, BIND provides the **named-checkconfig** and **named-checkzone** tools: **named-checkconfig** will check the syntax of DNS configuration file, **named.conf**, and **named-checkzone** will check a zone file's syntax. Other syntax checking tools are also available, such as **nslint**, which operates like the programming tool **lint**.

Numerous other DNS tools are also available. Check the DNS Resource Directory at **www.dns.net/dnsrd** for a listing. Table 38-3 lists several BIND administrative tools.

Tool	Description
dig *domain*	Domain Information Groper, tool to obtain information on a DNS server. Preferred over **nslookup**
host *hostname*	Simple lookup of hosts
nslookup *domain*	Tool to query DNS servers for information about domains and hosts
named-checkconf	BIND tool to check the syntax of your DNS configuration file, **/etc/named.conf**
named-checkzone	BIND tool to check the syntax of your DNS zone files
nslint	Tool to check the syntax of your DNS configuration and zone files
rndc *command*	Remote Name Daemon Controller, an administrative tool for managing a DNS server (version 9.x)
ndc	Name Daemon Controller (version 8.x)
system-config-bind	BIND DNS server configuration tool

TABLE 38-3   BIND Diagnostic and Administrative Tools

Starting and Stopping the BIND Server

On Fedora Core, the **named** daemon is started using a startup script in the **/etc/rc.d/init.d** directory called **named**. You can use this script to start, stop, and restart the daemon using the **stop**, **start**, and **restart** arguments. You can invoke the script with the **service** command as shown here:

```
service named restart
```

On most distributions, **named** runs as a stand-alone daemon, starting up when the system boots and constantly running. If you don't want **named** to start up automatically, you can use system-config-services or **chkconfig** to change its status.

Domain Name System Configuration

You configure a DNS server using a configuration file, several zone files, and a cache file. The part of a network for which the name server is responsible is called a zone. A *zone* is not the same as a domain, because in a large domain you could have several zones, each with its own name server. You could also have one name server service several zones. In this case, each zone has its own zone file.

DNS Zones

The zone files hold resource records that provide hostname and IP address associations for computers on the network for which the DNS server is responsible. Zone files exist for the server's network and the local machine. Zone entries are defined in the **named.conf** file. Here, you place zone entries for your master, slave, and forward DNS servers. The most commonly used zone types are described here:

- **Master zone**   This is the primary zone file for the network supported by the DNS server. It holds the mappings from domain names to IP addresses for all the hosts on that network.

- **Slave zone**   These are references to other DNS servers for your network. Your network can have a master DNS server and several slave DNS servers to help carry the workload. A slave DNS server automatically copies its configuration files, including all zone files, from the master DNS server. Any changes to the master configuration files trigger an automatic download of these files to the slave servers. In effect, you only have to manage the configuration files for the master DNS server, as they are automatically copied to the slave servers.

- **Forward zone**   The forward zone lists name servers outside your network that should be searched if your network's name server fails to resolve an address.

- **IN-ADDR.ARPA zone**   DNS can also provide reverse resolutions, where an IP address is used to determine the associated domain name address. Such lookups are provided by **IN-ADDR.ARPA** zone files. Each master zone file usually has a corresponding **IN-ADDR.ARPA** zone file to provide reverse resolution for that zone. For each master zone entry, a corresponding reverse mapping zone entry named **IN-ADDR.ARPA** also exists, as well as one for the localhost. This entry performs reverse mapping from an IP address to its domain name. The name of the zone entry uses the domain IP address, which is the IP address with segments listed starting from the host, instead of the network. So for the IP address 192.168.0.4, where 4 is the host address, the corresponding domain IP address is 4.0.168.192, listing the segments in reverse order. The reverse mapping for the localhost is 1.0.0.127.

- **IP6.ARPA zone**   This is the IPv6 equivalent of the **IN-ADDR.ARPA** zone, providing reverse resolution for that zone. The IP6.ARPA zone uses bit labels to provide a bit-level format that is easier to write, requiring no reverse calculation on the part of the DNS administrator.

- **IP6.INT zone**   This is the older form of the IPv6 IP6.ARPA zone, which is the equivalent of the IPv4 **IN-ADDR.ARPA** zone, providing reverse resolution for a zone. IP6.INT is meant to be used with the older AAAA IPv6 address records. IP6.INT uses a nibble format to specify a reverse zone. In this format, a hexadecimal IPv6 address is segmented into each of its 32 hexadecimal numbers and listed in reverse order, each segment separated by a period.

- **Hint zone**   A hint zone specifies the root name servers and is denoted by a period (.). A DNS server is normally connected to a larger network, such as the Internet, which has its own DNS servers. DNS servers are connected this way hierarchically, with each server having its root servers to which it can send resolution queries. The root servers are designated in the hint zone.

NOTE *On Fedora Core, you can use system-config-bind, the BIND Configuration Tool, to configure a DNS server for a simple local network (see Chapter 5). system-config-bind (accessible from Server Settings window or menu) provides a GNOME interface for setting up the master, slave, forward, and IN-ADDR.ARPA zones you would need for a server. Be aware, though, that it will overwrite your **named.conf** file. system-config-bind can be accessed from the Server Settings menu.*

DNS Server Types

There are several kinds of DNS servers, each designed to perform a different type of task under the Domain Name Service. The basic kind of DNS server is the *master* server. Each network must have at least one master server that is responsible for resolving names on the network. Large networks may need several DNS servers. Some of these can be slave servers that can be updated directly from a master server. Others may be *alternative master* servers that hosts in a network can use. Both are commonly referred to as *secondary* servers. For DNS requests a DNS server cannot resolve, the request can be forwarded to specific DNS servers outside the network, such as on the Internet. DNS servers in a network can be set up to perform this task and are referred to as *forwarder* servers. To help bear the workload, local DNS servers can be set up within a network to operate as caching servers. Such a server merely collects DNS lookups from previous requests it sent to the main DNS server. Any repeated requests can then be answered by the caching server.

A server that can answer DNS queries for a given zone with authority is known as an *authoritative* server. An authoritative server holds the DNS configuration records for hosts in a zone that will associate each host's DNS name with an IP address. For example, a master server is an authoritative server. So are slave and stealth servers (see the list that follows). A caching server is not authoritative. It only holds whatever associations it picked up from other servers and cannot guarantee that the associations are valid.

- **Master server**   This is the primary DNS server for a zone.
- **Slave server**   A DNS server that receives zone information from the master server.
- **Forwarder server**   A server that forwards unresolved DNS requests to outside DNS servers. Can be used to keep other servers on a local network hidden from the Internet.
- **Caching-only server**   Caches DNS information it receives from DNS servers and uses it to resolve local requests.
- **Stealth server**   A DNS server for a zone not listed as a name server by the master DNS server.

Location of BIND Server Files: /etc/named/chroot

On Fedora Core, both the configuration and zone files used by BIND are placed in a special subdirectory called **chroot** located within the **/var/named** directory, **/var/named/chroot**. The **chroot** directory sets up a chroot jail, creating a virtual root directory for any users of the DNS service. This prevents access by DNS users to any other part of the system. When the BIND server starts up, the **chroot** command is run on the **named** service making **/var/named/chroot** the root directory for any users of the DNS service. Check the Chroot-BIND HOWTO at the Linux Documentation site for more information (**www.tldp.org**).

Within the **/var/named/chroot** directory are subdirectories that hold the BIND files on your system. These include **var**, **etc**, and **dev**. The **var** subdirectory has a **named** subdirectory within which are the zone files used by the BIND DNS server. Links to these files are located in the **/var/named** directory. The **named.conf** configuration file is located in the **/var/named/chroot/etc** directory. The **/etc/named.conf** file is just a link to this file. The links allow your configuration files and tools to reference zone files using the standard BIND DNS directory names, as in **/etc/named**. For new configuration and zone files you would create new links.

```
/etc/named/chroot/etc/named.conf          BIND configuration file
/etc/named/chroot/var/named               BIND zone files
```

named.conf

The configuration file for the **named** daemon is **named.conf**. A link to it is located in the **/etc** directory, with the original file located in the **/var/named/chroot/etc** directory. It uses a flexible syntax similar to C programs. The format enables easy configuration of selected zones, enabling features such as access control lists and categorized logging. The **named.conf** file consists of BIND configuration statements with attached blocks within which specific options are listed. A configuration statement is followed by arguments and a block that is delimited with braces. Within the block are lines of option and feature entries. Each entry is terminated with a semicolon. Comments can use the C, C++, or Shell/Perl syntax: enclosing **/* */**, preceding **//**, or preceding **#**. The following example shows a **zone** statement followed by the zone name and a block of options that begin with an opening brace (**{**). Each option entry ends with a semicolon. The entire block ends with a closing brace, also followed by a semicolon. The format for a **named.conf** entry is show here, along with the different kinds of comments allowed. Tables 38-5, 38-6, and 38-7 list several commonly used statements and options.

```
// comments
/* comments */
# comments

statements {
 options and features; //comments
};
```

The following example shows a simple caching server entry:

```
// a caching only nameserver config
//
zone "." {
      type hint;
      file "named.ca";
      };
```

Once you have created your configuration file, you should check its syntax with the **named-checkconf** tool. Enter the command on a shell command line. If you do not specify a configuration file, it will default to **/etc/named.conf**.

```
named-checkconf
```

The zone Statement

The **zone** statement is used to specify the domains the name server will service. You enter the keyword **zone**, followed by the name of the domain placed within double quotes. Do not place a period at the end of the domain name. In the following example, a period is within the domain name, but not at the end, "**mytrek.com**"; this differs from the zone file, which requires a period at the end of a complete domain name.

After the zone name, you can specify the class **in**, which stands for Internet. You can also leave it out, in which case **in** is assumed (there are only a few other esoteric classes that are rarely used). Within the zone block, you can place several options (see Table 38-6). Two essential options are **type** and **file**. The **type** option is used to specify the zone's type. The **file** option is used to specify the name of the zone file to be used for this zone. You can choose from several types of zones: master, slave, stub, forward, and hint. *Master* specifies that the zone holds master information and is authorized to act on it. A master server was called a primary server in the older 4.*x* BIND configuration. *Slave* indicates that the zone needs to update its data periodically from a specified master name server. You use this entry if your name server is operating as a secondary server for another primary (master) DNS server. A *stub zone* copies only other name server entries, instead of the entire zone. A *forward zone* directs all queries to name servers specified in a **forwarders** statement. A *hint zone* specifies the set of root name servers used by all Internet DNS servers. You can also specify several options that can override any global options set with the **options** statement. Table 38-4 lists the BIND zone types. The following example shows a simple **zone** statement for the **mytrek.com** domain. Its class is Internet (in), and its type is master. The name of its zone file is usually the same as the zone name, in this case, "**mytrek.com**".

```
zone "mytrek.com" in {
      type master;
      file "mytrek.com";
      };
```

Configuration Statements

Other statements, such as **acl**, **server**, **options**, and **logging**, enable you to configure different features for your name server (see Table 38-5). The **server** statement defines the characteristics to be associated with a remote name server, such as the transfer method and key ID for transaction security. The **controls** statement defines special control channels. The **key** statement defines a key ID to be used in a **server** statement that associates an authentication method with a particular name server (see "DNSSEC" later in this chapter). The **logging** statement is used to configure logging options for the name server, such as the maximum size of the log file and a severity level for messages. Table 38-5 lists the BIND statements. The **sortlists** statement lets you specify preferences to be used when a query returns multiple responses. For example, you could give preference to your localhost network or to a private local network such as 192.168.0.0.

Type	Description
master	Primary DNS zone
slave	Slave DNS server; controlled by a master DNS server
hint	Set of root DNS Internet servers
forward	Forwards any queries in it to other servers
stub	Like a slave zone, but holds only names of DNS servers

TABLE 38-4 DNS BIND Zone Types

Statement	Description
/* comment */	BIND comment in C syntax.
// comment	BIND comment in C++ syntax.
# comment	BIND comment in Unix shell and Perl syntax.
acl	Defines a named IP address matching list.
include	Includes a file, interpreting it as part of the **named.conf** file.
key	Specifies key information for use in authentication and authorization.
logging	Specifies what the server logs and where the log messages are sent.
options	Global server configuration options and defaults for other statements.
controls	Declares control channels to be used by the ndc utility.
server	Sets certain configuration options for the specified server basis.
sortlists	Gives preference to specified networks according to a query's source.
trusted-keys	Defines DNSSEC keys preconfigured into the server and implicitly trusted.
zone	Defines a zone.
view	Defines a view.

TABLE 38-5   BIND Configuration Statements

Option	Description
type	Specifies a zone type.
file	Specifies the zone file for the zone.
directory	Specifies a directory for zone files.
forwarders	Lists hosts for DNS servers where requests are to be forwarded.
masters	Lists hosts for DNS master servers for a slave server.
notify	Allows master servers to notify their slave servers when the master zone data changes and updates are needed.
allow-transfer	Specifies which hosts are allowed to receive zone transfers.
allow-query	Specifies hosts that are allowed to make queries.
allow-recursion	Specifies hosts that are allowed to perform recursive queries on the server.

TABLE 38-6   Zone Options

The options Statement

The **options** statement defines global options and can be used only once in the configuration file. An extensive number of options cover such components as forwarding, name checking, directory pathnames, access control, and zone transfers, among others (see Table 38-7). A complete listing can be found in the BIND documentation.

Option	Description
`sortlist`	Gives preference to specified networks according to a query's source.
`directory`	Specifies a directory for zone files.
`forwarders`	Lists hosts for DNS servers where requests are to be forwarded.
`allow-transfer`	Specifies which hosts are allowed to receive zone transfers.
`allow-query`	Specifies hosts that are allowed to make queries.
`allow-recursion`	Specifies hosts that are allowed to perform recursive queries on the server.
`notify`	Allows master servers to notify their slave servers when the master zone data changes and updates are needed.
`blackhole`	Option to eliminate denial response by `allow-query`.

TABLE 38-7   BIND Options for the **options** Statement

The directory Option

A critically important option found in most configuration files is the **`directory`** option, which holds the location of the name server's zone and cache files on your system. The following example is based on the Fedora Core **/etc/named.conf** file. This example specifies that the zone files are located in the **/var/named** directory. In this directory, you can find your zone files, including those used for your local system. The example uses IPv4 addresses.

```
options {
        directory "/var/named";
        forwarders { 192.168.0.34;
                192.168.0.47;
                };
    };
```

The forwarders Option

Another commonly used global option is the **`forwarders`** option. With the **`forwarders`** option, you can list several DNS servers to which queries can be forwarded if they cannot be resolved by the local DNS server. This is helpful for local networks that may need to use a DNS server connected to the Internet. The **`forwarders`** option can also be placed in forward zone entries.

The notify Option

With the **`notify`** option turned on, the master zone DNS servers send messages to any slave DNS servers whenever their configuration has changed. The slave servers can then perform zone transfers in which they download the changed configuration files. Slave servers always use the DNS configuration files copied from their master DNS servers. The **`notify`** option takes one argument, **yes** or **no**, where **yes** is the default. With the **no** argument, you can have the master server not send out any messages to the slave servers, in effect preventing any zone transfers.

An IPv4 named.conf Example

The following example is a simple **named.conf** file based on the example provided in the BIND documentation. This example shows samples of several of the configuration statements. The file begins with comments using C++ syntax, **//**. The **options** statement has a directory entry that sets the directory for the zone and cache files to **/var/named**. Here, you find links to your zone files, such as **named.local** and reverse mapping files, along with the cache file, **named.ca**. The original files will be located in **/var/named/chroot/var/named**. The first **zone** statement (**.**) defines a hint zone specifying the root name servers. The cache file listing these servers is **named.ca**. The second **zone** statement defines a zone for the **mytrek.com** domain. Its type is master, and its zone file is named "**mytrek.com**". The next zone is used for reverse IP mapping of the previous zone. Its name is made up of a reverse listing of the **mytrek.com** domain's IP address with the term **IN-ADDR.ARPA** appended. The domain address for **mytrek.com** is 192.168.0, so the reverse is 1.168.192. The **IN-ADDR.ARPA** domain is a special domain that supports gateway location and Internet address–to–host mapping. The last **zone** statement defines a reverse mapping zone for the loopback interface, the method used by the system to address itself and enable communication between local users on the system. The zone file used for this local zone is **named.local**.

named.conf
```
//
// A simple BIND 9 configuration
//

logging {
        category cname { null; };
        };

options {
        directory "/var/named";
        };

zone "." {
        type hint;
        file "named.ca";
        };

zone "mytrek.com" {
                type master;
                file "mytrek.com";
                };
zone "1.168.192.IN-ADDR.ARPA" {
                        type master;
                        file "192.168.0";
                        };

zone "0.0.127.IN-ADDR.ARPA" {
                        type master;
                        file "named.local";
                        };
```

An IPv6 named.conf Example

The IPv6 version for the preceding **named.conf** file appears much the same, except that the IN-ADDR.ARPA domain is replaced by the IP6.ARPA domain in the reverse zone entries (IP6.INT is an older, deprecated version). IP6.ARPA uses bit labels providing bit-level specification for the address. This is simply the full hexadecimal address, including zeros, without intervening colons. You need to use the IP6.ARPA format of the IPv6 address for both the **mytrek.com** domain and the localhost domain. The IPv6 address for the localhost domain is 0000:0000:0000:0001, a special reserved address. IP6.INT is an older version of IP6.ARPA that uses a nibble format for reverse addresses (discussed later).

named.conf

```
//
// A simple BIND 9 configuration
//

logging {
        category cname { null; };
        };

options {
        directory "/var/named";
        };

zone "." {
        type hint;
        file "named.ca";
        };

zone "mytrek.com" {
                type master;
                file "mytrek.com";
                };
zone "\[xFEC0000000000000/64].IP6.ARPA" {
                        type master;
                        file "fec.ip6.arpa";
                        };

zone "\[x00000000000000000000000000000001/128].IP6.ARPA" {
                        type master;
                        file "named.local";
                        };
```

Caching-Only Server

When BIND is initially installed, it creates a default configuration for what is known as a caching-only server. A *caching-only* server copies queries made by users and saves them in a cache, for use later if the queries are repeated. This can save DNS lookup response times. The cache is held in memory and lasts only as long as **named** runs. The following example is the **named.conf** file initially installed for a caching-only server. Only the local and cache zones are defined.

named.conf (caching-only server)
```
// generated by named-bootconf.pl

options {
        directory "/var/named";
        };

//
// a caching only nameserver config
//
zone "." {
        type hint;
        file "named.ca";
        };

zone "0.0.127.IN-ADDR.ARPA" {
                        type master;
                        file "named.local";
                        };
```

Resource Records for Zone Files

Your name server holds domain name information about the hosts on your network in resource records placed in zone and reverse mapping files. Resource records are used to associate IP addresses with fully qualified domain names. You need a record for every computer in the zone that the name server services. A record takes up one line, though you can use parentheses to use several lines for a record, as is usually the case with SOA records. A resource record uses the Standard Resource Record Format as shown here:

```
name [<ttl>] [<class>] <type> <rdata> [<comment>]
```

Here, *name* is the name for this record. It can be a domain name or a hostname (fully qualified domain name). If you specify only the hostname, the default domain is appended. If no name entry exists, the last specific name is used. If the @ symbol is used, the name server's domain name is used. *ttl* (time to live) is an optional entry that specifies how long the record is to be cached ($TTL directive sets default). *class* is the class of the record. The class used in most resource record entries is IN, for Internet. By default, it is the same as that specified for the domain in the **named.conf** file. *type* is the type of the record. *rdata* is the resource record data. The following is an example of a resource record entry. The name is **rabbit.mytrek.com**, the class is Internet (IN), the type is a host address record (A), and the data is the IP address 192.168.0.2.

```
rabbit.mytrek.com.    IN   A   192.168.0.2
```

Resource Record Types

Different types of resource records exist for different kinds of hosts and name server operations (see Table 38-8 for a listing of resource record types). A, NS, MX, PTR, and CNAME are the types commonly used. A is used for host address records that match domain names with IP addresses. NS is used to reference a name server. MX specifies the host address of the mail server that services this zone. The name server has mail messages sent to that host. The PTR type is used for records that point to other resource records and is used for reverse mapping. CNAME is used to identify an alias for a host on your system.

Time To Live Directive and Field: $TTL

All zone files begin with a Time To Live directive, which specifies the time that a client should keep the provided DNS information before refreshing the information again from the DNS server. Realistically this should be at least a day, though if changes in the server are scheduled sooner, you can temporarily shorten the time, later restoring it. Each record, in fact, has a Time To Live value that can be explicitly indicated with the TTL field. This is the second field in a resource record. If no TTL field is specified in the record, then the default as defined by the $TLL directive can be used. The $TTL directive is placed at the beginning of each zone file. By default it will list the time in seconds, usually 86400 (24 hours).

```
$TTL 86400
```

You can also specify the time in days (d), hours (h), or minutes (m), as in

```
$TTL 2d3h
```

Type	Description
A	An IPv4 host address, maps hostname to IPv4 address
A6	An IPv6 host address
NS	Authoritative name server for this zone
CNAME	Canonical name, used to define an alias for a hostname
SOA	Start of Authority, starts DNS entries in zone file, specifies name server for domain, and other features such as server contact and serial number
WKS	Well-known service description
PTR	Pointer record, for performing reverse domain name lookups, maps IP address to hostname
RP	Text string that contains contact information about a host
HINFO	Host information
MINFO	Mailbox or mail list information
MX	Mail exchanger, informs remote site of your zone's mail server
TXT	Text strings, usually information about a host
KEY	Domain private key
SIG	Resource record signature
NXT	Next resource record

TABLE 38-8   Domain Name Service Resource Record Types

When used as a field in a resource record, the TTL will be a time specified as the second field. In the following example, the turtle resource record can be cached for three days. This will override the default time in the TTL time directive:

```
turtle    3d      IN    A     192.168.0.1
```

Start of Authority: SOA

A zone or reverse mapping file always begins with a special resource record called the Start of Authority (SOA) record. This record specifies that all the following records are authoritative for this domain. It also holds information about the name server's domain, which is to be given to other name servers. An SOA record has the same format as other resource records, though its data segment is arranged differently. The format for an SOA record follows:

```
name {ttl} class SOA Origin Person-in-charge (
                            Serial number
                            Refresh
                            Retry
                            Expire
                            Minimum )
```

Each zone has its own SOA record. The SOA begins with the zone name specified in the **named.conf** zone entry. This is usually a domain name. An @ symbol is usually used for the name and acts like a macro expanding to the domain name. The *class* is usually the Internet class, IN. *SOA* is the type. *Origin* is the machine that is the origin of the records, usually the machine running your name server daemon. The *person-in-charge* is the e-mail address for the person managing the name server (use dots, not @, for the e-mail address, as this symbol is used for the domain name). Several configuration entries are placed in a block delimited with braces. The first is the *serial number*. You change the serial number when you add or change records, so that it is updated by other servers. The serial number can be any number, as long as it is incremented each time a change is made to any record in the zone. A common practice is to use the year-month-day-number for the serial number, where number is the number of changes in that day. For example, 1999120403 would be the year 1999, December 4, for the third change. Be sure to update it when making changes.

Refresh specifies the time interval for refreshing SOA information. *Retry* is the frequency for trying to contact an authoritative server. *Expire* is the length of time a secondary name server keeps information about a zone without updating it. *Minimum* is the length of time records in a zone live. The times are specified in the number of seconds.

The following example shows an SOA record. The machine running the name server is **turtle.mytrek.com**, and the e-mail address of the person responsible for the server is **hostmaster.turtle.mytrek.com**. Notice the periods at the ends of these names. For names with no periods, the domain name is appended. **turtle** would be the same as **turtle.mytrek.com**. When entering full hostnames, be sure to add the period so that the domain is not appended.

```
@ IN SOA turtle.mytrek.com. hostmaster.turtle.mytrek.com. (
                            1997022700 ; Serial
                            28800 ; Refresh
                            14400 ; Retry
                            3600000 ; Expire
                            86400 ) ; Minimum
```

Name Server: NS

The name server record specifies the name of the name server for this zone. These have a resource record type of NS. If you have more than one name server, list them in NS records. These records usually follow the SOA record. As they usually apply to the same domain as the SOA record, their name field is often left blank to inherit the server's domain name specified by the @ symbol in the previous SOA record.

```
            IN   NS      turtle.mytrek.com.
```

You can, if you wish, enter the domain name explicitly as shown here:

```
mytrek.com.  IN   NS      turtle.mytrek.com.
```

Address Record: A and A6

Resource records of type A are address records that associate a fully qualified domain name with an IP address. Often, only their hostname is specified. Any domain names without a terminating period automatically have the domain appended to them. Given the domain **mytrek.com**, the **turtle** name in the following example is expanded to **turtle.mytrek.com**:

```
rabbit.mytrek.com. IN    A      192.168.0.2
turtle             IN    A      192.168.0.1
```

BIND versions 8.2.2 and 9.1 support IPv6 addresses. IPv6 IP addresses have a very different format from that of the IPv4 addresses commonly used (see Chapter 39). Instead of the numerals arranged in four segments, IPv6 uses hexadecimal numbers arranged in seven segments. In the following example, **turtle.mytrek.com** is associated with a site-local IPv6 address: **fec0::**. Recall that there are only three fields in a site-local address: format prefix, subnet identifier, and interface identifier. The empty segments of the subnet identifier can be represented by an empty colon pair (::). The interface identifier follows, **8:800:200C:417A**.

```
turtle.mytrek.com. IN    A6    FEC0::8:800:200C:417A
```

IPv6 also supports the use of IPv4 addresses as an interface identifier, instead of the MAC-derived identifier. The network information part of the IPv6 address would use IPv6 notation, and the remaining interface (host) identifier would use the full IPv4 address. These are known as mixed addresses. In the next example, **lizard.mytrek.com** is given a mixed address using IPv6 network information and IPv4 interface information. The IPv6 network information is for an IPv6 site-local address.

```
lizard.mytrek.com. IN     A6       fec0::192.168.0.3
```

The AAAA record is an older and deprecated version of an IPv6 record. It is still in use in many networks. An AAAA record operates much like a standard A address record, requiring a full IPv6 address. You can do the same with an A6 record. An A6 record, though, can be more flexible, in that it does not require a full address. Instead you chain A6 records together, specifying just part of the address in each. For example, you could specify just an interface identifier for a host, letting the network information be provided by another IPv6 record. In the next example, the first A6 record lists only the address for the interface identifier for the host **divit**. Following the address is the domain name, **mytrek.com**, whose address is to be used to complete **divit**'s address, providing network information. The next A6 record provides the network address information for **mytrek.com**.

```
divit.mygolf.com.  IN    A6    0:0:0:0:1234:5678:3466:af1f  mytrek.com.
mytrek.com.        IN    A6    3ffe:8050:201:1860::
```

Mail Exchanger: MX

The mail exchanger record, MX, specifies the mail server that is used for this zone or for a particular host. The mail exchanger is the server to which mail for the host is sent. In the following example, the mail server is specified as **turtle.mytrek.com**. Any mail sent to the address for any machines in that zone will be sent to the mail server, which in turn will send it to the specific machines. For example, mail sent to a user on **rabbit.mytrek.com** will first be sent to **turtle.mytrek.com**, which will then send it on to **rabbit.mytrek.com**. In the following example, the host 192.168.0.1 (**turtle.mytrek.com**) is defined as the mail server for the **mytrek.com** domain:

```
mytrek.com. IN    MX    10    turtle.mytrek.com.
```

You could also inherit the domain name from the SOA record, leaving the domain name entry blank.

```
            IN    MX    turtle.mytrek.com.
```

You could use the IP address instead, but in larger networks, the domain name may be needed to search for and resolve the IP address of a particular machine, which could change.

```
mytrek.com. IN    MX    10    192.168.0.1
```

An MX record recognizes an additional field that specifies the ranking for a mail exchanger. If your zone has several mail servers, you can assign them different rankings in their MX records. The smaller number has a higher ranking. This way, if mail cannot reach the first mail server, it can be routed to an alternate server to reach the host. In the following example, mail for hosts on the **mytrek.com** domain is first routed to the mail server at 192.168.0.1 (**turtle.mytrek.com**), and if that fails, it is routed to the mail server at 192.168.0.2 (**rabbit.mytrek.com**).

```
mytrek.com. IN MX 10 turtle.mytrek.com.
            IN MX 20 rabbit.mytrek.com.
```

You can also specify a mail server for a particular host. In the following example, the mail server for **lizard.mytrek.com** is specified as **rabbit.mytrek.com**:

```
lizard.mytrek.com. IN    A         192.168.0.3
                   IN    MX    10  rabbit.mytrek.com.
```

Aliases: CNAME

Resource records of type CNAME are used to specify alias names for a host in the zone. Aliases are often used for machines running several different types of servers, such as both Web and FTP servers. They are also used to locate a host when it changes its name. The old name becomes an alias for the new name. In the following example, **ftp.mytrek.com** is an alias for a machine actually called **turtle.mytrek.com**:

```
ftp.mytrek.com. IN CNAME turtle.mytrek.com.
```

The term CNAME stands for canonical name. The canonical name is the actual name of the host. In the preceding example, the canonical name is **turtle.mytrek.com**. The alias, also known as the CNAME, is **ftp.mytrek.com**. In a CNAME entry, the alias points to the canonical name. Aliases cannot be used for NS (name server) or MX (mail server) entries. For those records, you need to use the original domain name or IP address.

A more stable way to implement aliases is simply to create another address record for a host or domain. You can have as many hostnames for the same IP address as you want, provided they are certified. For example, to make **www.mytrek.com** an alias for **turtle.mytrek.com**, you only have to add another address record for it, giving it the same IP address as **turtle.mytrek.com**.

```
turtle.mytrek.com. IN A 192.168.0.1
www.mytrek.com. IN A 192.168.0.1
```

Pointer Record: PTR

A PTR record is used to perform reverse mapping from an IP address to a host. PTR records are used in the reverse mapping files. The name entry holds a reversed IP address, and the data entry holds the name of the host. The following example maps the IP address 192.168.0.1 to **turtle.mytrek.com**:

```
1.1.168.192 IN PTR turtle.mytrek.com.
```

In a PTR record, you can specify just that last number segment of the address (the host address) and let DNS fill in the domain part of the address. In the next example, 1 has the domain address, 1.168.192, automatically added to give 1.1.168.192:

```
1 IN PTR turtle.mytrek.com.
```

Host Information: HINFO, RP, MINFO, and TXT

The HINFO, RP, MINFO, and TXT records are used to provide information about the host. The RP record enables you to specify the person responsible for a certain host. The HINFO record provides basic hardware and operating system identification. The TXT record is used to enter any text you want. MINFO provides a host's mail and mailbox information. These are used sparingly, as they may give too much information out about the server.

Zone Files

A DNS server uses several zone files covering different components of the DNS. Each zone uses two zone files: the principal zone file and a reverse mapping zone file. The *zone file* contains the resource records for hosts in the zone. A *reverse mapping file* contains records that provide reverse mapping of your domain name entries, enabling you to map from IP addresses to domain names. The name of the file used for the zone file can be any name.

The name of the file is specified in the **zone** statement's file entry in the **named.conf** file. If your server supports several zones, you may want to use a name that denotes the specific zone. Most systems use the domain name as the name of the zone file. For example, the zone **mytrek.com** would have a zone file with the same name and the extension **zone**, as in **mytrek.com.zone** (system-config-bind saves the zone file using a **.db** extension). These could be placed in a subdirectory called **zones** or **master**. The zone file used in the following example is called **mytrek.com**. The reverse mapping file can also be any name, though it is usually the reverse IP address domain specified in its corresponding zone file. For example, in the case of the **mytrek.com.zone** zone file, the reverse mapping file might be called **192.168.0.zone**, the IP address of the **mytrek.com** domain defined in the **mytrek.com .zone** zone file. This file would contain reverse mapping of all the host addresses in the domain, allowing their hostname addresses to be mapped to their corresponding IP addresses. In addition, BIND sets up a cache file and a reverse mapping file for the localhost. The cache file holds the resource records for the root name servers to which your name server connects. The cache file can be any name, although it is usually called **named .ca**. The localhost reverse mapping file holds reverse IP resource records for the local loopback interface, localhost. Although localhost can be any name, it usually has the name **named .local**. The IPv6 version is **named.ip6.local**.

Once you have created your zone files, you should check their syntax with the **named-checkzone** tool. This tool requires that you specify both a zone and a zone file. In the following example, in the **/var/named** directory, the zone **mytrek.com** in the zone file **mytrek.com.zone** is checked:

```
named-checkzone  mytrek.com mytrek.com.zone
```

Zone Files for Internet Zones

A zone file holds resource records that follow a certain format. The file begins with general directives to define default domains or to include other resource record files. These are followed by a single SOA record, name server and domain resource records, and then resource records for the different hosts. Comments begin with a semicolon and can be placed throughout the file. The @ symbol operates like a special macro, representing the domain name of the zone to which the records apply. The @ symbol is used in the first field of a resource or SOA record as the zone's domain name. Multiple names can be specified using the * matching character. The first field in a resource record is the name of the domain to which it applies. If the name is left blank, the previous explicit name entry in another resource record is automatically used. This way, you can list several entries that apply to the same host without having to repeat the hostname. Any host or domain name used throughout this file that is not terminated with a period has the zone's domain appended to it. For example, if the zone's domain is **mytrek.com** and a resource record has only the name **rabbit** with no trailing period, the zone's domain is automatically appended to it, giving you **rabbit.mytrek.com**. Be sure to include the trailing period whenever you enter the complete fully qualified domain name, **turtle.mytrek.com.**, for example.

Directives

You can also use several directives to set global attributes. $ORIGIN sets a default domain name to append to address names that do not end in a period. $INCLUDE includes a file. $GENERATE can generate records whose domain or IP addresses differ only by an iterated number. The $ORIGIN directive is often used to specify the root domain to use in address records. Be sure to include the trailing period. The following example sets the domain origin to **mytrek.com** and will be automatically appended to the **lizard** hostname that follows:

```
$ORIGIN   mytrek.com.
lizard   IN   A   192.168.0.2
```

SOA Record

A zone file begins with an SOA record specifying the machine the name server is running on, among other specifications. The @ symbol is used for the name of the SOA record, denoting the zone's domain name. After the SOA, the name server resource records (NS) are listed. Just below the name server records are resource records for the domain itself. Resource records for host addresses (A), aliases (CNAME), and mail exchangers (MX) follow. The following example shows a sample zone file, which begins with an SOA record and is followed by an NS record, resource records for the domain, and then resource records for individual hosts:

```
; Authoritative data for turle.mytrek.com
;
$TTL 86400
@ IN SOA turtle.mytrek.com. hostmaster.turtle.mytrek.com.(
                            93071200 ; Serial number
                               10800 ; Refresh 3 hours
                                3600 ; Retry 1 hour
                             3600000 ; Expire 1000 hours
                               86400 ) ; Minimum 24 hours

              IN      NS         turtle.mytrek.com.
              IN      A          192.168.0.1
              IN      MX   10    turtle.mytrek.com.
              IN      MX   15    rabbit.mytrek.com.

turtle        IN      A          192.168.0.1
              IN      HINFO      PC-686 LINUX
gopher        IN      CNAME      turtle.mytrek.com.
ftp           IN      CNAME      turtle.mytrek.com.
www           IN      A          192.168.0.1

rabbit        IN      A          192.168.0.2

lizard        IN      A          192.168.0.3
              IN      HINFO      MAC MACOS
localhost     IN      A          127.0.0.1
```

The first two lines are comments about the server for which this zone file is used. Notice that the first two lines begin with a semicolon. The class for each of the resource records in this file is IN, indicating these are Internet records. The SOA record begins with an @ symbol that stands for the zone's domain. In this example, it is **mytrek.com**. Any host or domain name used throughout this file that is not terminated with a period has this domain appended to it. For example, in the following resource record, **turtle** has no period, so it automatically expands to **turtle.mytrek.com**. The same happens for **rabbit** and **lizard**. These are read as **rabbit.mytrek.com** and **lizard.mytrek.com**. Also, in the SOA, notice that the e-mail address for hostmaster uses a period instead of an @ symbol; @ is a special symbol in zone files and cannot be used for any other purpose.

Nameserver Record
The next resource record specifies the name server for this zone. Here, it is **mytrek.com**. Notice the name for this resource record is blank. If the name is blank, a resource record inherits the name from the previous record. In this case, the NS record inherits the value of @ in the SOA record, its previous record. This is the zone's domain, and the NS record specifies **turtle.mytrek.com** as the name server for this zone.

```
        IN    NS    turtle.mytrek.com.
```

Here the domain name is inherited. The entry can be read as the following. Notice the trailing period at the end of the domain name:

```
mytrek.com. IN    NS    turtle.mytrek.com.
```

Address Record
The following address records set up an address for the domain itself. This is often the same as the name server, in this case 192.168.0.1 (the IP address of **turtle.mytrek.com**). This enables users to reference the domain itself, rather than a particular host in it. A mail exchanger record follows that routes mail for the domain to the name server. Users can send mail to the **mytrek.com** domain and it will be routed to **turtle.mytrek.com.**

```
        IN    A    192.168.0.1
```

Here the domain name is inherited. The entry can be read as the following:

```
mytrek.com. IN    A    192.168.0.1
```

Mail Exchanger Record
The next records are mail exchanger (MX) records listing **turtle.mytrek.com** and **fast.mytrek .com** as holding the mail servers for this zone. You can have more than one mail exchanger record for a host. More than one host may exist through which mail can be routed. These can be listed in mail exchanger records for which you can set priority rankings (a smaller number ranks higher). In this example, if **turtle.mytrek.com** cannot be reached, its mail is routed through **rabbit.mytrek.com**, which has been set up also to handle mail for the **mytrek.com** domain:

```
        IN    MX    100    turtle.mytrek.com.
        IN    MX    150    rabbit.mytrek.com.
```

Again the domain name is inherited. The entries can be read as the following:

```
mytrek.com.    IN    MX    100    turtle.mytrek.com.
mytrek.com.    IN    MX    150    rabbit.mytrek.com.
```

Address Record with Hostname
The following resource record is an address record (A) that associates an IP address with the fully qualified domain name **turtle.mytrek.com**. The resource record name holds only **turtle**

with no trailing period, so it is automatically expanded to **turtle.mytrek.com.** This record provides the IP address to which **turtle.mytrek.com** can be mapped.

```
turtle   IN   A    192.168.0.1
```

Inherited Names

Several resource records immediately follow that have blank names. These inherit their names from the preceding full record—in this case, **turtle.mytrek.com.** In effect, these records also apply to that host. Using blank names is an easy way to list additional resource records for the same host (notice that an apparent indent occurs). The first record is an information record, providing the hardware and operating system for the machine.

```
         IN   HINFO   PC-686 LINUX
```

Alias Records

If you are using the same machine to run several different servers, such as Web, FTP, and Gopher servers, you may want to assign aliases to these servers to make accessing them easier for users. Instead of using the actual domain name, such as **turtle.mytrek.com**, to access the Web server running on it, users may find using the following is easier: for the Web server, **www.mytrek.com**; for the Gopher server, **gopher.mytrek.com**; and for the FTP server, **ftp.mytrek.com**. In the DNS, you can implement such a feature using alias records. In the example zone file, two CNAME alias records exist for the **turtle.mytrek.com** machine: FTP and Gopher. The next record implements an alias for **www** using another address record for the same machine. None of the name entries ends in a period, so they are appended automatically with the domain name **mytrek.com. www.mytrek.com**, **ftp.mytrek.com**, and **gopher.mytrek.com** are all aliases for **turtle.mytrek.com**. Users entering those URLs automatically access the respective servers on the **turtle.mytrek.com** machine.

Loopback Record

Address and mail exchanger records are then listed for the two other machines in this zone: **rabbit.mytrek.com** and **lizard.mytrek.com**. You could add HINFO, TXT, MINFO, or alias records for these entries. The file ends with an entry for localhost, the special loopback interface that allows your system to address itself.

IPv6 Zone File Example

This is the same zone file using IPv6 addresses. The addresses are site-local (FEC0), instead of global (3), providing private network addressing. The loopback device is represented by the IPv6 address ::1. The A6 IPv6 address records are used.

```
; Authoritative data for turtle.mytrek.com, IPv6 version
;
$TTL 1d
@ IN SOA turtle.mytrek.com. hostmaster.turtle.mytrek.com.(
                         93071200 ; Serial number
                            10800 ; Refresh 3 hours
                             3600 ; Retry 1 hour
                          3600000 ; Expire 1000 hours
                            86400 ) ; Minimum 24 hours

          IN     NS        turtle.mytrek.com.
```

```
              IN        A6          FEC0::8:800:200C:417A
              IN        MX    10    turtle.mytrek.com.
              IN        MX    15    rabbit.mytrek.com.

turtle        IN        A6          FEC0::8:800:200C:417A
              IN        HINFO       PC-686 LINUX
gopher        IN        CNAME       turtle.mytrek.com.
ftp           IN        CNAME       turtle.mytrek.com.
www           IN        A6          FEC0::8:800:200C:417A

rabbit        IN        A6          FEC0::FEDC:BA98:7654:3210

lizard        IN        A6          FEC0::E0:18F7:3466:7D
              IN        HINFO       MAC MACOS
localhost     IN        A6          ::1
```

Reverse Mapping File

Reverse name lookups are enabled using a reverse mapping file. *Reverse mapping* files map fully qualified domain names to IP addresses. This reverse lookup capability is unnecessary, but it is convenient to have. With reverse mapping, when users access remote hosts, their domain name addresses can be used to identify their own host, instead of only the IP address. The name of the file can be anything you want. On most current distributions, it is the zone's domain address (the network part of a zone's IP address). For example, the reverse mapping file for a zone with the IP address of 192.168.0.1 is 192.168.0. Its full pathname would be something like **/var/named/192.168.0**. On some systems using older implementations of BIND, the reverse mapping filename may consist of the root name of the zone file with the extension **.rev**. For example, if the zone file is called **mytrek.com**, the reverse mapping file would be called something like **mytrek.rev**.

IPv4 IN-ADDR.ARPA Reverse Mapping Format

In IPv4, the zone entry for a reverse mapping in the **named.conf** file uses a special domain name consisting of the IP address in reverse, with an **IN-ADDR.ARPA** extension. This reverse IP address becomes the zone domain referenced by the @ symbol in the reverse mapping file. For example, the reverse mapping zone name for a domain with the IP address of **192.168.43** would be **43.168.192.IN-ADDR.ARPA**. In the following example, the reverse domain name for the domain address **192.168.0** is **1.168.192.IN-ADDR.ARPA**:

```
zone "1.168.192.IN-ADDR.ARPA" in {
        type master;
        file "192.168.0";
        };
```

A reverse mapping file begins with an SOA record, which is the same as that used in a forward mapping file. Resource records for each machine defined in the forward mapping file then follow. These resource records are PTR records that point to hosts in the zone. These must be actual hosts, not aliases defined with CNAME records. Records for reverse mapping begin with a reversed IP address. Each segment in the IP address is sequentially reversed. Each segment begins with the host ID, followed by reversed network numbers. If you list only the host ID with no trailing period, the zone domain is automatically attached. In the case of a reverse mapping file, the zone domain as specified in the **zone** statement is the domain IP address backward. The 1 expands to 1.1.168.192. In the following example, **turtle** and **lizard** inherit the domain IP address, whereas **rabbit** has its address explicitly entered:

```
; reverse mapping of domain names 1.168.192.IN-ADDR.ARPA
;
$TTL 86400
@ IN SOA turtle.mytrek.com. hostmaster.turtle.mytrek.com. (
                          92050300 ; Serial (yymmddxx format)
                             10800 ; Refresh 3 hours
                              3600 ; Retry 1 hour
                           3600000 ; Expire 1000 hours
                             86400 ) ; Minimum 24 hours


@              IN     NS       turtle.mytrek.com.
1              IN     PTR      turtle.mytrek.com.
2.1.168.192    IN     PTR      rabbit.mytrek.com.
3              IN     PTR      lizard.mytrek.com.
```

IPv6 IP6.ARPA Reverse Mapping Format

In IPv6, reverse mapping can be handled either with the current IP6.ARPA domain format, or with the older IP6.INT format. With IP6.ARPA, the address is represented by a bit-level representation that places the hexadecimal address within brackets. The first bracket is preceded by a backslash. The address must be preceded by an x indicating that it is a hexadecimal address. Following the address is a number indicating the number of bits referenced. In a 128-bit address, usually the first 64 bits reference the network address and the last 64 bits are for the interface address. The following example shows the network and interface addresses for lizard.

```
FEC0:0000:0000:0000:00E0:18F7:3466:007D    lizard IPv6 address
\[xFEC0000000000000/64]                      lizard network address
\[x00E018F73466007D/64]                     lizard interface address
```

The zone entry for a reverse mapping in the **named.conf** file with an **IP6.ARPA** extension would use the bit-level representation for the network address.

```
zone "\[xfec0000000000000/64].IP6.ARPA" in {
        type master;
        file "fec.ip6.arpa";
        };
```

A reverse mapping file then uses the same bit-level format for the interface addresses.

```
$TTL 1d
@ IN SOA turtle.mytrek.com. hostmaster.turtle.mytrek.com. (
                          92050300 ; Serial (yymmddxx format)
                             10800 ; Refresh 3 hours
                              3600 ; Retry 1 hour
                           3600000 ; Expire 1000 hours
                             86400 ) ; Minimum 24 hours


@                            IN     NS       turtle.mytrek.com.
```

```
\[x00080800200C417A/64]      IN     PTR      turtle.mytrek.com.
\[xFEDCBA9876543210/64]      IN     PTR      rabbit.mytrek.com.
\[x00E018F73466007D/64]      IN     PTR      lizard.mytrek.com.
```

IPv6 IP6.INT Reverse Mapping Format

The older IP6.INT format uses a nibble format for the IPv6 address. This has since been replaced by the IPv6.ARPA format. The hexadecimal address is segmented into each hex number, separated by a period and written in reverse. This gives you 32 hex numbers in reverse order. The IP6.INT version for the lizard address is shown here:

```
FEC0:0000:0000:0000:00E0:18F7:3466:007D     lizard IPv6 address
0.0.0.0.0.0.0.0.0.0.0.0.0.c.e.f             lizard network address
D.7.0.0.6.6.4.3.7.F.8.1.0.E.0.0             lizard interface address
```

The zone entry for a reverse mapping in the **named.conf** file with an **IP6.INT** extension would use the reverse nibble format for the network address.

```
zone "0.0.0.0.0.0.0.0.0.0.0.0.0.c.e.f.IP6.INT" in {
        type master;
        file "fec.ip6.int";
        };
```

The reverse zone file then uses the reverse nibble format for each interface address.

```
$TTL 1d
@ IN SOA turtle.mytrek.com. hostmaster.turtle.mytrek.com.(
                        92050300 ; Serial (yymmddxx format)
                           10800 ; Refresh 3 hours
                            3600 ; Retry 1 hour
                         3600000 ; Expire 1000 hours
                           86400 ) ; Minimum 24 hours
$ORIGIN 0.0.0.0.0.0.0.0.0.0.0.0.0.c.e.f  IN   NS   turtle.mytrek.com.
A.7.1.4.C.0.0.2.0.0.8.0.8.0.0.0    IN     PTR      turtle.mytrek.com.
0.1.2.3.4.5.6.7.8.9.A.B.C.D.E.F    IN     PTR      rabbit.mytrek.com.
D.7.0.0.6.6.4.3.7.F.8.1.0.E.0.0    IN     PTR      lizard.mytrek.com.
```

Localhost Reverse Mapping

A localhost reverse mapping file implements reverse mapping for the local loopback interface known as *localhost*, whose network address is 127.0.0.1. This file can be any name. On Fedora Core, localhost is given the name **named.local** for IPv4 and **named.ip6.local** for IPv6 addressing. On other systems, localhost may use the network part of the IP address, 127.0.0. This file allows mapping the domain name localhost to the localhost IP address, which is always 127.0.0.1 on every machine. The address 127.0.0.1 is a special address that functions as the local address for your machine. It allows a machine to address itself. In the **zone** statement for this file, the name of the zone is **0.0.127.IN-ADDR.ARPA**. The domain part of the IP address is entered in reverse order, with **IN-ADDR.ARPA** appended to it, **0.0.127.IN-ADDR.ARPA**. The **named.conf** entry is shown here:

```
zone "0.0.127.IN-ADDR.ARPA" {
        type master;
        file "named.local";
        };
```

IPv4 Localhost

The name of the file used for the localhost reverse mapping file is usually **named.local**, though it can be any name. The NS record specifies the name server localhost should use. This file has a PTR record that maps the IP address to the localhost. The 1 used as the name expands to append the zone domain—in this case, giving you 1.0.0.127, a reverse IP address. The contents of the **named.local** file are shown here. Notice the trailing periods for localhost:

```
$TTL 1d
@ IN SOA localhost. root.localhost. (
                        1997022700 ; Serial
                            28800 ; Refresh
                            14400 ; Retry
                          3600000 ; Expire
                            86400 ) ; Minimum


            IN      NS      turtle.mytrek.com.
1           IN      PTR     localhost.
```

IPv6 Localhost

In IPv6, localhost reverse mapping is specified using the reverse of the IPv6 localhost address. This address consists of 31 zeros and a 1, which can be written in shorthand as **::1**, where :: represents the sequence of 31 zeros. With IPv6 IP6.ARPA format, these can be written in a bit-level format, where the first 64 bits consist of a network address of all zeros, and the interface address has the value 1.

```
0000:0000:0000:0000:0000:0000:0000:0001   locahost IPv6 address
\[x00000000000000000000000000000001/128]  localhost address
```

In the **named.conf** file, the IP6.ARPA localhost entry would look like this:

```
zone "\[x00000000000000000000000000000001/64].IP6.ARPA" in {
        type master;
        file "named.ip6.local";
        };
```

In the localhost reverse mapping file, the localhost entry would appear like this:

```
\[x0000000000000001/64]      IN      PTR     localhost.
```

Subdomains and Slaves

Adding a subdomain to a DNS server is a simple matter of creating an additional master entry in the **named.conf** file, and then placing name server and authority entries for that subdomain in your primary DNS server's zone file. The subdomain, in turn, has its own zone file with its SOA record and entries listing hosts, which are part of its subdomain, including any of its own mail and news servers.

Subdomain Zones

The name for the subdomain could be a different name altogether or a name with the same suffix as the primary domain. In the following example, the subdomain is called **beach**

.mytrek.com. It could just as easily be called **mybeach.com**. The name server to that domain is on the host **crab.beach.mytrek.com**, in this example. Its IP address is 192.168.0.33, and its zone file is **beach.mytrek.com**. The **beach.mytrek.com** zone file holds DNS entries for all the hosts being serviced by this name server. The following example shows zone entries for its **named.conf**:

```
zone "beach.mytrek.com" {
        type master;
        file "beach.mytrek.com";
        };

zone "1.168.192.IN-ADDR.ARPA" {
        type master;
        file "192.168.0";
        };
```

Subdomain Records

On the primary DNS server, in the example **turtle.mytrek.com**, you would place entries in the master zone file to identify the subdomain server's host and designate it as a name server. Such entries are also known as *glue records*. In this example, you would place the following entries in the **mytrek.com** zone file on **turtle.mytrek.com**:

```
beach.mytrek.com.    IN    NS    beach.mytrek.com.
beach.mytrek.com.    IN    A     192.168.0.33.
```

URL references to hosts serviced by **beach.mytrek.com** can now be reached from any host serviced by **mytrek.com**, which does not need to maintain any information about the **beach.mytrek.com** hosts. It simply refers such URL references to the **beach.mytrek.com** name server.

Slave Servers

A slave DNS server is tied directly to a master DNS server and periodically receives DNS information from it. You use a master DNS server to configure its slave DNS servers automatically. Any changes you make to the master server are automatically transferred to its slave servers. This transfer of information is called a *zone transfer*. Zone transfers are automatically initiated whenever the slave zone's refresh time is reached or the slave server receives a notify message from the master. The *refresh time* is the second argument in the zone's SOA entry. A notify message is automatically sent by the master whenever changes are made to the master zone's configuration files and the **named** daemon is restarted. In effect, slave zones are automatically configured by the master zone, receiving the master zone's zone files and making them their own.

Slave Zones

Using the previous examples, suppose you want to set up a slave server on **rabbit.mytrek.com**. Zone entries, as shown in the following example, are set up in the **named.conf** configuration file for the slave DNS server on **rabbit.mytrek.com**. The slave server is operating in the same domain as the master, and so it has the same zone name, **mytrek.com**. Its SOA file is named **slave.mytrek.com**. The term "slave" in the filename is merely a convention that helps identify it as a slave server configuration file. The **masters** statement lists its master DNS server—in this case, 192.168.0.1. Whenever the slave needs to make a zone transfer, it transfers data from that master DNS server. The entry for the reverse mapping file for this slave server lists its reverse mapping file as **slave.192.168.0**.

```
zone "mytrek.com" {
        type slave;
        file "slave.mytrek.com";
        masters { 192.168.0.1;
        };

zone "1.168.192.IN-ADDR.ARPA" {
        type slave;
        file "slave.192.168.0";
        masters { 192.168.0.1;
        };
```

Slave Records

On the master DNS server, the master SOA zone file has entries in it to identify the host that holds the slave DNS server and to designate it as a DNS server. In this example, you would place the following in the **mytrek.com** zone file:

```
        IN      NS      192.168.0.2
```

You would also place an entry for this name server in the **mytrek.com** reverse mapping file:

```
        2.0.168.192    IN      NS
```

Controlling Transfers

The master DNS server can control which slave servers can transfer zone information from it using the **allow-transfer** statement. Place the statement with the list of IP addresses for the slave servers to which you want to allow access. Also, the master DNS server should be sure its **notify** option is not disabled. The **notify** option is disabled by a "notify no" statement in the options or zone **named.conf** entries. Simply erase the "no" argument to enable **notify**.

Incremental Zone Transfers

With BIND versions 8.2.2 and 9.0, BIND now supports incremental zone transfers (IXFR). Previously, all the zone data would be replaced in an update, rather than changes such as the addition of a few resource records simply being edited in. With incremental zone transfers, a database of changes is maintained by the master zone. Then only the changes are transferred to the slave zone, which uses this information to update its own zone files. To implement incremental zone transfers, you have to turn on the **maintain-ixfr-base** option in the options section.

```
maintain-ixfr-base yes;
```

You can then use the **ixfr-base** option in a zone section to specify a particular database file to hold changes.

```
ixfr-base "db.mytrek.com.ixfr";
```

IP Virtual Domains

IP-based virtual hosting allows more than one IP address to be used for a single machine. If a machine has two registered IP addresses, either one can be used to address the machine. If you want to treat the extra IP address as another host in your domain, you need only create an address record for it in your domain's zone file. The domain name for the host would be the same as your domain name. If you want to use a different domain name for the extra IP, however, you have to set up a virtual domain for it. This entails creating a new **zone** statement for it with its own zone file. For example, if the extra IP address is 192.168.0.42 and you want to give it the domain name **sail.com**, you must create a new **zone** statement for it in your **named.conf** file with a new zone file. The **zone** statement would look something like this. The zone file is called **sail.com**:

```
zone "sail.com" in {
        type master;
        file "sail.com";
        };
```

In the **sail.com** file, the name server name is **turtle.mytrek.com** and the e-mail address is **hostmaster@turtle.mytrek.com**. In the name server (NS) record, the name server is **turtle .mytrek.com.** This is the same machine using the original address that the name server is running as. **turtle.mytrek.com** is also the host that handles mail addressed to **sail.com** (MX). An address record then associates the extra IP address 192.168.0.42 with the **sail.com** domain name. A virtual host on this domain is then defined as **jib.sail.com**. Also, **www** and **ftp** aliases are created for that host, creating **www.sail.com** and **ftp.sail.com** virtual hosts.

```
; Authoritative data for sail.com
;
$TTL 1d
@ IN SOA turtle.mytrek.com. hostmaster.turtle.mytrek.com. (
                             93071200 ; Serial (yymmddxx)
                                10800 ; Refresh 3 hours
                                 3600 ; Retry 1 hour
                              3600000 ; Expire 1000 hours
                                86400 ) ; Minimum 24 hours


        IN      NS         turtle.mytrek.com.
        IN      MX    10   turtle.mytrek.com.
        IN      A          192.168.0.42 ;address of the sail.com domain

jib     IN      A          192.168.0.42
www     IN      A          jib.sail.com.
ftp     IN      CNAME      jib.sail.com.
```

In your reverse mapping file (**/var/named/1.168.192**), add PTR records for any virtual domains.

```
42.1.168.192       IN      PTR      sail.com.
42.1.168.192       IN      PTR      jib.sail.com.
```

You also have to configure your network connection to listen for both IP addresses on your machine (see Chapter 5).

Cache File

The *cache file* is used to connect the DNS server to root servers on the Internet. The file can be any name. On many systems, the cache file is called **named.ca**. Other systems may call the cache file **named.cache** or **roots.hints**. The cache file is usually a standard file installed by your BIND software, which lists resource records for designated root servers for the Internet. You can obtain a current version of the **named.ca** file from the **rs.internic.net** FTP site. The following example shows sample entries taken from the **named.ca** file:

```
; formerly NS.INTERNIC.NET
;
. 3600000 IN NS A.ROOT-SERVERS.NET.
A.ROOT-SERVERS.NET. 3600000 A 198.41.0.4
;
; formerly NS1.ISI.EDU
;
. 3600000 NS B.ROOT-SERVERS.NET.
B.ROOT-SERVERS.NET. 3600000 A 128.9.0.107
```

If you are creating an isolated intranet, you need to create your own root DNS server until you connect to the Internet. In effect, you are creating a fake root server. This can be another server on your system pretending to be the root or the same name server.

Dynamic Update: DHCP and Journal Files

There are situations where you will need to have zones updated dynamically. Instead of your manually editing a zone file to make changes in a zone, an outside process updates the zone, making changes and saving the file automatically. Dynamic updates are carried out both by master zones updating slave zones and by DHCP servers providing IP addresses they generated for hosts to the DNS server.

A journal file is maintained recording all the changes made to a zone, having a **.jnl** extension. Should a system crash occur, this file is read to implement the most current changes. Should you want to manually update a dynamically updated zone, you will need to erase its journal file first; otherwise, your changes would be overwritten by the journal file entries.

You allow a zone to be automatically updated by specifying the **allow-update** option. This option indicates the host that can perform the update.

```
allow-update {turtle.mytrek.com;};
```

Alternatively, for master zones, you can create a more refined set of access rules using the **update-policy** statement. With the **update-policy** statement, you can list several grant and deny rules for different hosts and types of hosts.

TSIG Signatures and Updates

With BIND 9.*x*, TSIG signature names can be used instead of hostnames or IP addresses for both **allow-update** and **update-policy** statements (see the following sections on TSIG). Use of TSIG signatures implements an authentication of a host performing a dynamic update, providing a much greater level of security. For example, to allow a DHCP server to update a zone file, you would place an **allow-update** entry in the **zone** statement listed in the **named.conf** file.

The TSIG key is defined in a key statement, naming the key previously created by the **dnssec-keygen** command. The algorithm is HMAC-MD5, and the secret is the encryption key listed in the **.private** file generated by **dnssec-keygen**.

```
key mydhcpserver {
algorithm HMAC-MD5;
secret "ONQAfbBLnvWU9H8hRqq/WA==";
};
```

The key name can then be used in an **allow-update** or **allow-policy** statement to specify a TSIG key.

```
allow-update { key mydhcpserver;};
```

Manual Updates: nsupdate

You can use the update procedure to perform any kind of update you want. You can perform updates manually or automatically using a script. For DHCP updates, the DHCP server is designed to perform dynamic updates of the DNS server. You will need to configure the DHCP server appropriately, specifying the TSIG key to use and the zones to update.

You can manually perform an update using the **nsupdate** command, specifying the file holding the key with the **-k** option.

```
nsupdate -k myserver.private
```

At the prompt, you can use **nsupdate** commands to implement changes. You match on a record using its full or partial entry. To update a record, you would first delete the old one and then add the changed version, as shown here:

```
update delete rabbit.mytrek.com. A 192.168.0.2
update add rabbit.mytrek.com. A 192.168.0.44
```

DNS Security: Access Control Lists, TSIG, and DNSSEC

DNS security currently allows you to control specific access by hosts to the DNS server, as well as providing encrypted communications between servers and authentication of DNS servers. With access control lists, you can determine who will have access to your DNS server. The DNS Security Extensions (DNSSEC), included with BIND 9.*x*, provide private/public key-encrypted authentication and transmissions. TSIGs (transaction signatures) use shared private keys to provide authentication of servers to secure actions such as dynamic updates between a DNS server and a DHCP server.

Access Control Lists

To control access by other hosts, you use access control lists, implemented with the **acl** statement. **allow** and **deny** options with access control host lists enable you to deny or allow access by specified hosts to the name server. With **allow-query**, you can restrict queries to specified hosts or networks. Normally this will result in a response saying that access is denied. You can further eliminate this response by using the **blackhole** option in the **options** statement.

You define an ACL with the **acl** statement followed by the label you want to give the list and then the list of addresses. Addresses can be IP addresses, network addresses, or a range of addresses based on CNDR notation. You can also use an ACL as defined earlier. The following example defines an ACL called **mynet**:

```
acl mynet { 192.168.0.1; 192.168.0.2; };
```

If you are specifying a range, such as a network, you also add exceptions to the list by preceding such addresses with an exclamation point (!). In the following example, the mynetx ACL lists all those hosts in the 192.168.0.0 network, except for 192.168.0.3:

```
acl myexceptions {192.168.0.0; !192.168.0.3; };
```

Four default ACLs are already defined for you. You can use them wherever an option uses a list of addresses as an argument. These are **any** for all hosts, **none** for no hosts, **localhost** for all local IP addresses, and **localnet** for all hosts on local networks served by the DNS server.

Once a list is defined, you can then use it with the **allow-query**, **allow-transfer**, **allow-recursion**, and **blackhole** options in a **zone** statement to control access to a zone. **allow-query** specifies hosts that can query the DNS server. **allow-transfer** is used for master/slave zones, designating whether update transfers are allowed. **allow-recursion** specifies those hosts that can perform recursive queries on the server. The **blackhole** option will deny contact from any hosts in its list, without sending a denial response. In the next example, an ACL of mynet is created. Then in the **mytrek.com** zone, only these hosts are allowed to query the server. As the server has no slave DNS serves, zone transfers are disabled entirely. The **blackhole** option denies access from the myrejects list, without sending any rejection notice.

```
acl mynet { 192.168.0.0; };
acl myrejects { 10.0.0.44; 10.0.0.93; };

zone "mytrek.com" {
        type master;
        file "mytrek.com";
        allow-query { mynet; };
        allow-recursion { mynet; };
        allow-transfer { none; };
        blackhole {myrejects};
        };
```

Secret Keys

Different security measures will use encryption keys generated with the **dnssec-keygen** command. You can use **dnssec-keygen** to create different types of keys, including zone (ZONE), host (HOST), and user (USER) keys. You specify the type of key with the **-n** option. A zone key will require the name ZONE and the name of the zone's domain name.

A zone key is used in DNSSEC operations. The following example creates a zone key for the **mytrek.com** zone:

```
dnssec-keygen -n ZONE mytrek.com.
```

To create a host key, you would use the HOST type. HOST keys are often used in TSIG operations.

```
dnssec-keygen -n HOST turtle.mytrek.com.
```

You can further designate an encryption algorithm (**-a**) and key size (**-b**). Use the **-h** option to obtain a listing of the **dnssec-keygen** options. Currently you can choose from RSA, DSA, HMAC-MD5, and DH algorithms. The bit range will vary according to the algorithm. RSA ranges from 512 to 4096, and HMAC-MD5 ranges from 1 to 512. The following example creates a zone key using a 768-bit key and the DSA encryption algorithm:

```
dnssec-keygen -a DSA -b 768 -n ZONE mytrek.com.
```

The **dnssec-keygen** command will create public and private keys, each in corresponding files with the suffixes **.private** and **.key**. The **.key** file is a KEY resource record holding the public key. For DNSSEC, the private key is used to generate signatures for the zone, and the public key is used to verify the signatures. For TSIG, a shared private key generated by the HMAC-MD5 algorithm is used instead of a public/private key pair.

DNSSEC

DNSSEC provides encrypted authentication to DNS. With DNSSEC, you can create a signed zone that is securely identified with an encrypted signature. This form of security is used primarily to secure the connections between master and slave DNS servers, so that a master server transfers update records only to authorized slave servers and does so with a secure encrypted communication. Two servers that establish such a secure connection do so using a pair of public and private keys. In effect, you have a parent zone that can securely authenticate child zones, using encrypted transmissions. This involves creating zone keys for each child and having those keys used by the parent zone to authenticate the child zones.

Zone Keys

You generate a zone key using the **dnssec-keygen** command and specifying the zone type, ZONE, with the **-n** option. For the key name, you use the zone's domain name. The following example creates a zone key for the **mytrek.com** zone:

```
dnssec-keygen -n ZONE mytrek.com.
```

You can further designate an encryption algorithm (**-a**) and a key size (**-b**). Use the **-h** option to obtain a listing of the **dnssec-keygen** options. Since you are setting up a public/private key pair, you should choose either the RSA or DSA algorithm. The bit range will vary according to the algorithm. RSA ranges from 512 to 4096, and DSA ranges from 512 to 1024. The following example creates a zone key using a 768-bit key and the DSA encryption algorithm:

```
dnssec-keygen -a DSA -b 768 -n ZONE mytrek.com.
```

The **dnssec-keygen** command will create public and private keys, each in corresponding files with the suffixes **.private** and **.key**. The private key is used to generate signatures for the zone, and the public key is used to verify the signatures. The **.key** file is a KEY resource record holding the public key. This is used to decrypt signatures generated by the corresponding private key. You add the public key to the DNS configuration file, **named.conf**, using the **$INCLUDE** statement to include the **.key** file.

DNSSEC Resource Records

In the zone file, you then use three DNSSEC DNS resource records to implement secure communications for a given zone: KEY, SIG, and NXT. In these records, you use the signed keys for the zones you have already generated. The KEY record holds public keys associated with zones, hosts, or users. The SIG record stores digital signatures and expiration dates for a set of resource records. The NXT record is used to determine that a resource record for a domain does not exist. In addition, several utilities let you manage DNS encryption. With the **dnskeygen** utility, you generated the public and private keys used for encryption. **dnssigner** signs a zone using the zone's private key, setting up authentication.

To secure a DNS zone with DNSSEC, you first use **dnskeygen** to create public and private keys for the DNS zone. Then use **dnssigner** to create an authentication key. In the DNS zone file, you enter a KEY resource record in which you include the public key. The public key will appear as a lengthy string of random characters. For the KEY record, you enter in the domain name followed by the KEY and then the public key.

```
mytrek.com. KEY 0x4101 3 3 (
AvqyXgKk/uguxkJF/hbRpYzxZFG3x8EfNX389l7GX6w7rlLy
BJ14TqvrDvXr84XsShg+OFcUJafNr84U4ER2dg6NrlRAmZA1
jFfV0UpWDWcHBR2jJnvgV9zJB2ULMGJheDHeyztM1KGd2oGk
Aensm74NlfUqKzy/3KZ9KnQmEpj/EEBr48vAsgAT9kMjN+V3
NgAwfoqgS0dwj5OiRJoIR4+cdRt+s32OUKsclAODFZTdtxRn
vXF3qYV0S8oewMbEwh3trXi1c7nDMQC3RmoY8RVGt5U6LMAQ
KITDyHU3VmRJ36vn77QqSzbeUPz8zEnbpik8kHPykJZFkcyj
jZoHT1xkJ1tk )
```

For authentication, you can sign particular resource records for a given domain or host. Enter the domain or host followed by the term **SIG** and then the resource record's signature.

```
mytrek.com. SIG KEY 3 86400 19990321010705 19990218010705 4932 com. (
Am3tWJzEDzfU1xwg7hzkiJ0+8UQaPtlJhUpQx1snKpDUqZxm
igMZEVk= )
```

The NXT record lets you negatively answer queries.

```
mytrek.com. NXT ftp.mytrek.com. A NS SOA MX SIG KEY NXT
```

Signing Keys

To set up secure communications between a parent (master) and child (slave) DNS server, the public key then needs to be sent to the parent zone. There, the key can be signed by the parent. As you may have more than zone key, you create a keyset using the **dnssec-makekeyset** command. This generates a file with the extension **.keyset** that is then sent to the parent. The parent zone then uses the **dnssec-signkey** command to sign a child's keyset. This generates a file with the prefix **signedkey-**. This is sent back to the child and now contains both the child's keyset and the parent's signatures. Once the child has the **signedkey-** files, the `dnssec-signedzone` command can be used to sign the zone. The `dnssec-signedzone` command will generate a file with the extension **.signed**. This file is then included in the **named.conf** file with the INCLUDE operation. The `trusted-keys` statement needs to list the public key for the parent zone.

TSIG Keys

TSIG (transaction signatures) also provide secure DNS communications, but they share the private key instead of a private/public key pair. They are usually used for communications between two local DNS servers, and to provide authentication for dynamic updates such as those between a DNS server and a DHCP server.

NOTE *For BIND 8.0, you use* **dnskeygen** *instead of* **dnssec-keygen***.*

Generating TSIG Keys

To create a TSIG key for your DNS server, you use the **dnssec-keygen** command as described earlier. Instead of using the same keys you use for DNSSEC, you create a new set to use for transaction signatures. For TSIG, a shared private key is used instead of a public/private key pair. For a TSIG key you would use an HMAC-MD5 algorithm that generates the same key in the both the **.key** and **.private** files. Use the **-a** option to specify the HMAC-MD5 algorithm to use and the **-b** option for the bit size (HMAC-MD5 ranges from 1 to 512). The **-n** option specifies the key type, in this case HOST for the hostname. The bit range will vary according to the algorithm. The following example creates a host key using a 128-bit key and the HMAC-MD5 encryption algorithm:

```
dnssec-keygen -a HMAC-MD5 -b 128 -n HOST turtle.mytrek.com
```

This creates a private key and a public key, located in the **.key** and **.private** files. In a TSIG scheme, both hosts would use the same private key for authentication. For example, to enable a DHCP server to update a DNS server, both would need the private (secret) key for a TSIG authentication. The HMAC-MD5 key is used as a shared private key, generating both the same private and public keys in the **.key** and **.private** files.

The key Statement

You then specify a key in the **named.conf** file with the **key** statement. For the algorithm option, you list the HMAC-MD5 algorithm, and for the secret option, you list the private key. This key will be listed in both the **.private** and **.key** files. The preceding example would generate key and private files called **Kturtle.mytrek.com.+157.43080.key** and **Kturtle.mytrek.com.+157.43080.private**. The contents of the **.key** file consist of a resource record shown here:

```
turtle.mytrek.com. IN KEY 512 3 157 ONQAfbBLnvWU9H8hRqq/WA==
```

The contents of the private file show the same key along with the algorithm:

```
Private-key-format: v1.2
Algorithm: 157 (HMAC_MD5)
Key: ONQAfbBLnvWU9H8hRqq/WA==
```

Within the **named.conf** file, you then name the key using a **key** statement:

```
key myserver {
algorithm HMAC-MD5;
secret "ONQAfbBLnvWU9H8hRqq/WA==";
};
```

The key's name can then be used to reference the key in other named statements, such as **allow-update** statements:

```
allow-update myserver;
```

The DNS server or DHCP server with which you are setting up communication will also have to have the same key. See the earlier section "Dynamic Update: DHCP and Journal Files" and Chapter 39 for more information on DHCP and TSIG. For communication between two DNS servers, each would have a server statement specifying the shared key. In the following example, the **named.conf** file for the DNS server on 192.168.0.1 would have the following server statement to communicate with the DNS server on 10.0.0.1, using the shared myserver key. The **named.conf** file on the 10.0.0.1 DNS server would have a corresponding server statement for the 192.168.0.1 server.

```
server 10.0.0.1 {  keys (myserver;}; };
```

Split DNS: Views

BIND 9.*x* allows you to divide DNS space into internal and external views. This organization into separate views is referred to as *split DNS*. Such a configuration is helpful to manage a local network that is connected to a larger network, such as the Internet. Your internal view would include DNS information on hosts in the local network, whereas an external view would show only the part of the DNS space that is accessible to other networks. DNS views are often used when you have a local network that you want to protect from a larger network such as the Internet. In effect, you protect DNS information for hosts on a local network from a larger external network such as the Internet.

Internal and External Views

To implement a split DNS space, you need to set up different DNS servers for the internal and external views. The internal DNS servers will hold DNS information about local hosts. The external DNS server maintains connections to the Internet through a gateway as well as manages DNS information about any local hosts that allow external access, such as FTP or Web sites. The gateways and Internet-accessible sites make up the external view of hosts on the network. The internal servers handle all queries to the local hosts or subdomains. Queries to external hosts such as Internet sites are sent to the external servers, which then forward them on to the Internet. Queries sent to those local hosts that operate external servers such as Internet FTP and Web sites are sent to the external DNS servers for processing. Mail sent to local hosts from the Internet is handled first by the external servers, which then forward messages on to the internal servers. With a split DNS configuration, local hosts can access other local hosts, Internet sites, and local hosts maintaining Internet servers. Internet users, on the other hand, can access only those hosts open to the Internet (served by external servers) such as those with Internet servers like FTP and HTTP. Internet users can, however, send mail messages to any of the local hosts, internal and external.

You can also use DNS views to manage connections between a private network that may use only one Internet address to connect its hosts to the Internet. In this case, the internal view holds the private addresses (192.168...), and the external view connects a gateway host with an Internet address to the Internet. This adds another level of security, providing a result similar to IP masquerading (see Chapter 20).

Configuring Views

DNS views are configured with the allow statements such as **allow-query** and **allow-transfer**. With these statements, you can specify the hosts that a zone can send and receive queries and transfers to and from. For example, the internal zone could accept queries from other local hosts, but not from local hosts with external access such as Internet servers. The local Internet servers, though, can accept queries from the local hosts. All Internet queries are forwarded to the gateway. In the external configuration, the local Internet servers can accept queries from anywhere. The gateways receive queries from both the local hosts and the local Internet servers.

In the following example, a network of three internal hosts and one external host is set up into a split view. There are two DNS servers: one for the internal network and one for external access, based on the external host. In reality these make up one network but they are split into two views. The internal view is known as **mygolf.com**, and the external as **greatgolf.com**. In each configuration, the internal hosts are designated in ACL-labeled internals, and the external host is designated in ACL-labeled externals. Should you want to designate an entire IP address range as internal, you could simply use the network address, as in 192.168.0.0/24. In the options section, **allow-query**, **allow-recursion**, and **allow-transfers** restrict access within the network.

Split View Example

The following example shows only the configuration entries needed to implement an internal view. In the **mygolf.com** zone, queries and transfers are allowed only among internal hosts. The global **allow-recursion** option allows recursion among internals.

Internal DNS server

```
acl internals { 192.168.0.1; 192.168.0.2; 192.168.0.3; };
acl externals {10.0.0.1;};
options {
        forward only;
        forwarders {10.0.0.1;}; // forward to external servers
        allow-transfer { none; }; // allow-transfer to no one by dfault
        allow-query { internals; externals; };// restrict query access
        allow-recursion { internals; }; // restrict recursion to internals
            }
zone "mygolf.com" {
        type master;
        file "mygolf";
```

```
        forwarders { };
        allow-query { internals; };
        allow-transfer { internals; }
        };
```

In the configuration for the external DNS server, the same ACLs are set up for internals and externals. In the **options** statement, recursion is now allowed for both externals and internals. In the **mygolf.com** zone, queries are allowed from anywhere, and recursion is allowed for externals and internals. Transfers are not allowed at all.

External DNS server

```
acl internals { 192.168.0.1; 192.168.0.2; 192.168.0.3; };
acl externals {10.0.0.1;};
options {
        allow-transfer { none; }; // allow-transfer to no one
        allow-query { internals; externals; };// restrict query access
        allow-recursion { internals; externals }; // restrict recursion
        };

zone "greatgolf.com" {
        type master;
        file "greatgolf";
        allow-query { any; };
        allow-transfer { internals; externals; };
};
```

Network Autoconfiguration: IPv6, DHCPv6, and DHCP

Many networks now provide either IPv6 autoconfiguration or the DHCP (Dynamic Host Configuration Protocol) service, which automatically provides network configuration for all connected hosts. Autoconfiguration can be either stateless, as in the case of IPv6, or stateful, as with DHCP. Stateless IPv6 autoconfiguration requires no independent server or source to connect to a network. It is a direct plug-and-play operation, where the hardware network interfaces and routers can directly determine the correct addresses. DCHP is an older method that requires a separate server to manage and assign all addresses. Should this server ever fail, hosts could not connect.

With the DHCP protocol, an administrator uses a pool of IP addresses from which the administrator can assign an IP address to a host as needed. The protocol can also be used to provide all necessary network connection information such as the gateway address for the network or the netmask. Instead of having to configure each host separately, network configuration can be handled by a central DHCP server. The length of time that an address can be used can be controlled by means of leases, making effective use of available addresses. If your network is configuring your systems with DHCP, you will not have to configure it.

There are currently two versions of DHCP, one for the original IPv4 protocol and another, known as DHCPv6, for the IPv6 protocol. The IPv6 protocol includes information for dynamic configuration that the IPv4 protocol lacks. In this respect, the IPv4 protocol is much more dependent on DHCP than IPv6 is. As DHCPv6 is still under development, this chapter's DHCP coverage focuses on DHCP for the IPv4 protocol.

IPv6 Stateless Autoconfiguration

In an IPv6 network, the IPv6 protocol includes information that can directly configure a host. With IPv4 you either had to manually configure each host or rely on a DHCP server to provide configuration information. With IPv6 configuration information is integrated into the Internet protocol directly. IPv6 address autoconfiguration is described in detail in RFC 2462.

IPv6 autoconfiguration capabilities are known as stateless, meaning that it can directly configure a host without recourse to an external server. Alternatively, DHCP, including DHCPv6, is stateful, where the host relies on an external DHCP server to provide configuration information. Stateless autoconfiguration has the advantage of hosts not having to rely on a DHCP server to maintain connections to a network. Networks could even become mobile, hooking into one subnet or another, automatically generating addresses as needed. Hosts are no longer tied to a particular DHCP server.

Generating the Local Address

To autoconfigure hosts on a local network, IPv6 makes use of the each network device's hardware MAC address. This address is used to generate a temporary address, with which the host can be queried and configured.

The MAC address is used to create a link-local address, one with a link-local prefix, **FE80::0**, followed by an interface identifier. The link-local prefix is used for physically connected hosts such as those on a small local network.

A uniqueness test is then performed on the generated address. Using the Neighbor Discovery Protocol (NDP), other hosts on the network are checked to see if another host is already using the generated link-local address. If no other host is using the address, then the address is assigned for that local network. At this point the host has only a local address valid within the local physical network. Link-local addresses cannot be routed to a larger network.

Generating the Full Address: Router Advertisements

Once the link-local address has been determined, the router for the network is then queried for additional configuration information. The information can be either stateful or stateless, or both. For stateless configuration, information such as the network address is provided directly, whereas for stateful configuration, the host is referred to a DHCPv6 server where it can obtain configuration information. The two can work together. Often the stateless method is used for addresses, and the stateful DHCPv6 server is used to provide other configuration information such as DNS server addresses.

In the case of stateless addresses, the router provides the larger network address, such as the network's Internet address. This address is then added to the local address, replacing the original link-local prefix, giving either a complete global Internet address or, in the case of private networks, site-local addresses. Routers will routinely advertise this address information, though it can also be specifically requested. The NDP protocol is used to query the information. Before the address is officially assigned, a duplicate address detection procedure checks to see if the address is already in use. The process depends on the router's providing the appropriate addressing information in the form of router advertisements. For a Linux system that operates as a router, you can use the **radvd** router advertisement daemon to advertise addresses, specifying a network prefix in the **/etc/radvd.conf** file.

Figure 39-1 shows a network that is configured with stateless address autoconfiguration. First each host determines its interface identifier using its own MAC hardware address. This is used to create a temporary link-local address for each host using the **FE08::0** prefix. This allows initial communication with the network's router. The router then uses its network prefix to create full Internet addresses, replacing the link-local prefix.

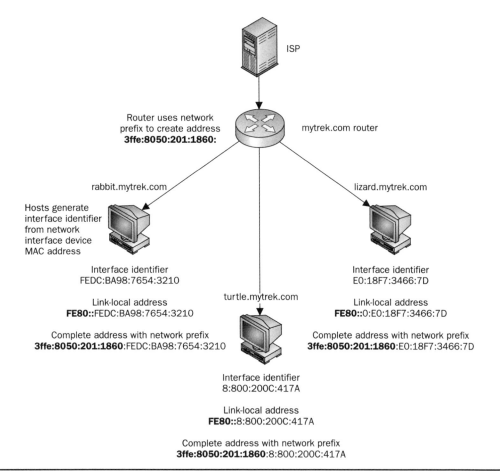

FIGURE 39-1   Stateless IPv6 address autoconfiguration

Router Renumbering

With IPv6, routers have the ability to renumber the addresses on their networks, by changing the network prefix. Renumbering is carried out through the Router Renumbering Protocol, RR. (See RFC 2894 for a description of router renumbering.) Renumbering is often used when a network changes ISP providers, requires that the net address for all hosts be changed (see Figure 39-2). It can also be used for mobile networks where a network can be plugged in to different larger networks, renumbering each time.

With renumbering, routers place a time limit on addresses, similar to the lease time in DHCP, by specifying an expiration limit for the network prefix when the address is generated. To ease transition, interfaces still keep their old addresses as deprecated addresses, while the new ones are first being used. The new ones will be the preferred addresses used for any new connections while deprecated ones are used for older connections. In effect a host could have two addresses, one deprecated and one preferred. This regeneration of addresses effectively renumbers the hosts.

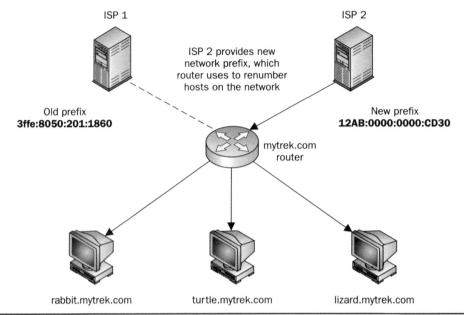

FIGURE 39-2   Router renumbering with IPv6 autoconfiguration

IPv6 Stateful Autoconfiguration: DHCPv6

The IPv6 version of DHCP (DHCPv6) provides stateful autoconfiguration to those networks that still want a DHCP-like service on IPv6 networks. DHCP IPv6 provides configuration information from a server, just like DHCP. But it is a completely different protocol from the IPv4 version, with different options and capabilities. As a stateful configuration process, information is provided by an independent server. DHCPv6 is still under development, though a version is distributed with Fedora Core 4.

DHCPv6 uses its own set of options for both the client and the server. The DHCP server for IPv6 is called **dhcp6s**, and the DHCP client for IPv6 is **dhcp6c**. Their corresponding configuration files are **/etc/dhcp6c** and **/etc/dhcp6s**. A service script, **/etc/init.d/dhcp6s**, can be used to manage the **dhcp6s** server.

As with IPv6 autoconfiguration, the host identifier for a local address is first automatically generated. This is a local-link address containing a host identifier address generated from the host interface's MAC address.

Once the local-link address is determined, the router is queried for the DHCPv6 server. This information is provided in router advertisements that are broadcast regularly. At this point the two different kinds of stateful information can be provided by the server: addresses and other configuration information. The host is notified which kinds of stateful information are provided. If address information is not given by the DHCPv6 server, then addresses will be determined using the stateless autoconfiguration method described in the preceding section. If address information is provided, then an address will be obtained from the server, instead of being directly generated. Before leasing an address, the server will run a duplicate address detection procedure to make sure the address is unique.

NOTE *DHCPv6 stateful addressing is useful for situations in which strict control needs to be maintained over the IP address of a host, whereas stateless IPv6 addressing is suitable for situations where the actual IP address is not important, just that connections be effective.*

DHCP for IPv4

DHCP provides configuration information to systems connected to an IPv4 TCP/IP network, whether the Internet or an intranet. The machines on the network operate as DHCP clients, obtaining their network configuration information from a DHCP server on their network. A machine on the network runs a DHCP client daemon that automatically receives its network configuration information from its network's DHCP server. The information includes its IP address, along with the network's name server, gateway, and proxy addresses, including the netmask. Nothing has to be configured manually on the local system, except to specify the DHCP server it should get its network configuration from. This has the added advantage of centralizing control over network configuration for the different systems on the network. A network administrator can manage the network configurations for all the systems on the network from the DHCP server.

A DHCP server also supports several methods for IP address allocation: automatic, dynamic, and manual. Automatic allocation assigns a permanent IP address for a host. Manual allocation assigns an IP address designated by the network administrator. With dynamic allocation, a DHCP server can allocate an IP address to a host on the network only when the host actually needs to use it. Dynamic allocation takes addresses from a pool of IP addresses that hosts can use when needed and release when they are finished.

The current version of DHCP now supports the DHCP failover protocol in which two DHCP servers support the same address pool. Should one fail, the other can continue to provide DHCP services for a network. Both servers are in synch and have the same copy of network support information for each host on the network. Primary and secondary servers in this scheme are designated with the primary and secondary statements.

A variety of DHCP servers and clients are available for different operating systems. For Linux, you can obtain DHCP software from the Internet Software Consortium (ISC) at **www.isc.org**. The software package includes a DHCP server, a client, and a relay agent. Linux includes a DHCP server and client. The DHCP client is called **dhclient**, and the IPv4 server is called **dhcpd**.

Configuring DHCP IPv4 Client Hosts

Configuring hosts to use a DHCP server is a simple matter of setting options for the host's network interface device, such as an Ethernet card. For a Linux host, you can use a distribution network tool to set the host to automatically access a DHCP server for network information. On a network tool's panel for configuring the Internet connection, you will normally find a check box for selecting DHCP. Clicking this box will enable DHCP. For Fedora Core, you can use the system-config-network tool: Select the network device on the Devices panel and edit it. On the General panel, click the entry labeled Automatically Obtain IP Address Settings With, and be sure DHCP is selected from the pop-up menu. If you are connecting to an Internet service provider (ISP), under DHCP Setting, click Automatically Obtain DNS Information From Provider. On Fedora Core, the **BOOTPROTO** entry to DHCP will be set in that interface's network script in the **/etc/sysconfig/network-scripts** directory, such as `ifcfg-eth0` for the first Ethernet card. You could also manually make this entry:

```
BOOTPROTO=dhcp
```

Be sure to restart your network devices with the network script to have the changes take effect.

Client support is carried out by the `dhclient` tool. When your network starts up, it uses `dhclient` to set up your DHCP connection. Though defaults are usually adequate, you can further configure the DHCP client using the **/etc/dhclient.conf** file. Consult the **dhclient.conf** Man page for a detailed list of configuration options. `dhclient` keeps lease information on the DCHP connection in the **/var/lib/dhcp/dhclient.leases** file. You can also directly run `dhclient` to configure DHCP connections.

```
dhclient
```

On a Windows client, locate the TCP/IP entry for your network interface card, then open its properties window. Click the box labeled Obtain IP Address Automatically. Then locate the WINS panel (usually by clicking the Advanced button) and select DHCP as the protocol you want to use.

Configuring the DHCP IPv4 Server

On Fedora Core systems, you can stop and start the DHCP server using the **dhcpd** command in the **/etc/rc.d/init.d** directory. Use the redhat-config-services tool or the **service** command with the **start**, **restart**, and **stop** options. The following example starts the DHCP server. Use the **stop** option to shut it down and **restart** to restart it.

```
service dhcpd start
```

Dynamically allocated IP addresses, known as *leases*, will be assigned for a given time. When a lease expires, it can be extended or a new one generated. Current leases are listed in the **dhcpd.leases** file located in the **/var/lib/dhcp** directory. A lease entry will specify the IP address and the start and end times of the lease along with the client's hostname.

On Fedora Core, DHCP server arguments and options can be specified in the **/etc/sysconfig/dhcpd** file. Network device arguments specify which network device the DHCP server should run on. You can also specify options such as the configuration file to use or the port to listen on. Network device arguments are needed should you have two or more network interfaces on your system but want the DHCP server to operate on only selected connections. Such arguments are listed in the **/etc/sysconf/dhcpd** file using the DHCPARGS setting. The following example says to run the DHCP server only on the Ethernet network device **eth0**:

```
DHPCARGS=eth0
```

This kind of configuration is useful for gateway systems that are connected to both a local network and a larger network such as the Internet through different network devices. On the Internet connection, you may want to run the DCHP client to receive an IP address from an ISP, and on the local network connection, you would want to run the DHCP server to assign IP addresses to local hosts.

The configuration file for the DHCP server is **/etc/dhcpd.conf**, where you specify parameters and declarations that define how different DHCP clients on your network are accessed by the DHCP server, along with options that define information passed to the clients by the DHCP server. These parameters, declarations, and options can be defined globally, for certain subnetworks, or for specific hosts. Global parameters, declarations, and options apply to all clients, unless overridden by corresponding declarations and options in subnet or host declarations. Technically, all entries in a **dhcpd.conf** file are statements that can be either declarations or parameters. All statements end with a semicolon. Options are specified in **options** parameter statements. Parameters differ from declarations in that they define if and how to perform tasks, such as how long a lease is allocated. Declarations describe network features such as the range of addresses to allocate or the networks that are accessible. See the **dhcpd.conf** Man page for a listing of commonly used declarations and options.

Declarations provide information for the DHCP server or designate actions it is to perform. For example, the **range** declaration is used to specify the range of IP addresses to be dynamically allocated to hosts:

```
range 192.168.0.5 192.168.0.128;
```

With parameters, you can specify how the server is to treat clients. For example, the **default-lease-time** declaration sets the number of seconds a lease is assigned to a client. The **filename** declaration specifies the boot file to be used by the client. The **server-name** declaration informs the client of the host from which it is booting. The **fixed-address** declaration can be used to assign a static IP address to a client. See the Man page for **dhcpd.conf** for a complete listing.

Options provide information to clients that they may need to access network services, such as the domain name of the network, the domain name servers that clients use, or the broadcast address. See the Man page for **dhcp-options** for a complete listing. This information is provided by **option** parameters as shown here:

```
option broadcast-address 192.168.0.255;
option domain-name-servers 192.168.0.1, 192.168.0.4;
option domain-name "mytrek.com";
```

Your **dhcpd.conf** file will usually begin with declarations, parameters, and options that you define for your network serviced by the DHCP server. The following example provides router (gateway), netmask, domain name, and DNS server information to clients. Additional parameters define the default and maximum lease times for dynamically allocated IP addresses.

```
option routers 192.168.0.1;
option subnet-mask 255.255.255.0;
option domain-name "mytrek.com";
option domain-name-servers 192.168.0.1;
default-lease-time 21600;
max-lease-time 43200;
```

With the subnet, host, and group declarations, you can reference clients in a specific network, particular clients, or different groupings of clients across networks. Within these declarations, you can enter parameters, declarations, or options that will apply only to those clients. Scoped declarations, parameters, and options are enclosed in braces. For example, to define a declaration for a particular host, you use the **host** declaration as shown here:

```
host rabbit {
        declarations, parameters, or options;
        }
```

You can collect different subnet, global, and host declarations into groups using the **group** declaration. In this case, the global declarations are applied only to those subnets and hosts declared within the group.

Dynamic IPv4 Addresses for DHCP

Your DHCP server can be configured to select IP addresses from a given range and assign them to different clients. Given a situation where you have many clients that may not always be connected to the network, you could effectively service them with a smaller pool of IP addresses. IP addresses are assigned only when they are needed. With the **range** declaration, you specify a range of addresses that can be dynamically allocated to clients. The declaration takes two arguments, the first and last addresses in the range.

```
range 192.168.1.5 192.168.1.128;
```

For example, if you are setting up your own small home network, you would use a network address beginning with 192.168. The range would specify possible IP addresses with that network. So for a network with the address 192.168.0.0, you would place a **range** declaration along with any other information you want to give to your client hosts. In the following example, a range of IP addresses extending from 192.168.0.5 to 192.168.0.128 can be allocated to the hosts on that network:

```
range 192.168.0.5 192.168.0.128;
```

You should also define your lease times, both a default and a maximum:

```
default-lease-time 21600;
max-lease-time 43200;
```

For a small, simple home network, you just need to list the **range** declaration along with any global options as shown here. If your DHCP server is managing several subnetworks, you will have to use the **subnet** declarations.

In order to assign dynamic addresses to a network, the DHCP server will require that your network topology be mapped. This means it needs to know what network addresses belong to a given network. Even if you use only one network, you will need to specify the address space for it. You define a network with the **subnet** declaration. Within this **subnet** declaration, you can specify any parameters, declarations, or options to use for that network. The **subnet** declaration informs the DHCP server of the possible IP addresses encompassed by a given subnet. This is determined by the network IP address and the netmask for that network. The next example defines a local network with address space from 192.168.0.0 to

192.168.0.255. The **range** declaration allows addresses to be allocated from 192.168.0.5 to 192.168.0.128.

```
subnet 192.168.1.0 netmask 255.255.255.0 {
        range 192.168.0.5 192.168.0.128;
 }
```

Versions of DHCP prior to 3.0 required that you even map connected network interfaces that are not being served by DHCP. Thus each network interface would have to have a corresponding **subnet** declaration. Those not being serviced by DHCP would have a **not authoritative** parameter as shown here (192.168.2.0 being a network not to be serviced by DHCP). In version 3.0 and later, DHCP simply ignores unmapped network interfaces:

```
subnet 192.168.2.0 netmask 255.255.255.0 {
      not authoritative;
}
```

The implementation of a very simple DHCP server for dynamic addresses is shown in the sample **dhcpd.conf** file that follows:

/etc/dhcpd.conf
```
option routers 192.168.0.1;
 option subnet-mask 255.255.255.0;
 option domain-name "mytrek.com";
 option domain-name-servers 192.168.0.1;

subnet 192.168.1.0 netmask 255.255.255.0 {
        range 192.168.0.5 192.168.0.128;
        default-lease-time 21600;
        max-lease-time 43200;
        }
```

DHCP Dynamic DNS Updates

For networks that also support a Domain Name System, dynamic allocation of IP addresses currently needs to address one major constraint: DHCP needs to sync with a DNS server. A DNS server associates hostnames with particular IP addresses, whereas in the case of dynamic allocation, the DHCP server randomly assigns its own IP addresses to different hosts. These may or may not be the same as the IP addresses that the DNS server expects to associate with a hostname. The solution to this problem is called Dynamic DNS. With Dynamic DNS, the DHCP server is able to automatically update the DNS server with the IP addresses the DHCP server has assigned to different hosts.

NOTE *Alternatively, if you want to statically sync your DHCP and DNS servers with fixed addresses, you would configure DHCP to assign those fixed addresses to hosts. You can then have the DHCP server perform a DNS lookup to obtain the IP address it should assign, or you can manually assign the same IP address in the DHCP configuration file. Performing a DNS lookup has the advantage of specifying the IP address in one place, the DNS server.*

The DHCP server has the ability to dynamically update BIND DNS server zone configuration files. As noted in Chapter 38, you enable dynamic updates on a DNS server for a zone file by specifying the **allow-update** option for it in the **named.conf** file. Furthermore, it is strongly encouraged that you use TSIG signature keys (see Chapter 38) to reference and authenticate the BIND and DHCP servers. Currently DHCP uses the Interim DNS Update Scheme to perform dynamic DNS updates, replacing an earlier Ad-Hoc DNS Update Scheme. A finalized version will be implemented in future DHCP releases. You can find detailed information about dynamic DNS in the **dhcpd.conf** Man page.

Enabling the use of a TSIG key involves syncing configurations for both your DHCP and DNS servers. Both have to be configured to use the same key for the same domains. First you need to create a shared secret TSIG signature key using **dnssec-keygen**, as described in Chapter 38. In the DNS server, you place TSIG key declarations and **allow-update** entries in the server's **named.conf** file, as shown in this example:

```
key mydhcpserver {
algorithm HMAC-MD5;
secret "ONQAfbBLnvWU9H8hRqq/WA==";
};


zone "mytrek.com" {
      type master;
      file "mytrek.com";
      allow-update {key mydhcpserver;};
 };

zone "1.168.192.IN-ADDR.ARPA" {
      type master;
      file "192.168.0";
      allow-update {key mydhcpserver;};
};
```

In the DHCP server, you place a corresponding TSIG key declaration and **allow-update** entries in the server's **dhcpd.conf** file, as shown in this example. The **key** declaration has the same syntax as the DNS server. DHCP **zone** statements are then used to specify the IP address of the domain and the TSIG key to use. The domain names and IP addresses need to match exactly in the configuration files for both the DNS and DHCP servers. Unlike in the **named.conf** file, there are no quotes around the domain name or IP addresses in the **dhcpd.conf** file. In the **dhcpd.conf** file, the domain names and IP addresses used in the **zone** statement also need to end with a period, as they do in the DNS zone files. The **key** statement lists the key to use. Though the DHCP server will try to determine the DNS servers to update, it is recommended that you explicitly identify them with a primary statement in a **zone** entry.

```
key mydhcpserver {
    algorithm HMAC-MD5;
    secret "ONQAfbBLnvWU9H8hRqq/WA==";
    };

zone mytrek.com. {                    #DNS domain zone to update
```

```
        primary 192.168.0.1;        #address of DNS server
        key mydhcpserver;           #TSIG signature key
};

zone 1.168.192.IN-ADDR.ARPA. {     #domain PTR zone to update
        primary 192.168.0.1;        #address of DNS server
        key mydhcpserver;           # TSIG signature key
};
```

To generate a fully qualified hostname to use in a DNS update, the DHCP server will normally use its own domain name and the hostname provided by a DHCP client (see the **dhcpd.conf** Man page for exceptions). Should you want to assign a specific hostname to a host, you can use the **ddns-hostname** statement to specify it in the host's hardware section. The domain name is specified in the **domain-name** option:

```
option domain-name "mytrek.com"
```

The DNS update capability can be turned on or off for all domains with the **ddns-update-style** statement. It is on by default. To turn off DNS updates for particular domains, you can use the **ddns-updates** statement. This is also on by default.

A simple DNS update configuration for a DHCP server in the **dhcpd.conf** file is shown here:

/etc/dhcpd.conf
```
option routers 192.168.0.1;
 option subnet-mask 255.255.255.0;
 option domain-name "mytrek.com";
 option domain-name-servers 192.168.0.1;
 key mydhcpserver {
         algorithm HMAC-MD5;
         secret "ONQAfbBLnvWU9H8hRqq/WA==";
         };

subnet 192.168.1.0 netmask 255.255.255.0 {
         range 192.168.0.5 192.168.0.128;
         default-lease-time 21600;
         max-lease-time 43200;
         zone mytrek.com. {
                 primary 192.168.0.1;
                 key mydhcpserver;
                 }
         zone 1.168.192.IN-ADDR.ARPA. {
                 primary 192.168.0.1;
                 key mydhcpserver;
                 }
}
```

DHCP Subnetworks

If you are dividing your network space into several subnetworks, you could use a single DHCP server to manage them. In that case, you would have a **subnet** declaration for each subnetwork. If you are setting up your own small network, you would use a network address beginning with 192.168. The range would specify possible IP addresses within that network. So for a network with the address 192.168.0.0, you would create a **subnet** declaration with the netmask 255.255.255.0. Within this declaration, you would place a **range** declaration along with any other information you want to give to your client hosts. In the following example, a range of IP addresses extending from 192.168.0.1 to 192.168.0.75 can be allocated to the hosts on that network:

```
subnet 192.168.0.0 netmask 255.255.255.0 {
 range 192.168.0.5 192.168.0.75;
}
```

You may want to specify different policies for each subnetwork, such as different lease times. Any entries in a **subnet** declaration will override global settings. So if you already have a global lease time set, a lease setting in a **subnet** declaration will override it for that subnet. The next example sets different lease times for different subnets, as well as different address allocations. The lease times for the first subnet are taken from the global lease time settings, whereas the second subnet defines its own lease times:

```
default-lease-time 21600;
max-lease-time 43200;

subnet 192.168.1.0 netmask 255.255.255.0 {
     range 192.168.0.5 192.168.0.75;
     }
subnet 192.168.1.128 netmask 255.255.255.252 {
     range 192.168.0.129 192.168.0.215;
     default-lease-time 56000;
     max-lease-time 62000;
      }
}
```

DHCP Fixed Addresses

Instead of using a pool of possible IP addresses for your hosts, you may want to give each one a specific address. Using the DHCP server still gives you control over which address will be assigned to a given host. However, to assign an address to a particular host, you need to know the hardware address for that host's network interface card (NIC). In effect, you have to inform the DHCP server that it has to associate a particular network connection device with a specified IP address. To do that, the DHCP server needs to know which network device you are referring to. You can identify a network device by its hardware address, known as its MAC address. To find out a client's hardware address, you log in to the client and use the **ifconfig** command to find out information about your network devices. To list all network devices, use the **-a** option. If you know your network device name, you can use that. The next example will list all information about the first Ethernet device, **eth0**:

```
ifconfig eth0
```

This will list information on all the client's network connection devices. The entry (usually the first) with the term **HWaddr** will display the MAC address. Once you have the MAC address, you can use it on the DHCP server to assign a specific IP address to that device.

In the **dhcpd.conf** file, you use a **host** declaration to set up a fixed address for a client. Within the **host** declaration, you place a **hardware** option in which you list the type of network connection device and its MAC address. Then you use the **fixed-address** parameter to specify the IP address to be assigned to that device. In the following example, the client's network device with a MAC address of 08:00:2b:4c:29:32 is given the IP address 192.168.0.2:

```
host rabbit {
          option host-name "rabbit.mytrek.com"
          hardware ethernet 08:00:2b:4c:29:32;
          fixed-address 192.168.0.2;
          }
```

CHAPTER

NFS, NIS, and GFS

Linux provides several tools for accessing files on remote systems connected to a network. The Network File System (NFS) enables you to connect to and directly access resources such as files or devices like CD-ROMs that reside on another machine. The Network Information Service (NIS) maintains configuration files for all systems on a network. With Samba, you can connect your Windows clients on a Microsoft Windows network to services such as shared files, systems, and printers controlled by the Linux Samba server (see Chapter 41).

Network File Systems: NFS and /etc/exports

NFS enables you to mount a file system on a remote computer as if it were local to your own system. You can then directly access any of the files on that remote file system. This has the advantage of allowing different systems on a network to access the same files directly, without each having to keep its own copy. Only one copy would be on a remote file system, which each computer could then access. You can find out more about NFS at its Web site at **nfs.sourceforge.net**.

Note *Mac OS X for Macintosh computers, which is based on BSD Unix, now supports NFS for file sharing. To access Apple file systems and printers using older Apple operating systems, you can use Netatalk. Netatalk implements the classic AppleTalk and AppleShare IP network protocols on Unix and Linux systems. The current Netatalk Web site is **netatalk.sourceforge .net**, with links to the FAQ and the HOW-TO sections.*

NFS Daemons

NFS operates over a TCP/IP network. The remote computer that holds the file system makes it available to other computers on the network. It does so by exporting the file system, which entails making entries in an NFS configuration file called **/etc/exports**, as well as by running several daemons to support access by other systems. These include **rpc.mountd**, **rpc.nfsd**, and **rpc.portmapper**. Access to your NFS server can be controlled by the **/etc/hosts.allow** and **/etc/hosts.deny** files. The NFS daemons are listed here:

- **rpc.nfsd**   Receives NFS requests from remote systems and translates them into requests for the local system.

- **rpc.mountd**   Performs requested mount and unmount operations.
- **rpc.portmapper**   Maps remote requests to the appropriate NFS daemon.
- **rpc.rquotad**   Provides user disk quote management.
- **rpc.statd**   Provides locking services when a remote host reboots.
- **rpc.lockd**   Handles lock recovery for systems that have gone down.

NOTE *It is advisable to use NFS on a local secure network only. If used over the Internet, NFS would open your system up to nonsecure access.*

Starting and Stopping NFS

On Fedora Core, you can start up and shut down the NFS daemons using the **/etc/rc.d/init. d/nfs** service, which you can invoke with the **service** command, **service nfs start**. To have NFS started automatically, you can use **chkconfig** or the system-config-services tool to specify the runlevels at which it will operate. The following example will have NFS start up automatically at runlevels 3 and 5 on Fedora Core:

```
chkconfig -level 35  nfs on
```

The **nfs** script will start up the **portmapper**, **nfsd**, **mountd**, and **rquotad** daemons. To enable NFS locking, you use the **nfslock** script. This will start up the **statd** and **lockd** daemons. NFS locking provides for better recovery from interrupted operations that can occur from system crashes on remote hosts.

To see if NFS is actually running, you can use the **rpcinfo** command with the **-p** option. You should see entries for **mountd** and **nfs**. If not, NFS is not running.

NFS Analytical Tools

The NFS package also includes analytical tools with which you can measure the performance of an NFS server. nhfsstone will generate performance data on specified test directories by generating an artificial load (demand on the server) based on a range of different NFS operations. nhfsrun will run nhfsstone with a variety of loads. You can use nhfsnum to generate a graph of the data, and nhfsgraph for a PostScript version. nfsstat will display current statistical information about NFS clients and servers. You can narrow your request to information on just the network activity, the NFS protocol, server usage, or RPC data.

Configuring NFS with the NFS Configuration Tool

Instead of manually mounting and configuring NFS directories, you can use the NFS configuration tool (system-config-nfs). Select NFS Server from the Server Settings window. This opens the NFS Server Configuration tool window as shown in Figure 40-1. Be sure your NFS server software is installed (system-config-packages) and that the NFS server is running (system-config-services).

To add a directory to share, click the Add button to open an Add NFS Share dialog window, similar to the Edit NFS Share window shown in Figure 40-1. You can browse for or enter the directory to be shared in the Directory box. You then list the host where it is located, and specify the access permissions. On the General Options tab, you can set basic

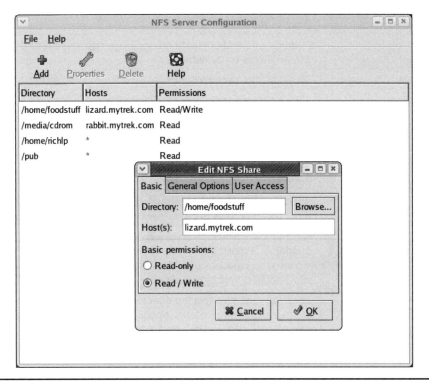

FIGURE 40-1   NFS configuration tool

security and update features such as insecure file locking or immediate syncing of write operations. By default, the Sync Write Operations On Request option is set. On the User Access tab, you can treat users as local root users or as anonymous users with specific user or group IDs.

When you click OK, the entry will be listed in the NFS Server Configuration window. Changes do not take effect until you click Apply. This will create an entry in the **/etc/exports** file for the shared directory. You can later change any of these settings by selecting the entry and clicking Properties to open an Edit dialog box. To save your settings, click Apply.

Figure 40-1 shows the same entries that are used in the **/etc/exports** file described in the next section. The **/etc/exports** file generated by the NFS Server Configuration tool using this example is shown here:

```
/home/foodstuff/        lizard.mytrek.com(rw,sync)
/media/cdrom            rabbit.mytrek.com(ro,sync)
/home/richlp            *(ro,sync)
/pub                    *(ro,insecure,sync,all_squash)
```

Options set in the Basic, General Options, and User Access panels show up as options listed for each entry. For example, Read access is ro and Read/Write access is rw. Check the NFS Server Configuration help documents for a complete listing. Options are listed in Table 40-1.

General Option	Description
secure	Requires request originate on secure ports, those less than 1024. This is on by default.
insecure	Turns off the **secure** option.
ro	Allows only read-only access. This is the default.
rw	Allows read/write access.
sync	Performs all writes when requested. This is the default.
async	Performs all writes when the server is ready.
no_wdelay	Performs writes immediately, not checking to see if they are related.
wdelay	Checks to see if writes are related, and, if so, waits to perform them together. Can degrade performance. This is the default.
hide	Automatically hides an exported directory that is the subdirectory of another exported directory. The subdirectory has to be explicitly mounted to be accessed. Mounting the parent directory does not allow access. This is the default.
no_hide	Does not hide an exported directory that is the subdirectory of another exported directory (opposite of **hide**). Only works for single hosts and can be unreliable.
subtree_check	Checks parent directories in a file system to validate an exported subdirectory. This is the default.
no_subtree_check	Does not check parent directories in a file system to validate an exported subdirectory.
insecure_locks	Does not require authentication of locking requests. Used for older NFS versions.
User ID Mapping	**Description**
all_squash	Maps all UIDs and GIDs to the anonymous user. Useful for NFS-exported public FTP directories, news spool directories, and so forth.
no_all_squash	The opposite option to **all_squash**. This is the default setting.
root_squash	Maps requests from remote root user to the anonymous UID/GID. This is the default.
no_root_squash	Turns off root squashing. Allows the root user to access as the remote root.
anonuid anongid	Sets explicitly the UID and GID of the anonymous account used for **all_squash** and **root_squash** options. The defaults are nobody and nogroup.

TABLE 40-1   The /etc/exports Options

NFS Configuration: /etc/exports

An entry in the **/etc/exports** file specifies the file system to be exported and the hosts on the network that can access it. For the file system, enter its *mountpoint,* the directory to which it was mounted on the host system. This is followed by a list of hosts that can access this file system along with options to control that access. A comma-separated list of export options placed within a set of parentheses may follow each host. For example, you might want to give one host read-only access and another read and write access. If the options are preceded by an * symbol, they are applied to any host. A list of options is provided in Table 40-1. The format of an entry in the **/etc/exports** file is shown here:

```
directory-pathname    host-designation(options)
```

NFS Host Entries
You can have several host entries for the same directory, each with access to that directory:

```
directory-pathname    host(options) host(options)   host(options)
```

You have a great deal of flexibility when specifying hosts. For hosts within your domain, you can just use the hostname, whereas for those outside, you need to use a fully qualified domain name. You could also just use the host's IP address. Instead of just a single host, you can reference all the hosts within a specific domain, allowing access by an entire network. A simple way to do this is to use the * for the host segment, followed by the domain name for the network, such as ***.mytrek.com** for all the hosts in the **mytrek.com** network. Instead of domain names, you could use IP network addresses using a CNDR format where you specify the netmask to indicate a range of IP addresses. You can also use an NIS netgroup name to reference a collection of hosts. The NIS netgroup name is preceded by a @ sign.

```
directory       host(options)
directory       *(options)
directory       *.domain(options)
directory       192.168.1.0/255.255.255.0(options)
directory       @netgroup(options)
```

NFS Options
Options in **/etc/exports** operate as permissions to control access to exported directories. Read-only access is set with the **ro** option, and read/write with the **rw** option. The **sync** and **async** options specify whether a write operation is performed immediately (**sync**) or when the server is ready to handle it (**async**). By default, write requests are checked to see if they are related, and if so, they are written together (**wdelay**). This can degrade performance. You can override this default with **no_wdelay** and have writes executed as they are requested. If two directories are exported, where one is the subdirectory of another, the subdirectory is not accessible unless it is explicitly mounted (**hide**). In other words, mounting the parent directory does not make the subdirectory accessible. The subdirectory remains hidden until also mounted. You can overcome this restriction with the **no_hide** option (though this can cause problems with some file systems). If an exported directory is actually a subdirectory in a larger file system, its parent directories are checked to make sure that the subdirectory is the valid directory (**subtree_check**). This option works well with read-only file systems but can cause problems for write-enabled file systems, where filenames and directories can be changed. You can cancel this check with the **no_subtree_check** option.

NFS User-Level Access

Along with general options, there are also options that apply to user-level access. As a security measure, the client's root user is treated as an anonymous user by the NFS server. This is known as *squashing* the user. In the case of the client root user, squashing prevents the client from attempting to appear as the NFS server's root user. Should you want a particular client's root user to have root-level control over the NFS server, you can specify the **no_root_squash** option. To prevent any client user from attempting to appear as a user on the NFS server, you can classify them as anonymous users (the **all_squash** option). Such anonymous users would only have access to directories and files that are part of the anonymous group.

Normally, if a user on a client system has a user account on the NFS server, that user can mount and access his or her files on the NFS server. However, NFS requires the User ID for the user be the same on both systems. If this is not the case, he or she is considered two different users. To overcome this problem, you could use an NIS service, maintaining User ID information in just one place, the NIS password file (see the later section "Network Information Service: NIS").

NFS /etc/exports Example

Examples of entries in an **/etc/exports** file are shown here. Read-only access is given to all hosts to the file system mounted on the **/pub** directory, a common name used for public access. Users, however, are treated as anonymous users (**all_squash**). Read and write access is given to the **lizard.mytrek.com** computer for the file system mounted on the **/home/foodstuff** directory. The next entry would allow access by **rabbit.mytrek.com** to the NFS server's CD-ROM, using only read access. The last entry allows anyone secure access to **/home/richlp**.

/etc/exports

```
/pub                 *(ro,insecure,all_squash,sync)
/home/foodstuff      lizard.mytrek.com(rw,sync)
/media/cdrom         rabbit.mytrek.com(ro,sync)
/home/richlp         *(secure,sync)
```

Applying Changes

Each time your system starts up the NFS server (usually when the system starts up), the **/etc/exports** file will be read and those directories specified will be exported. When a directory is exported, an entry for it is made in the **/var/lib/nfs/xtab** file. It is this file that NFS reads and uses to perform the actual exports. Entries are read from **/etc/exports** and corresponding entries made in **/var/lib/nfs/xtab**. The **xtab** file maintains the list of actual exports.

If you want to export added entries in the **/etc/exports** file immediately, without rebooting, you can use the **exportfs** command with the **-a** option. It is helpful to add the **-v** option to display the actions that NFS is taking. Use the same options to effect any changes you make to the **/etc/exports** file.

```
exportfs -a -v
```

If you later make changes to the **/etc/exports** file, you can use the **-r** option to re-export its entries. The **-r** option will resync the **/var/lib/nfs/xtab** file with the **/etc/exports** entries, removing any other exports or any with different options.

```
exportfs -r -v
```

To both export added entries and re-export changed ones, you can combine the **-r** and **-a** options.

```
exportfs -r -a -v
```

Manually Exporting File Systems

You can also use the **exportfs** command to manually export file systems instead of using entries for them in the **/etc/exports** file. Export entries will be added to the **/var/lib/nfs/xtab** file directly. With the **-o** option, you can list various permissions, and then follow them with the host and file system to export. The host and file system are separated by a colon. For example, to manually export the **/home/myprojects** directory to **golf.mytrek.com** with the permissions **ro** and **insecure**, you would use the following:

```
exportfs -o rw,insecure golf.mytrek.com:/home/myprojects
```

You can also use **exportfs** to unexport a directory that has already be exported, either manually or by the **/etc/exports** file. Just use the **-u** option with the host and the directory exported. The entry for the export will be removed from the **/var/lib/nfs/xtab** file. The following example will unexport the **/home/foodstuff** directory that was exported to **lizard.mytrek.com**:

```
exportfs -u lizard.mytrek.com:/home/foodstuff
```

NFS Security: /etc/hosts.allow and /etc/hosts.deny

The **/etc/hosts.allow** and **/etc/hosts.deny** files are used to restrict access to services provided by your server to hosts on your network or on the Internet (if accessible). For example, you can use the **hosts.allow** file to permit access by certain hosts to your FTP server. Entries in the **hosts.deny** file would explicitly deny access to certain hosts. For NFS, you can provide the same kind of security by controlling access to specific NFS daemons.

NOTE *You can further secure your NFS transmissions by having them operate over TCP instead of UDP. Use the **tcp** option to mount your NFS file systems (UDP is the default). However, performance does degrade for NFS when it uses TCP.*

Portmapper Service

The first line of defense is to control access to the portmapper service. The portmapper tells hosts where the NFS services can be found on the system. Restricting access does not allow a remote host to even locate NFS. For a strong level of security, you should deny access to all hosts except those that are explicitly allowed. In the **hosts.deny** file, you would place the following entry, denying access to all hosts by default. ALL is a special keyword denoting all hosts.

```
portmap:ALL
```

In the **hosts.allow** file, you would then enter the hosts on your network, or any others that you would want to permit access to your NFS server. Again, you would specify the portmapper service and then list the IP addresses of the hosts you are permitting access.

You can list specific IP addresses or a network range using a netmask. The following example allows access only by hosts in the local network, 192.168.0.0, and to the host 10.0.0.43. You can separate addresses with commas:

```
portmap: 192.168.0.0/255.255.255.0, 10.0.0.43
```

The portmapper is also used by other services such as NIS. If you close all access to the portmapper in **hosts.deny**, you will also need to allow access to NIS services in **hosts.allow**, if you are running them. These include ypbind and ypserver. In addition, you may have to add entries for remote commands like **ruptime** and **rusers**, if you are supporting them.

In addition, it is also advisable to add the same level of control for specific NFS services. In the **hosts.deny** file, you would add entries for each service, as shown here:

```
mountd:ALL
rquotad:ALL
statd:ALL
lockd:ALL
```

Then, in the **hosts.allow** file, you can add entries for each service:

```
mountd:   192.168.0.0/255.255.255.0, 10.0.0.43
rquotad:  192.168.0.0/255.255.255.0, 10.0.0.43
statd:    192.168.0.0/255.255.255.0, 10.0.0.43
lockd:    192.168.0.0/255.255.255.0, 10.0.0.43
```

Netfilter Rules

You can further control access using Netfilter to check transmissions from certain hosts on the ports used by NFS services. See Chapter 20 for an explanation of Netfilter. The portmapper uses port 111, and nfsd uses 2049. Netfilter is helpful if you have a private network that has an Internet connection, and you want to protect it from the Internet. Usually a specific network device, such as an Ethernet card, is dedicated to the Internet connection. The following examples assume that device **eth1** is connected to the Internet. Any packets attempting access on port 111 or 2049 are refused.

```
iptables -A INPUT -i eth1 -p 111 -j DENY
iptables -A INPUT -i eth1 -p 2049 -j DENY
```

To enable NFS for your local network, you will have to allow packet fragments. Assuming that **eth0** is the device used for the local network, you could use the following example:

```
iptables -A INPUT -i eth0 -f -j ACCEPT
```

NOTE *A root user on a remote host can try to access a remote NFS server as a root user with root-level permissions. The* **root_squash** *option (a default) will automatically change the remote root user to the nobody (anonymous) user.*

NFSv4

NFS version 4 is a new version of the NFS protocol with enhanced features like greater security, reliability, and speed. Currently it is supported in the Fedora Core 4 kernel as experimental, and is still under development. Most of the commands are the same with a few changes. For example, when you mount an NFSv4 file system you need to specify the **nfs4** file type. Also, for NFSv4, in the **/etc/exports** file, you can use the **fsid=0** option to specify the root export location.

```
/home/richlp          *(fsid=0,ro,sync)
```

The previous entry lets you then mount the file system to the **/home/richlp** directory without having to specify the root export directory in the mount operation.

```
# mount -t nfs4  rabbit.mytrek.com:/  /home/dylan/projects
```

See the NFSv4 sites at **developer.osdl.org** and **www.nfsv4.org** for the latest developments.

Mounting NFS File Systems: NFS Clients

Once NFS makes directories available to different hosts, those hosts can then mount those directories on their own systems and access them. The host needs to be able to operate as an NFS client. Current Linux kernels all have NFS client capability built in. This means that any NFS client can mount a remote NFS directory that it has access to by performing a simple mount operation.

Mounting NFS Automatically: /etc/fstab

You can mount an NFS directory either by an entry in the **/etc/fstab** file or by an explicit **mount** command. You have your NFS file systems mounted automatically by placing entries for them in the **/etc/fstab** file. An NFS entry in the **/etc/fstab** file has a mount type of NFS. An NFS file system name consists of the hostname of the computer it is located on, followed by the pathname of the directory where it is mounted. The two are separated by a colon. For example, **rabbit.trek.com:/home/project** specifies a file system mounted at **/home/project** on the **rabbit.trek.com** computer. The format for an NFS entry in the **/etc/fstab** file follows. Notice that the file type is **nfs**.

```
host:remote-directory    local-directory    nfs    options    0    0
```

You can also include several NFS-specific mount options with your NFS entry. You can specify the size of datagrams sent back and forth, and the amount of time your computer waits for a response from the host system. You can also specify whether a file system is to be hard-mounted or soft-mounted. For a *hard-mounted* file system, your computer continually tries to make contact if for some reason the remote system fails to respond. A *soft-mounted* file system, after a specified interval, gives up trying to make contact and issues an error message. A hard mount is the default. A system making a hard-mount attempt that continues to fail will stop responding to user input as it tries continually to achieve the mount. For this reason, soft mounts may be preferable, as they will simply stop attempting a mount that continually fails. Table 40-2 and the Man pages for **mount** contain a listing of these NFS client options. They differ from the NFS server options indicated previously.

Option	Description
`rsize=`n	The number of bytes NFS uses when reading files from an NFS server. The default is 1,024 bytes. A size of 8,192 can greatly improve performance.
`wsize=`n	The number of bytes NFS uses when writing files to an NFS server. The default is 1,024 bytes. A size of 8,192 can greatly improve performance.
`timeo=`n	The value in tenths of a second before sending the first retransmission after a timeout. The default value is seven-tenths of a second.
`retry=`n	The number of minutes to retry an NFS mount operation before giving up. The default is 10,000 minutes (one week).
`retrans=`n	The number of retransmissions or minor timeouts for an NFS mount operation before a major timeout (default is 3). At that time, the connection is cancelled or a "server not responding" message is displayed.
`soft`	Mount system using soft mount.
`hard`	Mount system using hard mount. This is the default.
`intr`	Allow NFS to interrupt the file operation and return to the calling program. The default is not to allow file operations to be interrupted.
`bg`	If the first mount attempt times out, continue trying the mount in the background. The default is to fail without backgrounding.
`tcp`	Mount the NFS file system using the TCP protocol, instead of the default UDP protocol.

TABLE 40-2 NFS Mount Options

An example of an NFS entry follows. The remote system is **rabbit.mytrek.com**, and the file system is mounted on **/home/projects**. This file system is to be mounted on the local system as the **/home/dylan/projects** directory. The **/home/dylan/projects** directory must already be created on the local system. The type of system is NFS, and the **timeo** option specifies the local system waits up to 20 tenths of a second (two seconds) for a response. The mount is a soft mount and can be interrupted by NFS.

```
rabbit.mytrek.com:/home/projects /home/dylan/projects  nfs  soft,intr,timeo=20
```

Mounting NFS Manually: mount

You can also use the **mount** command with the **-t nfs** option to mount an NFS file system explicitly. For a NFSv4 file system you would use **-t nfs4**. To mount the previous entry explicitly, use the following command:

```
# mount -t nfs -o soft,intr,timeo=20   \
        rabbit.mytrek.com:/home/projects   /home/dylan/projects
```

You can, of course, unmount an NFS directory with the **umount** command. You can specify either the local mountpoint or the remote host and directory, as shown here:

```
umount /home/dylan/projects
umount  rabbit.mytrek.com:/home/projects
```

NOTE *On Fedora Core systems, you can also mount and unmount all your NFS file systems at once with the /etc/rc.d/init.d/netfs script, which you can invoke with the **service** command. This script reads the NFS entries in the /etc/fstab file, using them to mount and unmount NFS remote directories. Using the **stop** argument unmounts the file systems, and with the **start** argument, you mount them again. The **restart** argument first unmounts and then remounts the file systems.*

Mounting NFS on Demand: autofs

You can also mount NFS file systems using the automount service, autofs. This requires added configuration on the client's part. The autofs service will mount a file system only when you try to access it. A directory change operation (**cd**) to a specified directory will trigger the mount operation, mounting the remote file system at that time.

The autofs service is configured using a master file to list map files, which in turn lists the file systems to be mounted. The **/etc/auto.master** file is the autofs master file. The master file will list the root pathnames where file systems can be mounted along with a map file for each of those pathnames. The map file will then list a key (subdirectory), mount options, and the file systems that can be mounted in that root pathname directory. On some distributions, the **/auto** directory is already implemented as the root pathname for file systems automatically mounted. You could add your own file systems in the **/etc/auto.master** file along with your own map files, if you wish. You will find that the **/etc/auto.master** file contains the following entry for the **/auto** directory, listing **auto.misc** as its map file:

```
/auto     auto.misc    --timeout 60
```

Following the map file, you can add options, as shown in the preceding example. The **timeout** option specifies the number of seconds of inactivity to wait before trying to automatically unmount.

In the map file, you list the key, the mount options, and the file system to be mounted. The key will be the subdirectory on the local system where the file system is mounted. For example, to mount the **/home/projects** directory on the **rabbit.mytrek.com** host to the **/auto/projects** directory, you would use the following entry:

```
projects   soft,intr,timeo=20    rabbit.mytrek.com:/home/projects
```

You could also create a new entry in the master file for an NFS file system, as shown here:

```
/myprojects     auto.myprojects    --timeout 60
```

You would then create an **/etc/auto.myprojects** file and place entries in it for NFS files system mounts, like the following:

```
dylan    soft,intr,rw    rabbit.mytrek.com:/home/projects
newgame  soft,intr,ro    lizard.mytrek.com:/home/supergame
```

NOTE *The autofs service can be used for any file systems, including floppy disks and CD-ROMs. See Chapter 32.*

Network Information Service: NIS

On networks supporting NFS, many resources and devices are shared by the same systems. Normally, each system would need its own configuration files for each device or resource. Changes would entail updating each system individually. However, NFS provides a special service called the Network Information System (NIS) that maintains such configuration files for the entire network. For changes, you only need to update the NIS files. NIS works for information required for most administrative tasks, such as those relating to users, network access, or devices. For example, you can maintain user and password information with an NIS service, having only to update those NIS password files.

NOTE *NIS+ is a more advanced form of NIS that provides support for encryption and authentication. However, it is more difficult to administer.*

NIS was developed by Sun Microsystems and was originally known as Sun's Yellow Pages (YP). NIS files are kept on an NIS server (NIS servers are still sometimes referred to as YP servers). Individual systems on a network use NIS clients to make requests from the NIS server. The NIS server maintains its information on special database files called *maps*. Linux versions exist for both NIS clients and servers. Linux NIS clients easily connect to any network using NIS.

The NIS client is installed as part of the initial installation on most Linux distributions. NIS client programs are ypbind (the NIS client daemon), ypwhich, ypcat, yppoll, ypmatch, yppasswd, and ypset. Each has its own Man page with details of its use. The NIS server programs are ypserv (the NIS server), ypinit, yppasswdd, yppush, ypxfr, and netgroup—each also with its own Man page. You can start and stop the **ypbind** client daemon and the **ypserv** NIS server with the `service` command. Alternatively, you can use system-config-services to start and stop the NIS client and server daemons.

```
service ypbind start
service ypserv start
```

NOTE *You can use system-config-authentication to specify the remote NIS server on your network.*

NIS Servers

You have significant flexibility when setting up NIS servers. If you have a small network, you may need only one NIS domain, for which you would have one NIS server. For larger networks, you can divide your network into several NIS domains, each with its own server. Even if you only have one domain, you may want several NIS slave servers. For an NIS domain, you can have a master NIS server and several NIS slave servers. The slave servers can act as backups, in case the master server goes down. A slave server only contains copies of the configuration files set up on the NIS master server.

Configuring an NIS server involves several steps, listed here:

1. Define the NIS domain name that the NIS server will work for.

2. Start the **ypserv** daemon.

3. In the **/var/yp/Makefile** file, set any NIS server options and specify the configuration files to manage.

4. Use ypinit to create the NIS versions of the configuration files.

Defining NIS Domain

You first have to define an NIS domain name. You can have the NIS domain defined whenever you start up your system, by defining the NIS_DOMAIN variable in the **/etc/sysconfig/network** file. To this variable, you assign the name you want to give your NIS domain. The following example defines the NIS domain called **myturtles.nis**:

```
NIS_DOMAIN=myturtles.nis
```

When first setting up the server, you may want to define your NIS domain name without having to restart your system. You can do so with the **domainname** command, as shown here:

```
domainname myturtles.nis
```

You can start the NIS server with the **ypserv** startup script:

```
service ypserv start
```

Setting NIS Server Options

Next edit the **/var/yp/Makefile** file to select the configuration files that the NIS server will maintain, along with setting any NIS server options. Standard options as well as most commonly used configuration files are usually already set up.

NIS server options are listed first. The **NOPUSH** option will be set to true, indicating that there are no slave NIS servers. If you are setting up any slave NIS servers for this domain, you will have to set this option to false:

```
NOPUSH = true
```

The minimum user and group IDs are set to 500. These are set using the **MINUID** and **MINGID** variables:

```
MINUID=500
MINGID=500
```

Most distributions use a shadow password and shadow group files to encrypt passwords and groups; the **MERGE_PASSWD** and **MERGE_GROUP** settings will be set to true. NIS will merge shadow password information into its password file:

```
MERGE_PASSWD=true
MERGE_GROUP=true
```

The directories where NIS will find password and other configuration files are then defined using the **YPSRCDIR** and **YPPWDIR** variables. Normally, the **/etc** directory holds your configuration files:

```
YPSRCDIR = /etc
YPPWDIR = /etc
```

Then the configuration files that NIS can manage are listed. Here, you will find entries like **PASSWD** for password, **GROUP** for your groups, and **PRINTCAP** for your printers. A sample of the entries are shown here:

```
GROUP        = $(YPPWDDIR)/group
PASSWD       = $(YPPWDDIR)/passwd
SHADOW       = $(YPPWDDIR)/shadow
GSHADOW      = $(YPPWDDIR)/gshadow
ALIASES      = /etc/aliases
ETHERS       = $(YPSRCDIR)/ethers       # ethernet addresses (for rarpd)
BOOTPARAMS   = $(YPSRCDIR)/bootparams # for booting Sun boxes (bootparamd)
HOSTS        = $(YPSRCDIR)/hosts
NETWORKS     = $(YPSRCDIR)/networks
PRINTCAP     = $(YPSRCDIR)/printcap
PROTOCOLS    = $(YPSRCDIR)/protocols
```

Specifying Shared Files
The actual files that are shared on the network are listed in the **all:** entry, which follows the list of configuration files. Only some of the files defined are listed as shared, those listed in the first line after **all:**. The remaining lines are automatically commented out (with a preceding **#** sign). You can add files by removing the **#** sign or moving their entries to the first line.

```
all:  passwd group hosts rpc services netid protocols mail \
      # netgrp shadow publickey networks ethers bootparams printcap \
      # amd.home auto.master auto.home auto.local passwd.adjunct \
      # timezone locale netmasks
```

Be sure not to touch the remainder of the Makefile.

Creating the NIS Database
You then enter the **ypinit** command with the **-m** option to create the NIS database consisting of the NIS configuration files. Your NIS server will be detected, and then you will be asked to enter the names of any slave NIS servers used on this NIS domain. If there are any, enter them. When you are finished, press CTRL-D. The NIS database files are then created.

```
ypinit -m
```

For an NIS slave server, you would use

```
ypinit -s masterhost
```

Should you receive the following error, it most likely means that your NIS server was not running. Be sure to start ypserv before you run ypinit.

```
failed to send 'clear' to local ypserv: RPC: Program not registeredUpdating
```

If you later need to update your NIS server files, you would change to the **/var/yp** directory and issue the **make** command.

```
cd /var/yp
make
```

Controlling Access

The **/var/yp/securenets** file enables access by hosts to your NIS server. Hosts can be referenced by network or individually. Entries consist of a subnet mask and an IP address. For example, you could give access to all the hosts in a local network with the following entry:

```
255.255.255.0  192.168.1.0
```

For individual hosts, you can use the mask 255.255.255.255 or just the term "host," as shown here:

```
host   192.168.1.4
```

Controlling how different hosts access NIS shared data is determined in **/etc/ypserv.conf**.

Netgroups

You can use NIS to set up netgroups, which allow you to create network-level groups of users. Whereas normal groups are created locally on separate hosts, an NIS netgroup can be used for network-wide services. For example, you can use NIS netgroups to control access to NFS file systems. Netgroups are defined in the **/etc/netgroup** file. Entries consist of a netgroup name followed by member identifiers consisting of three segments: the host, the user, and the NIS domain:

```
group    (host, user, NIS-domain) (host, user, NIS-domain) ...
```

For example, in the NIS domain **myturtles.nis**, to define a group called **myprojects** that consists of the user **chris** on the host **rabbit**, and the user **george** on the host **lizard.mytrek.com**, you would use the following:

```
myprojects (rabbit, chris, myturtles.nis) \
                    (lizard.mytrek.com, george, myturtles.nis)
```

A blank segment will match on any value. The following entry includes all users on the host **rabbit**:

```
newgame (rabbit,,myturtles.nis)
```

If your use of a group doesn't need either a user or a host segment, you can eliminate one or the other using a hyphen (-). The following example generates a netgroup consisting just of hostnames, with no usernames:

```
myservers (rabbit,-,) (turtle.mytrek.com,-,)
```

You can then reference different netgroups in various configuration files by prefixing the netgroup name with an @ sign, as shown here:

```
@newgame
```

NIS Clients

For a host to use NIS on your network, you first need to specify your NIS domain name on that host. In addition, your NIS clients need to know the name of your NIS server. If you installed Linux on a network already running NIS, you may have already entered this information during the installation process.

Specifying the NIS Domain and Server

On Fedora Core, you can specify your NIS domain name and server with the system-config-authentication tool, which you can access from the System Settings window. In that window, select Authentication. This opens the Authentication Configuration window. On the User Information panel, click the Configure NIS button to open a dialog where you can enter the name of the NIS domain as well as the NIS server. Be sure to also enable NIS on the User Information panel. The NIS domain will be saved in the **/etc/sysconfig/network** file, and the NIS server, in the **/etc/yp.conf** file.

Accessing the Server

Each NIS client host on your network then has to run the ypbind NIS client to access the server. In the client's **/etc/yp.conf** file, you need to specify the NIS server it will use. The following entry would reference the NIS server at 192.168.1.1:

```
ypserver 192.168.1.1
```

Alternatively, you can specify the NIS domain name and the server it uses:

```
domain mydomain.nis  server servername
```

The authconfg-gtk tool will make the following entry in **/etc/yp.conf** for the **myturtle .nis** NIS domain using the **turtle.mytrek.com** server:

```
domain myturtles.nis server turtle.mytrek.com
```

To start the NIS client, you run the **ypbind** script:

```
service ypbind start
```

Then, to check that all is working, you can use **ypcat** to try to list the NIS password file:

```
ypcat passwd.
```

You can use **ypcat** to list any of the NIS configuration files. The **ypwhich** command will display the name of the NIS server your client is using. **ypmatch** can be used to find a particular entry in a configuration file.

```
ypmatch cecelia passwd.
```

Users can change their passwords in the NIS **passwd** file by using the **yppasswd** command. It works the same as the **passwd** command. You will also have to have the **yppasswdd** daemon running.

Specifying Configuration Files with nsswitch.conf

To ensure that the client accesses the NIS server for a particular configuration file, you should specify **nisplus** in the file's entry in the **/etc/nsswitch.conf** file. The **nisplus** option refers to the NIS version 3 used currently on Fedora Core. The **nis** option is used to refer to the older NIS version 2. The **/etc/nsswitch.conf** file specifies where a host should look for certain kinds of information. For example, the following entry says to check the local configuration files (**files**) first and then the NIS server (**nisplus**) for passwords data:

```
passwd:   files nisplus
```

The **files** designation says to first use the system's own files, those on the local host. **nis** says to look up entries in the NIS files, accessing the NIS server. **nisplus** says to use NIS+ files maintained by the NIS+ server. **dns** says to perform DNS lookups; it can only be used on files like **hosts** that contain hostnames. These are some standard entries:

```
passwd:      files nisplus
shadow:      files nisplus
group:       files nisplus

hosts:       files nisplus dns
bootparams:  nisplus [NOTFOUND=return] files

ethers:      files
netmasks:    files
networks:    files
protocols:   files nisplus
rpc:         files
services:    files nisplus
netgroup:    files nisplus
publickey:   nisplus
automount:   files nisplus
aliases:     files nisplus
```

Distributed Network File Systems

For very large distributed systems like Linux clusters, Linux also supports distributed network file systems, such as Coda, Intermezzo, Red Hat Global File System (GFS), and the Parallel Virtual File System (PVFS2). These systems build on the basic concept of NFS as well as RAID techniques to create a file system implemented on multiple hosts across a large network, in effect, distributing the same file system among different hosts at a very low level (see Table 40-3). You can think of it as a kind of RAID array implemented across network hosts instead of just a single system. Instead of each host relying on its own file systems on its own hard drive, they all share the same distributed file system that uses hard drives collected on different distributed servers. This provides far greater efficient use of storage available to the hosts, as well as providing for more centralized management of file system use.

Web Site	Name
www.pvfs.org	Parallel Virtual File System, PVFS2 (open source)
www.redhat.com/software/rha/gfs **download.fedora.rehat.com**	Global File System (Fedora Core and commercial versions)
www.coda.cs.cmu.edu **ftp.coda.cs.cmu.edu/pub/coda/linux**	Coda file system, disconnected mobile access (experimental)
www.inter-mezzo.org	Intermezzo (open source)
clusterfs.com	Lustre

TABLE 40-3   Distributed File Systems

Red Hat Global File System (GFS)

The Red Hat Global File System (GFS) is an open source distributed file system included with Fedora Core 4. It is also supported as a commercial product for Red Hat Enterprise systems. GFS provides high-level support for hundreds of hosts, allowing them to use the same distributed file system, and, at the same time, providing redundancy to protect against storage failures. The file system easily integrates with the Linux virtual file system, letting you mount a GFS file system on your own Linux system.

For detailed information check the GFS Project Web site at **sources.redhat.com/cluster/gfs**, and the Clustering Project Web site at **sources.redhat.com/cluster**. There are corresponding sites under the sources.redhat.com.cluster prefix for different cluster tools used by GFS, such as **clvm**, **cman**, **gulm**, **ccs**, and **fence**. Check these sites for configuration details and examples. Red Hat GFS Administrators Guide can be helpful, but may be dated. The guide can be found on the Red Hat documentation page located at **www.redhat.com** (bear in mind that GFS now uses logical volumes instead of pools to set up physical volumes).

GFS can be run either directly connected to a SAN (Storage Area Network) or using GNBD (Global Network Block Device) storage connected over a LAN. The best performance is obtained from a SAN connection, whereas a GNBD format can be implemented easily using the storage on LAN (Ethernet) connected systems. Like RAID devices, mirroring, failover, and redundancy can help protect and recover data.

GFS separates the physical implementation from the logical format. A GFS file system appears as a set of logical volumes on one seamless logical device that can be mounted easily to any directory on your Linux file system. The logical volumes are created and managed by the Cluster Logical Volume Manager (CLVM) which is a cluster-enabled LVM (see Chapter 33). Physically, the file system is constructed from different storage resources known as cluster nodes distributed across your network. The administrator manages these nodes, providing needed mirroring or storage expansion. Should a node fail, GFS can fence a system off until it has recovered the node. Setting up a GFS file system requires planning. You have to determine ahead of time different settings like the number and names of your GFS file systems, the nodes will be able to mount the file systems, fencing methods, and the partitions and disks to use.

GFS Packages

To use GFS, you have to install a number of different packages that include the GFS tools, the locking method you want to use, and configuration tools. The GFS tools and locking methods also have several corresponding kernel module and header packages. Be sure to choose the kernel module for the kind of kernel you are running. There are kernel module packages for the different types of kernels: i586, i686, SMP, and Xen. There are also packages for both i586 and i686 kernel headers, needed for compiling other modules. The Fedora 4 GFS tools and the GFS SMP kernel module (used for hyperthreading Pentiums and dual processors) packages are shown here:

```
GFS-6.1-0.pre22.6.i386.rpm
GFS-kernel-smp-2.6.11.8-20050601.152643.FC4.0.i686.rpm
```

Cluster configuration tools and servers are kept in the Cluster Configuration System package, **ccs**. Fencing tools used to isolate failed resources are kept in the **fence** package. The tools and servers needed to implement a GNBD form of GFS are located in the **gnbd** package. In addition you need the kernel modules with the drivers to support GNBD devices, located in a **gnbd-kernel** package. Choose the one for your kernel. The Fedora Core 4 package names are listed here:

```
ccs
fence
gndb
gndb-kernel
```

To run a cluster, you need both a cluster manager and locking mechanism. You have two choices, the Cluster Manager (**cman**) with the Distributed Lock Manager (**dlm**) or the Grand Unified Lock Manager (**gulm**). **cman** with **dlm** implements cluster management and locking directly using modules, **cman** and **dlm**. **cman** manages connections between cluster devices and services, and uses **dlm** to provide locking. The **dlm** locking mechanism operates as a kernel module with supporting libraries and is invoked with the **cman** script. **gulm** operates as a server providing both cluster management and locking. **gulm** can be invoked by the **lock_gulmd** script. It is considered an alternative to **cman** and **dlm**. You need to only install either **gulm** or the **cman** and **dlm** packages.

```
cman
cman-kernel
dlm
dlm-kernel
gulm
gulm-kernel
```

You cannot run both **cman** and **gulm** at the same time. The **cman** script checks the **/etc/cluster.conf** file for **gulm** configuration, and if found will not load the **cman** kernel module. You can use **cman_tool** to have a node join a cluster or remove a node from the cluster.

Starting GFS File System Using Service Scripts

To start the GFS file system you run a series of scripts that start up the appropriate servers and load the needed modules. These are: the **ccsd** scripts which start up configuration detection, **fenced** for fencing support, **cman** for cluster management **dlm** locking, **clvmd** to detect activate the CLVM GFS devices, and finally **gfs** to mount your GFS file systems. The scripts will check for any GFS configuration settings in the **/etc/sysconfig/cluster** file.

```
service ccsd start
service cman start
service fenced start
service clvmd start
service gfs start
```

As noted previously, you have a choice between two different locking mechanisms, **gulm** and **dlm**. The **dlm** method is used in the previous example, which is invoked by the **cman** script.

The **clvmd** script both starts the **clvmd** server and uses LVM commands **vgscan** and **vgchange** to locate and activate your cluster devices.

The **gfs** service script will mount GFS file systems to the locations specified in the **/etd/ fstab** file. You will need entries for all the GFS file systems you want to mount in **/etc/fstab**. The stop option will unmount the file systems.

To shut down the GFS file system service, you would use a reverse sequence with the **stop** option, as shown here:

```
service gfs stop
service clvmd stop
service fenced stop
service cman stop
service ccsd stop
```

system-config-cluster

With the system-config-cluster tool you can configure and manage your GFS cluster. When you first start the tool it will create an **/etc/cluster.conf** file if one does not exist, and then prompt you for the locking method you want to use: DLM (preferred) or GULM (Grand Unified Lock Manager). On the Cluster Configuration tab you can create cluster nodes and fence devices. For the fence device you specify the fence method along with the name, IP address, and login and password. In the Managed Resources section you can specify the name, mountpoint, and device of your GFS file systems. system-config-cluster is currently under development.

Implementing a GFS File System

To set up a GFS file system you first need to create cluster devices using the physical volumes and organizing them into logical volumes. You use the CLVM (Clustering Logical Volume Manager) to set up logical volumes from physical partitions (in the past you used a volume manager called pool to do this). You can then install GFS file systems on these logical volumes directly. CLVM operates like LVM (see Chapter 33), using the same commands. It works over a distributed network and requires that the **clvmd** server be running.

You then configure your system with the Cluster Configuration System. Create a **cluster.conf** file and set up your configuration. The configuration will include information like the nodes used, fencing methods, and the locking method used (**gulm** or **dlm**). Consult the **cluster .conf** Man page for details. You then start the **ccsd** server and test the configuration with the **ccs_test** tool.

```
service ccsd start
ccs_test mygfs
```

You then use **ccs_tool** to create **cluster.ccs**, **fence.ccs**, and **node.ccs** configuration files. These files are organized into a CCS archive that is placed on each node and cluster device.

On each node, you then start the **ccsd** configuration, **fenced** fencing server, and the locking method you want to use like **dlm**. Check the respective Man pages for details on the locking servers. You can start the servers with their service scripts as noted previously.

To create new file systems on the cluster devices, you use the **gfs_mkfs** command, and then mount them with the **-t gfs** option. The following command creates a GFS file system on the **/dev/gv0/mgfs** and then mounts it to the **/gfs1** directory. For gfs_mkfs, the **-t** option indicates the lock table used and the **-p** option specifies the lock protocol. The **-j** option specifies the number of journals.

```
gfs_mkfs  -t mycluster:mygfs  -p lock_dlm  -j 2   /dev/vg0/mgfs
mount -t gfs /dev/vg0/mgfs /gfs1
```

To have the **gfs** service script mount the GFS file system for you, you need to place an entry for it in the **/etc/fstab** file. If you do not want the file system automatically mounted, add the **noauto** option.

```
/dev/vg0/mgfs   /gfs1   gfs   noauto,defaults   0   0
```

With GFS **/etc/fstab** entries, you can then use the **gfs** script to mount the GFS file system.

```
service gfs start
```

GFS Tools
GFS has several commands in different categories such as those that deal will fencing like **fence_node**, **gulm_tool** to manage gulm locking, and those used for configuration like **ccs_tool**. The GFS command for managing GFS file systems is listed in Table 40-4. Check their respective Man pages for detailed descriptions.

GFS File System Operations
To mount a GFS file system you use the **mount** command specifying **gfs** as the mount type, as in:

```
mount  -t gfs  /dev/vg0/mgfs  /gfs1
```

This will invoke the **gfs_mount** tool to perform the mount operation. Several GFS-specific mount options are also available, specified with the **-o** option, such as **lockproto** to specify a different lock protocol and **acl** to enable ACL support.

To check the status of a file system, you can use **gfs_fsck**. This tool operates much like fsck, checking for corrupt systems and attempting repairs. You must first unmount the file system before you can use **gfs_fsck** on it.

Should you add available space to the device on which a GFS file system resides, you can use **gfs_grow** to expand the file system to that available space. It can be run on just one node to expand the entire cluster. If you want journaling, you first have to add journal files with the **gfs_jadd** tool. **gfs_grow** can only be run on a mounted GFS file system.

Journal files for GFS are installed in space outside of the GFS file system, but on the same device. After creating a GFS file system, you can run **gfs_add** to add the journal files for it. If you are expanding a current GFS file system, you need to run **gfs_add** first. Like **gfs_grow**, **gfs_add** can only be run on mounted file systems.

As noted previously, to create a GFS file system you use the **gfs_mkfs** command. The **-t** option specifies the lock table to use, the **-j** options indicates the number of journals to create, and the **-p** option specifies the lock protocol to use.

Command	Description
ccs	CCS service script to start Cluster Configuration Service server. Also a Man page, CCS overview with steps to create configuration.
ccs_tool	CCS configuration update tool.
ccs_test	CCS diagnostic tool to test CCS configuration files.
ccsd	Daemon run on nodes to provide CCS configuration data to cluster software.
clvmd	Cluster Logical Volume Manager daemon, needed to create and manage LVM cluster devices, also a service script to start **clvmd**.
cman	The Cluster Manager, cman, start up script, uses dlm for locking (cman is run as kernel module directly).
cman_tool	Manages cluster nodes, requires cman.
dlm	Distributed Lock Manager, implemented as a kernel module, invoked by the **cman** script.
fence	Fence overview.
fenced	Fencing daemon, also a service script for starting the fenced daemon.
fence_tool	Manages fenced.
fence_node	Invokes a fence agent.
Fencing Agents	Numerous fencing agents available for different kinds of connections, see fence Man page.
fence_manual	Fence Agent for manual interaction.
fence_ack_manual	User interface for fence_manual.
gfs	GFS service script to mount GFS file systems, also a Man page overview.
gfs_mount	Invoked by mount. Use **-t gfs** mount option.
gfs_fsck	The GFS file system checker.
gfs_grow	Grow a GFS file system.
gfs_jadd	Add a journal to a GFS file system.
gfs_mkfs	Make a GFS file system.
gfs_quota	Manipulate GFS disk quotas.
gfs_tool	Manage a GFS file systems.
getfacl	Get the ACL permissions for a file or directory.
gulm_tool	Configure the **gulm** server.
lock_gulmd	The **gulm** alternative locking server, also service script.
setfacl	Set access controls (ACL) for a file or directory.

TABLE 40-4   GFS Commands, Daemons, and Service Scripts

GFS also supports access controls. You can restrict access by users or groups to certain files or directories, specifying read or write permissions. With the **setfacl** command you can set permissions for files and directories. You use the **-m** option to modify an ACL permission, and **−x** to delete it. **getfacl** obtains the current permissions for file or directory. The following sets read access by the user **dylan** to **myfile**.

```
setfacl -m u:dylan:r myfile
```

Parallel Virtual File System (PVFS)

The Parallel Virtual File System (PVFS) implements a distributed network file system using a management server that manages the files system on different I/0 servers. Management servers maintain the file system information, including access permissions, directory structure, and metadata information. Requests for access to a file are submitted by a client of the management server. The management server then sets up a connection between the client and the I/O servers that hold the requested file's data. Access operations such as read and write tasks are then carried out directly between the client and the I/O servers. PVFS can be implemented transparently using a kernel module to make use of the kernel's virtual file system. The PVFS file system can then be mounted by a client like any file system. In a PVFS implementation, the file system is organized into stripes of data, similar to a RAID array, but the stripes are distributed to different hosts on the network. Files are accessed as a collection of stripes that can be distributed across this network.

A new version of PVFS, known as PVFS2, is currently available from **www.pvfs.org**. You can download the source code from there. PVFS is a joint project with the Parallel Architecture Research Laboratory at Clemson University and the Mathematics and Computer Science Division at Argonne National Laboratory.

Coda

Coda is developed by Carnegie Mellon University as an experimental project, though freely available. Some of its features include support for mobile computing. access controls, and bandwidth adaptation. You can obtain information about Coda from **www.coda.cs.cmu.edu**. You can download Fedora Core RPM packages from **ftp.coda.cs.cmu.edu/pub/coda/linux**.

Using a kernel module to interface with the virtual file system, distributed Coda files can be accessed from the Coda directory on a client, usually **/coda**. Coda will maintain a cache of frequently accessed files on the client to improve efficiency. The cache is maintained by a cache manager called venus that handles all file system requests. The use of a cache allows for a disconnected operation on a file, letting users work on a file locally and then update it later with the main servers. A disconnected operation works well for mobile computing, where laptops may be disconnected from the network for periods of time. Corresponding databases for frequently used files by users, known as hoards, are also maintained on the server to facilitate updates.

To configure clients, you will need the coda-debug-client package. Use the **venus-setup** script to configure the client, and then start up Coda with the **venus** daemon. For the server, you will need to install the coda-dbug-server package and run **venus-setup** to configure your server.

Samba

With Samba, you can connect your Windows clients on a Microsoft Windows network to services such as shared files, systems, and printers controlled by the Linux Samba server and, at the same time, allow Linux systems to access shared files and printers on Windows systems. Samba is a collection of Linux tools that allow you to communicate with Windows systems over a Windows network. In effect, Samba allows a Linux system or network to act as if it were a Windows server, using the same protocols as used in a Windows network. Whereas most Unix and Linux systems use the TCP/IP protocol for networking, Microsoft networking with Windows uses a different protocol, called the Server Message Block (SMB) protocol, that implements a local area network (LAN) of PCs running Windows. SMB makes use of a network interface called Network Basic Input Output System (NetBIOS) that allows Windows PCs to share resources, such as printers and disk space. One Windows PC on such a network can access part of another Windows PC's disk drive as if it were its own. SMB was originally designed for small LANs. To connect it to larger networks, including those with Unix systems, Microsoft developed the Common Internet File System (CIFS). CIFS still uses SMB and NetBIOS for Windows networking. Wanting to connect his Linux system to a Windows PC, Andrew Tridgell wrote a SMB client and server that he called Samba. Samba allows Unix and Linux systems to connect to such a Windows network, as if they were Windows PCs. Unix systems can share resources on Windows systems as if they were just another Windows PC. Windows PCs can also access resources on Unix systems as if they were Windows systems. Samba, in effect, has become a professional-level, open source, and free version of CIFS. It also runs much faster than CIFS. Samba effectively enables you to use a Linux or Unix server as a network server for a group of Windows machines operating on a Windows network. You can also use it to share files on your Linux system with other Windows PCs, or to access files on a Windows PC from your Linux system, as well as between Windows PCs. On Linux systems, an **smbfs** file system enables you, in effect, to mount a remote SMB-shared directory on your own file system. You can then access it as if it were a directory on your local system.

Samba Documentation

You can obtain extensive documentation and current releases from the Samba Web and FTP sites at **www.samba.org** and **ftp.samba.org**. RPM packages for Red Hat Enterprise Linux and Fedora Core can be obtained from Red Hat and Fedora Core and RPM repositories (see Chapter 1). Samba is also included on most Linux distributions.

Other information can be obtained from the SMB newsgroup, **comp.protocols.smb**. Extensive documentation is provided with the software package and installed on your system, usually in the **/usr/share/doc** directory under a subdirectory bearing the name of the Samba release. Here, you can find extensive documentation in HTML and text format, as well as numerous examples and the current FAQs. Samba HOW-TO documentation is also available at **www.tldp.org**. The examples include sample **smb.conf** files for different kinds of configuration. The home page of the SWAT configuration utility also provides Web page–based Samba documentation, as well as context-level help for different features.

Samba Applications

The Samba software package consists of two server daemons and several utility programs (see Table 41-1). One daemon, **smbd**, provides file and printer services to SMB clients and other systems, such as Windows, that support SMB. The nmbd utility is a daemon that provides NetBIOS name resolution and service browser support. The smbclient utility provides FTP-like access by Linux clients to Samba services. smbmount and smbumount enable Linux clients to mount and unmount Samba shared directories (used by the **mount** command with the **-t smbfs** option). The smbstatus utility displays the current status of the SMB server and who is using it. You use testparm to test your Samba configuration. **smbtar** is a shell script that backs up SMB/CIFS-shared resources directly to a Unix tape drive. You use nmblookup to map the NetBIOS name of a Windows PC to its IP address. Also included with the package is the Samba Web administration tool (SWAT) and system-config-samba. This enables you to use a Web page or GUI interface to create and maintain your Samba configuration file, **/etc/samba/smb.conf**. Samba configuration files are kept in the **/etc/ samba** directory.

NOTE *To use system-config-packages to install Samba, select the Windows File Server entry.*

Samba provides four main services: file and printer services, authentication and authorization, name resolution, and service announcement. The SMB daemon, **smbd**, provides the file and printer services, as well as authentication and authorization for those services. This means users on the network can share files and printers. You can control access to these services by requiring users to provide a password. When users try to access a shared directory, they are prompted for a password. Control can be implemented in share mode or user mode. The *share* mode sets up one password for the shared resource and then enables any user who has that password to access it. The *user* mode provides a different password for each user. Samba maintains its own password file for this purpose: **/etc/samba/smbpasswd**.

Name resolution and service announcements are handled by the nmbd server. Name resolution essentially resolves NetBIOS names with IP addresses. Service announcements, also known as *browsing,* are the way a list of services available on the network is made known to the connected Windows PCs (and Linux PCs connected through Samba).

Samba also includes the **windbind** daemon, which allows Samba servers to use authentication services provided by a Windows domain. Instead of a Samba server maintaining its own set of users to allow access, it can make use of a Windows domain authentication service to authenticate users.

Application	Description
smbd	Samba server daemon that provides file and printer services to SMB clients
nmbd	Samba daemon that provides NetBIOS name resolution and service browser support
smbclient	Provides FTP-like access by Linux clients to Samba services
smbmount	Mounts Samba share directories on Linux clients (used by the **mount** command with the **-t smbfs** option)
smbumount	Unmounts Samba share directories mounted on Linux clients (used by the **mount** command with the **-t smbfs** option)
smbpasswd	Changes SMB-encrypted passwords on Samba servers
smbstatus	Displays the current status of the SMB network connections
smbrun	Interface program between smbd and external programs
testparm	Tests the Samba configuration file, **smb.conf**
smbtar	Backs up SMB/CIFS-shared resources directly to a Unix tape drive
nmblookup	Maps the NetBIOS name of a Windows PC to its IP address
system-config-samba	Samba GUI configuration tool (System Settings:Server Setttings: Samba Server)
SWAT	Samba Web administration tool for configuring **smb.conf** with a Web browser; enables you to use a Web page interface to create and maintain your Samba configuration file, **smb.conf**
windbind	Uses authentication services provided by Windows domain

TABLE 41-1   Samba Applications

NOTE *If you want to download source code or binaries in compressed archives (.tar.gz) from www .samba.org, the archive will extract to its own samba subdirectory. To use it, extract the archive in a software directory like /usr/local. Be sure to add /usr/local/samba/bin in your PATH. Alternatively, you could copy the samba/bin files to /usr/bin, except for nmb and smbd, which should be copied to /usr/sbin.*

Starting Up Samba

For a simple Samba setup, you should be able to use the default **smb.conf** file installed with the Linux distribution package of Samba. If you need to make changes, however, you must restart the Samba server to have the changes take effect. Starting, stopping, and restarting the Samba server is managed by the **/etc/rc.d/init.d/smb** script using the options **start**, **stop**, and **restart**. On Fedora Core, you can run the **smb** script directly as shown here:

```
service smb restart
```

On Fedora Core, you can also use the desktop Services configuration tool (system-config-services) to start and stop Samba.

To ensure name resolution, you can enter the name of your host and its IP address in the **/etc/lmhosts** file. On Windows systems, **lmhosts** entries consist of an IP address and the system's NetBIOS name, the name it is known by on a Microsoft network. For your Linux system, you can enter the IP address and the Linux system's hostname.

NOTE *On Fedora Core 4, the IPtables firewall prevents browsing Samba and Windows shares from your Linux desktop. To work around this restriction, you should download and install the latest version of system-config-security level (1.5.9-1 and above). Select the Samba Browsing entry in the Trusted Services section, as well as select your Ethernet connection as a trusted device. Alternatively you can either disable the firewall (system-config-securitylevel) or set up a Wins server and configure Samba to use it.*

Testing Samba from Linux

To test your connection from a Linux system, you can use the **smbclient** command to query the Samba server. To access the home directory of a user on the Samba server, use the IP or hostname address of the Samba server, along with the **homes** section. With the **-U** option, specify a user to connect to on the system, as shown here:

```
smbclient //turtle.mytrek.com/homes -U dylan
```

You are then prompted for a password. If the client password is different from the server password, use the server password. Once connected, you are presented with the SMB client prompt as shown here. You can then access the files on the user's home directory:

```
smb: \>
```

Configuring Samba Access from Windows

To set up a connection for a Windows client, you need to specify the Windows workgroup name and configure the password. The workgroup name is the name that appears in the My Network Places on Windows 2000, NT, and XP (the Entire Network window in the Network Neighborhood on earlier Windows versions). To set the workgroup name on Windows XP, open System on the Control Panel, and on the Computer Name panel, click the Change button for the Rename Or Change Domain Entry. This opens a dialog window with a setting for the Workgroup, where you can enter the workgroup name. The default is simply WORKGROUP.

On your Linux Samba server, in the **smb.conf** file, you specify the workgroup name in the **workgroup=** entry in the **global** section. The workgroup name should be uppercase and contain no spaces. The default name used on Windows XP systems is simple WORKGROUP. The **smb.conf workgroup** entry would then look like this:

```
workgroup = WORKGROUP
```

You can then restart the Samba server. On a Windows client, you see the Samba server listed when you select View Workgroups Computers from My Network Places. (On older Windows versions, use the Entire Network folder in your Network Neighborhood.) The Samba server will have as a name the description you gave it in your Samba configuration.

Opening the icon will display a window with all the configured shares and printers on that Samba server.

Samba Configuration File and Tools

Samba configuration options are kept in the **/etc/samba/smb.conf** file. You edit this file to make changes to the configuration. Once you finish making any changes, you should test your **smb.conf** file using the testparm program. The testparm program checks the validity of your configuration entries. By default, testparm uses the **/etc/samba/smb.conf** file, although you can supply a different configuration file as an argument:

```
testparm
```

To check your network connections, use the **smbstatus** command. This command returns a listing of all active SMB connections.

NOTE *The /etc/samba/smbusers file associates Windows network usernames with corresponding users on your Linux Samba server. For example, **admin** and **administrator** are made equivalent to the Linux root user.*

Passwords

Connections between Windows clients and Samba servers have been further complicated by the implementation of password encryption on Microsoft networks. Current versions of Windows operating systems, including upgraded versions of Windows NT, 2000, 98, and 95, now require the use of encrypted passwords by default. Samba, on the other hand, uses unencrypted passwords by default. To enable communication between Samba servers and Windows clients, you have to either change Windows clients to use unencrypted passwords or change the Samba server to use encrypted passwords. The more secure course is to implement encrypted passwords on Samba servers, though this entails more administrative work. Though not distributed by default, Samba can be built with SSL support. This SSL-enabled Samba provides support for encrypted SSL network communications. SSL-enabled Samba includes several SSL-specific configuration options, each preceded by the term **ssl**. For example, **ssl cipher** lets you determine the ciphers that can be used, and **ssl CA certFile** specifies the certificates file.

Samba also provides its own Samba password PAM module, **pam_smbpass.so**. With this module, you provide PAM authentication support for Samba passwords, enabling the use of Windows hosts on a PAM-controlled network. The module could be used for authentication and password management in your PAM **samba** file. The following entries in the PAM **samba** file would implement PAM authentication and passwords using the Samba password database:

```
auth required pam_smbpass.so nodelay
password required pam_smbpass.so nodelay
```

Be sure to enable PAM in the **smb.conf** file:

```
obey pam restrictions = yes
```

Samba Encrypted Passwords: smbpasswd

Encrypted passwords come into play if you are using user-level security instead of share-level security. With user-level security, access to Samba server resources by a Windows client is allowed only to users on that client. Each user on the Windows client has to have a corresponding user account on the Samba server. A user logs in to their Windows account and can then log into his or her Samba server account. Users have to log in providing their username and password, which have to be registered with the Samba server in the **/etc/samba/smbpasswd** file. You use the **smbpasswd** command to add these passwords.

Creating a Samba Password File

To implement encrypted passwords on Samba, the Samba server then needs to maintain an encrypted version of user passwords that can be used by Windows clients. This file of encrypted passwords is **/etc/samba/smbpasswd**. Samba passwords can be added or changed for different users with the **smbpasswd** command. Initially, you should generate the Samba password file so that it will have entries for all your current Samba users. For this task, you use the **mksmbpasswd.sh** script. You input to this script the contents of the Samba server's **/etc/passwd** file, and it generates entries that can be used for encrypted passwords. You use redirection (**>**) to create the encrypted file. In the following example, an **/etc/samba/smbpasswd** file is initially generated by the **mksmbpasswd** script. The **cat** command with a pipe operation is used to input the contents of the **/etc/passwd** file to the **mksmbpasswd.sh** script:

```
cat /etc/passwd | mksmbpasswd.sh > /etc/samba/smbpasswd
```

If your users and their passwords are being managed by NIS, you would use the **ypcat** command to access the user passwords, as shown here:

```
ypcat passwd | mksmbpasswd.sh > /etc/samba/smbpasswd
```

You then need to change the permissions on this file to protect it from unauthorized access. The 600 option allows only read and write access by the root user:

```
chmod 600 /etc/samba/smbpasswd
```

Adding and Changing Passwords

At this point, **/etc/samba/smbpasswd** will contain entries for all your current users with dummy fields for the passwords. You then use the **smbpasswd** command to add, or later change, encrypted passwords. To add a password for a particular user, you use the **smbpasswd** command with the username:

```
# smbpasswd dylan
New SMB Password: new-password
Repeat New SMB Password: new-password
```

Users can use **smbpasswd** to change their own password. The following example shows how you would use **smbpasswd** to change your Samba password. If the user has no Samba password, they can just press the ENTER key.

```
$ smbpasswd
```

```
Old SMB password: old-password
New SMB Password: new-password
Repeat New SMB Password: new-password
```

Configuring Encrypted Passwords
You also have to make sure that Samba is configured to use encrypted passwords. Set the **encrypt passwords** option to **yes** and specify the SMB password file. These options are already set in the **/etc/samba/smb.conf** file (described in the following section), but they are commented with a preceding ; symbol. Just locate the lines and remove the ; symbols at the beginnings of the lines:

```
encrypt passwords = yes
smb passwd file = /etc/samba/smbpasswd
```

You can also use SWAT to make this change. In the GLOBALS page, select Yes from the pop-up menu for the Encrypt Password entry. Then save your changes by clicking the Commit Changes button.

Be sure to restart the Samba server with the following command:

```
service smb restart
```

Configuring Samba with system-config-samba
Fedora Core provides a simple configuration tool for providing basic information about your Samba server, as well as adding Samba users and specifying Samba shares (see Figure 41-1). It will also automatically configure all the printers on your Linux system as Samba shared printers, allowing you to use them from a connected Windows system. You can start system-config-samba from the Samba entry in the Server Settings menu, accessible from the System Setting menu. The system-config-samba tool will list all the shares for your server. You can use buttons at the top to manage your shares, adding new ones or deleting current ones. If you delete, the actual directories are not removed; they just lose their status as shared directories. In Figure 41-1, a shared directory called **/groupics/vacation** has been set up with read-only access.

Server Configuration with system-config-samba
To configure your Samba server, select Server Settings from the Preferences menu. This opens a window with two panels, Basic and Security. On the Basic panel, you enter the Samba server workgroup name. This will be the same name used as the workgroup by all your Windows systems. For example, if you are using the default group name, WORKGROUP, for your Windows systems, you would enter WORKGROUP here. The description is the name you want displayed for your Samba server on your Windows systems. On the Security panel, you specify the authentication mode, the password encryption option, and the name of the guest account, along with the authentication server.

- As explained in detail later, the authentication mode specifies the access level, which can be user, share, server, or domain. User-level access restricts access by user password, whereas share access opens access to any guest.

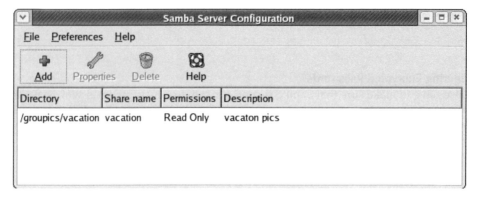

FIGURE 41-1   system-config-samba

- Normally, you would elect to encrypt passwords, rather than have them passed over your network in plain text.

- The Guest user is the name of the account used to allow access to shares or printers that you want open to any user, without having to provide a password. The pop-up menu will list all your current users, with nobody as the selected default.

Adding Samba Users with system-config-samba

With system-config-samba, you can add users and shares easily. User-level access restricts users to those that also have accounts on the Samba server. Samba maintains its own password listing for users. To provide a user Samba access, you need to register the user as a Samba user. Select Samba Users from the Preferences menu to open the Samba Users window, clicking the Add User button. Here you enter the Unix Username, the Windows Username, and the Samba Password. There is an additional box for confirming the Samba password. The Unix Username is a pop-up window listing all the users on your Samba server.

Specifying Samba Shares with system-config-samba

Click Add to add a share, or select Add Share from the File menu. On the Basic panel, you can then enter the directory on the Samba server that you want to share, specifying the full pathname. The Browse button lets you search and select a directory. You can also set permissions to either read-only or read/write. On the Access panel, you can restrict access to certain users or allow access to all users. All Samba users on your system will be listed with check boxes where you can select those you want to give access.

The Samba smb.conf Configuration File

You configure the Samba daemon using the **smb.conf** file located in the **/etc/samba** directory. The file is separated into two basic parts: one for global options and the other for shared services. A shared service, also known as *shares,* can be either filespace services (used by clients as an extension of their native file systems) or printable services (used by clients to access print services on the host running the server). The filespace service is a directory to which clients are given access; they can use the space in it as an extension of their local file system. A printable service provides access by clients to print services, such as printers managed by the Samba server.

The **/etc/samba/smb.conf** file holds the configuration for the various shared resources, as well as global options that apply to all resources. Linux installs an **smb.conf** file in your **/etc/samba** directory. The file contains default settings used for your distribution. You can edit the file to customize your configuration to your own needs. Many entries are commented with either a semicolon or a **#** sign, and you can remove the initial comment symbol to make them effective. Instead of editing the file directly, you may want to use the SWAT configuration utility, which provides an easy-to-use, full-screen Web page interface for entering configurations for shared resources. The SWAT configuration utility also provides extensive help features and documentation. For a complete listing of the Samba configuration parameters, check the Man page for **smb.conf**. An extensive set of sample **smb.conf** files is located in the **/usr/share/doc/samba*** directory in the **examples** subdirectory.

In the **smb.conf** file, global options are set first, followed by each shared resource's configuration. The basic organizing component of the **smb.conf** file is a section. Each resource has its own section that holds its service name and definitions of its attributes. Even global options are placed in a section of their own, labeled **global**. For example, each section for a filespace share consists of the directory and the access rights allowed to users of the filespace. The section of each share is labeled with the name of the shared resource. Special sections, called **printers** and **homes**, provide default descriptions for user directories and printers accessible on the Samba server. Following the special sections, sections are entered for specific services, namely access to specific directories or printers.

A section begins with a section label consisting of the name of the shared resource encased in brackets. Other than the special sections, the section label can be any name you want to give it. Following the section label, on separate lines, different parameters for this service are entered. The parameters define the access rights to be granted to the user of the service. For example, for a directory, you may want it to be browsable, but read-only, and to use a certain printer. Parameters are entered in the format *parameter name = value*. You can enter a comment by placing a semicolon at the beginning of the comment line.

A simple example of a section configuration follows. The section label is encased in brackets and followed by two parameter entries. The **path** parameter specifies the directory to which access is allowed. The **writeable** parameter specifies whether the user has write access to this directory and its filespace.

```
[mysection]
 path = /home/chris
 writeable = true
```

A printer service has the same format but requires certain other parameters. The **path** parameter specifies the location of the printer spool directory. The **read only** and **printable** parameters are set to **true**, indicating the service is read-only and printable. **public** indicates anyone can access it.

```
[myprinter]
 path = /var/spool/samba
 read only = true
 printable = true
 public = true
```

Parameter entries are often synonymous but different entries that have the same meaning. For example, **read only = no**, **writeable = yes**, and **write ok = yes** all mean the same thing, providing write access to the user. The **public** parameter is a synonym for **guest ok**. SWAT will use **guest ok** instead of **public**, and **read only** in place of **writeable**.

SWAT and smb.conf

SWAT is a network-based Samba configuration tool that uses a Web page interface to enable you to configure your **smb.conf** file. SWAT is an easy way to configure your Samba server, providing the full range of configuration options rather than the defaults provided by system-config-samba. SWAT provides a simple-to-use Web page interface with buttons, menus, and text boxes for entering values. A simple button bar across the top enables you to select the sections you want to configure. A button bar is even there to add passwords. To see the contents of the **smb.conf** file as SWAT changes it, click View. The initial screen (HOME) displays the index for Samba documentation. One of SWAT's more helpful features is its context-sensitive help. For each parameter and option SWAT displays, you can click a Help button to display a detailed explanation of the option and examples of its use.

Activating SWAT

SWAT is normally installed with Samba. SWAT is an xinetd service. As an xinetd service, it will be listed in the **/etc/services** and **/etc/xinetd.d/swat** files. The SWAT program uses port 901, as designated in the **/etc/services** file and shown here:

```
swat 901/tcp # Samba Web Administration Tool
```

As an xinetd service, SWAT will have its own xinetd file in the **/etc/xinetd.d** directory, **/etc/xinetd.d/swat**. SWAT is turned off by default, and its **disable** option is set to **yes**. To use SWAT, you will have to change the **disable** option to **no**.

You can do this by using either **chkconfig** or the Service Configuration tool to turn on the SWAT service or by manually editing the **/etc/xinetd.d/swat** file and changing the **disable** option to **no**. **chkconfig** will edit the **/etc/xinetd.d/swat** file for you, making this change (see Chapter 21 for more information about **chkconfig**). The following example shows how you would enable SWAT with the **chkconfig** command:

```
chkconfig swat on
```

With **chkconfig**, you will not have to manually restart the xinetd server. However, if you manually edit the file, you will also have to restart the server to have the change take effect. On Fedora Core, you can do this simply using the **xinetd** script, as shown here:

```
service xinetd restart
```

Before you use SWAT, back up your current **smb.conf** file. SWAT overwrites the original, replacing it with a shorter and more concise version of its own. The **smb.conf** file originally installed lists an extensive number of options with detailed explanations. This is a good learning tool, with excellent examples for creating various kinds of printer and directory sections. Simply make a backup copy:

```
cp /etc/samba/smb.conf /etc/samba/smb.bk
```

Accessing SWAT

You can start SWAT by selecting the Samba Configuration entry in the GNOME or KDE System menu. This will open your Web browser to the SWAT page using the localhost IP address 127.0.0.1 and port 901. You can also open your browser and enter the IP address 127.0.0.1 with port 901 to access SWAT.

```
http://127.0.0.1:901
```

You can start SWAT from a remote location by entering the address of the Samba server it is running on, along with its port (901), into a Web browser. However, you will first have to enable this feature in the **/etc/xinetd.d/swat** file. Currently, the **only_from** line in this file restricts access to just localhost. To enable access from any remote system, just remove this line. If you want to provide access to certain specific hosts, you can list them after 127.0.0.1 on the **only_from** line. Be sure to restart SWAT after any changes. The following example enables access from both 127.0.0.1 and **rabbit.mytrek.com**:

```
only_from  127.0.0.1  rabbit.mytrek.com
```

The following URL entered into a Web browser on a remote system would then display the Web page interface for SWAT on the **turtle.mytrek.com** Samba server:

```
http://turtle.mytrek.com:901
```

You are first asked to enter a username and a password. To configure Samba, you need to enter **root** and the root password. (If you are connecting from a remote system, it is *not* advisable to enter the root password in clear text—see Chapter 29.)

SWAT Configuration Pages

The main SWAT page is displayed with a button bar, with buttons for links for HOME, GLOBALS, SHARES, PRINTERS, STATUS, VIEW, and PASSWORD (see Table 41-2). You can use STATUS to list your active SMB network connections.

For the various sections, SWAT can display either a basic or advanced version. The basic version shows only those entries needed for a simple configuration, whereas the advanced version shows all the possible entries for that type of section. A button—labeled Advanced or Basic, depending on the current view—is at the top of the section page for toggling between the advanced or basic versions (see Figure 41-2). Section pages for printers and shares have added buttons and a menu for selecting the particular printer or share you want to configure. The term "share," as it's used here, refers to directories you want to make

Page	Description
HOME	SWAT home page listing documentation resources.
GLOBALS	Configures the Global section for Samba.
SHARES	Selects and configures directories to be shared (shares).
PRINTERS	Sets up access to printers.
WIZARD	Quick setup with default values.
STATUS	Checks the status of the Samba server, both smbd and nmbd; lists clients currently active and the actions they are performing. You can restart, stop, or start the Samba server from this page.
VIEW	Displays the **smb.conf** configuration file.
PASSWORD	Sets up password access for the server and users that have access.

TABLE 41-2   SWAT Configuration Pages

available through Samba. When you click the SHARES button, you initially see only a few buttons displayed at the top of the SHARES page. You use these buttons to create new sections or to edit sections already set up for shares. To set up a new Share section, you enter its name in the box next to the Create Share button and then click that button. The new share name appears in the drop-down menu next to the Choose Share button. Initially, this button is blank. Click it to display the list of current Share sections. Select the one you want, and then click the Choose Share button. The page then displays the entries for configuring a share. For a new share, these are either blank or default values. For example, to select the Homes section that configures the default setting for user home directories, click the drop-down menu, where you find a Homes entry. Select it, and then click the Choose Share button. The entries for the Homes section are displayed. The same process works for the Printers page, where you can select either the Printers section or Create sections for particular printers.

> **NOTE** *Samba automatically creates entries for any printer already configured for use on your system or network. It reads these from your **/etc/printcap** file. You will need to edit the printer entries to control access to your printers. For Samba to use a printer, it first has to be configured on your system as either a local or network printer (see system-config-printer in Chapter 4). Keep in mind that a network printer could be a printer connected to a Windows system.*

In Figure 41-2, notice the Help link next to each entry. Such a link displays a Web page showing the Samba documentation for **smb.conf**, positioned at the appropriate entry. In this figure, the Guest OK part of the documentation is displayed after the user clicks the Help link next to the Guest OK entry.

When you finish working on a section, click the Commit Changes button on its page to save your changes. Do this for each separate page you work on, including the GLOBALS page. Clicking Commit Changes generates a new version of the **smb.conf** file. To have the Samba server read these changes, you then have to restart it. You can do this by clicking the Restart SMB button on the Status page.

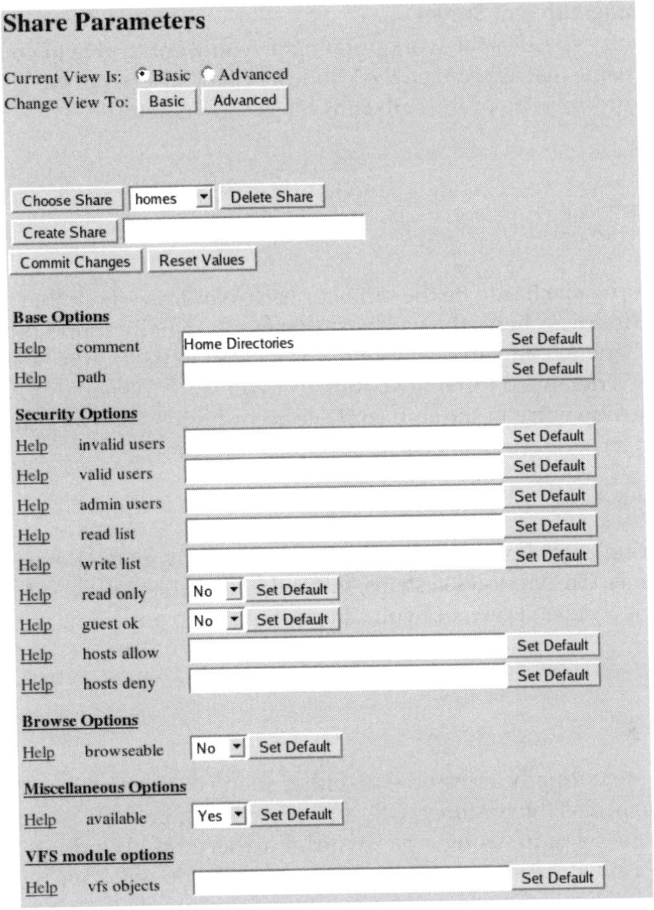

FIGURE **41-2**   SWAT Share page showing Homes section

You can, of course, edit the **/etc/samba/smb.conf** file directly. This is a simple text file you can edit with any text editor. You still must restart the SMB server to have the changes take effect, which you can do manually on Fedora Core with the following command:

```
service smb restart
```

Global Section

The Global section determines configuration for the entire server, as well as specifying default entries to be used in the home and directory segments. In this section, you find entries for the workgroup name, password configuration, and directory settings. Several of the more important entries are discussed here. The Basic View of this page lists the options you would most likely need.

Specifying the Workgroup and Server

The Workgroup entry specifies the workgroup name you want to give to your network. This is the workgroup name that appears on the Windows client's Network Neighborhood window. The default Workgroup entry in the **smb.conf** file is shown here:

```
[global]

# workgroup = NT-Domain-Name or Workgroup-Name
 workgroup = MYGROUP
```

The workgroup name has to be the same for each Windows client that the Samba server supports. On a Windows client, the workgroup name is usually found on the Network Identification or General panel in the System tool located in the Control Panel window. On many clients, this is defaulted to WORKGROUP. If you want to keep this name, you have to change the Workgroup entry in the **smb.conf** file accordingly. The Workgroup entry and the workgroup name on each Windows client have to be the same.

```
workgroup = WORKGROUP
```

The server string entry holds the descriptive name you want displayed for the server on the client systems. On Windows systems, this is the name displayed on the Samba server icon. The default is Samba Server, but you can change this to any name you want.

```
# server string is the equivalent of the NT Description field
 server string = Samba Server
```

Security Level

Samba resources are normally accessed with either share- or user-level security. On a share level, any user can access the resource without having to log in to the server. On a user level, each user has to log in, using a password. Furthermore, Windows 98, ME, NT, and XP clients use encrypted passwords for the login process. You will have to enable encrypted passwords for these clients. The default for encrypted passwords is **no**, so you will need to change it to **yes**. In the **smb.conf** file, the security option is set to the level you want and the **encrypt passwords** option is set to **yes** to enable encryption.

```
security = user
encrypt passwords = yes
```

If you want share-level security, specify **share** as the security option:

```
security = share
```

On the SWAT GLOBALS page, select the security level from the Security pop-up menu, either User or Share. Then select Yes for the encrypt passwords entry.

Network Access Control

As a security measure, you can restrict access to SMB services to certain specified local networks. On the host's network, type the network addresses of the local networks for which you want to permit access. To deny access to everyone in a network except a few particular hosts, you can use the EXCEPT option after the network address with the IP addresses of those hosts. The localhost (127) is always automatically included. The next example allows access to two local networks:

```
hosts allow = 192.168.1. 192.168.2.
```

Printing
To enable printing, allow Samba to load the printer descriptions from your **printcap** file.

```
printcap name = /etc/printcap
load printers = yes
```

To specify your printing system, you set the `printing` option. On Fedora Core, CUPS is the print server now supported. To set the printing system to CUPS, use the following:

```
printing = cups
```

Guest User Access
You can use a guest user login to make resources available to anyone without requiring a password. A guest user login would handle any users who log in without a specific account. On Linux systems, by default Samba will use the **nobody** user as the guest user. Alternatively, you can set up and designate a specific user to use as the guest user. You designate the guest user with the Guest Account entry in the **smb.conf** file. The commented **smb.conf** file provided with Samba currently lists a commented entry for setting up a guest user called **pcguest**. You can make this the user you want as the guest user. Be sure to add the guest user to the password file:

```
guest account = pcguest
```

On SWAT, you can specify a guest account entry on the GLOBALS page. By default, this is already set to the **nobody** user.

Passwords
As noted previously, user-level security requires that each user log into the Samba server using passwords. Samba can use either clear text or encrypted passwords, though current Windows clients support encrypted passwords. You can use the `smbpasswd` command to add and change Samba passwords. On SWAT, you enable password encryption on the GLOBALS page and manage passwords on the PASSWORDS page. In the Server Password Management section, you can add, change, remove, enable, or disable users. To add a new user, enter the username and password, and then click Add New User. As the root user on the Samba server, you can add new passwords as well as enable or disable current ones. Normal users can use the Client/Server Password Management section to change their own passwords.

Homes Section
The Homes section specifies default controls for accessing a user home directory through the SMB protocols by remote users. To access the Homes section on SWAT, you simply select the SHARES page, select the Homes entry from the drop-down menu, and click Choose Share. Setting the **browseable** entry to **no** prevents the client from listing the files

in a file browser. The **writeable** entry specifies whether users have read and write control over files in their home directories. The **create mode** and **directory mode** set default permissions for new files and directories (on SWAT, these are create mask and directory mask). The **valid users** entry uses the %S macro to map to the current service.

```
[homes]
 comment = Home Directories
 browseable = no
 writeable = yes
 valid users = %S
 create mode = yes
 directory mode = 775
```

Printers Section

The Printers section specifies the default controls for accessing printers. These are used for printers for which no specific sections exist. In this case, Samba uses printers defined in the server's **printcap** file.

In this context, setting **browseable** to **no** simply hides the Printers section from the client, not the printers. The **path** entry specifies the location of the spool directory Samba will use for printer files. To enable printing at all, the **printable** entry must be set to yes. To allow guest users to print, set the **guest ok** entry to **yes**. The **writeable** entry set to **no** prevents any kind of write access, other than the printer's management of spool files. On SWAT, select the PRINTERS page and the Printers entry in the drop-down menu, and then select Choose Printers. A standard implementation of the Printers section is shown here:

```
[printers]
 comment = All Printers
 path = /var/spool/samba
 browseable = no
 guest ok = yes
 writeable = no
 printable = yes
```

If you can't print, be sure to check the Default Print entry. This specifies the command the server actually uses to print documents.

Shares

Sections for specific shared resources, such as directories on your system, are usually placed after the Homes and Printers sections. For a section defining a shared directory, enter a label for the system. Then, on separate lines, enter options for its pathname and the different permissions you want to set. In the **path** = *option*, specify the full pathname for the directory. The **comment** = *option* holds the label to be given the share. You can make a directory writable, public, or read-only. You can control access to the directory with the Valid Users entry. With this entry, you can list those users permitted access. For those options not set, the defaults entered in the Global, Homes, and Printers segments are used.

On SWAT, you use the SHARES page to create and edit shared directories. Select the one you want to edit from the drop-down menu and click Choose Share. The Basic View shows the commonly used entries. For entries such as Valid Users, you need to select the Advanced

View. Be sure to click Commit Changes before you move on to another Share or Printer section (see Figure 41-2).

The following example is the **myprojects** share generated by SWAT from a share page. Here the **/myprojects** directory is defined as a share resource that is open to any user with guest access.

```
[myprojects]
     comment = Great Project Ideas
     path = /myprojects
     writeable = yes
     guest ok = yes
     printable = yes
```

To limit access to certain users, you can list a set of valid users. Setting the **guest ok** option to **no** closes it off from access by others.

```
[mynewmusic]
 comment =  Service
 path = //home/specialprojects
 valid users = mark
 guest ok = no
 writeable = yes
 printable = no
```

To allow complete public access, set the **guest ok** entry to **yes**, with no valid user's entry.

```
[newdocs]
 path = /home/newdocs
 guest ok = yes
 writeable = yes
 printable = yes
```

To set up a directory that can be shared by more than one user, where each user has control of the files they create, simply list the users in the Valid Users entry. Permissions for any created files are specified in the Advanced mode by the Create Mask entry (same as create mode). In this example, the permissions are set to 765, which provides read/write/execute access to owners, read/write access to members of the group, and only read/execute access to all others (the default is 744, read-only for group and other permission, see Chapter 30):

```
[myshare]
 comment = Writer's projects
 path = /usr/local/drafts
 valid users = justin chris dylan
 guest ok = no
 writeable = yes
 printable = no
 create mask = 0765
```

For more examples, check those in the original **smb.conf** file that shows a Shares section for a directory **fredsdir**.

Printers

Access to specific printers is defined in the Printers section of the **smb.conf** file. You can also configure printers in the SWAT PRINTERS page. For a printer, you need to include the Printer and Printable entries, as well as specify the type of Printing server used. With the Printer entry, you name the printer, and by setting the Printable entry to yes, you allow it to print. You can control access to specific users with the Valid Users entry and by setting the Public entry to no. For public access, set the Public entry to yes. For the CUPS server used on Fedora Core, set the printing option cups. On SWAT, you can create individual Printer sections on the PRINTERS page. Default entries are already set up for you.

The following example sets up a printer accessible to guest users. This opens the printer to use by any user on the network. Users need to have write access to the printer's spool directory, located in **/var/spool/samba**. Keep in mind that any printer has to first be installed on your system. The following printer was already installed as myhp and has an **/etc/printcap** entry with that name. On Fedora Core, you can use system-config-printer to install an LPRng printer, giving it a name and selecting its driver (see Chapters 4 and 26). You use the CUPS administrative tool to set up printers for the CUPS server (see Chapter 26). The Printing option can be inherited from general Printers share.

```
[myhp]
     path = /var/spool/samba
     writeable = yes
     guest ok = yes
     printable = yes
     printer = myhp
     oplocks = no
     share modes = no
     printing = cups
```

As with shares, you can restrict printer use to certain users, denying it to public access. The following example sets up a printer accessible only by the users **larisa** and **aleina** (you could add other users if you want). Users need to have write access to the printer's spool directory.

```
[larisalaser]
     path = /var/spool/samba
     writeable = yes
     valid users = larisa aleina
     guest ok = no
     printable = yes
     printing = cups
     printer = myhp
     oplocks = no
     share modes = no
```

Variable Substitutions

For string values assigned to parameters, you can incorporate substitution operators. This provides greater flexibility in designating values that may be context-dependent, such as usernames. For example, suppose a service needs to use a separate directory for each user who logs in. The path for such directories could be specified using the **%u** variable that substitutes in the name of the current user. The string **path = /tmp/%u** would become **path = /tmp/justin** for the **justin** user and **/tmp/dylan** for the **dylan** user. Table 41-3 lists several of the more common substitution variables.

Variable	Description
`%S`	Name of the current service
`%P`	Root directory of the current service
`%u`	Username of the current service
`%H`	Home directory of the user
`%h`	Internet hostname on which Samba is running
`%m`	NetBIOS name of the client machine
`%L`	NetBIOS name of the server
`%M`	Internet name of the client machine
`%I`	IP address of the client machine

TABLE 41-3 Samba Substitution Variables

Testing the Samba Configuration

After you make your changes to the **smb.conf** file, you can then use the testparm program to see if the entries are correctly entered. testparm checks the syntax and validity of Samba entries. By default, testparm checks the **/etc/samba/smb.conf** file. If you are using a different file as your configuration file, you can specify it as an argument to testparm. You can also have testparm check to see if a particular host has access to the service set up by the configuration file.

With SWAT, the STATUS page will list your connections and shares. From the command line, you can use the **smbstatus** command to check on current Samba connections on your network.

To check the real-time operation of your Samba server, you can log in to a user account on the Linux system running the Samba server and connect to the server.

Domain Logons

Samba also supports domain logons whereby a user can log on to the network. Logon scripts can be set up for individual users. To configure such netlogon capability, you need to set up a **netlogon** share in the **smb.conf** file. The following sample is taken from the original **smb .conf** file. This share holds the **netlogon** scripts—in this case, the **/home/netlogon** directory—which should not be writable but should be accessible by all users (Guest OK):

```
[netlogon]
 comment = Network Logon Service
 path = /home/netlogon
 guest ok = yes
 writeable = no
 share modes = no
```

The Global section would have the following parameters enabled:

```
domain logons = yes
```

With netlogon, you can configure Samba as an authentication server for both Linux and Windows hosts. A Samba username and password need to be set up for each host. In the Global section of the **smb.conf** file, be sure to enable encrypted passwords, user-level security, and domain logons, as well as an operating system level of 33 or more:

```
[global]
 encrypt passwords = yes
 security = user
 domain logons = yes
 os level = 33
```

NOTE *You can also configure Samba to be a Primary Domain Controller (PDC) for Windows NT networks. As a PDC, Samba can handle domain logons, retrieve lists of users and groups, and provide user-level security.*

Accessing Samba Services with Clients

Client systems connected to the SMB network can access the shared services provided by the Samba server. Windows clients should be able to access shared directories and services automatically through the Network Neighborhood and the Entire Network icons on a Windows desktop. For Linux systems connected to the same network, Samba services can be accessed using the GNOME Nautilus file manager and KDE file manager, as well as special Samba client programs.

With the Samba smbclient, a command line client, a local Linux system can connect to a shared directory on the Samba server and transfer files, as well as run shell programs. Using the **mount** command with the **-t smbfs** option, directories on the Samba server can be mounted to local directories on the Linux client. The **smbfs** option invokes **smbmount** to mount the directory.

Accessing Windows Samba Shares from GNOME

You can access your Samba shares directly from GNOME. On Fedora Core, you can open the My Computer icon and then the Network icon. This will display the icons for your network (see Chapter 3). The Windows Network icon will hold the Windows workgroups that your Windows hosts are part of. Opening up the Windows Network icon will list your Windows network groups, like WORKGROUP. Opening up the Windows group icon will list the hosts in that group. These will show host icons for your shared Windows hosts. Clicking a host icon will list all the shared resources on it. There is a conflict between Samba desktop browsing and the firewall on Fedora Core Linux systems. You will need to either disable the firewall, or upgrade the securitylevel package to version system-config-securitylevel-1.5.9-1 (if not in updates, check development directory). Then on the SecurityLevel Firewall Options panel select Samba browsing in the Trusted services section.

Alternatively, you can start Nautilus in browser mode and enter the **smb:** protocol to display all the Samba and Windows networks, from which you can access the Samba and Windows shares.

smbclient

The smbclient utility operates like FTP to access systems using the SMB protocols. Whereas with an FTP client you can access other FTP servers or Unix systems, with smbclient you can access SMB-shared services, either on the Samba server or on Windows systems. Many smbclient commands are similar to FTP, such as **mget** to transfer a file or **del** to delete a file. The smbclient program has several options for querying a remote system, as well as connecting to it. See the **smbclient** Man page for a complete list of options and commands. The smbclient program takes as its argument a server name and the service you want to access on that server. A double slash precedes the server name, and a single slash separates it from the service. The service can be any shared resource, such as a directory or a printer. The server name is its NetBIOS name, which may or may not be the same as its IP name. For example, to specify the **myreports** shared directory on the server named **turtle.mytrek.com**, use **//turtle.mytrek.com/myreports**. If you must specify a pathname, use backslashes for Windows files and forward slashes for Unix/Linux files:

```
//server-name/service
```

You can also supply the password for accessing the service. Enter it as an argument following the service name. If you do not supply the password, you are prompted to enter it.

Accessing Shares with smbclient

You can then add several options to access shares, such as the remote username or the list of services available. With the **-I** option, you can specify the system using its IP address. You use the **-U** option and a login name for the remote login name you want to use on the remote system. Attach **%** with the password if a password is required. With the **-L** option, you can obtain a list of the services provided on a server, such as shared directories or printers. The following command will list the shares available on the host **turtle.mytrek.com**:

```
smbclient -L turtle.mytrek.com
```

To access a particular directory on a remote system, enter the directory as an argument to the **smbclient** command, followed by any options. For Windows files, you use backslashes for the pathnames, and for Unix/Linux files, you use forward slashes. Once connected, an SMB prompt is displayed and you can use smbclient commands such as **get** and **put** to transfer files. The **quit** or **exit** commands quit the smbclient program. In the following example, smbclient accesses the directory **myreports** on the **turtle.mytrek.com** system, using the **dylan** login name:

```
smbclient //turtle.mytrek.com/myreports -I 192.168.0.1 -U dylan
```

In most cases, you can simply use the server name to reference the server, as shown here:

```
smbclient //turtle.mytrek.com/myreports -U dylan
```

If you are accessing the home directory of a particular account on the Samba server, you can simply specify the **homes** service. In the next example, the user accesses the home directory of the **aleina** account on the Samba server, after being prompted to enter that account's password:

```
smbclient //turtle.mytrek.com/homes -U aleina
```

You can also use smbclient to access shared resources located on Windows clients. Specify the computer name of the Windows client along with its shared folder. In the next example, the user accesses the **windata** folder on the Windows client named **lizard**. The folder is configured to allow access by anyone, so the user just presses the ENTER key at the password prompt.

```
$ smbclient //lizard/windata
added interface ip=192.168.0.2 bcast=192.168.0.255 nmask=255.255.255.0
Got a positive name query response from 192.168.0.3 ( 192.168.0.3 )
Password:
Domain=[WORKGROUP] OS=[Windows 5.1] Server=[Windows 2000 LAN Manager]
smb: \> ls
  .        D     0  Sat Sep  7 17:29:19 2002
  ..       D     0  Sat Sep  7 17:29:19 2002
  hi       A    10  Sat Sep  7 17:29:27 2002
  mynewdoc.doc  A     0  Sat Sep  7 16:59:13 2002
     39997 blocks of size 1048576. 39930 blocks available
smb: \> mget hi
Get file hi? y
getting file hi of size 10 as hi (1.22069 kb/s) (average 1.2207 kb/s)
smb: \> quit
```

smbclient Commands

Once logged in, you can execute smbclient commands to manage files and change directories. Shell commands can be executed with the **!** operator. To transfer files, you can use the **mget** and **mput** commands, much as they are used in the FTP program. The **recurse** command enables you to turn on recursion to copy whole subdirectories at a time. You can use file-matching operators, referred to here as *masks*, to select a certain collection of files. The file-matching (mask) operators are *****, **[]**, and **?** (see Chapter 8). The default mask is *****, which matches everything. The following example uses **mget** to copy all files with a .c suffix, as in **myprog.c**:

```
smb> mget *.c
```

During transfers, you can have smbclient either prompt you for each individual file or simply transfer all the selected ones. The **prompt** command toggles this file prompting on and off.

To access a particular printer on a remote system, enter the printer name as an argument to the **smbclient** command, followed by any options. In the following example, smbclient accesses the myepson printer on the **turtle.mytrek.com** system, using the **dylan** login name:

```
smbclient //turtle.mytrek.com/myepson -U dylan
```

Once connected, an smb prompt is displayed and you can use smbclient commands such as **print** to print files and **printmode** to specify graphics or text. In the next example, the user prints a file called **myfile**, after having accessed the myepson printer on **turtle.mytrek.com**:

```
smb> print myfile
```

smbmount: mount -t smbfs

Using the **mount** command with the **-t smbfs** option., a Linux or Unix client can mount a shared directory onto its local system. The **smbfs** option invokes the **smbmount** command to perform the mount operation. The syntax for the **smbmount** command is similar to that for the **smbclient** command, with many corresponding options. The **smbmount** command takes as its arguments the Samba server and shared directory, followed by the local directory where you want to mount the directory. The following example mounts the **myreports** directory onto the **/mnt/myreps** directory on the local system.

Instead of using **smbmount** explicitly, you use the **mount** command with the file system type **smbfs**. **mount** will then run the **/sbin/mount.smbfs** command, which will invoke smbclient to mount the file system:

```
mount -t smbfs //turtle.mytrek.com/myreports /mnt/myreps -U dylan
```

To unmount the directory, use the **smbumount** command with the local directory name, as shown here:

```
umount /mnt/myreps
```

To mount the home directory of a particular user on the server, specify the **homes** service and the user's login name. The following example mounts the home directory of the user **larisa** to the **/home/chris/larisastuff** directory on the local system:

```
mount -t smbfs //turtle.mytrek.com/homes /home/chris/larisastuff -U larisa
```

You can also mount shared folders on Windows clients. Just specify the computer name of the Windows client along with its folder. If the folder name contains spaces, enclose it in single quotes. In the following example, the user mounts the **windata** folder on **lizard** as the **/mylinux** directory. For a folder with access to anyone, just press ENTER at the password prompt:

```
$ mount -t smbfs //lizard/windata  /mylinux
Password:
$ ls /mylinux
hi mynewdoc.doc myreport.txt
```

To unmount the shared folder when you are finished with it, use the **umount** command.

```
umount /mylinux
```

You could also specify a username and password as options, if user-level access is required:

```
mount -t smbfs -o username=chris passwd=mypass //lizard/windata /mylinux
```

You can also use the **smbfs** type in an **/etc/fstab** entry to have a Samba file system mounted automatically:

```
//lizard/windata /mylinux smbfs defaults 0 0
```

Sharing Windows Directories and Printers with Samba Clients

To manage directory shares, open the Computer Management tool in the Administrative window in the Control Panel. Click Shared Folders and there you can see the Shares, Sessions, and Open folders. To add a new share, click the Shares folder and then click the Action menu and select New File Share. The Sessions and Open folders' Action menus let you disconnect active sessions and folders.

To allow share-level open access by users on other clients or on the Samba server, be sure to enable the guest user on your Windows client. It is not enabled by default. Access the Users and Passwords tool in the Control Panel to set up the guest user. Guest access is particularly important for providing access to a printer connected to a Windows client. The Linux system that wants to access a printer on a Windows system will configure the printer on its own system as a remote Samba printer. The user normally entered to access the printer is **guest**. For the Linux system to access the Windows printer, that Windows system has to have a guest user.

Sharing Windows Directories

To share a directory, right-click the directory and select Sharing from the pop-up menu (Sharing And Security on Windows XP). Click Share This Folder and then enter the share name, the name by which the directory will be known by Samba. You can specify whether you want to allow others to change files on the share. You can also specify a user limit (maximum allowed is the default). You can further click the Permissions button to control access by users. Here, you can specify which users will have access, as well as the type of access. For example, you could allow only read access to the directory.

Sharing Windows Printers

To share a printer, locate the printer in the Printers window and right-click it, selecting the Sharing As option. This opens the Sharing panel, where you can click the Shared As button and enter the name under which the printer will be known by other hosts. For example, on the Windows client named lizard, to have a printer called Epson Stylus Color shared as myepson, the Sharing panel for this printer would have the Shared As button selected and the name myepson entered. Then when the user double-clicks the lizard icon in the Computers Near Me window, the printer icon labeled myepson will appear.

For a Linux system to use this printer, it will have to be first configured as a remote Windows printer on that Linux system. For printers using the LPRng print server, you can do this easily with system-config-printer (Printing on the System Settings menu and window), and for printers using the CUPS print server, you use the CUPS Print Configuration tool (Extra System Tools menu).

To configure your remote printer, you give the printer a name by which it is known on your Linux system, the Windows client computer name, the name of the printer as it is accessed on the Windows client, along with the username for access (usually **guest**). Once configured, your printing commands can access it using just the printer name, as they would any other printer. For example, the myepson printer installed on the Windows client also has to be installed for CUPS on the Linux system operating as the Samba server. For the CUPS print server, you can use system-config-printer to configure your Windows printer. You can give the printer the same name, if you wish, and then in the Queue Type panel select Windows Printer (SMB). For the Share, you enter **//lizard/myepson**; for User, enter **guest**; and for Workgroup, enter the Windows client's workgroup (usually **WORKGROUP**).

For the CUPS print server, you can also use the CUPS Print Configuration tool and add the printer. For device, select Windows Printer via Samba. For the device URI, enter the share name with the smb: protocol, **smb://lizard/myepson** (to enable CUPS to use Samba, the CUPS smb directory, **/usr/lib/cups/backend/smb**, is linked to the Samba spool tool, **/usr/bin/smbspool**).

Once it is installed, you can restart the CUPS server. Then an **lpr** command can access the remote Windows printer directly. The next example prints the **mydoc** file on the Windows client's Epson printer:

```
lpr -P myepson mydoc
```

Windows Clients

To access Samba resources from a Windows system, you will need to make sure that your Windows system has enabled TCP/IP networking. This may already be the case if your Windows client is connected to a Microsoft network. If you need to connect a Windows system directly to a TCP/IP network that your Linux Samba server is running on, you should check that TCP/IP networking is enabled on that Windows system. This involves making sure that the Microsoft Network client and the TCP/IP protocol are installed, and that your network interface card (NIC adapter) is configured to use TCP/IP. The procedures differ slightly on Windows 2000 and XP, and Windows 95, 98, and ME.

Once connected, your Samba shares and printers will appear in the Windows network window. On Windows XP you can select My Network Places and it will list the Samba shares on your Linux Samba server. If you open View Workgroup Computers, it will list your Samba server (along with any other Samba or Windows systems in your workgroup). The Samba server will have the name given it in the **server string** option along with the netbios name (the hostname). Follow the instructions on your particular Windows system for accessing remote shared resources such as printers and directories.

About the DVD-ROM

The Linux distribution DVD-ROM, Fedora Core 4, is included in this book, featuring the complete Fedora Core 4 distribution. The Fedora Core 4 Linux distribution installs a professional-level and very stable Linux system along with the KDE and GNOME GUI interfaces, flexible and easy-to-use system configuration tools, an extensive set of Internet servers, a variety of different multimedia applications, and over 1,500 Linux applications of all kinds. You can find recent information about the Red Hat Fedora Project at **fedora.redhat.com**.

You will need a DVD-ROM drive on your computer to access the DVD-ROM disc. The DVD-ROM included with this book is the official Fedora Core 4 DVD with binary applications for Intel PC systems. The disk image is also available online at **FC4-i386-DVD.iso** from the Fedora download site in the i386 subdirectory, **download.fedora.redhat.com/pub/fedora/ linux/core/4/i386/iso** (the DVD image is only accessible with an FTP client, not a Web browser). The DVD includes all application binaries, but no source code. These can be downloaded separately. Also available from the Fedora site are the 64-bit version (**x86_64** directory) and Macintosh version (**ppc** directory), as well as the source code (**RPMS** directory). The DVD is bootable, letting you install your Fedora Core 4 system from the DVD-ROM directly.

Alternatively, you can also use a bootable CD to install Fedora Core 4 from the DVD-ROM, should your DVD drive not boot DVD discs. For details on how to create a boot CD for the DVD-ROM, see Chapter 2.

The DVD includes a comprehensive set of Linux software applications, including the GNU software packages (graphics, productivity, multimedia, communications, publishing, programming, and games), as well as development tools and Internet servers (FTP, Web, mail, news, and DNS). Both GNOME and the K Desktop Environment (KDE) GUI user interfaces are included, along with an extensive number of GNOME and KDE applications. Packages can be later installed or removed easily with the package management tool (system-config-packages).

Updates are now nearly automatic with the Red Hat Update Agent. Additional applications for Fedora Core 4, including many former Fedora Core applications, are now available from Fedora Extras at **download.fedora.redhat.com/pub/linux/fedora/extras**.

You can use the following command on a command line (terminal window) to automatically download and install Fedora Extras packages, along with any needed supporting packages. The following will install BitTorrent:

```
yum install bittorrent
```

You can also download additional software from Fedora Core–compatible repositories like **freshrpms.net** and **rpm.livna.org/fedora**. With either Firefox or Yum you can both download and install packages with a simple click or command (see Chapters 1, 4, 11, 12, and 31).

Index

GNU GENERAL PUBLIC LICENSE
Version 2, June 1991

Preamble

The licenses for most software are designed to take away your freedom to share and change it. By contrast, the GNU General Public License is intended to guarantee your freedom to share and change free software--to make sure the software is free for all its users. This General Public License applies to most of the Free Software Foundation's software and to any other program whose authors commit to using it. (Some other Free Software Foundation software is covered by the GNU Library General Public License instead.) You can apply it to your programs, too.

When we speak of free software, we are referring to freedom, not price. Our General Public Licenses are designed to make sure that you have the freedom to distribute copies of free software (and charge for this service if you wish), that you receive source code or can get it if you want it, that you can change the software or use pieces of it in new free programs; and that you know you can do these things.

To protect your rights, we need to make restrictions that forbid anyone to deny you these rights or to ask you to surrender the rights. These restrictions translate to certain responsibilities for you if you distribute copies of the software, or if you modify it.

For example, if you distribute copies of such a program, whether gratis or for a fee, you must give the recipients all the rights that you have. You must make sure that they, too, receive or can get the source code. And you must show them these terms so they know their rights.

We protect your rights with two steps: (1) copyright the software, and (2) offer you this license which gives you legal permission to copy, distribute and/or modify the software.

Also, for each author's protection and ours, we want to make certain that everyone understands that there is no warranty for this free software. If the software is modified by someone else and passed on, we want its recipients to know that what they have is not the original, so that any problems introduced by others will not reflect on the original authors' reputations. Finally, any free program is threatened constantly by software patents. We wish to avoid the danger that redistributors of a free program will individually obtain patent licenses, in effect making the program proprietary. To prevent this, we have made it clear that any patent must be licensed for everyone's free use or not licensed at all.

The precise terms and conditions for copying, distribution and modification follow.

GNU GENERAL PUBLIC LICENSE TERMS AND CONDITIONS FOR COPYING, DISTRIBUTION AND MODIFICATION

0. This License applies to any program or other work which contains a notice placed by the copyright holder saying it may be distributed under the terms of this General Public License. The "Program", below, refers to any such program or work, and a "work based on the Program" means either the Program or any derivative work under copyright law: that is to say, a work containing the Program or a portion of it, either verbatim or with modifications and/or translated into another language. (Hereinafter, translation is included without limitation in the term "modification".) Each licensee is addressed as "you".

Activities other than copying, distribution and modification are not covered by this License; they are outside its scope. The act of running the Program is not restricted, and the output from the Program is covered only if its contents constitute a work based on the Program (independent of having been made by running the Program). Whether that is true depends on what the Program does.

1. You may copy and distribute verbatim copies of the Program's source code as you receive it, in any medium, provided that you conspicuously and appropriately publish on each copy an appropriate copyright notice and disclaimer of warranty; keep intact all the notices that refer to this License and to the absence of any warranty; and give any other recipients of the Program a copy of this License along with the Program.

You may charge a fee for the physical act of transferring a copy, and you may at your option offer warranty protection in exchange for a fee.

2. You may modify your copy or copies of the Program or any portion of it, thus forming a work based on the Program, and copy and distribute such modifications or work under the terms of Section 1 above, provided that you also meet all of these conditions:

a) You must cause the modified files to carry prominent notices stating that you changed the files and the date of any change.

b) You must cause any work that you distribute or publish, that in whole or in part contains or is derived from the Program or any part thereof, to be licensed as a whole at no charge to all third parties under the terms of this License.

c) If the modified program normally reads commands interactively when run, you must cause it, when started running for such interactive use in the most ordinary way, to print or display an announcement including an appropriate copyright notice and a notice that there is no warranty (or else, saying that you provide a warranty) and that users may redistribute the program under these conditions, and telling the user how to view a copy of this License. (Exception: if the Program itself is interactive but does not normally print such an announcement, your work based on the Program is not required to print an announcement.)

These requirements apply to the modified work as a whole. If identifiable sections of that work are not derived from the Program, and can be reasonably considered independent and separate works in themselves, then this License, and its terms, do not apply to those sections when you distribute them as separate works. But when you distribute the same sections as part of a whole which is a work based on the Program, the distribution of the whole must be on the terms of this License, whose permissions for other licensees extend to the entire whole, and thus to each and every part regardless of who wrote it.

Thus, it is not the intent of this section to claim rights or contest your rights to work written entirely by you; rather, the intent is to exercise the right to control the distribution of derivative or collective works based on the Program.

In addition, mere aggregation of another work not based on the Program with the Program (or with a work based on the Program) on a volume of a storage or distribution medium does not bring the other work under the scope of this License.

3. You may copy and distribute the Program (or a work based on it, under Section 2) in object code or executable form under the terms of Sections 1 and 2 above provided that you also do one of the following:

a) Accompany it with the complete corresponding machine-readable source code, which must be distributed under the terms of Sections 1 and 2 above on a medium customarily used for software interchange; or,

b) Accompany it with a written offer, valid for at least three years, to give any third party, for a charge no more than your cost of physically performing source distribution, a complete machine-readable copy of the corresponding source code, to be distributed under the terms of Sections 1 and 2 above on a medium customarily used for software interchange; or,

c) Accompany it with the information you received as to the offer to distribute corresponding source code. (This alternative is allowed only for noncommercial distribution and only if you received the program in object code or executable form with such an offer, in accord with Subsection b above.)

The source code for a work means the preferred form of the work for making modifications to it. For an executable work, complete source code means all the source code for all modules it contains, plus any associated interface definition files, plus the scripts used to control compilation and installation of the executable. However, as a special exception, the source code distributed need not include anything that is normally distributed (in either source or binary form) with the major components (compiler, kernel, and so on) of the operating system on which the executable runs, unless that component itself accompanies the executable.

If distribution of executable or object code is made by offering access to copy from a designated place, then offering equivalent access to copy the source code from the same place counts as distribution of the source code, even though third parties are not compelled to copy the source along with the object code.

4. You may not copy, modify, sublicense, or distribute the Program except as expressly provided under this License. Any attempt otherwise to copy, modify, sublicense or distribute the Program is void, and will automatically terminate your rights under this License. However, parties who have received copies, or rights, from you under this License will not have their licenses terminated so long as such parties remain in full compliance.

5. You are not required to accept this License, since you have not signed it. However, nothing else grants you permission to modify or distribute the Program or its derivative works. These actions are prohibited by law if you do not accept this License. Therefore, by modifying or distributing the Program (or any work based on the Program), you indicate your acceptance of this License to do so, and all its terms and conditions for copying, distributing or modifying the Program or works based on it.

6. Each time you redistribute the Program (or any work based on the Program), the recipient automatically receives a license from the original licensor to copy, distribute or modify the Program subject to these terms and conditions. You may not impose any further restrictions on the recipients' exercise of the rights granted herein. You are not responsible for enforcing compliance by third parties to this License.

7. If, as a consequence of a court judgment or allegation of patent infringement or for any other reason (not limited to patent issues), conditions are imposed on you (whether by court order, agreement or otherwise) that contradict the conditions of this License, they do not excuse you from the conditions of this License. If you cannot distribute so as to satisfy simultaneously your obligations under this License and any other pertinent obligations, then as a consequence you may not distribute the Program at all. For example, if a patent license would not permit royalty-free redistribution of the Program by all those who receive copies directly or indirectly through you, then the only way you could satisfy both it and this License would be to refrain entirely from distribution of the Program.

If any portion of this section is held invalid or unenforceable under any particular circumstance, the balance of the section is intended to apply and the section as a whole is intended to apply in other circumstances.

It is not the purpose of this section to induce you to infringe any patents or other property right claims or to contest validity of any such claims; this section has the sole purpose of protecting the integrity of the free software distribution system, which is implemented by public license practices. Many people have made generous contributions to the wide range of software distributed through that system in reliance on consistent application of that system; it is up to the author/donor to decide if he or she is willing to distribute software through any other system and a licensee cannot impose that choice.

This section is intended to make thoroughly clear what is believed to be a consequence of the rest of this License.

8. If the distribution and/or use of the Program is restricted in certain countries either by patents or by copyrighted interfaces, the original copyright holder who places the Program under this License may add an explicit geographical distribution limitation excluding those countries, so that distribution is permitted only in or among countries not thus excluded. In such case, this License incorporates the limitation as if written in the body of this License.

9. The Free Software Foundation may publish revised and/or new versions of the General Public License from time to time. Such new versions will be similar in spirit to the present version, but may differ in detail to address new problems or concerns.

Each version is given a distinguishing version number. If the Program specifies a version number of this License which applies to it and "any later version", you have the option of following the terms and conditions either of that version or of any later version published by the Free Software Foundation. If the Program does not specify a version number of this License, you may choose any version ever published by the Free Software Foundation.

10. If you wish to incorporate parts of the Program into other free programs whose distribution conditions are different, write to the author to ask for permission. For software which is copyrighted by the Free Software Foundation, write to the Free Software Foundation; we sometimes make exceptions for this. Our decision will be guided by the two goals of preserving the free status of all derivatives of our free software and of promoting the sharing and reuse of software generally.

NO WARRANTY

11. BECAUSE THE PROGRAM IS LICENSED FREE OF CHARGE, THERE IS NO WARRANTY FOR THE PROGRAM, TO THE EXTENT PERMITTED BY APPLICABLE LAW. EXCEPT WHEN OTHERWISE STATED IN WRITING THE COPYRIGHT HOLDERS AND/OR OTHER PARTIES PROVIDE THE PROGRAM "AS IS" WITHOUT WARRANTY OF ANY KIND, EITHER EXPRESSED OR IMPLIED, INCLUDING, BUT NOT LIMITED TO, THE IMPLIED WARRANTIES OF MERCHANTABILITY AND FITNESS FOR A PARTICULAR PURPOSE. THE ENTIRE RISK AS TO THE QUALITY AND PERFORMANCE OF THE PROGRAM IS WITH YOU. SHOULD THE PROGRAM PROVE DEFECTIVE, YOU ASSUME THE COST OF ALL NECESSARY SERVICING, REPAIR OR CORRECTION.

12. IN NO EVENT UNLESS REQUIRED BY APPLICABLE LAW OR AGREED TO IN WRITING WILL ANY COPYRIGHT HOLDER, OR ANY OTHER PARTY WHO MAY MODIFY AND/OR REDISTRIBUTE THE PROGRAM AS PERMITTED ABOVE, BE LIABLE TO YOU FOR DAMAGES, INCLUDING ANY GENERAL, SPECIAL, INCIDENTAL OR CONSEQUENTIAL DAMAGES ARISING OUT OF THE USE OR INABILITY TO USE THE PROGRAM (INCLUDING BUT NOT LIMITED TO LOSS OF DATA OR DATA BEING RENDERED INACCURATE OR LOSSES SUSTAINED BY YOU OR THIRD PARTIES OR A FAILURE OF THE PROGRAM TO OPERATE WITH ANY OTHER PROGRAMS), EVEN IF SUCH HOLDER OR OTHER PARTY HAS BEEN ADVISED OF THE POSSIBILITY OF SUCH DAMAGES.

END OF TERMS AND CONDITIONS

How to Apply These Terms to Your New Programs

If you develop a new program, and you want it to be of the greatest possible use to the public, the best way to achieve this is to make it free software which everyone can redistribute and change under these terms.

To do so, attach the following notices to the program. It is safest to attach them to the start of each source file to most effectively convey the exclusion of warranty; and each file should have at least the "copyright" line and a pointer to where the full notice is found.

> <one line to give the program's name and a brief idea of what it does.> Copyright (C) <year> <name of author>
>
> This program is free software; you can redistribute it and/or modify it under the terms of the GNU General Public License as published by the Free Software Foundation; either version 2 of the License, or (at your option) any later version.
>
> This program is distributed in the hope that it will be useful, but WITHOUT ANY WARRANTY; without even the implied warranty of MERCHANTABILITY or FITNESS FOR A PARTICULAR PURPOSE. See the GNU General Public License for more details.
>
> You should have received a copy of the GNU General Public License along with this program; if not, write to the Free Software Foundation, Inc., 51 Franklin St, Fifth Floor, Boston, MA 02110-1301 USA

Also add information on how to contact you by electronic and paper mail.

If the program is interactive, make it output a short notice like this when it starts in an interactive mode:

> Gnomovision version 69, Copyright (C) year name of author Gnomovision comes with ABSOLUTELY NO WARRANTY; for details type `show w'. This is free software, and you are welcome to redistribute it under certain conditions; type `show c' for details.

The hypothetical commands `show w' and `show c' should show the appropriate parts of the General Public License. Of course, the commands you use may be called something other than `show w' and `show c'; they could even be mouse-clicks or menu items--whatever suits your program.

You should also get your employer (if you work as a programmer) or your school, if any, to sign a "copyright disclaimer" for the program, if necessary. Here is a sample; alter the names:

> Yoyodyne, Inc., hereby disclaims all copyright interest in the program `Gnomovision' (which makes passes at compilers) written by James Hacker.
>
> <signature of Ty Coon>, 1 April 1989
>
> Ty Coon, President of Vice

This General Public License does not permit incorporating your program into proprietary programs. If your program is a subroutine library, you may consider it more useful to permit linking proprietary applications with the library. If this is what you want to do, use the GNU Library General Public License instead of this License.